with MyFinanceLab™

- **Worked Solutions**—Provide step-by-step explanations on how to solve select problems using the exact numbers and data that were presented in the problem. Instructors will have access to the Worked Solutions in preview and review mode.

- **Algorithmic Test Bank**—Instructors have the ability to create multiple versions of a test or extra practice for students. Available with select titles.

- **Financial Calculator**—The Financial Calculator is available as a smartphone application, as well as on a computer, and includes important functions such as cash flow, net present value, and internal rate of return. Fifteen helpful tutorial videos show the many ways to use the Financial Calculator in MyFinanceLab.

- **Reporting Dashboard**—View, analyze, and report learning outcomes clearly and easily. Available via the Gradebook and fully mobile-ready, the Reporting Dashboard presents student performance data at the class, section, and program levels in an accessible, visual manner.

- **LMS Integration**—Link from any LMS platform to access assignments, rosters, and resources, and synchronize MyLab grades with your LMS gradebook. For students, new direct, single sign-on provides access to all the personalized learning MyLab resources that make studying more efficient and effective.

- **Mobile Ready**—Students and instructors can access multimedia resources and complete assessments right at their fingertips, on any mobile device.

COMMON SYMBOLS AND NOTATION

A	premerger total value of acquirer
APR	annual percentage rate
APY	annual percentage yield
β_i	beta of security i with respect to the market portfolio
C	cash flow
$CapEx$	capital expenditures
CCC	cash conversion cycle
C_{FC}	foreign currency cash flow
C_n, CF_n	cash flow that arrives at date n
$Corr(R_i, R_j)$	correlation between the returns of security i and security j
CPN	coupon payment on a bond
D	market value of debt
$D\%$	fraction of the firm financed with debt
Div_1	dividend due in one year
Div_{pfd}	dividend on preferred stock
Div_t	dividends paid in year t
E	market value of equity
$E[R_i]$	expected return of security i
$E[R_{Mkt}]$	expected return of the market portfolio
$E[R_P]$	expected return of a portfolio
$E\%$	fraction of the firm financed with equity
EAR	effective annual rate
$EBIT$	earnings before interest and taxes
$EBITDA$	earnings before interest, taxes, depreciation, and amortization
EPS_t	earnings per share on date t
F	forward exchange rate
FCF_t	free cash flow on date t
FV	future value; face value of a bond
FV_n	future value on date n
g	growth rate
IRR	internal rate of return
m	number of compounding periods per year
$MIRR$	modified internal rate of return
n	number of periods
N	date of the last cash flow in a stream of cash flows; terminal date
N_A	premerger number of shares of acquirer outstanding
NPV	net present value
N_T	premerger number of shares of target outstanding
NWC_t	net working capital in year t
P	price; initial principal or deposit, or equivalent present value

P/E	price-earnings ratio
$P\%$	fraction of the firm financed with preferred stock
P_A	premerger share price of acquirer
P_{cum}	cum-dividend (with dividend) stock price
P_E	price of common stock equity
P_{ex}	ex-dividend (without dividend) stock price
P_{pfd}	price of preferred stock
P_{rep}	stock price with share repurchase
P_T	premerger share price of target
P_t	price on date t
PV	present value
r	interest rate; discount rate; cost of capital
$\bar{R}$	average return
$r_\$$	dollar risk-free interest rate
$r_\$^*$	dollar cost of capital
r_D	expected return (cost of capital) of debt
r_E	expected return (cost of capital) of equity
r_f	risk-free interest rate
r_{FC}	foreign currency risk-free interest rate
r_{FC}^*	foreign currency cost of capital
R_i	return of security i
r_n	interest rate or discount rate for an n-year term
ROA	return on assets
ROE	return on equity
R_P	return of portfolio P
r_{pfd}	required return (cost of capital) for preferred stock
R_t	realized or total return of a security from date $t-1$ to t
r_U	expected return (cost of capital) of unlevered equity
r_{wacc}	weighted average cost of capital
S	spot exchange rate; value of all synergies
$SD(R_i)$	standard deviation (volatility) of the return of security i
SGR	sustainable growth rate
T	premerger total value of target
T_C	marginal corporate tax rate
$Var(R_i)$	variance of the return of security i
V^L	value of the firm with leverage
V_0^L	initial levered value
V_t	enterprise value on date t
V^U	value of the unlevered firm
w_i	fraction of the portfolio invested in security i (its relative *weight* in the portfolio)
x	number of new shares issued by acquirer to pay for target
y, YTM	yield to maturity
YTC	yield to call on a callable bond

Fundamentals of
Corporate Finance

FOURTH EDITION

Jonathan Berk
STANFORD UNIVERSITY

Peter DeMarzo
STANFORD UNIVERSITY

Jarrad Harford
UNIVERSITY OF WASHINGTON

New York, NY

The Pearson Series in Finance

*denotes titles with MyFinanceLab.   Log onto **www.myfinancelab.com** to learn more.

To Rebecca, Natasha, and Hannah for the love and for being there.   —J. B.

To Kaui, Pono, Koa, and Kai for all the love and laughter.   —P. D.

To Katrina, Evan, and Cole for your love and support.   —J. H.

Vice President, Business Publishing: Donna Battista
Director of Portfolio Management: Adrienne D'Ambrosio
Portfolio Manager: Kate Fernandes
Editorial Assistant: Kathryn Brightney
Vice President, Product Marketing: Roxanne McCarley
Director of Strategic Marketing: Brad Parkins
Strategic Marketing Manager: Deborah Strickland
Product Marketer: Kaylee Carlson
Field Marketing Manager: Ramona Elmer
Field Marketing Assistant: Kristen Compton
Product Marketing Assistant: Jessica Quazza
Vice President, Production and Digital Studio,
    Arts and Business: Etain O'Dea
Director of Production, Business: Jeff Holcomb
Managing Producer, Business: Alison Kalil
Content Producer: Nancy Freihofer
Operations Specialist: Carol Melville

Creative Director: Blair Brown
Manager, Learning Tools: Brian Surette
Content Developer, Learning Tools: Lindsey Sloan
Managing Producer, Digital Studio, Arts and Business:
    Diane Lombardo
Digital Studio Producer: Melissa Honig
Digital Studio Producer: Alana Coles
Digital Content Team Lead: Noel Lotz
Digital Content Project Lead: Miguel Leonarte
Full-Service Project Management and Composition:
    SPi Global
Interior Design: Gillian Hall, The Aardvark Group
Cover Design Manager: Laurie Entringer
Cover Art: designstock
Printer/Binder: LSC Communications
Cover Printer: LSC Communications

Microsoft and/or its respective suppliers make no representations about the suitability of the information contained in the documents and related graphics published as part of the services for any purpose. All such documents and related graphics are provided "as is" without warranty of any kind. Microsoft and/or its respective suppliers hereby disclaim all warranties and conditions with regard to this information, including all warranties and conditions of merchantability, whether express, implied or statutory, fitness for a particular purpose, title and non-infringement. In no event shall Microsoft and/or its respective suppliers be liable for any special, indirect or consequential damages or any damages whatsoever resulting from loss of use, data or profits, whether in an action of contract, negligence or other tortious action, arising out of or in connection with the use or performance of information available from the services.

The documents and related graphics contained herein could include technical inaccuracies or typographical errors. Changes are periodically added to the information herein. Microsoft and/or its respective suppliers may make improvements and/or changes in the product(s) and/or the program(s) described herein at any time. Partial screen shots may be viewed in full within the software version specified.

Microsoft® and Windows® are registered trademarks of the Microsoft Corporation in the U.S.A. and other countries. This book is not sponsored or endorsed by or affiliated with the Microsoft Corporation.

Acknowledgments of third-party content appear on the appropriate page within the text, which constitutes an extension of this copyright page. Photographs in the text courtesy of the following: p. 11, Anna Hoychuk/Shutterstock; p. 15, Gary/Fotolia; p. 17, Frank Hatheway; p. 29, Ruth Porat; p. 83, Xavier Subias/AGE Fotostock/Alamy; p. 146, Kevin M. Warsh; p. 180, Lisa Black; p. 246, Dick Grannis; p. 278, Denys Prykhodov/Shutterstock; p. 286, David Holland; p. 315, Douglas Kehring; p. 422, Shelagh Glaser; p. 437, Kevin Laws; p. 559, John Connors; p. 662, Tasos Katopodis/Getty Images; p. 665, Cristina99/Fotolia; p. 719, Chetianu/Fotolia; Web p. 60, Lawrence Harris.

PEARSON, ALWAYS LEARNING, and MYFINANCELAB™ are exclusive trademarks owned by Pearson Education, Inc. or its affiliates in the U.S. and/or other countries.

Unless otherwise indicated herein, any third-party trademarks, logos, or icons that may appear in this work are the property of their respective owners, and any references to third-party trademarks, logos, icons, or other trade dress are for demonstrative or descriptive purposes only. Such references are not intended to imply any sponsorship, endorsement, authorization, or promotion of Pearson's products by the owners of such marks, or any relationship between the owner and Pearson Education, Inc., or its affiliates, authors, licensees, or distributors.

Library of Congress Cataloging-in-Publication Data

Names: Berk, Jonathan B., 1962- author. | DeMarzo, Peter M., author. |
  Harford, Jarrad V. T., author.
Title: Fundamentals of corporate finance / Jonathan Berk, Peter DeMarzo,
  Jarrad Harford.
Description: 4th edition. | New York, NY : Prentice Hall, [2016]
Identifiers: LCCN 2016053928 | ISBN 9780134475561
Subjects: LCSH: Corporations--Finance.
Classification: LCC HG4026 .B464 2016 | DDC 658.15--dc23
LC record available at https://lccn.loc.gov/2016053928

26 2019

ISBN 10:   0-13-447556-9
ISBN 13: 978-0-13-447556-1

Brief Contents

Detailed Contents

CHAPTERS ON THE WEB

These Web Chapters are on MyFinanceLab at
www.myfinancelab.com

About the Authors

Jonathan Berk, Peter DeMarzo, and Jarrad Harford

Jonathan Berk is the A.P. Giannini Professor of Finance at the Graduate School of Business, Stanford University and is a Research Associate at the National Bureau of Economic Research. Before coming to Stanford, he was the Sylvan Coleman Professor of Finance at Haas School of Business at the University of California, Berkeley. Prior to earning his PhD, he worked as an Associate at Goldman Sachs (where his education in finance really began).

Professor Berk's research interests in finance include corporate valuation, capital structure, mutual funds, asset pricing, experimental economics, and labor economics. His work has won a number of research awards including the TIAA-CREF Paul A. Samuelson Award, the Smith Breeden Prize, Best Paper of the Year in *The Review of Financial Studies*, and the FAME Research Prize. His paper, "A Critique of Size-Related Anomalies," was selected as one of the two best papers ever published in *The Review of Financial Studies*. In recognition of his influence on the practice of finance he has received the Bernstein-Fabozzi/Jacobs Levy Award, the Graham and Dodd Award of Excellence, and the Roger F. Murray Prize. He served two terms as an Associate Editor of the *Journal of Finance*, and a term as a director of the American Finance Association, the Western Finance Association, and academic director of the Financial Management Association. He is a Fellow of the Financial Management Association and a member of the advisory board of the *Journal of Portfolio Management*.

Born in Johannesburg, South Africa, Professor Berk is married, with two daughters, and is an avid skier and biker.

Peter DeMarzo is the Mizuho Financial Group Professor of Finance at the Graduate School of Business, Stanford University. He is the current Vice President of the American Finance Association and a Research Associate at the National Bureau of Economic Research. He teaches MBA and PhD courses in Corporate Finance and Financial Modeling. In addition to his experience at the Stanford Graduate School of Business, Professor DeMarzo has taught at the Haas School of Business and the Kellogg Graduate School of Management, and he was a National Fellow at the Hoover Institution.

Professor DeMarzo received the Sloan Teaching Excellence Award at Stanford, and the Earl F. Cheit Outstanding Teaching Award at U.C. Berkeley. Professor DeMarzo has served as an Associate Editor for *The Review of Financial Studies*, *Financial Management*, and the *B.E. Journals in Economic Analysis and Policy*, as well as a Director of the American Finance Association. He has served as Vice President and President of the Western Finance Association. Professor DeMarzo's research is in the area of corporate investment and financing, asset securitization, and contracting, as well as market structure and regulation. His recent work has examined issues of the optimal design of contracts and securities, leverage dynamics and the role of bank capital regulation, and the influence of information asymmetries on stock prices and corporate investment. He has received numerous awards including the Western Finance Association Corporate Finance Award and the Barclays Global Investors/Michael Brennan best-paper award from *The Review of Financial Studies*.

Professor DeMarzo was born in Whitestone, New York, and is married with three boys. He and his family enjoy hiking, biking, and skiing.

Jarrad Harford is the Paul Pigott - PACCAR Professor of Finance at the University of Washington. Prior to Washington, Professor Harford taught at the Lundquist College of Business at the University of Oregon. He received his PhD in Finance with a minor in Organizations and Markets from the University of Rochester. Professor Harford has taught the core undergraduate finance course, Business Finance, for over nineteen years, as well as an elective in Mergers and Acquisitions, and "Finance for Non-financial Executives" in the executive education program. He has won numerous awards for his teaching, including the UW Finance Professor of the Year (2010, 2012, 2016), Panhellenic/Interfraternity Council Business Professor of the Year Award (2011, 2013), ISMBA Excellence in Teaching Award (2006), and the Wells Fargo Faculty Award for Undergraduate Teaching (2005). Professor Harford is currently a Managing Editor of the *Journal of Financial and Quantitative Analysis*, and serves as an Associate Editor for the *Journal of Financial Economics*, and *Journal of Corporate Finance*. His main research interests are understanding the dynamics of merger and acquisition activity as well as the interaction of corporate cash management policy with governance, payout and global tax considerations. Professor Harford was born in Pennsylvania, is married, and has two sons. He and his family enjoy traveling, hiking, and skiing.

Bridging Theory and Practice

EXAMPLE 7.1

Stock Prices
and Returns

MyFinanceLab

PROBLEM

Suppose you expect Longs Drug Stores to pay an annual dividend of $0.56 per share in the coming year and to trade for $45.50 per share at the end of the year. If investments with equivalent risk to Longs' stock have an expected return of 6.80%, what is the most you would pay today for Longs' stock? What dividend yield and capital gain rate would you expect at this price?

SOLUTION

PLAN

We can use Eq. 7.1 to solve for the beginning price we would pay now (P_0) given our expectations about dividends ($Div_1 = \$0.56$) and future price ($P_1 = \$45.50$) and the return we need to expect to earn to be willing to invest ($r_E = 0.068$). We can then use Eq. 7.2 to calculate the dividend yield and capital gain rate.

EXECUTE

Using Eq. 7.1, we have

$$P_0 = \frac{Div_1 + P_1}{1 + r_E} = \frac{\$0.56 + \$45.50}{1.0680} = \$43.13$$

Referring to Eq. 7.2, we see that at this price, Longs' dividend yield is $Div_1/P_0 = 0.56/43.13 = 1.30\%$. The expected capital gain is $\$45.50 - \$43.13 = \$2.37$ per share, for a capital gain rate of $2.37/43.13 = 5.50\%$.

EVALUATE

At a price of $43.13, Longs' expected total return is 1.30% + 5.50% = 6.80%, which is equal to its equity cost of capital (the return being paid by investments with equivalent risk to Longs'). This amount is the most we would be willing to pay for Longs' stock. If we paid more, our expected return would be less than 6.8% and we would rather invest elsewhere.

PROBLEM

Ellen is 35 years old and she has decided it is time to plan seriously for her retirement. At the end of each year until she is 65, she will save $10,000 in a retirement account. If the account earns 10% per year, how much will Ellen have in her account at age 65?

SOLUTION

PLAN

As always, we begin with a timeline. In this case, it is helpful to keep track of both the dates and Ellen's age:

35	36	37		65
0	1	2	...	30
	$10,000	$10,000		$10,000

Ellen's savings plan looks like an annuity of $10,000 per year for 30 years. (*Hint:* It is easy to become confused when you just look at age, rather than at both dates and age. A common error is to think there are only 65 − 36 = 29 payments. Writing down both dates and age avoids this problem.)

To determine the amount Ellen will have in her account at age 65, we'll need to compute the future value of this annuity.

EXECUTE

$$FV = \$10,000 \times \frac{1}{0.10}(1.10^{30} - 1)$$

$$= \$10,000 \times 164.49$$

$$= \$1.645 \text{ million at age 65}$$

Using a financial calculator or Excel:

	N	I/Y	PV	PMT	FV
Given:	30	10	0	−10,000	
Solve for:					1,644,940

Excel Formula: =FV(RATE,NPER, PMT, PV)=FV(0.10,30,−10000,0)

EVALUATE

By investing $10,000 per year for 30 years (a total of $300,000) and earning interest on those investments, the compounding will allow Ellen to retire with $1.645 million.

Study Aids with a Practical Focus

To be successful, students need to master the core concepts and learn to identify and solve problems that today's practitioners face.

- The **Valuation Principle** is presented as the foundation of all financial decision making: The central idea is that a firm should take projects or make investments that increase the *value* of the firm. The tools of finance determine the impact of a project or investment on the firm's value by comparing the costs and benefits in equivalent terms. The Valuation Principle is first introduced in Chapter 3, revisited in the part openers, and integrated throughout the text.

- **Guided Problem Solutions (GPS)** are Examples that accompany every important concept using a consistent problem-solving methodology that breaks the solution process into three steps: *Plan*, *Execute*, and *Evaluate*. This approach aids student comprehension, enhances their ability to model the solution process when tackling problems on their own, and demonstrates the importance of interpreting the mathematical solution.

- **Personal Finance GPS** Examples showcase the use of financial analysis in everyday life by setting problems in scenarios, such as purchasing a new car or house and saving for retirement.

- **Common Mistake** boxes alert students to frequently made mistakes stemming from misunderstanding of core concepts and calculations—in the classroom and in the field.

COMMON MISTAKE

Summing Cash Flows Across Time

Once you understand the time value of money, our first rule may seem straightforward. However, it is very common, especially for those who have not studied finance, to violate this rule, simply treating all cash flows as comparable regardless of when they are received. One example is in sports contracts. In 2011, Albert Pujols signed a contract with the Los Angeles Angels that was repeatedly referred to as a "$240 million" contract. The $240 million comes from simply adding up all the payments Pujols would receive over the 10 years of the contract—treating dollars received in 10 years the same as dollars received today. The same thing occurred when Lionel Messi signed a contract extension with FC Barcelona in 2013, giving him a "$150 million" contract through 2018, and in 2015 when Giancarlo Stanton signed a "$325 million" 13-year contract with the Florida Marlins.

Applications That Reflect Real Practice

Global Financial Crisis boxes reflect the reality of the recent financial crisis and sovereign debt crisis, noting lessons learned. Boxes interspersed through the book illustrate and analyze key details.

GLOBAL FINANCIAL CRISIS

2008–2009: A Very Cold IPO Market

The drop in IPO issues during the 2008 financial crisis was both global and dramatic. The bar graph shows the total worldwide dollar volume of IPO proceeds in billions of dollars (blue bars) and number of deals (red line) by quarter, from the last quarter of 2006 to the first quarter of 2009. Comparing the fourth quarter of 2007 (a record quarter for IPO issues) to the fourth quarter of 2008, dollar volume dropped a stunning 97% from $102 billion to just $3 billion. Things got even worse in the first quarter of 2009 with just $1.4 billion raised. The market for IPOs essentially dried up altogether.

During the 2008 financial crisis, IPO markets were not the only equity issue markets that saw a collapse in volume. Markets for seasoned equity offerings and leveraged buyouts also collapsed. The extreme market uncertainty at the time created a "flight to quality." Investors, wary of taking risk, sought to move their capital into risk-free investments like U.S. Treasury securities. The result was a crash in existing equity prices and a greatly reduced supply of new capital to risky asset classes.

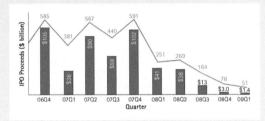

Source: Shifting Landscape—Are You Ready? Global IPO Trends report 2009, Ernst & Young.

Practitioner Interviews from notable professionals featured in many chapters highlight leaders in the field and address the effects of the financial crisis.

INTERVIEW WITH KEVIN M. WARSH

Kevin M. Warsh, *a lecturer at Stanford's Graduate School of Business and a distinguished visiting fellow at the Hoover Institution*, was a Federal Reserve governor from 2006 to 2011, serving as chief liaison to the financial markets.

QUESTION: *What are the main policy instruments used by central banks to control the economy?*

ANSWER: The Federal Reserve (Fed) deploys several policy tools to achieve its goals of price stability, maximum sustainable employment, and financial stability. Lowering the federal funds short-term interest rate, the primary policy instrument, stimulates the economy. Raising the federal funds rate generally slows the economy. Buying and selling short-term U.S. Treasury securities through *open market operations* is standard practice. Prior to the 2007–2009 financial crisis, the Fed's balance sheet ranged from $700–$900 billion. But when the Fed was unable to lower interest rates further because rates were so close to zero already, it resorted to large-scale, longer-term open market operations to increase liquidity in the financial system in the hopes of stimulating the economy further, thus growing its balance sheet significantly. With *open mouth operations*, the Fed's announcements of its intent to buy or sell assets indicates its desired degree of future policy accommodation, often prompting markets to react by adjusting interest rates immediately. The Fed's Lender-of-Last-Resort authority allows it to lend money against good collateral to troubled institutions under certain conditions.

QUESTION: *What factors limit the effectiveness of Fed policy?*

ANSWER: Monetary policy does not act in isolation. Fiscal (taxing and spending), trade, and regulatory policies have huge consequence on the state of economic and financial conditions. In the short term, monetary policy can help buy time for an economy to improve, but it cannot cure structural failings of an economy in isolation or compensate for the country's growing indebtedness.

QUESTION: *What tools did the Fed create to address the 2007–2009 financial crisis?*

ANSWER: During the darkest days of the crisis, markets did not operate effectively, prices for securities did not clear, and banks and other financial institutions lacked clarity and confidence in the financial wherewithal of each other. One effective, innovative tool, the *Term Auction Facility (TAF)*, stimulated the economy by providing cheap and readily available term funding to banks, large and small, on the front lines of the economy, thus encouraging them to extend credit to businesses and consumers. After reducing the policy rate to near zero to help revive the economy, the Fed instituted two *Quantitative Easing (QE)* programs—special purchases of government and agency securities—to increase money supply, promote lending, and according to some proponents, increase prices of riskier assets.

The Fed also addressed the global financial crisis by establishing temporary *central bank liquidity swap lines* with the European Central Bank and other major central banks. Using this facility, a foreign central bank is able to obtain dollar funding for its customers by swapping euros for dollars or another currency and agreeing to reverse the swap at a later date. The Fed does not take exchange rate risk, but it is subject to the credit risk of its central bank counterparty.

QUESTION: *What tools is the European Central Bank (ECB) using to address the sovereign debt crisis? How does its approach compare to the Fed's approach to the 2007–2009 financial crisis?*

ANSWER: As a novel economic federation, the ECB finds itself in a more difficult position than the Fed. The underlying economies and competitiveness are markedly different across the Eurozone—in Germany versus Greece, for example. From 2007 until mid-2010, many European financiers and policymakers believed that global financial crisis was largely American-made, with some strains exported to the continent. By mid-2010, however, they recognized that it was indeed a global crisis. The ECB is formally charged with a single mandate of ensuring price stability, rather than the broader mandate of the Fed. Still, its actions ultimately mirrored many of those undertaken by the Fed: lowering the effective policy rate to record lows, providing direct liquidity to the Eurozone's financial institutions to avoid a potential run on the banking system, and instituting the Security Market Purchase program (buying sovereign credit of some of its distressed countries).

General Interest boxes highlight timely material from current financial events that shed light on business problems and real company practices.

 The Credit Crisis and Bond Yields

The financial crisis that engulfed the world's economies in 2008 originated as a credit crisis that first emerged in August 2007. At that time, problems in the mortgage market had led to the bankruptcy of several large mortgage lenders. The default of these firms, and the downgrading of many of the bonds backed by mortgages these firms had made, caused many investors to reassess the risk of other bonds in their portfolios. As perceptions of risk increased, and investors attempted to move into safer U.S. Treasury securities, the prices of corporate bonds fell and so their credit spreads rose relative to Treasuries, as shown in Figure 6.7. Panel (a) shows the yield spreads for long-term corporate bonds, where we can see that spreads of even the highest-rated Aaa bonds increased dramatically, from a typical level of 0.5% to over 2% by the fall of 2008. Panel (b) shows a similar pattern for the rate banks had to pay on short-term loans compared to the yields of short-term Treasury bills. This increase in borrowing costs made it more costly for firms to raise the capital needed for new investment, slowing economic growth. The decline in these spreads in early 2009 was viewed by many as an important first step in mitigating the ongoing impact of the financial crisis on the rest of the economy.

Teaching Every Student to Think Finance

Simplified Presentation of Mathematics

Because one of the hardest parts of learning finance for non-majors is mastering the jargon, math, and non-standardized notation, *Fundamentals of Corporate Finance* systematically uses:

- **Notation Boxes.** Each chapter begins with a Notation box that defines the variables and the acronyms used in the chapter and serves as a "legend" for students' reference.

- **Numbered and Labeled Equations.** The first time a full equation is given in notation form it is numbered. Key equations are titled and revisited in the summary and in end papers.

- **Timelines.** Introduced in Chapter 3, timelines are emphasized as the important first step in solving *every* problem that involves cash flows over time.

- **Financial Calculator** instructions, including a box in Chapter 4 on solving for future and present values, and appendices to Chapters 4, 6, and 15 with keystrokes for HP-10BII and TI BAII Plus Professional calculators, highlight this problem-solving tool.

- **Spreadsheet Tables.** Select tables are available on MyFinanceLab as Excel® files, enabling students to change inputs and manipulate the underlying calculations. Icons in the text show students where spreadsheets are available in the eText.

- **Using Excel** boxes describe Excel techniques and include screenshots to serve as a guide for students using this technology.

Using a Financial Calculator

Financial calculators are programmed to perform most present and future value calculations. However, we recommend that you develop an understanding of the formulas before using the shortcuts. We provide a more extensive discussion of financial calculators on page 95 and in the appendix to Chapter 4, but we'll cover the relevant functions for this chapter here. To use financial calculator functions, you always enter the known values first and then the calculator solves for the unknown.

To answer Example 3.4 with a financial calculator, do the following:

Concept	Number of Periods	Interest Rate per Period	Recurring Payments	Future Value
Calculator Key	N	I/Y	PMT	FV
Enter	10	6	0	15000

Because you are solving for the present value (PV), press the **PV** key last (on an HP calculator), or press **CPT** then the **PV** key on a TI calculator. The calculator will return −8375.92. Note that the calculator balances inflows with outflows, so because the FV is positive (an inflow), it returns the PV as a negative (an outflow).

If you were solving for the future value instead, you would enter:

N	I/Y	PV	PMT
10	6	−8375.92	0

And finally, on an HP, press the **FV** key or on a TI, press **CPT** and then the **FV** key.

TABLE 18.18

Pro Forma Statement of Cash Flows for KMS, 2016–2021

	Year	2016	2017	2018	2019	2020	2021
1	Year	2016	2017	2018	2019	2020	2021
2	Statement of Cash Flows ($000s)						
3	Net Income		7,600	8,807	11,141	13,739	16,627
4	Depreciation		7,443	7,498	7,549	7,594	7,634
5	Changes in Working Capital						
6	Accounts Receivable		−2,561	−2,827	−3,144	−3,491	−3,872
7	Inventory		−2,696	−2,976	−3,309	−3,675	−4,076
8	Accounts Payable		2,157	2,381	2,647	2,940	3,261
9	Cash from Operating Activities		11,942	12,884	14,884	17,107	19,574
10	Capital Expenditures		−25,000	−8,000	−8,000	−8,000	−8,000
11	Other Investment		—	—	—	—	—
12	Cash from Investing Activities		−25,000	−8,000	−8,000	−8,000	−8,000
13	Net Borrowing		20,000	—	—	—	—
14	Dividends		−4,786	−2,503	−4,237	−6,167	−8,313
15	Cash from Financing Activities		15,214	−2,503	−4,237	−6,167	−8,313
16							
17	Change in Cash (9 + 12 + 15)		2,157	2,381	2,647	2,940	3,261

USING EXCEL

Capital Budgeting Using a Spreadsheet Program

Capital budgeting forecasts and analysis are most easily performed in a spreadsheet program. Here, we highlight a few best practices when developing your own capital budgets.

Create a Project Dashboard

All capital budgeting analyses begin with a set of assumptions regarding future revenues and costs associated with the investment. Centralize these assumptions within your spreadsheet in a project dashboard so they are easy to locate, review, and potentially modify. Here, we show an example for the HomeNet project.

	A	B	C	D	E	F	G	H	I	J
1	HomeNet Capital Budget									
2	Key Assumptions									
3	Revenues & Costs			Year 0	Year 1	Year 2	Year 3	Year 4	Year 5	
4	HomeNet Units Sold				50	50	50	50	50	
5	HomeNet Ave. Price/Unit				$ 260.00	$ 260.00	$ 260.00	$ 260.00		
6	HomeNet Cost/Unit				$ 110.00	$ 110.00	$ 110.00	$ 110.00		
7	Operating Expenses									
8	Marketing, Support & Rent				(2,800)	(2,800)	(2,800)	(2,800)		
9	Capital Expenditures									
10	Purchase Equipment			(7,500)						
11	Other Assumptions									
12	Depreciation Schedule			0.0%	20.0%	20.0%	20.0%	20.0%	20.0%	
13	Corporate Tax Rate			40.0%	40.0%	40.0%	40.0%	40.0%	40.0%	
14	Receivables (% sales)			15.0%	15.0%	15.0%	15.0%	15.0%	15.0%	
15	Payables (% expenses)			15.0%	15.0%	15.0%	15.0%	15.0%	15.0%	
16										

Practice Finance to Learn Finance

KEY POINTS AND EQUATIONS	KEY TERMS	ONLINE PRACTICE
4.1 Valuing a Stream of Cash Flows • The present value of a cash flow stream is: $$PV = C_0 + \frac{C_1}{(1+r)} + \frac{C_2}{(1+r)^2} + \cdots + \frac{C_N}{(1+r)^N} \quad (4.3)$$	stream of cash flows, p. 94	MyFinanceLab Study Plan 4.1
4.2 Perpetuities • A perpetuity is a stream of equal cash flows C paid every period, forever. The present value of a perpetuity is: $$PV(C \text{ in Perpetuity}) = \frac{C}{r} \quad (4.4)$$	consol, p. 98 perpetuity, p. 98	MyFinanceLab Study Plan 4.2
4.3 Annuities • An annuity is a stream of equal cash flows C paid every period for N periods. The present value of an annuity is: $$C \times \frac{1}{r}\left(1 - \frac{1}{(1+r)^N}\right) \quad (4.5)$$ • The future value of an annuity at the end of the annuity is: $$C \times \frac{1}{r}\left((1+r)^N - 1\right) \quad (4.6)$$	annuity, p. 101	MyFinanceLab Study Plan 4.3 Interactive Annuity Calculator Financial Calculator Tutorials: Calculating the Present Value of an Annuity and Solving for the Future Value of an Annuity

Working problems is the proven way to cement and demonstrate an understanding of finance.

- **Concept Check questions** at the end of each section enable students to test their understanding and target areas in which they need further review.

- **End-of-chapter problems written personally by Jonathan Berk, Peter DeMarzo, and Jarrad Harford** offer instructors the opportunity to assign first-rate materials to students for homework and practice with the confidence that the problems are consistent with the chapter content. All end-of-chapter problems are available in MyFinanceLab, the fully integrated homework and tutorial system. Both the problems and solutions, which were also prepared by the authors, have been class-tested and accuracy checked to ensure quality. Excel icons indicate the availability of instructor solutions and student templates in the Textbook Resources tab of MyFinanceLab.

End-of-Chapter Materials Reinforce Learning

Testing understanding of central concepts is crucial to learning finance.

- **MyFinanceLab Chapter Summary** presents the key points and conclusions from each chapter, provides a list of key terms with page numbers, and indicates online practice opportunities.

- **Data Cases** present in-depth scenarios in a business setting with questions designed to guide students' analysis. Many questions involve the use of Internet resources.

- **Integrative Cases** occur at the end of most parts and present a capstone extended problem for each part with a scenario and data for students to analyze based on that subset of chapters.

DATA CASE

This is your second interview with a prestigious brokerage firm for a job as an equity analyst. You survived the morning interviews with the department manager and the vice president of equity. Everything has gone so well that they want to test your ability as an analyst. You are seated in a room with a computer and a list with the names of two companies—Ford (F) and Microsoft (MSFT). You have 90 minutes to complete the following tasks:

1. Download the annual income statements, balance sheets, and cash flow statements for the last four fiscal years from Morningstar (www.morningstar.com). Enter each company's stock symbol and then go to "financials." Copy and paste the financial statements into Excel.

2. Find historical stock prices for each firm from Yahoo! Finance (finance.yahoo.com). Enter the stock symbol, click "Historical Prices" in the left column, and enter the proper date range to cover the last day of the month corresponding to the date of each financial statement. Use the closing stock prices (not the adjusted close). To calculate the firm's market capitalization at each date, multiply the number of shares outstanding by the firm's historic stock price. You can find the number of shares by using "Basic" under "Weighted average shares outstanding" at the bottom of the Income Statement.

Preface

Finance professors are united by their commitment to shaping future generations of financial professionals as well as instilling financial awareness and skills in non-majors. Our goal with *Fundamentals of Corporate Finance* is to provide an accessible presentation for both finance and non-finance majors. We know from experience that countless undergraduate students have felt that corporate finance is challenging. It is tempting to make finance *seem* accessible by de-emphasizing the core principles and instead concentrating on the results. In our over 50 years of combined teaching experience, we have found that emphasizing the core concepts in finance—which are clear and intuitive at heart—is what makes the subject matter accessible. What makes the subject challenging is that it is often difficult for a novice to distinguish between these core ideas and other intuitively appealing approaches that, if used in financial decision making, will lead to incorrect decisions.

The 2007–2009 financial crisis was fueled in part by many practitioners' poor decision making when they did not understand—or chose to ignore—the core concepts that underlie finance and the pedagogy in this book. With this point in mind, we present finance as one unified whole based on two simple, powerful ideas: (1) valuation drives decision making—the firm should take projects for which the value of the benefits exceeds the value of the costs, and (2) in a competitive market, market prices (rather than individual preferences) determine values. We combine these two ideas with what we call the *Valuation Principle*, and from it we establish all of the key ideas in corporate finance.

New to This Edition

All text discussions and figures, tables, and facts have been updated to accurately reflect exciting developments in the field of finance in the last three years. Specific highlights include the following:

- **New Interviews** with Frank Hatheway, Chief Economist and Senior VP for NASDAQ; Ruth Porat, Senior VP and CFO of Alphabet and Google; Kevin Laws, COO of Angel-List; and Douglas Kehring, Senior VP of Oracle.
- **Real-world examples** have been updated to reflect data through 2016.
- **New, Enhanced Media-Rich Pearson eText** includes Author Solution Videos that walk through the in-text examples using math, the financial calculator, and spreadsheets.
- **Using Excel boxes** have been updated and provide hands-on instruction of how to use Excel to solve financial problems and include screenshots to serve as a guide for students.
- **Added discussion of current issues** including negative interest rates, crowdfunding, new trading venues such as BATS and dark pools.

- **Added and revised end-of-chapter problems throughout the book,** once again personally writing and solving each one. In addition, every single problem is available in MyFinanceLab, the groundbreaking homework and tutorial system that accompanies the book.
- **We updated Data Cases and Integrative Cases** throughout the book, giving students a chance to apply the material with realistic data-analyzing exercises and problems that integrate material across chapters in each major part of the book.

Emphasis on Valuation

As painful as the financial crisis was, there is a silver lining: with the increasing focus on finance in the news, today's undergraduate students arrive in the classroom with an interest in finance. We strive to use that natural interest and motivation to overcome their fear of the subject and communicate time-tested core principles. Again, we take what has worked in the classroom and apply it to the text: By providing examples involving familiar companies such as Starbucks and Apple, making consistent use of real-world data, and demonstrating personal finance applications of core concepts, we strive to keep both non-finance and finance majors engaged.

By learning to apply the Valuation Principle, students develop the skills to make the types of comparisons—among loan options, investments, projects, and so on—that turn them into knowledgeable, confident financial consumers and managers. When students see how to apply finance to their personal lives and future careers, they grasp that finance is more than abstract, mathematically based concepts.

Table of Contents Overview

Fundamentals of Corporate Finance offers coverage of the major topical areas for introductory-level undergraduate courses. Our focus is on financial decision making related to the corporation's choice of which investments to make or how to raise the capital required to fund an investment. We designed the book with the need for flexibility and with consideration of time pressures throughout the semester in mind.

Part 1	Introduction	
	Ch. 1: Corporate Finance and the Financial Manager	Introduces the corporation and its governance; updated to include comparison of traditional trading venues, new electronic exchanges, and how the market for trading stocks is changing
	Ch. 2: Introduction to Financial Statement Analysis	Introduces key financial statements; Coverage of financial ratios has been centralized to prepare students to analyze financial statements holistically
Part 2	**Interest Rates and Valuing Cash Flows**	
	Ch. 3: Time Value of Money: An Introduction	Introduces the Valuation Principle and time value of money techniques for single-period investments
	Ch. 4: Time Value of Money: Valuing Cash Flow Streams	Introduces the mechanics of discounting; Includes examples with non-annual interest rates that provide time value of money applications in a personal loan context
	Ch. 5: Interest Rates	Presents how interest rates are quoted and compounding for all frequencies; Discusses key determinants of interest rates and their relation to the cost of capital; New discussion of negative interest rate

Ch. 22: Mergers and Acquisitions	Considers motives and methods for mergers and acquisitions, including leveraged buyouts
Ch. 23: International Corporate Finance	Analyzes the valuation of projects with foreign currency cash flows with integrated or segregated capital markets

Online Chapters
(on MyFinanceLab at www.myfinancelab.com)

Leasing Insurance and Risk Management Corporate Governance	Opportunities for course customization with online-only chapter offerings

A Complete Instructor and Student Support Package

MyFinanceLab

Not every student learns the same way or at the same rate. With the growing need for acceleration through many courses, it's more important than ever to meet students where they learn. Personalized learning in the MyFinanceLab gives you the flexibility to incorporate the approach that best suits your course and your students.

Study Plan

The **Study Plan** acts as a tutor, providing personalized recommendations for each of your students based on his or her ability to master the learning objectives in your course. This allows students to focus their study time by pinpointing the precise areas they need to review, and allowing them to use customized practice and learning aids—such as videos, eText, tutorials, and more—to get them back on track. Using the report available in the Gradebook, you can then tailor course lectures to prioritize the content where students need the most support—offering you better insight into classroom and individual performance.

Dynamic Study Modules

Dynamic Study Modules help students study effectively on their own by continuously assessing their activity and performance in real time. Here's how it works: students complete a set of questions with a unique answer format that also asks them to indicate their confidence level. Questions repeat until the student can answer them all correctly and confidently. Once completed, Dynamic Study Modules explain the concept using materials from the text. These are available as graded assignments prior to class, and accessible on smartphones, tablets, and computers. NEW! Instructors can now remove questions from Dynamic Study Modules to better fit their course.

Enhanced eText

The **Enhanced eText** keeps students engaged in learning on their own time, while helping them achieve greater conceptual understanding of course material. The worked examples bring learning to life, and algorithmic practice allows students to apply the very concepts they are reading about. Combining resources that illuminate content with accessible self-assessment, MyFinanceLab with Enhanced eText provides students with a complete digital learning experience—all in one place.

And with the **Pearson eText 2.0 mobile app** (available for select titles) students can now access the Enhanced eText and all of its functionality from their computer, tablet, or mobile phone. Because students' progress is synced across all of their devices, they can stop what they're doing on one device and pick up again later on another one—without breaking their stride.

Auto-Graded Excel Projects

Auto-graded Excel Projects allow instructors to seamlessly integrate Excel content into their course without having to manually grade spreadsheets. Students have the opportunity to practice important Finance skills in Microsoft Excel, helping them to master key concepts and gain proficiency with Excel.

Videos

Video clips available in MyFinanceLab profile well-known firms such as Boeing and Intel through interviews and analysis. The videos focus on core topical areas such as capital budgeting and risk and return. Author-created videos walk students through guided problem solutions for every in-text example.

Financial Calculator

The **Financial Calculator** is available as a smartphone application, as well as on a computer, and includes important functions such as cash flow, net present value, and internal rate of return. Fifteen helpful tutorial videos show the many ways to use the Financial Calculator in MyFinanceLab.

Interactive Figures

Select in-text graphs and figures have been digitally enhanced to allow students to interact with variables to affect outcomes and bring concepts to life.

Solutions Manual

The **Solutions Manual** provides students with detailed, accuracy-verified solutions to the problems in the book. The solutions, like the problems, were written by the authors themselves. Spreadsheet solutions in Excel, which allow the student to see the effect of changes in the input variables on the outcome, are also available to instructors for designated problems at the Instructor Resource Center (www.pearsonhighered.com/irc).

PowerPoint Presentations

The **PowerPoint Presentation**, authored by William Chittenden of Texas State University, is available in lecture form and includes art and tables from the book and additional examples. The PowerPoint presentation includes all tables and figures, examples, key terms, and spreadsheet tables from the textbook. All PowerPoint presentations are also available for download from the Instructor Resource Center at www.pearsonhighered.com/irc.

Test Bank

The **Test Bank** provides a wealth of accuracy-verified, algorithmic testing material. Each chapter offers a wide variety of true/false, short answer, and multiple-choice questions updated by Brian Nethercutt. Questions are verified by difficulty level and skill type, and correlated to the chapter topics. Numerical problems include step-by-step solutions and have been made algorithmic so they can be assigned for repeated practice.

TestGen

TestGen is a computerized test generation program, available exclusively from Pearson, that allows instructors to easily create and administer tests on paper, electronically, or online. Instructors can select test items from the publisher-supplied test bank, which is organized by chapter and based on the associated textbook material, or create their own questions from scratch. With both quick-and-simple test creation and flexible and robust editing tools, TestGen is a complete test generator system for today's educators.

Instructor's Manual

The **Instructor's Manual** was written by Mary R. Brown of the University of Illinois–Chicago, and contains annotated chapter outlines, lecture launchers, and questions for further class discussion. It also contains the solutions to the Data Cases and part-ending case problems, as well as answers to the end-of-chapter Critical Thinking questions in the book. As an additional resource to guide instructors with students who are planning to take the CFA exam, CFA learning outcomes met in each chapter are listed. A section also details how the end-of-chapter problems map to the accreditation standards set by the Association to Advance Collegiate Schools of Business (AACSB), so that instructors can track students' mastery of the AACSB standards. The Instructor's Manual is available for download as Microsoft Word files or as Adobe® PDF files from the Instructor Resource Center at www.pearsonhighered.com/irc.

Acknowledgments

Given the scope of this project, identifying the many people who made it happen is a tall order. This textbook was the product of the expertise and hard work of many talented colleagues. We are especially gratified with the work of those who developed the array of print supplements that accompany the book: William Chittenden for the PowerPoint presentations; Mary R. Brown, for the Instructor's Manual; James Linck, for serving as advisor for the videos; and our MyFinanceLab content development team, including Melissa Honig, Miguel Leonarte, Noel Lotz, and Sarah Peterson. We're also deeply appreciative of Susan White's contributions to the part-ending cases.

Creating a truly error-free text is a challenge we could not have lived up to without our team of expert error checkers. Jared Stanfield subjected the text and problem solutions to his exacting standards. We are also indebted to Jared for his adept research support throughout the writing process and Michael Wittry's assistance in providing updates.

At Pearson Education, we would like to single out Donna Battista, for her continued leadership and market insight; Kate Fernandes for her energy and fresh perspective as our new editor; Melissa Honig for her digital media expertise; and our production team, Meredith Gertz and especially Gillian Hall, for expertly managing the transformation of our files into a beautiful bound book. They were helped by Kalpana Arumugam at Spi Global, whose team provided the fantastic composition and artwork. We are truly thankful for the indispensable help provided by these and other professionals.

We are indebted to our colleagues for the time and expertise invested as manuscript reviewers, class testers, and focus group participants. We list all of these contributors on the following pages, but want to single out one group, our First Edition editorial board, for special notice: Tom Berry, *DePaul University*; Elizabeth Booth, *Michigan State University*; Julie Dahlquist, the *University of Texas–San Antonio*; Michaël Dewally, *Marquette University*; Robert M. Donchez, the *University of Colorado–Boulder*; Belinda Mucklow, the *University of Wisconsin–Madison*; Coleen Pantalone, *Northeastern University*; and Susan White, the *University of Maryland*. We strived to incorporate every contributor's input and are truly grateful for each comment and suggestion. The book has benefited enormously from this input.

Reviewers

Pankaj Agrrawal, *University of Maine*

Daniel Ahern, *California State University–Chico*

Paul Asabere, *Temple University*

Ajeyo Banerjee, *University of Colorado–Denver*

Tom Berry, *DePaul University*

Karan Bhanot, *University of Texas–San Antonio*

Rafiqul Bhuyan, *California State University–San Bernardino*

Eugene Bland, *Texas A&M University–Corpus Christi*

Matej Blasko, *University of Georgia*

Elizabeth Booth, *Michigan State University*

Mary Brown, *University of Illinois–Chicago*

Bill Brunsen, *Eastern New Mexico University*

David G. Cazier, *Brigham Young University–Provo*

Leo Chan, *Delaware State University*

Cindy Chen, *California State University–Long Beach*

Haiyu Chen, *Youngstown State University*

James F. Cotter, *Wake Forest University*

Vicentiu Covrig, *California State University–Northridge*

Julie Dahlquist, *University of Texas–San Antonio*

Pieter de Jong, *University of Texas–Arlington*

Andrea L. DeMaskey, *Villanova University*

Xiaohui Deng, *California State University–Fresno*

Michaël Dewally, *Marquette University*

Robert M. Donchez, *University of Colorado Boulder*

Gang Dong, *Rutgers University*

Dean Drenk, *Montana State University*

Robert Dubil, *University of Utah*

Hsing Fang, *California State University–Los Angeles*

David O. Fricke, *University of North Carolina–Pembroke*

Scott Fung, *California State University–East Bay*

Sharon Garrison, *University of Arizona*

Rakesh Gupta, *Central Queensland University*

Joseph D. Haley, *St. Cloud State University*

Thomas Hall, *Christopher Newport University*

Karen Hallows, *University of Maryland*

Karen L. Hamilton, *Georgia Southern University*

Robert Hanson, *Eastern Michigan University*

Mahfuzul Haque, *Indiana State University*

Edward C. Howell, *Northwood University*

Ping Hsiao, *San Francisco State University*

Xiaoqing Hu, *University of Illinois at Chicago*

Pankaj Jain, *University of Memphis*

Robert James, *Boston College*

Susan Ji, *Baruch College, City University of New York*

Domingo Joaquin, *Illinois State University*

Fred R. Kaen, *University of New Hampshire*

Terrill Keasler, *Appalachian State University*

Howard Keen, *Temple University*

Brett A. King, *University of North Alabama*

Daniel Klein, *Bowling Green State University*

Gregory Kuhlemeyer, *Carroll University*

Rose Neng Lai, *University of Macau*

Keith Lam, *University of Macau*

Reinhold P. Lamb, *University of North Florida*

Douglas Lamdin, *University of Maryland–Baltimore County*

Mark J. Laplante, *University of Georgia*

Sie Ting Lau, *Nanyang Technological University*

Richard LeCompte, *Wichita State University*

Adam Y.C. Lei, *Midwestern State University*

Qian Li, *Midwestern State University*

Chang Liu, *Washington State University*

Wei Liu, *Texas A&M University*

Hugh Marble III, *University of Vermont*

James Milanese, *University of North Carolina at Greensboro*

Sunil K. Mohanty, *University of St. Thomas*

Ted Moorman, *Northern Illinois University*

James Morris, *University of Colorado–Denver*

Belinda Mucklow, *University of Wisconsin–Madison*

Rick Nelson, *University of Minnesota*

Tom C. Nelson, *University of Colorado–Boulder*

Curtis Nicholls, *Bucknell University*

Anthony C. Ng, *Hong Kong Polytechnic University*

Coleen Pantalone, *Northeastern University*

Daniel Park, *Azusa Pacific University*

Janet Payne, *Texas State University*

Jay Peroni, *College of Charleston*

Lynn Pi, *Hong Kong University of Science and Technology*

J. Michael Pinegar, *Brigham Young University*

Annette Poulsen, *University of Georgia*

Eric Powers, *University of South Carolina*

Rose M. Prasad, *Central Michigan University*

Shoba Premkumar, *Iowa State University*

Mark K. Pyles, *College of Charleston*

A.A.B. Resing, *Hogeschool Van Amsterdam*

Greg Richey, *California State University, San Bernardino*

Scott Roark, *Boise State University*

David L. Robbins, *University of New Mexico*

Andrew Samwick, *Dartmouth College*

Salil K. Sarkar, *University of Texas–Arlington*

Oliver Schnusenberg, *University of North Florida*

Kenneth Scislaw, *University of Alabama–Huntsville*

Roger Severns, *Minnesota State University–Mankato*

Tatyana Sokolyk, *University of Wyoming*

Andrew C. Spieler, *Hofstra University*

Timothy G. Sullivan, *Bentley College*

Janikan Supanvanij, *St. Cloud State University*

Hugo Tang, *Purdue University*

Oranee Tawatnuntachai, *Pennsylvania State University–Harrisburg*

Robert Terpstra, *University of Macau*

Thomas Thomson, *University of Texas–San Antonio*
Olaf J. Thorp, *Babson College*
Ed Tiryakian, *Duke University*
Emery Trahan, *Northeastern University*
Joe Ueng, *University of St. Thomas*
Mo Vaziri, *California State University–San Bernardino*
Premal P. Vora, *Pennsylvania State University– Harrisburg*
Hefei Wang, *University of Illinois–Chicago*
Gwendolyn Webb, *Baruch College*
Paul M. Weinstock, *Ohio State University*
Susan White, *University of Maryland*
Annie Wong, *Western Connecticut State University*
Xiaoyan Xu, *San Jose State University*
Zhong-gou Zhou, *California State University–Northridge*
Kermit C. Zieg, Jr., *Florida Institute of Technology*

Focus Group Participants

Anne-Marie Anderson, *Lehigh University*
Sung Bae, *Bowling Green State University*
H. Kent Baker, *American University*
Steven Beach, *Radford University*
Rafiqul Bhuyan, *California State University–San Bernardino*
Deanne Butchey, *Florida International University*
Leo Chan, *Delaware State University*
George Chang, *Grand Valley State University*
Haiwei Chen, *California State University–San Bernardino*
Haiyu Chen, *Youngstown State University*
Massimiliano De Santis, *Dartmouth College*
Jocelyn Evans, *College of Charleston*
Kathleen Fuller, *University of Mississippi*
Xavier Garza Gomez, *University of Houston–Victoria*
William Gentry, *Williams College*
Axel Grossmann, *Radford University*
Pankaj Jain, *University of Memphis*
Zhenhu Jin, *Valparaiso University*
Steve Johnson, *University of Northern Iowa*
Steven Jones, *Samford University*
Yong-Cheol Kim, *University of Wisconsin–Milwaukee*
Robert Kiss, *Eastern Michigan University*
Ann Marie Klingenhagen, *DePaul University*
Thomas J. Krissek, *Northeastern Illinois University*
Olivier Maisondieu Laforge, *University of Nebraska–Omaha*
Douglas Lamdin, *University of Maryland–Baltimore County*
D. Scott Lee, *Texas A&M University*
Stanley A. Martin, *University of Colorado–Boulder*

Jamshid Mehran, *Indiana University, South Bend*
Sunil Mohanty, *University of St. Thomas*
Karyn L. Neuhauser, *State University of New York–Plattsburgh*
Thomas O'Brien, *University of Connecticut*
Hyuna Park, *Minnesota State University–Mankato*
G. Michael Phillips, *California State University–Northridge*
Wendy Pirie, *Valparaiso University*
Antonio Rodriguez, *Texas A&M International University*
Camelia S. Rotaru, *St. Edward's University*
Salil Sarkar, *University of Texas at Arlington*
Mark Sunderman, *University of Wyoming*
Chu-Sheng Tai, *Texas Southern University*
Oranee Tawatnuntachai, *Pennsylvania State University–Harrisburg*
Benedict Udemgba, *Alcorn State University*
Rahul Verma, *University of Houston–Downtown*
Angelo P. Vignola, *Loyola University–Chicago*
Premal Vora, *Pennsylvania State University–Harrisburg*
Eric Wehrly, *Seattle University*
Yan A. Xie, *University of Michigan–Dearborn*
Fang Zhao, *Siena College*
Sophie Zong, *California State University–Stanislaus*

Class Testers

Tom Berry, *DePaul University*
Eugene Bland, *Texas A&M University–Corpus Christi*
Charles Blaylock, *Murray State University*
Mary Brown, *University of Illinois–Chicago*
Bill Brunsen, *Eastern New Mexico University*
Sarah Bryant Bower, *Shippensburg University of Pennsylvania*
Alva Wright Butcher, *University of Puget Sound*
David G. Cazier, *Brigham Young University–Provo*
Asim G. Celik, *University of Nevada–Reno*
Michaël Dewally, *Marquette University*
Richard Gaddis, *Oklahoma Wesleyan University*
TeWhan Hahn, *Auburn University–Montgomery*
Matthew Hood, *University of Southern Mississippi*
Zhenhu Jin, *Valparaiso University*
Travis Jones, *Florida Gulf Coast University*
Francis E. Laatsch, *Bowling Green State University*
Diane Lander, *Saint Michael's College*
Vance Lesseig, *Texas State University*
Frances Maloy, *University of Washington*
Jamshid Mehran, *Indiana University–South Bend*
Belinda Mucklow, *University of Wisconsin–Madison*
Kuo-Chung Tseng, *California State University–Fresno*
Kermit C. Zieg, Jr., *Florida Institute of Technology*

Introduction

Valuation Principle Connection. What is *corporate finance*? No matter what your role in a corporation, an understanding of why and how financial decisions are made is essential. The focus of this book is how to make optimal corporate financial decisions. In Part 1, we lay the foundation for our study of corporate finance. In Chapter 1, we begin by introducing the corporation and related business forms. We then examine the role of financial managers and outside investors in decision making for the firm. To make optimal decisions, a decision maker needs information. As a result, in Chapter 2, we review and analyze an important source of information for corporate decision making—the firm's accounting statements. These chapters will introduce us to the role and objective of the financial manager and some of the information the financial manager uses in applying the Valuation Principle to make optimal decisions. Then, in Part 2, we will introduce and begin applying the Valuation Principle.

Chapter 1
Corporate Finance
and the Financial Manager

Chapter 2
Introduction to Financial
Statement Analysis

1

Corporate Finance and the Financial Manager

LEARNING OBJECTIVES

- Grasp the importance of financial information in both your personal and business lives

- Understand the important features of the four main types of firms and see why the advantages of the corporate form have led it to dominate economic activity

- Explain the goal of the financial manager and the reasoning behind that goal, as well as understand the three main types of decisions a financial manager makes

- Know how a corporation is managed and controlled, the financial manager's place in it, and some of the ethical issues financial managers face

- Understand the importance of financial markets, such as stock markets, to a corporation and the financial manager's role as liaison to those markets

- Recognize the role that financial institutions play in the financial cycle of the economy

This book focuses on how people in corporations make financial decisions. Despite its name, much of what we discuss in corporate finance applies to the financial decisions made within any organization, including not-for-profit entities such as charities and universities. In this chapter, we introduce the four main types of firms. We stress corporations, however, because they represent 85% of U.S. business revenue. We also highlight the financial manager's critical role inside any business enterprise. What products to launch, how to pay to develop those products, what profits to keep and how to return profits to investors—all of these decisions and many more fall within corporate finance. The financial manager makes these decisions with the goal of maximizing the value of the business, which is determined in the financial markets. In this chapter and throughout the book, we will focus on this goal, provide you with the tools to make financial management decisions, and show you how the financial markets provide funds to a corporation and produce market prices that are key inputs to any financial manager's investment analysis.

1.1 Why Study Finance?

Finance and financial thinking are everywhere in our daily lives. Consider your decision to go to college. You surely weighed alternatives, such as starting a full-time job immediately, and then decided that college provided you with the greatest net benefit. More and more, individuals are taking charge of their personal finances with decisions such as:

- When to start saving and how much to save for retirement.
- Whether a car loan or lease is more advantageous.
- Whether a particular stock is a good investment.
- How to evaluate the terms of a home mortgage.

Our career paths have become less predictable and more dynamic. In previous generations, it was common to work for one employer your entire career. Today, that would be highly unusual. Most of us will instead change jobs, and possibly even careers, many times. With each new opportunity, we must weigh all the costs and benefits, financial and otherwise.

Some financial decisions, such as whether to pay $2.00 for your morning coffee, are simple, but most are more complex. In your business career, you may face questions such as:

- Should your firm launch a new product?
- Which supplier should your firm choose?
- Should your firm produce a part of the product or outsource production?
- Should your firm issue new stock or borrow money instead?
- How can you raise money for your start-up firm?

In this book, you will learn how all of these decisions in your personal life and inside a business are tied together by one powerful concept, the *Valuation Principle*. The Valuation Principle shows how to make the costs and benefits of a decision comparable so that we can weigh them properly. Learning to apply the Valuation Principle will give you the skills to make the types of comparisons—among loan options, investments, and projects—that will turn you into a knowledgeable, confident financial consumer and manager.

From 2007 to 2009 we witnessed a credit freeze, a severe stock market decline, and the failures of well-known financial institutions. Attempts to understand these elements of the crisis, their origins, and how they affect our businesses and personal finances have highlighted the need for learning core financial principles and concepts.

Whether you plan to major in finance or simply take this one course, you will find the fundamental financial knowledge gained here to be essential in your personal and business lives.

1.2 The Four Types of Firms

We begin our study of corporate finance by examining the types of firms that financial managers run. As shown in Figure 1.1, There are four major types of firms: sole proprietorships, partnerships, limited liability companies, and corporations. We explain each organizational form in turn, but our primary focus is on the most important form—the corporation.

Sole Proprietorships

sole proprietorship A
business owned and run
by one person.

A **sole proprietorship** is a business owned and run by one person. Sole proprietorships are usually very small with few, if any, employees. Although they do not account for much sales revenue in the economy, they are the most common type of firm in the world. In 2012, an estimated 72% of businesses in the United States were sole proprietorships, although they generated only 3% of the revenue.[1]

We now consider the key features of a sole proprietorship.

1. Sole proprietorships have the advantage of being straightforward to set up. Consequently, many new businesses use this organizational form.

2. The principal limitation of a sole proprietorship is that there is no separation between the firm and the owner—the firm can have only one owner who runs the business. If there are other investors, they cannot hold an ownership stake in the firm.

3. The owner has unlimited personal liability for the firm's debts. That is, if the firm defaults on any debt payment, the lender can (and will) require the owner to repay the loan from personal assets. An owner who cannot afford to repay a loan for which he or she is personally liable must declare personal bankruptcy.

4. The life of a sole proprietorship is limited to the life of the owner. It is also difficult to transfer ownership of a sole proprietorship.

For most growing businesses, the disadvantages of a sole proprietorship outweigh the advantages. As soon as the firm reaches the point at which it can borrow without the owner agreeing to be personally liable, the owners typically convert the business into another form. Conversion also has other benefits that we will consider as we discuss the other forms below.

FIGURE 1.1

Types of U.S. Firms

There are four major types of firms in the United States. As (a) and (b) show, although the majority of U.S. firms are sole proprietorships, they generate only a small fraction of total revenue, in contrast to corporations.

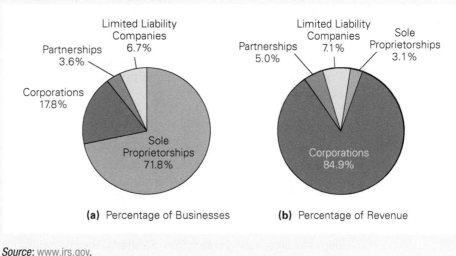

(a) Percentage of Businesses   (b) Percentage of Revenue

Source: www.irs.gov.

---

[1]U.S. Census Bureau National Data Book.

Partnerships

A **partnership** is a business owned and run by more than one owner. Key features include the following:

1. *All* partners are liable for the firm's debt. That is, a lender can require *any* partner to repay all the firm's outstanding debts.
2. The partnership ends in the event of the death or withdrawal of any single partner.
3. Partners can avoid liquidation if the partnership agreement provides for alternatives such as a buyout of a deceased or withdrawn partner.

Some old and established businesses remain as partnerships or sole proprietorships. Often these firms are the types of businesses in which the owners' personal reputations are the basis for the businesses. For example, law firms, medical practices, and accounting firms are frequently organized as partnerships. For such enterprises, the partners' personal liability increases the confidence of the firm's clients that the partners will strive to maintain the firm's reputation.

A **limited partnership** is a partnership with two kinds of owners: general partners and limited partners. In this case, the general partners have the same rights and privileges as partners in any general partnership—they are personally liable for the firm's debt obligations. Limited partners, however, have **limited liability**—that is, their liability is limited to their investment. Their private property cannot be seized to pay off the firm's outstanding debts. Furthermore, the death or withdrawal of a limited partner does not dissolve the partnership, and a limited partner's interest is transferable. However, a limited partner has no management authority and cannot legally be involved in the managerial decision making for the business.

Limited Liability Companies

A **limited liability company (LLC)** is like a limited partnership but without a general partner. That is, all the owners (referred to as *members*) have limited liability, but unlike limited partners, they can also run the business (as managing members). The LLC is a relatively new entity in the United States. The first state to pass a statute allowing the creation of an LLC was Wyoming in 1977; the last was Hawaii in 1997. Internationally, companies with limited liability are much older and established. LLCs first rose to prominence in Germany over 100 years ago as a *Gesellschaft mit beschränkter Haftung* (GmbH) and then in other European and Latin American countries. An LLC is known in France as a Société à responsabilité limitée (SAR), and by similar names in Italy (SRL) and Spain (SL).

Corporations

A **corporation** is a legally defined, artificial being (a legal entity), separate from its owners. As such, it has many of the legal powers that people have. It can enter into contracts, acquire assets, and incur obligations, and it enjoys protection under the U.S. Constitution against the seizure of its property. Because a corporation is a legal entity separate and distinct from its owners, it is solely responsible for its own obligations. Consequently, the owners of a corporation (or its employees, customers, etc.) are not liable for any obligations the corporation enters into. Similarly, the corporation is not liable for any personal obligations of its owners.

In the same way that it is difficult to imagine modern business life without e-mail and cell phones, the corporation revolutionized the economy. On February 2, 1819, the U.S. Supreme Court established the legal precedent that the property of a corporation, similar to that of a person, is private and entitled to protection under the U.S. Constitution.[2] This decision led to dramatic growth in the number of U.S. corporations from fewer than 1000 in 1830 to 50,000 in 1890. Today, the corporate structure is ubiquitous, not only in the United States (where it is responsible for 85% of business revenue), but all over the world.

Formation of a Corporation. A corporation must be legally formed, which means that the state in which it is incorporated must formally give its consent to the incorporation by chartering it. Setting up a corporation is therefore considerably more costly than setting up a sole proprietorship. The state of Delaware has a particularly attractive legal environment for corporations, so many corporations choose to incorporate there. For jurisdictional purposes, a corporation is a citizen of the state in which it is incorporated. Most firms hire lawyers to create a corporate charter that includes formal articles of incorporation and a set of bylaws. The corporate charter specifies the initial rules that govern how the corporation is run.

stock The ownership or equity of a corporation divided into shares.

equity The collection of all the outstanding shares of a corporation.

shareholder (also stockholder or equity holder) An owner of a share of stock or equity in a corporation.

dividend payments Payments made at the discretion of the corporation to its equity holders.

Ownership of a Corporation. There is no limit to the number of owners a corporation can have. Because most corporations have many owners, each owner owns only a fraction of the corporation. The entire ownership stake of a corporation is divided into shares known as **stock**. The collection of all the outstanding shares of a corporation is known as the **equity** of the corporation. An owner of a share of stock in the corporation is known as a **shareholder, stockholder, or equity holder**. Shareholders are entitled to **dividend payments**; that is, payments made at the discretion of the corporation to its equity holders. Shareholders usually receive a share of the dividend payments that is proportional to the amount of stock they own. For example, a shareholder who owns 25% of the firm's shares would be entitled to 25% of the total dividend payment.

An important feature of a corporation is that there is no limitation on who can own its stock. That is, an owner of a corporation need not have any special expertise or qualification. This feature allows free and anonymous trade in the shares of the corporation and provides one of the most important advantages of organizing a firm as a corporation. Corporations can raise substantial amounts of capital because they can sell ownership shares to anonymous outside investors.

The availability of outside funding has enabled corporations to dominate the economy. Let's look at one of the world's largest firms, Microsoft Corporation, as an example. Microsoft reported annual revenue of $93.6 billion over the 12 months from July 2014 through June 2015. The total value of the company (the owners' collective wealth in the company) as of June 2015 was $354 billion. The company employed 118,000 people. Putting these numbers into perspective, treating the sales of $93.6 billion as gross domestic product (GDP) in 2014 would rank Microsoft (just behind Slovak Republic) as the 62nd richest *country* (out of almost 200).[3] The Slovak Republic has almost 5.4 million people, about 45 times as many people as employees at Microsoft. Indeed, if the number of Microsoft employees were used as the "population" of the corporation, Microsoft would rank just above Curacao as the 28th least populous country on Earth!

---

[2]The case was Dartmouth v. Woodward and the full text of John Marshall's decision can be found at www.constitution.org/dwebster/dartmouth_decision.htm.

[3]World Development Indicators database, April 11, 2016. For quick reference tables on GDP, go to http://data.worldbank.org/indicator/NY.GDP.MKTP.CD.

Tax Implications for Corporate Entities

An important difference among the types of corporate organizational forms is the way they are taxed. Because a corporation is a separate legal entity, a corporation's profits are subject to taxation separate from its owners' tax obligations. In effect, shareholders of a corporation pay taxes twice. First, the corporation pays tax on its profits, and then when the remaining profits are distributed to the shareholders, the shareholders pay their own personal income tax on this income. This system is sometimes referred to as *double taxation*.

EXAMPLE 1.1

Taxation of
Corporate Earnings

MyFinanceLab

PROBLEM

You are a shareholder in a corporation. The corporation earns $5.00 per share before taxes. After it has paid taxes, it will distribute the rest of its earnings to you as a dividend (we make this simplifying assumption, but should note that most corporations retain some of their earnings for reinvestment). The dividend is income to you, so you will then pay taxes on these earnings. The corporate tax rate is 40% and your tax rate on dividend income is 15%. How much of the earnings remains after all taxes are paid?

SOLUTION

PLAN

Earnings before taxes: $5.00   Corporate tax rate: 40%   Personal dividend tax rate: 15%

To calculate the corporation's earnings after taxes, first we subtract the taxes paid at the corporate level from the pretax earnings of $5.00. The taxes paid will be 40% (the corporate tax rate) of $5.00. Since all of the after-corporate tax earnings will be paid to you as a dividend, you will pay taxes of 15% on that amount. The amount leftover is what remains after all taxes are paid.

EXECUTE

$5.00 per share $\times$ 0.40 = $2.00 in taxes at the corporate level, leaving $5.00 $-$ $2.00 = $3.00 in after-corporate tax earnings per share to distribute.

You will pay $3.00 $\times$ $2.00 = $0.45 in taxes on that dividend, leaving you with $2.55 from the original $5.00 after all taxes.

EVALUATE

As a shareholder, you keep $2.55 of the original $5.00 in earnings; the remaining $2.00 + $0.45 = $2.45 is paid as taxes. Thus, your total effective tax rate is 2.45/5 = 49%.

S corporations Those corporations that elect subchapter S tax treatment and are exempted by the U.S. Internal Revenue Service's tax code from double taxation.

S Corporations. The corporate organizational structure is the only organizational structure subject to double taxation. However, the U.S. Internal Revenue Code exempts **S corporations** from double taxation because they elect subchapter S tax treatment. Under subchapter S tax regulations, the firm's profits (and losses) are not subject to corporate taxes, but instead are allocated directly to shareholders based on their ownership share. The shareholders must include these profits as income on their individual tax returns (even if no money is distributed to them). However, after the shareholders have paid income taxes on these profits, no further tax is due.

Corporate Taxation Around the World

Most countries offer investors in corporations some relief from double taxation. Thirty countries make up the Organization for Economic Co-operation and Development (OECD), and of these countries, only Ireland offers no relief whatsoever. A few countries, including Australia, Finland, Mexico, New Zealand, and Norway, offer complete relief by effectively not taxing dividend income. The United States offers partial relief by having a lower tax rate on dividend income than on other sources of income. As of 2016, qualified dividends are taxed at 15% or 20%, depending on the investor's tax bracket, rates significantly below their personal income tax rate.

EXAMPLE 1.2

Taxation of S
Corporation Earnings

MyFinanceLab

PROBLEM

Rework Example 1.1, assuming the corporation in that example has elected subchapter S tax treatment and your tax rate on non-dividend income is 30%.

SOLUTION

PLAN

Earnings before taxes: $5.00   Corporate tax rate: 0%   Personal tax rate: 30%

In this case, the corporation pays no taxes. It earned $5.00 per share. In an S corporation, all income is treated as personal income to you, whether or not the corporation chooses to distribute or retain this cash. As a result, you must pay a 30% tax rate on those earnings.

EXECUTE

Your income taxes are $0.30 \times \$5.00 = \$1.50$, leaving you with $\$5.00 - \$1.50 = \$3.50$ in after-tax earnings.

EVALUATE

The $1.50 in taxes that you pay is substantially lower than the $2.45 you paid in Example 1.1. As a result, you are left with $3.50 per share after all taxes instead of $2.55. However, note that in a C corporation, you are only taxed when you receive the income as a dividend, whereas in an S corporation, you pay taxes on the income immediately regardless of whether the corporation distributes it as a dividend or reinvests it in the company.

C corporations
Corporations that have no restrictions on who owns their shares or the number of shareholders; they cannot qualify for subchapter S tax treatment and are subject to direct taxation.

C Corporations. The government places strict limitations on the qualifications for subchapter S tax treatment. In particular, the shareholders of such corporations must be individuals who are U.S. citizens or residents, and there can be no more than 100 of them. Because most corporations have no restrictions on who owns their shares or the number of shareholders, they cannot qualify for subchapter S tax treatment. Thus, most corporations are **C corporations**, which are corporations subject to corporate taxes.

As we have discussed, there are four main types of firms: sole proprietorships, partnerships (general and limited), limited liability companies, and corporations ("S" and "C"). To help you see the differences among them, Table 1.1 compares and contrasts the main characteristics of each.

TABLE 1.1

Characteristics of the
Different Types of Firms

	Number of Owners	Liability for Firm's Debts	Owners Manage the Firm	Ownership Change Dissolves Firm	Taxation
Sole Proprietorship	One	Yes	Yes	Yes	Personal
Partnership	Unlimited	Yes; each partner is liable for the entire amount	Yes	Yes	Personal
Limited Partnership	At least one general partner (GP), no limit on limited partners (LP)	GP-Yes LP-No	GP-Yes LP-No	GP-Yes LP-No	Personal
Limited Liability Company	Unlimited	No	Yes	No*	Personal
S Corporation	At most 100	No	No (but they legally may)	No	Personal
C Corporation	Unlimited	No	No (but they legally may)	No	Double

*However, most LLCs require the approval of the other members to transfer your ownership.

1. What is a limited liability company (LLC)? How does it differ from a limited partnership?
2. What are the advantages and disadvantages of organizing a business as a corporation?

1.3 The Financial Manager

As of December 2015, Apple, Inc. had over 5.5 *billion* shares of stock held by 26,000 owners.[4] Because there are many owners of a corporation, each of whom can freely trade their stock, it is often not feasible for the owners of a corporation to have direct control of the firm. It falls to the financial manager to make the financial decisions of the business for the stockholders. Within the corporation, the financial manager has three main tasks:

1. Make investment decisions.
2. Make financing decisions.
3. Manage short-term cash needs.

We will discuss each of these in turn, along with the financial manager's overarching goal.

Making Investment Decisions

The financial manager's most important job is to make the firm's investment decisions. The financial manager must weigh the costs and benefits of each investment or project and decide which ones qualify as good uses of the money stockholders have invested in the firm. These investment decisions fundamentally shape what the firm does and whether it will add value for its owners. For example, it may seem hard to imagine now, but there was a time when Apple's financial managers were evaluating whether to invest in the development of the first iPhone. They had to weigh the substantial development and production costs against uncertain future sales. Their analysis indicated that it was a good investment, and the rest is history. In this book, you will learn all the tools necessary to make these investment decisions.

GLOBAL FINANCIAL CRISIS

The Dodd-Frank Act

In response to the 2008 financial crisis, the U.S. federal government reevaluated its role in the control and management of financial institutions and private corporations. Signed into law on July 21, 2010, the **Dodd-Frank Wall Street Reform and Consumer Protection Act** brought a sweeping change to financial regulation in response to widespread calls for financial regulatory system reform after the near collapse of the world's financial system in the fall of 2008 and the ensuing global credit crisis. History indeed repeats itself: It was in the wake of the 1929 stock market crash and subsequent Great Depression that Congress passed the Glass-Steagall Act establishing the Federal Deposit Insurance Corporation (FDIC) and instituted significant bank reforms to regulate transactions between commercial banks and securities firms.

The Dodd-Frank Act aims to (1) promote U.S. financial stability by "improving accountability and transparency in the financial system," (2) put an end to the notion of "too big to fail," (3) "protect the American taxpayer by ending bailouts," and (4) "protect consumers from abusive financial services practices." Time will tell whether the Act will actually achieve these important goals.

Implementing the wide-ranging financial reforms in the Dodd-Frank Act requires the work of many federal agencies, either through rulemaking or other regulatory actions. As of mid-2015, five years since Dodd-Frank's passage, 247 of the reforms have been finalized, providing a clear picture of the Dodd-Frank regulatory framework. But another 143 rules or actions await completion. While only two-thirds of the rules have been finalized, many of the core reforms have been or are nearing completion. For instance, the Volcker Rule, which bars banks that take government-insured deposits from making speculative investments, took full effect in late July of 2015.

---

[4]Apple, Inc., Notice of 2016 Annual Meeting of Shareholders, December 28, 2015.

Making Financing Decisions

Once the financial manager has decided which investments to make, he or she also decides how to pay for them. Large investments may require the corporation to raise additional money. The financial manager must decide whether to raise more money from new and existing owners by selling more shares of stock (equity) or to borrow the money instead (bonds and other debt). A bond is a security sold by governments and corporations to raise money from investors today in exchange for a promised future payment. It can be viewed as a loan from those investors to the issuer. In this book, we will discuss the characteristics of each source of money and how to decide which one to use in the context of the corporation's overall mix of debt and equity.

Managing Short-Term Cash Needs

The financial manager must ensure that the firm has enough cash on hand to meet its obligations from day to day. This job, also commonly known as *managing working capital*,[5] may seem straightforward, but in a young or growing company, it can mean the difference between success and failure. Even companies with great products require a lot of money to develop and bring those products to market. Consider the costs to Starbucks of launching their VIA instant coffee, which included developing the instant coffee crystals and creating a big marketing campaign for them, or the costs to Boeing of producing the 787—billions of dollars were spent before the first 787 finally left the ground in December 2009. A company typically burns through a significant amount of cash before the sales of the product generate income. The financial manager's job is to make sure that limited access to cash does not hinder the firm's success.

The Goal of the Financial Manager

All of these decisions by the financial manager are made within the context of the over-riding goal of financial management—*to maximize the wealth of the owners, the stockholders*. The stockholders have invested in the corporation, putting their money at risk to become the owners of the corporation. Thus, the financial manager is a caretaker of the stockholders' money, making decisions in their interests. Many corporations have thousands of owners (shareholders). These shareholders vary from large institutions to small first-time investors, from retirees living off their investments to young employees just

starting to save for retirement. Each owner is likely to have different interests and priorities. Whose interests and priorities determine the goals of the firm? You might be surprised to learn that the interests of shareholders are aligned for many, if not most, important decisions. Regardless of their own personal financial position and stage in life, all the shareholders will agree that they are better off if the value of their investment in the corporation is maximized. For example, suppose the decision concerns whether to develop a new product that will be a profitable investment for the corporation. All shareholders will very likely agree that developing this product is a good idea. Returning to our iPhone example, by October 2010, Apple shares were worth three times as much as they were in January 2007, when the first iPhone was introduced. All Apple shareholders at the time of the development of

---

[5]*Working capital* refers to things such as cash on hand, inventories, raw materials, loans to suppliers, and payments from customers—the grease that keeps the wheels of production moving. We will discuss working capital in more detail in Chapter 2 and devote all of Chapter 19 to working capital management.

the first iPhone are clearly much better off because of it, whether they have since sold their shares of Apple to pay for retirement, or are still holding those shares in their retirement savings account.

Even when all the owners of a corporation agree on the goals of the corporation, these goals must be implemented. In the next section, we will discuss the financial manager's place in the corporation and how owners exert control over the corporation.

Shareholder Value Versus Stakeholder Value

While the goal of a financial manager is to increase the value of the firm to its shareholders, this responsibility does not imply that the impact of the firm's decisions on other stakeholders, such as employees or customers, can be ignored. By creating additional value for customers, the firm can raise prices and increase profits.

Similarly, if the firm makes decisions that benefit employees (for example, increasing their job security), it will be able to offer lower wages or benefit from increased productivity. On the other hand, if customers or employees anticipate that the firm is likely to exploit them, they will demand lower prices or higher wages. Thus, to maximize shareholder value, the financial manager must consider the impact of her decision on all stakeholders of the firm.

CONCEPT CHECK

3. What are the main types of decisions that a financial manager makes?

4. What is the goal of the financial manager?

1.4 The Financial Manager's Place in the Corporation

We've established that the stockholders own the corporation but rely on financial managers to actively manage the corporation. The *board of directors* and the management team headed by the *chief executive officer* possess direct control of the corporation. In this section, we explain how the responsibilities for the corporation are divided between these two entities and describe conflicts that arise between stockholders and the management team.

The Corporate Management Team

board of directors
A group of people elected by shareholders who have the ultimate decision-making authority in the corporation.

The shareholders of a corporation exercise their control by electing a **board of directors**, a group of people who have the ultimate decision-making authority in the corporation. In most corporations, each share of stock gives a shareholder one vote in the election of the board of directors, so investors with more shares have more influence. When one or two shareholders own a very large proportion of the outstanding stock, these shareholders might either be on the board of directors themselves, or they may have the right to appoint a number of directors.

chief executive officer (CEO) The person charged with running the corporation by instituting the rules and policies set by the board of directors.

The board of directors makes rules on how the corporation should be run (including how the top managers in the corporation are compensated), sets policy, and monitors the performance of the company. The board of directors delegates most decisions that involve the day-to-day running of the corporation to its management. The **chief executive officer (CEO)** is charged with running the corporation by instituting the rules and policies set by the board of directors. The size of the rest of the management team varies from corporation to corporation. In some corporations, the separation of powers between the board of directors and CEO is not always distinct. In fact, the CEO can also be the chairman of the board of directors. The most senior financial manager is the chief financial officer (CFO), often reporting directly to the CEO. Figure 1.2 presents part of a typical organizational chart for a corporation, highlighting the positions a financial manager may take.

FIGURE 1.2

The Financial
Functions Within a
Corporation

The board of directors, representing the stockholders, controls the corporation and hires the top management team. A financial manager might hold any of the green-shaded positions, including the Chief Financial Officer (CFO) role. The controller oversees accounting and tax functions. The treasurer oversees more traditional finance functions, such as capital budgeting (making investment decisions), risk management (managing the firm's exposure to movements in the financial markets), and credit management (managing the terms and policies of any credit the firm extends to its customers).

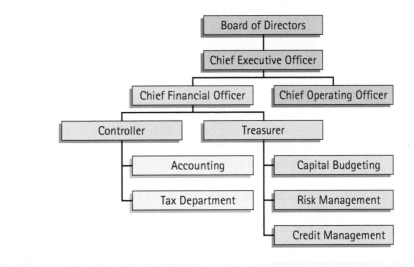

Ethics and Incentives in Corporations

A corporation is run by a management team, separate from its owners. How can the owners of a corporation ensure that the management team will implement their goals?

agency problem When managers, despite being hired as the agents of shareholders, put their self-interest ahead of the interests of those shareholders.

Agency Problems. Many people claim that because of the separation of ownership and control in a corporation, managers have little incentive to work in the interests of the shareholders when this means working against their self-interest. Economists call this an **agency problem**—when managers, despite being hired as the agents of shareholders, put their self-interest ahead of the interests of those shareholders. Managers face the ethical dilemma of whether to adhere to their responsibility to put the interests of shareholders first, or to do what is in their personal best interests. This problem is commonly addressed in practice by minimizing the number of decisions managers make that require putting their self-interest against the interests of the shareholders. For example, managers' compensation contracts are designed to ensure that most decisions in the shareholders' interest are also in the managers' interests; shareholders often tie the compensation of top managers to the corporation's profits or perhaps to its stock price. There is, however, a limitation to this strategy. By tying compensation too closely to performance, shareholders might be asking managers to take on more risk than they are comfortable taking. As a result, the managers may not make decisions that shareholders want them to, or it might be hard to find talented managers willing to accept the job. For example, biotech firms take big risks on drugs that fight cancer, AIDS, and other widespread diseases. The market for a successful drug is huge, but the risk of failure is high. Investors who put only some of their money in biotech may be comfortable with this risk, but managers who have all of their compensation tied to the success of such a drug might opt to develop a less risky drug that has a smaller market.

The Dodd-Frank Act on Corporate Compensation and Governance

Compensation is one of the most important conflicts of interest between corporate executives and shareholders. To limit senior corporate executives' influence over their own compensation and prevent excessive compensation, the Act directs the SEC to adopt new rules that:

- Mandate the independence of a firm's compensation committee and its advisers.
- Provide shareholders the opportunity to approve—in a nonbinding, advisory vote—the compensation of executive officers at least once every three years (referred to as a "Say-on-Pay" vote).
- Require firm disclosure and shareholder approval of large bonus payments (so-called "golden parachutes") to ousted senior executives as the result of a takeover.
- Require disclosure of the relationship of executive pay to the company's performance, as well as the ratio between the CEO's total compensation and that of the median employee.
- Create "clawback" provisions that allow firms to recoup compensation paid based on erroneous financial results.

Further potential for conflicts of interest and ethical considerations arise when some stakeholders in the corporation benefit and others lose from a decision. Shareholders and managers are two stakeholders in the corporation, but others include the regular employees and the communities in which the company operates, for example. Managers may decide to take the interests of other stakeholders into account in their decisions, such as keeping a loss-generating factory open because it is the main provider of jobs in a small town, paying above local market wages to factory workers in a developing country, or operating a plant at a higher environmental standard than local law mandates.

In some cases, these actions that benefit other stakeholders may also benefit the firm's shareholders by creating a more dedicated workforce, generating positive publicity with customers, or other indirect effects. In other instances, when these decisions benefit other stakeholders at shareholders' expense, they represent a form of corporate charity. Indeed, many if not most corporations explicitly donate (on behalf of their shareholders) to local and global causes. Shareholders often approve of such actions, even though they are costly and so reduce their wealth. While it is the manager's job to make decisions that maximize shareholder value, shareholders—who own the firm—also want the firm's actions to reflect their moral and ethical values. Of course, shareholders may not have identical preferences in these matters, leading to potential sources of conflict.

The CEO's Performance. Another way shareholders can encourage managers to work in the interests of shareholders is to discipline them if they do not. If shareholders are unhappy with a CEO's performance, they could, in principle, pressure the board to oust the CEO. Disney's Michael Eisner, Hewlett-Packard's Carly Fiorina, and Home Depot's Robert Nardelli were all forced to resign by their boards. Despite these high-profile examples, directors and top executives are rarely replaced through a grassroots shareholder uprising. Instead, dissatisfied investors often choose to sell their shares. Of course, somebody must be willing to buy the shares from the dissatisfied shareholders. If enough shareholders are dissatisfied, the only way to entice investors to buy (or hold) the shares is to offer them a low price. Similarly, investors who see a well-managed corporation, will want to purchase shares, which drives the stock price up. Thus, the stock price of the corporation

Citizens United v. Federal Election Commission

On January 21, 2010, the U.S. Supreme Court ruled on what some scholars have argued is the most important First Amendment case in many years. In *Citizens United v. Federal Election Commission*, the Court held, in a controversial 5–4 decision, that the First Amendment allows corporations and unions to make political expenditures in support of a particular candidate. This ruling overturned existing restrictions on political campaigning by corporations. Because it is highly unlikely that all shareholders of a corporation would unanimously support a particular candidate, allowing such activities effectively guarantees a potential conflict of interest.

is a barometer for corporate leaders that continuously gives them feedback on the shareholders' opinion of their performance.

When the stock performs poorly, the board of directors might react by replacing the CEO. In some corporations, however, the senior executives might be entrenched because boards of directors do not have the independence or motivation to replace them. Often, the reluctance to fire results when the board is comprised of people who are close friends of the CEO and lack objectivity. In corporations in which the CEO is entrenched and doing a poor job, the expectation of continued poor performance will cause the stock price to be low. Low stock prices create a profit opportunity. In a **hostile takeover**, an individual or organization—sometimes known as a *corporate raider*—purchases a large fraction of a company's stock and in doing so gets enough votes to replace the board of directors and the CEO. With a new superior management team, the stock is a much more attractive investment, which would likely result in a price rise and a profit for the corporate raider and the other shareholders. Although the words "hostile" and "raider" have negative connotations, corporate raiders provide an important service to shareholders. The mere threat of being removed as a result of a hostile takeover is often enough to discipline bad managers and motivate boards of directors to make difficult decisions. Consequently, the fact that a corporation's shares can be publicly traded creates a "market for corporate control" that encourages managers and boards of directors to act in the interests of their shareholders.

hostile takeover
A situation in which an individual or organization—sometimes referred to as a *corporate raider*—purchases a large fraction of a company's stock and in doing so gets enough votes to replace the board of directors and its CEO.

CONCEPT CHECK

5. How do shareholders control a corporation?

6. What types of jobs would a financial manager have in a corporation?

7. What ethical issues could confront a financial manager?

1.5   The Stock Market

stock market (also stock exchange or bourse) Organized market on which the shares of many corporations are traded.

liquid Describes an investment that can be easily turned into cash because it can be sold immediately at a competitive market price.

In Section 1.3, we established the goal of the financial manager: to maximize the wealth of the owners, the stockholders. The value of the owners' investments in the corporation is determined by the price of a share of the corporation's stock. Corporations can be private or public. A private corporation has a limited number of owners and there is no organized market for its shares, making it hard to determine the market price of its shares at any point in time. A public corporation has many owners and its shares trade on an organized market, called a **stock market** (or **stock exchange** or **bourse**). These markets provide *liquidity* for a company's shares and determine the market price for those shares. An investment is **liquid** if it can be easily turned into cash by selling it immediately at a competitive market price. An investor in a public company values the ability to turn his investment into cash easily and quickly by simply selling his shares on one of these markets. In this section, we provide an overview of the functioning of the major stock markets. The analysis and trading by participants in these markets provides an evaluation of the financial managers' decisions that determines the stock price and provides essential feedback to the managers on their decisions.

The Largest Stock Markets

The best known U.S. stock market and one of the largest stock markets in the world is the New York Stock Exchange (NYSE). Billions of dollars of stock are exchanged every day on the NYSE. The other well-known U.S. stock market is the NASDAQ (the National Association of Security Dealers Automated Quotation). Most other countries have at least one stock market. The biggest stock markets are the Shanghai and Shenzhen Stock Exchanges in China. Figure 1.3 ranks the world's largest stock exchanges by trading volume and reflects the recent rise in importance of electronic exchanges such as BATS Global Markets and BATS Chi-x, which we discuss later in this section.

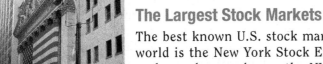

FIGURE 1.3

Worldwide Stock Markets Ranked by Volume of Trade

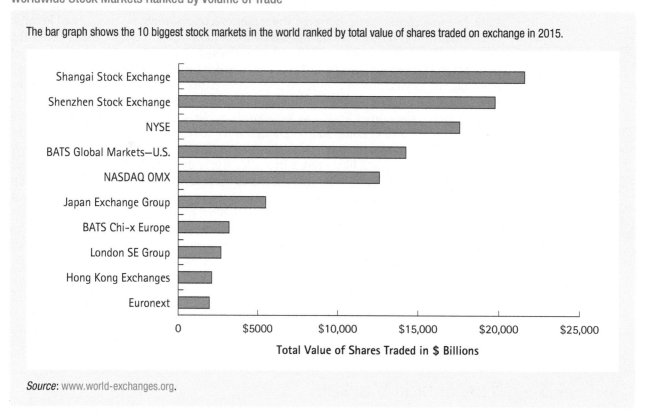

The bar graph shows the 10 biggest stock markets in the world ranked by total value of shares traded on exchange in 2015.

Source: www.world-exchanges.org.

Primary Versus Secondary Markets

primary market When a corporation issues new shares of stock and sells them to investors.

secondary market Markets, such as NYSE or NASDAQ, where shares of a corporation are traded between investors without the involvement of the corporation.

All of the markets in Figure 1.3 are secondary markets. The **primary market** refers to a corporation issuing new shares of stock and selling them to investors. After this initial transaction between the corporation and investors, the shares continue to trade in a **secondary market** between investors without the involvement of the corporation. For example, if you wish to buy 100 shares of Starbucks Coffee, you could place an order on the NASDAQ, where Starbucks trades under the ticker symbol SBUX. You would buy your shares from someone who already held shares of Starbucks, not from Starbucks itself. Because firms only occasionally issue new shares, secondary market trading accounts for the vast majority of trading in the stock market.

Traditional Trading Venues

market makers Individuals or companies at an exchange who match buyers with sellers.

specialists market makers at the NYSE.

bid price The price at which a market maker is willing to buy a security.

ask price The price at which a market maker is willing to sell a security.

Historically, firms would choose one stock exchange to list their stock, and almost all trade in the stock would occur on that exchange. In the U.S., the two most important exchanges are the New York Stock Exchange (NYSE) and the National Association of Security Dealers Automated Quotation (NASDAQ).

Prior to 2005, almost all trade on the NYSE took place on the exchange's trading floor in lower Manhattan. **Market makers** (known then on the NYSE as **specialists**) matched buyers and sellers. They posted two prices for every stock they made a market in: the price they stood willing to buy the stock at (the **bid price**) and the price they stood willing to sell the stock for (the **ask price**). When a customer arrived wanting to make a trade at these prices, they would honor the price (up to a limited number of shares) and would make the trade even if they did

INTERVIEW WITH FRANK HATHEWAY

As Chief Economist and Senior Vice President for NASDAQ, Dr. Frank Hatheway leads a team of 20 professionals who serve as an internal consultancy for the NASDAQ markets. Their work includes designing new features, evaluating operations markets, and advising on strategic initiatives.

QUESTION: *Compared to 15 years ago, the number of potential trading venues for investors has changed dramatically. Who have these changes benefited?*

ANSWER: The number of trading venues has increased dramatically. In 2000 you placed an order on NASDAQ or the NYSE, and the majority of trading activity in that stock occurred on the same market as your order. That's not the case anymore. Your trade may be executed on the National Stock Exchange, BATS, or one of 10 other exchanges. To deal with the soaring number of venues, trading became highly automated and highly competitive, benefiting both individual and institutional investors. A fast retail trade in the 1980s took about three minutes and cost over $100 (in 1980s money). Now it's a mouse click, browser refresh, and maybe $20 (in 2016 money). Trading costs for individual investors are down over 90 percent since 2000. Institutional-size block orders are also cheaper and easier to trade today.

Automation has virtually removed traditional equity traders like the market makers, specialists, and floor brokers at the exchanges. As the head of the trading desk for a major firm quipped around 2006, "I used to have 100 traders and 10 IT guys. I now have 100 IT guys and 10 traders." The once bustling New York Stock Exchange floor is now essentially a TV studio.

QUESTION: *How have these changes affected market liquidity?*

ANSWER: Liquidity is very transitory. The computer algorithms controlling trading constantly enter orders into the market and remove orders if the order fails to trade or if market conditions change. The algorithms quickly re-enter removed orders into the market, leading to rapidly changing prices and quantities. Also, numerous studies show that there is more liquidity in the market today. To control an order 15 years ago, you phoned your broker with your instructions. Today, the algorithm you selected controls the order and can change the order almost instantly. Because computers have more

control over orders than human traders did, there is less risk associated with placing an order. Consequently there are more orders and greater liquidity.

QUESTION: *How has NASDAQ been affected by these changes and what does the future hold?*

ANSWER: NASDAQ has become an innovative, technologically savvy company—much like the companies we list. Fifteen years ago we operated a single stock market in the United States. Thanks to increased technological efficiency, today we operate three stock markets, three listed-options markets, and a futures market. Operating these seven markets requires less than half the personnel required for a single market 15 years ago. To compete in this environment, NASDAQ had to develop a better trading system to handle our increased order volume. Order volume that took an entire day to process 15 years ago, today takes a few seconds. We've also transformed our culture from supporting an industry based on human traders to one based on algorithmic traders and the IT professionals who design those algorithms.

QUESTION: *Is High Frequency Trading a cause for concern in the market? Should it be limited?*

ANSWER: Specific concerns about High Frequency Trading are generally about market disruptions and manipulation, and cases center around the operation of trading algorithms. I believe market oversight is evolving to appropriately address disruptive or manipulative activity.

These days essentially every order in the United States is handled by a computer trading algorithm. Simply put, we are all High Frequency Traders. Consequently, limiting High Frequency Trading should not be a policy objective. What should be a policy objective is making sure that equity markets benefit investors and issuers by ensuring that the algorithms do not disrupt the markets and that they operate in a manner that is fair to investors. The market exists to support capital formation and economic growth. Market operators such as NASDAQ work with regulators and others to look after the interests of investors and issuers.

---

liquidity Extent to which the market for an asset is liquid, meaning that assets can be easily turned into cash because they can be sold immediately at competitive market prices.

bid-ask spread The amount by which the ask price exceeds the bid price.

not have another customer willing to take the other side of the trade. In this way, they provided **liquidity** by ensuring market participants that they always had somebody to trade with.

In contrast to the NYSE, the NASDAQ market never had a trading floor. Instead all trades were completed over the phone or on a computer network. An important difference between the NYSE and NASDAQ was that on the NYSE, each stock had only one market maker. On NASDAQ, stocks had multiple market makers who competed with each other. Each market maker posted bid and ask prices in the NASDAQ network which were viewed by all participants.

Market makers make money because ask prices exceed bid prices. This difference is called the **bid-ask spread**. Customers always buy at the ask (the higher price) and sell at

FIGURE 1.4

Distribution of trading volume for NYSE-listed (left panel) and NASDAQ-listed (right panel) stocks. NYSE Arca is the electronic trading platform of the NYSE. BATS and Direct Edge merged in 2014; these new electronic exchanges now handle about 20% of all trades. Other venues, including internal dealer platforms and so called "dark pools," accounted for almost 40% of all trades in 2015.

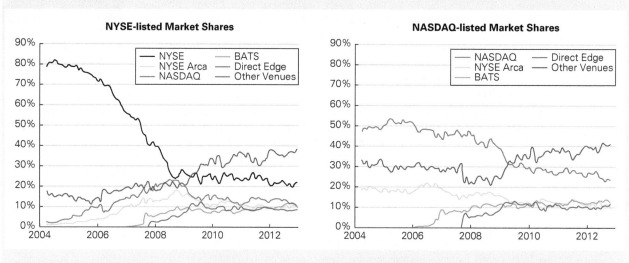

Source: J. Angel, L. Harris, and C. Spatt, "Equity Trading in the 21st Century: An Update," *Quarterly Journal of Finance* 5 (2015): 1–39.

---

transaction cost In most markets, an expense such as a broker commission and the bid-ask spread investors must pay in order to trade securities.

the bid (the lower price). The bid-ask spread is a **transaction cost** investors pay in order to trade. Because specialists on the NYSE took the other side of the trade from their customers, this cost accrued to them as a profit. This was the compensation they earned for providing a liquid market by standing ready to honor any quoted price. Investors also paid other forms of transactions costs like commissions.

New Competition and Market Changes

Stock markets have gone through enormous changes in the last decade. In 2005, the NYSE and NASDAQ exchanges accounted for over 75% of all trade in U.S. stocks. Since that time, however, they have faced increasing competition from new fully electronic exchanges as well as alternative trading systems. As Figure 1.4 shows, today these new entrants handle more than 50% of all trades.

With this change in market structure, the role of an official market maker has largely disappeared. Because all transactions occur electronically with computers matching buy and sell orders, anybody can make a market in a stock by posting a **limit order**. A limit order is an order to buy or sell a set amount at a fixed price. For example, an order to buy 100 shares of IBM at a price of $138/share is a limit buy order. The bid-ask spread of a stock is determined by the outstanding limit orders. The limit sell order with the lowest price is the ask price. The limit buy order with the highest price is the bid price. Traders make the market in the stock by posting limit buy and sell orders. The collection of all limit orders is known as the **limit order book**. Exchanges make their limit order books public so that investors (or their brokers) can see the best bid and ask prices when deciding where to trade.

Traders who post limit orders provide liquidity to the market. On the other hand, traders who place **market orders**—orders that trade immediately at the best outstanding limit order—are said to be "takers" of liquidity. Providers of liquidity earn the bid-ask spread, but in doing so they risk the possibility that their orders will become stale: When news about the stock arrives that causes the price of the stock to move, smart traders will quickly take advantage of the existing limit orders by executing trades at the old prices. To protect

limit order Order to buy or sell a set amount of a security at a fixed price.

limit order book Collection of all current limit orders for a given security.

market orders Orders to trade immediately at the best outstanding limit order available.

themselves against this possibility, liquidity providers need to constantly monitor the market, cancelling old orders and posting new orders when appropriate. So called **high frequency traders** (**HFTs**) are a class of traders who, with the aid of computers, place, update, cancel, and execute trades many times per second in response to new information as well as other orders, profiting by both providing liquidity and taking advantage of stale limit orders.

high frequency traders (HFTs) Traders who place, update, cancel, and execute trades many times per second.

Dark Pools

When trading on an exchange, investors are guaranteed the opportunity to trade immediately at the current bid or ask price, and transactions are visible to all traders when they occur. In contrast, alternative trading systems called **dark pools** do not make their limit order books visible. Instead, these dark pools offer investors the ability to trade at a better price (for example, the average of the bid and ask, thus saving the bid-ask spread) with the tradeoff that their order might not be filled if an excess of either buy or sell orders is received. Trading on a dark pool is therefore attractive to traders who do not want to reveal their demand and who are willing to sacrifice the guarantee of immediacy for potential price improvement.

dark pools Trading venues in which the size and price of orders are not disclosed to participants. Prices are within the best bid and ask prices available in public markets, but traders face the risk their orders may not be filled if an excess of either buy or sell orders is received.

When dark pools are included, researchers estimate that in the U.S. alone there could be as many 50 venues to trade stocks. These venues compete with one another for order volume. Because traders value liquid markets, an important area of competition is liquidity—exchanges try to ensure that their limit order books are deep, that is, contain many orders. As a result exchanges have been experimenting with different rules designed to encourage traders who provide liquidity and discourage traders who take advantage of stale limit orders. For example, some trading venues pay traders to post limit orders and charge traders who place market orders. Others pay for volume from retail investors, and impose additional charges on high frequency trading. The proliferation of exchange venues has generated a wide variety of different compensation schemes. Indeed, BATS (which stands for Better Alternative Trading System) operates different markets with different rules, essentially tailoring their markets to the perceived needs of their customers. It is highly unlikely that we have seen the end of these changes. Stock markets remain in a state of flux, and only time will tell what the eventual shakeout will look like.

Listing Standards

Each exchange has its own **listing standards**, outlines of the requirements a company must meet to be traded on the exchange. These standards usually require that the company has enough shares outstanding for shareholders to have a liquid market and to be of interest to a broad set of investors. The NYSE's standards are more stringent than those of NASDAQ; traditionally, there has been a certain pride in being listed on the NYSE. Many companies would start on the NASDAQ and then move to the NYSE as they grew. However, NASDAQ has retained many big, successful companies such as Starbucks, Apple, and Microsoft. The two exchanges compete actively over listings of larger companies (NASDAQ landed Facebook and the NYSE won Twitter's listing) and the decision of where to list often comes down to which exchange the company's board believes will give its stockholders the best execution and liquidity for their trades.

listing standards Outlines of the requirements a company must meet to be traded on the exchange.

Other Financial Markets

Of course, stock markets are not the only financial markets. There are markets to trade practically anything—some of them are physical places like the NYSE and others are purely electronic, like the NASDAQ. Two of the largest financial markets in the world, the bond market and the foreign exchange market, are simply networks of dealers connected by phone and computer. We will discuss these markets in more detail in later chapters (Chapters 6 and 15 for bonds and Chapter 23 for foreign exchange). Commodities like oil, wheat, and soybeans are traded on physical exchanges like the New York Mercantile Exchange. *Derivative securities*, which are complicated financial products used to hedge risks, are traded in locations like the Chicago Board Options Exchange (discussed in Chapter 21).

NYSE, BATS, DJIA, S&P 500: Awash in Acronyms

With all of these acronyms floating around, it's easy to get confused. You may have heard of the "Dow Jones" or "Dow Jones (Industrial) Average" and the "S&P 500" on news reports about the stock markets. The NYSE, BATS, and NASDAQ are all stock markets where the prices of stocks are determined through trading. However, when commentators talk about whether stocks are up or down in general in a given day, they often refer to the Dow Jones Industrial Average (DJIA) and the Standard and Poor's 500 (S&P 500). The DJIA and S&P 500 are simply measures of the aggregate price level of collections of preselected stocks—30 in the case of the DJIA and 500 in the case of the S&P 500. These stocks were selected by Dow Jones (the publisher of the *Wall Street Journal*) or Standard & Poor's as representative of the overall market. The S&P 500 consists of 500 of the highest-valued U.S. companies. While fewer in number, the 30 stocks in the DJIA include companies such as Microsoft, Walmart, Boeing, and 3M, and are selected to cover the important sectors in the U.S. economy. The table below shows the 30 stocks in the DJIA as of August 2016. Dow Jones editors choose these stocks to reflect the overall U.S. economy. The membership of the index has changed over time to reflect the U.S. economy's transition from being industrial-driven to being more services and technology based. For example, they added Chevron in 2008 to capture the growing importance of energy. In 2012, they added UnitedHealth, the United States' largest insurer, to reflect the importance of healthcare for an aging U.S. population. Both the DJIA and S&P 500 include stocks that are traded on the NYSE and stocks that are traded on NASDAQ and so are distinct from the exchanges themselves.

Composition of the Dow Jones Industrial Average (DJIA) as of October 2016

3M Co.	General Electric Co.	Nike Inc.
American Express Co.	Goldman Sachs Group Inc.	Pfizer Inc.
Apple Inc.	Home Depot Inc.	Procter & Gamble Co.
Boeing Co.	Intel Corp.	Travelers Co.
Caterpillar Inc.	International Business Machines	UnitedHealth Group Inc.
Chevron Corp.	Johnson & Johnson	United Technologies Corp.
Cisco Systems Inc.	J.P. Morgan Chase & Co.	Verizon Communications Inc.
Coca-Cola Co.	McDonald's Corp.	Visa Inc.
Du Pont	Merck & Co.	Walmart Stores Inc.
Exxon Mobil Co.	Microsoft Corp.	Walt Disney Co.

Source: djindexes.com.

CONCEPT CHECK

8. What advantage does a stock market provide to corporate investors? To financial managers?

9. What are the important changes that have occurred in stock markets over the last decade?

1.6   Financial Institutions

financial institutions
Entities that provide financial services, such as taking deposits, managing investments, brokering financial transactions, or making loans.

The spread of the 2008 financial crisis from subprime mortgages to Wall Street to traditional banks and businesses drew everyone's attention to *financial institutions* and their role in the economy. In general, **financial institutions** are entities that provide financial services, such as taking deposits, managing investments, brokering financial transactions, or making loans. In this section, we describe the key types of financial institutions and their functions.

The Financial Cycle

Keeping the names and roles of the different types of financial institutions straight can be challenging. It is helpful to think of the basic financial cycle, depicted in Figure 1.5, as context. In the financial cycle, (1) people invest and save their money, (2) that money, through loans and stock, flows to companies who use it to fund growth through new

FIGURE 1.5

The Financial Cycle

This figure depicts the basic financial cycle, which matches funds from savers to companies that have projects requiring funds and then returns the profits from those projects back to the savers and investors.

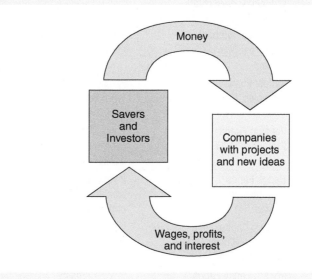

products, generating profits and wages, and (3) the money then flows back to the savers and investors. All financial institutions play a role at some point in this cycle of connecting money with ideas and returning the profits back to the savers and investors.

Types of Financial Institutions

Table 1.2 lists the major categories of financial institutions, provides examples of representative firms, and summarizes the institutions' sources and uses of funds.

Financial conglomerates, sometimes referred to as *financial services firms*, combine more than one type of institution. Examples include Bank of America, JPMorgan Chase, and Deutsche Bank, all of which engage in commercial banking (like Wells Fargo) as well as investment banking. Investment banking refers to the business of advising companies in major financial transactions. Examples include buying and selling companies or divisions, and raising new capital by issuing stock or bonds. Goldman Sachs and Morgan Stanley are financial institutions that are focused on investment banking activities.

Role of Financial Institutions

Financial institutions have a role beyond moving funds from those who have extra funds (savers) to those who need funds (borrowers and firms): They also move funds through time. For example, suppose you need a $20,000 car loan. You need $20,000 now, but do not have it. However, you will have it in the future as you earn a salary. The financial institution, in this case a bank or credit union, helps transfer your future salary into funds today by issuing you a loan.

Financial institutions also help spread out risk-bearing. Insurance companies essentially pool premiums together from policyholders and pay the claims of those who have an accident, fire, medical need, or who die. This process spreads the financial risk of these events out across a large pool of policyholders and the investors in the insurance company. Similarly, mutual funds and pension funds take your savings and spread them out among the stocks and bonds of many different companies, limiting your risk exposure to any one company.

TABLE 1.2

Financial Institutions
and Their Roles in the
Financial Cycle

Institution	Source of Money	Use of Money
Banks and Credit Unions Examples: *Wells Fargo, SunTrust*	Deposits (savings)	Loans to people and businesses
Insurance Companies Examples: *Liberty Mutual, Allstate*	Premiums and investment earnings	Invests mostly in bonds and some stocks, using the investment income to pay claims
Mutual Funds Examples: *Vanguard, Fidelity*	People's investments (savings)	Buys stocks, bonds, and other financial instruments on behalf of its investors
Pension Funds Examples: *CalPERS, REST*	Retirement savings contributed through the workplace	Similar to mutual funds, except with the purpose of providing retirement income
Hedge Funds Examples: *Bridgewater, Citadel*	Investments by wealthy individuals and endowments	Invests in any kind of investment in an attempt to maximize returns
Venture Capital Funds Examples: *Kleiner Perkins, Sequoia Capital*	Investments by wealthy individuals and endowments	Invests in start-up, entrepreneurial firms
Private Equity Funds Examples: *TPG Capital, KKR*	Investments by wealthy individuals and endowments	Purchases whole companies by using a small amount of equity and borrowing the rest

While you may have seen coverage of the stock markets and discussion of financial institutions on the news, it is unlikely that you have been exposed to the finance function within a firm. In this chapter, we provided a sense of what corporate finance is all about, what a financial manager does, and the importance of stock markets and financial institutions. In upcoming chapters, you will learn how to make financial management decisions and how to use financial market information. We will explore the tools of financial analysis hand-in-hand with a clear understanding of when to apply them and why they work.

CONCEPT CHECK

10. What is the basic financial cycle?
11. What are the three main roles financial institutions play?

MyFinanceLab

Here is what you should know after reading this chapter. MyFinanceLab will help you identify what you know, and where to go when you need to practice.

KEY POINTS AND EQUATIONS   **KEY TERMS**   **ONLINE PRACTICE**

1.1   Why Study Finance?
- Finance and financial decisions are everywhere in our daily lives.
- Many financial decisions are simple, but others are complex. All are tied together by the Valuation Principle—the foundation for financial decision making—which you will learn in this book.

1.2 The Four Types of Firms	C corporations, p. 9	MyFinanceLab
• There are four types of firms in the United States: sole proprietorships, partnerships, limited liability companies, and corporations.	corporation, p. 6 dividend payments, p. 7	Study Plan 1.2
• Firms with unlimited personal liability include sole proprietorships and partnerships.	equity, p. 7 equity holder, p. 7	
• Firms with limited liability include limited partnerships, limited liability companies, and corporations.	limited liability, p. 6 limited liability company (LLC), p. 6	
• A corporation is a legally defined artificial being (a judicial person or legal entity) that has many of the legal powers people have. It can enter into contracts, acquire assets, and incur obligations, and it enjoys protection under the U.S. Constitution against the seizure of its property.	limited partnership, p. 6 partnership, p. 6 S corporations, p. 8 shareholder, p. 7 sole proprietorship, p. 5	
• The shareholders in a C corporation effectively must pay tax twice. The corporation pays tax once and then investors must pay personal tax on any funds that are distributed. S corporations are exempt from the corporate income tax.	stock, p. 7 stockholder, p. 7	
• The ownership of a corporation is divided into shares of stock collectively known as equity. Investors in these shares are called shareholders, stockholders, or equity holders.		
1.3 The Financial Manager		MyFinanceLab
• The financial manager makes investing, financing, and cash flow management decisions.		Study Plan 1.3
• The goal of the financial manager is to maximize the wealth of the shareholders (maximize the stock price).		
1.4 The Financial Manager's Place in the Corporation	agency problem, p. 13	MyFinanceLab Study
• The ownership and control of a corporation are separate. Shareholders exercise their control indirectly through the board of directors.	board of directors, p. 12 chief executive officer (CEO), p. 12 hostile takeover, p. 15	Plan 1.4
1.5 The Stock Market	ask price, p. 16	MyFinanceLab
• The shares of public corporations are traded on stock markets. The shares of private corporations do not trade on a stock market.	auction market, p. 18 bid-ask spread, p. 17 bid price, p. 16	Study Plan 1.5
• When a firm sells shares to investors, that is a primary market. The stock markets, such as NYSE and NASDAQ, are secondary markets where investors trade shares among each other.	bourse, p. 15 dark pools, p. 19 high frequency traders (HFTs), p. 19	
• Traders provide liquidity in stock markets by posting limit orders.	limit order, p. 18 limit order book, p. 18 liquid, p. 15	
• The bid-ask spread is determined by the best bid and offer prices in the limit order book.	liquidity, p.17 listing standards, p. 19 market makers, p. 16 market orders, p. 18	

	primary market, p. 16 secondary market, p. 16 specialists, p. 16 stock exchange, p. 15 stock market, p. 15 transaction cost, p. 18	
1.6 Financial Institutions • In the basic financial cycle, money flows from savers and investors to companies and entrepreneurs with ideas, and then back to the savers and investors in the form of profits and interest. • Financial institutions all play some role in this cycle. • Financial institutions also help move money through time (e.g., loans against future wages) and spread risk across large investor bases.	financial institutions, p. 20	MyFinanceLab Study Plan 1.6

PROBLEMS

All problems are available in MyFinanceLab.

The Four Types of Firms

1. What is the most important difference between a corporation and *all* other organizational forms?

2. What does the phrase *limited liability* mean in a corporate context?

3. Which organizational forms give their owners limited liability?

4. What are the main advantages and disadvantages of organizing a firm as a corporation?

5. Explain the difference between an S and a C corporation.

6. You are a shareholder in a C corporation. The corporation earns $2.00 per share before taxes. Once it has paid taxes it will distribute the rest of its earnings to you as a dividend. Assume the corporate tax rate is 40% and the personal tax rate on (both dividend and non-dividend) income is 30%. How much is left for you after all taxes are paid?

7. Repeat Problem 6 assuming the corporation is an S corporation.

The Financial Manager

8. What is the most important type of decision that the financial manager makes?

9. Why do all shareholders agree on the same goal for the financial manager?

The Financial Manager's Place in the Corporation

10. Corporate managers work for the owners of the corporation. Consequently, they should make decisions that are in the interests of the owners, rather than in their own interests. What strategies are available to shareholders to help ensure that managers are motivated to act this way?

11. Recall the last time you ate at an expensive restaurant where you paid the bill. Now think about the last time you ate at a similar restaurant, but your parents paid the bill. Did you order more food (or more expensive food) when your parents paid? Explain how this relates to the agency problem in corporations.

12. Suppose you are considering renting an apartment. You, the renter, can be viewed as an agent while the company that owns the apartment can be viewed as the principal. What agency conflicts do you anticipate? Suppose, instead, that you work for the apartment company. What features would you put into the lease agreement that would give the renter incentives to take good care of the apartment?

13. You are the CEO of a company and you are considering entering into an agreement to have your company buy another company. You think the price might be too high, but you will be the CEO of the combined, much larger company. You know that when the company gets bigger, your pay and prestige will increase. What is the nature of the agency conflict here and how is it related to ethical considerations?

14. You are a financial manager in a public corporation. One of your engineers says that they can increase the profit margin on your flagship product by using a lower quality vendor. However, the product is likely to fail more often and will generally not last as long. Will taking your engineer's suggestion necessarily make shareholders better off? Why or why not?

15. You sit on the board of a public corporation. Your CEO has proposed taking steps to offset the carbon impact of your company's manufacturing process. Doing so will add to the company's overall expenses. Your CEO argues, however, that this action will actually increase the stock price, maximizing shareholder wealth. Why might socially-responsible activities also be value-maximizing?

The Stock Market

16. What is the difference between a public and a private corporation?

17. What is the difference between a primary and a secondary market?

18. How are limit orders and market orders different?

19. Explain why the bid-ask spread is a transaction cost.

20. What are the tradeoffs in using a dark pool?

21. The following quote on Yahoo! stock appeared on April 11, 2016, on Yahoo! Finance:

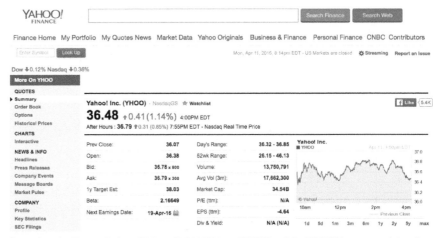

Reproduced with permission of Yahoo. © 2016 Yahoo. YAHOO! and the YAHOO! logo are registered trademarks of Yahoo.

If you wanted to buy Yahoo!, what price would you pay per share? How much would you receive per share if you wanted to sell Yahoo!?

Financial Institutions

22. What is the financial cycle?

23. How do financial institutions help with risk-bearing?

24. What role do investment banks play in the economy?

25. What are some of the similarities and differences among mutual funds, pension funds, and hedge funds?

2

Introduction to Financial Statement Analysis

LEARNING OBJECTIVES

- Know why the disclosure of financial information through financial statements is critical to investors

- Understand the function of the balance sheet

- Understand how the income statement is used

- Interpret a statement of cash flows

- Understand the management's discussion and analysis and the statement of stockholders' equity

- Analyze a firm through its financial statements, including using the DuPont Identity

- Understand the main purpose and aspects of the Sarbanes-Oxley reforms following Enron and other financial scandals

As we discussed in Chapter 1, anyone with money to invest is a potential investor who can own shares in a corporation. As a result, corporations are often widely held, with investors ranging from individuals who hold one share to large financial institutions that own millions of shares. For example, at the end of 2015, Microsoft Corporation had almost 8 billion shares outstanding held by hundreds of thousands of stockholders. Although the corporate organizational structure greatly facilitates the firm's access to investment capital, it also means that stock ownership is most investors' sole tie to the company. How, then, do investors learn enough about a company to know whether or not they should invest in it? One way firms evaluate their performance and communicate this information to investors is through their *financial statements*. Financial statements also enable financial managers to assess the success of their own firm and compare it to competitors.

Firms regularly issue financial statements to communicate financial information to the investment community. A detailed description of the preparation and analysis of these statements is sufficiently complicated that to do it justice would require an entire book. In this chapter, we briefly review the subject, emphasizing only the material that investors and corporate financial managers need in order to make the corporate finance decisions we discuss in the text.

We review the four main types of financial statements, present examples of these statements for a firm, and discuss where an investor or manager might find various types of information about the company. We also discuss some of the financial ratios used to assess a firm's performance and value. We close the chapter with a look at financial reporting abuses and the Sarbanes-Oxley regulatory response.

2.1 Firms' Disclosure of Financial Information

financial statements
Accounting reports issued by a firm quarterly and/or annually that present past performance information and a snapshot of the firm's assets and the financing of those assets.

annual report (10-K) The yearly summary of business, accompanying or including financial statements, sent by U.S. public companies to their shareholders.

Generally Accepted Accounting Principles (GAAP) A common set of rules and a standard format for public companies to use when they prepare their financial reports.

Financial statements are accounting reports issued by a firm periodically (usually quarterly and annually) that present past performance information and a snapshot of the firm's assets and the financing of those assets. Public companies in the United States are required to file their financial statements with the U.S. Securities and Exchange Commission (SEC) on a quarterly basis on form *10-Q* and annually on form *10-K*.[1] They must also send an **annual report (10-K)** with their financial statements to their shareholders each year. Often, private companies also prepare financial statements, but they usually do not have to disclose these reports to the public. Financial statements are important tools with which investors, financial analysts, and other interested outside parties (such as creditors) obtain information about a corporation. They are also useful for managers within the firm as a source of information for the corporate financial decisions we discussed in Chapter 1. In this section, we examine the guidelines for preparing financial statements and introduce the different types of financial statements.

Preparation of Financial Statements

Reports about a company's performance must be understandable and accurate. In the United States, the Financial Accounting Standards Board (FASB) establishes **Generally Accepted Accounting Principles (GAAP)** to provide a common set of rules and a standard format for public companies to use when they prepare their reports. This standardization also makes it easier to compare the financial results of different firms.

International Financial Reporting Standards

Generally Accepted Accounting Principles (GAAP) differ among countries. As a result, companies face tremendous accounting complexities when they operate internationally. Investors also face difficulty interpreting financial statements of foreign companies, which discourages them from investing abroad. As companies and capital markets become more global, however, interest in harmonization of accounting standards across countries has increased.

The most important harmonization project began in 1973 when representatives of 10 countries (including the United States) established the International Accounting Standards Committee. This effort led to the creation of the International Accounting Standards Board (IASB) in 2001, with headquarters in London. Now the IASB has issued a set of International Financial Reporting Standards (IFRS).

The IFRS are taking root throughout the world. The European Union (EU) approved an accounting regulation in 2002 requiring all publicly traded EU companies to follow IFRS in their consolidated financial statements starting in 2005. As of 2016, more than 130 jurisdictions either require or permit the use of IFRS, including the EU, Australia, Brazil, Canada, Russia, Hong Kong, Taiwan, and Singapore. China, India, and Japan will soon follow suit. In fact,

currently all major stock exchanges around the world accept IFRS except the United States and Japan, which maintain their local GAAP.

The main difference between U.S. GAAP and IFRS is conceptual—U.S. GAAP are based primarily on accounting rules with specific guidance in applying them, whereas IFRS are based more on principles requiring professional judgment by accountants, and specific guidance in application is limited. Even so, some differences in rules also exist. For example, U.S. GAAP generally prohibit the upward revaluation of non-financial assets, whereas the IFRS allow the revaluation of some such assets to fair value. U.S. GAAP also rely more heavily on historical cost, as opposed to "fair value," to estimate the value of assets and liabilities.

Effort to achieve convergence between U.S. GAAP and IFRS was spurred by the Sarbanes-Oxley Act of 2002 in the United States. It included a provision that U.S. accounting standards move toward international convergence on high-quality accounting standards. Currently, SEC regulations still require public U.S. firms to report using U.S. GAAP. That said, modifications to both IFRS and U.S. GAAP have brought the two closer together, with the key remaining differences in the areas of revenue recognition, impairment charges, leasing, insurance, and the treatment of financial instruments. As of the early 2016, the SEC looks likely to allow U.S. companies to use IFRS to provide supplemental information, but will still require them to file their financials in accordance with U.S. GAAP.

---

[1]The Securities and Exchange Commission was established by Congress in 1934 to regulate securities (for example, stocks and bonds) issued to the public and the financial markets (exchanges) on which those securities trade.

INTERVIEW WITH RUTH PORAT

Ruth Porat is Senior Vice President and Chief Financial Officer of Alphabet and Google. Previously she spent 27 years at Morgan Stanley, where she last was Executive Vice President and Chief Financial Officer. As Morgan Stanley's Vice Chairman of Investment Banking and Global Head of the Financial Institutions Group, she advised the U.S. Treasury and the New York Federal Reserve Bank.

QUESTION: *What best practices do you recommend for financial managers?*

ANSWER:

1. *Maintain a tight financial control environment with respect to accounting controls and process.* Incorporate a strategic approach to IT architecture to ensure data integrity, consistency, and process controls while reducing reliance on human, manual processes—a source of risk and errors.

2. *Ensure a robust budgeting and capital allocation process built on a strong Financial Planning & Analysis team that is well integrated into the business.* Push data transparency to business leaders. They are best positioned to make difficult tradeoffs in the budgeting process, but often lack data granularity to make those choices (and to see the imperative).

3. *Culture matters.* A culture of honest, frank debate that challenges the status quo and avoids homogeneity of thought makes the job more fun and leads to better results. A broad range of experience, and even some "battle scars," ensures the organization recognizes patterns to foresee emerging risks. In that regard, a diverse team with respect to gender, race, and socioeconomic background brings differentiated perspectives, contributing to effective risk management.

4. *Make tough calls early and, ideally, once.* Lead.

QUESTION: *How has the crisis shaped the role of the CFO, or your view of it?*

ANSWER: In financial services, it redefined the perception of a CFO. Beyond focusing on accounting and external reporting functions, the CFO is now also the firm's most senior global manager for guardianship and risk management. Guardianship includes accounting (the controller function) and overseeing a comprehensive approach to IT systems. Risk management requires identifying sources of vulnerability, stress testing, and planning against them. The CFO has become a trusted adviser to the CEO, board

and business leaders, which includes budgeting, capital allocation, and sensitivity analyses. Finally, in certain industries the CFO is the point person with regulators.

QUESTION: *What key lessons did you take from the financial crisis? What advice would you give future CFOs?*

ANSWER: I have three key takeaways from the financial crisis, relevant in both good and bad markets as well as across industries:

1. *Understand your greatest sources of vulnerability and defend against them.* For financial services, liquidity (access to cash) was a weak spot. In that period, we often said, "Liquidity is oxygen for a financial system: without it, you choke." Without sufficient liquidity, banks were forced into a negative cycle of selling assets to raise cash. As Morgan Stanley's CFO, I managed liquidity with the maxim that it was sacrosanct. We invested substantially in the amount and durability of the company's liquidity reserve. Similarly, regulators coming out of the crisis appropriately demanded higher capital, lower leverage, better liquidity, more durable funding, and rigorous stress testing, which imposed transparency on the banks and exposed their weaknesses.

2. *Build a robust control infrastructure ahead of needs, including financial and risk management controls, systems, and processes.* Just as one shouldn't drive a car at 100 mph with mud on the windshield, business leaders must have visibility about their business from accurate, insightful, and timely data consistent with strong financial controls. Rapid growth industries need to invest in infrastructure early because the business requirements continue to grow so rapidly.

3. *Recognize that time is your enemy.* Treasury Secretary Paulson told me during the financial crisis that you must have the will and the means to solve problems; too often, by the time you have the will, you no longer have the means. He was talking about policy, but that rule applies to any decision maker. The glaring examples, in retrospect, were the clear signs of crisis in August 2007 and the March 2008 collapse of Bear Stearns, but reactions were slow or nonexistent. Even in good times, business leaders must focus on resource optimization to maximize the potential for highest returns on investment.

auditor A neutral third party, which corporations are required to hire, that checks a firm's annual financial statements to ensure they are prepared according to GAAP, and provides evidence to support the reliability of the information.

Investors also need some assurance that the financial statements are prepared accurately. Publicly traded corporations are required to hire a neutral third party, known as an **auditor**, to check the annual financial statements, ensure they are prepared according to GAAP, and provide evidence to support the reliability of the information.

Types of Financial Statements

Every public company is required to produce four financial statements: the *balance sheet*, the *income statement*, the *statement of cash flows*, and the *statement of stockholders' equity*. These financial statements provide investors and creditors with an overview of the firm's financial performance. In the sections that follow, we take a close look at the content of these financial statements.

CONCEPT CHECK

1. What is the role of an auditor?
2. What are the four financial statements that all public companies must produce?

2.2 The Balance Sheet

balance sheet (or **statement of financial position**) A list of a firm's assets and liabilities that provides a snapshot of the firm's financial position at a given point in time.

assets The cash, inventory, property, plant, and equipment, and other investments a company has made.

liabilities A firm's obligations to its creditors.

shareholders' equity, stockholders' equity An accounting measure of a firm's net worth that represents the difference between the firm's assets and its liabilities.

common stock and paid-in surplus The amount that stockholders have directly invested in the firm through purchasing stock from the company.

retained earnings Profits made by the firm, but retained within the firm and reinvested in assets or held as cash.

The **balance sheet**, or **statement of financial position**,[2] lists the firm's *assets* and *liabilities*, providing a snapshot of the firm's financial position at a given point in time. Table 2.1 shows the balance sheet for a fictitious company, Global Corporation. Notice that the balance sheet is divided into two parts ("sides") with the assets on the left side and the liabilities on the right side.

1. The **assets** list the firm's cash, inventory, property, plant and equipment, and any other investments the company has made.
2. The **liabilities** show the firm's obligations to its creditors.
3. Also shown with liabilities on the right side of the balance sheet is the *stockholders' equity*. **Stockholders' equity** (also called **shareholders' equity**), the difference between the firm's assets and liabilities, is an accounting measure of the firm's net worth. For Global, the stockholders' equity has two parts: (1) **common stock and paid-in surplus**, the amount that stockholders have directly invested in the firm through purchasing stock from the company and (2) **retained earnings**, which are profits made by the firm, but retained within the firm and reinvested in assets or held as cash. We will take a more detailed look at retained earnings in our discussion of the statement of cash flows later in this chapter.

The assets on the left side show how the firm uses its capital (its investments), and the information on the right side summarizes the sources of capital, or how the firm raises the money it needs. Because of the way stockholders' equity is calculated, the left and right sides must balance:

The Balance Sheet Identity

$$\text{Assets} = \text{Liabilities} + \text{Stockholders' Equity} \qquad (2.1)$$

In Table 2.1, total assets for 2016 ($170.1 million) are equal to total liabilities ($147.9 million) plus stockholders' equity ($22.2 million).

Let's examine Global's assets, liabilities, and stockholders' equity in more detail.

---

[2]In IFRS and recent U.S. GAAP pronouncements, the balance sheet is referred to as the *statement of financial position*.

TABLE 2.1

Global Corporation Balance Sheet for 2016 and 2015 ($ millions)

Assets	2016	2015	Liabilities and Stockholders' Equity	2016	2015
Current Assets			Current Liabilities		
Cash	23.2	20.5	Accounts payable	29.2	26.5
Accounts receivable	18.5	13.2	Notes payable/short-term debt	5.5	3.2
Inventories	15.3	14.3			
Total current assets	57.0	48.0	Total current liabilities	34.7	29.7
Long-Term Assets			Long-Term Liabilities		
Net property, plant, and equipment	113.1	80.9	Long-term debt	113.2	78.0
Total long-term assets	113.1	80.9	Total long-term liabilities	113.2	78.0
			Total Liabilities	147.9	107.7
			Stockholders' Equity		
			Common stock and paid-in surplus	8.0	8.0
			Retained earnings	14.2	13.2
			Total Stockholders' Equity	22.2	21.2
Total Assets	170.1	128.9	Total Liabilities and Stockholders' Equity	170.1	128.9

current assets Cash or assets that can be converted into cash within one year.

marketable securities Short-term, low-risk investments that can be easily sold and converted to cash.

accounts receivable Amounts owed to a firm by customers who have purchased goods or services on credit.

inventories A firm's raw materials as well as its work-in-progress and finished goods.

long-term assets Assets that produce tangible benefits for more than one year.

depreciation A yearly deduction a firm makes from the value of its fixed assets (other than land) over time, according to a depreciation schedule that depends on an asset's life span.

book value The acquisition cost of an asset less its accumulated depreciation.

Assets

In Table 2.1, Global's assets are divided into *current* and *long-term assets*. We discuss each in turn.

Current Assets. **Current assets** are either cash or assets that can be converted into cash within one year. This category includes:

1. Cash and other **marketable securities**, which are short-term, low-risk investments that can be easily sold and converted to cash (such as money market investments, like government debt, that mature within a year);

2. **Accounts receivable**, which are amounts owed to the firm by customers who have purchased goods or services on credit;

3. **Inventories**, which are composed of raw materials as well as work-in-progress and finished goods; and

4. Other current assets, which is a catch-all category that includes items such as prepaid expenses (such as rent or insurance).

Long-Term Assets. Assets such as real estate or machinery that produce tangible benefits for more than one year are called **long-term assets**. If Global spends $2 million on new equipment, this $2 million will be included with net property, plant, and equipment under long-term assets on the balance sheet. Because equipment tends to wear out or become obsolete over time, Global will reduce the value recorded for this equipment through a yearly deduction called **depreciation** according to a depreciation schedule that depends on an asset's life span. Depreciation is not an actual cash expense that the firm pays; it is a way of recognizing that buildings and equipment wear out and thus become less valuable the older they get. The **book value** of an asset, which is the value shown in the firm's financial statements, is equal to its acquisition cost less accumulated depreciation. The figures for net property, plant, and equipment show the total book value of these assets.

Other long-term assets can include such items as property not used in business operations, start-up costs in connection with a new business, trademarks and patents, and property held for sale. The sum of all the firms' assets is the total assets at the bottom of the left side of the balance sheet in Table 2.1.

Liabilities

We now examine the liabilities, shown on the right side of the balance sheet, which are divided into *current* and *long-term liabilities*.

Current Liabilities. Liabilities that will be satisfied within one year are known as **current liabilities**. They include:

1. **Accounts payable**, the amounts owed to suppliers for products or services purchased with credit.
2. **Notes payable** and **short-term debt**, loans that must be repaid in the next year. Any repayment of long-term debt that will occur within the next year would also be listed here as current maturities of long-term debt.
3. Accrual items, such as salary or taxes, that are owed but have not yet been paid, and deferred or unearned revenue, which is revenue that has been received for products or services that have not yet been delivered.

The difference between current assets and current liabilities is the firm's **net working capital**, the capital available in the short term to run the business. While notes payable and short-term debt are included in current liabilities, they are different from accounts payable and accrual items. Notes payable and short-term debt are related to financing decisions of the firm, while accounts payable and accruals arise from operating decisions of the firm. This distinction is important later when we see that financial managers generally try to keep these two decisions (operating and financing) separate.

$$\text{Net Working Capital} = \text{Current Assets} - \text{Current Liabilities} \qquad (2.2)$$

For example, in 2016, Global's net working capital totaled $22.3 million ($57.0 million in current assets − $34.7 million in current liabilities). Firms with low (or negative) net working capital may face a shortage of funds. In such cases, the liabilities due in the short term exceed the company's cash and expected payments on receivables.

Long-Term Liabilities. Long-term liabilities are liabilities that extend beyond one year. When a firm needs to raise funds to purchase an asset or make an investment, it may borrow those funds through a long-term loan. That loan would appear on the balance sheet as **long-term debt**, which is any loan or debt obligation with a maturity of more than a year.

Stockholders' Equity

The sum of the current liabilities and long-term liabilities is total liabilities. The difference between the firm's assets and liabilities is the *stockholders' equity*; it is also called the **book value of equity** or *shareholders' equity*. As we stated earlier, it represents the net worth of the firm from an accounting perspective. The two main components are common stock and paid-in surplus and retained earnings. These two components form the book value of stockholders' ownership claims, stemming from their direct investment and reinvestment of profits.

Ideally, the balance sheet would provide us with an accurate assessment of the true value of the firm's equity. Unfortunately, this is unlikely to be the case. First, many of

current liabilities
Liabilities that will be satisfied within one year.

accounts payable The amounts owed to creditors for products or services purchased with credit.

notes payable, short-term debt Loans that must be repaid in the next year.

net working capital The difference between a firm's current assets and current liabilities that represents the capital available in the short term to run the business.

long-term debt Any loan or debt obligation with a maturity of more than a year.

book value of equity The difference between the book value of a firm's assets and its liabilities; also called *shareholders' equity* and *stockholders' equity*, it represents the net worth of a firm from an accounting perspective.

the assets listed on the balance sheet are valued based on their historical cost rather than their true value today. For example, an office building is listed on the balance sheet according to its historical cost less its accumulated depreciation. But the actual value of the office building today may be very different than this amount; in fact, if real estate prices went up it will be worth *more* than the amount the firm paid for it years ago. The same is true for other property, plant, and equipment: The true value today of an asset may be very different from, and even exceed, its book value. A second, and probably more important, problem is that *many of the firm's valuable assets are not captured on the balance sheet.* Consider, for example, the expertise of the firm's employees, the firm's reputation in the marketplace, the relationships with customers and suppliers, and the quality of the management team. All these assets add to the value of the firm but do not appear on the balance sheet. Although the book value of a firm's equity is not a good estimate of its true value as an ongoing firm, it is sometimes used as an estimate of the **liquidation value** of the firm, the value that would be left after its assets were sold and liabilities paid.

liquidation value The value of a firm after its assets are sold and liabilities paid.

Market Value Versus Book Value

For these reasons, the book value of equity is an inaccurate assessment of the actual value of the firm's equity. Thus, it is not surprising that it will often differ substantially from the amount investors are willing to pay for the equity. The total market value of a firm's equity equals the market price per share times the number of shares, referred to as the company's **market capitalization**. The market value of a stock does not depend on the historical cost of the firm's assets; instead, it depends on what investors expect those assets to produce in the future. To see the difference, think about what happens when a company like Boeing unveils a new plane. Investors' expectations about future cash flows from selling those planes increase the stock price immediately, elevating the market value of Boeing. However, the revenue from selling the planes will only be reflected in Boeing's financial statements when it actually sells them.

market capitalization The total market value of equity; equals the market price per share times the number of shares.

Finally, we note that the book value of equity can be negative (liabilities exceed assets), and that a negative book value of equity is not necessarily an indication of poor

EXAMPLE 2.1
Market Versus
Book Value

MyFinanceLab

PROBLEM

If Global has 3.6 million shares outstanding, and these shares are trading for a price of $10.00 per share, what is Global's market capitalization? How does the market capitalization compare to Global's book value of equity?

SOLUTION

PLAN

Market capitalization is equal to price per share times shares outstanding. We can find Global's book value of equity at the bottom of the right side of its balance sheet.

EXECUTE

Global's market capitalization is ($10.00/share) × (3.6 million shares) = $36 million. This market capitalization is significantly higher than Global's book value of equity of $22.2 million.

EVALUATE

Global must have sources of value that do not appear on the balance sheet. These include potential opportunities for growth, the quality of the management team, relationships with suppliers and customers, etc.

performance. Successful firms are often able to borrow in excess of the book value of their assets because creditors recognize that the market value of the assets is far higher. For example, in June 2005 Amazon.com had total liabilities of $2.6 billion and a book value of equity of −$64 million. At the same time, the market value of its equity was over $15 billion. Clearly, investors recognized that Amazon's assets were worth far more than the book value reported on the balance sheet. By 2016, several years of strong growth had brought its book value of equity to over $13 billion and its market value of equity to around $300 billion!

Market-to-Book Ratio

market-to-book ratio (price-to-book [P/B] ratio) The ratio of a firm's market (equity) capitalization to the book value of its stockholders' equity.

In Example 2.1, we compared the market and book values of Global's equity. A common way to make this comparison is to compute the **market-to-book ratio** (also called the **price-to-book [P/B] ratio**), which is the ratio of a firm's market capitalization to the book value of stockholders' equity.

$$\text{Market-to-Book Ratio} = \frac{\text{Market Value of Equity}}{\text{Book Value of Equity}} \qquad (2.3)$$

It is one of many financial ratios used to evaluate a firm. The market-to-book ratio for most successful firms substantially exceeds 1, indicating that the value of the firm's assets when put to use exceeds their historical cost (or liquidation value). The ratio will vary across firms due to differences in fundamental firm characteristics as well as the value added by management. Thus, this ratio is one way a company's stock price provides feedback to its managers on the market's assessment of their decisions.

value stocks Firms with low market-to-book ratios.

growth stocks Firms with high market-to-book ratios.

In early-2016, AmeriServ Financial, Inc. (ASRV) had a market-to-book ratio of 0.57, a reflection of investors' assessment that many of AmeriServ's assets were unlikely to be profitable and were worth less than their book value. Citigroup's market-to-book ratio of 0.59 tells a similar story. Figure 2.1 shows that at the same time, the average market-to-book ratio for the financial services industry was about 1.9 and for large U.S. firms it was close to 3. In contrast, consider that Amazon.com, Inc. (AMZN) had a market-to-book ratio of over 20, and the average for technology firms was over 8. Analysts often classify firms with low market-to-book ratios as **value stocks**, and those with high market-to-book ratios as **growth stocks**.

Enterprise Value

enterprise value The total market value of a firm's equity and debt, less the value of its cash and marketable securities. It measures the value of the firm's underlying business.

A firm's market capitalization measures the market value of the firm's equity, or the value that remains after the firm has paid its debts. So it includes any cash the firm holds. But what if you are interested in just the value of the business itself? The **enterprise value** of a firm assesses the value of the underlying business assets, unencumbered by debt and separate from any cash and marketable securities. We compute it as follows:

$$\text{Enterprise Value} = \text{Market Value of Equity} + \text{Debt} - \text{Cash} \qquad (2.4)$$

For example, given its market capitalization from Example 2.1, Global's enterprise value in 2016 is $36 + 118.7 − 23.2 = \$131.5$ million. We can interpret the enterprise value as the cost to take over the business. That is, it would cost $36 + 118.7 = \$154.7$ million to buy all of Global's equity and pay off its debts. Because we would acquire Global's $23.2 million in cash (which can be used to pay off Global's debt), the net cost is only $154.7 − 23.2 = \$131.5$ million.

FIGURE 2.1

Market-to-Book
Ratios in 2016

This figure presents market-to-book ratios of different firms and groups of firms in 2016. Firms that might be classified as value stocks (low market-to-book ratios) are in red and those that might be classified as growth stocks (high market-to-book ratios) are in blue.

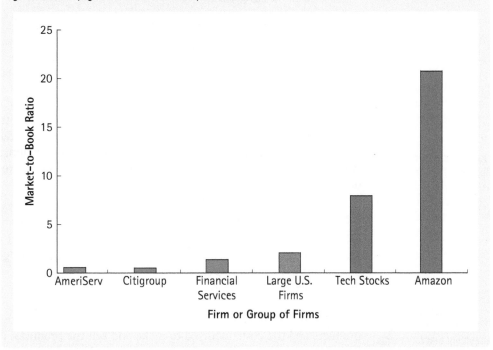

EXAMPLE 2.2

Computing
Enterprise Value

MyFinanceLab

PROBLEM

In June 2013, H.J. Heinz Co. (HNZ) had 320.7 million shares outstanding, a share price of $72.36, a book value of debt of $4.98 billion, and cash of $1.1 billion. What was Heinz's market capitalization (its market value of equity)? What was its enterprise value?

SOLUTION

PLAN

Share Price	$72.36
Shares Outstanding	320.7 million
Cash	$1.10 billion
Debt (book)	$4.98 billion

We will solve the problem using Eq. 2.4: Enterprise Value = Market Value of Equity + Debt − Cash. We can compute the market capitalization by multiplying the share price times the number of shares outstanding. We are given the amount of cash and the amount of debt.

EXECUTE

Heinz had a market capitalization of $72.36/share × 320.7 million shares = $23.21 billion. Thus, Heinz's enterprise value was 23.21 + 4.98 − 1.10 = $27.09 billion.

EVALUATE

The value of Heinz's underlying business, separate from any cash it holds, should be equal to the total value of the financial claims (equity and debt) on that business, which is its enterprise value of $27.09 billion.

CONCEPT CHECK

3. What is depreciation designed to capture?
4. The book value of a company's assets usually does not equal the market value of those assets. What are some reasons for this difference?

2.3 The Income Statement

income statement A list of a firm's revenues and expenses over a period of time.

net income or earnings The last or "bottom" line of a firm's income statement that is a measure of the firm's income over a given period of time.

When you want someone to get to the point, you might ask them for the "bottom line." This expression comes from the *income statement*. The **income statement** lists the firm's revenues and expenses over a period of time. The last or "bottom" line of the income statement shows the firm's **net income**, which is a measure of its profitability during the period. The income statement is sometimes called a *profit and loss* or *P&L statement*, and the net income is also referred to as the firm's **earnings**. In this section, we examine the components of the income statement in detail and introduce ratios we can use to analyze this data.

Earnings Calculations

Whereas the balance sheet shows the firm's assets and liabilities at a given point in time, the income statement shows the flow of revenues and expenses generated by those assets and liabilities between two dates. Table 2.2 shows Global's income statement for 2016 and 2015. We examine each category on the statement.

gross profit The third line of an income statement that represents the difference between a firm's sales revenues and its costs.

Gross Profit. The first two lines of the income statement list the revenues from sales of products and the costs incurred to make and sell the products. Note that in accounting, the terms *revenues* and *net sales* are equivalent. Net sales is simply gross sales minus any returns, discounts, and allowances. We will simply use the term *sales* from here forward. The third line is **gross profit**, the difference between sales revenues and the cost of sales.

TABLE 2.2

Global Corporation's Income Statement Sheet for 2016 and 2015

GLOBAL CORPORATION Income Statement Year ended December 31 (in $ millions)		
	2016	**2015**
Net sales	186.7	176.1
Cost of sales	−153.4	−147.3
Gross Profit	33.3	28.8
Selling, general, and administrative expenses	−13.5	−13
Research and development	−8.2	−7.6
Depreciation and amortization	−1.2	−1.1
Operating Income	10.4	7.1
Other income	—	—
Earnings Before Interest and Taxes (EBIT)	10.4	7.1
Interest income (expense)	−7.7	−4.6
Pretax Income	2.7	2.5
Taxes	−0.7	−0.6
Net Income	2.0	1.9
Earnings per share:	$0.56	$0.53
Diluted earnings per share:	$0.53	$0.50

Operating Expenses. The next group of items is operating expenses. These are expenses from the ordinary course of running the business that are not directly related to producing the goods or services being sold. They include administrative expenses and overhead, salaries, marketing costs, and research and development expenses. The third type of operating expense, depreciation and amortization (a charge that captures the change in value of acquired assets), represents an estimate of the costs that arise from wear and tear or obsolescence of the firm's assets.[3] It is not an actual cash expense. The firm's gross profit less its operating expenses is called **operating income**.

operating income
A firm's gross profit less its operating expenses.

EBIT A firm's earnings before interest and taxes are deducted.

earnings per share (EPS) A firm's net income divided by the total number of shares outstanding.

stock options The right to buy a certain number of shares of stock by a specific date at a specific price.

convertible bonds Corporate bonds with a provision that gives the bondholder an option to convert each bond owned into a fixed number of shares of common stock.

dilution An increase in the total number of shares that will divide a fixed amount of earnings.

diluted EPS The earnings per share a company would have based on the total number of shares including the effects of all stock options and convertible bonds.

Earnings Before Interest and Taxes. We next include other sources of income or expenses that arise from activities that are not the central part of a company's business. Cash flows from the firm's financial investments are one example of other income that would be listed here. After we have adjusted for other sources of income or expenses, we have the firm's earnings before interest and taxes, or **EBIT**.

Pretax and Net Income. From EBIT, we deduct the interest paid on outstanding debt to compute Global's pretax income, and then we deduct corporate taxes to determine the firm's net income.

Net income represents the total earnings of the firm's equity holders. It is often reported on a per-share basis as the firm's **earnings per share (EPS)**, which we compute by dividing net income by the total number of shares outstanding:

$$\text{EPS} = \frac{\text{Net Income}}{\text{Shares Outstanding}} = \frac{\$2.0 \text{ million}}{3.6 \text{ million shares}} = \$0.56 \text{ per share} \qquad (2.5)$$

Although Global has only 3.6 million shares outstanding as of the end of 2016 (from Example 2.1), the number of shares outstanding may grow if Global has made commitments that would cause it to issue more shares. Consider these two examples:

1. Suppose Global compensates its employees or executives with **stock options** that give the holder the right to buy a certain number of shares by a specific date at a specific price. If employees "exercise" these options, the company issues new stock and the number of shares outstanding would grow.

2. The number of shares may also grow if the firm issues **convertible bonds**, a form of debt that can be converted into shares of common stock.

In the cases of stock options and convertible bonds, because there will be more total shares to divide the same earnings, this growth in the number of shares is referred to as **dilution**. Firms disclose the potential for dilution from options they have awarded by reporting **diluted EPS**, which shows the earnings per share the company would have if the stock options were exercised. For example, if Global has awarded options for 200,000 shares of stock to its key executives, its diluted EPS is $2.0 million/3.8 million shares = $0.53.

EBITDA

As will become clear when we discuss the Statement of Cash Flows in the next section, neither EBIT nor net income are the same as the firm's cash flow. So, financial analysts often compute a firm's earnings before interest, taxes, depreciation, and amortization, or **EBITDA**. Because depreciation and amortization are not cash expenses for the firm,

---

[3]Only certain types of amortization are deductible as a pretax expense (e.g., amortization of the cost of an acquired patent). Amortization of goodwill is not a pretax expense and is generally included as an extraordinary item after taxes are deducted.

EBITDA A computation of a firm's earnings before interest, taxes, depreciation, and amortization are deducted.

EBITDA reflects the cash a firm has earned from its operations. If we add back Global's depreciation and amortization to its EBIT, we find that its EBITDA in 2016 was $10.4 + 1.2 = \$11.6$ million.

CONCEPT CHECK

5. What do a firm's earnings measure?

6. What is dilution?

2.4   The Statement of Cash Flows

The income statement provides a measure of the firm's profit over a given time period. However, it does not indicate the amount of *cash* the firm has earned. There are two reasons that net income does not correspond to cash earned. First, there are non-cash entries on the income statement, such as depreciation and amortization. Second, certain uses, such as the purchase of a building or expenditures on inventory, and sources of cash, such as the collection of accounts receivable, are not reported on the income statement. The firm's **statement of cash flows** utilizes the information from the income statement and balance sheet to determine how much cash the firm has generated, and how that cash has been allocated, during a set period. Cash is important: It is needed to pay bills and maintain operations and is the source of any return of investment for investors. Thus, from the perspective of an investor attempting to value the firm or a financial manager concerned about cash flows (vs. earnings), the statement of cash flows provides what may be the most important information of the four financial statements.

statement of cash flows An accounting statement that shows how a firm has used the cash it earned during a set period.

The statement of cash flows is divided into three sections: operating activities, investment activities, and financing activities. These sections roughly correspond to the three major jobs of the financial manager.

1. *Operating activities* starts with net income from the income statement. It then adjusts this number by adding back all non-cash entries related to the firm's operating activities.

2. *Investment activities* lists the cash used for investment.

3. *Financing activities* shows the flow of cash between the firm and its investors.

Global's statement of cash flows is shown in Table 2.3. In this section, we take a close look at each component of the statement of cash flows.

Operating Activity

The first section of Global's statement of cash flows adjusts net income by all non-cash items related to operating activity. For instance, depreciation is deducted when computing net income, but it is not an actual cash expense. Thus, we add it back to net income when determining the amount of cash the firm has generated. Similarly, we add back any other non-cash expenses (for example, deferred taxes).

Next, we adjust for changes to net working capital that arise from changes to accounts receivable, accounts payable, or inventory. When a firm sells a product, it records the revenue as income even though it may not receive the cash from that sale immediately. Instead, it may grant the customer credit and let the customer pay in the future. The customer's obligation adds to the firm's accounts receivable. We use the following guidelines to adjust for changes in working capital:

1. **Accounts receivable:** When a sale is recorded as part of net income, but the cash has not yet been received from the customer, we must adjust the cash flows by *deducting* the increases in accounts receivable. This increase represents additional lending by the firm to its customers and it reduces the cash available to the firm.

2. **Accounts payable:** We *add* increases in accounts payable. Accounts payable represents borrowing by the firm from its suppliers. This borrowing increases the cash available to the firm.

3. **Inventory:** Finally, we *deduct* increases in inventory. Increases in inventory are not recorded as an expense and do not contribute to net income (the cost of the goods are only included in net income when the goods are actually sold). However, the cost of increasing inventory is a cash expense for the firm and must be deducted.

Working capital adjustments address the difference between the time when sales and costs are recorded on the income statement and when the cash actually goes in and out of the firm. For example, Table 2.3 shows that in 2016 we *subtracted* the $5.3 million increase in accounts receivable from net income as part of the operating cash flow calculation. What happened? From Table 2.2, we see that Global had $10.6 million more in sales in 2016 than

TABLE 2.3

Global Corporation's Statement of Cash Flows for 2016 and 2015

GLOBAL CORPORATION Statement of Cash Flows Year ended December 31 (in $ millions)		
	2016	**2015**
Operating activities		
Net income	2.0	1.9
Depreciation and amortization	1.2	1.1
Cash effect of changes in		
Accounts receivable	−5.3	−0.3
Accounts payable	2.7	−0.5
Inventory	−1.0	−1.0
Cash from operating activities	−0.4	1.2
Investment activities		
Capital expenditures	−33.4	−4.0
Acquisitions and other investing activity	—	—
Cash from investing activities	−33.4	−4.0
Financing activities		
Dividends paid	−1.0	−1.0
Sale or purchase of stock	—	—
Increase in short-term borrowing	2.3	3.0
Increase in long-term borrowing	35.2	2.5
Cash from financing activities	36.5	4.5
Change in cash and cash equivalents	2.7	1.7

in 2015. However, from Table 2.1, we also see that Global's accounts receivable increased from $13.2 million in 2015 to $18.5 million in 2016. So, even though Global's sales were up considerably, it has not yet collected all the cash flow for those sales—instead, Global's customers owe it $5.3 million more at the end of 2016 than they did at the end of 2015. Because the statement of cash flows starts with net income, which includes sales for which Global has not yet been paid, we deduct the additional $5.3 million in sales Global is still owed when computing the actual cash flows it generated.

We must make a similar adjustment for inventory. Global does not record the cost of the inventory until it is sold, when it is included in the cost of goods sold. However, when it actually pays for the inventory, cash has flowed out of Global, decreasing operating cash flow. The opposite is true for accounts payable—Global has recorded additional expenses without actually paying for them yet. Those expenses reduce net income, but do not represent cash outflows.

Finally, we add depreciation to net income before calculating operating cash flow. Depreciation is an accounting adjustment to book value that is an expense, but not a cash outflow. That is, when Global's property, plant, and equipment depreciate by $1.2 million, it does not literally cost Global $1.2 million in cash flow. Because this is an expense that reduces net income, but not an actual cash outflow, we must add it back to calculate cash flow. We will talk more about depreciation when we do capital budgeting in Chapter 9. All these adjustments mean that cash flow can be very different from net income. Although Global showed positive net income on the income statement, it actually had a negative $0.4 million cash flow from operating activity, in large part because of the increase in accounts receivable.

EXAMPLE 2.3

The Impact of Depreciation on Cash Flow

MyFinanceLab

PROBLEM
Suppose Global had an additional $1 million depreciation expense in 2016. If Global's tax rate on pretax income is 26%, what would be the impact of this expense on Global's earnings? How would it impact Global's cash at the end of the year?

SOLUTION

PLAN

Depreciation is an operating expense, so Global's operating income, EBIT, and pretax income would be affected. With a tax rate of 26%, Global's tax bill will decrease by 26 cents for every dollar that pretax income is reduced. In order to determine how Global's cash would be impacted, we have to determine the effect of the additional depreciation on cash flows. Recall that depreciation is not an actual cash outflow, even though it is treated as an expense, so the only effect on cash flow is through the reduction in taxes.

EXECUTE

Global's operating income, EBIT, and pretax income would fall by $1 million because of the $1 million in additional operating expense due to depreciation.

This $1 million decrease in pretax income would reduce Global's tax bill by 26% × $1 million = $0.26 million. Therefore, net income would fall by $1 − $0.26 = $0.74 million.

On the statement of cash flows, net income would fall by $0.74 million, but we would add back the additional depreciation of $1 million because it is not a cash expense. Thus, cash from operating activities would rise by −$0.74 + 1 = $0.26 million. Therefore, Global's cash balance at the end of the year would increase by $0.26 million, the amount of the tax savings that resulted from the additional depreciation deduction.

EVALUATE

The increase in cash balance comes completely from the reduction in taxes. Because Global pays $0.26 million less in taxes even though its cash expenses have not increased, it has $0.26 million more in cash at the end of the year.

Investment Activity

capital expenditures
Purchases of new property, plant, and equipment.

The next section of the statement of cash flows shows the cash required for investment activities. Purchases of new property, plant, and equipment are **capital expenditures**. Recall that capital expenditures do not appear immediately as expenses on the income statement. Instead, the firm depreciates these assets and deducts depreciation expenses over time. To determine the firm's cash flow, we already added back depreciation because it is not an actual cash expense. Now, we subtract the actual capital expenditure that the firm made. Similarly, we also deduct other assets purchased or investments made by the firm, such as acquisitions. In Table 2.3, we see that in 2016, Global spent $33.4 million in cash on investing activities. This can be confirmed by adding the depreciation amount of $1.2 from Table 2.2 to the change in long-term assets of ($113.1 – $80.9) from Table 2.1.

Financing Activity

The last section of the statement of cash flows shows the cash flows from financing activities. Dividends paid to shareholders are a cash outflow. Global paid $1 million to its shareholders as dividends in 2016.

The difference between a firm's net income and the amount it spends on dividends is referred to as the firm's retained earnings for that year:

$$\text{Retained Earnings} = \text{Net Income} - \text{Dividends} \tag{2.6}$$

payout ratio The ratio of a firm's dividends to its net income.

Global retained $2 million − $1 million = $1 million, or 50% of its earnings in 2016. This makes its *payout ratio* for 2016 equal to 50%. A firm's **payout ratio** is the ratio of its dividends to its net income:

$$\text{Payout Ratio} = \frac{\text{Dividends}}{\text{Net Income}} \tag{2.7}$$

Also listed under financing activity is any cash the company received from the sale of its own stock, or cash spent buying (repurchasing) its own stock. Global did not issue or repurchase stock during this period.

The last items to include in this section result from changes to Global's short-term and long-term borrowing. Global raised money by issuing debt, so the increases in short-term and long-term borrowing represent cash inflows. The last line of the statement of cash flows combines the cash flows from these three activities to calculate the overall change in the firm's cash balance over the period of the statement. In this case, Global had cash inflows of $2.7 million in 2016, which matches the change in cash from 2015 to 2016 shown earlier in the balance sheet. By looking at the statement in Table 2.3 as a whole, we can determine that Global chose to borrow (mainly in the form of long-term debt) to cover the cost of its investment and operating activities. Although the firm's cash balance has increased, Global's negative operating cash flows and relatively high expenditures on investment activities might give investors some reasons for concern. If this pattern continues, Global will need to raise new external capital to remain in business.

CONCEPT CHECK

7. Why does a firm's net income not correspond to cash earned?

8. What are the components of the statement of cash flows?

2.5 Other Financial Statement Information

The most important elements of a firm's financial statements are the balance sheet, income statement, and the statement of cash flows, which we have already discussed. Several other pieces of information contained in the financial statements warrant brief mention: the *statement of stockholders' equity*, the *management discussion and analysis*, and *notes to the financial statements*.

Statement of Stockholders' Equity

statement of stockholders' equity An accounting statement that breaks down the stockholders' equity computed on the balance sheet into the amount that came from issuing new shares versus retained earnings.

The **statement of stockholders' equity** breaks down the stockholders' equity computed on the balance sheet into the amount that came from issuing shares (par value plus paid-in capital) versus retained earnings. Because the book value of stockholders' equity is not a useful assessment of value for financial purposes, financial managers use the statement of stockholders' equity infrequently (so we will skip the computational details here). We can, however, determine the change in stockholders' equity using information from the firm's other financial statements as follows:[4]

$$\text{Change in Stockholders' Equity} = \text{Retained Earnings} + \text{Net Sales of Stock}$$
$$= \text{Net Income} - \text{Dividends} + \text{Sales of Stock}$$
$$- \text{Repurchases of Stock} \qquad (2.8)$$

For example, because Global had no stock sales or repurchases, its stockholders' equity increased by the amount of its retained earnings, or $1.0 million, in 2016. Note that this result matches the change in stockholders' equity shown earlier on Global's balance sheet.

Management Discussion and Analysis

management discussion and analysis (MD&A) A preface to the financial statements in which a company's management discusses the recent year (or quarter), providing a background on the company and any significant events that may have occurred.

The **management discussion and analysis (MD&A)** is a preface to the financial statements in which the company's management discusses the recent year (or quarter), providing a background on the company and any significant events that may have occurred. Management may also discuss the coming year, and outline goals and new projects.

Management must also discuss any important risks that the firm faces or issues that may affect the firm's liquidity or resources. Management is also required to disclose any **off-balance sheet transactions**, which are transactions or arrangements that can have a material impact on the firm's future performance yet do not appear on the balance sheet. For example, if a firm has made guarantees that it will compensate a buyer for losses related to an asset purchased from the firm, these guarantees represent a potential future liability for the firm that must be disclosed as part of the MD&A.

off-balance sheet transactions Transactions or arrangements that can have a material impact on a firm's future performance yet do not appear on the balance sheet.

Notes to the Financial Statements

In addition to the four financial statements, companies provide extensive notes with additional details on the information provided in the statements. For example, the notes document important accounting assumptions that were used in preparing the statements. They often provide information specific to a firm's subsidiaries or its separate product lines. They show the details of the firm's stock-based compensation plans for employees and the different types of debt the firm has outstanding. Details of acquisitions, spin-offs, leases, taxes, and risk management activities are also given. The information provided in the notes is often very important to a full interpretation of the firm's financial statements.

CONCEPT CHECK

9. Where do off-balance sheet transactions appear in a firm's financial statements?

10. What information do the notes to financial statements provide?

2.6   Financial Statement Analysis

Investors often use accounting statements to evaluate a firm in one of two ways:

1. Compare the firm with itself by analyzing how the firm has changed over time.
2. Compare the firm to other similar firms using a common set of financial ratios.

---

[4]Sales of stock would also include any stock-based compensation.

In this section, we will describe the most commonly used ratios—related to profitability, liquidity, asset efficiency, working capital, interest coverage, leverage, valuation, and operating returns—and explain how each one is used in practice.

Profitability Ratios

We introduce three profitability ratios: *gross margin, operating margin*, and *net profit margin*.

gross margin The ratio of gross profit to revenues (sales), it reflects the ability of the company to sell a product for more than the sum of the direct costs of making it.

Gross Margin. The **gross margin** of a firm is the ratio of gross profit to revenues (sales):

$$\text{Gross Margin} = \frac{\text{Gross Profit}}{\text{Sales}} \tag{2.9}$$

The gross margin simply reflects the ability of the company to sell a product for more than the sum of the direct costs of making it. All of the firm's other expenses of doing business (those not directly related to producing the goods sold) must be covered by this margin. In 2016, Global's gross profit was $33.3 million and its sales were $186.7 million, for a gross margin of 33.3/186.7 = 17.84%.

operating margin The ratio of operating income to revenues, it reveals how much a company has earned from each dollar of sales before deducting interest and taxes.

Operating Margin. Because operating income reflects all of the expenses of doing business, another important profitability ratio is the **operating margin**, the ratio of operating income to revenues:

$$\text{Operating Margin} = \frac{\text{Operating Income}}{\text{Sales}} \tag{2.10}$$

The operating margin reveals how much a company earns before interest and taxes from each dollar of sales. Global's operating margin in 2016 was 10.4/186.7 = 5.57%, an increase from its 2015 operating margin of 7.1/176.1 = 4.03%. By comparing operating margins across firms within an industry, we can assess the relative efficiency of firms' operations. For example, in 2015, United Continental Holdings (UAL) had an operating margin of 13.64% (i.e., they gained 13.64 cents for each dollar in revenues). However, competitor Alaska Air Group (ALK) had an operating margin of 23.19%.

Differences in operating margins can also result from differences in strategy. For example, in 2016, Walmart Stores had an operating margin of 5% while higher-end retailer Macy's had an operating margin of 9%. In this case, Walmart's lower operating margin is not a result of its inefficiency but is part of its strategy of offering lower prices to sell common products in high volume. Indeed, Walmart's sales were more than 17 times higher than those of Macy's.

net profit margin The ratio of net income to revenues, it shows the fraction of each dollar in revenues that is available to equity holders after the firm pays its expenses, plus interest and taxes.

Net Profit Margin. A firm's **net profit margin** is the ratio of net income to revenues:

$$\text{Net Profit Margin} = \frac{\text{Net Income}}{\text{Sales}} \tag{2.11}$$

The net profit margin shows the fraction of each dollar in revenues that is available to equity holders after the firm pays its expenses, interest, and taxes. Global's net profit margin in 2016 was 2.0/186.7 = 1.07%. Differences in net profit margins can be due to differences in efficiency, but they can also result from differences in leverage (the firm's reliance on debt financing), which determines the amount of interest payments.

Liquidity Ratios

current ratio The ratio of current assets to current liabilities.

quick ratio ("acid-test ratio") The ratio of current assets other than inventory to current liabilities.

Creditors often compare a firm's current assets and current liabilities to assess whether the firm has sufficient working capital to meet its short-term needs. This comparison is sometimes summarized in the firm's **current ratio**, the ratio of current assets to current liabilities. A more stringent test of the firm's liquidity is the **quick ratio ("acid-test" ratio)**, which compares only cash and "near cash" assets, such as short-term investments and accounts receivable, to current liabilities.

$$\text{Current Ratio} = \frac{\text{Current Assets}}{\text{Current Liabilities}} \qquad (2.12)$$

$$\text{Quick Ratio} = \frac{\text{Current Assets} - \text{Inventory}}{\text{Current Liabilities}} \qquad (2.13)$$

In 2016, Global's quick ratio was $(57.0 - 15.3)/34.7 = 1.20$. A higher current or quick ratio implies less risk of the firm experiencing a cash shortfall in the near future. A reason to exclude inventory is that an increase in the current ratio that results from an unusual increase in inventory could be an indicator that the firm is having difficulty selling its products.

Ultimately, firms need cash to pay employees and meet other obligations. Running out of cash can be very costly for a firm, so firms often gauge their cash position by calculating the **cash ratio**, which is the most stringent liquidity ratio:

cash ratio The ratio of cash to current liabilities.

$$\text{Cash Ratio} = \frac{\text{Cash}}{\text{Current Liabilities}} \qquad (2.14)$$

Asset Efficiency

A financial manager can use the combined information in the firm's income statement and balance sheet to gauge how efficiently his or her firm is utilizing its assets. A first broad measure of efficiency is **asset turnover**, the ratio of sales to total assets:

asset turnover The ratio of sales to total assets.

$$\text{Asset Turnover} = \frac{\text{Sales}}{\text{Total Assets}} \qquad (2.15)$$

Low values of asset turnover indicate that the firm is not generating much revenue (sales) per dollar of assets. In 2016, Global's $170.1 million in assets generated $186.7 million in sales, for an asset turnover ratio of 1.1 ($= \$186.7/\$170.1$). Since total assets includes assets, such as cash, that are not directly involved in generating sales, Global's manager might also look at Global's fixed asset turnover, which is equal to sales divided by fixed assets:

$$\text{Fixed Asset Turnover} = \frac{\text{Sales}}{\text{Fixed Assets}} \qquad (2.16)$$

accounts receivable days (average collection period or days sales outstanding) An expression of a firm's accounts receivable in terms of the number of days' worth of sales that the accounts receivable represents.

Global's fixed assets in 2016 were $113.1 million worth of property, plant, and equipment, yielding a fixed asset turnover of 1.7 ($= \$186.7/\$113.1$). Low asset turnover ratios indicate that the firm is generating relatively few sales given the amount of assets it employs.

Working Capital Ratios

Global's managers might be further interested in how efficiently they are managing their net working capital. We can express the firm's accounts receivable in terms of the number of days' worth of sales that it represents, called the **accounts receivable days**, **average collection period**, or **days sales outstanding**:[5]

$$\text{Accounts Receivable Days} = \frac{\text{Accounts Receivable}}{\text{Average Daily Sales}} \tag{2.17}$$

accounts payable days An expression of a firm's accounts payable in terms of the number of days' worth of cost of goods sold that the accounts payable represents.

Given average daily sales of $186.7 million/365 = $0.51 million in 2016, Global's receivables of $18.5 million represent 18.5/0.51 = 36 days' worth of sales. In other words, Global takes a little over one month to collect payment from its customers, on average. In 2015, Global's accounts receivable represented only 27.5 days worth of sales. Although the number of receivable days can fluctuate seasonally, a significant unexplained increase could be a cause for concern (perhaps indicating the firm is doing a poor job collecting from its customers or is trying to boost sales by offering generous credit terms). Similar ratios exist for accounts payable and inventory. Those ratios are called **accounts payable days** (accounts payable divided by average daily cost of goods sold) and **inventory days** (inventory divided by average daily cost of goods sold).

inventory days An expression of a firm's inventory in terms of the number of days' worth of cost of goods sold that the inventory represents.

We can also compute how efficiently firms use inventory. The **inventory turnover ratio** is equal to the cost of goods sold divided by either the latest cost of inventory or the average inventory over the year. We use the cost of goods sold because that is how inventory costs are reflected on the income statement. It is also common to use sales in the numerator to make the ratio more like the asset turnover ratios.

inventory turnover ratio The cost of goods sold divided by either the latest cost of inventory or the average inventory over the year, it shows how efficiently companies turn their inventory into sales.

$$\text{Inventory Turnover} = \frac{\text{Cost of Goods Sold}}{\text{Inventory}} \tag{2.18}$$

As with the other ratios in this section, a normal level for this ratio can vary substantially for different industries, although a higher level (more dollars of sales per dollar of inventory) is generally better.

EXAMPLE 2.4

Computing Working Capital Ratios

MyFinanceLab

PROBLEM

Compute Global's accounts payable days, inventory days, and inventory turnover for 2016.

SOLUTION

PLAN AND ORGANIZE

Working capital ratios require information from both the balance sheet and the income statement. For these ratios, we need inventory and accounts payable from the balance sheet and cost of goods sold from the income statement (often listed as cost of sales).

Inventory = 15.3, Accounts payable = 29.2, Cost of goods sold (cost of sales) = 153.4

EXECUTE

$$\text{Accounts payable days} = \frac{\text{Accounts Payable}}{\text{Average Daily Cost of Goods Sold}} = \frac{29.2}{(153.4/365)} = 69.48$$

$$\text{Inventory days} = \frac{\text{Inventory}}{\text{Average Daily Cost of Goods Sold}} = \frac{15.3}{(153.4/365)} = 36.40$$

$$\text{Inventory turnover} = \frac{\text{Cost of Goods Sold}}{\text{Inventory}} = \frac{153.4}{15.3} = 10.03$$

(Continued)

---

[5]Accounts receivable days can also be calculated based on the average accounts receivable at the end of the current and prior years.

EVALUATE

Assuming that Global's accounts payable at year-end on its balance sheet is representative of the normal amount during the year, Global is able, on average, to take about 69.5 days to pay its suppliers. This compares well with the 27.5 days we calculated that it waits on average to be paid (its accounts receivable days). Global typically takes 36 days to sell its inventory. Note that inventory turnover and inventory days tell us the same thing in different ways—if it takes Global about 36 days to sell its inventory, then it turns over its inventory about 10 times per 365-day year. In Chapter 19 on working capital management, we'll see how a company's receivable, inventory, and payable days make up its operating cycle.

Interest Coverage Ratios

interest coverage ratio or times interest earned (TIE) ratio An assessment by lenders of a firm's leverage, it is equal to a measure of earnings divided by interest.

Lenders often assess a firm's leverage by computing an **interest coverage ratio**, also known as a **times interest earned (TIE) ratio**, which is equal to a measure of earnings divided by interest. Financial managers watch these ratios carefully because they assess how easily the firm will be able to cover its interest payments. There is no one accepted measure of earnings for these ratios; it is common to consider operating income, EBIT, or EBITDA as a multiple of the firm's interest expenses. When this ratio is high, it indicates that the firm is earning much more than is necessary to meet its required interest payments.

EXAMPLE 2.5

Computing Interest Coverage Ratios

MyFinanceLab

PROBLEM

Assess Global's ability to meet its interest obligations by calculating interest coverage ratios using both EBIT and EBITDA.

SOLUTION

PLAN AND ORGANIZE

Gather the EBIT, depreciation, and amortization and interest expense for each year from Global's income statement.

$$2015: \text{EBIT} = 7.1, \quad \text{EBITDA} = 7.1 + 1.1, \quad \text{Interest expense} = 4.6$$

$$2016: \text{EBIT} = 10.4, \quad \text{EBITDA} = 10.4 + 1.2, \quad \text{Interest expense} = 7.7$$

EXECUTE

In 2015 and 2016, Global had the following interest coverage ratios:

$$2015: \frac{\text{EBIT}}{\text{Interest}} = \frac{7.1}{4.6} = 1.54 \quad \text{and} \quad \frac{\text{EBITDA}}{\text{Interest}} = \frac{7.1 + 1.1}{4.6} = 1.78$$

$$2016: \frac{\text{EBIT}}{\text{Interest}} = \frac{10.4}{7.7} = 1.35 \quad \text{and} \quad \frac{\text{EBITDA}}{\text{Interest}} = \frac{10.4 + 1.2}{7.7} = 1.51$$

EVALUATE

The coverage ratios indicate that Global is generating enough cash to cover its interest obligations. However, Global's low—and declining—interest coverage could be a source of concern for its creditors.

Leverage Ratios

leverage A measure of the extent to which a firm relies on debt as a source of financing.

Another important piece of information that we can learn from a firm's balance sheet is the firm's **leverage**, or the extent to which it relies on debt as a source of financing. The **debt-equity ratio** is a common ratio used to assess a firm's leverage that we calculate by

debt-equity ratio The ratio of a firm's total amount of short- and long-term debt (including current maturities) to the value of its equity, which may be calculated based on market or book values.

dividing the total amount of short- and long-term debt (including current maturities) by the total stockholders' equity:

$$\text{Debt-Equity Ratio} = \frac{\text{Total Debt}}{\text{Total Equity}} \tag{2.19}$$

We can calculate this ratio using either book or market values for equity and debt. From Table 2.1, Global's debt in 2016 includes notes payable ($5.5 million) and long-term debt ($113.2 million), for a total of $118.7 million. Therefore, using the book value of equity, its *book* debt-equity ratio is 118.7/22.2 = 5.3. Note the large increase from 2015, when the book debt-equity ratio was only (3.2 + 78)/21.2 = 3.8.

Because of the difficulty interpreting the book value of equity, the book debt-equity ratio is not especially useful. It is more informative to compare the firm's debt to the market value of its equity. Global's debt-equity ratio in 2016, using the market value of equity (from Example 2.1), is 118.7/36 = 3.3, which means Global's debt is a bit more than triple the market value of its equity.[6] As we will see later in the text, a firm's *market* debt-equity ratio has important consequences for the risk and return of its stock.

debt-to-capital ratio The ratio of total debt to total debt plus total equity.

We can also calculate the fraction of the firm financed by debt in terms of its **debt-to-capital ratio**:

$$\text{Debt-to-Capital Ratio} = \frac{\text{Total Debt}}{\text{Total Equity} + \text{Total Debt}} \tag{2.20}$$

Again, this ratio can be computed using book or market values.

While leverage increases the risk to the firm's equity holders, firms may also hold cash reserves in order to reduce risk. Thus, another useful measure to consider is the firm's **net debt**, or debt in excess of its cash reserves:

net debt Debt in excess of a firm's cash reserves.

$$\text{Net Debt} = \text{Total Debt} - \text{Excess Cash \& Short-Term Investments} \tag{2.21}$$

To understand why net debt may be a more relevant measure of leverage, consider a firm with more cash than debt outstanding: Because such a firm could pay off its debts immediately using its available cash, it has not increased its risk and has no effective leverage.

Analogous to the debt-to-capital ratio, we can use the concept of net debt to compute the firm's **debt-to-enterprise value ratio**:

debt-to-enterprise value ratio The ratio of a firm's net debt to its enterprise value.

$$\text{Debt-to-Enterprise Value Ratio} = \frac{\text{Net Debt}}{\text{Market Value of Equity} + \text{Net Debt}}$$

$$= \frac{\text{Net Debt}}{\text{Enterprise Value}} \tag{2.22}$$

Given Global's 2016 cash balance of $23.2 million, and total long- and short-term debt of $118.7 million, its net debt is 118.7 − 23.2 = $95.5 million.[7] Given its market value of equity of $36.0 million, Global's enterprise value in 2016 is 36.0 + 95.5 = $131.5 million, and thus its debt-to-enterprise value ratio is 95.5/131.5 = 72.6%. That is, 72.6% of Global's underlying business activity is financed via debt.

---

[6]In this calculation, we have compared the market value of equity to the book value of debt. Strictly speaking, it would be best to use the market value of debt. But because the market value of debt is generally not very different from its book value, this distinction is often ignored in practice.

[7]While net debt should ideally be calculated by deducting cash in excess of the firm's operating needs, absent additional information, it is typical in practice to deduct all cash on the balance sheet.

equity multiplier A measure of leverage equal to total assets divided by total equity.

A final measure of leverage is a firm's **equity multiplier**, measured in book value terms as Total Assets/Book Value of Equity. As we will see shortly, this measure captures the amplification of the firm's accounting returns that results from leverage. The market value equity multiplier, which is generally measured as Enterprise Value/Market Value of Equity, indicates the amplification of shareholders' financial risk that results from leverage.

Valuation Ratios

price-earnings ratio (P/E) The ratio of the market value of equity to the firm's earnings, or its share price to its earnings per share.

Analysts and investors use a number of ratios to gauge the market value of a firm. The most important is the firm's **price-earnings ratio (P/E)**:

$$\text{P/E Ratio} = \frac{\text{Market Capitalization}}{\text{Net Income}} = \frac{\text{Share Price}}{\text{Earnings per Share}} \qquad (2.23)$$

That is, the P/E ratio is the ratio of the value of equity to the firm's earnings, either on a total basis or on a per-share basis. Following Eq. 2.23, Global's P/E ratio in 2016 was $36/2.0 = 10/0.56 = 18$. The P/E ratio is a simple measure that is often used to assess whether a stock is over- or under-valued, based on the idea that the value of a stock should be proportional to the level of earnings it can generate for its shareholders. P/E ratios can vary widely across industries and tend to be higher for industries with high growth rates. For example, in 2016, the average large U.S. firm had a P/E ratio of about 25. But software firms, which tend to have above-average growth rates, had an average P/E ratio of 38. One way to capture the idea that a higher P/E ratio can be justified by a higher growth rate is to compare it to the company's expected earnings growth rate. For example, if Global's expected growth rate is 18%, then it would have a P/E to Growth, or **PEG ratio**, of 1. Some investors consider PEG ratios of 1 or below as indicating the stock is fairly priced, but would question whether the company is potentially overvalued if the PEG is higher than 1.

PEG ratio The ratio of a firm's P/E to its expected earnings growth rate.

The P/E ratio considers the value of the firm's equity and so depends on its leverage. Recall that the amount of assets controlled by the equity holders can be increased through the use of leverage. To assess the market value of the underlying business, it is common to consider valuation ratios based on the firm's enterprise value. Typical ratios include the ratio of enterprise value to revenue, or enterprise value to operating income, or EBITDA. These ratios compare the value of the business to its sales, operating profits, or cash flow. Similar to the P/E ratio, managers use these ratios to make intra-industry comparisons of how firms are priced in the market.

COMMON MISTAKE

Mismatched Ratios

When considering valuation (and other) ratios, be sure that the items you are comparing both represent amounts related to the entire firm or that both represent amounts related solely to equity holders. For example, a firm's share price and market capitalization are values associated with the firm's equity. Thus, it makes sense to compare them to the firm's earnings per share or net income, which are amounts to equity holders after interest has been paid to debt holders. We must be careful, however, if we compare a firm's market capitalization to its revenues, operating income, or EBITDA. These amounts are related to the whole firm, and both debt and equity holders have a claim to them. Therefore, it is better to compare revenues, operating income, or EBITDA to the enterprise value of the firm, which includes both debt and equity.

The P/E ratio is not useful when the firm's earnings are negative. In this case, it is common to look at the firm's enterprise value relative to sales. The risk in doing so, however, is that earnings might be negative because the firm's underlying business model is fundamentally flawed, as was the case for many Internet firms in the late 1990s.

EXAMPLE 2.6

Computing Profitability and Valuation Ratios

MyFinanceLab

PROBLEM

Consider the following data for Walmart Stores and Target Corporation ($ billions):

	Walmart Stores (WMT)	**Target Corporation (TGT)**
Sales	469	73
Operating Income	28	5
Net Income	17	3
Market Capitalization	222	38
Cash	8	1
Debt	54	18

Compare Walmart's and Target's operating margin, net profit margin, P/E ratio, and the ratio of enterprise value to operating income and sales.

SOLUTION

PLAN

The table contains all of the raw data, but we need to compute the ratios using the inputs in the table.

Operating Margin = Operating Income/Sales
Net Profit Margin = Net Income/Sales
P/E Ratio = Price/Earnings = Market Capitalization/Net Income
Enterprise Value to Operating Income = Enterprise Value/Operating Income
Enterprise Value to Sales = Enterprise Value/Sales

EXECUTE

Walmart had an operating margin of 28/469 = 6.0%, a net profit margin of 17/469 = 3.6%, and a P/E ratio of 222/17 = 13.1. Its enterprise value was 222 + 54 − 8 = $268 billion. Its ratio to operating income is 268/28 = 9.6, and its ratio to sales is 268/469 = 0.57.

Target had an operating margin of 5/73 = 6.8%, a net profit margin of 3/73 = 4.1%, and a P/E ratio of 38/3 = 12.7. Its enterprise value was 38 + 18 − 1 = $55 billion. Its ratio to operating income is 55/5 = 11, and its ratio to sales is 55/73 = 0.75.

EVALUATE

Target has a slightly higher operating margin, net profit margin, and enterprise value ratio, but a slightly lower P/E ratio. This suggests that the market expects similar growth rates from Target and Walmart, despite large differences in size.

Operating Returns

return on equity (ROE) The ratio of a firm's net income to the book value of its equity.

Analysts and financial managers often evaluate the firm's return on investment by comparing its income to its investment using ratios such as the firm's **return on equity (ROE):**[8]

$$\text{Return on Equity} = \frac{\text{Net Income}}{\text{Book Value of Equity}} \qquad (2.24)$$

Global's ROE in 2016 was 2.0/22.2 = 9.0%. The ROE provides a measure of the return that the firm has earned on its past investments. A high ROE may indicate the firm is able to find investment opportunities that are very profitable. Of course, one weakness of this measure is the difficulty in interpreting the book value of equity.

---

[8]Because net income is measured over the year, the ROE can also be calculated based on the average book value of equity at the end of the current and prior years.

Another common measure is the **return on assets (ROA)**, which is net income plus interest expense divided by the total assets. The ROA calculation includes interest expense in the numerator because the assets in the denominator have been funded by both debt and equity investors. A firm must earn both a positive ROE and ROA to grow.

As a performance measure, ROA has the benefit that it is less sensitive to leverage than ROE. However, it is sensitive to working capital—for example, an equal increase in the firm's receivables and payables will increase total assets and thus lower ROA. To avoid this problem, we can consider the firm's **return on invested capital (ROIC)**:

$$\text{Return on Invested Capital} = \frac{\text{EBIT} \, (1 - \text{Tax Rate})}{\text{Book Value of Equity} + \text{Net Debt}} \quad (2.25)$$

The return on invested capital measures the after-tax profit generated by the business itself, excluding any interest expenses (or interest income), and compares it to the capital raised from equity and debt holders that has already been deployed (i.e., is not held as cash). Of the three measures of operating returns, ROIC is the most useful in assessing the performance of the underlying business.

PROBLEM

Assess how Global's ability to use its assets effectively has changed in the last year by computing the change in its return on assets.

SOLUTION

PLAN AND ORGANIZE

In order to compute ROA, we need net income, interest expense, and total assets.

	2015	2016
Net Income	1.9	2.0
Interest Expense	4.6	7.7
Total Assets	128.9	170.1

EXECUTE

In 2016, Global's ROA was $(2.0 + 7.7)/170.1 = 5.7\%$, compared to an ROA in 2015 of $(1.9 + 4.6)/128.9 = 5.0\%$.

EVALUATE

The improvement in Global's ROA from 2015 to 2016 suggests that Global was able to use its assets more effectively and increase its return over this period.

The DuPont Identity

Global's financial manager will need to know that its ROE is 9%, but that financial manager would also need to understand the drivers of his or her firm's return on equity. High margins, efficient use of assets, or even simply high leverage could all lead to a higher return on equity. By delving deeper into the sources of return on equity, the financial manager can gain a clear sense of the firm's financial picture. One common tool for doing so is the **DuPont Identity**, named for the company that popularized it, which expresses return on equity as the product of profit margin, asset turnover, and a measure of leverage.

To understand the DuPont Identity, we start with ROE and decompose it in steps into the drivers identified in the identity. First, we simply multiply ROE by (sales/sales), which is just 1, and rearrange terms:

$$\text{ROE} = \left(\frac{\text{Net Income}}{\text{Total Equity}}\right)\left(\frac{\text{Sales}}{\text{Sales}}\right) = \left(\frac{\text{Net Income}}{\text{Sales}}\right)\left(\frac{\text{Sales}}{\text{Total Equity}}\right) \quad (2.26)$$

This expression says that ROE can be thought of as net income per dollar of sales (profit margin) times the amount of sales per dollar of equity. For example, Global's ROE comes from its profit margin of 1.07% multiplied by its sales per dollar of equity $(186.7/22.2 = 8.41)$: $1.07\% \times 8.41 = 9\%$. We can take the decomposition further by multiplying Eq. 2.26 by (total assets/total assets), which again is just 1, and rearranging the terms:

DuPont Identity

$$\text{ROE} = \left(\frac{\text{Net Income}}{\text{Sales}}\right)\left(\frac{\text{Sales}}{\text{Total Equity}}\right)\left(\frac{\text{Total Assets}}{\text{Total Assets}}\right)$$

$$= \left(\frac{\text{Net Income}}{\text{Sales}}\right)\left(\frac{\text{Sales}}{\text{Total Assets}}\right)\left(\frac{\text{Total Assets}}{\text{Total Equity}}\right) \quad (2.27)$$

This final expression says that ROE is equal to net income per dollar of sales (profit margin) times sales per dollar of assets (asset turnover) times assets per dollar of equity (equity multiplier). Equation 2.27 is the DuPont Identity, expressing return on equity as the product of profit margin, asset turnover, and the equity multiplier. Turning to Global, its equity multiplier is 7.7($=170.1/22.2$). A financial manager at Global looking for ways to increase ROE could assess the drivers behind its current ROE with the DuPont Identity. With a profit margin of 1.07%, asset turnover of 1.1, and an equity multiplier of 7.7, we have:

$$\text{ROE} = 9\% = (1.07\%)(1.1)(7.7)$$

This decomposition of ROE shows that leverage is already high (confirmed by the fact that the book debt-to-equity ratio shows that Global's debt is more than five times its equity). However, Global is operating with only 1% profit margins and relatively low asset turnover. Thus, Global's managers should focus on utilizing the firm's existing assets more efficiently and lowering costs to increase the profit margin.[9]

EXAMPLE 2.8

DuPont Analysis

MyFinanceLab

PROBLEM

The following table contains information about Walmart (WMT) and Nordstrom (JWN). Compute their respective ROEs and then determine how much Walmart would need to increase its profit margin in order to match Nordstrom's ROE.

	Profit Margin	Asset Turnover	Equity Multiplier
Walmart	3.6%	2.3	2.7
Nordstrom	6.1%	1.5	4.2

(Continued)

---

[9]Although the DuPont Identity makes it look like you can increase ROE just by increasing leverage, it is not quite that simple. An increase in leverage will increase your interest expense, decreasing your profit margin.

SOLUTION

PLAN AND ORGANIZE

The table contains all the relevant information to use the DuPont Identity to compute the ROE. We can compute the ROE of each company by multiplying together its profit margin, asset turnover, and equity multiplier. In order to determine how much Walmart would need to increase its profit margin to match Nordstrom's ROE, we can set Walmart's ROE equal to Nordstrom's, keep its turnover and equity multiplier fixed, and solve for the profit margin.

EXECUTE

Using the DuPont Identity, we have:

$$ROE_{WMT} = 3.6\% \times 2.3 \times 2.7 = 22.4\%$$
$$ROE_{JWN} = 6.1\% \times 1.5 \times 4.2 = 38.4\%$$

Now, using Nordstrom's ROE, but Walmart's asset turnover and equity multiplier, we can solve for the profit margin that Walmart needs to achieve Nordstrom's ROE:

$$38.4\% = \text{Margin} \times 2.3 \times 2.7$$
$$\text{Margin} = 38.4\%/6.21 = 6.2\%$$

EVALUATE

Walmart would have to increase its profit margin from 3.6% to 6.2% in order to match Nordstrom's ROE. It would be able to achieve Nordstrom's ROE with much lower leverage and around the same profit margin as Nordstrom (6.2% vs. 6.1%) because of its higher turnover.

Table 2.4 summarizes financial ratios and provides typical values of those ratios for the manufacturing, retail, and service sectors along with the 500 firms in the S&P 500 index. Because many companies with debt also held high levels of cash over the period, leverage ratios based on Net Debt are much lower than those based on Total Debt.

TABLE 2.4

A Summary of Key Financial Ratios

Ratio	Formula	Manufacturing	Retail	Service	S&P 500
Profitability Ratios					
Gross Margin	$\dfrac{\text{Gross Profit}}{\text{Sales}}$	33.8%	30.1%	51.4%	39.0%
Operating Margin	$\dfrac{\text{Operating Income}}{\text{Sales}}$	8.1%	7.3%	12.2%	16.2%
Net Profit Margin	$\dfrac{\text{Net Income}}{\text{Sales}}$	1.3%	2.6%	2.5%	4.5%
Liquidity Ratios					
Current Ratio	$\dfrac{\text{Current Assets}}{\text{Current Liabilities}}$	2.6	1.5	1.8	2.1
Quick Ratio	$\dfrac{\text{Current Assets} - \text{Inventory}}{\text{Current Liabilities}}$	1.9	0.8	1.7	1.6
Cash Ratio	$\dfrac{\text{Cash}}{\text{Current Liabilities}}$	0.9	0.3	0.9	0.7
Efficiency and Working Capital Ratios					
Accounts Receivable Days	$\dfrac{\text{Accounts Receivable}}{\text{Average Daily Sales}}$	57.6	7.8	63.0	60.2
Fixed Asset Turnover	$\dfrac{\text{Sales}}{\text{Fixed Assets}}$	5.4	6.6	10.6	4.8

Ratio	Formula	Manufacturing	Retail	Service	S&P 500
Total Asset Turnover	$\dfrac{\text{Sales}}{\text{Total Assets}}$	0.7	1.7	0.6	0.5
Inventory Turnover	$\dfrac{\text{Cost of Goods Sold}}{\text{Inventory}}$	4.2	6.9	26.9	5.7
Interest Coverage Ratios					
EBIT/Interest Coverage	$\dfrac{\text{EBIT}}{\text{Interest Expense}}$	3.2	5.5	2.3	3.9
EBITDA/Interest Coverage	$\dfrac{\text{EBITDA}}{\text{Interest Expense}}$	6.0	9.3	5.3	6.7
Leverage Ratios					
Book Debt-to-Equity Ratio	$\dfrac{\text{Total Debt}}{\text{Book Value of Total Equity}}$	27.1%	44.2%	21.5%	46.6%
Market Debt-to-Equity Ratio	$\dfrac{\text{Total Debt}}{\text{Market Value of Total Equity}}$	10.0%	17.2%	6.2%	21.8%
Debt-to-Capital Ratio	$\dfrac{\text{Total Debt}}{\text{Total Equity} + \text{Total Debt}}$	20.9%	30.6%	17.6%	32.0%
Debt-to-Enterprise Value	$\dfrac{\text{Net Debt}}{\text{Enterprise Value}}$	0.0%	4.7%	0.0%	2.0%
Equity Multiplier	$\dfrac{\text{Total Assets}}{\text{Total Equity}}$	1.8	2.4	1.98	2.4
Operating Returns					
Return on Equity	$\dfrac{\text{Net Income}}{\text{Book Value of Equity}}$	4.2%	10.4%	3.6%	7.1%
Return on Assets	$\dfrac{\text{Net Income} + \text{Interest Expense}}{\text{Total Assets}}$	3.6%	5.8%	3.3%	4.1%
Return on Invested Capital (ROIC)	$\dfrac{\text{EBIT}(1-\text{Tax Rate})}{\text{Book Value of Equity} + \text{Net Debt}}$	18.0%	20.1%	18.3%	17.0%
Valuation Ratios					
Market-to-Book Ratio	$\dfrac{\text{Market Value of Equity}}{\text{Book Value of Equity}}$	2.7	2.7	3.5	2.1
Price-to-Earnings Ratio	$\dfrac{\text{Share Price}}{\text{Earnings per Share}}$	21.5	21.6	28.8	21.2
Enterprise Value Ratios (typical values shown are based on EV/EBITDA)	$\dfrac{\text{Enterprise Value}}{\text{EBIT or EBITDA or Sales}}$	8.3	11.7	10.5	12.1

Source: Standard and Poors' Compustat based on averages of fiscal years 2012 to 2015.

CONCEPT CHECK

11. What does a high debt-to-equity ratio tell you?

12. What is a firm's enterprise value?

13. How can a financial manager use the DuPont Identity to assess the firm's ROE?

14. How do you use the price-earnings (P/E) ratio to gauge the market value of a firm?

Financial Reporting in Practice

The various financial statements we have examined are of critical importance to investors and financial managers alike. Even with safeguards such as GAAP and auditors, financial reporting abuses unfortunately do take place. We now review one of the most infamous recent examples and offer some concluding thoughts to guide financial managers through the complexities of financial statements.

Enron

Enron is the most well-known of the accounting scandals of the early 2000s. Enron started as an operator of natural gas pipelines but evolved into a global trader dealing in a range of products including gas, oil, electricity, and even broadband Internet capacity. A series of events unfolded that led Enron to file what was at the time the largest bankruptcy filing in U.S. history in December 2001. By the end of 2001, the market value of Enron's shares had fallen by over $60 billion.

Interestingly, throughout the 1990s and up to late 2001, Enron was touted as one of the most successful and profitable companies in America. *Fortune* rated Enron "The Most Innovative Company in America" for six straight years, from 1995 to 2000. But while many aspects of Enron's business were successful, subsequent investigations suggest that Enron executives had been manipulating Enron's financial statements to mislead investors and artificially inflate the price of Enron's stock and to maintain its credit rating. In 2000, for example, 96% of Enron's reported earnings were the result of accounting manipulation.[10]

Although the accounting manipulation that Enron used was quite sophisticated, the essence of most of the deceptive transactions was surprisingly simple. Enron sold assets at inflated prices to other firms (or, in many cases, business entities that Enron's CFO Andrew Fastow had created), together with a promise to buy back those assets at an even higher future price. Thus, Enron was effectively borrowing money, receiving cash today in exchange for a promise to pay more cash in the future. But Enron recorded the incoming cash as revenue and then hid the promises to buy the assets back in a variety of ways.[11] In the end, much of their revenue growth and profits in the late 1990s were the result of this type of manipulation.

The Sarbanes-Oxley Act

Sarbanes-Oxley Act (SOX) Legislation passed by Congress in 2002, intended to improve the accuracy of financial information given to both boards and shareholders.

Accurate and up-to-date financial statements are essential to investors evaluating investment opportunities. In 2002, Congress passed the **Sarbanes-Oxley Act (SOX)**. While SOX contains many provisions, the overall intent of the legislation was to improve the accuracy of information given to both boards and shareholders. SOX attempted to achieve this goal in three ways: (1) by overhauling incentives and independence in the auditing process, (2) by stiffening penalties for providing false information, and (3) by forcing companies to validate their internal financial control processes.

Many of the problems at Enron and elsewhere were kept hidden from boards and shareholders until it was too late. In the wake of these scandals, many people felt that the

---

[10]John R. Kroger, "Enron, Fraud and Securities Reform: An Enron Prosecutor's Perspective," *University of Colorado Law Review*, December 2005, pp. 57–138.

[11]In some cases, these promises were called "price risk management liabilities" and hidden with other trading activities; in other cases they were off-balance sheet transactions that were not fully disclosed.

accounting statements of these companies, while often remaining true to the letter of GAAP, did not present an accurate picture of the financial health of the companies.

Auditing firms are supposed to ensure that a company's financial statements accurately reflect the financial state of the firm. In reality, most auditors have a long-standing relationship with their audit clients; this extended relationship and the auditors' desire to keep the lucrative auditing fees make auditors less willing to challenge management. More importantly, perhaps, most accounting firms have developed large and extremely profitable consulting divisions. Obviously, if an audit team refuses to accommodate a request by a client's management, that client will be less likely to choose the accounting firm's consulting division for its next consulting contract. SOX addressed this concern by putting strict limits on the amount of non-audit fees (consulting or otherwise) that an accounting firm can earn from the same firm that it audits. It also required that audit partners rotate every five years to limit the likelihood that auditing relationships become too cozy over time. Finally, SOX called on the SEC to force companies to have audit committees that are dominated by outside directors, and required that at least one outside director has a financial background.

SOX also stiffened the criminal penalties for providing false information to shareholders. It required both the CEO and the CFO to personally attest to the accuracy of the financial statements presented to shareholders and to sign a statement to that effect. Penalties for providing false or misleading financial statements were increased under SOX—fines of as much as $5 million and imprisonment of a maximum of 20 years are permitted. Further, CEOs and CFOs must return bonuses or profits from the sale of stock or the exercise of options during any period covered by statements that are later restated.

Finally, Section 404 of SOX requires senior management and the boards of public companies to attest to the effectiveness and validity of the process through which funds are allocated and controlled, and outcomes monitored throughout the firm. Section 404 has arguably garnered more attention than any other section in SOX because of the potentially enormous burden it places on every firm to validate its entire financial control system. When the SEC estimated the cost of implementing Section 404, its staff economists put the total cost at $1.24 billion. In 2005, surveys by Financial Executives International and the American Electronics Association predicted that the actual cost would be between $20 billion and $35 billion.[12] The burden of complying with this provision is greater, as a fraction of revenue, for smaller companies. The surveys cited earlier found that multibillion-dollar companies would pay less than 0.05% of their revenues to comply, whereas small companies with less than $20 million in revenues would pay more than 3% of their revenues to comply.

Dodd-Frank Act

To mitigate the compliance burden on small firms, the Dodd-Frank Wall Street Reform and Consumer Protection Act passed in 2010 exempts firms with less than $75 million in publicly held shares from the SOX Section 404 requirements. It also requires the SEC to study how it might reduce cost for medium-sized firms with a public float of less than $250 million, and to assess whether such measures would encourage more firms to list on U.S. exchanges.

Dodd-Frank also broadened the whistleblower provisions of SOX, so that an individual who provides "information related to a possible violation of the federal securities laws (including any rules or regulations thereunder)" that results in penalties or recoveries by the SEC or agencies is eligible to receive from 10 to 30% of that penalty or recovery.

---

[12]American Electronics Association, "Sarbanes-Oxley Section 404: The 'Section' of Unintended Consequences and Its Impact on Small Business" (2005).

Bernard Madoff's Ponzi Scheme

"It's only when the tide goes out that you learn who's been swimming naked."
—Warren Buffett

On December 11, 2008, federal agents arrested Bernie Madoff, one of the largest and most successful hedge fund managers. It turned out that the $65 billion[13] fund he ran was in fact a fraud. His spectacular performance of the last 17 years, generating consistent annual returns between 10% and 15%, was actually a complete fabrication. Madoff had been running the world's largest Ponzi scheme: That is, he used the capital contributed by new investors to pay off old investors. His strategy was so successful that for more than a decade investors ranging from Steven Spielberg to New York University, as well as a number of large banks and investment advisors, lined up to invest with him. Indeed, Madoff quite likely would have been able to hide the fraud until his deathbed had not the global financial crisis spurred many investors to seek to withdraw funds from their Madoff accounts in order to raise cash and cover losses elsewhere in their portfolios. In addition, the financial crisis meant there were fewer new investors with both the cash and the willingness to invest. As a result, Madoff did not have enough new capital to pay off the investors who wanted to withdraw their capital, and the scheme finally collapsed.

How was Madoff able to hide perhaps the largest fraud of all time for so long? Rather than simply manipulate his accounting statements, Madoff *made them up* with the assistance of a virtually unknown accounting firm with only one active accountant. Although many investors may have questioned why such a large fund, with $65 billion in assets, would choose an unknown and tiny audit firm, not enough of them recognized this choice as a potential red flag. In addition, because Madoff's firm was private, it was not subject to the strict regulatory requirements for public companies (such as the Sarbanes-Oxley Act) and so had weak reporting requirements. As this case makes clear, when making an investment decision, it is important not only to review the firm's financial statements, but also to consider the reliability and reputation of the auditors who prepared them.

The Financial Statements: A Useful Starting Point

In this chapter, we have highlighted the role of the financial statements in informing outside analysts, investors, and the financial managers themselves about the performance, position, and financial condition of the firm. However, especially from the financial manager's perspective, financial statements are only a starting point. For example, we have emphasized the importance of market values over book values. We have also shown that while much can be learned through ratio analysis, these ratios are only markers that point the financial manager toward areas where the firm is doing well or where he or she needs to focus an effort toward improvement. No single ratio tells the whole story. However, by studying all of the financial statements and considering ratios that assess profitability, leverage, and efficiency, you should be able to develop a clear sense of the health and performance of the firm. Finally, the usefulness of the financial statements to investors relies on the ethics of those constructing them. However, even in cases of deception, an informed reader of the financial statements could have spotted the warning signs by focusing on the statement of cash flows and carefully reading the notes to the financial statements.

CONCEPT CHECK

15. Describe the transactions Enron used to increase its reported earnings.

16. What is the Sarbanes-Oxley Act?

---

[13]$65 billion is the total amount Madoff had reported to his investors, including (fictitious) returns; investigators are still trying to determine the exact amount that investors had actually contributed to the fund, but it appears to be in excess of $17 billion (see www.madoff.com).

MyFinanceLab

Here is what you should know after reading this chapter. MyFinanceLab will help you identify what you know, and where to go when you need to practice.

KEY POINTS AND EQUATIONS	KEY TERMS	ONLINE PRACTICE

2.1 Firms' Disclosure of Financial Information
- Financial statements are accounting reports that a firm issues periodically to describe its past performance.
- Investors, financial analysts, managers, and other interested parties, such as creditors, rely on financial statements to obtain reliable information about a corporation.
- The main types of financial statements are the balance sheet, the income statement, the statement of cash flows, and the statement of stockholders' equity.
- While the U.S. maintains its own GAAP, most countries in the world are standardizing their accounting systems around International Financial Reporting Standards.

Key terms: annual report (10-K), p. 28; auditor, p. 30; financial statements, p. 28; Generally Accepted Accounting Principles (GAAP), p. 28

Online Practice: MyFinanceLab Study Plan 2.1

2.2 The Balance Sheet
- The balance sheet shows the current financial position (assets, liabilities, and stockholders' equity) of the firm at a single point in time.
- The two sides of the balance sheet must balance:

$$\text{Assets} = \text{Liabilities} + \text{Stockholders' Equity} \quad (2.1)$$

- Stockholders' equity is the book value of the firm's equity. It differs from the market value of the firm's equity, its market capitalization, because of the way assets and liabilities are recorded for accounting purposes.
- A successful firm's market-to-book ratio typically exceeds 1.
- The enterprise value of a firm is the total value of its underlying business operations:

$$\text{Enterprise Value} = \text{Market Value of Equity} + \text{Debt} - \text{Cash} \quad (2.4)$$

Key terms: accounts payable, p. 32; accounts receivable, p. 31; assets, p. 30; balance sheet, p. 30; book value, p. 31; book value of equity, p. 32; common stock and paid-in surplus, p. 30; current assets, p. 31; current liabilities, p. 32; depreciation, p. 31; enterprise value, p. 34; growth stocks, p. 34; inventories, p. 31; liabilities, p. 30; liquidation value, p. 33; long-term assets, p. 31; long-term debt, p. 32; market capitalization, p. 33; marketable securities, p. 31; market-to-book ratio (price-to-book [P/B] ratio), p. 34; net working capital, p. 32; notes payable, p. 32; retained earnings, p. 30; shareholders' equity, p. 30; short-term debt, p. 32; statement of financial position, p. 30; stockholders' equity, p. 30; value stocks, p. 34

Online Practice: MyFinanceLab Study Plan 2.2

2.3   The Income Statement

- The income statement reports the firm's revenues and expenses, and it computes the firm's bottom line of net income, or earnings.
- Net income is often reported on a per-share basis as the firm's earnings per share:

  Earnings per Share (EPS) = Net Income/
  $$\text{Shares Outstanding} \quad (2.5)$$

- We compute diluted EPS by adding to the number of shares outstanding the possible increase in the number of shares from the exercise of stock options the firm has awarded.

convertible bonds, p. 37
diluted EPS, p. 37
dilution, p. 37
earnings per share (EPS), p. 37
EBIT, p. 37
EBITDA, p. 38
gross profit, p. 36
income statement, p. 36
net income or earnings, p. 36
operating income, p. 37
stock options, p. 37

MyFinanceLab
Study Plan 2.3

2.4   The Statement of Cash Flows

- The statement of cash flows reports the sources and uses of the firm's cash. It shows the adjustments to net income for non-cash expenses and changes to net working capital, as well as the cash used (or provided) from investing and financing activities.

capital expenditures, p. 41
payout ratio, p. 41
statement of cash flows, p. 38

MyFinanceLab
Study Plan 2.4

2.5   Other Financial Statement Information

- The management discussion and analysis section of the financial statement contains management's overview of the firm's performance, as well as disclosure of risks the firm faces, including those from off-balance sheet transactions.
- The statement of stockholders' equity breaks down the stockholders' equity computed on the balance sheet into the amount that came from issuing new shares versus retained earnings. It is not particularly useful for financial valuation purposes.
- The notes to a firm's financial statements generally contain important details regarding the numbers used in the main statements.

management discussion and analysis (MD&A), p. 42
off-balance sheet transactions, p. 42
statement of stockholders' equity, p. 42

MyFinanceLab
Study Plan 2.5

2.6   Financial Statement Analysis

- Profitability ratios show the firm's operating or net income as a fraction of sales, and they are an indication of a firm's efficiency and its pricing strategy.
- Liquidity ratios help creditors assess whether the firm has enough cash to meet its short-term needs.
- Asset efficiency ratios assess how efficiently the firm is using its assets by showing how many dollars of revenues the firm produces per dollar of assets.
- Working capital ratios express the firm's working capital as a number of days of sales (for receivables) or cost of sales (for inventory or payables).

accounts payable days, p. 45
accounts receivable days, p. 44
asset turnover, p. 44
average collection period or days sales outstanding, p. 44
cash ratio, p. 44
current ratio, p. 44
debt-equity ratio, p. 47
debt-to-capital ratio, p. 47
debt-to-enterprise value ratio, p. 47
DuPont Identity, p. 50
equity multiplier, p. 48
gross margin, p. 43
interest coverage ratio, p. 46

MyFinanceLab
Study Plan 2.6

- Interest coverage ratios indicate the ratio of the firm's income or cash flows to its interest expenses, and they are a measure of financial strength.
- A common ratio used to assess a firm's leverage is:

$$\text{Debt-Equity Ratio} = \frac{\text{Total Debt}}{\text{Total Equity}} \quad (2.19)$$

- This ratio is most informative when computed using the market value of equity. It indicates the degree of leverage of the firm.
- Valuation ratios compute market capitalization or enterprise value of the firm relative to its earnings or operating income.
- The P/E ratio computes the value of a share of stock relative to the firm's EPS. P/E ratios tend to be high for fast-growing firms.
- When comparing valuation ratios, it is important to be sure both the numerator and denominator match in terms of whether they include debt.
- ROE and ROA are typical operating return ratios. ROE expresses the firm's net income as a return on the book value of its equity. ROA expresses net income plus interest as a return on total assets.
- The DuPont Identity says that

$$\text{ROE} = \left(\frac{\text{Net Income}}{\text{Sales}} \right) \times \left(\frac{\text{Sales}}{\text{Total Assets}} \right)$$
$$\times \left(\frac{\text{Total Assets}}{\text{Total Equity}} \right) \quad (2.27)$$

inventory days, p. 45
inventory turnover ratio, p. 45
leverage, p. 46
net debt, p. 47
net profit margin, p. 43
operating margin, p. 43
PEG ratio, p. 48
price-earnings ratio (P/E), p. 48
quick ratio ("acid-test ratio"), p. 44
return on assets (ROA), p. 50
return on invested capital (ROIC), p. 50
return on equity (ROE), p. 49
times interest earned (TIE) ratio, p. 46

2.7 Financial Reporting in Practice

- Recent accounting scandals have drawn attention to the importance of financial statements. New legislation has increased the penalties for fraud, and tightened the procedures firms must use to ensure that statements are accurate.

Sarbanes-Oxley Act (SOX), p. 54

MyFinanceLab Study Plan 2.7

CRITICAL THINKING

1. Why do firms disclose financial information?

2. Who reads financial statements? List at least three different categories of people. For each category, provide an example of the type of information they might be interested in and discuss why?

3. What is the purpose of the balance sheet?

4. What is the purpose of the income statement?

5. How does the statement of cash flows differ from the income statement?

6. Can a firm with positive net income run out of cash? Explain.

7. How can you use the balance sheet to assess the health of a firm?

8. How are the balance sheet and the income statement related?

9. What is the DuPont Identity and how can a financial manager use it?

10. What can you learn from the management's discussion in the financial statements or the notes to the financial statements?

11. How did accounting fraud contribute to the collapse of Enron?

PROBLEMS

All problems are available in MyFinanceLab. *The* ⊞×⊞ *icon indicates problems that are easier to solve using Excel and have data in an Excel format available in* MyFinanceLab. *An asterisk * indicates problems with a higher level of difficulty.*

Firms' Disclosure of Financial Information

1. What four financial statements can be found in a firm's 10-K filing? What checks are there on the accuracy of these statements?

2. What is GAAP and who oversees it?

3. Confirm that you can find the most recent financial statements for Starbucks Corporation (SBUX) using the following sources:
   a. From the company's Web page. (*Hint*: Search their Web site for "investor relations.")
   b. From the SEC Web site (www.sec.gov). (*Hint*: Search for company filings in the EDGAR database.)
   c. From the Yahoo! Finance Web site (finance.yahoo.com).
   d. From at least one other source. (*Hint*: Enter "SBUX 10K" at www.bing.com.)

The Balance Sheet

4. Consider the following potential events that might have occurred to Global on December 30, 2016. For each one, indicate which line items in Global's balance sheet would be affected and by how much. Also indicate the change to Global's book value of equity.
   a. Global used $20 million of its available cash to repay $20 million of its long-term debt.
   b. A warehouse fire destroyed $5 million worth of uninsured inventory.
   c. Global used $5 million in cash and $5 million in new long-term debt to purchase a $10 million building.
   d. A large customer owing $3 million for products it already received declared bankruptcy, leaving no possibility that Global would ever receive payment.
   e. Global's engineers discover a new manufacturing process that will cut the cost of its flagship product by more than 50%.
   f. A key competitor announces a radical new pricing policy that will drastically undercut Global's prices.

5. What was the change in Global's book value of equity from 2015 to 2016 according to Table 2.1? Does this imply that the market price of Global's shares increased in 2016? Explain.

6. Use EDGAR (www.sec.gov) to find Qualcomm's 10K filing for 2014. From the balance sheet, answer the following questions:
   a. How much did Qualcomm have in cash and short-term investments?
   b. What were Qualcomm's total accounts receivable?
   c. What were Qualcomm's total assets?
   d. What were Qualcomm's total liabilities? How much of this was long-term debt?
   e. What was the book value of Qualcomm's equity?

7. Find the annual 10-K report for Costco Wholesale Corporation (COST) for fiscal year 2015 (filed in October 2015). Answer the following questions from its balance sheet:
   a. How much cash did Costco have?
   b. What were Costco's total assets?
   c. What were Costco's total liabilities? How much debt did Costco have?
   d. What was the book value of Costco equity?

Income Statement

8. Find online the annual 10-K report for Costco Wholesale Corporation (COST) for fiscal year 2015 (filed in October 2015). Answer the following questions from the income statement:
   a. What were Costco revenues for 2015? By what percentage did revenues grow from the prior year?
   b. What were Costco operating and net profit margins in 2015? How do they compare with its margins in the prior year?
   c. What were Costco diluted earnings per share in 2015? What number of shares is this EPS based on?

TABLE 2.5

2012–2016 Financial Statement Data and Stock Price Data for Mydeco Corp.

Mydeco Corp. 2012–2016	(All data as of fiscal year end; $ in millions)				
Income Statement	**2012**	**2013**	**2014**	**2015**	**2016**
Revenue	404.3	363.8	424.6	510.7	604.1
Cost of Goods Sold	(188.3)	(173.8)	(206.2)	(246.8)	(293.4)
Gross Profit	215.9	190.0	218.3	263.9	310.7
Sales and Marketing	(66.7)	(66.4)	(82.8)	(102.1)	(120.8)
Administration	(60.6)	(59.1)	(59.4)	(66.4)	(78.5)
Depreciation & Amortization	(27.3)	(27.0)	(34.3)	(38.4)	(38.6)
EBIT	61.3	37.4	41.8	57.0	72.8
Interest Income (Expense)	(33.7)	(32.9)	(32.2)	(37.4)	(39.4)
Pretax Income	27.7	4.5	9.6	19.6	33.4
Income Tax	(9.7)	(1.6)	(3.4)	(6.9)	(11.7)
Net Income	18.0	2.9	6.2	12.7	21.7
Shares Outstanding (millions)	55.0	55.0	55.0	55.0	55.0
Earnings per Share	$0.33	$0.05	$0.11	$0.23	$0.39
Balance Sheet	**2012**	**2013**	**2014**	**2015**	**2016**
<u>Assets</u>					
Cash	48.8	68.8	86.2	77.4	84.9
Accounts Receivable	88.6	69.8	69.8	76.9	86.1
Inventory	33.7	30.9	28.4	31.7	35.3
Total Current Assets	171.1	169.4	184.4	186.1	206.3
Net Property, Plant, & Equipment	245.3	243.2	308.9	345.5	347.0
Goodwill & Intangibles	361.7	361.7	361.7	361.7	361.7
Total Assets	778.1	774.3	855.0	893.3	914.9

(Continued)

Mydeco Corp. 2012–2016	(All data as of fiscal year end; $ in millions)				
Balance Sheet (continued)	**2012**	**2013**	**2014**	**2015**	**2016**
Liabilities & Stockholders' Equity					
Accounts Payable	18.7	17.9	22.0	26.8	31.7
Accrued Compensation	6.7	6.4	7.0	8.1	9.7
Total Current Liabilities	25.5	24.2	29.0	34.9	41.4
Long-Term Debt	500.0	500.0	575.0	600.0	600.0
Total Liabilities	525.5	524.2	604.0	634.9	641.4
Stockholders' Equity	252.6	250.1	251.0	258.3	273.5
Total Liabilities & Stock-holders' Equity	778.1	774.3	855.0	893.3	914.9
Statement of Cash Flows	**2012**	**2013**	**2014**	**2015**	**2016**
Net Income	18.0	2.9	6.2	12.7	21.7
Depreciation & Amortization	27.3	27.0	34.3	38.4	38.6
Change in Accounts Receivable	3.9	18.8	(0.0)	(7.2)	(9.1)
Change in Inventory	(2.9)	2.9	2.5	(3.3)	(3.6)
Change in Payables & Accrued Compensation	2.2	(1.3)	4.8	5.9	6.5
Cash from Operations	48.4	50.4	47.8	46.6	54.0
Capital Expenditures	(25.0)	(25.0)	(100.0)	(75.0)	(40.0)
Cash from Investing Activities	(25.0)	(25.0)	(100.0)	(75.0)	(40.0)
Dividends Paid	(5.4)	(5.4)	(5.4)	(5.4)	(6.5)
Sale (or Purchase) of Stock	—	—	—	—	—
Debt Issuance (Pay Down)	—	—	75.0	25.0	—
Cash from Financing Activities	(5.4)	(5.4)	69.6	19.6	(6.5)
Change in Cash	18.0	20.0	17.4	(8.8)	7.5
Mydeco Stock Price	*$7.90*	*$3.29*	*$5.23*	*$8.70*	*$10.87*

 9. See Table 2.5 showing financial statement data and stock price data for Mydeco Corp.
   a. By what percentage did Mydeco's revenues grow each year from 2013–2016?
   b. By what percentage did net income grow each year?
   c. Why might the growth rates of revenues and net income differ?

 10. See Table 2.5 showing financial statement data and stock price data for Mydeco Corp. Suppose Mydeco repurchases 2 million shares each year from 2013–2016. What would its earnings per share be in 2016?

 11. See Table 2.5 showing financial statement data and stock price data for Mydeco Corp. Suppose Mydeco had purchased additional equipment for $12 million at the end of 2013, and this equipment was depreciated by $4 million per year in 2014, 2015, and 2016. Given Mydeco's tax rate of 35%, what impact would this additional purchase have had on Mydeco's net income in years 2013–2016?

 12. See Table 2.5 showing financial statement data and stock price data for Mydeco Corp. Suppose Mydeco's costs and expenses had been the same fraction of revenues in 2013–2016 as they were in 2012. What would Mydeco's EPS have been each year in this case?

13. Suppose a firm's tax rate is 35%.
    a. What effect would a $10 million operating expense have on this year's earnings? What effect would it have on next year's earnings?
    b. What effect would a $10 million capital expense have on this year's earnings if the capital is depreciated at a rate of $2 million per year for five years? What effect would it have on next year's earnings?

*14. Quisco Systems has 6.5 billion shares outstanding and a share price of $18. Quisco is considering developing a new networking product in house at a cost of $500 million. Alternatively, Quisco can acquire a firm that already has the technology for $900 million worth (at the current price) of Quisco stock. Suppose that absent the expense of the new technology, Quisco will have EPS of $0.80.
    a. Suppose Quisco develops the product in house. What impact would the development cost have on Quisco's EPS? Assume all costs are incurred this year and are treated as an R&D expense, Quisco's tax rate is 35%, and the number of shares outstanding is unchanged.
    b. Suppose Quisco does not develop the product in house but instead acquires the technology. What effect would the acquisition have on Quisco's EPS this year? (Note that acquisition expenses do not appear directly on the income statement. Assume the firm was acquired at the start of the year and has no revenues or expenses of its own, so that the only effect on EPS is due to the change in the number of shares outstanding.)
    c. Which method of acquiring the technology has a smaller impact on earnings? Is this method cheaper? Explain.

The Statement of Cash Flows

15. Find online the annual 10-K report for Costco Wholesale Corporation (COST) for fiscal year 2015 (filed in October 2015). Answer the following questions from its cash flow statement:
    a. How much cash did Costco generate from operating activities in 2015?
    b. What was Costco depreciation expense in 2015?
    c. How much cash was invested in new property and equipment (net of any sales) in 2015?
    d. How much did Costco raise from the sale of shares of its stock (net of any purchases) in 2015?

16. See the cash flow statement below (all values in thousands of dollars) (*see* MyFinanceLab *for the data in Excel format*):
    a. What were the company's cumulative earnings over these four quarters? What were its cumulative cash flows from operating activities?

Quarter	4	3	2	1
Net income	276,710	228,964	194,062	218,532
Operating Activities, Cash Flows Provided by or Used in				
Depreciation	69,997	75,733	74,570	73,173
Adjustments to net income	14,359	(13,142)	48,826	(47,993)
Changes in accounts receivable	(38,869)	(53,218)	100,732	(84,711)
Changes in liabilities	82,816	(111,577)	201,725	39,949
Changes in inventories	(195,186)	(114,121)	85,028	57,681
Changes in other operating activities	17,675	(26,574)	12,692	(2,097)

(Continued)

Quarter	4	3	2	1
Total Cash Flow from Operating Activities	227,502	(13,935)	717,635	254,534
Investing Activities, Cash Flows Provided by or Used in				
Capital expenditures	(82,584)	(41,634)	(100,109)	(69,170)
Investments	(5,465)	5,465	(93,153)	(48,330)
Other cash flows from investing activities	(108,903)	732	(58,069)	20,652
Total Cash Flows from Investing Activities	(196,952)	(35,437)	(251,331)	(96,848)
Financing Activities, Cash Flows Provided by or Used in				
Dividends paid	(131,483)	(131,333)	(119,452)	(121,404)
Sale purchase of stock	78,774	1,210	(76,807)	(79,288)
Net borrowings	515,709	114,766	(283,696)	64,885
Other cash flows from financing activities	(282)	2,000	(46,234)	39,763
Total Cash Flows from Financing Activities	462,718	(13,357)	(526,189)	(96,044)
Effect of exchange rate changes	(119,960)	(610)	32,807	6,890
Change in Cash and Cash Equivalents	$373,308	(63,339)	(27,078)	$68,532

b. What fraction of the cash from operating activities was used for investment over the four quarters?

c. What fraction of the cash from operating activities was used for financing activities over the four quarters?

17. Suppose your firm receives a $5 million order on the last day of the year. You fill the order with $2 million worth of inventory. The customer picks up the entire order the same day and pays $1 million up front in cash; you also issue a bill for the customer to pay the remaining balance of $4 million within 40 days. Suppose your firm's tax rate is 0% (i.e., ignore taxes). Determine the consequences of this transaction for each of the following:

a. Revenues
b. Earnings
c. Receivables
d. Inventory
e. Cash

18. Nokela Industries purchases a $40 million cyclo-converter. The cyclo-converter will be depreciated by $10 million per year over four years, starting this year. Suppose Nokela's tax rate is 40%.

a. What impact will the cost of the purchase have on earnings for each of the next four years?

b. What impact will the cost of the purchase have on the firm's cash flow for the next four years?

Financial Statement Analysis

19. In December 2015, General Electric (GE) had a book value of equity of $98 billion, 9.4 billion shares outstanding, and a market price of $31 per share. GE also had cash of $102 billion, and total debt of $199 billion.
    a. What was GE's market capitalization? What was GE's market-to-book ratio?
    b. What was GE's book debt-equity ratio? What was GE's market debt-equity ratio?
    c. What was GE's enterprise value?

20. In December 2015, Apple had cash of $38.07 billion, current assets of $76.22 billion, and current liabilities of $76.09 billion. It also had inventories of $2.45 billion.
    a. What was Apple's current ratio?
    b. What was Apple's quick ratio?
    c. In January 2016, Hewlett-Packard had a quick ratio of 0.66 and a current ratio of 0.90. What can you say about the asset liquidity of Apple relative to Hewlett-Packard?

21. In early-2016, the following information was true about Abercrombie and Fitch (ANF) and The Gap (GPS), both clothing retailers. Values (except price per share) are in millions of dollars.

	Book Equity	Price per Share	Number of Shares (millions)
ANF	1,291	26.35	67.59
GPS	2,545	24.74	397.14

    a. What is the market-to-book ratio of each company?
    b. What conclusions do you draw from comparing the two ratios?

22. In fiscal year 2015, Walmart Stores. (WMT) had revenue of $485.65 billion, gross profit of $120.57 billion, and net income of $16.36 billion. Costco Wholesale Corporation (COST) had revenue of $116.20 billion, gross profit of $15.13 billion, and net income of $2.38 billion.
    a. Compare the gross margins for Walmart and Costco.
    b. Compare the net profit margins for Walmart and Costco.
    c. Which firm was more profitable in 2015?

23. Local Co. has sales of $10 million and cost of sales of $6 million. Its selling, general, and administrative expenses are $500,000 and its research and development is $1 million. It has annual depreciation charges of $1 million and a tax rate of 35%.
    a. What is Local's gross margin?
    b. What is Local's operating margin?
    c. What is Local's net profit margin?

24. If Local Co., the company in Problem 23, had an increase in selling expenses of $300,000, how would that affect each of its margins?

25. If Local Co., the company in Problem 23, had interest expense of $800,000, how would that affect each of its margins?

26. Chutes & Co. has interest expense of $1 million and an operating margin of 10% on total sales of $30 million. What is Chutes' interest coverage ratio?

27. Ladders, Inc. has a net profit margin of 5% on sales of $50 million. It has book value of equity of $40 million and total liabilities with a book value of $30 million. What is Ladders' ROE? ROA?

28. JPJ Corp has sales of $1 million, accounts receivable of $50,000, total assets of $5 million (of which $3 million are fixed assets), inventory of $150,000, and cost of goods sold of $600,000. What is JPJ's accounts receivable days? Fixed asset turnover? Total asset turnover? Inventory turnover?

29. If JPJ Corp (the company in Problem 28) is able to increase sales by 10% but keep its total and fixed asset growth to only 5%, what will its new asset turnover ratios be?

*30. Suppose that in 2016, Global launched an aggressive marketing campaign that boosted sales by 15%. However, their operating margin fell from 5.57% to 4.50%. Suppose that they had no other income, interest expenses were unchanged, and taxes were the same percentage of pretax income as in 2015.
    a. What was Global's EBIT in 2016?
    b. What was Global's income in 2016?
    c. If Global's P/E ratio and number of shares outstanding remained unchanged, what was Global's share price in 2016?

31. You are analyzing the leverage of two firms and you note the following (all values in millions of dollars):

	Debt	Book Equity	Market Equity	Operating Income	Interest Expense
Firm A	500	300	400	100	50
Firm B	80	35	40	8	7

    a. What is the market debt-to-equity ratio of each firm?
    b. What is the book debt-to-equity ratio of each firm?
    c. What is the interest coverage ratio of each firm?
    d. Which firm will have more difficulty meeting its debt obligations?

32. For 2015, Walmart and Target had the following information (all values are in millions of dollars):

	Sales (Income Statement)	Cost of Goods Sold (Income Statement)	Accounts Receivable (Balance Sheet)	Inventory (Balance Sheet)
Walmart	482,130	360,984	5,624	44,469
Target	73,785	51,997	779	8,601

    a. What is each company's accounts receivable days?
    b. What is each company's inventory turnover?
    c. Which company is managing its accounts receivable and inventory more efficiently?

33. In January 2016, United Airlines (UAL) had a market capitalization of $20.6 billion, debt of $11.9 billion, and cash of $5.2 billion. United Airlines had revenues of $37.9 billion. Southwest Airlines (LUV) had a market capitalization of $27.5 billion, debt of $3.2 billion, cash of $3.0 billion, and revenues of $19.8 billion.
    a. Compare the market capitalization-to-revenue ratio (also called the price-to-sales ratio) for United Airlines and Southwest Airlines.
    b. Compare the enterprise value-to-revenue ratio for United Airlines and Southwest Airlines.
    c. Which of these comparisons is more meaningful? Explain.

34. Consider a retail firm with a net profit margin of 3.5%, a total asset turnover of 1.8, total assets of $44 million, and a book value of equity of $18 million.
    a. What is the firm's current ROE?
    b. If the firm increased its net profit margin to 4%, what would its ROE be?
    c. If, in addition, the firm increased its revenues by 20% (while maintaining this higher profit margin and without changing its assets or liabilities), what would its ROE be?

*35. Find online the annual 10-K report for Costco Wholesale Corporation (COST) for fiscal year 2015 (filed in October 2015).
    a. Compute Costco's net profit margin, total asset turnover, and equity multiplier.
    b. Verify the DuPont Identity for Costco ROE.
    c. If Costco managers wanted to increase its ROE by 1 percentage point, how much higher would their asset turnover need to be?

36. Repeat the analysis from parts a and b in Problem 35 using Walmart Stores (WMT) instead. Specifically, use Walmart's 2015 fiscal data, filed in October 2015. Based on the DuPont Identity, what explains the difference between the two firms' ROEs?

Other Financial Statement Information

37. Some balance sheet information is shown here (all values in millions of dollars) (*see* MyFinanceLab *for the data in Excel format*):

Balance Sheet: Assets	31-Mar-16	31-Dec-15	30-Sep-15	30-Jun-15
Assets				
Current Assets				
Cash and cash equivalents	293	300	255	232
Net receivables	401	362	385	460
Inventory	374	342	437	306
Other current assets	60	43	53	45
Total Current Assets	1,128	1,047	1,130	1,043
Long-term investments	128	97	—	200
Property, plant, and equipment	979	991	995	1,052
Goodwill	744	748	736	742
Other assets	777	827	911	797
Total Assets	3,756	3,710	3,772	3,834
Liabilities				
Current Liabilities				
Accounts payable	876	1,467	922	980
Short/current long-term debt	410	2	173	288
Other current liabilities	—	—	—	—
Total Current Liabilities	1,286	1,469	1,095	1,268
Long-term debt	2,381	2,124	474	475
Other liabilities	435	574	559	551
Total Liabilities	4,102	4,167	2,128	2,294
Total Stockholder Equity	−346	−457	1,644	1,540
Total Liabilities and Stockholder Equity	$3,756	$3,710	$3,772	$3,834

   a. What change in the book value of the company's equity took place at the end of 2015?

   b. Is the company's market-to-book ratio meaningful? Is its book debt-equity ratio meaningful? Explain.

   c. Find the company's other financial statements from that time online. What was the cause of the change to its book value of equity at the end of 2015?

   d. Does the company's book value of equity in 2016 imply that it is unprofitable? Explain.

Financial Reporting in Practice

38. Find online the annual 10-K report for Costco Wholesale Corporation (COST) for fiscal year 2015 (filed in October 2015).

   a. Which auditing firm certified the financial statements?

   b. Which officers of Costco certified the financial statements?

DATA CASE

This is your second interview with a prestigious brokerage firm for a job as an equity analyst. You survived the morning interviews with the department manager and the vice president of equity. Everything has gone so well that they want to test your ability as an analyst. You are seated in a room with a computer and a list with the names of two companies—Ford (F) and Microsoft (MSFT). You have 90 minutes to complete the following tasks:

1. Download the annual income statements, balance sheets, and cash flow statements for the last four fiscal years from Morningstar (www.morningstar.com). Enter each company's stock symbol and then go to "financials." Copy and paste the financial statements into Excel.

2. Find historical stock prices for each firm from Yahoo! Finance (finance.yahoo.com). Enter the stock symbol, click "Historical Prices" in the left column, and enter the proper date range to cover the last day of the month corresponding to the date of each financial statement. Use the closing stock prices (not the adjusted close). To calculate the firm's market capitalization at each date, multiply the number of shares outstanding by the firm's historic stock price. You can find the number of shares by using "Basic" under "Weighted average shares outstanding" at the bottom of the Income Statement.

3. For each of the four years of statements, compute the following ratios for each firm:

   Valuation Ratios
   Price-earnings ratio (for EPS use diluted EPS total)
   Market-to-book ratio
   Enterprise value-to-EBITDA
   (For debt, include long-term and short-term debt; for cash, include marketable securities.)

   Profitability Ratios
   Operating margin
   Net profit margin
   Return on equity

   Financial Strength Ratios
   Current ratio
   Book debt–equity ratio
   Market debt–equity ratio
   Interest coverage ratio (EBIT ÷ interest expense)

4. Obtain industry averages for each firm from Reuters (www.reuters.com/finance/stocks). Enter the stock symbol at the top of the page in the "Symbol lookup" and then click the "Financials" button, and then click "Search."

   a. Scroll down to "Valuation Ratios," and compare each firm's ratios to the available industry ratios for the most recent year. (Ignore the "Company" column as your calculations will be different.)

   b. Analyze the performance of each firm versus the industry and comment on any trends in each individual firm's performance. Identify any strengths or weaknesses you find in each firm.

5. Examine the market-to-book ratios you calculated for each firm. Which, if either, of the two firms can be considered "growth firms" and which, if either, can be considered "value firms"?

6. Compare the valuation ratios across the two firms. How do you interpret the difference between them?

7. Consider the enterprise value of both firms for each of the four years. How have the values of both firms changed over the time period?

Interest Rates and Valuing Cash Flows

Valuation Principle Connection. In this part of the text, we introduce the basic tools for making financial decisions. Chapter 3 presents the most important idea in this book, the *Valuation Principle*. The Valuation Principle states that we can use market prices to determine the value of an investment opportunity to the firm. As we progress through our study of corporate finance, we will demonstrate that the Valuation Principle is the one unifying principle that underlies all of finance and links all the ideas throughout this book.

Every day, managers in companies all over the world make financial decisions. These range from relatively minor decisions such as a local hardware store owner's determination of when to restock inventory, to major decisions such as Starbucks' 2008 closing of more than 600 stores, Apple's 2010 launch of the iPad, and Microsoft's 2015 software overhaul launching Windows 10. What do these diverse decisions have in common? They all were made by comparing the costs of the action against the value to the firm of the benefits. Specifically, a company's managers must determine what it is worth to the company today to receive the project's future cash inflows while paying its cash outflows.

In Chapter 3, we start to build the tools to undertake this analysis with a central concept in financial economics—the *time value of money.* In Chapter 4, we explain how to value any series of future cash flows and derive a few useful shortcuts for valuing various types of cash flow patterns. Chapter 5 discusses how interest rates are quoted in the market and how to handle interest rates that compound more frequently than once per year. In Chapter 6, we will apply what we have learned about interest rates and the present value of cash flows to the task of valuing bonds. In the last chapter of Part 2, Chapter 7, we discuss the features of common stocks and learn how to calculate an estimate of their value.

3

Time Value of Money: An Introduction

LEARNING OBJECTIVES

- Identify the roles of financial managers and competitive markets in decision making

- Understand the Valuation Principle, and how it can be used to identify decisions that increase the value of the firm

- Assess the effect of interest rates on today's value of future cash flows

- Calculate the value of distant cash flows in the present and of current cash flows in the future

notation

r	interest rate		C	cash flow
PV	present value		n	number of periods
FV	future value			

In 2011, Amazon.com managers decided to more directly compete in the tablet market with the launch of the Kindle Fire, and they priced it at $199, which by some estimates was either at or below the cost to build it. How did Amazon's managers decide this was the right decision for the company? Similarly, how did Apple's managers decide to enter the wearable technology market with the Apple Watch in 2015?

Every decision has future consequences that will affect the value of the firm. These consequences will generally include both benefits and costs. For example, in addition to the up-front cost of developing its own mobile phone and software, Amazon will also incur ongoing costs associated with future software and hardware development for the Fire, marketing efforts, and customer support. The benefits to Amazon include the revenues from the sales as well as additional content purchased through the device. This decision will increase Amazon's value if these benefits outweigh the costs.

More generally, a decision is good for the firm's investors if it increases the firm's value by providing benefits whose value exceeds the costs. But how do we compare costs and benefits that occur at different points in time, or are in different currencies, or have different risks associated with them? To make a valid comparison, we must use the tools of finance to express all costs and benefits in common terms. We convert all costs and benefits into a common currency and common point of time, such as dollars today. In this chapter, we learn (1) how to use market information to evaluate costs and benefits and (2) why market prices are so important. Then, we will start to build the critical tools relating to the time value of money. These tools will allow you to correctly compare the costs and benefits of a decision no matter when they occur.

3.1   Cost-Benefit Analysis

The first step in decision making is to identify the costs and benefits of a decision. In this section, we look at the role of financial managers in evaluating costs and benefits and the tools they use to quantify them.

Role of the Financial Manager

A financial manager's job is to make decisions on behalf of the firm's investors. Our objective in this book is to explain how to make decisions that increase the value of the firm to its investors. In principle, the idea is simple and intuitive: For good decisions, the benefits exceed the costs. Of course, real-world opportunities are usually complex and the costs and benefits are often difficult to quantify. Quantifying them often means using skills from other management disciplines, as in the following examples:

> *Marketing*: to determine the increase in revenues resulting from an advertising campaign
> *Economics*: to determine the increase in demand from lowering the price of a product
> *Organizational Behavior*: to determine the effect of changes in management structure on productivity
> *Strategy*: to determine a competitor's response to a price increase
> *Operations*: to determine production costs after the modernization of a manufacturing plant

For the remainder of this text, we will assume we can rely on experts in these areas to provide this information so the costs and benefits associated with a decision have already been identified. With that task done, the financial manager's job is to compare the costs and benefits and determine the best decision for the value of the firm.

Quantifying Costs and Benefits

Any decision in which the value of the benefits exceeds the costs will increase the value of the firm. To evaluate the costs and benefits of a decision, we must value the options in the same terms—cash today. Let's make this concrete with a simple example.

Suppose a jewelry manufacturer has the opportunity to trade 200 ounces of silver for 10 ounces of gold today. An ounce of silver differs in value from an ounce of gold. Consequently, it is incorrect to compare 200 ounces to 10 ounces and conclude that the larger quantity is better. Instead, to compare the cost of the silver and the benefit of the gold, we first need to quantify their values in equivalent terms—cash today.

Consider the silver. What is its cash value today? Suppose silver can be bought and sold for a current market price of $20 per ounce. Then the 200 ounces of silver we would give up has a cash value of:[1]

$$(200 \text{ ounces of silver}) \times (\$20/\text{ounce of silver}) = \$4000$$

If the current market price for gold is $1000 per ounce, then the 10 ounces of gold we would receive has a cash value of

$$(10 \text{ ounces of gold}) \times (\$1000/\text{ounce of gold}) = \$10{,}000$$

We have now quantified the decision. The jeweler's opportunity has a benefit of $10,000 and a cost of $4000. The net benefit of the decision is $10,000 − $4000 = $6000 today.

---

[1]You might wonder whether commissions and other transactions costs need to be included in this calculation. For now, we will ignore transactions costs, but we will discuss their effect in later chapters.

The net value of the decision is positive, so by accepting the trade, the jewelry firm will be richer by $6000.

Role of Competitive Market Prices. Suppose the jeweler works exclusively on silver jewelry or thinks the price of silver should be higher. Should his decision change? The answer is no—he can always make the trade and then buy silver at the current market price. Even if he has no use for the gold, he can immediately sell it for $10,000, buy back the 200 ounces of silver at the current market price of $4000, and pocket the remaining $6000. Thus, independent of his own views or preferences, the value of the silver to the jeweler is $4000.

Because the jeweler can both buy and sell silver at its current market price, his personal preferences or use for silver and his opinion of the fair price are irrelevant in evaluating the value of this opportunity. This observation highlights an important general principle related to goods trading in a **competitive market**, a market in which a good can be bought *and* sold at the same price. Whenever a good trades in a competitive market, that price determines the value of the good. This point is one of the central and most powerful ideas in finance. It will underlie almost every concept we develop throughout the text.

competitive market
A market in which a good can be bought *and* sold at the same price.

EXAMPLE 3.1

Competitive Market Prices Determine Value

MyFinanceLab

PROBLEM

You have just won a radio contest and are disappointed to learn that the prize is four tickets to the Def Leppard reunion tour (face value $40 each). Not being a fan of 1980s power rock, you have no intention of going to the show. However, the radio station offers you another option: two tickets to your favorite band's sold-out show (face value $45 each). You notice that, on eBay, tickets to the Def Leppard show are being bought and sold for $30 apiece and tickets to your favorite band's show are being bought and sold at $50 each. What should you do?

SOLUTION

PLAN

Market prices, not your personal preferences (or the face value of the tickets), are relevant here:

> 4 Def Leppard tickets at $30 apiece

> 2 of your favorite band's tickets at $50 apiece

You need to compare the market value of each option and choose the one with the highest market value.

EXECUTE

The Def Leppard tickets have a total value of $120 (4 × $30) versus the $100 total value of the other 2 tickets (2 × $50). Instead of taking the tickets to your favorite band, you should accept the Def Leppard tickets, sell them on eBay, and use the proceeds to buy 2 tickets to your favorite band's show. You'll even have $20 left over to buy a T-shirt.

EVALUATE

Even though you prefer your favorite band, you should still take the opportunity to get the Def Leppard tickets instead. As we emphasized earlier, whether this opportunity is attractive depends on its net value using market prices. Because the value of Def Leppard tickets is $20 more than the value of your favorite band's tickets, the opportunity is appealing.

CONCEPT CHECK

1. When costs and benefits are in different units or goods, how can we compare them?

2. If crude oil trades in a competitive market, would an oil refiner that has a use for the oil value it differently than another investor would?

Market Prices and the Valuation Principle

In the previous examples, the right decisions for the firms were clear because the costs and benefits were easy to evaluate and compare. They were easy to evaluate because we were able to use current market prices to convert them into equivalent cash values. Once we can express costs and benefits in terms of cash today, it is a straightforward process to compare them and determine whether the decision will increase the firm's value.

The Valuation Principle

Our discussion so far establishes competitive market prices as the way to evaluate the costs and benefits of a decision in terms of cash today. Once we do this, it is a simple matter to determine the best decision for the firm. The best decision makes the firm and its investors wealthier, because the value of its benefits exceeds the value of its costs. We call this idea the Valuation Principle:

> **The Valuation Principle:**
>
> *The value of a commodity or an asset to the firm or its investors is determined by its competitive market price. The benefits and costs of a decision should be evaluated using those market prices. When the value of the benefits exceeds the value of the costs, the decision will increase the market value of the firm.*

The Valuation Principle provides the basis for decision making throughout this text. In the remainder of this chapter, we apply it to decisions whose costs and benefits occur at different points in time.

EXAMPLE 3.2

Applying the
Valuation Principle

MyFinanceLab

PROBLEM

You are the operations manager at your firm. Due to a pre-existing contract, you have the opportunity to acquire 200 barrels of oil and 3000 pounds of copper for a total of $25,000. The current market price of oil is $90 per barrel and for copper is $3.50 per pound. You are not sure that you need all the oil and copper, so you are wondering whether you should take this opportunity. How valuable is it? Would your decision change if you believed the value of oil or copper would plummet over the next month?

SOLUTION

PLAN

We need to quantify the costs and benefits using market prices. We are comparing $25,000 with:

  200 barrels of oil at $90 per barrel

  3000 pounds of copper at $3.50 per pound

EXECUTE

Using the competitive market prices we have:

$$(200 \text{ barrels of oil}) \times (\$90/\text{barrel today}) = \$18,000 \text{ today}$$
$$(3000 \text{ pounds of copper}) \times (\$3.50/\text{pound today}) = \$10,500 \text{ today}$$

The value of the opportunity is the value of the oil plus the value of the copper less the cost of the opportunity, or $18,000 + $10,500 − $25,000 = $3500 today. Because the value is positive, we should take it. This value depends only on the *current* market prices for oil and copper. If we do not need all of the oil and copper, we can sell the excess at current market prices. Even if we thought the value of oil or copper was about to plummet, the value of this investment would be unchanged. (We can always exchange them for dollars immediately at the current market prices.)

EVALUATE

Since we are transacting today, only the current prices in a competitive market matter. Our own use for or opinion about the future prospects of oil or copper do not alter the value of the decision today. This decision is good for the firm and will increase its value by $3500.

Why There Can Be Only One Competitive Price for a Good

The Valuation Principle and finance in general rely on using a competitive market price to value a cost or benefit. We cannot have two different competitive market prices for the same good—otherwise we would arrive at two different values. Fortunately, powerful market forces keep competitive prices the same. To illustrate, imagine what you would do if you saw gold simultaneously trading for two different prices. You and everyone else who noticed the difference would buy at the low price and sell at the high price for as many ounces of gold as possible, making instant risk-free profits. The flood of buy and sell orders would push the two prices together until the profit was eliminated. These forces establish the **Law of One Price**, which states that in competitive markets, the same good or securities must have the same price. More generally, securities that produce exactly the same cash flows must have the same price.

Law of One Price In competitive markets, securities with the same cash flows must have the same price.

In general, the practice of buying and selling equivalent goods in different markets to take advantage of a price difference is known as **arbitrage**. We refer to any situation in which it is possible to make a profit without taking any risk or making any investment as an **arbitrage opportunity**. Because an arbitrage opportunity's benefits are more valuable than its costs, whenever an arbitrage opportunity appears in financial markets, investors will race to take advantage of it and their trades will eliminate the opportunity.

arbitrage The practice of buying and selling equivalent goods to take advantage of a price difference.

arbitrage opportunity Any situation in which it is possible to make a profit without taking any risk or making any investment.

Retail stores often quote different prices for the same item in different countries. *The Economist* magazine has long compared prices for a McDonald's Big Mac around the world. Here, we compare Big Mac prices from January 2016. The price in the local currency and converted to U.S. dollars is listed. Of course, these prices are not examples of competitive market prices, because you can only buy a Big Mac at these prices. Hence, they do not present an arbitrage opportunity. Even if shipping were free, you could buy as many Big Macs as you could get your hands on in Venezuela but you would not be able to sell those rotten Big Macs in Switzerland for a profit!

Country	Local Cost	U.S. Dollar Cost
Switzerland	6.50 Swiss francs	$6.44
Sweden	45 Swedish Krona	$5.23
United States	4.93 US dollars	$4.93
Britain	2.89 pounds	$4.22
Canada	5.84 Canadian dollars	$4.14
Australia	5.30 Australian dollars	$3.74
U.A.E.	13 dirhams	$3.54
Brazil	13.50 reals	$3.35
Japan	370 yen	$3.12
Mexico	49 pesos	$2.81
China	17.60 yuan	$2.68
Hong Kong	19.20 HK dollars	$2.48
Poland	960 zlotys	$2.37
Indonesia	30,500 rupiahs	$2.19
Russia	114 rubles	$1.53
Venezuela	132 bolivares fuertes	$0.66

Source: Economist.com.

Your Personal Financial Decisions

While the focus of this text is on the decisions a financial manager makes in a business setting, you will soon see that concepts and skills you will learn here apply to personal decisions as well. As a normal part of life we all make decisions that trade off benefits and costs across time. Going to college, purchasing this book, saving for a new car or house down payment, taking out a car loan or home loan, buying shares of stock, and deciding between jobs are just a few examples of decisions you have faced or could face in the near future. As you read through this book, you will see that the Valuation Principle is the foundation of *all* financial decision making—whether in a business or in a personal context.

**CONCEPT
CHECK**
3. How do investors' profit motives keep competitive market prices correct?

4. How do we determine whether a decision increases the value of the firm?

3.3   The Time Value of Money and Interest Rates

Unlike the examples presented so far, most financial decisions have costs and benefits that occur at different points in time. For example, typical investment projects incur costs up front and provide benefits in the future. In this section, we show how to account for this time difference when using the Valuation Principle to make a decision.

The Time Value of Money

Your company has an investment opportunity with the following cash flows:

Cost: $100,000 today
Benefit: $105,000 in one year

Both are expressed in dollar terms, but are the cost and benefit directly comparable? No. Calculating the project's net value as $105,000 − $100,000 = $5000 is incorrect because it ignores the *timing* of the costs and benefits. That is, it treats money today as equivalent to money in one year. In general, a dollar received today is worth *more* than a dollar received in one year: If you have $1 today, you can invest it now and have more money in the future. For example, if you deposit it in a bank account paying 10% interest, you will have $1.10 at the end of one year. We call the difference in value between money today and money in the future the **time value of money**.

time value of money The difference in value between money received today and money received in the future; also, the observation that two cash flows at two different points in time have different values.

Figure 3.1 illustrates how we use competitive market prices and interest rates to convert between dollars today and other goods, or dollars in the future. Just like silver and gold, money today and money tomorrow are not the same thing. We compare them just like we did with silver and gold—using competitive market prices. But in the case of money, what is the price? It is the interest rate, the price for exchanging money today for money in a year. We can use the interest rate to determine values in the same way we used competitive market prices. Once we quantify all the costs and benefits of an investment

FIGURE 3.1

Converting Between Dollars Today and Gold or Dollars in the Future

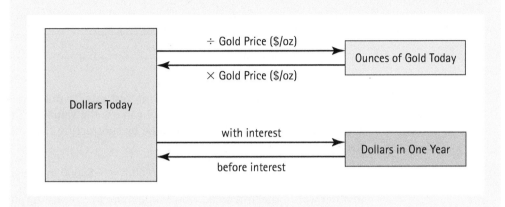

We can convert dollars today to different goods or points in time by using the competitive market price or interest rate. Once values are in equivalent terms, we can use the Valuation Principle to make a decision.

in terms of dollars today, we can rely on the Valuation Principle to determine whether the investment will increase the firm's value.

The Interest Rate: Converting Cash Across Time

We now develop the tools needed to value our $100,000 investment opportunity correctly. By depositing money into a savings account, we can convert money today into money in the future with no risk. Similarly, by borrowing money from the bank, we can exchange money in the future for money today. Suppose the current annual interest rate is 10%. By investing $1 today we can convert this $1 into $1.10 in one year. Similarly, by borrowing at this rate, we can exchange $1.10 in one year for $1 today. More generally, we define the **interest rate**, r, for a given period as the interest rate at which money can be borrowed or lent over that period. In our example, the interest rate is 10% and we can exchange 1 dollar today for $(1 + .10)$ dollars in one year. In general, we can exchange 1 dollar today for $(1 + r)$ dollars in one year, and vice versa. We refer to $(1 + r)$ as the **interest rate factor** for cash flows; it defines how we convert cash flows across time, and has units of "$ in one year/$ today."

Like other market prices, the interest rate ultimately depends on supply and demand. In particular, the interest rate equates the supply of savings to the demand for borrowing. But regardless of how it is determined, once we know the interest rate, we can apply the Valuation Principle and use it to evaluate other decisions in which costs and benefits are separated in time.

interest rate The rate at which money can be borrowed or lent over a given period.

interest rate factor One plus the interest rate, it is the rate of exchange between dollars today and dollars in the future. It has units of "$ in the future/$ today."

Value of $100,000 Investment in One Year. Let's reevaluate the investment we considered earlier, this time taking into account the time value of money. If the interest rate is 10%, then your company faces a choice: use $1 today, or deposit it and have $1.10 in one year. That means we can think of $1.10 as the cost of every dollar used today. So, we can express the cost of the investment as:

$$\text{Cost} = (\$100,000 \text{ today}) \times \left(\frac{\$1.10 \text{ in one year}}{\$1 \text{ today}} \right)$$

$$= \$110,000 \text{ in one year}$$

Think of this amount as the opportunity cost of spending $100,000 today: The firm gives up the $110,000 it would have had in one year if it had left the money in the bank. Alternatively, by borrowing the $100,000 from the same bank, the firm would owe $110,000 in one year.

	Today		One Year
Investment	−$100,000		+$105,000
Bank	−$100,000		+$110,000

We have used a market price, the interest rate, to put both the costs and benefits in terms of "dollars in one year," so now we can use the Valuation Principle to compare them and compute the investment's net value by subtracting the cost of the investment from the benefit in one year:

$$\$105,000 - \$110,000 = -\$5000 \text{ in one year}$$

In other words, the firm could earn $5000 more in one year by putting the $100,000 in the bank rather than making this investment. Because the net value is negative, we should reject the investment: If we took it, the firm would be $5000 poorer in one year than if we didn't.

Value of $100,000 Investment Today. The preceding calculation expressed the value of the costs and benefits in terms of dollars in one year. Alternatively, we can use the interest rate factor to convert to dollars today. Consider the benefit of $105,000 in one year. What is the equivalent amount in terms of dollars today? That is, how much would we need to have in the bank today so we end up with $105,000 in the bank in one year? We find this amount by dividing $105,000 by the interest rate factor:

$$\text{Benefit} = (\$105,000 \text{ in one year}) \div \left(\frac{\$1.10 \text{ in one year}}{\$1 \text{ today}} \right)$$

$$= \$95,454.55 \text{ today}$$

This is also the amount the bank would lend to us today if we promised to repay $105,000 in one year.[2] Thus, it is the competitive market price at which we can "buy" or "sell" today an amount of $105,000 in one year.

	Today		One Year
Value of Cost Today	−$100,000		+$105,000
Value of Benefit Today	+$95,454.55 ⟵	$\frac{105{,}000}{1.10}$ ⟵	

Now we are ready to compute the net value of the investment today (as opposed to its net value in one year) by subtracting the cost from the benefit:

$$\$95,454.55 - \$100,000 = -\$4545.45 \text{ today}$$

Because this net value is calculated in terms of dollars today (in the present), it is typically called the *net present value*. We will formally introduce this concept in Chapter 8. Once again, the negative result indicates that we should reject the investment. Taking the investment would make the firm $4,545.45 poorer today because it gave up $100,000 for something worth only $95,454.55.

---

[2]We are assuming the bank is willing to lend at the same 10% interest rate, which would be the case if there were no risk associated with the cash flow.

Present Versus Future Value. This calculation demonstrates that our decision is the same whether we express the value of the investment in terms of dollars in one year or dollars today: We should reject the investment. Indeed, if we convert from dollars today to dollars in one year,

$$(-\$4545.45 \text{ today}) \times (\$1.10 \text{ in one year}/\$1 \text{ today}) = -\$5000 \text{ in one year}$$

we see that the two results are equivalent, but expressed as values at different points in time. When we express the value in terms of dollars today, we call it the **present value (PV)** of the investment. If we express it in terms of dollars in the future, we call it the **future value (FV)** of the investment.

present value (PV) The value of a cost or benefit computed in terms of cash today.

future value (FV) The value of a cash flow that is moved forward in time.

discount factor The value today of a dollar received in the future.

discount rate The appropriate rate to discount a cash flow to determine its value at an earlier time.

Discount Factors and Rates. In the preceding calculation, we can interpret

$$\frac{1}{1 + r} = \frac{1}{1.10} = 0.90909$$

as the *price* today of $1 in one year. In other words, for just under 91 cents, you can "buy" $1 to be delivered in one year. Note that the value is less than $1—money in the future is worth less today, so its price reflects a discount. Because it provides the discount at which we can purchase money in the future, the amount $1/(1 + r)$ is called the one-year **discount factor**. The interest rate is also referred to as the **discount rate** for an investment.

EXAMPLE 3.3

Comparing Revenues at Different Points in Time

MyFinanceLab

PROBLEM

The launch of Sony's PlayStation 3 was delayed until November 2006, giving Microsoft's Xbox 360 a full year on the market without competition. Sony did not repeat this mistake in 2013 when PS4 launched at the same time as Xbox One. Imagine that it is November 2005 and you are the marketing manager for the PlayStation. You estimate that if PlayStation 3 were ready to be launched immediately, you could sell $2 billion worth of the console in its first year. However, if your launch is delayed a year, you believe that Microsoft's head start will reduce your first-year sales by 20% to $1.6 billion. If the interest rate is 8%, what is the cost of a delay of the first year's revenues in terms of dollars in 2005?

SOLUTION

PLAN

Revenues if released today: $2 billion   Revenue if delayed: $1.6 billion   Interest rate: 8%

We need to compute the revenues if the launch is delayed and compare them to the revenues from launching today. However, in order to make a fair comparison, we need to convert the future revenues of the PlayStation if they are delayed into an equivalent present value of those revenues today.

EXECUTE

If the launch is delayed to 2006, revenues will drop by 20% of $2 billion, or $400 million, to $1.6 billion. To compare this amount to revenues of $2 billion if launched in 2005, we must convert it using the interest rate of 8%:

$$\$1.6 \text{ billion in 2006} \div (\$1.08 \text{ in 2006}/\$1 \text{ in 2005}) = \frac{\$1.6 \text{ billion}}{(1.08)} = \$1.481 \text{ billion in 2005}$$

Therefore, the cost of a delay of one year is

$$\$2 \text{ billion} - \$1.481 \text{ billion} = \$0.519 \text{ billion} (\$519 \text{ million}).$$

(Continued)

> **EVALUATE**
>
> Delaying the project for one year was equivalent to giving up $519 million in cash. In this example, we focused only on the effect on the first year's revenues. However, delaying the launch delays the entire revenue stream by one year, so the total cost would be calculated in the same way by summing the cost of delay for each year of revenues.

Timelines

timeline A linear representation of the timing of (potential) cash flows.

Our visual representation of the cost and benefit of the $100,000 investment in this section is an example of a **timeline**, a linear representation of the timing of the expected cash flows. Timelines are an important first step in organizing and then solving a financial problem. We use them throughout this text.

Constructing a Timeline. To understand how to construct a timeline, assume a friend owes you money. He has agreed to repay the loan by making two payments of $10,000 at the end of each of the next two years. We represent this information on a timeline as follows:

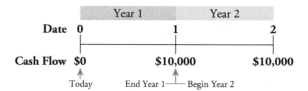

Identifying Dates on a Timeline. To track cash flows, we interpret each point on the timeline as a specific date. The space between date 0 and date 1 represents the first year of the loan. Date 0 is today, the beginning of the first year, and date 1 is the end of the first year. The $10,000 cash flow below date 1 is the payment you will receive at the end of the first year. Similarly, date 1 is the beginning of the second year, date 2 is the end of the second year, and the $10,000 cash flow below date 2 is the payment you will receive at the end of the second year. Note that date 1 signifies *both* the end of year 1 *and* the beginning of year 2, which makes sense since those dates are effectively the same point in time.[3]

Distinguishing Cash Inflows from Outflows. In this example, both cash flows are inflows. In many cases, however, a financial decision will include inflows and outflows. To differentiate between the two types of cash flows, we assign a different sign to each: Inflows (cash flows received) are positive cash flows, whereas outflows (cash flows paid out) are negative cash flows.

To illustrate, suppose you have agreed to lend your brother $10,000 today. Your brother has agreed to repay this loan with interest by making payments of $6000 at the end of each of the next two years. The timeline is:

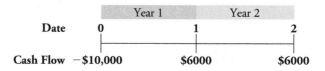

---

[3]That is, there is no real time difference between a cash flow paid at 11:59 P.M. on December 31 and one paid at 12:01 A.M. on January 1, although there may be some other differences such as taxation, which we will overlook for now.

Notice that the first cash flow at date 0 (today) is represented as −$10,000 because it is an outflow. The subsequent cash flows of $6000 are positive because they are inflows.

Representing Various Time Periods. So far, we have used timelines to show the cash flows that occur at the end of each year. Actually, timelines can represent cash flows that take place at any point in time. For example, if you pay rent each month, you could use a timeline such as the one in our first example to represent two rental payments, but you would replace the "year" label with "month."

Many of the timelines included in this chapter are simple. Consequently, you may feel that it is not worth the time or trouble to construct them. As you progress to more difficult problems, however, you will find that timelines identify events in a transaction or investment that are easy to overlook. If you fail to recognize these cash flows, you will make flawed financial decisions. Therefore, approach *every* problem by drawing the timeline as we do in this chapter and the next.

CONCEPT CHECK

5. How is an interest rate like a price?

6. Is the value today of money to be received in one year higher when interest rates are high or when interest rates are low?

3.4   Valuing Cash Flows at Different Points in Time

The example of the $100,000 investment in the previous section laid the groundwork for how we will compare cash flows that happen at different points in time. In this section, we will generalize from the example by introducing three important rules central to financial decision making that allow us to compare or combine values across time.

Rule 1: Comparing and Combining Values

Our first rule is that it is only possible to compare or combine values at the same point in time. This rule restates a conclusion from the last section: Only cash flows in the same units can be compared or combined. A dollar today and a dollar in one year are not equivalent. Having money now is more valuable than having money in the future; if you have the money today you can invest it and earn interest.

To compare or combine cash flows that occur at different points in time, you first need to convert the cash flows into the same units by moving them to the same point in time. The next two rules show how to move the cash flows on the timeline.

COMMON MISTAKE

Summing Cash Flows Across Time

Once you understand the time value of money, our first rule may seem straightforward. However, it is very common, especially for those who have not studied finance, to violate this rule, simply treating all cash flows as comparable regardless of when they are received. One example is in sports contracts. In 2011, Albert Pujols signed a contract with the Los Angeles Angels that was repeatedly referred to as a "$240 million" contract. The $240 million comes from simply adding up all the payments Pujols would receive over the 10 years of the contract—treating dollars received in 10 years the same as dollars received today. The same thing occurred when Lionel Messi signed a contract extension with FC Barcelona in 2013, giving him a "$150 million" contract through 2018, and in 2015 when Giancarlo Stanton signed a "$325 million" 13-year contract with the Florida Marlins.

Rule 2: Compounding

Suppose we have $1000 today, and we wish to determine the equivalent amount in one year's time. If the current market interest rate is 10%, we saw in the last section that we can use that rate as an exchange rate, meaning the rate at which we exchange money today for money in one year, to move the cash flow forward in time. That is:

$$(\$1000 \text{ today}) \times (\$1.10 \text{ in one year}/\$1 \text{ today}) = \$1100 \text{ in one year}$$

compounding Computing the return on an investment over a long horizon by multiplying the return factors associated with each intervening period.

In general, if the market interest rate for the year is r, then we multiply by the interest rate factor, $(1 + r)$ to move the cash flow from the beginning to the end of the year. We multiply by $(1 + r)$ because at the end of the year you will have $(1 \times$ your original investment$)$ plus interest in the amount of $(r \times$ your original investment$)$. This process of moving forward along the timeline to determine a cash flow's value in the future (its future value) is known as **compounding**. *Our second rule stipulates that to calculate a cash flow's future value, you must compound it.*

We can apply this rule repeatedly. Suppose we want to know how much the $1000 is worth in two years' time. If the interest rate for year 2 is also 10%, then we convert as we just did:

$$(\$1100 \text{ in one year}) \times (\$1.10 \text{ in two years}/\$1 \text{ in one year}) = \$1210 \text{ in two years}$$

Let's represent this calculation on a timeline:

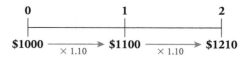

Given a 10% interest rate, all of the cash flows—$1000 at date 0, $1100 at date 1, and $1210 at date 2—are equivalent. They have the same value but are expressed in different units (different points in time). An arrow that points to the right indicates that the value is being moved forward in time—that is, compounded.

In the preceding example, $1210 is the future value of $1000 two years from today. Note that the value grows as we move the cash flow further in the future. In the last section, we defined the time value of money as the difference in value between money today and money in the future. Here, we can say that $1210 in two years is equivalent to $1000 today. The reason money is more valuable to you today is that you have opportunities to invest it. As in this example, by having money sooner, you can invest it (here at a 10% return) so that it will grow to a larger amount in the future. Note also that the equivalent amount grows by $100 the first year, but by $110 the second year. In the second year, we earn interest on our original $1000, plus we earn interest on the $100 interest we received in the first year. This effect of earning interest on both the original principal plus the accumulated interest, so that you are earning "interest on interest," is known as **compound interest**. Figure 3.2 shows how over time the amount of money you earn from interest on interest grows so that it will eventually exceed the amount of money that you earn as interest on your original deposit.

compound interest The effect of earning "interest on interest."

How does the future value change in the third year? Continuing to use the same approach, we compound the cash flow a third time. Assuming the competitive market interest rate is fixed at 10%, we get:

$$\$1000 \times (1.10) \times (1.10) \times (1.10) = \$1000 \times (1.10)^3 = \$1331$$

FIGURE 3.2

The Composition of
Interest over Time

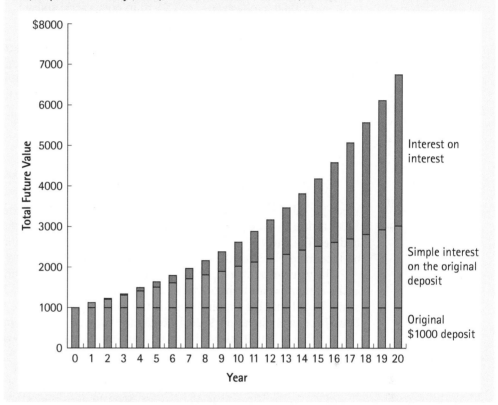

This bar graph shows how the account balance and the composition of the interest changes over time when an investor starts with an original deposit of $1000, represented by the red area, in an account earning 10% interest over a 20-year period. The green (middle) bars show the effect of **simple interest**, interest earned only on the initial deposit. The blue (top) bars show the effect of compound interest, where interest is also earned on prior interest payments. Over time, the effect of compounding is more pronounced, and by year 20, simple interest is only $2000, whereas interest on interest is $3727.50.

simple interest Interest earned only on the initial deposit

In general, to compute a cash flow C's value n periods into the future, we must compound it by the n intervening interest rate factors. If the interest rate r is constant, this calculation yields:

Future Value of a Cash Flow

$$FV_n = C \times \underbrace{(1 + r) \times (1 + r) \times \cdots \times (1 + r)}_{n \text{ times}} = C \times (1 + r)^n \quad (3.1)$$

 Rule of 72

Another way to think about the effect of compounding is to consider how long it will take your money to double given different interest rates. Suppose you want to know how many years it will take for $1 to grow to a future value of $2. You want the number of years, n, to solve:

$$FV_n = \$1 \times (1 + r)^n = \$2$$

If you solve this formula for different interest rates, you will find the following approximation:

Years to double ≈ 72 ÷ (interest rate in percent)

This simple "Rule of 72" is fairly accurate (that is, within one year of the exact doubling time) for interest rates higher than 2%. For example, if the interest rate is 9%, the doubling time should be about 72 ÷ 9 = 8 years. Indeed, $1.09^8 = 1.99$! So, given a 9% interest rate, your money will approximately double every 8 years.

Rule 3: Discounting

The third rule describes how to put a value today on a cash flow that comes in the future. Suppose you would like to compute the value today of $1000 that you anticipate receiving in one year. If the current market interest rate is 10%, you can compute this value by converting units as we did in the last section:

($1000 in one year) ÷ ($1.10 in one year/$1 today) = $909.09 today

That is, to move the cash flow back along the timeline, we divide it by the interest rate factor, $(1 + r)$, where r is the interest rate. This process of finding the equivalent value today of a future cash flow is known as **discounting**. *Our third rule stipulates that to calculate the value of a future cash flow at an earlier point in time, we must discount it.*

discounting Finding the equivalent value today of a future cash flow by multiplying by a discount factor, or equivalently, dividing by 1 plus the discount rate.

Suppose that you anticipate receiving the $1000 two years from today rather than in one year. If the interest rate for both years is 10%, you can prepare the following timeline:

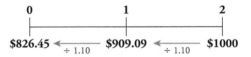

When the interest rate is 10%, all of the cash flows—$826.45 at date 0, $909.09 at date 1, and $1000 at date 2—are equivalent. They represent the same value in different units (different points in time). The arrow points to the left to indicate that the value is being moved backward in time or discounted. Note that the value decreases the further in the future is the original cash flow.

The value of a future cash flow at an earlier point on the timeline is its present value at the earlier point in time. That is, $826.45 is the present value at date 0 of $1000 in two years. Recall that the present value is the "do-it-yourself" price to produce a future cash flow. Thus, if we invested $826.45 today for two years at 10% interest, we would have a future value of $1000, using the second rule of valuing cash flows:

Suppose the $1000 were three years away and you wanted to compute the present value. Again, if the interest rate is 10%, we have:

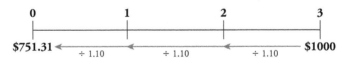

That is, the present value today of a cash flow of $1000 in three years is given by:

$1000 ÷ (1.10) ÷ (1.10) ÷ (1.10) = $1000 ÷ (1.10)^3 = $751.31

In general, to compute the present value of a cash flow C that comes n periods from now, we must discount it by the n intervening interest rate factors. If the interest rate r is constant, this yields:

Present Value of a Cash Flow

$$PV = C \div (1 + r)^n = \frac{C}{(1 + r)^n} \qquad (3.2)$$

PROBLEM

You are considering investing in a savings bond that will pay $15,000 in 10 years. If the competitive market interest rate is fixed at 6% per year, what is the bond worth today?

SOLUTION

PLAN

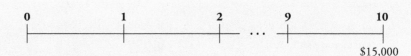

First, set up your timeline. The cash flows for this bond are represented by the following timeline:
Thus, the bond is worth $15,000 in 10 years. To determine the value today, we compute the present value using Equation 3.2 and our interest rate of 6%.

EXECUTE

$$PV = \frac{15,000}{1.06^{10}} = \$8375.92 \text{ today}$$

EVALUATE

The bond is worth much less today than its final payoff because of the time value of money.

As we've seen in this section, we can compare cash flows at different points in time as long as we follow the Three Rules of Valuing Cash Flows, summarized in Table 3.1. Armed with these three rules, a financial manager can compare an investment's costs and benefits that are spread out over time and apply the Valuation Principle to make the right decision. In Chapter 4, we will show you how to apply these rules to situations involving multiple cash flows at different points in time.

TABLE 3.1

The Three Rules of
Valuing Cash Flows

Rule	Formula
1: Only values at the same point in time can be compared or combined.	None
2: To calculate a cash flow's future value, we must compound it.	Future value of a cash flow: $FV_n = C \times (1 + r)^n$
3: To calculate the present value of a future cash flow, we must discount it.	Present value of a cash flow: $PV = C \div (1 + r)^n = \dfrac{C}{(1 + r)^n}$

**CONCEPT
CHECK**

7. Can you compare or combine cash flows at different times?

8. What do you need to know to compute a cash flow's present or future value?

Using a Financial Calculator

Financial calculators are programmed to perform most present and future value calculations. However, we recommend that you develop an understanding of the formulas before using the shortcuts. We provide a more extensive discussion of financial calculators on page 95 and in the appendix to Chapter 4, but we'll cover the relevant functions for this chapter here. To use financial calculator functions, you always enter the known values first and then the calculator solves for the unknown.

To answer Example 3.4 with a financial calculator, do the following:

Concept	Number of Periods	Interest Rate per Period	Recurring Payments	Future Value
Calculator Key	N	I/Y	PMT	FV
Enter	10	6	0	15000

Because you are solving for the present value (PV), press the PV key last (on an HP calculator), or press CPT then the PV key on a TI calculator. The calculator will return −8375.92. Note that the calculator balances inflows with outflows, so because the FV is positive (an inflow), it returns the PV as a negative (an outflow).

If you were solving for the future value instead, you would enter:

N	I/Y	PV	PMT
10	6	−8375.92	0

And finally, on an HP, press the FV key or on a TI, press CPT and then the FV key.

MyFinanceLab

Here is what you should know after reading this chapter. MyFinanceLab will help you identify what you know, and where to go when you need to practice.

KEY POINTS AND EQUATIONS	KEY TERMS	ONLINE PRACTICE
3.1 Cost-Benefit Analysis • To evaluate a decision, we must value the incremental costs and benefits associated with that decision. A good decision is one for which the value of the benefits exceeds the value of the costs. • To compare costs and benefits that occur at different points in time we must put all costs and benefits in common terms. Typically, we convert costs and benefits into cash today. • A competitive market is one in which a good can be bought and sold at the same price. We use prices from competitive markets to determine the cash value of a good.	competitive market, p. 75	MyFinanceLab Study Plan 3.1

3.2 Market Prices and the Valuation Principle

- Arbitrage is the process of trading to take advantage of equivalent goods that have different prices in different competitive markets.
- If equivalent goods or securities trade simultaneously in different competitive markets, they will trade for the same price in each market. This is equivalent to saying that no arbitrage opportunities should exist.
- The Valuation Principle states that the value of a commodity or an asset to the firm or its investors is determined by its competitive market price. The benefits and costs of a decision should be evaluated using those market prices. When the value of the benefits exceeds the value of the costs, the decision will increase the market value of the firm.

arbitrage, p. 77
arbitrage opportunity, p. 77
Law of One Price, p. 77

MyFinanceLab
Study Plan 3.2

3.3 The Time Value of Money and Interest Rates

- The time value of money is the difference in value between money today and money in the future.
- The rate at which we can exchange money today for money in the future by borrowing or investing is the current market interest rate.
- The present value (PV) of a cash flow is its value in terms of cash today.
- Timelines are a critical first step in organizing the cash flows in a financial problem.

discount factor, p. 81
discount rate, p. 81
future value (FV), p. 81
interest rate, p. 79
interest rate factor, p. 79
present value (PV), p. 81
time value of money, p. 78
timeline, p. 82

MyFinanceLab
Study Plan 3.3

3.4 Valuing Cash Flows at Different Points in Time

- There are three rules of valuing cash flows:
  a. Only cash flows that occur at the same point in time can be compared or combined.
  b. To calculate a cash flow's future value, you must compound it.
  c. To calculate a cash flow's present value, you must discount it.
- The future value in n years of a cash flow C today is:
$$C \times (1 + r)^n \qquad (3.1)$$
- The present value today of a cash flow C received in n years is:
$$C \div (1 + r)^n \qquad (3.2)$$

compounding, p. 84
compound interest, p. 84
discounting, p. 86
simple interest, p. 85

MyFinanceLab
Study Plan 3.4

Financial Calculator Tutorials:
Calculating the Future Value of a Lump Sum and Solving for the Present Value of a Single Future Cash Flow

CRITICAL THINKING

1. What makes an investment decision a good one?

2. How important are our personal preferences in valuing an investment decision?

3. Why are market prices useful to a financial manager?

4. Why is arbitrage important to competitive market prices?

5. How does the Valuation Principle help a financial manager make decisions?

6. Can we directly compare dollar amounts received at different points in time?

7. Why is a cash flow in the future worth less than the same amount today?

8. What is a discount rate?

9. What is compound interest?

10. What is the intuition behind the geometric growth in interest?

PROBLEMS

All problems are available in MyFinanceLab. *An asterisk * indicates problems with a higher level of difficulty.*

Cost-Benefit Analysis

1. Honda Motor Company is considering offering a $2000 rebate on its minivan, lowering the vehicle's price from $30,000 to $28,000. The marketing group estimates that this rebate will increase sales over the next year from 40,000 to 55,000 vehicles. Suppose Honda's profit margin with the rebate is $6000 per vehicle. If the change in sales is the only consequence of this decision, what are its costs and benefits? Is it a good idea?

2. You are an international shrimp trader. A food producer in the Czech Republic offers to pay you 2 million Czech koruna today in exchange for a year's supply of frozen shrimp. Your Thai supplier will provide you with the same supply for 3 million Thai baht today. If the current competitive market exchange rates are 25.50 koruna per dollar and 41.25 baht per dollar, what is the value of this exchange to you?

3. Suppose your employer offers you a choice between a $5000 bonus and 100 shares of the company's stock. Whichever one you choose will be awarded today. The stock is currently trading at $63 per share.
   a. Suppose that if you receive the stock bonus, you are free to trade it. Which form of the bonus should you choose? What is its value?
   b. Suppose that if you receive the stock bonus, you are required to hold it for at least one year. What can you say about the value of the stock bonus now? What will your decision depend on?

4. Suppose Big Bank offers an interest rate of 5.5% on both savings and loans, and Bank Enn offers an interest rate of 6% on both savings and loans.
   a. What profit opportunity is available?
   b. Which bank would experience a surge in the demand for loans? Which bank would receive a surge in deposits?
   c. What would you expect to happen to the interest rates the two banks are offering?

5. If the cost of buying a CD and ripping the tracks to your iPod (including your time) is $25, what is the most Apple could charge on iTunes for a whole 15-track CD?

6. Some companies cross-list their shares, meaning that their stock trades on more than one stock exchange. For example, Restaurant Brands International (QSR), the parent company of Burger King and Tim Hortons, trades on both the Toronto Stock Exchange and NYSE. If its price in Toronto is 50 Canadian dollars per share and anyone can exchange Canadian dollars for U.S. dollars at the rate of US$0.85 per C$1.00, what must QSR's price be on NYSE?

Market Prices and the Valuation Principle

7. Bubba is a shrimp farmer. In an ironic twist, Bubba is allergic to shellfish, so he cannot eat any shrimp. Each day he has a one-ton supply of shrimp. The market price of shrimp is $10,000 per ton.
   a. What is the value of a ton of shrimp to him?
   b. Would this value change if he were not allergic to shrimp? Why or why not?

8. Brett has almond orchards, but he is sick of almonds and prefers to eat walnuts instead. The owner of the walnut orchard next door has offered to swap this year's crop with him. Assume he produces 1000 tons of almonds and his neighbor produces 800 tons of walnuts. If the market price of almonds is $100 per ton and the market price of walnuts is $110 per ton:
   a. Should he make the exchange?
   b. Does it matter whether he prefers almonds or walnuts? Why or why not?

The Time Value of Money and Interest Rates

9. You have $100 and a bank is offering 5% interest on deposits. If you deposit the money in the bank, how much will you have in one year?

10. You expect to have $1000 in one year. A bank is offering loans at 6% interest per year. How much can you borrow today?

11. Due to your good credit, your bank reduces the interest rate on your $12,000 loan from 9% to 7.5% per year. Thanks to the change, how much will you save in interest this year?

12. A friend asks to borrow $55 from you and in return will pay you $58 in one year. If your bank is offering a 6% interest rate on deposits and loans:
   a. How much would you have in one year if you deposited the $55 instead?
   b. How much money could you borrow today if you pay the bank $58 in one year?
   c. Should you loan the money to your friend or deposit it in the bank?

13. What is the discount factor that is equivalent to a 6% discount rate?

14. If your discount factor is 0.9009, what is your discount rate?

15. You plan to borrow $1000 from a bank. In exchange for $1000 today, you promise to pay $1080 in one year. What does the cash flow timeline look like from your perspective? What does it look like from the bank's perspective?

16. The local electronics store is offering a promotion "1-year: same as cash," meaning that you can buy a TV now, and wait a year to pay (with no interest). So, if you take home a $1000 TV today, you will owe them $1000 in one year. If your bank is offering 4% interest, what is the true cost of the TV to you today?

Valuing Cash Flows at Different Points in Time

17. Suppose the interest rate is 4%.
   a. Having $200 today is equivalent to having what amount in one year?
   b. Having $200 in one year is equivalent to having what amount today?
   c. Which would you prefer, $200 today or $200 in one year? Does your answer depend on when you need the money? Why or why not?

18. You are considering a savings bond that will pay $100 in 10 years. If the interest rate is 2%, what should you pay today for the bond?

19. If your bank pays you 1.5% interest and you deposit $500 today, what will your balance be in 5 years?

20. Consider the following alternatives:
   i. $100 received in one year
   ii. $200 received in 5 years
   iii. $300 received in 10 years
   a. Rank the alternatives from most valuable to least valuable if the interest rate is 10% per year.
   b. What is your ranking if the interest rate is only 5% per year?
   c. What is your ranking if the interest rate is 20% per year?

*21. Suppose you invest $1000 in an account paying 8% interest per year.
   a. What is the balance in the account after 3 years? How much of this balance corresponds to "interest on interest"?
   b. What is the balance in the account after 25 years? How much of this balance corresponds to "interest on interest"?

22. Calculate the future value of $2000 in
   a. 5 years at an interest rate of 5% per year.
   b. 10 years at an interest rate of 5% per year.
   c. 5 years at an interest rate of 10% per year.
   *d. Why is the amount of interest earned in part (a) less than half the amount of interest earned in part (b)?

23. What is the present value of $10,000 received
   a. 12 years from today when the interest rate is 4% per year?
   b. 20 years from today when the interest rate is 8% per year?
   c. 6 years from today when the interest rate is 2% per year?

24. Your brother has offered to give you either $5000 today or $10,000 in 10 years. If the interest rate is 7% per year, which option is preferable?

25. Your bank pays 2.5% interest per year. You put $1000 in the bank today and $500 more in the bank in one year. How much will you have in the bank in 2 years?

26. Your cousin is currently 12 years old. She will be going to college in 6 years. Your aunt and uncle would like to have $100,000 in a savings account to fund her education at that time. If the account promises to pay a fixed interest rate of 4% per year, how much money do they need to put into the account today to ensure that they will have $100,000 in 6 years?

27. Your mom is thinking of retiring. Her retirement plan will pay her either $250,000 immediately on retirement or $350,000 five years after the date of her retirement. Which alternative should she choose if the interest rate is
   a. 0% per year?
   b. 8% per year?
   c. 20% per year?

28. You just won a prize that comes with two payout choices. The first option is to get $100,000 right now and nothing hereafter. The second option is to get $94,000 right now and $10,000 three years from now (and nothing after that). If your discount rate is 8%, which should you take?

29. You are planning to invest $5000 in an account earning 9% per year for retirement.
   a. If you put the $5000 in an account at age 23, and withdraw it 42 years later, how much will you have?
   b. If you wait 10 years before making the deposit, so that it stays in the account for only 32 years, how much will you have at the end?

*30. Your grandfather put some money in an account for you on the day you were born. You are now 18 years old and are allowed to withdraw the money for the first time. The account currently has $3996 in it and pays an 8% interest rate.
   a. How much money would be in the account if you left the money there until your 25th birthday?
   b. What if you left the money until your 65th birthday?
   c. How much money did your grandfather originally put in the account?

4

Time Value of Money: Valuing Cash Flow Streams

LEARNING OBJECTIVES

- Value a series of many cash flows

- Value a perpetual series of regular cash flows called a *perpetuity*

- Value a common set of regular cash flows called an *annuity*

- Value both perpetuities and annuities when the cash flows grow at a constant rate

- Compute the number of periods, cash flow, or rate of return of a loan or investment

- Value cash flow streams with non-annual payments

notation

C	cash flow
C_n	cash flow at date n
FV	future value
FV_n	future value on date n
g	growth rate

N	date of the last cash flow in a stream of cash flows
P	initial principal or deposit, or equivalent present value
PV	present value
r	interest rate or rate of return

As we have discussed, to evaluate a project a financial manager must compare its costs and benefits. In most cases, the cash flows in financial investments involve more than one future period. Thus, the financial manager is faced with the task of trading off a known up-front cost against a series of uncertain future benefits. We learned to value those costs and benefits by computing their cash values today—their present values.

In financial management, as well as your personal finances, you will need to evaluate series of cash flows occurring across time. In this chapter, we build on the tools we developed in Chapter 3 to value any series of cash flows. We will develop shortcuts for valuing *annuities*, *perpetuities*, and other special cases of assets with cash flows that follow regular patterns.

In Chapter 5, we will learn how interest rates are quoted and determined. Once we understand how interest rates are quoted, it will be straightforward to extend the tools of this chapter to cash flows that occur more frequently than once per year.

4.1   Valuing a Stream of Cash Flows

stream of cash flows
A series of cash flows lasting several periods.

We refer to a series of cash flows lasting several periods as a **stream of cash flows**. As with single cash flows, we can represent a stream of cash flows on a timeline. In this chapter, we will continue to use timelines and the rules of cash flow valuation introduced in Chapter 3 to organize and then solve financial problems.

Applying the Rules of Valuing Cash Flows to a Cash Flow Stream

Most investment opportunities have multiple cash flows that occur at different points in time. In Chapter 3, we learned the rules to value such cash flows:

Rule 1: Only values at the same point in time can be compared or combined.

Rule 2: To calculate a cash flow's future value, we must compound it using Eq. 3.1 from Chapter 3.

$$FV_n = C \times (1 + r)^n \tag{4.1}$$

Rule 3: To calculate the present value of a future cash flow, we must discount it using Eq. 3.2 from Chapter 3.

$$PV = C \div (1 + r)^n = \frac{C}{(1 + r)^n} \tag{4.2}$$

The rules of cash flow valuation allow us to compare and combine cash flows that occur at different points in time. Suppose we plan to save $1000 today and $1000 at the end of each of the next two years. If we earn a fixed 10% interest rate on our savings, how much will we have three years from today?

Again, we start with a timeline:

The timeline shows the three deposits we plan to make. We need to compute their value at the end of three years.

We can use the cash flow valuation rules in a number of ways to solve this problem. First, we can take the deposit at date 0 and move it forward to date 1. Because it is then in the same time period as the date 1 deposit, we can combine the two amounts to find out the total in the bank on date 1:

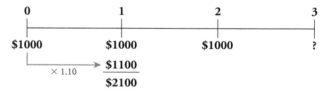

Using the first two rules, we find that our total savings on date 1 will be $2100. Continuing in this fashion, we can solve the problem as follows:

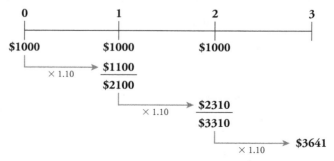

The total amount we will have in the bank at the end of three years is $3641. This amount is the future value of our $1000 savings deposits.

Another approach to the problem is to compute the future value in year 3 of each cash flow separately. Once all three amounts are in year 3 dollars, we can then combine them.

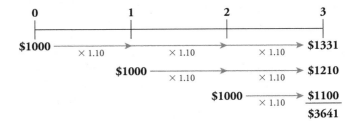

Both calculations give the same future value of $3641. As long as we follow the rules, we get the same result. The order in which we apply the rules does not matter. The calculation we choose depends on which is more convenient for the problem at hand.

Now we formalize this approach by deriving a general formula for valuing a stream of cash flows.

Consider a stream of cash flows: C_0 at date 0, C_1 at date 1, and so on, up to C_N at date N. We represent this cash flow stream on a timeline as follows:

Using the rules of cash flow valuation, we compute the present value of this cash flow stream in two steps. First, we compute the present value of each individual cash flow. Then, once the cash flows are in common units of dollars today, we can combine them.

For a given interest rate r, we represent this process on the timeline as follows:

$$C_0 + \frac{C_1}{(1+r)} + \frac{C_2}{(1+r)^2} + \ldots + \frac{C_N}{(1+r)^N}$$

This timeline provides the general formula for the present value of a cash flow stream:

$$PV = C_0 + \frac{C_1}{(1+r)} + \frac{C_2}{(1+r)^2} + \cdots + \frac{C_N}{(1+r)^N} \tag{4.3}$$

That is, the present value of the cash flow stream is the sum of the present values of each cash flow. Recall from Chapter 3 that we defined the present value as the dollar amount you would need to invest today to produce the single cash flow in the future. The same idea holds in this context. The present value is the amount you need to invest today to generate the cash flows stream $C_0, C_1, \ldots, C_N$. That is, receiving those cash flows is equivalent to having their present value in the bank today.

PERSONAL FINANCE

EXAMPLE 4.1

Present Value of a
Stream of Cash Flows

MyFinanceLab

PROBLEM

You have just graduated and need money to buy a new car. Your rich Uncle Henry will lend you the money as long as you agree to pay him back within four years, and you offer to pay him the rate of interest that he would otherwise get by putting his money in a savings account. Based on your earnings and living expenses, you think you will be able to pay him $5000 in one year, and then $8000 each year for the next three years. If Uncle Henry would otherwise earn 6% per year on his savings, how much can you borrow from him?

SOLUTION

PLAN

The cash flows you can promise Uncle Henry are as follows:

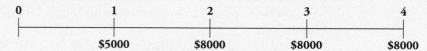

How much money should Uncle Henry be willing to give you today in return for your promise of these payments? He should be willing to give you an amount that is equivalent to these payments in present value terms. This is the amount of money that it would take him to produce these same cash flows. We will (1) solve the problem using Eq. 4.3 and then (2) verify our answer by calculating the future value of this amount.

EXECUTE

1. We can calculate the PV as follows:

$$PV = \frac{5000}{1.06} + \frac{8000}{1.06^2} + \frac{8000}{1.06^3} + \frac{8000}{1.06^4}$$
$$= 4716.98 + 7119.97 + 6716.95 + 6336.75$$
$$= \$24{,}890.65$$

Now suppose that Uncle Henry gives you the money, and then deposits your payments to him in the bank each year. How much will he have four years from now?

We need to compute the future value of the annual deposits. One way to do this is to compute the bank balance each year:

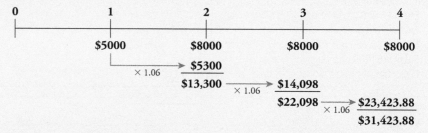

2. To verify our answer, suppose your uncle kept his $24,890.65 in the bank today earning 6% interest. In four years he would have:
$$FV = \$24{,}890.65 \times (1.06)^4 = \$31{,}423.87 \text{ in 4 years}$$

We get the same answer both ways (within a penny, which is due to rounding).

EVALUATE

Thus, Uncle Henry should be willing to lend you $24,890.65 in exchange for your promised payments. This amount is less than the total you will pay him ($5000 + $8000 + $8000 + $8000 = $29,000) due to the time value of money.

Example 4.1 illustrates that if you want to compute the future value of a stream of cash flows, you can do it directly (the first approach), or you can first compute the present value and then move it to the future (the second approach). As always, we use Eq. 4.1 to calculate the future value of any present value. Because we obey the rules of valuing cash flows in both cases, we get the same result.

Using a Financial Calculator: Solving for Present and Future Values of Cash Flow Streams

So far, we have used formulas to compute present values and future values of cash flow streams. As we discussed at the end of Chapter 3, both financial calculators and spreadsheets have these formulas preprogrammed to quicken the process. In this box, we focus on financial calculators, but spreadsheets such as Excel have very similar shortcut functions.

Financial calculators have a set of functions that perform the calculations that finance professionals do most often. These functions are all based on the following timeline, which among other things can handle most types of loans:

$$
\begin{array}{ccccc}
0 & 1 & 2 & & NPER \\
\mid & \mid & \mid & \cdots & \mid \\
PV & PMT & PMT & & PMT + FV
\end{array}
$$

There are a total of five variables: number of periods (N or $NPER$), present value (PV), cash flow or "payment" (PMT), future value (FV), and the interest rate, denoted I/Y. Each function takes four of these variables as inputs and returns the value of the fifth one that ensures that the sum of the present value of the cash flows is zero.

By setting the recurring payments equal to 0, you could compute present and future values of single cash flows such as we have done above using Eqs. 4.2 and 4.1. In the examples shown in Sections 4.2 through 4.4, we will calculate cash flows using the **PMT** button. The best way to learn to use a financial calculator is by practicing. We present one example below. We will also show the calculator buttons for any additional examples in this chapter that can be solved with financial calculator functions. Finally, the appendix to this chapter contains step-by-step instructions for using the two most popular financial calculators.

Example

Suppose you plan to invest $20,000 in an account paying 8% interest. You will invest an additional $1000 at the end of each year for 15 years. How much will you have in the account in 15 years? We represent this problem with the following timeline:

$$
\begin{array}{ccccc}
0 & 1 & 2 & & NPER = 15 \\
\mid & \mid & \mid & \cdots & \mid \\
PV = -\$20{,}000 & PMT = -\$1000 & -\$1000 & & FV = ?
\end{array}
$$

To compute the solution, we enter the four variables we know, $N = 15$, $I/Y = 8$, $PV = -20{,}000$, $PMT = -\$1000$, and solve for the one we want to determine: FV. Specifically, for the HP-10BII or TI-BAII Plus calculators:

1. Enter 15 and press the **N** button.
2. Enter 8 and press the **I/Y** button (**I/YR** for the HP calculator).
3. Enter −20,000 and press the **PV** button.
4. Enter −$1000 and press the **PMT** button.
5. Press the **FV** button (for the Texas Instruments calculator, press **CPT** and then **FV**).

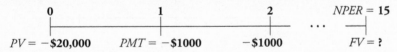

	N	I/Y	PV	PMT	FV
Given:	15	8	−20,000	−1000	
Solve for:					90,595.50
Excel Formula: =FV(0.08,15,−1000,−20000)					

The calculator then shows a future value of $90,595.50.

Note that we entered PV and PMT as negative numbers (the amounts we are putting *into* the bank), and FV is shown as a positive number (the amount we can take *out* of the bank). It is important to use signs correctly to indicate the direction in which the money is flowing when using the calculator functions. You will see more examples of getting the sign of the cash flows correct throughout the chapter.

Excel has the same functions, but it calls "N," "NPER" and "I/Y," "RATE." ***Also, it is important to note that you enter an interest rate of 8% as "8" in a financial calculator, but as "0.08" in Excel.***

PERSONAL FINANCE

EXAMPLE 4.2

Computing the
Future Value

MyFinanceLab

PROBLEM

Let's revisit the savings plan we considered earlier: We plan to save $1000 today and at the end of each of the next two years. At a fixed 10% interest rate, how much will we have in the bank three years from today?

SOLUTION

PLAN

We'll start with the timeline for this savings plan:

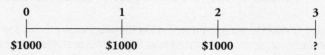

Let's solve this problem in a different way than we did in the text, while still following the rules we established. First, we'll compute the present value of the cash flows. Then, we'll compute its value three years later (its future value).

EXECUTE

There are several ways to calculate the present value of the cash flows. Here, we treat each cash flow separately and then combine the present values.

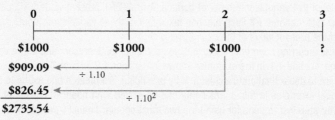

Saving $2735.54 today is equivalent to saving $1000 per year for three years. Now let's compute future value in year 3 of that $2735.54:

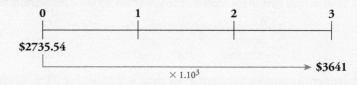

EVALUATE

This answer of $3641 is precisely the same result we found earlier. As long as we apply the three rules of valuing cash flows, we will always get the correct answer.

**CONCEPT
CHECK**

1. How do you calculate the present value of a cash flow stream?
2. How do you calculate the future value of a cash flow stream?

4.2   Perpetuities

The formulas we have developed so far allow us to compute the present or future value of any cash flow stream. In this section and the next one, we consider two types of cash flow streams, *perpetuities* and *annuities*, and learn shortcuts for valuing them. These shortcuts are possible because the cash flows follow a regular pattern.

Perpetuities

perpetuity A stream of equal cash flows that occurs at regular intervals and lasts forever.

consol A bond that promises its owner a fixed cash flow every year, forever.

A **perpetuity** is a stream of equal cash flows that occur at regular intervals and last forever. One example is the British government bond called a **consol** (or *perpetual bond*). Consol bonds promise the owner a fixed cash flow every year, forever.

Here is the timeline for a perpetuity:

Note from the timeline that the first cash flow does not occur immediately; *it arrives at the end of the first period*. This timing is sometimes referred to as *payment in arrears* and is a standard convention in loan payment calculations and elsewhere, so we adopt it throughout this text.

Using the formula for the present value, the present value of a perpetuity with payment C and interest rate r is given by:

$$PV = \frac{C}{(1+r)} + \frac{C}{(1+r)^2} + \frac{C}{(1+r)^3} + \cdots$$

Notice that all the cash flows (C in the formula) are the same because the cash flow for a perpetuity is constant. Also, because the first cash flow is in one period, there is no cash flow at time 0 ($C_0 = 0$).

To find the value of a perpetuity by discounting one cash flow at a time would take forever—literally! You might wonder how, even with a shortcut, the sum of an infinite number of positive terms could be finite. The answer is that the cash flows in the future are discounted for an ever-increasing number of periods, so their contribution to the sum eventually becomes negligible.

To derive the shortcut, we calculate the value of a perpetuity by creating our own perpetuity. The Valuation Principle tells us that the value of a perpetuity must be the same as the cost we incurred to create our own identical perpetuity. To illustrate, suppose you could invest $100 in a bank account paying 5% interest per year, forever. At the end of one year, you will have $105 in the bank—your original $100 plus $5 in interest. Suppose you withdraw the $5 interest and reinvest the $100 for a second year. Again, you will have $105 after one year, and you can withdraw $5 and reinvest $100 for another year. By doing this year after year, you can withdraw $5 every year in perpetuity:

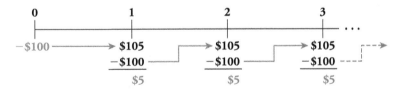

By investing $100 in the bank today, you can, in effect, create a perpetuity paying $5 per year. Because the bank will "sell" us (allow us to create) the perpetuity for $100, the present value of the $5 per year in perpetuity is this "do-it-yourself" cost of $100.

Now let's generalize this argument. Suppose we invest an amount P in a bank account with an interest rate r. Every year we can withdraw the interest we have earned, $C = r \times P$, leaving the principal, P, in the bank. Because our cost for creating the perpetuity is only the initial investment of principal (P), the value of receiving C in perpetuity is therefore the upfront cost P. Rearranging $C = r \times P$ to solve for P we have $P = C/r$. Therefore:

Present Value of a Perpetuity

$$PV(C \text{ in Perpetuity}) = \frac{C}{r} \qquad (4.4)$$

By depositing the amount $\dfrac{C}{r}$ today, we can withdraw interest of $\dfrac{C}{r} \times r = C$ each period in perpetuity.

Note the logic of our argument. To determine the present value of a cash flow stream, we computed the "do-it-yourself" cost of creating those same cash flows at the bank. This is an extremely useful and powerful approach—and is much simpler and faster than summing those infinite terms![1]

Historical Examples of Perpetuities

Companies sometimes issue bonds that they call perpetuities, but in fact are not really perpetuities. For example, in mid-2010, Europe's largest bank, HSBC, sold $3.4 billion of "perpetual" bonds that promise investors a fixed amount each year with no maturity date. But while the bonds have no fixed maturity, they are not exactly true perpetuities as HSBC has the right to pay off the bonds after 5½ years. Thus, the bond's payments might not last forever. Perpetual bonds were some of the first bonds ever issued. The oldest perpetuities that are still making interest payments were issued in 1624 by the *Hoogheemraadschap Lekdijk Bovendams*, a seventeenth-century Dutch water board responsible for upkeep of the local dikes. To verify that these bonds continue to pay interest, two finance professors at Yale University,

William Goetzmann and Geert Rouwenhorst, purchased one of these bonds on July 1, 2003, and collected 26 years of back interest. On its issue date in 1648, this bond originally paid interest in Carolus guilders. Over the next 355 years, the currency of payment changed to Flemish pounds, Dutch guilders, and most recently euros. Recently, the bond was paying interest of €11.34 annually.

Although the Dutch bonds are the oldest perpetuities still in existence, the first perpetuities date from much earlier times. For example, *cencus agreements* and *rentes*, which were forms of perpetuities and annuities, were issued in the twelfth century in Italy, France, and Spain. They were initially designed to circumvent the usury laws of the Catholic Church: Because they did not require the repayment of principal, in the eyes of the church they were not considered loans.

PERSONAL FINANCE

EXAMPLE 4.3

Endowing a
Perpetuity

MyFinanceLab

PROBLEM

You want to endow an annual graduation party at your alma mater. You want the event to be memorable, so you budget $30,000 per year forever for the party. If the university earns 8% per year on its investments, and if the first party is in one year's time, how much will you need to donate to endow the party?

SOLUTION

PLAN

The timeline of the cash flows you want to provide is:

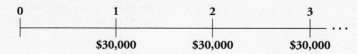

This is a standard perpetuity of $30,000 per year. The funding you would need to give the university in perpetuity is the present value of this cash flow stream.

EXECUTE

Use the formula for a perpetuity:

$$PV = C/r = \$30,000/0.08 = \$375,000 \text{ today}$$

EVALUATE

If you donate $375,000 today, and if the university invests it at 8% per year forever, then the graduates will have $30,000 every year to fund their graduation party.

---

[1]Another mathematical derivation of this result exists (see the online appendix), but it is less intuitive.

COMMON MISTAKE

Discounting One Too Many Times

The perpetuity formula assumes that the first payment occurs at the end of the first period (at date 1). Sometimes perpetuities have cash flows that start later. In this case, we can adapt the perpetuity formula to compute the present value, but we need to do so carefully to avoid a common mistake.

To illustrate, consider the graduation party described in Example 4.3. Rather than starting in one year, suppose the first party will be held two years from today. How would this delay change the amount of the donation required?

Now the timeline looks like this:

We need to determine the present value of these cash flows, as it tells us the amount of money needed in the bank today to finance the future parties. We cannot apply the perpetuity formula directly, however, because these cash flows are not *exactly* a perpetuity as we defined it. Specifically, the cash flow in the first period is "missing." But consider the situation on date 1—at that point, the first party is one period away and then the cash flows occur regularly. From the perspective of date 1, this *is* a perpetuity, and we can apply the formula. From the preceding calculation, we know we need $375,000 on date 1 to have enough to start the parties on date 2. We rewrite the timeline as follows:

Our goal can now be restated more simply: How much do we need to invest today to have $375,000 in one year? This is a simple present value calculation:

$$PV = \$375{,}000/1.08 = \$347{,}222 \text{ today}$$

A common mistake is to discount the $375,000 twice because the first party is in two periods. *Remember—the present value formula for the perpetuity already discounts the cash flows to one period prior to the first cash flow.* Keep in mind that this common mistake may be made with perpetuities, annuities, and all the other special cases discussed in this chapter. All these formulas discount the cash flows to one period prior to the first cash flow.

CONCEPT CHECK

3. What are some examples of perpetuities?

4. What is the intuition behind the fact that an infinite stream of cash flows has a finite present value?

4.3 Annuities

annuity A stream of equal cash flows arriving at a regular interval and ending after a specified time period.

An **annuity** is a stream consisting of a fixed number of equal cash flows paid at regular intervals. So the difference between an annuity and a perpetuity is that an annuity ends after some fixed number of payments whereas a perpetuity continues forever. Most car loans, mortgages, and some bonds are annuities. We represent the cash flows of an annuity on a timeline as follows:

Note that just as with the perpetuity, we adopt the convention that the first payment takes place at date 1, one period from today. The present value of an N-period annuity with payment C and interest rate r is:

$$PV = \frac{C}{(1+r)} + \frac{C}{(1+r)^2} + \frac{C}{(1+r)^3} + \cdots + \frac{C}{(1+r)^N}$$

Present Value of an Annuity

To find a simpler formula, we use the same approach we followed with the perpetuity: Find a way to create your own annuity. To illustrate, suppose you invest $100 in a bank account paying 5% interest. At the end of one year, you will have $105 in the bank—your original

$100 plus $5 in interest. Using the same strategy as you did for calculating the value of a perpetuity, suppose you withdraw the $5 interest and reinvest the $100 for a second year. Once again you will have $105 after one year. You can repeat the process, withdrawing $5 and reinvesting $100, every year. For a perpetuity, you left the principal in the bank forever. Alternatively, you might decide after 20 years to close the account and withdraw the principal. In that case, your cash flows will look like this:

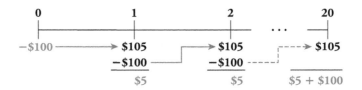

With your initial $100 investment, you have created a 20-year annuity of $5 per year, plus you will receive an extra $100 at the end of 20 years. The Valuation Principle's Law of One Price tells us that things that produce exactly the same cash flows must have the same value. Because it only took an initial investment of $100 to create the cash flows on the timeline, the present value of these cash flows is $100, or:

$$\$100 = PV(\text{20-year annuity of \$5 per year}) + PV(\$100 \text{ in 20 years})$$

So if we invest $100 now, we can receive $5 per year for 20 years as well as $100 in the 20th year, representing the following cash flows:

Rearranging the equation above shows that the cost of a 20-year annuity of $5 per year is $100 minus the present value of $100 in 20 years.

$$PV(\text{20-year annuity of \$5 per year}) = \$100 - PV(\$100 \text{ in 20 years})$$

$$= 100 - \frac{100}{(1.05)^{20}} = \$100 - \$37.69 = \$62.31$$

```
     0              1              2              20
     |              |              |        ...   |
  -$100            $5             $5           $5 + $100

              Removing the $100 in 20 years and its present
              value ($37.69) leaves the following cash flows:

  -$62.31         $5             $5      ...     $5
```

So the present value of $5 for 20 years is $62.31. Intuitively, the value of the annuity is the initial investment in the bank account minus the present value of the principal that will be left in the account after 20 years.

The $5 we receive every year is the interest on the $100 and can be written as $100(.05) = $5. Rearranging this equation, we have $100 = $5/.05. If we substitute $5/.05 into our formula above, we can represent the PV of the annuity as a function of its cash flow ($5), the discount rate (5%) and the number of years (20):

$$PV(\text{20-year annuity of \$5 per year}) = \frac{\$5}{.05} - \frac{\frac{\$5}{.05}}{(1.05)^{20}} = \frac{\$5}{.05}\left(1 - \frac{1}{(1.05)^{20}}\right)$$

$$= \$5 \times \frac{1}{.05}\left(1 - \frac{1}{(1.05)^{20}}\right)$$

This method is very useful because we will most often want to know the PV of the annuity given its cash flow, discount rate, and number of years. We can write this as a general formula for the present value of an annuity of C for N periods:

Present Value of an Annuity

$$PV(\text{Annuity of } C \text{ for } N \text{ Periods with Interest Rate } r) = C \times \frac{1}{r}\left(1 - \frac{1}{(1+r)^N}\right) \quad (4.5)$$

PERSONAL FINANCE

EXAMPLE 4.4

Present Value of
a Lottery Prize
Annuity

MyFinanceLab

PROBLEM

You are the lucky winner of a $30 million state lottery. You can take your prize money either as (a) 30 payments of $1 million per year (starting today), or (b) $15 million paid today. If the interest rate is 8%, which option should you choose?

SOLUTION

PLAN

Option (a) provides $30 million in prize money but paid over time. To evaluate it correctly, we must convert it to a present value. Here is the timeline:

0	1	2	29
$1 million	$1 million	$1 million	$1 million

Because the first payment starts today, the last payment will occur in 29 years (for a total of 30 payments).[2] The $1 million at date 0 is already stated in present value terms, but we need to compute the present value of the remaining payments. Fortunately, this case looks like a 29-year annuity of $1 million per year, so we can use the annuity formula.

EXECUTE

We use the annuity formula:

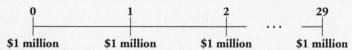

$$PV(\text{29-year annuity of \$1 million at 8\% annual interest}) = \$1 \text{ million} \times \frac{1}{0.08}\left(1 - \frac{1}{1.08^{29}}\right)$$

$$= \$1 \text{ million} \times 11.16$$

$$= \$11.16 \text{ million today}$$

(Continued)

---

[2]An annuity in which the first payment occurs immediately is sometimes called an *annuity due*. Throughout this text, we always use the term "annuity" to mean one that is paid in arrears.

Thus, the total present value of the cash flows is $1 million + $11.16 million = $12.16 million. In timeline form:

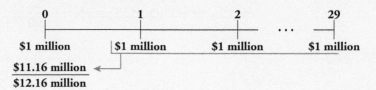

Option (b), $15 million upfront, is more valuable—even though the total amount of money paid is half that of option (a).

Financial calculators or Excel can handle annuities easily—just enter the cash flow in the annuity as the PMT:

	N	I/Y	PV	PMT	FV
Given:	29	8		1,000,000	0
Solve for:			−11,158,406		
Excel Formula: =PV(RATE,NPER,PMT,FV)=PV(0.08,29,1000000,0)					

Both the financial calculator and Excel will give you the PV of the 29 payments ($11,158,406, or 11.16 million), to which you must add the first payment of $1 million just as shown.

EVALUATE

The reason for the difference is the time value of money. If you have the $15 million today, you can use $1 million immediately and invest the remaining $14 million at an 8% interest rate. This strategy will give you $14 million × 8% = $1.12 million per year in perpetuity! Alternatively, you can spend $15 million − $11.16 million = $3.84 million today, and invest the remaining $11.16 million, which will still allow you to withdraw $1 million each year for the next 29 years before your account is depleted.

Future Value of an Annuity

Now that we have derived a simple formula for the present value of an annuity, it is easy to find a simple formula for the future value. If we want to know the value N years in the future, we move the present value N periods forward on the timeline.

$$PV = \frac{C}{r}\left(1 - \frac{1}{(1+r)^N}\right) \qquad \longrightarrow \qquad FV = \frac{C}{r}\left(1 - \frac{1}{(1+r)^N}\right) \times (1+r)^N$$

As the timeline shows, we compound the present value for N periods at interest rate r:

Future Value of an Annuity

$$FV(\text{Annuity}) = PV \times (1+r)^N$$

$$= \frac{C}{r}\left(1 - \frac{1}{(1+r)^N}\right) \times (1+r)^N$$

$$= C \times \frac{1}{r}\left((1+r)^N - 1\right) \tag{4.6}$$

This formula is useful if we want to know how a savings account will grow over time if the investor deposits the same amount every period.

PERSONAL FINANCE

EXAMPLE 4.5

Retirement Savings Plan Annuity

MyFinanceLab

PROBLEM

Ellen is 35 years old and she has decided it is time to plan seriously for her retirement. At the end of each year until she is 65, she will save $10,000 in a retirement account. If the account earns 10% per year, how much will Ellen have in her account at age 65?

SOLUTION

PLAN

As always, we begin with a timeline. In this case, it is helpful to keep track of both the dates and Ellen's age:

35	36	37	65
0	1	2	30
	$10,000	$10,000	$10,000

Ellen's savings plan looks like an annuity of $10,000 per year for 30 years. (*Hint*: It is easy to become confused when you just look at age, rather than at both dates and age. A common error is to think there are only $65 - 36 = 29$ payments. Writing down both dates and age avoids this problem.)

To determine the amount Ellen will have in her account at age 65, we'll need to compute the future value of this annuity.

EXECUTE

$$FV = \$10,000 \times \frac{1}{0.10}(1.10^{30} - 1)$$

$$= \$10,000 \times 164.49$$

$$= \$1.645 \text{ million at age 65}$$

Using a financial calculator or Excel:

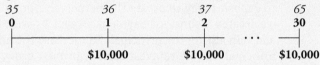

	N	I/Y	PV	PMT	FV
Given:	30	10	0	−10,000	
Solve for:					1,644,940
	Excel Formula: =FV(RATE,NPER, PMT, PV)=FV(0.10,30,−10000,0)				

EVALUATE

By investing $10,000 per year for 30 years (a total of $300,000) and earning interest on those investments, the compounding will allow Ellen to retire with $1.645 million.

CONCEPT CHECK

5. What are some examples of annuities?

6. What is the difference between an annuity and a perpetuity?

4.4 Growing Cash Flows

So far, we have considered only cash flow streams that have the same cash flow every period. If, instead, the cash flows are expected to grow at a constant rate in each period, we can also derive a simple formula for the present value of the future stream.

Growing Perpetuity

A **growing perpetuity** is a stream of cash flows that occur at regular intervals and grow at a constant rate forever. For example, a growing perpetuity with a first payment of $100 that grows at a rate of 3% has the following timeline:

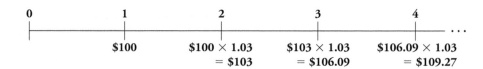

To derive the formula for the present value of a growing perpetuity, we follow the same logic used for a regular perpetuity: Compute the amount you would need to deposit today to create the perpetuity yourself. In the case of a regular perpetuity, we created a constant payment forever by withdrawing the interest earned each year and reinvesting the principal. To increase the amount we can withdraw each year, the principal that we reinvest each year must grow. Therefore, we withdraw less than the full amount of interest earned each period, using the remaining interest to increase our principal.

Let's consider a specific case. Suppose you want to create a perpetuity growing at 2%, so you invest $100 in a bank account that pays 5% interest. At the end of one year, you will have $105 in the bank—your original $100 plus $5 in interest. If you withdraw only $3, you will have $102 to reinvest—2% more than the amount you had initially. This amount will then grow to $102 × 1.05 = $107.10 in the following year, and you can withdraw $3 × 1.02 = $3.06, which will leave you with principal of $107.10 − $3.06 = $104.04. Note that $102 × 1.02 = $104.04. That is, both the amount you withdraw and the principal you reinvest grow by 2% each year. On a timeline, these cash flows look like this:

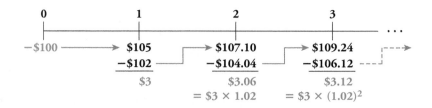

By following this strategy, you have created a growing perpetuity that starts at $3 and grows 2% per year. This growing perpetuity must have a present value equal to the cost of $100.

We can generalize this argument. If we want to increase the amount we withdraw from the bank each year by g, then the principal in the bank will have to grow by the same factor g. That is, instead of reinvesting P in the second year, we should reinvest $P(1 + g) = P + gP$. In order to increase our principal by gP, we need to leave gP of the interest in the account, so of the total interest of rP, we can only withdraw $rP - gP = P(r - g)$. We demonstrate this for the first year of our example:

Initial amount deposited	$100	P
Interest earned	(.05)($100)	rP
Amount needed to increase principal	(.02)($100)	gP
Amount withdrawn	(.05)($100) − (.02)($100)	$rP - gP$
	= $100(.05 − .02)	= $P(r - g)$

Denoting our withdrawal as C, we have $C = P(r - g)$. Solving this equation for P, the initial amount deposited in the bank account, gives the present value of a growing perpetuity with initial cash flow C:[3]

Present Value of a Growing Perpetuity

$$PV(\text{Growing Perpetuity}) = \frac{C}{r - g} \qquad (4.7)$$

To understand intuitively the formula for a growing perpetuity, start with the formula for a perpetuity. In the earlier case, you had to put enough money in the bank to ensure that the interest earned matched the cash flows of the regular perpetuity. In the case of a growing perpetuity, you need to put more than that amount in the bank because you have to finance the growth in the cash flows. How much more? If the bank pays interest at a rate of 5%, then all that is left to take out, if you want to make sure the principal grows 2% per year, is the difference: 5% − 2% = 3%. So instead of the present value of the perpetuity being the first cash flow divided by the interest rate, it is now the first cash flow divided by the *difference* between the interest rate and the growth rate.

PERSONAL FINANCE

EXAMPLE 4.6

Endowing a Growing Perpetuity

MyFinanceLab

PROBLEM

In Example 4.3, you planned to donate money to your alma mater to fund an annual $30,000 graduation party. Given an interest rate of 8% per year, the required donation was the present value of:

$$PV = \$30,000/0.08 = \$375,000 \text{ today}$$

Before accepting the money, however, the student association has asked that you increase the donation to account for the effect of inflation on the cost of the party in future years. Although $30,000 is adequate for next year's party, the students estimate that the party's cost will rise by 4% per year thereafter. To satisfy their request, how much do you need to donate now?

SOLUTION

PLAN

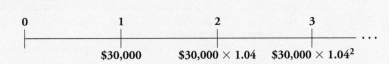

The cost of the party next year is $30,000, and the cost then increases 4% per year forever. From the timeline, we recognize the form of a growing perpetuity and can value it that way.

EXECUTE

To finance the growing cost, you need to provide the present value today of:

$$PV = \$30,000/(0.08 - 0.04) = \$750,000 \text{ today}$$

EVALUATE

You need to double the size of your gift!

---

[3]Suppose $g \geq r$. Then the cash flows grow even faster than they are discounted; each term in the sum of discounted cash flows gets larger, rather than smaller. In this case, the sum is infinite! What does an infinite present value mean? Remember that the present value is the "do-it-yourself" cost of creating the cash flows. An infinite present value means that no matter how much money you start with, it is *impossible* to sustain a growth rate of g forever and reproduce those cash flows on your own. Growing perpetuities of this sort cannot exist in practice because no one would be willing to offer one at any finite price. A promise to pay an amount that forever grew faster than the interest rate is also unlikely to be kept (or believed by any savvy buyer). The only viable growing perpetuities are those where the perpetual growth rate is less than the interest rate, so we assume that $g < r$ for a growing perpetuity.

Growing Annuity

growing annuity A stream of cash flows, growing at a constant rate and paid at regular intervals, that end after a specified number of periods.

A **growing annuity** is a stream of N growing cash flows, paid at regular intervals. It is a growing perpetuity that eventually comes to an end. The following timeline shows a growing annuity with initial cash flow C, growing at rate g every period until period N:

The conventions used earlier still apply: (1) The first cash flow arrives at the end of the first period and (2) the first cash flow is before growth. The last cash flow therefore reflects only $N - 1$ periods of growth.

The present value of an N-period growing annuity with initial cash flow C, growth rate g, and interest rate r is given by

Present Value of a Growing Annuity

$$PV = C \times \frac{1}{r-g}\left(1 - \left(\frac{1+g}{1+r}\right)^{N}\right) \tag{4.8}$$

Because the annuity has a finite number of terms, Eq. 4.8 also works when $g > r$.[4] The process of deriving this simple expression for the present value of a growing annuity is the same as for a regular annuity. Interested readers may consult the online appendix for details.

EXAMPLE 4.7

Retirement Savings with a Growing Annuity

MyFinanceLab

PROBLEM

In Example 4.5, Ellen considered saving $10,000 per year for her retirement. Although $10,000 is the most she can save in the first year, she expects her salary to increase each year so that she will be able to increase her savings by 5% per year. With this plan, if she earns 10% per year on her savings, how much will Ellen have in her account at age 65?

SOLUTION

PLAN

Her new savings plan is represented by the following timeline:

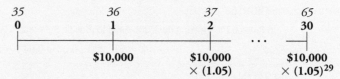

This example involves a 30-year growing annuity, with a growth rate of 5%, and an initial cash flow of $10,000. We can use Eq. 4.8 to solve for the present value of this growing annuity. Then we can use Eq. 4.1 to calculate the future value.

---

[4]Equation 4.8 does not work for $g = r$. But in that case, growth and discounting cancel out, and the present value is equivalent to receiving all the cash flows at date 1: $PV = C \times N/(1 + r)$.

EXECUTE

The present value of Ellen's growing annuity is given by

$$PV = \$10,000 \times \frac{1}{0.10 - 0.05}\left(1 - \left(\frac{1.05}{1.10}\right)^{30}\right)$$

$$= \$10,000 \times 15.0463$$

$$= \$150,463 \text{ today}$$

Ellen's proposed savings plan is equivalent to having $150,463 in the bank *today*. To determine the amount she will have at age 65, we need to move this amount forward 30 years:

$$FV = \$150,463 \times 1.10^{30}$$

$$= \$2.625 \text{ million in 30 years}$$

EVALUATE

Ellen will have $2.625 million at age 65 using the new savings plan. This sum is almost $1 million more than she had without the additional annual increases in savings. Because she is increasing her savings amount each year and the interest on the cumulative increases continues to compound, her final savings is much greater.

CONCEPT CHECK

7. How can an infinitely growing stream of cash flows have a finite value?

8. What is an example of a growing perpetuity?

4.5 Solving for Variables Other Than Present Value or Future Value

So far, we have calculated the present value or future value of a stream of cash flows. Sometimes, however, we know the present value or future value, but do not know one of the variables that so far we have been given as an input. For example, when you take out a loan, you may know the amount you would like to borrow, but may not know the loan payments that will be required to repay it. Or, if you make a deposit into a bank account, you may want to calculate how long it will take before your balance reaches a certain level. In such situations, we use the present and/or future values as inputs, and solve for the variable we are interested in. We examine several special cases in this section.

Solving for the Cash Flows

Let's consider an example where we know the present value of an investment, but do not know the cash flows. The best example is a loan—you know how much you want to borrow (the present value) and you know the interest rate, but you do not know how much you need to repay each year. Suppose you are opening a business that requires an initial investment of $100,000. Your bank manager has agreed to lend you this money. The terms of the loan state that you will make equal annual payments for the next 10 years and will pay an interest rate of 8% with the first payment due one year from today. What is your annual payment?

From the bank's perspective, the timeline looks like this:

0	1	2	10
−$100,000	+C	+C	+C

The bank will give you $100,000 today in exchange for 10 equal payments over the next decade. You need to determine the size of the payment C that the bank will require. For the bank to be willing to lend you $100,000, the loan cash flows must have a present value of $100,000 when evaluated at the bank's interest rate of 8%. That is:

$100,000 = PV$(10-year annuity of C per year, evaluated at the loan rate)

Using the formula for the present value of an annuity (Eq. 4.5),

$$100,000 = C \times \frac{1}{0.08}\left(1 - \frac{1}{1.08^{10}}\right) = C \times 6.71$$

Solving this equation for C gives:

$$C = \frac{100,000}{6.71} = 14,903$$

You will be required to make 10 annual payments of $14,903 in exchange for $100,000 today.

We can also solve this problem with a financial calculator or Excel (from your standpoint the $100,000 is positive and the payments are negative):

	N	I/Y	PV	PMT	FV
Given:	10	8	100,000		0
Solve for:				−14,903	
Excel Formula: =PMT(RATE,NPER,PV,FV)=PMT(0.08,10,100000,0)					

In general, when solving for a loan payment, think of the amount borrowed (the loan principal) as the present value of the payments. If the payments of the loan are an annuity, we can solve for the payment of the loan by inverting the annuity formula. Writing the equation for the payments formally for a loan with principal P, requiring N periodic payments of C and interest rate r, we have:

Cash Flow in an Annuity (Loan Payment)

$$C = \frac{P}{\dfrac{1}{r}\left(1 - \dfrac{1}{(1+r)^{N}}\right)} \tag{4.9}$$

EXAMPLE 4.8
Computing a Loan Payment

MyFinanceLab

PROBLEM

Your firm plans to buy a warehouse for $100,000. The bank offers you a 30-year loan with equal annual payments and an interest rate of 8% per year. The bank requires that your firm pays 20% of the purchase price as a down payment, so you can borrow only $80,000. What is the annual loan payment?

SOLUTION

PLAN

We start with the timeline (from the bank's perspective):

Using Eq. 4.9, we can solve for the loan payment, C, given N = 30, r = 0.08, and P = $80,000.

EXECUTE

Equation 4.9 gives the following payment (cash flow):

$$C = \frac{P}{\frac{1}{r}\left(1 - \frac{1}{(1+r)^N}\right)} = \frac{80{,}000}{\frac{1}{0.08}\left(1 - \frac{1}{(1.08)^{30}}\right)}$$

$$= \$7106.19$$

Using a financial calculator or Excel:

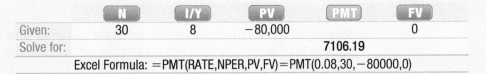

	N	I/Y	PV	PMT	FV
Given:	30	8	−80,000		0
Solve for:				7106.19	

Excel Formula: =PMT(RATE,NPER,PV,FV)=PMT(0.08,30,−80000,0)

EVALUATE

Your firm will need to pay $7106.19 each year to repay the loan. The bank is willing to accept these payments because the PV of 30 annual payments of $7106.19 at 8% interest rate per year is exactly equal to the $80,000 it is giving you today.

We can use this same idea to solve for the cash flows when we know the future value rather than the present value. As an example, suppose you have just graduated from college and you decide to be prudent and start saving for a down payment on a house. You would like to have $60,000 saved in 10 years. If you can earn 7% per year on your savings, how much do you need to save each year to meet your goal?

The timeline for this example is:

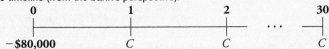

That is, you plan to save some amount C per year, and then withdraw $60,000 from the bank in 10 years. Therefore, we need to find the annuity payment that has a future value of $60,000 in 10 years. Use the formula for the future value of an annuity from Eq. 4.6:

$$60{,}000 = FV(\text{annuity}) = C \times \frac{1}{0.07}(1.07^{10} - 1) = C \times 13.816$$

Therefore, $C = \dfrac{60{,}000}{13.816} = \$4343$. Thus, you need to save $4343 per year. If you do, then at a 7% interest rate your savings will grow to $60,000 in 10 years when you are ready to buy a house.

Now let's solve this problem using a financial calculator or Excel:

	N	I/Y	PV	PMT	FV
Given:	10	7	0		60,000
Solve for:				−4343	
Excel Formula: =PMT(RATE,NPER,PV,FV)=PMT(0.07,10,0,60000)					

Once again, we find that you need to save $4343 per year for 10 years to accumulate $60,000.

Rate of Return

In some situations, you know the cost of an investment opportunity and the expected cash flows from it, but you do not know the rate of return. The rate of return on the investment opportunity is the rate at which the present value of the benefits exactly offsets the cost.

For example, suppose you have an investment opportunity that requires a $1000 investment today and will have a $2000 payoff in six years. This would appear on a timeline as:

$$
\begin{array}{ccccc}
0 & 1 & 2 & & 6 \\
\vdash & \vdash & \vdash & \cdots & \dashv \\
-\$1000 & & & & \$2000
\end{array}
$$

One way to analyze this investment is to ask the question: What interest rate, r, would you need so that the present value of what you get is exactly equal to the present value of what you give up?

$$1000 = \frac{2000}{(1+r)^6}$$

Rearranging this calculation gives the following:

$$1000 \times (1+r)^6 = 2000$$

That is, r is the interest rate you would need to earn on your $1000 to have a future value of $2000 in six years. We can solve for r as follows:

$$1 + r = \left(\frac{2000}{1000}\right)^{\frac{1}{6}} = 1.1225$$

Or, $r = 0.1225$. This rate is the rate of return of this investment opportunity. Making this investment is like earning 12.25% per year on your money for six years.

When there are just two cash flows, as in the preceding example, it is straightforward to compute the rate of return. Consider the general case in which you invest an amount P today, and receive FV in N years:

$$P \times (1+r)^N = FV$$

$$1 + r = (FV/P)^{1/N}$$

That is, we take the total return of the investment over N years, FV/P, and convert it to an equivalent one-year rate by raising it to the power $1/N$.

Now let's consider a more sophisticated example. Suppose your firm needs to purchase a new forklift. The dealer gives you two options: (1) a price for the forklift if you pay cash and (2) the annual payments if you take out a loan from the dealer. To evaluate the loan that the dealer is offering, you will want to compare the rate on the loan with the rate that your bank is willing to offer you. Given the loan payment that the dealer quotes, how do you compute the interest rate charged by the dealer?

In this case, we need to compute the rate of return of the dealer's loan. Suppose the cash price of the forklift is $40,000, and the dealer offers financing with no down payment and four annual payments of $15,000. This loan has the following timeline:

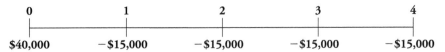

From the timeline, it is clear that the loan is a four-year annuity with a payment of $15,000 per year and a present value of $40,000. Setting the present value of the cash flows equal to zero requires that the present value of the payments equals the purchase price:

$$40,000 = 15,000 \times \frac{1}{r}\left(1 - \frac{1}{(1+r)^4}\right)$$

The value of r that solves this equation is the interest rate charged on the loan. Unfortunately, in this case, there is no simple way to solve for the interest rate r.[5] The only way to solve this equation is to guess at values of r until you find the right one.

Start by guessing $r = 10\%$. In this case, the value of the annuity is:

$$15,000 \times \frac{1}{0.10}\left(1 - \frac{1}{(1.10)^4}\right) = 47,548$$

The present value of the payments is too large. To lower it, we need to use a higher interest rate. This time we guess 20%:

$$15,000 \times \frac{1}{0.20}\left(1 - \frac{1}{(1.20)^4}\right) = 38,831$$

Now the present value of the payments is too low, so we must pick a rate between 10% and 20%. We continue to guess until we find the right rate. Let's try 18.45%:

$$15,000 \times \frac{1}{0.1845}\left(1 - \frac{1}{(1.1845)^4}\right) = 40,000$$

The interest rate charged by the dealer is 18.45%.

An easier solution than guessing the rate of return and manually calculating values is to use a spreadsheet or calculator to automate the guessing process. When the cash flows are an annuity, as in this example, we can use a financial calculator or Excel to compute the rate of return. Both solve (with slightly varying notation—recall that I/Y is the discount rate and PMT is the cash flow or payment) the following equation:

$$0 = PV + PMT \times \frac{1}{I/Y}\left(1 - \frac{1}{(1+I/Y)^N}\right) + \frac{FV}{(1+I/Y)^N}$$

The equation ensures that the value of investing in the annuity is zero in that the present value of the costs and benefits exactly offset each other. When the unknown variable is the

---

[5]With five or more periods and general cash flows, there is *no* general formula to solve for *r*; trial and error (by hand or computer) is the *only* way to compute it.

interest rate, it will solve for the interest rate that sets the equation equal to zero. For this case, you could use a financial calculator or Excel, as follows:

	N	I/Y	PV	PMT	FV
Given:	4		40,000	−15,000	0
Solve for:		18.45			
Excel Formula: =RATE(NPER,PMT,PV,FV)=RATE(4,−15000,40000,0)					

Both the financial calculator and Excel correctly compute a rate of return of 18.45%. Note that the calculator returns *I/Y* as 18.45, but it should be read as 18.45%, which is 0.1845, the number Excel returns.

PERSONAL FINANCE

EXAMPLE 4.9

Computing the
Rate of Return
with a Financial
Calculator

MyFinanceLab

PROBLEM

Let's return to the lottery prize in Example 4.4. How high of a rate of return do you need to earn by investing on your own in order to prefer the $15 million payout?

SOLUTION

PLAN

Recall that the lottery offers you the following deal: take either (a) 30 payments of $1 million per year starting immediately, or (b) a $15 million lump sum payment immediately. The first option is an annuity of 29 payments of $1 million plus an initial $1 million payment.

0	1	2		29
$1 million	$1 million	$1 million	...	$1 million

We need to solve for the rate of return that makes the two offers equivalent. Anything above that rate of return would make the present value of the annuity lower than the $15 million lump sum payment, and anything below that rate of return would make it greater than the $15 million payment.

EXECUTE

We set the present value of option (a) equal to option (b), which is already in present value since it is an immediate payment of $15 million:

$$\$15 \text{ million} = \$1 \text{ million} + \$1 \text{ million} \times \frac{1}{r}\left(1 - \frac{1}{(1+r)^{29}}\right)$$

$$\$14 \text{ million} = \$1 \text{ million} \times \frac{1}{r}\left(1 - \frac{1}{(1+r)^{29}}\right)$$

Using a financial calculator to solve for *r*:

	N	I/Y	PV	PMT	FV
Given:	29		−14,000,000	1,000,000	0
Solve for:		5.72			
Excel Formula: =RATE(NPER,PMT,PV,FV)=RATE(29,1000000,−14000000,0)					

The rate of return equating the two options is 5.72%.

EVALUATE

5.72% is the rate of return that makes giving up the $15 million payment and taking the 30 installments of $1 million an even trade in terms of present value. If you could earn more than 5.72% investing on your own, then you could take the $15 million, invest it and generate 30 installments that are each more than $1 million. If you could not earn at least 5.72% on your investments, you would be unable to replicate the $1 million installments on your own and would be better off choosing the installment plan.

Solving for the Number of Periods

In addition to solving for cash flows or the interest rate, we can solve for the amount of time it will take a sum of money to grow to a known value. In this case, the interest rate, present value, and future value are all known. We need to compute how long it will take for the present value to grow to the future value.

Suppose we invest $10,000 in an account paying 10% interest, and we want to know how long it will take for the amount to grow to $20,000.
We want to determine N.

In terms of our formulas, we need to find N so that the future value of our investment equals $20,000:

$$FV = \$10,000 \times 1.10^N = \$20,000 \tag{4.10}$$

One approach is to use trial and error to find N, as with the rate of return we calculated earlier. For example, with $N = 7$ years, $FV = \$19,487$, so it will take longer than 7 years. With $N = 8$ years, $FV = \$21,436$, so it will take between 7 and 8 years.

Alternatively, this problem can be solved on a financial calculator or Excel. In this case, we solve for N:

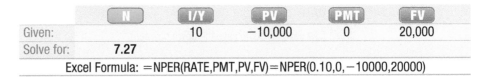

	N	I/Y	PV	PMT	FV
Given:		10	−10,000	0	20,000
Solve for:	7.27				
Excel Formula: =NPER(RATE,PMT,PV,FV)=NPER(0.10,0,−10000,20000)

It will take about 7.3 years for our savings to grow to $20,000. The problem of solving for the number of periods can also be solved mathematically using logarithms.

PERSONAL FINANCE

EXAMPLE 4.10

Solving for the Number of Periods in a Savings Plan

MyFinanceLab

PROBLEM

Let's return to your savings for a down payment on a house. Imagine that some time has passed and you have $10,050 saved already, and you can now afford to save $5000 per year at the end of each year. Also, interest rates have increased so that you now earn 7.25% per year on your savings. How long will it take to reach your goal of $60,000?

SOLUTION

PLAN

The timeline for this problem is:

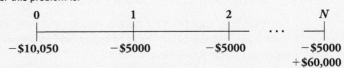

We need to find N so that the future value of your current savings plus the future value of your planned additional savings (which is an annuity) equals your desired amount. There are two contributors to the future value: the initial lump sum of $10,050 that will continue to earn interest, and the annuity contributions of $5000 per year that will earn interest as they are contributed. Thus, we need to find the future value of the lump sum plus the future value of the annuity.

(Continued)

EXECUTE

We can solve this problem using a financial calculator or Excel:

	N	I/Y	PV	PMT	FV
Given:		7.25	−10,050	−5000	60,000
Solve for:	7.00				

Excel Formula: =NPER(RATE,PMT,PV,FV)=NPER(0.0725,−5000,−10050,60000)

There is also a mathematical solution. We can calculate the future value of the initial cash flow by using Eq. 4.1 and the future value of the annuity using Eq. 4.6:

$$10{,}050 \times 1.0725^N + 5000 \times \frac{1}{0.0725}(1.0725^N - 1) = 60{,}000$$

Rearranging the equation to solve for N,

$$1.0725^N = \frac{60{,}000 \times 0.0725 \; + \; 5000}{10{,}050 \times 0.0725 \; + \; 5000} = 1.632$$

we can then solve for N:

$$N = \frac{\ln(1.632)}{\ln(1.0725)} = 7 \text{ years}$$

EVALUATE

It will take seven years to save the down payment.

CONCEPT CHECK

9. What are examples of times you would need to solve for the cash flow in an annuity?

10. When you are solving for the interest rate, if you keep PV and FV constant, but extend the time period, will the interest rate be higher or lower?

4.6   Non-Annual Cash Flows

Until now, we have only considered cash flow streams that occur at annual intervals. Do the same tools apply if the cash flows occur at another interval, say monthly? The answer is yes: Everything we have learned about annual cash flow streams applies to monthly cash flow streams as long as:

1. The interest rate is specified as a monthly rate.
2. The number of periods is expressed in months.

For example, suppose you have a credit card that charges 2% interest per month. If you have a $1000 balance on the card today, and make no payments for six months, your future balance in one year's time will be

$$FV = C \times (1 + r)^n = \$1000 \times (1.02)^6 = \$1126.16$$

We apply the future value formula exactly as before, but with r equal to the *monthly* interest rate and n equal to the number of *months*.

The same logic applies to annuities, as shown in Example 4.11.

EXAMPLE 4.11

Evaluating an
Annuity with Monthly
Cash Flows

MyFinanceLab

PROBLEM

You are about to purchase a new car and have two payment options. You can pay $20,000 in cash immediately, or you can get a loan that requires you to pay $500 each month for the next 48 months (four years). If the monthly interest rate you earn on your cash is 0.5%, which option should you choose?

SOLUTION

Let's start by writing down the timeline of the loan payments:

The timeline shows that the loan is a 48-period annuity. Using the annuity formula, the present value is

$$PV(\text{48-period annuity of \$500}) = \$500 \times \frac{1}{0.005}\left(1 - \frac{1}{1.005^{48}}\right)$$

$$= \$21,290$$

Alternatively, we may use the annuity spreadsheet to solve the problem:

	NPER	RATE	PV	PMT	FV
Given:	48	0.50%		500	0
Solve for:			(21,290)		
Excel Formula: =PV(0.005,48,500,0)

EVALUATE

Thus, taking the loan is equivalent to paying $21,290 today, which is costlier than paying cash. You should pay cash for the car.

What should you do if you aren't given a monthly rate? In Chapter 5, we will discuss how interest rates are quoted and you will learn how to convert between annual and monthly (or quarterly) rates.

The Big Picture

We began this chapter with the goal of further developing the tools a financial manager needs to be able to apply the Valuation Principle by valuing the costs and benefits of a decision. Starting from Chapter 3's fundamental concept of the time value of money—a dollar today is worth more than a dollar tomorrow—we learned how to calculate the equivalent value of a stream of future cash flows today and today's cash flows in the future. We then learned some shortcuts for handling common sets of regular cash flows such as those found in perpetuities and loans. As we have seen, the discount rate is a critical input to any of our present value or future value calculations. Throughout this chapter, we have taken the discount rate as given.

What determines these discount rates? The Valuation Principle shows us that we must rely on market information to assess the value of cash flows across time. In Chapter 5, we will learn the drivers of market interest rates as well as how they are quoted. Understanding interest rate quoting conventions will also allow us to extend the tools we developed in this chapter to situations where the interest rate is compounded more frequently than once per year.

**CONCEPT
CHECK**

11. Do the present and future value formulas depend upon the cash flows occurring at annual intervals?

12. When cash flows occur at a non-annual interval, what interest rate must you use? What number of periods must you use?

MyFinanceLab

Here is what you should know after reading this chapter. MyFinanceLab will help you identify what you know, and where to go when you need to practice.

KEY POINTS AND EQUATIONS	KEY TERMS	ONLINE PRACTICE
4.1 Valuing a Stream of Cash Flows • The present value of a cash flow stream is: $$PV = C_0 + \frac{C_1}{(1+r)} + \frac{C_2}{(1+r)^2} + \cdots + \frac{C_N}{(1+r)^N} \quad (4.3)$$	stream of cash flows, p. 94	MyFinanceLab Study Plan 4.1
4.2 Perpetuities • A perpetuity is a stream of equal cash flows C paid every period, forever. The present value of a perpetuity is: $$PV(C \text{ in Perpetuity}) = \frac{C}{r} \quad (4.4)$$	consol, p. 98 perpetuity, p. 98	MyFinanceLab Study Plan 4.2
4.3 Annuities • An annuity is a stream of equal cash flows C paid every period for N periods. The present value of an annuity is: $$C \times \frac{1}{r}\left(1 - \frac{1}{(1+r)^N}\right) \quad (4.5)$$ • The future value of an annuity at the end of the annuity is: $$C \times \frac{1}{r}\left((1+r)^N - 1\right) \quad (4.6)$$	annuity, p. 101	MyFinanceLab Study Plan 4.3 Interactive Annuity Calculator Financial Calculator Tutorials: Calculating the Present Value of an Annuity and Solving for the Future Value of an Annuity
4.4 Growing Cash Flows • In a growing perpetuity, the cash flows grow at a constant rate g each period. The present value of a growing perpetuity is: $$\frac{C}{r-g} \quad (4.7)$$ • A growing annuity is like a growing perpetuity, but with an ending point. The present value of a growing annuity is: $$PV = C \times \frac{1}{r-g}\left(1 - \left(\frac{1+g}{1+r}\right)^N\right) \quad (4.8)$$	growing annuity, p. 108 growing perpetuity, p. 106	MyFinanceLab Study Plan 4.4
4.5 Solving for Variables Other Than Present Value or Future Value • The annuity and perpetuity formulas can be used to solve for the annuity payments when either the present value or the future value is known.		MyFinanceLab Study Plan 4.5

- The periodic payment on an *N*-period loan with principal *P* and interest rate *r* is:

$$C = \frac{P}{\frac{1}{r}\left(1 - \frac{1}{(1+r)^N}\right)} \qquad (4.9)$$

- The rate of return of an investment opportunity is the interest rate at which the PV of the benefits of the investment opportunity exactly offset the PV of the costs.
- The annuity formulas can be used to solve for the number of periods it takes to save a fixed amount of money.

4.6 Non-Annual Cash Flows

- Monthly cash flow streams (or any other period length) can be evaluated in exactly the same way as annual cash flow streams as long as the interest rate and number of periods are expressed in monthly terms.

MyFinanceLab Study Plan 4.6

CRITICAL THINKING

1. What is the intuition behind the fact that the present value of a stream of cash flows is just the sum of the present values of each individual cash flow?

2. What must be true about a cash flow stream in order for us to be able to use the shortcut formulas?

3. What is the difference between an annuity and a perpetuity?

4. What are some examples of perpetuities?

5. How can a perpetuity have a finite value?

6. What are some examples of annuities?

7. What must be true about the growth rate in order for a growing perpetuity to have a finite value?

8. In what types of situations would it be useful to solve for the number of periods or the rate of return?

PROBLEMS

All problems are available in MyFinanceLab. *The* ⊞ *icon indicates problems that are easier to solve using Excel and have data in an Excel format available in* MyFinanceLab. *An asterisk * indicates problems with a higher level of difficulty.*

Valuing a Stream of Cash Flows

1. a. What is the present value of the following set of cash flows, discounted at 10% per year?

Year	1	2	3	4	5
CF	10	20	30	40	50

b. What is the present value of the following set of cash flows, discounted at 10% per year?

Year	1	2	3	4	5
CF	50	40	30	20	10

c. Each set contains the same cash flows (10, 20, 30, 40, 50), so why is the present value different?

2. What is the present value of the following set of cash flows, discounted at 15% per year?

Year	1	2	3	4
CF	100	−100	200	−200

3. You want to borrow $10,000. You figure that you can make the following payments. If the interest rate on the loan is 8.5% per year, will your payments be enough to pay off the $10,000 loan?

Year	1	2	3	4
Payment	2000	3000	3500	3975

4. You have a balance of $5000 on your credit card, which charges an interest rate of 1.5% per month. Looking at your budget, you figure you can make the following payments. Will they be enough to pay off your credit card?

Month	1	2	3	4	5	6	7	8
Payment	500	550	600	650	700	750	800	850

5. You have just taken out a five-year loan from a bank to buy an engagement ring. The ring costs $5000. You plan to put down $1000 and borrow $4000. You will need to make annual payments of $1000 at the end of each year. Show the timeline of the loan from your perspective. How would the timeline differ if you created it from the bank's perspective?

6. You currently have a one-year-old loan outstanding on your car. You make monthly payments of $300. You have just made a payment. The loan has four years to go (i.e., it had an original term of five years). Show the timeline from your perspective. How would the timeline differ if you created it from the bank's perspective?

7. You plan to deposit $500 in a bank account now and $300 at the end of one year. If the account earns 3% interest per year, what will the balance be in the account right after you make the second deposit?

8. You have just received a windfall from an investment you made in a friend's business. She will be paying you $10,000 at the end of this year, $20,000 at the end of next year, and $30,000 at the end of the year after that (three years from today). The interest rate is 3.5% per year.
a. What is the present value of your windfall?
b. What is the future value of your windfall in three years (on the date of the last payment)?

9. Suppose you receive $100 at the end of each year for the next three years.
a. If the interest rate is 8%, what is the present value of these cash flows?

   b. What is the future value in three years of the present value you computed in (a)?

   c. Suppose you deposit the cash flows in a bank account that pays 8% interest per year. What is the balance in the account at the end of each of the next three years (after your deposit is made)? How does the final bank balance compare with your answer in (b)?

10. You have a loan outstanding. It requires making three annual payments of $1000 each at the end of the next three years. Your bank has offered to allow you to skip making the next two payments in lieu of making one large payment at the end of the loan's term in three years. If the interest rate on the loan is 5%, what final payment will the bank require you to make so that it is indifferent to the two forms of payment?

11. Assume you can earn 9% per year on your investments.
   a. If you invest $100,000 for retirement at age 30, how much will you have 35 years later for retirement?
   b. If you wait until age 40 to invest the $100,000, how much will you have 25 years later for retirement?
   c. Why is the difference so large?

Perpetuities

12. You want to endow a scholarship that will pay $10,000 per year forever, starting one year from now. If the school's endowment discount rate is 7%, what amount must you donate to endow the scholarship?

13. How would your answer to Problem 12 change if you endow it now, but it makes the first award to a student 10 years from today?

14. The British government has a consol bond outstanding paying £100 per year forever. Assume the current interest rate is 4% per year.
   a. What is the value of the bond immediately after a payment is made?
   b. What is the value of the bond immediately before a payment is made?

15. You are offered the right to receive $1000 per year forever, starting in one year. If your discount rate is 5%, what is this offer worth to you?

16. You have $100,000 to donate to your college. You want to endow a perpetual scholarship that makes its first payment in 1 year. If the college's discount rate is 4%, how large will the annual scholarship payment be?

17. If you still donate the $100,000 from Problem 16 today, but ask the college to delay the scholarship payment so that the first scholarship payment is made 10 years from today, then how large will the annual payment be?

Annuities

18. What is the present value of $1000 paid at the end of each of the next 100 years if the interest rate is 7% per year?

19. Your grandmother has been putting $1000 into a savings account on every birthday since your first (that is, when you turned one). The account pays an interest rate of 3%. How much money will be in the account immediately after your grandmother makes the deposit on your 18th birthday?

20. Assume that your parents wanted to have $160,000 saved for college by your 18th birthday and they started saving on your first birthday. They saved the same amount each year on your birthday and earned 8% per year on their investments.
   a. How much would they have to save each year to reach their goal?

b. If they think you will take five years instead of four to graduate and decide to have $200,000 saved just in case, how much more would they have to save each year to reach their new goal?

*21. When you purchased your car, you took out a five-year annual-payment loan with an interest rate of 6% per year. The annual payment on the car is $5000. You have just made a payment and have now decided to pay off the loan by repaying the outstanding balance. What is the payoff amount for the following scenarios?
  a. You have owned the car for one year (so there are four years left on the loan)?
  b. You have owned the car for four years (so there is one year left on the loan)?

22. You figure that the total cost of college will be $100,000 per year 18 years from today. If your discount rate is 8% compounded annually, what is the present value today of four years of college costs starting 18 years from today?

23. Assume that Social Security promises you $40,000 per year starting when you retire 45 years from today (the first $40,000 will be paid 45 years from now). If your discount rate is 7%, compounded annually, and you plan to live for 15 years after retiring (so that you will receive a total of 16 payments including the first one), what is the value today of Social Security's promise? (*See* MyFinanceLab *for the data in Excel Format.*)

*24. When Alex Rodriguez moved to the Texas Rangers in 2001, he received a lot of attention for his "$252 million" contract (the total of the payments promised was $252 million). He later moved to the Yankees, but assume the following in order to determine the value of his contract when he signed it:

Rodriguez earns $16 million in the first year, $17 million in years 2 through 4, $19 million in years 5 and 6, $23 million in year 7, and $27 million in years 8 through 10. He also receives his $10 million signing bonus spread equally over the first 5 years ($2 million per year). His deferred payments begin in 2011. The deferred payment amounts total $33 million and are $5 million, then $4 million, then eight amounts of $3 million (ending in 2020). However, the actual payouts will be different. All of the deferred payments will earn 3% per year until they are paid. For example, the $5 million is deferred from 2001 to 2011, or 10 years, meaning that it will actually be $6.7196 million when paid. Assume that the $4 million payment deferred to 2012 is deferred from 2002 (each payment is deferred 10 years).

The contract is a 10-year contract, but each year has a deferred component so that cash flows are paid out over a total of 20 years. The contractual payments, signing bonus, and deferred components are given below. Note that, by contract, the deferred components are not paid in the year they are earned, but instead are paid (plus interest) 10 years later.

2001	2002	2003	2004	2005	2006	2007	2008	2009	2010
$16M	$17M	$17M	$17M	$19M	$19M	$23M	$27M	$27M	$27M
$2M	$2M	$2M	$2M	$2M					
Deferred									
$5M	$4M	$3M	$3M	$3M	$3M	$3M	$3M	$3M	$3M

Assume that an appropriate discount rate for A-Rod to apply to the contract payments is 7% per year.
  a. Calculate the true promised payments under this contract, including the deferred payments with interest.
  b. Draw a timeline of all of the payments.
  c. Calculate the present value of the contract.

    d. Compare the present value of the contract to the quoted value of $252 million. What explains the difference?

 *25. You are trying to decide how much to save for retirement. Assume you plan to save $5000 per year with the first investment made one year from now. You think you can earn 10% per year on your investments and you plan to retire in 43 years, immediately after making your last $5000 investment.

    a. How much will you have in your retirement account on the day you retire?

    b. If, instead of investing $5000 per year, you wanted to make one lump-sum investment today for your retirement that will result in the same retirement saving, how much would that lump sum need to be?

    c. If you hope to live for 20 years in retirement, how much can you withdraw every year in retirement (starting one year after retirement) so that you will just exhaust your savings with the 20th withdrawal (assume your savings will continue to earn 10% in retirement)?

    d. If, instead, you decide to withdraw $300,000 per year in retirement (again with the first withdrawal one year after retiring), how many years will it take until you exhaust your savings? (Use trial-and-error, a financial calculator: solve for "N," or Excel: function NPER)

    e. Assuming the most you can afford to save is $1000 per year, but you want to retire with $1 million in your investment account, how high of a return do you need to earn on your investments? (Use trial-and-error, a financial calculator: solve for the interest rate, or Excel: function RATE)

Growing Cash Flows

26. A rich relative has bequeathed you a growing perpetuity. The first payment will occur in a year and will be $1000. Each year after that, you will receive a payment on the anniversary of the last payment that is 8% larger than the last payment. This pattern of payments will go on forever. Assume that the interest rate is 12% per year.

    a. What is today's value of the bequest?

    b. What is the value of the bequest immediately after the first payment is made?

*27. You are thinking of building a new machine that will save you $1000 in the first year. The machine will then begin to wear out so that the savings decline at a rate of 2% per year forever. What is the present value of the savings if the interest rate is 5% per year?

28. When Alfred Nobel died, he left the majority of his estate to fund five prizes, each to be awarded annually in perpetuity starting one year after he died (the sixth one, in economics, was added later).

    a. If he wanted the cash award of each of the five prizes to be $45,000 and his estate could earn 7% per year, how much would he need to fund his prizes?

    b. If he wanted the value of each prize to grow by 4% per year (perhaps to keep up with inflation), how much would he need to leave? Assume that the first amount was still $45,000.

    c. His heirs were surprised by his will and fought it. If they had been able to keep the amount of money you calculated in (b), and had invested it at 7% per year, how much would they have in 2014, 118 years after his death?

29. You work for a pharmaceutical company that has developed a new drug. The patent on the drug will last 17 years. You expect that the drug's profits will be $2 million in its first year and that this amount will grow at a rate of 5% per year for the next 17 years. Once the patent expires, other pharmaceutical companies will be able to produce the same drug and competition will likely drive profits to zero. What is the present value of the new drug if the interest rate is 10% per year?

30. A rich aunt has promised you $5000 one year from today. In addition, each year after that, she has promised you a payment (on the anniversary of the last payment) that is 3% larger than the last payment. She will continue to show this generosity for 20 years, giving a total of 20 payments. If the interest rate is 5%, what is her promise worth today?

Solving for Variables Other Than Present Value or Future Value

31. You are thinking about buying a savings bond. The bond costs $50 today and will mature in 10 years with a value of $100. What annual interest rate will the bond earn?

32. You have an investment account that started with $1000 10 years ago and which now has grown to $5000.
    a. What annual rate of return have you earned (you have made no additional contributions to the account)?
    b. If the savings bond earns 15% per year from now on, what will the account's value be 10 years from now?

33. You have an investment opportunity that requires an initial investment of $5000 today and will pay $6000 in one year. What is the rate of return of this opportunity?

34. You have decided to buy a perpetual bond. The bond makes one payment at the end of every year forever and has an interest rate of 5%. If the bond initially costs $1000, what is the payment every year?

35. You are thinking of purchasing a house. The house costs $350,000. You have $50,000 in cash that you can use as a down payment on the house, but you need to borrow the rest of the purchase price. The bank is offering a 30-year mortgage that requires annual payments and has an interest rate of 7% per year. What will your annual payment be if you sign this mortgage?

*36. You are thinking about buying a piece of art that costs $50,000. The art dealer is proposing the following deal: He will lend you the money, and you will repay the loan by making the same payment every two years for the next 20 years (i.e., a total of 10 payments). If the interest rate is 4% per year, how much will you have to pay every two years?

 *37. You would like to buy the house and take the mortgage described in Problem 35. You can afford to pay only $23,500 per year. The bank agrees to allow you to pay this amount each year, yet still borrow $300,000. At the end of the mortgage (in 30 years), you must make a balloon payment; that is, you must repay the remaining balance on the mortgage. How much will this balloon payment be?

*38. You are saving for retirement. To live comfortably, you decide you will need to save $2 million by the time you are 65. Today is your 22nd birthday, and you decide, starting today and continuing on every birthday up to and including your 65th birthday, that you will put the same amount into a savings account. If the interest rate is 5%, how much must you set aside each year to ensure that you will have $2 million in the account on your 65th birthday?

 39. You receive a $10,000 check from your grandparents for graduation. You decide to save it toward a down payment on a house. You invest it earning 10% per year and you think you will need to have $20,000 saved for the down payment. How long will it be before the $10,000 has grown to $20,000?

40. A local bank is running the following advertisement: "For just $1000 we will pay you $100 forever!" The fine print says that for a $1000 deposit, the bank will pay $100 every year in perpetuity, starting one year after the deposit is made. What interest rate is the bank advertising (what is the rate of return of this investment)?

*41. You are thinking of making an investment in a new factory. The factory will generate revenues of $1 million per year for as long as you maintain it. You expect that the maintenance costs will start at $50,000 per year and will increase 5% per year thereafter. Assume that all revenue and maintenance costs occur at the end of the year. You intend to run the factory as long as it continues to make a positive cash flow (as long as the cash generated by the plant exceeds the maintenance costs). The factory can be built and become operational immediately and the interest rate is 6% per year.

    a. What is the present value of the revenues?

    b. What is the present value of the maintenance costs?

    c. If the plant costs $10 million to build, should you invest in the factory?

*42. You have just turned 22 years old, received your bachelor's degree, and accepted your first job. Now you must decide how much money to put into your retirement plan. The plan works as follows: Every dollar in the plan earns 7% per year. You cannot make withdrawals until you retire on your 65th birthday. After that, you can make withdrawals as you see fit. You decide that you will plan to live to 100 and work until you turn 65. You estimate that to live comfortably in retirement, you will need $100,000 per year, starting at the end of the first year of retirement and ending on your 100th birthday. You will contribute the same amount to the plan at the end of every year that you work. How much do you need to contribute each year to fund your retirement?

Non-Annual Cash Flows

43. Suppose you currently have $5000 in your savings account, and your bank pays interest at a rate of 0.5% per month. If you make no further deposits or withdrawals, how much will you have in the account in five years?

44. Your firm spends $5000 every month on printing and mailing costs, sending statements to customers. If the interest rate is 0.5% per month, what is the present value of eliminating this cost by sending the statements electronically?

45. You are looking to buy a car and can afford to pay $200 per month. If the interest rate on a car loan is 0.75% per month for a 60-month loan, what is the most expensive car you can afford to buy?

46. You have just entered college and have decided to pay for your living expenses using a credit card that has no minimum monthly payment. You intend to charge $1000 per month on the card for the next 45 months. The card carries a monthly interest rate of 1%. How much money will you owe on the card 46 months from now, when you receive your first statement post-graduation?

47. You intend to endow a scholarship that pays $5000 every 6 months, starting 6 months from now. If the appropriate discount rate is 2% per 6-month period, how much money will you have to donate today to endow the scholarship?

48. You have just deposited $1000 in an unusual bank account that pays interest biannually (once every 2 years). If the 2-year interest rate is 8% (total interest over 2 years is 8%, not 8% per year), how much will you have in the account after 6 years?

DATA CASE   Assume that today is August 5, 2015. Natasha Kingery is 30 years old and has a Bachelor of Science degree in computer science. She is currently employed as a Tier 2 field service representative for a telephony corporation located in Seattle, Washington, and earns $38,000 a year that she anticipates will grow at 3% per year. Natasha hopes to retire at age 65 and has just begun to think about the future.

Natasha has $75,000 that she recently inherited from her aunt. She invested this money in 10-year Treasury bonds. She is considering whether she should further her education and would use her inheritance to pay for it.

She has investigated a couple of options and is asking for your help as a financial planning intern to determine the financial consequences associated with each option. Natasha has already been accepted to two programs and could start either one soon.

One alternative that Natasha is considering is attaining a certification in network design. This certification would automatically promote her to a Tier 3 field service representative in her company. The base salary for a Tier 3 representative is $10,000 more than the salary of a Tier 2 representative, and she anticipates that this salary differential will grow at a rate of 3% a year for as long as she remains employed. The certification program requires the completion of 20 Web-based courses and a score of 80% or better on the final exam. She has learned that the average amount of time necessary to finish the program is one year. The total cost of the program is $5000, due when she enrolls in the program. Because she will do all the work for the certification on her own time, Natasha does not expect to lose any income during the certification process.

Another option is going back to school for an MBA degree. With an MBA degree, Natasha expects to be promoted to a managerial position in her current firm. The managerial position pays $20,000 a year more than her current position. She expects that this salary differential will also grow at a rate of 3% per year for as long as she keeps working. The evening program, which will take three years to complete, costs $25,000 per year, due at the beginning of each of her three years in school. Because she will attend classes in the evening, Natasha doesn't expect to lose any income while she is earning her MBA if she chooses to undertake it.

1. Determine the interest rate Natasha is currently earning on her inheritance by going to Yahoo! Finance (http://finance.yahoo.com) and clicking the 10 Yr Bond link in the Market Summary section or enter ^TNX in the symbol lookup field. Then go to the Historical Prices link and enter the appropriate date, August 5, 2015, to obtain the closing yield or interest rate that she is earning. Use this interest rate as the discount rate for the remainder of this problem.

2. Create a timeline in Excel for Natasha's current situation, as well as the certification program and MBA degree options, using the following assumptions:
   a. Salaries for the year are paid only once, at the end of the year.
   b. The salary increase becomes effective immediately upon graduating from the MBA program or being certified. That is, because the increases become effective immediately but salaries are paid at the end of the year, the first salary increase will be paid exactly one year after graduation or certification.

3. Calculate the present value of the salary differential for completing the certification program. Subtract the cost of the program to get the value of undertaking the certification program.

4. Calculate the present value of the salary differential for completing the MBA degree. Calculate the present value of the cost of the MBA program. Based on your calculations, determine the value of undertaking the MBA.

5. Based on your answers to Questions 3 and 4, what advice would you give to Natasha? What if the two programs are mutually exclusive? If Natasha undertakes one of the programs, there is no further benefit to undertaking the other program. Would your advice change?

Chapter 4 Appendix	Using a Financial Calculator

Specifying Decimal Places

Make sure you have plenty of decimal places displayed!

HP-10BII

      [　]　[DISP]　[4]

TI BAII Plus Professional

      [2ND]　[•]　[4]　[ENTER]

Toggling Between the Beginning and End of a Period

You should always make sure that your calculator is in *end-of-period* mode.

HP-10BII

      [　]　[MAR]

TI BAII Plus Professional

      [2ND]　[PMT]

Set the Number of Periods per Year

To avoid a lot of confusion later, always set your periods per year (P/Y) to 1:

HP-10BII

      [　]　[PMT]　[1]

TI BAII Plus Professional

      [2ND]　[I/Y]　[1]　[ENTER]

General TVM Buttons

HP-10BII

      [N]　[I/YR]　[PV]　[PMT]　[FV]

TI BAII Plus Professional

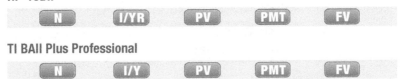

      [N]　[I/Y]　[PV]　[PMT]　[FV]

Solving for the Future Value of an Annuity (Example 4.5)

Ellen is 35 years old, and she has decided it is time to plan seriously for her retirement. At the end of each year until she is 65, she will save $10,000 in a retirement account. If the account earns 10% per year, how much will Ellen have in her account at age 65? [*Answer*: $1,644,940]

HP-10BII

Press [Orange Shift] and then the [C] button to clear all previous entries.

Enter the Number of periods.

Enter the market annual interest rate.

Enter the Payment amount per period.

Indicate that there is no initial amount in the retirement account.

Solve for the Future Value.

TI-BAII Plus Professional

Press [2ND] and then the [FV] button to clear all previous entries.

Enter the Number of periods.

Enter the market annual interest rate.

Enter the payment amount per period.

Indicate that there is no initial amount in the retirement account.

Solve for the Future Value.

Solving for the Rate of Return

If you have an initial cash outflow of $2000 and one cash inflow per year for the following four years of $1000, $400, $400, and $800, what is the rate of return on the project per year (sometimes called the *Internal Rate of Return* or *IRR* on the calculators)? [*Answer*: 12.12%]

HP-10BII

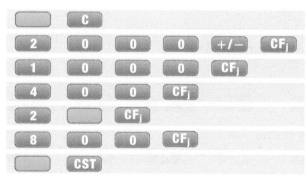

Press [Orange Shift] and then the [C] button to clear all previous entries.

Enter the initial cash outflow.

Enter the first cash inflow.

Enter the second cash inflow.

Enter the number of consecutive periods the second cash inflow occurs.

Enter the fourth cash inflow.

Press [Orange Shift] and then the [CST] button to calculate the IRR/year.

TI-BAII Plus Professional

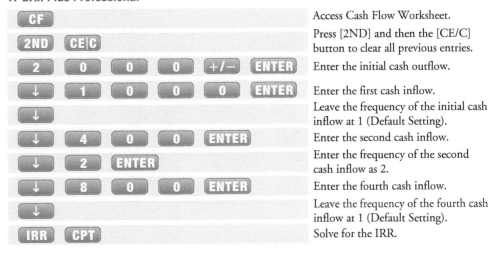

CF	Access Cash Flow Worksheet.
2ND CE|C	Press [2ND] and then the [CE/C] button to clear all previous entries.
2 0 0 0 +/− ENTER	Enter the initial cash outflow.
↓ 1 0 0 0 ENTER	Enter the first cash inflow.
↓	Leave the frequency of the initial cash inflow at 1 (Default Setting).
↓ 4 0 0 ENTER	Enter the second cash inflow.
↓ 2 ENTER	Enter the frequency of the second cash inflow as 2.
↓ 8 0 0 ENTER	Enter the fourth cash inflow.
↓	Leave the frequency of the fourth cash inflow at 1 (Default Setting).
IRR CPT	Solve for the IRR.

5

Interest Rates

LEARNING OBJECTIVES

- Understand the different ways interest rates are quoted

- Use quoted rates to calculate loan payments and balances

- Know how inflation, expectations, and risk combine to determine interest rates

- See the link between interest rates in the market and a firm's opportunity cost of capital

notation

APR	annual percentage rate
APY	annual percentage yield
C	cash flow
C_n	cash flow that arrives in period n
EAR	effective annual rate
FV	future value

m	number of compounding periods per year
n	number of periods
N	date of the last cash flow in a stream of cash flows
PV	present value
r	interest rate or discount rate
r_n	interest rate or discount rate for an n-year term

In Chapters 3 and 4, we explored the mechanics of computing present values and future values given a market interest rate. Recall that an interest rate allows us to convert money at one point in time to another. But how do we determine that interest rate? In this chapter, we consider the factors that affect interest rates and discuss how to determine the appropriate discount rate for a set of cash flows. We begin by looking at the way interest is paid and interest rates are quoted, and we show how to calculate the effective interest paid in one year given different quoting conventions. We then consider some of the main determinants of interest rates—namely, inflation and economic growth. Because interest rates tend to change over time, investors will demand different interest rates for different investment horizons, based on their expectations and the risk involved in longer time horizons.

5.1 Interest Rate Quotes and Adjustments

If you spend some time looking through a newspaper, you will find literally dozens of interest rates discussed and advertised, from savings deposit rates to auto loan rates to interest rates being paid on the government's debt. Interest rates are clearly central to the functioning of any financial system. To understand interest rates, it's important to think of interest rates as a price—the price of using money. When you borrow money to buy a car, you are using the bank's money now to get the car and paying the money back over time. The interest rate on your loan is the price you pay to be able to convert your future loan payments into a car today. Similarly, when you deposit money into a savings account, you are letting the bank use your money until you withdraw it later. The interest the bank pays you on your deposit is the price it pays to use your money (for things like making car loans).

Just like any other price, interest rates are set by market forces, in particular the supply of and demand for funds. When the supply (savings) is high and the demand (borrowing) is low, interest rates are low, other things being equal. Additionally, as we discuss later in the chapter, interest rates are also influenced by expected inflation and risk.

In order to be able to study and use interest rates, we have to understand how they are quoted. In practice, interest is paid, and interest rates are quoted, in different ways. For example, in early-2016, Ally Bank offered savings accounts with a rate of 1.00% annually with interest paid on a daily basis, while other banks offered savings rates with interest paid on a quarterly or annual basis. Interest rates can also differ depending on the investment horizon. In April 2016, investors earned around 0.60% on one-year risk-free U.S. Treasury Bills, but could earn around 2.20% on 20-year Treasuries. Interest rates can also vary due to risk or tax consequences: The U.S. government is able to borrow at a lower interest rate than Johnson & Johnson, which in turn can borrow at a lower rate than American Airlines.

Because interest rates may be quoted for different time intervals, such as monthly, semi-annually, or annually, it is often necessary to adjust the interest rate to a time period that matches that of our cash flows. We explore these mechanics of interest rates in this section.

The Effective Annual Rate

effective annual rate (EAR) or annual percentage yield (APY) The total amount of interest that will be earned at the end of one year.

Interest rates are often reported as an **effective annual rate (EAR)** or **annual percentage yield (APY)**, which indicates the total amount of interest that will be earned at the end of one year.[1] We have used this method of quoting the interest rate thus far in this book, and in Chapters 3 and 4 we used the EAR as the discount rate r in our time value of money calculations. For example, with an EAR of 5%, a $100 investment grows to

$$\$100 \times (1 + r) = \$100 \times (1.05) = \$105$$

in one year. After two years it will grow to:

$$\$100 \times (1 + r)^2 = \$100 \times (1.05)^2 = \$110.25$$

Month:	0		1		2
Cash flow:	$100	× (1.05)	= $105	× (1.05)	= $110.25
	$100	×	$(1.05)^2$	=	$110.25
	$100	×	(1.1025)	=	$110.25

---

[1]The effective annual rate is also referred to as the *effective annual yield* (EAY).

Adjusting the Discount Rate to Different Time Periods

The preceding example shows that earning an effective annual rate of 5% for two years is equivalent to earning 10.25% in total interest over the entire period:

$$\$100 \times (1.05)^2 = \$100 \times 1.1025 = \$110.25$$

In general, by raising the interest rate factor $(1 + r)$ to the appropriate power, we can compute an equivalent interest rate for a longer time period.

We can use the same method to find the equivalent interest rate for periods shorter than one year. In this case, we raise the interest rate factor $(1 + r)$ to the appropriate fractional power. For example, earning 5% interest in one year is equivalent to receiving

$$(1 + r)^{0.5} = (1.05)^{0.5} = \$1.0247$$

for each \$1 invested every six months (0.5 years). That is, a 5% effective annual rate is equivalent to an interest rate of approximately 2.47% earned every six months. We can verify this result by computing the interest we would earn in one year by investing for two six-month periods at this rate:

$$(1 + r)^2 = (1.0247)^2 = \$1.05$$

Month:	0	$\frac{1}{2}$	1

Cash flow:	\$1	$\times (1.0247)$	$= \$1.0247 \times (1.0247)$	$= \$1.05$
	\$1	$\times$	$(1.0247)^2$	$= \$1.05$
	\$1	$\times$	(1.05)	$= \$1.05$

In general, we can convert a discount rate of r for one period to an equivalent discount rate for n periods using the following formula:

$$\text{Equivalent } n\text{-period Discount Rate} = (1 + r)^n - 1 \qquad (5.1)$$

In this formula, n can be larger than 1 (to compute a rate over more than one period) or smaller than 1 (to compute a rate over a fraction of a period).

When computing present or future values, you should adjust the discount rate to match the time period of the cash flows.

This adjustment is necessary to apply the perpetuity or annuity formulas to non-annual cash flows, as shown in Example 5.1.

PERSONAL FINANCE

EXAMPLE 5.1

Valuing Monthly
Cash Flows

MyFinanceLab

PROBLEM

Suppose your bank account pays interest monthly with an effective annual rate of 6%. What amount of interest will you earn each month?

If you have no money in the bank today, how much will you need to save at the end of each month to accumulate \$100,000 in 10 years?

SOLUTION

PLAN

We can use Eq. 5.1 to convert the EAR to a monthly rate, answering the first question. The second question is a future value of an annuity question. It is asking how big a monthly annuity we would have to deposit in order to end up with \$100,000 in 10 years. However, in order to solve this problem, we need to write the timeline in terms of monthly periods because our cash flows (deposits) will be monthly:

(Continued)

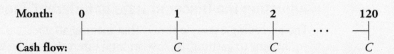

That is, we can view the savings plan as a monthly annuity with $10 \times 12 = 120$ monthly payments. We have the future value of the annuity ($100,000), the length of time (120 months), and we will have the monthly interest rate from the answer to the first part of the question. We can then use the future value of an annuity formula (Eq. 4.6) to solve for the monthly deposit.

EXECUTE

From Eq. 5.1, a 6% EAR is equivalent to earning $(1.06)^{1/12} - 1 = 0.4868\%$ per month. The exponent in this equation is $1/12$ because the period is $1/12$ th of a year (a month).

To determine the amount to save each month to reach the goal of $100,000 in 120 months, we must determine the amount C of the monthly payment that will have a future value of $100,000 in 120 months, given an interest rate of 0.4868% per month. Now that we have all of the inputs in terms of months (monthly payment, monthly interest rate, and total number of months), we use the future value of annuity formula from Chapter 4 to solve this problem:

$$FV\,(\text{annuity}) = C \times \frac{1}{r}\left[\,(1+r)^n - 1\,\right]$$

We solve for the payment C using the equivalent monthly interest rate $r = 0.4868\%$, and $n = 120$ months:

$$C = \frac{FV\,(\text{Annuity})}{\dfrac{1}{r}\left[\,(1+r)^n - 1\,\right]} = \frac{\$100{,}000}{\dfrac{1}{0.004868}\left[\,(1.004868)^{120} - 1\,\right]} = \$615.47 \text{ per month}$$

We can also compute this result using a financial calculator or spreadsheet:

	N	I/Y	PV	PMT	FV
Given:	120	0.4868	0		100,000
Solve for:				−615.47	
	Excel Formula: = PMT(RATE,NPER,PV,FV)=PMT(0.004868,120,0,100000)				

EVALUATE

Thus, if we save $615.47 per month and we earn interest monthly at an effective annual rate of 6%, we will have $100,000 in 10 years. Notice that the timing in the annuity formula must be consistent for all of the inputs. In this case, we had a monthly deposit, so we needed to convert our interest rate to a monthly interest rate and then use total number of months (120) instead of years.

Annual Percentage Rates

annual percentage rate (APR) Indicates the amount of interest earned in one year without the effect of compounding.

The most common way to quote interest rates is in terms of an **annual percentage rate (APR)**, which indicates the amount of simple interest earned in one year, that is, the amount of interest earned *without* the effect of compounding. Because it does not include the effect of compounding, the APR quote is typically less than the actual amount of interest that you will earn. To compute the actual amount that you will earn in one year, you must first convert the APR to an effective annual rate.

For example, suppose Granite Bank advertises savings accounts with an interest rate of "6% APR with monthly compounding." When it quotes a rate this way, Granite Bank really means that you will earn 6%/12 = 0.5% every month. That is, an APR with monthly compounding is actually a way of quoting a *monthly* interest rate, rather than an annual interest rate. In this case, the actual rate being quoted is 0.5% *per month*, and by convention,

COMMON MISTAKE

Using the EAR in the Annuity Formula

At this point, many students make the mistake of trying to use the EAR in the annuity formula. The interest rate in the annuity formula must match the frequency of the cash flows. That's why in Example 5.1, we first converted the EAR into a monthly rate and then used the annuity formula to compute the monthly loan payments. The common mistake in this case would be to use the EAR in the annuity formula to obtain annual cash flows, and then divide those cash flows by 12 to obtain the monthly payments.

This process will produce the wrong answer. To see why, consider the timing of the first deposit in Example 5.1. With a monthly rate and monthly payments, the annuity formula assumes that the first payment will be made one month from now. It then assumes that you will be making 11 more monthly deposits before the end of the first year. Each of those deposits will start earning interest as soon as you make it. In contrast, if you use an EAR and calculate an annual cash flow, the formula assumes that you will make your first deposit one *year* from now, so that you will forgo a whole year of interest before you start earning anything. Thus, you can see that the EAR approach misses the fact that you are making deposits earlier and more often than annually, so you are adding to your interest-earning principal more frequently than once per year.

the bank states it as an APR by multiplying by 12 months. Because the interest compounds each month, you will actually have

$$\$1 \times (1.005)^{12} = \$1.061678$$

at the end of one year, for an effective annual rate of 6.1678%. The 6.1678% that you earn on your deposit is higher than the quoted 6% APR due to compounding: In later months, you earn interest on the interest paid in earlier months. To summarize, an actual rate of 0.5% *per month* can be stated in either of the following ways:

- 6% APR, compounded monthly
- EAR of 6.1678%, which is the actual rate earned *per year*

It is important to remember that because the APR does not reflect the true amount you will earn over one year, *the APR itself cannot be used as a discount rate.* Instead, the APR is a way of quoting the actual interest earned each compounding period:

$$\text{Interest Rate per Compounding Period} = \frac{APR}{m}$$

$$(m = \text{number of compounding periods per year}) \tag{5.2}$$

Once we have computed the interest earned per compounding period from Eq. 5.2, we can compute the equivalent interest rate for any other time interval using Eq. 5.1. Thus, the effective annual rate corresponding to an APR is given by the following conversion formula:

Converting an APR to an EAR

$$1 + EAR = \left(1 + \frac{APR}{m}\right)^m$$

$$(m = \text{number of compounding periods per year}) \tag{5.3}$$

Table 5.1 shows the effective annual rates that correspond to an APR of 6% with different compounding intervals. The EAR increases with the frequency of compounding because of the ability to earn interest on interest sooner. Investments can compound even more frequently than daily. In principle, the compounding interval could be hourly or every second. As a practical matter, compounding more frequently than daily has a negligible impact on the effective annual rate and is rarely observed.

When working with APRs, we must first convert the APR to a discount rate per compounding interval using Eq. 5.2, or to an EAR using Eq. 5.3, before evaluating the present or future value of a set of cash flows.

TABLE 5.1

Effective Annual Rates
for a 6% APR
with Different
Compounding Periods

Compounding Interval	Effective Annual Rate
Annual	$\left(1 + \dfrac{0.06}{1}\right)^1 - 1 = 6\%$
Semiannual	$\left(1 + \dfrac{0.06}{2}\right)^2 - 1 = 6.09\%$
Monthly	$\left(1 + \dfrac{0.06}{12}\right)^{12} - 1 = 6.1678\%$
Daily	$\left(1 + \dfrac{0.06}{365}\right)^{365} - 1 = 6.1831\%$

EXAMPLE 5.2

Converting the APR
to a Discount Rate

MyFinanceLab

PROBLEM

Your firm is purchasing a new telephone system that will last for four years. You can purchase the system for an up-front cost of $150,000, or you can lease the system from the manufacturer for $4000 paid at the end of each month. The lease price is offered for a 48-month lease with no early termination—you cannot end the lease early. Your firm can borrow at an interest rate of 6% APR with monthly compounding. Should you purchase the system outright or pay $4000 per month?

SOLUTION

PLAN

The cost of leasing the system is a 48-month annuity of $4000 per month:

Month:	0	1	2	48
Payment:		$4000	$4000	$4000

... (between month 2 and 48)

We can compute the present value of the lease cash flows using the annuity formula, but first we need to compute the discount rate that corresponds to a period length of one month. To do so, we convert the borrowing cost of 6% APR with monthly compounding to a monthly discount rate using Eq. 5.2. Once we have a monthly rate, we can use the present value of annuity formula Eq. 4.5 to compute the present value of the monthly payments and compare it to the cost of buying the system.

EXECUTE

As Eq. 5.2 shows, the 6% APR with monthly compounding really means 6%/12 = 0.5% every month. The 12 comes from the fact that there are 12 monthly compounding periods per year. Now that we have the true rate corresponding to the stated APR, we can use that discount rate in the annuity formula Eq. 4.5 to compute the present value of the monthly payments:

$$PV = 4000 \times \frac{1}{0.005}\left(1 - \frac{1}{1.005^{48}}\right) = \$170,321.27$$

Using a financial calculator or spreadsheet:

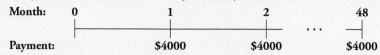

	N	I/Y	PV	PMT	FV
Given:	48	0.5		−4000	0
Solve for:			170,321.27		
	Excel Formula: =PV(RATE,NPER,PMT,FV)=PV(0.005,48,−4000,0)				

EVALUATE

Thus, paying $4000 per month for 48 months is equivalent to paying a present value of $170,321.27 today. This cost is $170,321.27 − $150,000 = $20,321.27 higher than the cost of purchasing the system, so it is better to pay $150,000 for the system rather than lease it. One way to interpret this result is as follows: At a 6% APR with monthly compounding, by promising to repay $4000 per month your firm can borrow $170,321 today. With this loan it could purchase the phone system and have an additional $20,321 to use for other purposes.

1. What is the difference between an EAR and an APR quote?

2. Why can't the APR be used as a discount rate?

5.2 Application: Discount Rates and Loans

Now that we have explained how to compute the discount rate from an interest rate quote, let's apply the concept to solve two common financial problems: calculating a loan payment and calculating the remaining balance on a loan.

Computing Loan Payments

amortizing loan A loan on which the borrower makes monthly payments that include interest on the loan plus some part of the loan balance.

Many loans, such as mortgages and car loans, have monthly payments and are quoted in terms of an APR with monthly compounding. These types of loans are **amortizing loans**, which means that each month you pay interest on the loan plus some part of the loan balance. Each monthly payment is the same, and the loan is fully repaid with the final payment. Typical terms for a new car loan might be "6.75% APR for 60 months." When the compounding interval for the APR is not stated explicitly, it is equal to the interval between the payments, or one month in this case. Thus, this quote means that the loan will be repaid with 60 equal monthly payments, computed using a 6.75% APR with monthly compounding. It sometimes helps to look at the loan from the bank's point of view: The bank will give you $30,000 in cash today to use to buy the car. In return, you will give the bank 60 equal payments each month for 60 months, starting one month from now. In order for the bank to be willing to accept this exchange, it must be true that the present value of what you will give the bank, discounted at the loan's interest rate, is equal to the amount of cash the bank is giving you now. Consider the timeline for a $30,000 car loan with these terms:

Month:	0	1	2	⋯	60
Cash flow:	$30,000	$-C$	$-C$		$-C$

The payment, C, is set so that the present value of the cash flows, evaluated using the loan interest rate, equals the original principal amount of $30,000. In this case, the 6.75% APR with monthly compounding corresponds to a one-month discount rate of $6.75\%/12 = 0.5625\%$. It is important that the discount rate matches the frequency of the cash flows—here we have a monthly discount rate and a monthly loan payment, so we can proceed. Because the loan payments are an annuity, we can use Eq. 4.9 to find C:

$$C = \frac{P}{\frac{1}{r}\left(1 - \frac{1}{(1+r)^N}\right)} = \frac{30{,}000}{\frac{1}{0.005625}\left(1 - \frac{1}{(1+0.005625)^{60}}\right)} = \$590.50$$

Alternatively, we can solve for the payment C using a financial calculator or spreadsheet:

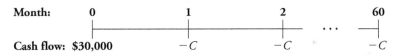

	N	I/Y	PV	PMT	FV
Given:	60	0.5625	30,000		0
Solve for:				−590.50	
Excel Formula: =PMT(RATE,NPER,PV,FV)=PMT(0.005625,60,30000,0)					

Your loan payment each month includes interest and repayment of part of the principal, reducing the amount you still owe. Because the loan balance (the amount you still owe) is decreasing each month, the interest that accrues on that balance is decreasing. As a result, even though your payment stays the same over the entire 60-month life of the loan, the part of that payment needed to cover interest each month is constantly decreasing and the part left over to reduce the principal further is constantly increasing. We illustrate this effect in Panel (a) of Figure 5.1, where we show the proportion of each

FIGURE 5.1

Amortizing Loan

Panel (a) shows how the interest (red) and principal portions (blue) of the monthly payment on the $30,000 car loan change over the life of the loan. Panel (b) illustrates the effect on the outstanding balance (principal) of the loan. Note that as the balance decreases, the amount of the payment needed to cover interest on that balance decreases, allowing more of the payment to be used to reduce the principal.

Panel (a)

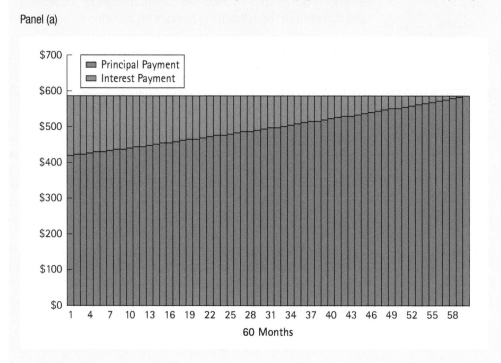

Panel (b)

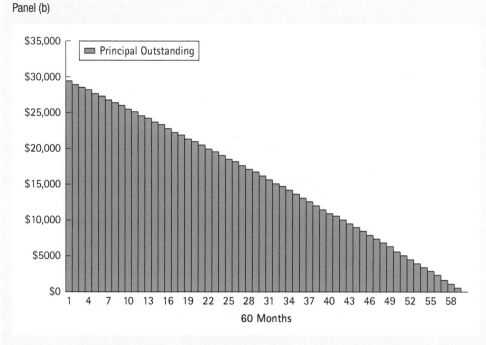

Teaser Rates and Subprime Loans

Some loans, such as adjustable rate mortgages (ARMs), have interest rates that are not constant over the life of the loan. When the interest rate on such a loan changes, the loan payments are recalculated based on the loan's current outstanding balance, the new interest rate, and the remaining life of the loan.

Adjustable rate mortgages were the most common type of so-called "subprime" loans made to homebuyers with poor credit histories. These loans often featured low initial rates, aptly named teaser rates. After a short period (often 2 to 5 years) the interest rate would jump to a higher rate, implying that the monthly payment would also jump. For example, a $500,000 30-year mortgage with a teaser rate of 4.8% would have monthly payments of $2623.33 initially. If, after 2 years, the rate increased to 7.2%, the new monthly interest rate would be 7.2%/12 = 0.6% per month. With the higher rate, the monthly payment would jump to $3355.62!

While the loan might have been affordable at the initial teaser rate, many subprime borrowers could not afford the higher payments that were required after the loan rate adjusted. Prior to 2007, while interest rates remained low and home prices were high (and increasing), such borrowers were able to avoid default simply by refinancing their loans into new loans that also featured low initial teaser rates. In this way, they were able to keep their payments low. But as mortgage rates increased and housing prices began to decline in 2007, this strategy for keeping their loan payments low was no longer possible. In many cases, the outstanding loan balance exceeded the market value of the home, making lenders unwilling to refinance the loans. Stuck with a loan at a now unaffordable interest rate, many homeowners defaulted, and the rate of foreclosure on subprime loans skyrocketed.

To prevent future lenders from using teaser rates to get borrowers into loans they might not ultimately be able to afford, the Dodd-Frank Act requires lenders to verify that borrowers have sufficient income to repay their loans even after the teaser rate expires.

monthly loan payment that covers interest (red) and the portion left over to reduce the principal (blue). As you can see, $168.75 of your first $590.50 payment is needed just to cover interest accrued over the first month ($30,000 \times 0.005625 = $168.75). However, this amount steadily decreases so that by the end of the loan, nearly all of your payment is going toward principal.

Panel (b) of Figure 5.1 shows the effect of your payments on the loan balance. When you make your first payment of $590.50, $168.75 covers interest on the loan, leaving $421.75 to reduce the principal to $30,000 − $421.75 = $29,578.25. The next month, you owe interest only on the $29,578.25 loan balance, which is $166.38, leaving more of your $590.50 payment to reduce the principal further. This effect continues so that each month more of your payment is available to reduce the principal, causing the principal to decrease rapidly toward the end of the loan as you are taking bigger and bigger chunks out of the balance.

Computing the Outstanding Loan Balance

As Figure 5.1 shows, the outstanding balance on an amortizing loan is different each month. The amount you owe at any point can be calculated as the present value of your future obligations on the loan. So, the outstanding balance, also called the *outstanding principal,* is equal to the present value of the remaining future loan payments, again evaluated using the loan interest rate. We calculate the outstanding loan balance by determining the present value of the remaining loan payments using the loan rate as the discount rate.

PROBLEM

Let's say that you are now three years into your $30,000 car loan from the previous section and you decide to sell the car. When you sell the car, you will need to pay whatever the remaining balance is on your car loan. After 36 months of payments, how much do you still owe on your car loan?

SOLUTION

PLAN

We have already determined that the monthly payments on the loan are $590.50. The remaining balance on the loan is the present value of the remaining two years, or 24 months, of payments. Thus, we can just use the annuity formula with the monthly rate of 0.5625%, a monthly payment of $590.50, and 24 months remaining.

EXECUTE

$$\text{Balance with 24 months remaining} = \$590.50 \times \frac{1}{0.005625}\left(1 - \frac{1}{1.005625^{24}}\right) = \$13,222.32$$

Thus, after three years, you owe $13,222.32 on the loan.
Using a financial calculator or spreadsheet:

	N	I/Y	PV	PMT	FV
Given:	24	0.5625		−590.50	0
Solve for:			13,222.32		
Excel Formula: =PV(RATE,NPER,PMT,FV)=PV(0.005625,24,−590.50,0)					

You could also compute this as the FV of the original loan amount after deducting payments:

	N	I/Y	PV	PMT	FV
Given:	36	0.5625	30,000	−590.50	
Solve for:					13,222.56
Excel Formula: =FV(RATE,NPER,PMT,PV)=FV(0.005625,36,−590.50,30000)					

The 24 cent difference is due to rounding on the payment amount.

EVALUATE

At any point in time, including when you first take out the loan, you can calculate the balance of the loan as the present value of your remaining payments. Recall that when the bank gave you the $30,000 in the first place, it was willing to take 60 monthly payments of $590.50 in return only because the present value of those payments was equivalent to the cash it was giving you. Any time that you want to end the loan, the bank will charge you a lump sum equal to the present value of what it would receive if you continued making your payments as planned. As the second approach shows, the amount you owe can also be thought of as the future value of the original amount borrowed after deducting payments made along the way.

CONCEPT CHECK

3. How is the principal repaid in an amortizing loan?

4. Why does the part of your loan payment covering interest change over time?

5.3 The Determinants of Interest Rates

Now that we understand how interest rates are quoted and used in loans, we turn to a broader question: How are interest rates determined? Fundamentally, interest rates are determined by market forces based on the relative supply and demand of funds. This supply and demand is in turn determined by the willingness of individuals, banks, and firms to borrow, save, and lend. Changes in interest rates affect consumer decisions, such as how much you can borrow for a car loan or mortgage. Because they change the present value of future cash flows, changes in interest rates also have a broad impact on capital budgeting decisions within the firm. In this section, we look at some of the factors that may influence interest rates, such as inflation, current economic activity, and expectations of future growth.

Inflation and Real Versus Nominal Rates

Inflation measures how the purchasing power of a given amount of currency declines due to increasing prices. How many times have you heard the expression, "A dollar just doesn't buy what it used to"? We've all witnessed the steady upward climb of prices—for example, your morning coffee probably costs a little more today than it did five years ago. Inflation affects how we evaluate the interest rates being quoted by banks and other financial institutions. Those interest rates, and the ones we have used for discounting cash flows in this book, are **nominal interest rates**, which indicate the rate at which your money will grow if invested for a certain period. Of course, if prices in the economy are also increasing due to inflation, the nominal interest rate does not represent the true increase in purchasing power that will result from investing.

nominal interest rates Interest rates quoted by banks and other financial institutions that indicate the rate at which money will grow if invested for a certain period of time.

For example, let's say that a cup of coffee costs $1 this year. If you have $100, you could buy 100 coffees. Instead, if you put that $100 in a bank account earning 5.06% per year, you will have $105.06 at the end of the year. But how much better off will you really be? That depends on how much prices have increased over the same year. If inflation was 3% over the year, then that cup of coffee would cost 3% more, or $1.03 at the end of the year. Thus, you could take your $105.06 and buy $105.06/$1.03 = 102 coffees, so you're really only 2% better off.

real interest rate The rate of growth of purchasing power, after adjusting for inflation.

That 2% is your **real interest rate**: the rate of growth of your purchasing power, after adjusting for inflation. Just as in the example, we can calculate the rate of growth of purchasing power as follows:

$$\text{Growth in Purchasing Power} = 1 + \text{Real Rate} = \frac{1 + \text{Nominal Rate}}{1 + \text{Inflation Rate}}$$

$$= \frac{\text{Growth of Money}}{\text{Growth of Prices}} \tag{5.4}$$

We can rearrange Eq. 5.4 to find the following formula for the real interest rate, together with a convenient approximation for the real interest rate when inflation rates are low:

The Real Interest Rate

$$\text{Real Rate} = \frac{\text{Nominal Rate} - \text{Inflation Rate}}{1 + \text{Inflation Rate}} \approx \text{Nominal Rate} - \text{Inflation Rate} \tag{5.5}$$

That is, the real interest rate is approximately equal to the nominal interest rate less the rate of inflation.[2]

---

[2]The real interest rate should not be used as a discount rate for future cash flows. It can be used as a discount rate only if the cash flows are not the expected cash flows that will be paid, but are the equivalent cash flows before adjusting them for growth due to inflation (in that case, we say the cash flows are in *real terms*). This approach is error prone, however, so throughout this book we will always forecast cash flows including any growth due to inflation, and discount using nominal interest rates.

EXAMPLE 5.4

Calculating the Real
Interest Rate

MyFinanceLab

PROBLEM

At the start of 2008, one-year U.S. government bond rates were about 3.3%, while the inflation rate that year was 0.1%. At the start of 2011, one-year interest rates were about 0.3%, and the inflation rate that year was about 3.0%. What were the real interest rates in 2008 and in 2011?

SOLUTION

Using Eq. 5.5, the real interest rate in 2008 was $(3.3\% - 0.1\%)/(1.001) = 3.20\%$. In 2011, the real interest rate was $(0.3\% - 3.0\%)/(1.03) = -2.62\%$.

EVALUATE

Note that the real interest rate was negative in 2011, indicating that interest rates were insufficient to keep up with inflation: Investors in U.S. government bonds were able to buy less at the end of the year than they could have purchased at the start of the year. On the other hand, there was hardly any inflation.

Figure 5.2 shows the history of nominal interest rates and inflation rates in the United States since 1955. Note that the nominal interest rate tends to move with inflation. Intuitively, individuals' willingness to save will depend on the growth in purchasing power they can expect (given by the real interest rate). Thus, when the inflation rate is high, a higher nominal interest rate is needed to induce individuals to save. This was evident in the late 1970s and early 1980s when inflation reached double-digits in the United States, and nominal rates increased in response.

Investment and Interest Rate Policy

Interest rates affect not only individuals' propensity to save, but also firms' incentive to raise capital and invest. Consider an opportunity that requires an up-front investment of

FIGURE 5.2

U.S. Interest Rates
and Inflation Rates,
1962–2016

The graph shows U.S. nominal interest rates (in blue) and inflation rates (in red) from 1962–2016. Note that interest rates tend to be high when inflation is high. The interest rates we graph here are one-year Treasury rates, and the inflation rates are the increase in the U.S. Bureau of Labor Statistics' consumer price index over the coming year, with both series computed on a monthly basis. The difference between them thus reflects the approximate real interest rate earned by holding Treasuries.

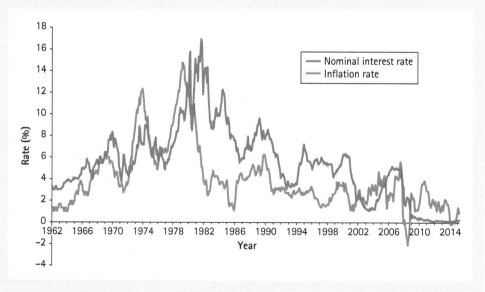

Source: St. Louis Federal Reserve Economic Data (FRED).

$10 million and generates a cash flow of $3 million per year for four years. If the interest rate is 5%, this investment's benefits have a PV of:

$$PV = \frac{3}{1.05} + \frac{3}{1.05^2} + \frac{3}{1.05^3} + \frac{3}{1.05^4} = \$10.638 \text{ million}$$

If the interest rate is 9%, the PV falls to

$$PV = \frac{3}{1.09} + \frac{3}{1.09^2} + \frac{3}{1.09^3} + \frac{3}{1.09^4} = \$9.719 \text{ million}$$

and the investment is no longer profitable given its $10 million cost. The reason, of course, is that we are discounting the positive cash flows at a higher rate, which reduces their present value. The cost of $10 million occurs today, however, so its present value is independent of the discount rate.

More generally, when the costs of an investment precede the benefits, an increase in the interest rate will make the investment less attractive. All else being equal, higher interest rates will therefore tend to shrink the set of good investments available to firms. The Federal Reserve in the United States and central banks in other countries attempt to use this relationship between interest rates and investment incentives when trying to guide the economy. They will often lower interest rates in an attempt to stimulate investment if the economy is slowing, and they will raise interest rates to reduce investment if the economy is "overheating" and inflation is on the rise.

Monetary Policy, Deflation, and the 2008 Financial Crisis. When the 2008 financial crisis struck the economy, the U.S. Federal Reserve responded quickly to mitigate its impact on the broader economy by cutting its short-term interest rate target to 0% by year's end. But while this use of monetary policy is generally quite effective, because consumer prices were falling in late 2008, the inflation rate was negative, and so even with a 0% nominal interest rate the real interest rate remained positive initially. The consequence of this deflation, and the risk that it might continue, meant that the Federal Reserve was "out of

How Is Inflation Actually Calculated?

Inflation is calculated as the rate of change in the *Consumer Price Index* (CPI). The CPI measures what it costs each month to purchase a standard set of goods that the average consumer would buy. How controversial can price data be?

To gather the price information, data collectors visit stores and gather 80,000 retail price quotes and 5000 housing rent quotes. The data is sent daily to Washington, DC, where analysts at the Bureau of Labor Statistics seek to determine if part of a price change captures a change in quality or inflation. Because this adjustment can be subjective, herein lies the controversy in the CPI calculation. The *Wall Street Journal*, covering the controversy, reported the following examples:

- A 57-inch television in which the price dropped from $2238.99 to $1909.97. Going over the checklist, the data gatherer in the field discovered the old version had a built-in high-definition tuner. The new one did not. The analyst estimated that the tuner was valued at $513.69. This turned what appeared to be a 14.7% price decrease into a 10.7% increase.

- A 27-inch television where the price appeared to stay the same, but an analyst determined that the price had declined. The latest model had a flat screen, something that consumers value more than the curved screen in the old model. The newer TV also had a 10-watt stereo, compared with the weaker 6-watt stereo in the older model.

Critics argue that this quality adjustment most often ends up making a price increase look smaller or even turning it into a decline. Thus, they conclude that the government underestimates the true rate of inflation. Supporters argue that these adjustments are necessary because paying more for a better product is not equivalent to paying more for the same product. This debate is important because many union contracts, for example, have wages linked to inflation, and investors need good inflation data to determine what interest rate to demand.

WSJ Source: Aeppel, T., "New and Improved: An Inflation Debate Brews Over Intangibles at the Mall—Critics Say U.S. Plays Down CPI Through Adjustments For Quality, Not Just Price—Value of a TV's Flat Screen," 9 May 2005, A1.

ammunition" with regard to its usual weapon against an economic slowdown—it could not lower rates further. This problem was one of the reasons the United States and other governments began to consider other measures, such as increased government spending and investment, to stimulate their economies. Former Federal Reserve Governor Kevin Warsh further discusses monetary policy responses to the economic crisis in both the United States and Europe in the interview box on page 146.

Why couldn't the Federal Reserve go further and make nominal interest rates negative? Since individuals can always hold cash and earn at least a zero return, the nominal interest rate can never be *significantly* negative. But because storing cash is costly, and because investors viewed many banks as unsafe, short-term U.S. Treasury interest rates were actually slightly negative (down to –0.05%) at several points throughout this period! Perhaps more notable is the fact that in 2016, several central banks, including the European Central Bank and the Bank of Japan set negative deposit rates to encourage banks to lend in order to boost economic growth. As we stated above, negative rates are hard to sustain and in fact, in response to the Bank of Japan announcement, there was a run on safes by Japanese savers! So, while we correctly think of zero as the appropriate floor for interest rates (you would not choose to pay to give someone the use of your money), the global financial crisis and its aftermath have produced several examples of special cases of negative rates being driven by depositor risk-aversion, costly substitutes, and the ability of monetary authorities to impose such rates on their member banks. (See Chapter 6 for further discussion.)

The Yield Curve and Discount Rates

The interest rates that banks offer on investments or charge on loans depend on the horizon, or *term*, of the investment or loan. For example, suppose you are willing to put your

FIGURE 5.3

Term Structure of Risk-Free U.S. Interest Rates, November 2006, 2007, and 2008

The figure shows the interest rate available from investing in risk-free U.S. Treasury securities with different investment terms. In each case, the interest rates differ depending on the horizon. For example, in 2008, the interest rate on a 10-year loan (3.41%) was more than three times the rate on a 1-year loan (0.91%).

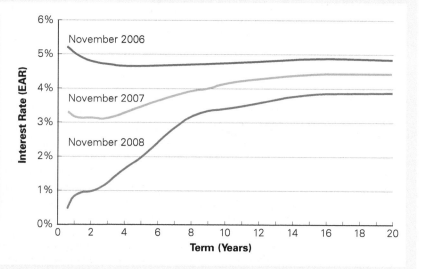

Term	Date		
(years)	Nov-06	Nov-07	Nov-08
0.5	5.23%	3.32%	0.47%
1	4.99%	3.16%	0.91%
2	4.80%	3.16%	0.98%
3	4.72%	3.12%	1.26%
4	4.63%	3.34%	1.69%
5	4.64%	3.48%	2.01%
6	4.65%	3.63%	2.49%
7	4.66%	3.79%	2.90%
8	4.69%	3.96%	3.21%
9	4.70%	4.00%	3.38%
10	4.73%	4.18%	3.41%
15	4.89%	4.44%	3.86%
20	4.87%	4.45%	3.87%

(Data from U.S. Treasury securities.)

money in a CD (certificate of deposit)[3] that matures in two years (meaning that you cannot get the money back before then without a penalty). The bank will offer you a higher rate of interest for this CD than if you put your money in a statement savings account, where you can withdraw your funds at any time. The relationship between the investment term and the interest rate is called the **term structure** of interest rates. We can plot this relationship on a graph called the **yield curve**. Figure 5.3 shows the term structure and corresponding yield curve of U.S. interest rates that were available to investors in November 2006, 2007, and 2008. In each case, note that the interest rate depends on the horizon, and that the difference between short-term and long-term interest rates was especially pronounced in 2008. The rates plotted are interest rates for U.S. Treasury securities, which are considered to be free of any risk of default (the U.S. government will not default on its loans). Thus, each of these rates is a **risk-free interest rate**, which is the interest rate at which money can be borrowed or lent without risk over a given period.

> **term structure** The relationship between the investment term and the interest rate.

> **yield curve** A plot of bond yields as a function of the bonds' maturity date.

> **risk-free interest rate** The interest rate at which money can be borrowed or lent without risk over a given period.

We can use the term structure to compute the present and future values of a risk-free cash flow over different investment horizons. For example, $100 invested for one year at the one-year interest rate in November 2008 would grow to a future value of

$$\$100 \times 1.0091 = \$100.91$$

at the end of one year, and $100 invested for 10 years at the 10-year interest rate in November 2008 would grow to:[4]

$$\$100 \times (1.0341)^{10} = \$139.84$$

We can apply the same logic when computing the present value of cash flows with different maturities. A risk-free cash flow received in two years should be discounted at the two-year interest rate, and a cash flow received in 10 years should be discounted at the 10-year interest rate. In general, a risk-free cash flow of C_n received in n years has the present value

$$PV = \frac{C_n}{(1+r_n)^n} \tag{5.6}$$

where r_n is the risk-free interest rate for an n-year term. In other words, when computing a present value we must match the term of the cash flow and term of the discount rate.

Combining Eq. 5.6 for cash flows in different years leads to the general formula for the present value of a cash flow stream:

Present Value of a Cash Flow Stream Using a Term Structure of Discount Rates

$$PV = \frac{C_1}{1+r_1} + \frac{C_2}{(1+r_2)^2} + \cdots + \frac{C_N}{(1+r_N)^N} \tag{5.7}$$

Note the difference between Eq. 5.7 and Eq. 4.3. Here, we use a different discount rate for each cash flow, based on the rate from the yield curve with the same term. When interest rates are very similar across maturities, we say that the yield curve is flat, because it is close to a flat line. When the yield curve is relatively flat, as it was in November 2006, the distinction of using different rates for each cash flow is relatively minor and is often ignored by discounting using a single "average" interest rate r. But when short-term and long-term interest rates vary widely, as they did in November 2008, Eq. 5.7 should be used.

---

[3]A certificate of deposit is a short- or medium-term debt instrument offered by banks. You deposit money in the bank for a stated period of time and normally receive a fixed rate of interest. The rate is higher than it would be on a savings account because you cannot withdraw your money early without paying a penalty.
[4]We could also invest for 10 years by investing at the one-year interest rate for 10 years in a row. However, because we do not know what future interest rates will be, our ultimate payoff would not be risk free.

Warning: All of our shortcuts for computing present values (annuity and perpetuity formulas, and financial calculators) are based on discounting all of the cash flows *at the same rate*. They *cannot* be used in situations in which cash flows need to be discounted at different rates.

KEVIN M. WARSH

Kevin M. Warsh, *a lecturer at Stanford's Graduate School of Business and a distinguished visiting fellow at the Hoover Institution*, was a Federal Reserve governor from 2006 to 2011, serving as chief liaison to the financial markets.

QUESTION: *What are the main policy instruments used by central banks to control the economy?*

ANSWER: The Federal Reserve (Fed) deploys several policy tools to achieve its goals of price stability, maximum sustainable employment, and financial stability. Lowering the federal funds short-term interest rate, the primary policy instrument, stimulates the economy. Raising the federal funds rate generally slows the economy. Buying and selling short-term U.S. Treasury securities through *open market operations* is standard practice. Prior to the 2007–2009 financial crisis, the Fed's balance sheet ranged from $700–$900 billion. But when the Fed was unable to lower interest rates further because rates were so close to zero already, it resorted to large-scale, longer-term open market operations to increase liquidity in the financial system in the hopes of stimulating the economy further, thus growing its balance sheet significantly. With *open mouth operations*, the Fed's announcements of its intent to buy or sell assets indicates its desired degree of future policy accommodation, often prompting markets to react by adjusting interest rates immediately. The Fed's Lender-of-Last-Resort authority allows it to lend money against good collateral to troubled institutions under certain conditions.

QUESTION: *What factors limit the effectiveness of Fed policy?*

ANSWER: Monetary policy does not act in isolation. Fiscal (taxing and spending), trade, and regulatory policies have huge consequence on the state of economic and financial conditions. In the short term, monetary policy can help buy time for an economy to improve, but it cannot cure structural failings of an economy in isolation or compensate for the country's growing indebtedness.

QUESTION: *What tools did the Fed create to address the 2007–2009 financial crisis?*

ANSWER: During the darkest days of the crisis, markets did not operate effectively, prices for securities did not clear, and banks and other financial institutions lacked clarity and confidence in the financial wherewithal of each other. One effective, innovative tool, the *Term Auction Facility (TAF)*, stimulated the economy by providing cheap and readily available term funding to banks, large and small, on the front lines of the economy, thus encouraging them to extend credit to businesses and consumers. After reducing the policy rate to near zero to help revive the economy, the Fed instituted two *Quantitative Easing (QE)* programs—special purchases of government and agency securities—to increase money supply, promote lending, and according to some proponents, increase prices of riskier assets.

The Fed also addressed the global financial crisis by establishing temporary *central bank liquidity swap lines* with the European Central Bank and other major central banks. Using this facility, a foreign central bank is able to obtain dollar funding for its customers by swapping euros for dollars or another currency and agreeing to reverse the swap at a later date. The Fed does not take exchange rate risk, but it is subject to the credit risk of its central bank counterparty.

QUESTION: *What tools is the European Central Bank (ECB) using to address the sovereign debt crisis? How does its approach compare to the Fed's approach to the 2007–2009 financial crisis?*

ANSWER: As a novel economic federation, the ECB finds itself in a more difficult position than the Fed. The underlying economies and competitiveness are markedly different across the Eurozone—in Germany versus Greece, for example. From 2007 until mid-2010, many European financiers and policymakers believed that global financial crisis was largely American-made, with some strains exported to the continent. By mid-2010, however, they recognized that it was indeed a global crisis. The ECB is formally charged with a single mandate of ensuring price stability, rather than the broader mandate of the Fed. Still, its actions ultimately mirrored many of those undertaken by the Fed: lowering the effective policy rate to record lows, providing direct liquidity to the Eurozone's financial institutions to avoid a potential run on the banking system, and instituting the Security Market Purchase program (buying sovereign credit of some of its distressed countries).

EXAMPLE 5.5

Using the Term Structure to Compute Present Values

MyFinanceLab

PROBLEM

Compute the present value of a risk-free five-year annuity of $1000 per year, given the yield curve for November 2008 in Figure 5.3.

SOLUTION

PLAN

The timeline of the cash flows of the annuity is:

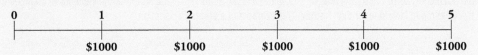

We can use the table next to the yield curve to identify the interest rate corresponding to each length of time: 1, 2, 3, 4, and 5 years. With the cash flows and those interest rates, we can compute the PV.

EXECUTE

From Figure 5.3, we see that the interest rates are: 0.91%, 0.98%, 1.26%, 1.69%, and 2.01%, for terms of 1, 2, 3, 4, and 5 years, respectively.

To compute the present value, we discount each cash flow by the corresponding interest rate:

$$PV = \frac{1000}{1.0091} + \frac{1000}{1.0098^2} + \frac{1000}{1.0126^3} + \frac{1000}{1.0169^4} + \frac{1000}{1.0201^5} = \$4775$$

EVALUATE

The yield curve tells us the market interest rate per year for each different maturity. In order to correctly calculate the PV of cash flows from five different maturities, we need to use the five different interest rates corresponding to those maturities. Note that we cannot use the annuity formula here because the discount rates differ for each cash flow.

COMMON MISTAKE

Using the Annuity Formula When Discount Rates Vary

When computing the present value of an annuity, a common mistake is to use the annuity formula with a single interest rate even though interest rates vary with the investment horizon. For example, we *cannot* compute the present value of the five-year annuity in Example 5.5 using the five-year interest rate from November 2008:

$$PV \neq \$1000 \times \frac{1}{0.0201}\left(1 - \frac{1}{1.0201^5}\right) = \$4712$$

If we want to find the single interest rate that we could use to value the annuity, we must first compute the present value of the annuity using Eq. 5.7 and then solve for its rate of return. For the annuity in Example 5.5, we use a financial calculator or spreadsheet to find its rate of return of 1.55%. The rate of return of the annuity is always between the highest and lowest discount rates used to calculate its present value, as is the case in this example.

	N	I/Y	PV	PMT	FV
Given:	5		−4775	1000	0
Solve for:		1.55			
Excel Formula: =RATE(NPER,PMT,PV,FV)=RATE(5,1000,−4775,0)					

The Yield Curve and the Economy

As Figure 5.4 illustrates, the yield curve changes over time. Sometimes, short-term rates are close to long-term rates, and at other times they may be very different. What accounts for the changing shape of the yield curve?

FIGURE 5.4

Yield Curve Shapes

The figure shows three different yield curve shapes. The blue line represents a "normal" yield curve. Most of the time the yield curve has this shape—moderately upward sloping. The red line depicts a steep yield curve—note the larger than normal difference between short-term rates (2%) and long-term rates (7%), making the yield curve look steeper than normal. This example of a steep yield curve is from October 1991. Finally, the green line depicts an inverted yield curve, so called because it slopes downward instead of upward. This happens when short-term rates are higher than long-term rates as they were in January 1981. We discuss why the shape of the yield curve changes over time in the rest of this section.

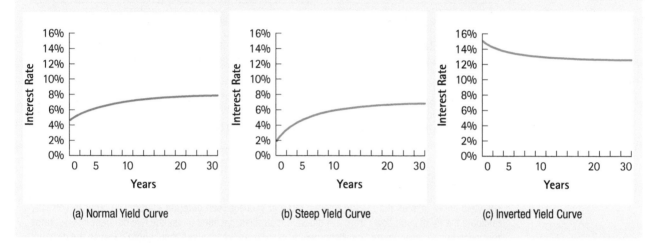

(a) Normal Yield Curve   (b) Steep Yield Curve   (c) Inverted Yield Curve

Interest Rate Determination. The Federal Reserve determines very short-term interest rates through its influence on the **federal funds rate**, which is the rate at which banks can borrow cash reserves on an overnight basis. All other interest rates on the yield curve are set in the market and are adjusted until the supply of lending matches the demand for borrowing at each loan term. As we shall see, expectations of future interest rate changes have a major effect on investors' willingness to lend or borrow for longer terms and, therefore, on the shape of the yield curve.

federal funds rate The overnight loan rate charged by banks with excess reserves at a Federal Reserve bank (called *federal funds*) to banks that need additional funds to meet reserve requirements.

Suppose short-term interest rates are equal to long-term interest rates. If interest rates are expected to rise in the future, investors would not want to make long-term investments. Instead, they could do better by investing on a short-term basis and then reinvesting after interest rates rise. Thus, if interest rates are expected to rise, long-term interest rates will tend to be higher than short-term rates to attract investors.

Similarly, if interest rates are expected to fall in the future, then borrowers would not wish to borrow at long-term rates that are equal to short-term rates. They would do better by borrowing on a short-term basis, and then taking out a new loan after rates fall. So, if interest rates are expected to fall, long-term rates will tend to be lower than short-term rates to attract borrowers.

Yield Curve Shape. These arguments indicate that the shape of the yield curve will be strongly influenced by interest rate expectations. A sharply increasing (*steep*) yield curve, with long-term rates much higher than short-term rates, generally indicates that interest rates are expected to rise in the future. A decreasing (*inverted*) yield curve, with long-term rates lower than short-term rates, generally signals an expected decline in future interest rates. Because interest rates tend to drop in response to a slowdown in the economy, an inverted yield curve is often interpreted as a negative forecast for economic growth. Indeed, as Figure 5.5 illustrates, each of the last seven recessions in the United States was preceded by a period in which the yield curve was inverted (note the red shaded areas before the gray

FIGURE 5.5

Short-Term Versus Long-Term U.S. Interest Rates and Recessions

One-year and 10-year U.S. Treasury rates are plotted, with the spread between them shaded in green if the shape of the yield curve is increasing (the one-year rate is below the 10-year rate) and in red if the yield curve is inverted (the one-year rate exceeds the 10-year rate). Gray bars show the dates of U.S. recessions as determined by the National Bureau of Economic Research. Note that inverted yield curves tend to precede recessions as determined by the National Bureau of Economic Research. In recessions, interest rates tend to fall, with short-term rates dropping further. As a result, the yield curve tends to be steep coming out of a recession.

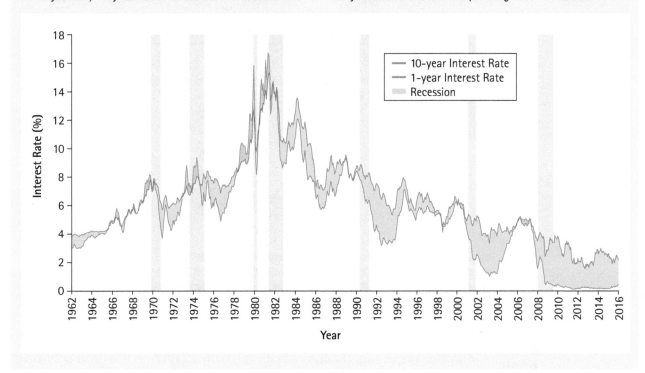

bars indicating a recession). Conversely, the yield curve tends to be steep (shaded green) as the economy comes out of a recession and interest rates are expected to rise.

The normal shape of the yield curve is moderately upward sloping. This would be the case if investors almost always believed that interest rates were going to rise in the future. But that is unlikely, so there have to be other forces at work to cause long-term interest rates normally to be higher than short-term rates. The most commonly cited reason is that long-term loans are riskier than short-term loans. If you make a 30-year loan today and lock in the interest rate, the present value of the payments you receive on the loan is very sensitive to even small changes in market interest rates. This sensitivity is due to the effect of compounding a change in interest rates over a 30-year period. To see this effect, consider Example 5.6.

EXAMPLE 5.6

Long-Term Versus Short-Term Loans

MyFinanceLab

PROBLEM

You work for a bank that has just made two loans. In one, you lent $909.09 today in return for $1000 in one year. In the other, you lent $909.09 today in return for $15,863.08 in 30 years. The difference between the loan amount and repayment amount is based on an interest rate of 10% per year. Imagine that immediately after you make the loans, news about economic growth is announced that increases inflation expectations, so that the market interest rate for loans like these jumps to 11%. Loans make up a major part of a bank's assets, so you are naturally concerned about the value of these loans. What is the effect of the interest rate change on the value to the bank of the promised repayment of these loans?

(Continued)

SOLUTION

PLAN

Each of these loans has only one repayment cash flow at the end of the loan. They differ only by the time to repayment:

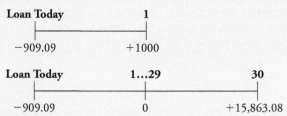

The effect on the value of the future repayment to the bank today is just the PV of the loan repayment, calculated at the new market interest rate.

EXECUTE

For the one-year loan:

$$PV = \frac{\$1000}{(1.11)^1} = \$900.90$$

For the 30-year loan:

$$PV = \frac{\$15,863.08}{(1.11)^{30}} = \$692.94$$

EVALUATE

The value of the one-year loan decreased by $909.09 − $900.90 = $8.19, or 0.9%, but the value of the 30-year loan decreased by $909.09 − $692.94 = $216.15, or almost 24%! The small change in market interest rates, compounded over a longer period, resulted in a much larger change in the present value of the loan repayment. You can see why investors and banks view longer-term loans as being riskier than short-term loans.

In addition to specifying the discount rates for risk-free cash flows that occur at different horizons, it is also a potential leading indicator of future economic growth. Due to these qualities, the yield curve provides extremely important information for a business manager.

5. What is the difference between a nominal and real interest rate?

6. How are interest rates and the level of investment made by businesses related?

5.4 The Opportunity Cost of Capital

**opportunity cost of capital
or cost of capital** The best
available expected return
offered in the market on an
investment of comparable
risk and term to the cash
flow being discounted; the
return the investor forgoes
on an alternative investment
of equivalent risk and term
when the investor takes on
a new investment.

As we have seen in this chapter, the interest rates we observe in the market will vary based on quoting conventions, the term of the investment, and risk. In this chapter, we have developed the tools to account for these differences and gained insights into how interest rates are determined. This knowledge will provide the foundation for our study of bonds in Chapter 6.

In Chapter 3, we argued that the Valuation Principle tells us to use the "market interest rate" to compute present values and evaluate an investment opportunity. But with so many interest rates to choose from, the term "market interest rate" is inherently ambiguous. Therefore, going forward in the book, we will base the discount rate that we use to evaluate cash flows on the investor's **opportunity cost of capital** (or more simply, the **cost of capital**), which is *the best available expected return offered in the market on an investment of comparable risk and term to the cash flow being discounted.*

Interest Rates, Discount Rates, and the Cost of Capital

By now, you may have noticed that we are using three terms to refer to rates of return. While many people use these terms interchangeably, they are distinct. Throughout this book, we will use "interest rate" to mean a quoted rate in the market. A "discount rate" is the appropriate rate for discounting a given cash flow, *matched to the frequency of the cash flow*. Finally, we use "cost of capital" to indicate the rate of return on an investment of similar risk.

In order to understand the definition of opportunity cost of capital, it helps to think of yourself as a financial manager competing with financial managers at other firms to attract investors' funds (capital). In order to attract investors to invest in your firm or creditors to lend to your firm, you have to be able to offer them an expected return at least as good as what they could get elsewhere in the market for the same risk and length of investment. Now it is easier to see where the term (opportunity) cost of capital comes from—investors in your firm are giving up the opportunity to invest their funds elsewhere. This is an opportunity cost to them and to overcome it you must offer them a return equal to or better than their opportunity cost of capital. Even if you already have the funds internally in the firm to invest, the logic still applies. You could either return the funds to your shareholders to invest elsewhere, or reinvest them in a new project; however, you should only reinvest them if doing so provides a better return than the shareholders' other opportunities.

The opportunity cost of capital is the return the investor forgoes when the investor takes on a new investment. For a risk-free project, it will typically correspond to the interest rate on U.S. Treasury securities with a similar term. But the cost of capital is a much more general concept that can be applied to risky investments as well.

EXAMPLE 5.7
The Opportunity Cost of Capital

MyFinanceLab

PROBLEM

Suppose a friend offers to borrow $100 from you today and in return pay you $110 one year from today. Looking in the market for other options for investing the $100, you find your best alternative option that you view as equally risky as lending it to your friend. That option has an expected return of 8%. What should you do?

SOLUTION

PLAN

Your decision depends on what the opportunity cost is of lending your money to your friend. If you lend her the $100, then you cannot invest it in the alternative with an 8% expected return. Thus, by making the loan, you are giving up the opportunity to invest for an 8% expected return. You can make your decision by using your 8% opportunity cost of capital to value the $110 in one year.

EXECUTE

The value of the $110 in one year is its present value, discounted at 8%:

$$PV = \frac{\$110}{(1.08)^1} = \$101.85$$

The $100 loan is worth $101.85 to you today, so you make the loan.

EVALUATE

The Valuation Principle tells us that we can determine the value of an investment by using market prices to value the benefits net of the costs. As this example shows, market prices determine what our best alternative opportunities are, so that we can decide whether an investment is worth the cost.

Chapter 3 introduced the Valuation Principle as a unifying theme in finance. In this and the preceding chapters, we have developed the fundamental tools a financial manager needs to value cash flows at different points in time. In this last section, we reiterated the importance of using market information to determine the opportunity cost of capital, which is your discount rate in valuation calculations. In Chapter 6, we will study bonds and how they are priced, which provides us with an immediate application of the knowledge we have built so far.

States Dig a $3 Trillion Hole by Discounting at the Wrong Rate

Almost all states in the United States offer their employees a defined benefit pension plan guaranteeing a retirement income based on the duration of their employment with the state and their final salary. These promised payments are the plan's liabilities—and because the payouts are guaranteed, they are comparable to a risk-free bond. To meet these liabilities, states put aside funds and invest them in risky assets like stocks and corporate bonds.

Unfortunately, states make a critical, but common, mistake when determining their funding requirements: They compute the present value of the liabilities using an arbitrary discount rate (typically 8%) that is unrelated to the riskiness of the plan's liabilities.

Because of their guaranteed nature, the risk-free rate, which is currently well below 8%, is the correct discount rate for plan liabilities.[5] This error has led states to grossly underestimate the value of their liabilities—and underfunded pension plans impose a potential future obligation on taxpayers. How large is this obligation? Professors Robert Novy-Marx and Joshua Rauh[6] found that total state pension underfunding in 2008 amounted to at least $3 *trillion*. They also estimated that there is less than a 5% probability that, over the next 15 years, states will be able to meet their pension obligations without turning to taxpayers. Worse still, states are most likely to need the money in market downturns, precisely when taxpayers are least able to pay.

CONCEPT CHECK

7. What is the opportunity cost of capital?
8. Can you ignore the cost of capital if you already have the funds inside the firm?

MyFinanceLab

Here is what you should know after reading this chapter. MyFinanceLab will help you identify what you know, and where to go when you need to practice.

KEY POINTS AND EQUATIONS	KEY TERMS	ONLINE PRACTICE
5.1 Interest Rate Quotes and Adjustments • Just like any other price, interest rates are set by market forces, in particular the supply and demand of funds. • The effective annual rate (EAR) (or annual percentage yield—APY) indicates the actual amount of interest earned in one year. The EAR can be used as a discount rate for annual cash flows. • Given an EAR r, the equivalent discount rate for an n-year time interval, where n may be more than one year or less than or equal to one year (a fraction), is: Equivalent n-period Discount Rate $$= (1 + r)^n - 1 \qquad (5.1)$$ • An annual percentage rate (APR) is a common way of quoting interest rates. The actual interest rate per period is the APR/number of compounding periods per year. APRs cannot be used as discount rates.	annual percentage rate (APR), p. 134 annual percentage yield (APY), 132 effective annual rate (EAR), p. 132 simple interest, p. 134	MyFinanceLab Study Plan 5.1

---

[5]States often justify the 8% rate as the return they expect to earn on their investments. But the risks of their investments and of their liabilities are not comparable (for example, the return on stocks is not guaranteed), so this argument is fundamentally flawed.

[6]R. Novy-Marx and J. Rau, The Liabilities and Risks of State-Sponsored Pension Plans, *Journal of Economic Perspectives* (Fall 2009) Vol. 23, No. 4.

- We need to know the compounding interval of an APR to determine the EAR:

$$1 + EAR = \left(1 + \frac{APR}{m}\right)^m \qquad (5.3)$$

m = number of compounding periods per year.
- For a given APR, the EAR increases with the compounding frequency.

5.2 Application: Discount Rates and Loans	amortizing loan, p. 137	MyFinanceLab Study Plan 5.2

5.2 Application: Discount Rates and Loans
- Loan rates are typically stated as APRs. The outstanding balance of a loan is equal to the present value of the loan cash flows, when evaluated using the actual interest rate per payment interval based on the loan rate.
- In each loan payment on an amortizing loan, you pay interest on the loan plus some part of the loan balance.

amortizing loan, p. 137

MyFinanceLab Study Plan 5.2

5.3 The Determinants of Interest Rates
- Quoted interest rates are nominal interest rates, which indicate the rate of growth of the money invested. The real interest rate indicates the rate of growth of one's purchasing power after adjusting for inflation.
- Given a nominal interest rate and an inflation rate, the real interest rate is:

$$\text{Real Rate} = \frac{\text{Nominal Rate} - \text{Inflation Rate}}{1 + \text{Inflation Rate}}$$

$$\approx \text{Nominal} - \text{Inflation Rate} \qquad (5.5)$$

- Nominal interest rates tend to be high when inflation is high and low when inflation is low.
- Higher interest rates tend to reduce the attractiveness of typical investment projects. The U.S. Federal Reserve raises interest rates to moderate investment and combat inflation and lowers interest rates to stimulate investment and economic growth.
- Interest rates differ with the investment horizon according to the term structure of interest rates. The graph plotting interest rates as a function of the horizon is called the yield curve.
- Cash flows should be discounted using the discount rate that is appropriate for their horizon. Thus, the PV of a cash flow stream is:

$$PV = \frac{C_1}{1 + r_1} + \frac{C_2}{(1 + r_2)^2} + \cdots + \frac{C_N}{(1 + r_N)^N} \qquad (5.7)$$

- Annuity and perpetuity formulas cannot be applied when discount rates vary with the horizon.

federal funds rate, p. 148
nominal interest rates, p. 141
real interest rate, p. 141
risk-free interest rate, p. 145
term structure, p. 145
yield curve, p. 145

MyFinanceLab Study Plan 5.3

Interactive Yield Curve

- The shape of the yield curve tends to vary with investors' expectations of future economic growth and interest rates. It tends to be inverted prior to recessions and to be steep coming out of a recession. Because investors view long-term loans as riskier, long-term rates are generally higher than short-term rates.

5.4 The Opportunity Cost of Capital	(opportunity) cost of	MyFinanceLab
• An investor's opportunity cost of capital (or simply, the cost of capital) is the best available expected return offered in the market on an investment of comparable risk and term to the cash flow being discounted.	capital, p. 150	Study Plan 5.4

CRITICAL THINKING

1. Explain how an interest rate is just a price.

2. Why is the EAR for 6% APR, with semiannual compounding, higher than 6%?

3. Why is it so important to match the frequency of the interest rate to the frequency of the cash flows?

4. Why aren't the payments for a 15-year mortgage twice the payments for a 30-year mortgage at the same rate?

5. What mistake do you make when you discount real cash flows with nominal discount rates?

6. How do changes in inflation expectations impact interest rates?

7. Can the nominal interest rate available to an investor be negative? (*Hint*: Consider the interest rate earned from saving cash "under the mattress.") Can the real interest rate be negative?

8. In the early 1980s, inflation was in the double-digits and the yield curve sloped sharply downward. What did the yield curve say about investors' expectations about future inflation rates?

9. What do we mean when we refer to the "opportunity cost" of capital?

PROBLEMS

All problems are available in MyFinanceLab. *The* icon *indicates problems that are easier to solve using Excel and have data in an Excel format available in* MyFinanceLab. *An asterisk * indicates problems with a higher level of difficulty.*

Interest Rate Quotes and Adjustments

1. You are considering a car loan with a stated APR of 6% based on monthly compounding. What is the effective annual rate of this loan?

2. Your bank is offering you an account that will pay 20% interest in total for a two-year deposit. Determine the equivalent discount rate for a period length of
   a. six months.
   b. one year.
   c. one month.

3. You are looking to buy a car and you have been offered a loan with an APR of 6%, compounded monthly.
   a. What is the true monthly rate of interest?
   b. What is the EAR?

4. You are considering two ways of financing a spring break vacation. You could put it on your credit card, at 15% APR, compounded monthly, or borrow the money from your parents, who want an 8% interest payment every six months. Which is the lower rate?

5. An online bank is offering to pay 0.25% interest per month on deposits. Your local bank offers to pay 0.75% interest quarterly (every 3 months). Which is the higher interest rate?

6. Which do you prefer: a bank account that pays 5% per year (EAR) for three years or
   a. an account that pays 2.5% every six months for three years?
   b. an account that pays 7.5% every 18 months for three years?
   c. an account that pays 0.5% per month for three years?

*7. You have been offered a job with an unusual bonus structure. As long as you stay with the firm, you will get an extra $70,000 every seven years, starting seven years from now. What is the present value of this incentive if you plan to work for the company for 42 years and the interest rate is 6% (EAR)?

8. You have found three investment choices for a one-year deposit: 10% APR compounded monthly, 10% APR compounded annually, and 9% APR compounded daily. Compute the EAR for each investment choice. (Assume that there are 365 days in the year.)

9. Your bank account pays interest with an EAR of 5%. What is the APR quote for this account based on semiannual compounding? What is the APR with monthly compounding?

10. Suppose the interest rate is 8% APR with monthly compounding. What is the present value of an annuity that pays $100 every six months for five years?

11. A payday loan is structured to obscure the true interest rate you are paying. For example, in Washington, you pay a $30 "fee" for a two-week $200 payday loan (when you repay the loan, you pay $230). What is the effective annual interest rate for this loan?

12. You have been accepted into college. The college guarantees that your tuition will not increase for the four years you attend. The first $10,000 tuition payment is due in six months. After that, the same payment is due every six months until you have made a total of eight payments. The college offers a bank account that allows you to withdraw money every six months and has a fixed APR of 4% (semiannual) guaranteed to remain the same over the next four years. How much money must you deposit today if you intend to make no further deposits and would like to make all the tuition payments from this account, leaving the account empty when the last payment is made?

Application: Discount Rates and Loans

13. You make monthly payments on your car loan. It has a quoted APR of 5% (monthly compounding). What percentage of the outstanding principal do you pay in interest each month?

14. Suppose Capital One is advertising a 60-month, 5.99% APR motorcycle loan. If you need to borrow $8000 to purchase your dream Harley-Davidson, what will your monthly payment be?

15. Assume you graduate from college with $30,000 in student loans. If your interest rate is fixed at 4.66% APR with monthly compounding and you will repay the loans over a 10-year period, what will be your monthly payment?

16. Ironwood Bank is offering a 30-year mortgage with an APR of 6.00% based on monthly compounding. If you plan to borrow $160,000, what will be your monthly payment?

17. You have just taken out a $20,000 car loan with a 6% APR, compounded monthly. The loan is for five years. When you make your first payment in one month, how much of the payment will go toward the principal of the loan and how much will go toward interest?

*18. Consider the loan from the previous question: a 60-month, $20,000 car loan with a 6% APR, compounded monthly. Assume that right after you make your 50th payment, the balance on the loan is $3,762.32. How much of your next payment goes toward principal and how much goes toward interest? Compare this with your answer in the last question—what is happening?

*19. You are buying a house and the mortgage company offers to let you pay a "point" (1% of the total amount of the loan) to reduce your APR from 6.5% to 6.25% on your $400,000, 30-year mortgage with monthly payments. If you plan to be in the house for at least five years, should you do it?

20. You have decided to refinance your mortgage. You plan to borrow whatever is outstanding on your current mortgage. The current monthly payment is $2356 and you have made every payment on time. The original term of the mortgage was 30 years, and the mortgage is exactly four years and eight months old. You have just made your monthly payment. The mortgage interest rate is 6.375% (APR). How much do you owe on the mortgage today?

*21. You have just sold your house for $1,000,000 in cash. Your mortgage was originally a 30-year mortgage with monthly payments and an initial balance of $800,000. The mortgage is currently exactly 18½ years old, and you have just made a payment. If the interest rate on the mortgage is 5.25% (APR), how much cash will you have from the sale once you pay off the mortgage?

22. You have just purchased a car and taken out a $50,000 loan. The loan has a five-year term with monthly payments and an APR of 6%.
    a. How much will you pay in interest, and how much will you pay in principal, during the first month, second month, and first year? (*Hint*: Compute the loan balance after one month, two months, and one year.)
    b. How much will you pay in interest, and how much will you pay in principal, during the fourth year (i.e., between three and four years from now)?

23. You are thinking about leasing a car. The purchase price of the car is $30,000. The residual value (the amount you could pay to keep the car at the end of the lease) is $15,000 at the end of 36 months. Assume the first lease payment is due one month after you get the car. The interest rate implicit in the lease is 6% APR, compounded monthly. What will your lease payments be for a 36-month lease?

*24. You have some extra cash this month and you are considering putting it toward your car loan. Your interest rate is 7%, your loan payments are $600 per month, and you have 36 months left on your loan. If you pay an additional $1000 with your next regular $600 payment (due in one month), how much will it reduce the amount of time left to pay off your loan?

*25. You have an outstanding student loan with required payments of $500 per month for the next four years. The interest rate on the loan is 9% APR (monthly). You are considering making an extra payment of $100 today (i.e., you will pay an extra $100 that you are not required to pay). If you are required to continue to make payments of $500 per month until the loan is paid off, what is the amount of your final payment? What rate of return (expressed as an APR with monthly compounding) have you earned on the $100?

*26. Consider again the setting of Problem 25. Now that you realize your best investment is to prepay your student loan, you decide to prepay as much as you can each month.

Looking at your budget, you can afford to pay an extra $250 per month in addition to your required monthly payments of $500, or $750 in total each month. How long will it take you to pay off the loan?

*27. Oppenheimer Bank is offering a 30-year mortgage with an APR of 5.25% based on monthly compounding. With this mortgage your monthly payments would be $2,000 per month. In addition, Oppenheimer Bank offers you the following deal: Instead of making the monthly payment of $2,000 every month, you can make half the payment every two weeks (so that you will make 52/2 = 26 payments per year). With this plan, how long will it take to pay off the mortgage if the EAR of the loan is unchanged?

*28. Your friend tells you he has a very simple trick for taking one-third off the time it takes to repay your mortgage: Use your Christmas bonus to make an extra payment on January 1 of each year (that is, pay your monthly payment due on that day twice). Assume that the mortgage has an original term of 30 years and an APR of 12%.
   a. If you take out your mortgage on January 1, so that your first payment is due on February 1, and you make your first extra payment at the end of the first year, in what year will you finish repaying your mortgage?
   b. If you take out your mortgage on July 1 (so the first payment is August 1) and make the extra payment each January, in how many months will you pay off your mortgage?
   c. How will the amount of time it takes to pay off the loan given this strategy vary with the interest rate on the loan?

29. The mortgage on your house is five years old. It required monthly payments of $1402, had an original term of 30 years, and had an interest rate of 10% (APR). In the intervening five years, interest rates have fallen and so you have decided to refinance—that is, you will roll over the outstanding balance into a new mortgage. The new mortgage has a 30-year term, requires monthly payments, and has an interest rate of $6\,5/8$% (APR).
   a. What monthly repayments will be required with the new loan?
   b. If you still want to pay off the mortgage in 25 years, what monthly payment should you make after you refinance?
   c. Suppose you are willing to continue making monthly payments of $1402. How long will it take you to pay off the mortgage after refinancing?
   d. Suppose you are willing to continue making monthly payments of $1402, and want to pay off the mortgage in 25 years. How much additional cash can you borrow today as part of the refinancing?

30. You have credit card debt of $25,000 that has an APR (monthly compounding) of 15%. Each month you pay the minimum monthly payment. You are required to pay only the outstanding interest. You have received an offer in the mail for an otherwise identical credit card with an APR of 12%. After considering all your alternatives, you decide to switch cards, roll over the outstanding balance on the old card into the new card, and borrow additional money as well. How much can you borrow today on the new card without changing the minimum monthly payment you will be required to pay?

31. Your firm has taken out a $500,000 loan with 9% APR (compounded monthly) for some commercial property. As is common in commercial real estate, the loan is a five-year loan based on a 15-year amortization. This means that your loan payments will be calculated as if you will take 15 years to pay off the loan, but you actually must do so in five years. To do this, you will make 59 equal payments based on the 15-year amortization schedule and then make a final 60th payment to pay the remaining balance.
   a. What will your monthly payments be?
   b. What will your final payment be?

*32. Five years ago you took out a 5/1 adjustable rate mortgage and the five-year fixed rate period has just expired. The loan was originally for $300,000 with 360 payments at 4.2% APR, compounded monthly.
   a. Now that you have made 60 payments, what is the remaining balance on the loan?
   b. If the interest rate increases by 1%, to 5.2% APR, compounded monthly, what will your new payments be?

The Determinants of Interest Rates

33. In 1975, interest rates were 7.85% and the rate of inflation was 12.3% in the United States. What was the real interest rate in 1975? How would the purchasing power of your savings have changed over the year?

34. If the rate of inflation is 5%, what nominal interest rate is necessary for you to earn a 3% real interest rate on your investment?

35. Assume the inflation rate is 3% APR, compounded annually. Would you rather earn a nominal return of 5% APR, compounded semiannually, or a real return of 2% APR, compounded quarterly?

36. Assume inflation is 0.2% per month. Would you rather earn a nominal return of 0.75% per month, or a real return of 6.5% APR, compounded annually?

37. You are pleased to see that you have been given a 5% raise this year. However, you read on the *Wall Street Journal* Web site that inflation over the past year has been 2%. How much better off are you in terms of real purchasing power?

38. What is the shape of the yield curve given in the following term structure? What expectations are investors likely to have about future interest rates?

Term (in years)	1	2	3	5	7	10	20
Rate (EAR, %)	1.99	2.41	2.74	3.32	3.76	4.13	4.93

39. See the Treasury Yield Curve from June 2013 below. At the time, some were concerned about whether the Federal Reserve's stimulus activities would lead to high inflation. Based on the Yield Curve, can you tell whether the bond market was concerned about inflation? Explain.

Term (in years)	1	2	3	5	7	10	30
Rate (EAR, %)	0.13	0.32	0.53	1.12	1.62	2.21	3.36

The Opportunity Cost of Capital

40. You are thinking about investing $5000 in your friend's landscaping business. Even though you know the investment is risky and you can't be sure, you expect your investment to be worth $5750 next year. You notice that the rate for one-year Treasury bills is 1%. However, you feel that other investments of equal risk to your friend's landscape business offer a 10% expected return for the year. What should you do?

41. You have invested in a business that proudly reports that it is profitable. Your investment of $5000 has produced a profit of $300. The managers think that if you leave your $5000 invested with them, they should be able to generate $300 per year in profits for you in perpetuity. Evaluating other investment opportunities, you note that other long-term investments of similar risk offer an expected return of 8%. Should you remain invested in this firm?

6

Bonds

LEARNING OBJECTIVES

- Understand bond terminology
- Compute the price and yield to maturity of a zero-coupon bond
- Compute the price and yield to maturity of a coupon bond
- Analyze why bond prices change over time
- Know how credit risk affects the expected return from holding a corporate bond

notation				
	CPN	coupon payment on a bond	*y*	yield to maturity
	FV	face value of a bond	*YTM*	yield to maturity
	n	number of periods	YTM_n	yield to maturity on a zero-coupon bond with n periods to maturity
	P	initial price of a bond		
	PV	present value		

In this chapter, we introduce bonds and apply our tools for valuing cash flows to them. Bonds are simply loans. When an investor buys a bond from an issuer, the investor is lending money to the bond issuer. Who are the issuers of bonds? Federal and local governments issue bonds to finance long-term projects, and many companies issue bonds as part of their debt financing.

Understanding bonds and their pricing is useful for several reasons. First, we can use the prices of risk-free government bonds to determine the risk-free interest rates that produce the yield curves discussed in Chapter 5. As we saw there, the yield curve provides important information for valuing risk-free cash flows and assessing expectations of inflation and economic growth. Second, firms often issue bonds to fund their own investments. The return investors receive on those bonds is one factor that determines a firm's cost of capital. Finally, bonds provide an opportunity to begin our study of how securities are priced in a competitive market. The bond markets are very large and very liquid; there are more than $39 *trillion* of bonds outstanding in the U.S. markets alone.[1] Further, the ideas we develop in this chapter will be helpful when we turn to the topic of valuing stocks in Chapter 7.

Pricing bonds gives us an opportunity to apply what we've learned in the last three chapters about valuing cash flows using competitive market prices. As we explained in Chapter 3, the Valuation Principle implies that the price of a security in a competitive market should be the present value of the cash flows an investor will receive from owning it. Thus, we begin the chapter by evaluating the promised cash flows for different types of bonds. If a bond is risk-free, so that the promised cash flows will be paid with certainty, we can use the Law of One Price to directly relate the return of a bond and its price. We then discuss how and why bond prices change over time. Once we have a firm understanding of the pricing of bonds in the absence of risk, we add the risk of default, where cash flows are not known with certainty. The risk of default and its implications are important considerations for a financial manager who is considering issuing corporate bonds. (In Chapter 15, we will discuss the details of issuing debt financing and cover some additional corporate bond features.)

6.1   Bond Terminology

bond certificate States the terms of a bond as well as the amounts and dates of all payments to be made.

maturity date The final repayment date of a bond.

term The time remaining until the final repayment date of a bond.

face value, par value, principal amount The notional amount of a bond used to compute its interest payments. The face value of the bond is generally due at the bond's maturity.

coupons The promised interest payments of a bond, paid periodically until the maturity date of the bond.

coupon rate Determines the amount of each coupon payment of a bond. The coupon rate, expressed as an APR, is set by the issuer and stated on the bond certificate.

Recall from Chapter 1 that a bond is a security sold by governments and corporations to raise money from investors today in exchange for a promised future payment. The terms of the bond are described as part of the **bond certificate**, which indicates the amounts and dates of all payments to be made. A bond certificate is shown in Figure 6.1. Payments on the bond are made until a final repayment date called the **maturity date** of the bond. The time remaining until the repayment date is known as the **term** of the bond.

Bonds typically make two types of payments to their holders. The principal or **face value** (also known as **par value** or **principal amount**) of a bond is the notional amount we use to compute the interest payments. Typically, the face value is repaid at maturity. It is generally denominated in standard increments such as $1000. A bond with a $1000 face value, for example, is often referred to as a "$1000 bond."

In addition to the face value, some bonds also promise additional payments called **coupons**. The bond certificate typically specifies that the coupons will be paid periodically (for example, semiannually) until the maturity date of the bond. As you can see from Figure 6.1, historically, on a payment date, the holder of the bond would clip off the next coupon for the next payment and present it for payment. It follows that the interest payments on the bond are called *coupon payments*. Today, the majority of bonds are registered electronically but the term remains.

The amount of each coupon payment is determined by the **coupon rate** of the bond. This coupon rate is set by the issuer and stated on the bond certificate. By convention, the coupon rate is expressed as an APR, so the amount of each coupon payment, *CPN*, is:

Coupon Payment

$$CPN = \frac{\text{Coupon Rate} \times \text{Face Value}}{\text{Number of Coupon Payments per Year}} \tag{6.1}$$

For example, a "$1000 bond with a 10% coupon rate and semiannual payments" will pay coupon payments of $(10\% \times \$1000)/2 = \$50$ every six months.

Table 6.1 summarizes the bond terminology we have presented thus far.

---

[1] Outstanding U.S. Bond Market Debt, www.sifma.org. December 2009.

FIGURE 6.1

A Bearer Bond and Its Unclipped Coupons Issued by the Elmira and Williamsport Railroad Company for $500

Source: Courtesy Heritage Auctions, Inc. © 1999–2006.

TABLE 6.1

Review of Bond Terminology

Bond Certificate	States the terms of a bond as well as the amounts and dates of all payments to be made.
Coupons	The promised interest payments of a bond. Usually paid semiannually, but the frequency is specified in the bond certificate. They are determined by the coupon rate, which is stated on the bond certificate. The amount paid is equal to: $$\frac{\text{Coupon Rate} \times \text{Face Value}}{\text{Number of Coupon Payments per Year}}$$
Maturity Date	Final repayment date of the bond. Payments continue until this date.
Principal or Face Value	The notional amount used to compute the interest payment. It is usually repaid on the maturity date. Also called *par value*.
Term	The time remaining until the repayment date.

CONCEPT CHECK

1. What types of cash flows does a bond buyer receive?

2. How are the periodic coupon payments on a bond determined?

6.2 Zero-Coupon Bonds

zero-coupon bond A bond that makes only one payment at maturity.

Treasury bills Zero-coupon bonds, issued by the U.S. government, with a maturity of up to one year.

Not all bonds have coupon payments. Bonds without coupons are called **zero-coupon bonds**. As these are the simplest type of bond, we shall analyze them first. The only cash payment an investor in a zero-coupon bond receives is the face value of the bond on the maturity date. **Treasury bills**, which are U.S. government bonds with a maturity of up to one year, are zero-coupon bonds. The general name for risk-free zero coupon bonds is "STRIPS," which is an abbreviation of Separately Tradable Registered Interest and Principal Securities.

Zero-Coupon Bond Cash Flows

There are only two cash flows if we purchase and hold a zero-coupon bond. First, we pay the bond's current market price at the time we make the purchase. Then, at the maturity date, we receive the bond's face value. For example, suppose that a one-year, risk-free, zero-coupon bond with a $100,000 face value has an initial price of $96,618.36. If you purchased this bond and held it to maturity, you would have the following cash flows:

discount A price at which bonds trade that is less than their face value.

pure discount bonds Zero-coupon bonds.

Note that although the bond pays no "interest" directly, as an investor you are compensated for the time value of your money by purchasing the bond at a discount to its face value. Recall from Chapter 3 that the present value of a future cash flow is less than the cash flow itself. As a result, prior to its maturity date, the price of a zero-coupon bond is always less than its face value. That is, zero-coupon bonds always trade at a **discount** (a price lower than the face value), so they are also called **pure discount bonds**.

Yield to Maturity of a Zero-Coupon Bond

yield to maturity (YTM) The rate of return of an investment in a bond that is held to its maturity date, or the discount rate that sets the present value of the promised bond payments equal to the current market price of the bond.

Now that we understand the cash flows associated with a zero-coupon bond, we can calculate the rate of return of buying a bond and holding it until maturity. Recall from Chapter 4 that we can always find the rate of return of an investment opportunity as the discount rate that equates the present value of the investment to its costs. With a zero-coupon bond, the price is the cost of the bond. So, the rate of return on the zero-coupon bond is the discount rate that makes the present value of the future cash flow received (that is, the bond principal) equal to the cost of the bond. We can extend this concept to a coupon bond: the rate of return is the discount rate at which the present value of all future cash flows from the bond equals the price of the bond. The rate of return of an investment in a bond is given a special name, the **yield to maturity (YTM)** or just the *yield*:

> *The yield to maturity of a bond is the discount rate that sets the present value of the promised bond payments equal to the current market price of the bond.*

Intuitively, the yield to maturity for a zero-coupon bond is the return you will earn as an investor by buying the bond at its current market price, holding the bond to maturity, and receiving the promised face value payment.

Let's determine the yield to maturity of the one-year zero-coupon bond discussed earlier. According to the definition, the yield to maturity of the one-year bond solves the following equation:

$$96{,}618.36 = \frac{100{,}000}{1 + YTM_1}$$

In this case:

$$1 + YTM_1 = \frac{100{,}000}{96{,}618.36} = 1.035$$

That is, the yield to maturity for this bond is 3.5%. Because the bond is risk free, investing in this bond and holding it to maturity is like earning 3.5% interest on your initial investment:

$$\$96{,}618.36 \times 1.035 = \$100{,}000$$

GLOBAL FINANCIAL CRISIS

Negative Bond Yields

On December 9, 2008, in the midst of one of the worst financial crises in history, the unthinkable happened: For the first time since the Great Depression, U.S. Treasury Bills traded at a negative yield. That is, these risk-free pure discount bonds traded at premium. As Bloomberg.com reported: "If you invested $1 million in three-month bills at today's negative discount rate of 0.01%, for a price of 100.002556, at maturity you would receive the par value for a loss of $25.56."

A negative yield on a Treasury bill implies that investors have an arbitrage opportunity: By selling the bill, and holding the proceeds in cash, they would have a risk-free profit of $25.56. Why did investors not rush to take advantage of the arbitrage opportunity and thereby eliminate it?

Well, first, the negative yields did not last very long, suggesting that, in fact, investors did rush to take advantage of this opportunity. But second, after closer consideration, the opportunity might not have been a sure risk-free arbitrage. When selling a Treasury security, the investor must choose where to invest, or at least hold, the proceeds. In normal times, investors would be happy to deposit the proceeds with a bank, and consider this deposit to be risk free. But these were not normal times—many investors had great concerns about the financial stability of banks and other financial intermediaries. Perhaps investors shied away from this "arbitrage" opportunity because they were worried that the cash they would receive could not be held safely anywhere (even putting it "under the mattress" has a risk of theft!). Thus, we can view the $25.56 as the price investors were willing to pay to have the U.S. Treasury hold their money safely for them at a time when no other investments seemed truly safe.

This phenomenon repeated itself in Europe starting in mid-2012. In this case, negative yields emerged due to a concern about the both the safety of European banks as well as the stability of the euro as a currency. As investors in Greece or other countries began to worry their economies might depart from the euro, they were willing to hold German and Swiss government bonds even at negative yields as a way to protect themselves against the Eurozone unraveling. By mid-2015, almost 25% of European government bonds had negative yields, with some Swiss bonds having yields close to −1%!

These persistent and significantly negative yields are challenging to explain. Most of the holders of these bonds are institutions and pension funds who are restricted to hold very safe assets. And while they could hold currency instead, obtaining, storing, and securing large quantities of cash would also be very costly. (Indeed, Swiss banks have reportedly refused large currency withdrawals by hedge funds attempting to exploit the arbitrage opportunity.) Bonds are also much easier to trade, and use as collateral, than giant vaults of cash. Together, the safety and convenience of these bonds must be worth the nearly 1% per year these investors are willing to sacrifice.

We can use a similar method to find the yield to maturity for any maturity zero-coupon bond:

Yield to Maturity of an n-Year Zero-Coupon Bond

$$1 + YTM_n = \left(\frac{\text{Face Value}}{\text{Price}} \right)^{1/n} \tag{6.2}$$

The yield to maturity (YTM_n) in Eq. 6.2 is the per-period rate of return for holding the bond from today until maturity on date n.

EXAMPLE 6.1

Yields for Different Maturities

MyFinanceLab

PROBLEM

Suppose the following zero-coupon bonds are trading at the prices shown below per $100 face value. Determine the corresponding yield to maturity for each bond.

Maturity	1 year	2 years	3 years	4 years
Price	$96.62	$92.45	$87.63	$83.06

SOLUTION

PLAN

We can use Eq. 6.2 to solve for the YTM of the bonds. The table gives the prices and number of years to maturity and the face value is $100 per bond.

EXECUTE

Using Eq. 6.2, we have

$$YTM_1 = (100/96.62)^{1/1} - 1 = 3.50\%$$
$$YTM_2 = (100/92.45)^{1/2} - 1 = 4.00\%$$

(Continued)

$$YTM_3 = (100/87.63)^{1/3} - 1 = 4.50\%$$

$$YTM_4 = (100/83.06)^{1/4} - 1 = 4.75\%$$

EVALUATE

Solving for the YTM of a zero-coupon bond is the same process we used to solve for the rate of return in Chapter 4. Indeed, the YTM is the rate of return of buying the bond.

Risk-Free Interest Rates

Above, we calculated the yield to maturity of the one-year risk-free bond as 3.5%. But recall that the Valuation Principle's Law of One Price implies that all one-year risk-free investments must earn this same return of 3.5%. That is, 3.5% must be *the* competitive-market risk-free interest rate.

More generally, in Chapter 5, we discussed the competitive market interest rate r_n available from today until date n for risk-free cash flows. Recall that we used this interest rate as the cost of capital for a risk-free cash flow that occurs on date n. A default-free zero-coupon bond that matures on date n provides a risk-free return over the same period. So the Law of One Price guarantees that the risk-free interest rate equals the yield to maturity on such a bond. Consequently, we will often refer to the yield to maturity of the appropriate maturity, zero-coupon risk-free bond as *the* risk-free interest rate. Some financial professionals also use the term **spot interest rates** to refer to these default-free, zero-coupon yields because these rates are offered "on the spot" at that point in time.

In Chapter 5, we introduced the yield curve, which plots the risk-free interest rate for different maturities. These risk-free interest rates correspond to the yields of risk-free zero-coupon bonds. Thus, the yield curve we introduced in Chapter 5 is also referred to as the **zero-coupon yield curve**. Figure 6.2 illustrates the yield curve consistent with the zero-coupon bond prices in Example 6.1.

spot interest rates
Default-free, zero-coupon yields.

zero-coupon yield curve A plot of the yield of risk-free zero-coupon bonds (STRIPS) as a function of the bond's maturity date.

FIGURE 6.2

Zero-Coupon Yield Curve Consistent with the Bond Prices in Example 6.1

Recall from Chapter 5 that a yield curve simply plots the yield to maturity of investments of different maturities. In this figure, we show the yield curve that would be produced by plotting the yield to maturities determined by the bond prices in Example 6.1. Note that as in this figure, the longer maturities generally have higher yields.

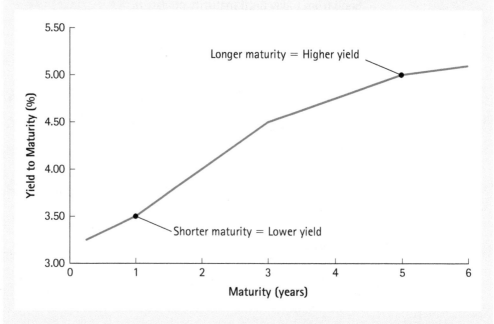

In Example 6.1, we used the bond's price to compute its yield to maturity. But from the definition of the yield to maturity, we can also use a bond's yield to compute its price. In the case of a zero-coupon bond, the price is simply equal to the present value of the bond's face value, discounted at the bond's yield to maturity.

EXAMPLE 6.2

Computing the Price of a Zero-Coupon Bond

MyFinanceLab

PROBLEM

Given the yield curve shown in Figure 6.2, what is the price of a five-year risk-free zero-coupon bond with a face value of $100?

SOLUTION

PLAN

We can compute the bond's price as the present value of its face amount, where the discount rate is the bond's yield to maturity. From the yield curve, the yield to maturity for five-year risk-free zero-coupon bonds is 5.0%.

EXECUTE

$$P = 100/(1.05)^5 = 78.35$$

EVALUATE

We can compute the price of a zero-coupon bond simply by computing the present value of the face amount using the bond's yield to maturity. Note that the price of the five-year zero-coupon bond is even lower than the price of the other zero-coupon bonds in Example 6.1, because the face amount is the same but we must wait longer to receive it.

CONCEPT CHECK

3. Why would you want to know the yield to maturity of a bond?

4. What is the relationship between a bond's price and its yield to maturity?

6.3 Coupon Bonds

coupon bonds Bonds that pay regular coupon interest payments up to maturity, when the face value is also paid.

Treasury notes A type of U.S. Treasury coupon security, currently traded in financial markets, with original maturities from one to ten years.

Treasury bonds A type of U.S. Treasury coupon security, currently traded in financial markets, with original maturities of more than ten years.

Similar to zero-coupon bonds, **coupon bonds** pay investors their face value at maturity. In addition, these bonds make regular coupon interest payments. As Table 6.2 indicates, two types of U.S. Treasury coupon securities are currently traded in financial markets: **Treasury notes**, which have original maturities from one to ten years, and **Treasury bonds**, which have original maturities of more than ten years. The original maturity is the term of the bond at the time it was originally issued.

TABLE 6.2

Existing U.S. Treasury Securities

Treasury Security	Type	Original Maturity
Bills	Discount	4, 13, 26, and 52 weeks
Notes	Coupon	2, 3, 5, and 10 year
Bonds	Coupon	20 and 30 year

Coupon Bond Cash Flows

While an investor's return on a zero-coupon bond comes from buying it at a discount to its principal value, the return on a coupon bond comes from two sources: (1) any difference between the purchase price and the principal value, and (2) its periodic coupon payments. Before we can compute the yield to maturity of a coupon bond, we need to know all of its cash flows, including the coupon interest payments and when they are paid. In Example 6.3, we take a bond description and translate it into the bond's cash flows.

EXAMPLE 6.3

The Cash Flows of a
Coupon Bond or Note

MyFinanceLab

PROBLEM

Assume that it is May 15, 2010, and the U.S. Treasury has just issued securities with a May 2015 maturity, $1000 par value, and a 2.2% coupon rate with semiannual coupons. Since the original maturity is only five years, these would be called "notes" as opposed to "bonds." The first coupon payment will be paid on November 15, 2010. What cash flows will you receive if you hold this note until maturity?

SOLUTION

PLAN

The description of the note should be sufficient to determine all of its cash flows. The phrase "May 2015 maturity, $1000 par value" tells us that this is a note with a face value of $1000 and five years to maturity. The phrase "2.2% coupon rate with semiannual coupons" tells us that the note pays a total of 2.2% of its face value each year in two equal semiannual installments. Finally, we know that the first coupon is paid on November 15, 2010.

EXECUTE

The face value of this note is $1000. Because this note pays coupons semiannually, using Eq. 6.1 you can compute that you will receive a coupon payment every six months of $CPN = (2.2\% \times \$1000)/2 = \$11$. Here is the timeline based on a six-month period and there are a total of 10 cash flows:

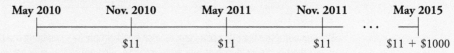

May 2010	Nov. 2010	May 2011	Nov. 2011		May 2015
	$11	$11	$11	...	$11 + $1000

Note that the last payment occurs five years (10 six-month periods) from now and is composed of both a coupon payment of $11 and the face value payment of $1000.

EVALUATE

Since a note is just a package of cash flows, we need to know those cash flows in order to value the note. That's why the description of the note contains all of the information we would need to construct its cash flow timeline.

The U.S. Treasury Market

In most years, the U.S. Federal Government spends more than it takes in through taxes and other revenue sources. To finance this deficit, the U.S. Department of the Treasury issues debt instruments, commonly known as "Treasuries." The market for Treasury securities is huge and extremely liquid. At the end of 2015, the total amount of public debt outstanding was over $18.15 *trillion*. Treasury securities are held by institutional investors such as insurance companies, pension funds and bond mutual funds, individual investors, and even other governmental agencies (such as the Federal Reserve) as shown in the pie chart below. The figures are in *billions* of dollars (7489 billion is 7.489 trillion).

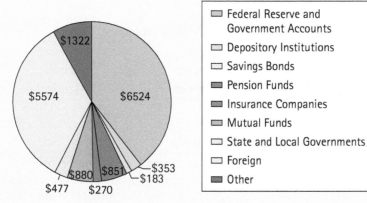

- Federal Reserve and Government Accounts
- Depository Institutions
- Savings Bonds
- Pension Funds
- Insurance Companies
- Mutual Funds
- State and Local Governments
- Foreign
- Other

Source: Treasury Bulletin Ownership of Federal Securities, https://www.fiscal.treasury.gov/fsreports/rpt/treasBulletin/treasBulletin_home.htm, September 2015.

Yield to Maturity of a Coupon Bond

Once we have determined the coupon bond's cash flows, given its market price we can determine its yield to maturity. Recall that the yield to maturity for a bond is the rate of return of investing in the bond and holding it to maturity. This investment has the cash flows shown in the timeline below:

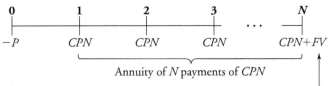

The yield to maturity of the bond is the *single* discount rate that equates the present value of the bond's remaining cash flows to its current price. For zero-coupon bonds, there were only two cash flows. But coupon bonds have many cash flows, complicating the yield to maturity calculation. From the timeline, we see that the coupon payments represent an annuity, so the yield to maturity is the interest rate y that solves the following equation:

Yield to Maturity of a Coupon Bond

$$P = CPN \times \frac{1}{y}\left(1 - \frac{1}{(1+y)^N}\right) + \frac{FV}{(1+y)^N} \qquad (6.3)$$

Present Value of all of the periodic coupon payments — Present Value of the Face Value repayment using the YTM (y)

Annuity Factor using the YTM (y)

Unfortunately, unlike zero-coupon bonds, there is no simple formula to solve for the yield to maturity directly. Instead, we need to use either trial and error or, more commonly, a financial calculator or a spreadsheet (both of which we demonstrate in Example 6.4).

When we calculate a bond's yield to maturity by solving Eq. 6.3, the yield we compute will be a rate *per coupon interval*. However, yields are typically quoted as APRs, so we multiply by the number of coupons per year, thereby converting the answer into an APR quote with the same compounding interval as the coupon rate.

EXAMPLE 6.4

Computing the Yield to Maturity of a Coupon Bond

MyFinanceLab

PROBLEM

Consider the five-year, $1000 bond with a 2.2% coupon rate and semiannual coupons described in Example 6.3. If this bond is currently trading for a price of $963.11, what is the bond's yield to maturity?

SOLUTION

PLAN

We worked out the bond's cash flows in Example 6.3. From the cash flow timeline, we can see that the bond consists of an annuity of 10 payments of $11, paid every six months, and one lump-sum payment of $1000 in five years (in 10 six-month periods). We can use Eq. 6.3 to solve for the yield to maturity. However, we must use six-month intervals consistently throughout the equation.

EXECUTE

Because the bond has 10 remaining coupon payments, we compute its yield y by solving Eq. 6.3 for this bond:

$$963.11 = 11 \times \frac{1}{y}\left(1 - \frac{1}{(1+y)^{10}}\right) + \frac{1000}{(1+y)^{10}}$$

(Continued)

We can solve it by trial and error, a financial calculator, or a spreadsheet. To use a financial calculator, we enter the price we pay as a negative number for the PV (it is a cash outflow), the coupon payments as the PMT, and the bond's par value as its FV. Finally, we enter the number of coupon payments remaining (10) as N.

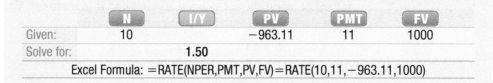

	N	I/Y	PV	PMT	FV
Given:	10		−963.11	11	1000
Solve for:		1.50			

Excel Formula: =RATE(NPER,PMT,PV,FV)=RATE(10,11,−963.11,1000)

Therefore, $y = 1.5\%$. Because the bond pays coupons semiannually, this yield is for a six-month period. We convert it to an APR by multiplying by the number of coupon payments per year. Thus, the bond has a yield to maturity equal to a 3% APR with semiannual compounding.

EVALUATE

As the equation shows, the yield to maturity is the discount rate that equates the present value of the bond's cash flows with its price. Note that the YTM is higher than the coupon rate and the price is lower than the par value. We will discuss why in the next section.

We can also use Eq. 6.3 to compute a bond's price based on its yield to maturity. We simply discount the cash flows using the yield, as in Example 6.5.

PROBLEM

Consider again the five-year, $1000 bond with a 2.2% coupon rate and semiannual coupons in Example 6.4. Suppose interest rates drop and the bond's yield to maturity decreases to 2% (expressed as an APR with semiannual compounding). What price is the bond trading for now? And what is the effective annual yield on this bond?

SOLUTION

PLAN

Given the yield, we can compute the price using Eq. 6.3. First, note that a 2% APR is equivalent to a semiannual rate of 1%. Also, recall that the cash flows of this bond are an annuity of 10 payments of $11, paid every six months, and one lump-sum cash flow of $1000 (the face value), paid in five years (10 six-month periods). In Chapter 5, we learned how to compute an effective annual rate from an APR using Eq. 5.3. We do the same here to compute the effective annual yield from the bond's yield to maturity expressed as an APR.

EXECUTE

Using Eq. 6.3 and the six-month yield of 1%, the bond price must be:

$$P = 11 \times \frac{1}{0.01}\left(1 - \frac{1}{1.01^{10}}\right) + \frac{1000}{1.01^{10}} = \$1009.47$$

We can also use a financial calculator or spreadsheet:

	N	I/Y	PV	PMT	FV
Given:	10	1		11	1000
Solve for:			−1009.47		

Excel Formula: =PV(RATE,NPER,PMT,FV)=PV(.01,10,11,1000)

The effective annual yield corresponding to 1% every six months is:

$$(1 + .01)^2 - 1 = .0201, \text{ or } 2.01\%$$

EVALUATE

The bond's price has risen to $1009.47, lowering the return from investing in it from 1.5% to 1% per six-month period. Interest rates have dropped, so the lower return brings the bond's yield into line with the lower competitive rates being offered for similar risk and maturity elsewhere in the market.

 Finding Bond Prices on the Web

Unlike the NYSE where many stocks are traded, there is no particular physical location where bonds are traded. Instead, they are traded electronically. Recently, the Financial Industry Regulatory Authority (FINRA) has made an effort

to make bond prices more widely available. Their Web site, http://finra-markets.morningstar.com/BondCenter/Default.jsp, allows anyone to search for the most recent trades and quotes for bonds. Here, we show a screenshot from the Web site displaying the pricing information for one of Procter and Gamble's (PG) bonds.

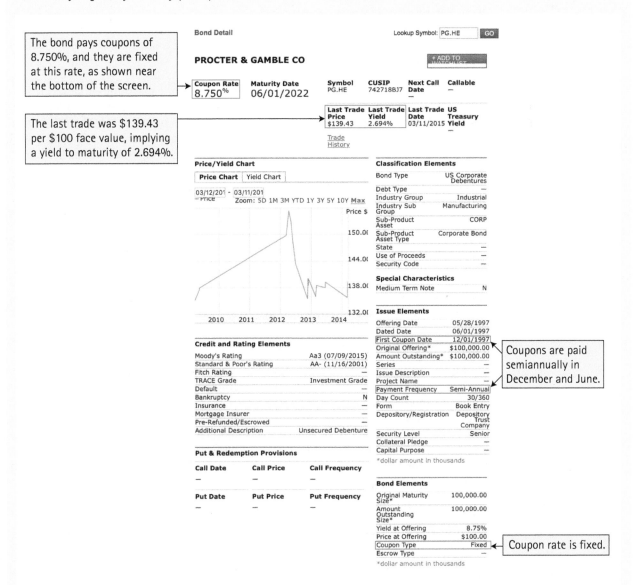

The bond pays coupons of 8.750%, and they are fixed at this rate, as shown near the bottom of the screen.

The last trade was $139.43 per $100 face value, implying a yield to maturity of 2.694%.

Coupons are paid semiannually in December and June.

Coupon rate is fixed.

Coupon Bond Price Quotes

Because we can convert any price into a yield, and vice versa, prices and yields are often used interchangeably. For example, the bond in Example 6.5 could be quoted as having a yield of 2% or a price of $1009.47 per $1000 face value. Indeed, bond traders generally quote bond yields rather than bond prices. One advantage of quoting the yield to maturity rather than the price is that the yield is independent of the face value of the bond. When prices are quoted in the bond market, they are conventionally quoted per $100 face value. Thus, the bond in Example 6.5 would be quoted as having a price of $100.947 (per $100 face value), which would imply an actual price of $1009.47 given the $1000 face value of the bond.

<table>
<tr><td>**CONCEPT CHECK**</td><td>5. What cash flows does a company pay to investors holding its coupon bonds?</td></tr>
<tr><td></td><td>6. What do we need in order to value a coupon bond?</td></tr>
</table>

6.4 Why Bond Prices Change

premium A price at which coupon bonds trade that is greater than their face value.

As we mentioned earlier, zero-coupon bonds always trade for a discount—that is, prior to maturity, their price is less than their face value. But as shown in Examples 6.4 and 6.5, coupon bonds may trade at a discount, or at a **premium** (a price greater than their face value). In this section, we identify when a bond will trade at a discount or premium, as well as how the bond's price will change due to the passage of time and fluctuations in interest rates.

par A price at which coupon bonds trade that is equal to their face value.

Most issuers of coupon bonds choose a coupon rate so that the bonds will *initially* trade at, or very close to, **par** (that is, at the bond's face value). For example, the U.S. Treasury sets the coupon rates on its notes and bonds in this way. After the issue date, the market price of a bond generally changes over time for two reasons. First, as time passes, the bond gets closer to its maturity date. Holding fixed the bond's yield to maturity, the present value of the bond's remaining cash flows changes as the time to maturity decreases. Second, at any point in time, changes in market interest rates affect the bond's yield to maturity and its price (the present value of the remaining cash flows). We explore these two effects in the remainder of this section.

Interest Rate Changes and Bond Prices

If a bond sells at par (at its face value), the only return investors will earn is from the coupons that the bond pays. Therefore, the bond's coupon rate will exactly equal its yield to maturity. As interest rates in the economy fluctuate, the yields that investors demand to invest in bonds will also change. Imagine that your company issues a bond when market interest rates imply a YTM of 8%, setting the coupon rate to be 8%. Suppose interest rates then rise so that new bonds have a YTM of 9%. These new bonds would have a coupon rate of 9% and sell for $1000. So, for $1000, the investor would get $90 per year until the bond matured. Your existing bond was issued when rates were lower such that its coupon is fixed at 8%, so it offers payments of $80 per year until maturity. Because its cash flows are lower, the 8% bond must have a lower price than the 9% bond.[2] Thus, the price of the 8% bond will fall until the investor is indifferent between buying the 8% bond and buying the 9% bond. Figure 6.3 illustrates the relationship between the bond's price and its yield to maturity.

---

[2]Otherwise, if the 8% bond had the same or higher price, there would be an arbitrage opportunity: One could sell the 8% bond and buy the 9% bond, receiving cash today and higher coupons going forward.

In our example, the price of the 8% bond will drop to below face value ($1000), so it will be trading at a discount (also called trading *below par*). If the bond trades at a discount, an investor who buys the bond will earn a return both from receiving the coupons *and* from receiving a face value that exceeds the price paid for the bond. As a result, if a bond trades at a discount, its yield to maturity will exceed its coupon rate.

A bond that pays a coupon can also trade at a premium to its face value (trading *above par*). Imagine what would have happened in our example if interest rates had gone down to 7% instead of up to 9%. Then, the holder of the existing 8% bond would not part with it for $1000. Instead, its price would have to rise until the yield to maturity from buying it at that price would be 7%. In this case, an investor's return from the coupons is diminished by receiving a face value less than the price paid for the bond. *Thus, a bond trades at a premium whenever its yield to maturity is less than its coupon rate.*[3]

FIGURE 6.3

A Bond's Price Versus Its Yield to Maturity

At a price of $1000, the 8% semiannual coupon bond offers an 8% YTM. In order for the 8% coupon bond to offer a competitive yield to maturity, its price must fall until its yield to maturity rises to the 9% yield being offered by otherwise similar bonds. In the example depicted here, for a bond with five years left to maturity, its price must fall to $960.44 before investors will be indifferent between buying it and the 9% coupon bond priced at $1000. The curve depicts this bond's price at yields to maturity between 6% and 10%.

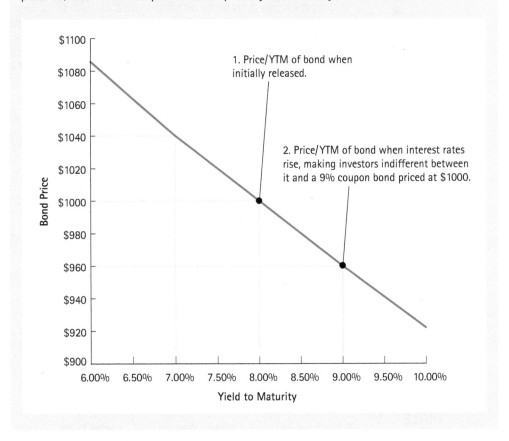

---

[3]The terms "discount" and "premium" are simply descriptive and are not meant to imply that you should try to buy bonds at a discount and avoid buying bonds at a premium. In a competitive market, the Law of One Price ensures that all similar bonds are priced to earn the same return. When you buy a bond, the price exactly equals the present value of the bond's cash flows, so that you earn a fair return, but not an abnormally good (or bad) return.

This example illustrates a general phenomenon. A higher yield to maturity means that investors demand a higher return for investing. They apply a higher discount rate to the bond's remaining cash flows, reducing their present value and hence the bond's price. The reverse holds when interest rates fall. Investors then demand a lower yield to maturity, reducing the discount rate applied to the bond's cash flows and raising the price. Therefore, *as interest rates and bond yields rise, bond prices will fall, and vice versa, so that interest rates and bond prices always move in the opposite direction.*

Table 6.3 summarizes the relationship between interest rates and bond prices.

EXAMPLE 6.6

Determining the Discount or Premium of a Coupon Bond

MyFinanceLab

PROBLEM

Consider three 30-year bonds with annual coupon payments. One bond has a 10% coupon rate, one has a 5% coupon rate, and one has a 3% coupon rate. If the yield to maturity of each bond is 5%, what is the price of each bond per $100 face value? Which bond trades at a premium, which trades at a discount, and which trades at par?

SOLUTION

PLAN

From the description of the bonds, we can determine their cash flows. Each bond has 30 years to maturity and pays its coupons annually. Therefore, each bond has an annuity of coupon payments, paid annually for 30 years, and then the face value paid as a lump sum in 30 years. They are all priced so that their yield to maturity is 5%, meaning that 5% is the discount rate that equates the present value of the cash flows to the price of the bond. Therefore, we can use Eq. 6.3 to compute the price of each bond as the PV of its cash flows, discounted at 5%.

EXECUTE

For the 10% coupon bond, the annuity cash flows are $10 per year (10% of each $100 face value). Similarly, the annuity cash flows for the 5% and 3% bonds are $5 and $3 per year. We use a $100 face value for all of the bonds.

Using Eq. 6.3 and these cash flows, the bond prices are:

$$P(10\% \text{ coupon}) = 10 \times \frac{1}{0.05}\left(1 - \frac{1}{1.05^{30}}\right) + \frac{100}{1.05^{30}} = \$176.86 \text{ (trades at a premium)}$$

$$P(5\% \text{ coupon}) = 5 \times \frac{1}{0.05}\left(1 - \frac{1}{1.05^{30}}\right) + \frac{100}{1.05^{30}} = \$100.00 \text{ (trades at par)}$$

$$P(3\% \text{ coupon}) = 3 \times \frac{1}{0.05}\left(1 - \frac{1}{1.05^{30}}\right) + \frac{100}{1.05^{30}} = \$69.26 \text{ (trades at a discount)}$$

EVALUATE

The prices reveal that when the coupon rate of the bond is higher than its yield to maturity, it trades at a premium. When its coupon rate equals its yield to maturity, it trades at par. When its coupon rate is lower than its yield to maturity, it trades at a discount.

TABLE 6.3

Bond Prices Immediately After a Coupon Payment

When the bond price is ...	greater than the face value	equal to the face value	less than the face value
We say the bond trades ...	"above par" or "at a premium"	"at par"	"below par" or "at a discount"
This occurs when ...	Coupon Rate > Yield to Maturity	Coupon Rate = Yield to Maturity	Coupon Rate < Yield to Maturity

Time and Bond Prices

Let's consider the effect of time on the price of a bond. As the next payment from a bond grows nearer, the price of the bond increases to reflect the increasing present value of that cash flow. Take a bond paying semiannual coupons of $50 and imagine tracking the price of the bond starting on the day after the last coupon payment was made. The price would slowly rise over the following six months as the next $50 coupon payment grows closer and closer. It will peak right before the coupon payment is made, when buying the bond still entitles you to receive the $50 payment immediately. If you buy the bond right after the coupon payment is made, you do not have the right to receive that $50 coupon. The price you are willing to pay for the bond will therefore be $50 less than it was right before the coupon was paid. This pattern—the price slowly rising as a coupon payment nears and then dropping abruptly after the payment is made—continues for the life of the bond. Figure 6.4 illustrates this phenomenon.

FIGURE 6.4

The Effect of Time on Bond Prices

The graph illustrates the effects of the passage of time on bond prices when the yield remains constant, in this case 5%. The price of a zero-coupon bond rises smoothly. The prices of the coupon bonds are indicated by the zigzag lines. Notice that the prices rise between coupon payments, but tumble on the coupon date, reflecting the amount of the coupon payment. For each coupon bond, the gray line shows the trend of the bond price just after each coupon is paid.

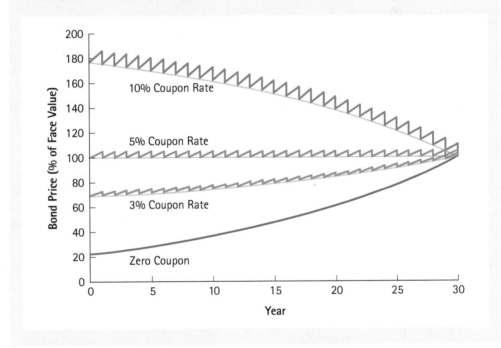

EXAMPLE 6.7

The Effect of Time on the Price of a Bond

MyFinanceLab

PROBLEM

Suppose you purchase a 30-year, zero-coupon bond with a yield to maturity of 5%. For a face value of $100, the bond will initially trade for:

$$P(\,30\ \text{years to maturity}\,) = \frac{100}{1.05^{30}} = \$23.14$$

If the bond's yield to maturity remains at 5%, what will its price be five years later? If you purchased the bond at $23.14 and sold it five years later, what would the rate of return of your investment be?

(Continued)

SOLUTION

PLAN

If the bond was originally a 30-year bond and five years have passed, then it has 25 years left to maturity. If the yield to maturity does not change, then you can compute the price of the bond with 25 years left exactly as we did for 30 years, but using 25 years of discounting instead of 30.

Once you have the price in five years, you can compute the rate of return of your investment just as we did in Chapter 4. The FV is the price in five years, the PV is the initial price ($23.14), and the number of years is five.

EXECUTE

$$P(\text{25 years to maturity}) = \frac{100}{1.05^{25}} = \$29.53$$

If you purchased the bond for $23.14 and then sold it after five years for $29.53, the rate of return of your investment would be

$$\left(\frac{29.53}{23.14}\right)^{1/5} - 1 = 5.0\%$$

That is, your return is the same as the yield to maturity of the bond.

EVALUATE

Note that the bond price is higher, and hence the discount from its face value is smaller, when there is less time to maturity. The discount shrinks because the yield has not changed, but there is less time until the face value will be received. This example illustrates a more general property for bonds: *If a bond's yield to maturity does not change, then the rate of return of an investment in the bond equals its yield to maturity even if you sell the bond early.*

Interest Rate Risk and Bond Prices

While the effect of time on bond prices is predictable, unpredictable changes in interest rates will also affect bond prices. Further, bonds with different characteristics will respond differently to changes in interest rates—some bonds will react more strongly than others. We showed in Chapter 5 that investors view long-term loans to be riskier than short-term loans. Because bonds are just loans, the same is true of short- versus long-term bonds.

The example illustrates how bonds of different maturity will have different sensitivities to interest rate changes. However, even bonds with the same maturity will differ in

EXAMPLE 6.8

The Interest Rate Sensitivity of Bonds

MyFinanceLab

PROBLEM

Consider a 10-year coupon bond and a 30-year coupon bond, both with 10% annual coupons. By what percentage will the price of each bond change if its yield to maturity increases from 5% to 6%?

SOLUTION

PLAN

We need to compute the price of each bond for each yield to maturity and then calculate the percentage change in the prices. For both bonds, the cash flows are $10 per year for $100 in face value and then the $100 face value repaid at maturity. The only difference is the maturity: 10 years and 30 years. With those cash flows, we can use Eq. 6.3 to compute the prices.

EXECUTE

YTM	10-Year, 10% Annual Coupon Bond	30-Year, 10% Annual Coupon Bond
5%	$10 \times \dfrac{1}{0.05}\left(1 - \dfrac{1}{1.05^{10}}\right) + \dfrac{100}{1.05^{10}} = \$138.61$	$10 \times \dfrac{1}{0.05}\left(1 - \dfrac{1}{1.05^{30}}\right) + \dfrac{100}{1.05^{30}} = \$176.86$
6%	$10 \times \dfrac{1}{0.06}\left(1 - \dfrac{1}{1.06^{10}}\right) + \dfrac{100}{1.06^{10}} = \$129.44$	$10 \times \dfrac{1}{0.06}\left(1 - \dfrac{1}{1.06^{30}}\right) + \dfrac{100}{1.06^{30}} = \$155.06$

The price of the 10-year bond changes by $(129.44 - 138.61)/138.61 = -6.6\%$ if its yield to maturity increases from 5% to 6%.

For the 30-year bond, the price change is $(155.06 - 176.86)/176.86 = -12.3\%$.

EVALUATE

The 30-year bond is almost twice as sensitive to a change in the yield than is the 10-year bond. In fact, if we graph the price and yields of the two bonds, we can see that the line for the 30-year bond, shown in blue, is steeper throughout than the green line for the 10-year bond, reflecting its heightened sensitivity to interest rate changes.

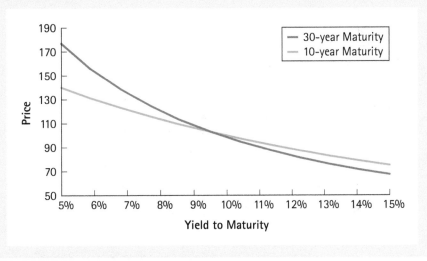

interest rate sensitivity if their coupon rates are different. Bonds with higher coupon rates—because they pay higher cash flows up-front—are less sensitive to interest rate changes than otherwise identical bonds with lower coupon rates.[4] Table 6.4 summarizes this conclusion.

TABLE 6.4

Bond Prices and Interest Rates

Bond Characteristic	Effect on Interest Rate Risk
Longer term to maturity	Increase
Higher coupon payments	Decrease

[4]The *duration* of a bond measures its sensitivity to interest rate changes. A full discussion of the concept of duration is beyond the scope of this book.

EXAMPLE 6.9

Coupons
and Interest Rate
Sensitivity

MyFinanceLab

PROBLEM

Consider two bonds, each of which pays semiannual coupons and has five years left until maturity. One has a coupon rate of 5% and the other has a coupon rate of 10%, but both currently have a yield to maturity of 8%. By what percentage will the price of each bond change if its yield to maturity decreases from 8% to 7%?

SOLUTION

PLAN

As in Example 6.8, we need to compute the price of each bond at 8% and 7% yield to maturities and then compute the percentage change in price. Each bond has 10 semiannual coupon payments remaining along with the repayment of par value at maturity. The cash flows per $100 of face value for the first bond are $2.50 every six months and then $100 at maturity. The cash flows per $100 of face value for the second bond are $5 every six months and then $100 at maturity. Since the cash flows are semiannual, the yield to maturity is quoted as a semiannually compounded APR, so we convert the yields to match the frequency of the cash flows by dividing by two. With semiannual rates of 4% and 3.5%, we can use Eq. 6.3 to compute the prices.

EXECUTE

YTM	Five-Year, 5% Coupon Bond	Five-Year, 10% Coupon Bond
8%	$2.50 \times \dfrac{1}{0.04}\left(1 - \dfrac{1}{1.04^{10}}\right) + \dfrac{100}{1.04^{10}} = \$87.83$	$5 \times \dfrac{1}{0.04}\left(1 - \dfrac{1}{1.04^{10}}\right) + \dfrac{100}{1.04^{10}} = \$108.11$
7%	$2.50 \times \dfrac{1}{0.035}\left(1 - \dfrac{1}{1.035^{10}}\right) + \dfrac{100}{1.035^{10}} = \$91.68$	$5 \times \dfrac{1}{0.035}\left(1 - \dfrac{1}{1.035^{10}}\right) + \dfrac{100}{1.035^{10}} = \$112.47$

The 5% coupon bond's price changed from $87.83 to $91.68, or 4.4%, but the 10% coupon bond's price changed from $108.11 to $112.47, or 4.0%. You can calculate the price change very quickly with a financial calculator or spreadsheet. For example, take the 5% coupon bond at 8% YTM (4% per 6 months):

	N	I/Y	PV	PMT	FV
Given:	10	4		2.50	100
Solve for:			−87.83		
	Excel Formula: =PV(RATE,NPER,PMT,FV)=PV(.04,10,2.5,100)				

With all of the basic bond information entered, you can simply change the I/Y by entering 3.5 and pressing I/Y and then solve for PV again. So, with just a few keystrokes, you will have the new price of $91.68.

EVALUATE

The bond with the smaller coupon payments is more sensitive to changes in interest rates. Because its coupons are smaller relative to its par value, a larger fraction of its cash flows are received later. As we learned in Example 6.8, later cash flows are affected more greatly by changes in interest rates, so compared to the 10% coupon bond, the effect of the interest change is greater for the cash flows of the 5% coupon bond.

Clean and Dirty Prices for Coupon Bonds

As Figure 6.4 illustrates, coupon bond prices fluctuate around the time of each coupon payment in a sawtooth pattern: The value of the coupon bond rises as the next coupon payment gets closer and then drops after it has been paid. This fluctuation occurs even if there is no change in the bond's yield to maturity.

Bond traders are more concerned about changes in the bond's price that arise due to changes in the bond's yield, rather than these predictable patterns around coupon payments. As a result, they often do not quote the price of a bond in terms of its actual cash price, which is also called the **dirty price** or **invoice price** of the bond. Instead, bonds are often quoted in terms of a **clean price**, which is the bond's cash price less an adjustment for accrued interest, the amount of the next coupon payment that has already accrued:

$$\text{Clean Price} = \text{Cash (Dirty) Price} - \text{Accrued Interest}$$

$$\text{Accrued Interest} = \text{Coupon Amount} \times \left(\frac{\text{Days Since Last Coupon Payment}}{\text{Days in Current Coupon Period}} \right)$$

Note that immediately before a coupon payment is made, the accrued interest will equal the full amount of the coupon. Immediately after the coupon payment is made, the accrued interest will be zero. Thus, accrued interest will rise and fall in a sawtooth pattern as each coupon payment passes.

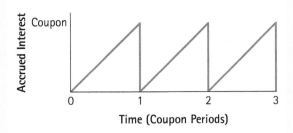

If we subtract accrued interest from the bond's cash price and compute the clean price, the sawtooth pattern is eliminated.

---

dirty price or invoice price A bond's actual cash price.

clean price A bond's cash price less an adjustment for accrued interest, the amount of the next coupon payment that has already accrued.

Bond Prices in Practice

In actuality, bond prices are subject to the effects of both the passage of time and changes in interest rates. Bond prices converge to the bond's face value due to the time effect, but simultaneously move up and down due to unpredictable changes in bond yields. Figure 6.5 illustrates this behavior by demonstrating how the price of the 30-year, zero-coupon bond might change over its life. Note that the bond price tends to converge to the face value as the bond approaches the maturity date, but also moves higher when its yield falls and lower when its yield rises.

As the fluctuating price in Figure 6.5 demonstrates, prior to maturity the bond is exposed to interest rate risk. If an investor chooses to sell and the bond's yield to maturity has decreased, then the investor will receive a high price and earn a high return. If the yield to maturity has increased, the bond price is low at the time of sale and the investor will earn a low return.

CONCEPT CHECK

7. Why do interest rates and bond prices move in opposite directions?

8. If a bond's yield to maturity does not change, how does its cash price change between coupon payments?

FIGURE 6.5

Yield to Maturity
and Bond Price
Fluctuations
over Time

The graphs illustrate changes in price and yield for a 30-year zero-coupon bond over its life. Panel (a) illustrates the changes in the bond's yield to maturity (YTM) over its life. In Panel (b), the actual bond price is shown in blue. Because the YTM does not remain constant over the bond's life, the bond's price fluctuates as it converges to the face value over time. Also shown is the price if the YTM remained fixed at 4%, 5%, or 6%. Panel (a) shows that the bond's YTM mostly remained between 4% and 6%. The broken lines in Panel (b) show the price of the bond if its YTM had remained constant at those levels. Note that in all cases, the bond's price must eventually converge to $100 on its maturity date.

Panel (a) The Bond's Yield to Maturity over Time

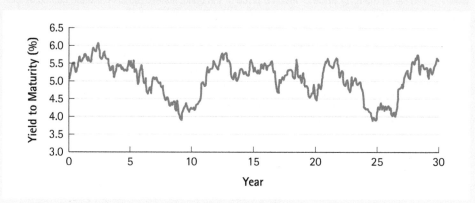

Panel (b) The Bond's Price over Time (Price = $100 on Maturity Date)

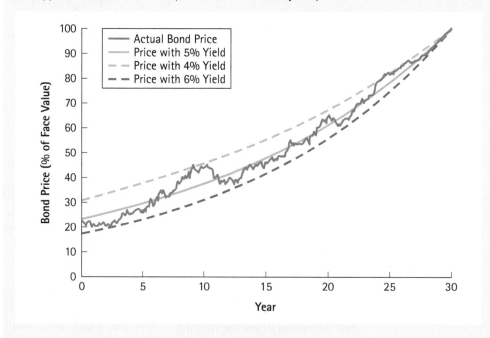

6.5 Corporate Bonds

In the previous sections, we developed the basics of bond pricing in the context of U.S. Treasury bonds, which have no risk of default. In this section, our focus is on **corporate bonds**, which are bonds issued by corporations. We will examine the role of default risk in the price and yield to maturity of corporate bonds. As we will see, corporations with higher default risk will need to pay higher coupons to attract buyers to their bonds.

corporate bonds Bonds
issued by corporations.

TABLE 6.5

Interest Rates on
Five-Year Bonds for
Various Borrowers,
December 2015

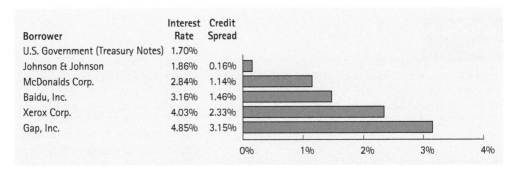

Borrower	Interest Rate	Credit Spread
U.S. Government (Treasury Notes)	1.70%	
Johnson & Johnson	1.86%	0.16%
McDonalds Corp.	2.84%	1.14%
Baidu, Inc.	3.16%	1.46%
Xerox Corp.	4.03%	2.33%
Gap, Inc.	4.85%	3.15%

Credit Risk

Table 6.5 lists the interest rates paid by a number of different borrowers at the end of 2015 for a five-year bond. Why do these interest rates vary so widely? The lowest interest rate is the 1.70% rate paid on U.S. Treasury notes. United States Treasury securities are widely regarded to be risk-free because there is virtually no chance the government will fail to pay the interest and default on these bonds. Thus, as we noted in Section 6.2, when we refer to the "risk-free interest rate," we mean the rate on U.S. Treasuries.

The remaining bonds are all corporate bonds. With corporate bonds, the bond issuer may default—that is, it might not pay back the full amount promised in the bond prospectus. For example, a company with financial difficulties may be unable to fully repay the loan. This risk of default, which is known as the **credit risk** of the bond, means that the bond's cash flows are not known with certainty. To compensate for the risk that the firm may default, investors demand a higher interest rate than the rate on U.S. Treasuries.[5] The difference between the interest rate of the loan and the Treasury rate will depend on investors' assessment of the likelihood that the firm will default. For example, investors place a higher probability of default on Gap than on Johnson & Johnson, forcing Gap to pay a larger credit spread, which is reflected in a higher interest rate.

credit risk The risk of default by the issuer of any bond that is not default free; it is an indication that the bond's cash flows are not known with certainty.

 Are Treasuries Really Default-Free Securities?

Most investors treat U.S. Treasury securities as risk free, meaning that they believe there is no chance of default (a convention we follow in this book). But are Treasuries really risk free? The answer depends on what you mean by "risk free."

No one can be certain that the U.S. government will never default on its bonds—but most people believe the probability of such an event is very small. More importantly, the default probability is smaller than for any other bond. So saying that the yield on a U.S. Treasury security is risk free really means that the Treasury security is the lowest-risk investment denominated in U.S. dollars in the world.

That said, there have been occasions in the past where Treasury holders did not receive exactly what they were promised: In 1790,

Treasury Secretary Alexander Hamilton lowered the interest rate on outstanding debt and in 1933 President Franklin Roo-sevelt suspended bondholders' right to be paid in gold rather than currency.

A new risk emerged in mid-2011 when a series of large budget deficits brought the United States up against the debt ceiling, a constraint imposed by Congress limiting the overall amount of debt the government can incur. An act of Congress was required by August 2011 for the Treasury to meet its obligations and avoid a default. In response to the political uncertainty about whether Congress would raise the ceiling in time, Standard & Poor's downgraded its rating of U.S. Government bonds. Congress ultimately raised the debt ceiling and no default occurred. Given persistent budget deficits, however, similar debt ceiling debates recurred in 2013 and 2015. These incidents serve as a recurring reminder that perhaps no investment is truly "risk free."

---

[5]Because trading in corporate bonds is much less liquid than trading in Treasuries, part of the increased interest rate is to compensate investors for this lack of liquidity.

LISA BLACK

Lisa Black is Managing Director at Teachers Insurance and Annuity Association, a major financial services company. A Chartered Financial Analyst, she oversees a variety of fixed income funds, including money market, intermediate bond, high-yield, emerging market debt, and inflation-linked bond funds.

QUESTION: *When people think about the financial markets, many of them picture the equity markets. How big and how active are the bond markets compared to the equity markets?*

ANSWER: The dollar volume of bonds traded daily is about 10 times that of equity markets. For example, a single $15 billion issue of 10-year Treasury bonds will sell in one day. The market value of the Barclays Capital U.S. Universal Bond Index of dollar-denominated debt as of June 30, 2009, was $13.8 trillion, with the U.S. Aggregate Index (investment-grade debt) accounting for almost 90%. It includes Treasuries, agencies, corporate bonds, and mortgage-backed securities. Other major sectors of the Universal Index include corporate high-yield bonds, Eurodollar bonds, emerging markets, and private placements.

QUESTION: *How do the bond markets operate?*

ANSWER: Firms and governments turn to bond markets when they need to borrow money to fund new construction projects, finance acquisitions, and for general corporate purposes. On the other side, institutions like TIAA-CREF, endowments, and foundations have funds to invest. Wall Street investment bankers serve as intermediaries, matching up borrowers with creditors in terms of maturity needs and risk appetite. Because we provide annuities for college professors, for example, we invest money for longer periods of time than an insurance company that needs funds to pay claims. In the institutional world, bond funds typically trade in blocks of bonds ranging from $5 million to $50 million at a time.

QUESTION: *What drives changes in the values of Treasury bonds?*

ANSWER: The simple answer is that when interest rates rise, bond prices fall. The key is to dig below that reality to see *why* interest rates rise and fall. A major factor is investors' expectations for inflation and economic growth. Interest rates generally rise when the expectation is that growth will accelerate, because inflation won't be far behind. During the 2008–2009 recession, interest rates dropped as the Federal Reserve injected liquidity into the system. There was also a flight to quality after the bankruptcy of Lehman Brothers. The value of The Reserve Fund fell drastically as its holdings of about $785 million of Lehman's short-term debt securities became all but worthless. Worried retail and institutional investors sold their money market funds and purchased U.S. Treasury bills and notes to protect their principal. With increased demand, interest rates on risk-free Treasury securities fell sharply. At one point, T-bills even had a negative yield.

QUESTION: *What impact did the 2008–2009 financial crisis have on the bond market? What changes do you anticipate going forward as a result?*

ANSWER: While the effects of the crisis on equity markets have been widely discussed, the effects on the bond market have been just as profound. Particularly noteworthy is the role governments and central bankers have played—and likely will continue to play—to stabilize financial institutions deemed too big or important to fail. The Fed introduced an unprecedented number of stimulus programs to unfreeze credit markets, including programs to guarantee money funds. The challenge will be how and when the various support programs and financial infusions will end and/or be paid back. In addition, the rating agencies' role and ratings methodologies will likely be subject to greater scrutiny, both from regulators and investors.

In the corporate sector, many borrowers—the automotive industries, for example—could not raise debt financing during the crisis. Credit spreads widened dramatically as investors shunned even AAA- and AA-rated credits. Major institutional investors sat on the sidelines for several months, and the corporate bond new-issue market was essentially nonexistent. Not until the federal government announced programs to increase liquidity did institutional investors reenter the market, first buying only the highest credit-quality instruments, such as first mortgage bonds issued by utilities and government-guaranteed mortgage-backed securities. Investors then began to move down the credit-quality chain, selectively focusing on issuers that could weather an economic downturn.

Corporate Bond Yields

How does the credit risk of default affect bond prices and yields? The cash flows promised by the bond are the most that bondholders can hope to receive. Due to credit risk, the cash flows that a purchaser of a corporate bond actually *expects* to receive may be less than that amount. For example, GM struggled financially in 2006 and 2007, substantially increasing the chance that they would default on their bonds, and GM subsequently did in 2009. Realizing this risk, investors in GM bonds incorporated an increased probability that the bond payments would not be made as promised and prices of the bonds fell. Because the yield to maturity of GM's bonds is computed by comparing the price to the *promised* cash flows, the yield to maturity *increased* as the probability of being paid as promised decreased. This example highlights the following general truths:

1. Investors pay less for bonds with credit risk than they would for an otherwise identical default-free bond.

2. Because the yield to maturity for a bond is calculated using the promised cash flows instead of the *expected* cash flows, the yield of bonds with credit risk will be higher than that of otherwise identical default-free bonds.

These two points lead us to an important conclusion: *the yield to maturity of a defaultable bond is not equal to the expected return of investing in the bond.* The promised cash flows used to determine the yield to maturity are always higher than the expected cash flows investors use to calculate the expected return. As a result, the yield to maturity will always be higher than the expected return of investing in the bond. *Moreover, a higher yield to maturity does not necessarily imply that a bond's expected return is higher.*

Bond Ratings

investment-grade bonds Bonds in the top four categories of creditworthiness with a low risk of default.

The probability of default is clearly important to the price you are willing to pay for a corporate bond. How do you assess a firm's likelihood of default? Several companies rate the creditworthiness of bonds and make this information available to investors. By consulting these ratings, investors can assess the creditworthiness of a particular bond issue. The ratings therefore encourage widespread investor participation and relatively liquid markets. The two best-known bond-rating companies are Standard & Poor's and Moody's. Table 6.6 summarizes the rating classes each company uses. Bonds with the highest rating (Aaa or AAA) are judged to be least likely to default.

speculative bonds, junk bonds, or high-yield bonds Bonds in one of the bottom five categories of creditworthiness (below investment grade) that have a high risk of default.

Bonds in the top four categories are often referred to as **investment-grade bonds** because of their low default risk. Bonds in the bottom five categories are often called **speculative bonds**, **junk bonds**, **or high-yield bonds** because their likelihood of default is higher and so they promise higher yields. The rating depends on the risk of bankruptcy as well as the bondholders' ability to lay claim to the firm's assets in the event of such a bankruptcy. Thus, debt issues with a low-priority claim in bankruptcy will have a lower rating than issues from the same company that have a high priority in bankruptcy or that are backed by a specific asset such as a building or a plant.

Corporate Yield Curves

default spread or credit spread The difference between the risk-free interest rate on U.S. Treasury notes and the interest rates on all other loans. The magnitude of the credit spread will depend on investors' assessment of the likelihood that a particular firm will default.

Just as we can construct a yield curve from risk-free Treasury securities, we can plot a similar yield curve for corporate bonds. Figure 6.6 shows the average yields of U.S. corporate coupon bonds with three different Standard & Poor's bond ratings: two curves are for investment-grade bonds (AAA and BBB) and one is for junk bonds (B). Figure 6.6 also includes the U.S. (coupon-paying) Treasury yield curve. We refer to the difference between the yields of the corporate bonds and the Treasury yields as the **default spread** or **credit spread**. This difference can be seen in Figure 6.6 as the distance between the bottom blue line for Treasuries and each of the red, green, and purple lines as default probability increases. Credit spreads fluctuate as perceptions regarding the probability of default change. Note that the credit spread is high for bonds with low ratings and therefore a greater likelihood of default.

TABLE 6.6

Bond Ratings and the Number of U.S. Public Firms with Those Ratings in March 2016

Moody's	Standard & Poor's	Number of Public Firms	Description (Moody's)
Investment Grade Debt			
Aaa	AAA	3*	Judged to be of the best quality. They carry the smallest degree of investment risk and are generally referred to as "gilt edged."
Aa	AA	29	Judged to be of high quality by all standards. Together with the Aaa group, they constitute what are generally known as high-grade bonds.
A	A	221	Possess many favorable investment attributes and are considered as upper-medium-grade obligations. Factors giving security to principal and interest are considered adequate at present, but may not remain that way.
Baa	BBB	515	Are considered as medium-grade obligations (i.e., they are neither highly protected nor poorly secured).
Speculative Bonds ("Junk Bonds")			
Ba	BB	363	Judged to have speculative elements; their future cannot be considered as well assured.
B	B	255	Generally lack characteristics of the desirable investment. Assurance of interest and principal payments over any long period may be small.
Caa	CCC	41	Are of poor standing. Such issues may be in default or there may be present elements of danger with respect to principal or interest.
Ca	CC	5	Are speculative to a high degree. Such issues are often in default or have other marked shortcomings.
C	C, D	10	Lowest-rated class of bonds, and issues so rated can be regarded as having extremely poor prospects of ever attaining any real investment standing.

*The three AAA-rated companies were Microsoft, Johnson & Johnson, and ExxonMobil. However, ExxonMobil was downgraded at the end of April, 2016.

Source: www.moodys.com and S&P Compustat.

FIGURE 6.6

Corporate Yield Curves for Various Ratings, May 2016

This figure shows the yield curve for U.S. Treasury securities (in yellow) and yield curves for corporate securities with ratings AA (in blue), and BBB (in green). Note how the yield to maturity is higher for the corporate bonds, which have a higher probability of default than the U.S. Treasury securities.

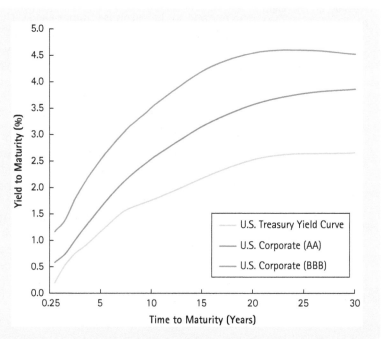

Source: Bloomberg.

EXAMPLE 6.10

Credit Spreads and
Bond Prices

PROBLEM

Your firm has a credit rating of AA. You notice that the credit spread for 10-year maturity AA debt is 90 basis points (0.90%). Your firm's 10-year debt has a coupon rate of 5%. You see that new 10-year Treasury notes are being issued at par with a coupon rate of 4.5%. What should be the price of your outstanding 10-year bonds?

SOLUTION

PLAN

If the credit spread is 90 basis points, then the yield to maturity (YTM) on your debt should be the YTM on similar Treasuries plus 0.9%. The fact that new 10-year Treasuries are being issued at par with coupons of 4.5% means that with a coupon rate of 4.5%, these notes are selling for $100 per $100 face value. Thus, their YTM is 4.5% and your debt's YTM should be 4.5% + 0.9% = 5.4%. The cash flows on your bonds are $5 per year for every $100 face value, paid as $2.50 every six months. The six-month rate corresponding to a 5.4% yield is 5.4%/2 = 2.7%. Armed with this information, you can use Eq. 6.3 to compute the price of your bonds.

EXECUTE

$$2.50 \times \frac{1}{0.027}\left(1 - \frac{1}{1.027^{20}}\right) + \frac{100}{1.027^{20}} = \$96.94$$

EVALUATE

Your bonds offer a higher coupon (5% vs. 4.5%) than Treasuries of the same maturity, but sell for a lower price ($96.94 vs. $100). The reason is the credit spread. Your firm's higher probability of default leads investors to demand a higher YTM on your debt. To provide a higher YTM, the purchase price for the debt must be lower. If your debt paid 5.4% coupons, it would sell at $100, the same as the Treasuries. But to get that price, you would have to offer coupons that are 90 basis points higher than those on the Treasuries—exactly enough to offset the credit spread.

 ### The Credit Crisis and Bond Yields

The financial crisis that engulfed the world's economies in 2008 originated as a credit crisis that first emerged in August 2007. At that time, problems in the mortgage market had led to the bankruptcy of several large mortgage lenders. The default of these firms, and the downgrading of many of the bonds backed by mortgages these firms had made, caused many investors to reassess the risk of other bonds in their portfolios. As perceptions of risk increased, and investors attempted to move into safer U.S. Treasury securities, the prices of corporate bonds fell and so their credit spreads rose relative to Treasuries, as shown in Figure 6.7. Panel (a) shows the yield spreads for long-term corporate bonds, where we can see that spreads of even the highest-rated Aaa bonds increased dramatically, from a typical level of 0.5% to over 2% by the fall of 2008. Panel (b) shows a similar pattern for the rate banks had to pay on short-term loans compared to the yields of short-term Treasury bills. This increase in borrowing costs made it more costly for firms to raise the capital needed for new investment, slowing economic growth. The decline in these spreads in early 2009 was viewed by many as an important first step in mitigating the ongoing impact of the financial crisis on the rest of the economy.

As we indicated at the beginning of this chapter, the bond market, while less well-known than the stock markets, is large and important. Because debt is a substantial part of the financing of most corporations, a financial manager needs to understand bonds and how investors price the company's bonds. In this chapter, we have introduced the major types of bonds, how bonds repay investors, and how they are priced. In Chapter 15, we will discuss the bond markets further, including the process a firm goes through to issue debt.

FIGURE 6.7

Yield Spreads and the Financial Crisis

Panel (a) shows the yield spread between long-term (30-year) U.S. corporate and Treasury bonds. Panel (b) shows the yield spread of short-term loans to major international banks (called LIBOR) and U.S. Treasury bills (also referred to as the *Treasury-Eurodollar* or *"TED" spread*). Note the dramatic increase in these spreads beginning in August 2007 and again in September 2008, before beginning to decline in late 2008 and early 2009. While spreads returned to pre-crisis levels by mid-2011, note the increase in spreads in 2012 in response to the European debt crisis. Spreads began rising again in 2015, partly in response to a surge in corporate borrowing, as well as declining demand from banks facing tighter regulation of their trading activities.

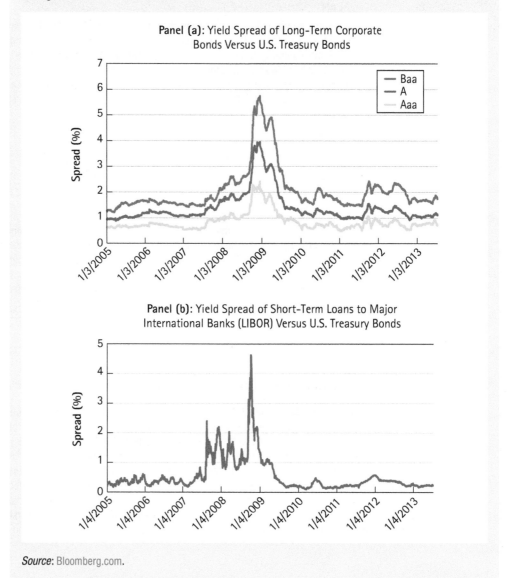

Source: Bloomberg.com.

CONCEPT CHECK

9. What is a junk bond?

10. How will the yield to maturity of a bond vary with the bond's risk of default?

MyFinanceLab

Here is what you should know after reading this chapter. MyFinanceLab will help you identify what you know, and where to go when you need to practice.

KEY POINTS AND EQUATIONS	KEY TERMS	ONLINE PRACTICE
6.1 Bond Terminology • Bonds pay both coupon and principal or face value payments to investors. By convention, the coupon rate of a bond is expressed as an APR, so the amount of each coupon payment, CPN, is: $$CPN = \frac{\text{Coupon Rate} \times \text{Face Value}}{\text{Number of Coupon Payments per Year}} \quad (6.1)$$	bond certificate, p. 160 coupon rate, p. 160 coupons, p. 160 face value, p. 160 maturity date, p. 160 par value, p. 160 principal amount, p. 160 term, p. 160	MyFinanceLab Study Plan 6.1
6.2 Zero-Coupon Bonds • Zero-coupon bonds make no coupon payments, so investors receive only the bond's face value. • The rate of return of a bond is called its yield to maturity (or yield). The yield to maturity of a bond is the discount rate that sets the present value of the promised bond payments equal to the current market price of the bond. • The yield to maturity for a zero-coupon bond is given by: $$1 + YTM_n = \left(\frac{\text{Face Value}}{\text{Price}} \right)^{1/n} \quad (6.2)$$ • The risk-free interest rate for an investment until date n equals the yield to maturity of a risk-free zero-coupon bond that matures on date n. A plot of these rates against maturity is called the zero-coupon yield curve.	discount, p. 162 pure discount bond, p. 162 spot interest rates, p. 164 Treasury bills, p. 161 yield to maturity (YTM), p. 162 zero-coupon bond, p. 161 zero-coupon yield curve, p. 164	MyFinanceLab Study Plan 6.2 Financial Calculator Tutorial: Solving for the Yield to Maturity of a Bond
6.3 Coupon Bonds • The yield to maturity for a coupon bond is the discount rate, y, that equates the present value of the bond's future cash flows with its price: $$P = CPN \times \frac{1}{y} \left(1 - \frac{1}{(1+y)^N} \right) + \frac{FV}{(1+y)^N} \quad (6.3)$$	coupon bonds, p. 165 Treasury bonds, p. 165 Treasury notes, p. 165	MyFinanceLab Study Plan 6.3 Financial Calculator Tutorial: Bond Valuation with Interest Compounded Semiannually

6.4 Why Bond Prices Change
- A bond will trade at a premium if its coupon rate exceeds its yield to maturity. It will trade at a discount if its coupon rate is less than its yield to maturity. If a bond's coupon rate equals its yield to maturity, it trades at par.
- As a bond approaches maturity, the price of the bond approaches its face value.
- Bond prices change as interest rates change. When interest rates rise, bond prices fall, and vice versa.
- Long-term zero-coupon bonds are more sensitive to changes in interest rates than are short-term zero-coupon bonds.
- Bonds with low coupon rates are more sensitive to changes in interest rates than are similar maturity bonds with high coupon rates.

clean price, p. 177
dirty price, p. 177
invoice price, p. 177
par, p. 170
premium, p. 170

MyFinanceLab
Study Plan 6.4

Interactive
Interest Rate
Sensitivity
Analysis

6.5 Corporate Bonds
- When a bond issuer does not make a bond payment in full, the issuer has defaulted.
- The risk that default can occur is called default or credit risk. United States Treasury securities are free of default risk.
- The expected return of a corporate bond, which is the firm's debt cost of capital, equals the risk-free rate of interest plus a risk premium. The expected return is less than the bond's yield to maturity because the yield to maturity of a bond is calculated using the promised cash flows, not the expected cash flows.
- Bond ratings summarize the creditworthiness of bonds for investors.
- The difference between yields on Treasury securities and yields on corporate bonds is called the credit spread or default spread. The credit spread compensates investors for the difference between promised and expected cash flows and for the risk of default.

corporate bonds, p. 178
credit risk, p. 179
default (credit) spread, p. 181
high-yield bonds, p. 181
investment-grade bonds, p. 181
junk bonds, p. 181
speculative bonds, p. 181

MyFinanceLab
Study Plan 6.5

CRITICAL THINKING

1. How is a bond like a loan?
2. How does an investor receive a return from buying a bond?
3. How is yield to maturity related to the concept of rate of return?
4. Does a bond's yield to maturity determine its price or does the price determine the yield to maturity?
5. Explain why the yield of a bond that trades at a discount exceeds the bond's coupon rate.

6. Explain the relationship between interest rates and bond prices.

7. Why are longer-term bonds more sensitive to changes in interest rates than shorter-term bonds?

8. Explain why the expected return of a corporate bond does not equal its yield to maturity.

PROBLEMS

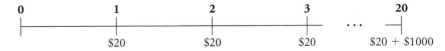

All problems are available in MyFinanceLab. *The* icon *indicates problems that are easier to solve using Excel and have data in an Excel format available in* MyFinanceLab.

Bond Terminology

1. Consider a 10-year bond with a face value of $1000 that has a coupon rate of 5.5%, with semiannual payments.
   a. What is the coupon payment for this bond?
   b. Draw the cash flows for the bond on a timeline.

2. Assume that a bond will make payments every six months as shown on the following timeline (using six-month periods):

0	1	2	3	...	20
	$20	$20	$20		$20 + $1000

   a. What is the maturity of the bond (in years)?
   b. What is the coupon rate (in percent)?
   c. What is the face value?

3. Your company wants to raise $10 million by issuing 20-year zero-coupon bonds. If the yield to maturity on the bonds will be 6% (annually compounded APR), what total principal amount of bonds must you issue?

Zero-Coupon Bonds

4. The following table summarizes prices of various default-free zero-coupon bonds (expressed as a percentage of face value):

Maturity (years)	1	2	3	4	5
Price (per $100 face value)	$95.51	$91.05	$86.38	$81.65	$76.51

   a. Compute the yield to maturity for each bond.
   b. Plot the zero-coupon yield curve (for the first five years).
   c. Is the yield curve upward sloping, downward sloping, or flat?

Use the following information for Problems 5–7. The current zero-coupon yield curve for risk-free bonds is as follows:

Maturity (years)	1	2	3	4	5
YTM	5.00%	5.50%	5.75%	5.95%	6.05%

5. What is the price per $100 face value of a two-year, zero-coupon, risk-free bond?

6. What is the price per $100 face value of a four-year, zero-coupon, risk-free bond?

7. What is the risk-free interest rate for a five-year maturity?

8. In the Global Financial Crisis box in Section 6.2, Bloomberg.com reported that the three-month Treasury bill sold for $100.002556 per $100 face value. What is the yield to maturity of this bond, expressed as an EAR?

Coupon Bonds

9. For each of the following pairs of Treasury securities (each with $1000 par value), identify which will have the higher price:
   a. A three-year zero-coupon bond or a five-year zero coupon bond?
   b. A three-year zero-coupon bond or a three-year 4% coupon bond?
   c. A two-year 5% coupon bond or a two-year 6% coupon bond?

10. The yield to maturity of a $1000 bond with a 7% coupon rate, semiannual coupons, and two years to maturity is 7.6% APR, compounded semiannually. What must its price be?

11. Assume the current Treasury yield curve shows that the spot rates for six months, one year, and 1½ years are 1%, 1.1%, and 1.3%, all quoted as semiannually compounded APRs. What is the price of a $1000 par, 4% coupon bond maturing in 1½ years (the next coupon is exactly six months from now)?

12. Suppose a 10-year, $1000 bond with an 8% coupon rate and semiannual coupons is trading for $1034.74.
   a. What is the bond's yield to maturity (expressed as an APR with semiannual compounding)?
   b. If the bond's yield to maturity changes to 9% APR, what will the bond's price be?

13. Suppose a five-year, $1000 bond with annual coupons has a price of $900 and a yield to maturity of 6%. What is the bond's coupon rate?

14. Assume that the six-month Treasury spot rate is 1.6% APR, and the one-year rate is 2% APR, both compounded semiannually. What is the price of a one-year $1000 par Treasury bond with 2% coupons?

Why Bond Prices Change

15. The prices of several bonds with face values of $1000 are summarized in the following table:

Bond	A	B	C	D
Price	$972.50	$1040.75	$1150.00	$1000.00

For each bond, state whether it trades at a discount, at par, or at a premium.

16. You have purchased a 10% coupon bond for $1040. What will happen to the bond's price if market interest rates rise?

17. Suppose a seven-year, $1000 bond with an 8% coupon rate and semiannual coupons is trading with a yield to maturity of 6.75%.
   a. Is this bond currently trading at a discount, at par, or at a premium? Explain.
   b. If the yield to maturity of the bond rises to 7.00% (APR with semiannual compounding), what price will the bond trade for?

Suppose that General Motors Acceptance Corporation issued a bond with 10 years until maturity, a face value of $1000, and a coupon rate of 7% (annual payments). The yield to maturity on this bond when it was issued was 6%. Use this information to solve Problems 18–20.

18. What was the price of this bond when it was issued?

19. Assuming the yield to maturity remains constant, what is the price of the bond immediately before it makes its first coupon payment?

 20. Assuming the yield to maturity remains constant, what is the price of the bond immediately after it makes its first coupon payment?

21. Your company currently has $1000 par, 6% coupon bonds with 10 years to maturity and a price of $1078. If you want to issue new 10-year coupon bonds at par, what coupon rate do you need to set? Assume that for both bonds, the next coupon payment is due in exactly six months.

22. Suppose you purchase a 10-year bond with 6% annual coupons. You hold the bond for four years, and sell it immediately after receiving the fourth coupon. If the bond's yield to maturity was 5% when you purchased and sold the bond, what cash flows will you pay and receive from your investment in the bond per $100 face value?

Consider the following bonds for Problems 23 and 24:

Bond	Coupon Rate (annual payments)	Maturity (years)
A	0%	15
B	0%	10
C	4%	15
D	8%	10

 23. What is the percentage change in the price of each bond if its yield to maturity falls from 6% to 5%?

24. Which of the bonds A–D is most sensitive to a 1% drop in interest rates from 6% to 5% and why? Which bond is least sensitive? Provide an intuition explanation for your answer.

 25. Suppose you purchase a 30-year, zero-coupon bond with a yield to maturity of 6%. You hold the bond for five years before selling it.
    a. If the bond's yield to maturity is 6% when you sell it, what is the annualized rate of return of your investment?
    b. If the bond's yield to maturity is 7% when you sell it, what is the annualized rate of return of your investment?
    c. If the bond's yield to maturity is 5% when you sell it, what is the annualized rate of return of your investment?
    d. Even if a bond has no chance of default, is your investment risk free if you plan to sell it before it matures? Explain.

Corporate Bonds

26. The following table summarizes the yields to maturity on several one-year, zero-coupon securities:

Security	Yield (%)
Treasury	3.1
AAA corporate	3.2
BBB corporate	4.2
B corporate	4.9

    a. What is the price (expressed as a percentage of the face value) of a one-year, zero-coupon corporate bond with an AAA rating?

    b. What is the credit spread on AAA-rated corporate bonds?

    c. What is the credit spread on B-rated corporate bonds?

    d. How does the credit spread change with the bond rating? Why?

27. Andrew Industries is contemplating issuing a 30-year bond with a coupon rate of 7% (annual coupon payments) and a face value of $1000. Andrew believes it can get a rating of A from Standard & Poor's. However, due to recent financial difficulties at the company, Standard & Poor's is warning that it may downgrade Andrew Industries bonds to BBB. Yields on A-rated, long-term bonds are currently 6.5%, and yields on BBB-rated bonds are 6.9%.

    a. What is the price of the bond if Andrew Industries maintains the A rating for the bond issue?

    b. What will the price of the bond be if it is downgraded?

28. Your firm has a credit rating of A. You notice that the credit spread for five-year maturity A debt is 85 basis points (0.85%). Your firm's five-year debt has a coupon rate of 6%. You see that new five-year Treasury notes are being issued at par with a coupon rate of 2.0%. What should the price of your outstanding five-year bonds be per $100 of face value?

29. HMK Enterprises would like to raise $10 million to invest in capital expenditures. The company plans to issue five-year bonds with a face value of $1000 and a coupon rate of 6.5% (annual payments). The following table summarizes the yield to maturity for five-year (annual-pay) coupon corporate bonds of various ratings:

Rating	AAA	AA	A	BBB	BB
YTM	6.20%	6.30%	6.50%	6.90%	7.50%

    a. Assuming the bonds will be rated AA, what will the price of the bonds be?

    b. How much of the total principal amount of these bonds must HMK issue to raise $10 million today, assuming the bonds are AA rated? (Because HMK cannot issue a fraction of a bond, assume that all fractions are rounded to the nearest whole number.)

    c. What must the rating of the bonds be for them to sell at par?

    d. Suppose that when the bonds are issued, the price of each bond is $959.54. What is the likely rating of the bonds? Are they junk bonds?

30. A BBB-rated corporate bond has a yield to maturity of 8.2%. A U.S. Treasury security has a yield to maturity of 6.5%. These yields are quoted as APRs with semiannual compounding. Both bonds pay semiannual coupons at a rate of 7% and have five years to maturity.

    a. What is the price (expressed as a percentage of the face value) of the Treasury bond?

    b. What is the price (expressed as a percentage of the face value) of the BBB-rated corporate bond?

    c. What is the credit spread on the BBB bonds?

DATA CASE

You are an intern with Ford Motor Company in its corporate finance division. The firm is planning to issue $50 million of 12% annual coupon bonds with a 10-year maturity. The firm anticipates an increase in its bond rating. Your boss wants you to determine the gain in the proceeds of the new issue if it is rated above the firm's current bond rating. To prepare this information, you will have to determine Ford's current debt rating and the yield curve for its particular rating.

1. Begin by finding the current U.S. Treasury yield curve. At the Treasury Web site (www.treas.gov), search using the term "yield curve" and select "US Treasury—Daily Treasury Yield Curve." *Beware*: There will likely be two links with the same title. Look at the description below the link and select the one that does NOT say "Real Yield . . ." You want the nominal rates. Copy the table into Excel.

2. Find the current yield spreads for the various bond ratings. Unfortunately, the current spreads are available only for a fee, so you will use old ones. Go to BondsOnline (www.bondsonline.com) and click "Today's Market." Next, click "US Corporate Bond Spreads." Copy this table to the same Excel file as the Treasury yields.

3. Find the current bond rating for Ford Motor Co. Go to Standard & Poor's Web site. Select your country. Look for the "Find a Rating" box under "Ratings" and enter Ford Motor Co. and select Ford Motor Co. from the list it returns. At this point you will have to register (it's free) or enter the username and password provided by your instructor. Use the issuer credit rating for "local long term."

4. Return to Excel and create a timeline with the cash flows and discount rates you will need to value the new bond issue.
   a. To create the required spot rates for Ford's issue, add the appropriate spread to the Treasury yield of the same maturity.
   b. The yield curve and spread rates you have found do not cover every year that you will need for the new bonds. Specifically, you do not have yields or spreads for four-, six-, eight-, and nine-year maturities. Fill these in by linearly interpolating the given yields and spreads. For example, the four-year spot rate and spread will be the average of the three- and five-year rates. The six-year rate and spread will be the average of the five- and seven-year rates. For years eight and nine you will have to spread the difference between years seven and ten across the two years.
   c. To compute the spot rates for Ford's current debt rating, add the yield spread to the Treasury rate for each maturity. However, note that the spread is in basis points, which are 1/100th of a percentage point.
   d. Compute the cash flows that would be paid to bondholders each year and add them to the timeline.

5. Use the spot rates to calculate the present value of each cash flow paid to the bondholders.

6. Compute the issue price of the bond and its initial yield to maturity.

7. Repeat steps 4–6 based on the assumption that Ford is able to raise its bond rating by one full-step (for example, BBB to A). Compute the new yield based on the higher rating and the new bond price that would result.

8. Compute the additional cash proceeds that could be raised from the issue if the rating were improved.

Chapter 6
APPENDIX A
Solving for the Yield to Maturity of a Bond Using a Financial Calculator

You are looking to purchase a three-year, $1000 par, 10% annual coupon bond. Payments begin one year from now. The price of the bond is $1074.51 per $1000 par value. What is the yield to maturity of the bond? [answer: 7.15%]

HP-10BII

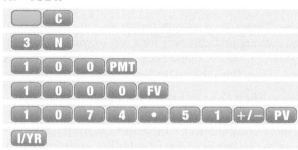

Press [Orange Shift] and then the [C] button to clear all previous entries.

Enter the number of periods.

Enter the payment amount per period.

Enter the par value of the bond you will receive in year 3.

Enter present value or price of the bond you solved for earlier.

Solves for the yield to maturity.

TI-BAII Plus Professional

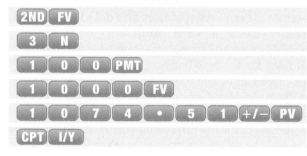

Press [2ND] and then the [FV] button to clear all previous entries.

Enter the number of periods.

Enter the payment amount per period.

Enter the par value of the bond you will receive in year 3.

Enter present value or price of the bond you solved for earlier.

Solves for the yield to maturity.

Chapter 6
APPENDIX B

The Yield Curve and the Law of One Price

Thus far, we have focused on the relationship between the price of an individual bond and its yield to maturity. In this section, we explore the relationship between the prices and yields of different bonds. In Chapter 3, we saw how market forces keep the same asset from having two prices at the same time—we call this the Valuation Principle's *Law of One Price*. Using the Law of One Price, we show that given the spot interest rates, which are the yields of default-free zero-coupon bonds, we can determine the price and yield of any other default-free bond. As a result, the yield curve provides sufficient information to evaluate all such bonds.

Valuing a Coupon Bond with Zero-Coupon Prices

We begin with the observation that it is possible to replicate the cash flows of a coupon bond using zero-coupon bonds. Therefore, we can use the Law of One Price to compute the price of a coupon bond from the prices of zero-coupon bonds. For example, we can replicate a three-year, $1000 bond that pays 10% annual coupons using three zero-coupon bonds as follows:

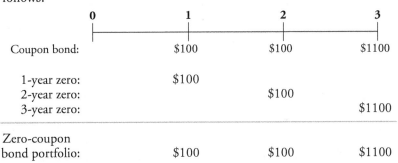

We match each coupon payment to a zero-coupon bond with a face value equal to the coupon payment and a term equal to the time remaining to the coupon date. Similarly, we match the final bond payment (final coupon plus return of face value) in three years to a three-year zero-coupon bond with a corresponding face value of $1100. Because the coupon bond cash flows are identical to the cash flows of the portfolio of zero-coupon bonds, the Law of One Price states that the price of the portfolio of zero-coupon bonds must be the same as the price of the coupon bond.

To illustrate, assume that current zero-coupon bond yields and prices are as shown in Table 6.7 (they are the same as in Example 6.1).

We can calculate the cost of the zero-coupon bond portfolio that replicates the three-year coupon bond as follows:

Zero-Coupon Bond	Face Value Required	Cost
1 Year	100	96.62
2 Years	100	92.45
3 Years	1100	11 × 87.63 = 963.93
		Total Cost: $1153.00

TABLE 6.7

Yields and Prices (per
$100 Face Value) for
Zero-Coupon Bonds

Maturity	1 Year	2 Years	3 Years	4 Years
YTM	3.50%	4.00%	4.50%	4.75%
Price	$96.62	$92.45	$87.63	$83.06

By the Law of One Price, the three-year coupon bond must trade for a price of $1153. If the price of the coupon bond were higher, you could earn an arbitrage profit by selling the coupon bond and buying the zero-coupon bond portfolio. If the price of the coupon bond were lower, you could earn an arbitrage profit by buying the coupon bond and selling the zero-coupon bonds.

Valuing a Coupon Bond Using Zero-Coupon Yields

To this point, we have used the zero-coupon bond *prices* to derive the price of the coupon bond. Alternatively, we can use the zero-coupon bond *yields*. Recall that the yield to maturity of a zero-coupon bond is the competitive market interest rate for a risk-free investment with a term equal to the term of the zero-coupon bond. Since the cash flows of the bond are its coupon payments and face value repayment, the price of a coupon bond must equal the present value of its coupon payments and face value discounted at the competitive market interest rates (see Eq. 5.7 in Chapter 5):

Price of a Coupon Bond

$$P = PV(\text{Bond Cash Flows})$$

$$= \frac{CPN}{1 + YTM_1} + \frac{CPN}{(1 + YTM_2)^2} + \cdots + \frac{CPN + FV}{(1 + YTM_n)^n} \tag{6.4}$$

where CPN is the bond coupon payment, YTM_n is the yield to maturity of a *zero-coupon* bond that matures at the same time as the nth coupon payment, and FV is the face value of the bond. For the three-year, $1000 bond with 10% annual coupons considered earlier, we can use Eq. 6.4 to calculate its price using the zero-coupon yields in Table 6.7:

$$P = \frac{100}{1.035} + \frac{100}{1.04^2} + \frac{100 + 1000}{1.045^3} = \$1153$$

This price is identical to the price we computed earlier by replicating the bond. Thus, we can determine the no-arbitrage price of a coupon bond by discounting its cash flows using the zero-coupon yields. In other words, the information in the zero-coupon yield curve is sufficient to price all other risk-free bonds.

Coupon Bond Yields

Given the yields for zero-coupon bonds, we can use Eq. 6.4 to price a coupon bond. In Section 6.3, we saw how to compute the yield to maturity of a coupon bond from its price. Combining these results, we can determine the relationship between the yields of zero-coupon bonds and coupon-paying bonds.

Consider again the three-year, $1000 bond with 10% annual coupons. Given the zero-coupon yields in Table 6.7, we calculate a price for this bond of $1153. From Eq. 6.3, the yield to maturity of this bond is the rate y that satisfies:

$$P = 1153 = \frac{100}{(1 + y)} + \frac{100}{(1 + y)^2} + \frac{100 + 1000}{(1 + y)^3}$$

We can solve for the yield by using a financial calculator or spreadsheet:

	N	I/Y	PV	PMT	FV
Given:	3		−1153	100	1000
Solve for:		**4.44**			
Excel Formula:	=RATE(NPER,PMT,PV,FV)=RATE(3,100,−1153,1000)				

Therefore, the yield to maturity of the bond is 4.44%. We can check this result directly as follows:

$$P = \frac{100}{1.0444} + \frac{100}{1.0444^2} + \frac{100 + 1000}{1.0444^3} = \$1153$$

Because the coupon bond provides cash flows at different points in time, the yield to maturity of a coupon bond is a weighted average of the yields of the zero-coupon bonds of equal and shorter maturities. The weights depend (in a complex way) on the magnitude of the cash flows each period. In this example, the zero-coupon bonds yields were 3.5%, 4.0%, and 4.5%. For this coupon bond, most of the value in the present value calculation comes from the present value of the third cash flow because it includes the principal, so the yield is closest to the three-year zero-coupon yield of 4.5%.

EXAMPLE 6.11

Yields on Bonds with the Same Maturity

MyFinanceLab

PROBLEM

Given the following zero-coupon yields, compare the yield to maturity for a three-year zero-coupon bond, a three-year coupon bond with 4% annual coupons, and a three-year coupon bond with 10% annual coupons. All of these bonds are default free.

Maturity	1 Year	2 Years	3 Years	4 Years
Zero-Coupon YTM	3.50%	4.00%	4.50%	4.75%

SOLUTION

PLAN

From the information provided, the yield to maturity of the three-year zero-coupon bond is 4.50%. Also, because the yields match those in Table 6.7, we already calculated the yield to maturity for the 10% coupon bond as 4.44%. To compute the yield for the 4% coupon bond, we first need to calculate its price, which we can do using Eq. 6.4. Since the coupons are 4%, paid annually, they are $40 per year for three years. The $1000 face value will be repaid at that time. Once we have the price, we can use Eq. 6.3 to compute the yield to maturity.

EXECUTE

Using Eq. 6.4, we have:

$$P = \frac{40}{1.035} + \frac{40}{1.04^2} + \frac{40 + 1000}{1.045^3} = \$986.98$$

The price of the bond with a 4% coupon is $986.98. From Eq. 6.4:

$$\$986.98 = \frac{40}{(1 + y)} + \frac{40}{(1 + y)^2} + \frac{40 + 1000}{(1 + y)^3}$$

We can calculate the yield to maturity using a financial calculator or spreadsheet:

	N	I/Y	PV	PMT	FV
Given:	3		−986.98	40	1000
Solve for:		**4.47**			
Excel Formula:	=RATE(NPER,PMT,PV,FV)=RATE(3,40,−986.98,1000)				

(*Continued*)

To summarize, for the three-year bonds considered:

Coupon Rate	0%	4%	10%
YTM	4.50%	4.47%	4.44%

EVALUATE

Note that even though the bonds all have the same maturity, they have different yields. In fact, holding constant the maturity, the yield decreases as the coupon rate increases. We discuss why below.

Example 6.11 shows that coupon bonds with the same maturity can have different yields depending on their coupon rates. The yield to maturity of a coupon bond is a weighted average of the yields on the zero-coupon bonds. As the coupon increases, earlier cash flows become relatively more important than later cash flows in the calculation of the present value. The shape of the yield curve keys us in on trends with the yield to maturity:

1. If the yield curve is upward sloping (as it is for the yields in Example 6.11), the resulting yield to maturity decreases with the coupon rate of the bond.
2. When the zero-coupon yield curve is downward sloping, the yield to maturity will increase with the coupon rate.
3. With a flat yield curve, all zero-coupon and coupon-paying bonds will have the same yield, independent of their maturities and coupon rates.

Treasury Yield Curves

As we have shown in this section, we can use the zero-coupon yield curve to determine the price and yield to maturity of other risk-free bonds. The plot of the yields of coupon bonds of different maturities is called the *coupon-paying yield curve*. When U.S. bond traders refer to "the yield curve," they are often referring to the coupon-paying Treasury yield curve. As we showed in Example 6.11, two coupon-paying bonds with the same maturity may have different yields. By convention, practitioners always plot the yield of the most recently issued bonds, termed the *on-the-run bonds*. Using similar methods to those employed in this section, we can apply the Law of One Price to determine the zero-coupon bond yields using the coupon-paying yield curve. Thus, either type of yield curve provides enough information to value all other risk-free bonds.

7

Stock Valuation

LEARNING OBJECTIVES

- Understand the tradeoff between dividends and growth in stock valuation

- Appreciate the limitations of valuing a stock based on expected dividends

- Value a stock as the present value of the company's total payout

- Describe the basics of common stock, preferred stock, and stock quotes

- Compare how trades are executed on the NYSE and NASDAQ

- Value a stock as the present value of its expected future dividends

notation

Div_t	dividends paid in year t	P_t	stock price at the end of year t
EPS_t	earnings per share on date t	PV	present value
g	expected dividend growth rate	r_E	equity cost of capital
N	terminal date or forecast horizon		

At 5:00 P.M. on March 21, 2013, footwear and apparel maker Nike, Inc., announced that its quarterly earnings would be higher than expected and that orders for the following year would be strong as well. The next day, Nike's stock price increased by 11% on the New York Stock Exchange to $59.53, with more than 19 million shares being traded—more than four times its average daily volume.

How might an investor decide whether to buy or sell a stock such as Nike at this price? Why would the stock suddenly be worth 11% more after the announcement of this news? What actions can Nike's managers take to further increase the stock price?

To answer these questions, we turn to the Valuation Principle. The Valuation Principle indicates that the price of a security should equal the present value of the expected cash flows an investor will receive from owning it. In this chapter, we apply this idea to stocks. Thus, to value a stock, we need to know the expected cash flows an investor will receive and the appropriate cost of capital with which to discount those cash flows. Both these quantities can be challenging to estimate, and we will develop many of the details needed to do so throughout the remainder of this text.

We begin our study of stock valuation by contrasting the different types of stocks, interpreting a stock quote, and explaining how specialists execute stock trades. We then turn to our first model of stock valuation, the *dividend-discount model*, which considers the dividends and capital gains received by investors who hold the stock for different periods.

7.1 Stock Basics

As discussed in Chapter 1, the ownership of a corporation is divided into shares of stock. A public corporation has many owners and its shares trade on a stock market that provides liquidity for a company's shares and determines the market price for those shares. In this section, we explain what a stock market quote is and introduce the two types of stocks, *common* and *preferred*.

Stock Market Reporting: Stock Quotes

common stock A share of ownership in the corporation, which confers rights to any common dividends as well as rights to vote on election of directors, mergers, and other major events.

ticker symbol A unique abbreviation assigned to a publicly traded company.

Figure 7.1 shows a stock quote with basic information about Nike's stock from Google Finance (www.google.com/finance) for June 25, 2013.[1] Nike's stock is **common stock**, which means a share of ownership in the corporation gives its owner rights to any common dividends as well as rights to vote on the election of directors, mergers, and other major events. The Web page notes that the company is a public corporation (its shares are widely held and traded in a market) and that its shares trade on the NYSE (New York Stock Exchange) under the *ticker symbol* NKE. A **ticker symbol** is a unique abbreviation assigned to a publicly traded company used when its trades are reported on the ticker (a real-time electronic display of trading activity). Traditionally, shares on the NYSE have ticker symbols consisting of three or fewer characters, while shares on the NASDAQ generally have four or more characters in their ticker symbols. However, for recent listings, such as Facebook, which goes by FB on the NASDAQ and Twitter (TWTR on the NYSE), this convention no longer applies.

During the period mid-February through late June 2013, Nike paid two quarterly dividends to its common shareholders, on February 28, and May 30. The dividends are marked by a "D" and the amount of the dividend. In this case, the dividend was 21 cents per share. Thus, if you owned 1000 shares of NKE, you would have received $0.21 \times 1000 = $210 when Nike paid each dividend. The chart also clearly shows the jump in the price of NKE shares in March 2013 that we discussed in the chapter introduction.

Finally, the Web page displays some basic information about the performance of NKE stock. Notice the price of the last trade of NKE shares in the market ($60.39), the price that shares started at when the market opened that day ($60.42), the range of low to high prices reached during trading that day ($59.95 to $60.99), and the volume of trading for the day (5.45 million shares). The total value of all the equity of NKE is its market capitalization, equal to the price per share multiplied by the number of shares outstanding: on June 25, 2013, it was $60.39 \times 893.61 million = $53.97 billion. Over the preceding 52 weeks, NKE achieved a high price of $66.07 and a low price of $42.55 and had an average daily volume of shares traded of 3.54 million shares. Also, note some basic information about the company: the price-earnings ratio (P/E) and earnings per share (EPS), both of which we discussed in Chapter 2. The Web page also notes that NKE's *beta* is 0.88.[2]

---

[1]There are many places on the Internet to get free stock information, such as Google Finance (http://www.google.com/finance), MSN Money (http://www.msn.com/money), the *Wall Street Journal*'s Web site (www.wsj.com), and the exchange sites www.nyse.com and www.nasdaq.com.

[2]*Beta* is a measure of risk that we will discuss in Chapter 12.

FIGURE 7.1

Stock Price Quote
for Nike (NKE)

This screenshot from Google Finance shows the basic stock price information and price history charting for the common stock of Nike. The historical price chart covers the period mid-February through late June 2013. The price of $60.39 is for June 25, 2013.

Source: www.google.com/finance?q=nke.

In preceding chapters, we have learned how financial managers make decisions that affect the value of their company. Although the current price of NKE is $60.39, the stock's price has varied over time, reflecting the expected effects of new decisions and the results of past decisions.

Common Stock

We now examine the rights of common stockholders, including their voice in the running of the corporation. All rights accruing to the shareholders are in proportion to the number of shares they hold.

straight voting Voting for directors where shareholders must vote for each director separately, with each shareholder having as many votes as shares held.

Shareholder Voting. To illustrate the shareholder voting process, consider an election of 10 directors at a company with only two shareholders: Donna and Jonathan. Donna has 600 shares and Jonathan has 400, but they have very different views of how the company should be run. If the company has **straight voting**, each shareholder has as many votes for each director as shares held. That is, for each director, Donna will have 600 votes and

cumulative voting Voting for directors where each shareholder is allocated votes equal to the number of open spots multiplied by his or her number of shares.

Jonathan 400, so Jonathan will lose every vote and have no representation on the board. If the company has **cumulative voting**, each shareholder's total vote allocation for all directors is equal to the number of open spots multiplied by his or her number of shares. With 10 directors up for election, Jonathan is allocated a total of 10×400 votes (4000 votes) and Donna is allocated 10×600 votes (6000 votes) to use across the 10 director spots. Jonathan could allocate all his votes to four directors, ensuring that he has four directors representing his views on the board. Donna would do the same for six directors, ensuring her representation. With cumulative voting, even shareholders with minority blocks (less than 50%) have a chance at representation on the board.

classes Different types of common stock for the same company, often carrying different voting rights.

This example is based on the concept of one share, one vote. Some companies have different types of common stock, called **classes**, which carry different voting rights. This is typical in companies that are family run, or where the founder is still active. For example, Nike has Class A and Class B stock. Phil Knight, Nike's founder, owns almost all the Class A stock, which carries the rights to elect 9 of the company's 12 directors. Alphabet Inc. (Google) has Class A, Class B, and Class C stock. Class A stock has been sold to the public, while Google's founders and managers hold all the Class B stock, each share of which carries 10 times the voting power of a share of Class A stock. Class C stock, which was split from Class A stock in April 2014, has no voting rights.

annual meeting Meeting held once per year where shareholders vote on directors and other proposals as well as ask managers questions.

proxy A written authorization for someone else to vote your shares.

proxy contest When two or more groups are competing to collect proxies to prevail in a matter up for shareholder vote (such as election of directors).

Shareholder Rights. Each year, companies hold an **annual meeting** at which managers and directors answer questions from shareholders, and shareholders vote on the election of directors and other proposals. All shareholders have the right to attend the annual meeting and cast their votes directly. In practice, though, most either allow the board to vote for them or direct that their shares be voted for them via **proxy**, or explicit instructions on how they should be voted. Typically, matters at the annual meeting are uncontested, but occasionally a dissident shareholder group will propose an alternative slate of directors or oppose a management proposal. In that case, each side will actively solicit the proxies of all the shareholders so they may win the vote in a **proxy contest**.

As an ownership claim, common stock carries the right to share in the profits of the corporation through dividend payments. Recall from Chapter 1 that dividends are periodic payments, usually in the form of cash, that firms make to shareholders as a partial return on their investment in the corporation. The board of directors decides the timing and amount of each dividend. Shareholders are paid dividends in proportion to the number of shares they own. If the company is liquidated through bankruptcy and there are assets left over after satisfying the claims of the creditors, shareholders divide the remaining assets proportionally based on each shareholder's number of shares.

Preferred Stock

preferred stock Stock with preference over common shares in payment of dividends and in liquidation.

Some companies have an additional issue of stock called **preferred stock**, which has preference over common shares in the distribution of dividends or cash during liquidation. While the directors can, at their discretion, choose not to pay the preferred shareholders a dividend, they cannot pay a dividend to common stockholders unless they pay the promised dividend to preferred shareholders first. For example, Nike has preferred shares that pay a $0.10 dividend per share each year. The firm must pay this dividend before common shareholders can receive a dividend.

cumulative preferred stock Preferred stock where all missed preferred dividends must be paid before any common dividends can be paid.

non-cumulative preferred stock Preferred stock where missed dividends do not accumulate. Only the current dividend is owed before common dividends can be paid.

Cumulative Versus Non-Cumulative Preferred Stock. There are two types of preferred stock: *cumulative* and *non-cumulative*. With **cumulative preferred stock**, any unpaid dividends are carried forward. For example, if DuPont fails to pay its preferred dividend for several years, its obligation to its cumulative preferred shareholders accumulates, and it cannot pay any dividends to common shareholders until it has paid all the unpaid preferred dividends. With **non-cumulative preferred stock**, missed dividends do not accumulate, and the firm can pay current dividend payments first to preferred and then to common stock shareholders. Almost all preferred stock is cumulative. Some preferred stock also gives preferred shareholders the right to elect one or more directors to the board if the firm is substantially in arrears on preferred dividends.

Preferred Stock: Equity or Debt? You may be wondering how to think about preferred stock—is it equity or is it debt? Economically, it is like a perpetual bond because it has a promised cash flow to holders and there are consequences if those cash flows are not paid. However, unlike debtholders, preferred shareholders cannot force the firm into bankruptcy. Preferred shareholders stand in line in front of common shareholders for annual dividends, but behind regular bondholders, because interest is paid before dividends. If the firm is bankrupt, the same priority is followed in settling claims: bondholders, preferred shareholders, and then common shareholders. Finally, as long as the firm is meeting its preferred dividend obligations, the preferred shareholders have none of the control rights of owners, such as voting on directors or other important matters. However, despite all these similarities to debt, preferred shares are, for all tax and legal purposes, treated as equity.

CONCEPT CHECK

1. What is a share of stock and what are dividends?
2. What are some key differences between preferred and common stock?

7.2 The Mechanics of Stock Trades

Suppose you decide to invest in Nike (NKE), and so you place a market order to buy 100 shares of its stock. A *market order* means you do not specify a price, rather you want the order to execute immediately at the most favorable price available. If instead you wanted to specify a maximum price you were willing to pay, and you were willing to wait until the shares were available at that price, you would place a *limit order*.

What actually happens when you place this market order to buy Nike stock? In market parlance, 100 shares is a "round lot" and would be considered a small order. Small orders such as this would typically be transmitted electronically to the stock exchange via a system called the *Super Display Book System* (which replaced the old SuperDOT system in 2009). Upon reaching the exchange, it would go directly to the workstation of the specialist who oversees trading in Nike stock. Recall from Chapter 1 that a specialist holds a trading license at the NYSE and acts as a market maker for a particular stock, maintaining orderly trading and stepping in to provide liquidity when needed. The small order would automatically execute against the specialist's inventory in a few *milliseconds*.

If you were making a very large or complex trade, the process would involve people. At a physical stock market such as the NYSE, your trade would still be transmitted electronically to the exchange, but it would be sent to the wireless handheld terminal of a *floor broker*. A **floor broker** holds a trading license at the NYSE and works to get the best execution possible for investors. In this case, the floor broker would find the best way to execute the trade, which may be electronically, or may mean going to the physical location where the NKE's designated market maker is. The floor broker would take note of the bid and ask and then negotiate with any selling brokers to buy 15,000 shares at as low a price as possible. Depending on how many shares are offered for sale at the best (lowest) ask price, the trade may need to execute above the ask price in order to clear the full order. So, depending on the size of your order and the current market conditions, an order on the NYSE may be executed very quickly through electronic algorithms or through traditional interaction between floor brokers.

floor broker A person at the NYSE with a trading license who represents orders on the floor, balancing speed and price to get the best execution.

If you were buying a stock on an electronic exchange such as NASDAQ, the trade would proceed slightly differently. Recall from Chapter 1 that NASDAQ is a computer network with no physical location. Also, each stock listed on NASDAQ has multiple dealers posting bid and ask quotes and trading at those prices for their own accounts and for customer accounts. The NASDAQ Market Center integrates these bids and asks with the limit orders of all market participants. If you place an order through your broker or online brokerage account to buy 100 shares of Facebook (FB), the order will be transmitted electronically to the NASDAQ Market Center where it automatically executes against the best (lowest) ask quote for Facebook. If you are trying to buy a very large block of shares, then you can proceed the same way, transmitting your order and having it execute against the limit order book. Depending on the depth of the limit order book (the number of shares for sale close to the best ask price), you may prefer to split your order into smaller trades over a longer period, or even use a dark pool.

But how do you decide whether to buy or sell a stock in the first place? You must estimate the value of the stock and compare it to the current market price. In the rest of this chapter, we discuss one traditional approach to valuing a stock, the *dividend-discount model*.[3]

CONCEPT   3. What is the role of a floor broker at the NYSE?
CHECK   4. What is the role of a dealer at the NASDAQ?

7.3   The Dividend-Discount Model

The Valuation Principle implies that to value any security, we must determine the expected cash flows that an investor will receive from owning it. We begin our analysis of stock valuation by considering the cash flows for an investor with a one-year investment horizon. We will show how the stock's price and the investor's return from the investment are related. We then consider the perspective of investors with a long investment horizon. Finally, we will reach our goal of establishing the first stock valuation method: the *dividend-discount model*.

A One-Year Investor

There are two potential sources of cash flows from owning a stock:

1. The firm might pay out cash to its shareholders in the form of a dividend.
2. The investor might generate cash by selling the shares at some future date.

The total amount received in dividends and from selling the stock will depend on the investor's investment horizon. Let's begin by considering the perspective of a one-year investor.

When an investor buys a stock, she will pay the current market price for a share, P_0. While she continues to hold the stock, she will be entitled to any dividends the stock pays. Let Div_1 be the total dividends the investor expects to be paid per share during the year. At the end of the year, the investor will sell her share at the new market price. Let P_1 be the price the investor expects to sell her share at at the end of the year. Assuming for simplicity that all dividends are paid at the end of the year, we have the following timeline for this investment:

$$\begin{array}{ccc} 0 & & 1 \\ \vdash & \! & \dashv \\ -P_0 & & Div_1 + P_1 \end{array}$$

---

[3]In Chapter 10, we return to the question of stock valuation with a discussion of additional approaches. As you will see, when estimating the value of a stock, it is best to try several different approaches to increase the confidence in your estimate.

Of course, the future dividend payment and stock price in this timeline are not known with certainty. Rather, these values are based on the investor's expectations at the time the stock is purchased. Given these expectations, the investor will be willing to pay a price today up to the point at which the benefits equal the cost—that is, up to the point at which the current price equals the present value of the expected future dividend and sale price.

Because these cash flows are risky, we cannot discount them using the risk-free interest rate, but instead must use the cost of capital for the firm's equity. We have previously defined the cost of capital of any investment to be the expected return that investors could earn on their best alternative investment with similar risk and maturity. Thus, we must discount the equity cash flows based on the **equity cost of capital**, r_E, for the stock, which is the expected return of other investments available in the market with equivalent risk to the firm's shares. Doing so leads to the following equation for the stock price:

equity cost of capital The expected rate of return available in the market on other investments that have equivalent risk to the risk associated with the firm's shares.

$$P_0 = \frac{Div_1 + P_1}{1 + r_E} \qquad (7.1)$$

If the current stock price were less than this amount, the cost would be less than the PV of the benefits, so investors would rush in and buy it, driving up the stock's price. If the stock price exceeded this amount, selling would be attractive and the stock price would quickly fall.

Dividend Yields, Capital Gains, and Total Returns

A critical part of Eq. 7.1 for determining the stock price is the firm's equity cost of capital, r_E. At the beginning of this section, we pointed out that an investor's return from holding a stock comes from dividends and cash generated from selling the stock. We can rewrite Eq. 7.1 to show these two return components. If we multiply by $(1 + r_E)$, divide by P_0, and subtract 1 from both sides, we have

Total Return

$$r_E = \underbrace{\frac{Div_1 + P_1}{P_0} - 1}_{} = \underbrace{\frac{Div_1}{P_0}}_{\text{Dividend Yield}} + \underbrace{\frac{P_1 - P_0}{P_0}}_{\text{Capital Gain Rate}} \qquad (7.2)$$

dividend yield The expected annual dividend of a stock divided by its current price; the percentage return an investor expects to earn from the dividend paid by the stock.

The first term on the right side of Eq. 7.2 is the stock's **dividend yield**, which is the expected annual dividend of the stock divided by its current price. The dividend yield is the percentage return the investor expects to earn from the dividend paid by the stock. The second term on the right side of Eq. 7.2 reflects the **capital gain** the investor will earn on the stock, which is the difference between the expected sale price and the original purchase price for the stock, $P_1 - P_0$. We divide the capital gain by the current stock price to express the capital gain as a percentage return, called the **capital gain rate**.

capital gain The amount by which the selling price of an asset exceeds its initial purchase price.

The sum of the dividend yield and the capital gain rate is called the **total return** of the stock. The total return is the expected return the investor will earn for a one-year investment in the stock. Equation 7.2 states that the stock's total return should equal the equity cost of capital. In other words, *the expected total return of the stock should equal the expected return of other investments available in the market with equivalent risk.*

capital gain rate An expression of capital gain as a percentage of the initial price of the asset.

This result is exactly what we would expect: The firm must pay its shareholders a return commensurate with the return they can earn elsewhere while taking the same risk. If the stock offered a higher return than other securities with the same risk, investors would sell those other investments and buy the stock instead. This activity would then drive up the stock's current price, lowering its dividend yield and capital gain rate until Eq. 7.2 holds true. If the stock offered a lower expected return, investors would sell the stock and drive down its price until Eq. 7.2 was again satisfied.

total return The sum of a stock's dividend yield and its capital gain rate.

EXAMPLE 7.1

Stock Prices
and Returns

MyFinanceLab

PROBLEM

Suppose you expect Longs Drug Stores to pay an annual dividend of $0.56 per share in the coming year and to trade for $45.50 per share at the end of the year. If investments with equivalent risk to Longs' stock have an expected return of 6.80%, what is the most you would pay today for Longs' stock? What dividend yield and capital gain rate would you expect at this price?

SOLUTION

PLAN

We can use Eq. 7.1 to solve for the beginning price we would pay now (P_0) given our expectations about dividends ($Div_1 = \$0.56$) and future price ($P_1 = \$45.50$) and the return we need to expect to earn to be willing to invest ($r_E = 0.068$). We can then use Eq. 7.2 to calculate the dividend yield and capital gain rate.

EXECUTE

Using Eq. 7.1, we have

$$P_0 = \frac{Div_1 + P_1}{1 + r_E} = \frac{\$0.56 + \$45.50}{1.0680} = \$43.13$$

Referring to Eq. 7.2, we see that at this price, Longs' dividend yield is $Div_1/P_0 = 0.56/43.13 = 1.30\%$. The expected capital gain is $\$45.50 - \$43.13 = \$2.37$ per share, for a capital gain rate of $2.37/43.13 = 5.50\%$.

EVALUATE

At a price of $43.13, Longs' expected total return is $1.30\% + 5.50\% = 6.80\%$, which is equal to its equity cost of capital (the return being paid by investments with equivalent risk to Longs'). This amount is the most we would be willing to pay for Longs' stock. If we paid more, our expected return would be less than 6.8% and we would rather invest elsewhere.

A Multiyear Investor

We now extend the intuition we developed for the one-year investor's return to a multiyear investor. Equation 7.1 depends upon the expected stock price in one year, P_1. But suppose we planned to hold the stock for two years. Then we would receive dividends in both year 1 and year 2 before selling the stock, as shown in the following timeline:

Setting the stock price equal to the present value of the future cash flows in this case implies:[4]

$$P_0 = \frac{Div_1}{1 + r_E} + \frac{Div_2 + P_2}{(1 + r_E)^2} \tag{7.3}$$

Equations 7.1 and 7.3 are different: As a two-year investor we care about the dividend and stock price in year 2, but these terms do not appear in Eq. 7.1. Does this difference imply that a two-year investor will value the stock differently than a one-year investor?

---

[4]In using the same equity cost of capital for both periods, we are assuming that the equity cost of capital does not depend on the term of the cash flows; that is, r_E is not different for year 2 (or any other year). Otherwise, we would need to adjust for the term structure of the equity cost of capital (as we did with the yield curve for risk-free cash flows in Chapter 5). This step would complicate the analysis but would not change its results.

The answer to this question is no. A one-year investor does not care about the dividend and stock price in year 2 directly. She will care about them indirectly, however, because they will affect the price for which she can sell the stock at the end of year 1. For example, suppose the investor sells the stock to another one-year investor with the same expectations. The new investor will expect to receive the dividend and stock price at the end of year 2, so he will be willing to pay

$$P_1 = \frac{Div_2 + P_2}{1 + r_E}$$

for the stock. Substituting this expression for P_1 into Eq. 7.1, we get the same result as in Eq. 7.3:

$$P_0 = \frac{Div_1 + P_1}{1 + r_E} = \frac{Div_1}{1 + r_E} + \frac{1}{1 + r_E} \overbrace{\left(\frac{Div_2 + P_2}{1 + r_E} \right)}^{P_1}$$

$$= \frac{Div_1}{1 + r_E} + \frac{Div_2 + P_2}{(1 + r_E)^2}$$

Thus, the formula for the stock price for a two-year investor is the same as that for a sequence of two one-year investors.

Dividend-Discount Model Equation

dividend-discount model A model that values shares of a firm according to the present value of the future dividends the firm will pay.

We can continue this process for any number of years by replacing the final stock price with the value that the next holder of the stock would be willing to pay. Doing so leads to the general **dividend-discount model** for the stock price, where the horizon N is arbitrary:

Dividend-Discount Model

$$P_0 = \frac{Div_1}{1 + r_E} + \frac{Div_2}{(1 + r_E)^2} + \cdots + \frac{Div_N}{(1 + r_E)^N} + \frac{P_N}{(1 + r_E)^N} \qquad (7.4)$$

Equation 7.4 applies to a single N-year investor, who will collect dividends for N years and then sell the stock, or to a series of investors who hold the stock for shorter periods and then resell it. Note that Eq. 7.4 holds for *any* horizon N. As a consequence, all investors (with the same expectations) will attach the same value to the stock, independent of their investment horizons. How long they intend to hold the stock and whether they collect their return in the form of dividends or capital gains is irrelevant. For the special case in which the firm eventually pays dividends and is never acquired or liquidated, it is possible to hold the shares forever. In this scenario, rather than having a stopping point where we sell the shares, we rewrite Eq. 7.4 to show that the dividends go on into the future:

$$P_0 = \frac{Div_1}{1 + r_E} + \frac{Div_2}{(1 + r_E)^2} + \frac{Div_3}{(1 + r_E)^3} + \cdots \qquad (7.5)$$

That is, *the price of the stock is equal to the present value of all of the expected future dividends it will pay.*

CONCEPT CHECK

5. How do you calculate the total return of a stock?

6. What discount rate do you use to discount the future cash flows of a stock?

7.4   Estimating Dividends in the Dividend-Discount Model

Equation 7.5 expresses the value of a stock in terms of the expected future dividends the firm will pay. Of course, estimating these dividends—especially for the distant future—is difficult. A commonly used approximation is to assume that in the long run, dividends will grow at a constant rate. In this section, we consider the implications of this assumption for stock prices and explore the tradeoff between dividends and growth.

Constant Dividend Growth

The simplest forecast for the firm's future dividends states that they will grow at a constant rate, g, forever. That case yields the following timeline for the cash flows for an investor who buys the stock today and holds it:

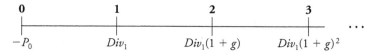

Because the expected dividends are a constant growth perpetuity, we can use Eq. 4.7 to calculate their present value. We then obtain the following simple formula for the stock price:[5]

Constant Dividend Growth Model

$$P_0 = \frac{Div_1}{r_E - g} \qquad (7.6)$$

constant dividend growth model A model for valuing a stock by viewing its dividends as a constant growth perpetuity.

According to the **constant dividend growth model**, the value of the firm depends on the dividend level next year, divided by the equity cost of capital adjusted by the growth rate.

EXAMPLE 7.2

Valuing a Firm with Constant Dividend Growth

MyFinanceLab

PROBLEM

Consolidated Edison, Inc. (Con Ed) is a regulated utility company that services the New York City area. Suppose Con Ed plans to pay $2.30 per share in dividends in the coming year. If its equity cost of capital is 7% and dividends are expected to grow by 2% per year in the future, estimate the value of Con Ed's stock.

SOLUTION

PLAN

Because the dividends are expected to grow perpetually at a constant rate, we can use Eq. 7.6 to value Con Ed. The next dividend (Div_1) is expected to be $2.30, the growth rate ($g$) is 2%, and the equity cost of capital (r_E) is 7%.

EXECUTE

$$P_0 = \frac{Div_1}{r_E - g} = \frac{\$2.30}{0.07 - 0.02} = \$46.00$$

EVALUATE

You would be willing to pay 20 times this year's dividend of $2.30 to own Con Ed stock because you are buying a claim to this year's dividend *and* to an infinite growing series of future dividends.

---

[5]As discussed in Chapter 4, this formula requires that $g < r_E$. Otherwise, the present value of the growing perpetuity is infinite. The implication here is that it is impossible for a stock's dividends to grow at a rate $g > r_E$ *forever*. If the growth rate does exceed r_E, the situation must be temporary, and the constant growth model cannot be applied in such a case.

For another interpretation of Eq. 7.6, note that we can rearrange it as follows:

$$r_E = \frac{Div_1}{P_0} + g \tag{7.7}$$

Comparing Eq. 7.7 with Eq. 7.2, we see that g equals the expected capital gain rate. In other words, with constant expected dividend growth, the expected growth rate of the share price matches the growth rate of the dividends.

Dividends Versus Investment and Growth

In Eq. 7.6, the firm's share price increases with the current dividend level, Div_1, and the expected growth rate, g. To maximize its share price, a firm would like to increase both these quantities. Often, however, the firm faces a tradeoff: Increasing growth may require investment, and money spent on investment cannot be used to pay dividends. The constant dividend growth model provides insight into this tradeoff.

dividend payout rate
The fraction of a firm's earnings that the firm pays out as dividends each year.

A Simple Model of Growth. What determines the rate of growth of a firm's dividends? If we define a firm's **dividend payout rate** as the fraction of its earnings that the firm pays as dividends each year, then we can write the firm's dividend per share at date t as follows:

$$Div_t = \underbrace{\frac{Earnings_t}{Shares\ Outstanding_t}}_{EPS_t} \times Dividend\ Payout\ Rate_t \tag{7.8}$$

That is, the dividend each year is equal to the firm's earnings per share (EPS) multiplied by its dividend payout rate. The firm can, therefore, increase its dividend in three ways:

1. It can increase its earnings (net income).
2. It can increase its dividend payout rate.
3. It can decrease its number of shares outstanding.

Suppose for now that the firm does not issue new shares (or buy back its existing shares), so that the number of shares outstanding remains fixed. We can then explore the tradeoff between options 1 and 2.

A firm can do one of two things with its earnings: It can pay them out to investors, or it can retain and reinvest them. By investing cash today, a firm can increase its future dividends. For simplicity, let's assume that absent reinvesting its retained earnings, the firm does not grow, so the current level of earnings generated by the firm remains constant. If all increases in future earnings result exclusively from new investment made with retained earnings, then

$$Change\ in\ Earnings = New\ Investment \times Return\ on\ New\ Investment \tag{7.9}$$

retention rate The fraction of a firm's current earnings that the firm retains.

New investment equals the firm's earnings multiplied by its **retention rate**, or the fraction of current earnings that the firm retains:

$$New\ Investment = Earnings \times Retention\ Rate \tag{7.10}$$

Substituting Eq. 7.10 into Eq. 7.9 and dividing by earnings gives an expression for the growth rate of earnings:

$$Earnings\ Growth\ Rate = \frac{Change\ in\ Earnings}{Earnings}$$

$$= Retention\ Rate \times Return\ on\ New\ Investment \tag{7.11}$$

If the firm chooses to keep its dividend payout rate constant, then the growth in its dividends will equal the growth in its earnings:

$$g = \text{Retention Rate} \times \text{Return on New Investment} \qquad (7.12)$$

Profitable Growth. Equation 7.12 shows that a firm can increase its growth rate by retaining more of its earnings. But if the firm retains more earnings, and as a result pays out a smaller fraction of those earnings as dividends, then according to Eq. 7.8 the firm may have to cut its dividend in the short run. If a firm wants to increase its share price, should it cut its dividend and invest more, or should it cut its investments and increase its dividend? Not surprisingly, the answer to this question will depend on the profitability of the firm's investments. Let's consider an example.

EXAMPLE 7.3

Cutting Dividends
for Profitable Growth

MyFinanceLab

PROBLEM

Crane Sporting Goods expects to have earnings per share of $6 in the coming year. Rather than reinvest these earnings and grow, the firm plans to pay out all of its earnings as a dividend. With these expectations of no growth, Crane's current share price is $60.

Suppose Crane could cut its dividend payout rate to 75% for the foreseeable future and use the retained earnings to open new stores. The return on its investment in these stores is expected to be 12%. If we assume that the risk of these new investments is the same as the risk of its existing investments, then the firm's equity cost of capital is unchanged. What effect would this new policy have on Crane's stock price?

SOLUTION

PLAN

To figure out the effect of this policy on Crane's stock price, we need to know several things. First, we need to compute its equity cost of capital. Next, we must determine Crane's dividend and growth rate under the new policy.

Because we know that Crane currently has a growth rate of 0 ($g = 0$), a dividend of $6, and a price of $60, we can use Eq. 7.7 to estimate r_E. Next, the new dividend will simply be 75% of the old dividend of $6. Finally, given a retention rate of 25% and a return on new investment of 12%, we can use Eq. 7.12 to compute the new growth rate (g). Finally, armed with the new dividend, Crane's equity cost of capital, and its new growth rate, we can use Eq. 7.6 to compute the price of Crane's shares if it institutes the new policy.

EXECUTE

Using Eq. 7.7 to estimate r_E, we have

$$r_E = \frac{Div_1}{P_0} + g = \frac{\$6}{\$60} + 0\% = 0.10 + 0$$

In other words, to justify Crane's stock price under its current policy, the expected return of other stocks in the market with equivalent risk must be 10%.

Next, we consider the consequences of the new policy. If Crane reduces its dividend payout rate to 75%, then from Eq. 7.8 its dividend this coming year will fall to $Div_1 = EPS_1 \times 75\% = \$6 \times 75\% = \$4.50$.

At the same time, because the firm will now retain 25% of its earnings to invest in new stores, from Eq. 7.12 its growth rate will increase to

$$g = \text{Retention Rate} \times \text{Return on New Investment} = 0.25 \times 0.12 = 0.03 = 3\%$$

Assuming Crane can continue to grow at this rate, we can compute its share price under the new policy using the constant dividend growth model of Eq. 7.6:

$$P_0 = \frac{Div_1}{r_E - g} = \frac{\$4.50}{0.10 - 0.03} = \$64.29$$

EVALUATE

Crane's share price should rise from $60 to $64.29 if the company cuts its dividend in order to increase its investment and growth. By using its earnings to invest in projects that offer a rate of return (12%) greater than its equity cost of capital (10%), Crane has created value for its shareholders.

In Example 7.3, cutting the firm's dividend in favor of growth raised the firm's stock price. This is not always the case, however, as Example 7.4 demonstrates.

EXAMPLE 7.4

Unprofitable Growth

MyFinanceLab

PROBLEM

Suppose Crane Sporting Goods decides to cut its dividend payout rate to 75% to invest in new stores, as in Example 7.3. But now suppose that the return on these new investments is 8%, rather than 12%. Given its expected earnings per share this year of $6 and its equity cost of capital of 10% (we again assume that the risk of the new investments is the same as its existing investments), what will happen to Crane's current share price in this case?

SOLUTION

PLAN

We will follow the steps in Example 7.3, except that in this case, we assume a return on new investments of 8% when computing the new growth rate (g) instead of 12% as in Example 7.3.

EXECUTE

Just as in Example 7.3, Crane's dividend will fall to $6 \times 0.75 = \$4.50$. Its growth rate under the new policy, given the lower return on new investment, will now be $g = 0.25 \times 0.08 = 0.02 = 2\%$. The new share price is therefore

$$P_0 = \frac{Div_1}{r_E - g} = \frac{\$4.50}{0.10 - 0.02} = \$56.25$$

EVALUATE

Even though Crane will grow under the new policy, the return on its new investments is too low. The company's share price will fall if it cuts its dividend to make new investments with a return of only 8%. By reinvesting its earnings at a rate (8%) that is lower than its equity cost of capital (10%), Crane has reduced shareholder value.

Comparing Example 7.3 with Example 7.4, we see that the effect of cutting the firm's dividend to grow crucially depends on the value of the new investments the firm plans to make. In Example 7.3, the return on new investment of 12% exceeds the firm's equity cost of capital of 10%, so the investment is a good one. In Example 7.4, however, the return on new investment is only 8%, so the new investment's return is below the firm's cost of capital. In that case, the new investment is not worthwhile even though it will lead to earnings growth. In this example, we can check that cutting the firm's dividend to increase investment will create value and raise the stock price if, and only if, the new investments generate a return greater than their cost of capital. In Chapter 8, we will consider more generally how to identify projects that create value and thus increase the stock price.

Changing Growth Rates

Successful young firms often have very high initial earnings growth rates. During this period of high growth, firms often retain 100% of their earnings to exploit profitable investment opportunities. As they mature, their growth slows to rates more typical of established companies. At that point, their earnings exceed their investment needs and they begin to pay dividends.

We cannot use the constant dividend growth model to value the stock of such a firm for two reasons:

1. These firms often pay *no* dividends when they are young.
2. Their growth rate continues to change over time until they mature.

However, we can use the general form of the dividend-discount model to value such a firm by applying the constant growth model to calculate the future share price of the stock P_N once the firm matures and its expected growth rate stabilizes:

Specifically, if the firm is expected to grow at a long-term rate g after year $N + 1$, then from the constant dividend growth model:

$$P_N = \frac{Div_{N+1}}{r_E - g} \tag{7.13}$$

We can then use this estimate of P_N as a final cash flow in the dividend-discount model. Intuitively, we value the stock as the present value of the dividends we will receive plus the present value of the price we expect to be able to sell the stock for in the future. For example, consider a company with expected dividends of $2.00, $2.50, and $3.00 in each of the next three years. After that point, its dividends are expected to grow at a constant rate of 5%. If its equity cost of capital is 12%, we can find the current price. Using Eq. 7.13, we can compute the price in year 3:

$$P_N = \frac{Div_{N+1}}{r_E - g} = \left(\frac{\$3.00\,(1.05)}{0.12 - 0.05} \right) = 45.00$$

Now, using Eq. 7.4, we calculate the current price as the PV of the first 3 years' dividends and then the price at the end of year 3:

$$P_0 = \frac{\$2.00}{1.12} + \frac{\$2.50}{(1.12)^2} + \frac{\$3.00}{(1.12)^3} + \frac{\$45.00}{(1.12)^3} = \$37.94$$

This example also reinforces an important point: The constant dividend growth model (Eq. 7.13) is just a special case of the general dividend-discount formula (Eq. 7.4). We can always value all the stream of dividends using Eq. 7.4. However, if we assume constant growth, we can apply the growing perpetuity shortcut to all or part of the dividend stream, depending on whether the constant growth starts now or at some point in the future.

COMMON MISTAKE

Forgetting to "Grow" This Year's Dividend

The most common mistake in handling growing dividends is to use the current period's dividend in the numerator of the growing perpetuity formula. In the example just discussed in the text above, the dividends reached $3 in year 3, and then grew by 5% per year thereafter. A common mistake is to calculate the growing stream of dividends as

$$\frac{3.00}{0.12 - 0.05},$$

forgetting that next year's dividend (the numerator) has already grown by 5%! As we show in the example, the correct calculation is

$$\frac{3.00 \times (1.05)}{0.12 - 0.05} = \$45.$$

Also, remember to avoid the common mistake from Chapter 4: The growing perpetuity formula gives the value in year N for dividends starting in year $N + 1$. In the example above, the formula gives the value in year 3 of the growing dividend stream starting in year 4. That is why we discount the $45 back only three years.

EXAMPLE 7.5

Valuing a Firm
with Two Different
Growth Rates

MyFinanceLab

PROBLEM

Small Fry, Inc., has just invented a potato chip that looks and tastes like a french fry. Given the phenomenal market response to this product, Small Fry is reinvesting all of its earnings to expand its operations. Earnings were $2 per share this past year and are expected to grow at a rate of 20% per year until the end of year 4. At that point, other companies are likely to bring out competing products. Analysts project that at the end of year 4, Small Fry will cut its investment and begin paying 60% of its earnings as dividends. Its growth will also slow to a long-run rate of 4%. If Small Fry's equity cost of capital is 8%, what is the value of a share today?

SOLUTION

PLAN

We can use Small Fry's projected earnings growth rate and payout rate to forecast its future earnings and dividends. After year 4, Small Fry's dividends will grow at a constant 4%, so we can use the constant dividend growth model (Eq. 7.13) to value all dividends after that point. Finally, we can pull everything together with the dividend-discount model (Eq. 7.4).

EXECUTE

The following spreadsheet projects Small Fry's earnings and dividends:

Year	0	1	2	3	4	5	6
Earnings							
1 EPS Growth Rate (versus prior year)		20%	20%	20%	20%	4%	4%
2 EPS	$2.00	$2.40	$2.88	$3.46	$4.15	$4.31	$4.49
Dividends							
3 Dividend Payout Rate		0%	0%	0%	60%	60%	60%
4 Div		$ —	$ —	$ —	$2.49	$2.59	$2.69

Starting from $2.00 in year 0, EPS grows by 20% per year until year 4, after which growth slows to 4%. Small Fry's dividend payout rate is zero until year 4, when competition reduces its investment opportunities and its payout rate rises to 60%. Multiplying EPS by the dividend payout ratio, we project Small Fry's future dividends in line 4.

After year 4, Small Fry's dividends will grow at the constant expected long-run rate of 4% per year. Thus, we can use the constant dividend growth model to project Small Fry's share price at the end of year 3. Given its equity cost of capital of 8%,

$$P_3 = \frac{Div_4}{r_E - g} = \frac{\$2.49}{0.08 - 0.04} = \$62.25$$

We then apply the dividend-discount model (Eq. 7.4) with this terminal value:

$$P_0 = \frac{Div_1}{1 + r_E} + \frac{Div_2}{(1 + r_E)^2} + \frac{Div_3}{(1 + r_E)^3} + \frac{P_3}{(1 + r_E)^3} = \frac{\$62.25}{(1.08)^3} = \$49.42$$

EVALUATE

The dividend-discount model is flexible enough to handle any forecasted pattern of dividends. Here, the dividends were zero for several years and then settled into a constant growth rate, allowing us to use the constant dividend growth model as a shortcut.

TABLE 7.1

The Dividend-Discount Model

General formula	$P_0 = \dfrac{Div_1}{1 + r_E} + \dfrac{Div_2}{(1 + r_E)^2} + \cdots + \dfrac{Div_N}{(1 + r_E)^N} + \dfrac{P_N}{(1 + r_E)^N}$
If dividend growth is constant	$P_0 = \dfrac{Div_1}{r_E - g}$
If early growth is variable followed by constant growth	$P_0 = \dfrac{Div_1}{1 + r_E} + \dfrac{Div_2}{(1 + r_E)^2} + \cdots + \dfrac{Div_N}{(1 + r_E)^N} + \left(\dfrac{1}{(1 + r_E)^N} \right) \left(\dfrac{Div_{N+1}}{r_E - g} \right)$

Table 7.1 summarizes the dividend-discount model, including how to apply the shortcut for constant growth.

Value Drivers and the Dividend-Discount Model

Now that we have fully developed the dividend-discount model, it is worth assessing how well it does capturing the intuitive drivers of stock value. When we think about how valuable a company is, we usually focus on how profitable it is now and how that profitability will grow or decline in the future, along with the risk of investing in the company. Where are these measures captured in the dividend-discount model? Profitability determines the company's ability to pay dividends, so, implicitly in the forecasted dividend stream, we are forecasting the company's profitability. As for the risk, that is captured in the equity cost of capital we use to discount those forecasted dividends. Riskier investments require higher expected returns, which enter the dividend-discount model as higher equity cost of capital.

CONCEPT CHECK
7. What are three ways that a firm can increase the amount of its future dividends per share?

8. Under what circumstances can a firm increase its share price by cutting its dividend and investing more?

7.5 Limitations of the Dividend-Discount Model

The dividend-discount model has two fundamental limitations that we will now address: its reliance on dividend forecasts and lack of applicability to non-dividend-paying stocks.

Uncertain Dividend Forecasts

The dividend-discount model values a stock based on a forecast of the future dividends paid to shareholders. But unlike a Treasury bond, whose cash flows are known with virtual certainty, a firm's future dividends carry a tremendous amount of uncertainty.

Let's reconsider the example of Nike (NKE). In 2013, NKE paid annual dividends of $0.84 (by paying four quarterly dividends of $0.21 each). If we assume an equity cost of capital of 10% and expected dividend growth of 8.5%, the constant dividend growth model implies a share price for NKE of

$$P_0 = \frac{Div_1}{r_E - g} = \frac{\$0.84 \, (1 + 0.085)}{0.10 - 0.085} = \$60.76$$

which is quite close to the $60.39 share price that the stock had at the time. With a 9% dividend growth rate, however, this estimate would rise to more than $91 per share; with a 6% dividend growth rate, the estimate falls to less than $23 per share. As we see in Figure 7.2, even small changes in the assumed dividend growth rate can lead to large changes in the estimated stock price.

FIGURE 7.2

Implied NKE Stock
Prices for Different
Expected Growth
Rates

The figure shows what the price of Nike would be in 2013 for different dividend growth expectations. Stock prices are based on the constant dividend growth model. We assume a dividend in 2013 of $0.84 and an equity cost of capital of 10%. The expected dividend growth rate varies from 0% to 9%. Note how even a small change in the expected growth rate produces a large change in the stock price, especially at higher growth rates.

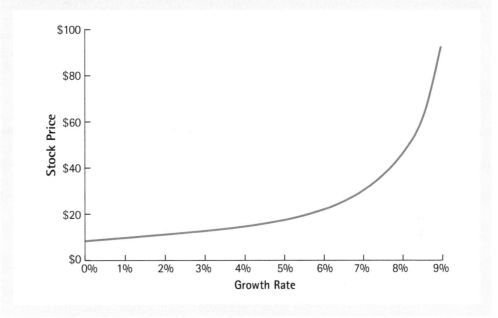

Furthermore, it is difficult to know which estimate of the dividend growth rate is more reasonable. NKE more than doubled its dividend between 2005 and 2010, but its earnings growth then moderated. Consequently, that rate of increase was not sustainable and its dividend increased by about 40% from 2010 to 2013. However, continued strong growth allowed Nike to increase dividends by over 50% from 2013 to the end of 2015 and the stock price increased to nearly $130 per share. From Eq. 7.8, forecasting dividends requires forecasting the firm's earnings, dividend payout rate, and future share count. Future earnings, however, will depend on interest expenses (which, in turn, depend on how much the firm borrows), and the firm's share count and dividend payout rate will depend on whether NKE uses a portion of its earnings to repurchase shares. Because borrowing and repurchase decisions are at management's discretion, they are more difficult to forecast reliably than other fundamental aspects of the firm's cash flows.[6]

Non-Dividend-Paying Stocks

Many companies do not pay dividends—Facebook, Amazon.com, and Google are just a few examples. How then do we value those stocks? In the next section, we discuss a small modification to the dividend-discount model to capture total payouts to shareholders, whether the payouts are dividends or not. In Chapter 10, we will discuss other valuation approaches that do not rely on payouts. Those approaches will be more meaningful once we have covered how financial managers create value within the firm through decisions about which projects to approve. So, in Chapters 8 and 9, we will cover investment decision rules and project evaluation.

**CONCEPT
CHECK**

9. What are the main limitations of the dividend-discount model?

10. What pieces of information are needed to forecast dividends?

---

[6]We discuss management's decision to borrow funds or repurchase shares in Part 6 of the text.

7.6 Share Repurchases and the Total Payout Model

share repurchase A transaction in which a firm uses cash to buy back its own stock.

In our discussion of the dividend-discount model, we implicitly assumed that any cash paid out by the firm to shareholders takes the form of a dividend. In recent years, an increasing number of firms have replaced dividend payouts with *share repurchases*. In a **share repurchase**, the firm uses excess cash to buy back its own stock. Share repurchases have two consequences for the dividend-discount model. First, the more cash the firm uses to repurchase shares, the less cash it has available to pay dividends. Second, by repurchasing shares, the firm decreases its share count, which increases its earnings and dividends on a per-share basis.

In the dividend-discount model, we valued a share from the perspective of a single shareholder, discounting the dividends the shareholder will receive:

$$P_0 = PV(\text{Future Dividends per Share}) \tag{7.14}$$

total payout model A method that values shares of a firm by discounting the firm's total payouts to equity holders (that is, all the cash distributed as dividends and stock repurchases) and then dividing by the current number of shares outstanding.

An alternative method that may be more reliable when a firm repurchases shares is the **total payout model**, which values *all* of the firm's equity, rather than a single share. To use this model, we discount the total payouts that the firm makes to shareholders, which is the total amount spent on both dividends *and* share repurchases (net of new share issuance).[7] This gives the total value of the firm's equity. We then divide by the current number of shares outstanding to determine the share price:

Total Payout Model

$$P_0 = \frac{PV(\text{Future Total Dividends and Net Repurchases})}{\text{Shares Outstanding}_0} \tag{7.15}$$

We can apply the same simplifications to the total payout method that we obtained by assuming constant growth in Section 7.3. The only change is that *we discount total dividends and share repurchases and use the growth rate of earnings (rather than earnings per share) when forecasting the growth of the firm's total payouts.* When the firm uses share repurchases, this method can be more reliable and easier to apply than the dividend-discount model.

EXAMPLE 7.6
Valuation with Share Repurchases

MyFinanceLab

PROBLEM
Titan Industries has 217 million shares outstanding and expects earnings at the end of this year of $860 million. Titan plans to pay out 50% of its earnings in total, paying 30% as a dividend and using 20% to repurchase shares. If Titan's earnings are expected to grow by 7.5% per year and these payout rates remain constant, determine Titan's share price assuming an equity cost of capital of 10%.

SOLUTION

PLAN
Based on the equity cost of capital of 10% and an expected earnings growth rate of 7.5%, we can compute the present value of Titan's future payouts as a constant growth perpetuity. The only input missing here is Titan's total payouts this year, which we can calculate as 50% of its earnings. The present value of all of Titan's future payouts is the value of its total equity. To obtain the price of a share, we divide the total value by the number of shares outstanding (217 million).

EXECUTE
Titan will have total payouts this year of 50% × $860 million = $430 million. Using the constant growth perpetuity formula, we have

[7]You can think of the total payouts as the amount you would receive if you owned 100% of the firm's shares: You would receive all the dividends, plus the proceeds from selling shares back to the firm in the share repurchase.

$$PV(\text{Future Total Dividends and Repurchases}) = \frac{\$430 \text{ million}}{0.10 - 0.075} = \$17.2 \text{ billion}$$

This present value represents the total value of Titan's equity (i.e., its market capitalization). To compute the share price, we divide by the current number of shares outstanding:

$$P_0 = \frac{\$17.2 \text{ billion}}{217 \text{ million shares}} = \$79.26 \text{ per share}$$

EVALUATE

Using the total payout method, we did not need to know the firm's split between dividends and share repurchases. To compare this method with the dividend-discount model, note that Titan will pay a dividend of $30\% \times (\$860 \text{ million}/217 \text{ million shares}) = \$1.19$ per share, for a dividend yield of $1.19/79.26 = 1.50\%$. From Eq. 7.7, we can solve for Titan's expected growth rates of EPS, dividend, and share price:

$$g = r_E - \frac{Div_1}{P_0} = .10 - \frac{1.19}{79.26} = 0.085 = 8.5\%.$$

This growth rate exceeds the 7.50% growth rate of earnings because Titan's share count will decline over time owing to its share repurchases.[8]

CONCEPT CHECK

11. How does the total payout model address part of the dividend-discount model's limitations?

12. How does the growth rate used in the total payout model differ from the growth rate used in the dividend-discount model?

7.7 Putting It All Together

We now return to the questions posed at the beginning of the chapter. First, how would an investor decide whether to buy or sell Nike stock? She would value the stock using her own expectations. We showed one set of expectations about dividend growth that would be consistent with the price. If her expectations were substantially different, she might conclude that the stock was over- or under-priced at $60.39 in 2013. Based on that conclusion, she would sell or buy the stock, and time would reveal whether her expectations were better than the market's.

Second, how could Nike stock suddenly be worth 11% more after Nike's announcement in March of 2013? As investors digested the news in Nike's announcement and updated their expectations, they would have determined that the previous day's closing price was too low based on the new information about future earnings growth. Buying pressure would then drive the stock price up until the buys and sells came into balance.

Third, what should Nike's managers do to raise the stock price further? The only way to raise the stock price is to make value-increasing decisions. We turn to this task in the next section of the book. As shown in Chapters 8 and 9, through capital budgeting analysis, managers can identify projects that add value to the company. By increasing the value of the company through good investment decisions, Nike's managers can increase the stock price. Chapter 10 returns to the question of stock valuation and extends the techniques developed here to incorporate the lessons of the next two chapters on project selection.

---

[8]We can check that an 8.5% EPS growth rate is consistent with 7.5% earnings growth and Titan's repurchase plans as follows: Given an expected share price of $79.26 \times 1.085 = \$86.00$ next year, Titan will repurchase $20\% \times \$860 \text{ million} \div (\$86.00 \text{ per share}) = 2$ million shares next year. With the decline in the number of shares from 217 million to 215 million, EPS grows by a factor of $1.075 \times (217/215) = 1.085$ or by 8.5%.

MyFinanceLab

Here is what you should know after reading this chapter. MyFinanceLab will help you identify what you know, and where to go when you need to practice.

KEY POINTS AND EQUATIONS	KEY TERMS	ONLINE PRACTICE
7.1 Stock Basics • Ownership in a corporation is divided into shares of stock. These shares carry rights to share in the profits of the firm through future dividend payments. • The shares also come with rights to vote to elect directors and decide on other important matters. • Some firms issue preferred stock, which has preference over common stock in the payment of dividends and in liquidation, but typically carries no voting rights.	annual meeting, p. 200 classes, p. 200 common stock, p. 198 cumulative preferred stock, p. 200 cumulative voting, p. 200 non-cumulative preferred stock, p. 200 preferred stock, p. 200 proxy, p. 200 proxy contest, p. 200 straight voting, p. 199 ticker symbol, p. 198	MyFinanceLab Study Plan 7.1
7.2 The Mechanics of Stock Trades • The NYSE has a physical trading location, but many small trades execute electronically. • NASDAQ is a computer network without a specific trading location. Many trades execute automatically, while larger trades must be negotiated with one or more of the stock's dealers.	floor broker, p. 201	MyFinanceLab Study Plan 7.2
7.3 The Dividend-Discount Model • The Valuation Principle states that the value of a stock is equal to the present value of the dividends and future sale price the investor will receive. Because these cash flows are risky, they must be discounted at the equity cost of capital, which is the expected return of other securities available in the market with equivalent risk to the firm's equity. The total return of a stock is equal to the dividend yield plus the capital gain rate. The expected total return of a stock should equal its equity cost of capital:	capital gain, p. 203 capital gain rate, p. 203 dividend-discount model, p. 205 dividend yield, p. 203 equity cost of capital, p. 203 total return, p. 203	MyFinanceLab Study Plan 7.3 Using Excel: Building a Dividend-Discount Model

$$r_E = \frac{Div_1 + P_1}{P_0} - 1 = \underbrace{\frac{Div_1}{P_0}}_{\text{Dividend Yield}} + \underbrace{\frac{P_1 - P_0}{P_0}}_{\text{Capital Gain Rate}} \quad (7.2)$$

• When investors have the same beliefs, the dividend-discount model states that, for any horizon N, the stock price satisfies the following equation:

$$P_0 = \frac{Div_1}{1 + r_E} + \frac{Div_2}{(1 + r_E)^2} + \cdots + \frac{Div_N}{(1 + r_E)^N} + \frac{P_N}{(1 + r_E)^N}$$

$$(7.4)$$

• If the stock eventually pays dividends and is never acquired, the dividend-discount model implies that the stock price equals the present value of all future dividends.

7.4 Estimating Dividends in the Dividend-Discount Model
- The constant dividend growth model assumes that dividends grow at a constant expected rate, g. In that case, g is also the expected capital gain rate, and

$$P_0 = \frac{Div_1}{r_E - g} \quad (7.6)$$

- Future dividends depend on earnings, shares outstanding, and the dividend payout rate:

$$Div_t = \underbrace{\frac{Earnings_t}{Shares\ Outstanding_t}}_{EPS_t} \times Dividend\ Payout\ Rate_t \quad (7.8)$$

- If all increases in future earnings result exclusively from new investments made with retained earnings, then earnings growth can be found as:

$$Earnings\ Growth\ Rate = \frac{Change\ in\ Earnings}{Earnings} \quad (7.11)$$

$$= Retention\ Rate \times Return\ on\ New\ Investment$$

(where Retention Rate = 1 − Payout Rate)

- If the dividend payout rate and the number of shares outstanding is constant, and if earnings change only as a result of new investment from retained earnings, then the growth rate of the firm's earnings, dividends, and share price is calculated as follows:

$$g = Retention\ Rate \times Return\ on\ New\ Investment \quad (7.12)$$

- Cutting the firm's dividend to increase investment will raise the stock price if, and only if, the new investments generate a return greater than their cost of capital.
- If the firm has a long-term growth rate of g after the period $N + 1$, then we can apply the dividend-discount model and use the constant dividend growth formula to estimate the terminal stock value P_N.

constant dividend growth model, p. 206
dividend payout rate, p. 207
retention rate, p. 207

MyFinanceLab
Study Plan 7.4

7.5 Limitations of the Dividend-Discount Model
- The dividend-discount model is sensitive to the dividend growth rate, which is difficult to estimate accurately.
- The dividend-discount model is not practical for valuing the majority of stocks not paying dividends. In Chapter 10, we discuss alternative approaches.

MyFinanceLab
Study Plan 7.5

7.6 Share Repurchases and the Total Payout Model
- If the firm undertakes share repurchases, it is more reliable to use the total payout model to value the firm. In this model, the value of equity equals the present value of future total dividends and repurchases. To determine the stock price, we divide the equity value by the initial number of shares outstanding of the firm:

$$P_0 = \frac{PV(Future\ Total\ Dividends\ and\ Repurchases)}{Shares\ Outstanding_0} \quad (7.15)$$

- The growth rate of the firm's total payout is governed by the growth rate of earnings, not earnings per share.

share repurchase, p. 214
total payout model, p. 214

MyFinanceLab
Study Plan 7.6

CRITICAL THINKING

1. What rights come with a share of stock?

2. Which two components make up the total return to an investor in a share of stock?

3. What does the dividend-discount model say about valuing shares of stock?

4. What is the relationship between the return from reinvesting cash flows and the change in the price of the stock?

5. How can the dividend-discount model be used with changing growth rates in future dividends?

6. What are some of the drawbacks of the dividend-discount model?

7. What are share repurchases, and how can they be incorporated into the valuation of a stock?

PROBLEMS

All problems are available in MyFinanceLab. *An asterisk * indicates problems with a higher level of difficulty.*

Stock Basics

1. If you own 15,000 shares of stock of Nike and it pays a dividend of $0.21 per share, then what is the total dividend you will receive?

2. You own 20% of the stock of a company that has 10 directors on its board. How much representation can you get on the board if the company has cumulative voting? How much representation can you ensure if the company has straight voting?

3. Anzio, Inc., has two classes of shares. Class B has 10 times the voting rights as Class A. If you own 10% of the class A shares and 20% of the Class B shares, what percentage of the total voting rights do you hold?

The Dividend-Discount Model

4. Assume Evco, Inc., has a current stock price of $50 and will pay a $2 dividend in one year; its equity cost of capital is 15%. What price must you expect Evco stock to sell for immediately after the firm pays the dividend in one year to justify its current price?

5. You just purchased a share of SPCC for $100. You expect to receive a dividend of $5 in one year. If you expect the price after the dividend is paid to be $110, what total return will you have earned over the year? What was your dividend yield? Your capital gain rate?

6. Assume Coleco pays an annual dividend of $1.50 and has a share price of $37.50. It announces that its annual dividend will increase to $1.75. If its dividend yield is to stay the same, what should its new share price be?

7. Anle Corporation has a current stock price of $20 and is expected to pay a dividend of $1 in one year. Its expected stock price right after paying that dividend is $22.
   a. What is Anle's equity cost of capital?
   b. How much of Anle's equity cost of capital is expected to be satisfied by dividend yield and how much by capital gain?

8. Achi Corp. has preferred stock with an annual dividend of $3. If the required return on Achi's preferred stock is 8%, what is its price? (*Hint*: For a preferred stock, the dividend growth rate is zero.)

9. Ovit, Inc., has preferred stock with a price of $20 and a dividend of $1.50 per year. What is its dividend yield?

10. Suppose Acap Corporation will pay a dividend of $2.80 per share at the end of this year and a dividend of $3 per share next year. You expect Acap's stock price to be $52 in two years. Assume that Acap's equity cost of capital is 10%.
    a. What price would you be willing to pay for a share of Acap stock today, if you planned to hold the stock for two years?
    b. Suppose instead you plan to hold the stock for one year. For what price would you expect to be able to sell a share of Acap stock in one year?
    c. Given your answer to (b), what price would you be willing to pay for a share of Acap stock today, if you planned to hold the stock for one year? How does this price compare to your answer in (a)?

11. Krell Industries has a share price of $22.00 today. If Krell is expected to pay a dividend of $0.88 this year and its stock price is expected to grow to $23.54 at the end of the year, what is Krell's dividend yield and equity cost of capital?

Estimating Dividends in the Dividend-Discount Model

12. NoGrowth Corporation currently pays a dividend of $0.50 per quarter, and it will continue to pay this dividend forever. What is the price per share of NoGrowth stock if the firm's equity cost of capital is 15%?

13. Summit Systems will pay a dividend of $1.50 this year. If you expect Summit's dividend to grow by 6% per year, what is its price per share if the firm's equity cost of capital is 11%?

14. Dorpac Corporation has a dividend yield of 1.5%. Its equity cost of capital is 8%, and its dividends are expected to grow at a constant rate.
    a. What is the expected growth rate of Dorpac's dividends?
    b. What is the expected growth rate of Dorpac's share price?

15. Laurel Enterprises expects earnings next year of $4 per share and has a 40% retention rate, which it plans to keep constant. Its equity cost of capital is 10%, which is also its expected return on new investment. Its earnings are expected to grow forever at a rate of 4% per year. If its next dividend is due in one year, what do you estimate the firm's current stock price to be?

*16. DFB, Inc., expects earnings at the end of this year of $5 per share, and it plans to pay a $3 dividend to shareholders (assume that is one year from now). DFB will retain $2 per share of its earnings to reinvest in new projects that have an expected return of 15% per year. Suppose DFB will maintain the same dividend payout rate, retention rate, and return on new investments in the future and will not change its number of outstanding shares.
    a. What growth rate of earnings would you forecast for DFB?
    b. If DFB's equity cost of capital is 12%, what price would you estimate for DFB stock today?
    c. Suppose instead that DFB paid a dividend of $4 per share at the end of this year and retained only $1 per share in earnings. That is, it chose to pay a higher dividend instead of reinvesting in as many new projects. If DFB maintains this higher payout rate in the future, what stock price would you estimate for the firm now? Should DFB raise its dividend?

17. Cooperton Mining just announced it will cut its dividend from $4 to $2.50 per share and use the extra funds to expand. Prior to the announcement, Cooperton's dividends

were expected to grow at a 3% rate, and its share price was $50. With the planned expansion, Cooperton's dividends are expected to grow at a 5% rate. What share price would you expect after the announcement? (Assume that the new expansion does not change Cooperton's risk.) Is the expansion a good investment?

18. Assume Gillette Corporation will pay an annual dividend of $0.65 one year from now. Analysts expect this dividend to grow at 12% per year thereafter until the fifth year. After then, growth will level off at 2% per year. According to the dividend-discount model, what is the value of a share of Gillette stock if the firm's equity cost of capital is 8%?

19. CX Enterprises has the following expected dividends: $1 in one year, $1.15 in two years, and $1.25 in three years. After that, its dividends are expected to grow at 4% per year forever (so that year 4's dividend will be 4% more than $1.25 and so on). If CX's equity cost of capital is 12%, what is the current price of its stock?

20. Assume Highline Company has just paid an annual dividend of $0.96. Analysts are predicting an 11% per year growth rate in earnings over the next five years. After then, Highline's earnings are expected to grow at the current industry average of 5.2% per year. If Highline's equity cost of capital is 8.5% per year and its dividend payout ratio remains constant, for what price does the dividend-discount model predict Highline stock should sell?

*21. Halliford Corporation expects to have earnings this coming year of $3 per share. Halliford plans to retain all of its earnings for the next two years. Then, for the subsequent two years, the firm will retain 50% of its earnings. It will retain 20% of its earnings from that point onward. Each year, retained earnings will be invested in new projects with an expected return of 25% per year. Any earnings that are not retained will be paid out as dividends. Assume Halliford's share count remains constant and all earnings growth comes from the investment of retained earnings. If Halliford's equity cost of capital is 10%, what price would you estimate for Halliford stock?

Share Repurchases and the Total Payout Model

22. Shatin Intl. has 10 million shares, an equity cost of capital of 13% and is expected to pay a total dividend of $20 million each year forever. It announces that it will increase its payout to shareholders. Instead of increasing its dividend, it will keep it constant and will start repurchasing $10 million of stock each year as well. How much will its stock price increase?

23. Zoom Enterprises expects that one year from now it will pay a total dividend of $5 million and repurchase $5 million worth of shares. It plans to spend $10 million on dividends and repurchases every year after that forever, although it may not always be an even split between dividends and repurchases. If Zoom's equity cost of capital is 13% and it has 5 million shares outstanding, what is its share price today?

24. Tolo Co. plans the following repurchases: $10 million in one year, nothing in two years, and $20 million in three years. After that, it will stop repurchasing and will issue dividends totaling $25 million in four years. The total paid in dividends is expected to increase by 3% per year thereafter. If Tolo has 2 million shares outstanding and an equity cost of capital of 11%, what is its price per share today?

25. AFW Industries has 200 million shares outstanding and expects earnings at the end of this year of $700 million. AFW plans to pay out 60% of its earnings in total, paying 40% as a dividend and using 20% to repurchase shares. If AFW's earnings are expected to grow by 8% per year and these payout rates remain constant, determine AFW's share price assuming an equity cost of capital of 12%.

26. Suppose Compco Systems pays no dividends but spent $5 billion on share repurchases last year. If Compco's equity cost of capital is 12%, and if the amount spent on repurchases is expected to grow by 8% per year, estimate Compco's market capitalization. If Compco has 6 billion shares outstanding, to what stock price does this correspond?

*27. Maynard Steel plans to pay a dividend of $3 this year. The company has an expected earnings growth rate of 4% per year and an equity cost of capital of 10%.
   a. Assuming that Maynard's dividend payout rate and expected growth rate remain constant, and that the firm does not issue or repurchase shares, estimate Maynard's share price.
   b. Suppose Maynard decides to pay a dividend of $1 this year and to use the remaining $2 per share to repurchase shares. If Maynard's total payout rate remains constant, estimate Maynard's share price.
   c. If Maynard maintains the dividend and total payout rate given in (b), at what rates are Maynard's dividends and earnings per share expected to grow?

2 Integrative Case

This case draws on material from Chapters 3–7.

Adam Rust looked at his mechanic and sighed. The mechanic had just pronounced a death sentence on his road-weary car. The car had served him well—at a cost of $500 it had lasted through four years of college with minimal repairs. Now, he desperately needs wheels. He has just graduated, and has a good job at a decent starting salary. He hopes to purchase his first new car. The car dealer seems very optimistic about his ability to afford the car payments, another first for him.

The car Adam is considering is $35,000. The dealer has given him three payment options:

1. *Zero percent financing.* Make a $4000 down payment from his savings and finance the remainder with a 0% APR loan for 48 months. Adam has more than enough cash for the down payment, thanks to generous graduation gifts.

2. *Rebate with no money down.* Receive a $4000 rebate, which he would use for the down payment (and leave his savings intact), and finance the rest with a standard 48-month loan, with an 8% APR. He likes this option, as he could think of many other uses for the $4000.

3. *Pay cash.* Get the $4000 rebate and pay the rest with cash. While Adam doesn't have $35,000, he wants to evaluate this option. His parents always paid cash when they bought a family car; Adam wonders if this really was a good idea.

Adam's fellow graduate, Jenna Hawthorne, was lucky. Her parents gave her a car for graduation. Okay, it was a little Hyundai, and definitely not her dream car, but it was serviceable, and Jenna didn't have to worry about buying a new car. In fact, Jenna has been trying to decide how much of her new salary she could save. Adam knows that with a hefty car payment, saving for retirement would be very low on his priority list. Jenna believes she could easily set aside $3000 of her $45,000 salary. She is considering putting her savings in a stock fund. She just turned 22 and has a long way to go until retirement at age 65, and she considers this risk level reasonable. The fund she is looking at has earned an average of 9% over the past 15 years and could be expected to continue earning this amount, on average. While she has no current retirement savings, five years ago Jenna's grandparents gave her a new 30-year U.S. Treasury bond with a $10,000 face value.

Jenna wants to know her retirement income if she both (1) sells her Treasury bond at its current market value and invests the proceeds in the stock fund and (2) saves an additional $3000 at the end of each year in the stock fund from now until she turns 65. Once she retires, Jenna wants those savings to last for 25 years until she is 90.

Both Adam and Jenna need to determine their best options.

Case Questions

1. What are the cash flows associated with each of Adam's three car financing options?

2. Suppose that, similar to his parents, Adam had plenty of cash in the bank so that he could easily afford to pay cash for the car without running into debt now or in the foreseeable future. If his cash earns interest at a 5.4% APR (based on monthly compounding) at the bank, what would be his best purchase option for the car?

3. In fact, Adam doesn't have sufficient cash to cover all his debts including his (substantial) student loans. The loans have a 10% APR, and any money spent on the car could not be used to pay down the loans. What is the best option for Adam now? (*Hint*: Note that having an extra $1 today saves Adam roughly $1.10 next year because he can pay down the student loans. So, 10% is Adam's time value of money in this case.)

4. Suppose instead Adam has a lot of credit card debt, with an 18% APR, and he doubts he will pay off this debt completely before he pays off the car. What is Adam's best option now?

5. Suppose Jenna's Treasury bond has a coupon interest rate of 6.5%, paid semiannually, while current Treasury bonds with the same maturity date have a yield to maturity of 5.4435% (expressed as an APR with semiannual compounding). If she has just received the bond's 10th coupon, for how much can Jenna sell her treasury bond?

6. Suppose Jenna sells the bond, reinvests the proceeds, and then saves as she planned. If, indeed, Jenna earns a 9% annual return on her savings, how much could she withdraw each year in retirement? (Assume she begins withdrawing the money from the account in equal amounts at the end of each year once her retirement begins.)

7. Jenna expects her salary to grow regularly. While there are no guarantees, she believes an increase of 4% a year is reasonable. She plans to save $3000 the first year, and then increase the amount she saves by 4% each year as her salary grows. Unfortunately, prices will also grow due to inflation. Suppose Jenna assumes there will be 3% inflation every year. In retirement, she will need to increase her withdrawals each year to keep up with inflation. In this case, how much can she withdraw at the end of the first year of her retirement? What amount does this correspond to in today's dollars? (*Hint*: Build a spreadsheet in which you track the amount in her retirement account each year.)

8. Should Jenna sell her Treasury bond and invest the proceeds in the stock fund? Give at least one reason for and against this plan.

9. At the last minute, Jenna considers investing in Coca-Cola stock at a price of $55.55 per share instead. The stock just paid an annual dividend of $1.76 and she expects the dividend to grow at 4% annually. If the next dividend is due in one year, what expected return is Coca-Cola stock offering?

Valuation and the Firm

Valuation Principle Connection. One of the most important decisions facing a financial manager is choosing which investments the corporation should make. These decisions fundamentally drive value in the corporation. In Chapter 8 we learn how the Valuation Principle allows us to apply the concept of *net present value (NPV)* to compare the costs and benefits of a project in terms of a common unit—namely, dollars today. We will then be able to evaluate a decision by answering this question: *Does the cash value today of its benefits exceed the cash value today of its costs?* In addition, we will see that the difference between the cash values of the benefits and costs indicates the net amount by which the decision will increase the value of the firm and therefore the wealth of its investors.

After establishing the usefulness of the NPV decision rule for making investment decisions, we discuss alternative rules found in practice and their drawbacks. The process of allocating the firm's capital for investment is known as *capital budgeting*. In Chapter 9, we outline how to estimate a project's incremental cash flows, which then become the inputs to the NPV decision rule. Chapter 9 also provides a practical demonstration of the power of the discounting tools that were introduced in Chapters 3 and 4. Capital budgeting drives value in the firm, so in Chapter 10, Stock Valuation: A Second Look, we return to valuing the ownership claim in the firm—its stock. In Chapter 7, we valued a stock by discounting its future dividends or total payments. In Chapter 10, we consider alternative methods such as discounting free cash flows or comparing its value to that of similar, publicly traded companies.

8

Investment Decision Rules

LEARNING OBJECTIVES

- Calculate Net Present Value

- Use the NPV rule to make investment decisions

- Understand alternative decision rules and their drawbacks

- Choose between mutually exclusive alternatives

- Evaluate projects with different lives

- Rank projects when a company's resources are limited so that it cannot take all positive-NPV projects

notation

CF_n	cash flow that arrives at date n	NPV	net present value
g	growth rate	PV	present value
IRR	internal rate of return	r	discount rate
$MIRR$	modified internal rate of return		

Managers are constantly faced with major investment decisions. In 2007, Apple decided to introduce its first mobile phone. In 2013, Microsoft tried to jumpstart its own phone business with a $7 billion acquisition of Nokia's phone unit. Amazon.com entered the mobile phone business in 2014 and exited it in 2015. That same year, Tesla started offering a mid-market sedan for pre-sale, priced at less than half of its popular premium S-series. Amazon.com decided to start flying its own cargo planes, leasing 20 Boeing 767 freighters in 2016. How did Apple, Microsoft, Amazon, and Tesla managers decide to commit substantial capital to these initiatives? In this chapter, we focus on the decision-making tools managers use to evaluate investment decisions. Examples of these decisions include new products, equipment purchases, and marketing campaigns.

We begin by introducing the *net present value (NPV) rule*. Although the NPV investment rule maximizes the value of the firm, some firms nevertheless use other techniques to evaluate investments and decide which projects to pursue. As a result, it is important to understand those techniques, so we will explain some commonly used alternative techniques—namely, the *payback rule* and the *internal rate of return (IRR) rule*. In each case, we define the decision rule and compare decisions based on this rule to decisions based on the NPV rule. We also illustrate the circumstances in which each of the alternative rules is likely to lead to bad investment decisions.

After establishing these rules in the context of a single, stand-alone project, we broaden our perspective to include evaluating multiple opportunities to select the best one. We conclude with a look at project selection when the firm faces limits on capital or managers' time.

8.1 The NPV Decision Rule

In the previous chapters, we learned how to convert between cash today and cash in the future using the discount rate. As long as we convert costs and benefits to the same point in time, we can use the Valuation Principle to make a decision. In practice, most corporations prefer to measure values in terms of their present value—that is, in terms of cash today. In this section, we apply the Valuation Principle to derive the concept of the *net present value* or *NPV*, which we can use to define the "golden rule" of financial decision making, the *NPV rule*.

Net Present Value

net present value (NPV)
The difference between the present value of a project's or investment's benefits and the present value of its costs.

When the value of a cost or benefit is computed in terms of cash today, we refer to it as the present value (PV). Similarly, we define the **net present value (NPV)** of a project or investment as the difference between the present value of its benefits and the present value of its costs:

$$\textbf{Net Present Value}$$
$$NPV = PV(\,\text{Benefits}\,) - PV(\,\text{Costs}\,) \tag{8.1}$$

Let's consider a simple example. Suppose your firm is offered the following investment opportunity: In exchange for $500 today, you will receive $550 in one year. If the interest rate is 8% per year, then:

$$PV(\,\text{Benefit}\,) = (\,\$550 \text{ in one year}\,) \div (\,\$1.08 \text{ in one year/\$1 today}\,)$$
$$= \$509.26 \text{ today}$$

This PV is the amount you would need to put in the bank today to generate $550 in one year ($509.26 \times 1.08 = 550). In other words, *the present value is the amount you need to invest at the current interest rate to recreate the cash flow.* We can think of this as the cash cost today of generating the cash flow ourselves.

Once the costs and benefits are in present value terms, we can compare them by computing the investment's NPV:

$$NPV = \$509.26 - \$500 = \$9.26 \text{ today}$$

The NPV is positive, so the benefits outweigh the costs, which means the firm should undertake this investment opportunity.

But what if you don't have the $500 needed to cover the initial cost of the project? Does the project still have the same value? Because we computed the value using competitive market prices, it should not depend on your tastes or the amount of cash you have in the bank. If you don't have the $500, suppose you borrow $509.26 from the bank at the 8% interest rate and then take the project. What are your cash flows in this case?

Today: $509.26 (loan) − $500 (invested in the project) = $9.26

In one year: $550 (from project) − $509.26 × 1.08 (loan balance) = $0

This transaction leaves you with exactly $9.26 extra cash in your pocket today and no future net obligations. So taking the project is similar to having an extra $9.26 in cash upfront. Thus, the NPV expresses the value of an investment decision as an amount of cash received today. *As long as the NPV is positive, the decision increases the value of the firm and is a good decision regardless of your current cash needs or preferences regarding when to spend the money.*

<table>
<tr><td>

EXAMPLE 8.1

The NPV Is Equivalent to Cash Today

MyFinanceLab

</td><td>

PROBLEM

After saving $1500 by waiting tables, you are about to buy a 50-inch TV. You notice that the store is offering a "one year same as cash" deal. You can take the TV home today and pay nothing until one year from now, when you will owe the store the $1500 purchase price. If your savings account earns 5% per year, what is the NPV of this offer? Show that its NPV represents cash in your pocket.

SOLUTION

PLAN

You are getting something worth $1500 today (the TV) and in exchange will need to pay $1500 in one year. Think of it as getting back the $1500 you thought you would have to spend today to get the TV. We treat it as a positive cash flow.
Cash flows:

Today	In one year
+$1500	−$1500

The discount rate for calculating the present value of the payment in one year is your interest rate of 5%. You need to compare the present value of the cost ($1500 in one year) to the benefit today (a $1500 TV).

EXECUTE

$$NPV = +1500 - \frac{1500}{(1.05)} = 1500 - 1428.57 = \$71.43$$

You could take $1428.57 of the $1500 you had saved for the TV and put it in your savings account. With interest, in one year it would grow to $1428.57 × (1.05) = $1500, enough to pay the store. The extra $71.43 is money in your pocket to spend as you like (or put toward the speaker system for your new media room).

EVALUATE

By taking the delayed payment offer, we have extra net cash flows of $71.43 today. If we put $1428.57 in the bank, it will be just enough to offset our $1500 obligation in the future. Therefore, this offer is equivalent to receiving $71.43 today, without any future net obligations.

</td></tr>
</table>

The NPV Decision Rule

As shown in Example 8.1, the Valuation Principle implies that we should undertake projects with a positive NPV because undertaking those projects increases wealth. That is, good projects are those for which the present value of the benefits exceeds the present value of the costs. As a result, the value of the firm increases and investors are wealthier. Projects with negative NPVs have costs that exceed their benefits. Accepting them is equivalent to losing money today.

NPV decision rule When choosing among investment alternatives, take the alternative with the highest NPV. Choosing this alternative is equivalent to receiving its NPV in cash today.

We capture this logic in the **NPV Decision Rule**:

When making an investment decision, take the alternative with the highest NPV. Choosing this alternative is equivalent to receiving its NPV in cash today.

Because NPV is expressed in terms of cash today, using the NPV decision rule is a simple way to apply the Valuation Principle. Decisions that increase wealth are superior to those that decrease wealth. We don't need to know anything about the investor's preferences to reach this conclusion. As long as we have correctly captured all the cash flows of a project and applied the appropriate discount rate, we can determine whether the project makes us wealthier. Being wealthier increases our options and makes us better off, whatever our preferences are.

A common way companies apply the NPV rule in financial practices is when deciding whether to accept or reject a project. Because rejecting the project generally has $NPV = 0$ (there are no new costs or benefits from not doing the project), the NPV decision rule implies that we should

- Accept positive-NPV projects; accepting them is equivalent to receiving their NPV in cash today, and

- Reject negative-NPV projects; accepting them would reduce the value of the firm, whereas rejecting them has no cost $(NPV = 0)$.

If the NPV is exactly zero, then you will neither gain nor lose by accepting the project instead of rejecting it, which also has an NPV of zero. It is not a bad project because it does not reduce the firm's value, but it does not add value to the firm either.

CONCEPT CHECK

1. What is the NPV decision rule? How is it related to the Valuation Principle?
2. Why doesn't the NPV decision rule depend on the investor's preferences?

8.2 Using the NPV Rule

We continue our discussion of investment decision rules by considering a take-it-or-leave-it decision about a single, stand-alone project. By undertaking this project, the firm does not constrain its ability to take other projects. In the case of a stand-alone project, the alternatives we are considering are to accept or reject a project. The NPV rule then implies that we should compare the project's NPV to zero (the NPV of rejecting the project and doing nothing). Thus, we should accept the project if its NPV is positive.[1]

Organizing the Cash Flows and Computing the NPV

Researchers at Fredrick's Feed and Farm have made a breakthrough. They believe they can produce a new, environmentally friendly fertilizer at a substantial cost saving over the company's existing line of fertilizer. The fertilizer will require a new plant that can be built immediately at a cost of $81.6 million. Financial managers estimate that the benefits of the new fertilizer will be $28 million per year, starting at the end of the first year and lasting for four years, as shown by the following timeline:

Year:	0	1	2	3	4
Cash flow (in millions):	−$81.60	+$28	+$28	+$28	+$28

Thus, the cash flows are an immediate $81.6 million outflow followed by an annuity inflow of $28 million per year for four years. Therefore, given a discount rate r, the NPV of this project is:

---

[1]Some prefer to state the rule that the project should be accepted if its NPV is non-negative. Since the firm should be indifferent at an NPV of exactly zero (you will neither gain nor lose by accepting the project instead of rejecting it), we prefer to state it this way. A zero NPV project is not a bad project because it does not reduce the firm's value, but it does not add value to the firm either.

$$NPV = -81.6 + \frac{28}{1+r} + \frac{28}{(1+r)^2} + \frac{28}{(1+r)^3} + \frac{28}{(1+r)^4} \qquad (8.2)$$

We can also use the annuity formula from Chapter 4 to write the NPV as:

$$NPV = -81.6 + \frac{28}{r}\left(1 - \frac{1}{(1+r)^4}\right) \qquad (8.3)$$

To apply the NPV rule, we need to know the cost of capital. The financial managers responsible for this project estimate a cost of capital of 10% per year. If we replace r in Eq. 8.2 or 8.3 with the project's cost of capital of 10%, we get an NPV of $7.2 million, which is positive. Recall that a net present value tells us the present value of the benefits (positive cash flows) net of the costs (negative cash flows) of the project. By putting everything into present values, it puts all the costs and benefits on an equal footing for comparison. In this case, the benefits outweigh the costs by $7.2 million in present value. The NPV investment rule indicates that by making the investment, Fredrick's will increase the value of the firm today by $7.2 million, so Fredrick's should undertake this project.

The NPV Profile

NPV profile A graph of a project's NPV over a range of discount rates.

The NPV of the project depends on its appropriate cost of capital. Often, there may be some uncertainty regarding the project's cost of capital. In that case, it is helpful to compute an **NPV profile**, which graphs the project's NPV over a range of discount rates. It is easiest to prepare the NPV profile using a spreadsheet such as Excel. We simply repeat our calculation of the NPV above using a range of different discount rates instead of only 10%. Figure 8.1 presents the NPV profile for Fredrick's project by plotting the NPV as a function of the discount rate, r.[2]

FIGURE 8.1

NPV of Fredrick's
New Project

The graph in Panel (b) shows the NPV as a function of the discount rate based on the data in Panel (a). The NPV is positive, represented by the green-shaded area, only for discount rates that are less than 14%, the *internal rate of return (IRR)*. Given the cost of capital of 10%, the project has a positive NPV of $7.2 million. The red-shaded area indicates discount rates above the 14% IRR with negative NPVs.

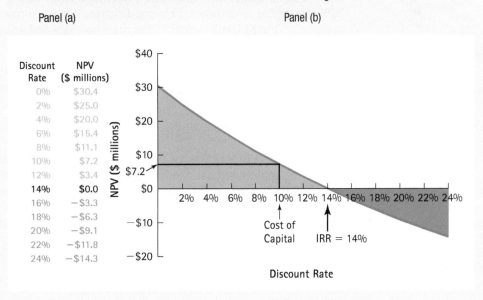

Panel (a)

Discount Rate	NPV ($ millions)
0%	$30.4
2%	$25.0
4%	$20.0
6%	$15.4
8%	$11.1
10%	$7.2
12%	$3.4
14%	**$0.0**
16%	−$3.3
18%	−$6.3
20%	−$9.1
22%	−$11.8
24%	−$14.3

Panel (b)

---

[2]In the online appendix to this chapter, we show you how to create an NPV profile in Excel. You can find this in the chapter resources section of MyFinanceLab.

internal rate of return (IRR) The interest rate that sets the net present value of the cash flows equal to zero.

Notice that the NPV is positive only for discount rates that are less than 14% (the green shaded area in Figure 8.1). Referring to the graph and the accompanying data table, we see that at 14% the NPV is zero. The discount rate that sets the net present value of the cash flows equal to zero is an investment's **internal rate of return (IRR)**. Thus, by constructing the NPV profile, we have determined that Fredrick's project has an IRR of 14%. We can also compute the IRR without graphing the NPV by using a financial calculator or a spreadsheet's IRR function (see the appendix to Chapter 4. The calculator instructions for solving for the rate of return can be used to solve for the IRR).

	N	I/Y	PV	PMT	FV
Given:	4		−81.6	28	0
Solve for:		14			
Excel Formula: =RATE(NPER,PMT,PV,FV)=RATE(4,28,−81.6,0)					

Measuring Sensitivity with IRR

In our Fredrick's example, the firm's managers provided the cost of capital. If you are unsure of your cost of capital estimate, it is important to determine how sensitive your analysis is to errors in this estimate. The IRR can provide this information. For Fredrick's, if the cost of capital estimate is more than the 14% IRR, the NPV will be negative (see the red shaded area in Figure 8.1). Therefore, as long as our estimate of the cost of capital of 10% is within 4% of the true cost of capital, our decision to accept the project is correct. In general, the difference between the cost of capital and the IRR tells us the amount of estimation error in the cost of capital estimate that can exist without altering the original decision.

Alternative Rules Versus the NPV Rule

The NPV rule indicates that Fredrick's should undertake the investment in fertilizer technology. As we evaluate alternative rules for project selection in the subsequent sections, keep in mind that sometimes other investment rules may give the same answer as the NPV rule, but at other times they may disagree. When the rules conflict, always base your decision on the NPV rule, which is the most accurate and reliable decision rule.

CONCEPT CHECK

3. Explain the NPV rule for stand-alone projects.

4. How can you interpret the difference between the cost of capital and the IRR?

8.3   Alternative Decision Rules

Even though the NPV rule is the most accurate and reliable rule, in practice a wide variety of rules are applied, often in tandem with the NPV rule. In a 2001 study, John Graham and Campbell Harvey[3] found that 75% of the firms they surveyed used the NPV rule for making investment decisions. This result is substantially different from that found in a similar study in 1977 by L. J. Gitman and J. R. Forrester,[4] who found that only 10% of firms used

---

[3]John Graham and Campbell Harvey, "The Theory and Practice of Corporate Finance: Evidence from the Field," *Journal of Financial Economics* 60 (2001): 187–243.

[4]L. J. Gitman and J. R. Forrester, Jr., "A Survey of Capital Budgeting Techniques Used by Major U.S. Firms," *Financial Management* 6 (1977): 66–71.

USING EXCEL

Computing NPV
and IRR

Here we discuss how to use Microsoft Excel to solve for NPV and IRR. We also identify some pitfalls to avoid when using Excel.

NPV Function: Leaving Out Date 0

Excel's NPV function has the format *NPV (rate, value1, value2, . . .)*, where "rate" is the interest rate per period used to discount the cash flows, and "value1", "value2", etc., are the cash flows (or ranges of cash flows). The NPV function computes the present value of the cash flows *assuming the first cash flow occurs at date 1.* Therefore, if a project's first cash flow occurs at date 0, we cannot use the NPV function by itself to compute the NPV. We can use the NPV function to compute the present value of the cash flows from date 1 onward, and then we must add the date 0 cash flow to that result to calculate the NPV. The screenshot below shows the difference. The first NPV calculation (outlined in blue) is correct: we used the NPV function for all of the cash flows occurring at time 1 and later and then added on the first cash flow occurring at time 0 since it is already in present value. The second calculation (outlined in green) is incorrect: we used the NPV function for all of the cash flows, but the function assumed that the first cash flow occurs in period 1 instead of immediately.

NPV Function: Ignoring Blank Cells

Another pitfall with the NPV function is that cash flows that are left blank are treated differently from cash flows that are equal to zero. If the cash flow is left blank, *both the cash flow and the period are ignored.* For example, the second set of cash flows below is equivalent to the first—we have simply left the cash flow for date 2 blank instead of entering a "0." However, the NPV function ignores the blank cell at date 2 and assumes the cash flow is 10 at date 1 and 110 at date 2, which is clearly not what is intended and produces an incorrect answer (outlined in red).

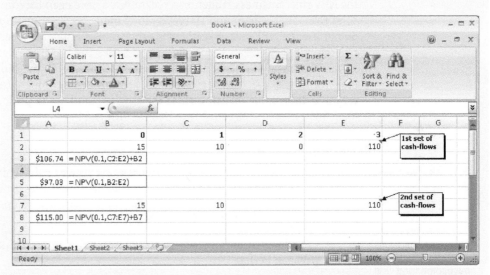

Because of these idiosyncrasies, we avoid using Excel's NPV function. It is more reliable to compute the present value of each cash flow separately in Excel, and then sum them to determine the NPV.

IRR FUNCTION

Excel's IRR function has the format *IRR (values, guess)*, where "values" is the range containing the cash flows, and "guess" is an optional starting guess where Excel begins its search for an IRR. Two things to note about the IRR function:

1. The values given to the IRR function should include all of the cash flows of the project, including the one at date 0. In this sense, the IRR and NPV functions in Excel are inconsistent.

2. Like the NPV function, the IRR ignores the period associated with any blank cells.

FIGURE 8.2

The Most Popular
Decision Rules
Used by CFOs

The bar graph shows the most popular decision rules used by CFOs in Professors Graham and Harvey's 2001 survey. Many CFOs used more than one method, but no other methods were mentioned by more than half of CFOs.

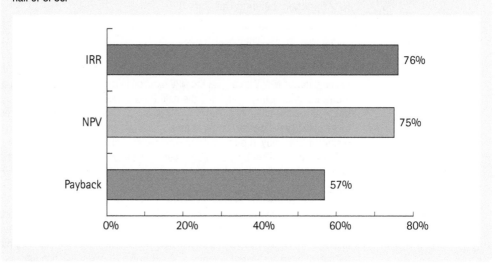

the NPV rule. Business students in recent years have been listening to their finance professors! Even so, Graham and Harvey's study indicates that one-fourth of U.S. corporations do not use the NPV rule. Exactly why other capital budgeting techniques are used in practice is not always clear. Figure 8.2 summarizes the top three decision rules given in the survey. Because you may encounter these techniques in the business world, you should know what they are, how they are used, and how they compare to NPV. In this section, we examine alternative decision rules for single, stand-alone projects within the firm. The focus here is on *the payback rule* and *the IRR rule*.

The Payback Rule

payback investment rule Only projects that pay back their initial investment within a prespecified period are undertaken.

The simplest investment rule is the **payback investment rule**, which states that you should only accept a project if its cash flows pay back its initial investment within a prespecified period. The rule is based on the notion that an opportunity that pays back its initial investment quickly is a good idea. To apply the payback rule,

payback period The amount of time until the cash flows from a project offset the initial investment. The time it takes to pay back the initial investment.

1. Calculate the amount of time it takes to pay back the initial investment, called the **payback period**.
2. Accept the project if the payback period is less than a prespecified length of time—usually a few years.
3. Reject the project if the payback period is greater than that prespecified length of time.

For example, a firm might adopt any project with a payback period of less than two years.

EXAMPLE 8.2

Using the
Payback Rule

MyFinanceLab

PROBLEM
Assume Fredrick's requires all projects to have a payback period of two years or less. Would the firm undertake the fertilizer project under this rule?

SOLUTION

PLAN

In order to implement the payback rule, we need to know whether the sum of the inflows from the project will exceed the initial investment before the end of two years. The project has inflows of $28 million per year and an initial investment of $81.6 million.

EXECUTE

The sum of the cash flows for years 1 and 2 is $28 \times 2 = $56 million, which will not cover the initial investment of $81.6 million. In fact, it will not be until year 3 that the cash inflows exceed the initial investment ($28 \times 3 = $84 million). Because the payback period for this project exceeds two years, Fredrick's will reject the project.

EVALUATE

While simple to compute, the payback rule requires us to use an arbitrary cutoff period in summing the cash flows. Furthermore, note that the payback rule does not discount future cash flows. Instead, it simply sums the cash flows and compares them to a cash outflow in the present. In this case, Fredrick's would have rejected a project that would have increased the value of the firm.

Relying on the payback rule analysis in Example 8.2, Fredrick's will reject the project. However, as we saw earlier, with a cost of capital of 10%, the NPV is $7.2 million. Following the payback rule would be a mistake because Fredrick's will pass up a project worth $7.2 million.

The payback rule is not as reliable as the NPV rule because it (1) ignores the time value of money, (2) ignores cash flows after the payback period, and (3) lacks a decision criterion grounded in economics (what is the right number of years to require for a payback period?). Some companies have addressed the first failing by computing the payback period using discounted cash flows, called the **discounted payback rule**. However, this does not solve the fundamental problem because the other two failings remain. Despite these failings, Graham and Harvey found that about 57% of the firms they surveyed reported using the payback rule as part of the decision-making process.

discounted payback rule Only accept projects where the sum of the discounted cash flows within the payback period is greater than or equal to the initial investment.

Why do some companies consider the payback rule? The answer probably relates to its simplicity. This rule is typically used for small investment decisions—for example, whether to purchase a new copy machine or to service the old one. In such cases, the cost of making an incorrect decision might not be large enough to justify the time required to calculate the NPV. The appeal of the payback rule is that it favors short-term projects. Some firms are unwilling to commit capital to long-term investments. Also, if the required payback period is short (one to two years), then most projects that satisfy the payback rule will have a positive NPV.

The Internal Rate of Return Rule

internal rate of return (IRR) investment rule A decision rule that accepts any investment opportunity where the IRR exceeds the opportunity cost of capital and otherwise rejects the opportunity.

Similar to NPV, the **internal rate of return (IRR) investment rule** is based on the concept that if the return on the investment opportunity you are considering is greater than the return on other alternatives in the market with equivalent risk and maturity (i.e., the project's cost of capital), you should undertake the investment opportunity. We state the rule formally as follows:

> *IRR investment rule: Take any investment opportunity whose IRR exceeds the opportunity cost of capital. Turn down any opportunity whose IRR is less than the opportunity cost of capital.*

The IRR investment rule will give the correct answer (that is, the same answer as the NPV rule) in many—but not all—situations. For instance, it gives the correct answer for Fredrick's fertilizer opportunity. From Figure 8.1, whenever the cost of capital is in the green area below the IRR (14%), the project has a positive NPV and you should undertake the investment. Table 8.1 summarizes our analysis of Fredrick's new project. The NPV and IRR rules agree, but using the payback rule with a required payback period of two years or less would cause Fredrick's to reject the project.

TABLE 8.1

Summary of NPV, IRR, and Payback for Fredrick's New Project

NPV at 10%	$7.2 million	Accept ($7.2 million > 0)
Payback Period	3 years	Reject (3 years $>$ 2 year required payback)
IRR	14%	Accept (14% $>$ 10% cost of capital)

In general, the IRR rule works for a stand-alone project if all of the project's negative cash flows precede its positive cash flows. But in other cases, the IRR rule may disagree with the NPV rule and thus be incorrect. Let's examine several situations in which the IRR fails.

Delayed Investments. Star basketball player Evan Cole is graduating from college with a degree in finance and preparing for the NBA draft. Several companies have already approached him with endorsement contracts. Two competing sports drink companies are pursuing him. QuenchIt offers him a single up-front payment of $1 million to exclusively endorse their sports drink for three years. PowerUp offers $500,000 per year, payable at the end of each of the next three years, to endorse their product exclusively. Which offer is better? One direct way to compare the two contracts is to realize that signing with QuenchIt causes Evan to forgo the PowerUp contract, or $500,000 per year. Considering the risk of his alternative income sources and available investment opportunities, Evan estimates his opportunity cost of capital to be 10%. The timeline of Evan's investment opportunity is:

The NPV of Evan's investment opportunity is:

$$NPV = 1,000,000 - \frac{500,000}{1+r} - \frac{500,000}{(1+r)^2} - \frac{500,000}{(1+r)^3}$$

By setting the NPV equal to zero and solving for r, we find the IRR. We can use either a financial calculator or a spreadsheet to find the IRR:

	N	I/Y	PV	PMT	FV
Given:	3		1,000,000	−500,000	0
Solve for:		23.38			
Excel Formula:	=RATE(NPER,PMT,PV,FV)=RATE(3,−500000,1000000,0)				

The 23.38% IRR is larger than the 10% opportunity cost of capital. According to the IRR rule, Evan should sign the deal. But what does the NPV rule say?

$$NPV = 1,000,000 - \frac{500,000}{1.1} - \frac{500,000}{1.1^2} - \frac{500,000}{1.1^3} = -\$243,426$$

At a 10% discount rate, the NPV is negative, so signing the deal would reduce Evan's wealth. He should not sign the endorsement deal with QuenchIt, and should sign with PowerUp instead.

To resolve this conflict, we can prepare an NPV profile for the QuenchIt contract. Figure 8.3 plots the NPV of the investment opportunity for a range of discount rates. It shows that, no matter what the cost of capital is, the IRR rule and the NPV rule will give exactly opposite recommendations. That is, the NPV is positive only when the opportunity cost of capital is *above* 23.38% (the IRR). Evan should accept the investment only when the opportunity cost of capital is greater than the IRR, the opposite of what the IRR rule recommends.

Figure 8.3 also illustrates the problem with using the IRR rule in this case. For most investment opportunities, expenses occur initially and cash is received later. In this case, Evan receives cash *upfront* from QuenchIt but the forgone cash flows from PowerUp occurred later. It is as if Evan borrowed money, and when you borrow money you prefer as *low* a rate as possible. Evan's optimal rule is to borrow money as long as the rate at which he borrows is *less* than the cost of capital.

Even though the IRR rule fails to give the correct answer in this case, the IRR itself still provides useful information *in conjunction* with the NPV rule. As mentioned earlier, the IRR provides information on how sensitive the investment decision is to uncertainty in the cost of capital estimate. In this case, the difference between the cost of capital and the IRR is large—10% versus 23.38%. Evan would have to have underestimated the cost of capital by 13.38% to make the NPV positive.

Multiple IRRs. Evan has informed QuenchIt that it needs to sweeten the deal before he will accept it. In response, the company has agreed to make an additional payment of $600,000 in 10 years as deferred compensation for the long-term increase in sales that

FIGURE 8.3

NPV of Evan Cole's $1 Million QuenchIt Deal

When all the benefits of an investment occur at time zero and before the costs, the NPV is an *increasing* function of the discount rate. The NPV is positive in the green-shaded areas and negative in the red-shaded areas. Notice that the NPV is positive when the cost of capital is above 23.38%, the IRR, so the NPV and IRR rules conflict.

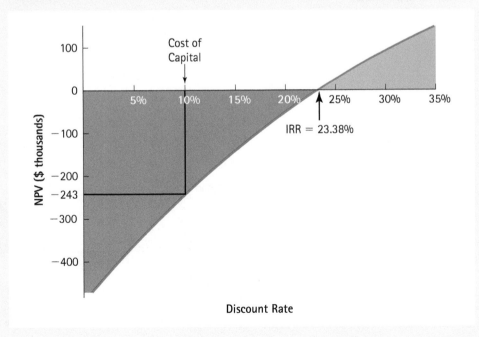

even a short-term endorsement by Evan would bring. Should he accept or reject the new offer?

We begin with the new timeline:

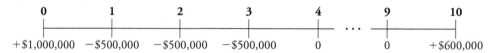

0	1	2	3	4	9	10
+$1,000,000	−$500,000	−$500,000	−$500,000	0	0	+$600,000

The NPV of Evan's new investment opportunity is:

$$NPV = 1,000,000 - \frac{500,000}{1+r} - \frac{500,000}{(1+r)^2} - \frac{500,000}{(1+r)^3} + \frac{600,000}{(1+r)^{10}}$$

We can find the IRR for this investment opportunity by creating an NPV profile and noting where it crosses zero. Figure 8.4 plots the NPV of the opportunity at different discount rates. In this case, there are *two* IRRs—that is, there are two values of r that set the NPV equal to zero. You can verify this fact by substituting IRRs of 5.79% and 13.80% for r into the equation. Because there is more than one IRR, we cannot apply the IRR rule. It is also worth noting that you should take special care when using a spreadsheet or financial calculator to determine the IRR. Both solve for the IRR through trial and error because you cannot calculate the IRR directly. In cases where there is more than one IRR, the spreadsheet or calculator will simply produce the first one that it finds, with no indication that there could be others! Some financial calculators will return an error message if there are multiple IRRs. Thus, it always pays to create the NPV profile.

For guidance, let's turn to the NPV rule. If the cost of capital were *either* below 5.79% or above 13.80%, Evan should undertake the opportunity. But given his cost of capital of 10%, he should still turn it down. Notice that even though the IRR rule fails in this case,

FIGURE 8.4

NPV of Evan's Sports Drink Deal with Additional Deferred Payments

The graph in Panel (b) shows the NPV of Evan's deal with additional deferred payment based on the data in Panel (a). In this case, there are two IRRs, invalidating the IRR rule. If the opportunity cost of capital is *either* below 5.79% or above 13.80%, Evan should accept the deal because the NPV is then positive, as indicated by the green-shaded areas. At any point between the two IRRs, the NPV is negative (see the red-shaded area).

Panel (a) Panel (b)

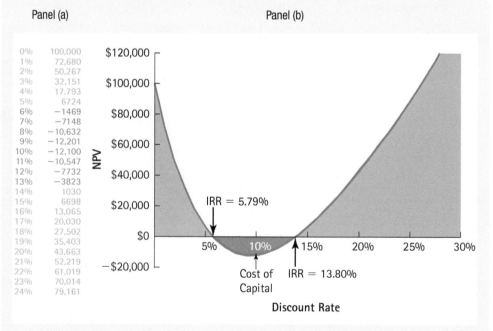

0%	100,000
1%	72,680
2%	50,267
3%	32,151
4%	17,793
5%	6724
6%	−1469
7%	−7148
8%	−10,632
9%	−12,201
10%	−12,100
11%	−10,547
12%	−7732
13%	−3823
14%	1030
15%	6698
16%	13,065
17%	20,030
18%	27,502
19%	35,403
20%	43,663
21%	52,219
22%	61,019
23%	70,014
24%	79,161

COMMON MISTAKE

IRR Versus the IRR Rule

Throughout this subsection, we have distinguished between the IRR itself and the IRR rule. While we have pointed out the shortcomings of using the IRR rule to make investment decisions, *the IRR*

itself remains a very useful tool. The IRR measures the average return of the investment and indicates the sensitivity of the NPV to estimation error in the cost of capital. Thus, knowing the IRR can be very useful, but relying on it to make investment decisions can be hazardous.

the two IRRs are still useful as bounds on the cost of capital estimate. If the cost of capital estimate is wrong, and it is actually smaller than 5.79% or larger than 13.80%, the decision not to pursue the project will change because it will have a positive NPV.

There is no easy fix for the IRR rule when there are multiple IRRs. Although the NPV is negative between the IRRs in this example, the reverse is also possible (see Figure 8.5). In that case, the project would have a positive NPV for discount rates between the IRRs rather than for discount rates lower or higher than the IRRs. Furthermore, there are situations in which more than two IRRs exist.[5] In such situations, our only choice is to rely on the NPV rule.

modified internal rate of return (MIRR) The discount rate that sets the NPV of modified cash flows of a project equal to zero. Cash flows are modified so there is only one negative cash flow (and one sign change) to ensure that only one IRR exists.

Modified Internal Rate of Return

The fact that there can be multiple IRRs for the cash flows from a project is a clear disadvantage for the IRR. To overcome this, some have proposed various ways of modifying the cash flows before computing the IRR. All these modifications have the common feature that they group the cash flows so that there is only one negative cash flow, occurring at either the beginning or the end. In that case, there is only one sign change for the cash flows as a whole and hence only one IRR. This new IRR, computed as the discount rate that sets the NPV of the modified cash flows of the project equal to zero, is called the **modified internal rate of return (MIRR)**.

FIGURE 8.5

NPV Profile for a Project with Multiple IRRs

The graph shows the NPV profile for a multiple-IRR project with cash flows of −$1000, $2500, and −$1540 in years 0, 1, and 2, respectively. As the NPV profile shows, the project has two IRRs: 10% and 40%.

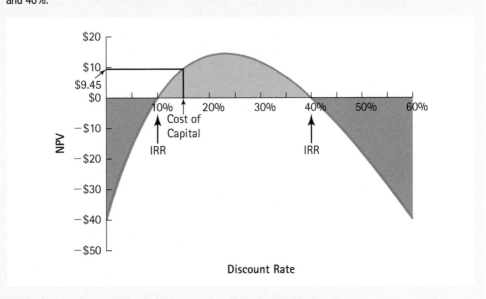

---

[5]In general, there can be as many IRRs as the number of times the project's cash flows change sign over time.

Why Do Rules Other Than the NPV Rule Persist?

Professors Graham and Harvey found that a sizable minority of firms (25%) in their study do not use the NPV rule at all. In addition, about 50% of firms surveyed used the payback rule. Furthermore, it appears that most firms use *both* the NPV rule and the IRR rule. Why do firms use rules other than NPV if they can lead to erroneous decisions?

One possible explanation for this phenomenon is that Graham and Harvey's survey results might be misleading. CFOs who were using the IRR as a sensitivity measure in conjunction with the NPV rule might have checked both the IRR box and the NPV box on the survey. The question they were asked was, "How frequently does your firm use the following techniques when deciding which projects or acquisitions to pursue?" By computing the IRR and using it in conjunction with the NPV rule to estimate the sensitivity of their results, they might have felt they were using *both* techniques.

Nevertheless, a significant minority of managers surveyed replied that they used only the IRR rule, so this explanation cannot be the whole story.

One common reason that managers give for using the IRR rule exclusively is that you do not need to know the opportunity cost of capital to calculate the IRR. On a superficial level, this is true: The IRR does not depend on the cost of capital. You may not need to know the cost of capital to *calculate* the IRR, but you certainly need to know the cost of capital when you *apply* the IRR rule. Consequently, the opportunity cost is as important to the IRR rule as it is to the NPV rule.

Nonetheless, part of the appeal of the IRR rule is that the IRR seems to sum up the attractiveness of an investment without requiring an assumption about the cost of capital. However, a more useful summary is the project's NPV profile, showing the NPV as a function of the discount rate. The NPV profile also does not require knowing the cost of capital, but it has the distinct advantage of being much more informative and reliable.

MIRR Technique. Let's clarify this with an example. You are considering a project that has the following three cash flows:

The NPV profile for this project, shown in Figure 8.5, identifies the two IRRs for this project as 10% and 40%.

Assume that your discount rate for this project is 15%. As Figure 8.5 shows, the NPV of the project at 15% is $9.45. We could modify the cash flows of the project to eliminate the multiple IRR problem. By discounting all of the negative cash flows to the present and compounding all of the positive cash flows to the end of the project, we have only two cash flows, yielding a single IRR. What discount rate and compounding rate should we use? One natural choice is our cost of capital for this project, which is 15%.

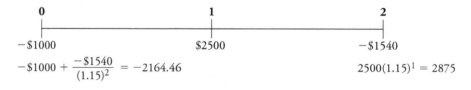

Figure 8.6 presents the NPV profile for our modified cash flows. As Figure 8.6 shows, there is now only a single IRR, at 15.25%. Because our cost of capital is 15%, we would properly accept the project using the IRR rule. Also note that the advantage of using 15% as our discount and compounding rates when modifying the cash flows is that the NPV of the modified cash flows at 15% is the same as the NPV of the true cash flows at 15%. Figure 8.6 also makes an important point: We are no longer evaluating the true cash flows of the project. Instead, we have modified them to force them to produce a single IRR. The NPV profile of the true cash flows of the project is given earlier in Figure 8.5 and is clearly different from the one produced by the modified cash flows in Figure 8.6.

FIGURE 8.6

NPV Profile of Modified
Cash Flows for the
Multiple-IRR Project
from Figure 8.5

The graph presents the NPV profile for the modified project cash flows of −2164.46 in year 0 and 2875 in year 2. The modified cash flows have only one IRR: 15.25%. Given the 15% cost of capital, the IRR rule confirms that we should accept the project.

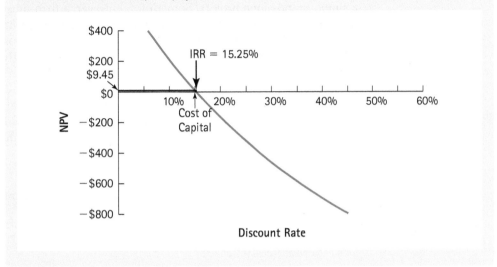

There is no set way to modify project cash flows to produce an MIRR. Two other approaches that each solve the multiple IRR problem are:

1. Discount all the negative cash flows to time 0 and leave the positive cash flows alone.

2. Leave the initial cash flow alone and compound all the remaining cash flows to the final period of the project. In this approach, you are implicitly reinvesting all the cash flows from the project at your compound rate until the project is complete.

Again, in either case, if you use the project's cost of capital as your discount and compounding rate, you will not alter the NPV of the project at that discount rate. Furthermore, a decision to accept or reject the project based on the modified IRR will be the same as the one based on the NPV decision rule.

MIRR: A Final Word. There is considerable debate about whether MIRR is actually better than IRR. Most of the argument centers on whether it is advisable to modify the cash flows of the project. The IRR is truly an internal rate of return based solely on the actual cash flows of the project. However, the IRR implicitly assumes that all cash flows generated by the project are reinvested at the project's IRR rather than at the firm's cost of capital until the project ends. For a project with a high IRR, this may be an unrealistic assumption. Furthermore, there may be more than one IRR, which complicates its use. The MIRR avoids these problems, but is based on a set of cash flows modified through the use of a chosen discount and compounding rate. Thus, it is not really an internal rate of return and is no longer based solely on the actual cash flows of the project. Finally, MIRR still does not solve some of the other problems associated with using IRR when choosing among projects.

CONCEPT
CHECK

5. How do you apply the payback rule?

6. Under what conditions will the IRR rule lead to the same decision as the NPV rule?

8.4 Choosing Among Projects

Thus far, we have considered only decisions where the choice is either to accept or to reject a single, stand-alone project. Sometimes, however, a firm must choose just one project from among several possible projects. For example, a manager may be evaluating alternative package designs for a new product. The manager must choose only one of the designs. When choosing any one project excludes us from taking the other projects, we are facing **mutually exclusive projects**.

mutually exclusive projects Projects that compete with one another; by accepting one, you exclude the others.

When projects, such as the package designs, are mutually exclusive, it is not enough to determine which projects have positive NPVs. With mutually exclusive projects, the manager's goal is to rank the projects and choose the best one. In this situation, the NPV rule provides a straightforward answer: *Pick the project with the highest NPV.*

EXAMPLE 8.3

NPV and Mutually Exclusive Projects

MyFinanceLab

PROBLEM

You own a small piece of commercial land near a university. You are considering what to do with it. You have been approached with an offer to buy it for $220,000. You are also considering three alternative uses yourself: a bar, a coffee shop, and an apparel store. You assume that you would operate your choice indefinitely, eventually leaving the business to your children. You have collected the following information about the uses. What should you do?

	Initial Investment	Cash Flow in the First Year (CF_1)	Growth Rate (g)	Cost of Capital (r)
Bar	$400,000	$60,000	3.5%	12%
Coffee Shop	$200,000	$40,000	3%	10%
Apparel Store	$500,000	$75,000	3%	13%

SOLUTION

PLAN

Since you can develop only one project (you only have one piece of land), these are mutually exclusive projects. In order to decide which project is most valuable, you need to rank them by NPV. Each of these projects (except for selling the land) has cash flows that can be valued as a growing perpetuity, so from Chapter 4, the present value of the inflows is $CF_1/(r-g)$. The NPV of each investment will be:

$$\frac{CF_1}{r-g} - \text{Initial Investment}$$

EXECUTE

The NPVs are:

$$\text{Bar: } \frac{\$60,000}{0.12-0.035} - \$400,000 = \$305,882$$

$$\text{Coffee Shop: } \frac{\$40,000}{0.10-0.03} - \$200,000 = \$371,429$$

$$\text{Apparel Store: } \frac{\$75,000}{0.13-0.03} - \$500,000 = \$250,000$$

So, the ranking is

Alternative	NPV
Coffee Shop	$371,429
Bar	$305,882
Apparel Store	$250,000
Sell the Land	$220,000

You should choose the coffee shop.

EVALUATE

All the alternatives have positive NPVs, but you can take only one of them, so you should choose the one that creates the most value. Even though the coffee shop has the lowest cash flows, its lower start-up cost coupled with its lower cost of capital (it is less risky) make it the best choice.

Because the IRR is a measure of the expected return of investing in the project, you might be tempted to extend the IRR investment rule to the case of mutually exclusive projects by picking the project with the highest IRR. Unfortunately, picking one project over another simply because it has a larger IRR can lead to mistakes. Problems arise when the mutually exclusive investments have differences in scale (require different initial investments) and when they have different cash flow patterns. We discuss each of these situations in turn.

Differences in Scale

Would you prefer a 200% return on $1 or a 10% return on $1 million? The former return certainly sounds impressive and gives you great bragging rights, but at the end of the day you make only $2. The latter opportunity may sound much more mundane, but you make $100,000. This comparison illustrates an important shortcoming of IRR: Because it is a return, you cannot tell how much value has actually been created without knowing the basis for the return—a 10% IRR can have very different value implications for an initial investment of $1 million versus an initial investment of $100 million.

If a project has a positive NPV, then if we can double its size, its NPV will double: By the Valuation Principle, doubling the cash flows of an investment opportunity must make it worth twice as much. However, the IRR rule does not have this property—it is unaffected by the scale of the investment opportunity because the IRR measures the average return of the investment. Thus, the IRR rule cannot be used to compare projects of different scales. Let's illustrate this concept in the context of an example.

Identical Scale. We begin by considering two mutually exclusive projects with the same scale. Maria is evaluating two investment opportunities. If she goes into business with her boyfriend, she would need to invest $10,000 and the business would generate incremental cash flows of $6000 per year for three years. Alternatively, she could start a courier/delivery service using two high-end drones. The drone setup will cost $10,000 and will generate $5000 per year for three years. The opportunity cost of capital for both opportunities is 12% and both will require all her time, so Maria must choose between them. How valuable is each opportunity, and which one should she choose?

Let's consider both the NPV and IRR of each project. The timeline for the investment with Maria's boyfriend is:

The NPV of the investment opportunity when $r = 0.12$ is:

$$NPV = -10{,}000 + \frac{6000}{1.12} + \frac{6000}{1.12^2} + \frac{6000}{1.12^3} = \$4411$$

We can determine the IRR of this investment by using a financial calculator or spreadsheet:

	N	I/Y	PV	PMT	FV
Given:	3		−10,000	6000	0
Solve for:		**36.3**			

Excel Formula: =RATE(NPER,PMT,PV,FV)=RATE(3,6000,−10000,0)

Thus, the IRR for Maria's investment in her boyfriend's business is 36.3%. The timeline for her investment in the drone delivery business is:

0	1	2	3
−10,000	+5000	+5000	+5000

The NPV of the investment opportunity when $r = 0.12$ is:

$$NPV = -10{,}000 + \frac{5000}{1.12} + \frac{5000}{1.12^2} + \frac{5000}{1.12^3} = \$2009$$

The \$2009 NPV of the delivery business is lower than the \$4411 NPV for her boyfriend's business, so Maria should join her boyfriend in business. Luckily, it appears that Maria does not need to choose between her money and her relationship!

We could also compare IRRs. For the delivery business, we would find that the IRR is 23.4%. The delivery business has a lower IRR than the investment in her boyfriend's business. As Figure 8.7 shows, in this case the project with the higher IRR has the higher NPV.

Change in Scale. What happens if we change the scale of one of the projects? Maria's finance professor points out that, given the potential for automation, she could manage

FIGURE 8.7

NPV of Maria's Investment Opportunities with the Two-Drone Delivery Service

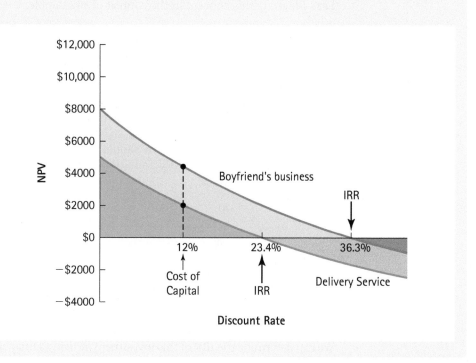

The NPV of her boyfriend's business is always larger than the NPV of the delivery service. The same is true for the IRR; the IRR of her boyfriend's business is 36.3%, while the IRR for the delivery service is 23.4%.

five times as many drones in her courier and delivery business. Her setup cost would now be $50,000 and her annual cash flows would be $25,000. What should Maria do now?

Note that the IRR is unaffected by the scale. Because we are scaling all the cash flows

	N	I/Y	PV	PMT	FV
Given:	3		−50,000	25,000	0
Solve for:		**23.4**			
Excel Formula: =RATE(NPER,PMT,PV,FV)=RATE(3,25000,−50000,0)					

up by a factor of 5, a 10-drone delivery service has exactly the same IRR as a 2-drone service, so her boyfriend's business still has a higher IRR than the delivery service:

However, the NPV of the delivery service does grow by the scale—it is five times larger:

$$NPV = -50,000 + \frac{25,000}{1.12} + \frac{25,000}{1.12^2} + \frac{25,000}{1.12^3} = \$10,046$$

Now Maria should invest in the 10-drone delivery service. As Figure 8.8 shows, the NPV of the 10-drone delivery service exceeds the NPV of going into business with her boyfriend whenever the cost of capital is less than 20%. In this case, even though the IRR of going into business with her boyfriend exceeds the IRR of the delivery service, picking the investment opportunity with the higher IRR does not result in taking the opportunity with the higher NPV.

Percentage Return Versus Dollar Impact on Value. This result might seem counterintuitive and you can imagine Maria having a difficult time explaining to her boyfriend why

FIGURE 8.8

NPV of Maria's Investment Opportunities with the Ten-Drone Delivery Service

As in Figure 8.7, the IRR of her boyfriend's business is 36.3%, while the IRR for the delivery service is 23.4%. But in this case, the NPV of her boyfriend's business is larger than the NPV of the 10-drone delivery service only for discount rates over 20%.

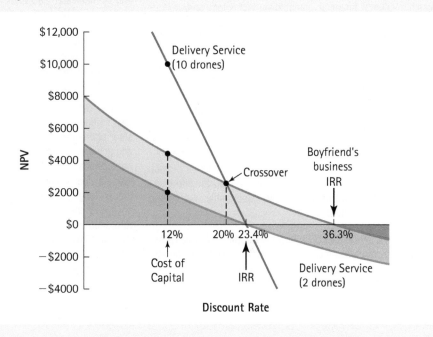

she is choosing a lower return over going into business with him. Why would anyone turn down an investment opportunity with a 36.3% return (IRR) in favor of one with only a 23.4% return? The answer is that the latter opportunity, the delivery service, makes more money. Recall the comparison at the beginning of this section: a 200% return on $1 versus a 10% return on $1 million. We agreed that ranking the returns was not the same as ranking the value created. The IRR is a measure of the average return, which can be valuable information. When you are comparing mutually exclusive projects of different scale, however, you need to know the dollar impact on value—the NPV.

INTERVIEW WITH DICK GRANNIS

Dick Grannis is Senior Vice President and Treasurer of QUALCOMM Incorporated, a world leader in digital wireless communications technology and semiconductors, headquartered in San Diego. He joined the company in 1991 and oversees the company's $10 billion cash investment portfolio. He works primarily on investment banking, capital structure, and international finance.

QUESTION: *QUALCOMM has a wide variety of products in different business lines. How does your capital budgeting process for new products work?*

ANSWER: QUALCOMM evaluates new projects (such as new products, equipment, technologies, research and development, acquisitions, and strategic investments) by using traditional financial measurements including DCF models, IRR levels, peak funding requirements, the time needed to reach cumulative positive cash flows, and the short-term impact of the investment on our reported net earnings. For strategic investments, we consider the possible value of financial, competitive, technology and/or market value enhancements to our core businesses—even if those benefits cannot be quantified. Overall, we make capital budgeting decisions based on a combination of objective analyses and our own business judgment.

We do not engage in capital budgeting and analysis if the project represents an immediate and necessary requirement for our business operations. One example is new software or production equipment to start a project that has already received approval.

We are also mindful of the opportunity costs of allocating our internal engineering resources on one project vs. another project. We view this as a constantly challenging but worthwhile exercise, because we have many attractive opportunities but limited resources to pursue them.

QUESTION: *How often does QUALCOMM evaluate its hurdle rates and what factors does it consider in setting them? How do you allocate capital across areas and regions and assess the risk of non-U.S. investments?*

ANSWER: QUALCOMM encourages its financial planners to utilize hurdle (or discount) rates that vary according to the risk of the particular project. We expect a rate of return commensurate with the project's risk. Our finance staff considers a wide range of discount rates and chooses one that fits the project's expected risk profile and time horizon. The range can be from 6.00% to 8.00% for relatively safe investments in the domestic market to 50% or more for equity investments in foreign markets that may be illiquid and difficult to predict. We re-evaluate our hurdle rates at least every year.

We analyze key factors including: (i) market adoption risk (whether or not customers will buy the new product or service at the price and volume we expect), (ii) technology development risk (whether or not we can develop and patent the new product or service as expected), (iii) execution risk (whether we can launch the new product or service cost effectively and on time), and (iv) dedicated asset risk (the amount of resources that must be consumed to complete the work).

QUESTION: *How are projects categorized and how are the hurdle rates for new projects determined? What would happen if QUALCOMM simply evaluated all new projects against the same hurdle rate?*

ANSWER: We primarily categorize projects by risk level, but we also categorize projects by the expected time horizon. We consider short-term and long-term projects to balance our needs and achieve our objectives. For example, immediate projects and opportunities may demand a great amount of attention, but we also stay focused on long-term projects because they often create greater long-term value for stockholders.

If we were to evaluate all new projects against the same hurdle rate, then our business planners would, by default, consistently choose to invest in the highest risk projects because those projects would appear to have the greatest expected returns in DCF models or IRR analyses. That approach would probably not work well for very long.

EXAMPLE 8.4

Computing the
Crossover Point

MyFinanceLab

PROBLEM

Solve for the crossover point for Maria from Figure 8.8.

SOLUTION

PLAN

The *crossover point* is the discount rate that makes the NPV of the two alternatives equal. We can find the discount rate by setting the equations for the NPV of each project equal to each other and solving for the discount rate. In general, we can always compute the effect of choosing the delivery service over her boyfriend's business as the difference of the NPVs. At the crossover point the difference is 0.

EXECUTE

Setting the difference equal to 0:

$$NPV = -50,000 + \frac{25,000}{1+r} + \frac{25,000}{(1+r)^2} + \frac{25,000}{(1+r)^3}$$

$$-\left(-10,000 + \frac{6000}{(1+r)} + \frac{6000}{(1+r)^2} + \frac{6000}{(1+r)^3}\right) = 0$$

combining terms, we have

$$-40,000 + \frac{19,000}{(1+r)} + \frac{19,000}{(1+r)^2} + \frac{19,000}{(1+r)^3} = 0$$

As you can see, solving for the crossover point is just like solving for the IRR, so we will need to use a financial calculator or spreadsheet:

	N	I/Y	PV	PMT	FV
Given:	3		−40,000	19,000	0
Solve for:		20.04			

Excel Formula: =RATE(NPER,PMT,PV,FV)=RATE(3,19000,−40000,0)

We find that the crossover occurs at a discount rate of 20.04%.

EVALUATE

Just as the NPV of a project tells us the value impact of taking the project, so the difference of the NPVs of two alternatives tells us the *incremental* impact of choosing one project over another. The crossover point is the discount rate at which we would be indifferent between the two projects because the incremental value of choosing one over the other would be zero.

Timing of the Cash Flows

Even when projects have the same scale, the IRR may lead you to rank them incorrectly due to differences in the timing of the cash flows. The reason for this is that the IRR is expressed as a return, but the dollar value of earning a given return—and therefore the NPV—depends on how long the return is earned. Consider a high-IRR project with cash flows paid back quickly. It may have a lower NPV than a project with a lower IRR whose cash flows are paid back over a longer period. This sensitivity to timing is another reason why you cannot use the IRR to choose between mutually exclusive investments. To see this in the context of an example, let's return to Maria's delivery business.

Maria believes that after starting the delivery business, she may be able to sell her stake in the business at the end of the first year for $40,000 (she will stay on and manage the business after she sells). Thus, counting her first-year profit of $25,000, she would earn a total of $65,000 after one year. In that case, the timeline is:

```
        0            1
        ├────────────┤
    −$50,000     +$65,000
```

FIGURE 8.9

NPV with and
without Selling

The IRR from selling after one year (30%) is larger than the IRR without selling (23.4%). However, the NPV from selling after one year exceeds the NPV without selling only for discount rates that are in excess of 16.3% (see the yellow-shaded area versus the blue-shaded area). Thus, given a cost of capital of 12%, it is better not to sell the delivery service after one year, despite the higher IRR.

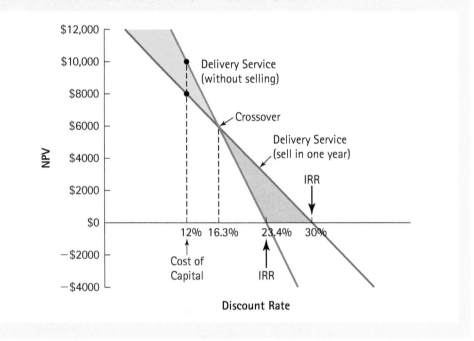

Figure 8.9 plots the NPV profile for the delivery service with and without selling it after one year. If Maria sells, the NPV profile crosses the *x*-axis at 30%, which is its IRR. The IRR for the delivery service if she does not sell is still 23.4%. Therefore, if Maria picks the alternative with the higher IRR, she will sell. However, since the height of each line indicates the NPV of that decision, we can see that his NPV given a 12% cost of capital is higher if she chooses not to sell. (In fact, the NPV is higher as long as the cost of capital is less than 16.3%.) The intuition is as follows: While the 30% IRR from selling is high, this return is only earned in the first year. While the 23.4% IRR from not selling is not as high, it is still attractive relative to the cost of capital, and it is earned over a longer period. Again, only by comparing the NPV can we determine which option is truly more valuable.

The Bottom Line on IRR. As these examples make clear, picking the investment opportunity with the largest IRR can lead to mistakes. In general, it is dangerous to use the IRR in cases where you are choosing between projects, or anytime when your decision to accept or reject one project would affect your decision on another project. In such a situation, always rely on NPV.

**CONCEPT
CHECK**

7. What is the most reliable way to choose between mutually exclusive projects?

8. For mutually exclusive projects, explain why picking one project over another because it has a larger IRR can lead to mistakes.

8.5 Evaluating Projects with Different Lives

Often, a company will need to choose between two solutions to the same problem. A complication arises when those solutions last for different periods of time. For example, a firm could be considering two vendors for its internal network servers. Each vendor offers the same level of service, but they use different equipment. Vendor A offers a more expensive server with lower per-year operating costs that it guarantees for three years. Vendor B offers a less expensive server with higher per-year operating costs that it guarantees for two years. The costs are shown in Table 8.2 along with the present value of the costs of each option, discounted at the 10% cost of capital for this project.

TABLE 8.2

Cash Flows ($ thousands) for Network Server Options

Year	PV at 10%	0	1	2	3
A	−12.49	−10	−1	−1	−1
B	−10.47	−7	−2	−2	

Note that all of the cash flows are negative, and so is the present value. This is a choice of an internal server, where the project must be taken and the benefits are diffuse (the company could not function effectively without an internal network). Thus, we are trying to minimize the cost of providing this service for the company. Table 8.2 shows that option A is more expensive on a present value basis (−$12,487 versus −$10,471). However, the comparison is not that simple: Option A lasts for three years while option B lasts for two. The decision comes down to whether it is worth paying $2000 more for option A to get the extra year. One method that is used to evaluate alternatives such as these that have different lives is to compute the **equivalent annual annuity (EAA)** for each project, which is the level annual cash flow with the same present value as the cash flows of the project. The intuition is that we can think of the cost of each solution as the constant annual cost that gives us the same present value of the lumpy cash flows of buying and operating the server. On a timeline, equivalent annual annuity cash flows would appear as follows:

equivalent annual annuity (EAA) The level annual cash flow that has the same present value as the cash flows of a project. Used to evaluate alternative projects with different lives.

When you have a level cash flow at a constant interval, you are dealing with an annuity and that is exactly how to approach this problem. We know the present value (−$12.49) the number of years (3), and the discount rate (10%). We need to solve for the cash flow, of an equivalent annuity. Recall from Chapter 4 that the formula (Eq. 4.9) for solving for the cash flow in an annuity is:

$$\text{Cash Flow} = \frac{\text{Present Value}}{\frac{1}{r}\left(1 - \frac{1}{(1+r)^N}\right)} = \frac{-12.49}{\frac{1}{0.10}\left(1 - \frac{1}{(1.10)^3}\right)} = -5.02$$

So, buying and operating server A is equivalent to spending $5020 per year to have a network server. We can repeat the calculation for server B, but for a two-year annuity because server B has only a two-year life (the change in exponent is highlighted):

$$\text{Cash Flow} = \frac{\text{Present Value}}{\frac{1}{r}\left(1 - \frac{1}{(1+r)^N}\right)} = \frac{-10.47}{\frac{1}{0.10}\left(1 - \frac{1}{(1.10)^2}\right)} = -6.03$$

Therefore, we can reinterpret the cost of each alternative as shown in Table 8.3:

Now we are ready to choose between the two servers. Server A is equivalent to spending $5020 per year and server B is equivalent to spending $6030 per year to have a network server. Seen in this light, server A appears to be the less expensive solution.

TABLE 8.3

Cash Flows ($ thousands) for Network Server Options, Expressed as Equivalent Annual Annuities

Year	PV at 10%	0	1	2	3
A	−12.49	0	−5.02	−5.02	−5.02
B	−10.47	0	−6.03	−6.03	

EXAMPLE 8.5

Computing an Equivalent Annual Annuity

MyFinanceLab

PROBLEM

You are about to sign the contract for server A from Table 8.2 when a third vendor approaches you with another option that lasts for four years. The cash flows for server C are given below. Should you choose the new option or stick with server A?

Server C ($ thousands)

0	1	2	3	4
−14	−1.2	−1.2	−1.2	−1.2

SOLUTION

PLAN

In order to compare this new option to server A, we need to put server C on an equal footing by computing its annual cost. We can do this by:

1. Computing its NPV at the 10% discount rate we used above.
2. Computing the equivalent four-year annuity with the same present value.

EXECUTE

$$PV = -14 - 1.2\left(\frac{1}{0.10}\right)\left[1 - \frac{1}{(1.10)^4}\right] = -17.80$$

$$\text{Cash Flow} = \frac{PV}{\frac{1}{r}\left[1 - \frac{1}{(1+r)^N}\right]} = \frac{-17.80}{\frac{1}{0.10}\left[1 - \frac{1}{(1.10)^4}\right]} = -5.62$$

Server C's annual cost of $5620 is greater than the annual cost of server A ($5020), so we should still choose server A.

EVALUATE

In this case, the additional cost associated with purchasing and maintaining server C is not worth the extra year we get from choosing it. By putting all of these costs into an equivalent annuity, the EAA tool allows us to see that.

Important Considerations When Using the Equivalent Annual Annuity

Although server A appears to be the lowest-cost alternative, there are several factors to consider before making our decision.

Required Life. We computed the equivalent annual cost of server A assuming we would use it for three years. But suppose it is likely that we will not need the server in the third year. Then we would be paying for something that we would not use. In that case, it may be cheaper to purchase server B, which provides coverage for the years we will need it at a lower total cost.[6]

---

[6]In this scenario, we should also consider any salvage value that server A might have if we sold it after two years.

Replacement Cost. When we compare servers A and B based on their equivalent annual cost, we are assuming that the cost of servers will not change over time. But suppose we believe a dramatic change in technology will reduce the cost of servers by the third year to an annual cost of $2000 per year. Then server B has the advantage that we can upgrade to the new technology sooner. The cost of three years of service from either server in this case can be represented as follows:

Year	PV at 10%	0	1	2	3
A	−12.49	0	−5.02	−5.02	−5.02
B	−11.97	0	−6.03	−6.03	−2.00

Therefore, when cost or performance is expected to change significantly over time, it may be cheaper to purchase server B despite its higher equivalent annual cost because it gives us the option to switch to the new technology sooner.

CONCEPT CHECK

9. Explain why choosing the option with the highest NPV is not always correct when the options have different lives.

10. What issues should you keep in mind when choosing among projects with different lives?

8.6 Choosing Among Projects When Resources Are Limited

In the previous sections, we compared projects that had *identical* resource needs. For example, in Maria's case, we assumed that both the delivery service and her boyfriend's business demanded all of her time. In this section, we develop an approach for situations where the choices have differing resource needs.

Evaluating Projects with Different Resource Requirements

In some situations, different investment opportunities demand different amounts of a particular resource. If there is a fixed supply of the resource so that you cannot undertake all possible opportunities, simply picking the highest NPV opportunity might not lead to the best decision.

We usually assume that you will be able to finance all positive NPV projects that you have. In reality, managers work within the constraint of a budget that restricts the amount of capital they may invest in a given period. Such a constraint would force a manager to choose among positive NPV projects to maximize the total NPV while staying within her budget. For example, assume you are considering the three projects in Table 8.4, and that you have a budget of $200 million. Table 8.4 shows the NPV of each project and the initial investment that each project requires. Project A has the highest NPV but it uses up the entire budget. Projects B and C can *both* be undertaken (together they use the entire budget), and their combined NPV exceeds the NPV of project A; thus, you should initiate them both. Together, their NPV is $145 million compared to $100 million for project A alone.

TABLE 8.4

Possible Projects for $200 Million Budget

Project	NPV ($ millions)	Initial Investment ($ millions)	NPV/Initial Investment
A	100	200	0.500
B	75	120	0.625
C	70	80	0.875

Profitability Index. Note that in the last column of Table 8.4 we included the ratio of the project's NPV to its initial investment. We can interpret this as telling us that for every dollar invested in project A, we will generate 50 cents in value (over and above the dollar investment).[7] Both projects B and C generate higher NPVs per dollar invested than project A, consistent with the fact that given our budget of $200 million, the two of them together created a higher NPV than project A alone.

In this simple example, identifying the optimal combination of projects to undertake is straightforward. In actual situations replete with many projects and resources, finding the optimal combination can be difficult. Practitioners often use the **profitability index (PI)** to help identify the optimal combination of projects to undertake in such situations:

profitability index (PI) Measures the NPV per unit of resource consumed.

Profitability Index

$$\text{Profitability Index} = \frac{\text{Value Created}}{\text{Resource Consumed}} = \frac{NPV}{\text{Resource Consumed}} \tag{8.4}$$

The profitability index measures the "bang for your buck"—that is, the value created in terms of NPV per unit of resource consumed. After computing the profitability index, we can rank projects based on it. Starting with the project with the highest index, we move down the ranking, taking all projects until the resource is consumed. In Table 8.4, the ratio in the last column is the profitability index. Note how the profitability index rule would correctly select projects B and C.

EXAMPLE 8.6

Profitability Index with a Human Resource Constraint

MyFinanceLab

PROBLEM

Your division at NetIt, a large networking company, has put together a project proposal to develop a new home networking router. The expected NPV of the project is $17.7 million, and the project will require 50 software engineers. NetIt has 190 engineers available, and is unable to hire additional qualified engineers in the short run. Therefore, the router project must compete with the following other projects for these engineers:

Project	NPV ($ millions)	Engineering Headcount (EHC)
Router	17.7	50
Project A	22.7	47
Project B	8.1	44
Project C	14.0	40
Project D	11.5	61
Project E	20.6	58
Project F	12.9	32
Total	107.5	332

How should NetIt prioritize these projects?

SOLUTION

PLAN

The goal is to maximize the total NPV that we can create with 190 engineers (at most). We can use Eq. 8.4 to determine the profitability index for each project. In this case, since engineers are our limited resource, we will use Engineering Headcount in the denominator. Once we have the profitability index for each project, we can sort them based on the index.

---

[7]Sometimes, practitioners add 1 to this ratio such that the interpretation would be that every dollar invested returned $1.50. Leaving off the additional 1 allows the ratio to be applied to resources other than budgets as we show in Example 8.6.

EXECUTE

Project	NPV ($ millions)	Engineering Headcount (EHC)	Profitability Index (NPV per EHC)	Cumulative EHC Required
Project A	22.7	47	0.483	47
Project F	12.9	32	0.403	79 (47 + 32)
Project E	20.6	58	0.355	137 (79 + 58)
Router	17.7	50	0.354	187 (137 + 50)
Project C	14.0	40	0.350	
Project D	11.5	61	0.189	
Project B	8.1	44	0.184	

As shown in the table above, we assigned the resource to the projects in descending order according to the profitability index. The final column shows the cumulative use of the resource as each project is taken on until the resource is used up. To maximize NPV within the constraint of 190 engineers, NetIt should choose the first four projects on the list.

EVALUATE

By ranking projects in terms of their NPV per engineer, we find the most value we can create, given our 190 engineers. There is no other combination of projects that will create more value without using more engineers than we have. This ranking also shows us exactly what the engineering constraint costs us—this resource constraint forces NetIt to forgo three otherwise valuable projects (C, D, and B) with a total NPV of $33.6 million.

Shortcomings of the Profitability Index. Although the profitability index is simple to compute and use, in some situations it does not give an accurate answer. For example, suppose in Example 8.6 that NetIt has an additional small project with an NPV of only $100,000 that requires three engineers. The profitability index in this case is $0.1/3 = 0.03$, so this project would appear at the bottom of the ranking. However, notice that three of the 190 employees are not being used after the first four projects are selected. As a result, it would make sense to take on this project even though it would be ranked last because it would exactly use up our constraint.

In general, because the profitability index already includes the cost of capital (in computing the NPV), it would be better if the firm could raise additional funding to relieve the constraint. If the constraint is something else (such as engineers or physical capacity), there may be no way to relieve the constraint quickly enough to avoid having to choose among projects. Nonetheless, because all of the projects being ranked are value-increasing positive NPV projects, it is still better to focus on relieving the constraint.

A more serious problem occurs when multiple resource constraints apply. In this case, the profitability index can break down completely. The only surefire way to find the best combination of projects is to search through all of them. Although this process may sound exceedingly time-consuming, there are more advanced techniques that can tackle this specific kind of problem.[8] By using these techniques on a computer, the solution can usually be obtained almost instantaneously.

CONCEPT CHECK

11. Explain why picking the project with the highest NPV might not be optimal when you evaluate projects with different resource requirements.

12. What does the profitability index tell you?

---

[8]Specifically, there are techniques called *integer and linear programming* that can be used to find the combination with the highest NPV when there are multiple constraints that must be satisfied. These methods are available, for example, in many spreadsheet programs.

8.7 Putting It All Together

In Table 8.5, we summarize the decision rules outlined in this chapter. As a financial manager, you are likely to run into many different types of investment decision rules in your career. In fact, in the interview in this chapter, the Treasurer of QUALCOMM mentions five

TABLE 8.5

Summary of
Decision Rules

NPV	
Definition	• The difference between the present value of an investment's benefits and the present value of its costs
Rule	• Take any investment opportunity where the NPV is positive; turn down any opportunity where it is negative
Advantages	• Corresponds directly to the impact of the project on the firm's value • Direct application of the Valuation Principle
Disadvantages	• Relies on an accurate estimate of the discount rate • Can be time-consuming to compute
IRR	
Definition	• The interest rate that sets the net present value of the cash flows equal to zero; the average return of the investment
Rule	• Take any investment opportunity where its IRR exceeds the opportunity cost of capital; turn down any opportunity where its IRR is less than the opportunity cost of capital
Advantages	• Related to the NPV rule and usually yields the same (correct) decision
Disadvantages	• Hard to compute • Multiple IRRs lead to ambiguity • Cannot be used to choose among projects • Can be misleading if inflows come before outflows
Payback Period	
Definition	• The amount of time it takes to pay back the initial investment
Rule	• Accept the project if the payback period is less than a prespecified length of time—usually a few years; otherwise, turn it down
Advantages	• Simple to compute • Favors liquidity
Disadvantages	• No guidance as to correct payback cutoff • Ignores cash flows after the cutoff completely • Not necessarily consistent with maximizing shareholder wealth
Profitability Index	
Definition	• NPV/Resource Consumed
Rule	• Rank projects according to their PI based on the constrained resource and move down the list accepting value-creating projects until the resource is exhausted
Advantages	• Uses the NPV to measure the benefit • Allows projects to be ranked on value created per unit of resource consumed
Disadvantages	• Breaks down when there is more than one constraint • Requires careful attention to make sure the constrained resource is completely utilized

different decision rules used by his company when evaluating investments. We have demonstrated that while alternative decision rules may sometimes (or even often) agree with the NPV decision rule, only the NPV decision rule is always correct. This is because the NPV provides you with a dollar-value measure of the impact of the project on shareholder wealth. Thus, it is the only rule that is directly tied to your goal of maximizing shareholder wealth. Computing the IRR can be a useful supplement to the NPV because knowing the IRR allows you to gauge how sensitive your decision is to errors in your discount rate. And some decision metrics are much simpler to calculate, such as the payback period. However, you should never rely on an alternative rule to make investment decisions.

If you are employed by a firm that uses the IRR rule (or another rule) exclusively, our advice is to always calculate the NPV. If the two rules agree, you can feel comfortable reporting the IRR rule recommendation. If they do not agree, you should investigate why the IRR rule failed by using the concepts in this chapter. Once you have identified the problem, you can alert your superiors to it and perhaps persuade them to adopt the NPV rule.

MyFinanceLab

Here is what you should know after reading this chapter. MyFinanceLab will help you identify what you know, and where to go when you need to practice.

KEY POINTS AND EQUATIONS	KEY TERMS	ONLINE PRACTICE
8.1 The NPV Decision Rule • The net present value (NPV) of a project is $$PV(\text{Benefits}) - PV(\text{Costs}) \qquad (8.1)$$ • A good project is one with a positive net present value. • The NPV decision rule states that when choosing from among a set of alternatives, choose the one with the highest NPV. The NPV of a project is equivalent to the cash value today of the project. • Regardless of our preferences for cash today versus cash in the future, we should always first maximize NPV. We can then borrow or lend to shift cash flows through time and find our most preferred pattern of cash flows.	net present value (NPV), p. 228 NPV decision rule, p. 229	MyFinanceLab Study Plan 8.1 Financial Calculator Tutorial: Calculating the Net Present Value of a Series of Uneven Cash Flows
8.2 Using the NPV Rule • If your objective is to maximize wealth, the NPV rule always gives the correct answer. • The difference between the cost of capital and the IRR is the maximum amount of estimation error that can exist in the cost of capital estimate without altering the original decision.	internal rate of return (IRR), p. 232 NPV profile, p. 231	MyFinanceLab Study Plan 8.2 Using Excel: Making an NPV Profile

8.3 Alternative Decision Rules

- Payback investment rule: Calculate the amount of time it takes to pay back the initial investment (the payback period). If the payback period is less than a prespecified length of time, accept the project. Otherwise, turn it down.
- IRR investment rule: Take any investment opportunity whose IRR exceeds the opportunity cost of capital. Turn down any opportunity whose IRR is less than the opportunity cost of capital.
- The IRR rule may give the wrong answer if the cash flows have an up-front payment (negative investment). When there are multiple IRRs or the IRR does not exist, the IRR rule cannot be used.
- Project cash flows can be modified to eliminate the multiple IRR problem. The modified IRR is calculated based on these modified cash flows.

discounted payback rule, p. 235
internal rate of return (IRR) investment rule, p. 235
modified internal rate of return (MIRR), p. 239
payback investment rule, p. 234
payback period, p. 234

MyFinanceLab Study Plan 8.3

Interactive IRR Analysis

Financial Calculator Tutorial: Solving for the Internal Rate of Return

8.4 Choosing Between Projects

- When choosing among mutually exclusive investment opportunities, pick the opportunity with the highest NPV. Do not use IRR to choose among mutually exclusive investment opportunities.

mutually exclusive projects, p. 242

MyFinanceLab Study Plan 8.4

8.5 Evaluating Projects with Different Lives

- When choosing among projects with different lives, you need a standard basis of comparison. First, compute an annuity with an equivalent present value to the NPV of each project. Then the projects can be compared on their cost or value created *per year*.

equivalent annual annuity (EAA), p. 249

MyFinanceLab Study Plan 8.5

8.6 Choosing Among Projects When Resources Are Limited

- When choosing among projects competing for the same resource, rank the projects by their profitability indices and pick the set of projects with the highest profitability indices that can still be undertaken given the limited resource.

$$\text{Profitability Index} = \frac{\text{Value Created}}{\text{Resource Consumed}}$$
$$= \frac{NPV}{\text{Resource Consumed}} \quad (8.4)$$

profitability index (PI), p. 252

MyFinanceLab Study Plan 8.6

CRITICAL THINKING

1. What is the NPV rule?

2. How is the NPV rule related to the goal of maximizing shareholder wealth?

3. What is the intuition behind the payback rule? What are some of its drawbacks?

4. What is the intuition behind the IRR rule? What are some of its drawbacks?

5. Under what conditions will the IRR rule and the NPV rule give the same accept/reject decision?

6. When is it possible to have multiple IRRs?

7. How does the MIRR solve the problem of multiple IRRs?

8. Why is it generally a bad idea to use IRR to choose between mutually exclusive projects?

9. When should you use the equivalent annual annuity?

10. What is the intuition behind the profitability index?

PROBLEMS

All problems are available in MyFinanceLab. The *icon indicates problems that are easier to solve using Excel and have data in an Excel format available in MyFinanceLab. An asterisk * indicates problems with a higher level of difficulty.*

The NPV Decision Rule

1. You have an opportunity to invest $50,000 now in return for $60,000 in one year. If your cost of capital is 8%, what is the NPV of this investment?

2. You have an opportunity to invest $100,000 now in return for $80,000 in one year and $30,000 in two years. If your cost of capital is 9%, what is the NPV of this investment?

3. Your storage firm has been offered $100,000 in one year to store some goods for one year. Assume your costs are $95,000, payable immediately, and the cost of capital is 8%. Should you take the contract?

4. You are preparing to produce some goods for sale. You will sell them in one year and you will incur costs of $80,000 immediately. If your cost of capital is 7%, what is the minimum dollar amount you need to expect to sell the goods for in order for this to be a non-negative NPV?

5. You run a construction firm. You have just won a contract to build a government office building. Building it will require an investment of $10 million today and $5 million in one year. The government will pay you $20 million in one year upon the building's completion. Assume the cost of capital is 10%.
   a. What is the NPV of this opportunity?
   b. How can your firm turn this NPV into cash today?

6. You have been offered a unique investment opportunity. If you invest $10,000 today, you will receive $500 one year from now, $1500 two years from now, and $10,000 ten years from now.
   a. What is the NPV of the opportunity if the cost of capital is 6% per year? Should you take the opportunity?
   b. What is the NPV of the opportunity if the cost of capital is 2% per year? Should you take it now?

7. Marian Plunket owns her own business and is considering an investment. If she undertakes the investment, it will pay $4000 at the end of each of the next three years. The opportunity requires an initial investment of $1000 plus an additional investment at the end of the second year of $5000. What is the NPV of this opportunity if the cost of capital is 2% per year? Should Marian take it?

Using the NPV Rule

8. Your factory has been offered a contract to produce a part for a new printer. The contract would be for three years and your cash flows from the contract would be $5 million per year. Your up-front setup costs to be ready to produce the part would

be $8 million. Your cost of capital for this contract is 8%.

a. What does the NPV rule say you should do?

b. If you take the contract, what will be the change in the value of your firm?

9. You are considering opening a new plant. The plant will cost $100 million up front and will take one year to build. After that, it is expected to produce profits of $30 million at the end of every year of production. The cash flows are expected to last forever. Calculate the NPV of this investment opportunity if your cost of capital is 8%. Should you make the investment? Calculate the IRR and use it to determine the maximum deviation allowable in the cost of capital estimate to leave the decision unchanged.

10. Bill Clinton reportedly was paid $10 million to write his book *My Life*. The book took three years to write. In the time he spent writing, Clinton could have been paid to make speeches. Given his popularity, assume that he could earn $8 million per year (paid at the end of the year) speaking instead of writing. Assume his cost of capital is 10% per year.

a. What is the NPV of agreeing to write the book (ignoring any royalty payments)?

b. Assume that, once the book was finished, it was expected to generate royalties of $5 million in the first year (paid at the end of the year) and these royalties were expected to decrease at a rate of 30% per year in perpetuity. What is the NPV of the book with the royalty payments?

*11. FastTrack Bikes, Inc., is thinking of developing a new composite road bike. Development will take six years and the cost is $200,000 per year. Once in production, the bike is expected to make $300,000 per year for 10 years. The cash inflows begin at the end of year 7.

Assuming the cost of capital is 10%:

a. Calculate the NPV of this investment opportunity. Should the company make the investment?

b. Calculate the IRR and use it to determine the maximum deviation allowable in the cost of capital estimate to leave the decision unchanged.

c. How long must development last to change the decision?

Assuming the cost of capital is 14%:

a. Calculate the NPV of this investment opportunity. Should the company make the investment?

b. How much must this cost of capital estimate deviate to change the decision?

c. How long must development last to change the decision?

12. OpenSeas, Inc., is evaluating the purchase of a new cruise ship. The ship will cost $500 million, and will operate for 20 years. OpenSeas expects annual cash flows from operating the ship to be $70 million and its cost of capital is 12%.

a. Prepare an NPV profile of the purchase.

b. Identify the IRR on the graph.

c. Should OpenSeas proceed with the purchase?

d. How far off could OpenSeas' cost of capital estimate be before your purchase decision would change?

13. You are CEO of Rivet Networks, maker of ultra-high performance network cards for gaming computers, and you are considering whether to launch a new product. The product, the Killer X3000, will cost $900,000 to develop upfront (year 0), and you expect revenues the first year of $800,000, growing to $1.5 million the second year, and then declining by 40% per year for the next 3 years before the product is fully obsolete. In years 1 through 5, you will have fixed costs associated with the product of $100,000 per year, and variable costs equal to 50% of revenues.

    a. What are the cash flows for the project in years 0 through 5?

    b. Plot the NPV profile for this investment using discount rates from 0% to 40% in 10% increments.

    c. What is the project's NPV if the project's cost of capital is 10%?

    d. Use the NPV profile to estimate the cost of capital at which the project would become unprofitable; that is, estimate the project's IRR.

Alternative Decision Rules

14. You are a real estate agent thinking of placing a sign advertising your services at a local bus stop. The sign will cost $5000 and will be posted for one year. You expect that it will generate additional free cash flow of $500 per month. What is the payback period?

 15. Does the IRR rule agree with the NPV rule in Problem 8?

 16. How many IRRs are there in part (a) of Problem 10? Does the IRR rule give the correct answer in this case?

 17. How many IRRs are there in part (b) of Problem 10? Does the IRR rule work in this case?

 18. Professor Wendy Smith has been offered the following deal: A law firm would like to retain her for an up-front payment of $50,000. In return, for the next year the firm would have access to eight hours of her time every month. Smith's rate is $550 per hour and her opportunity cost of capital is 15% per year. What does the IRR rule advise regarding this opportunity? What about the NPV rule?

 19. Innovation Company is thinking about marketing a new software product. Up-front costs to market and develop the product are $5 million. The product is expected to generate profits of $1 million per year for 10 years. The company will have to provide product support expected to cost $100,000 per year in perpetuity. Assume all profits and expenses occur at the end of the year.

    a. What is the NPV of this investment if the cost of capital is 6%? Should the firm undertake the project? Repeat the analysis for discount rates of 2% and 11%.

    b. How many IRRs does this investment opportunity have?

    c. What does the IRR rule indicate about this investment?

20. You have 3 projects with the following cash flows:

Year	0	1	2	3	4
Project 1	−150	20	40	60	80
Project 2	−825	0	0	7000	−6500
Project 3	20	40	60	80	−245

    a. For which of these projects is the IRR rule reliable?

    b. Estimate the IRR for each project (to the nearest 1%).

    c. What is the NPV of each project if the cost of capital is 5%? 20%? 50%?

 21. You own a coal mining company and are considering opening a new mine. The mine will cost $120 million to open. If this money is spent immediately, the mine will generate $20 million for the next 10 years. After that, the coal will run out and the site must be cleaned and maintained at environmental standards. The cleaning and maintenance are expected to cost $2 million per year in perpetuity. What does the IRR rule say about whether you should accept this opportunity? If the cost of capital is 8%, what does the NPV rule say?

22. Your firm is considering a project that will cost $4.55 million upfront, generate cash flows of $3.5 million per year for three years, and then have a cleanup and shutdown cost of $6 million in the fourth year.
  a. How many IRRs does this project have?
  b. Calculate a modified IRR for this project discounting the outflows and leaving the inflows unchanged. Assume a discount and compounding rate of 10%.
  c. Using the MIRR and a cost of capital of 10%, would you take the project?

23. You have just been offered a contract worth $1 million per year for five years. However, to take the contract, you will need to purchase some new equipment. Your discount rate for this project is 12%. You are still negotiating the purchase price of the equipment. What is the most you can pay for the equipment and not have a negative NPV?

*24. You are getting ready to start a new project that will incur some cleanup and shutdown costs when it is completed. The project costs $5.4 million up front and is expected to generate $1.1 million per year for 10 years and then have some shutdown costs in year 11. Use the MIRR approach to find the maximum shutdown costs you could incur and still meet your cost of capital of 15% on this project.

*25. You are considering investing in a new gold mine in South Africa. Gold in South Africa is buried very deep, so the mine will require an initial investment of $250 million. Once this investment is made, the mine is expected to produce revenues of $30 million per year for the next 20 years. It will cost $10 million per year to operate the mine. After 20 years, the gold will be depleted. The mine must then be stabilized on an ongoing basis, which will cost $5 million per year in perpetuity. Calculate the IRR of this investment. (*Hint:* Plot the NPV as a function of the discount rate.)

26. You are evaluating a project that will cost $500,000, but is expected to produce cash flows of $125,000 per year for 10 years, with the first cash flow in one year. Your cost of capital is 11% and your company's preferred payback period is three years or less.
  a. What is the payback period of this project?
  b. Should you take the project if you want to increase the value of the company?

27. You are considering making a movie. The movie is expected to cost $10 million upfront and take a year to produce. After that, it is expected to make $5 million in the year it is released and $2 million for the following four years. What is the payback period of this investment? If you require a payback period of two years, will you make the movie? Does the movie have positive NPV if the cost of capital is 10%?

Choosing Between Projects

28. You are choosing between two projects, but can only take one. The cash flows for the projects are given in the following table:

	0	1	2	3	4
A	−$50	25	20	20	15
B	−$100	20	40	50	60

  a. What are the IRRs of the two projects?
  b. If your discount rate is 5%, what are the NPVs of the two projects?
  c. Why do IRR and NPV rank the two projects differently?

29. You are deciding between two mutually exclusive investment opportunities. Both require the same initial investment of $10 million. Investment A will generate $2 million per year (starting at the end of the first year) in perpetuity. Investment B will generate $1.5 million at the end of the first year and its revenues will grow at 2% per year for every year after that.

a. Which investment has the higher IRR?

b. Which investment has the higher NPV when the cost of capital is 7%?

c. In this case, when does picking the higher IRR give the correct answer as to which investment is the better opportunity?

30. You are considering the following projects and can take only one. Your cost of capital is 11%.

	0	1	2	3	4
A	−100	25	30	40	50
B	−100	50	40	30	20

a. What is the NPV of each project at your cost of capital?

b. What is the IRR of each project?

c. At what cost of capital are you indifferent between the two projects?

d. What should you do?

31. You need a particular piece of equipment for your production process. An equipment-leasing company has offered to lease you the equipment for $10,000 per year if you sign a guaranteed five-year lease. The company would also maintain the equipment for you as part of the lease. Alternatively, you could buy and maintain the equipment yourself. The cash flows (in thousands) from doing so are listed below (the equipment has an economic life of five years). If your discount rate is 7%, what should you do?

0	1	2	3	4	5
−40	−2	−2	−2	−2	−2

Evaluating Projects with Different Lives

32. You are trying to decide between two mobile phone carriers. Carrier A requires you to pay $200 for the phone and monthly charges of $60 for 24 months. Carrier B wants you to pay $100 for the phone and monthly charges of $70 for 12 months. Assume you will keep replacing the phone after your contract expires. Your cost of capital is 4%. Based on cost alone, which carrier should you choose?

33. Gateway Tours is choosing between two bus models. One is more expensive to purchase and maintain, but lasts much longer than the other. Its discount rate is 11%. It plans to continue with one of the two models for the foreseeable future; which should it choose? Based on the costs of each model shown below, which should it choose?

Model	0	1	2	3	4	5...	7
Old Reliable	−200	−4	−4	−4	−4	−4...	−4
Short and Sweet	−100	−2	−2	−2	−2		

34. Hassle-Free Web is bidding to provide Web hosting services for Hotel Lisbon. Hotel Lisbon pays its current provider $10,000 per year for hosting its Web page, handling transactions, etc. Hassle-Free figures that it will need to purchase equipment worth $15,000 upfront and then spend $2000 per year on monitoring, updates, and bandwidth to provide the service for three years. If Hassle-Free's cost of capital is 10%, can it bid less than $10,000 per year to provide the service and still increase its value by doing so?

35. You have to buy a new copier. The cost of the copier is $2000, plus $400 per year in maintenance costs. The copier will last for five years. Alternatively, a local company offers to lease the copier to you and do the maintenance as well. If your discount rate is 6%, what is the most you would be willing to pay per year to lease the copier (your first lease payment is due in one year)?

Choosing Among Projects When Resources Are Limited

36. Fabulous Fabricators needs to decide how to allocate space in its production facility this year. It is considering the following contracts:

	NPV	Use of Facility
A	$2 million	100%
B	$1 million	60%
C	$1.5 million	40%

    a. What are the profitability indexes of the projects?
    b. What should Fabulous Fabricators do?

37. Kartman Corporation is evaluating four real estate investments. Management plans to buy the properties today and sell them three years from today. The annual discount rate for these investments is 15%. The following table summarizes the initial cost and the sale price in three years for each property:

	Cost Today	Sale Price in Year 3
Parkside Acres	$650,000	$1,150,000
Real Property Estates	800,000	1,400,000
Lost Lake Properties	650,000	1,050,000
Overlook	150,000	350,000

    Kartman has a total capital budget of $800,000 to invest in properties. Which properties should it choose?

38. Orchid Biotech Company is evaluating several development projects for experimental drugs. Although the cash flows are difficult to forecast, the company has come up with the following estimates of the initial capital requirements and NPVs for the projects. Given a wide variety of staffing needs, the company has also estimated the number of research scientists required for each development project (all cost values are given in millions of dollars).

Project Number	Initial Capital	Number of Research Scientists	NPV
I	$10	2	$10.1
II	15	3	19.0
III	15	4	22.0
IV	20	3	25.0
V	30	12	60.2

    a. Suppose that Orchid has a total capital budget of $60 million. How should it prioritize these projects?
    b. Suppose that Orchid currently has 12 research scientists and does not anticipate being able to hire more in the near future. How should Orchid prioritize these projects?

DATA CASE

You have just purchased a house for $500,000 that is located very close to the university you attend. You plan to put $100,000 down and borrow $400,000. You need to decide which mortgage deal to take. To find out what your choices are, go to www.bankrate.com and select the appropriate buttons to get a quote for a 30-year fixed rate mortgage on a new purchase (not a refinancing). Assume your FICO score is very high and you are looking for a zero point mortgage. Find the best coupon rate on a mortgage that requires paying no upfront fees or points.[9] We will refer to this mortgage as the no-fee mortgage and assume that the rate on this mortgage is your cost of capital.

You are going to make the decision about which mortgage to consider by calculating the NPV of switching from the no-fee mortgage to each of the top six mortgages listed (sorted by their coupon). To calculate the NPV of this decision, calculate the difference in payments today, and over the life of the mortgage, by subtracting the alternative mortgage payments from the no-fee mortgage payments and calculating the NPV. For good measure, calculate the IRR as well.[10] Assume that you will be living in the house for the next 30 years for certain and you will never repay the mortgage early. Which mortgage should you undertake? Do the NPV and IRR rules agree?

Next, assume that the bank will allow you to borrow any fees and points, so the loan amount will increase by these charges. Repeat the above calculations.

Finally, repeat the calculations assuming that you will repay the outstanding balance on the mortgage after 5 years, using the same cost of capital. What can you say about which mortgage you should choose if you have a long horizon versus a shorter horizon?

Of course, the choice of cost of capital will vary by individual. Because your cost of capital might be different to the one used above, for both horizons, pick the option with the largest NPV and plot the NPV profile.

---

[9]The mortgage coupon is listed in the *rate* field (*not* the *APR*) and is quoted as a monthly APR. Both fees and "points" refer to money that must be paid upfront. Fees are specified in dollars, while points refer to a percentage of the amount borrowed. So, a $1000 fee together with a 1% point implies that you must pay $400,000 \times 1\% + 1000 = \$5000$ upfront. This means that although the loan amount will be $400,000 you will actually only borrow $395,000 (so you need to put down an extra $5000).

[10]Hint: If you are having trouble calculating the IRR, make sure it exists by first plotting the NPV profile.

9

Fundamentals of Capital Budgeting

LEARNING OBJECTIVES

- Identify the types of cash flows needed in the capital budgeting process

- Forecast incremental earnings in a pro forma earnings statement for a project

- Convert forecasted earnings to free cash flows and compute a project's NPV

- Recognize common pitfalls that arise in identifying a project's incremental free cash flows

- Assess the sensitivity of a project's NPV to changes in your assumptions

- Identify the most common options available to managers in projects and understand why these options can be valuable

notation

CapEx	capital expenditures	*NPV*	net present value
EBIT	earnings before interest and taxes	NWC_t	net working capital in year t
FCF_t	free cash flow in year t	*PV*	present value
IRR	internal rate of return	r	projected cost of capital

An important responsibility of corporate financial managers is determining which projects or investments a firm should undertake. *Capital budgeting*, the focus of this chapter, is the process of analyzing investment opportunities and deciding which ones to accept. In doing so, we are allocating the firm's funds to various projects—we are budgeting its capital. Chapter 8 covered the various methods for evaluating projects and proved that NPV will be the most reliable and accurate method for doing so. In retrospect, this may not be surprising as it is the only rule directly tied to the Valuation Principle. To implement the NPV rule, we must compute the NPV of our projects and accept only those projects for which the NPV is positive. In the last chapter, we spoke about Sony and Toshiba each using investment decision rules to pursue competing high-definition DVD standards (and eventually for Toshiba, to decide to abandon HD-DVD). In order to implement the investment decision rules, financial managers from Toshiba, for example, first had to forecast the incremental cash flows associated with the investments and later had to forecast the incremental cash flows associated with the decision to stop investing in HD-DVD. The process of forecasting those cash flows, crucial inputs in the investment decision process, is our focus in this chapter.

We begin by estimating the project's expected cash flows by forecasting the project's revenues and costs. Using these cash flows, we can compute the project's NPV—its contribution to shareholder value. Then, because the cash flow forecasts almost always contain uncertainty, we demonstrate how to compute the sensitivity of the NPV to the uncertainty in the forecasts. Finally, we examine the relationship between a project's flexibility and its NPV.

9.1 The Capital Budgeting Process

capital budget Lists the projects and investments that a company plans to undertake during the next period.

capital budgeting The process of analyzing projects and investment opportunities and deciding which ones to accept.

The first step in analyzing various investment opportunities is compiling a list of potential projects. A **capital budget** lists the projects and investments that a company plans to undertake during the next period. To create this list, firms analyze projects and investment opportunities and decide which ones to accept through a process called **capital budgeting**. This process begins with forecasts of each project's future consequences for the firm. Some of these consequences will affect the firm's revenues; others will affect its costs. Our ultimate goal is to determine the effect of the decision to accept or reject a project on the firm's cash flows, and evaluate the NPV of these cash flows to assess the consequences of the decision for the firm's value. Figure 9.1 depicts the types of cash flows found in a typical project. We will examine each of these as we proceed through our discussion of capital budgeting.

Of course, forecasting these cash flows is frequently challenging. We will often need to rely on different experts within the firm to obtain estimates for many of them. For example, the marketing department may provide sales forecasts, the operations manager may provide information about production costs, and the firm's engineers may estimate the up-front research and development expenses that are required to launch the project. Another important source of information comes from looking at past projects of the firm, or those of other firms in the same industry. In particular, practitioners often base their assessments of a project's revenues and costs using information on revenues and costs that can be learned from the historical financial statements of the firm or its competitors.

Once we have these estimates, how do we organize them? One common starting point is to consider the consequences of the project for the firm's earnings. Thus, we will *begin*

FIGURE 9.1

Cash Flows in a Typical Project

The diagram shows some typical cash flows in project analysis and their timing.

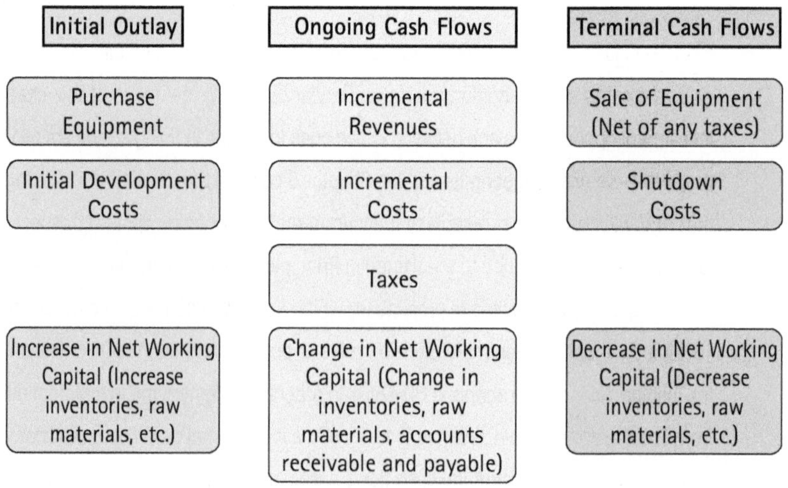

Initial Outlay	Ongoing Cash Flows	Terminal Cash Flows
Purchase Equipment	Incremental Revenues	Sale of Equipment (Net of any taxes)
Initial Development Costs	Incremental Costs	Shutdown Costs
	Taxes	
Increase in Net Working Capital (Increase inventories, raw materials, etc.)	Change in Net Working Capital (Change in inventories, raw materials, accounts receivable and payable)	Decrease in Net Working Capital (Decrease inventories, raw materials, etc.)

incremental earnings
The amount by which a firm's earnings are expected to change as a result of an investment decision.

our analysis in Section 9.2 by determining the **incremental earnings** of a project—that is, the amount by which a firm's earnings are expected to change as a result of an investment decision. The incremental earnings forecast tells us how the decision will affect the firm's reported profits from an accounting perspective. However, as we emphasized in Chapter 2, *earnings are not actual cash flows.* We need to estimate the project's cash flows to determine its NPV and decide whether it is a good project for the firm. Therefore, in Section 9.3, we demonstrate how to use the incremental earnings to forecast the actual cash flows of the project. Understanding how to compute the cash flow consequences of an investment based on its earning consequences is important for a number of reasons. First, as a practical matter, financial managers often begin by forecasting earnings. Second, if we are looking at historical data, accounting information is often the only information that is readily available.

CONCEPT CHECK

1. What is capital budgeting, and what is its goal?
2. Why is computing a project's effect on the firm's earnings insufficient for capital budgeting?

9.2 Forecasting Incremental Earnings

Let's begin our discussion of incremental earnings with a simple example that we will examine throughout this section. Suppose you are considering whether to upgrade your manufacturing plant to increase its capacity by purchasing a new piece of equipment. The equipment costs $1 million, plus an additional $20,000 to transport it and install it. You will also spend $50,000 on engineering costs to redesign the plant to accommodate the increased capacity. What are the initial earnings consequences of this decision?

Operating Expenses Versus Capital Expenditures

Most projects require some form of up-front investment—we may need to conduct a marketing survey, develop a prototype, or launch an ad campaign. These types of costs are accounted for as operating expenses in the year that they are incurred. However, many projects also include investments in plant, property, and/or equipment, called *capital expenditures.* Recall from Chapter 2 that while investments in plant, property, and equipment are cash expenses, they are not directly listed as expenses when calculating *earnings.* Instead, the firm deducts a fraction of the cost of these items each year as depreciation. Financial managers use several different methods to compute depreciation. The simplest method is **straight-line depreciation**, in which an asset's cost is divided equally over its depreciable life (we discuss another common method in Section 9.4).

straight-line depreciation A method of depreciation in which an asset's cost is divided equally over its life.

In our example, the up-front costs associated with the decision to increase capacity have two distinct consequences for the firm's earnings. First, the $50,000 spent on redesigning the plant is an operating expense reported in year 0. For the $1,020,000 spent to buy, ship, and install the machine, accounting principles as well as tax rules require you to depreciate the $1,020,000 over the depreciable life of the equipment. Assuming that the equipment has a five-year depreciable life and that we use the straight-line method, we would expense $1,020,000/5 = $204,000 per year for five years. (The motivation for this accounting treatment is to match the cost of acquiring the machine to the timing of the revenues it will generate.)

1	Year	0	1	2	3	4	5
2	Operating Expenses (Plant Redesign)	−$50,000					
3	Depreciation (New Equipment)		−$204,000	−$204,000	−$204,000	−$204,000	−$204,000

As the timeline shows, the up-front cash outflow of $1,020,000 to purchase and set up the machine is not recognized as an expense in year 0. Instead, it appears as depreciation expenses in years 1 through 5. Remember that these *depreciation expenses do not correspond to actual cash outflows*. This accounting and tax treatment of capital expenditures is one of the key reasons why earnings are not an accurate representation of cash flows. We will return to this issue in Section 9.3.[1]

Incremental Revenue and Cost Estimates

Our next step is to estimate the ongoing revenues and costs for the project. Forecasting future revenues and costs is challenging. The most successful practitioners collect as much information as possible before tackling this task—they will talk to members of marketing and sales teams as well as company economists to develop an estimate of sales, and they will talk to engineering and production teams to refine their estimate of costs.

There are several factors to consider when estimating a project's revenues and costs, including the following:

1. A new product typically has lower sales initially, as customers gradually become aware of the product. Sales will then accelerate, plateau, and ultimately decline as the product nears obsolescence or faces increased competition.

2. The average selling price of a product and its cost of production will generally change over time. Prices and costs tend to rise with the general level of inflation in the economy. The prices of technology products, however, often fall over time as newer, superior technologies emerge and production costs decline.

3. For most industries, competition tends to reduce profit margins over time.

Our focus here is on how to get from these forecasts to incremental earnings and then to cash flows. Chapter 18 discusses forecasting methods in more detail.

All our revenue and cost estimates should be *incremental*, meaning that we only account for additional sales and costs generated by the project. For example, if we are evaluating the purchase of a faster manufacturing machine, we are only concerned with how many additional units of the product we will be able to sell (and at what price) and any additional costs created by the new machine. We do not forecast total sales and costs because those include our production using the old machine. *Remember, we are evaluating how the project will change the cash flows of the firm. That is why we focus on incremental revenues and costs.*

Let's return to our plant upgrade example. Assume that after we have bought and installed the machine and redesigned the plant, our additional capacity will allow us to generate incremental revenues of $500,000 per year for five years. Those incremental revenues will be associated with $150,000 per year in incremental costs. In that case, our revenue, cost, and depreciation estimates for the project are as shown below (in thousands of dollars):

1	Year	0	1	2	3	4	5
2	Incremental Revenues		500	500	500	500	500
3	Incremental Costs	−50	−150	−150	−150	−150	−150
4	Depreciation		−204	−204	−204	−204	−204

Now that we have these estimates, we are ready to compute the consequences of our project for the firm's earnings. As we saw in Chapter 2, both depreciation expenses and

---

[1]Some students might note that for financial reporting, the asset should be depreciated to salvage value. For tax purposes, salvage value is always treated as zero, so this is the relevant method for capital budgeting.

the actual costs of producing (e.g., cost of goods sold) must be subtracted from revenues, so that:

$$\text{Incremental Earnings Before Interest and Taxes (EBIT)} = \text{Incremental Revenue}$$
$$- \text{Incremental Costs} - \text{Depreciation} \qquad (9.1)$$

Taxes

The final expense we must account for is corporate taxes. The correct tax rate to use is the firm's **marginal corporate tax rate**, which is the tax rate it will pay on an *incremental* dollar of pretax income. The incremental income tax expense is calculated as:

marginal corporate tax rate The tax rate a firm will pay on an incremental dollar of pretax income.

$$\text{Income Tax} = \text{EBIT} \times \text{The Firm's Marginal Corporate Tax Rate} \qquad (9.2)$$

Incremental Earnings Forecast

We're now ready to put the pieces together for an incremental earnings forecast. Assume our firm faces a marginal tax rate of 40% and that the firm as a whole has at least $50,000 in profits in year 0 for the incremental costs in that year to offset. Then the incremental earnings (or net income) are as follows (in thousands of dollars):[2]

	Year	0	1	2	3	4	5
1	**Year**	0	1	2	3	4	5
2	Incremental Revenues		500	500	500	500	500
3	Incremental Costs	−50	−150	−150	−150	−150	−150
4	Depreciation		−204	−204	−204	−204	−204
5	**EBIT**	−50	146	146	146	146	146
6	Income Tax at 40%	20	−58.4	−58.4	−58.4	−58.4	−58.4
7	**Incremental Earnings**	**−30**	**87.6**	**87.6**	**87.6**	**87.6**	**87.6**

We can combine Eqs. 9.1 and 9.2 to compute incremental earnings directly. For example, in years 1 through 5 we have:

$$\text{Incremental Earnings} = (\text{Incremental Revenues} - \text{Incremental Cost}$$
$$- \text{Depreciation}) \times (1 - \text{Tax Rate}) \qquad (9.3)$$
$$\text{Incremental Earnings} = (500,000 - 150,000 - 204,000)$$
$$\times (1 - 0.4) = 87,600$$

EXAMPLE 9.1

Incremental Earnings

MyFinanceLab

PROBLEM

Suppose that the managers of the router division of Cisco Systems are considering the development of a wireless home networking appliance, called HomeNet, that will provide both the hardware and the software necessary to run an entire home from any Internet connection. In addition to connecting computers and smartphones, HomeNet will control Internet-capable televisions, streaming video services, heating and air-conditioning units, major appliances, security systems, office equipment, and so on. The major competitor for HomeNet is a product being developed by Brandt-Quigley Corporation.

Based on extensive marketing surveys, the sales forecast for HomeNet is 50,000 units per year. Given the pace of technological change, Cisco expects the product will have a four-year life and an expected

(Continued)

---

[2]While revenues and costs occur throughout the year, the standard convention, which we adopt here, is to list revenues and costs in the year in which they occur. Thus, cash flows that occur at the end of one year will be listed in a different column than those that occur at the start of the next year, even though they may occur only weeks apart. When additional precision is required, cash flows are often estimated on a quarterly or monthly basis.

wholesale price of $260 (the price Cisco will receive from stores). Actual production will be outsourced at a cost (including packaging) of $110 per unit.

To verify the compatibility of new consumer Internet-ready appliances, as they become available, with the HomeNet system, Cisco must also establish a new lab for testing purposes. It will rent the lab space, but will need to purchase $7.5 million of new equipment. The equipment will be depreciated using the straight-line method over a five-year life. Cisco's marginal tax rate is 40%.

The lab will be operational at the end of one year. At that time, HomeNet will be ready to ship. Cisco expects to spend $2.8 million per year on rental costs for the lab space, as well as marketing and support for this product. Forecast the incremental earnings from the HomeNet project.

SOLUTION

PLAN

We need four items to calculate incremental earnings: (1) incremental revenues, (2) incremental costs, (3) depreciation, and (4) the marginal tax rate:

Incremental revenues are: Additional units sold × price = 50,000 × $260 = $13,000,000

Incremental costs are: Additional units sold × production costs
= 50,000 × $110 = $5,500,000

Selling, general, and administrative = $2,800,000 for rent, marketing, and support

Depreciation is: Depreciable basis/Depreciable life = $7,500,000/5 = $1,500,000

Marginal tax rate is: 40%

Note that even though the project lasts for four years, the equipment has a five-year life, so we must account for the final depreciation charge in the fifth year.

EXECUTE (IN $000S)

1	Year	0	1	2	3	4	5
2	Revenues		13,000	13,000	13,000	13,000	–
3	Cost of Goods Sold		−5,500	−5,500	−5,500	−5,500	–
4	**Gross Profit**		7,500	7,500	7,500	7,500	–
5	Selling, General, and Administrative		−2,800	−2,800	−2,800	−2,800	–
6	Depreciation		−1,500	−1,500	−1,500	−1,500	−1,500
7	**EBIT**		3,200	3,200	3,200	3,200	−1,500
8	Income Tax at 40%		−1,280	−1,280	−1,280	−1,280	600
9	**Incremental Earnings**		1,920	1,920	1,920	1,920	−900

EVALUATE

These incremental earnings are an intermediate step on the way to calculating the incremental cash flows that would form the basis of any analysis of the HomeNet project. The cost of the equipment does not affect earnings in the year it is purchased, but does so through the depreciation expense in the following five years. Note that the depreciable life, which is based on accounting rules, does not have to be the same as the economic life of the asset—the period over which it will have value. Here, the firm will use the equipment for four years, but will depreciate it over five years.

Pro Forma Statement. The table calculating incremental earnings that we produced for our plant upgrade, and again in Example 9.1, is often referred to as a **pro forma** statement, because it is not based on actual data but rather depicts the firm's financials under a given set of hypothetical assumptions. In the HomeNet example, the firm's forecasts of revenues and costs were assumptions that allowed Cisco to forecast incremental earnings in a pro forma statement.

pro forma Describes a statement that is not based on actual data but rather depicts a firm's financials under a given set of hypothetical assumptions.

Taxes and Negative EBIT. Notice that in year 0 of our plant upgrade project, and in year 5 of the HomeNet example, EBIT is negative. Why are taxes relevant in this case? Consider the HomeNet example. HomeNet will reduce Cisco's taxable income in year 5 by $1.5

million. As long as Cisco earns taxable income elsewhere in year 5 against which it can offset HomeNet's losses, Cisco will owe $1.5 million $\times$ 40% = $600,000 *less* in taxes in year 5 than if it were not undertaking the project. Because the tax savings come from the depreciation expense on equipment for the HomeNet project, the firm should credit this tax savings to the HomeNet project.

EXAMPLE 9.2

Taxing Losses
for Projects
in Profitable
Companies

MyFinanceLab

PROBLEM

Suppose that Kellogg Company plans to launch a new line of high-fiber, gluten-free breakfast pastries. The heavy advertising expenses associated with the new product launch will generate operating losses of $15 million next year for the product. Kellogg expects to earn pretax income of $460 million from operations other than the new pastries next year. If Kellogg pays a 40% tax rate on its pretax income, what will it owe in taxes next year without the new pastry product? What will it owe with the new product?

SOLUTION

PLAN

We need Kellogg's pretax income with and without the new product losses and its tax rate of 40%. We can then compute the tax without the losses and compare it to the tax with the losses.

EXECUTE

Without the new product, Kellogg will owe $460 million $\times$ 40% = $184 million in corporate taxes next year. With the new product, Kellogg's pretax income next year will be only $460 million − $15 million = $445 million, and it will owe $445 million $\times$ 40% = $178 million in tax.

EVALUATE

Thus, launching the new product reduces Kellogg's taxes next year by $184 million − $178 million = $6 million. Because the losses on the new product reduce Kellogg's taxable income dollar for dollar, it is the same as if the new product had a tax bill of *negative* $6 million.

What About Interest Expenses? In Chapter 2, we saw that to compute a firm's net income, we must first deduct interest expenses from EBIT. When evaluating a capital budgeting decision, however, we generally *do not include interest expenses*. Any incremental interest expenses will be related to the firm's decision regarding how to finance the project, which is a separate decision. Here, we wish to evaluate the earnings contributions from the project on its own, separate from the financing decision. Ultimately, managers may also look at the additional earnings consequences associated with different methods of financing the project.

Thus, we evaluate a project *as if* the company will not use any debt to finance it (whether or not that is actually the case), and we postpone the consideration of alternative financing choices until Parts 5 and 6 of the book. Because we calculate the net income assuming no debt (no leverage), we refer to the net income we compute using Eq. 9.3, as in the pro forma in Example 9.1, as the **unlevered net income** of the project, to indicate that it does not include any interest expenses associated with debt.

unlevered net income Net income that does not include interest expenses associated with debt.

CONCEPT CHECK

3. How are operating expenses and capital expenditures treated differently when calculating incremental earnings?

4. Why do we focus only on incremental revenues and costs, rather than all revenues and costs of the firm?

9.3 Determining Incremental Free Cash Flow

As discussed in Chapter 2, earnings are an accounting measure of the firm's performance. They do not represent real profits: The firm cannot use its earnings to buy goods, pay employees, fund new investments, or pay dividends to shareholders. To do those things,

free cash flow The incremental effect of a project on a firm's available cash.

the firm needs cash. Thus, to evaluate a capital budgeting decision, we must determine its consequences for the firm's available cash. The incremental effect of a project on the firm's available cash is the project's incremental **free cash flow**.

Converting from Earnings to Free Cash Flow

As discussed in Chapter 2, there are important differences between earnings and cash flow. Earnings include non-cash charges, such as depreciation, but do not include expenditures on capital investment. To determine a project's free cash flow from its incremental earnings, we must adjust for these differences.

Capital Expenditures and Depreciation. As we have noted, depreciation is not a cash expense that is paid by the firm. Rather, it is a method used for accounting and tax purposes to allocate the original purchase cost of the asset over its life. Because depreciation is not a cash flow, we do not include it in the cash flow forecast. However, that does not mean we can ignore depreciation. The depreciation expense reduces our taxable earnings and in doing so reduces our taxes. Taxes are cash flows, so because depreciation affects our cash flows, it still matters. Our approach for handling depreciation is to add it back to the incremental earnings to recognize the fact that we still have the cash flow associated with it.

For example, a project has incremental gross profit (revenues minus costs) of $1 million and a $200,000 depreciation expense. If the firm's tax rate is 40%, then the incremental earnings will be $(\$1,000,000 - \$200,000) \times (1 - 0.40) = \$480,000$. However, the firm will still have $680,000 because the $200,000 depreciation expense is not an actual cash outflow. Table 9.1 shows the calculation to get the incremental free cash flow in this case. Blue boxes indicate all of the actual cash flows in the column labeled "Correct." A good way to check to make sure the incremental free cash flow is correct is to sum the actual cash flows. In this case, the firm generated $1,000,000 in gross profit (a positive cash flow), paid $320,000 in taxes (a negative cash flow), and was left with $1,000,000 - \$320,000 = \$680,000$, which is the amount shown as the incremental free cash flow. In the last column, labeled "Incorrect," we show what would happen if you just ignored depreciation altogether. Because EBIT would be too high, the taxes would be too high as well and consequently, the incremental free cash flow would be too low. (Note that the difference of $80,000 between the two cases is entirely due to the difference in tax payments.)

TABLE 9.1

Deducting and Then Adding Back Depreciation

	Correct	Incorrect
Incremental Gross Profit	$1,000,000	$1,000,000
Depreciation	−200,000	
EBIT	$800,000	$1,000,000
Tax at 40%	−$320,000	−$400,000
Incremental Earnings	$480,000	$600,000
Add Back Depreciation	$200,000	
Incremental Free Cash Flow	$680,000	$600,000

EXAMPLE 9.3

Incremental Free Cash Flows

MyFinanceLab

PROBLEM

Let's return to the HomeNet example. In Example 9.1, we computed the incremental earnings for HomeNet, but we need the incremental free cash flows to decide whether Cisco should proceed with the project.

SOLUTION

PLAN

The difference between the incremental earnings and incremental free cash flows in the HomeNet example will be driven by the equipment purchased for the lab. We need to recognize the $7.5 million cash outflow associated with the purchase in year 0 and add back the $1.5 million depreciation expenses from year 1 to 5 as they are not actually cash outflows.

EXECUTE (IN $000S)

We recognize the outflow for the equipment in row 11 and we add back the depreciation expenses in row 10.

1	Year	0	1	2	3	4	5
2	Revenues		13,000	13,000	13,000	13,000	–
3	Cost of Goods Sold		−5,500	−5,500	−5,500	−5,500	–
4	**Gross Profit**		7,500	7,500	7,500	7,500	–
5	Selling, General, and Administrative		−2,800	−2,800	−2,800	−2,800	–
6	Depreciation		−1,500	−1,500	−1,500	−1,500	−1,500
7	**EBIT**		3,200	3,200	3,200	3,200	−1,500
8	Income Tax at 40%		−1,280	−1,280	−1,280	−1,280	600
9	**Incremental Earnings**		1,920	1,920	1,920	1,920	−900
10	Add Back Depreciation		1,500	1,500	1,500	1,500	1,500
11	Purchase of Equipment	−7,500					
12	**Incremental Free Cash Flows**	**−7,500**	**3,420**	**3,420**	**3,420**	**3,420**	**600**

EVALUATE

By recognizing the outflow from purchasing the equipment in year 0, we account for the fact that $7.5 million left the firm at that time. By adding back the $1.5 million depreciation expenses in years 1 through 5, we adjust the incremental earnings to reflect the fact that the depreciation expense is not a cash outflow.

Net Working Capital (NWC). Another way that incremental earnings and free cash flows can differ is if there are changes in net working capital. We defined net working capital in Chapter 2 as the difference between current assets and current liabilities. The main components of net working capital are cash, inventory, receivables, and payables:

$$\text{Net Working Capital} = \text{Current Assets} - \text{Current Liabilities}$$
$$= \text{Cash} + \text{Inventory} + \text{Receivables} - \text{Payables} \quad (9.4)$$

Note that as discussed in Chapter 2, we do not include short-term financing such as notes payable or short-term debt because those represent financing decisions that we keep separate from our investment decisions. Most projects will require the firm to invest in net working capital. Firms may need to maintain a minimum cash balance[3] to meet unexpected expenditures, and inventories of raw materials and finished product to accommodate production uncertainties and demand fluctuations. Also, customers may not pay for the goods they purchase immediately. While sales are immediately counted as part of earnings, the firm does not receive any cash until the customers actually pay. In the interim, the firm includes the amount that customers owe in its receivables. Thus, the firm's receivables measure the total credit that the firm has extended to its customers. In the same way, payables measure the credit the firm has received from its suppliers. The difference between receivables and payables is the net amount of the firm's capital that is consumed as a result of these credit transactions, known as **trade credit**.

trade credit The difference between receivables and payables (the net amount of a firm's capital consumed as a result of these credit transactions); the credit that a firm extends to its customers.

---

[3] The cash included in net working capital is cash that is *not* invested to earn a market rate of return. It includes cash held in the firm's checking account, in a company safe or cash box, in cash registers (for retail stores), and other sites.

We care about net working capital because it reflects a short-term investment that ties up cash flow that could be used elsewhere. For example, when a firm holds a lot of unsold inventory or has a lot of outstanding receivables, cash flow is tied up in the form of inventory or in the form of credit extended to customers. It is costly for the firm to tie up that cash flow because it delays the time until the cash flow is available for reinvestment or distribution to shareholders. Since we know that money has time value, we cannot ignore this delay in our forecasts for the project. Thus, whenever net working capital increases, reflecting additional investment in working capital, it represents a reduction in cash flow that year.

It is important to note that only changes in net working capital impact cash flows. For example, consider a three-year project that causes the firm to build up initial inventory by $20,000 and maintain that level of inventory in years 1 and 2, before drawing it down as the project ends and the last product is sold. It is often necessary for the initial increase in inventory to occur prior to the first sale so that the higher level of inventory would be achieved by the end of year 0. The level of the incremental net working capital in each year, the associated change in net working capital, and the cash flow implications, would be:

	Year	0	1	2	3
1					
2	Level of Incremental NWC	20,000	20,000	20,000	0
3	*Change* in Incremental NWC	+20,000	0	0	−20,000
4	**Cash Flow from Change in NWC**	**−20,000**	**0**	**0**	**+20,000**

Note that the cash flow effect from a change in net working capital is always equal and opposite in sign to the change in net working capital. For example, an increase in inventory represents an investment or cash outflow, while a reduction in that inventory frees up that investment of capital and represents a cash inflow. Thus, in capital budgeting we subtract changes in net working capital to arrive at the cash flows. Also notice that since the level of incremental net working capital did not change in years 1 and 2, there was no new cash flow effect. Intuitively, as the firm is using up inventory and replenishing it, the net new investment in inventory is zero, so no additional cash outflow is required. Finally, note that over the life of the project, the incremental net working capital returns to zero so that the changes ($+20,000$ in year 0 and $−20,000$ in year 3) sum to zero. Accounting principles ensure this by requiring the recapture of working capital over the life of the project.

More generally, we define the change in net working capital in year t as:

$$\text{Change in } NWC \text{ in Year } t = NWC_t - NWC_{t-1} \tag{9.5}$$

When a project causes a change in NWC, that change must be subtracted from incremental earnings to arrive at incremental free cash flows.

EXAMPLE 9.4

Incorporating Changes in Net Working Capital

MyFinanceLab

PROBLEM

Suppose that HomeNet will have no incremental cash or inventory requirements (products will be shipped directly from the contract manufacturer to customers). However, receivables related to HomeNet are expected to account for 15% of annual sales, and payables are expected to be 15% of the annual cost of goods sold (COGS). Fifteen percent of $13 million in sales is $1.95 million and 15% of $5.5 million in COGS is $825,000. HomeNet's net working capital requirements are shown in the following table:

	Year	0	1	2	3	4	5
1							
2	**Net Working Capital Forecast ($000s)**						
3	Cash Requirements	0	0	0	0	0	0
4	Inventory	0	0	0	0	0	0
5	Receivables (15% of Sales)	0	1,950	1,950	1,950	1,950	0
6	Payables (15% of COGS)	0	−825	−825	−825	−825	0
7	**Net Working Capital**	**0**	**1,125**	**1,125**	**1,125**	**1,125**	**0**

How does this requirement affect the project's free cash flow?

SOLUTION

PLAN

Any increases in net working capital represent an investment that reduces the cash available to the firm and so reduces free cash flow. We can use our forecast of HomeNet's net working capital requirements to complete our estimate of HomeNet's free cash flow. In year 1, net working capital increases by $1.125 million. This increase represents a cost to the firm. This reduction of free cash flow corresponds to the fact that in year 1, $1.950 million of the firm's sales and $0.825 million of its costs have not yet been paid.

In years 2–4, net working capital does not change, so no further contributions are needed. In year 5, when the project is shut down, net working capital falls by $1.125 million as the payments of the last customers are received and the final bills are paid. We add this $1.125 million to free cash flow in year 5.

EXECUTE (IN $000S)

	Year	0	1	2	3	4	5
1							
2	Net Working Capital	0	1,125	1,125	1,125	1,125	0
3	Change in NWC		+1,125	0	0	0	−1,125
4	Cash Flow Effect		−1,125	0	0	0	+1,125

The incremental free cash flows would then be:

	Year	0	1	2	3	4	5
1							
2	Revenues		13,000	13,000	13,000	13,000	0
3	Costs of Goods Sold		−5,500	−5,500	−5,500	−5,500	0
4	**Gross Profit**		7,500	7,500	7,500	7,500	0
5	Selling, General, and Administrative		−2,800	−2,800	−2,800	−2,800	0
6	Depreciation		−1,500	−1,500	−1,500	−1,500	−1,500
7	**EBIT**		3,200	3,200	3,200	3,200	−1,500
8	Income Tax at 40%		−1,280	−1,280	−1,280	−1,280	600
9	**Incremental Earnings**		1,920	1,920	1,920	1,920	−900
10	Add Back Depreciation		1,500	1,500	1,500	1,500	1,500
11	Purchase of Equipment	−7,500					
12	Subtract Changes in NWC		−1,125	0	0	0	1,125
13	**Incremental Free Cash Flows**	**−7,500**	**2,295**	**3,420**	**3,420**	**3,420**	**1,725**

EVALUATE

The free cash flows differ from unlevered net income by reflecting the cash flow effects of capital expenditures on equipment, depreciation, and changes in net working capital. Note that in the first year, free cash flow is lower than unlevered net income, reflecting the up-front investment in equipment. In later years, free cash flow exceeds unlevered net income because depreciation is not a cash expense. In the last year, the firm ultimately recovers the investment in net working capital, further boosting the free cash flow.

Calculating Free Cash Flow Directly

As we noted at the outset of this chapter, because practitioners usually begin the capital budgeting process by first forecasting earnings, we have chosen to do the same. However, we can calculate a project's free cash flow directly by using the following shorthand formula:

Free Cash Flow

$$\text{Free Cash Flow} = \overbrace{(\text{Revenues} - \text{Costs} - \text{Depreciation}) \times (1 - \text{Tax Rate})}^{\text{Unlevered Net Income}} \quad (9.6)$$
$$+ \text{Depreciation} - \text{CapEx} - \text{Change in } NWC$$

Note that we first deduct depreciation when computing the project's incremental earnings and then add it back (because it is a non-cash expense) when computing free cash flow.

Thus, the only effect of depreciation is to reduce the firm's taxable income. Indeed, we can rewrite Eq. 9.6 as:

$$\text{Free Cash Flow} = (\text{Revenues} - \text{Costs}) \times (1 - \text{Tax Rate}) - \text{CapEx}$$
$$- \text{Change in } NWC + \text{Tax Rate} \times \text{Depreciation} \qquad (9.7)$$

depreciation tax shield The tax savings that result from the ability to deduct depreciation.

The last term in Eq. 9.7, Tax Rate × Depreciation, is called the **depreciation tax shield**, which is the tax savings that result from the ability to deduct depreciation. As a consequence, depreciation expenses have a *positive* impact on free cash flow. Returning to our example in Table 9.1, if the firm ignored depreciation, its taxes were $400,000 instead of $320,000, leaving it with incremental free cash flow of $600,000 instead of $680,000. Notice that the $80,000 difference is exactly equal to the tax rate (40%) multiplied by the depreciation expense ($200,000). Every dollar of depreciation expense saves the firm 40 cents in taxes, so the $200,000 depreciation expense translates into an $80,000 tax savings.

Firms often report a different depreciation expense for accounting and for tax purposes. Because only the tax consequences of depreciation are relevant for free cash flow, we should use the depreciation expense that the firm will use for tax purposes in our forecast. For tax purposes, many firms use a system called *Modified Accelerated Cost Recovery System*, which we will discuss in the next section.

Calculating the NPV

The goal of forecasting the incremental free cash flows is to have the necessary inputs to calculate the project's NPV. To compute a project's NPV, we must discount its free cash flow at the appropriate cost of capital. As discussed in Chapter 5, the cost of capital for a project is the expected return that investors could earn on their best alternative investment with similar risk and maturity. We will develop the techniques needed to estimate the cost of capital in Part 4 of the text, when we discuss risk and return. For now, we take the cost of capital as given.

We compute the present value of each free cash flow in the future by discounting it at the project's cost of capital. As explained in Chapter 3, using r to represent the cost of capital, the present value of the free cash flow in year t (or FCF_t) is:

$$PV(FCF_t) = \frac{FCF_t}{(1+r)^t} = FCF_t \times \underbrace{\frac{1}{(1+r)^t}}_{t\text{-year discount factor}} \qquad (9.8)$$

EXAMPLE 9.5

Calculating the Project's NPV

MyFinanceLab

PROBLEM

Assume that Cisco's managers believe that the HomeNet project has risks similar to its existing projects, for which it has a cost of capital of 12%. Compute the NPV of the HomeNet project.

SOLUTION

PLAN

From Example 9.4, the incremental free cash flows for the HomeNet project are (in $000s):

	Year	0	1	2	3	4	5
1							
2	Incremental Free Cash Flows	−7,500	2,295	3,420	3,420	3,420	1,725

To compute the NPV, we sum the present values of all of the cash flows, noting that the year 0 cash outflow is already a present value.

EXECUTE

Using Eq. 9.8,

$$NPV = -7500 + \frac{2295}{(1.12)^1} + \frac{3420}{(1.12)^2} + \frac{3420}{(1.12)^3} + \frac{3420}{(1.12)^4} + \frac{1725}{(1.12)^5} = 2862$$

EVALUATE

Based on our estimates, HomeNet's NPV is $2.862 million. While HomeNet's up-front cost is $7.5 million, the present value of the additional free cash flow that Cisco will receive from the project is $10.362 million. Thus, taking the HomeNet project is equivalent to Cisco having an extra $2.862 million in the bank today.

USING EXCEL

Capital Budgeting Using a Spreadsheet Program

Capital budgeting forecasts and analysis are most easily performed in a spreadsheet program. Here, we highlight a few best practices when developing your own capital budgets.

Create a Project Dashboard

All capital budgeting analyses begin with a set of assumptions regarding future revenues and costs associated with the investment. Centralize these assumptions within your spreadsheet in a project dashboard so they are easy to locate, review, and potentially modify. Here, we show an example for the HomeNet project.

	A	B	C	D	E	F	G	H	I	J
1	**HomeNet Capital Budget**									
2	**Key Assumptions**									
3		*Revenues & Costs*		**Year 0**	**Year 1**	**Year 2**	**Year 3**	**Year 4**	**Year 5**	
4		HomeNet Units Sold			50	50	50	50		
5		HomeNet Ave. Price/Unit			$ 260.00	$ 260.00	$ 260.00	$ 260.00		
6		HomeNet Cost/Unit			$ 110.00	$ 110.00	$ 110.00	$ 110.00		
7		*Operating Expenses*								
8		Marketing, Support & Rent			(2,800)	(2,800)	(2,800)	(2,800)		
9		*Capital Expenditures*								
10		Purchase Equipment		(7,500)						
11		*Other Assumptions*								
12		Depreciation Schedule		0.0%	20.0%	20.0%	20.0%	20.0%	20.0%	
13		Corporate Tax Rate		40.0%	40.0%	40.0%	40.0%	40.0%	40.0%	
14		Receivables (% sales)		15.0%	15.0%	15.0%	15.0%	15.0%	15.0%	
15		Payables (% expenses)		15.0%	15.0%	15.0%	15.0%	15.0%	15.0%	
16										

Color Code for Clarity

In spreadsheet models, use a blue font to distinguish numerical assumptions from formulas. For example, HomeNet's revenue and cost estimates are set to a numerical value in year 1, whereas estimates in later years are set to equal the year 1 estimates. It is therefore clear which cells contain the main assumptions, should we wish to change them later.

Maintain Flexibility

In the HomeNet dashboard, note that we state all assumptions on an annual basis even if we expect them to remain constant. For example, we specify HomeNet's unit volume and average sale price for each year. We can then calculate HomeNet revenues each year based on the corresponding annual assumptions. Doing so provides flexibility if we later determine that HomeNet's adoption rate might vary over time or if we expect prices to follow a trend.

Never Hardcode

So that your assumptions are clear and easy to modify, reference any numerical values you need to develop your projections in the project dashboard. Never "hardcode," or enter numerical values directly into formulas. For example, in the computation of taxes in cell E24 below, we use the formula "=−E23*E13" rather than "=−E23*0.40". While the latter formula would compute the same answer, because the tax rate is hardcoded it would be difficult to update the model if the forecast for the tax rate were to change.

	A	B	C	D	E	F	G	H	I	J
22		*Incremental Earnings Forecast*		**Year 0**	**Year 1**	**Year 2**	**Year 3**	**Year 4**	**Year 5**	
23		EBIT			$3,200	$3,200	$3,200	$3,200	($1,500)	
24		Income Tax			=−E23*E13	($1,280)	($1,280)	($1,280)	$600	
25		Net Income			$1,920	$1,920	$1,920	$1,920	($900)	

5. If depreciation expense is not a cash flow, why do we have to subtract it and add it back? Why not just ignore it?

6. Why does an increase in net working capital represent a cash outflow?

9.4 Other Effects on Incremental Free Cash Flows

When computing the incremental free cash flows of an investment decision, we should include *all* changes between the firm's free cash flows with the project versus without the project. These include opportunities forgone due to the project and effects of the project on other parts of the firm. In this section, we discuss these other effects, some of the pitfalls and common mistakes to avoid, and the complications that can arise when forecasting incremental free cash flows.

Opportunity Costs

opportunity cost The value a resource could have provided in its best alternative use.

Many projects use a resource that the company already owns. Because the firm does not need to pay cash to acquire this resource for a new project, it is tempting to assume that the resource is available for free. However, in many cases, the resource could provide value for the firm in another opportunity or project. The **opportunity cost** of using a resource is the value it could have provided in its best alternative use.[4] Because this value is lost when the resource is used by another project, we should include the opportunity cost as an incremental cost of the project. For example, your company may be considering building a retail store on land that it owns. Even though it already owns the land, it is not free to the store project. If it does not put its store on the land, the company could sell the land, for example. This forgone market price for the land is an opportunity cost of the retail store project.

COMMON MISTAKE

The Opportunity Cost of an Idle Asset

A common mistake is to conclude that if an asset is currently idle, its opportunity cost is zero. For example, the firm might have a warehouse that is currently empty or a machine that is not being used. Often, the asset may have been idled in anticipation of taking on the new project, and would have otherwise been put to use by the firm. Even if the firm has no alternative use for the asset, the firm could choose to sell or rent the asset. The value obtained from the asset's alternative use, sale, or rental represents an opportunity cost that must be included as part of the incremental cash flows.

Project Externalities

project externalities
Indirect effects of a project that may increase or decrease the profits of other business activities of a firm.

Project externalities are indirect effects of a project that may increase or decrease the profits of other business activities of the firm. For instance, some purchasers of Apple's larger iPad Pro would otherwise have bought Apple's iPad Air. When sales of a new product displace sales of an existing product, the situation is often referred

---

[4]In Chapter 5, we defined the opportunity cost of capital as the rate you could earn on an alternative investment with equivalent risk. We similarly define the opportunity cost of using an existing asset in a project as the cash flow generated by the next-best alternative use for the asset.

cannibalization When sales of a firm's new product displace sales of one of its existing products.

to as **cannibalization**. The lost sales of the existing product are an incremental cost to the company of going forward with the new product.

Sunk Costs

sunk cost Any unrecoverable cost for which a firm is already liable.

A **sunk cost** is any unrecoverable cost for which the firm is already liable. Sunk costs have been or will be paid regardless of the decision whether or not to proceed with the project. Therefore, they are not incremental with respect to the current decision and should not be included in its analysis. You may hire a market research firm to determine whether there is demand for a new product you are considering and the analysis may show that there is not enough demand, so you decide not to go forward with the project. Does that mean you do not have to pay the research firm's bill? Of course you still have to pay the bill, emphasizing that the cost is sunk and incurred whether you move forward with the project or not.

A good rule to remember is that *if your decision does not affect a cash flow, then the cash flow should not affect your decision.* If the cash flow is the same regardless of the decision, then it is not relevant to your decision. The following are some common examples of sunk costs you may encounter.

overhead expenses Expenses associated with activities that are not directly attributable to a single business activity but instead affect many different areas of a corporation.

Fixed Overhead Expenses. **Overhead expenses** are associated with activities that are not directly attributable to a single business activity but instead affect many different areas of a corporation. Examples include the cost of maintaining the company's headquarters and the salary of the CEO. These expenses are often allocated to the different business activities for accounting purposes. To the extent that these overhead costs are fixed and will be incurred in any case, they are not incremental to the project and should not be included. Only include as incremental expenses the *additional* overhead expenses that arise because of the decision to take on the project.

COMMON MISTAKE

The Sunk Cost Fallacy

Being influenced by sunk costs is such a widespread mistake that it has a special name: sunk cost fallacy. The most common problem is that people "throw good money after bad." That is, people sometimes continue to invest in a project that has a negative NPV because they have already invested a large amount in the project and feel that by not continuing it, the prior investment will be wasted. The sunk cost fallacy is also sometimes called the "Concorde effect," which refers to the British and French

governments' decision to continue funding the joint development of the Concorde aircraft even after it was clear that sales of the plane would fall far short of what was necessary to justify its continued development. The project was viewed by the British government as a commercial and financial disaster. However, the political implications of halting the project—and thereby publicly admitting that all past expenses on the project would result in nothing—ultimately prevented either government from abandoning the project.

Past Research and Development Expenditures. A pharmaceutical company may spend tens of millions of dollars developing a new drug, but if it fails to produce an effect in trials (or worse, has only negative effects), should it proceed? The company cannot get its development costs back and the amount of those costs should have no bearing on whether to continue developing a failed drug.

When a firm has already devoted significant resources to develop a new product, there may be a tendency to continue investing in the product even if market conditions have changed and the product is unlikely to be viable. The rationale that is sometimes given is that if the product is abandoned, the money that has already been invested will be "wasted." In other cases, a decision is made to abandon a project because it cannot possibly be successful enough to recoup the investment that has already been made. In fact, neither argument is correct: Any money that has already been spent is a sunk cost and therefore irrelevant. The decision to continue or abandon should be based only on the incremental costs and benefits of the product going forward.

Unavoidable Competitive Effects. When developing a new product, firms often worry about the cannibalization of their existing products. But if sales are likely to decline in any case as a result of new products introduced by competitors, then these lost sales are a sunk cost and we should not include them in our projections.

Adjusting Free Cash Flow

Here, we describe a number of complications that can arise when estimating a project's free cash flow.

Timing of Cash Flows. For simplicity, we have treated the cash flows in our examples as if they occur at annual intervals. In reality, cash flows are spread throughout the year. While it is common to forecast at the annual level, we can forecast free cash flow on a quarterly or monthly basis when greater accuracy is required. In practice, firms often choose shorter intervals for riskier projects so that they might forecast cash flows at the monthly level for projects that carry considerable risk. For example, cash flows for a new facility in Europe may be forecasted at the quarterly or annual level, but if that same facility were located in a politically unstable country, the forecasts would likely be at the monthly level.

Accelerated Depreciation. Because depreciation contributes positively to the firm's cash flow through the depreciation tax shield, it is in the firm's best interest to use the most accelerated method of depreciation that is allowable for tax purposes. By doing so, the firm will accelerate its tax savings and increase their present value. In the United States, the most accelerated depreciation method allowed by the IRS is *MACRS (Modified Accelerated Cost Recovery System) depreciation*. With **MACRS depreciation**, the firm first categorizes assets according to their recovery period. Based on the recovery period, MACRS depreciation tables assign a fraction of the purchase price that the firm can recover each year. We provide MACRS tables and recovery periods for common assets in the appendix to this chapter. As we explain in the appendix, MACRS allows for partial depreciation in the year when the asset is purchased and put into service.

MACRS depreciation The most accelerated cost recovery system allowed by the IRS. Based on the recovery period, MACRS depreciation tables assign a fraction of the purchase price that the firm can depreciate each year.

EXAMPLE 9.6
Computing Accelerated Depreciation

MyFinanceLab

PROBLEM

What depreciation deduction would be allowed for HomeNet's $7.5 million lab equipment using the MACRS method, assuming the lab equipment is designated to have a five-year recovery period? For clarity, assume that the lab equipment is purchased and put into use in December of year 0, allowing the partial year depreciation in year 0. This means that year 0 is the first year of the MACRS schedule (year 1) in the appendix. (See the appendix to this chapter for information on MACRS depreciation schedules.)

SOLUTION

PLAN

Table 9.4 (in the appendix) provides the percentage of the cost that can be depreciated each year. Under MACRS, we take the percentage in the table for each year and multiply it by the original purchase price of the equipment to calculate the depreciation for that year.

EXECUTE

Based on the table, the allowable depreciation expense for the lab equipment is shown below (in thousands of dollars):

	Year	0	1	2	3	4	5
1							
2	**MACRS Depreciation**						
3	Lab Equipment Cost	−7,500					
4	MACRS Depreciation Rate	20.00%	32.00%	19.20%	11.52%	11.52%	5.76%
5	Depreciation Expense	−1,500	−2,400	−1,440	−864	−864	−432

EVALUATE

As long as the equipment is put into use by the end of year 0, the tax code allows us to take our first depreciation expense in the same year. Compared with straight-line depreciation, the MACRS method allows for larger depreciation deductions earlier in the asset's life, which increases the present value of the depreciation tax shield and so will raise the project's NPV. In the case of HomeNet, computing the NPV using MACRS depreciation leads to an NPV of $3.179 million.

Now compare what would happen if we put the machine into use at the very beginning of year 1 (the same year as we first recognize revenues in this example). Then, all of our depreciation expenses would shift by one year. Because we put the equipment *into use in year 1*, then the first time we can take a depreciation expense is in year 1. In that case, the table would be:

	Year	0	1	2	3	4	5	6
1	**MACRS Depreciation**							
2								
3	Lab Equipment Cost	−7,500						
4	MACRS Depreciation Rate		20.00%	32.00%	19.20%	11.52%	11.52%	5.76%
5	Depreciation Expense		−1,500	−2,400	−1,440	−864	−864	−432

In this case, the NPV would be $2.913 million because all of the depreciation tax shields are delayed by one year relative to the case where the equipment is put into use before year 1. Nonetheless, the NPV is still higher than in the case of straight-line depreciation because a larger percentage of the depreciation comes earlier.

Liquidation or Salvage Value. Assets that are no longer needed often have a resale value, or some salvage value if the parts are sold for scrap. Some assets may have a negative liquidation value. For example, it may cost money to remove and dispose of the used equipment.

In the calculation of free cash flow, we include the liquidation value of any assets that are no longer needed and may be disposed of. When an asset is liquidated, any capital gain is taxed as income. We calculate the capital gain as the difference between the sale price and the book value of the asset:

$$\text{Capital Gain} = \text{Sale Price} - \text{Book Value} \qquad (9.9)$$

The book value is equal to the asset's original cost less the amount it has already been depreciated for tax purposes:

$$\text{Book Value} = \text{Purchase Price} - \text{Accumulated Depreciation} \qquad (9.10)$$

We must adjust the project's free cash flow to account for the after-tax cash flow that would result from an asset sale:

$$\text{After-Tax Cash Flow from Asset Sale} = \text{Sale Price} - (\text{Tax Rate} \times \text{Capital Gain}) \quad (9.11)$$

EXAMPLE 9.7
Computing After-Tax Cash Flows from an Asset Sale

MyFinanceLab

PROBLEM

As production manager, you are overseeing the shutdown of a production line for a discontinued product. Some of the equipment can be sold for $50,000. The equipment was originally purchased and put into use five years ago for $500,000 and is being depreciated according to the five-year MACRS schedule (so that you are five years into the six years of the 5-year MACRS schedule). If your marginal tax rate is 35%, what is the after-tax cash flow you can expect from selling the equipment?

SOLUTION

PLAN

In order to compute the after-tax cash flow, you will need to compute the capital gain, which, as Eq. 9.9 shows, requires you to know the book value of the equipment. The book value is given in Eq. 9.10 as the original purchase price of the equipment less accumulated depreciation. Thus, you need to follow these steps:
1. Use the MACRS schedule to determine the accumulated depreciation.

(*Continued*)

2. Determine the book value as purchase price minus accumulated depreciation.
3. Determine the capital gain as the sale price less the book value.
4. Compute the tax owed on the capital gain and subtract it from the sale price, following Eq. 9.11, and then subtract the tax owed from the sale price.

EXECUTE

From the appendix, we see that the first five rates of the five-year MACRS schedule (including year 0) are:

1	Year	1	2	3	4	5
2	Depreciation Rate	20.00%	32.00%	19.20%	11.52%	11.52%
3	Depreciation Amount	100,000	160,000	96,000	57,600	57,600

Thus, the accumulated depreciation is $100,000 + 160,000 + 96,000 + 57,600 + 57,600 = 471,200$, such that the remaining book value is $500,000 − $471,200 = $28,800$. (Note we could have also calculated this by summing the rates for years remaining on the MACRS schedule: Year 6 is 5.76%, so $.0576 \times 500,000 = 28,800$).
The capital gain is then $50,000 − $28,800 = $21,200$ and the tax owed is
$$0.35 \times \$21,200 = \$7,420.$$
Your after-tax cash flow is then found as the sale price minus the tax owed:
$$\$50,000 − \$7,420 = \$42,580.$$

EVALUATE

Because you are only taxed on the capital gain portion of the sale price, figuring the after-tax cash flow is not as simple as subtracting the tax rate multiplied by the sale price. Instead, you have to determine the portion of the sale price that represents a gain and compute the tax from there. The same procedure holds for selling equipment at a loss relative to book value—the loss creates a deduction for taxable income elsewhere in the company.

Tax Loss Carryforwards and Carrybacks. A firm generally identifies its marginal tax rate by determining the tax bracket that it falls into based on its overall level of pretax income. Two features of the tax code, called **tax loss carryforwards** and **carrybacks**, allow corporations to take losses during a current year and offset them against gains in nearby years. Since 1997, companies can "carry back" losses for two years and "carry forward" losses for 20 years. This tax rule means that a firm can offset losses during one year against income for the last two years, or save the losses to be offset against income during the next 20 years. When a firm can carry back losses, it receives a refund for back taxes in the current year. Otherwise, the firm must carry forward the loss and use it to offset future taxable income. When a firm has tax loss carryforwards well in excess of its current pretax income, then additional income it earns today will simply increase the taxes it owes after it exhausts its carryforwards.

tax loss carryforwards and carrybacks Two features of the U.S. tax code that allow corporations to take losses during a current year and offset them against gains in nearby years. Since 1997, companies can "carry back" losses for two years and "carry forward" losses for 20 years.

Replacement Decisions

Often, the financial manager must decide whether to replace an existing piece of equipment. The new equipment may allow increased production, resulting in incremental revenue, or it may simply be more efficient, lowering costs. The typical incremental effects associated with such a decision are salvage value from the old machine, purchase of the new machine, cost savings and revenue increases, and depreciation effects.

EXAMPLE 9.8

Replacing an Existing Machine

MyFinanceLab

PROBLEM

You are trying to decide whether to replace a machine on your production line. The new machine will cost $1 million, but will be more efficient than the old machine, reducing costs by $500,000 per year. Your old machine is fully depreciated, but you could sell it for $50,000. You would depreciate the new machine over a five-year life using MACRS. The new machine will not change your working capital needs. Your tax rate is 35%, and your cost of capital is 9%. Should you replace the machine?

SOLUTION

PLAN

Incremental revenues: 0

Incremental costs: −500,000 (a reduction in costs will appear as a positive number in the costs line of our analysis)

Depreciation schedule (from the appendix):

1	Year	1	2	3	4	5	6
2	Depreciation Rate	20.00%	32.00%	19.20%	11.52%	11.52%	5.76%
3	Depreciation Amount	200,000	320,000	192,000	115,200	115,200	57,600

Capital gain on salvage = $50,000 − $0 = $50,000

Cash flow from salvage value: +50,000 − (50,000)(.35) = 32,500

EXECUTE

(values in thousands)

1	Year	0	1	2	3	4	5	6
2	Incremental Revenues							
3	Incremental Costs of Goods Sold		500	500	500	500	500	
4	**Incremental Gross Profit**		500	500	500	500	500	
5	Depreciation		−200	−320	−192	−115.2	−115.2	−57.6
6	EBIT		300	180	308	384.8	384.8	−57.6
7	Income Tax at 35%		−105	−63	−107.8	−134.68	−134.68	20.16
8	**Incremental Earnings**		195	117	200.2	250.12	250.12	−37.44
9	Add Back Depreciation		200	320	192	115.2	115.2	57.6
10	Purchase of Equipment	−1000						
11	Salvage Cash Flow	32.5						
12	**Incremental Free Cash Flows**	**−967.5**	**395**	**437**	**392.2**	**365.32**	**365.32**	**20.16**

$$NPV = -967.5 + \frac{395}{1.09} + \frac{437}{1.09^2} + \frac{392.2}{1.09^3} + \frac{365.32}{1.09^4} + \frac{365.32}{1.09^5} + \frac{20.16}{1.09^6} = 573.81$$

EVALUATE

Even though the decision has no impact on revenues, it still matters for cash flows because it reduces costs. Furthermore, both selling the old machine and buying the new machine involve cash flows with tax implications. The NPV analysis shows that replacing the machine will increase the value of the firm by almost $574,000.

CONCEPT CHECK

7. Should we include sunk costs in the cash flows of a project? Why or why not?

8. Explain why it is advantageous for a firm to use the most accelerated depreciation schedule possible for tax purposes.

9.5   Analyzing the Project

When evaluating a capital budgeting project, financial managers should make the decision that maximizes NPV. As we have discussed, to compute the NPV for a project you need to estimate the incremental free cash flows and choose a discount rate. Given these inputs, the NPV calculation is relatively straightforward. The most difficult part of capital budgeting is deciding how to estimate the cash flows and cost of capital. These estimates are often subject to significant uncertainty. In this section, we look at methods that assess the importance of this uncertainty and identify the drivers of value in the project.

sensitivity analysis An important capital budgeting tool that determines how the NPV varies as underlying assumptions change one at a time.

Sensitivity Analysis

An important capital budgeting tool for assessing the effect of uncertainty in forecasts is *sensitivity analysis*. **Sensitivity analysis** breaks the NPV calculation into its component assumptions and shows how the NPV varies as underlying assumptions change. In this way, sensitivity analysis allows us to explore the effects of errors in our NPV estimates for a project. By conducting a sensitivity analysis, we learn which assumptions are the most important; we can then invest further resources and effort to refine these assumptions. Such an analysis also reveals which aspects of a project are most critical when we are actually managing the project.

In fact, we have already performed a type of sensitivity analysis in Chapter 8 when we constructed an NPV profile. By graphing the NPV of a project as a function of the discount rate, we are assessing the sensitivity of our NPV calculation to uncertainty about the correct cost of capital to use as a discount rate. In practice, financial managers explore the sensitivity of their NPV calculation to many more factors than just the discount rate.

To illustrate, consider the assumptions underlying the calculation of HomeNet's NPV in Example 9.5. There is likely to be significant uncertainty surrounding each revenue and cost assumption. In addition to the base case assumptions about units sold, sale price, cost of goods sold, net working capital, and cost of capital, Cisco's managers would also identify best- and worst-case scenarios for each. For example, assume that they identified the best- and worst-case assumptions listed in Table 9.2. Note that these are best- and worst-case scenarios for each parameter rather than representing one worst-case scenario and one best-case scenario.

To determine the importance of this uncertainty, we recalculate the NPV of the HomeNet project under the best- and worst-case assumptions for each parameter. For example, if the number of units sold is only 35,000 per year, the NPV of the project falls to −$1.13 million. We repeat this calculation for each parameter. The result is shown in Figure 9.2, which reveals that the parameter assumptions with the largest effect on NPV are the number of units sold and the sale price per unit. As a result, these assumptions deserve the greatest scrutiny during the estimation process. In addition, as the most important drivers of the project's value, these factors deserve close attention when managing the project after it starts.

Break-Even Analysis

break-even The level of a parameter for which an investment has an NPV of zero.

A natural extension of the sensitivity analysis is to ask at what level of each parameter would the project have an NPV of zero. For each parameter, this level is its **break-even**. One example that we have already considered is the calculation of the internal rate of return (IRR). Recall from Chapter 8 that the difference between the IRR of a project and the cost of capital tells you how much error in the cost of capital it would take to change the investment decision. By either graphing the NPV profile or using the Excel IRR function, we would find that the incremental cash flows of HomeNet given in Example 9.5 imply an IRR of 26.6%. Thus, the true cost of capital can be as high as 26.6% and the project will still have a positive NPV.

break-even analysis A calculation of the value of each parameter for which the NPV of the project is zero.

We can determine the uncertainty of other parameters as well. In a **break-even analysis**, for each parameter we calculate the value at which the NPV of the project is zero. This would be tedious to do by hand, so in practice it is always done with a spreadsheet. As with the NPV profile for the discount rate, we can graph the NPV as a function of each of the critical assumptions. In each case, we keep all of the other parameters fixed at their initially assumed values and vary only the parameter in question. Figure 9.3 does this for HomeNet.

TABLE 9.2

Best- and Worst-Case Assumptions for Each Parameter in the HomeNet Project

Parameter	Initial Assumption	Worst Case	Best Case
Units Sold (thousands)	50	35	65
Sale Price ($/unit)	260	240	280
Cost of Goods ($/unit)	110	120	100
NWC ($ thousands)	1125	1525	725
Cost of Capital	12%	15%	10%

FIGURE 9.2

HomeNet's NPV Under Best- and Worst- Case Parameter Assumptions

Bars show the change in NPV going from the best-case assumption to the worst-case assumption for each parameter. For example, the NPV of the project ranges from −$1.13 million if only 35,000 units are sold to $6.85 million if 65,000 units are sold. Under the initial assumptions, HomeNet's NPV is $2.862 million.

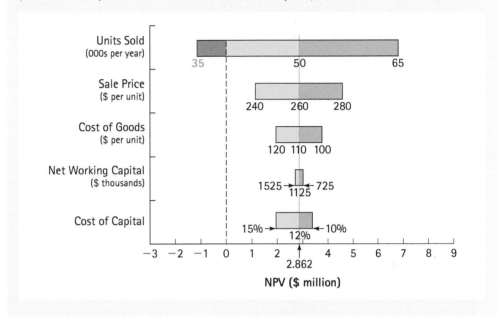

EBIT break-even The level of a particular parameter for which a project's EBIT is zero.

Accounting Break-Even. We have examined the break-even levels in terms of the project's NPV, which is the most useful perspective for decision making. Other accounting notions of break-even are sometimes considered, however. For example, we could compute the **EBIT break-even** for sales, which is the level of sales for which a project's EBIT is zero.

FIGURE 9.3

Break-Even Analysis Graphs

The graphs in Panels (a) and (b) relate two of the key parameters to the project's NPV to identify the parameters' break-even points. For example, based on the initial assumptions, the HomeNet project will break even with a sales level of 39,242 units per year. Similarly, holding sales and the other parameters constant at their initial assumed values, the project will break even at a cost of goods sold of just over $142 per unit.

Panel (a) Break-Even Point Based on Units Sold

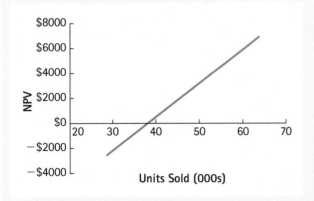

Panel (b) Break-Even Point Based on Costs of Goods Sold

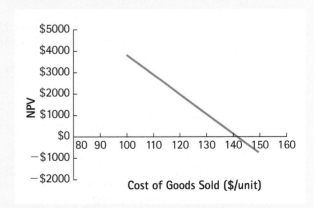

Recall from Eq. 9.1 that the project's EBIT is Revenues − Costs − Depreciation. Costs include cost of goods sold, and selling, general, and administrative expense (SG&A). Revenues equal Units Sold × Sale Price, and cost of goods sold equals Units Sold × Cost per Unit, so we have EBIT = (Units Sold × Sale Price) − (Units Sold × Cost per Unit) − SG&A − Depreciation. Setting this equal to zero and solving for units sold:

$$\text{Units Sold} \times (\text{Sale Price} - \text{Cost per Unit}) - \text{SG\&A} - \text{Depreciation} = 0$$

$$\text{Units Sold} = \frac{\text{SG\&A} + \text{Depreciation}}{\text{Sales Price} - \text{Cost per Unit}} = \frac{2{,}800{,}000 + 1{,}500{,}000}{260 - 110} = 28{,}667$$

INTERVIEW WITH DAVID HOLLAND

David Holland is currently Senior Vice President of Sports and Entertainment Solutions where he is responsible for accelerating development and adoption of Cisco solutions in that market. He was previously Senior Vice President and Treasurer of Cisco, and was responsible for managing all funding, risk, and capital market activities related to the firm's $50 billion balance sheet.

QUESTION: *What is the importance of considering free cash flow, as opposed to just the earnings implications of a financial decision?*

ANSWER: There is an adage saying, "Cash flow is a fact and earnings are an opinion." Earnings use an accounting framework and are governed by many rules, making it hard to know what earnings tell the investor. The economics of cash flow are clear: We can't dispute whether cash has come in or gone out. Cisco's investment decisions are based primarily on cash flow models because they take project risk into account and show the impact on value creation for owners of the business.

QUESTION: *What key financial metrics does Cisco use to make investment decisions?*

ANSWER: Cisco focuses primarily on net present value (NPV) for investment decisions. Robust NPV analysis goes beyond simply accepting projects with positive NPVs and rejecting those with negative NPVs. It identifies the key drivers that affect project success and demonstrates the interplay between factors that affect cash flow. For example, running a model using a lower margin approach shows us the impact on revenue growth and on operating cost structures. We can compare that to a higher margin (premium pricing) approach. The business unit manager learns how to control aspects of the business model to alleviate risk or accelerate the upside potential.

We prefer NPV to internal rate of return (IRR), which may return multiple answers or give false signals as to an investment's profitability, depending on the organization of cash flows. An attraction of IRR analysis is the ease of comparing percentage returns. However, this method hides the scope of a project. A project with a 25% return may generate $1 million in shareholder value, while another with a 13% IRR might produce $1 billion. NPV captures the size of the return in dollar terms and shows a project's impact on share price. NPV also creates an ownership framework for employees whose compensation package includes some form of stock ownership, directly tying the decision-making criteria to stock price.

QUESTION: *When developing a model to analyze a new investment, how do you deal with the uncertainty surrounding estimates, especially for new technologies?*

ANSWER: Cisco relies on strong financial modeling for the thousands of investment decisions we make every year. Our 2500 finance people worldwide work with the internal client—the business lead—to understand the assumptions in the model and to check the model's result against alternative assumptions. Evaluating the cash flows for technology projects, especially new technology, is difficult. When you buy an oil refinery, you can see the throughput and the cash flows. Identifying the relevant savings from a component technology for a larger router or switch product or a strategic move into a new area is more complex and intangible. Scenario and sensitivity analyses and game theory help us control risk by adjusting our strategy. We also look at the qualitative aspects, such as how the strategy fits into the customer sector and the directions customers are moving with their tech platforms.

QUESTION: *How does Cisco adjust for risk?*

ANSWER: To stay competitive in the technology space, we must be prepared to take some level of risk, even in down markets. We apply the same discount rate to all projects in a category, based on their market risk (i.e., sensitivity to market conditions). We do not adjust the discount rate to account for project-specific risks, because our required return has not changed and that would distort the true value of the company. To assess a project's unique risks, we model the upside or downside of cash flows with scenario and sensitivity analysis. We might analyze the sensitivity of a project's NPV to a 1% change in both revenue growth and operating costs. Then we run the model with other assumptions, developing base, optimistic, and bearish cases. We discuss these models with the business lead and rerun the models based on their input. This process improves our potential outcome and project profitability.

However, this EBIT break-even number is misleading. While HomeNet's EBIT break-even level of sales is only 28,667 units per year, given the large up-front investment required in HomeNet, its NPV is −$2.81 million at that sales level.

Scenario Analysis

scenario analysis
An important capital budgeting tool that determines how the NPV varies as multiple project parameters are changed simultaneously.

In the analysis thus far, we have considered the consequences of varying only one parameter at a time. In reality, certain factors may affect more than one parameter. **Scenario analysis** considers the effect on NPV of changing multiple project parameters simultaneously. For example, lowering HomeNet's price may increase the number of units sold. We can use scenario analysis to evaluate alternative pricing strategies for the HomeNet product in Table 9.3. In this case, the current strategy is optimal. Figure 9.4 shows the combinations of price and volume that lead to the same NPV of $2.862 million for HomeNet as the current strategy. Only strategies with price and volume combinations above the curve will lead to a higher NPV.

TABLE 9.3

Scenario Analysis of Alternative Pricing Strategies

Strategy	Sale Price ($/unit)	Expected Units Sold (thousands)	NPV ($ thousands)
Current Strategy	260	50	2862
Price Reduction	245	55	2729
Price Increase	275	45	2729

FIGURE 9.4

Price and Volume Combinations for HomeNet with Equivalent NPV

The graph shows alternative price per unit and annual volume combinations that lead to an NPV of $2.862 million. Pricing strategies with combinations above the curve will lead to a higher NPV and are superior. For example, if Cisco managers think they will be able to sell 48,000 units at a price of $275, this strategy would yield a higher NPV ($3,607 million).

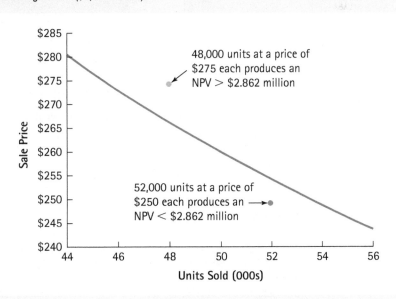

Here, we describe several useful Excel tools that assist with project analysis.

Goal Seek for Break-Even Analysis

Excel's goal seek function determines the break-even point for key assumptions in our model. For example, to determine the break-even level of units for annual sales, use the Goal Seek window (see the Data > What-If Analysis menu, or keyboard shortcut Alt-A-W-G). The set cell is the cell in which we calculated NPV (in this case, cell D31). To set its value to 0 (break-even), we change the average sale price (cell E5). Excel will then use trial and error to find the sale price at which the project's NPV is zero—in this case $227.73.

	A	B	C	D	E	F	G	H	I
1	**HomeNet Capital Budget**								
2	**Key Assumptions**			**Year 0**	**Year 1**	**Year 2**	**Year 3**	**Year 4**	**Year 5**
5		HomeNet Ave. Price/Unit			$ 260.00	$ 260.00	$ 260.00	$ 260.00	
30									
31		NPV		2,862					

Goal Seek

Set cell: D31
To value: 0
By changing cell: E5

OK   Cancel

Data Tables for Sensitivity Analysis

Data tables, which we introduced in the online appendix to Chapter 7 to construct the NPV profile, allow us to compute the sensitivity of NPV to any other input variable in our financial model. Excel can also compute a two-dimensional data table showing the sensitivity of NPV to two inputs simultaneously. For example, the data table below shows NPVs for different combinations of testing equipment cost and HomeNet's manufacturing costs.

	C	D	E	F	G	H
39	NPV			**HomeNet Cost/Unit**		
40		2,862	$110	$105	$100	$95
41		-7500	2,862	3,305	3,749	4,192
42		-7750	2,684	3,128	3,571	4,014
43		-8000	2,506	2,950	3,393	3,836
44	Equipment Cost	-8250	2,328	2,772	3,215	3,659
45		-8500	2,150	2,594	3,037	3,481
46		-8750	1,973	2,416	2,859	3,303
47		-9000	1,795	2,238	2,681	3,125
48		-9250	1,617	2,060	2,504	2,947
49		-9500	1,439	1,882	2,326	2,769
50		-9750	1,261	1,704	2,148	2,591
51		-10000	1,083	1,526	1,970	2,413

Data Table

Row input cell: E6
Column input cell: D10

OK   Cancel

To construct this data table, we put the values of each input along the sides of the table (shown in blue), and a formula for the value we want to compute in the upper-left corner (cell D36, which in this case is just a link to the cell in which we computed the NPV). We select the entire table (D36:H47), bring up the Data Table window (see the Data > What-If Analysis menu or keyboard shortcut Alt-D-T), and input the locations in our project dashboard (see page 277) of the cost assumption (row input cell E6) and equipment cost (column input cell D10). The data table shows, for example, that NPV increases if we lower our manufacturing cost to $100 per unit by spending an additional $1 million on equipment to test the design.

Scenarios in the Project Dashboard

The project dashboard on page 277 shows only our base-case assumptions. We can build multiple scenarios into our project dashboard by adding additional rows with alternative assumptions, and then using Excel's index function to select the scenario we would like to use in our analysis. For example, rows 5–7 on page 289 show alternative annual sales assumptions for HomeNet. We then select the scenario to analyze by entering the appropriate number (in this case 1, 2, or 3) in the highlighted cell (C4), and use the index function to pull the appropriate data into row 4.

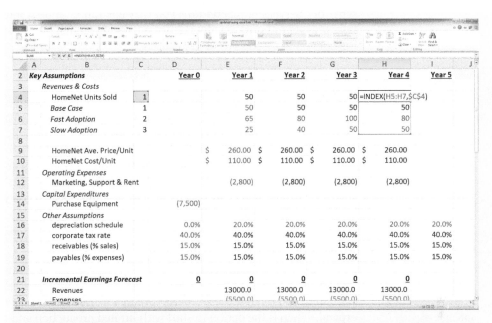

		Year 0	Year 1	Year 2	Year 3	Year 4	Year 5
2	**Key Assumptions**						
3	*Revenues & Costs*						
4	HomeNet Units Sold	1		50	50	50	=INDEX(H5:H7,C4)	
5	*Base Case*	1		50	50	50	50
6	*Fast Adoption*	2		65	80	100	80
7	*Slow Adoption*	3		25	40	50	50
8							
9	HomeNet Ave. Price/Unit		$	260.00 $	260.00 $	260.00 $	260.00
10	HomeNet Cost/Unit		$	110.00 $	110.00 $	110.00 $	110.00
11	*Operating Expenses*						
12	Marketing, Support & Rent			(2,800)	(2,800)	(2,800)	(2,800)
13	*Capital Expenditures*						
14	Purchase Equipment		(7,500)				
15	*Other Assumptions*						
16	depreciation schedule		0.0%	20.0%	20.0%	20.0%	20.0%	20.0%
17	corporate tax rate		40.0%	40.0%	40.0%	40.0%	40.0%	40.0%
18	receivables (% sales)		15.0%	15.0%	15.0%	15.0%	15.0%	15.0%
19	payables (% expenses)		15.0%	15.0%	15.0%	15.0%	15.0%	15.0%
20							
21	**Incremental Earnings Forecast**		0	0	0	0	0
22	Revenues			13000.0	13000.0	13000.0	13000.0
23	Expenses			(5500.0)	(5500.0)	(5500.0)	(5500.0)

We can then analyze the consequences for each scenario using the one-dimensional data table in C54:D57 below, with column input cell C4.

	A	B	C	D
53				NPV
54		**HomeNet Units Sold**		2,862
55		*Base Case*	1	2,862
56		*Fast Adoption*	2	11,029
57		*Slow Adoption*	3	319

CONCEPT CHECK

9. What is sensitivity analysis?

10. How does scenario analysis differ from sensitivity analysis?

9.6 Real Options in Capital Budgeting

Our approach to capital budgeting thus far has focused on the initial investment decision without explicitly considering future decisions that may need to be made over the life of a project. Rather, we assumed that our forecast of a project's expected future cash flows already incorporated the effect of future decisions that would be made. In truth, most projects contain *real options*. A **real option** is the right, but not the obligation, to make a particular business decision. Because you are not obligated to take the action, you will do so only if it increases the NPV of the project. In particular, because real options allow a decision maker to choose the most attractive alternative after new information has been learned, the presence of real options adds value to an investment opportunity. The tools to estimate the actual value created by real options are beyond the scope of this chapter and are contained later in the book. However, we introduce the concept here to give you a

real option The right to make a particular business decision, such as a capital investment.

sense of the types of real options you may encounter and establish the intuition that flexibility (more options) is valuable. Let's look at some of the most common real options in the context of Cisco's HomeNet project.

Option to Delay

option to delay commitment The option to time a particular investment

The **option to delay commitment** (the option to time an investment) is almost always present. Cisco could wait to commit to the HomeNet project. Waiting could be valuable if Cisco expects prices of the components to decrease substantially, soon-to-be-released new technology that will make the existing components obsolete, or increased sales of Web-ready appliances (heightening the demand for HomeNet). In addition, Cisco may simply want more time to gather information about the potential market for HomeNet. As with any other capital budgeting decision, Cisco would only choose to delay if doing so would increase the NPV of the project.

Option to Expand

option to expand The option to start with limited production and expand only if the product is successful.

In the section on sensitivity analysis, we looked at changes in our assumptions about units sold. All of the analysis was performed, however, under the assumption that Cisco would fully commit to and roll out the HomeNet product worldwide. We did not consider the **option to expand**, which is the option to start with limited production and expand only if the product is successful. Cisco could, instead, test market the product in limited release before committing to it fully. Doing so would create an option to expand worldwide only if HomeNet were successful in limited release. It is possible that, by reducing its up-front commitment and choosing to expand only if the product is successful, Cisco will increase the NPV of the HomeNet product. However, in this particular case, there are large costs of development that would be paid whether Cisco sells one or one million units, so limiting the initial market does not reduce the financial commitment substantially. Thus, in the case of HomeNet, it is unlikely that Cisco would choose a limited release with an option to expand.

Option to Abandon

abandonment option The option for an investor to cease investing in a project. Abandonment options can add value to a project because a firm can drop a project if it turns out to be unsuccessful.

An **abandonment option** is the option to walk away. Abandonment options can add value to a project because a firm can drop a project if it turns out to be unsuccessful. Imagine that a competitor developed new technology that allowed it to introduce a successful competing product priced at $170. At that price, HomeNet would produce negative cash flows every year. But would Cisco continue to sell HomeNet if it had to do so at a loss? Probably not. Cisco has an option to abandon the project. It could stop producing HomeNet and sell the equipment. Depending on how much Cisco believes the equipment would sell for if it abandoned the project, the abandonment option could make HomeNet attractive even if there was a substantial risk of a competing product.

All these options point to the same conclusion: *If you can build greater flexibility into your project, you will increase its NPV.* In Chapter 21, we will discuss how to value options so that you can estimate just how much more valuable the project is with greater flexibility. Many industries regularly make use of real options. For example, most movie producers build in an option for a sequel if the first movie does well. Pharmaceutical developers like Merck develop new drugs in stages, allowing them to abandon development if tests do not go well.

CONCEPT CHECK

11. What are real options?

12. Why do real options increase the NPV of a project?

MyFinanceLab

Here is what you should know after reading this chapter. MyFinanceLab will help you identify what you know, and where to go when you need to practice.

KEY POINTS AND EQUATIONS	KEY TERMS	ONLINE PRACTICE
9.1 The Capital Budgeting Process • Capital budgeting is the process of analyzing investment opportunities and deciding which ones to accept. A capital budget is a list of all projects that a company plans to undertake during the next period. • We use the NPV rule to evaluate capital budgeting decisions, making decisions that maximize NPV. When deciding to accept or reject a project, we accept projects with a positive NPV.	capital budget, p. 266 capital budgeting, p. 266 incremental earnings, p. 267	MyFinanceLab Study Plan 9.1
9.2 Forecasting Incremental Earnings • The incremental earnings of a project comprise the amount by which the project is expected to change the firm's earnings. • Incremental earnings should include all incremental revenues and costs associated with the project. $$\text{Incremental Earnings} = (\text{Incremental Revenues} - \text{Incremental Cost} - \text{Depreciation}) \times (1 - \text{Tax Rate}) \quad (9.3)$$ • Interest and other financing-related expenses are excluded to determine the project's unlevered net income.	marginal corporate tax rate, p. 269 pro forma, p. 270 straight-line depreciation, p. 267 unlevered net income, p. 271	MyFinanceLab Study Plan 9.2
9.3 Determining Incremental Free Cash Flow • We compute free cash flow from incremental earnings by eliminating all non-cash expenses and including all capital investment. • Depreciation is not a cash expense, so it is added back. • Actual capital expenditures are deducted. • Increases in net working capital are deducted and decreases are added. Net working capital is defined as: $$\text{Cash} + \text{Inventory} + \text{Receivables} - \text{Payables} \quad (9.4)$$ • The basic calculation for free cash flow is: $$\text{Free Cash Flow} = (\text{Revenues} - \text{Costs} - \text{Depreciation}) \times (1 - \text{Tax Rate}) + \text{Depreciation} - \text{CapEx} - \text{Change in } NWC \quad (9.6)$$	depreciation tax shield, p. 276 free cash flow, p. 272 trade credit, p. 273	MyFinanceLab Study Plan 9.3

9.4 Other Effects on Incremental Free Cash Flows
- An opportunity cost is the cost of using an existing asset.
- Project externalities are cash flows that occur when a project affects other areas of the company's business.
- A sunk cost is an unrecoverable cost that has already been incurred.
- Depreciation expenses affect free cash flow only through the depreciation tax shield. The firm should use the most accelerated depreciation schedule possible.
- The discount rate for a project is its cost of capital: the expected return of securities with comparable risk and horizon.
- When you sell an asset, the portion of the proceeds above its book value is taxed:

$$\text{After-Tax Cash Flow from Asset Sale} = \text{Sale Price} - (\text{Tax Rate} \times \text{Capital Gain}) \quad (9.11)$$

cannibalization, p. 279
MACRS depreciation, p. 280
opportunity cost, p. 278
overhead expenses, p. 278
project externalities, p. 278
sunk cost, p. 279
tax loss carryforwards and carrybacks, p. 282

MyFinance Lab Study Plan 9.4

HomeNet Example Spreadsheet

9.5 Analyzing the Project
- Sensitivity analysis breaks the NPV calculation into its component assumptions, showing how the NPV varies as the values of the underlying assumptions change.
- Break-even analysis computes the level of a parameter that makes the project's NPV equal zero.
- Scenario analysis considers the effect of changing multiple parameters simultaneously.

break-even, p. 284
break-even analysis, p. 284
EBIT break-even, p. 285
scenario analysis, p. 287
sensitivity analysis, p. 283

MyFinanceLab Study Plan 9.5

Interactive Sensitivity Analysis, Using Excel: Performing Sensitivity Analysis

9.6 Real Options in Capital Budgeting
- Real options are options to make a business decision, often after gathering more information. The presence of real options in a project increases the project's NPV.

abandonment option, p. 290
option to delay commitment, p. 290
option to expand, p. 290
real option, p. 289

MyFinanceLab Study Plan 9.6

CRITICAL THINKING

1. What are pro forma incremental earnings?

2. What is the difference between pro forma incremental earnings and pro forma free cash flow?

3. Why do we convert from incremental earnings to free cash flow when performing capital budgeting?

4. What is the role of net working capital in projects?

5. How does net working capital affect the cash flows of a project?

6. Why is it important to adjust project sales and costs for externalities?

7. Does accelerated depreciation generally increase or decrease NPV relative to straight-line depreciation?

8. How is sensitivity analysis performed and what is its purpose?

PROBLEMS

All problems are available in MyFinanceLab. *The* 🔲 *icon indicates problems that are easier to solve using Excel and have data in an Excel format available in* MyFinanceLab. *An asterisk * indicates problems with a higher level of difficulty.*

Forecasting Incremental Earnings

1. Daily Enterprises is purchasing a $10 million machine. It will cost $50,000 to transport and install the machine. The machine has a depreciable life of five years and will have no salvage value. If Daily uses straight-line depreciation, what are the depreciation expenses associated with this machine?

2. The machine in Problem 1 will generate incremental revenues of $4 million per year along with incremental costs of $1.2 million per year. If Daily's marginal tax rate is 35%, what are the incremental earnings associated with the new machine?

3. You are upgrading to better production equipment for your firm's only product. The new equipment will allow you to make more of your product in the same amount of time. Thus, you forecast that total sales will increase next year by 20% over the current amount of 100,000 units. If your sales price is $20 per unit, what are the incremental revenues next year from the upgrade?

4. Pisa Pizza, a seller of frozen pizza, is considering introducing a healthier version of its pizza that will be low in cholesterol and contain no trans fats. The firm expects that sales of the new pizza will be $20 million per year. While many of these sales will be to new customers, Pisa Pizza estimates that 40% will come from customers who switch to the new, healthier pizza instead of buying the original version.
   a. Assume customers will spend the same amount on either version. What level of incremental sales is associated with introducing the new pizza?
   b. Suppose that 50% of the customers who would switch from Pisa Pizza's original pizza to its healthier pizza will switch to another brand if Pisa Pizza does not introduce a healthier pizza. What level of incremental sales is associated with introducing the new pizza in this case?

5. Kokomochi is considering the launch of an advertising campaign for its latest dessert product, the Mini Mochi Munch. Kokomochi plans to spend $5 million on TV, radio, and print advertising this year for the campaign. The ads are expected to boost sales of the Mini Mochi Munch by $9 million this year and by $7 million next year. In addition, the company expects that new consumers who try the Mini Mochi Munch will be more likely to try Kokomochi's other products. As a result, sales of other products are expected to rise by $2 million each year.

   Kokomochi's gross profit margin for the Mini Mochi Munch is 35%, and its gross profit margin averages 25% for all other products. The company's marginal corporate tax rate is 35% both this year and next year. What are the incremental earnings associated with the advertising campaign?

6. Hyperion, Inc., currently sells its latest high-speed color printer, the Hyper 500, for $350. It plans to lower the price to $300 next year. Its cost of goods sold for the Hyper 500 is $200 per unit, and this year's sales are expected to be 20,000 units.
   a. Suppose that if Hyperion drops the price to $300 immediately, it can increase this year's sales by 25% to 25,000 units. What would be the incremental impact on this year's EBIT of such a price drop?
   b. Suppose that for each printer sold, Hyperion expects additional sales of $75 per year on ink cartridges for the next three years, and Hyperion has a gross profit margin of 70% on ink cartridges. What is the incremental impact on EBIT for the next three years of a price drop this year?

Determining Incremental Free Cash Flow

7. You have a depreciation expense of $500,000 and a tax rate of 35%. What is your depreciation tax shield?

8. You have forecast pro forma earnings of $1,000,000. This includes the effect of $200,000 in depreciation. You also forecast a decrease in working capital of $100,000 that year. What is your forecast of free cash flows for that year?

9. Your pro forma income statement shows sales of $1,000,000, cost of goods sold as $500,000, depreciation expense of $100,000, and taxes of $160,000 due to a tax rate of 40%. What are your pro forma earnings? What is your pro forma free cash flow?

10. You are evaluating a new product. In year 3 of your analysis, you are projecting pro forma sales of $5 million and cost of goods sold of $3 million. You will be depreciating a $1 million machine for 5 years using straight-line depreciation. Your tax rate is 35%. Finally, you expect working capital to increase from $200,000 in year 2 to $300,000 in year 3. What are your pro forma earnings for year 3? What are your pro forma free cash flows for year 3?

11. You are forecasting incremental free cash flows for Daily Enterprises. Based on the information in Problems 1 and 2, what are the incremental free cash flows associated with the new machine?

12. Castle View Games would like to invest in a division to develop software for a soon-to-be-released video game console. To evaluate this decision, the firm first attempts to project the working capital needs for this operation. Its chief financial officer has developed the following estimates (in millions of dollars) (see MyFinanceLab *for the data in Excel format*):

	Year	1	2	3	4	5
2	Cash	6	12	15	15	15
3	Accounts Receivable	21	22	24	24	24
4	Inventory	5	7	10	12	13
5	Accounts Payable	18	22	24	25	30

Assuming that Castle View currently does not have any working capital invested in this division, calculate the cash flows associated with changes in working capital for the first five years of this investment.

13. In the HomeNet example from the chapter, its receivables are 15% of sales and its payables are 15% of COGS. Forecast the required investment in net working capital for HomeNet assuming that sales and cost of goods sold (COGS) will be as follows (see MyFinanceLab *for the data in Excel format*):

	Year	0	1	2	3	4
2	Sales		23,500	26,438	23,794	8,566
3	COGS		9,500	10,688	9,619	3,483

14. Elmdale Enterprises is deciding whether to expand its production facilities. Although long-term cash flows are difficult to estimate, management has projected the following cash flows for the first two years (in millions of dollars) (see MyFinanceLab *for the data in Excel format*):

a. What are the incremental earnings for this project for years 1 and 2?

b. What are the free cash flows for this project for years 1 and 2?

Year	1	2
Revenues	125	160
Operating Expenses (other than depreciation)	40	60
Depreciation	25	36
Increase in Net Working Capital	2	8
Capital Expenditures	30	40
Marginal Corporate Tax Rate	35%	35%

15. Cellular Access, Inc., a cellular telephone service provider, reported net income of $250 million for the most recent fiscal year. The firm had depreciation expenses of $100 million, capital expenditures of $200 million, and no interest expenses. Net working capital increased by $10 million. Calculate the free cash flow for Cellular Access for the most recent fiscal year.

16. Recall the HomeNet example from the chapter. Suppose HomeNet's lab will be housed in warehouse space that the company could have otherwise rented out for $200,000 per year during years 1 through 4. How does this opportunity cost affect HomeNet's incremental earnings?

*17. One year ago, your company purchased a machine used in manufacturing for $110,000. You have learned that a new machine is available that offers many advantages and you can purchase it for $150,000 today. It will be depreciated on a straight-line basis over 10 years and has no salvage value. You expect that the new machine will produce a gross margin (revenues minus operating expenses other than depreciation) of $40,000 per year for the next 10 years. The current machine is expected to produce a gross margin of $20,000 per year. The current machine is being depreciated on a straight-line basis over a useful life of 11 years, and has no salvage value, so depreciation expense for the current machine is $10,000 per year. The market value today of the current machine is $50,000. Your company's tax rate is 45%, and the opportunity cost of capital for this type of equipment is 10%. Should your company replace its year-old machine?

*18. Beryl's Iced Tea currently rents a bottling machine for $50,000 per year, including all maintenance expenses. It is considering purchasing a machine instead and is comparing two options:
a. Purchase the machine it is currently renting for $150,000. This machine will require $20,000 per year in ongoing maintenance expenses.
b. Purchase a new, more advanced machine for $250,000. This machine will require $15,000 per year in ongoing maintenance expenses and will lower bottling costs by $10,000 per year. Also, $35,000 will be spent upfront to train the new operators of the machine.

Suppose the appropriate discount rate is 8% per year and the machine is purchased today. Maintenance and bottling costs are paid at the end of each year, as is the rental cost of the machine. Assume also that the machines will be depreciated via the straight-line method over seven years and that they have a 10-year life with a negligible salvage value. The marginal corporate tax rate is 35%. Should Beryl's Iced Tea continue to rent, purchase its current machine, or purchase the advanced machine?

Other Effects on Incremental Free Cash Flows

19. You have just completed a $20,000 feasibility study for a new coffee shop in some retail space you own. You bought the space two years ago for $100,000, and if you sold it today, you would net $115,000 after taxes. Outfitting the space for a coffee shop would require

a capital expenditure of $30,000 plus an initial investment of $5,000 in inventory. What is the correct initial cash flow for your analysis of the coffee shop opportunity?

20. After spending a year and $50,000, you finally have the design of your new product ready. In order to start production, you will need $30,000 in raw materials and you will also need to use some existing equipment that you've fully depreciated, but which has a market value of $100,000. Your colleague notes that the new product could represent 10% of the company's overall sales and that 10% of overhead is $60,000. Your tax rate is 40%. As you start your analysis of the product, what should be your initial incremental free cash flow?

21. You purchased a machine for $1 million three years ago and have been applying straight-line depreciation to zero for a seven-year life. Your tax rate is 35%. If you sell the machine today (after three years of depreciation) for $700,000, what is your incremental cash flow from selling the machine?

22. The Jones Company has just completed the third year of a five-year MACRS recovery period for a piece of equipment it originally purchased for $300,000.
    a. What is the book value of the equipment?
    b. If Jones sells the equipment today for $180,000 and its tax rate is 35%, what is the after-tax cash flow from selling it?

23. Just before it is about to sell the equipment from Problem 22, Jones receives a new order. It can take the new order if it keeps the old equipment. Is there a cost to taking the order and if so, what is it? Explain.

24. Home Builder Supply, a retailer in the home improvement industry, currently operates seven retail outlets in Georgia and South Carolina. Management is contemplating building an eighth retail store across town from its most successful retail outlet. The company already owns the land for this store, which currently has an abandoned warehouse located on it. Last month, the marketing department spent $10,000 on market research to determine the extent of customer demand for the new store. Now Home Builder Supply must decide whether to build and open the new store.

    Which of the following should be included as part of the incremental earnings for the proposed new retail store?
    a. The original purchase price of the land where the store will be located.
    b. The cost of demolishing the abandoned warehouse and clearing the lot.
    c. The loss of sales in the existing retail outlet, if customers who previously drove across town to shop at the existing outlet become customers of the new store instead.
    d. The $10,000 in market research spent to evaluate customer demand.
    e. Construction costs for the new store.
    f. The value of the land if sold.
    g. Interest expense on the debt borrowed to pay the construction costs.

25. Nirvana Chip Designs has finished designing its next generation of chips, the XJ5000 series and is getting ready to start production. As the analyst on the project, you are required to prepare pro forma free cash flows. Which of the following are relevant to your analysis?
    a. Design costs for the chips.
    b. Potential lost sales of the XJ4000 chips.
    c. Proportional cost of the corporate jet lease.
    d. Start-up investment in raw materials.
    e. Upgrades to the chip fabrication facility required if the chip is produced.
    f. Market research done to guide the development of the new chip.
    g. Market value of land and buildings where new chip will be produced.

26. If Daily Enterprises uses MACRS instead of straight-line depreciation, which incremental free cash flows from Problem 11 would increase and which would decrease?

27. Markov Manufacturing recently spent $15 million to purchase some equipment used in the manufacture of disk drives. The firm expects that this equipment will have a useful life of five years, and its marginal corporate tax rate is 35%. The company plans to use straight-line depreciation.
    a. What is the annual depreciation expense associated with this equipment?
    b. What is the annual depreciation tax shield?
    c. Rather than straight-line depreciation, suppose Markov will use the MACRS depreciation method for the five-year life of the property. Calculate the depreciation tax shield each year for this equipment under this accelerated depreciation schedule.
    d. If Markov has a choice between straight-line and MACRS depreciation schedules, and its marginal corporate tax rate is expected to remain constant, which schedule should it choose? Why?
    e. How might your answer to part (d) change if Markov anticipates that its marginal corporate tax rate will increase substantially over the next five years?

28. Your company has been doing well, reaching $1 million in earnings, and is considering launching a new product. Designing the new product has already cost $500,000. The company estimates that it will sell 800,000 units per year for $3 per unit and variable non-labor costs will be $1 per unit. Production will end after year 3. New equipment costing $1 million will be required. The equipment will be depreciated to zero using the 7-year MACRS schedule. You plan to sell the equipment for book value at the end of year 3. Your current level of working capital is $300,000. The new product will require the working capital to increase to a level of $380,000 immediately, then to $400,000 in year 1, in year 2 the level will be $350,000, and finally in year 3 the level will return to $300,000. Your tax rate is 35%. The discount rate for this project is 10%. Do the capital budgeting analysis for this project and calculate its NPV.

29. You work for Apple. After toiling away on $10 million worth of prototypes, you have finally produced your answer to Google Glasses: iGlasses (the name alone is genius). iGlasses will instantly transport the wearer into the world as Apple wants you to experience it: iTunes with the wink of an eye and apps that can be activated just by looking at them. You think that these will sell for 5 years until the next big thing comes along (or until users are unable to interact with actual human beings). Revenues are projected to be $450 million per year along with expenses of $350 million. You will need to spend $60 million immediately on additional equipment that will be depreciated using the 5-year MACRS schedule. Additionally, you will use some fully depreciated existing equipment that has a market value of $10 million. As iGlasses are an outcome of the R&D center, Apple plans to charge $5 million of the annual costs of the center to the iGlasses product for 5 years. Finally, Apple's working capital levels will increase from their current level of $120 million to $140 million immediately. They will remain at the elevated level until year 5, when they will return to $120 million. Apple's discount rate for this project is 15% and its tax rate is 35%. Calculate the free cash flows and determine the NPV of this project.

30. After spending $10,000 on client development, you have just been offered a big production contract by a new client. The contract will add $200,000 to your revenues for each of the next 5 years and it will cost you $100,000 per year to make the additional product. You will have to use some existing equipment and buy new equipment as well. The existing equipment is fully depreciated, but could be sold for $50,000 now. If you use it in the project, it will be worthless at the end of the project. You will buy new equipment valued at $30,000 and use the 5-year MACRS schedule to depreciate it.

It will be worthless at the end of the project. Your current production manager earns $80,000 per year. Since she is busy with ongoing projects, you are planning to hire an assistant at $40,000 per year to help with the expansion. You will have to increase your inventory immediately from $20,000 to $30,000. It will return to $20,000 at the end of the project. Your company's tax rate is 35% and your discount rate is 15%. What is the NPV of the contract?

31. You are a manager at Percolated Fiber, which is considering expanding its operations in synthetic fiber manufacturing. Your boss comes into your office, drops a consultant's report on your desk, and complains, "We owe these consultants $1 million for this report, and I am not sure their analysis makes sense. Before we spend the $25 million on new equipment needed for this project, look it over and give me your opinion." You open the report and find the following estimates (in thousands of dollars) (*see* MyFinanceLab *for the data in Excel format*):

	Year	1	2	...	9	10
1	Year	1	2	...	9	10
2	Sales Revenue	30,000	30,000		30,000	30,000
3	Costs of Goods Sold	18,000	18,000		18,000	18,000
4	**Gross Profit**	12,000	12,000		12,000	12,000
5	Selling, General, and Administrative Expenses	2,000	2,000		2,000	2,000
6	Depreciation	2,500	2,500		2,500	2,500
7	**EBIT**	7,500	7,500		7,500	7,500
8	Income Tax	2,625	2,625		2,625	2,625
9	**Net Income**	4,875	4,875		4,875	4,875

All of the estimates in the report seem correct. You note that the consultants used straight-line depreciation for the new equipment that will be purchased today (year 0), which is what the accounting department recommended. They also calculated the depreciation assuming no salvage value for the equipment, which is the company's assumption in this case. The report concludes that because the project will increase earnings by $4.875 million per year for 10 years, the project is worth $48.75 million. You think back to your glory days in finance class and realize there is more work to be done!

First, you note that the consultants have not included the fact that the project will require $10 million in working capital up front (year 0), which will be fully recovered in year 10. Next, you see they have attributed $2 million of selling, general, and administrative expenses to the project, but you know that $1 million of this amount is overhead that will be incurred even if the project is not accepted. Finally, you know that accounting earnings are not the right thing to focus on!

a. Given the available information, what are the free cash flows in years 0 through 10 that should be used to evaluate the proposed project?

b. If the cost of capital for this project is 14%, what is your estimate of the value of the new project?

Analyzing the Project

32. Bauer Industries is an automobile manufacturer. Management is currently evaluating a proposal to build a plant that will manufacture lightweight trucks. Bauer plans to use a cost of capital of 12% to evaluate this project. Based on extensive research, it has prepared the incremental free cash flow projections shown on page 299 (in millions of dollars) (*see* MyFinanceLab *for the data in Excel format*).

a. For this base-case scenario, what is the NPV of the plant to manufacture lightweight trucks?

	Year	0	1–9	10
1	Year	0	1–9	10
2	Revenues		100.0	100.0
3	Manufacturing Expenses (other than depreciation)		−35.0	−35.0
4	Marketing Expenses		−10.0	−10.0
5	Depreciation		−15.0	−15.0
6	**EBIT**		40.0	40.0
7	Taxes at 35%		−14.0	−14.0
8	**Unlevered Net Income**		26.0	26.0
9	Depreciation		+15.0	+15.0
10	Additions to Net Working Capital		−5.0	−5.0
11	Capital Expenditures	−150.0		
12	Continuation Value			+12.0
13	**Free Cash Flow**	−150.0	36.0	48.0

b. Based on input from the marketing department, Bauer is uncertain about its revenue forecast. In particular, management would like to examine the sensitivity of the NPV to the revenue assumptions. What is the NPV of this project if revenues are 10% higher than forecast? What is the NPV if revenues are 10% lower than forecast?

c. Rather than assuming that cash flows for this project are constant, management would like to explore the sensitivity of its analysis to possible growth in revenues and operating expenses. Specifically, management would like to assume that revenues, manufacturing expenses, and marketing expenses are as given in the table for year 1 and grow by 2% per year every year starting in year 2. Management also plans to assume that the initial capital expenditures (and therefore depreciation), additions to working capital, and continuation value remain as initially specified in the table. What is the NPV of this project under these alternative assumptions? How does the NPV change if the revenues and operating expenses grow by 5% per year rather than by 2%?

d. To examine the sensitivity of this project to the discount rate, management would like to compute the NPV for different discount rates. Create a graph, with the discount rate on the *x*-axis and the NPV on the *y*-axis, for discount rates ranging from 5% to 30%. For what ranges of discount rates does the project have a positive NPV?

 *33. Billingham Packaging is considering expanding its production capacity by purchasing a new machine, the XC-750. The cost of the XC-750 is $2.75 million. Unfortunately, installing this machine will take several months and will partially disrupt production. The firm has just completed a $50,000 feasibility study to analyze the decision to buy the XC-750, resulting in the following estimates:

- *Marketing*: Once the XC-750 is operational next year, the extra capacity is expected to generate $10 million per year in additional sales, which will continue for the 10-year life of the machine.
- *Operations*: The disruption caused by the installation will decrease sales by $5 million this year. As with Billingham's existing products, the cost of goods for the products produced by the XC-750 is expected to be 70% of their sale price. The increased production will also require increased inventory on hand of $1 million during the life of the project, including year 0.
- *Human Resources*: The expansion will require additional sales and administrative personnel at a cost of $2 million per year.
- *Accounting*: The XC-750 will be depreciated via the straight-line method over the 10-year life of the machine. The firm expects receivables from the new sales to be 15% of revenues and payables to be 10% of the cost of goods sold. Billingham's marginal corporate tax rate is 35%.
  a. Determine the incremental earnings from the purchase of the XC-750.

    b. Determine the free cash flow from the purchase of the XC-750.

    c. If the appropriate cost of capital for the expansion is 10%, compute the NPV of the purchase.

    d. While the expected new sales will be $10 million per year from the expansion, estimates range from $8 million to $12 million. What is the NPV in the worst case? In the best case?

    e. What is the break-even level of new sales from the expansion? What is the break-even level for the cost of goods sold?

    f. Billingham could instead purchase the XC-900, which offers even greater capacity. The cost of the XC-900 is $4 million. The extra capacity would not be useful in the first two years of operation, but would allow for additional sales in years 3 through 10. What level of additional sales (above the $10 million expected for the XC-750) per year in those years would justify purchasing the larger machine?

Real Options in Captial Budgeting

34. Why must real options have positive value?

35. What kind of real option does the XC-900 machine provide to Billingham in Problem 33?

36. If Billingham knows that it can sell the XC-750 to another firm for $2 million in two years, what kind of real option would that provide?

DATA CASE

You have just been hired by Intel in its finance division. Your first assignment is to determine the net cash flows and NPV of a proposed new generation of mobile chips.

    Capital expenditures to produce the new chips will initially require an investment of $1.2 billion. The R&D that will be required to finish the chips is $500 million this year. Any ongoing R&D for upgrades will be covered in the margin calculation in 2a below. The product family is expected to have a life of five years. First-year revenues for the new chip are expected to be $2,000,000,000 ($2,000 million). The chip family's revenues are expected to grow by 20% for the second year, and then decrease by 10% for the third, decrease by 20% for the 4th and finally decrease by 50% for the 5th (final) year of sales. Your job is to determine the rest of the cash flows associated with this project. Your boss has indicated that the operating costs and net working capital requirements are similar to the rest of the company's products. Since your boss hasn't been much help, here are some tips to guide your analysis:

1. Obtain Intel's financial statements. Download the annual income statements and balance sheets for the last four fiscal years from Google Finance (finance.google .com). Enter Intel's ticker symbol (INTC) and then go to "Financials." Click "Annual," to ensure you're getting annual, instead of quarterly, data. Next, copy and paste the income statements and balance sheets into Excel.

2. You are now ready to determine the free cash flow. Compute the free cash flow for each year using Eq. 9.6 from this chapter:

$$\overbrace{\text{Free Cash Flow} = (\text{Revenues} - \text{Costs} - \text{Depreciation}) \times (1 - \text{Tax Rate})}^{\text{Unlevered Net Income}}$$
$$+ \text{ Depreciation} - \text{CapEx} - \text{Change in } NWC$$

Set up the timeline and computation of the free cash flow in separate, contiguous columns for each year of the project life. Be sure to make outflows negative and inflows positive.

a. Assume that the project's profitability will be similar to Intel's existing projects in 2015 and estimate costs each year by using the 2015 ratio of non-depreciation costs to revenue:

[(Cost of Revenue + SG&A + R&D)/ Total Revenue]

You should assume that this ratio will hold for this project as well. You do not need to break out the individual components of operating costs in your forecast. Simply forecast the total of Cost of Revenue + SG&A + R&D for each year.

b. Determine the annual depreciation by assuming Intel depreciates these assets by the straight-line method over a 5-year life.

c. Determine Intel's tax rate as $[1 - (\text{Income After Tax/Income Before Tax})]$ in 2015. Note that on Intel's income statement on Google Finance, there is a difference between operating income and income before tax. That difference is due to small adjustments. Ignore this issue and simply focus on the Income Before Tax line.

d. Calculate the net working capital required each year by assuming that the level of NWC will be a constant percentage of the project's sales. Use Intel's 2015 NWC/Sales to estimate the required percentage. (Use only accounts receivable, accounts payable, and inventory to measure working capital. Other components of current assets and liabilities are harder to interpret and are not necessarily reflective of the project's required NWC—e.g., Intel's cash holdings.)

e. To determine the free cash flow, calculate the *additional* capital investment and the *change* in net working capital each year.

3. Determine the IRR of the project and the NPV of the project at a cost of capital of 12% using the Excel functions. For the calculation of NPV, include cash flows 1 through 5 in the NPV function and then subtract the initial cost (i.e., $= NPV(\text{rate}, CF_1 : CF_5) + CF_0)$. For IRR, include cash flows 0 through 5 in the cash flow range.

Chapter 9 APPENDIX — MACRS Depreciation

The U.S. tax code allows for accelerated depreciation of most assets. The depreciation method that you use for any particular asset is determined by the tax rules in effect at the time you place the asset into service. (Congress has changed the depreciation rules many times over the years, so many firms that have held property for a long time may have to use several depreciation methods simultaneously.)

For most business property placed in service after 1986, the IRS allows firms to depreciate the asset using the MACRS (Modified Accelerated Cost Recovery System) method. Under this method, you categorize each business asset into a recovery class that determines the time period over which you can write off the cost of the asset. The most commonly used items are classified as shown below:

- *3-year property*: Tractor units, race horses over 2 years old, and horses over 12 years old.

- *5-year property*: Automobiles, buses, trucks, computers and peripheral equipment, office machinery, and any property used in research and experimentation. Also includes breeding and dairy cattle.

- *7-year property*: Office furniture and fixtures, and any property that has not been designated as belonging to another class.
- *10-year property*: Water transportation equipment, single-purpose agricultural or horticultural structures, and trees or vines bearing fruit or nuts.
- *15-year property*: Depreciable improvements to land such as fences, roads, and bridges.
- *20-year property*: Farm buildings that are not agricultural or horticultural structures.
- *27.5-year property*: Residential rental property.
- *39-year property*: Nonresidential real estate, including home offices. (Note that the value of land may not be depreciated.)

Generally speaking, residential and nonresidential real estate is depreciated via the straight-line method, but other classes can be depreciated more rapidly in early years. Table 9.4 shows the standard depreciation rates for assets in the other recovery classes; refinements of this table can be applied depending on the month that the asset was placed into service (consult IRS guidelines). The table indicates the percentage of the asset's cost that may be depreciated each year, with year 1 indicating the year the asset was first put into use (typically year 0 in your spreadsheet as in Example 9.8).

The lower amount in year 1 reflects a "half-year convention" in which the asset is presumed to be in use (and thus depreciated) for half of the first year, no matter when it was actually put into use. After year 1, it is assumed that the asset depreciates more rapidly in earlier years.

TABLE 9.4

MACRS Depreciation Table Showing the Percentage of the Asset's Cost That May Be Depreciated Each Year Based on Its Recovery Period

		Depreciation Rate for Recovery Period				
Year	3 Years	5 Years	7 Years	10 Years	15 Years	20 Years
1	33.33	20.00	14.29	10.00	5.00	3.750
2	44.45	32.00	24.49	18.00	9.50	7.219
3	14.81	19.20	17.49	14.40	8.55	6.677
4	7.41	11.52	12.49	11.52	7.70	6.177
5		11.52	8.93	9.22	6.93	5.713
6		5.76	8.92	7.37	6.23	5.285
7			8.93	6.55	5.90	4.888
8			4.46	6.55	5.90	4.522
9				6.56	5.91	4.462
10				6.55	5.90	4.461
11				3.28	5.91	4.462
12					5.90	4.461
13					5.91	4.462
14					5.90	4.461
15					5.91	4.462
16					2.95	4.461
17						4.462
18						4.461
19						4.462
20						4.461
21						2.231

10

Stock Valuation: A Second Look

LEARNING OBJECTIVES

- Value a stock as the present value of the company's free cash flows

- Value a stock by applying common multiples based on the values of comparable firms

- Understand how information is incorporated into stock prices through competition in efficient markets

- Describe some of the behavioral biases that influence the way individual investors trade

notation

Div_t	dividends paid in year t
$EBIT$	earnings before interest and taxes
$EBITDA$	earnings before interest, taxes, depreciation, and amortization
EPS_t	earnings per share on date t
FCF_t	free cash flow on date t
g	expected dividend growth rate
g_{FCF}	expected free cash flow growth rate

N	terminal date or forecast horizon
P_t	stock price at the end of year t
PV	present value
r_E	equity cost of capital
r_{wacc}	weighted average cost of capital
V_t	enterprise value on date t

In early-2016, the four most valuable U.S. companies were Alphabet (Google), Apple, Microsoft, and Facebook. Google and Facebook do not pay dividends, and until 2012, neither did Apple (yet in 2011 it was the most valuable company in the world). In Chapter 7, we discussed the basics of stocks and valued them using the dividend-discount model. As we pointed out at the end of that chapter, the dividend-discount model is not a practical approach for valuing the stock of the thousands of companies like Google and Facebook that do not pay dividends. We then modified the dividend-discount model to include other forms of payout such as repurchases.

Some companies, especially young ones, neither repurchase shares nor pay dividends. In this chapter, we develop a more broadly applicable method to value companies—it can even be used to value companies that currently make no cash payouts to investors. Termed the *Discounted Free Cash Flow* model, it is very closely linked to the concepts we just learned for capital budgeting. In fact, you will see that just as the discounted cash flows of a project determine the value of a project to the firm, the discounted cash flows of the firm as a whole determine its value to its investors.

The final valuation method we discuss in this chapter, the method of comparables, or "comps," is also broadly applicable to all types of companies. This method, in which we compare the firm to others in the same line of business, is based on the intuitive idea that similar companies should be valued similarly. We will learn how to use the market's valuation of one company to estimate a value of a similar company.

We close the chapter with a discussion of the role of competition in markets. We explain how information is reflected in stock prices through investor competition and discuss the implication for investors and corporate managers. Finally, we describe some common trading biases of individual investors.

10.1   The Discounted Free Cash Flow Model

In Chapter 7, we developed the dividend-discount model to value the stock of a dividend-paying firm. In this section, we outline an alternative approach to valuing the firm's shares that avoids some of the difficulties of the dividend-discount model. Specifically, we consider the *discounted free cash flow model*, which focuses on the cash flows to all of the firm's investors, both debt and equity holders. This model allows us to avoid the difficulties associated with estimating the impact of the firm's borrowing decisions on earnings. It also demonstrates the important connection between the capital budgeting analysis we did in Chapter 9 and its implications for the firm's stock price.

discounted free cash flow model A method for estimating a firm's enterprise value by discounting its future free cash flow.

The dividend-discount model values a single share of stock. In the total payout model, we first value the firm's equity, rather than just a single share. The **discounted free cash flow model** goes one step further and begins by determining the total value of the firm to all investors—both equity holders *and* debt holders. We begin by estimating the firm's enterprise value, which we defined in Chapter 2 as follows:[1]

$$\text{Enterprise Value} = \text{Market Value of Equity} + \text{Debt} - \text{Cash} \qquad (10.1)$$

Because the enterprise value is the value of the firm's underlying business, unencumbered by debt and separate from any cash or marketable securities, it is also the value of the underlying business to all investors. We can interpret the enterprise value as the net cost of acquiring the firm's equity, paying off all debt, and taking its cash; in essence, it is equivalent to owning the unlevered business. The advantage of the discounted free cash flow model is that it allows us to value a firm without explicitly forecasting its dividends, share repurchases, or use of debt.

Valuing the Enterprise

How can we estimate a firm's enterprise value? To estimate the value of the firm's equity, we compute the present value of the firm's total payouts to equity holders. Likewise, to estimate a firm's enterprise value, we compute the present value of the *free cash flow* (FCF) that the firm has available to pay all investors, both debt and equity holders. We saw how to compute the free cash flow for a project in Chapter 9; we now perform the same calculation for the entire firm:

$$\text{Free Cash Flow} = EBIT \times (1 - \text{Tax Rate}) + \text{Depreciation}$$
$$- \text{Capital Expenditures} - \text{Increases in Net Working Capital} \qquad (10.2)$$

Free cash flow measures the cash generated by the firm before any payments to debt or equity holders are considered.

---

[1]To be precise, when we say "cash," we are referring to the firm's cash in excess of its working capital needs, which is the amount of cash it has invested at a competitive market interest rate.

Thus, just as we determine the value of a project by calculating the NPV of the project's free cash flow, we estimate a firm's current enterprise value, V_0, by computing the present value of the firm's free cash flow:

Discounted Free Cash Flow Model

$$V_0 = PV(\text{Future Free Cash Flow of Firm})\qquad(10.3)$$

Given the enterprise value, we can estimate the share price by using Eq. 10.1 to solve for the value of equity and then divide by the total number of shares outstanding:

$$P_0 = \frac{V_0 + \text{Cash}_0 - \text{Debt}_0}{\text{Shares Outstanding}_0}\qquad(10.4)$$

In the dividend-discount model, the firm's cash and debt are included indirectly through the effect of interest income and expenses on earnings. By contrast, in the discounted free cash flow model, we ignore interest income and expenses because free cash flow is based on EBIT (Earnings *Before* Interest and Taxes), but we then adjust for cash and debt directly (in Eq. 10.4).

Implementing the Model

A key difference between the discounted free cash flow model and the earlier models we have considered is the discount rate. In previous calculations, we used the firm's equity cost of capital, r_E, because we were discounting the cash flows to equity holders. Here, we are discounting the free cash flow that will be paid to both debt and equity holders. Thus, we should use the firm's **weighted average cost of capital (WACC)**, denoted by r_{wacc}. It is the cost of capital that reflects the risk of the overall business, which is the combined risk of the firm's equity *and* debt. We interpret r_{wacc} as the expected return the firm must pay to investors to compensate them for the risk of holding the firm's debt and equity together. If the firm has no debt, then $r_{wacc} = r_E$. We will develop methods to calculate the WACC explicitly in Part 4 of the text.

weighted average cost of capital (WACC) The cost of capital that reflects the risk of the overall business, which is the combined risk of the firm's equity and debt.

Given the firm's weighted average cost of capital, we implement the discounted free cash flow model in much the same way as we did the dividend-discount model. That is, we forecast the firm's free cash flow up to some horizon, together with a terminal (continuation) value of the enterprise:

$$V_0 = \frac{FCF_1}{1 + r_{wacc}} + \frac{FCF_2}{(1 + r_{wacc})^2} + \cdots + \frac{FCF_N}{(1 + r_{wacc})^N} + \frac{V_N}{(1 + r_{wacc})^N}\qquad(10.5)$$

Often, we estimate the terminal value by assuming a constant long-run growth rate g_{FCF} for free cash flows beyond year N, so that

$$V_N = \frac{FCF_{N+1}}{r_{wacc} - g_{FCF}} = \left(\frac{1 + g_{FCF}}{r_{wacc} - g_{FCF}}\right) \times FCF_N\qquad(10.6)$$

The long-run growth rate g_{FCF} is typically based on the expected long-run growth rate of the firm's revenues.

EXAMPLE 10.1

Valuing Nike, Inc., Stock Using Free Cash Flow

MyFinanceLab

PROBLEM

Recall our example of Nike, Inc., from Chapter 7. Nike had sales of $25.3 billion in 2012. Suppose you expected its sales to grow at a rate of 10% in 2013, but then slow by 1% per year to the long-run growth rate that is characteristic of the apparel industry—5%—by 2018. Based on Nike's past profitability and investment needs, you expected EBIT to be 10% of sales, increases in net working capital requirements to be 10% of any increase in sales, and capital expenditures to equal depreciation expenses. If Nike had $3.3 billion in cash, $1.2 billion in debt, 893.6 million shares outstanding, a tax rate of 24%, and a weighted average cost of capital of 10%, what would have been your estimate of the value of Nike stock in early 2013?

(Continued)

SOLUTION

PLAN

We can estimate Nike's future free cash flow by constructing a pro forma statement as we did for HomeNet in Chapter 9. The only difference is that the pro forma statement is for the whole company, rather than just one project. Furthermore, we need to calculate a terminal (or continuation) value for Nike at the end of our explicit projections. Because we expected Nike's free cash flow to grow at a constant rate after 2018, we can use Eq.10.6 to compute a terminal enterprise value. The present value of the free cash flows during the years 2013–2018 and the terminal value will be the total enterprise value for Nike. From that value, we can subtract the debt, add the cash, and divide by the number of shares outstanding to compute the price per share (Eq. 10.4).

EXECUTE

The following spreadsheet presents a simplified pro forma for Nike based on the information we have:

	Year	2012	2013	2014	2015	2016	2017	2018
2	**FCF Forecast ($ million)**							
3	Sales	25,300.0	27,830.0	30,334.7	32,761.5	35,054.8	37,158.1	39,016.0
4	*Growth Versus Prior Year*		*10.0%*	*9.0%*	*8.0%*	*7.0%*	*6.0%*	*5.0%*
5	**EBIT** (10% of sales)		2,783.0	3,033.5	3,276.1	3,505.5	3,715.8	3,901.6
6	Less: Income Tax (24%)		667.9	728.0	786.3	841.3	891.8	936.4
7	Plus: Depreciation		—	—	—	—	—	—
8	Less: Capital Expenditures		—	—	—	—	—	—
9	Less: Increase in NWC (10% ΔSales)		253.0	250.5	242.7	229.3	210.3	185.8
10	**Free Cash Flow**		1,862.1	2,055.0	2,247.2	2,434.8	2,613.7	2,779.4

Because capital expenditures are expected to equal depreciation, lines 7 and 8 in the spreadsheet cancel out. We can set them both to zero rather than explicitly forecast them.

Given our assumption of constant 5% growth in free cash flows after 2018 and a weighted average cost of capital of 10%, we can use Eq. 10.6 to compute a terminal enterprise value:

$$V_{2018} = \left(\frac{1 + g_{FCF}}{r_{wacc} - g_{FCF}} \right) \times FCF_{2018} = \left(\frac{1.05}{0.10 - 0.05} \right) \times 2,779.4 = \$58,367.9 \text{ million}$$

From Eq. 10.5, Nike's 2013 enterprise value is the present value of its free cash flows plus the present value of the firm's terminal value:

$$V_0 = \frac{1,862.1}{1.10} + \frac{2,055.0}{1.10^2} + \frac{2,247.2}{1.10^3} + \frac{2,434.8}{1.10^4} + \frac{2,613.7}{1.10^5} + \frac{2,779.4}{1.10^6} + \frac{58,367.9}{1.10^6} = \$42,881.5 \text{ million}$$

We can now estimate the value of a share of Nike stock using Eq. 10.4:

$$P_0 = \frac{\$42,881.5 + \$3,300 - \$1,200}{893.6} = \$50.34$$

EVALUATE

The total value of all of the claims, both debt and equity, on the firm must equal the total present value of all cash flows generated by the firm, in addition to any cash it currently has. The total present value of all cash flows to be generated by Nike is $42,881.5 million and it has $3,300 million in cash. Subtracting off the value of the debt claims ($1,200 million), leaves us with the total value of the equity claims and dividing by the number of shares produces the value per share.

Connection to Capital Budgeting

There is an important connection between the discounted free cash flow model and the NPV rule for capital budgeting we developed in Chapter 9. Because the firm's free cash flow is equal to the sum of the free cash flows from the firm's current and future investments, we can interpret the firm's enterprise value as the sum of the present value of its existing projects and the NPV of future ones. Hence, the NPV of any investment decision represents its contribution to the firm's enterprise value. To maximize the firm's share price, we should therefore accept those projects that have a positive NPV.

Recall also from Chapter 9 that many forecasts and estimates were necessary to estimate the free cash flows of a project. The same is true for the firm: We must forecast its future sales, operating expenses, taxes, capital requirements, and other factors to obtain its free cash flow. On the one hand, estimating free cash flow in this way gives us flexibility to incorporate many specific details about the future prospects of the firm. On the other hand, some uncertainty inevitably surrounds each assumption. Given this fact, it is important to conduct a sensitivity analysis, as described in Chapter 9, to translate this uncertainty into a range of potential values for the stock.

EXAMPLE 10.2

Sensitivity Analysis for Stock Valuation

MyFinanceLab

PROBLEM

In Example 10.1, Nike's EBIT was assumed to be 10% of sales. If Nike can reduce its operating expenses and raise its EBIT to 11% of sales, how would the estimate of the stock's value change?

SOLUTION

PLAN

In this scenario, EBIT will increase by 1% of sales compared to Example 10.1. From there, we can use the tax rate (24%) to compute the effect on the free cash flow for each year. Once we have the new free cash flows, we repeat the approach in Example 10.1 to arrive at a new stock price.

EXECUTE

In year 1, EBIT will be 1% × $27,830 million = $278.3 million higher. After taxes, this increase will raise the firm's free cash flow in year 1 by $(1 - 0.24) \times \$278.3 = \$211.5$ million, to $2,073.6 million. Doing the same calculation for each year, we get the following revised FCF estimates:

Year	2013	2014	2015	2016	2017	2018
FCF	2,073.6	2,285.5	2,496.2	2,701.2	2,896.1	3,075.9

We can now reestimate the stock price as in Example 10.1. The terminal value is $V_{2018} = [\,1.05/(0.10 - 0.05)\,] \times 3,075.9 = \$65,594.8$ million, so

$$V_0 = \frac{2,073.6}{1.10} + \frac{2,285.5}{1.10^2} + \frac{2,496.2}{1.10^3} + \frac{2,701.2}{1.10^4} + \frac{2,896.1}{1.10^5} + \frac{3,075.9}{1.10^6} + \frac{64,594.8}{1.10^6} = \$47,491 \text{ million}$$

The new estimate for the value of the stock is $P_0 = (\,47,491 + 3,300 - 1,200\,)/893.6 = \$55.50$ per share, a difference of about 10% compared to the result found in Example 10.1.

EVALUATE

Nike's stock price is fairly sensitive to changes in the assumptions about its profitability. A 1% permanent change in its margins affects the firm's stock price by 10%.

Figure 10.1 summarizes the different valuation methods we have discussed so far. We use the present value of a stock's future dividends to determine its value. We can estimate the total market capitalization of the firm's equity from the present value of the firm's total payouts, which includes dividends and share repurchases. Finally, the present value of the firm's free cash flow, which is the amount of cash the firm has available to make payments to equity or debt holders, determines the firm's enterprise value.

By computing the present value of the firm's dividends, total payouts, or free cash flows, we can estimate the value of the stock, the total value of the firm's equity, or the firm's enterprise value. The final column details what adjustment is necessary to obtain the stock price.

Present Value of...	Determines the...	To Get Stock Price Estimate...
Dividend Payments	Stock Price	No adjustment necessary
Total Payouts (all dividends and repurchases)	Equity Value	Divide by shares oustanding
Free Cash Flow (cash available to pay all security holders)	Enterprise Value	Subtract what does not belong to equity holders (debt and preferred stock), add cash and marketable securities, and divide by shares outstanding

1. What is the relation between capital budgeting and the discounted free cash flow model?
2. Why do we ignore interest payments on the firm's debt in the discounted free cash flow model?

10.2 Valuation Based on Comparable Firms

So far, we have valued a firm or its stock by considering the expected future cash flows it will provide to its owner. The Valuation Principle then tells us that its value is the present value of its future cash flows, because the present value is the amount we would need to invest elsewhere in the market to replicate the cash flows with the same risk.

method of comparables An estimate of the value of a firm based on the value of other, comparable firms or other investments that are expected to generate very similar cash flows in the future.

Another application of the Valuation Principle is the *method of comparables*. In the **method of comparables** (or "comps"), rather than value the firm's cash flows directly, we estimate the value of the firm based on the value of other, comparable firms or investments that we expect will generate very similar cash flows in the future. For example, consider the case of a new firm that is *identical* to an existing publicly traded company. Recall that from competitive market prices, the Valuation Principle implies that two securities with identical cash flows must have the same price. Thus, if these firms will generate identical cash flows, we can use the market value of the existing company to determine the value of the new firm.

Of course, identical companies do not really exist. Even two firms in the same industry selling the same types of products, while similar in many respects, are likely to be of a different size or scale. For example, Intel Corporation and Advanced Micro Devices (AMD) both develop and sell semiconductor chips. In 2015, Intel had sales of $55 billion, whereas AMD had less than $4 billion. In this section, we consider ways to adjust for scale differences to use comparables to value firms with similar businesses and then discuss the strengths and weaknesses of this approach.

Valuation Multiples

valuation multiple A ratio of a firm's value to some measure of the firm's scale or cash flow.

We can adjust for differences in scale between firms by expressing their value in terms of a **valuation multiple**, which is a ratio of the value to some measure of the firm's scale.

As an analogy, consider valuing an office building. A natural measure to consider would be the price per square foot for other buildings recently sold in the area. Multiplying the size of the office building under consideration by the average price per square foot would typically provide a reasonable estimate of the building's value. We can apply this same idea to stocks, replacing square footage with some more appropriate measure of the firm's scale.

The Price-Earnings Ratio. The most common valuation multiple is the price-earnings ratio, which we introduced in Chapter 2. The P/E ratio is so common that it is almost always part of the basic statistics computed for a stock (as shown in Figure 10.2, the screenshot from Google Finance for Nike). A firm's P/E ratio is equal to the share price divided by its earnings per share. The intuition behind its use is that, when you buy a stock, you are in a sense buying the rights to the firm's future earnings. If differences in the scale of firms' earnings are likely to persist, you should be willing to pay proportionally more for a stock with higher current earnings. Using this idea, we can estimate the value of a share of stock of a firm by using the P/E ratios of other firms. For example, we can estimate the stock price of a private firm by multiplying its current earnings per share (EPS) by the average P/E ratio of comparable public firms.

FIGURE 10.2

Stock Price Quote for Nike (NKE)

This screenshot from Google Finance shows the basic stock price information and price history charting for the common stock of Nike. The historical price chart covers the period March through late June 2013. Notice that the price-earnings (P/E) ratio is listed as part of the basic information.

EXAMPLE 10.3
Valuation Using
the Price-Earnings
Ratio

MyFinanceLab

PROBLEM

Suppose furniture manufacturer Herman Miller, Inc., has earnings per share of $1.38. If the average P/E of comparable furniture stocks is 21.3, estimate a value for a share of Herman Miller stock using the P/E as a valuation multiple. What are the assumptions underlying this estimate?

SOLUTION

PLAN

We estimate a share price for Herman Miller by multiplying its EPS by the P/E of comparable firms:

$$\text{EPS} \times \text{P/E} = \text{Earnings per Share} \times (\text{Price per Share} \div \text{Earnings per Share}) = \text{Price per Share}$$

EXECUTE

$P_0 = \$1.38 \times 21.3 = \$29.39$. This estimate assumes that Herman Miller will have similar future risk, payout rates, and growth rates to comparable firms in the industry.

EVALUATE

Although valuation multiples are simple to use, they rely on some very strong assumptions about the similarity of the comparable firms to the firm you are valuing. It is important to consider whether these assumptions are likely to be reasonable—and thus to hold—in each case.

---

trailing earnings A firm's earnings over the prior 12 months.

forward earnings A firm's expected earnings over the coming 12 months.

trailing P/E A firm's price-earnings (P/E) ratio calculated using trailing (past) earnings.

forward P/E A firm's price-earnings (P/E) ratio calculated using forward (expected) earnings.

We can compute a firm's P/E ratio by using either **trailing earnings**—earnings over the prior 12 months—or **forward earnings**—expected earnings over the coming 12 months—with the resulting ratio being called the **trailing P/E** or the **forward P/E**, respectively. For valuation purposes, the forward P/E is generally preferred, as we are most concerned about future earnings.

To understand how P/E ratios relate to the other valuation techniques we have discussed, consider the dividend discount model introduced in Chapter 7.[2] For example, in the case of constant dividend growth (see Eq. 7.6), we had

$$P_0 = \frac{Div_1}{r_E - g}$$

Dividing through by EPS_1, we find that

$$\text{Forward P/E} = \frac{P_0}{EPS_1} = \frac{Div_1/EPS_1}{r_E - g} = \frac{\text{Dividend Payout Rate}}{r_E - g} \qquad (10.7)$$

In Chapter 7, we showed that Nike's current price is consistent with an equity cost of capital of 10% and an expected dividend growth rate of 8.5%. From the Nike quote, we can also see that Nike has earnings per share (EPS) of $2.52 and a dividend of $0.21 per quarter, or $0.84 per year which gives a dividend payout rate of $0.84/2.52 = 0.333$. Assuming that earnings growth and payout rates remain at this level for the foreseeable future, then we could compute the forward P/E as:

$$\text{Forward P/E} = \frac{0.84/2.52}{.10 - 0.085} = 22.22, \text{ which is not far off its reported P/E of 24.00.}$$

Equation 10.7 suggests that firms and industries that have high growth rates, and that generate cash well in excess of their investment needs so that they can maintain high payout rates, should have high P/E multiples. Taking the example of Nike we showed that at

---

[2]We use the dividend discount model rather than discounted cash flows because price and earnings are variables associated exclusively with equity.

FIGURE 10.3

Relating the P/E Ratio to Expected Future Growth

The graph shows the expected growth in earnings under two growth scenarios for Nike: 8.5% and 5%. In 2013, earnings per share were $2.52. Higher growth increases the PV of the earnings stream, which means that the price increases. The result is that the higher price divided by current earnings yields a higher P/E ratio. We found that a growth rate of 8.5% implied a P/E ratio of 22.22 while a growth rate of 5% implied a P/E ratio of 6.67. The graph shows how higher expected growth translates into a higher P/E.

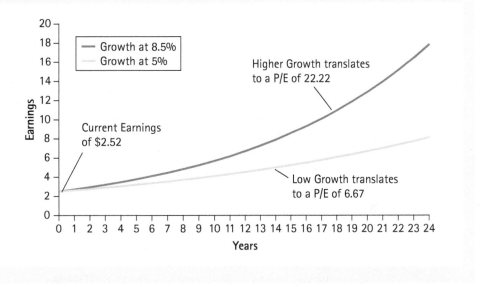

an expected growth rate of 8.5%, it would have a P/E ratio of 22.22. If our growth expectations were lower, its P/E would drop. Holding current earnings, dividends, and equity cost of capital constant, but decreasing the growth rate to 5%, we would have:

$$\text{Forward P/E} = \frac{0.84/2.52}{.10 - 0.05} = 6.67$$

This result is much lower than its current P/E of 24.00 making it clear that simply comparing P/E ratios without taking into account growth prospects can be highly misleading.

Figure 10.3 shows the relationship between expected earnings growth and P/E ratios.

EXAMPLE 10.4

Growth Prospects and the Price-Earnings Ratio

MyFinanceLab

PROBLEM

Amazon.com and Macy's are retailers. In 2016, Amazon had a price of $717.93 and forward earnings per share of $9.78. Macy's had a price of $31.21 and forward earnings per share of $3.77. Calculate their forward P/E ratios and explain the difference.

SOLUTION

PLAN

We can calculate their P/E ratios by dividing each company's price per share by its forward earnings per share. The difference we find is most likely due to different growth expectations.

EXECUTE

Forward P/E for Amazon = $717.93/$9.78 = 73.4. Forward P/E for Macy's = $31.21/$3.77 = 8.28. Amazon's P/E ratio is higher because investors expect its earnings to grow more than Macy's.

(Continued)

EVALUATE

Although both companies are retailers, they have very different growth prospects, as reflected in their P/E ratios. Investors in Amazon.com are willing to pay 73.4 times this year's expected earnings because they are also buying the present value of high future earnings created by expected growth.

Enterprise Value Multiples. The P/E ratio has the same limitations as the dividend discount model—because it relates exclusively to equity, it ignores the effect of debt. Consequently, it is also common practice to use valuation multiples based on the firm's enterprise value. By representing the total value of the firm's underlying business rather than just the value of equity, the enterprise value allows us to compare firms with different amounts of leverage.

Because the enterprise value represents the entire value of the firm before the firm pays its debt, to form an appropriate multiple, we divide it by a measure of earnings or cash flows before interest payments are made. Common multiples to consider are enterprise value to EBIT, EBITDA (earnings before interest, taxes, depreciation, and amortization), and free cash flow. However, because capital expenditures can vary substantially from period to period (e.g., a firm may need to add capacity and build a new plant one year, but then may not need to expand further for many years), most practitioners rely on enterprise value to EBITDA (EV/EBITDA) multiples.

Enterprise value multiples value the entire firm, and so they are most closely related to the discount cash flow model. When expected free cash flow growth is constant, we can use Eq. 10.6 to write enterprise value to EBITDA as

$$\frac{V_0}{EBITDA_1} = \frac{\frac{FCF_1}{r_{wacc} - g_{FCF}}}{EBITDA_1} = \frac{FCF_1/EBITDA_1}{r_{wacc} - g_{FCF}} \tag{10.8}$$

As with the P/E multiple, this valuation multiple is higher for firms with high growth rates and low capital requirements (which means that free cash flow is high in proportion to EBITDA).

EXAMPLE 10.5

Valuation Using the Enterprise Value Multiple

MyFinanceLab

PROBLEM

Fairview, Inc., is an ocean transport company with EBITDA of $50 million, cash of $20 million, debt of $100 million, and 10 million shares outstanding. The ocean transport industry as a whole has an average EV/EBITDA ratio of 8.5. What is one estimate of Fairview's enterprise value? What is a corresponding estimate of its stock price?

SOLUTION

PLAN

To estimate Fairview's enterprise value, we multiply its EBITDA by the average EV/EBITDA ratio of its industry. From there, we can subtract Fairview's debt and add its cash to calculate its equity value. Finally, we can divide by the number of shares outstanding to arrive at its stock price.

EXECUTE

Fairview's enterprise value estimate is $50 million × 8.5 = $425 million.

Next, subtract the debt from its enterprise value and add in its cash:

$425 million − $100 million + $20 million = $345 million, which is an estimate of the equity value.

Its stock price estimate is equal to its equity value estimate divided by the number of shares outstanding:

$345 million ÷ 10 million = $34.50.

EVALUATE

If we assume that Fairview should be valued similarly to the rest of the industry, then $425 million is a reasonable estimate of its enterprise value and $34.50 is a reasonable estimate of its stock price. However, we are relying on the assumption that Fairview's expected free cash flow growth is similar to the industry average. If that assumption is wrong, so is our valuation.

Other Multiples. Many other valuation multiples are used. Looking at the enterprise value as a multiple of sales can be useful if it is reasonable to assume the firm will maintain a similar margin in the future. For firms with substantial tangible assets, the ratio of price-to-book value of equity per share is sometimes used as a valuation multiple. Some multiples are specific to an industry. In the cable TV industry, for example, analysts compare enterprise value per subscriber.

Limitations of Multiples

If comparable firms were identical to the firm being valued, the firms' multiples would match precisely. Of course, firms are not identical, so the usefulness of a valuation multiple will inevitably depend on the nature of the differences between firms and the sensitivity of the multiples to these differences.

Table 10.1 lists several valuation multiples, as of July 2013, for firms in the footwear industry that could be used as comparables for Nike. Also shown in the table is the average for each multiple, together with the range around the average (in percentage terms). The bottom rows showing the range make it clear that the footwear industry has a lot of dispersion for all the multiples (for example, Wolverine has a price-to-book (P/B) of 4.13,

TABLE 10.1
Stock Prices and Multiples for the Footwear Industry (excluding Nike), July 2013

Name	Market Capitalization ($ million)	Enterprise Value ($ million)	P/E	Price/Book	Enterprise Value/Sales	Enterprise Value/EBITDA
Nike, Inc.	55,970	54,023	23.29	5.07	2.03	15.71
Adidas AG	23,105	23,317	32.33	3.06	1.20	11.88
Puma AG	4,330	4,085	70.56	1.96	0.96	9.34
Wolverine World Wide	2,910	3,981	37.6	4.13	1.22	9.28
Steve Madden, Ltd.	2,320	2,140	18.4	3.68	1.74	10.70
Deckers Outdoor Corp.	1,990	1,923	16.74	2.67	1.36	8.73
Crocs, Inc.	1,470	1,240	11.46	2.4	1.10	6.74
Skechers U.S.A.	1,340	1,213	67.41	1.54	0.78	18.16
Weyco Group, Inc.	301	325	16.53	1.71	1.11	9.69
R. G. Barry Corp.	197	174	14.92	2.31	1.19	6.44
Rocky Brands, Inc.	113	132	12.46	0.89	0.58	6.61
		Average	29.84	2.44	1.12	9.76
		Maximum	+136%	+70%	+55%	+86%
		Minimum	−62%	−63%	−48%	−34%

while Rocky Brands, Inc. has a P/B of only 0.89). While the Enterprise Value/Sales multiple shows the smallest variation, even with it we cannot expect to obtain a precise estimate of a firm's value.

The differences in these multiples most likely reflect differences in expected future growth rates, risk (and therefore costs of capital), and, in the case of Puma and Adidas, differences in accounting conventions between the United States and Germany. Investors in the market understand that these differences exist, so the stocks are priced accordingly. When valuing a firm using multiples, however, there is no clear guidance about how to adjust for these differences other than by narrowing the set of comparables used.

Another limitation of comparables is that they provide only information regarding the value of the firm *relative to* the other firms in the comparison set. Using multiples will not help us determine whether an entire industry is overvalued, for example. This issue became especially important during the Internet boom of the late 1990s. Because many of these firms did not have positive cash flows or earnings, new multiples were created to value them (for instance, price to "page views"). While these multiples could justify the value of these firms in relationship to one another, it was much more difficult to justify the stock prices of many of these firms using a realistic estimate of cash flows and the discounted free cash flow approach.

Comparison with Discounted Cash Flow Methods

The use of a valuation multiple based on comparables is best viewed as a shortcut. Rather than separately estimate the firm's cost of capital and future earnings or free cash flows, we rely on the market's assessment of the value of other firms with similar future prospects. In addition to its simplicity, the multiples approach has the advantage of being based on actual stock prices of real firms, rather than on what may be unrealistic forecasts of future cash flows.

The most important shortcoming of the comparables approach is that it does not take into account materially important differences among firms. For example, the approach ignores the fact that some firms have exceptionally talented managers, others have developed more efficient manufacturing processes, and still others might hold a patent on a new technology. Discounted cash flow methods have an advantage because they allow us to incorporate specific information about the firm's cost of capital or future growth. Thus, because the true driver of value for any firm is its ability to generate cash flows for its investors, the discounted cash flow methods have the potential to be more accurate than the use of a valuation multiple.

CONCEPT CHECK

3. What are some common valuation multiples?

4. What implicit assumptions do we make when valuing a firm using multiples based on comparable firms?

10.3 Stock Valuation Techniques: A Final Word

In the end, no single technique provides a final answer regarding a stock's true value. Indeed, all approaches inevitably require assumptions or forecasts that are too uncertain to provide a definitive assessment of the firm's value. Most real-world practitioners use a combination of these approaches and gain confidence in the outcome if the results are consistent across a variety of methods.

Figure 10.4 compares the ranges of values for Nike stock using the different valuation methods discussed in this chapter and in Chapter 7. The firm's stock price of $60.39 on June 25, 2013 was within the range of some methods, but higher than the range suggested by some of the multiples. Hence, based on this evidence alone, we would not conclude that the stock is obviously under- or over-priced. But if this were not the case—what if these valuation techniques produce valuations markedly different to what the stock is trading at in the market? In the next section, we tackle this question.

FIGURE 10.4

Range of Valuations
for Nike Stock Using
Various Valuation
Methods

Valuations from multiples are based on the low, high, and average values of the comparable firms from Table 10.1 (see Problems 17 and 18 at the end of this chapter). The constant dividend growth model is based on a 10% equity cost of capital and dividend growth rates of 6% to 9%, as discussed at the beginning of Section 7.5. The discounted free cash flow model is based on Example 10.1 with the range of parameters in Problem 9 at the end of this chapter. Midpoints are based on average multiples or base-case assumptions. Red and blue regions show the variation between the lowest-multiple/worst-case scenario and the highest-multiple/best-case scenario. Nike's actual share price of $60.39 is indicated by the gray line.

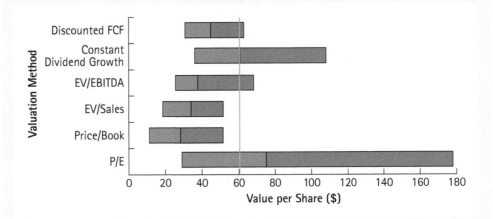

DOUGLAS KEHRING

INTERVIEW WITH

Since 2005, Douglas Kehring has been Senior Vice President of Oracle Corporation's Corporate Development and Strategic Planning group, providing planning, advisory, execution, and integration management services to Oracle on mergers and acquisitions and related transactions.

QUESTION: *How does Oracle target companies to acquire?*

ANSWER: Oracle uses an ongoing strategic planning process to identify potential acquisition targets. Top-down, the corporate development group works with the CEO's office looking for large, game-changing acquisitions. We also work bottom-up with engineering executives who sponsor potential acquisitions to fill customer needs and product gaps. Together we identify prospects, engage with targets, perform due diligence, develop business plans, and proceed with feasible transactions. Our group also provides the CEO's office with objective opinions of sponsor proposals, based on Oracle's overall needs and priorities. The CEO's office approves all transactions.

We see about 300 to 400 opportunities a year and show all to the appropriate product group executives, including those from venture capital firms and investment bankers. Typically, they express an interest in about 20 to 40, and we sign confidentiality agreements to proceed with a thorough analysis. About 12 of those reach the letter of intent stage, where we issue a term sheet and an exclusivity period to complete the transaction.

QUESTION: *Once you decide to try to acquire a company, how do you determine how much to pay for it?*

ANSWER: The pricing occurs after due diligence but before the letter of intent. From a practical standpoint, we negotiate the price point with the seller—that's where the art comes into play. Our DCF analysis is the most important part in justifying the value. We take into account what we believe we can do with the business from an income statement perspective, to determine the break-even valuation at the chosen hurdle rate. If we pay less, we'll earn a higher rate of return, and vice versa.

QUESTION: *Discuss the role of both discounted cash flow and comparables analysis in determining the price to pay.*

ANSWER: We use 5-year DCFs, because it takes that long to get to a steady state and predicting beyond that is difficult. The hardest part is determining the income statement inputs. The fifth-year numbers dominate value. Getting to that point depends on how fast you grow the business and how profitable it is. Assumptions are the key. We take a conservative approach, leveraging available information. Overly aggressive sponsor assumptions lead to extreme valuations, creating an acquirer's biggest problems.

(Continued)

The hurdle rate for a project varies. We might use cost of equity or the WACC. Then we ask, "What is right risk/return profile for this transaction?" and adjust the rate accordingly—for example, possibly requiring a higher return for a smaller, more volatile company.

Oracle's 80 completed transactions give us actual experience on which to base more realistic assumptions. We look at variables and attributes—was it a product line, a specific feature, a stand-alone acquisition?—and assess how well we did based on our models, to improve our cash flow analysis for future acquisitions. Then we benchmark using common valuation multiples based on comparable publicly traded companies and similar M&A transactions.

QUESTION: *How does your analysis differ for private versus public companies?*

ANSWER: The basic DCF analysis is no different: We perform the same due diligence for private and public companies and receive the same types of information. Typically, the larger the public company's revenues, the more stable it is and the more professional its orientation and systems. We feel more confident in our risk attributes and the information we receive. In acquiring a public company, we prepare a pro forma statement for the combined entity to determine whether it will increase or decrease our earnings per share.

Of greater concern to us is the target's size. A $2 billion company, whether public or private, has multiple product lines and larger installed bases, reducing its risk profile. A $100 million company may have only one product line and thus, higher risk and volatility. On the other hand, the small company may grow faster than a large one.

10.4   Information, Competition, and Stock Prices

As shown in Figure 10.5, the models described in this chapter and in Chapter 7 link the firm's expected future cash flows, its cost of capital (determined by its risk), and the value of its shares. But what conclusions should we draw if the actual market price of a stock does not appear to be consistent with our estimate of its value? Is it more likely that the stock is mispriced or that we are mistaken about its risk and future cash flows?

Information in Stock Prices

Suppose you are a new junior analyst assigned to research Nike stock and assess its value. You scrutinize the company's recent financial statements, look at the trends in the industry, and forecast the firm's future earnings, dividends, and free cash flows. After you carefully crunch the numbers, you estimate the stock's value to be $85 per share. On your way to present your analysis to your boss, you run into a slightly more experienced colleague in the elevator. It turns out that your colleague has been researching the same stock. But according to her analysis, the value of Nike stock is only $65 per share. What would you do?

Although you could just assume your colleague is wrong, most of us would reconsider our own analysis. The fact that someone else who has carefully studied the same stock has come to a very different conclusion is powerful evidence that you might be mistaken. In the face of this information from our colleague, you would probably adjust your assessment

FIGURE 10.5

The Valuation Triad

Valuation models determine the relationship among the firm's future cash flows, its cost of capital, and the value of its shares. We can use the stock's expected cash flows and cost of capital to assess its market price (share value). Conversely, we can use the market price to assess the firm's future cash flows or cost of capital.

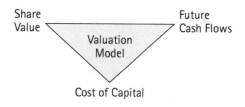

of the stock's value downward. Of course, your colleague might also revise her opinion upward based on your assessment. After sharing the analyses, we would likely end up with a consensus estimate somewhere between $65 and $85 per share.

This type of encounter happens millions of times every day in the stock market. When a buyer seeks to buy a stock, the willingness of other parties to sell the same stock suggests that they value the stock differently. This information should lead both buyers and sellers to revise their valuations. Ultimately, investors trade until they reach a consensus regarding the value (market price) of the stock. In this way, stock markets aggregate the information and views of many different investors.

Thus, if your valuation model suggests a stock is worth $30 per share when it is trading for $20 per share in the market, the discrepancy is equivalent to knowing that thousands of investors—many of them professionals who have access to the best information about the stock available—disagree with your assessment. This knowledge should make you reconsider your original analysis. You would need a very compelling reason to trust your own estimate in the face of such contrary opinions.

What conclusion can we draw from this discussion? Recall Figure 10.5, in which a valuation model links the firm's future cash flows, its cost of capital, and its share price. In other words, given accurate information about any two of these variables, a valuation model allows us to make inferences about the third variable. Thus, the way we use a valuation model will depend on the quality of our information: The model will tell us the most about the variable for which our prior information is the least reliable.

For a publicly traded firm, its market price should already provide very accurate information, aggregated from a multitude of investors, regarding the true value of its shares. In these situations, the best use of a valuation model is to inform us about the things we cannot observe directly—the firm's future cash flows or cost of capital. Only in the relatively rare case in which we have some superior information that other investors lack regarding the firm's cash flows and cost of capital would it make sense to second-guess the stock price.

EXAMPLE 10.6

Using the Information in Market Prices

MyFinanceLab

PROBLEM

Suppose Tecnor Industries will have free cash flows next year of $40 million. Its weighted average cost of capital is 11%, and you expect its free cash flows to grow at a rate of approximately 4% per year, though you are somewhat unsure of the precise growth rate. Tecnor has 10 million shares outstanding, no debt, and $20 million in cash. If Tecnor stock is currently trading for $55.33 per share, how would you update your beliefs about its dividend growth rate?

SOLUTION

PLAN

If we apply the growing perpetuity formula for the growing FCF based on a 4% growth rate, we can estimate a stock price using Eqs.10.3 and 10.4. If the market price is higher than our estimate, it implies that the market expects higher growth in FCF than 4%. Conversely, if the market price is lower than our estimate, the market expects FCF growth to be less than 4%.

EXECUTE

Applying the growing perpetuity formula, we have $PV(FCF) = 40 \div (0.11 - 0.04) = \$571.43$ million. Applying Eq. 10.4, the price per share would be ($571.43 million $-$ 0 $+$ $20 million) $\div$ 10 million shares $=$ $59.14 per share. The market price of $55.33, however, implies that most investors expect FCF to grow at a somewhat slower rate.

EVALUATE

Given the $55.33 market price for the stock, we should lower our expectations for the FCF growth rate from 4% unless we have very strong reasons to trust our own estimate.

**efficient markets
hypothesis** The idea that
competition among inves-
tors works to eliminate
all positive-NPV trading
opportunities. It implies
that securities will be fairly
priced, based on their
future cash flows, given all
information that is available to investors.

Competition and Efficient Markets

The notion that market prices reflect the information of many investors is a natural consequence of investor competition. If information were available that indicated buying a stock
had a positive NPV, investors with that information would choose to buy the stock; their
attempts to purchase it would then drive up the stock's price. By a similar logic, investors
with information that selling a stock had a positive NPV would sell it, so the stock's price
would fall.

The idea that competition among investors works to eliminate *all* positive-NPV trading
opportunities is the **efficient markets hypothesis**. It implies that securities will be fairly
priced, based on their future cash flows, given all information that is available to investors.

Forms of Market Efficiency

The type of market efficiency we describe here, where all publicly available information is incorporated very quickly into stock
prices, is often called *semistrong form market efficiency*. The term
"semistrong" indicates that it is not as complete as *strong form
market efficiency*, where prices immediately incorporate *all* information, including private information known, for example, only to
managers. Finally, the term *weak form market efficiency* means
that only the history of past prices is already reflected in the stock
price. It helps to think of the different forms of market efficiency
as meaning that prices incorporate a steadily increasing set of
information, each of which encompasses all the lower forms. For
example, since the history of past prices is public information,
semistrong form efficiency encompasses weak form. The diagram
illustrates the idea. In the diagram, the information sets of weak
form, semistrong form, and strong form efficiency are represented
by the blue, green, and yellow circles, respectively.

Not all market participants believe that the stock market is
semistrong form efficient. Technical analysts, who look for patterns in stock prices, do not believe the market is even weak form
efficient. Mutual fund managers and fundamental analysts, such
as those who work for brokerages and make stock recommendations, believe that mispricing can be uncovered by careful analysis

of company fundamentals. There is evidence that traders with
inside information about upcoming merger or earnings announcements can make abnormal returns by trading (illegally) on that
information, so the market is clearly not strong form efficient.

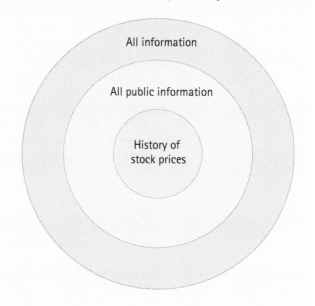

What happens when new information about a stock arrives? The answer depends on
the degree of competition, that is, on the number of investors who have access to this new
information. Consider two important cases.

Public, Easily Interpretable Information. Information that is available to all investors
includes information in news reports, financial statements, corporate press releases, or
other public data sources. If investors can readily ascertain the effects of this information
on the firm's future cash flows, then all investors can determine how this information will
change the firm's value.

In this situation, we expect competition among investors to be fierce and the stock
price to react nearly instantaneously to such news. A few lucky investors might be able to
trade a small quantity of shares before the price has fully adjusted. Most investors, however,
would find that the stock price already reflected the new information before they were able
to trade on it. In other words, the efficient markets hypothesis holds very well with respect
to this type of information.

EXAMPLE 10.7

Stock Price Reactions
to Public Information

MyFinanceLab

PROBLEM

Myox Labs announces that it is pulling one of its leading drugs from the market, owing to the potential side effects associated with the drug. As a result, its future expected free cash flow will decline by $85 million per year for the next 10 years. Myox has 50 million shares outstanding, no debt, and an equity cost of capital of 8%. If this news came as a complete surprise to investors, what should happen to Myox's stock price upon the announcement?

SOLUTION

PLAN

In this case, we can use the discounted free cash flow method. With no debt, $r_{wacc} = r_E = 8\%$. The effect on the Myox's enterprise value will be the loss of a 10-year annuity of $85 million. We can compute the effect today as the present value of that annuity.

EXECUTE

Using the annuity formula, the decline in expected free cash flow will reduce Myox's enterprise value by

$$\$85 \text{ million} \times \frac{1}{0.08}\left(1 - \frac{1}{1.08^{10}}\right) = \$570.36 \text{ million}$$

Thus, the stock price should fall by 570.36 = $11.41 per share.

EVALUATE

Because this news is public and its effect on the firm's expected free cash flow is clear, we would expect the stock price to drop by $11.41 per share nearly instantaneously.

Private or Difficult-to-Interpret Information. Of course, some information is not publicly available. For example, an analyst might spend considerable time and effort gathering information from a firm's employees, competitors, suppliers, or customers that is relevant to the firm's future cash flows. This information is not available to other investors who have not devoted a similar effort to gathering it.

Even when information is publicly available, it may be difficult to interpret. Non-experts in the field may find it challenging to evaluate research reports on new technologies, for example. It may take a great deal of legal and accounting expertise and effort to understand the full consequences of a highly complicated business transaction. Certain consulting experts may have greater insight into consumer tastes and the likelihood of a product's acceptance. In these cases, while the fundamental information may be public, the *interpretation* of how that information will affect the firm's future cash flows is itself private information.

As an example, imagine that Phenyx Pharmaceuticals has announced the development of a new drug for which the company is seeking approval from the U.S. Food and Drug Administration (FDA). If the drug is approved and subsequently launched in the U.S. market, the future profits from the new drug will increase Phenyx's market value by $750 million, or $15 per share given its 50 million shares outstanding. Assume that the development of this drug comes as a surprise to investors, and that the average likelihood of FDA approval is 10%. In that case, because many investors probably know the chance of FDA approval is 10%, competition should lead to an immediate jump in Phenyx's stock price of 10% × $15 = $1.50 per share. Over time, however, analysts and experts in the field will likely make their own assessments of the probable efficacy of the drug. If they conclude that the drug looks more promising than average, they will begin to trade on their private information and buy the stock, and the firm's price will tend to drift higher over time. However, if the experts conclude that the drug looks less promising than average, they will tend to sell the stock, and the firm's price will drift lower over time. Of course, at the time of the announcement, uninformed investors do not know which way it will go. Examples of possible price paths are shown in Figure 10.6.

FIGURE 10.6

Possible Stock Price
Paths for Phenyx
Pharmaceuticals

Phenyx's stock price jumps on the announcement based on the average likelihood of FDA approval. The stock price then drifts up (green path) or down (orange path) as informed traders trade on their more accurate assessment of the drug's likelihood of approval and hence entry into the U.S. market. At the time of the announcement, uninformed investors do not know which way the stock will go.

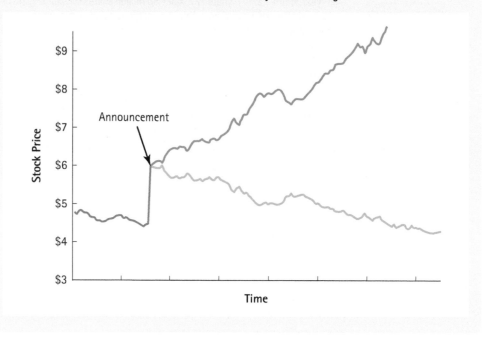

When private information is in the hands of a relatively small number of investors, these investors may be able to profit by trading on their information.[3] In this case, the efficient markets hypothesis will not hold in the strict sense. However, as these informed traders begin to trade, their actions will tend to move prices, so over time prices will begin to reflect their information as well.

If the profit opportunities from having this type of information are large, other individuals will attempt to gain the expertise and devote the resources needed to acquire it. As more individuals become better informed, competition to exploit this information will increase. Thus, in the long run, we should expect that the degree of "inefficiency" in the market will be limited by the costs of obtaining the information.

Lessons for Investors and Corporate Managers

The effect of competition based on information about stock prices has important consequences for both investors and corporate managers.

Consequences for Investors. As in other markets, investors should be able to identify positive-NPV trading opportunities in securities markets only if some barrier or restriction to free competition exists. An investor's competitive advantage may take several forms. For instance, the investor may have expertise or access to information known only to a few

---

[3]Even with private information, informed investors may find it difficult to profit from that information, because they must find others who are willing to trade with them; that is, the market for the stock must be sufficiently *liquid*. A liquid market requires that other investors in the market have alternative motives to trade (for example, selling shares of a stock to purchase a house) and so are willing to trade even when facing the risk that other traders may be better informed.

The 2013 Prize: An Enigma?

When the 2013 Nobel Prize in Economics was awarded to three financial economists, most people were surprised. The surprise was not that Eugene Fama, Robert Shiller, and Lars Peter Hansen had won the prize—most economists would agree they certainly deserved the prize for their contributions—rather it was that they won it *together*. After all, Fama is most well-known for what he termed the *efficient market hypothesis*, the assertion that markets are so competitive it is impossible to make money by trying to predict stock price movements. On the other hand, Robert Shiller argued the opposite, that the excess volatility in markets results from irrational behavior that can be exploited. Lars Peter Hansen is credited with developing statistical tools that can help distinguish these opposing views. Here is how the Nobel Prize committee justified its decision:

"Beginning in the 1960s, Eugene Fama and several collaborators demonstrated that stock prices are extremely difficult to predict in the short run, and that new information is very quickly incorporated into prices. . . . If prices are nearly impossible to predict over days or weeks, then shouldn't they be even harder to predict over several years? The answer is no, as Robert Shiller discovered in the early 1980s. He found that stock prices fluctuate much more than corporate dividends, and that the ratio of prices to dividends tends to fall when it is high, and to increase when it is low. This pattern holds not only for stocks, but also for bonds and other assets. Lars Peter Hansen developed a statistical method that is particularly well suited to testing rational theories of asset pricing. Using this method, Hansen and other researchers have found that modifications of these theories go a long way toward explaining asset prices."

Source: "The Prize in Economic Sciences 2013—Press Release." Nobelprize.org.

people. Alternatively, the investor may have lower trading costs than other market participants and so can exploit opportunities that others would find unprofitable. In all cases, the source of the positive-NPV trading opportunity must be something that is difficult to replicate; otherwise, any gains would be competed away in short order.

While the fact that positive-NPV trading opportunities are hard to come by may be disappointing, there is some good news as well. If stocks are fairly priced according to our valuation models, then investors who buy stocks can expect to receive future cash flows that fairly compensate them for the risk of their investment. In such cases, the average investor can invest with confidence, even if he or she is not fully informed.

Implications for Corporate Managers. If stocks are fairly valued according to the models we have described in this chapter and in Chapter 7, then the value of the firm is determined by the cash flows that it can pay to its investors. This result has several key implications for corporate managers:

- *Focus on NPV and free cash flow.* A manager seeking to boost the price of her firm's stock should make investments that increase the present value of the firm's free cash flow. Thus, the capital budgeting methods outlined in Chapter 9 are fully consistent with the objective of maximizing the firm's share price.

- *Avoid accounting illusions.* Many managers make the mistake of focusing on accounting earnings as opposed to free cash flows. According to the efficient markets hypothesis, the accounting consequences of a decision do not directly affect the value of the firm and should not drive decision making.

- *Use financial transactions to support investment.* With efficient markets, the firm can sell its shares at a fair price to new investors. As a consequence, the firm should not be constrained from raising capital to fund positive-NPV investment opportunities.

The Efficient Markets Hypothesis Versus No Arbitrage

There is an important distinction between the efficient markets hypothesis and the notion of no arbitrage that we introduced in Chapter 3. An arbitrage opportunity is a situation in which two securities (or portfolios) with *identical* cash flows have different prices. Because anyone can earn a sure profit in this situation by buying the low-priced security and selling the high-priced one, we expect investors to exploit and eliminate these opportunities immediately. Thus, arbitrage opportunities will not be found.

The efficient markets hypothesis states that the best estimate of the value of a share of stock is its market price. That is, investors' own estimates of value are not as accurate as the market price. But that does not mean that the market price always correctly estimates the value of a share of stock. There is a difference between the best estimate and being correct. Thus, there is no reason to expect the market price to always assess value accurately; rather, the price is best viewed as an approximation. However, because the price is the best estimate, the efficient market hypothesis implies that you cannot tell which prices overestimate and which underestimate the true value of the stock.

CONCEPT CHECK

5. State the efficient markets hypothesis.

6. What are the implications of the efficient markets hypothesis for corporate managers?

10.5 Individual Biases and Trading

Not all investors accept the notion that second guessing the stock prices requires specialized knowledge and unusual skills. Instead, they attempt to make money by trading and in most cases end up losing money. In this next section, we will briefly discuss some common psychological biases and consider how they affect individuals' trading behavior. In an efficient market, these biases can be costly, resulting in lower realized returns and reduced wealth.

Excessive Trading and Overconfidence

Trading is expensive; you must pay commissions on top of the difference between the bid and ask price, called the *spread*. Given how hard it should be to identify over- and undervalued stocks, you might then expect individual investors to take a conservative approach to trading. However, in an influential study of the trading behavior of individual investors that held accounts at a discount brokerage, researchers Brad Barber and Terrance Odean found that individual investors tend to trade very actively, with average turnover almost 50% above the average of all investors including institutions during the time period of their study.[4]

What might explain this trading behavior? Psychologists have known since the 1960s that uninformed individuals tend to overestimate the precision of their knowledge. For example, many sports fans sitting in the stands confidently second-guess the coaching decisions on the field, truly believing that they can do a better job. In finance we call investors' presumptuousness of their ability to beat the market by overtrading the **overconfidence hypothesis**. Barber and Odean hypothesized that this kind of behavior also characterizes individual investment decision making: Like sports fans, individual investors believe they can pick winners and losers when, in fact, they cannot; this overconfidence leads them to trade too much.

An implication of this overconfidence hypothesis is that, assuming they have no true ability, investors who trade more will not earn higher returns. Instead, their performance will be worse once we take into account the costs of trading (due to both commissions and bid-ask spreads). Figure 10.7 documents precisely this result, showing that much investor trading appears not to be based on rational assessments of performance.

Hanging On to Losers and the Disposition Effect

Investors tend to hold on to stocks that have lost value and sell stocks that have risen in value since the time of purchase. We call this tendency to keep losers and sell winners the **disposition effect**. Researchers Hersh Shefrin and Meir Statman, building on the work of

overconfidence hypothesis The tendency of individual investors to trade too much based on the mistaken belief that they can pick winners and losers better than investment professionals.

disposition effect The tendency to hold on to stocks that have lost value and sell stocks that have risen in value since the time of purchase.

---

[4]B. Barber and T. Odean, "Trading Is Hazardous to Your Wealth: The Common Stock Investment Performance of Individual Investors," *Journal of Finance*, 55 (2000) 773–806.

FIGURE 10.7

Individual Investor
Returns Versus
Portfolio Turnover

The plot shows the average annual return (net of commissions and trading costs) for individual investors at a large discount brokerage from 1991–1997. Investors are grouped into quintiles based on their average annual turnover. While the least-active investors had slightly (but not significantly) better performance than the S&P 500, performance declined with the rate of turnover.

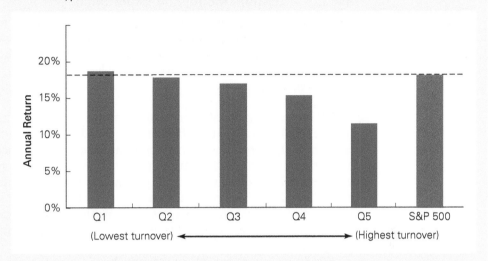

Source: B. Barber and T. Odean, "Trading Is Hazardous to Your Wealth: The Common Stock Investment Performance of Individual Investors," *Journal of Finance*, 55 (2000): 773–806.

psychologists Daniel Kahneman and Amos Tversky, suggest that this effect arises due to investors' increased willingness to take on risk in the face of possible losses.[5] It may also reflect a reluctance to admit a mistake by taking the loss.

Researchers have verified the disposition effect in many studies. For example, in a study of all trades in the Taiwanese stock market from 1995–1999, investors in aggregate were twice as likely to realize gains as they were to realize losses. Also, nearly 85% of individual investors were subject to this bias.[6] On the other hand, mutual funds and foreign investors did not exhibit the same tendency, and other studies have shown that more sophisticated investors appear to be less susceptible to the disposition effect.[7]

This behavioral tendency to sell winners and hang on to losers is costly from a tax perspective. Because capital gains are taxed only when the asset is sold, it is optimal for tax purposes to postpone taxable gains by continuing to hold profitable investments; delaying the tax payment reduces its present value. On the other hand, investors should capture tax losses by selling their losing investments, especially near the year's end, in order to accelerate the tax write-off.

Of course, keeping losers and selling winners might make sense if investors forecast that the losing stocks would ultimately "bounce back" and outperform the winners going forward. While investors may in fact have this belief, it does not appear to be justified—if anything, the losing stocks that investors continue to hold tend to *underperform* the

---

[5]H. Shefrin and M. Statman, "The Disposition to Sell Winners Too Early and Ride Losers Too Long: Theory and Evidence," *Journal of Finance* 40 (1985): 777–790, and D. Kahneman and A. Tversky, "Prospect Theory: An Analysis of Decision under Risk," *Econometrica*, 47 (1979): 263–291.

[6]B. Barber, Y. T. Lee, Y. J. Liu, and T. Odean, "Is the Aggregate Investor Reluctant to Realize Losses? Evidence from Taiwan," *European Financial Management*, 13 (2007): 423–447.

[7]R. Dhar and N. Zhu, "Up Close and Personal: Investor Sophistication and the Disposition Effect," *Management Science*, 52 (2006): 726–740.

winners they sell. According to one study, losers underperformed winners by 3.4% over the year after the winners were sold.[8]

Investor Attention, Mood, and Experience

Individual investors generally are not full-time traders. As a result, they have limited time and attention to spend on their investment decisions and may be influenced by attention-grabbing news stories or other events. Studies show that individuals are more likely to buy stocks that have recently been in the news, engaged in advertising, experienced exceptionally high trading volume, or have had extreme (either positive or negative) returns.[9]

Investment behavior also seems to be affected by investors' moods. For example, sunshine generally has a positive effect on mood, and studies have found that stock returns tend to be higher when it is a sunny day at the location of the stock exchange. In New York City, the annualized market return on perfectly sunny days is approximately 24.8% per year versus 8.7% per year on perfectly cloudy days.[10] Further evidence of the link between investor mood and stock returns comes from the effect of major sports events on returns. One recent study estimates that a loss in the World Cup elimination stage lowers the next day's stock returns in the losing country by about 0.50%, presumably due to investors' poor moods.[11]

Finally, investors appear to put too much weight on their own experience rather than considering all the historical evidence. As a result, people who grow up and live during a time of high stock returns are more likely to invest in stocks than people who grow up and live during a time of low stock returns.[12]

Why would investors continue to make such mistakes? Even if they started with such misconceptions, wouldn't they be able to learn over time the cost of these errors? The challenge is that stock returns are extremely volatile, and this volatility masks the small differences in returns from different trading strategies. We will start Chapter 11 with a review of the historical evidence on average stock returns and their volatility. You will see how variable returns are and how there have been long stretches of good returns, as in the 1990s, and stretches in which the total return was negative, as in the 2000s.

CONCEPT CHECK

7. What are several systematic behavioral biases that individual investors fall prey to?

8. Why would excessive trading lead to lower realized returns?

---

[8]T. Odean, "Are Investors Reluctant to Realize Their Losses?" *Journal of Finance*, 53 (1998): 1775–1798.

[9]See G. Grullon, G. Kanatas, and J. Weston, "Advertising, Breadth of Ownership, and Liquidity," *Review of Financial Studies*, 17 (2004): 439–461; M. Seasholes and G. Wu, "Predictable Behavior, Profits, and Attention," *Journal of Empirical Finance*, 14 (2007): 590–610; B. Barber and T. Odean, "All That Glitters: The Effect of Attention and News on the Buying Behavior of Individual and Institutional Investors," *Review of Financial Studies*, 21 (2008): 785–818.

[10]Based on data from 1982–1997; see D. Hirshleifer and T. Shumway, "Good Day Sunshine: Stock Returns and the Weather," *Journal of Finance*, 58 (2003): 1009–1032.

[11]A. Edmans, D. Garcia, and O. Norli, "Sports Sentiment and Stock Returns," *Journal of Finance*, 62 (2007): 1967–1998.

[12]U. Malmendier and S. Nagel, "Depression Babies: Do Macroeconomic Experiences Affect Risk-Taking?" NBER working paper no. 14813.

MyFinanceLab

Here is what you should know after reading this chapter. MyFinanceLab will help you identify what you know, and where to go when you need to practice.

KEY POINTS AND EQUATIONS	KEY TERMS	ONLINE PRACTICE
10.1 The Discounted Free Cash Flow Model • When a firm has leverage, it is more reliable to use the discounted free cash flow model. In this model, the enterprise value of the firm equals the present value of the firm's future free cash flow: $$V_0 = PV(\text{Future Free Cash Flow of Firm}) \quad (10.3)$$ • We discount cash flows using the weighted average cost of capital, which is the expected return the firm must pay to investors to compensate them for the risk of holding the firm's debt and equity together. • We can estimate a terminal enterprise value by assuming free cash flow grows at a constant rate (typically equal to the rate of long-run revenue growth). • We determine the stock price by subtracting debt and adding cash to the enterprise value, and then dividing by the initial number of shares outstanding of the firm: $$P_0 = \frac{V_0 + \text{Cash}_0 - \text{Debt}_0}{\text{Shares Outstanding}_0} \quad (10.4)$$	discounted free cash flow model, p. 304 weighted average cost of capital (WACC), p. 305	MyFinanceLab Study Plan 10.1 Interactive Discounted Cash Flow Valuation
10.2 Valuation Based on Comparable Firms • We can also value stocks by using valuation multiples based on comparable firms. Multiples commonly used for this purpose include the P/E ratio and the ratio of enterprise value (EV) to EBITDA. When we use multiples, we assume that comparable firms have the same risk and future growth as the firm being valued. • No valuation model provides a definitive value for the stock. It is best to use several methods to identify a reasonable range for the value.	forward earnings, p. 310 forward P/E, p. 310 method of comparables, p. 308 trailing earnings, p. 310 trailing P/E, p. 310 valuation multiple, p. 308	MyFinanceLab Study Plan 10.2
10.3 Stock Valuation Techniques: A Final Word • All valuation approaches require assumptions or forecasts that are too uncertain to provide a definitive assessment of the firm's value. • You can be more confident if the valuation is consistent across a variety of methods.		
10.4 Information, Competition, and Stock Prices • Stock prices aggregate the information of many investors. Therefore, if our valuation disagrees with the stock's market price, it is most likely an indication that our assumptions about the firm's cash flows are wrong.	efficient markets hypothesis, p. 318	MyFinanceLab Study Plan 10.3

- Competition between investors tends to eliminate positive-NPV trading opportunities. Competition will be strongest when information is public and easy to interpret. Privately informed traders may be able to profit from their information, which is reflected in prices only gradually.
- The efficient markets hypothesis states that competition eliminates all positive-NPV trades, which is equivalent to stating that securities with equivalent risk have the same expected returns.
- In an efficient market, investors will not find positive-NPV trading opportunities without some source of competitive advantage. By contrast, the average investor will earn a fair return on his or her investment.
- In an efficient market, to raise the stock price, corporate managers should focus on maximizing the present value of the free cash flow from the firm's investments, rather than accounting consequences or financial policy.

10.5 Individual Biases and Trading • Individual investors display many biases, including overconfidence, disposition effect, limited attention, and mood affects. • In an efficient market, these biases can lead to trading losses through excessive trading or biases in valuations.	disposition effect, p. 322 overconfidence hypothesis, p. 322	MyFinanceLab Study Plan 10.4

CRITICAL THINKING

1. What are the advantages of valuing a stock based on discounted free cash flows?

2. Explain the connection between the FCF valuation model and capital budgeting.

3. What is the intuition behind valuation by multiples and what are the major assumptions?

4. What are the limitations of valuation by multiples?

5. What is an efficient market?

6. How do interactions in a market lead to information being incorporated into stock prices?

7. Why does market efficiency lead a manager to focus on NPV and free cash flow?

8. Why don't investors always trade rationally?

9. What are some of the major behavioral trading biases?

PROBLEMS

All problems are available in MyFinanceLab. *The* 📊 *icon indicates problems that are easier to solve using Excel and have data in an Excel format available in* MyFinanceLab. *An asterisk * indicates problems with a higher level of difficulty.*

The Discounted Free Cash Flow Model

1. This year, FCF, Inc., has earnings before interest and taxes of $10 million, depreciation expenses of $1 million, capital expenditures of $1.5 million, and has increased its net working capital by $500,000. If its tax rate is 35%, what is its free cash flow?

2. Victoria Enterprises expects earnings before interest and taxes (EBIT) next year of $1 million. Its depreciation and capital expenditures will both be $300,000, and it expects its capital expenditures to always equal its depreciation. Its working capital will increase by $50,000 over the next year. Its tax rate is 40%. If its WACC is 10% and its FCFs are expected to increase at 4% per year in perpetuity, what is its enterprise value?

3. The present value of JECK Co.'s expected free cash flows is $100 million. If JECK has $30 million in debt, $6 million in cash, and 2 million shares outstanding, what is its share price?

4. Portage Bay Enterprises has $1 million in excess cash, no debt, and is expected to have free cash flow of $10 million next year. Its FCF is then expected to grow at a rate of 3% per year forever. If Portage Bay's equity cost of capital is 11% and it has 5 million shares outstanding, what should be the price of Portage Bay stock?

5. River Enterprises has $500 million in debt and 20 million shares of equity outstanding. Its excess cash reserves are $15 million. They are expected to generate $200 million in free cash flows next year with a growth rate of 2% per year in perpetuity. River Enterprises' cost of equity capital is 12%. After analyzing the company, you believe that the growth rate should be 3% instead of 2%. How much higher (in dollars) would the price per share of stock be if you are right?

6. Heavy Metal Corporation is expected to generate the following free cash flows over the next five years:

Year	1	2	3	4	5
FCF ($ million)	53	68	78	75	82

After 5 years, the free cash flows are expected to grow at the industry average of 4% per year. Using the discounted free cash flow model and a weighted average cost of capital of 14%:
a. Estimate the enterprise value of Heavy Metal.
b. If Heavy Metal has no excess cash, debt of $300 million, and 40 million shares outstanding, estimate its share price.

*7. Covan, Inc., is expected to have the following free cash flows:

Year	1	2	3	4	...
FCF	10	12	13	14	Grow by 4% per year

a. Covan has 8 million shares outstanding, $3 million in excess cash, and it has no debt. If its cost of capital is 12%, what should its stock price be?
b. Covan reinvests all its FCF and has no plans to add debt or change its cash holdings. If you plan to sell Covan at the beginning of year 2, what should you expect its price to be?
c. Assume you bought Covan stock at the beginning of year 1. What is your expected return from holding Covan stock until year 2?

8. Sora Industries has 60 million outstanding shares, $120 million in debt, $40 million in cash, and the following projected free cash flow for the next four years (*see* MyFinanceLab *for the data in Excel format*):

1	Year	0	1	2	3	4
2	**Earnings and FCF Forecast ($ million)**					
3	Sales	433.0	468.0	516.0	547.0	574.3
4	*Growth Versus Prior Year*		*8.1%*	*10.3%*	*6.0%*	*5.0%*
5	Cost of Goods Sold		−313.6	−345.7	−366.5	−384.8
6	**Gross Profit**		154.4	170.3	180.5	189.5
7	Selling, General, and Administrative		−93.6	−103.2	−109.4	−114.9
8	Depreciation		−7.0	−7.5	−9.0	−9.5
9	**EBIT**		53.8	59.6	62.1	65.2
10	Less: Income Tax at 40%		−21.5	−23.8	−24.8	−26.1
11	Plus: Depreciation		7.0	7.5	9.0	9.5
12	Less: Capital Expenditures		−7.7	−10.0	−9.9	−10.4
13	Less: Increase in NWC		−6.3	−8.6	−5.6	−4.9
14	**Free Cash Flow**		**25.3**	**24.6**	**30.8**	**33.3**

a. Suppose Sora's revenues and free cash flow are expected to grow at a 5% rate beyond year 4. If Sora's weighted average cost of capital is 10%, what is the value of Sora stock based on this information?

b. Sora's cost of goods sold was assumed to be 67% of sales. If its cost of goods sold is actually 70% of sales, how would the estimate of the stock's value change?

c. Return to the assumptions of part (a) and suppose Sora can maintain its cost of goods sold at 67% of sales. However, the firm reduces its selling, general, and administrative expenses from 20% of sales to 16% of sales. What stock price would you estimate now? (Assume no other expenses, except taxes, are affected.)

*d. Sora's net working capital needs were estimated to be 18% of sales (their current level in year 0). If Sora can reduce this requirement to 12% of sales starting in year 1, but all other assumptions remain as in part (a), what stock price do you estimate for Sora? (*Hint*: This change will have the largest effect on Sora's free cash flow in year 1.)

9. Consider the valuation of Nike given in Example 10.1.

a. Suppose you believe Nike's initial revenue growth rate will be between 7% and 11% (with growth always slowing linearly to 5% by year 2018). What range of prices for Nike stock is consistent with these forecasts?

b. Suppose you believe Nike's initial revenue EBIT margin will be between 9% and 11% of sales. What range of prices for Nike stock is consistent with these forecasts?

c. Suppose you believe Nike's weighted average cost of capital is between 9.5% and 12%. What range of prices for Nike stock is consistent with these forecasts?

d. What range of stock prices is consistent if you vary the estimates as in parts (a), (b), and (c) simultaneously?

Valuation Based on Comparable Firms

10. You are evaluating the stock price of Kroger, a grocery store chain. It has forward earnings per share of $3. You notice that its competitor Safeway has a P/E ratio of 13. What is a good estimate of Kroger's stock price?

11. You notice that Coca-Cola has a stock price of $41.09 and EPS of $1.89. Its competitor PepsiCo has EPS of $3.90. But, Jones Soda, a small batch Seattle-based soda producer has a P/E ratio of 35. Based on this information, what is one estimate of the value of a share of PepsiCo stock?

12. CSH has EBITDA of $5 million. You feel that an appropriate EV/EBITDA ratio for CSH is 9. CSH has $10 million in debt, $2 million in cash, and 800,000 shares outstanding. What is your estimate of CSH's stock price?

13. Next year, BHH Co. is expected to pay a dividend of $3 per share from earnings of $5 per share. The equity cost of capital for BHH is 12%. What should BHH's forward P/E ratio be if its dividend growth rate is expected to be 4% for the foreseeable future?

14. GHL, Inc., has a dividend payout ratio of 50%. Its cost of equity is 11% and its dividend growth rate is 5%. If its forward EPS is $6, what is your estimate of its stock price?

15. SLYMN Enterprises has a P/E ratio of 12 and a dividend payout ratio of 40%. If its equity cost of capital is 13%, what growth rate is its P/E ratio consistent with?

16. After researching the competitors of EJH Enterprises, you determine that most comparable firms have the following valuation ratios (*see* MyFinanceLab *for the data in Excel format*):

	Comp 1	Comp 2	Comp 3	Comp 4
EV/EBITDA	12	11	12.5	10
P/E	19	18	20	17

EJH Enterprises has EPS of $2, EBITDA of $300 million, $30 million in cash, $40 million in debt, and 100 million shares outstanding. What range of prices is consistent with both sets of multiples?

17. Suppose that in July 2013, Nike had EPS of $2.52 and a book value of equity of $12.48 per share.
    a. Using the average P/E multiple in Table 10.1, estimate Nike's share price.
    b. What range of share prices do you estimate based on the highest and lowest P/E multiples in Table 10.1?
    c. Using the average price-to-book value multiple in Table 10.1, estimate Nike's share price.
    d. What range of share prices do you estimate based on the highest and lowest price-to-book value multiples in Table 10.1?

18. Suppose that in July 2013, Nike had sales of $25,313 million, EBITDA of $3,254 million, excess cash of $3,337 million, $1,390 million of debt, and 893.6 million shares outstanding.
    a. Using the average enterprise value to sales multiple in Table 10.1, estimate Nike's share price.
    b. What range of share prices do you estimate based on the highest and lowest enterprise value to sales multiples in Table 10.1?
    c. Using the average enterprise value to EBITDA multiple in Table 10.1, estimate Nike's share price.
    d. What range of share prices do you estimate based on the highest and lowest enterprise value to EBITDA multiples in Table 10.1?

*19. Suppose Rocky Brands has earnings per share of $2.30 and EBITDA of $30.7 million. The firm also has 5.4 million shares outstanding and debt of $125 million (net of cash). You believe Deckers Outdoor Corporation is comparable to Rocky Brands in terms of its underlying business, but Deckers has no debt. If Deckers has a P/E of 13.3 and an enterprise value to EBITDA multiple of 7.4, estimate the value of Rocky Brands stock using both multiples. Which estimate is likely to be more accurate?

20. Consider the following data for the airline industry for December 2015 (EV = enterprise value, Book = equity book value). Discuss the potential challenges of using multiples to value an airline.

Company Name	Market Capitalization	Enterprise Value (EV)	EV/Sales	EV/EBITDA	EV/EBIT	P/E	P/Book
Delta Air Lines (DAL)	40,857	45,846	1.1x	6.0x	7.6x	15.0x	4.0x
American Airlines (AAL)	27,249	38,937	0.9x	4.5x	5.5x	6.2x	7.5x
United Continental (UAL)	22,000	28,522	0.7x	4.2x	5.6x	3.4x	2.6x
Southwest Airlines (LUV)	28,499	28,125	1.5x	6.0x	7.4x	16.1x	4.1x
Alaska Air (ALK)	10,396	9,870	1.8x	6.3x	7.9x	13.4x	4.4x
JetBlue Airways (JBLU)	7,338	8,189	1.3x	6.1x	7.9x	13.8x	2.4x
SkyWest (SKYW)	1,039	2,590	0.8x	5.2x	11.1x	21.2x	0.7x
Hawaiian (HA)	1,974	2,281	1.0x	5.3x	6.9x	15.1x	5.3x

Source: Capital IQ and Yahoo! Finance.

21. Suppose Hawaiian Airlines (HA) has 53 million shares outstanding. Estimate Hawaiian's share value using each of the five valuation multiples in Problem 20, based on the median valuation multiple of the other seven airlines shown.

Information, Competition, and Stock Prices

22. Summit Systems has an equity cost of capital of 11%, will pay a dividend of $1.50 in one year and its dividends had been expected to grow by 6% per year. You read in the paper that Summit has revised its growth prospects and now expects its dividends to grow at a rate of 3% per year forever.
    a. What is the drop in the value of a share of Summit Systems stock based on this information?
    b. If you tried to sell your Summit Systems stock after reading this news, what price would you be likely to get? Why?

23. Assume that Cola Co. has a share price of $43. The firm will pay a dividend of $1.24 in one year, and you expect Cola Co. to raise this dividend by approximately 7% per year in perpetuity.
    a. If Cola Co.'s equity cost of capital is 8%, what share price would you expect based on your estimate of the dividend growth rate?
    b. Given Cola Co.'s share price, what would you conclude about your assessment of Cola Co.'s future dividend growth?

24. Roybus, Inc., a manufacturer of flash memory, just reported that its main production facility in Taiwan was destroyed in a fire. Although the plant was fully insured, the loss of production will decrease Roybus's free cash flow by $180 million at the end of this year and by $60 million at the end of next year.
    a. If Roybus has 35 million shares outstanding and a weighted average cost of capital of 13%, what change in Roybus's stock price would you expect upon this announcement? (Assume the value of Roybus's debt is not affected by the event.)
    b. Would you expect to be able to sell Roybus stock on hearing this announcement and make a profit? Explain.

*25. Apnex, Inc., is a biotechnology firm that is about to announce the results of its clinical trials of a potential new cancer drug. If the trials were successful, Apnex stock will be worth $70 per share. If the trials were unsuccessful, Apnex stock will be worth

$18 per share. Suppose that the morning before the announcement is scheduled, Apnex shares are trading for $55 per share.

a. Based on the current share price, what sort of expectations do investors seem to have about the success of the trials?

b. Suppose hedge fund manager Paul Kliner has hired several prominent research scientists to examine the public data on the drug and make their own assessment of the drug's promise. Would Kliner's fund be likely to profit by trading the stock in the hours prior to the announcement?

c. Which factors would limit the ability of Kliner's fund to profit on its information?

Individual Biases and Trading

26. You have a $100,000 portfolio made up of 15 stocks. You trade each stock five times this year and each time you trade, you pay about $30 in commissions and spread. You have no special knowledge, so you earn only the average market return of 12% on your investments. How much lower will your total return be because of your trades?

27. Assume the annual return for the lowest turnover portfolio is 18% and the annual return for the highest turnover portfolio is 12%. If you invest $100,000 and have the highest turnover, how much lower will the value of your portfolio be at the end of 10 years than if you had had the lowest turnover?

DATA CASE

As a new junior analyst for a large brokerage firm, you are excited to demonstrate the skills you learned in college and prove that you are worth your attractive salary. Your first assignment is to analyze Johnson & Johnson stock. Your boss recommends determining prices based on both the discounted free cash flow valuation method and the comparable P/E ratio method. You are a little concerned about your boss's recommendation because your finance professor explained that these two valuation methods can result in widely differing estimates when applied to real data. You are really hoping the two methods will reach similar prices. Good luck with that!

1. Go to Reuters (http://www.reuters.com) and enter the symbol for Johnson & Johnson (JNJ) in the "Search" box, then select Johnson and Johnson. From the main page for JNJ, gather the following information, and enter it into a spreadsheet:
   a. The current stock price (on the left side of the page)
   b. The EPS (TTM)
   c. The number of shares of stock outstanding
   d. The industry P/E (TTM) ratio

2. Click the "Analysts" tab. On the Analyst page, scroll down to find the LT (Long-Term) Growth Rate and enter the Mean value into your spreadsheet.

3. Go to Morningstar (http://www.morningstar.com) and enter "JNJ" into the "Quote" box.

4. Under "Financials," Click Income Statement. Copy and paste (or use the Export to Excel button to create a new file with the data) the most recent three years' worth of income statements into a new worksheet in your existing Excel file. Repeat this process for both the balance sheet and the cash flow statement for Johnson and Johnson. Keep all of the different statements in the same Excel worksheet. *Note*: Make sure you are collecting annual data, rather than quarterly or interim data.

5. To determine the stock value based on the discounted free cash flow method:
   a. Forecast the free cash flows. Start by using the historical data from the financial statements downloaded from Morningstar to compute the three-year average of the following ratios:
      i. EBIT/sales
      ii. Tax rate (income tax expense/income before tax)
      iii. Property plant and equipment/sales
      iv. Depreciation/property plant and equipment
      v. Net working capital/sales
   b. Create an empty timeline for the next five years.
   c. Forecast future sales based on the most recent year's total revenue growing at the LT growth rate from Reuters for the first five years.
   d. Use the average ratios computed in part (a) to forecast EBIT, property, plant and equipment, depreciation, and net working capital for the next five years.
   e. Forecast the free cash flow for the next five years using Eq. 10.2.
   f. Determine the horizon enterprise value for year 5 using Eq. 10.6 and a long-run growth rate of 4% and a cost of capital for JNJ of 11%.
   g. Determine the enterprise value of the firm as the present value of the free cash flows.
   h. Determine the stock price using Eq. 10.4. Note that your enterprise value is in $ thousands and the number of shares outstanding is in billions.

6. To calculate an estimate of JNJ price based on a comparable P/E ratio, multiply the industry average P/E ratio by JNJ EPS.

7. Compare the stock prices produced by the two methods to the actual stock price. What recommendations can you make as to whether clients should buy or sell JNJ stock based on your price estimates?

8. Explain to your boss why the estimates from the two valuation methods differ. Specifically address the assumptions implicit in the models themselves as well as the assumptions you made in preparing your analysis. Why do these estimates differ from the actual stock price of JNJ?

3

Integrative Case

This case draws on material from this and earlier chapters.

Nanovo, Inc., is a manufacturer of low-cost micro batteries for use in a wide variety of compact electronic devices such as children's toys, wireless transmitters, and sensors. The growth in the use of these devices has steadily increased, leading to an ever greater demand for Nanovo's products. Nanovo has responded to this increase in demand by expanding its production capacity, more than doubling the firm's size over the last decade. Despite this growth, however, Nanovo does not have sufficient capacity to meet the current demand for its ultra-long-life, low-voltage batteries. You have been asked to evaluate two proposals to expand one of Nanovo's existing plants, and make a recommendation.

Proposal 1

The current plant has a capacity of 25,000 cases per month. The first proposal is for a major expansion that would double the plant's current capacity to 50,000 cases per month. After talking with the firm's design engineers, sales managers, and plant operators, you have prepared the following estimates:

- Expanding the plant will require the purchase of $3.6 million in new equipment, and entail up-front design and engineering expenses of $3.9 million. These costs will be paid immediately when the expansion begins.
- Installing the new equipment and redesigning the plant to accommodate the higher capacity will require shutting down the plant for nine months. During that time, the plant's production will cease. After the expansion is finished, the plant will operate at double its original capacity.
- Marketing and selling the additional volume will lead to $1 million per year in additional sales, marketing, and administrative costs. These costs will begin in the first year (even while the plant is under construction and shut down).

Proposal 2

The engineers have put forth a second proposal for a minor expansion that will increase the firm's capacity by only 50%, to 37,500 cases per month. While the capacity is smaller, such an expansion would be cheaper and less disruptive:

- The smaller expansion will require only $2.4 million in new equipment, and $1.5 million in design and engineering expenses.
- The existing plant will need to be shut down for only four months.
- Sales, marketing, and administrative costs will only increase by $500,000.

Nanovo believes that with or without any expansion, the technology used at the plant will be obsolete after six years and will have no salvage value, and the plant itself will need to be completely overhauled at that time. You also have the following additional general information:

- With or without either proposed expansion, Nanovo will be able to sell all it can produce at an average wholesale price of $80 per case. This price is not expected to change during the next six years.
- Nanovo has a gross profit margin of 55% on these batteries.
- Nanovo's average net working capital at the end of each year will equal 15% of its annual revenue.
- Nanovo pays a 40% corporate tax rate.
- While all design and engineering costs are immediately deductible as operating expenses, all capital expenditures will be straight-line depreciated for tax purposes over the subsequent six years.

Management believes the risk of the expansion is similar to the risk of Nanovo's existing projects, and because Nanovo is all equity financed, the risk of the expansion is also similar to the risk of Nanovo stock. You have the following additional information about the stock:

- Nanovo has no debt and has 2 million shares outstanding. The firm's current share price is $75 per share.
- Analysts are expecting Nanovo to pay a $3 dividend at the end of this year, and to raise its dividend at an average rate of 8% per year in the future.

Based on this information, you have been tasked with preparing expansion recommendations for Nanovo (using Excel is optional but recommended).

Case Questions

1. Determine the annual incremental free cash flow associated with each expansion proposal relative to the status quo (no expansion).
2. Compute the IRR and payback period of each expansion proposal. Which plan has a higher IRR? Which has a shorter payback period?
3. Estimate Nanovo's equity cost of capital. Use it to determine the NPV associated with each expansion proposal. Which plan has a higher NPV?
4. Should Nanovo expand the plant? If so, which proposal should Nanovo adopt? Explain.
5. Suppose Nanovo decides to do the major expansion. If investors are not expecting this expansion, and if they agree with the forecasts above, how will the stock price change when the expansion is announced?
6. Suppose Nanovo announces the major expansion and the stock price reacts as in Question 5. Nanovo then issues new shares at this price to cover the up-front free cash flow required to launch the expansion, and thereafter pays out as dividends the total amount it expected to pay prior to the expansion, plus the additional free cash flow associated with the expansion. What dividend per share will Nanovo pay over the next eight years? What is the fair price today for Nanovo stock given these dividends?

PART 4

Risk and Return

Valuation Principle Connection. To apply the Valuation Principle, we must be able to discount the future costs and benefits of a decision. To do so, we need a discount rate that should reflect the risk, or uncertainty, surrounding those future costs and benefits. Our objective in this part of the book is to explain how to measure and compare risks across investment opportunities and use that knowledge to determine a discount rate, or cost of capital, for each investment opportunity. Chapter 11 introduces the key insight that investors only demand a risk premium for risk they cannot costlessly remove themselves by diversifying their portfolios. Hence, only non-diversifiable risk will matter when comparing investment opportunities. In Chapter 12, we quantify this idea, leading to the Capital Asset Pricing Model (CAPM), the central model of financial economics that quantifies what an equivalent risk is and in doing so provides the relation between risk and return. In Chapter 13, we apply what we've learned to estimate a company's overall cost of capital.

11

Risk and Return in Capital Markets

LEARNING OBJECTIVES

- Identify which types of securities have historically had the highest returns and which have been the most volatile

- Compute the average return and volatility of returns from a set of historical asset prices

- Understand the tradeoff between risk and return for large portfolios versus individual stocks

- Describe the difference between common and independent risk

- Explain how diversified portfolios remove independent risk, leaving common risk as the only risk requiring a risk premium

notation

Div_t	dividend paid on date t
P_t	price on date t
R_t	realized or total return of a security from date $t-1$ to t

$\bar{R}$	average return
$SD(R)$	standard deviation of return R
$Var(R)$	variance of return R

Over the 10-year period of 2006 through 2015, investors in Consolidated Edison, Inc. (an electric utility) earned an average return of over 9% per year. Within this period there was considerable variation, with the annual return ranging from −16% in 2008 to nearly 31% in 2011. Over the same period, investors in Microsoft Corporation earned an average return of nearly 13%. However, the road was more rocky—these investors gained 60% in 2009, but lost 44% in 2008. At the same time, investors in three-month U.S. Treasury bills earned an average return of 1% during the period, with a high of nearly 5% in 2006 and a low of 0.02% in 2014. Thus, these three investments offered investors returns that were very different in terms of their average level and their variability. While Microsoft stock paid the highest return on average, its returns were also the most volatile.

In this chapter, our goal is to develop an understanding of how risk relates to return. In the last three chapters, we established that value in projects, and hence in the firm, is determined by the present value of free cash flows. Up until now, we have focused on how to forecast and discount those cash flows. In this chapter and the two that follow, we turn our attention to the discount rate. As we have emphasized, the discount rate should be our cost of capital, and our cost of capital is determined by the risk of the project. But how exactly do we measure risk and how does a particular level of risk imply a specific cost of capital?

We will see how holding many assets together affects our risk exposure. In Chapter 12, we will build on this foundation to develop a theory that explains how to determine the cost of capital for any investment opportunity. Then, in Chapter 13, we will apply what we've learned about the relation between risk and return to the cost of capital for a company as a whole.

We begin our investigation of the relationship between risk and return by looking at historical data for publicly traded securities. We will see, for example, that while stocks are riskier investments than bonds, they have also earned higher average annual returns. We interpret the higher average return on stocks versus bonds as compensation to investors for the greater risk they are taking. But we will also find that not all risk needs to be compensated. By holding a portfolio of many different investments, investors can eliminate risks that are specific to individual securities. Only risks that cannot be eliminated by holding a large portfolio determine the risk premium investors will require.

11.1   A First Look at Risk and Return

If your great-grandparents had invested only $100 in a portfolio of small companies in 1925, your family could be worth over $3 million today! As we will see, however, such a decision would have carried considerable risk and it is only with 20/20 hindsight that we know it would have been a profitable one.

We begin our look at risk and return by illustrating how the risk premium affects investor decisions and returns. Suppose your great-grandparents had indeed invested $100 on your behalf at the end of 1925. They instructed their broker to reinvest any dividends or interest earned in the account until the end of 2015. How would that $100 have grown if it were invested in one of the following?

1. Standard & Poor's 500 (S&P 500): A portfolio, constructed by Standard & Poor's, comprising 90 U.S. stocks up to 1957 and 500 U.S. stocks after that. The firms represented are leaders in their respective industries and are among the largest firms, in terms of market capitalization (share price times the number of shares in the hands of the shareholders), traded on U.S. markets.

2. Small stocks: A portfolio, updated quarterly, of U.S. stocks traded on the NYSE with market capitalizations in the bottom 20%.

3. World portfolio: A portfolio of international stocks from all of the world's major stock markets in North America, Europe, and Asia.

4. Corporate bonds: A portfolio of long-term, AAA-rated U.S. corporate bonds with maturities of approximately 20 years.[1]

5. Treasury bills: An investment in one-month U.S. Treasury bills (reinvested as the bills mature).

Figure 11.1 shows the result, through the end of 2015, of investing $100 at the end of 1925 for each of these five different investment portfolios. The results are striking—had your great-grandparents invested $100 in the small-stock portfolio, the investment would have been worth over $3.5 million at the end of 2015! On the other hand, if they had invested in Treasury bills, the investment would have been worth only $2043.

For comparison, consider how prices have changed during the same period based on the Consumer Price Index (CPI), the bottom line in Figure 11.1. From 1925–2015, small stocks

---

[1] Based on Moody's AAA Corporate Bond Index.

FIGURE 11.1

Value of $100 Invested at the End of 1925 in Small Stocks, U.S. Large Stocks (S&P 500),
World Portfolio, Corporate Bonds, and Treasury Bills

Note that the investments that performed the best in the long run also had the greatest fluctuations from year to year. The change in the Consumer Price Index (CPI) is shown as a reference point. The vertical scale is such that a given vertical distance is always the same *percentage* change (going from 10 to 100 is 10 times, just like going from $10,000 to $100,000).

Source: Global Financial Data and CRSP.

in the United States experienced the highest long-term return, followed by the large stocks in the S&P 500, the international stocks in the world portfolio, corporate bonds, and finally Treasury bills. All of the investments grew faster than inflation (as measured by the CPI).

There is a second pattern evident in Figure 11.1. While the small-stock portfolio performed the best in the long run, its value also experienced the largest fluctuations. For example, investors in small stocks had the largest loss during the Depression era of the 1930s. To illustrate, suppose that in 1925 your great-grandparents put the $100 in a small-stock portfolio intended for their own retirement 15 years later in 1940. They would have had only $144 with which to retire, compared with $217 from an investment in corporate bonds. Moreover, during the 15-year period, they would have seen the value of their investment drop as low as $15. Yet if they had invested in Treasury bills, they would not have experienced any losses during the Depression period, but would have enjoyed steady—though modest—gains each year. Indeed, when ranking the investments by the size of their increases and decreases in value, we have the same ranking as before: small stocks had the most variable returns, followed by the S&P 500, the world portfolio, corporate bonds, and finally Treasury bills.

Investors are averse to fluctuations in the value of their investments, so they demand that riskier investments have higher expected returns. But even more importantly, when times are bad, investors do not like to have their problems exacerbated by experiencing losses on their investments. In fact, even if your great-grandparents had actually put the $100 into a small-stock portfolio in 1925, it is unlikely you would have received the proceeds. More likely, in the depths of the Great Depression your great-grandparents would have turned to their investments to supplement their income. Table 11.1 presents the first 10 years of returns that correspond to several of the investments in Figure 11.1. Negative returns (losses) are in red. Notice the string of large, negative returns from 1929–1931 for small stocks. Unfortunately, your great-grandparents' small-stock portfolio would have been of little help to them in the Great Depression—in June 1932 their original $100 investment would have been worth only $15. With the benefit of 85 years of hindsight, the small-stock portfolio looks like a great investment, but in 1932 it would have seemed like a huge mistake. Perhaps this is the reason your great-grandparents did not actually invest money for you in small stocks. The pleasure of knowing that their great-grandchild might one day be a millionaire does not really make up for the pain of the investment going bust at precisely the time that the money is needed for other things.

TABLE 11.1

Realized Returns, in Percent (%) for Small Stocks, the S&P 500, Corporate Bonds, and Treasury Bills, 1926–1935

Year	Small Stocks	S&P 500	Corp Bonds	Treasury Bills
1926	−7.20	11.14	6.29	3.19
1927	25.75	37.13	6.55	3.12
1928	46.87	43.31	3.38	3.82
1929	−50.47	−8.91	4.32	4.74
1930	−45.58	−25.26	6.34	2.35
1931	−50.22	−43.86	−2.38	1.02
1932	8.70	−8.86	12.20	0.81
1933	187.20	52.89	5.26	0.29
1934	25.21	−2.34	9.73	0.15
1935	64.74	47.21	6.86	0.17

Source: Global Financial Data.

We have established the general principle that investors do not like risk and therefore demand a risk premium to bear it. Our goal in this chapter is to further understand that because investors can eliminate some risk by holding large portfolios of stocks, not all risk is entitled to a risk premium. To show this, we must first develop tools that will allow us to measure risk and return.

CONCEPT CHECK

1. Historically, which types of investments have had the highest average returns and which have been the most volatile from year to year? Is there a relation?

2. Why do investors demand a higher return when investing in riskier securities?

11.2 Historical Risks and Returns of Stocks

In this section, we explain how to compute average returns and a measure of risk, or volatility, using historical stock market data. The distribution of past returns can be useful in estimating the possible future returns for investors. We start by explaining how to compute historical returns.

Computing Historical Returns

realized return The total return that occurs over a particular time period.

We begin with *realized returns* for an individual investment and a portfolio. The **realized return** is the total return that occurs over a particular time period.

Individual Investment Realized Return. Suppose you invested $10 in a stock a month ago. Today, it paid a dividend of $0.50 and you then sold it for $11. What was your return? Your return came from two sources: the dividend and the change in price. You earned $0.50 on your $10 investment through the dividend, for a return of $0.50/$10 = 5%, and you earned $1 from the increase in price, for a return of $1/$10 or 10%. Your total return was 15%:

$$\text{Return} = \frac{\$0.50}{\$10} + \frac{(\$11 - \$10)}{\$10} = 5\% + 10\% = 15\%$$

In general, assume you buy a stock on date t for price P_t. If the stock pays a dividend, Div_{t+1}, on date $t + 1$, and you sell the stock at that time for price P_{t+1}, then the timeline of your cash flows for the stock looks like this:

The realized return from your investment in the stock from t to $t + 1$ is:

$$R_{t+1} = \frac{Div_{t+1} + P_{t+1} - P_t}{P_t} = \frac{Div_{t+1}}{P_t} + \frac{P_{t+1} - P_t}{P_t}$$

$$= \text{Dividend Yield} + \text{Capital Gain Yield} \qquad (11.1)$$

Your realized return for the period from t to $t + 1$ is the total of the dividend yield and the capital gain (as a percentage of the initial price); as discussed in Chapter 7, it is also called the *total return*. For each dollar invested at date t, you will have $1 + R_{t+1}$ at date $t + 1$. We can compute the total return for any security in the same way, by replacing the dividend payments with any cash flows paid by the security (for example, with a bond, coupon payments would replace dividends).

EXAMPLE 11.1
Realized Return

MyFinanceLab

PROBLEM

Microsoft paid a one-time special dividend of $3.08 on November 15, 2004. Suppose you bought Microsoft stock for $28.08 on November 1, 2004, and sold it immediately after the dividend was paid for $27.39. What was your realized return from holding the stock?

SOLUTION

PLAN

We can use Eq. 11.1 to calculate the realized return. We need the purchase price ($28.08), the selling price ($27.39), and the dividend ($3.08) and we are ready to proceed.

EXECUTE

Using Eq. 11.1, the return from Nov 1, 2004, until Nov 15, 2004, is equal to:

$$R_{t+1} = \frac{Div_{t+1} + P_{t+1} - P_t}{P_t} = \frac{3.08 + (27.39 - 28.08)}{28.08} = 0.0851, \text{ or } 8.51\%$$

(Continued)

This 8.51% can be broken down into the dividend yield and the capital gain yield:

$$\text{Dividend Yield} = \frac{Div_{t+1}}{P_t} = \frac{3.08}{28.08} = .1097, \text{ or } 10.97\%$$

$$\text{Capital Gain Yield} = \frac{P_{t+1} - P_t}{P_t} = \frac{27.39 - 28.08}{28.08} = -0.0246, \text{ or } -2.46\%$$

EVALUATE

These returns include both the capital gain (or in this case a capital loss) and the return generated from receiving dividends. Both dividends and capital gains contribute to the total realized return—ignoring either one would give a very misleading impression of Microsoft's performance.

If you hold the stock beyond the date of the first dividend, then to compute your return we must specify how you invest any dividends you receive in the interim. To focus on the returns of a single security, we assume that *all dividends are immediately reinvested and used to purchase additional shares of the same stock or security*. In this case, we can use Eq. 11.1 to compute a stock's return between dividend payments and then compound the returns from each dividend interval to compute the return over a longer horizon. If a stock pays dividends at the end of each quarter, with realized returns $R_1, \ldots, R_4$ each quarter, then we show the four quarterly returns for this stock as:

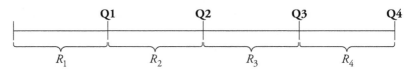

Its annual realized return, R_{annual}, is:

$$1 + R_{\text{annual}} = (1 + R_1)(1 + R_2)(1 + R_3)(1 + R_4) \tag{11.2}$$

EXAMPLE 11.2

Compounding
Realized Returns

MyFinanceLab

PROBLEM

Suppose you purchased Microsoft stock (MSFT) on Nov 1, 2004, and held it for one year, selling on Oct 31, 2005. What was your annual realized return?

SOLUTION

PLAN

We need to analyze the cash flows from holding MSFT stock for each quarter. In order to obtain the cash flows, we must look up MSFT's stock price data at the purchase date and selling date, as well as at any dividend dates (see Chapter 7 and the book's Web site for online sources of stock price and dividend data). From the data, we can construct the following table to fill out our cash flow timeline:

Date	Price	Dividend
Nov 01 04	28.08	
Nov 15 04	27.39	3.08
Feb 15 05	25.93	0.08
May 16 05	25.49	0.08
Aug 15 05	27.13	0.08
Oct 31 05	25.70	

Next, compute the realized return between each set of dates using Eq. 11.1. Then determine the annual realized return similarly to Eq. 11.2 by compounding the returns for all of the periods in the year.

EXECUTE

In Example 11.1, we already computed the realized return for November 1, 2004, to November 15, 2004, as 8.51%. We continue as in that example, using Eq. 11.1 for each period until we have a series of realized returns. For example, from November 15, 2004, to February 15, 2005, the realized return is:

$$R_{t+1} = \frac{Div_{t+1} + P_{t+1} - P_t}{P_t} = \frac{0.08 + (25.93 - 27.39)}{27.39} = -0.0504, \text{ or } -5.04\%$$

The following table includes the realized return in each period

Date	Price	Dividend	Return
Nov 01 04	28.08		
Nov 15 04	27.39	3.08	8.51%
Feb 15 05	25.93	0.08	−5.04%
May 16 05	25.49	0.08	−1.39%
Aug 15 05	27.13	0.08	6.75%
Oct 31 05	25.70		−5.27%

We then determine the one-year return by compounding.

Note that to use the method in Eq. 11.2, we must have an investment to compound, so just as in Chapter 3, when we compounded interest, we add 1 as if we are computing the outcome of investing $1. The first return is 8.51%, giving us $1 + .0851$ or 1.0851. The same is true when the return is negative: The second return is −5.04%, giving us $1 + (-.0504)$ or 0.9496. To compute the annual realized return, we simply subtract the initial $1, leaving only the return:

$$1 + R_{annual} = (1 + R_1)(1 + R_2)(1 + R_3)(1 + R_4)(1 + R_5)$$
$$1 + R_{annual} = (1.0851)(0.9496)(0.9861)(1.0675)(0.9473) = 1.0275$$
$$R_{annual} = 1.0275 - 1 = 0.0275 \text{ or } 2.75\%$$

EVALUATE

By repeating these steps, we have successfully computed the realized returns for an investor holding MSFT stock over this one-year period. From this exercise we can see that returns are risky. MSFT fluctuated up and down over the year and ended only slightly up (2.75%) at the end.

It is unlikely that anyone investing in Microsoft on November 1, 2004, expected to receive exactly the realized return we calculated in Example 11.2. In any given year we only observe one actual realized return from all of the possible returns that could have been realized. However, we can observe realized returns over many years. By counting the number of times the realized return falls in a particular range, we can start to graph the distribution of possible returns. Let's illustrate this process with the data in Table 11.1.

In Figure 11.2, we plot the annual returns for each U.S. investment in Table 11.1 in a histogram. In this histogram, the height of each bar represents the number of years that the annual returns were in each range indicated on the x-axis. Notice how much more variable stock returns are compared to Treasury bills.

Average Annual Returns

average annual return
The arithmetic average of an investment's realized returns for each year.

Out of the distribution of possible returns for each security depicted in Figure 11.2, we want to know the most likely return, represented by the average. The **average annual return** of an investment during some historical period is simply the average of the realized returns

FIGURE 11.2

The Distribution of
Annual Returns for U.S.
Large Company Stocks
(S&P 500), Small
Stocks, Corporate
Bonds, and Treasury
Bills, 1926–2015

The height of each bar represents the number of years that the annual returns were in each range. For example, the bar in the T-bills chart indicates that in more than 50% of the years, the annual return on one-month Treasury bills was between 0 and 5%. Note the greater variability of stock returns (especially small stocks) compared to the returns of corporate bonds or Treasury bills.

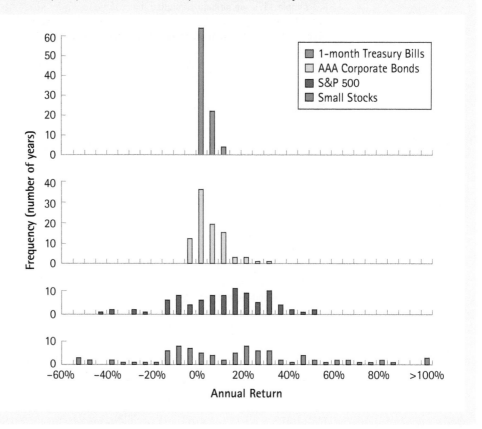

for each year. That is, if R_t is the realized return of a security in each year t, then the average annual return for years 1 through T is:

Average Annual Return of a Security

$$\overline{R} = \frac{1}{T}(R_1 + R_2 + \cdots + R_T) \qquad (11.3)$$

If we assume that the distribution of possible returns is the same over time, the average return provides an estimate of the return we should expect in any given year—the expected return. This idea is not unique to returns. For example, a Starbucks manager cannot know exactly how many customers she will have today, but by looking at the average number of customers who have come in historically, she can form an expectation to use in staffing and stocking.

We can use Eq. 11.3 to calculate the average return for the S&P 500 for the years 2005–2009. The returns are:

2005	2006	2007	2008	2009
4.9%	15.8%	5.5%	−37.0%	26.5%

and the average return is:

$$\frac{1}{5}\left(4.9\% + 15.8\% + 5.5\% - 37.0\% + 26.5\%\right) = 3.1\%$$

The average Treasury bill return during the same period was 2.0%. Therefore, investors earned 1.1% $(3.1\% - 2.0\%)$ more on average holding the S&P 500 than investing in Treasury bills during this period. This average is computed over just five years of data. Naturally, our estimate of the true average of the distribution is more precise the more data we use. We display the average returns for different U.S. investments from 1926–2012 in Figure 11.3.

Arithmetic Average Returns Versus Compound Annual Returns

In Figure 11.1, we saw that $100 invested in the S&P 500 at the end of 1925 would have grown to $487,210 by the end of 2015. What if we wanted to know the average compound annual return for that investment? That's the same as asking what return, earned each year for 90 years, would have caused our $100 to grow into $487,210. We know that the formula for future value tells us that:

$$FV = PV(1 + R)^n$$

Thus:

$$\$487,210 = \$100(1 + R)^{90}$$

Solving for R, we get 9.894% (rounded).

But Figure 11.3 shows that the average annual return for the S&P 500 for this period was 11.84%. How can the two answers be different?

The difference is due to the fact that returns are volatile. To see the effect of volatility, suppose an investment has annual returns of +20% one year and −20% the next. The average annual return is:

$$\frac{20\% + (-20\%)}{2} = 0\%$$

But the value of $1 invested after two years is:

$$\$1 \times (1 + 0.20) \times (1 - 0.20) = \$0.96$$

This tells us that an investor would have lost money. Why? Because the 20% gain happens on a $1 investment for a total of 20 cents, whereas the 20% loss happens on a larger investment of $1.20. The loss is 20% of $1.20, or 24 cents.

$$+20\%(\$1) = +\$0.20 \qquad \overset{\$1.20}{\diagup} \qquad -20\%(\$1.20) = -\$0.24$$
$$\$1.00 \text{\textemdash\textemdash\textemdash\textemdash\textemdash\textemdash\textemdash\textemdash\textemdash\textemdash\textemdash\textemdash\textemdash\textemdash} \searrow$$
$$\$0.96$$

In this case, the compound annual return is

$$\$0.96 = \$1(1 + R)^2$$

so solving for R:

$$R = (0.96)^{1/2} - 1 = -2\%$$

We calculated the 11.84% average for the S&P 500 as a simple arithmetic average of the realized returns, while we calculated 9.9% as the average annual compound return that corresponds to the total gain on our $100 investment (called the *geometric average*).

Which is a better description of an investment's return? The compound annual return is a better description of the long-term *historical performance* of an investment. It describes the average annual compound return for that particular history of returns. The ranking of the long-term performance of different investments coincides with the ranking of their compound annual returns. Thus, the compound annual return is the return that is most often used for comparison purposes. For example, mutual funds generally report their compound annual returns over the last five or ten years.

On the other hand, the arithmetic average return should be used when trying to estimate an investment's *expected* return over a *future* horizon based on its past performance. If we view past annual returns as independent realizations of actual returns from the same set of possible returns, then we know from statistics that the arithmetic average provides the best estimate of the true mean. If the investment above is equally likely to have annual returns of +20% and −20% in the future, then the payoff from a $1 investment after two years will be:

25% of the time: $1 × (1.20) × (1.20) = $1.44
50% of the time: $1 × (1.20) × (0.80)
$$= (0.80) \times (1.20) = \$0.96$$
25% of the time: $1 × (0.80) × (0.80) = $0.64

The expected payoff is

$$25\% (1.44) + 50\% (0.96) + 25\% (0.64) = \$1$$

which is consistent with the arithmetic average return of 0%.

FIGURE 11.3

Average Annual
Returns of U.S. Small
Stocks, Large Stocks
(S&P 500), Corporate
Bonds, and Treasury
Bills, 1926–2015

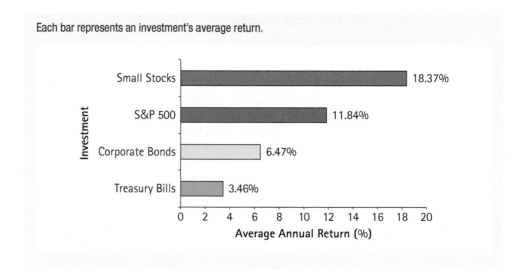

Each bar represents an investment's average return.

Small Stocks — 18.37%
S&P 500 — 11.84%
Corporate Bonds — 6.47%
Treasury Bills — 3.46%

Investment (vertical axis)
Average Annual Return (%) (horizontal axis: 0 2 4 6 8 10 12 14 16 18 20)

The Variance and Volatility of Returns

Looking at Figure 11.2, we can see that the variability of the returns is very different for each investment. The distribution of small stocks' returns is the most widely dispersed—if you had invested in these stocks, you would have lost more than 50% in some years and gained more than 100% in some years! The large company stocks in the S&P 500 have returns that vary less than small company stocks, but much more than corporate bonds or Treasury bills. While we can see these differences in variability in the chart, we need a way to formally quantify them. To determine the variability of returns, we calculate the *standard deviation* of the distribution of realized returns. The **standard deviation** is the square root of the *variance* of the distribution of realized returns. **Variance** measures the variability in returns by taking the differences of the returns from the average return and squaring those differences. We have to square the difference of each return from the average because, by definition, the unsquared differences from an average must sum to zero. Because we square the returns, the variance is in units of "%^{2}" or percent-squared. That is not very useful to us, so we take the square root, to get the standard deviation, in units of %.

While that sounds a bit abstract, standard deviation simply indicates the tendency of the historical returns to be different from their average and how far from the average they tend to be. Standard deviation therefore captures our intuition of risk: How often will we miss the mark and how far off will we be? Formally, we calculate the variance with the following equation:[2]

standard deviation A common method used to measure the risk of a probability distribution; it is the square root of the variance.

variance A method to measure the variability of returns; it is the expected squared deviation of returns from the mean.

Variance Estimate Using Realized Returns

$$Var(R) = \frac{1}{T-1}[(R_1 - \overline{R})^2 + (R_2 - \overline{R})^2 + \cdots + (R_T - \overline{R})^2] \qquad (11.4)$$

[2]You may wonder why we divide by $T - 1$ rather than T here. The reason is that we are not computing deviations from the true expected return; instead, we are computing deviations from the estimated average return $\overline{R}$. Because the average return is derived from the same data, we lose a degree of freedom (in essence, we have used up one of the data points), so that when computing the variance there are really only $T - 1$ additional data points on which to base it.

The standard deviation, which we will call the *volatility*, is the square root of the variance:[3]

$$SD(R) = \sqrt{Var(R)} \tag{11.5}$$

EXAMPLE 11.3

Computing Historical Volatility

MyFinanceLab

PROBLEM

Using the following data, what is the standard deviation of the S&P 500's returns for the years 2005–2009?

2005	2006	2007	2008	2009
4.9%	15.8%	5.5%	−37.0%	26.5%

SOLUTION

PLAN

With the five returns, compute the average return using Eq. 11.3 because it is an input to the variance equation. Next, compute the variance using Eq. 11.4 and then take its square root to determine the standard deviation, as shown in Eq. 11.5.

EXECUTE

In the previous section we computed the average annual return of the S&P 500 during this period as 3.1%, so we have all of the necessary inputs for the variance calculation:
Applying Eq.11.4, we have:

$$Var(R) = \frac{1}{T-1}[(R_1 - \bar{R})^2 + (R_2 - \bar{R})^2 + \ldots + (R_T - \bar{R})^2]$$

$$= \frac{1}{5-1}[(.049 - .031)^2 + (.158 - .031)^2 + (.055 - .031)^2$$

$$+ (-.370 - .031)^2 + (.265 - .031)^2]$$

$$= .058$$

Alternatively, we can break out the calculation of this equation as follows:

	2005	2006	2007	2008	2009
Return	0.049	0.158	0.055	−0.370	0.265
Average	0.031	0.031	0.031	0.031	0.031
Difference	0.018	0.127	0.024	−0.401	0.234
Squared	0.000	0.016	0.001	0.161	0.055

Summing the squared differences in the last row, we get 0.233.

Finally, dividing by $(5 - 1 = 4)$ gives us 0.233/4 = 0.058. The standard deviation is therefore:

$$SD(R) = \sqrt{Var(R)} = \sqrt{.058} = 0.241, \text{ or } 24.1\%$$

EVALUATE

Our best estimate of the expected return for the S&P 500 is its average return, 3.1%, but it is risky, with a standard deviation of 24.1%.

---

[3]If the returns used in Eq. 11.4 are not annual returns, it is conventional to convert the variance to annual terms by multiplying the number of returns per year. Thus, when using monthly returns, we multiply the variance by 12, and equivalently, the standard deviation by $\sqrt{12}$.

Mistakes When Computing Standard Deviation

Example 11.3 highlights two missteps often made in computing standard deviations.

1. Remember to divide by ONE LESS than the number of returns you have ($T-1$, NOT T).

2. Don't forget to take the square root of the variance to obtain the standard deviation. You are not done when you calculate the variance—you have one more step to go.

We began our review of statistics with the goal of being able to quantify the difference in the variability of the distributions that we observed in Figure 11.2. We can now do so with the standard deviation of the returns on the U.S. investments as shown in Figure 11.4.

Comparing the standard deviations in Figure 11.4 we see that, as expected, small companies have had the most variable historical returns, followed by large companies. The returns of corporate bonds and Treasury bills are much less variable than stocks, with Treasury bills being the least volatile investment category.

USING EXCEL

Computing the
Standard Deviation
of Historical
Returns

1. Enter or import the historical returns into Excel.
2. Next, highlight the cell where you want to produce the standard deviation and select **Function** from the **Insert** tab.
3. Select the "**STDEV**" function, highlight the returns for which you want to compute the average, and click **OK**.

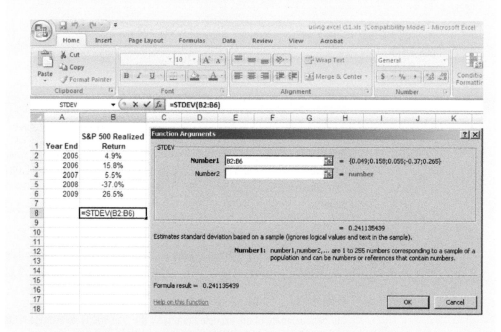

4. *Make sure that you use the STDEV function and NOT the STDEVP function.* STDEV calculates the sample standard deviation as in Eqs. 11.4 and 11.5, by dividing by $T-1$. STDEVP assumes that you know with certainty the true mean and calculates the standard deviation by dividing by T. See footnote 2 for more discussion of this important distinction.

FIGURE 11.4

Volatility (Standard Deviation) of U.S. Small Stocks, Large Stocks (S&P 500), Corporate Bonds, and Treasury Bills, 1926–2015

Each bar represents the standard deviation of the investment's returns.

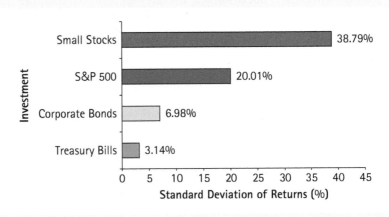

The Normal Distribution

normal distribution A symmetric probability distribution that is completely characterized by its average and standard deviation. About 95% of all possible outcomes fall within two standard deviations above and below the average.

The standard deviations that we have computed in Figure 11.4 are useful for more than just ranking the investments from most to least risky. The standard deviation also plays an important role in describing a **normal distribution**, shown in Figure 11.5, which is a symmetric probability distribution that is completely characterized by its average and standard deviation. Importantly, about two-thirds of all possible outcomes fall within one standard deviation above or below the average, and about 95% of all possible outcomes fall within two standard deviations above and below the average. Figure 11.5 shows these outcomes for small company stocks.

FIGURE 11.5

Normal Distribution

The height of the line reflects the likelihood of each return occurring. Using the data from Figures 11.3 and 11.4, if the returns of small companies are normally distributed, then about two-thirds of all possible outcomes should lie within one standard deviation of the average return of 18.37% (given in Figure 11.3) and about 95% should lie within two standard deviations. Figure 11.4 shows the standard deviation to be 38.79%, so that puts 95% of possible outcomes between −59.21% and +95.95% (the shaded area of the distribution).

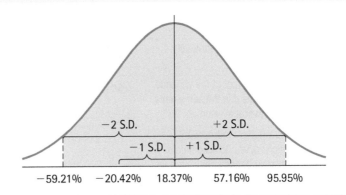

prediction interval A range of values that is likely to include a future observation. A 95% prediction interval should have a 95% chance of including the observed future observation.

Because about 95% of the time, next year's return will be within two standard deviations of the average, we say that the 95% **prediction interval** runs from [the average − 2 × standard deviation] to [the average + 2 × standard deviation]:

$$\text{Average} \pm (2 \times \text{standard deviation})$$
$$\bar{R} \pm (2 \times SD(R)) \tag{11.6}$$

Table 11.2 summarizes the central concepts and equations that we developed in this section. Calculating historical averages and volatilities indicates how investments performed in the past and might perform in the future. Of course, using the past to predict the future is fraught with uncertainty. In the next section, we will discuss that uncertainty.

EXAMPLE 11.4

Prediction Intervals

MyFinanceLab

PROBLEM

In Example 11.3, we found the average return for the S&P 500 from 2005 to 2009 to be 3.1% with a standard deviation of 24.1%. What is a 95% prediction interval for 2010's return?

SOLUTION

PLAN

We can use Eq. 11.6 to compute the prediction interval.

EXECUTE

Using Eq. 11.6, we have:

$$\text{Average} \pm (2 \times \text{standard deviation}) = 3.1\% - (2 \times 24.1\%) \text{ to } 3.1\% + (2 \times 24.1\%)$$
$$= -45.1\% \text{ to } 51.3\%.$$

EVALUATE

Even though the average return from 2005 to 2009 was 3.1%, the S&P 500 was volatile, so if we want to be 95% confident of 2010's return, the best we can say is that it will lie between −45.1% and +51.3%.

TABLE 11.2

Summary of Tools for Working with Historical Returns

Concept	Definition	Formula
Realized Returns	Total return earned over a particular period of time	$R_{t+1} = \dfrac{Div_{t+1} + P_{t+1} - P_t}{P_t}$
Average Annual Return	Average of realized returns for each year	$\bar{R} = \dfrac{1}{T}(R_1 + R_2 + \cdots + R_T)$
Variance of Returns	A measure of the variability of returns	$Var(R) = \dfrac{1}{T-1}[(R_1 - \bar{R})^2 + (R_2 - \bar{R})^2 + \cdots + (R_T - \bar{R})^2]$
Standard Deviation or Volatility of Returns	The square root of the variance (which puts it in the same units as the average—namely "%")	$SD(R) = \sqrt{Var(R)}$
95% Prediction Interval	The range of returns within which we are 95% confident that next period's return will lie	$\bar{R} \pm 2 \times SD(R)$

CONCEPT CHECK

3. For what purpose do we use the average and standard deviation of historical stock returns?

4. How does the standard deviation of historical returns affect our confidence in predicting the next period's return?

11.3 The Historical Tradeoff Between Risk and Return

Would you intentionally choose to accept additional risk without additional reward? In other words, are you willing to pursue riskier investments if they do not have the potential to generate higher returns? The answer to both of these questions is most likely "no." In this section, we will examine the historical tradeoff between risk (as measured by price volatility) and reward (as measured by returns) to see if historically investors behaved as you would.

The Returns of Large Portfolios

In Figures 11.3 and 11.4, we showed the historical average returns and volatilities for a number of different types of investments. In Figure 11.6, we plot the average return versus the volatility of each type of investment from those tables. We also include the world portfolio from Figure 11.1. Note that the investments with higher volatility, measured here with standard deviation, have rewarded investors with higher average returns. Figure 11.6 is consistent with our view that investors are risk averse. Riskier investments must offer investors higher average returns to compensate for the risk they are taking.

The Returns of Individual Stocks

Figure 11.6 suggests the following simple model of the risk premium: Investments with higher volatility should have a higher risk premium and therefore higher returns. Indeed, looking at the dotted line in Figure 11.6, it is tempting to conclude that all investments should lie on or near this line—that is, expected return should rise proportionately with volatility. This conclusion appears to be approximately true for the large portfolios we have looked at so far. Is it correct? Does it apply to individual stocks?

FIGURE 11.6

The Historical Tradeoff Between Risk and Return in Large Portfolios, 1926–2014

Note the general increasing relationship between historical volatility and average return for these large portfolios. In addition to the portfolios in Figure 11.1, also included is a mid-cap portfolio composed of the 10% of U.S. stocks whose size is just above the median of all U.S. stocks. (Data from 1926–2014.)

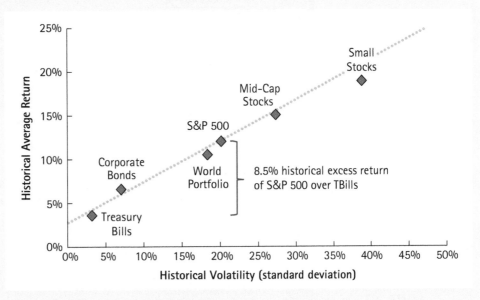

Source: CRSP, Morgan Stanley Capital International.

Actually, the answer to both questions is no. There is no clear relationship between volatility and returns for individual stocks. Figure 11.7 shows that, if we look at the volatility and return of individual stocks, we do not see any clear relationship between them. Each point represents the volatility and average return from investing in the *N*th largest stock traded in the United States (updated annually) for *N* = 1 to 500. Although it will take more work to establish the relation between risk and return for individual stocks, the following is true:

1. There is a relationship between size and risk—on average larger stocks have lower volatility than smaller stocks.

2. Even the largest stocks are typically more volatile than a portfolio of large stocks, such as the S&P 500.

3. All individual stocks have lower returns and/or higher risk than the portfolios in Figure 11.6.

Thus, while volatility (standard deviation) seems to be a reasonable measure of risk when evaluating a large portfolio, the volatility of an individual security doesn't explain the size of its average return. What are we to make of this? Why wouldn't investors demand a higher return from stocks with a higher volatility? And how is it that the S&P 500, a portfolio of 500 large stocks, is so much less risky than almost all of the 500 stocks individually? To answer these questions, we need to think more carefully about how to measure risk for an investor.

FIGURE 11.7

Historical Volatility and Return for 500 Individual Stocks, Ranked Annually by Size

Unlike the case for large portfolios, there is no precise relationship between volatility and average return for individual stocks. Individual stocks have higher volatility and lower average returns than the relationship shown for large portfolios. (Annual data from 1926–2014.)

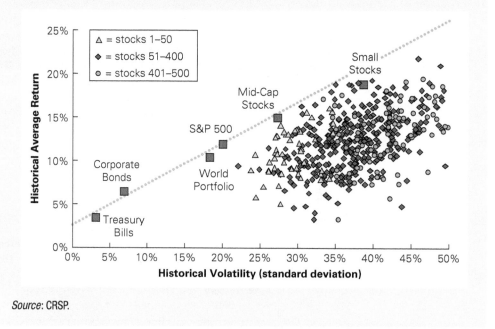

Source: CRSP.

CONCEPT CHECK

5. What is the relation between risk and return for large portfolios? How are individual stocks different?

6. Do portfolios or the stocks in the portfolios tend to have the lower volatility?

11.4 Common Versus Independent Risk

In this section, we explain why the risk of an individual security differs from the risk of a portfolio composed of similar securities. We begin with an example from the insurance industry to understand how the portfolio of insurance products performs for the insurance company offering them.

Theft Versus Earthquake Insurance: An Example

Consider two types of home insurance an insurance company might offer: theft insurance and earthquake insurance. Let's assume, for the purpose of illustration, that the risk of each of these two hazards is similar for a given home in the San Francisco area—each year there is about a 1% chance the home will be robbed and also a 1% chance that the home will be damaged by an earthquake. In this case, the chance the insurance company will pay a claim for a single home is the same for the two types of insurance policies. Suppose an insurance company writes 100,000 policies of each type for homeowners in San Francisco. We know the risks of the individual policies are similar, but are the risks of the portfolios of 100,000 policies similar?

First consider theft insurance. Because the chance of a theft for any given home is 1%, we would expect about 1% of the 100,000 homes to experience a robbery. Thus, the number of theft claims will be about 1000 per year. The actual number of claims may be a bit higher or lower each year, but not by much. In this case, if the insurance company holds reserves sufficient to cover 1200 claims, it will almost certainly have enough to cover its obligations on its theft insurance policies.

Now consider earthquake insurance. There is a 99% chance that an earthquake will not occur. All the homes are in the same city, so if an earthquake does occur, all homes are likely to be affected and the insurance company can expect 100,000 claims. As a result, the insurance company can expect either 0 claims or 100,000 claims. Because it may have 100,000 claims, it will have to hold reserves of cash (or other investments) sufficient to cover claims on all 100,000 policies it wrote in order to meet its obligations if an earthquake occurs.

Thus, earthquake and theft insurance lead to portfolios with very different risk characteristics. For earthquake insurance, the percentage of claims is very risky—it will most likely be 0, but there is a 1% chance that the insurance company will have to pay claims on *all* the policies it wrote. So the risk of the portfolio of earthquake insurance policies is no different from the risk of any single policy. On the other hand, we've seen that for theft insurance the number of claims in a given year is quite predictable. Year in and year out, it will be very close to 1% of the total number of policies, or 1000 claims. The portfolio of theft insurance policies has almost no risk! That is, the insurance company's payouts are quite stable and predictable over time.

common risk Risk that is linked across outcomes.

Types of Risk

Why are the portfolios of insurance policies so different when the individual policies themselves are quite similar? Intuitively, the key difference between them is that an earthquake affects all houses simultaneously, and so the risk is linked across homes, meaning either all homes are damaged or all homes are not damaged. We call risk that is linked in this way **common risk**. In contrast, we have assumed that thefts in different houses are not related to each other—whether one house is burglarized has no effect on another house's chance of being burglarized. **Independent risk**, such as the risk of theft, is not linked across homes. When risks are independent, some individual homeowners are unlucky, others are lucky, but overall the number of claims is similar. The averaging out of risks in a large portfolio is called **diversification**.[4] Table 11.3 summarizes our discussion of common and independent risk.

independent risk Risks that bear no relation to each other. If risks are independent, then knowing the outcome of one provides no information about the other.

diversification The averaging of independent risks in a large portfolio.

---

[4]Harry Markowitz was the first to formalize the benefits from diversification. See H.M. Markowitz, "Portfolio Selection," *Journal of Finance*, 7(1) (1952): 77–91.

TABLE 11.3

Summary of Types of Risk

Type of Risk	Definition	Example	Risk Diversified in Large Portfolio?
Common Risk	Linked across outcomes	Risk of earthquake	No
Independent Risk	Risks that bear no relation to each other	Risk of theft	Yes

The principle of diversification is used routinely in the insurance industry. In addition to theft insurance, many other forms of insurance (life, health, auto) rely on the fact that the number of claims is relatively predictable in a large portfolio. Even in the case of earthquake insurance, insurers can achieve some diversification by selling policies in different geographical regions, or by combining different types of policies. Diversification is used to reduce risk in many other settings. For example, many systems are designed with redundancy to decrease the risk of a disruption. For example, firms often add redundancy to critical parts of the manufacturing process: NASA puts more than one antenna on its space probes, and automobiles contain spare tires.

In many settings, the risks lie somewhere between the common risks and independent risks. For example, you probably applied to more than one college. Your chances of being accepted (or rejected) at any one school are not perfectly linked across schools because schools have different admissions criteria and are looking for different types of students. However, your risk of rejection is not completely independent, either; all schools look at your high school grades and SAT/ACT scores, so their decisions will be related.

EXAMPLE 11.5

Diversification

MyFinanceLab

PROBLEM

You are playing a very simple gambling game with your friend: a $1 bet based on a coin flip. That is, you each bet $1 and flip a coin: heads you win your friend's $1, tails you lose and your friend takes your dollar. How is your risk different if you play this game 100 times versus just betting $100 (instead of $1) on a single coin flip?

SOLUTION

PLAN

The risk of losing one coin flip is independent of the risk of losing the next one: Each time you have a 50% chance of losing, and one coin flip does not affect any other coin flip. We can compute the expected outcome of any flip as a weighted average by weighting your possible winnings (+$1) by 50% and your possible losses (−$1) by 50%. We can then compute the probability of losing all $100 under either scenario.

EXECUTE

If you play the game 100 times, you should lose 50 times and win 50 times, so your expected outcome is $50 \times (+\$1) + 50 \times (-\$1) = \$0$. You should break even. But even if you don't win exactly half of the time, the probability that you would lose all 100 coin flips (and thus lose $100) is exceedingly small (in fact, it is 0.50^{100}, which is far less than even 0.0001%). If it happens, you should take a very careful look at the coin!

If instead you make a single $100 bet on the outcome of one coin flip, you have a 50% chance of winning $100 and a 50% chance of losing $100, so your expected outcome will be the same: break-even. However, there is a 50% chance you will lose $100, so your risk is far greater than it would be for 100 one-dollar bets.

EVALUATE

In each case, you put $100 at risk, but by spreading out that risk across 100 different bets, you have diversified much of your risk away, compared to placing a single $100 bet.

CONCEPT CHECK

7. What is the difference between common and independent risk?

8. How does diversification help with independent risk?

11.5 Diversification in Stock Portfolios

As the insurance example indicates, the risk of a portfolio depends upon whether the individual risks within it are common or independent. Independent risks are diversified in a large portfolio, whereas common risks are not. Our goal is to understand the relation between risk and return in the capital markets, so let's consider the implication of this distinction for the risk of stock portfolios.

Unsystematic Versus Systematic Risk

Over any given time period, the risk of holding a stock is that the dividends plus the final stock price will be higher or lower than expected, which makes the realized return risky. What causes dividends or stock prices, and therefore returns, to be higher or lower than we expect? Usually, stock prices and dividends fluctuate due to two types of news:

1. *Company or industry-specific news*: This is good or bad news about a company (or industry) itself. For example, a firm might announce that it has been successful in gaining market share within its industry. Or, the home-building industry may be damaged by a real estate slowdown.

2. *Market-wide news*: This is news that affects the economy as a whole and therefore affects all stocks. For instance, the Federal Reserve might announce that it will lower interest rates in an attempt to boost the economy.

Fluctuations of a stock's return that are due to company- or industry-specific news are independent risks. Similar to theft across homes, these are unrelated across stocks. This type of risk is also referred to as **unsystematic risk.**

unsystematic risk
Fluctuations of a stock's return that are due to company- or industry-specific news and are independent risks unrelated across stocks.

On the other hand, fluctuations of a stock's return that are due to market-wide news represent common risk. As with earthquakes, all stocks are affected simultaneously. This type of risk is also called **systematic risk**.

When we combine many stocks in a large portfolio, the unsystematic risks for each stock will average out and be eliminated by diversification. Good news will affect some stocks and bad news will affect others, but the amount of good or bad news overall will be relatively constant. The systematic risk, however, will affect all firms—and therefore the entire portfolio—and will not be eliminated by diversification.

systematic risk
Fluctuations of a stock's return that are due to market-wide news representing common risk.

Let's consider a hypothetical example. Suppose type S firms are *only* affected by the systematic risk of the strength of the economy, which has a 50-50 chance of being either strong or weak. If the economy is strong, type S stocks will earn a return of 40%, and if the economy is weak, their return will be −20%. Because the risk these firms face (the strength of the economy) is systematic risk, holding a large portfolio of type S stocks will not diversify the risk. When the economy is strong, the portfolio will have the same return of 40% as each type S firm. When the economy is weak, the portfolio will also have a return of −20%.

Now consider type U firms, which are only affected by unsystematic risks. Their returns are equally likely to be 35% or −25%, based on factors specific to each firm's local market. Because these risks are firm-specific, if we hold a portfolio of many type U stocks, the risk is diversified. About half of the firms will have returns of 35%, and half will have returns of −25%. The return of the portfolio will be the average return of 50% $(0.35) + 50% (-0.25) = .05$ or 5%, no matter whether the economy is strong or weak.

Figure 11.8 illustrates how volatility, measured by standard deviation, declines with the size of the portfolio for type S and type U firms. Type S firms have only systematic risk. Similar to earthquake insurance, the volatility of the portfolio does not change as we increase the number of firms. Type U firms have only unsystematic risk. As with theft insurance, the risk is diversified as the number of firms increases, and volatility declines. As is evident from Figure 11.8, with a large number of firms, Type U firms' risk is, essentially, completely eliminated.

Of course, actual firms are not similar to type S or type U firms. Firms are affected by both systematic, market-wide risks, as well as unsystematic risks. Figure 11.8 also shows

FIGURE 11.8

Volatility of
Portfolios of Type S
and Type U Stocks

Because type S firms have only systematic risk, the volatility of the portfolio does not change. Type U firms have only unsystematic risk, which is diversified and eliminated as the number of firms in the portfolio grows. Typical stocks carry a mix of both types of risk, so that the risk of the portfolio declines as unsystematic risk is diversified, but systematic risk remains.

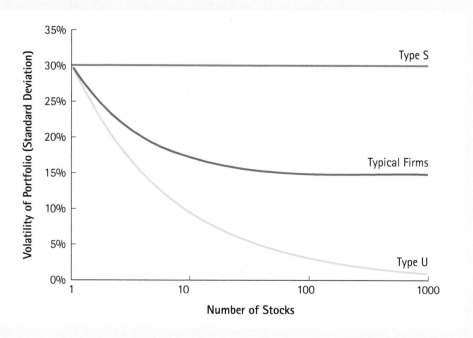

how the volatility changes with the number of stocks in a portfolio of typical firms. *When firms carry both types of risk, only the unsystematic risk will be eliminated by diversification when we combine many firms into a portfolio. The volatility will therefore decline until only the systematic risk, which affects all firms, remains.*

This example explains one of the puzzles from Section 11.3. There we saw that the S&P 500 had much lower volatility than any of the individual stocks. Now we can see why—the individual stocks each contain unsystematic risk, which is eliminated when we combine them into a large portfolio. Thus, the portfolio can have lower volatility than each of the stocks within it. Figure 11.9 illustrates this fact. The dotted lines show the extremes of the range of returns of a portfolio of Intel and Ford. The returns of each of the two stocks in the portfolio cross each of these extremes. Thus, the volatility of the portfolio is lower than the volatility of both of the stocks in the portfolio.

GLOBAL FINANCIAL CRISIS

Diversification Benefits During Market Crashes

The figure on page 357 illustrates the benefits of diversification over the last 40 years. The blue graph shows the historical volatility of the S&P 500 portfolio (annualized based on daily returns each quarter). The pink graph is the average volatility of the individual stocks in the portfolio (weighted according to the size of each stock). Thus, the pink shaded area is idiosyncratic risk—risk that has been diversified away by holding the portfolio. The blue area is market risk which cannot be diversified.

Market volatility clearly varies, increasing dramatically during times of crisis. But notice also that the fraction of risk that can be diversified away also varies, and seems to decline during times

of crisis. For example, since 1970, on average about 50% of the volatility of individual stocks is diversifiable (i.e., the pink area is about 50% of the total). But as the figure demonstrates, during the 1987 stock market crash, the 2008 financial crisis, and the recent Eurozone debt crisis, this fraction fell dramatically, so that only about 20% of the volatility of individual stocks could be diversified. The combined effect of increased volatility and reduced diversification during the 2008 financial crisis was so severe that the risk that investors care about—market risk—increased *seven*-fold, from 10% to 70%, between 2006 and the last quarter of 2008.

Although you are always better off diversifying, it is important to keep in mind that the benefits of diversification depend on economic conditions. In times of extreme crisis, the benefits may go down, making downturns in the market particularly painful for investors.

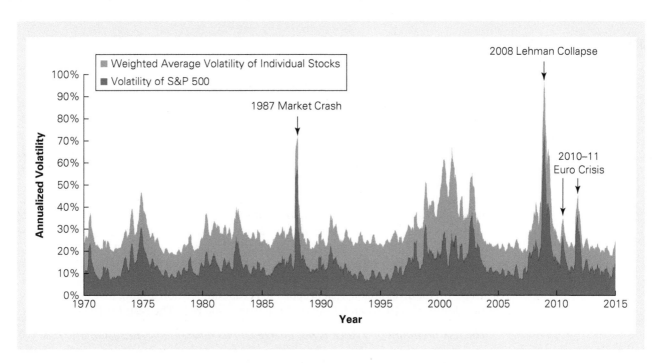

FIGURE 11.9

The Effect of
Diversification on
Portfolio Volatility

While Ford and Intel are each very volatile, some of their movements offset each other. If they are in a portfolio together, as represented by the green bars, the total movement of the portfolio is muted relative to the movement of either of the individual stocks. The dotted lines show the highest and lowest returns of the portfolio—note that the portfolio's worst return is better than the worst return of either stock on its own.

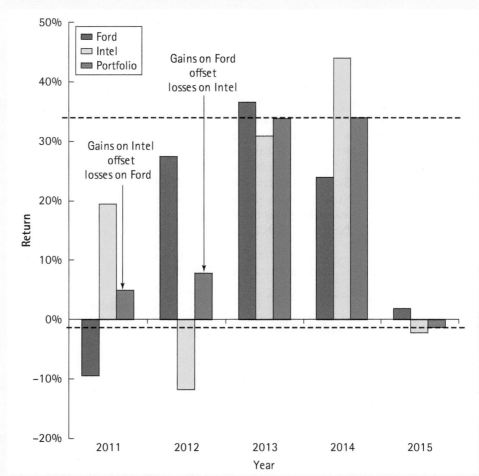

Diversifiable Risk and the Risk Premium

What if you hold only one or two stocks—wouldn't you be exposed to unsystematic risk and demand a premium for it? If the market compensated you with an additional risk premium for choosing to bear diversifiable risk, then other investors could buy the same stocks, earn the additional premium, while putting them in a portfolio so that they could diversify and eliminate the unsystematic risk. By doing so, investors could earn an additional premium without taking additional risk!

This opportunity to earn something for nothing is an arbitrage opportunity as we discussed in Chapter 3, and so it is something investors would find very attractive. As more and more investors take advantage of this situation and purchase shares that pay a risk premium for diversifiable, unsystematic risk, the current share price of those firms would rise, lowering their expected return—recall that the current share price P_t is the denominator when computing the stock's return as in Eq. 11.1. This trading would stop only when the risk premium for diversifiable risk dropped to zero. Competition among investors ensures that no additional return can be earned for diversifiable risk. The result is that

The risk premium of a stock is not affected by its diversifiable, unsystematic risk.

This argument is essentially an application of the Valuation Principle's Law of One Price. Imagine a large portfolio of type U firms, which have no systematic risk. As depicted in Figure 11.8, a large portfolio of type U firms eliminates all unsystematic risk, leaving no additional risk. Since that portfolio has no risk, it cannot earn a risk premium and instead must earn the risk-free interest rate. This line of reasoning suggests the following more general principle:

The risk premium for diversifiable risk is zero. Thus, investors are not compensated for holding unsystematic risk.

The Importance of Systematic Risk

Because investors can eliminate unsystematic risk "for free" by diversifying their portfolios, they will not require (nor deserve) a reward or risk premium for bearing it. On the other hand, diversification does not reduce systematic risk: Even when holding a large portfolio, an investor will be exposed to risks that affect the entire economy and therefore affect all securities. We can reduce the systematic risk of a portfolio by selling stocks and investing in risk-free bonds, but at the cost of giving up the higher expected return of stocks. Because unsystematic risk can be eliminated for free by diversifying, whereas systematic risk can only be eliminated by sacrificing expected returns, it is a security's systematic risk that determines the risk premium investors require to hold it. This fact, summarized in Table 11.4, leads to the second key principle:

The risk premium of a security is determined by its systematic risk and does not depend on its diversifiable risk.

TABLE 11.4

Systematic Risk Versus Unsystematic Risk

	Diversifiable?	Requires a Risk Premium?
Systematic Risk	No	Yes
Unsystematic Risk	Yes	No

This principle implies that a stock's volatility, which is a measure of total risk (that is, systematic risk + unsystematic risk), is not useful in determining the risk premium that investors will earn. For example, consider again type S and type U firms. As shown in Figure 11.8, the volatility (standard deviation) of a single type S or type U firm is 30%. However, as Table 11.5 shows, although they have the same volatility, type S firms have an expected return of 10% and type U firms have an expected return of 5%.

TABLE 11.5

The Expected Return of Type S and Type U Firms, Assuming the Risk-Free Rate Is 5%

	S Firm	U Firm
Volatility (standard deviation)	30%	30%
Risk-Free Rate	5%	5%
Risk Premium	5%	0%
Expected Return	10%	5%

The difference in expected returns is due to the difference in the kind of risk each firm bears. Type U firms have only unsystematic risk, which does not require a risk premium, and so the expected return of 5% for type U firms equals the risk-free interest rate. Type S firms have only systematic risk. Because investors will require compensation for this risk, the expected return of 10% for type S firms provides investors with a 5% risk premium above the risk-free interest rate.

We now have an explanation for the second puzzle from Section 11.3. While volatility or standard deviation might be a reasonable measure of risk for a large portfolio, it is not appropriate for an individual security.

Thus, there is no relationship between volatility and average returns for individual securities.

Consequently, to estimate a security's expected return we need to find a measure of a security's systematic risk.

We began this chapter by showing in Figure 11.1 that your great-grandparents' investment in small stocks would have lost a lot of money in the Depression, potentially leaving them in dire straits. Thus, risk-averse investors will demand a premium to invest in securities that will do poorly in bad times. This idea coincides with the notion of systematic risk we have defined in this chapter. Economy-wide risk, the risk of recessions and booms, is systematic risk that cannot be diversified. Therefore, an asset that moves with the economy contains systematic risk and so requires a risk premium. In Chapter 12, we will discuss how to measure an investment's systematic risk and then use that measure to compute its expected return. We can then apply that return expected by investors as our cost of capital.

COMMON MISTAKE

A Fallacy of Long-Run Diversification

We have seen that investors can greatly reduce risk by dividing their investment dollars over many different investments, eliminating the diversifiable risk in their portfolios. It is sometimes argued that the same logic applies over time: By investing for many years, we can also diversify the risk we face during any particular year. Thus, young investors should choose risky portfolios because they have more time to make up their losses. Is this correct? In the long run, does risk still matter?

It is true that if returns each year are independent, the volatility of the average annual return does decline with the number of years that we invest. But, as long-term investors, we don't care about the volatility of our *average* return; instead we care about the volatility of our *cumulative* return over the period. This volatility grows with the investment horizon, as illustrated in the following example.

In 1925, large U.S. stocks increased in value by about 30%. So, a $77 investment at the start of 1925 would have grown to $77 × 1.30 = $100 by the end of the year. We see from Figure 11.1 that if that $100 were invested in the S&P 500 from 1926 onward, it would have grown to about $487,210 by the start of 2016. But suppose instead that mining and transportation strikes had caused stocks to drop by 35% in 1925. Then the initial $77 invested would only be worth $77 × (1 − 0.35) = $50 at the start of 1926. If returns from then on were unchanged, the investment would be worth half as much in 2016, or $243,605.

Thus, if future returns are not affected by today's return, then an increase or decline in the value of our portfolio today will translate into the same percentage increase or decrease in the value of our portfolio in the future, and so there is no diversification over time. The only way the length of the time horizon can reduce risk is if a below-average return this year implies that returns are

(Continued)

more likely to be above average in the future (and vice versa). If this were true, past low returns can be used to predict future high returns in the stock market.

For short horizons of a few years, there is no evidence of this predictability in the stock market. For longer horizons, there is some evidence of this historically, but it is not clear how reliable this evidence is (there are not enough decades of accurate stock market data available) or whether the pattern will continue. But even if there is long-run reversal in stock returns, a buy-and-hold diversification strategy is still not optimal: If past returns can be used to predict future returns, it is optimal to invest more in stocks when returns are predicted to be high, and less when they are predicted to be low. Note that this strategy is very different from the diversification we achieve by holding many stocks, where we cannot predict which stocks will have good or bad unsystematic shocks.

CONCEPT CHECK

9. Why is the risk of a portfolio usually less than the average risk of the stocks in the portfolio?

10. Does systematic or unsystematic risk require a risk premium? Why?

MyFinanceLab

Here is what you should know after reading this chapter. MyFinanceLab will help you identify what you know, and where to go when you need to practice.

KEY POINTS AND EQUATIONS	KEY TERMS	ONLINE PRACTICE
11.1 A First Look at Risk and Return • While in hindsight some investments have had very high returns, they have also had the most volatility over time.		MyFinanceLab Study Plan 11.1
11.2 Historical Risks and Returns of Stocks • The realized return from investing in a stock from time t to $t + 1$ is: $$R_{t+1} = \frac{Div_{t+1} + P_{t+1} - P_t}{P_t} = \frac{Div_{t+1}}{P_t} + \frac{P_{t+1} - P_t}{P_t}$$ $$= \text{Dividend Yield} + \text{Capital Gain Yield} \quad (11.1)$$	average annual return, p. 343 normal distribution, p. 349 prediction interval, p. 350 realized return, p. 341 standard deviation, p. 346 variance, p. 346	MyFinanceLab Study Plan 11.2 Using Excel: Standard Deviation of Historical Returns
• We can calculate the average annual return and variance of realized returns: $$\bar{R} = \frac{1}{T}(R_1 + R_2 + \cdots + R_T) \quad (11.3)$$ $$Var(R) = \frac{1}{T-1}[(R_1 - \bar{R})^2 + (R_2 - \bar{R})^2 + \cdots + (R_T - \bar{R})^2] \quad (11.4)$$ • The square root of the estimated variance is the standard deviation, an estimate of the volatility of returns. • Based on historical data, small stocks have had higher volatility and higher average returns than large stocks, which have higher volatility and higher average returns than bonds. • About 95% of possible outcomes lie within two standard deviations above or below the average outcome.		

11.3 The Historical Tradeoff Between Risk and Return • There is no clear relationship between the volatility (standard deviation) and return of individual stocks. • Larger stocks tend to have lower overall volatility, but even the largest stocks are typically more risky than a portfolio of large stocks. • All stocks seem to have higher risk and lower returns than would be predicted based on extrapolation of data for large portfolios.	MyFinanceLab Study Plan 11.3
11.4 Common Versus Independent Risk • Common risk is risk that is perfectly linked across investments. • Independent risks are unrelated across investments. • Diversification is the averaging of risks in a large portfolio.	common risk, p. 353 diversification, p. 353 independent risk, p. 353	MyFinanceLab Study Plan 11.4
11.5 Diversification in Stock Portfolios • The total risk of a security represents both unsystematic risk and systematic risk. • Variation in a stock's return due to industry-specific or a firm's news is called unsystematic risk. • Systematic risk is risk due to market-wide news that affects all stocks simultaneously. • Diversification eliminates unsystematic risk but does not eliminate systematic risk. • Because investors can eliminate unsystematic risk, they do not require a risk premium for it. • Because investors cannot eliminate systematic risk, they must be compensated for it. So, the risk premium for a stock depends upon the amount of its systematic risk rather than its total risk.	systematic risk, p. 355 unsystematic risk, p. 355	MyFinanceLab Study Plan 11.5 Interactive Risk and Portfolio Diversification Analysis

CRITICAL THINKING

1. What does the historical relation between volatility and return tell us about investors' attitude toward risk?

2. What are the components of a stock's realized return?

3. What is the intuition behind using the average annual return as a measure of expected return?

4. How does standard deviation relate to the general concept of risk?

5. How does the relationship between the average return and the historical volatility of individual stocks differ from the relationship between the average return and the historical volatility of large, well-diversified, portfolios?

6. Consider two local banks. Bank A has 100 loans outstanding, each for $1 million, that it expects will be repaid today. Each loan has a 5% probability of default, in which case the bank is not repaid anything. The chance of default is independent across all the loans. Bank B has only one loan of $100 million outstanding that it also expects will be repaid today. It also has a 5% probability of not being repaid. Explain the difference between the type of risk each bank faces. Assuming you are averse to risk, which bank would you prefer to own?

7. What is meant by diversification and how does it relate to common versus independent risk?

8. Which of the following risks of a stock are likely to be unsystematic, diversifiable risks and which are likely to be systematic risks? Which risks will affect the risk premium that investors will demand?
   a. The risk that the founder and CEO retires
   b. The risk that oil prices rise, increasing production costs
   c. The risk that a product design is faulty and the product must be recalled
   d. The risk that the economy slows, reducing demand for the firm's products
   e. The risk that your best employees will be hired away
   f. The risk that the new product you expect your R&D division to produce will not materialize

9. What is the difference between systematic and unsystematic risk?

10. There are three companies working on a new approach to customer-tracking software. You work for a software company that thinks this could be a good addition to its software line. If you invest in one of them versus all three of them:
    a. Is your systematic risk likely to be very different?
    b. Is your unsystematic risk likely to be very different?

11. If you randomly select 10 stocks for a portfolio and 20 other stocks for a different portfolio, which portfolio is likely to have the lower standard deviation? Why?

12. Why doesn't the risk premium of a stock depend on its diversifiable risk?

13. Your spouse works for Southwest Airlines and you work for a grocery store. Is your company or your spouse's company likely to be more exposed to systematic risk?

PROBLEMS

All problems are available in MyFinanceLab. *The* icon *indicates problems that are easier to solve using Excel and have data in an Excel format available in* MyFinanceLab. *An asterisk * indicates problems with a higher level of difficulty.*

Historical Risks and Returns of Stocks

1. You bought a stock one year ago for $50 per share and sold it today for $55 per share. It paid a $1 per share dividend today. What was your realized return?

2. How much of the return in Problem 1 came from dividend yield and how much came from capital gain?

3. Repeat Problems 1 and 2 assuming instead that the stock fell $5 to $45.
   a. Is your capital gain different? Why or why not?
   b. Is your dividend yield different? Why or why not?

4. Your portfolio consists of 100 shares of CSH and 50 shares of EJH, which you just bought at $20 and $30 per share, respectively.
   a. What fraction of your portfolio is invested in CSH? In EJH?
   b. If CSH increases to $23 and EJH decreases to $29, what is the return on your portfolio?

5. You have just purchased a share of stock for $20. The company is expected to pay a dividend of $0.50 per share in exactly one year. If you want to earn a 10% return on your investment, what price do you need if you expect to sell the share immediately after it pays the dividend?

6. You expect KStreet Co's trade at $100 per share right after paying a $2 dividend per share in one year. What is the most you would pay to buy the stock now if you want to earn at least a 15% return?

7. The following table contains prices and dividends for a stock. All prices are after the dividend has been paid. If you bought the stock on January 1 and sold it on December 31, what is your realized return?

	Price	Dividend
Jan 1	10.00	
Mar 31	11.00	0.20
Jun 30	10.50	0.20
Sep 30	11.10	0.20
Dec 31	11.00	0.20

 8. Using the data in the following table, calculate the return for investing in Boeing stock (BA) from January 2, 2008, to January 2, 2009, and also from January 3, 2011, to January 3, 2012, assuming all dividends are reinvested in the stock immediately.

Historical Stock and Dividend Data for Boeing

Date	Price	Dividend	Date	Price	Dividend
1/2/2008	86.62		1/3/2011	66.40	
2/6/2008	79.91	0.40	2/9/2011	72.63	0.42
5/7/2008	84.55	0.40	5/11/2011	79.08	0.42
8/6/2008	65.40	0.40	8/10/2011	57.41	0.42
11/5/2008	49.55	0.40	11/8/2011	66.65	0.42
1/2/2009	45.25		1/3/2012	74.22	

 9. The last four years of returns for a stock are as follows:

1	2	3	4
−4%	+28%	+12%	+4%

a. What is the average annual return?
b. What is the variance of the stock's returns?
c. What is the standard deviation of the stock's returns?

 10. Use the data in SBUX_GOOG.xlsx on MFL to answer the following questions:
a. What is the return for SBUX over the period without including its dividends? With the dividends?
b. What is the return for GOOG over the period?
c. If you have 30% of your portfolio in SBUX and 70% in GOOG, what was the return on your portfolio?

 11. Download the spreadsheet from the book's Web site containing the data for Figure 11.1.
a. Compute the average return for each of the assets from 1929 to 1940 (the Great Depression).
b. Compute the variance and standard deviation for each of the assets from 1929 to 1940.
c. Which asset was riskiest during the Great Depression? How does that fit with your intuition?

 12. Ten annual returns are listed in the following table.

−19.9%	16.6%	18.0%	−50.0%	43.3%	1.2%	−16.5%	45.6%	45.2%	−3.0%

a. What is the arithmetic average return over the 10-year period?

*b. What is the geometric average return over the 10-year period?

c. If you invested $100 at the beginning, how much would you have at the end?

13. Using the data in the following table, calculate the return for investing in this stock from January 1 to December 31. Prices are after the dividend has been paid (*see* MyFinanceLab *for the data in Excel format*).

Stock and Dividend Data

Date	Price	Dividend
Jan 1	33.88	
Feb 5	30.67	0.17
May 14	29.49	0.17
Aug 13	32.38	0.17
Nov 12	39.07	0.17
Dec 31	41.99	

14. What was your dividend yield from investing in the stock in Problem 12? What was your capital gain?

15. Using the data in the following table, calculate the return for investing in this stock from January 1 to December 31. Prices are after the dividend has been paid (*see* MyFinanceLab *for the data in Excel format*).

	Stock Price	Dividend
Jan 1	$50.00	
Mar 31	$51.00	$0.55
Jun 30	$49.47	$0.55
Sep 30	$51.94	$0.75
Dec 31	$52.46	$0.75

16. Consider the following five monthly returns:

a. Calculate the arithmetic average monthly return over this period.

*b. Calculate the geometric average monthly return over this period.

c. Calculate the monthly variance over this period.

d. Calculate the monthly standard deviation over this period.

0.05	−0.02	0.04	0.08	−0.01

17. Explain the difference between the arithmetic average return you calculated in Problem 16a and the geometric average return you calculated in Problem 16b. Are both numbers useful? If so, explain why.

18. The last four years of returns for a stock are as follows:

1	2	3	4
−4%	+28%	+12%	+4%

a. What is the average annual return?

b. What is the variance of the stock's returns?

c. What is the standard deviation of the stock's returns?

19. Calculate the 95% prediction intervals for the four different investments included in Figures 11.3 and 11.4.

20. You are choosing between the four investments from Problem 18 and you want to be 95% certain that you do not lose more than 8% on your investment. Which investments should you choose?

21. If returns of S&P 500 stocks are normally distributed, what range of returns would you expect to see 95% of the time? Base your answer on Figures 11.3 and 11.4.

22. You observe a portfolio for five years and determine that its average return is 12% and the standard deviation of its returns is 20%. Can you be 95% confident that this portfolio will not lose more than 30% of its value next year?

Common Versus Independent Risk

*23. Using the data in Critical Thinking Question 6, calculate the following:
   a. The expected overall payoff of each bank
   b. The standard deviation of the overall payoff of each bank

Diversification in Stock Portfolios

24. You are a risk-averse investor who is considering investing in one of two economies. The expected return and volatility of all stocks in both economies are the same. In the first economy, all stocks move together—in good times all prices rise together and in bad times they all fall together. In the second economy, stock returns are independent—one stock increasing in price has no effect on the prices of other stocks. Which economy would you choose to invest in? Explain.

25. Consider the following 6 months of returns for 2 stocks and a portfolio of those 2 stocks.

	Jan	Feb	Mar	Apr	May	Jun
Stock A	2%	5%	−6%	3%	−2%	4%
Stock B	0%	−3%	8%	−1%	4%	−2%
Portfolio	1%	1%	1%	1%	1%	1%

   a. What is the expected return and standard deviation of returns for each of the two stocks?
   b. What is the expected return and standard deviation of return for the portfolio?
   c. Is the portfolio more or less risky than the two stocks? Why?

DATA CASE

Today is April 30, 2016, and you have just started your new job with a financial planning firm. In addition to studying for all your license exams, you have been asked to review a portion of a client's stock portfolio to determine the risk/return profiles of 12 stocks in the portfolio. Unfortunately, your small firm cannot afford the expensive databases that would provide all this information with a few simple keystrokes, but that's why they hired you. Specifically, you have been asked to determine the monthly average returns and standard deviations for the 12 stocks for the past five years.

The stocks (with their symbols in parentheses) are:

Archer Daniels Midland (ADM)
Boeing (BA)
Caterpillar (CAT)
Deere & Co. (DE)

General Mills, Inc. (GIS)
eBay, Inc. (EBAY)
Hershey (HSY)
International Business Machines Corporation (IBM)
JPMorgan Chase & Co. (JPM)
Microsoft (MSFT)
Procter and Gamble (PG)
Walmart (WMT)

1. Collect price information for each stock from Yahoo! Finance (finance.yahoo.com) as follows:
   a. Enter the stock symbol. On the page for that stock, click "Historical Prices" on the left side of the page.
   b. Enter the "start date" as April 1, 2011, and the "end date" as April 30, 2016, to cover the five-year period. Make sure you click "monthly" next to the date.
   c. After hitting "Get Prices," scroll to the bottom of the first page and click "Download to Spreadsheet." If you are asked if you want to open or save the file, click open.
   d. Copy the entire spreadsheet, open Excel, and paste the Web data into a spreadsheet. Delete all the columns except the date and the adjusted close (the first and last columns).
   e. Keep the Excel file open and go back to the Yahoo! Finance Web page and hit the back button. If you are asked if you want to save the data, click no.
   f. When you return to the prices page, enter the next stock symbol and hit "Get Prices" again. Do not change the dates or frequency, but make sure you have the same dates for all the stocks you will download. Again, click "Download to Spreadsheet" and then open the file. Copy the last column, "Adj. Close," paste it into the Excel file and change "Adj. Close" to the stock symbol. Make sure that the first and last prices are in the same rows as the first stock.
   g. Repeat these steps for the remaining 10 stocks, pasting each closing price right next to the other stocks, again making sure that the correct prices on the correct dates all appear on the same rows.

2. Convert these prices to monthly returns as the percentage change in the monthly prices. (*Hint*: Create a separate worksheet within the Excel file.) Note that to compute a return for each month, you need a beginning and ending price, so you will not be able to compute the return for the first month.

3. Compute the mean monthly returns and standard deviations for the monthly returns of each of the stocks.[5] Convert the monthly statistics to annual statistics for easier interpretation (muliply the mean monthly return by 12, and multiply the monthly standard deviation by $\sqrt{12}$).

4. Add a column in your Excel worksheet with the average return across stocks for each month. This is the monthly return to an equally weighted portfolio of these 12 stocks. Compute the mean and standard deviation of monthly returns for the equally weighted portfolio. Double-check that the average return on this equally weighted portfolio is

---

[5]In Eq. 11.1, we showed how to compute returns with stock price and dividend data. The "adjusted close" series from Yahoo! Finance is already adjusted for dividends and splits, so we may compute returns based on the percentage change in monthly adjusted prices.

equal to the average return of all of the individual stocks. Convert these monthly statistics to annual statistics (as described in step 3) for interpretation.

5. Using the annual statistics, create an Excel plot with standard deviation (volatility) on the *x*-axis and average return on the *y*-axis as follows:
   a. Create three columns on your spreadsheet with the statistics you created in Questions 3 and 4 for each of the individual stocks and the equally weighted portfolio. The first column will have the ticker, the second will have annual standard deviation, and the third will have the annual mean return.
   b. Highlight the data in the last two columns (standard deviation and mean), choose > Insert > Chart > XY Scatter Plot. Complete the chart wizard to finish the plot.

6. What do you notice about the average of the volatilities of the individual stocks, compared to the volatility of the equally weighted portfolio?

12

Systematic Risk and the Equity Risk Premium

LEARNING OBJECTIVES

- Calculate the expected return and volatility (standard deviation) of a portfolio

- Understand the relation between systematic risk and the market portfolio

- Measure systematic risk

- Use the Capital Asset Pricing Model (CAPM) to compute the cost of equity capital for a stock

notation

β_i	beta of security i with respect to the market portfolio
$Corr(R_i, R_j)$	correlation between the returns of security i and security j
$E[R_i]$	expected return of security i
$E[R_{Mkt}]$	expected return of the market portfolio
$E[R_P]$	expected return of a portfolio

r_f	risk-free interest rate
R_i	return of security i
R_P	return of portfolio P
$SD(R_i)$	standard deviation (volatility) of the return of security i
$Var(R_i)$	variance of the return of security i
w_i	fraction of the portfolio invested in security i (its relative *weight* in the portfolio)

In Chapter 11, we started our exploration of the tradeoff between risk and return. We found that for large portfolios, while investors should expect to experience higher returns for higher risk, the same does not hold true for individual stocks. Stocks have both unsystematic, diversifiable risk and systematic, undiversifiable risk; only the systematic risk is rewarded with higher expected returns. With no reward for bearing unsystematic risk, rational investors should choose to diversify.

Put yourself in the role of a financial manager at a company such as Cisco. One part of your job would be to calculate Cisco's cost of equity capital so that its managers know what return its equity investors require. Recall that in Chapter 5 we defined the cost of capital as the best available expected return offered in the market on an investment of comparable risk and term. Since only systematic risk contributes to expected returns, we need to measure the systematic risk of Cisco and map it into an expected return for Cisco. To do so, we need to think about Apple's stock the way our investors would—as part of a portfolio. As a result, we begin where we left off in Chapter 11: with portfolios. After learning how to calculate the risk and expected return of a portfolio, we will focus on the biggest portfolio of them all: the portfolio of *all* risky securities. This portfolio has no diversifiable risk left and can be used as a baseline for measuring systematic risk. From there, we will develop a simple, powerful model that relates the systematic risk of an investment to its expected return. In other words, the model says that the return we should expect on any investment is equal to the risk-free rate of return plus a risk premium proportional to the amount of systematic risk in the investment.

12.1   The Expected Return of a Portfolio

In Chapter 11, we learned the important role that portfolios play in reducing unsystematic risk. As financial managers, we have to be mindful that investors hold our company's stock as part of a larger portfolio. Thus, it is important to understand how portfolios work and the implications for the return our investors expect on the stock of our company and the projects we undertake in that company.

Portfolio Weights

We begin by calculating the return and expected return of a portfolio. For example, consider a portfolio with 200 shares of Apple worth $200 per share ($40,000 total), and 1000 shares of Coca-Cola worth $60 per share ($60,000 total). The total value of the portfolio is $100,000, so Apple is 40% of the portfolio and Coca-Cola is 60% of the portfolio. More generally, we can describe a portfolio by its **portfolio weights**, which are the fractions of the total investment in a portfolio held in each individual investment in the portfolio:

portfolio weights The fraction of the total investment in a portfolio held in each individual investment in the portfolio.

$$w_i = \frac{\text{Value of Investment } i}{\text{Total Value of Portfolio}} \qquad (12.1)$$

These portfolio weights add up to 100% (that is, $w_1 + w_2 + \ldots + w_N = 100\%$), so that they represent the way we have divided our money between the different individual investments in the portfolio. We can confirm the portfolio weights for our portfolio of Apple and Coca-Cola:

$$w_{Apple} = \frac{200 \times \$200}{\$100,000} = 40\% \text{ and } w_{Coca\text{-}Cola} = \frac{1000 \times \$60}{\$100,000} = 60\%$$

Portfolio Returns

Once you know the portfolio weights, you can calculate the return on the portfolio. For example, take the portfolio of Apple and Coca-Cola. If Apple earns a 10% return and Coca-Cola earns a 15% return, then 40% of the portfolio earns 10% and 60% of the portfolio earns 15%, so the portfolio as a whole earns: $(0.40)(10\%) + (0.60)(15\%) = 13\%$.

return of a portfolio The weighted average of the returns on the investments in a portfolio, where the weights correspond to the portfolio weights.

The **return of a portfolio** *is the weighted average of the returns on the investments in the portfolio, where the weights correspond to the portfolio weights.*

Formally, suppose $w_1, \ldots, w_n$ are the portfolio weights of the n investments in a portfolio and these investments have returns $R_1, \ldots, R_n$, then the formula for the return on the portfolio is:

$$R_p = w_1 R_1 + w_2 R_2 + \ldots + w_n R_n \qquad (12.2)$$

EXAMPLE 12.1

Calculating Portfolio Returns

MyFinanceLab

PROBLEM

Suppose you invest $100,000 and buy 200 shares of Apple at $200 per share ($40,000) and 1000 shares of Coca-Cola at $60 per share ($60,000). If Apple's stock rises to $240 per share and Coca-Cola stock falls to $57 per share and neither paid dividends, what is the new value of the portfolio? What return did the portfolio earn? Show that Eq. 12.2 is true by calculating the individual returns of the stocks and multiplying them by their weights in the portfolio. If you don't buy or sell any shares after the price change, what are the new portfolio weights?

SOLUTION

PLAN

Your portfolio: 200 shares of Apple: $200 → $240 ($40 capital gain per share)
                1000 shares of Coca-Cola: $60 → $57 ($3 capital loss per share)

A. To calculate the return on your portfolio, compute its value using the new prices and compare it to the original $100,000 investment.
B. To confirm that Eq. 12.2 is true, compute the return on each stock individually using Eq. 11.1 from Chapter 11, multiply those returns by their original weights in the portfolio, and compare your answer to the return you just calculated for the portfolio as a whole.

EXECUTE

The new value of your Apple stock is $200 \times \$240 = \$48,000$ and the new value of your Coca-Cola stock is $1000 \times \$57 = \$57,000$. So, the new value of your portfolio is $\$48,000 + 57,000 = \$105,000$, for a gain of $5000 or a 5% return on your initial $100,000 investment.

Since neither stock paid any dividends, we calculate their returns simply as the capital gain or loss divided by the purchase price. The return on Apple stock was $40/$200 = 20%, and the return on Coca-Cola stock was −$3/$60 = −5%.

The initial portfolio weights were $40,000/$100,000 = 40% for Apple and $60,000/$100,000 = 60% for Coca-Cola, so we can also compute the return of the portfolio from Eq. 12.2 as:

$$R_p = w_{Apple} R_{Apple} + w_{Coke} R_{Coke} = 0.40 \,(20\%) + 0.60 \,(-5\%) = 5\%$$

After the price change, the new portfolio weights are equal to the value of your investment in each stock divided by the new portfolio value:

$$w_{Apple} = \frac{200 \times \$240}{105,000} = 45.71\% \text{ and } w_{Coca\text{-}Cola} = \frac{1000 \times \$57}{105,000} = 54.29\%$$

As a check on your work, always make sure that your portfolio weights sum to 100%!

EVALUATE

The $3000 loss on your investment in Coca-Cola was offset by the $8000 gain in your investment in Apple, for a total gain of $5,000 or 5%. The same result comes from giving a 40% weight to the 20% return on Apple and a 60% weight to the −5% loss on Coca-Cola—you have a total net return of 5%.

After a year, the portfolio weight on Apple has increased and the weight on Coca-Cola has decreased. Note that without trading, the portfolio weights will increase for the stock(s) in the portfolio whose returns are above the overall portfolio return. The charts below show the initial and ending weights on Apple (shown in yellow) and Coca-Cola (shown in red).

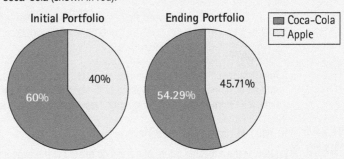

Expected Portfolio Return

expected return of a portfolio The weighted average of the expected returns of the investments in a portfolio, where the weights correspond to the portfolio weights.

As we showed in Chapter 11, you can use the historical average return of a security as its expected return. With these expected returns, you can compute the **expected return of a portfolio**, which is simply the weighted average of the expected returns of the investments within it, using the portfolio weights:

$$E[R_P] = w_1E[R_1] + w_2E[R_2] + \ldots + w_nE[R_n] \tag{12.3}$$

We started by stating that you can describe a portfolio by its weights. These weights are used in computing both a portfolio's return and its expected return. Table 12.1 summarizes these concepts.

TABLE 12.1
Summary of Portfolio Concepts

Term	Concept	Equation
Portfolio weight	The relative investment in your portfolio	$w_i = \dfrac{\text{Value of Investment } i}{\text{Total Value of Portfolio}}$
Portfolio return	The total return earned on your portfolio, accounting for the returns of all of the securities in the portfolio and their weights	$R_P = w_1R_1 + w_2R_2 + \cdots + w_nR_n$
Portfolio expected return	The return you can expect to earn on your portfolio, given the expected returns of the securities in that portfolio and the relative amount you have invested in each	$E[R_P] = w_1E[R_1] + w_2E[R_2] + \cdots + w_nE[R_n]$

EXAMPLE 12.2
Portfolio Expected Return

MyFinanceLab

PROBLEM
Suppose you invest $10,000 in Boeing (BA) stock, and $30,000 in Merck (MRK) stock. You expect a return of 10% for Boeing and 16% for Merck. What is the expected return for your portfolio?

SOLUTION

PLAN
You have a total of $40,000 invested:

$$\$10,000/\$40,000 = 25\% \text{ in Boeing and:} \quad E[R_{BA}] = 10\%$$
$$\$30,000/\$40,000 = 75\% \text{ in Merck and:} \quad E[R_{MRK}] = 16\%$$

Using Eq. 12.3, compute the expected return on your whole portfolio by multiplying the expected returns of the stocks in your portfolio by their respective portfolio weights.

EXECUTE
The expected return on your portfolio is:

$$E[R_P] = w_{BA}E[R_{BA}] + w_{MRK}E[R_{MRK}]$$
$$E[R_P] = 0.25 \times 10\% + 0.75 \times 16\% = 14.5\%$$

EVALUATE
The importance of each stock for the expected return of the overall portfolio is determined by the relative amount of money you have invested in it. Most (75%) of your money is invested in Merck, so the overall expected return of the portfolio is much closer to Merck's expected return than it is to Boeing's.

CONCEPT CHECK

1. What do the weights in a portfolio tell us?

2. How is the expected return of a portfolio related to the expected returns of the stocks in the portfolio?

12.2   The Volatility of a Portfolio

Investors in a company such as Apple care not only about the return, but also about the risk of their portfolios. Understanding how Apple's investors think about risk requires us to understand how to calculate the risk of a portfolio. As we explained in Chapter 11, when we combine stocks in a portfolio, some of their risk is eliminated through diversification. The amount of risk that will remain depends upon the degree to which the stocks share common risk. The **volatility of a portfolio** is the total risk, measured as standard deviation, of the portfolio. In this section, we describe the tools to quantify the degree to which two stocks share risk and to determine the volatility of a portfolio.

volatility of a portfolio
The total risk, measured as standard deviation, of a portfolio.

Diversifying Risks

Let's begin with a simple example of how risk changes when stocks are combined in a portfolio. Table 12.2 shows returns for three hypothetical stocks, along with their average returns and volatilities. Note that while the three stocks have the same volatility and average return, the pattern of returns differs. In years when the airline stocks performed well, the oil stock tended to do poorly (see 2011–2012), and when the airlines did poorly, the oil stock tended to do well (2014–2015).

Table 12.2 also shows the returns for two portfolios of the stocks. The first portfolio is an equal investment in the two airlines, North Air and West Air. The second portfolio is an equal investment in West Air and Texas Oil. The bottom two rows display the average return and volatility for each stock and portfolio of stocks. Note that the 10% average return of both portfolios is equal to the 10% average return of the stocks, consistent with Eq. 12.3. However, as Figure 12.1 illustrates, their volatilities (standard deviations)—12.1% for portfolio 1 and 5.1% for portfolio 2—are very different from the 13.4% volatility for the individual stocks *and* from each other.

This example demonstrates two important things that we learned in Chapter 11. *First, by combining stocks into a portfolio, we reduce risk through diversification.* Because the stocks do not move identically, some of the risk is averaged out in a portfolio. As a result, both portfolios have lower risk than the individual stocks.

Second, the amount of risk that is eliminated in a portfolio depends upon the degree to which the stocks face common risks and move together. Because the two airline stocks tend to perform well or poorly at the same time, the portfolio of airline stocks has a volatility that is only slightly lower than the volatility of the individual stocks. The airline and

TABLE 12.2

Returns for Three Stocks, and Portfolios of Pairs of Stocks

		Stock Returns		Portfolio Returns	
				(1)	**(2)**
				Half N.A. and Half W.A.	**Half W.A. and Half T.O.**
Year	**North Air**	**West Air**	**Texas Oil**		
2011	21%	9%	−2%	15.0%	3.5%
2012	30%	21%	−5%	25.5%	8.0%
2013	7%	7%	9%	7.0%	8.0%
2014	−5%	−2%	21%	−3.5%	9.5%
2015	−2%	−5%	30%	−3.5%	12.5%
2016	9%	30%	7%	19.5%	18.5%
Avg. Return	10.0%	10.0%	10.0%	10.0%	10.0%
Volatility	13.4%	13.4%	13.4%	12.1%	5.1%

FIGURE 12.1

Volatility of Airline and Oil Portfolios

The figures graph the portfolio returns from Table 12.2. In Panel (a), we see that the airline stocks move in synch, so that a portfolio made up of the two airline stocks does not achieve much diversification. In Panel (b), because the airline and oil stocks often move opposite each other, a portfolio of West Air and Texas Oil achieves greater diversification and lower portfolio volatility. Because both stocks have an average return of 10%, so does the portfolio, but it achieves that return with much less volatility than either of the individual stocks.

Panel (a): Portfolio split equally between West Air and North Air

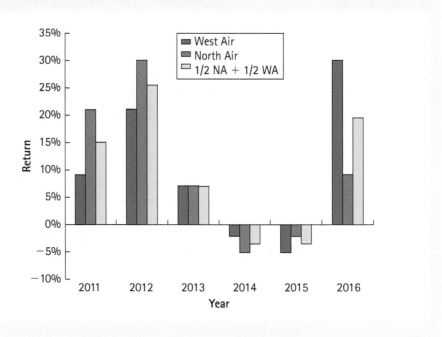

Panel (b): Portfolio split equally between West Air and Texas Oil

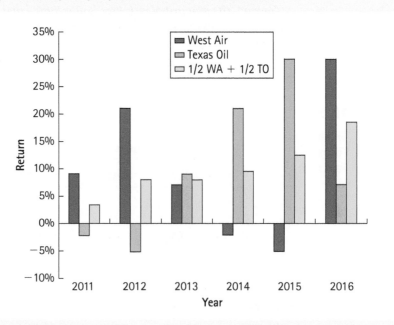

oil stocks, on the other hand, do not move together. Indeed, they tend to move in opposite directions. As a result, more risk is canceled out, making that portfolio much less risky.

Measuring Stocks' Co-Movement: Correlation

Figure 12.1 emphasizes the fact that to find the risk of a portfolio, we need to know more than just the risk of the component stocks: We need to know the degree to which the stocks' returns move together. The stocks' *correlation* is such a measure, ranging from -1 to $+1$.[1]

As Figure 12.2 shows, **correlation** is a barometer of the degree to which the returns share common risk. The closer the correlation is to $+1$, the more the returns tend to move together as a result of common risk. When the correlation equals 0, the returns are *uncorrelated*; that is, they have no tendency to move together or opposite of one another. Independent risks are uncorrelated. Finally, the closer the correlation is to -1, the more the returns tend to move in opposite directions.

When will stock returns be highly correlated with each other? Stock returns will tend to move together if they are affected similarly by economic events. Thus, stocks in the same industry tend to have more highly correlated returns than stocks in different industries. This tendency is illustrated in Table 12.3, which shows the volatility (standard deviation) of individual stock returns and the correlation between them for several common stocks. The blue-shaded boxes along the diagonal show the correlation of a stock with itself—which has to be 1 (a stock is perfectly correlated with itself). The table can be read across the rows or down the columns. Each correlation appears twice. For example, reading across the Coca-Cola row, the correlation between Coca-Cola and McDonald's (red box) is 0.59, which you could also find by reading across the McDonald's row for the correlation between McDonald's and Coca-Cola. McDonald's and Coca-Cola have the highest correlation in the table, 0.59, because both companies do

correlation A measure of the degree to which returns share common risk. It is calculated as the covariance of the returns divided by the product of the standard deviations of each return.

FIGURE 12.2

Correlation

The correlation measures how returns move in relation to each other. The correlation is between $+1$ (returns always move together) and -1 (returns always move oppositely). Independent risks have no tendency to move together and have zero correlation. The correlations of Microsoft with Boeing and Cisco are indicated on the continuum. Note that software company Microsoft is more correlated with a computer network infrastructure company than with an airplane manufacturer. See Table 12.3 for more examples of correlations.

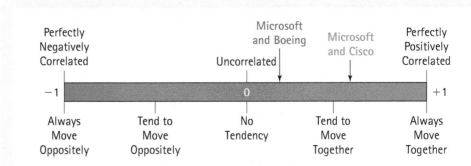

Source: Authors' calculations based on data from The Center for Research in Security Prices.

---

[1]Correlation is scaled covariance and is defined as:

$$Corr(R_i, R_j) = \frac{Covariance(R_i, R_j)}{SD(R_i)SD(R_j)}$$

TABLE 12.3

Estimated Annual Volatilities and Correlations for Selected Stocks
(Based on Monthly Returns, January 2006–December 2015)

Standard Deviation	Microsoft 25%	Starbucks 29%	Netflix 61%	Coca-Cola 16%	McDonald's 14%	Cisco 28%	Boeing 26%
Microsoft	1	0.35	0.18	0.40	0.43	0.52	0.28
Starbucks	0.35	1	0.19	0.23	0.17	0.52	0.48
Netflix	0.18	0.19	1	0.00	0.13	0.10	0.10
Coca-Cola	0.40	0.23	0.00	1	0.59	0.27	0.34
McDonald's	0.43	0.17	0.13	0.59	1	0.28	0.37
Cisco	0.52	0.52	0.10	0.27	0.28	1	0.46
Boeing	0.28	0.48	0.10	0.34	0.37	0.46	1

Source: Authors' calculations based on data from The Center for Research in Security Prices.

well when people buy more fast-food (and McDonald's serves only Coca-Cola products). None of the correlations are negative, however, showing the general tendency of stocks to move together. The lowest correlation is shown in the green boxes for Coca-Cola and Netflix, which is <0.01 (it is actually 0.004), showing that there is little relation between a soft drink company and an Internet television provider. Figure 12.3 shows scatter plots of monthly returns for Coca-Cola and Netflix and for Coca-Cola and McDonald's. While there is a clear positive relation between the returns of Coca-Cola and McDonald's, the plot for Coca-Cola and Netflix looks like an unrelated cloud of returns.

FIGURE 12.3

Scatter Plots of Returns

Plots of pairs of monthly returns for Coca-Cola and Netflix and for Coca-Cola and McDonald's. Notice the clear positive relation between Coca-Cola and McDonald's, which tend to move up and down together, versus the lack of a relation between Coca-Cola and Netflix.

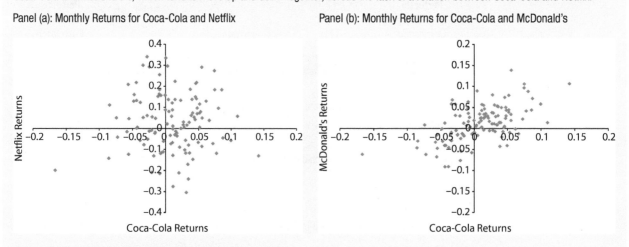

Panel (a): Monthly Returns for Coca-Cola and Netflix

Panel (b): Monthly Returns for Coca-Cola and McDonald's

Source: Authors' calculations based on data from The Center for Research in Security Prices.

USING EXCEL

Calculating the
Correlation Between
Two Sets of Returns

The correlations presented in Table 12.3 were calculated by comparing the returns of two stocks. Here we describe how you can use Excel to calculate these correlations.

1. Enter or import the historical returns for the two stocks into Excel.
2. Next, from the Data Group, select **Data Analysis**, and then select **Correlation**.
3. For the "Input Range" field, highlight the two columns of returns, as shown in the screenshot.
4. Click **OK**.
5. The answer will appear in a new worksheet as the correlation between "column 1" and "column 2."

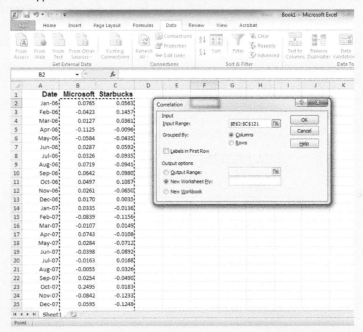

Note that if you don't have the Analysis Toolpak installed, you can use the CORREL function. In this case, you would type: =CORREL(B2:B145,C2:C145) into any empty cell. The function would return the correlation. The cell ranges B2:B145 and C2:C145 are the returns of Microsoft and Starbucks, respectively.

Computing a Portfolio's Variance and Standard Deviation

We now have the tools to formally compute portfolio variance. The formula for the variance of a two-stock portfolio is:

$$Var(R_p) = \overbrace{w_1^2 SD(R_1)^2}^{\substack{\text{Accounting} \\ \text{for the risk} \\ \text{of stock 1}}} + \overbrace{w_2^2 SD(R_2)^2}^{\substack{\text{Accounting} \\ \text{for the risk} \\ \text{of stock 2}}} + \overbrace{2w_1 w_2 Corr(R_1, R_2) SD(R_1) SD(R_2)}^{\substack{\text{Adjustment for} \\ \text{how much the two stocks move together}}} \quad (12.4)$$

Each part of Eq. 12.4 accounts for an important determinant of the overall variance of the portfolio: the risk of stock 1, the risk of stock 2, and an adjustment for how much the two stocks move together (their correlation, given as $Corr(R_1, R_2)$.[2] The equation demonstrates

---

[2]For three stocks, the formula is

$$Var(R_p) = w_1^2 SD(R_1)^2 + w_2^2 SD(R_2)^2 + w_3^2 SD(R_3)^2 + 2w_1 w_2 Corr(R_1, R_2) SD(R_1) SD(R_2)$$
$$+ 2w_2 w_3 Corr(R_2, R_3) SD(R_2) SD(R_3) + 2w_1 w_3 Corr(R_1, R_3) SD(R_1) SD(R_3)$$

and for n stocks, it is:

$$\sum_{i=1}^{n} \sum_{j=1}^{n} w_i w_j Corr(R_i, R_j) SD(R_i) SD(R_j)$$

that with a positive amount invested in each stock, the more the stocks move together and the higher their correlation, the more volatile the portfolio will be. The portfolio will have the greatest variance if the stocks have a perfect positive correlation of +1. In fact, when combining stocks into a portfolio, unless the stocks all have a perfect positive correlation of +1 with each other, the risk of the portfolio will be lower than the weighted average volatility of the individual stocks (as shown in Figure 12.1). Contrast this fact with a portfolio's expected return. The expected return of a portfolio is equal to the weighted average expected return of its stocks, but the volatility of a portfolio is less than the weighted average volatility. As a result, it is clear that we can eliminate some volatility by diversifying. Equation 12.4 formalized the concept of diversification introduced in Chapter 11. In the following example, we use it to compute the volatility of a portfolio.

EXAMPLE 12.3

Computing the Volatility of a Two-Stock Portfolio

MyFinanceLab

PROBLEM

Using the data from Table 12.3, what is the volatility (standard deviation) of a portfolio with equal amounts invested in Microsoft and Cisco stock? What is the standard deviation of a portfolio with equal amounts invested in Microsoft and Starbucks stock?

SOLUTION

PLAN

	Weight	Volatility	Correlation with Microsoft
Microsoft	0.50	0.25	1
Cisco	0.50	0.28	0.52
Microsoft	0.50	0.25	1
Starbucks	0.50	0.29	0.35

A. With the portfolio weights, volatility, and correlations of the stocks in the two portfolios, we have all the information we need to use Eq. 12.4 to compute the variance of each portfolio.
B. After computing the portfolio's variance, we can take the square root to get the portfolio's standard deviation.

EXECUTE

For Microsoft and Cisco, from Eq. 12.4 the portfolio's variance is:

$$Var(R_P) = w_{MSFT}^2 SD(R_{MSFT})^2 + w_{CSCO}^2 SD(R_{CSCO})^2$$
$$+ 2w_{MSFT}w_{CSCO}Corr(R_{MSFT}, R_{CSCO})SD(R_{MSFT})SD(R_{CSCO})$$
$$= (.50)^2(.25)^2 + (.50)^2(.28)^2 + 2(.50)(.50)(.52)(.25)(.28)$$
$$= 0.05343$$

The standard deviation is therefore:

$$SD(R_P) = \sqrt{Var(R_P)} = \sqrt{0.05343} = 0.231, \text{ or } 23.1\%$$

For the portfolio of Microsoft and Starbucks:

$$Var(R_P) = w_{MSFT}^2 SD(R_{MSFT})^2 + w_{SBUX}^2 SD(R_{SBUX})^2$$
$$+ 2w_{MSFT}w_{SBUX}Corr(R_{MSFT}, R_{SBUX})SD(R_{MSFT})SD(R_{SBUX})$$
$$= (.50)^2(.25)^2 + (.50)^2(.29)^2 + 2(.50)(.50)(.35)(.25)(.29)$$
$$= 0.04934$$

The standard deviation in this case is:

$$SD(R_P) = \sqrt{Var(R_P)} = \sqrt{0.04934} = 0.222, \text{ or } 22.2\%.$$

EVALUATE

The weights, standard deviations, and correlation of the two stocks are needed to compute the variance and then the standard deviation of the portfolio. Here, we computed the standard deviation of the portfolio of Microsoft and Cisco to be 23.1% and of Microsoft and Starbucks to be 22.2%. Note that both portfolios are less volatile than any of the individual stocks in the portfolios. The portfolio of Microsoft and Starbucks is actually less volatile than the portfolio of Microsoft and Cisco. Even though Starbucks is more volatile than Cisco, its lower correlation with Microsoft leads to greater diversification benefits in the portfolio, which offsets Starbuck's higher volatility.

In the next example, we show how portfolios can be used to reduce risk without giving up too much expected return.

EXAMPLE 12.4

Reducing Risk Without
Sacrificing Return

MyFinanceLab

PROBLEM

Based on historical data, your expected annual return for Boeing is 13% and for Coca-Cola is 12%. What is the expected return and risk (standard deviation) of your portfolio if you hold only Boeing? If you split your money evenly between Boeing and Coca-Cola, what is the expected return and risk of your portfolio?

SOLUTION

PLAN

A. From Table 12.3 we can get the standard deviations of Boeing (BA) and Coca-Cola (KO) stock along with their correlation:
$$SD(R_{BA}) = 0.26, \quad SD(R_{KO}) = .16 \quad Corr(R_{BA}, R_{KO}) = 0.34$$

B. With this information and the information from the problem, we can compute the expected return of the portfolio using Eq. 12.3 and its variance using Eq. 12.4.

EXECUTE

For the all-Boeing portfolio, we have 100% of our money in Boeing stock, so the expected return and standard deviation of our portfolio is simply the expected return and standard deviation of that stock:
$$E[R_{BA}] = .13, \quad SD(R_{BA}) = 0.26$$

However, when we invest our money 50% in Coca-Cola and 50% in Boeing, the expected return is:
$$E[R_P] = w_{KO} E[R_{KO}] + w_{BA} E[R_{BA}] = 0.5(.12) + 0.5(.13) = 0.125$$

and the variance is:
$$Var(R_P) = w_{KO}^2 SD(R_{KO})^2 + w_{BA}^2 SD(R_{BA})^2$$
$$+ 2w_{KO} w_{BA} Corr(R_{KO}, R_{BA}) SD(R_{KO}) SD(R_{BA})$$
$$= (.50)^2(.16)^2 + (.50)^2(.26)^2 + 2(.50)(.50)(.34)(.16)(.26)$$
$$= 0.0304$$

The standard deviation is therefore:
$$SD(R_P) = \sqrt{Var(R_P)} = \sqrt{0.0304} = 0.174$$

EVALUATE

For a very small reduction in expected return, we gain a large reduction in risk. This is the advantage of portfolios: By selecting stocks with low correlation but similar expected returns, we achieve our desired expected return at the lowest possible risk.

The Volatility of a Large Portfolio

We can gain additional benefits of diversification by holding more than two stocks in our portfolio. As we add more stocks to our portfolio, the diversifiable firm-specific risk for each stock matters less and less. Only risk that is common to all of the stocks in the portfolio continues to matter.

In Figure 12.4, we graph the volatility for an *equally weighted portfolio* with different numbers of stocks. In an **equally weighted portfolio**, the same amount of money is invested in each stock. Note that the volatility declines as the number of stocks in the portfolio grows. In fact, nearly half the volatility of the individual stocks is eliminated in a large portfolio by diversification. The benefit of diversification is most dramatic initially—the decrease in volatility going from one to two stocks is much larger than the decrease going from 100 to 101 stocks. Even for a very large portfolio, however, we cannot eliminate all of the risk—the systematic risk remains.

equally weighted portfolio A portfolio in which the same amount of money is invested in each stock.

FIGURE 12.4

Volatility of an Equally Weighted Portfolio Versus the Number of Stocks

The graph in Panel (b) is based on the data in Panel (a). Note that the volatility declines as we increase the number of stocks in the portfolio. Yet even in a very large portfolio, systematic (market) risk remains. Also note that the volatility declines at a decreasing rate (the effect of going from one to two stocks—an 8-percentage point decrease in volatility—is bigger than the effect of going from four to five stocks, which is a 1.1-percentage point decrease). The graph is formed based on the assumption that each stock has a volatility of 40% and a correlation with other stocks of 0.28. Both are average for large stocks in the United States.

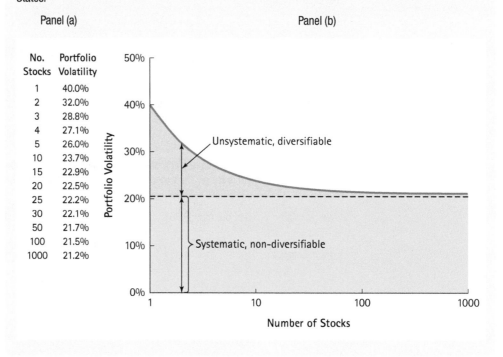

CONCEPT CHECK

3. What determines how much risk will be eliminated by combining stocks in a portfolio?

4. When do stocks have more or less correlation?

12.3 Measuring Systematic Risk

Our goal is to understand the impact of risk on the firm's investors. By understanding how they view risk, we can quantify the relation between risk and required return to produce a discount rate for our present value calculations. In Chapter 11, we established that the only risk that is related to return is systematic risk, but standard deviation measures *total* risk, including the unsystematic part. We need a way to measure just the systematic risk of an investment opportunity. The previous section contains two important insights that we will now build on to determine the sensitivity of individual stocks to risk. To recap:

1. *The amount of a stock's risk that is removed by diversification depends on its correlation with other stocks in the portfolio.* For example, in Example 12.3 we showed that much less of Microsoft's risk is diversified away in a portfolio with Cisco than in a portfolio with Starbucks.

2. *If you build a large enough portfolio, you can remove all unsystematic risk by diversification, but you will still be left with systematic risk.* Figure 12.4 shows that as the number of stocks in your portfolio grows, the unsystematic positive and negative events affecting only a few stocks will cancel out, leaving systematic events as the only source of risk for the portfolio.

Role of the Market Portfolio

As we explained in Chapter 11, investors should diversify their portfolios in order to reduce their risk. If investors choose their portfolios optimally, they will do so until no further diversifiable risk is present, and only systematic risk remains. Let's assume that all investors behave in this way; that is

Suppose all investors hold portfolios that contain only systematic risk.

If that is the case, then consider the portfolio we obtain by combining the portfolios of every investor. Because each investor's portfolio contains only systematic risk, the same is true for this "aggregate" portfolio. So, the aggregate portfolio held by all investors is a fully diversified, optimal portfolio. Moreover, we can identify this portfolio: Because all securities are held by someone, the aggregate portfolio contains all shares outstanding of every risky security. We call this portfolio the **market portfolio**.

market portfolio The portfolio of all risky investments, held in proportion to their value.

To illustrate, imagine that there are only two companies in the world, each with 1000 shares outstanding:

	Number of Shares Outstanding	Price per Share	Market Capitalization
Company A	1000	$40	$40,000
Company B	1000	$10	$10,000

market capitalization The total market value of a firm's equity; equals the market price per share times the number of shares.

In this simple setting, the market portfolio consists of 1000 shares of each stock and has a total value of $50,000. Stock A's portfolio weight is therefore 80% ($40,000/$50,000) and B's is 20% ($10,000/$50,000). Because all of the shares of A and all of the shares of B must be held by someone, the sum of all investors' portfolios must equal this market portfolio. Note from this example that the portfolio weight of each stock is proportional to the total market value of its outstanding shares, which is called its **market capitalization**:

$$\text{Market Capitalization} = (\text{Number of Shares Outstanding}) \times (\text{Price per Share}) \qquad (12.5)$$

Generally, the market portfolio will consist of all risky securities in the market, with portfolio weights proportional to their market capitalization. Thus, for example, if Microsoft's market capitalization were equal to 3% of the total market value of all securities, then it would have a 3% weight in the market portfolio. Because stocks are held in proportion to their market capitalization (value), we say that the market portfolio is **value weighted**.

value-weighted portfolio A portfolio in which each security is held in proportion to its market capitalization.

Because the market portfolio only contains systematic risk, we can use it to measure the amount of systematic risk of other securities in the market. In particular, any risk that is correlated with the market portfolio must be systematic risk. Therefore, by looking at the sensitivity of a stock's return to the overall market, we can calculate the amount of systematic risk the stock has.

Stock Market Indexes as the Market Portfolio

While the market portfolio is easy to identify, actually constructing it is a different matter. Because it should contain all risky securities, we need to include all stocks, bonds, real estate, commodities, etc., both in the United States and around the world. Clearly, it would be impractical, if not impossible, to collect and update returns on all risky assets everywhere. In practice, we use a **market proxy**—a portfolio whose return should track the underlying, unobservable market portfolio. The most common proxy portfolios are *market indexes*, which are broadly used to represent the performance of the stock market. A **market index** reports the value of a particular portfolio of securities. We list the most popular indexes below, but you can also read the box on page 16 in Section 1.5 of Chapter 1 that compares the different market indexes.

market proxy A portfolio whose return should closely track the true market portfolio.

market index The market value of a broad-based portfolio of securities.

Dow Jones Industrial Average. The most familiar stock index in the United States is the Dow Jones Industrial Average, or DJIA. This index consists of a portfolio of 30 large stocks. While these stocks are chosen to be representative of different sectors of the economy, they clearly do not represent the entire market. Despite being non-representative of the entire market, the DJIA remains widely cited because it is one of the oldest stock market indexes (it was first published in 1884).

S&P 500. A better representation of the entire U.S. stock market is the S&P 500, a value-weighted portfolio of 500 of the largest U.S. stocks.[3] The S&P 500 was the first widely publicized value-weighted index (S&P began publishing its index in 1923), and it is a standard benchmark for professional investors. This index is the most commonly cited index when evaluating the overall performance of the U.S. stock market. It is also the standard portfolio used to represent "the market" in practice. As we show in Figure 12.5, even though the S&P 500 includes only 500 of more than 7000 individual U.S. stocks, because the S&P 500 includes the largest stocks, it represents more than 70% of the U.S. stock market in terms of market capitalization.

Market Risk and Beta

Now that we have established that the market portfolio is a good basis for measuring systematic risk, we can use the relation between an individual stock's returns and the market portfolio's returns to measure the amount of systematic risk present in that stock. The intuition is that if a stock's returns are highly sensitive to the market portfolio's returns,

---

[3]There is no precise formula for determining which stocks will be included in the S&P 500. Standard & Poor's periodically replaces stocks in the index (on average about seven or eight stocks per year). While size is one criterion, Standard & Poor's also tries to maintain appropriate representation of different segments of the economy and chooses firms that are leaders in their industries.

FIGURE 12.5

The S&P 500

The Panel (a) pie chart shows the 500 firms in the S&P 500 as a fraction of the approximately 3600 U.S. public operating firms. Panel (b) shows the S&P 500 firms' importance in terms of market capitalization—these 500 firms represent approximately 80% of the total capitalization of the 3600 public firms.

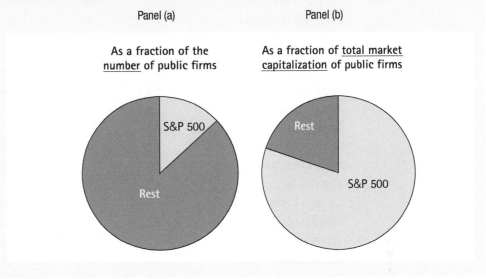

Index Funds

One easy way investors can buy (an approximation of) the market portfolio is to invest in an *index fund*, which invests in stocks and other securities with the goal of matching the performance of a particular market index. The Vanguard Group was the largest mutual fund company in 2013 and it specializes in index funds. Vanguard was founded in 1974 by John Bogle, who advocates the benefits of index funds for individual investors. Comparing index funds to the strategy

of trying to pick hot stocks, Bogle reportedly said, "What's the point of looking for the needle in the haystack? Why not own the haystack?"

In August of 1976, Vanguard created its well-known S&P 500 Index Fund, which tries to match the performance of the S&P 500 index as closely as possible. As of April 2016, this fund had nearly $230 billion in assets. Vanguard's Total Stock Market Index Fund is designed to track the performance of the MSCI US Broad Market index, an index that measures the performance of all U.S. stocks with available price data.

then that stock is highly sensitive to systematic risk. That is, events that are systematic and affect the whole market are also strongly reflected in that stock's returns. If a stock's returns do not depend on the market's returns, then it has little systematic risk—when systematic events happen, they are not strongly reflected in its returns. So stocks whose returns are volatile *and* are highly correlated with the market's returns are the riskiest in the sense that they have the most systematic risk.

Specifically, we can measure a stock's systematic risk by estimating the stock's sensitivity to the market portfolio, which we refer to as its **beta** (β):

beta (β) The expected percentage change in the excess return of a security for a 1% change in the excess return of the market (or other benchmark) portfolio.

A stock's beta (β) is the percentage change in its return that we expect for each 1% change in the market's return.

There are many data sources that provide estimates of beta based on historical data. Typically, these data sources estimate betas using two-to-five years of weekly or monthly returns and use the S&P 500 as the market portfolio. Table 12.4 shows estimates of betas for a number of large stocks and their industries. You can find the betas of other companies

TABLE 12.4

Average Betas for Stocks by Industry and the Betas of a Selected Company in Each Industry

Industry	Average Beta	Ticker	Company	Beta
Electric Utilities	0.8	EIX	Edison International	0.2
Personal & Household Prods.	0.5	PG	The Procter & Gamble Company	0.5
Food Processing	0.9	CPB	Campbell Soup Co.	0.4
Restaurants	0.5	SBUX	Starbucks Corporation	0.8
Beverages (Nonalcoholic)	0.2	KO	The Coca-Cola Company	0.5
Retail (Grocery)	0.6	KR	Kroger Co	0.8
Major Drugs	0.7	PFE	Pfizer Inc.	0.9
Beverages (Alcoholic)	0.6	SAM	Boston Beer Company Inc.	0.7
Apparel/Accessories	1.2	ANF	Abercrombie & Fitch	1.2
Retail (Home Improvement)	0.7	HD	Home Depot Inc.	0.9
Software & Programming	0.9	MSFT	Microsoft Corporation	1.0
Consumer (Discretionary)	0.5	TRIP	TripAdvisor Inc.	2.3
Auto & Truck Manufacturers	1.2	F	Ford Motor Company	1.4
Communications Equipment	1.1	CSCO	Cisco Systems Inc.	1.3
Forestry & Wood Products	0.6	WY	Weyerhaeuser Company	1.4
Computer Services	1.0	GOOGL	Alphabet Inc. (Google)	0.9
Computer Hardware	0.8	HPQ	Hewlett Packard	1.7
Semiconductors	1.3	INTC	Intel Corporation	1.0

Source: Reuters, May 2016.

by going to http://finance.google.com or http://finance.yahoo.com. Note that because different Web sites use different time frames for estimating betas, they can display different betas from each other and from your own calculation for a stock's beta.

As we explain below, the beta of the overall market portfolio is 1, so you can think of a beta of 1 as representing average exposure to systematic risk. However, as the table demonstrates, many industries and companies have betas much higher or lower than 1. The differences in betas by industry are related to the sensitivity of each industry's profits to the general health of the economy. For example, Hewlett Packard, Abercrombie & Fitch, and TripAdvisor all have high betas (near or above 1.2) because demand for their products usually varies with the business cycle (cyclical stocks): People tend to indulge in new computers, new clothes, and travel when times are good, but cut back on these purchases when the economy slows. Thus, systematic events have a greater-than-average impact on these firms and their exposure to systematic risk is greater than average. On the other hand, the demand for personal and household products such as shampoo has very little relation to the state of the economy (stocks of companies providing these types of products are often called *defensive stocks*). Firms producing these types of goods, such as Procter & Gamble, tend to have low betas (near 0.5). Note also that even within an industry, each company's specific strategy and focus can lead to different exposures to systematic events, so that there is variation in beta even within industries (see, for example, how different Weyerhaeuser's beta is than the average beta in the forestry and wood products industry).

COMMON MISTAKE

Mixing Standard Deviation and Beta

Volatility (standard deviation) and beta are measured in different units (standard deviation is measured in % and beta is unitless). So even though total risk (volatility) is equal to the sum of systematic risk (measured by beta) and firm-specific risk, our measure of volatility does not have to be a bigger number than our measure for beta. To illustrate, consider Microsoft. It has total risk (volatility), measured as standard deviation, of 25% or 0.25 (see Table 12.3),

but Table 12.4 shows that it has systematic risk, measured as a beta, of 1.0, which is greater than 0.25. Volatility (standard deviation) is measured in percentage terms, but beta is not, so 0.25 does not have to be greater than 1.0. For the same reason, it is possible for Boston Beer Company to have a higher standard deviation than Microsoft (35%), but a lower beta (0.7). Figure 12.6 illustrates one possible breakdown of total risk for Microsoft and Boston Beer Company that would be consistent with these data.

FIGURE 12.6

Systematic Versus Firm-Specific Risk in Boston Beer and Microsoft

Beta, measuring systematic risk, and standard deviation, measuring total risk, are in different units. Even though Microsoft's total risk (standard deviation) is 0.25 (25%), its beta, measuring only systematic risk, is 1.0. In this case, the beta of 1.0 corresponds to a breakdown in total risk as depicted in the figure. Formally, the portion of Microsoft's total risk that is in common with the market is calculated by multiplying the correlation between Microsoft and the market by the standard deviation (total risk) of Microsoft. We can do a similar breakdown of Boston Beer's risk. Note that Boston Beer has more total, but less systematic, risk than Microsoft.

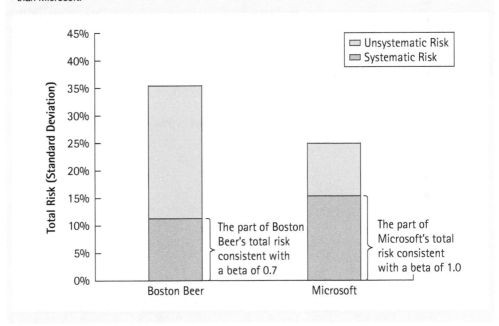

EXAMPLE 12.5

Total Risk Versus Systematic Risk

MyFinanceLab

PROBLEM

Suppose that in the coming year, you expect SysCo's stock to have a standard deviation of 30% and a beta of 1.2, and UniCo's stock to have a standard deviation of 41% and a beta of 0.6. Which stock carries more total risk? Which has more systematic risk?

SOLUTION

PLAN

	Standard Deviation (Total Risk)	Beta (β) (Systematic Risk)
SysCo	30%	1.2
UniCo	41%	0.6

(Continued)

EXECUTE

Total risk is measured by standard deviation; therefore, UniCo's stock has more total risk. Systematic risk is measured by beta. SysCo has a higher beta, and so has more systematic risk.

EVALUATE

As we discuss in the Common Mistake box on p. 385, a stock can have high total risk, but if a lot of it is diversifiable, it can still have low or average systematic risk.

Estimating Beta from Historical Returns

A security's beta is the expected percentage change in the return of the security for a 1% change in the return of the market portfolio. That is, beta represents the amount by which risks that affect the overall market are amplified or dampened in a given stock or investment. As demonstrated in Table 12.4, securities whose returns tend to move one for one with the market on average have a beta of one. Securities that tend to move more than the market have higher betas, while those that move less than the market have lower betas.

For example, let's look at Cisco's stock. Figure 12.7 shows the monthly returns for Cisco and the monthly returns for the S&P 500 from January 2011 through December 2015. Note the overall tendency for Cisco to have a high return when the market is up and a low return when the market is down. Indeed, Cisco tends to move in the same direction as the market, but its movements are larger. The pattern suggests that Cisco's beta is greater than one.

FIGURE 12.7

Monthly Excess Returns for Cisco Stock and for the S&P 500, January 2011 through December 2015

Note that Cisco's returns tend to move in the same direction but farther than those of the S&P 500.

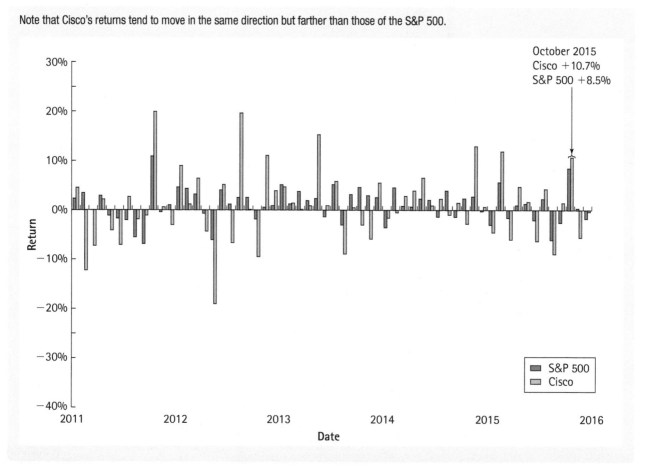

We can see Cisco's sensitivity to the market even more clearly by plotting Cisco's return as a function of the S&P 500 return, as shown in Figure 12.8. Each point in this figure represents the returns of Cisco and the S&P 500 for one of the months in Figure 12.7. For example, in October 2015, Cisco's return was 10.7% and the S&P 500's was 8.5%.

As the scatter plot makes clear, Cisco's returns have a positive correlation with the market: Cisco tends to be up when the market is up, and vice versa. In practice, we use linear regression to estimate the relation between Cisco's returns and the market's return. The output of the linear regression analysis is the best-fitting line that represents the historical relation between the stock and the market. The slope of this line is our estimate of its beta. That slope tells us how much, on average, the stock's return changes for a 1% change in the market's return.[4]

For example, in Figure 12.8, the best-fitting line shows that a 1% change in the market's return corresponds to about a 1.3% change in Cisco's return. That is, Cisco's return moves about 1.3 times the overall market's movement, and so Cisco's beta is about 1.3.

To fully understand this result, recall that beta measures the systematic, market risk of a security. The best-fitting line in Figure 12.8 captures the components of a security's returns that can be explained by market-risk factors. In any individual month, the security's returns will be higher or lower than the best-fitting line. Such deviations from the best-fitting line result from risk that is not related to the market as a whole. This risk is diversifiable risk that averages out in a large portfolio.

But what is the beta of the market portfolio? Imagine plotting the returns of the S&P 500 against themselves. You would have a line with a slope of one and no deviations from that line. Thus, the beta of the market portfolio is 1. What about a risk-free investment?

FIGURE 12.8

Scatter Plot of Monthly Returns for Cisco Versus the S&P 500, January 2011 through December 2015

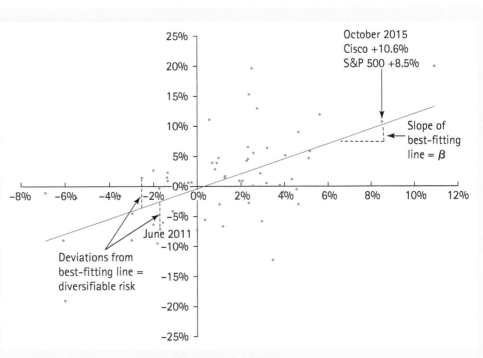

Beta corresponds to the slope of the best-fitting line. Beta measures the expected change in Cisco's return per 1% change in the market's return. Deviations from the best-fitting line, such as in June 2011, correspond to diversifiable, unsystematic risk.

---

[4]Formally, the beta of an investment is defined as:

Volatility of i that is common with the market

$$\beta_i = \frac{\overbrace{SD\,(R_i) \times Corr\,(R_i, R_{Mkt})}}{SD\,(R_{Mkt})} = \frac{Covariance\,(R_i, R_{Mkt})}{Var\,(R_{Mkt})}$$

Because the risk-free return is the return earned on a Treasury bond and is therefore known in advance, it has no volatility and hence no correlation with the market. Therefore, the beta of the risk-free investment is 0.

1. Enter or import the historical returns for the stock and the S&P 500 into Excel.
2. Next, from the Data Tab, select **Data Analysis**, and then select **Regression**.
3. For the "Input Y Range" box, highlight the stock's returns.
4. For the "Input X Range" box, highlight the S&P 500's returns, as shown in the screenshot.
5. Click **OK**.

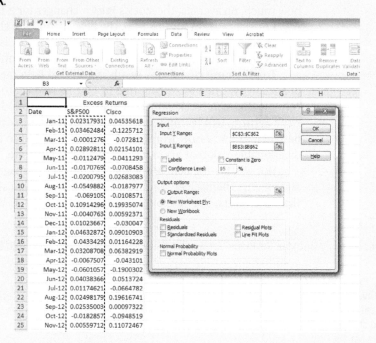

6. The output will appear in a separate sheet. The stock's beta is the coefficient on "X Variable 1." In this case, the beta is 1.247, circled in the screenshot.

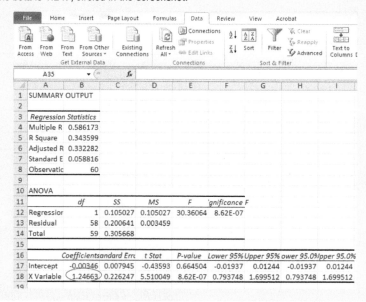

5. What is the market portfolio?

6. What does beta (β) tell us?

12.4 Putting It All Together: The Capital Asset Pricing Model

One of our goals in this chapter is to compute the cost of equity capital for Apple, which is the best available expected return offered in the market on an investment of comparable risk and term. Thus, in order to compute the cost of capital, we need to know the relation between Apple's risk and its expected return. In the last three sections, we have laid the foundation for a practical way of measuring this relation. In this section, we put all the pieces together to build a model for determining the expected return of any investment.

The CAPM Equation Relating Risk to Expected Return

As we have learned, only common, systematic risk determines expected returns—firm-specific risk is diversifiable and does not warrant extra return. In the introduction to this chapter, we stated that, intuitively, the expected return on any investment should come from two components:

1. A baseline risk-free rate of return that we would demand to compensate for inflation and the time value of money, even if there were no risk of losing our money.

2. A risk premium that varies with the amount of systematic risk in the investment.

Expected Return = Risk-Free Rate + Risk Premium for Systematic Risk

We devoted the last section to measuring systematic risk. Beta is our measure of the amount of systematic risk in an investment:

Expected Return for Investment i =
Risk-Free Rate + β_i × Risk Premium per Unit of Systematic Risk (per unit of β).

But what is the risk premium per unit of systematic risk? Well, we know that the market portfolio, by definition, has exactly one unit of systematic risk (it has a beta of 1). So, a natural estimate of the risk premium per unit of systematic risk is the historical average excess return on the market portfolio, also known as the **market** or **equity risk premium**. Historically, the average excess return of the S&P 500 over the return on U.S. Treasury bonds (the risk-free rate) has been 5% to 7%, depending on the period of measurement (we'll discuss issues in determining the risk premium and risk-free rate in Chapter 13). With this last piece of the puzzle, we can write the equation for the expected return of an investment:

market risk premium (equity risk premium) The historical average excess returns on the market portfolio.

Capital Asset Pricing Model

$$E[R_i] = r_f + \underbrace{\beta_i(E[R_{Mkt}] - r_f)}_{\text{Risk premium for security } i}$$

(12.6)

Capital Asset Pricing Model (CAPM) An equilibrium model of the relationship between risk and return that characterizes a security's expected return based on its beta with the market portfolio.

This equation for the expected return of any investment is the **Capital Asset Pricing Model (CAPM)**. In words, the CAPM simply says that the return we should expect on any investment is equal to the risk-free rate of return plus a risk premium proportional to the amount of systematic risk in the investment. Specifically, the risk premium of an investment is equal to the market risk premium $(E[R_{Mkt}] - r_f)$ multiplied by the amount of systematic (market) risk present in the investment, measured by its beta with the market (β_i).

Why Not Estimate Expected Returns Directly?

If we have to use historical data to estimate beta and determine a security's expected return (or an investment's cost of capital), why not just use the security's historical average return as an estimate for its expected return instead? This method would certainly be simpler and more direct.

The answer is that it is extremely difficult to infer the average return of individual stocks from historical data. Because stock returns are so volatile, even with 100 years of data we would have little confidence in our estimate of the true average. (Imagine drawing 100 numbers from a swimming pool full of widely ranging

numbers and being asked to guess the average of all of the numbers in the pool.) Worse, few stocks have existed for 100 years, and those that have probably bear little resemblance today to what they were like 100 years ago. If we use less than ten years of data, we would have very little confidence in our estimate at all. In fact, if the volatility of the stock's return is 20%, it turns out that we would need 1600 years of data to be 95% confident that our estimate of its true average return was within +/−1% of being correct!

On the other hand, the linear regression technique allows us to infer beta from historical data reasonably accurately with just a few years of data. Thus, in theory at least, using beta and the CAPM can provide much more accurate estimates of expected returns for stocks than we could obtain from their historical average return.

required return The expected return of an investment that is necessary to compensate for the risk of undertaking the investment.

Because investors will not invest in this security unless they can expect at least the return given in Eq. 12.6, we also call this return the investment's **required return**.

The CAPM is the main method used by most major corporations to determine the equity cost of capital. In a survey of CFOs, Graham and Harvey found that more than 70% rely on the CAPM, and Bruner, Eades, Harris, and Higgins reported that 85% of a sample of large firms rely on it.[5] It has become the most important model of the relationship between risk and return, and for his contributions to the theory, William Sharpe was awarded the Nobel Prize in Economics in 1990.

EXAMPLE 12.6

Computing the Expected Return of a Stock

MyFinanceLab

PROBLEM

Suppose the risk-free return is 3% and you measure the market risk premium to be 6%. Cisco has a beta of 1.3. According to the CAPM, what is its expected return?

SOLUTION

PLAN

We can use Eq. 12.6 to compute the expected return according to the CAPM. For that equation, we will need the market risk premium, the risk-free return, and the stock's beta. We have all of these inputs, so we are ready to go.

EXECUTE

Using Eq. 12.6:

$$E[R_{CSCO}] = r_f + \beta_{CSCO}(E[R_{Mkt}] - r_f) = 3\% + 1.3(6\%)$$

$$= 10.8\%$$

EVALUATE

Because of Cisco's beta of 1.3, investors will require a risk premium of 7.8% over the risk-free rate for investments in its stock to compensate for the systematic risk of Cisco stock. This leads to a total expected return of 10.8%.

---

[5]J. Graham and C. Harvey, "The Theory and Practice of Corporate Finance: Evidence from the Field," *Journal of Financial Economics*, 60 (2001): 187–243; and R. Bruner, K. Eades, R. Harris, and R. Higgins, "Best Practices in Estimating the Cost of Capital: Survey and Synthesis," *Financial Practice and Education*, 8 (1998): 13–28.

William Sharpe

The CAPM was proposed as a model of risk and return by William Sharpe in a 1964 paper, and in related papers by Jack Treynor (1961), John Lintner (1965), and Jan Mossin (1966).*

Below is an excerpt from a 1998 interview with William Sharpe:

Portfolio Theory focused on the actions of a single investor with an optimal portfolio. I said what if everyone was optimizing? They've all got their copies of Markowitz and they're doing what he says. Then some people decide they want to hold more IBM, but there aren't enough shares to satisfy demand. So they put price pressure on IBM and up it goes, at which point they have to change their estimates of risk and return, because now they're paying more for the stock. That process of upward and downward pressure on prices continues until prices reach an equilibrium and everyone collectively wants to hold what's available. At that point, what can you say about the relationship between risk and return? The answer is that expected return is proportionate to beta relative to the market portfolio.

The CAPM was and is a theory of equilibrium. Why should anyone expect to earn more by investing in one security as opposed to another? You need to be compensated for doing badly when times are bad. The security that is going to do badly just when you need money when

times are bad is a security you have to hate, and there had better be some redeeming virtue or else who will hold it? That redeeming virtue has to be that in normal times you expect to do better. The key insight of the Capital Asset Pricing Model is that higher expected returns go with the greater risk of doing badly in bad times. Beta is a measure of that. Securities or asset classes with high betas tend to do worse in bad times than those with low betas.

Source: Jonathan Burton, "Revisiting the Capital Asset Pricing Model." *Dow Jones Asset Manager* (May/June 1998): 20–28.

---

*W. F. Sharpe: "Capital Asset Prices: A Theory of Market Equilibrium Under Conditions of Risk." *Journal of Finance*, 19 (September 1964): 425–442.

Jack Treynor, "Toward a Theory of the Market Value of Risky Assets." Unpublished manuscript (1961).

J. Lintner: "The Valuation of Risk Assets and the Selection of Risky Investments in Stock Portfolios and Capital Budgets." *Review of Economics and Statistics*, 47 (February 1965): 13–37.

J. Mossin "Equilibrium in a Capital Asset Market." *Econometrica*, 34 (4) (1966): 768–783.

The Security Market Line

Figure 12.9 graphs the relations between expected return and both total risk and systematic risk (beta) for the stocks in Table 12.4. Recall from Chapter 11 that there is no clear relation between a stock's standard deviation (total risk) and its expected return, as shown in Panel (a). However, the CAPM equation (Eq. 12.6) implies that there is a linear relation between a stock's beta and its expected return. This line is graphed in Panel (b) as the line through the risk-free investment (with a beta of zero) and the market (with a beta of one); it is called **security market line** the **security market line (SML)**. We see that the relation between risk and return for indi- **(SML)** The pricing impli- vidual securities is only evident when we measure market risk as in Panel (b), rather than cation of the CAPM; it total risk as in Panel (a).

specifies a linear relation The security market line in Figure 12.9 raises the subject of negative beta stocks. While between the risk premium the vast majority of stocks have a positive beta, it is possible to have returns that co-vary of a security and its beta negatively with the market. Firms that provide goods or services that are in greater demand with the market portfolio. in economic contractions than in booms fit this description.

FIGURE 12.9

Expected Return, Volatility, and Beta

Panel (a) Expected Return and Total Risk (Standard Deviation)
The graph compares the standard deviation and expected returns of the stocks in Table 12.4. There is no relation between total risk and expected return. Some of the stocks are identified. It is clear that we could not predict Boston Beer's expected return using its total risk (volatility).

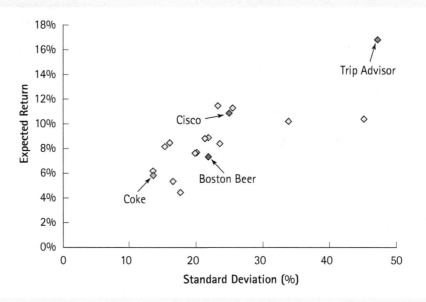

Panel (b) Expected Return and Beta
The security market line shows the expected return for each security in Table 12.4 as a function of its beta with the market. According to the CAPM, all stocks and portfolios (including the market portfolio) should lie on the security market line. Thus, Boston Beer's expected return can be determined by its beta, which measures its systematic risk.

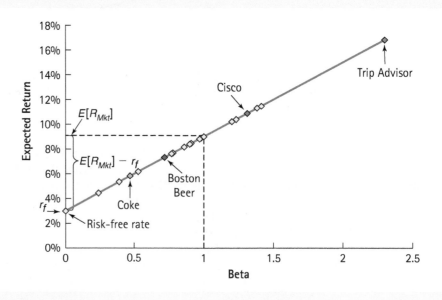

EXAMPLE 12.7

A Negative Beta Stock

MyFinanceLab

PROBLEM

Suppose the stock of Bankruptcy Auction Services Inc. (BAS) has a negative beta of -0.30. How does its expected return compare to the risk-free rate, according to the CAPM? Does your result make sense?

SOLUTION

PLAN

We can use the CAPM equation, Eq. 12.6, to compute the expected return of this negative beta stock just as we would with a positive beta stock. We don't have the risk-free rate or the market risk premium, but the problem doesn't ask us for the exact expected return, just whether or not it will be more or less than the risk-free rate. Using Eq. 12.6, we can answer that question.

EXECUTE

Because the expected return of the market is higher than the risk-free rate, Eq. 12.6 implies that the expected return of Bankruptcy Auction Services (BAS) will be *below* the risk-free rate. As long as the market risk premium is positive (as long as people demand a higher return for investing in the market than for a risk-free investment), then the second term in Eq. 12.6 will have to be negative if the beta is negative. For example, if the risk-free rate is 4% and the market risk premium is 6%:

$$E[R_{BAS}] = 4\% - 0.30\,(6\%) = 2.2\%.$$

(See Figure 12.9—the security market line drops below r_f for $\beta < 0$.)

EVALUATE

This result seems odd—why would investors be willing to accept a 2.2% expected return on this stock when they can invest in a safe investment and earn 4%? The answer is that a savvy investor will not hold BAS alone; instead, the investor will hold it in combination with other securities as part of a well-diversified portfolio. These other securities will tend to rise and fall with the market. But because BAS has a negative beta, its correlation with the market is negative, which means that BAS tends to perform well when the rest of the market is doing poorly. Therefore, by holding BAS, an investor can reduce the overall market risk of the portfolio. In a sense, BAS is "recession insurance" for a portfolio, and investors will pay for this insurance by accepting a lower expected return.

The CAPM and Portfolios

Because the security market line applies to all securities, we can apply it to portfolios as well. For example, the market portfolio is on the SML, and according to the CAPM, other portfolios (such as mutual funds) are also on the SML. Therefore, the expected return of a portfolio should correspond to the portfolio's beta. We calculate the beta of a portfolio made up of securities each with weight w_i as follows:

$$\beta_P = w_1\beta_1 + w_2\beta_2 + \cdots + w_n\beta_n \tag{12.7}$$

That is, the *beta of a portfolio is the market value weighted average beta of the securities in the portfolio.*

EXAMPLE 12.8

The Expected Return of a Portfolio

MyFinanceLab

PROBLEM

Suppose drug-maker Pfizer (PFE) has a beta of 0.9, whereas the beta of Abercrombie & Fitch (ANF) is 1.2. If the risk-free interest rate is 3% and the market risk premium is 6%, what is the expected return of an equally weighted portfolio of Pfizer and Abercrombie & Fitch, according to the CAPM?

SOLUTION

PLAN

We have the following information:

$$r_f = 3\%, \qquad E[R_{Mkt}] - r_f = 6\%$$

PFE: $\quad \beta_{PFE} = 0.9, \quad w_{PFE} = 0.50$

ANF: $\quad \beta_{ANF} = 1.2, \quad w_{ANF} = 0.50$

(Continued)

We can compute the expected return of the portfolio two ways. First, we can use the CAPM (Eq. 12.6) to compute the expected return of each stock and then compute the expected return of the portfolio using Eq. 12.3.

Or, we can compute the beta of the portfolio using Eq. 12.7 and then use the CAPM (Eq. 12.6) to find the portfolio's expected return.

EXECUTE

Using the first approach, we compute the expected return for PFE and GOOG:

$$E[R_{PFE}] = r_f + \beta_{PFE}(E[R_{Mkt}] - r_f) \qquad E[R_{ANF}] = r_f + \beta_{GOOG}(E[R_{Mkt}] - r_f)$$

$$E[R_{PFE}] = 3\% + 0.9(6\%) = 8.4\% \qquad E[R_{ANF}] = 3\% + 1.2(6\%) = 10.2\%$$

Then the expected return of the equally weighted portfolio *P* is:

$$E[R_P] = 0.5(8.4\%) + 0.5(10.2\%) = 9.3\%$$

Alternatively, we can compute the beta of the portfolio using Eq.12.7:

$$\beta_P = w_{PFE}\beta_{PFE} + w_{ANF}\beta_{ANF}$$
$$\beta_P = (0.5)(0.9) + (0.5)(1.2) = 1.05$$

We can then find the portfolio's expected return from the CAPM:

$$E[R_P] = r_f + \beta_P(E[R_{Mkt}] - r_f)$$
$$E[R_P] = 3\% + 1.05(6\%) = 9.3\%$$

EVALUATE

The CAPM is an effective tool for analyzing securities and portfolios of those securities. You can compute the expected return of each security using its beta and then compute the weighted average of those expected returns to determine the portfolio's expected return. Or, you can compute the weighted average of the securities' betas to get the portfolio's beta and then compute the expected return of the portfolio using the CAPM. Either way, you will get the same answer.

Summary of the Capital Asset Pricing Model

The CAPM is a powerful tool that is widely used to estimate the expected return on stocks and investments within companies. To summarize the model and its use:

- Investors require a risk premium proportional to the amount of *systematic* risk they are bearing.
- We can measure the systematic risk of an investment by its β, which is the sensitivity of the investment's return to the market's return. For each 1% change in the market portfolio's return, the investment's return is expected to change by β percent due to risks that it has in common with the market.
- The most common way to estimate a stock's beta is to regress its historical returns on the market's historical returns. The stock's beta is the slope of the line that best explains the relation between the market's return and the stock's return.
- The CAPM says that we can compute the expected, or required, return for any investment using the following equation:

$$E[R_i] = r_f + \beta_i(E[R_{Mkt}] - r_f)$$

which when graphed is called the *security market line*.

The Big Picture

The CAPM marks the culmination of our examination of how investors in capital markets trade off risk and return. It provides a powerful and widely used tool to quantify the return that should accompany a particular amount of systematic risk. We have already reached our goal (in Example 12.6) of estimating the cost of equity capital for Cisco. While our finding that equity investors in Cisco should reasonably expect (and therefore require) a return of 10.8% on their investments is an important piece of information to Cisco's managers, it is not the whole picture. While some firms have only equity investors, most have debt investors as well. In Chapters 13, we will apply what we have learned here and in Chapters 6, 7, and 10 on bonds and stocks to develop the overall cost of capital for a company. The Valuation Principle tells us to use this cost of capital to discount the future expected cash flows of a firm to arrive at the value of the firm. Thus, the cost of capital is an essential input to the financial manager's job of analyzing investment opportunities, and so knowing this overall cost of capital is critical to the company's success at creating value for its investors.

CONCEPT
CHECK

7. What does the CAPM say about the required return of a security?

8. What is the security market line?

MyFinanceLab

Here is what you should know after reading this chapter. MyFinanceLab will help you identify what you know, and where to go when you need to practice.

KEY POINTS AND EQUATIONS	KEY TERMS	ONLINE PRACTICE
12.1 The Expected Return of a Portfolio • The portfolio weight is the initial fraction w_i of an investor's money invested in each asset. Portfolio weights add up to one: $$w_i = \frac{\text{Value of Investment } i}{\text{Total Value of Portfolio}} \quad (12.1)$$ • The expected return of a portfolio is the weighted average of the expected returns of the investments within it, using the portfolio weights: $$E[R_P] = w_1 E[R_1] + w_2 E[R_2] + \cdots + w_n E[R_n] (12.3)$$	expected return of a portfolio, p. 372 portfolio weights, p. 370 return of a portfolio, p. 370	MyFinanceLab Study Plan 12.1
12.2 The Volatility of a Portfolio • To find the risk of a portfolio, we need to know the degree to which stock returns move together. Correlation measures the co-movement of returns. The correlation is always between -1 and $+1$. It represents the fraction of the volatility due to risk that is common to the securities. • The variance of a portfolio depends on the correlation of the stocks. For a portfolio with two stocks, the portfolio variance is: $$Var(R_p)$$ $$= w_1^2 SD(R_1)^2 + w_2^2 SD(R_2)^2$$ $$+ 2w_1 w_2 Corr(R_1, R_2) SD(R_1) SD(R_2) \ (12.4)$$ • As we lower the correlation between the two stocks in a portfolio, we lower the portfolio variance. • Diversification eliminates independent, firm-specific risks, and the volatility of a large portfolio results from the common systematic risk between the stocks in the portfolio.	correlation, p. 375 equally weighted portfolio, p. 380 volatility of a portfolio, p. 373	MyFinanceLab Study Plan 12.2 Using Excel: Correlation Between Two Sets of Returns

12.3 Measuring Systematic Risk

- The market portfolio in theory is a value-weighted index of all risky investments. In practice, we often use a stock market index such as the S&P 500 to represent the market.
- A stock's beta is the percentage change in its return that we expect for each 1% change in the market's return.
- To estimate beta, we often use historical returns. Most data sources use five years of monthly returns to estimate beta.
- Beta also corresponds to the slope of the best-fitting line in the plot of a security's excess returns versus the market's excess returns. We use linear regression to find the best-fitting line.
- The beta of a portfolio is the weighted-average beta of the securities in the portfolio.

beta (β), p. 383
market capitaliza-
  tion, p. 381
market index,
  p. 382
market portfolio,
  p. 381
market proxy,
  p. 382
value-weighted
  portfolio, p. 382

MyFinanceLab
Study Plan 12.3

Interactive Beta
Calculation, Using
Excel: Calculating
a Stock's Beta

12.4 Putting It All Together: The Capital Asset Pricing Model

- According to the CAPM, the risk premium of any security is equal to the market risk premium multiplied by the beta of the security. This relationship is called the security market line (SML), and it determines the expected or required return for an investment:

$$E[R_i] = r_f + \underbrace{\beta_i(E[R_{Mkt}] - r_f)}_{\text{Risk premium for security } i} \qquad (12.6)$$

Capital Asset
  Pricing Model
  (CAPM), p. 389
market or equity risk
  premium, p. 389
required return,
  p. 390
security market line
  (SML), p. 391

MyFinanceLab
Study Plan 12.4

CRITICAL THINKING

1. What information do you need to compute the expected return of a portfolio?

2. What does correlation tell us?

3. Why isn't the total risk of a portfolio simply equal to the weighted average of the risks of the securities in the portfolio?

4. What does beta measure? How do we use beta?

5. What, intuitively, does the CAPM say drives expected return?

6. What relation is described by the security market line?

PROBLEMS

All problems are available in MyFinanceLab. *The* 🔲 *icon indicates problems that are easier to solve using Excel and have data in an Excel format available in* MyFinanceLab. *An asterisk * indicates problems with a higher level of difficulty.*

The Expected Return of a Portfolio

1. You buy 100 shares of Tidepool Co. for $40 each and 200 shares of Madfish, Inc., for $15 each. What are the weights in your portfolio?

2. Fremont Enterprises has an expected return of 15% and Laurelhurst News has an expected return of 20%. If you put 70% of your portfolio in Laurelhurst and 30% in Fremont, what is the expected return of your portfolio?

3. HNL has an expected return of 18% and KOA has an expected return of 22%. If you create a portfolio that is 60% HNL and 40% KOA, what is the expected return of the portfolio?

4. You are considering how to invest part of your retirement savings. You have decided to put $200,000 into three stocks: 50% of the money in GoldFinger (currently

$25/share), 25% of the money in Moosehead (currently $80/share), and the remainder in Venture Associates (currently $2/share). If GoldFinger stock goes up to $30/share, Moosehead stock drops to $60/share, and Venture Associates stock rises to $3 per share,

a. What is the new value of the portfolio?

b. What return did the portfolio earn?

c. If you don't buy or sell shares after the price change, what are your new portfolio weights?

5. You have $70,000. You put 20% of your money in a stock with an expected return of 12%, $30,000 in a stock with an expected return of 15%, and the rest in a stock with an expected return of 20%. What is the expected return of your portfolio?

6. There are two ways to calculate the expected return of a portfolio: Either calculate the expected return using the value and dividend stream of the portfolio as a whole, or calculate the weighted average of the expected returns of the individual stocks that make up the portfolio. Which return is higher?

The Volatility of a Portfolio

7. If the returns of two stocks have a correlation of 1, what does this imply about the relative movements in the stock prices?

 8. Stocks A and B have the following returns (*see* MyFinanceLab *for the data in Excel format*):

	Stock A	Stock B
1	0.10	0.06
2	0.07	0.02
3	0.15	0.05
4	−0.05	0.01
5	0.08	−0.02

a. What are the expected returns of the two stocks?

b. What are the standard deviations of the returns of the two stocks?

c. If their correlation is 0.46, what is the expected return and standard deviation of a portfolio of 70% stock A and 30% stock B?

 9. Using the data in the following table, estimate the average return and volatility for each stock (*see* MyFinanceLab *for the data in Excel format*).

	Realized Returns	
Year	Stock A	Stock B
2008	−10%	21%
2009	20%	30%
2010	5%	7%
2011	−5%	−3%
2012	2%	−8%
2013	9%	25%

10. Using your estimates from Problem 9 and the fact that the correlation of A and B is 0.48, calculate the volatility (standard deviation) of a portfolio that is 70% invested in stock A and 30% invested in stock B.

11. The following spreadsheet contains monthly returns for Cola Co. and Gas Co. for 2013. Using these data, estimate the average monthly return and volatility for each stock (*see* MyFinanceLab *for the data in Excel format*).

Date	Cola Co.	Gas Co.
Jan	−10.84%	−6.00%
Feb	2.36%	1.28%
Mar	6.60%	−1.86%
Apr	2.01%	−1.90%
May	18.36%	7.40%
June	−1.22%	−0.26%
July	2.25%	8.36%
Aug	−6.89%	−2.46%
Sep	−6.04%	−2.00%
Oct	13.61%	0.00%
Nov	3.51%	4.68%
Dec	0.54%	2.22%

12. Using the spreadsheet from Problem 11 and the fact that Cola Co. and Gas Co. have a correlation of 0.6083, calculate the volatility (standard deviation) of a portfolio that is 55% invested in Cola Co. stock and 45% invested in Gas Co. stock. Calculate the volatility by
    a. Using Eq. 12.4.
    b. Calculating the monthly returns of the portfolio and computing its volatility directly.
    c. How do your results compare?

13. Using the data in Table 12.2,
    a. Compute the annual returns for a portfolio with 25% invested in North Air, 25% invested in West Air, and 50% invested in Texas Oil.
    b. What is the lowest annual return for your portfolio in part a? How does it compare with the lowest annual return of the individual stocks or portfolios in Table 12.2?

14. Using the data from Table 12.3, what is the volatility of an equally weighted portfolio of Microsoft and Coca-Cola stock?

15. Suppose Johnson & Johnson and the Walgreen Company have the expected returns and volatilities shown below, with a correlation of 22%.

	E[R]	SD[R]
Johnson & Johnson	7%	16%
Walgreen Company	10%	20%

For a portfolio that is equally invested in Johnson & Johnson's and Walgreen's stock, calculate
    a. The expected return.
    b. The volatility (standard deviation).

16. Arbor Systems and Gencore stocks both have a volatility of 40%. Compute the volatility of a portfolio with 50% invested in each stock if the correlation between the stocks is (a) +1, (b) 0.50, (c) 0, (d) −0.50, and (e) −1.0. In which cases is the volatility lower than that of the original stocks?

17. Suppose Wesley Publishing stock has a volatility of 60%, while Addison Printing stock has a volatility of 30%. If the correlation between these stocks is 25%, what is the volatility of the following portfolios of Addison and Wesley: (a) 100% Addison, (b) 75% Addison and 25% Wesley, and (c) 50% Addison and 50% Wesley?

18. You have a portfolio with a standard deviation of 30% and an expected return of 18%. You are considering adding one of the two stocks in the following table. If after adding the stock you will have 20% of your money in the new stock and 80% of your money in your existing portfolio, which one should you add?

	Expected Return	Standard Deviation	Correlation with Your Portfolio's Returns
Stock A	15%	25%	0.2
Stock B	15%	20%	0.6

19. Your client has $100,000 invested in stock A. She would like to build a two-stock portfolio by investing another $100,000 in either stock B or C. She wants a portfolio with an expected return of at least 14% and as low a risk as possible, but the standard deviation must be no more than 40%. What do you advise her to do, and what will be the portfolio's expected return and standard deviation?

	Expected Return	Standard Deviation	Correlation with A
A	15%	50%	1
B	13%	40%	0.2
C	13%	40%	0.3

Measuring Systematic Risk

20. Suppose all possible investment opportunities in the world are limited to the five stocks listed in the following table. What are the market portfolio weights (*see* MyFinanceLab *for the data in Excel format*)?

Stock	Price/Share ($)	Number of Shares Outstanding (millions)
A	10	10
B	20	12
C	8	3
D	50	1
E	45	20

21. Given the information below, construct a value-weighted portfolio of the four stocks if you have $500,000 to invest. That is, how much of your $500,000 would you invest in each stock?

Stock	Market Cap
OGG	$50 million
HNL	$75 million
KOA	$20 million
LIH	$10 million

22. Given $100,000 to invest, construct a value-weighted portfolio of the four stocks listed below (*see* MyFinanceLab *for the data in Excel format*).

Stock	Price/Share ($)	Number of Shares Outstanding (millions)
Golden Seas	13	1.00
Jacobs and Jacobs	22	1.25
MAG	43	30
PDJB	5	10

23. If one stock in a value-weighted portfolio goes up in price and all other stock prices remain the same, what trades are necessary to keep the portfolio value weighted?

24. You hear on the news that the S&P 500 was down 2% today relative to the risk-free rate (the market's excess return was −2%). You are thinking about your portfolio and your investments in Zynga and Procter & Gamble.
    a. If Zynga's beta is 1.4, what is your best guess as to Zynga's excess return today?
    b. If Procter & Gamble's beta is 0.5, what is your best guess as to P&G's excess return today?

25. The risk-free rate is 3% and you believe that the S&P 500's excess return will be 10% over the next year. If you invest in a stock with a beta of 1.2 (and a standard deviation of 30%), what is your best guess as to its expected return over the next year?

26. Go to Chapter Resources on MyFinanceLab and use the data in the spreadsheet provided to estimate the beta of Nike stock using linear regression.

27. The Chapter Resources section of MyFinanceLab has data on Microsoft and the S&P 500 from 1986 to 2006.
    a. Estimate Microsoft's beta using linear regression over the periods 1987–1991, 1992–1996, 1997–2001, and 2002–2006.
    b. Compare the four estimated betas. What do you conclude about how Microsoft's exposure to systematic risk changed over that 20-year period? What do you think explains the change?

Putting It All Together: The Capital Asset Pricing Model

28. Suppose the risk-free return is 4% and the market portfolio has an expected return of 10% and a standard deviation of 16%. Johnson & Johnson Corporation stock has a beta of 0.32. What is its expected return?

29. What is the sign of the risk premium of a negative-beta stock? Explain. (Assume the risk premium of the market portfolio is positive.)

30. EJH has a beta of 1.2, CSH has a beta of 0.6, and KMS has a beta of 1.0. If you put 25% of your money in EJH, 25% in CSH, and 50% in KMS, what is the beta of your portfolio?

31. Suppose Autodesk stock has a beta of 2.16, whereas Costco stock has a beta of 0.69. If the risk-free interest rate is 4% and the expected return of the market portfolio is 10%, what is the expected return of a portfolio that consists of 60% Autodesk stock and 40% Costco stock, according to the CAPM?

32. Suppose Intel stock has a beta of 1.6, whereas Boeing stock has a beta of 1. If the risk-free interest rate is 4% and the expected return of the market portfolio is 10%, according to the CAPM,
    a. What is the expected return of Intel stock?
    b. What is the expected return of Boeing stock?

    c. What is the beta of a portfolio that consists of 60% Intel stock and 40% Boeing stock?

    d. What is the expected return of a portfolio that consists of 60% Intel stock and 40% Boeing stock? (Show both ways to solve this.)

*33. You are thinking of buying a stock priced at $100 per share. Assume that the risk-free rate is about 4.5% and the market risk premium is 6%. If you think the stock will rise to $117 per share by the end of the year, at which time it will pay a $1 dividend, what beta would it need to have for this expectation to be consistent with the CAPM?

*34. You are analyzing a stock that has a beta of 1.2. The risk-free rate is 5% and you estimate the market risk premium to be 6%. If you expect the stock to have a return of 11% over the next year, should you buy it? Why or why not?

35. You have risen through the ranks of a coffee company, from the lowly green-apron barista to the coveted black apron, and all the way to CFO. A quick Internet check shows that your company's beta is 0.6. The risk-free rate is 5% and you believe the market risk premium to be 5.5%. What is your best estimate of investors' expected return on your company's stock (its cost of equity capital)?

36. At the beginning of 2007 (the year the iPhone was introduced), Apple's beta was 1.4 and the risk-free rate was about 4.5%. Apple's price was $84.84. Apple's price at the end of 2007 was 198.08. If you estimate the market risk premium to have been 6%, did Apple's managers exceed their investors' required return as given by the CAPM?

*37. You want to invest $50,000 in a portfolio with a beta of no more than 1.4 and an expected return of 12.4%. Bay Corp. has a beta of 1.2 and an expected return of 11.2%, and City Inc. has a beta of 1.8 and an expected return of 14.8%. The risk-free rate is 4%. You can invest in Bay Corp. and City Inc. How much will you invest in each?

**Chapter 12
APPENDIX**

Alternative Models of Systematic Risk

While the CAPM is the most widely used model for estimating the cost of capital in practice, recently some practitioners have tried to improve on the CAPM.

Problems with the CAPM in Practice

Researchers have found that using only the S&P 500, or some other simple proxy for the true market portfolio, has led to consistent pricing errors from the CAPM. That is, some stocks and portfolios of stocks earn consistently higher or lower returns than the CAPM would predict. For example, researchers have found that small stocks, stocks with high ratios of book-to-market value of equity, and stocks that have recently performed very well have consistently earned higher returns than the CAPM would predict using a simple stock market proxy for the market portfolio.

Multi-Factor Models

These findings have led researchers to add new portfolios to the CAPM pricing equation in an attempt to construct a better proxy for the true market portfolio. The goal is a proxy that captures the components of systematic risk that just using the S&P 500 alone misses.

Although we might not be able to identify a perfect proxy for the true market portfolio, the market portfolio can be constructed from other portfolios. This observation implies that as long as the market portfolio can be constructed from a collection of portfolios, the collection itself can be used to measure risk. *Thus, it is not actually necessary to identify the market portfolio itself.* All that is required is to identify a collection of portfolios from which it can be constructed.

Thus, we can use a collection of portfolios to capture the components of systematic risk, referred to as **risk factors**. A model with more than one portfolio to capture risk is known as a **multi-factor model**. Each portfolio can be thought of as either the risk factor itself or a portfolio of stocks correlated with an unobservable risk factor. This particular form of the multi-factor model was originally developed by Professor Stephen Ross, but Professor Robert Merton developed an alternative multi-factor model earlier.[6] The model is also referred to as the **Arbitrage Pricing Theory (APT)**.

Fama-French-Carhart Factor Specification

Practitioners have added portfolios specifically to address the CAPM pricing errors. One such portfolio is constructed by buying small firms and selling large firms. This portfolio is widely known as the *small-minus-big (SMB) portfolio*. A second portfolio buys high book-to-market firms and sells low book-to-market firms, and we call it the *high-minus-low (HML) portfolio*. A third portfolio buys stocks that have recently done extremely well and sells those that have done extremely poorly. Since this portfolio addresses the problem that this extremely good and bad performance continues in the short run, it is called the *prior 1-year (PR1YR) momentum portfolio*.

The collection of these four portfolios—the stock market (Mkt), SMB, HML, and PR1YR—is the most popular collection of portfolios used as an alternative model to the CAPM and is one example of a multi-factor model. Using this collection, the expected return of security i is given by:

$$E[R_i] = r_f + \beta_i^{Mkt}(E[R_{Mkt}] - r_f) + \beta_i^{SMB}E[R_{SMB}] + \beta_i^{HML}E[R_{HML}] + \beta_i^{PR1YR}E[R_{PR1YR}] \tag{12.8}$$

where β_i^{Mkt}, β_i^{SMB}, β_i^{HML}, and β_i^{PR1YR} are the factor betas of stock i and measure the sensitivity of the stock to each portfolio. Because the collection of portfolios in Eq. 12.8 (Mkt, SMB, HML, and PR1YR) were identified by Professors Eugene Fama, Kenneth French, and Mark Carhart, we refer to this collection of portfolios as the **Fama-French-Carhart (FFC) factor specification**.

The average monthly returns for each of the four portfolios in the FFC factor specification are given in Table 12.5.

TABLE 12.5

FFC Portfolio Average Monthly Returns (1926–2008)

	Average Monthly Return (%)
Mkt$-r_f$	0.61
SMB	0.25
HML	0.38
PR1YR	0.70

Source: Kenneth French: http://mba.tuck.dartmouth.edu/pages/faculty/ken.french/data_library.html.

---

[6]See Stephen A. Ross, "The Arbitrage Theory of Capital Asset Pricing," *Journal of Economic Theory*, 3 (December 1976): 343–362, and Robert C. Merton "An Intertemporal Capital Asset Pricing Model," *Econometrica*, 41(1973): 867–887.

EXAMPLE 12.9

Using the FFC Factor
Specification to
Calculate the
Cost of Capital

MyFinanceLab

PROBLEM

You are currently considering making an investment in the fast food industry. You determine the project has the same level of non-diversifiable risk as investing in McDonald's stock. You use data over the past nine years to estimate the factor betas of McDonald's stock (ticker symbol: MCD). Specifically, you regress the monthly excess return (the realized return in each month minus the risk-free rate) of McDonald's stock on the return of each of the four-factor portfolios. You determine that the factor betas for MCD are:

$$\beta_{MCD}^{Mkt} = 0.687$$

$$\beta_{MCD}^{SMB} = -0.299$$

$$\beta_{MCD}^{HML} = -0.156$$

$$\beta_{MCD}^{PR1YR} = 0.123$$

The current risk-free monthly rate is 1.5%/12 = 0.125%. Determine the cost of capital by using the FFC factor specification.

SOLUTION

PLAN

First, gather the information you have. Combining the information in the problem with the data in Table 12.5, you have:

	Average Monthly Return (%)	MCD's β with Factor
Mkt$-r_f$	0.61	0.687
SMB	0.25	−0.299
HML	0.38	−0.156
PR1YR	0.70	0.123

Using the information you have collected along with the monthly risk-free rate of 0.125%, you can use Eq. 12.8 to calculate the monthly expected return for investing in McDonald's. From there, you can multiply by 12 to get the annual expected return, represented as an APR.

EXECUTE

Using Eq. 12.8, the monthly expected return of investing in McDonald's is:

$$E[R_{MCD}] = r_f + \beta_{MCD}^{Mkt}(E[R_{Mkt}] - r_f) + \beta_{MCD}^{SMB}E[R_{SMB}] + \beta_{MCD}^{HML}E[R_{HML}] + \beta_{MCD}^{PR1YR}E[R_{PR1YR}]$$

$$= 0.125\% + 0.687 \times 0.61\% - 0.299 \times 0.25\% - 0.156 \times 0.38\% + 0.123 \times 0.70\%$$

$$= 0.496\%$$

Expressed as an APR, the expected return is 0.496% × 12 = 5.95%

EVALUATE

By gathering all of the inputs and applying the FFC factor specification in the same way we would apply the CAPM, we can calculate this alternative estimate of the cost of capital for McDonald's stock. According to this approach, we would conclude that the annual cost of capital of the investment opportunity is about 5.95%.

As a comparison, a standard CAPM regression over the same time period leads to an estimated market beta of 0.54 for McDonald's—the market beta differs from the estimate of 0.687 above because we are using only a single factor in the CAPM regression. Using the historical excess return on the market implies an expected return of 0.125% + 0.54 × 0.61% = 0.454% per month, or about 5.5% per year.

13

The Cost of Capital

LEARNING OBJECTIVES

- Understand the drivers of the firm's overall cost of capital

- Measure the costs of debt, preferred stock, and common stock

- Compute a firm's overall, or weighted average, cost of capital

- Apply the weighted average cost of capital to value projects

- Adjust the cost of capital for the risk associated with the project

- Account for the direct costs of raising external capital

notation

$D\%$	fraction of the firm financed with debt	P_E	price of common stock equity
Div_1	dividend due in one year	P_{pfd}	price of preferred stock
Div_{pfd}	dividend on preferred stock	r_D	required return (cost of capital) for debt
$E\%$	fraction of the firm financed with equity	r_E	required return (cost of capital) of levered equity
FCF_t	incremental free cash flow in year t	r_{pfd}	required return (cost of capital) for preferred stock
g	expected growth rate for dividends	r_{wacc}	weighted average cost of capital
$P\%$	fraction of the firm financed with preferred stock	T_C	marginal corporate tax rate
		V_0^L	initial levered value

In Chapter 12, we learned how to determine a firm's equity cost of capital. In reality, most firms are financed with a combination of equity, debt, and other securities such as preferred stock. As a result, financial managers must determine their firm's overall cost of capital based on all sources of financing. This overall cost of capital is a critical input into the capital budgeting process. The Valuation Principle tells us that the value of a project is the present value of its benefits net of the present value of its costs. In capital budgeting, we implement this important concept with net present value (NPV). To calculate a project's NPV, we need a cost of capital to use as a discount rate.

In this chapter, we will learn how to calculate and use the firm's overall cost of capital, which is typically referred to as its *weighted average cost of capital (WACC)*. We will see that the WACC is a weighted average of the costs of capital from each of the firm's different financing sources. After we have learned how to estimate the WACC, we will apply it in capital budgeting. As part of that discussion, we will learn the conditions under which we can use the firm's overall cost of capital as a discount rate and identify those situations in which we will instead need to determine a cost of capital specific to a project or division of the firm.

13.1   A First Look at the Weighted Average Cost of Capital

Most firms draw on some combination of equity, debt, and other securities to raise the funds they need for investment. In this section, we examine the role of financing sources in determining the firm's overall cost of capital. We begin by stepping back to assess these financing sources in the context of the firm's balance sheet.

The Firm's Capital Structure

capital A firm's sources of financing—debt, equity, and other securities that it has outstanding.

A firm's sources of financing, which usually consist of debt and equity, represent its **capital**. The typical firm raises funds to invest by selling shares to stockholders (its equity) and borrowing from lenders (its debt). Recall the most basic form of the balance sheet, as represented in Figure 13.1. The left side of the balance sheet lists the firm's assets, and the right side describes the firm's capital.

capital structure The relative proportions of debt, equity, and other securities that a firm has outstanding.

The relative proportions of debt, equity, and other securities that a firm has outstanding constitute its **capital structure**. When corporations raise funds from outside investors, they must choose which type of security to issue. The most common choices are financing through equity alone and financing through a combination of debt and equity. Figure 13.2 shows the capital structures of Facebook, Apple, and UnitedContinental Holdings. Capital structures vary widely across firms. In Chapter 16, we will discuss how a firm sets its capital structure.

Opportunity Cost and the Overall Cost of Capital

Financial managers take into account each component of the firm's capital structure when determining the firm's overall cost of capital. Throughout the discussion that follows, keep in mind the intuition behind the term "cost of capital." When investors buy the stock

FIGURE 13.1

A Basic Balance Sheet

This figure provides a very basic balance sheet for reference. As discussed in Chapter 2, the two sides of the balance sheet must equal each other: Assets = Liabilities + Equity. The right side represents the way the assets are financed. In this chapter, we will focus on the required returns for the different forms of financing found on the right side of the balance sheet.

Assets	Liabilities and Equity
Current Assets	Debt
Long-Term Assets	Preferred Stock
	Equity

FIGURE 13.2

Two Capital Structures

This figure shows the capital structures of three real firms. Facebook is financed almost 100% with equity (shown in blue), Apple is financed 89% with equity, while United Continental Holdings is financed 56% with equity and 44% with debt, shaded in beige.

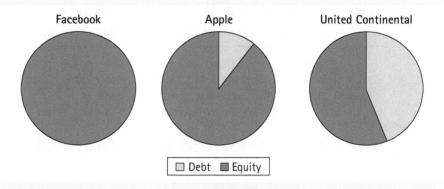

Source: Authors' calculations based on publicly available data in 2016. Percentages are based on market value of equity.

or bonds of a company, they forgo the opportunity to invest that money elsewhere. The expected return from those alternative investments constitutes an opportunity cost to them. Thus, to attract their investments as capital to the firm, the firm must offer potential investors an expected return equal to what they could expect to earn elsewhere for assuming the same level of risk. Providing this return is the cost a company bears in exchange for obtaining capital from investors.

Weighted Averages and the Overall Cost of Capital

Intuitively, the firm's overall cost of capital should be a blend of the costs of the different sources of capital. In fact, we calculate the firm's overall cost of capital as a weighted average of its equity and debt costs of capital, known as the firm's **weighted average cost of capital (WACC)**.

weighted average cost of capital (WACC) The average of a firm's equity and debt costs of capital, weighted by the fractions of the firm's value that correspond to equity and debt, respectively.

But what should the weights be? Imagine you owned all of the stock and all of the debt of the firm. If that was all you had in your portfolio, the return on your portfolio would be the total return of the firm. As we showed in Chapter 12, a portfolio return is the weighted average of the returns of the securities in the portfolio. In this case, the return on your portfolio—the total return of the firm—is a weighted average of the return you earn holding all the stock of the firm and the return you earn holding all of the debt. Since you hold all of each, your portfolio weights are just the relative amount of debt and equity issued by the firm. Thus, the weights we use in the WACC are the proportions of debt and equity used in the firm's capital structure. For example, if the firm is financed 30% by debt and 70% by equity, then the weights used in its WACC would be 30% on the debt cost of capital and 70% on the equity cost of capital.

This example suggests that you can determine the weights by looking at the right side of the firm's balance sheet. That assumption is correct, with one important modification: You must use the *market values* of the debt and equity to determine the proportions, not the accounting-based *book values* listed on the balance sheet. Recall from Chapter 2 that book values reflect historical costs, but market values are forward-looking, based on what the assets are expected to produce in the future. Holders of the firm's financial claims—equity and, if the firm has it, debt—assess the firm based on the market value of its assets, not the book value.

market-value balance sheet Similar to an accounting balance sheet, but all values are current market values rather than historical costs.

In fact, it is useful to think about the **market-value balance sheet**, where the assets, debt, and equity are all listed in terms of their market values, instead of their book values. Of course, the market-value balance sheet must still balance:

$$\text{Market Value of Equity} + \text{Market Value of Debt} = \text{Market Value of Assets} \qquad (13.1)$$

Equation 13.1 states that the total market value of all the claims (equity and debt) issued by the firm must be equal to the total market value of all its assets. This equality drives home the point that the equity and debt issued by the firm derive their value from the underlying assets they claim. The risk, and hence the required return, of the debt and equity of the firm are determined by the risk of the firm's assets. This point will be useful as we derive the firm's WACC.

Weighted Average Cost of Capital Calculations

In this section, we will develop the intuition behind the use of market-value weights as well as the link between the risk of the assets and the risk of the debt and equity claims on those assets.

unlevered A firm that does not have debt outstanding.

We begin with the straightforward case of the firm that does not issue debt—the **unlevered** firm that pays out all of the free cash flows generated by its assets to its equity holders. When some of a firm's financing comes from debt, we say the firm is **levered**. Just as a lever allows you to lift a heavy object by exerting relatively little force, so borrowing money through debt allows equity holders to control highly valued assets with relatively little investment of their own money. We refer to the relative amount of debt on the balance sheet as the firm's **leverage**.

levered A firm that has debt outstanding.

leverage The relative amount of debt on a firm's balance sheet.

The Weighted Average Cost of Capital: Unlevered Firm. If a firm is unlevered, so that it has no debt, all of the free cash flows generated by its assets are ultimately paid out to its equity holders. Because the free cash flows to the equity holders are the same as the free cash flows from the assets, the Valuation Principle tells us that the market value, risk, and cost of capital for the firm's equity are equal to the corresponding amounts for its assets. Given this relationship, we can estimate the firm's equity cost of capital using the Capital Asset Pricing Model (CAPM). The resulting estimate is the cost of capital for the firm as a whole. For example, Zynga does do not issue debt, so the cost of capital for Zynga's assets is the same as Zynga's cost of equity.

The Weighted Average Cost of Capital: Levered Firm. But what if the firm has debt? How should we incorporate the cost of this debt to determine the cost of capital for the firm's assets as a whole? The market-value balance sheet provides the answer. We can interpret the equality in Eq. 13.1 in terms of a portfolio: By holding a portfolio of the firm's equity and debt, we can get the same cash flows as if we held the assets directly. Because the return of a portfolio is equal to the weighted average of the returns of the securities in it, this equality implies the following relationship between the required returns (costs) of equity, debt, and assets:

$$\textbf{Weighted Average Cost of Capital (Pretax)}$$

$$
\begin{aligned}
r_{wacc} &= \left(\begin{array}{c} \text{Fraction of Firm Value} \\ \text{Financed by Equity} \end{array} \right) \left(\begin{array}{c} \text{Equity} \\ \text{Cost of Capital} \end{array} \right) \\
&+ \left(\begin{array}{c} \text{Fraction of Firm Value} \\ \text{Financed by Debt} \end{array} \right) \left(\begin{array}{c} \text{Debt} \\ \text{Cost of Capital} \end{array} \right) \\
&= \left(\begin{array}{c} \text{Asset} \\ \text{Cost of Capital} \end{array} \right) \qquad (13.2)
\end{aligned}
$$

We now have the justification for our intuition that the overall cost of capital for a firm should be a weighted average of its equity and debt costs of capital. Eq. 13.2 shows that we can calculate the cost of capital of the firm's assets by computing the weighted average of the firm's equity and debt cost of capital. In the next section, we explore how to estimate the firm's costs of equity and debt capital.

EXAMPLE 13.1

Calculating the Weights in the WACC

MyFinanceLab

PROBLEM

Suppose Kenai Corp. has debt with a book (face) value of $10 million, trading at 95% of face value. It also has book equity of $10 million, and 1 million shares of common stock trading at $30 per share. What weights should Kenai use in calculating its WACC?

SOLUTION

PLAN

Equation 13.2 tells us that the weights are the fractions of Kenai financed with debt and financed with equity. Furthermore, these weights should be based on market values because the cost of capital is based on investors' current assessment of the value of the firm, not on accounting-based book values. As a consequence, we can ignore the book values of debt and equity.

EXECUTE

$10 million in debt trading at 95% of face value is $9.5 million in market value. One million shares of stock at $30 per share is $30 million in market value. So, the total market value of the firm is $39.5 million.
The weights are

$$9.5 \div 39.5 = 24.1\% \text{ for debt and } 30 \div 39.5 = 75.9\% \text{ for equity.}$$

EVALUATE

When calculating its overall cost of capital, Kenai will use a weighted average of the cost of its debt capital and the cost of its equity capital, giving a weight of 24.1% to its cost of debt and a weight of 75.9% to its cost of equity.

CONCEPT CHECK

1. Why does a firm's capital have a cost?
2. Why do we use market-value weights in the weighted average cost of capital?

13.2 The Firm's Costs of Debt and Equity Capital

Section 13.1 made it clear that to measure the firm's overall cost of capital, we need to start by determining the cost of each type of capital a firm might use. We now turn to how a company measures the costs of its debt, preferred stock, and common stock. We will use General Electric (GE) as an example.

Cost of Debt Capital

We will start at the top of the right side of the balance sheet with the cost of the firm's debt. A firm's cost of debt is the interest rate it would have to pay to refinance its existing debt, such as through new bond issues. This rate differs from the coupon rate on the firm's existing debt, which reflects the interest rate the firm had to offer at the time the debt was issued.

Yield to Maturity and the Cost of Debt. Existing debt trades in the marketplace, so its price fluctuates to reflect both changes in the overall credit environment and changes in the risk specifically associated with the firm. As we learned in Chapter 6, the market price of the firm's existing debt implies a yield to maturity, which is the return that current purchasers of the debt would earn if they held the debt to maturity and received all of the payments as promised. So, we can use the yield to maturity to estimate the firm's current cost of debt: It is the yield that investors demand to hold the firm's debt (new or existing).[1]

Suppose General Electric has debt due in 2021 with a coupon rate of 5.3% priced at $1147.93 per $1000 face value. Because the market price of the debt is above its face value, investors in debt earn a yield that is lower than the 5.3% coupon rate. In fact, based on the timing of the remaining payments, this price implies a yield to maturity of 1.98%, which is an estimate of General Electric's current cost of debt. You would not need to actually compute the yield to maturity yourself because prices and their implied yields to maturity are always quoted together in the bond market.[2]

COMMON MISTAKE

Using the Coupon Rate as the Cost of Debt

A common mistake in estimating a company's overall cost of capital is to use the coupon rate on its existing debt as its debt cost of capital. The company's cost of capital is forward-looking and based on current conditions. By contrast, the coupon rate on existing debt is historical and set under potentially very different conditions. A better estimate of the firm's debt cost of capital is the yield to maturity of its existing debt, which is the promised return its lenders currently demand. As we mention in the text, it would be even better to adjust the promised yield to maturity for expected losses to get an estimate of investors' actual expected return.

Consider KB Homes as an example. KB had bonds due in 2014 that were originally issued in 2004; these bonds had a coupon rate of 5.75%. With the collapse of the U.S. real estate market in 2008, KB Homes' performance suffered and the risk that it might not be able to meet all of its debt obligations increased. By mid-2010, those 5.75% coupon bonds were rated BB (below investment grade) and trading at a yield to maturity of about 8.6%. Thus, to be willing to take a creditor position in KB, investors demanded a yield to maturity of 8.6%. Taking into account the probability of default and the expected loss in default, BB-rated bonds had an average expected loss of 1.3%. Thus, the true expected return was closer to 7.3% (8.6% promised minus 1.3% expected loss).

So, which is a better estimate of the cost of debt capital for KB in 2010: the 5.75% coupon or something based on the 8.6% yield to maturity? It would be a mistake for KB to use 5.75% as its cost of debt capital. The 5.75% rate, which was set under different circumstances, is not a relevant measure of KB's debt holders' required return in 2010, so it should not enter into the WACC calculation. Because of the default risk, the 7.3% we calculated would be a much better estimate of KB's cost of debt capital.

Taxes and the Cost of Debt. In the case of debt, the return paid to the debt holders is not the same as the cost to the firm. How could this be? The difference arises because interest paid on debt is a tax-deductible expense. When a firm uses debt financing, the cost of the interest it must pay is offset to some extent by the tax savings from the tax deduction.

For example, suppose a firm with a 35% tax rate borrows $100,000 at 10% interest per year. Then its net cost at the end of the year is calculated as follows:

		Year-End
Interest expense	$r_D \times \$100,000 =$	$10,000
Tax savings	$- \text{Tax Rate} \times r_D \times \$100,000 =$	−$3500
Effective after-tax interest expense	$r_D \times (1 - \text{Tax Rate}) \times \$100,000 =$	$6500

effective cost of the debt A firm's net cost of interest on its debt after accounting for the interest tax deduction.

The **effective cost of the debt**—the firm's net cost of interest on its debt after taxes—is only $6500/$100,000 = 6.50% of the loan amount, rather than the full 10% interest. Thus, the tax deductibility of interest lowers the effective cost of debt financing for the firm.

---

[1]In fact, the yield to maturity is the *most* the firm will pay because there is some risk the firm may not repay its debt. The expected return on the bond can be significantly less than the *promised* yield to maturity during times when the firm might be close to financial distress. However, outside of these times, the yield on an A-rated bond such as General Electric's provides a reasonable estimate of its expected return.

[2]Chapter 6 demonstrated how to find current prices and yields to maturity for corporate bonds online using the Web site http://www.finra.org/marketdata.

More generally, with tax-deductible interest and denoting the corporate tax rate as T_C, the effective after-tax borrowing rate is

$$r_D(1 - T_C) \tag{13.3}$$

EXAMPLE 13.2

Effective Cost of Debt

MyFinanceLab

PROBLEM
By using the yield to maturity on General Electric's debt, we found that its pretax cost of debt is 1.98%. If General Electric's tax rate is 35%, what is its effective cost of debt?

SOLUTION

PLAN

We can use Eq. 13.3 to calculate General Electric's effective cost of debt:

$$r_D = 0.0198 \, (\text{pretax cost of debt})$$
$$T_C = 0.35 \, (\text{corporate tax rate})$$

EXECUTE

General Electric's effective cost of debt is $0.0198\,(1 - 0.35) = 0.01287 = 1.287\%$.

EVALUATE

For every new $1000 it borrows, General Electric would pay its bondholders $0.0198\,(\$1000) = \$19.80$ in interest every year. Because it can deduct that $19.80 in interest from its income, every dollar in interest saves General Electric 35 cents in taxes, so the interest tax deduction reduces the firm's tax payment to the government by $0.35\,(\$19.80) = \$6.93$. Thus, General Electric's net cost of $1000 of debt is the $19.80 it pays minus the $6.93 in reduced tax payments, which is $12.87 per $1000 or 1.287%.

We have used corporate bonds as an example for estimating the cost of debt. Many smaller companies do not have access to the bond market and use bank debt instead. In their case, they typically have a good sense of their cost of debt from discussions with their banker about interest rates on new loans.

Cost of Preferred Stock Capital

Firms may also raise capital by issuing preferred stock. Typically, holders of the preferred stock are promised a fixed dividend, which must be paid "in preference to" (i.e., before) any dividends can be paid to common stockholders.

If the preferred dividend is known and fixed, we can estimate the preferred stock's cost of capital using Eq. 7.7 of Chapter 7,

$$r_E = \frac{Div_1}{P_0} + g$$

where the growth rate $g = 0$. Thus,

$$\text{Cost of Preferred Stock Capital} = \frac{\text{Preferred Dividend}}{\text{Preferred Stock Price}} = \frac{Div_{pfd}}{P_{pfd}} \tag{13.4}$$

For example, assume General Electric's series D preferred stock has a price of $85.83 and an annual dividend of $3.50. Its cost of preferred stock, therefore, is $3.50 \div 85.83 = 4.08\%$.[3]

---

[3]General Electric previously had three sets of outstanding preferred shares, but exchanged them for Series D in early 2016.

Cost of Common Stock Capital

As we learned in Chapter 12, a company cannot directly observe its cost of common stock (equity), but must instead estimate it. We now present and compare the two major methods for doing so.

Capital Asset Pricing Model. The most common approach is to use the CAPM as presented in Chapter 12. To summarize that approach:

1. Estimate the firm's beta of equity, typically by regressing 60 months of the company's returns against 60 months of returns for a market proxy such as the S&P 500.
2. Determine the risk-free rate, typically by using the yield on Treasury bills or bonds.
3. Estimate the market risk premium, typically by comparing historical returns on a market proxy to historical risk-free rates.
4. Apply the CAPM:

$$\text{Cost of Equity} = \text{Risk-Free Rate} + \text{Equity Beta} \times \text{Market Risk Premium}$$

For example, suppose the equity beta of General Electric is 1.30, the yield on 10-year Treasury notes is 3%, and you estimate the market risk premium to be 6%. General Electric's cost of equity is $3\% + 1.30 \times 6\% = 10.8\%$.

Constant Dividend Growth Model. Another way to estimate a company's cost of equity comes from the constant dividend growth model (CDGM) introduced in Chapter 7. Equation 7.7 from Chapter 7 shows that

$$\text{Cost of Equity} = \frac{\text{Dividend (in one year)}}{\text{Current Price}} + \text{Dividend Growth Rate} = \frac{Div_1}{P_E} + g \quad (13.5)$$

Thus, to estimate the cost of equity, we need the current price of the stock, the expected dividend in one year, and an estimate of the dividend growth rate. The current price of the stock is easy to obtain online. We may even have a reasonable estimate of next year's dividend. However, as we discussed in Chapter 7, estimating the future dividend growth rate can be very difficult. For example, General Electric's recent annual dividend history is $0.58 (2011), $0.68 (2012), $0.76 (2013), $0.88 (2014), and $0.92 (2015). Perhaps it is reasonable to assume that 2016's dividend will also be $0.92 per year, but what about the dividend's long-term growth rate? The historical growth has been uneven.

Rather than looking backward at historical growth, one common approach is to use estimates produced by stock analysts, as these estimates are forward-looking. As discussed in Chapter 7, if General Electric keeps its dividend payout rate constant, then the long-run growth in dividends will equal the long-run growth in earnings. In early-2016, the average forecast for GE's long-run earnings growth rate was 12.7%. Thus, with an expected dividend in one year of $0.92, a price of $30.05, and long-run dividend growth of 12.7%, the CDGM estimates GE's cost of equity as follows (using Eq. 13.5):

$$\text{Cost of Equity} = \frac{Div_1}{P_E} + g = \frac{\$0.92}{\$30.05} + 0.127 = 0.158, \text{ or } 15.8\%$$

We should not be surprised that the two estimates of General Electric's cost of equity (10.8% and 15.8%) do not match, because each was based on different assumptions. Furthermore, even given an estimate of future growth of dividends, Eq. 13.5 makes an assumption that future dividend growth will continue at a constant rate. This assumption is unlikely to be valid for most firms. For example, even though General Electric's dividend has grown steadily over 5 years, it was forced to reduce its dividend substantially in 2009 during the financial crisis. Also note that many young, growing firms do not pay a dividend and have no plans to do so in the near future.

TABLE 13.1

Estimating the Cost of Equity

	Capital Asset Pricing Model	**Constant Dividend Growth Model**
Inputs	Equity beta	Current stock price
	Risk-free rate	Expected dividend next year
	Market risk premium	Future dividend growth rate
Major Assumptions	Estimated beta is correct	Dividend estimate is correct
	Market risk premium is accurate	Growth rate matches market expectations
	CAPM is the correct model	Future dividend growth is constant

We could use any model relating a firm's stock price to its future cash flows to estimate its cost of equity—the CDGM is just one of the possible models. For example, we could use the discounted free cash flow model from Chapter 10 to solve for the firm's cost of equity.

CAPM and CDGM Comparison. Because of the difficulties with the CDGM, the CAPM is the most popular approach for estimating the cost of equity. Table 13.1 compares the two approaches.

EXAMPLE 13.3

Estimating the Cost of Equity

MyFinanceLab

PROBLEM

Assume the equity beta for Johnson & Johnson (ticker: JNJ) is 0.55. The yield on 10-year treasuries is 3%, and you estimate the market risk premium to be 6%. Furthermore, Johnson & Johnson issues dividends at an annual rate of $2.81. Its current stock price is $92.00, and you expect dividends to increase at a constant rate of 4% per year. Estimate J&J's cost of equity in two ways.

SOLUTION

PLAN

The two ways to estimate J&J's cost of equity are to use the CAPM and the CDGM.
1. The CAPM requires the risk-free rate, an estimate of the equity's beta, and an estimate of the market risk premium. We can use the yield on 10-year Treasury notes as the risk-free rate.
2. The CDGM requires the current stock price, the expected dividend next year, and an estimate of the constant future growth rate for the dividend.

Risk-free rate: 3%	Current price: $92.00
Equity beta: 0.55	Expected dividend: $2.81
Market risk premium: 6%	Estimated future dividend growth rate: 4%

We can use the CAPM from Chapter 12 to estimate the cost of equity using the CAPM approach and Eq. 13.5 to estimate it using the CDGM approach.

EXECUTE

1. The CAPM says that

$$\text{Cost of Equity} = \text{Risk-Free Rate} + \text{Equity Beta} \times \text{Market Risk Premium}$$

For J&J, this implies that its cost of equity is $3\% + 0.55 \times 6\% = 6.3\%$.

2. The CDGM says

$$\text{Cost of Equity} = \frac{\text{Dividend (in one year)}}{\text{Current Price}} + \text{Dividend Growth Rate} = \frac{\$2.81}{\$92.00} + 4\% = 7.1\%$$

EVALUATE

According to the CAPM, the cost of equity capital is 6.3%; the CDGM produces a result of 7.1%. Because of the different assumptions we make when using each method, the two methods do not have to produce the same answer—in fact, it would be highly unlikely that they would. When the two approaches produce

(Continued)

different answers, we must examine the assumptions we made for each approach and decide which set of assumptions is more realistic. We can also see what assumption about future dividend growth would be necessary to make the answers converge. By rearranging the CDGM and using the cost of equity we estimated from the CAPM, we have

$$\text{Dividend Growth Rate} = \text{Cost of Equity} - \frac{\text{Dividend (in one year)}}{\text{Current Price}} = 6.3\% - 3.1\% = 3.2\%$$

Thus, if we believe that J&J's dividends will grow at a rate of 3.2% per year, the two approaches would produce the same cost of equity estimate.

CONCEPT CHECK

3. How can you measure a firm's cost of debt?

4. What are the major tradeoffs in using the CAPM versus the CDGM to estimate the cost of equity?

13.3   A Second Look at the Weighted Average Cost of Capital

Now that we have estimated the costs of General Electric's different sources of capital, we are ready to calculate the firm's overall WACC. The weights are the percentage of the firm's value financed by equity, preferred stock, and debt. We can represent these as $E\%$, $P\%$, and $D\%$, respectively, and note that they must sum to 100% (i.e., we must account for all the sources of financing).

WACC Equation

Formally, denoting the cost of equity, preferred and debt capital as r_E, r_{pfd}, and r_D, and the corporate tax rate as T_C, the WACC is

Weighted Average Cost of Capital

$$r_{wacc} = r_E E\% + r_{pfd} P\% + r_D (1 - T_C) D\% \tag{13.6}$$

For a company that does not have preferred stock, the WACC condenses to

$$r_{wacc} = r_E E\% + r_D (1 - T_C) D\% \tag{13.7}$$

For example, in 2016, the market values of General Electric's common stock, preferred stock, and debt were \$276,880 million, \$6,000 million, and \$198,270 million, respectively. Its total value was, therefore, \$276,880 million + \$6,000 million + \$198,270 million = \$481,150 million. Given the costs of common stock (CAPM estimate), preferred stock, and debt we have already computed, General Electric's WACC in 2016 was

$$r_{wacc} = r_E E\% + r_{pfd} P\% + r_D (1 - T_C) D\%$$

$$r_{wacc} = 10.8\% \left(\frac{276,880}{481,150} \right) + 4.08\% \left(\frac{6,000}{481,150} \right) + 1.98\% (1 - 0.35) \left(\frac{198,270}{481,150} \right)$$

$$r_{wacc} = 6.8\%$$

EXAMPLE 13.4

Computing the WACC

MyFinanceLab

PROBLEM

Assume the expected return on Target's equity is 11.5%, and the firm has a yield to maturity on its debt of 6%. Debt accounts for 18% and equity for 82% of Target's total market value. If its tax rate is 35%, what is an estimate of this firm's WACC?

SOLUTION

PLAN

We can compute the WACC using Eq. 13.7. To do so, we need to know the costs of equity and debt, their proportions in Target's capital structure, and the firm's tax rate. We have all that information, so we are ready to proceed.

EXECUTE

$$r_{wacc} = r_E E\% + r_D(1 - T_C)D\% = (0.115)(0.82) + (0.06)(1 - 0.35)(0.18)$$
$$= 0.101, \text{ or } 10.1\%$$

EVALUATE

Even though we cannot observe the expected return of Target's investments directly, we can use the expected return on its equity and debt and the WACC formula to estimate it, adjusting for the tax advantage of debt. Target needs to earn at least a 10.1% return on its investment in current and new stores to satisfy both its debt and equity holders.

Weighted Average Cost of Capital in Practice

The WACC is driven by the risk of a company's line of business and, because of the tax effect of interest, its leverage. As a result, WACCs vary widely across industries and companies. Figure 13.3 presents the WACC for several real companies to provide a sense of the degree to which the cost of capital can vary. Some lines of business are clearly riskier than others.

FIGURE 13.3

WACCs for Real Companies

The cost of equity is computed using the company's equity beta, a risk-free rate of 3%, and a market risk premium of 6%. The cost of debt is based on market yield to maturities of the debt. The percent equity and percent debt are determined from the company's market capitalization and balance sheet. The WACC is computed using Eq. 13.7 with a 35% tax rate and is shown in the accompanying bar graph. "N/A" means that the cost of debt is not applicable and refers to companies that have no debt.

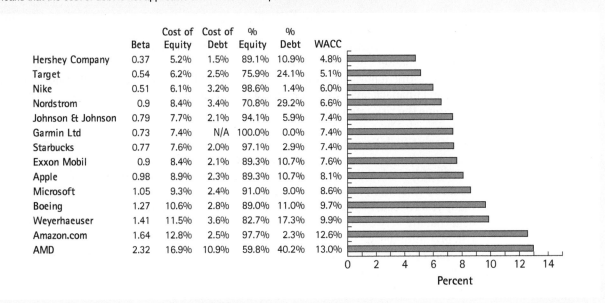

	Beta	Cost of Equity	Cost of Debt	% Equity	% Debt	WACC
Hershey Company	0.37	5.2%	1.5%	89.1%	10.9%	4.8%
Target	0.54	6.2%	2.5%	75.9%	24.1%	5.1%
Nike	0.51	6.1%	3.2%	98.6%	1.4%	6.0%
Nordstrom	0.9	8.4%	3.4%	70.8%	29.2%	6.6%
Johnson & Johnson	0.79	7.7%	2.1%	94.1%	5.9%	7.4%
Garmin Ltd	0.73	7.4%	N/A	100.0%	0.0%	7.4%
Starbucks	0.77	7.6%	2.0%	97.1%	2.9%	7.4%
Exxon Mobil	0.9	8.4%	2.1%	89.3%	10.7%	7.6%
Apple	0.98	8.9%	2.3%	89.3%	10.7%	8.1%
Microsoft	1.05	9.3%	2.4%	91.0%	9.0%	8.6%
Boeing	1.27	10.6%	2.8%	89.0%	11.0%	9.7%
Weyerhaeuser	1.41	11.5%	3.6%	82.7%	17.3%	9.9%
Amazon.com	1.64	12.8%	2.5%	97.7%	2.3%	12.6%
AMD	2.32	16.9%	10.9%	59.8%	40.2%	13.0%

Source: Authors' calculations based on publicly available information in 2016.

For example, selling chocolate, as Hershey does, is a fairly low-risk proposition, but being an online retailer (Amazon) or semiconductor company (AMD) is much riskier.

Methods in Practice

We now turn to some issues that arise for financial managers when they are estimating the WACC in practice.

net debt Total debt outstanding minus any cash balances.

Net Debt. When calculating the weights for the WACC, it is increasingly common practice to make an adjustment to the debt. Many practitioners now use **net debt**, the total debt outstanding minus any cash balances:

$$\text{Net Debt} = \text{Debt} - \text{Cash and Risk-Free Securities} \qquad (13.8)$$

Why subtract a company's cash from its debt? The assets on a firm's balance sheet include any holdings of cash or risk-free securities. If a firm holds $1 in cash and has $1 of risk-free debt, then the interest earned on the cash will equal the interest paid on the debt. The cash flows from each source cancel each other, just as if the firm held no cash and no debt. In fact, we can view cash as being equivalent to negative debt. Significant excess cash on a firm's balance sheet can complicate the assessment of the risk (and hence the cost of capital) of the assets the firm actually uses in the course of business. Thus, when trying to evaluate a firm's business assets separate from any cash holdings, practitioners often measure the leverage of the firm in terms of its net debt and measure the market value of a firm's business assets using its enterprise value. Recall Chapter 2's definition of the enterprise value as the market value of its equity plus its net debt.

Using this approach, the weights in the WACC would then be

$$\left(\frac{\text{Market Value of Equity}}{\text{Enterprise Value}}\right) \text{ and } \left(\frac{\text{Net Debt}}{\text{Enterprise Value}}\right)$$

For firms with substantial excess cash reserves, this adjustment could be important. For firms with relatively low levels of cash, it will not have a large effect on the overall WACC estimate.

The Risk-Free Interest Rate. Estimating the equity cost of capital using the CAPM requires the risk-free interest rate. The risk-free interest rate is generally determined using the yields of U.S. Treasury securities, which are free from default risk. But which horizon should we choose? The CAPM states that we should use the risk-free interest corresponding to the investment horizon of the firm's investors. When surveyed, the vast majority of large firms and financial analysts report using the yields of long-term (10- to 30-year) bonds to determine the risk-free rate.[4]

The Market Risk Premium. Using the CAPM also requires an estimate of the market risk premium. As mentioned in Chapter 11, one way to estimate the market risk premium is to look at historical data. Because we are interested in the *future* market risk premium, we face a tradeoff in terms of the amount of data we use. As noted in Chapter 11, it takes many years of data to produce even moderately accurate estimates of expected returns—yet data that are very old may have little relevance for investors' expectations of the market risk premium today.

Table 13.2 reports excess returns of the S&P 500 versus one-year and 10-year Treasury rates. Since 1926, the S&P 500 has produced an average return of 7.7% above the rate

---

[4]See Robert Bruner, et al., "Best Practices in Estimating the Cost of Capital: Survey and Synthesis," *Financial Practice and Education* 8 (1998): 13–28.

TABLE 13.2

Historical Excess
Returns of the S&P 500
Compared to One-Year
Treasury Bills
and 10-Year U.S.
Treasury Securities

| S&P 500 Excess | Period | |
Return Versus	1926–2015	1965–2015
One-year Treasury	7.7%	5.0%
10-year Treasury*	5.9%	3.9%

*Based on a comparison of compounded returns over a 10-year holding period.

for one-year Treasury securities. However, some evidence indicates that the market risk premium has declined over time. Since 1965, the S&P 500 has shown an excess return of only 5.0% over the rate for one-year Treasury securities. Compared with 10-year Treasury securities, the S&P 500 had an average excess return of only 3.9% (due primarily to the fact that 10-year Treasury bond rates tend to be higher than one-year rates).

How can we explain this decline? One explanation may be that as more investors have begun to participate in the stock market and the costs of constructing a diversified portfolio have declined, investors have tended to hold less risky portfolios. As a result, the return they require as compensation for taking on that risk has diminished. In addition, the overall volatility of the market has declined over time. Some researchers believe that the future expected returns for the market are likely to be even lower than these historical numbers, in a range of 3% to 5% over Treasury bills.[5] Consequently, many financial managers currently use market risk premiums closer to 5%, rather than 7%.

CONCEPT CHECK

5. Why do different companies have different WACCs?

6. What are the tradeoffs in estimating the market risk premium?

13.4   Using the WACC to Value a Project

A project's cost of capital depends on its risk. When the market risk of the project is similar to the average market risk of the firm's investments, then its cost of capital is equivalent to the cost of capital for a portfolio of all the firm's securities. In other words, the project's cost of capital is equal to the firm's WACC. As shown in Eq. 13.6, the WACC incorporates the benefit of the interest tax deduction by using the firm's *after-tax* cost of capital for debt.

Because the WACC incorporates the tax savings from debt, we can compute the value of an investment including the benefit of the interest tax deduction given the firm's leverage policy, sometimes called the investment's **levered value**. To do so, we discount the firm's future incremental free cash flow using the WACC, a process we refer to as the **WACC method**. Specifically, if FCF_t is the expected incremental free cash flow of an investment at the end of year t, then the Valuation Principle tells us that the investment's levered value, V_0^L, is

levered value The value of an investment, including the benefit of the interest tax deduction, given the firm's leverage policy.

WACC method Discounting future incremental free cash flows using the firm's WACC. This method produces the levered value of a project.

$$V_0^L = FCF_0 + \frac{FCF_1}{1 + r_{wacc}} + \frac{FCF_2}{\left(1 + r_{wacc}\right)^2} + \frac{FCF_3}{\left(1 + r_{wacc}\right)^3} + \cdots \qquad (13.9)$$

The intuition for the WACC method is that the firm's WACC represents the average return the firm must pay to its investors (both debt and equity holders) on an after-tax basis. Thus, to have a positive NPV, a project with the same risk as the average risk for the firm's projects should generate an expected return of at least the firm's WACC.

---

[5]See I. Welch, "Views of Financial Economists on the Equity Premium and Other Issues," *Journal of Business* 73 (2000): 501–537 (with 2009 update), and J. Graham and C. Harvey, "The Equity Risk Premium in 2008: Evidence from the Global CFO Outlook Survey," SSRN 2008, "The Equity Risk Premium in 2008: Evidence from the Global CFO Outlook Survey," SSRN 2008, and Ivo Welch and Amit Goyal, "A Comprehensive Look at The Empirical Performance of Equity Premium Prediction," Review of Financial Studies 21 (2008): 1455–1508.

EXAMPLE 13.5

The WACC Method

MyFinanceLab

PROBLEM

Suppose Anheuser-Busch InBev is considering introducing a new ultra-light beer with zero calories to be called BudZero. The firm believes that the beer's flavor and appeal to calorie-conscious drinkers will make it a success. The cost of bringing the beer to market is $200 million, but Anheuser-Busch InBev expects first-year incremental free cash flows from BudZero to be $100 million and to grow at 3% per year thereafter. If Anheuser-Busch InBev's WACC is 5.7%, should it go ahead with the project?

SOLUTION

PLAN

We can use the WACC method shown in Eq. 13.9 to value BudZero and then subtract the up-front cost of $200 million. We will need Anheuser-Busch InBev's WACC, which is 5.7%.

EXECUTE

The cash flows for BudZero are a growing perpetuity. Applying the growing perpetuity formula with the WACC method, we have

$$V_0^L = FCF_0 + \frac{FCF_1}{r_{wacc} - g} = -\$200 \text{ million} + \frac{\$100 \text{ million}}{0.057 - 0.03} = \$3,503.7 \text{ million} \ (\$3.5 \text{ billion})$$

EVALUATE

The BudZero project has a positive NPV because it is expected to generate a return on the $200 million far in excess of Anheuser-Busch InBev's WACC of 5.7%. As discussed in Chapter 8, taking positive-NPV projects adds value to the firm. Here, we can see that the value is created by exceeding the required return of the firm's investors.

Key Assumptions

While it is common practice to use the WACC as the discount rate in capital budgeting, it is important to be aware of the underlying assumptions. We examine the critical assumptions here and then explore these assumptions further in the context of an application.

Assumption 1: Average Risk. We assume initially that the market risk of the project is equivalent to the average market risk of the firm's investments. In that case, we assess the project's cost of capital based on the risk of the firm.

debt-equity ratio A ratio of the market value of debt to the market value of equity.

Assumption 2: Constant Debt-Equity Ratio. We assume that the firm adjusts its leverage continuously to maintain a constant ratio of the market value of debt to the market value of equity—a relationship referred to as the **debt-equity ratio**. This policy determines the amount of debt the firm will take on when it accepts a new project. It also implies that the risk of the firm's equity and debt, and therefore its WACC, will not fluctuate owing to leverage changes.

Assumption 3: Limited Leverage Effects. We assume initially that the main effect of leverage on valuation follows from the interest tax deduction. We assume that any other factors (such as possible financial distress) are not significant at the level of debt chosen. We discuss these other factors in detail in Chapter 16.

Assumptions in Practice. These assumptions are reasonable for many projects and firms. The first assumption is likely to fit typical projects of firms with investments concentrated in a single industry. In that case, the market risk of both the project and the firm will primarily depend on the sensitivity of the industry to the overall economy. The second assumption, while unlikely to hold exactly, reflects the fact that firms tend to increase their levels of debt as they grow larger; some may even have an explicit target for their debt-equity ratio.[6] Finally, for firms without very high levels of debt, the interest tax deduction is likely to be the most important factor affecting the capital budgeting decision. Hence, the third assumption is a reasonable starting point to begin our analysis.

Of course, while these three assumptions may be a reasonable approximation in many situations, there are certainly projects and firms for which they do not apply. In the following section, we apply the WACC method under all three assumptions. Next, we relax the first assumption, which states that the project has average risk. (We will relax the other two assumptions in later chapters.)

WACC Method Application: Extending the Life of a GE Facility

Let's apply the WACC method to value a project. Suppose GE is considering an investment that would extend the life of one of its facilities for four years. The project would require up-front costs of $6.67 million plus a $24 million investment in equipment. The equipment will be obsolete in four years and will be depreciated via the straight-line method over that period. During the next four years, however, GE expects annual sales of $60 million per year from this facility. Material costs and operating expenses are expected to total $25 million and $9 million, respectively, per year. Finally, GE expects no net working capital requirements for the project, and it pays a corporate tax rate of 35%.

Using this information, the spreadsheet in Table 13.3 forecasts the project's expected free cash flow. Assume that the market risk of the project of extending the life of the facility is the same as that for GE's overall business. As a consequence, we can use GE's WACC to compute the NPV of the project.

We can determine the value of the project, including the present value of the interest tax deduction from the debt, by calculating the present value of its future free cash flows, V_0^L, using the WACC method and GE's WACC of 6.8%, which we computed in Section 13.3:

$$V_0^L = \frac{19}{1.068} + \frac{19}{1.068^2} + \frac{19}{1.068^3} + \frac{19}{1.068^4} = \$64.65 \text{ million}$$

TABLE 13.3

Expected Free Cash Flow from GE's Facility Project

1	Year	0	1	2	3	4
2	**Incremental Earnings Forecast ($million)**					
3	Sales	—	60.00	60.00	60.00	60.00
4	Cost of Goods Sold	—	−25.00	−25.00	−25.00	−25.00
5	**Gross Profit**	—	35.00	35.00	35.00	35.00
6	Operating Expenses	−6.67	−9.00	−9.00	−9.00	−9.00
7	Depreciation	—	−6.00	−6.00	−6.00	−6.00
8	**EBIT**	−6.67	20.00	20.00	20.00	20.00
9	Income Tax at 35%	2.33	−7.00	−7.00	−7.00	−7.00
10	**Unlevered Net Income**	−4.34	13.00	13.00	13.00	13.00
11	**Incremental Free Cash Flow ($ million)**					
12	Plus: Depreciation	—	6.00	6.00	6.00	6.00
13	Less: Capital Expenditures	−24.00	—	—	—	—
14	Less: Increases in NWC	—	—	—	—	—
15	**Incremental Free Cash Flow**	−28.34	19.00	19.00	19.00	19.00

---

[6]We discuss the tradeoff between debt and equity and the concept of a target debt-equity ratio in Chapter 16.

Because the up-front after-tax cost of extending the facility's life is only $28.34 million, this project is a good idea. Taking the project results in an NPV of $64.65 million − $28.34 million = $36.31 million for the firm.

Summary of the WACC Method

To summarize, the key steps in the WACC valuation method are as follows:

1. Determine the incremental free cash flow of the investment.
2. Compute the weighted average cost of capital using Eq. 13.6.
3. Compute the value of the investment, including the tax benefit of leverage, by discounting the incremental free cash flow of the investment using the WACC.

In many firms, the corporate treasurer performs the second step, calculating the firm's WACC. This rate can then be used throughout the firm as the companywide cost of capital for new investments *that are of comparable risk to the rest of the firm and that will not alter the firm's debt-equity ratio*. Employing the WACC method in this way is very simple and straightforward. As a result, this method is the most commonly used in practice for capital budgeting purposes.

CONCEPT CHECK

7. What are the main assumptions you make when you use the WACC method?
8. What inputs do you need to be ready to apply the WACC method?

13.5 Project-Based Costs of Capital

Up to this point we have assumed that both the risk and the leverage of the project under consideration matched those characteristics for the firm as a whole. This assumption allowed us, in turn, to assume that the cost of capital for a project matched the firm's cost of capital.

In reality, specific projects often differ from the average investment made by the firm. Consider again General Electric Company (GE), a large firm with many divisions that operate in completely different lines of business. Projects in GE's health-care division are likely to have different market risk than projects in its air transportation equipment division or in its appliance division. Projects may also vary in terms of the amount of leverage they will support—for example, acquisitions of real estate or capital equipment are often highly levered, while investments in intellectual property are not. We will study the effect of leverage on the cost of capital when we cover the leverage decision in Chapter 16. In this section, we show how to calculate the cost of capital for the project's cash flows when a project's risk differs from the firm's overall risk.

COMMON MISTAKE

Using a Single Cost of Capital in Multi-Divisional Firms

Many firms combine business units with widely different market risk. Yet some of them use a single cost of capital to evaluate projects throughout the organization. Using the same cost of capital for projects that have different riskiness, is, of course, a mistake, and will result in the firm taking on too many risky projects and too few safer projects. That is, when the same cost of capital is used for all investment opportunities, regardless of their riskiness, riskier projects will be discounted at too low a cost of capital, making negative NPV investments appear to be positive NPV and be accepted. Similarly, less risky projects will be discounted at too high a cost of capital, and so may be erroneously rejected.

Because survey evidence suggests that this mistake is quite common, Professors Philipp Krüger, Augustin Landier, and David Thesmar* looked at the behavior of conglomerates and found evidence that they were making this mistake. For each conglomerate, they identified the most important division, what they termed the *core-division*. They then demonstrated that, on average, conglomerates invest relatively less in divisions that are less risky than the core-division, and relatively more in divisions that are more risky than the core-division.

*"The WACC Fallacy: The Real Effects of Using a Unique Discount Rate," *Journal of Finance*, 70 (2015): 1253–1285.

Cost of Capital for a New Acquisition

We begin by explaining how to calculate the cost of capital of a project with market risk that is different from the risk for the rest of the firm. Suppose GE wants to enter the athletic shoe business. To do so, it is considering acquiring Nike, a company that is focused on that business. Nike faces different market risks than GE does in GE's broad range of businesses. What cost of capital should GE use to value a possible acquisition of Nike?

Because the risks are different, GE's WACC would be inappropriate for valuing Nike. Instead, GE should calculate and use Nike's WACC when assessing the acquisition. In Figure 13.3, we find the following information for Nike, where the WACC is based on a tax rate of 35%:

	Beta	Cost of Equity	Cost of Debt	% Equity	% Debt	WACC
Nike	0.51	6.1%	3.2%	99%	1%	6.0%

Assuming that GE will find it appropriate to continue to finance Nike with the same mix of debt and equity after it buys Nike,[7] we can use Nike's WACC as the cost of capital for acquiring it. Thus, GE would use a cost of capital of 6.0% to value Nike for purchase.

Divisional Costs of Capital

Now assume GE makes a different decision: It decides to create an athletic shoes division internally, rather than buying Nike. What should the cost of capital for the new division be? If GE plans to finance the division with the same proportion of debt as is used by Nike, then GE would use Nike's WACC as the WACC for its new division. Because Nike's WACC is the right cost of capital given the risks of athletic shoes and 1% debt financing, it has to be the right cost of capital for an internally created athletic shoes division that is financed 1% with debt.

In most cases, firms with more than one division should not use a single companywide WACC to evaluate projects. More typically, they perform analyses similar to GE's analysis of Nike. Multidivisional firms benchmark their own divisions off of companies that compete with their division and are focused in that single line of business. By performing the same analysis as we did in Figure 13.3, the multidivisional firm can estimate the WACCs of its divisions' competitors—adjusting for different financing if necessary—to estimate the cost of capital for each division.

EXAMPLE 13.6

A Project in a New Line of Business

MyFinanceLab

PROBLEM

You are working for Microsoft evaluating the possibility of selling digital video recorders (DVRs). Microsoft's WACC is 8.6%. DVRs would be a new line of business for Microsoft, however, so the systematic risk of this business would likely differ from the systematic risk of Microsoft's current business. As a result, the assets of this new business should have a different cost of capital. You need to find the cost of capital for the DVR business. Assuming that the risk-free rate is 3% and the market risk premium is 6%, how would you estimate the cost of capital for this type of investment?

SOLUTION

PLAN

The first step is to identify a company operating in Microsoft's targeted line of business. TiVo, Inc., is a well-known marketer of DVRs. In fact, that is its sole business. Thus, the cost of capital for TiVo would be a good estimate of the cost of capital for Microsoft's proposed DVR business. Many Web sites are available that provide betas for traded stocks, including http://finance.yahoo.com. Suppose you visit that site and find that the beta of TiVo stock is 1.45. With this beta, the risk-free rate, and the market risk premium, you can use the CAPM to estimate the cost of equity for TiVo. Fortunately for us, TiVo has no debt, so its cost of equity is the same as its cost of capital for its assets.

(Continued)

---

[7]We consider what to do if GE wants to change Nike's financing mix in Chapter 16.

EXECUTE

Using the CAPM, we have

TiVo's Cost of Equity = Risk-Free Rate + TiVo's Equity Beta × Market Risk Premium

$$= 3\% + 1.45 \times 6\% = 11.7\%$$

Because TiVo has no debt, its WACC is equivalent to its cost of equity.

EVALUATE

The correct cost of capital for evaluating a DVR investment opportunity is 11.7%. If we had used the 8.6% cost of capital that is associated with Microsoft's *existing* business, we would have mistakenly used too low of a cost of capital. That could lead us to go ahead with the investment, even if it truly had a negative NPV.

INTERVIEW WITH SHELAGH GLASER

Shelagh M. Glaser is vice president of Finance and Group Controller of the Client Computing Group at Intel Corporation. Her responsibilities include profit and loss forecasting, reporting and controls.

QUESTION: *Does Intel set the discount rate at the corporate or project level?*

ANSWER: We typically set the discount rate at the corporate level. As a company, Intel makes a broad set of products that sell into similar markets, so one hurdle rate makes sense for our core business. To justify an investment, every project has to earn or exceed that level of return for our shareholders.

We may use a different discount rate for mergers and acquisitions. For example, recently we've done more software acquisitions. That industry is very different from semiconductors and has different risk factors, so we take those considerations into account to set the hurdle rate.

QUESTION: *How does Intel compute the cost of capital for new investment opportunities?*

ANSWER: We reexamine our weighted average cost of capital (WACC) each year to see that we have the right inputs and if any have changed: What is the current market risk premium? Are we using the right risk-free rate? How should we weight historical data? We use the CAPM to determine beta but consider whether to continue using the five-year weekly beta or to change to a daily or monthly beta in the calculation. We also look at the latest studies from academia on what the inputs should be.

Once we have estimated the WACC, we think about the appropriate hurdle rate for our circumstances. We have not changed the hurdle rate in recent years—even though the WACC may have changed—and continue to use a hurdle rate that is above the WACC. This higher hurdle rate reflects our ability to time our investments and helps us choose projects that maximize our expected returns. Intel has more projects with returns above our hurdle than we can invest in, so assessing opportunity cost is a significant aspect of decision making. We may invest in some projects with NPVs below the hurdle rate if they are of strategic importance.

QUESTION: *How do project-specific considerations affect Intel's cost of capital calculation?*

ANSWER: When deciding whether to invest billions in wafer fabrication plants, Intel considers both the physical plant and the product line. We calculate the margin we would need from the product and develop a comprehensive set of metrics to justify the large capital investment. Typically we use our standard hurdle rate and also look at risk factors and the timing of the product launch. Intel's business is driven by the economics of Moore's Law, allowing us to double transistors every two years. Each generation of new technology creates cost reductions that enable new fabrication plants to clear the hurdle rate. These plants produce our leading-edge product, which earn our highest margins. To get a premium price, our customers require a product that takes advantage of the performance and power efficiency of the latest technology.

QUESTION: *Did the 2008 financial crisis affect how you evaluate investment opportunities?*

ANSWER: In 2008, the market was very depressed. We continued making R&D investments and reduced spending in other areas, such as marketing and short-term promotion. Cutting R&D would have left us with a gap in our product line in several years, because product development cycles typically run four years. In this industry, not keeping the R&D machine flowing, to boost short-term earnings, will harm the company's long-term viability. R&D is critical to our fundamental business model, which may require long-term decisions that negatively impact short-term results.

Intel has a long history of investing to maintain performance leadership during downturns. Intel carries almost no debt. Our capital policy is to maintain sufficient cash for fabrication plants and multiple years of R&D expenses, to avoid depending on capital markets to finance ongoing operations. A painful experience in the 1980s, when Intel's access to capital markets was curtailed, highlighted how this conservative capital policy pays off. Going into this crisis with no debt and an extremely strong cash position has served us well.

9. When evaluating a project in a new line of business, which assumptions for the WACC method are most likely to be violated?

10. How can you estimate the WACC to be used in a new line of business?

13.6 When Raising External Capital Is Costly

So far, we have assumed that there are no important factors to consider in seeking capital other than taxes. Among other things, this implies that we can raise external capital without any extra costs associated with the capital-raising transaction. As a consequence, we have no reason to treat a project financed with new external funds any differently than a project financed with internal funds (retained earnings).

In reality, issuing new equity or bonds carries a number of costs. These costs include the costs of filing and registering with the Securities and Exchange Commission and the fees charged by investment bankers to place the securities. We will discuss the process for issuing equity and bonds in detail in Chapters 14 and 15. Here, we mention it briefly in the context of the cost of capital.

Because of these issuing costs, a project that can be financed from internal funds will be less costly overall than the same project if it were financed with external funds. One approach would be to adjust the costs of equity and debt capital in the WACC to incorporate the issuing costs. A better and far more direct route is to simply treat the issuing costs as what they are—cash outflows that are necessary to the project. We can then incorporate this additional cost as a negative cash flow in the NPV analysis.

EXAMPLE 13.7

Evaluating an Acquisition with Costly External Financing

MyFinanceLab

PROBLEM

You are analyzing GE's potential acquisition of Nike. GE plans to offer $100 billion as the purchase price for Nike, and it will need to issue additional debt and equity to finance such a large acquisition. You estimate that the issuance costs will be $800 million and will be paid as soon as the transaction closes. You estimate the incremental free cash flows from the acquisition will be $3.3 billion in the first year and will grow at 3% per year thereafter. What is the NPV of the proposed acquisition?

SOLUTION

PLAN

We know from Section 13.5 that the correct cost of capital for this acquisition is Nike's WACC. We can value the incremental free cash flows as a growing perpetuity:

$$PV = \frac{FCF_1}{r - g}$$

where

$$FCF_1 = \$3.3 \text{ billion}$$

$$r = \text{Nike's WACC} = 0.06 \text{ (from Figure 13.3)}$$

$$g = 0.03$$

The NPV of the transaction, including the costly external financing, is the present value of this growing perpetuity net of both the purchase cost and the transaction costs of using external financing.

EXECUTE

Noting that $800 million is $0.8 billion,

$$NPV = -\$100 - \$0.8 + \frac{\$3.3}{0.06 - 0.03} = \$9.2 \text{ billion}$$

> **EVALUATE**
>
> It is not necessary to try to adjust Nike's WACC for the issuance costs of debt and equity. Instead, we can subtract the issuance costs from the NPV of the acquisition to confirm that the acquisition remains a positive-NPV project even if it must be financed externally.

In this chapter, we learned what a firm's cost of capital is, where it comes from, and how it is used in capital budgeting. The role of capital budgeting is to identify positive-NPV projects that allow a firm to cover the costs of its various types of capital. Now, we turn to another aspect of capital financing—where the firm gets that capital. In Chapters 14 through 16, we explore how a firm raises equity and debt capital and how it decides the proportion of each to have in its capital structure.

CONCEPT CHECK

11. What types of additional costs does a firm incur when accessing external capital?
12. What is the best way to incorporate these additional costs into capital budgeting?

MyFinanceLab

Here is what you should know after reading this chapter. MyFinanceLab will help you identify what you know, and where to go when you need to practice.

KEY POINTS AND EQUATIONS	KEY TERMS	ONLINE PRACTICE
13.1 A First Look at the Weighted Average Cost of Capital • A firm's debt and equity represent its capital. The relative proportions of debt, equity, and other securities that a firm has outstanding constitute its capital structure. • Investors of each type of capital have a required return. Providing this return is the cost a company bears to obtain capital from investors. • We calculate the firm's overall cost of capital as a weighted average of its equity and debt costs of capital, referred to as the firm's weighted average cost of capital. • The weights in the WACC must be based on the market values of both the firm's debt and equity, not the book values.	capital, p. 406 capital structure, p. 406 leverage, p. 408 levered, p. 408 market-value balance sheet, p. 408 unlevered, p. 408 weighted average cost of capital (WACC), p. 407	MyFinanceLab Study Plan 13.1
13.2 The Firm's Costs of Debt and Equity Capital • To estimate the cost of capital for a company as a whole, we usually start by estimating the cost of each of the company's sources of capital. • The cost of debt is the interest a firm would need to pay on *new* debt. Generally, it will differ from the coupon rate on existing debt, but can be estimated from the yield to maturity on existing debt. • The cost of preferred stock is straightforward to estimate because of its constant and known dividend: $$\text{Cost of Preferred Stock Capital} = \frac{Div_{pfd}}{P_{pfd}} \quad (13.4)$$	effective cost of the debt, p. 410	MyFinanceLab Study Plan 13.2

- The Capital Asset Pricing Model (CAPM) is the most common approach for estimating the cost of equity capital. To apply the CAPM, we need an estimate of the firm's equity beta, the market risk premium, and the risk-free rate:

$$\text{Cost of Equity} = \text{Risk-Free Rate} + \text{Equity Beta} \times \text{Market Risk Premium}$$

- Another approach to estimating the cost of equity is to use the constant dividend growth model (CDGM). To apply this model, we need the current stock price, the expected future dividend, and an estimate of the dividend's constant growth rate:

$$\text{Cost of Equity} = \frac{Div_1}{P_E} + g \qquad (13.5)$$

13.3 A Second Look at the Weighted Average Cost of Capital - The WACC equation is $$r_{wacc} = r_E E\% + r_{pfd} P\% + r_D(1 - T_C)D\% \quad (13.6)$$ - For a company that does not have preferred stock, the WACC equation condenses to $$r_{wacc} = r_E E\% + r_D(1 - T_C)D\% \qquad (13.7)$$ - The WACC is driven by the risk of a company's line of business and, because of the tax effect of interest, its leverage. As a result, WACCs vary widely across industries and companies.	net debt, p. 416	MyFinanceLab Study Plan 13.3
13.4 Using the WACC to Value a Project - Assuming a project has average risk for the firm, that the firm will maintain its current leverage ratio, and that a firm's leverage affects its value only through taxes, the WACC can be used to value the cash flows from a new project.	debt-equity ratio, p. 418 levered value, p. 417 WACC method, p. 417	MyFinanceLab Study Plan 13.4 Spreadsheet Table 13.3
13.5 Project-Based Costs of Capital - If the project's risk differs from the average risk for the firm, the WACC will not be the appropriate discount rate for the project. Instead, you must estimate the WACC from the WACC of other firms operating in the same line of business as the new project.		MyFinanceLab Study Plan 13.5
13.6 When Raising External Capital Is Costly - The WACC is calculated without accounting for the direct costs of raising external financing. Rather than adjusting the WACC, the correct way to account for these costs is to subtract their present value from the NPV of the project.		MyFinanceLab Study Plan 13.6

CRITICAL THINKING

1. What does the WACC measure?

2. Why are market-based weights important?

3. Why is the coupon rate of existing debt irrelevant for finding the cost of debt capital?

4. Why is it easier to determine the costs of preferred stock and of debt than it is to determine the cost of common equity?

5. Describe the steps involved in the CAPM approach to estimating the cost of equity.

6. Why would the CDGM and CAPM produce different estimates of the cost of equity capital?

7. Under what assumptions can the WACC be used to value a project?

8. What possible problems might be associated with the assumptions used in applying the WACC method?

9. How should you value a project in a line of business with risk that is different than the average risk of your firm's projects?

10. What is the right way to adjust for the costs of raising external financing?

PROBLEMS

All problems are available in MyFinanceLab.

A First Look at the Weighted Average Cost of Capital

1. MV Corporation has debt with market value of $100 million, common equity with a book value of $100 million, and preferred stock worth $20 million outstanding. Its common equity trades at $50 per share, and the firm has 6 million shares outstanding. What weights should MV Corporation use in its WACC?

2. Andyco, Inc., has the following balance sheet and an equity market-to-book ratio of 1.5. Assuming the market value of debt equals its book value, what weights should it use for its WACC calculation?

Assets	Liabilities and Equity	
1000	Debt	400
	Equity	600

3. Book Co. has 1 million shares of common equity with a par (book) value of $1, retained earnings of $30 million, and its shares have a market value of $50 per share. It also has debt with a par value of $20 million that is trading at 101% of par.
   a. What is the market value of its equity?
   b. What is the market value of its debt?
   c. What weights should it use in computing its WACC?

4. Consider a simple firm that has the following market-value balance sheet:

Assets	Liabilities and Equity	
1000	Debt	400
	Equity	600

Next year, there are two possible values for its assets, each equally likely: $1200 and $960. Its debt will be due with 5% interest. Because all of the cash flows from the assets must go either to the debt or the equity, if you hold a portfolio of the debt and equity in the same proportions as the firm's capital structure, your portfolio should earn exactly the expected return on the firm's assets. Show that a portfolio invested 40% in the firm's debt and 60% in its equity will have the same expected return as the assets of the firm. That is, show that the firm's pretax WACC is the same as the expected return on its assets.

The Firm's Costs of Debt and Equity Capital

5. Aluminum maker Alcoa has a beta of about 2.0, whereas Hormel Foods has a beta of 0.45. If the expected excess return of the marker portfolio is 5%, which of these firms has a higher equity cost of capital, and how much higher is it?

6. Avicorp has a $10 million debt issue outstanding, with a 6% coupon rate. The debt has semiannual coupons, the next coupon is due in six months, and the debt matures in five years. It is currently priced at 95% of par value.
   a. What is Avicorp's pretax cost of debt?
   b. If Avicorp faces a 40% tax rate, what is its after-tax cost of debt?

7. Laurel, Inc., has debt outstanding with a coupon rate of 6% and a yield to maturity of 7%. Its tax rate is 35%. What is Laurel's effective (after-tax) cost of debt?

8. Dewyco has preferred stock trading at $50 per share. The next preferred dividend of $4 is due in one year. What is Dewyco's cost of capital for preferred stock?

9. Steady Company's stock has a beta of 0.20. If the risk-free rate is 6% and the market risk premium is 7%, what is an estimate of Steady Company's cost of equity?

10. Wild Swings Inc.'s stock has a beta of 2.5. If the risk-free rate is 6% and the market risk premium is 7%, what is an estimate of Wild Swings' cost of equity?

11. HighGrowth Company has a stock price of $20. The firm will pay a dividend next year of $1, and its dividend is expected to grow at a rate of 4% per year thereafter. What is your estimate of HighGrowth's cost of equity capital?

12. Slow 'n Steady, Inc., has a stock price of $30, will pay a dividend next year of $3, and has expected dividend growth of 1% per year. What is your estimate of Slow 'n Steady's cost of equity capital?

13. Mackenzie Company has a price of $36 and will issue a dividend of $2 next year. It has a beta of 1.2, the risk-free rate is 5.5%, and it estimates the market risk premium to be 5%.
   a. Estimate the equity cost of capital for Mackenzie.
   b. Under the CGDM, at what rate do you need to expect Mackenzie's dividends to grow to get the same equity cost of capital as in part (a)?

A Second Look at the Weighted Average Cost of Capital

14. CoffeeCarts has a cost of equity of 15%, has an effective cost of debt of 4%, and is financed 70% with equity and 30% with debt. What is this firm's WACC?

15. AllCity, Inc., is financed 40% with debt, 10% with preferred stock, and 50% with common stock. Its pretax cost of debt is 6%, its preferred stock pays an annual dividend of $2.50 and is priced at $30. It has an equity beta of 1.1. Assume the risk-free rate is 2%, the market risk premium is 7% and AllCity's tax rate is 35%. What is its after-tax WACC?

16. Pfd Company has debt with a yield to maturity of 7%, a cost of equity of 13%, and a cost of preferred stock of 9%. The market values of its debt, preferred stock, and equity are $10 million, $3 million, and $15 million, respectively, and its tax rate is 40%. What is this firm's after-tax WACC?

17. Growth Company's current share price is $20 and it is expected to pay a $1 dividend per share next year. After that, the firm's dividends are expected to grow at a rate of 4% per year.

    a. What is an estimate of Growth Company's cost of equity?
    b. Growth Company also has preferred stock outstanding that pays a $2 per share fixed dividend. If this stock is currently priced at $28, what is Growth Company's cost of preferred stock?
    c. Growth Company has existing debt issued three years ago with a coupon rate of 6%. The firm just issued new debt at par with a coupon rate of 6.5%. What is Growth Company's pretax cost of debt?
    d. Growth Company has 5 million common shares outstanding and 1 million preferred shares outstanding, and its equity has a total book value of $50 million. Its liabilities have a market value of $20 million. If Growth Company's common and preferred shares are priced as in parts (a) and (b), what is the market value of Growth Company's assets?
    e. Growth Company faces a 35% tax rate. Given the information in parts (a) through (d), and your answers to those problems, what is Growth Company's WACC?

Using the WACC to Value a Project

18. A retail coffee company is planning to open 100 new coffee outlets that are expected to generate $15 million in free cash flows per year, with a growth rate of 3% in perpetuity. If the coffee company's WACC is 10%, what is the NPV of this expansion?

19. RiverRocks, Inc., is considering a project with the following projected free cash flows:

0	1	2	3	4
−50	10	20	20	15

    The firm believes that, given the risk of this project, the WACC method is the appropriate approach to valuing the project. RiverRocks' WACC is 12%. Should it take on this project? Why or why not?

Project-Based Costs of Capital

20. RiverRocks (whose WACC is 12%) is considering an acquisition of Raft Adventures (whose WACC is 15%). What is the appropriate discount rate for RiverRocks to use to evaluate the acquisition? Why?

21. RiverRocks' purchase of Raft Adventures (from Problem 20) will cost $100 million, and will generate cash flows that start at $15 million in one year and then grow at 4% per year forever. What is the NPV of the acquisition?

22. Your firm is planning to invest in an automated packaging plant. Harburtin Industries is an all-equity firm that specializes in this business. Suppose Harburtin's equity beta is 0.85, the risk-free rate is 4%, and the market risk premium is 5%. If your firm's project is all equity financed, estimate its cost of capital.

23. CoffeeStop primarily sells coffee. It recently introduced a premium coffee-flavored liquor. Suppose the firm faces a tax rate of 35% and collects the following information. If it plans to finance 11% of the new liquor-focused division with debt and the rest with equity, what WACC should it use for its liquor division? Assume a cost of debt of 4.8%, a risk-free rate of 3%, and a risk premium of 6%.

	Beta	% Equity	% Debt
CoffeeStop	0.61	96%	4%
BF Liquors	0.26	89%	11%

24. Your company has two divisions: One division sells software and the other division sells computers through a direct sales channel, primarily taking orders over the Internet. You have decided that Dell Computer is very similar to your computer division, in terms of both risk and financing. You go online and find the following information: Hewlett Packard's beta is 1.21, the risk-free rate is 4.5%, its market value of equity is $67 billion, and it has $700 million worth of debt with a yield to maturity of 6%. Your tax rate is 35% and you use a market risk premium of 5% in your WACC estimates.
    a. What is an estimate of the WACC for your computer sales division?
    b. If your overall company WACC is 12% and the computer sales division represents 40% of the value of your firm, what is an estimate of the WACC for your software division?

When Raising External Capital Is Costly

25. RiverRocks realizes that it will have to raise the financing for the acquisition of Raft Adventures (described in Problem 21) by issuing new debt and equity. The firm estimates that the direct issuing costs will come to $7 million. How should it account for these costs in evaluating the project? Should RiverRocks go ahead with the project?

26. You are planning to issue debt to finance a new project. The project will require $20 million in financing and you estimate its NPV to be $15 million. The issue costs for the debt will be 3% of face value. Taking into account the costs of external financing, what is the NPV of the project?

DATA CASE

You work in Walt Disney Company's corporate finance and treasury department and have been assigned to the team estimating Disney's WACC. You must estimate this WACC in preparation for a team meeting later today. You quickly realize that the information you need is readily available online.

1. Go to http://finance.yahoo.com. Under "Market Data" you will find the yield to maturity for 10-year Treasury bonds listed as "10 Yr Bond(%)." Collect this number as your risk-free rate.

2. In the box next to the "Look Up" button, type Walt Disney's ticker symbol (DIS), and click "Search." Once you see the basic information for Disney, find and click "Key Statistics" on the left side of the screen. From the key statistics, collect Disney's market capitalization (its market value of equity), enterprise value (market value equity + net debt), cash, and beta.

3. To get Disney's cost of debt and the market value of its long-term debt, you will need the price and yield to maturity on the firm's existing long-term bonds. Go to http://finra-markets.morningstar.com/BondCenter/Default.jsp?, click "Search," click "Corporate," type Disney's ticker symbol (DIS), and click "Show Results." A list of Disney's outstanding bond issues will appear. Assume that Disney's policy is to use the yield to maturity on non-callable 10-year obligations as its cost of debt. Find the non-callable bond issue that is as close to 10 years from maturity as possible. (*Hint*: You will see a column titled "Callable"; make sure the issue you choose has "No" in this column.) You may have to choose a bond issued by one of its subsidiaries, like ABC. Find the yield to maturity for your chosen bond issue (it is in the column titled "Yield") and enter that yield as your pretax cost of debt into your spreadsheet. Next, copy and paste the data in the entire table into Excel.

4. You now have the price for each bond issue, but you need to know the size of the issue. Returning to the Web page, go to the row of the bond you chose and click the Issuer Name in the first column (this will either be Walt Disney Company or ABC or another subsidiary). This brings up a Web page with all of the information

about the bond issue. Scroll down until you find "Amount Outstanding" on the right side. Noting that this amount is quoted in thousands of dollars (e.g., $60,000 means $60 million = $60,000,000), record the issue amount in the appropriate row of your spreadsheet. Repeat this step for all of the bond issues.

5. The price for each bond issue in your spreadsheet is reported as a percentage of the bond's par value. For example, 104.50 means that the bond issue is trading at 104.5% of its par value. You can calculate the market value of each bond issue by multiplying the amount outstanding by (Price ÷ 100). Do so for each issue and then calculate the total of all the bond issues. This is the market value of Disney's debt.

6. Compute the weights for Disney's equity and debt based on the market value of equity and Disney's market value of debt, computed in step 5.

7. Calculate Disney's cost of equity capital using the CAPM, the risk-free rate you collected in step 1, and a market risk premium of 5%.

8. Assuming that Disney has a tax rate of 35%, calculate its effective cost of debt capital.

9. Calculate Disney's WACC.

10. Calculate Disney's net debt by subtracting its cash (collected in step 2) from its debt. Recalculate the weights for the WACC using the market value of equity, net debt, and enterprise value. Recalculate Disney's WACC using the weights based on the net debt. How much does it change?

11. How confident are you of your estimate? Which implicit assumptions did you make during your data collection efforts?

Integrative Case

This case draws on material from Chapters 11–13.

You work for HydroTech, a large manufacturer of high-pressure industrial water pumps. The firm specializes in natural disaster services, ranging from pumps that draw water from lakes, ponds, and streams in drought-stricken areas to pumps that remove high water volumes in flooded areas. You report directly to the CFO. Your boss has asked you to calculate HydroTech's WACC in preparation for an executive retreat. Too bad you're not invited, as water pumps and skiing are on the agenda in Sun Valley, Idaho. At least you have an analyst on hand to gather the following required information:

1. The risk-free rate of interest, in this case, the yield of the 10-year government bond, which is 3%
2. HydroTech's:
   a. Market capitalization (its market value of equity), $100 million
   b. CAPM beta, 1.2
   c. Total book value of debt outstanding, $50 million
   d. Cash, $10 million
3. The cost of debt (using the quoted yields on HydroTech's outstanding bond issues), which is 5%

With this information in hand, you are now prepared to undertake the analysis.

Case Questions

1. Calculate HydroTech's net debt.
2. Compute HydroTech's equity and (net) debt weights based on the market value of equity and the book value of net debt.
3. Calculate the cost of equity capital using the CAPM, assuming a market risk premium of 5%.
4. Using a tax rate of 35%, calculate HydroTech's effective cost of debt capital.
5. Calculate HydroTech's WACC.
6. When is it appropriate to use this WACC to evaluate a new project?

Long-Term Financing

Valuation Principle Connection. How should a firm raise the funds it needs to undertake its investments? In Part 5, we explain the mechanics of raising equity and issuing debt. Chapter 14 describes the process a company goes through when it raises equity capital. In Chapter 15, we will review firms' use of debt markets to raise capital. Later, in the capital structure section of the text, we will discuss the financial manager's choice between these two major categories of financing. A firm's ability to raise capital depends on the value the market applies to its securities. The Valuation Principle tells us that the price of any securities issued by the firm will be the present value of the cash flows accruing to them. Thus, while we discuss the process for raising capital in the following two chapters, it is important to remember that the price investors are willing to pay for a firm's securities depends on the financial manager making investment decisions that maximize the value of the firm.

14

Raising Equity Capital

LEARNING OBJECTIVES

- Contrast the different ways to raise equity capital for a private company

- Understand the process of taking a company public

- Gain insight into puzzles associated with initial public offerings

- Explain how to raise additional equity capital once the company is public

As we pointed out in Chapter 1, most U.S. businesses are small, sole proprietorships and partnerships. That said, these firms as a whole generate less than 15% of total U.S. sales. Sole proprietorships are not allowed to access outside equity capital, so these businesses have relatively little capacity for growth. Sole proprietors are also forced to hold a large fraction of their wealth in a single asset—the company—and therefore are likely to be undiversified. By incorporating, businesses can gain access to capital and founders can reduce the risk of their portfolios by selling some of their equity and diversifying. Consequently, even though corporations make up only about 20% of U.S. businesses, they account for about 85% of sales in the U.S. economy.

In this chapter, we discuss how companies raise equity capital. To illustrate this concept, we follow the case of an actual company, Facebook, Inc. (ticker: FB). Facebook is a leading social network company whose products include Instagram, WhatsApp, and Oculus. Facebook was founded in 2004. Using the example of Facebook, we first discuss the alternative ways new companies can raise capital and then examine the impact of these funding alternatives on current and new investors.

14.1   Equity Financing for Private Companies

The initial capital that is required to start a business is usually provided by the entrepreneur and her immediate family. Few families, however, have the resources to finance a growing business, so growth almost always requires outside capital. In this section, we examine the sources that can provide a private company this capital and the effect of the infusion of outside capital on the control of the company.

Sources of Funding

When a private company decides to raise outside equity capital, it can seek funding from several potential sources: *angel investors*, *venture capital firms*, *institutional investors*, and *corporate investors*.

angel investors
Individual investors who buy equity in small private firms.

Angel Investors. Individual investors who buy equity in small private firms are called **angel investors**. For many start-ups, the first round of outside private equity financing is often obtained from angels. The term originated 100 years ago in New York when wealthy investors came to the rescue of new Broadway productions by providing critical funding. These investors are frequently friends or acquaintances of the entrepreneur. Because their capital investment is often large relative to the amount of capital already in place at the firm, they typically receive a sizable equity share in the business in return for their funds. As a result, these investors may have substantial influence in the business decisions of the firm. Angels may also bring expertise to the firm that the entrepreneur lacks.

In most cases, firms need more capital than what a few angels can provide. Finding angels is difficult—often it is a function of how well connected the entrepreneur is in the local community. Most entrepreneurs, especially those launching their first start-up company, have few relationships with people who have substantial capital to invest. At some point, many firms that require equity capital for growth must turn to the *venture capital* industry.

venture capital firm
A limited partnership that specializes in raising money to invest in the private equity of young firms.

Venture Capital Firms. A **venture capital firm** is a limited partnership that specializes in raising money to invest in the private equity of young firms. Figure 14.1 lists the twelve most active U.S. venture capital firms in 2015 as well as the split between various stages of financing in 2016, based on the number of deals completed.

FIGURE 14.1

Most Active U.S. Venture Capital Firms in 2015 (by Number of Deals Completed)

Venture Capital Firm	Number of Deals	Avg. Deal Size ($m)
Sequoia Capital	265	36.3
500 Startups	164	2.1
New Enterprise Associates	163	25.7
Accel Partners	158	31.1
Matrix Partners	143	19.8
Y Combinator	113	3.5
Intel Capital	111	16.1
Tiger Global Management	96	73.4
Kleiner Perkins Caufield & Byers	96	53.4
Silicon Valley Bank	94	29.0
Andreessen Horowitz	93	39.3
Bessemer Venture Partners	92	42.0

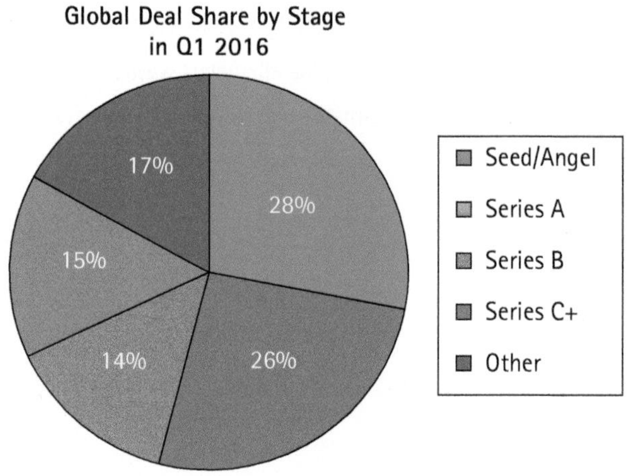

Global Deal Share by Stage in Q1 2016

- 28% Seed/Angel
- 26% Series A
- 14% Series B
- 15% Series C+
- 17% Other

Source: Venture Pulse, Q1'16, Global Analysis of Venture Funding, KPMG International and CB Insigts April 13, 2016

KEVIN LAWS

Kevin Laws is an active angel investor, partner at Maiden Lane Ventures, and Chief Operating Officer of AngelList, an online platform where start-up companies can meet investors and recruit talent.

QUESTION: *How has angel investing changed over the last decade?*

ANSWER: Historically, angel investors typically grouped together in regions and markets not well covered by venture capital (VC) or would dispense cash along with advice at the earliest stages of a few technology companies. Often investors viewed funding start-ups as a sideline rather than a full-time business.

The cost of starting a technology company today has dropped significantly. Cloud services, social marketing, Search Engine Optimization, and other platforms and tools allow entrepreneurs to launch for $500,000 rather than $5 million. Because venture investors prefer to invest several million dollars, angels are now the dominant form of fundraising for the earliest (seed stage) cash needs of the company.

QUESTION: *How has angel investing affected the venture capital industry?*

ANSWER: The lines between angel investing and venture capital are blurring. Today's angels ask for terms they didn't when angel investing was more of a hobby—for example, pro rata investment rights (to maintain their level of percentage ownership during later financing rounds) and information rights. The venture industry is adjusting to a host of new players and is responding primarily by ceding the earliest stage markets to angel investors and engaging at Series A (the first round of financing after seed capital) and beyond.

QUESTION: *How do the returns from angel investing compare with other investment classes?*

ANSWER: Historically, angel investing encompassed a wide range of investments (from investing in your nephew's doomed dry cleaner to early Google investors), making it hard to define the returns. An Angel Capital Association's study found that returns of more "professional" angel investors outstripped venture capital investor returns. It is too early to say whether that will continue as angel investing in technology jumps dramatically, because most investments take 7 to 10 years to come to fruition. Early indicators are that it will likely converge with early stage venture returns.

QUESTION: *Is angel investing only for wealthy investors with domain expertise? Or is it accessible/attractive even for smaller investors?*

ANSWER: Currently, active angel investing with large checks is still for wealthy investors with domain expertise. Although a typical angel check is $25,000, the risk profile of each individual investment is such that you want 30 to 50 investments in a good portfolio. You also need domain expertise to recognize good deals and be familiar enough with the management team and markets to move quickly.

While angel investing is still an asset class for sophisticated investors, it no longer requires as much wealth or start-up experience to participate. Services like AngelList allow investors to invest as little as $1,000 per company across hundreds of companies behind the wealthy, experienced investors. This means that the standard for wealth has dropped (because your friends can combine their money with yours to make the appropriate check size), plus by investing behind experienced investors you can get access without having the same expertise. That has broadened the investor base significantly.

QUESTION: *On what basis do angel investors make the decision to invest?*

ANSWER: Team, traction, and social proof, in that order, based on a recent study I co-authored with several economists. The characteristics of the founding team were the most important factor, followed by how much progress the company had made (which varies by industry—downloads, paying customers, pre-orders, etc.). The third factor, social proof, is who else is involved as investor or advisor to the company. When you are writing small checks for companies whose most likely failure reason is "running out of cash too soon," you want to be sure you're investing with many other investors. A successful investor is a lot more likely to be followed by other investors than an unknown one, much as investors buy a stock after Warren Buffett does. Investing in a company that only manages to raise your $25,000 will lose you money for certain, no matter how "right" you were about its product or market.

---

venture capitalists The general partners who work for and run a venture capital firm.

Typically, institutional investors, such as pension funds, are the limited partners in the venture capital firm. The general partners are known as **venture capitalists** and they work for and run the venture capital firm. Venture capital firms offer limited partners a number of advantages over investing directly in start-ups themselves as angel investors. Because these firms invest in many start-ups, limited partners are more diversified than if they invested on their own. They also benefit from the expertise of the general partners. However, these advantages come at a cost. General partners usually charge substantial fees, taken mainly as a percentage of the positive returns they generate. Most firms charge 20% of any positive returns they make, but the successful firms may charge more than 30%. They also generally charge an annual management fee of about 2% of the fund's committed capital.

Venture capital firms can provide substantial capital for young companies. For example, even in 2009 during the global financial crisis, venture capital firms invested $17.8 billion in 2868 deals, for an average investment of about $6.2 million per deal.[1] In return, venture capitalists often demand a great deal of control. Paul Gompers and Josh Lerner[2] report that venture capitalists typically control about one-third of the seats on a start-up's board of directors, and often represent the single largest voting block on the board. Although entrepreneurs generally view this control as a necessary cost of obtaining venture capital, it can actually be an important benefit of accepting venture financing. Venture capitalists use their control to protect their investments, so they may therefore perform a key nurturing and monitoring role for the firm.

The importance of the venture capital sector has grown enormously in the last 50 years. As Figure 14.2 shows, growth in the sector increased in the 1990s and peaked at the height of the Internet boom. Although the size of the industry has decreased substantially since then, it remains larger than it was in 1996 and is the highest it has been since 2001.

Institutional Investors. Institutional investors such as pension funds, insurance companies, endowments, and foundations manage large quantities of money. They are major investors in many different types of assets, so, not surprisingly, they are also active investors in private companies. Institutional investors may invest directly in private firms, or they may invest indirectly by becoming limited partners in venture capital firms. Institutional interest in private equity grew dramatically in the early 2000s. For example, in 2016, the California Public Employees' Retirement System (CalPERS) reported that it had

FIGURE 14.2

Venture Capital Funding in the United States

Panel (a) indicates the total number of venture capital deals by year. Panel (b) shows the total dollar amount of venture capital investment.

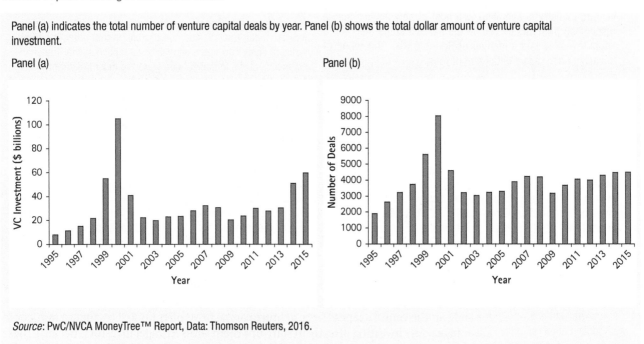

Source: PwC/NVCA MoneyTree™ Report, Data: Thomson Reuters, 2016.

---

[1]"MoneyTree Report," PricewaterhouseCoopers. Data provided by Thomson Financial.

[2]Paul A. Gompers and Josh Lerner, *The Venture Capital Cycle* (Cambridge, MA: MIT Press, 1999).

Crowdfunding: The Wave of the Future?

The last 10 years has seen growth in an entirely new kind of funding for start-ups, known as **crowdfunding**, in which the firm raises very small amounts of money from a large number of people. Investment levels can be minute, in some cases less than $100.

Historically in the U.S., the SEC has enforced strict rules that only allowed "qualified investors" (investors with a high net worth) to invest in private equity issues. These rules effectively barred U.S. crowdfunding sites from offering equity to investors. As a result, companies like Kickstarter and Indiegogo offered investors other payoffs such as the products the company would ultimately produce. In many cases these "financing" contracts looked more like advanced purchase orders.

However, in 2012 the landscape changed dramatically when Congress passed the JOBS Act that exempted crowdfunding from the historical restrictions on private equity investments. The act allowed equity investment by non-qualified individuals so long as the crowdfunding sites did not charge a commission for the transaction. In the wake of this act, a number of equity-based platforms such as AngelList emerged that charged fees based on the performance of the investment. Recently the SEC announced specific restrictions on the size of an equity investment via crowdfunding. For example, in any year, companies may raise no more than $1 million through crowdfunding, and individuals whose annual income or net worth is less than $100,000 can invest no more than $2000, or up to 5% of their annual income or net worth (whichever is less) in crowdfunding-based equity.

$27 billion of its $294 billion portfolio invested in private equity, with another $12 billion in capital committed to the sector.

Corporate Investors. Many established corporations purchase equity in younger, private companies. A corporation that invests in private companies is referred to by many different names, including **corporate investor**, **corporate partner**, **strategic partner**, and **strategic investor**. Most of the other types of investors in private firms that we have considered so far are primarily interested in the financial return that they will earn on their investments. Corporate investors, by contrast, might invest for corporate strategic objectives in addition to the desire for investment returns. For example, in 2007 Microsoft Corporation, as part of a strategic partnership, invested $240 million in Facebook. The deal gave Microsoft a 1.6% stake in Facebook and control over its banner ad placement outside the United States.

corporate investor, corporate partner, strategic partner, strategic investor A corporation that invests in private companies.

Securities and Valuation

When a company founder decides to sell equity to outside investors for the first time, it is common practice for private companies to issue preferred stock rather than common stock to raise capital. **Preferred stock** issued by mature companies such as banks usually has a preferential dividend and seniority in any liquidation, and sometimes special voting rights. Conversely, while retaining its seniority, the preferred stock issued by young companies typically does not pay regular cash dividends. However, this preferred stock usually gives the owner an option to convert it into common stock on some future date, so it is often called **convertible preferred stock**. In short, it will have all of the future rights and benefits of common stock if things go well. On the other hand, if the company runs into financial difficulties, the preferred stockholders have a senior claim on the assets of the firm relative to any common stockholders (who are often the employees of the firm).

preferred stock Preferred stock issued by mature companies such as banks usually has a preferential dividend and seniority in any liquidation and sometimes special voting rights. Preferred stock issued by young companies has seniority in any liquidation but typically does not pay cash dividends and contains a right to convert to common stock.

convertible preferred stock A preferred stock that gives the owner an option to convert it into common stock on some future date.

To illustrate, let's consider Facebook, which was founded by Mark Zuckerberg, Dustin Moskovitz, Chris Hughes, and Eduardo Saverin from their dorm room in 2004. Facebook's initial funding came from $15,000 (Saverin) and another $85,000 (Zuckerberg and his father). By July of 2004, Facebook had caught the attention of angel investors Peter Thiel (co-founder of Paypal), Mark Pincus (co-founder of Zynga) and Reid Hoffman (co-founder of LinkedIn). They invested about $500,000 of new capital into the young firm in return for 10% ownership.

As Facebook grew rapidly (reaching over 1 million users by the end of 2004), it needed more capital. Its first round of venture capital financing came in May 2005 with $12.7 million worth of Series A preferred stock sold to Accel Partners (Facebook's angel investors also invested more capital at this point). A year later, in April 2006, Facebook closed its series B funding round with $27.5 million from a group of 5 venture capital firms.[3] It is important to understand that Facebook remained a private company after this transaction. Simply selling equity to outside investors does not cause a company to be public. Companies may remain private, meaning their shares are not listed on an exchange and they are not required to file their financial statements with the SEC, as long as the number of shareholders remains small. Later in this chapter we discuss the process of offering shares to the general public and thereby transitioning to public status. After this funding round the distribution of ownership was:

Funding Round	Date	Capital Raised	Ownership Sold to Investors	Founder Ownership	Implied Valuation of Facebook
Angel	Mid-2004	$500,000	10%	90%	$5,000,000
Series A	May 2005	$12,700,000	12.7%	77.3%	$100,000,000
Series B	April 2006	$27,500,000	5%	72.3%	$550,000,000

pre-money valuation
The value of a firm's prior shares outstanding at the price in the funding round.

post-money valuation
The value of the whole firm (old plus new shares) at the price at which the new equity is sold.

The Series B preferred shares were new shares of stock being sold by Facebook. At the price the new shares were sold for, Series A and the founders' shares were now worth 397.65 million and represented 72.3% of the shares of the $550 million company. It is important to note that the increase in the value of Zuckerberg's and the other founders' shares was very uncertain when they founded the company. The value of the prior shares outstanding at the price in the funding round ($397.65 million in this example) is called the **pre-money valuation**. The value of the whole firm (old plus new shares) at the funding round price ($550 million) is known as the **post-money valuation**. The difference between the pre- and post-money valuation is the amount invested. In other words,

$$\text{Post-Money Valuation} = \text{Pre-Money Valuation} + \text{Amount Invested} \qquad (14.1)$$

EXAMPLE 14.1

Funding and Ownership

MyFinanceLab

PROBLEM

You founded your own firm two years ago. Initially you contributed $100,000 of your own money and, in return, received 1.5 million shares of stock. Since then, you have sold an additional 500,000 shares to angel investors. Now you are considering raising even more capital from a venture capitalist (VC). This VC would invest $6 million and would receive 3 million newly issued shares. What is the post-money valuation? Assuming that this is the VC's first investment in your company, what percentage of the firm will she end up owning? What percentage will you own? What is the value of your shares?

SOLUTION

PLAN

After this funding round, there will be a total of 5 million shares outstanding:

Your shares	1,500,000
Angel investors' shares	500,000
Newly issued shares	3,000,000
Total	5,000,000

The VC would be paying $6,000,000/3,000,000 = $2 per share. The post-money valuation will be the total number of shares multiplied by the price paid by the VC. The percentage of the firm owned by the VC is the number of her shares divided by the total number of shares. Your percentage will be the number of your shares divided by the total number of shares, and the value of your shares will be the number of shares you own multiplied by the price the VC paid.

---

[3]The information given here for this and subsequent funding comes from the IPO prospectus (available on EDGAR at www.sec.gov/edgar/searchedgar/webusers.htm).

EXECUTE

There are 5 million shares and the VC paid $2 per share. Therefore, the post-money valuation would be 5,000,000 × $2 = $10 million, which, by Eq. 14.1 equals the pre-money valuation ($4 million) plus the amount invested ($6 million).

Because she is buying 3 million shares, and there will be 5 million total shares outstanding after the funding round, the VC will end up owning 3,000,000/5,000,000 = 60% of the firm.

You will own 1,500,000/5,000,000 = 30% of the firm, and the post-money valuation of your shares is 1,500,000 × $2 = $3,000,000.

EVALUATE

Funding your firm with new equity capital, whether it is from an angel or a venture capitalist, involves a tradeoff—you must give up part of the ownership of the firm in return for the money you need to grow. If you can negotiate a higher price per share, the percentage of your firm that you will have to give up for a specified amount of capital will be smaller.

Over the next few years, Facebook raised several more rounds of outside equity in addition to the Series B funding round:[4]

Funding Round	Date	Capital Raised	Ownership Sold to Investors	Founder/Employee Ownership	Implied Valuation of Facebook
Series C	Oct 2007–April 2008	$375,000,000	2.5%	69.8%	$15,000,000,000
Series D	May–Nov 2009	$290,000,000	2.9%	66.9%	$10,000,000,000
Series E	June 2010	$120,000,000	0.6%	66.1%	$20,000,000,000
Common	Jan 2011	$1,500,000,000	3.0%	63.1%	$50,000,000,000

In each case, investors bought preferred stock in the private company. These investors were very similar to the profile of typical investors in private firms that we described earlier. Angel investors invested early and some continued to invest in later rounds as well. The other investors were primarily venture capital funds and wealthy individuals, like Li Ka-shing and Bono. Microsoft purchased most of the Series C stock as a corporate investor.

Exiting an Investment in a Private Company

Like any relationship, the one between a firm and its investors is subject to change as needs and resources develop. An important consideration for investors in private companies is their **exit strategy**—how they will eventually realize the return from their investment. Investors exit in two main ways: through an acquisition or through a public offering. Often, large corporations purchase successful start-up companies. In such a case, the acquiring company purchases the outstanding stock of the private company, allowing all investors to cash out. Roughly 86% of venture capital exits from 2011–2015 occurred through mergers or acquisitions with typical deal sizes in the range of $100 million to $150 million.[5] The alternative way for the company to allow its investors to liquidate their investment is to become a publicly traded company.

Over time, the value of a share of Facebook's stock and the size of its funding rounds increased. Because Goldman Sachs and its investors were willing to pay $1.5 billion for just 3% of the company in January 2011, the valuation of existing stock had increased significantly, representing a substantial capital gain for early investors. Because Facebook was still a private company, however, investors could not realize this gain by selling their stock in the public stock markets. In the next section, we discuss the process a firm goes through to sell shares to the public and have its shares traded on a public market.

exit strategy An important consideration for investors in private companies, it details how they will eventually realize the return from their investment.

---

[4]Funding terms were private. Details are authors' estimates based on media reporting.

[5]The National Venture Capital Association.

CONCEPT CHECK

1. What are the main sources of funding for private companies to raise outside equity capital?
2. What is a venture capital firm?

14.2 Taking Your Firm Public: The Initial Public Offering

initial public offering (IPO) The process of selling stock to the public for the first time.

The process of selling stock to the public for the first time is called an **initial public offering (IPO)**. Recent headline-grabbing IPOs by Facebook, Alibaba, and Twitter have highlighted this stage in a company's growth. In this section, we look at the mechanics of IPOs in two cases—the traditional setup and recent innovations.

Advantages and Disadvantages of Going Public

Going public provides companies with greater liquidity and better access to capital. By going public, companies give their private equity investors the ability to diversify. In addition, public companies typically have access to much larger amounts of capital through the public markets, both in the initial public offering and in subsequent offerings. For example, the 29 largest equity issues in the world each raised $7 billion or more, as shown in Table 14.1. In Facebook's case, its last round of private equity funding raised about $1.5 billion in January 2011. It sold $16 billion in shares in its May 2012 IPO, with $6.8 billion in new financing and $9 billion to selling shareholders. Thus, as a public company, Facebook was able to raise substantially more money.

The major advantage of undertaking an IPO is also one of the major disadvantages of an IPO: When investors sell their stake and thereby diversify their holdings, the equity holders of the corporation become more widely dispersed. This undermines investors' ability to monitor the company's management and thus represents a loss of control. Furthermore, once a company goes public, it must satisfy all of the requirements of public companies. Several high-profile corporate scandals during the early part of the twenty-first century prompted tougher regulations designed to address corporate abuses. Organizations such as the Securities and Exchange Commission (SEC), the securities exchanges (including the New York Stock Exchange and the NASDAQ), and Congress (through the Sarbanes-Oxley Act of 2002 and other legislation) adopted new standards that focused on more thorough financial disclosure, greater accountability, and more stringent requirements for the makeup and responsibilities of a board of directors. In general, these standards were designed to provide better protection for investors. However, compliance with the new standards is costly and time-consuming for public companies.

underwriter An investment banking firm that manages a security issuance and designs its structure.

primary offering New shares available in a public offering that raise new capital.

secondary offering An equity offering of shares sold by existing shareholders (as part of their exit strategy).

Primary and Secondary IPO Offerings

After deciding to go public, managers of the company work with an **underwriter**, an investment banking firm that manages the security issuance and designs its structure. In this case, the underwriter is managing the company's offering of securities to the public. Choices for the offering's structure include the type of shares to be sold and the mechanism the underwriter will use to sell the stock.

At an IPO, a firm offers a large block of shares for sale to the public for the first time. The shares that are sold in the IPO may either be new shares that raise new capital, known as a **primary offering**, or existing shares that are sold by current shareholders (as part of their exit strategy), known as a **secondary offering**.

The traditional IPO process follows a standardized form. We will explore the steps that underwriters go through during an IPO.

TABLE 14.1

Largest Global IPOs

Company Name	Offer Date	Exchange	Industry	Underwriter	Deal Size (US $ Millions)
Alibaba Group Holding	09/18/2014	NYSE	Technology	Credit Suisse	$21,767
ABC Bank	07/07/2010	Hong Kong / Shanghai	Financial	Goldman Sachs (Asia)	$19,228
ICBC Bank	10/20/2006	Hong Kong / Shanghai	Financial	Merrill Lynch	$19,092
NTT Mobile	10/22/1998	Tokyo Stock Exchange	Communications	Goldman Sachs (Asia)	$18,099
Visa	03/18/2008	NYSE	Financial	J.P. Morgan	$17,864
AIA	10/21/2010	Hong Kong	Financial	Citi	$17,816
ENEL SpA	11/01/1999	NYSE	Utilities	Merrill Lynch	$16,452
Facebook	05/17/2012	NASDAQ	Technology	Morgan Stanley	$16,007
General Motors	11/17/2010	NYSE	Capital Goods & Services	Morgan Stanley	$15,774
Nippon Tel	02/09/1987	Tokyo Stock Exchange	Communications	Nomura Securities	$15,301
Deutsche Telekom	11/17/1996	NYSE	Communications	Goldman, Sachs & Co	$13,034
Bank of China	05/24/2006	Hong Kong/Shanghai	Financial	Goldman, Sachs & Co.	$11,186
Dai-ichi Mutual Life Insurance	03/23/2010	Tokyo Stock Exchange	Financial	BofA Merrill Lynch	$10,986
AT&T Wireless Group	04/26/2000	NYSE	Communications	Goldman, Sachs & Co.	$10,620
Rosneft Oil Company	07/13/2006	Russian Trading System	Energy	ABN AMRO	$10,421
Glencore International	05/19/2011	LSE Main/Hong Kong	Basic Resources	Citi	$10,316
Japan Tobacco Inc. (JT)	10/27/1994	Tokyo Stock Exchange	Consumer	Nomura Securities	$9,576
China Construction Bank	10/20/2005	Hong Kong/Shanghai	Financial	Morgan Stanley	$9,227
Kraft Foods	06/12/2001	NYSE	Consumer	Credit Suisse	$8,680
Electricite De France	11/18/2005	Euronext/Paris	Utilities	ABN AMRO	$8,328
Water Holding Co	11/22/1989	LSE Main	Utilities	Credit Suisse	$8,199
VTB Bank	05/10/2007	LSE Main	Financial	Citi	$7,988
Banader Hotels Co	11/20/2005	Bahrain Stock Exchange	Consumer	KPMG Corporate	$7,958
Telia AB	06/13/2000	OMX Nordic Exchange	Communications	Morgan Stanley	$7,728
British Gas PLC	12/08/1986	LSE Main	Energy	Goldman, Sachs & Co.	$7,610
DDI Corp	09/03/1993	Tokyo Stock Exchange	Communications	Daiwa Securities	$7,592
China Engineering	07/23/2009	Shanghai	Capital Goods & Services	China International Capital	$7,343
France Telecom	10/17/1997	NYSE	Communications	Merrill Lynch	$7,289
Banco Santander Brasil	10/06/2009	NYSE/Bovespa	Financial	Santander Investment	$7,026

Source: www.renaissancecapital.com, June 2016.

lead underwriter The primary banking firm responsible for managing a security issuance.

Underwriters and the Syndicate. Many IPOs, especially the larger offerings, are managed by a group of underwriters. The **lead underwriter** is the primary banking firm responsible for managing the security issuance. The lead underwriter provides most of the advice on

syndicate A group of underwriters who jointly underwrite and distribute a security issuance.

the sale and arranges for a group of other underwriters, called the **syndicate**, to help market and sell the issue. Table 14.2 shows the lead underwriters who were responsible for the largest value of IPOs globally during 2015, as well as their rankings for 2012–2015. As you can see, the major U.S. and European investment and commercial banks dominate the underwriting business.

Underwriters market the IPO, and they help the company with all the necessary filings. More importantly, as we discuss below, they actively participate in determining the offer price. In many cases, the underwriter will also commit to making a market in the stock by matching buyers and sellers after the issue, thereby guaranteeing that the stock will be liquid.

registration statement A legal document that provides financial and other information about a company to investors prior to a security issuance.

preliminary prospectus (red herring) Part of the registration statement prepared by a company prior to an IPO that is circulated to investors before the stock is offered.

SEC Filings. The SEC requires that companies prepare a **registration statement**, a legal document that provides financial and other information about the company to investors prior to a security issuance. Company managers work closely with the underwriters to prepare this registration statement and submit it to the SEC. Part of the registration statement, called the **preliminary prospectus** or **red herring**, circulates to investors before the stock is offered. The term "red herring" derives from the warning in red ink on the front of the prospectus stating that it is preliminary and is not an offer to sell the shares. (Interestingly, the term "red herring" originates from the sport of fox hunting, where traditionally a red [smoked] herring was used to distract the dogs and throw them off the scent of their prey.)

The SEC reviews the registration statement to make sure that the company has disclosed all of the information necessary for investors to decide whether to purchase the

TABLE 14.2

International IPO Underwriter Ranking Report for 2015

	Proceeds (US $ millions)	No. of Issues	Market Share (Proceeds)	Rank			
				2015	2014	2013	2012
Morgan Stanley	14,360.6	92	7.6	1	1	3	1
Goldman, Sachs & Co	11,026.2	87	5.9	2	2	1	7
JP Morgan	10,114.1	72	5.4	3	3	2	2
UBS	8,991.7	55	4.8	4	7	8	8
Bank of America Merrill Lynch	8,610.2	69	4.6	5	8	4	4
Citi	8,134.0	75	4.3	6	6	7	5
Deutsche Bank	7,408.2	61	3.9	7	4	5	3
Credit Suisse	5,670.3	61	3.0	8	5	6	6
Barclays	5,094.6	43	2.7	9	9	9	9
HSBC Holdings PLC	4,659.5	27	2.5	10	10	14	18
Nomura	3,516.9	45	1.9	11	11	10	15
CITIC	3,428.6	23	1.8	12	16	-	-
Jefferies LLC	3,043.8	43	1.6	13	14	13	-
Sumitomo Mitsui Finl Grp Inc	2,158.6	30	1.2	14	-	19	14
Everbright Securities Co Ltd	2,075.3	7	1.1	15	-	-	-
Daiwa Securities Group Inc	2,061.5	18	1.1	16	-	-	-
Ping An Securities Ltd	2,028.0	20	1.1	17	-	-	-
China International Capital Co	2,001.3	18	1.1	18	-	-	-
Mizuho Financial Group	1,924.1	18	1.0	19	-	-	18
China Merchants Securities Co	1,924.1	22	1.0	20	15	-	-

Source: ThomsonReuters.

final prospectus Part of the final registration statement prepared by a company prior to an IPO that contains all the details of the offering, including the number of shares offered and the offer price.

stock. Once the company has satisfied the SEC's disclosure requirements, the SEC approves the stock for sale to the general public. Prior to the IPO, the company prepares the final registration statement, which includes the **final prospectus** that contains all the details of the IPO, including the number of shares offered and the offer price.[6]

To illustrate this process, let's return to Facebook. Figure 14.3 shows the cover page for the final prospectus for Facebook's IPO. This cover page includes the name of the company, the list of underwriters (with the co-lead underwriters shown first), and summary information about the pricing of the deal. This was a primary offering of 180 million shares and a secondary offering of 241 million shares.

FIGURE 14.3

The Cover Page of Facebook's IPO Prospectus

The cover page includes the name of the company, a list of underwriters, and summary information about the pricing of the offering.

PROSPECTUS

421,233,615 Shares

CLASS A COMMON STOCK

Facebook, Inc. is offering 180,000,000 shares of its Class A common stock and the selling stockholders are offering 241,233,615 shares of Class A common stock. We will not receive any proceeds from the sale of shares by the selling stockholders. This is our initial public offering and no public market currently exists for our shares of Class A common stock.

We have two classes of common stock, Class A common stock and Class B common stock. The rights of the holders of Class A common stock and Class B common stock are identical, except voting and conversion rights. Each share of Class A common stock is entitled to one vote. Each share of Class B common stock is entitled to ten votes and is convertible at any time into one share of Class A common stock. The holders of our outstanding shares of Class B common stock will hold approximately 96.0% of the voting power of our outstanding capital stock following this offering, and our founder, Chairman, and CEO, Mark Zuckerberg, will hold or have the ability to control approximately 55.9% of the voting power of our outstanding capital stock following this offering.

Our Class A common stock has been approved for listing on the NASDAQ Global Select Market under the symbol "FB."

We are a "controlled company" under the corporate governance rules for NASDAQ-listed companies, and our board of directors has determined not to have an independent nominating function and instead to have the full board of directors be directly responsible for nominating members of our board.

Investing in our Class A common stock involves risks. See "Risk Factors" beginning on page 12.

PRICE $38.00 A SHARE

	Price to Public	Underwriting Discounts and Commissions	Proceeds to Facebook	Proceeds to Selling Stockholders
Per share	$38.00	$0.418	$37.582	$37.582
Total	$16,006,877,370	$176,075,651	$6,764,760,000	$9,066,041,719

We and the selling stockholders have granted the underwriters the right to purchase up to an additional 63,185,042 shares of Class A common stock to cover over-allotments.

The Securities and Exchange Commission and state regulators have not approved or disapproved of these securities, or determined if this prospectus is truthful or complete. Any representation to the contrary is a criminal offense.

The underwriters expect to deliver the shares of Class A common stock to purchasers on May 22, 2012.

MORGAN STANLEY   *J.P. MORGAN*   *GOLDMAN, SACHS & CO.*

BofA MERRILL LYNCH   *BARCLAYS*   *ALLEN & COMPANY LLC*

CITIGROUP   *CREDIT SUISSE*   *DEUTSCHE BANK SECURITIES*

RBC CAPITAL MARKETS   *WELLS FARGO SECURITIES*

Source: SEC filings.

[6]Registration statements may be found at EDGAR, the SEC Web site providing registration information to investors: www.sec.gov/edgar/searchedgar/webusers.htm.

road show During an
IPO, when a company's
senior management and
its lead underwriters travel
to promote the company
and explain their rationale
for an offer price to institutional investors such as
mutual funds and pension
funds.

Valuation. Before the offer price is set, the underwriters work closely with the company to come up with a price range that they believe provides a reasonable valuation for the firm using the techniques described in Chapters 7 and 10. As we pointed out in those chapters, there are two ways to value a company: estimate the future cash flows and compute the present value, or estimate the value by examining comparable companies. Most underwriters use both techniques. However, when these techniques give substantially different answers, underwriters often rely on comparables based on recent IPOs.

Once an initial price range is established, the underwriters try to determine what the market thinks of the valuation. They begin by arranging a **road show**, in which senior management and the lead underwriters travel around the country (and sometimes around the world) promoting the company and explaining their rationale for the offer price to the underwriters' largest customers—mainly institutional investors such as mutual funds and pension funds.

EXAMPLE 14.2

Valuing an IPO Using
Comparables

MyFinanceLab

PROBLEM

Wagner, Inc., is a private company that designs, manufactures, and distributes branded consumer products. During its most recent fiscal year, Wagner had revenues of $325 million and earnings of $15 million. Wagner has filed a registration statement with the SEC for its IPO. Before the stock is offered, Wagner's investment bankers would like to estimate the value of the company using comparable companies. The investment bankers have assembled the following information based on data for other companies in the same industry that have recently gone public. In each case, the ratios are based on the IPO price.

Company	Price/Earnings	Price/Revenues
Ray Products Corp.	18.8 ×	1.2 ×
Byce-Frasier Inc.	19.5 ×	0.9 ×
Fashion Industries Group	24.1 ×	0.8 ×
Recreation International	22.4 ×	0.7 ×
Average	21.2 ×	0.9 ×

After the IPO, Wagner will have 20 million shares outstanding. Estimate the IPO price for Wagner using the price/earnings ratio and the price/revenues ratio.

SOLUTION

PLAN

If the IPO price of Wagner is based on a price/earnings ratio that is similar to those for recent IPOs, then this ratio will equal the average of recent deals. Thus, to compute the IPO price based on the P/E ratio, we will first take the average P/E ratio from the comparison group and multiply it by Wagner's total earnings. This will give us a total value of equity for Wagner. To get the per share IPO price, we need to divide the total equity value by the number of shares outstanding after the IPO (20 million). The approach will be the same for the price/revenues ratio.

EXECUTE

The average P/E ratio for recent deals is 21.2. Given earnings of $15 million, the total market value of Wagner's stock will be $15 million × 21.2 = $318 million. With 20 million shares outstanding, the price per share should be $318 million/20 million = $15.90.

Similarly, if Wagner's IPO price implies a price/revenues ratio equal to the recent average of 0.9, then using its revenues of $325 million, the total market value of Wagner will be $325 million × 0.9 = $292.5 million, or $14.63 per share ($292.5/20).

EVALUATE

As we found in Chapter 10, using multiples for valuation always produces a range of estimates—you should not expect to get the same value from different ratios. Based on these estimates, the underwriters will probably establish an initial price range for Wagner stock of $13 to $17 per share to take on the road show.

At the end of the road show, customers inform the underwriters of their interest by telling the underwriters how many shares they may want to purchase. Although these commitments are nonbinding, the underwriters' customers value their long-term relationships with the underwriters, so they rarely go back on their word. The underwriters then add up the total demand and adjust the price until it is unlikely that the issue will fail. This process for coming up with the offer price based on customers' expressions of interest is called **book building**.

book building A process used by underwriters for coming up with an offer price based on customers' expressions of interest.

Pricing the Deal and Managing Risk. In the most common arrangement, an underwriter and an issuing firm agree to a **firm commitment** IPO, in which the underwriter guarantees that it will sell all of the stock at the offer price. The underwriter purchases the entire issue (at a slightly lower price than the offer price) and then resells it at the offer price. If the entire issue does not sell out, the underwriter is on the hook: The remaining shares must be sold at a lower price and the underwriter must take the loss. The most notorious loss in the industry happened when the British government privatized British Petroleum. In a highly unusual deal, the company was taken public gradually. The British government sold its final stake in British Petroleum at the time of the October 1987 stock market crash. The offer price was set just before the crash, but the offering occurred after the crash.[7] At the end of the first day's trading, the underwriters were facing a loss of $1.29 billion. The price then fell even further, until the Kuwaiti Investment Office stepped in and started purchasing a large stake in the company.

firm commitment An agreement between an underwriter and an issuing firm in which the underwriter guarantees that it will sell all of the stock at the offer price.

In the Facebook's IPO, the final offer price was $38.00 per share. The company agreed to pay the underwriters a fee, called a **spread**, which is a percentage of the issue price of a share of stock, in this case $0.418 per share—1.1% of the issue price. Because this was a firm commitment deal, the underwriters bought the stock from Facebook and the selling shareholders for $38.00 − $0.418 = $37.582 per share and then resold it to their customers for $38.00 per share.

spread The fee a company pays to its underwriters that is a percentage of the issue price of a share of stock.

Recall that when an underwriter provides a firm commitment, it is potentially exposing itself to the risk that the banking firm might have to sell the shares at less than the offer price and take a loss. However, according to Tim Loughran and Jay Ritter, between 1990 and 1998, just 9% of U.S. IPOs experienced a fall in share price on the first day.[8] For another 16% of firms, the price at the end of the first day was the same as the offer price. Therefore, the vast majority of IPOs experienced a price increase on the first day of trading, indicating that the initial offer price was generally lower than the price that stock market investors were willing to pay.

Underwriters appear to use the information they acquire during the book-building stage to intentionally underprice the IPO, thereby reducing their exposure to losses. Furthermore, once the issue price (or offer price) is set, underwriters may invoke another mechanism that allows them to sell extra shares of more successful offerings—the **over-allotment allocation**, or **greenshoe provision**.[9] This option allows the underwriter to issue more stock, amounting to 15% of the original offer size, at the IPO offer price. In the case of Facebook, the underwriters had the option to purchase additional shares to cover over-allotments, up to 63 million shares, at the underwriter discount price of $37.582 for 30 days after the stock started trading.

over-allotment allocation (greenshoe provision) In an IPO, an option that allows the underwriter to issue more stock, usually amounting to 15% of the original offer size, at the IPO offer price.

---

[7]This deal was exceptional in that the offer price was determined more than a week before the issue date. In the United States, the underwriter usually sets the final offer price within a day of the IPO date.

[8]"Why Don't Issuers Get Upset About Leaving Money on the Table in IPOs?" *Review of Financial Studies*, 15 (2) (2002): 413–443.

[9]The name derives from the Green Shoe Company, the first issuer to have an over-allotment option in its IPO.

Once the IPO process is complete, the company's shares trade publicly on an exchange. The lead underwriter usually makes a market in the stock by matching buyers and sellers and assigns an analyst to cover it. By doing so, the underwriter increases the liquidity of the stock in the secondary market. This service is of value to both the issuing company and the underwriter's customers. A liquid market ensures that investors who purchased shares via the IPO are able to trade those shares easily. If the stock is actively traded, the issuer will have continued access to the equity markets in the event that the company decides to issue more shares in a new offering. In most cases, the existing shareholders are subject to a **lockup**, a restriction that prevents them from selling their shares for some period (usually 180 days) after the IPO. Once the lockup period expires, they are free to sell their shares.

lockup A restriction that prevents existing share-holders from selling their shares for some period (usually 180 days) after an IPO.

Other IPO Types

Now that we have established the traditional method for IPOs, we will discuss three other ways shares may be sold during an IPO.

best-efforts basis For smaller initial public offerings (IPOs), a situation in which the underwriter does not guarantee that the stock will be sold, but instead tries to sell the stock for the best possible price.

Best-Efforts Basis. For smaller IPOs, the underwriter commonly accepts the deal on a **best-efforts basis**. In this case, the underwriter does not guarantee that the stock will be sold, but instead tries to sell the stock for the best possible price. Often such deals have an all-or-none clause: Either all of the shares are sold in the IPO, or the deal is called off.

auction IPO An online method for selling new issues directly to the public that lets the market determine the price through bids from potential investors.

Auction IPO. In the late 1990s, the investment banking firm of WR Hambrecht + Company attempted to change the U.S. IPO process by selling new issues directly to the public using an online **auction IPO** mechanism called *OpenIPO*. Rather than setting the price itself in the traditional way, Hambrecht lets the market determine the price of the stock by auction-ing off the company.[10] Investors place bids over a set period of time. An auction IPO then sets the highest price such that the number of bids at or above that price equals the number of offered shares. All winning bidders pay this price, even if their bids were higher. The first OpenIPO was the $11.55 million IPO for Ravenswood Winery, completed in 1999.

It's easier to understand how an auction IPO works by considering an example. Your firm is planning an auction IPO for 3 million shares. Potential buyers submit bids at various prices and their bids are then aggregated. Table 14.3 summarizes those bids. The column "Shares Sought at This Price" shows the total number of shares from investors' bids at each price. The last column contains the total number of shares bid at *or above* each price. Because investors are willing to buy at prices lower than the amount they bid, this total represents the number of shares that can be sold at each price. For example, while investors were only willing to buy a total of 75,000 shares at a price of $19.50, at a price of $19.00 a total of 225,000 (150,000 + 75,000) can be sold.

TABLE 14.3

Bids Received to Purchase Shares in a Hypothetical Auction IPO

Price	Shares Sought at This Price (in thousands)	Total Shares Sought at or Above This Price (in thousands)
$16.50	3,200	11,800
$17.00	2,900	8,600
$17.50	2,700	5,700
$18.00	1,925	3,000
$18.50	850	1,075
$19.00	150	225
$19.50	75	75

[10]While the auction IPO method had been used in many other countries earlier, Hambrecht was instru-mental in bringing the method to the U.S. You can find details about Hambrecht's auction IPO process at http://www.wrhambrecht.com/ind/auctions/openipo/.

FIGURE 14.4

Aggregating the
Shares Sought in
the Hypothetical
Auction IPO

The figure graphs the last column in Table 14.3, which indicates the total number of shares that can be sold at each price. In this case, investors are willing to buy a total of 3 million shares at or above a price of $18. So, you would set your IPO price at $18 to give you the highest price at which you could place 3 million shares.

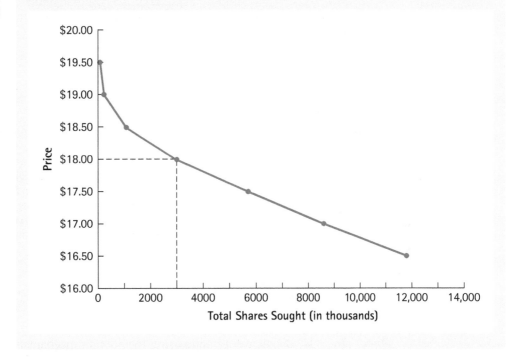

You are interested in selling a total of 3 million shares at the highest price possible. This suggests that you should look in the left column of Table 14.3 to find the highest price at which the total demand is at least 3 million shares. In this case, the highest price at which we can sell 3 million shares is $18. Figure 14.4 shows this graphically.

EXAMPLE 14.3
Auction IPO Pricing

MyFinanceLab

PROBLEM
Fleming Educational Software, Inc., is selling 500,000 shares of stock in an auction IPO. At the end of the bidding period, Fleming's investment bank has received the following bids:

Price ($)	Number of Shares Bid
8.00	25,000
7.75	100,000
7.50	75,000
7.25	150,000
7.00	150,000
6.75	275,000
6.50	125,000

What will the offer price of the shares be?

SOLUTION

PLAN
First, we must compute the total number of shares demanded at or above any given price. Then, we pick the highest price that will allow us to sell the full issue (500,000 shares).

(Continued)

EXECUTE

Converting the table of bids into a table of cumulative demand, we have:

Price ($)	Cumulative Demand
8.00	25,000
7.75	125,000
7.50	200,000
7.25	350,000
7.00	500,000
6.75	775,000
6.50	900,000

For example, the company has received bids for a total of 125,000 shares at $7.75 per share or higher (25,000 + 100,000 = 125,000).

Fleming is offering a total of 500,000 shares. The winning auction price would be $7 per share, because investors have placed orders for a total of 500,000 shares at a price of $7 or higher. All investors who placed bids of at least this price will be able to buy the stock for $7 per share, even if their initial bid was higher.

In this example, the cumulative demand at the winning price exactly equals the supply. If the total demand at this price were greater than the supply, all auction participants who bid prices higher than the winning price would receive their full bid (at the winning price). Shares would be awarded on a pro rata basis to bidders who bid exactly the winning price.

EVALUATE

Although the auction IPO does not provide the certainty of the firm commitment, it has the advantage of using the market to determine the offer price. It also reduces the underwriter's role and, consequently, fees.

In 2004, Google went public using the auction mechanism (see the box describing Google's IPO), which generated renewed interest in this alternative. In May 2007, Interactive Brokers Group raised $1.2 billion in its IPO using a Hambrecht OpenIPO auction. Although the auction IPO mechanism seems to represent an attractive alternative to traditional IPO procedures, it has not been widely adopted either in the United States or abroad. After completing fewer than 30 transactions between 1999 and 2008, Hambrecht has not completed another auction IPO since.

Because no offer price is set in an auction IPO, book building is not as important in that venue as it is in traditional IPOs. In a recent paper, Professors Ravi Jagannathan and Ann Sherman examine why auctions have failed to become a popular IPO method and why they have been plagued by inaccurate pricing and poor performance following the issue. They suggest that because auctions do not use the book-building process, which aids in collecting large investors' valuations of the stock, investors are discouraged from participating in auctions.[11] Table 14.4 summarizes the methods a firm can use for an initial public offering of its stock.

TABLE 14.4

Summary of IPO Methods

Firm Commitment	Best-Efforts Basis	Auction IPO
Underwriter purchases the entire issue at an agreed price and sells it to investors at a higher price.	Underwriter makes its "best effort" to sell the issue to investors at an agreed price.	Firm or underwriter solicits bids (price and quantity) from investors, and chooses the highest price at which there is sufficient demand to sell the entire issue.

[11]For a comparison of auction and traditional IPOs, see A. Sherman, "Global Trends in IPO Methods: Book Building versus Auctions with Endogenous Entry," *Journal of Financial Economics*, 78 (3) (2005): 615–649.

Google's IPO

On April 29, 2004, Google, Inc., announced plans to go public. Breaking with tradition, Google startled Wall Street by declaring its intention to rely heavily on the auction IPO mechanism for distributing its shares. Google had been profitable since 2001, so according to Google executives, access to capital was not the only motive to go public. The company also wanted to provide employees and private equity investors with liquidity.

One of the major attractions of the auction mechanism was the possibility of allocating shares to more individual investors. Google also hoped to set an accurate offer price by letting market bidders set the IPO price. After the Internet stock market boom, there were many lawsuits related to the way underwriters allocated shares. Google hoped to avoid the allocation scandals by letting the auction allocate shares.

Investors who wanted to bid opened a brokerage account with one of the deal's underwriters and then placed their bids with the brokerage house. Google and its underwriters identified the highest bid that allowed the company to sell all of the shares being offered. They also had the flexibility to choose to offer shares at a lower price.

On August 18, 2004, Google sold 19.6 million shares at $85 per share. At the time, the $1.67 billion raised was the largest U.S. auction IPO ever. Google stock (ticker: GOOG) opened trading on the NASDAQ market the next day at $100 per share. Although the Google IPO sometimes stumbled along the way, it represents a significant example of the use of the auction mechanism as an alternative to the traditional IPO mechanism.

Sources: Kevin Delaney and Robin Sidel, "Google IPO Aims to Change the Rules," *Wall Street Journal*, April 30, 2004, p. C1; Ruth Simon and Elizabeth Weinstein, "Investors Eagerly Anticipate Google's IPO," *Wall Street Journal*, April 30, 2004, p. C1; and Gregory Zuckerman, "Google Shares Prove Big Winners—for a Day," *Wall Street Journal*, August 20, 2004, p. C1.

CONCEPT CHECK

3. What services does the underwriter provide in a traditional IPO?

4. Explain the mechanics of an auction IPO.

14.3   IPO Puzzles

Four characteristics of IPOs puzzle financial economists, and all are relevant to the financial manager:

1. On average, IPOs appear to be underpriced: The price at the end of trading on the first day is often substantially higher than the IPO price.

2. The number of IPOs is highly cyclical. When times are good, the market is flooded with IPOs; when times are bad, the number of IPOs dries up.

3. The transaction costs of the IPO are very high, and it is unclear why firms willingly incur such high costs.

4. The long-run performance of a newly public company (three to five years from the date of issue) is poor. That is, on average, a three- to five-year buy-and-hold strategy appears to be a bad investment.

We will now examine each of these puzzles that financial economists seek to understand.

Underpriced IPOs

For Facebook, the underwriters offered the stock at an IPO price of $38.00 per share on May 18, 2012. Facebook stock opened trading on the NASDAQ at a price of $42.05 per share, and traded as high as $45 before closing at $38.23. This lack of underpricing is atypical. For example, Twitter closed more than 72% above its offer price on its first day of trading. On average, between 1960 and 2016, the price in the U.S. aftermarket was 17% higher than the IPO price at the end of the first day of trading.[12] As is evident in Figure 14.5, the one-day average return for IPOs has historically been very large around the world. Note that

[12]See https://site.warrington.ufl.edu/ritter/ipo-data/.

FIGURE 14.5

International Comparison of First-Day IPO Returns

The bars show the average initial returns from the offer price to the first closing market price. For China, the bar shows the average initial return on A share IPOs, available only to residents of China. The date in parentheses indicates the sample period for each country.

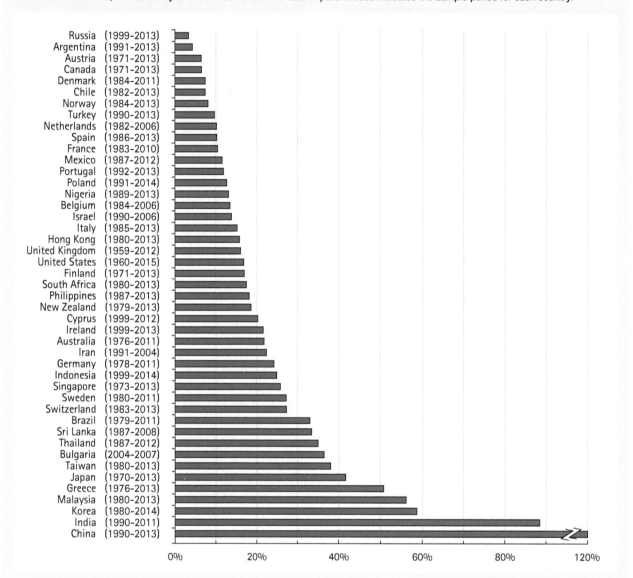

Source: Adapted courtesy of Jay Ritter (https://site.warrington.ufl.edu/ritter/ipo-data/).

although underpricing is a persistent and global phenomenon, it is generally smaller in more developed capital markets.

Who benefits from the offer price being set below the market price at the end of the first day of trading (underpricing)? We have already explained how the underwriters benefit by controlling their risk—it is much easier to sell the firm's shares if the price is set low.

Of course, investors who are able to buy stock from underwriters at the IPO price also gain from the first-day underpricing. Who bears the cost? The pre-IPO shareholders of the issuing firms do. In effect, these owners are selling stock in their firm for less than they could get in the aftermarket.

"Hot" and "Cold" IPO Markets

Figure 14.6 shows the number of IPOs by year from 1980 to 2015. As the figure makes clear, the dollar volume of IPOs grew significantly in the early 1990s, reaching a peak in 1999–2000. An even more important feature of the data is that the trends related to the number of issues are cyclical. Sometimes, as in 1996, the volume of IPOs is unprecedented by historical standards, yet within a year or two the volume of IPOs may decrease significantly. This cyclicality by itself is not particularly surprising. We would expect there to be a greater need for capital in times with more growth opportunities than in times with fewer growth opportunities. What is surprising is the magnitude of the swings. For example, it is difficult to explain the almost seven-fold increase in IPOs from the early to mid-1990s, and the nearly 75% drop from 2000 to 2001 and a 45% drop from 2014 to 2015. It appears that the number of IPOs is not solely driven by the demand for capital. Sometimes firms and investors seem to favor IPOs; at other times firms appear to rely on alternative sources of capital.

FIGURE 14.6

Cyclicality of Initial Public Offerings in the United States (1975–2015)

The graph shows the number of IPOs by year. The number of IPOs reached a peak in 1996, demonstrating that trends related to the number of issues are highly cyclical.

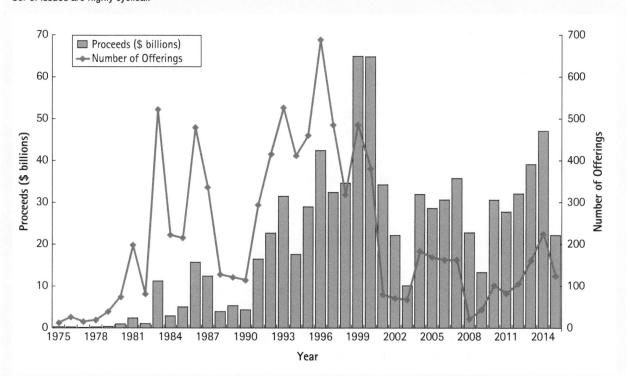

Source: Adapted courtesy of Jay R. Ritter (https://site.warrington.ufl.edu/ritter/ipo-data/).

GLOBAL FINANCIAL CRISIS

2008–2009: A Very Cold IPO Market

The drop in IPO issues during the 2008 financial crisis was both global and dramatic. The bar graph shows the total worldwide dollar volume of IPO proceeds in billions of dollars (blue bars) and number of deals (red line) by quarter, from the last quarter of 2006 to the first quarter of 2009. Comparing the fourth quarter of 2007 (a record quarter for IPO issues) to the fourth quarter of 2008, dollar volume dropped a stunning 97% from $102 billion to just $3 billion. Things got even worse in the first quarter of 2009 with just $1.4 billion raised. The market for IPOs essentially dried up altogether.

During the 2008 financial crisis, IPO markets were not the only equity issue markets that saw a collapse in volume. Markets for seasoned equity offerings and leveraged buyouts also collapsed. The extreme market uncertainty at the time created a "flight to quality." Investors, wary of taking risk, sought to move their capital into risk-free investments like U.S. Treasury securities. The result was a crash in existing equity prices and a greatly reduced supply of new capital to risky asset classes.

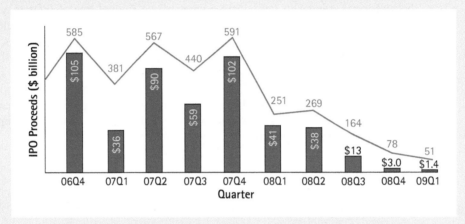

Source: Shifting Landscape—Are You Ready? Global IPO Trends report 2009, Ernst & Young.

High Cost of Issuing an IPO

In the United States, a typical spread—that is, the discount below the issue price at which the underwriter purchases the shares from the issuing firm—is 7% of the issue price. For an issue size of $50 million, this amounts to $3.5 million. This fee covers the cost to the underwriter of managing the syndicate and helping the company prepare for the IPO, as well as providing it with a return on the capital employed to purchase and market the issue. By most standards, however, this fee is large, especially considering the additional cost to the firm associated with underpricing. Internationally, spreads are generally about half this amount. As Figure 14.7 shows, compared to other security issues, the total cost of issuing stock for the first time is substantially larger than the costs for other securities.

Even more puzzling is the seeming lack of sensitivity of fees to issue size. Although a large issue requires some additional effort, one would not expect the increased effort to be rewarded as lucratively. For example, Hsuan-Chi Chen and Jay Ritter found that almost all issues ranging in size from $20 million to $80 million paid underwriting fees of about 7% (in addition to other direct costs).[13] It is difficult to understand how a $20 million issue can be profitably done for "only" $1.4 million, while an $80 million issue requires paying fees of $5.6 million. Some have argued that these fees are kept artificially high by the small number of "top" underwriters in the United States who often work together, though others view the 7% as an "insurance premium" that may reflect the greater risk underwriters face in larger deals.

---

[13]Hsuan-Chi Chen and Jay R. Ritter, "The Seven Percent Solution," *Journal of Finance*, 55 (3) (2000): 1105–1131.

FIGURE 14.7

Relative Costs of
Issuing Securities

This figure shows the total direct costs (all underwriting, legal, and auditing costs) of issuing securities as a percentage of the amount of money raised. The figure reports results for IPOs, seasoned equity offerings (subsequent equity offerings), convertible bonds, and standard bonds for issues of different sizes from 1990–1994.

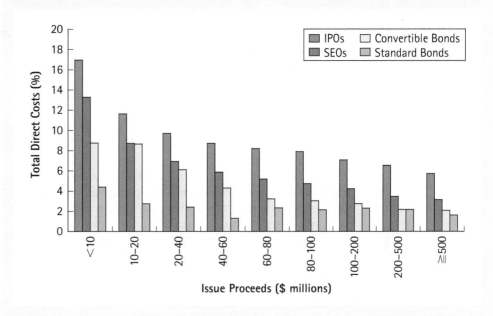

Source: Adapted from I. Lee, S. Lochhead, J. Ritter, and Q. Zhao, "The Costs of Raising Capital," *Journal of Financial Research*, 19 (1) (1996): 59–74.

Poor Post-IPO Long-Run Stock Performance

We know that the shares of IPOs generally perform very well immediately following the public offering. It's perhaps surprising, then, that Jay Ritter found that newly listed firms subsequently appear to perform relatively poorly over the following three to five years after their IPOs.[14] This creates a puzzle as to why investors are willing to pay as much as they do for the shares when they begin trading after the IPO.

As we will see in the next section, underperformance is not unique to an initial public issuance of equity—it is associated with subsequent issuances as well, raising the possibility that underperformance might not result from the issue of equity itself, but rather from the conditions that motivated the equity issuance in the first place. We will explain this idea in more detail in the next section after we explain how a public company issues additional equity.

CONCEPT CHECK

5. List and discuss four characteristics about IPOs that are puzzling.

6. For each of the characteristics, identify its relevance to financial managers.

---

[14]Jay R. Ritter, "The Long-Run Performance of Initial Public Offerings," *Journal of Finance*, 46 (1) (1991): 3–27.

14.4

Raising Additional Capital: The Seasoned Equity Offering

A firm's need for outside capital rarely ends at the IPO. Usually, profitable growth opportunities occur throughout the life of the firm, and in some cases it is not feasible to finance these opportunities out of retained earnings. Thus, a public company more often than not returns to the equity markets and offers new shares for sale in a type of offering called a **seasoned equity offering (SEO)**.

seasoned equity offering (SEO) When a public company returns to the equity markets and offers new shares for sale.

SEO Process

When a firm issues stock using an SEO, it follows many of the same steps as for an IPO. The main difference is that a market price for the stock already exists, so the price-setting process is not necessary.

Facebook has conducted one SEO as of mid-2016. On December 19, 2013, the firm offered 70 million shares in an SEO at a price of $55.05 per share. Of these shares, 27 million were **primary shares**—new shares issued by the company. The remaining 43 million shares were **secondary shares**—shares sold by existing shareholders, including the company's founder, Mark Zuckerberg, who sold 41 million of his 485 million shares.

primary shares New shares issued by a company in an equity offering.

Historically, underwriters would advertise the sale of stock (both IPOs and SEOs) by taking out newspaper advertisements called **tombstones**. Through these ads, investors would know who to call to buy stock. Today, investors become informed about the impending sale of stock by the news media, from the Internet, via a road show, or through the book-building process, so these tombstones are not as common and are purely ceremonial. Figure 14.8 shows the prospectus for the Facebook SEO.

secondary shares Shares sold by existing shareholders in an equity offering.

tombstone Newspaper advertisements in which underwriters advertise a security issuance.

Two types of seasoned equity offerings exist: a *cash offer* and a *rights offer*. In a **cash offer**, the firm offers the new shares to investors at large. In a **rights offer**, the firm offers the new shares only to existing shareholders. In the United States, most offers are cash offers, but the same is not true internationally. For example, in the United Kingdom, most seasoned offerings of new shares are rights offers.

cash offer A type of seasoned equity offering (SEO) in which a firm offers the new shares to investors at large.

Rights offers protect existing shareholders from underpricing. To illustrate, suppose a company holds $100 in cash as its sole asset and has 50 shares outstanding. Each share is worth $2. The company announces a cash offer for 50 shares at $1 per share. Once this offer is complete, the company will have $150 in cash and 100 shares outstanding. The price per share is now $1.50 to reflect the fact that the new shares were sold at a discount. The new shareholders therefore receive a $0.50 per share windfall at the expense of the old shareholders.

rights offer A type of seasoned equity offering (SEO) in which a firm offers the new shares only to existing shareholders.

The old shareholders would be protected if, instead of a cash offer, the company did a rights offer. In this case, rather than offer the new shares for general sale, every shareholder would have the right to purchase an additional share for $1 per share. If all shareholders chose to exercise their rights, then after the sale the value of the company would be the same as with a cash offer: It would be worth $150 with 100 shares outstanding and a price of $1.50 per share. In this case, however, the $0.50 windfall accrues to existing shareholders, which exactly offsets the drop in the stock price. Thus, if a firm's management is concerned that its equity may be underpriced in the market, by using a rights offer the firm can continue to issue equity without imposing a loss on its current shareholders.

FIGURE 14.8

Prospectus for the
Facebook SEO

PROSPECTUS

70,000,000 Shares

Class A Common Stock

Facebook, Inc. is offering 27,004,761 shares of its Class A common stock and the selling stockholders are offering 42,995,239 shares of Class A common stock. We will not receive any proceeds from the sale of shares by the selling stockholders.

We have two classes of common stock, Class A common stock and Class B common stock. The rights of the holders of Class A common stock and Class B common stock are identical, except voting and conversion rights. Each share of Class A common stock is entitled to one vote. Each share of Class B common stock is entitled to ten votes and is convertible at any time into one share of Class A common stock. The holders of our outstanding shares of Class B common stock will hold approximately 75.4% of the voting power of our outstanding capital stock following this offering, and our Chairman and CEO, Mark Zuckerberg, will hold or have the ability to control approximately 62.8% of the voting power of our outstanding capital stock following this offering.

Our Class A common stock is listed on the NASDAQ Global Select Market under the symbol "FB." On December 20, 2013, the reported closing sale price of our Class A common stock on the NASDAQ Global Select Market was $55.10 per share.

Investing in our Class A common stock involves risks. See "Risk Factors" beginning on page 4.

PRICE $55.05 A SHARE

	Price to Public	Underwriting Discounts and Commissions (1)	Proceeds to Facebook	Proceeds to Selling Stockholders
Per share	$55.05	$0.2752	$54.7748	$54.7748
Total	$3,853,500,000	$19,264,000	$1,479,180,383	$2,355,055,617

(1) See "Underwriting."

The Securities and Exchange Commission and state regulators have not approved or disapproved of these securities, or determined if this prospectus is truthful or complete. Any representation to the contrary is a criminal offense.

The underwriters expect to deliver the shares of Class A common stock to purchasers on December 26, 2013.

J.P. MORGAN   BofA MERRILL LYNCH   MORGAN STANLEY   BARCLAYS

BNP PARIBAS   CITIGROUP   RBC CAPITAL MARKETS

CREDIT SUISSE   HSBC

RBS   STANDARD CHARTERED   PIPER JAFFRAY

ALLEN & COMPANY LLC

Source: SEC Filings.

EXAMPLE 14.4

Raising Money with
Rights Offers

MyFinanceLab

PROBLEM

You are the CFO of a company that has a market capitalization of $1 billion. The firm has 100 million shares outstanding, so the shares are trading at $10 per share. You need to raise $200 million and have announced a rights issue. Each existing shareholder is sent one right for every share he or she owns. You have not decided how many rights you will require to purchase a share of new stock. You will require either four rights to purchase one share at a price of $8 per share, or five rights to purchase two new shares at a price of $5 per share. Which approach will raise more money?

(Continued)

SOLUTION

PLAN

In order to know how much money will be raised, we need to compute how many total shares would be purchased if everyone exercises their rights. Then we can multiply it by the price per share to calculate the total amount of capital raised.

EXECUTE

There are 100 million shares, each with one right attached. In the first case, four rights will be needed to purchase a new share, so 100 million/4 = 25 million new shares will be purchased. At a price of $8 per share, that would raise $8 × 25 million = $200 million.

In the second case, for every five rights, two new shares can be purchased, so there will be 2 × (100 million/5) = 40 million new shares. At a price of $5 per share, that would also raise $200 million. If all shareholders exercise their rights, both approaches will raise the same amount of money.

EVALUATE

In both cases, the value of the firm after the issue is $1.2 billion. In the first case, there are 125 million shares outstanding after the issue, so the price per share after the issue is $1.2 billion/125 million = $9.60. This price exceeds the issue price of $8, so the shareholders will exercise their rights. Because exercising will yield a profit of ($9.60 − $8.00)/4 = $0.40 per right, the total value per share to each shareholder is $9.60 + 0.40 = $10.00. In the second case, the number of shares outstanding will grow to 140 million, resulting in a post-issue stock price of $1.2 billion/140 million shares = $8.57 per share (also higher than the issue price). Again, the shareholders will exercise their rights, and receive a total value per share of $8.57 + (2 × ($8.57 − $5.00)/5) = $10.00. Thus, in both cases the same amount of money is raised and shareholders are equally well off.

SEO Price Reaction

Researchers have found that, on average, the market greets the news of an SEO with a price decline. Often, the value lost due to the price decline can be a significant fraction of the new money raised. Figure 14.9 shows the typical stock price reaction when an SEO is announced. To see why the market price of the stock drops when an SEO is announced, consider the following situation: Suppose a used-car dealer tells you he is willing to sell you a nice-looking sports car for $5000 less than its typical price. Rather than feel lucky, perhaps your first thought is that there must be something wrong with the car—it is probably a "lemon." Buyers will be skeptical of a seller's motivation for selling because the seller has private information about the quality of the car. Thus, his *desire to sell* reveals the car is probably of low quality. Buyers are therefore reluctant to buy except at heavily discounted prices. Owners of high-quality cars are reluctant to sell because they know buyers will think they are selling a lemon and offer only a low price. Consequently, the quality and prices of cars sold in the used-car market are both low. This lemons principle—that when quality is hard to judge, the average quality of goods being offered for sale will be low—is referred to as **adverse selection**.

adverse selection
Reflects the lemons principle or the idea that when quality is hard to judge, the average quality of goods being offered for sale will be low.

The lemons problem is very real for financial managers contemplating selling new equity. Because managers concerned about protecting their existing shareholders will tend to sell only at a price that correctly values or overvalues the firm, investors infer from the decision to sell that the company is likely to be overvalued. As a result, the price drops with the announcement of the SEO.

As with IPOs, there are several puzzles surrounding SEOs. First, by offering a rights issue a company can mitigate the problem leading to the price decline. The price decline

FIGURE 14.9

Price Reaction to an SEO Announcement

The figure shows the typical stock price reaction to the announcement of an SEO. The days are relative to the announcement day, so that day 0 is the announcement day. Notice that the stock price is typically increasing prior to the announcement—managers do not like to issue stock when its price has been dropping. Also note that the stock drops by about 1.5% when the SEO is announced and remains relatively flat afterward. The data include all SEOs from 2004 to 2007.

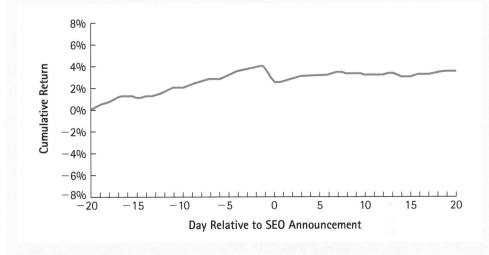

Source: CRSP and authors' calculations.

occurs because of the likelihood that the shares are overvalued, but in a rights offering the shares are being offered directly to existing shareholders. A firm would not benefit its shareholders by issuing shares that are overvalued, so it has no motivation to do so. It is not clear, at least in the United States, why companies do not initiate more rights issues. Second, as with IPOs, evidence suggests that companies underperform following a seasoned offering. This underperformance appears to suggest that the stock price decrease is not large enough, because underperformance implies that the price following the issue was too high.

SEO Costs

Although not as costly as IPOs, seasoned offerings are still expensive, as Figure 14.7 shows. In addition to the price drop when the SEO is announced, the firm must pay direct costs as well. Underwriting fees amount to 5% of the proceeds of the issue and, as with IPOs, the variation across issues of different sizes is relatively small. Furthermore, rights offers have lower costs than cash offers.[15] Given the other advantages of a rights offer, it is a puzzle why the majority of offers in the United States are cash offers. The one advantage of a cash offer is that the underwriter takes on a larger role and, therefore, can credibly attest to the issue's quality.

CONCEPT CHECK

7. What is the difference between a cash offer and a rights offer for a seasoned equity offering?

8. What is the typical stock price reaction to an SEO?

---

[15]In the United Kingdom, Myron Slovin, Marie Sushka, and Kam Wah Lai [*Journal of Financial Economics*, 57 (2) (2000)] found that the average fee for a cash offer is 6.1% versus 4.6% for an underwritten rights offer.

MyFinanceLab

Here is what you should know after reading this chapter. MyFinanceLab will help you identify what you know, and where to go when you need to practice.

KEY POINTS AND EQUATIONS	KEY TERMS	ONLINE RACTICE
14.1 Equity Financing for Private Companies • Private companies can raise outside equity capital from angel investors, venture capital firms, institutional investors, or corporate investors. • When a company founder sells stock to an outsider to raise capital, the founder's ownership share and control over the company are reduced. $$\text{Post-Money Valuation} = \text{Pre-Money Valuation} + \text{Amount Invested} \quad (14.1)$$ • Equity investors in private companies plan to sell their stock eventually through one of two main exit strategies: an acquisition or a public offering.	angel investors, p. 436 convertible preferred stock, p. 439 corporate investor, corporate partner, strategic partner, strategic investor, p. 439 exit strategy, p. 441 post-money valuation, p. 440 preferred stock, p. 439 pre-money valuation, p. 440 venture capital firm, p. 436 venture capitalists, p. 437	MyFinanceLab Study Plan 14.1
14.2 Taking Your Firm Public: The Initial Public Offering • An initial public offering (IPO) is the first time a company sells its stock to the public. • The main advantages of going public are greater liquidity and better access to capital. Disadvantages include regulatory and financial reporting requirements and the undermining of the investors' ability to monitor the company's management. • During an IPO, the shares sold may represent either a primary offering (if the shares are being sold to raise new capital) or a secondary offering (if the shares are sold by earlier investors). • An underwriter is an investment bank that manages the IPO process and helps the company sell its stock. • The lead underwriter is responsible for managing the IPO. • The lead underwriter forms a group of underwriters, called the syndicate, to help sell the stock. • The SEC requires that a company file a registration statement prior to an IPO. The preliminary prospectus is part of the registration statement that circulates to investors before the stock is offered. After the deal is completed, the company files a final prospectus. • Underwriters value a company before an IPO using valuation techniques and by book building. • Stock may be sold during an IPO on a best-efforts basis, as a firm commitment IPO, or using an auction IPO. The firm commitment process is the most common practice in the United States.	auction IPO, p. 448 best-efforts basis, p. 448 book building, p. 447 final prospectus, p. 445 firm commitment, p. 447 initial public offering (IPO), p. 442 lead underwriter, p. 443 lockup, p. 448 over-allotment allocation (greenshoe provision), p. 447 preliminary prospectus (red herring), p. 444 primary offering, p. 442 registration statement, p. 444 road show, p. 446 secondary offering, p. 442 spread, p. 447 syndicate, p. 444 underwriter, p. 442	MyFinanceLab Study Plan 14.2

14.3 IPO Puzzles		MyFinanceLab

14.3 IPO Puzzles

- Several puzzles are associated with IPOs.
  1. IPOs are underpriced on average.
  2. New issues are highly cyclical.
  3. The transaction costs of an IPO are very high.
  4. Long-run performance (three to five years) after an IPO is poor on average.

MyFinanceLab
Study Plan 14.3

14.4 Raising Additional Capital: The Seasoned Equity Offering

- A seasoned equity offering (SEO) is the sale of stock by a company that is already publicly traded.
- Two kinds of SEOs exist: a cash offer (when new shares are sold to investors at large) and a rights offer (when new shares are offered only to existing shareholders).
- The stock price reaction to an SEO is negative on average.

adverse selection, p. 458
cash offer, p. 456
primary shares, p. 456
rights offer, p. 456
seasoned equity offering (SEO), p. 456
secondary shares, p. 456
tombstone, p. 456

MyFinanceLab
Study Plan 14.4

CRITICAL THINKING

1. What are some of the alternative sources from which private companies can raise equity capital?
2. What are the advantages and the disadvantages to a private company of raising money from a corporate investor?
3. What are the main advantages and disadvantages of going public?
4. What are the main differences between a firm commitment IPO and an auction IPO?
5. Do underwriters face the most risk from a best-efforts IPO, a firm commitment IPO, or an auction IPO?
6. How is the price set in an auction IPO?
7. Why should a financial manager be concerned about underpricing?
8. IPOs are very cyclical. In some years, there are large numbers of IPOs; in other years, there are very few. Why is this cyclicality a puzzle?
9. What are the advantages of a rights offer?
10. What are the advantages to a company of selling stock in an SEO using a cash offer?
11. Why does the stock price typically decrease when a firm announces an SEO?

PROBLEMS

All problems are available in MyFinanceLab. An asterisk * indicates problems with a higher level of difficulty.

Equity Financing for Private Companies

1. You have started a company and are in luck—a venture capitalist has offered to invest. You own 100% of the company with 5 million shares. The VC offers $1 million for 800,000 new shares.
   a. What is the implied price per share?
   b. What is the post-money valuation?
   c. What fraction of the firm will you own after the investment?

2. Starware Software was founded last year to develop software for gaming applications. The founder initially invested $800,000 and received 8 million shares of stock. Starware now needs to raise a second round of capital, and it has identified a venture capitalist who is interested in investing. This venture capitalist will invest $1 million and wants to own 20% of the company after the investment is completed.
   a. How many shares must the venture capitalist receive to end up with 20% of the company? What is the implied price per share of this funding round?
   b. What will the value of the whole firm be after this investment (the post-money valuation)?

3. Your start-up company needs capital. Right now, you own 100% of the firm with 10 million shares. You have received two offers from venture capitalists. The first offers to invest $3 million for 1 million new shares. The second offers $2 million for 500,000 new shares.
   a. What is the first offer's post-money valuation of the firm?
   b. What is the second offer's post-money valuation of the firm?
   c. What is the difference in the percentage dilution caused by each offer?
   d. What is the dilution per dollar invested for each offer?

4. Three years ago, you founded your own company. You invested $100,000 of your own money and received 5 million shares of Series A preferred stock. Your company has since been through three additional rounds of financing.

Round	Price ($)	Number of Shares
Series B	0.50	1,000,000
Series C	2.00	500,000
Series D	4.00	500,000

   a. What is the pre-money valuation for the Series D funding round?
   b. What is the post-money valuation for the Series D funding round?

5. Based on the information in Problem 4 (and that each share of all series of preferred stock is convertible into one share of common stock), what fractions of the firm do the Series B, C, and D investors each own in your firm?

6. Assuming that you own only the Series A preferred stock in Problem 4 (and that each share of all series of preferred stock is convertible into one share of common stock), what percentage of the firm do you own after the last funding round?

Taking Your Firm Public: The Initial Public Offering

7. Roundtree Software is going public using an auction IPO. The firm has received the following bids:

Price ($)	Number of Shares
14.00	100,000
13.80	200,000
13.60	500,000
13.40	1,000,000
13.20	1,200,000
13.00	800,000
12.80	400,000

Assuming Roundtree would like to sell 1.8 million shares in its IPO, what will be the winning auction offer price?

8. If Roundtree from Problem 7 decides to issue an extra 500,000 shares (for a total of 2.3 million shares), how much total money will it raise?

9. Three years ago, you founded Outdoor Recreation, Inc., a retailer specializing in the sale of equipment and clothing for recreational activities such as camping, skiing, and hiking. So far, your company has gone through three funding rounds:

Round	Date	Investor	Shares	Share Price ($)
Series A	Feb. 2013	You	500,000	1.00
Series B	Aug. 2014	Angels	1,000,000	2.00
Series C	Sept. 2015	Venture capital	2,000,000	3.50

It is now 2016 and you need to raise additional capital to expand your business. You have decided to take your firm public through an IPO. You would like to issue an additional 6.5 million new shares through this IPO. Assuming that your firm successfully completes its IPO, you forecast that 2016 net income will be $7.5 million.
   a. Your investment banker advises you that the prices of other recent IPOs have been set such that the P/E ratios based on 2016 forecasted earnings average 20.0. Assuming that your IPO is set at a price that implies a similar multiple, what will your IPO price per share be?
   b. What percentage of the firm will you own after the IPO?

10. Your investment bankers price your IPO at $15 per share for 10 million shares. If the price at the end of the first day of trading is $17 per share,
   a. What was the percentage underpricing?
   b. How much money did the firm miss out on due to underpricing?

11. Margoles Publishing recently completed its IPO. The stock was offered at $14 per share. On the first day of trading, the stock closed at $19 per share.
   a. What was the initial return on Margoles?
   b. Who benefited from this underpricing? Who lost, and why?

12. If Margoles Publishing from Problem 11 paid an underwriting spread of 7% for its IPO and sold 10 million shares, what was the total cost (exclusive of underpricing) to it of going public?

13. Chen Brothers, Inc., sold 4 million shares in its IPO, at a price of $18.50 per share. Management negotiated a fee (the underwriting spread) of 7% on this transaction. What was the dollar cost of this fee?

14. You are negotiating with your underwriters in a firm commitment offering of 10 million primary shares. You have two options: set the IPO price at $20.00 per share with a spread of 7%, or set the price at $19.50 per share with a spread of 4%. Which option raises more money for your firm?

15. Your firm is selling 3 million shares in an IPO. You are targeting an offer price of $17.25 per share. Your underwriters have proposed a spread of 7%, but you would like to lower it to 5%. However, you are concerned that if you do so, they will argue for a lower offer price. Given the potential savings from a lower spread, how much lower can the offer price go before you would have preferred to pay 7% to get $17.25 per share?

Use the following information for Problems 16 through 18: The firm you founded currently has 12 million shares, of which you own 7 million. You are considering an IPO where you would sell 2 million shares for $20 each.

16. If all of the shares sold are primary shares, how much will the firm raise? What will be your percentage ownership of the firm after the IPO?

17. If all of the shares sold are from your holdings, how much will the firm raise? What will be your percentage ownership of the firm after the IPO?

18. What is the maximum number of secondary shares you could sell and still retain more than 50% ownership of the firm? How much would the firm raise in that case?

Raising Additional Capital: The Seasoned Equity Offering

19. YVR, Inc. just announced a 10 million share SEO at $50 per share. If all of the SEO shares are primary shares and its underwriter charges 7% of the gross proceeds, how much new capital will YVR raise?

20. On January 20, Metropolitan, Inc., sold 8 million shares of stock in an SEO. The market price of Metropolitan at the time was $42.50 per share. Of the 8 million shares sold, 5 million shares were primary shares being sold by the company, and the remaining 3 million shares were being sold by the venture capital investors. Assume the underwriter charges 5% of the gross proceeds as an underwriting fee.
    a. How much money did Metropolitan raise?
    b. How much money did the venture capitalists receive?
    c. If the stock price dropped 3% on announcement of the SEO and the new shares were sold at that price, how much money would Metropolitan receive?

*21. Foster Enterprises' stock is trading for $50 per share and there are currently 10 million shares outstanding. It would like to raise $100 million. If its underwriter charges 5% of gross proceeds,
    a. How many shares must it sell?
    b. If it expects the stock price to drop by 2% upon announcement of the SEO, how many shares should it plan to sell?
    c. If all of the shares are primary shares and are sold to new investors, what percentage reduction in ownership will all of the existing shareholders experience?

22. MacKenzie Corporation currently has 10 million shares of stock outstanding at a price of $40 per share. The company would like to raise money and has announced a rights issue. Every existing shareholder will be sent one right per share of stock that he or she owns. The company plans to require 10 rights to purchase one share at a price of $40 per share. How much money will it raise if all rights are exercised?

DATA CASE   Few IPOs have garnered as much attention as social media giant Facebook's public offering on May 18, 2012. It was the biggest IPO in Internet history, easily topping Google's initial public offering eight years earlier. Let's take a closer look at the IPO itself, as well as the payoffs to some of Facebook's early investors.

1. Begin by navigating to the SEC EDGAR Web site, which provides access to company filings: http://www.sec.gov/edgar.shtml. Choose "Search for Company Filings" and pick search by company name. Enter "Facebook" and then search for its IPO prospectus, which was filed on the date of the IPO and is listed as filing "424B4" (this acronym

derives from the rule number requiring the firm to file a prospectus, Rule 424(b)(4)). From the prospectus, calculate the following information:

  a. The underwriting spread in percentage terms. How does this spread compare to a typical IPO?

  b. The fraction of the offering that comprised primary shares and the fraction that comprised secondary shares.

  c. The size, in number of shares, of the greenshoe provision. What percent of the deal did the greenshoe provision represent?

2. Next, navigate to Google Finance and search for "Facebook." Determine the closing price of the stock on the day of the IPO (use the "Historical prices" link). What was the first day return? How does this return compare to the typical IPO?

3. Using the data provided by Google Finance, calculate the performance of Facebook in the three-month post-IPO period. That is, calculate the annualized return an investor would have received if he had invested in Facebook at the closing price on the IPO day and sold the stock three months later. What was the return for a one-year holding period?

4. Prior to the public offering, Facebook was able to raise capital from all the sources mentioned in the chapter. Let's concentrate on one particular source, Microsoft Corporation.

  a. Microsoft made one investment in Facebook, during October 2007. Go to Facebook's corporate news Web site (http://newsroom.fb.com) and locate the press release announcing this investment. Using the information in that press release and the number of shares owned by Microsoft listed in the IPO prospectus, calculate the per share price Microsoft paid.

  b. Calculate the return (expressed on an annual basis) Microsoft earned on its investment up to the IPO (using the IPO price).

  c. How much money did Microsoft receive from the IPO?

5. Facebook had only one angel investor, Peter Thiel (the founder of PayPal). Mr. Thiel invested more than once in Facebook, both as an angel and, in later rounds, on behalf of investors in his venture capital firm, Founders Fund. As an angel, Mr. Thiel invested $500,000 in September 2004. Assuming that all the shares he received in the angel round were registered under the name Rivendell One LLC,[16] use the information in the prospectus to calculate:

  a. The per share price he paid as an angel.

  b. The annualized return (using the IPO price) he made on his investment.

  c. The amount of angel money Mr. Thiel received from the proceeds of the IPO (that is, from his Rivendell investments alone).

---

[16]How Mr. Thiel holds his investments in Facebook is private information, so there is no substantive basis on which to make this assumption. That said, Mr. Thiel is reported to be a fan of *The Lord of the Rings*.

15

Debt Financing

LEARNING OBJECTIVES

- Identify different types of debt financing available to a firm

- Understand limits within bond contracts that protect the interests of bondholders

- Describe the various options available to firms for the early repayment of debt

notation

PV	present value	*YTM*	yield to maturity on a bond
YTC	yield to call on a callable bond		

In Chapter 14, we discussed the process a firm uses to raise equity capital, starting with angel investors for a young private firm and continuing through to seasoned equity offerings for an established public firm. We noted that each round of new equity financing dilutes the founder's ownership of the firm. An alternative financing source is to borrow the money—debt financing. In fact, debt is the most important source of financing; American corporations had over $8.7 *trillion* dollars in debt outstanding at the end of 2015. In 2013, Verizon issued a record $49 billion in bonds to partially finance the purchase of the 45% of Verizon Wireless it did not own from Vodaphone PLC. While debt financing does not dilute the ownership of the firm, the disadvantage is that loans must be repaid. That is, the firm is legally obligated to make interest and principal payments on its debt. If it fails to do so, it is in default and can be forced into bankruptcy. We discuss the relative advantages and disadvantages of debt versus equity financing in the next chapter, "Capital Structure." Here, we focus on the process for financing part of the firm with debt and on the features of corporate debt.

In mid-2005, Ford Motor Company decided to put one of its subsidiaries, Hertz Corporation, up for competitive bid. On September 13, 2005, the *Wall Street Journal* reported that a group of private investors led by Clayton, Dubilier & Rice (CDR), a private equity firm, had reached a deal with Ford to purchase Hertz's outstanding equity for $5.6 billion. In addition, Hertz had $9.1 billion in existing debt that it needed to refinance as part of the deal. CDR planned to finance the transaction in part by raising over $11 billion in new debt. Because almost all of the purchase would be financed with debt (leverage), the transaction is called a leveraged buyout. We will examine the details of this transaction throughout this chapter to illustrate debt financing.

When companies raise capital by issuing debt, they have several potential sources from which to seek funds. To complete the Hertz purchase, the group led by CDR relied on at least four different kinds of debt: domestic- and foreign-denominated high-yield bonds, bank loans, and *asset-backed securities*. In addition, each debt issue has its own specific terms determined at the time of issue. Building on the discussion of bond valuation in Chapter 6, we begin our exploration of debt financing by explaining the process of issuing debt and the types of debt available to companies. We continue by discussing restrictions on company actions in the debt agreement. Finally, we discuss some of the more advanced features of bonds such as the call provision.

15.1   Corporate Debt

Corporate debt can be *private debt*, which is negotiated directly with a bank or a small group of investors, or *public debt*, which trades in a public market. As we will see, the Hertz example described in the introduction included both.

Private Debt

private debt Debt that is not publicly traded.

The first debt financing many young firms undertake is a bank loan. However, even very large, established firms use bank loans as part of their debt financing. Bank loans are an example of **private debt**, debt that is not publicly traded. The private debt market is larger than the public debt market. Private debt has the advantage that it avoids the cost and delay of registration with the U.S. Securities and Exchange Commission (SEC). The disadvantage is that because it is not publicly traded, it is illiquid, meaning that it is hard for a holder of the firm's private debt to sell it in a timely manner.

 Debt Financing at Hertz: Bank Loans

As part of the transaction with CDR, Hertz took out more than $2 billion in bank loans. Hertz negotiated a $1.7 billion syndicated term loan with a seven-year term. Deutsche Bank AG negotiated the loan and then sold portions of it off to other banks—mostly smaller regional banks that had excess cash but lacked the resources to negotiate a loan of this magnitude by themselves. In addition to the term loan, Hertz negotiated an asset-backed revolving line of credit (for five years and $1.6 billion), which it could use as needed. Hertz's initial draw on the line of credit was $400 million.

term loan A bank loan that lasts for a specific term.

There are several segments of the private debt market: *bank loans* (*term loans* and *lines of credit*) and *private placements*.

syndicated bank loan A single loan that is funded by a group of banks rather than a single bank.

revolving line of credit A credit commitment for a specific time period, typically two to three years, which a company can use as needed.

Bank Loans. A **term loan** is a bank loan that lasts for a specific term. When a single loan is funded by a group of banks rather than a single bank, it is called a **syndicated bank loan**. Usually, one member of the syndicate (the lead bank) negotiates the terms of the bank loan. Many companies establish a **revolving line of credit**, a credit commitment for a specific time period up to some limit, typically two to three years, which a company can use as needed. A company may be able to get a larger line of credit or a lower interest rate if it secures the line of credit by pledging an asset as collateral. Such a line of credit is referred to as an **asset-backed line of credit**.

Private Placements. Recall from Chapter 6 that corporate bonds are securities issued by corporations. They account for a significant amount of invested capital. At the beginning

asset-backed line of credit A type of credit commitment, in which the borrower secures a line of credit by pledging an asset as collateral.

private placement A bond issue that does not trade on a public market but rather is sold to a small group of investors.

of 2013, the value of outstanding U.S. corporate bonds was about $9.2 trillion. Bonds can be issued publicly or placed privately. A **private placement** is a bond issue that does not trade on a public market but rather is sold to a small group of investors. Because a private placement does not need to be registered with the SEC, it is less costly to issue and often a simple promissory note is sufficient. Privately placed debt also need not conform to the same standards as public debt; as a consequence, it can be tailored to the particular situation.

In 1990, the SEC issued Rule 144A, which significantly increased the liquidity of certain privately placed debt. Private debt issued under this rule can be traded by large financial institutions among themselves. The rule was motivated by a desire to increase the access of foreign corporations to U.S. debt markets. Bonds that are issued under this rule are nominally private debt, but because they are tradable between financial institutions they are only slightly less liquid than public debt. Many firms issue debt under Rule 144A with the explicit promise to publicly register the debt within a certain time frame. The advantage of this approach to debt financing is that companies can raise the capital quickly and then spend the time it takes to comply with all of the filing requirements.

Debt Financing at Hertz: Private Placements

Hertz privately placed an additional $4.2 billion of U.S. asset-backed securities and $2.1 billion of international asset-backed securities. In this case, the assets backing the debt were the fleet of rental cars Hertz owned; hence, this debt was termed "fleet debt."

Hertz had an additional $2.7 billion bond issue that it issued under Rule 144A. As part of the offering, it agreed to publicly register the bonds within 390 days.* Because the debt was marketed and sold with the understanding that it would become public debt, we classified that issue as public debt.

*If Hertz failed to fulfill this commitment, the interest rate on all the outstanding bonds would increase by 0.5%.

Public Debt

In Chapter 6 we discussed several aspects of the public bond markets for corporate debt. In particular, we discussed default risk, bond ratings, and the role of ratings agencies. Here we expand our discussion to include the different types of public corporate debt and the markets in which they are offered.

indenture Included in a prospectus, it is a formal contract between a bond issuer and a trust company, which represents the bondholders' interests.

The Prospectus. A public bond issue is similar to a stock issue. A prospectus or offering memorandum must be produced that describes the details of the offering. Figure 15.1 shows the front page of the Hertz offering memorandum. In addition, the prospectus for a public offering must include an **indenture**, a formal contract that specifies the firm's obligations to the bondholders. This contract is actually written between the bond issuer and a trust company that represents the bondholders and makes sure that the terms of the indenture are enforced. In the case of default, the trust company represents the bondholders' interests.

While corporate bonds almost always pay coupons semiannually, a few corporations (for instance, Coca-Cola) have issued zero-coupon bonds. Corporate bonds have historically been issued with a wide range of maturities. Most corporate bonds have maturities of 30 years or less, although in the past there have been original maturities of up to 999 years. In July 1993, for example, Walt Disney Company issued $150 million in bonds with a maturity of 100 years that soon became known as the "Sleeping Beauty" bonds.

The face value or principal amount of the bond is denominated in standard increments, usually $1000. The face value does not always correspond to the actual money raised

FIGURE 15.1

Front Cover of the
Offering Memorandum
for the Hertz Junk
Bond Issue

OFFERING MEMORANDUM   CONFIDENTIAL

CCMG Acquisition Corporation
to be merged with and into The Hertz Corporation
$1,800,000,000 8.875% Senior Notes due 2014
$600,000,000 10.5% Senior Subordinated Notes due 2016
€225,000,000 7.875% Senior Notes due 2014

The Company is offering $1,800,000,000 aggregate principal amount of its 8.875% Senior Notes due 2014 (the "Senior Dollar Notes"), $600,000,000 aggregate principal amount of its 10.5% Senior Subordinated Notes due 2016 (the "Senior Subordinated Notes" and, together with the Senior Dollar Notes, the "Dollar Notes"), and €225,000,000 aggregate principal amount of its 7.875% Senior Notes due 2014 (the "Senior Euro Notes"). The Senior Dollar Notes and the Senior Euro Notes are collectively referred to as the "Senior Notes," and the Dollar Notes and the Senior Euro Notes are collectively referred to as the "Notes."

The Senior Notes will mature on January 1, 2014 and the Senior Subordinated Notes will mature on January 1, 2016. Interest on the Notes will accrue from December 21, 2005. We will pay interest on the Notes on January 1 and July 1 of each year, commencing July 1, 2006.

We have the option to redeem all or a portion of the Senior Notes and the Senior Subordinated Notes at any time (1) before January 1, 2010 and January 1, 2011, respectively, at a redemption price equal to 100% of their principal amount plus the applicable make-whole premium set forth in this offering memorandum and (2) on or after January 1, 2010 and January 1, 2011, respectively, at the redemption prices set forth in this offering memorandum. In addition, on or before January 1, 2009, we may, on one or more occasions, apply funds equal to the proceeds from one or more equity offerings to redeem up to 35% of each series of Notes at the redemption prices set forth in this offering memorandum. If we undergo a change of control or sell certain of our assets, we may be required to offer to purchase Notes from holders.

The Senior Notes will be senior unsecured obligations and will rank equally with all of our senior unsecured indebtedness. The Senior Subordinated Notes will be unsecured obligations and subordinated in right of payment to all of our existing and future senior indebtedness. Each of our domestic subsidiaries that guarantees specified bank indebtedness will guarantee the Senior Notes with guarantees that will rank equally with all of the senior unsecured indebtedness of such subsidiaries and the Senior Subordinated Notes with guarantees that will be unsecured and subordinated in right of payment to all existing and future senior indebtedness of such subsidiaries.

We have agreed to make an offer to exchange the Notes for registered, publicly tradable notes that have substantially identical terms as the Notes. The Dollar Notes are expected to be eligible for trading in the Private Offering, Resale and Trading Automated Linkages (PORTAL℠) market. This offering memorandum includes additional information on the terms of the Notes, including redemption and repurchase prices, covenants and transfer restrictions.

Investing in the Notes involves a high degree of risk. See "Risk Factors" beginning on page 23.

We have not registered the Notes under the federal securities laws of the United States or the securities laws of any other jurisdiction. The Initial Purchasers named below are offering the Notes only to qualified institutional buyers under Rule 144A and to persons outside the United States under Regulation S. See "Notice to Investors" for additional information about eligible offerees and transfer restrictions.

Price for each series of Notes: 100%

We expect that (i) delivery of the Dollar Notes will be made to investors in book-entry form through the facilities of The Depository Trust Company on or about December 21, 2005 and (ii) delivery of the Senior Euro Notes will be made to investors in book-entry form through the facilities of the Euroclear System and Clearstream Banking, S.A. on or about December 21, 2005.

Joint Book-Running Managers

Deutsche Bank Securities   **Lehman Brothers**

Merrill Lynch & Co.   **Goldman, Sachs & Co.**   **JPMorgan**

Co-Lead Managers

BNP PARIBAS   **RBS Greenwich Capital**   **Calyon**

The date of this offering memorandum is December 15, 2005.

Source: Courtesy of Hertz Corporation.

**original issue discount
(OID) bond** A coupon
bond issued at a discount.

because of underwriting fees and the possibility that the bond might not actually sell for its face value when it is offered for sale initially. If a coupon bond is issued at a discount, it is called an **original issue discount (OID) bond.**

unsecured debt A type of corporate debt that, in the event of a bankruptcy, gives bondholders a claim to only the assets of the firm that are not already pledged as collateral on other debt.

notes A type of unsecured corporate debt with maturities of less than 10 years.

Secured and Unsecured Corporate Debt. Four types of corporate debt are typically issued: *notes*, *debentures*, *mortgage bonds*, and *asset-backed bonds* (see Table 15.1). These types of debt fall into two categories: *unsecured debt* and *secured debt*. With **unsecured debt**, in the event of a bankruptcy bondholders have a claim to only the assets of the firm that are not already pledged as collateral on other debt. **Notes** are a type of unsecured debt, typically with maturities of less than 10 years, and **debentures** are a type of unsecured debt with maturities of 10 years or longer. With **secured debt**, specific assets are pledged as collateral that bondholders have a direct claim to in the event of a bankruptcy. **Mortgage bonds** are secured by real property, but **asset-backed bonds** can be secured by any kind of asset. Although the word "bond" is commonly used to mean any kind of debt security, technically a corporate bond must be secured.

TABLE 15.1

Types of Corporate Debt

debentures A type of unsecured corporate debt with maturities of 10 years or longer.

Secured Debt	Unsecured Debt
Mortgage bonds (secured with real property)	Notes (original maturity of less than 10 years)
Asset-backed bonds (secured with any asset)	Debentures

secured debt A type of corporate loan or debt security in which specific assets are pledged as a firm's collateral that bondholders have a direct claim to in the event of a bankruptcy.

mortgage bonds A type of secured corporate debt in which real property is pledged as collateral.

 Debt Financing at Hertz: Public Debt

As part of the transaction's financing, Hertz planned to issue $2.7 billion worth of unsecured debt—in this case, high-yield notes known as *junk bonds*. Recall from Chapter 6 that bonds rated below investment grade are called junk bonds. Furthermore, remember that companies such as Standard & Poor's and Moody's rate the creditworthiness of bonds and make this information available to investors (see Table 6.6 for the specific ratings). The high-yield issue for the Hertz transaction was divided into three kinds of debt or **tranches**, different classes of securities comprising a single bond issue and paid from the same cash flow source (see Table 15.2), all of which made semiannual coupon payments and were issued at par. The largest tranche was a $1.8 billion face-value note maturing in eight years. It paid a coupon of 8.875%, which at the time represented a 4.45% spread over Treasuries.

TABLE 15.2

Hertz's December 2005 Junk Bond Issues

	Tranche 1: Senior Dollar-Denominated Note	Tranche 2: Senior Euro-Denominated Note	Tranche 3: Senior Subordinated Dollar-Denominated Note
Face value	$1.8 billion	€225 million	$600 million
Maturity	December 1, 2014	December 1, 2014	December 1, 2016
Coupon	8.875%	7.875%	10.5%
Issue price	Par	Par	Par
Yield	8.875%	7.875%	10.5%
Rating:			
Standard and Poor's	B	B	B
Moody's	B1	B1	B3
Fitch	BB−	BB−	BB+

asset-backed bonds A type of secured corporate debt in which specific assets are pledged as collateral.

tranches Different classes of securities that comprise a single bond issuance.

seniority A bondholder's priority, in the event of a default, in claiming assets not already securing other debt.

subordinated debenture A debenture issue that has a lower priority claim to the firm's assets than other outstanding debt.

domestic bonds Bonds issued by a local entity, denominated in the local currency, and traded in a local market, but purchased by foreigners.

foreign bonds Bonds issued by a foreign company in a local market and intended for local investors. They are also denominated in the local currency.

Eurobonds International bonds that are not denominated in the local currency of the country in which they are issued.

global bonds Bonds that are offered for sale in several different markets simultaneously.

Seniority. Debentures and notes are unsecured. Because more than one debenture might be outstanding, the bondholder's priority in claiming assets in the event of default, known as the bond's **seniority**, is important. As a result, most debenture issues contain clauses restricting the company from issuing new debt with equal or higher priority than existing debt.

When a firm conducts a subsequent debenture issue that has lower priority than its outstanding debt, the new debt is known as a **subordinated debenture**. In the event of default, the assets not pledged as collateral for outstanding bonds cannot be used to pay off the holders of subordinated debentures until all more senior debt has been paid off. In Hertz's case, one tranche of the junk bond issue is a note that is subordinated to the other two tranches. In the event of bankruptcy, this note has a lower-priority claim on the firm's assets. Because holders of this tranche are likely to receive less in the event Hertz defaults, the yield on this debt is higher than that of the other tranches—10.5% compared to 8.875% for the first tranche.

International Bond Markets. The second tranche of Hertz's junk bond issue is a note that is denominated in euros rather than U.S. dollars—it is an international bond. International bonds are classified into four broadly defined categories.

1. **Domestic bonds** are bonds issued by a local entity and traded in a local market, but purchased by foreigners. They are denominated in the local currency of the country in which they are issued.

2. **Foreign bonds** are bonds issued by a foreign company in a local market and intended for local investors. They are also denominated in the local currency. Foreign bonds in the United States are known as *Yankee bonds*. In other countries, foreign bonds also have special names; for example, in Japan they are called Samurai bonds; in the United Kingdom, they are known as Bulldogs.

3. **Eurobonds** are international bonds that are not denominated in the local currency of the country in which they are issued. Consequently, there is no connection between the physical location of the market on which they trade and the location of the issuing entity. They can be denominated in any number of currencies that might or might not be connected to the location of the issuer. The trading of these bonds is not subject to any particular nation's regulations. In Chapter 6, we mentioned Eurodollar bonds, which are Eurobonds denominated in dollars.

4. **Global bonds** combine the features of domestic, foreign, and Eurobonds, and are offered for sale in several different markets simultaneously. Unlike Eurobonds, global bonds can be offered for sale in the same currency as the country of issuance. The Hertz junk bond issue is an example of a global bond issue: It was simultaneously offered for sale in the United States and Europe.

A bond that makes its payments in a foreign currency contains the risk of holding that currency and, therefore, is priced off the yields of similar bonds in that currency. Hence, the euro-denominated note of the Hertz junk bond issue has a different yield from the dollar-denominated note, even though both bonds have the same seniority and maturity. While they have the same default risk, they differ in their *exchange rate risk*—the risk that the foreign currency will depreciate in value relative to the local currency. (For further discussion of exchange rate risk, see Chapter 23.)

Table 15.3 summarizes Hertz's debt after the leveraged buyout (LBO) transaction. About $2.7 billion of the $11.1 billion total was public debt and the rest was private debt consisting of a term loan, a revolving line of credit, and fleet debt. Both the fleet debt and the line of credit were backed by specific assets of the firm.

TABLE 15.3

Summary of New Debt Issued as Part of the Hertz LBO

Type of Debt	Amount ($ million)
Public Debt	
Senior dollar-denominated	1800.0
Senior euro-denominated (€225 million)	268.9
Subordinated dollar-denominated	600.0
Private Debt	
Term loan	1707.0
Asset-backed revolving line of credit	400.0
Asset-backed "fleet debt"*	6348.0
Total	**$11,123.9**

* The collateral for this debt was Hertz's fleet of rental cars.

CONCEPT CHECK

1. List the four types of corporate public debt that are typically issued.
2. What are the four categories of international bonds?

15.2 Other Types of Debt

Corporations are not the only entities that use debt. We begin with the largest debt sector—loans to government entities.

Sovereign Debt

sovereign debt Debt issued by national governments.

Sovereign debt is debt issued by national governments. Recall from Chapter 6 that bonds issued by the U.S. government are called Treasury securities. Treasury securities represent the single largest sector of the U.S. bond market. On June 30, 2015, the market value of outstanding Treasury securities was $12.70 trillion. These bonds enable the U.S. government to borrow money so that it can engage in deficit spending (that is, spending more than what is received in tax revenues).

long bonds Bonds issued by the U.S. Treasury with the longest outstanding maturities (30 years).

The U.S. Treasury issues four kinds of securities (see Table 15.4). Treasury bills are pure discount bonds with maturities ranging from a few days to one year. Currently, the Treasury issues bills with original maturities of 4, 13, 26, and 52 weeks. Treasury notes are semiannual coupon bonds with original maturities of between 1 and 10 years. The Treasury issues notes with maturities of 2, 3, 5, 7, and 10 years at the present time. Treasury bonds are semiannual coupon bonds with maturities longer than 10 years. The Treasury currently issues bonds with maturities of 30 years (often called **long bonds**). All of these Treasury securities trade in the bond market.

TABLE 15.4

Existing U.S. Treasury Securities

Treasury Security	Type	Original Maturity
Bills	Discount	4, 13, 26, and 52 weeks
Notes	Coupon	2, 3, 5, 7, and 10 years
Bonds	Coupon	30 years
Inflation indexed	Coupon	5, 10, and 30 years

**TIPS (Treasury Inflation-
Protected Securities)**
An inflation-indexed bond
issued by the U.S. Treasury
with maturities of 5, 10,
and 20 years. They are
standard coupon bonds
with one difference: The
outstanding principal is
adjusted for inflation.

EXAMPLE 15.1
Coupon Payments
on Inflation-Indexed
Bonds

MyFinanceLab

The last type of security that the U.S. Treasury is currently issuing is inflation-indexed bonds called **TIPS** (Treasury Inflation-Protected Securities) with maturities of 5, 10, and 30 years. These bonds are standard coupon bonds with one difference: The outstanding principal is adjusted for inflation. Thus, although the coupon *rate* is fixed, the dollar coupon varies because the semiannual coupon payments are a fixed rate of the inflation-adjusted principal. In addition, the final repayment of principal at maturity (but not the interest payments) is protected against deflation. That is, if the final inflation-adjusted principal amount is less than the original principal amount, the original principal amount is repaid.

PROBLEM

On January 15, 2008, the U.S. Treasury issued a 10-year inflation-indexed note with a coupon of 1⅝%. On the date of issue, the consumer price index (CPI) was 209.49645. On January 15, 2015, the CPI had increased to 236.85403. What coupon payment was made on January 15, 2015?

SOLUTION

Between the issue date and January 15, 2015, the CPI appreciated by $226.33474/184.77419 = 1.13059$. Consequently, the principal amount of the bond increased by this amount; that is, the original face value of $1000 increased to $1130.59. Because the bond pays semiannual coupons, the coupon payment was $1130.59 \times 0.01625/2 = \$9.19$.

stop-out yield The highest yield competitive bid that will fund a particular U.S. Treasury security issue when all successful bidders (including the noncompetitive bidders) are awarded this yield.

STRIPS (Separate Trading of Registered Interest and Principal Securities)
Zero-coupon Treasury securities with maturities longer than one year that trade in the bond market.

municipal bonds Bonds issued by state and local governments. They are not taxable at the federal level (and sometimes not at the state or local level either) and so are sometimes also referred to as tax-exempt bonds.

serial bonds A single issue of municipal bonds that are scheduled to mature serially over a period of years.

Treasury securities are initially sold to the public by auction. Two kinds of bids are allowed: competitive bids and noncompetitive bids. Noncompetitive bidders (usually individuals) just submit the amount of bonds they wish to purchase and are guaranteed to have their orders filled at the auction. All competitive bidders submit sealed bids in terms of yields and the amount of bonds they are willing to purchase. The Treasury then accepts the lowest-yield (highest-price) competitive bids up to the amount required to fund the deal. The highest yield accepted is termed the **stop-out yield**. All successful bidders (including the noncompetitive bidders) are awarded this yield. In the case of a Treasury bill offering, the stop-out yield is used to set the price of the bill and all bidders then pay this price. In the case of a Treasury note or Treasury bond offering, this yield determines the coupon of the bond and then all bidders pay the par value for the bond or note.[1] All income from Treasury securities is taxable at the federal level. This income, however, is not taxable at the state or local level.[2]

Zero-coupon Treasury securities with maturities longer than one year also trade in the bond market. They are called **STRIPS** (Separate Trading of Registered Interest and Principal Securities). The Treasury itself does not issue STRIPS. Instead, investors (or, more commonly, investment banks) purchase Treasury notes and bonds and then resell each coupon and principal payment separately as a zero-coupon bond.

Municipal Bonds

Municipal bonds ("munis") are issued by state and local governments. Their distinguishing characteristic is that the income on municipal bonds is not taxable at the federal level. Consequently, municipal bonds are sometimes also referred to as tax-exempt bonds. Some issues are also exempt from state and local taxes.

Most municipal bonds pay semiannual coupons. A single issue will often contain a number of different maturity dates. Such issues are often called **serial bonds** because the bonds

[1]Because coupons are specified in eighths, if the winning yield is not divisible by eight, the coupon is set at the rate that produces a price closest to, but not over, par.
[2]For more details, see the U.S. Treasury Web site: www.treasurydirect.gov/.

Detroit's Art Museum at Risk

In July 2013, the city of Detroit filed for Chapter 9 bankruptcy protection, making history as the largest-ever municipal default. The city emerged from bankruptcy 15 months later, defaulting on $7 billion of its debt and cutting pension payments by 4.5%. But the cuts might have been worse, had not the city effectively "sold" its art museum.

The trouble for the city's art museum began prior to the bankruptcy filing when Kevyn Orr was appointed as an emergency manager of the city and demanded that the art museum sell $500 million of its art to help pay off city debts. The museum responded by raising $800 million from donors and using the money to buy its independence from the city. Following the bankruptcy, the ownership of the art museum transferred from the city to an independent trust.

Compared to a corporate bankruptcy, which allows the debtors to claim all the assets of the corporation, the ability of the debtors to claim assets in a municipal bankruptcy is very limited. Although the museum did ultimately contribute to the bankruptcy settlement, the amount of the contribution was far less than the $4.6 billion appraised value of its art. Similarly, although the pensioners did take cuts, the assets that backed their pensions were left intact in the pension plans and were not used to pay off debt holders. In the end, the debt holders took losses even when city assets existed, that if liquidated, could have covered some, if not all, of those losses.

Source: Slate 11/7/2014 "Detroit Exits Bankruptcy, Thanks to Its Art Museum" and *New York Times*, 11/7/2014, "'Grand Bargain' Saves the Detroit Institute of Arts."

---

revenue bonds Municipal bonds for which the local or state government can pledge as repayment revenues generated by specific projects.

general obligation bonds Bonds backed by the full faith and credit of a local government.

double-barreled Describes municipal bonds for which the issuing local or state government has strengthened its promise to pay by committing itself to using general revenue to pay off the bonds.

asset-backed security (ABS) A security whose cash flows come from an underlying pool of financial securities that "back" it.

asset securitization The process of creating an asset-backed security by packaging a portfolio of financial securities and issuing an asset-backed security backed by this portfolio.

mortgage-backed security (MBS) An asset-backed security backed by home mortgages.

are scheduled to mature serially over a number of years. The coupons on municipal bonds can be either *fixed* or *floating*. A fixed-coupon bond has the same coupon over the life of the bond. In a floating-rate issue, the coupon of the bond is adjusted periodically. The reset formula is a spread over a reference rate like the rate on Treasury bills that is established when the bond is first issued. There are also a few zero-coupon municipal bond issues.

Municipal bonds can differ in terms of the source of funds that guarantee them. **Revenue bonds** pledge specific revenues generated by projects that were initially financed by the bond issue. For example, the State of Nevada issued revenue bonds to finance the Las Vegas Monorail, to be repaid from fare revenues. Bonds backed by the full faith and credit of a local government are known as **general obligation bonds**. Sometimes local governments strengthen the commitment further by tying the promise to a particular revenue source, such as a special fee. Because a local government can always use its general revenue to repay such bonds, this commitment is over and above the usual commitment, so these bonds are called **double-barreled**. Despite these protections, municipal bonds are not nearly as secure as bonds backed by the federal government. Since 1970, about 4% of municipal bonds have defaulted, with the frequency and magnitude of default increasing in the aftermath of the 2008 financial crisis (including the aforementioned Las Vegas Monorail bonds).[3] The largest municipal bond defaults in U.S. history were Detroit's default in 2013 on over $7 billion in debt, soon surpassed by Puerto Rico's 2016 default on as much as $72 billion in debt.

Asset-Backed Securities

An **asset-backed security (ABS)** is a security that is made up of other financial securities; that is, the security's cash flows come from the cash flows of the underlying financial securities that "back" it. We refer to the process of creating an asset-backed security—packaging a portfolio of financial securities and issuing an asset-backed security backed by this portfolio—as **asset securitization**.

By far, the largest sector of the asset-backed security market is the *mortgage-backed security* market. A **mortgage-backed security (MBS)** is an asset-backed security backed by home mortgages. U.S. government agencies and sponsored enterprises, such as The Government National Mortgage Association (GNMA, or "Ginnie Mae") are the largest issuers in this sector. When homeowners in the underlying mortgages make their

---

[3]M. Walsh, "Muni Bonds Not as Safe as Thought," *The New York Times*, August 15, 2012.

GLOBAL FINANCIAL CRISIS

CDOs, Subprime Mortgages, and the Financial Crisis

GNMA and the other government agencies that issue mortgage-backed securities restrict the type of mortgages that they are prepared to securitize. For example, they will only securitize mortgages below a certain face value and, more importantly, that meet certain credit criteria. Mortgages that do not satisfy these criteria and have a high default probability are known as **subprime mortgages**. Part of the housing boom in the mid-2000s can be attributed to the increased availability of subprime mortgages. As the number of subprime mortgages exploded so, too, did the incentives to securitize them. Private institutions, such as banks, issued large amounts of mortgage-backed securities backed by subprime mortgages.

To understand the origins of the crisis, it is helpful to understand how subprime loans were securitized. Banks originating these loans first combined them into large **asset pools**. The cash flows from these mortgage-backed security pools were then used to back promises to different tranches of securities, distinguished by their seniority, known as **collateralized mortgage obligations (CMOs)**. By first pooling and diversifying the mortgages, and then tranching them into senior and subordinated securities, it is possible to create senior securities that have much lower risk than the underlying mortgages themselves. For example, consider a security with a senior claim to any principal repayments, for up to one half of the total principal outstanding. This security would be impaired only if more than 50% of the mortgages in the pool defaulted.

The figure below illustrates this idea, showing the flow of mortgage cash flows, first into MBS pools, and then into buckets representing the CMO security tranches. The buckets that are first in line are very likely to be filled. These senior tranches received AAA ratings and were attractive to investors because of

their high yields given their perceived safety. Of course, as we move further down, the later buckets face a much higher risk of not filling completely. The most junior tranches had low ratings (or were even unrated), and were much riskier than the original pools (if even one mortgage in the entire pool defaulted, these securities would be affected). As a result, these junior tranches appealed only to very sophisticated investors with an appetite for, and an ability to assess, their risk.

As the subprime market grew, finding investors willing to hold the junior tranches became more problematic. To resolve this problem, investment banks created pools of these junior securities, which they then tranched into a new series of senior and junior securities (CDOs). By the same reasoning as before, the senior tranches of these new CDOs were perceived to be very low risk and received AAA ratings, making them easy to sell to a wide range of investors. (Note also that, due to diversification, the CDO securities can have a higher average rating than the individual assets backing them.)

What went wrong? From 2002 through 2005, default rates on subprime mortgages were quite low, dropping to below 6%. As a result, ratings agencies relaxed their requirements and increased the size of the tranches that received AAA ratings. However, these low default rates occurred because house prices were rising, making it easy for subprime borrowers to refinance their loans and avoid default. Once the housing market slowed and began to decline in 2006–2007, refinancing was no longer possible (as banks would not lend more than the house was worth), and the default rate skyrocketed to over 40%.

The increased default rate had two important consequences. First, the original mortgage-backed securities turned out to be riskier than anticipated: Securities that were protected against default rates in excess of 20%, which seemed extremely safe in 2005, began to experience losses. But the damage was even more dramatic in the CDO securities that were created from the junior

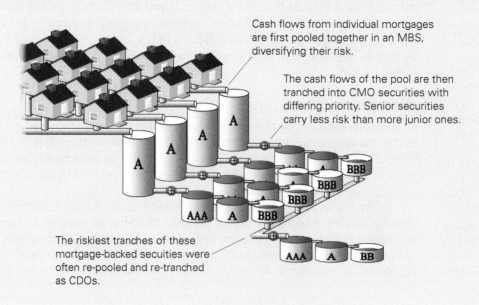

Cash flows from individual mortgages are first pooled together in an MBS, diversifying their risk.

The cash flows of the pool are then tranched into CMO securities with differing priority. Senior securities carry less risk than more junior ones.

The riskiest tranches of these mortgage-backed secuities were often re-pooled and re-tranched as CDOs.

mortgage-backed securities. The safety of the senior tranches of these CDOs relied on diversification—if no more than 20% of the junior mortgage-backed securities defaulted, these securities would be fully repaid. But the unexpectedly pervasive nature of the housing crisis meant that almost all of the securities that were backing these CDOs were running dry. As a result, many of the most senior, AAA-rated, CDO tranches were virtually wiped out, with their values declining to pennies on the dollar. This outcome was an extreme shock for the many investors who held them believing they were safe investments.

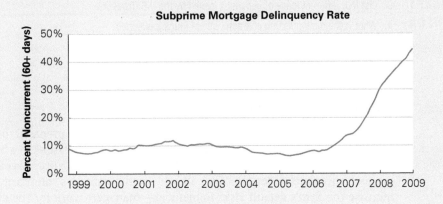

Subprime Mortgage Delinquency Rate

mortgage payments, this cash is passed through (minus servicing fees) to the holders of the mortgage-backed security. The cash flows of mortgage-backed securities therefore mirror the cash flows of home mortgages.

In the case of GNMA-issued mortgage-backed securities, the U.S. government provides an explicit guarantee to investors against default risk. This guarantee does not mean that these securities are risk-free, however. A mortgage borrower always has an option to repay some or all of the mortgage loan early (often because the borrower moves or refinances), and this early repayment of principal is passed through to owners of mortgage-backed securities. Thus, holders of mortgage-backed securities face **prepayment risk**—the risk that the bond will be partially (or wholly) repaid earlier than expected.

Other government-sponsored enterprises issuing mortgage-backed securities are the Federal National Mortgage Association (FNMA or "Fannie Mae") and the Federal Home Loan Mortgage Corporation (FHLMC or "Freddie Mac"). The Student Loan Marketing Association ("Sallie Mae") issues asset-backed securities backed by student loans. While, unlike Ginnie Mae, these enterprises are not explicitly backed by the full faith and credit of the U.S. government, most investors doubt that the government would allow any of its agencies to default and so believe these issues contain an implicit guarantee. In September 2008, this confidence was borne out when both Fannie Mae and Freddie Mac, which were both on the brink of failure, were placed into conservatorship of the Federal Housing Finance Agency, effectively bailing them out. On June 16, 2010, Fannie Mae's and Freddie Mac's stocks were delisted from the NYSE.

Private organizations, such as banks, also issue asset-backed securities. These securities can be backed by home mortgages (typically loans that do not meet the criteria to be included in the asset-backed securities issued by the government agencies) or other kinds of consumer loans such as automobile loans and credit card receivables. In addition, private asset-backed securities can be backed by other asset-backed securities. When banks re-securitize asset-backed and other fixed income securities, the new asset-backed security is known as a **collateralized debt obligation (CDO)**. CDO cash flows are usually divided into different tranches that are assigned different priorities. For example, investors in the

prepayment risk The risk faced by an investor in a callable bond or loan that the principal may be prepaid prior to maturity. This risk is the most important risk for holders of agency-backed mortgages.

collateralized debt obligation (CDO) The security that results when banks re-securitize other asset-backed securities.

junior tranche of an asset-backed security do not receive any cash flows until investors in the senior tranche have received their promised cash flows. Because of this prioritization, different CDO securities can have very different risk characteristics from each other, and from the underlying assets themselves (see the box on pages 476 and 477).

(see the box on pages 476 and 477)

CONCEPT CHECK

3. List four different kinds of securities issued by the U.S. Treasury.

4. What is the distinguishing characteristic of municipal bonds?

5. What is an asset-backed security?

15.3   Bond Covenants

covenants Restrictive clauses in a bond contract that limit the issuer from taking actions that may undercut its ability to repay the bonds.

Now that we have established the main types of debt, we are prepared to take a closer look at the bond contract provisions. **Covenants** are restrictive clauses in a bond contract that limit the issuer from taking actions that may undercut its ability to repay the bonds. Why are such covenants necessary? After all, why would managers voluntarily take actions that increase the firm's default risk? Remember—managers work for the equity holders and sometimes there are actions they can take that benefit the equity holders at the expense of debt holders. Covenants are there to protect debt holders in such cases.

Types of Covenants

Once bonds are issued, equity holders have an incentive to increase dividends at the expense of debt holders. Think of an extreme case in which a company issues a bond, and then immediately liquidates its assets, pays out the proceeds (including those from the bond issue) in the form of a dividend to equity holders, and declares bankruptcy. In this case, the equity holders receive the value of the firm's assets plus the proceeds from the bond, while bondholders are left with nothing. Consequently, bond agreements often contain covenants that restrict the ability of management to pay dividends. Other covenants may restrict how much more debt the firm can issue or they may specify that the firm must maintain a minimum amount of working capital. If the firm fails to live up to any covenant, the bond goes into technical default and the bondholder can demand immediate repayment or force the company to renegotiate the terms of the bond. Table 15.5 summarizes typical bond covenants. All of the covenants are designed to limit the company's (the borrower's) ability to increase the risk of the bond. For example, without restrictions on the issuance of new debt, the company could issue new debt of equal or greater seniority than the existing bonds, thus increasing the risk that it will not repay the existing bonds.

Advantages of Covenants

You might expect that equity holders would try to include as few covenants as possible in a bond agreement. In fact, this is not necessarily the case. The stronger the covenants in the bond contract, the less likely the firm will default on the bond, and thus the lower the interest rate investors will require to buy the bond. That is, by including more covenants, firms can reduce their costs of borrowing. The reduction in the firm's borrowing costs can more than outweigh the cost of the loss of flexibility associated with covenants.

TABLE 15.5

Typical Bond Covenants

Restrictions on:	Typical Restrictions
Issuing new debt	New debt must be subordinate to existing debt
	No new debt unless firm maintains specific leverage or interest coverage ratios
Dividends and share repurchases	Payouts can be made only from earnings generated after the bond issue
	Payouts can be made only if earnings exceed some threshold
Mergers and acquisitions	Mergers are allowed only if the combined firm has a minimum ratio of net tangible assets to debt
Asset disposition	Maximum amount of assets that can be sold, and/or minimum amount of assets that must be maintained
	Restrictions on making loans or any other provision of credit
Requiring Maintenance of:	
Accounting measures	Minimum retained earnings, working capital, and/or net assets
	Maximum leverage ratios

Source: Adapted from the American Bar Association's *Commentaries on Debentures*.

Application: Hertz's Covenants

Covenants in the Hertz junk bond issue limited Hertz's ability to incur more debt, make dividend payments, redeem stock, make investments, transfer or sell assets, and merge or consolidate. They also included a requirement that Hertz offer to repurchase the bonds at 101% of face value if the corporation experiences a change in control.

CONCEPT CHECK

6. What happens if an issuer fails to live up to a bond covenant?
7. Why can bond covenants reduce a firm's borrowing costs?

15.4 Repayment Provisions

A firm repays its bonds by making coupon and principal payments as specified in the bond contract. However, this is not the only way a firm can repay bonds. For example, the firm can repurchase a fraction of the outstanding bonds in the market, or it can make a tender offer for the entire issue, as Hertz did on its existing bonds. In this section, we explain the three main features affecting the repayment of the bond: *call provisions*, *sinking funds*, and *convertible provisions*.

Call Provisions

callable bonds Bonds containing a call provision that allows the issuer to repurchase the bonds at a predetermined price.

call date The date in the call provision on or after which the bond issuer has the right to retire the bond.

call price A price specified at the issuance of a bond for which the issuer can redeem the bond.

Firms can repay bonds by exercising a *call* provision. **Callable bonds** allow the issuer of the bond to repurchase the bonds at a predetermined price. A call feature also allows the issuer the right (but not the obligation) to retire all outstanding bonds on (or after) a specific date known as the **call date**, for the **call price** that is specified at the issuance of the bond. The call price is expressed as a percentage of the bond's face value and is generally set at or above the face value. The difference (in dollars) between the call price and the par value is the *call premium*. For example, a bond might have a call price of 105%, implying a call premium of $5 per $100 of par value.

Hertz's Callable Bonds. Hertz's junk bonds are examples of callable bonds. Table 15.6 lists the call features in each tranche. In Hertz's case, the call dates of the two senior tranches are at the end of the fourth year. For the duration of 2010, the first tranche has a call price of 104.438% of the bond's face value. In the following years, the call price is gradually reduced until in 2012 the bond became callable at par (100% of face value). The euro-denominated bond has similar terms at slightly different call prices. The subordinated tranche's call date is a year later and has a different call-price structure.

The Hertz bonds are also partially callable in the first three years. Hertz has the option to retire up to 35% of the outstanding principal at the call prices listed in Table 15.6, as long as the funds needed to repurchase the bonds are derived from the proceeds of an equity issuance.

Call Provisions and Bond Prices. When would a financial manager choose to exercise the firm's right to call the bond? A firm can always retire one of its bonds early by repurchasing the bond in the open market. If the call provision offers a cheaper way to retire the bond, however, the firm will forgo the option of purchasing the bond in the open market and call the bond instead. Thus, when the market price of the bond exceeds the call price, the firm will call the bond.

We know from Chapter 6 that bond prices rise when market interest rates fall. If market interest rates have decreased since the bond was issued and are now less than the bond's coupon rate, the bond will be trading at a premium. If the firm has the option to call the bond at less than the premium, it could do so and refinance its debt at the new, lower market interest rates.

Given the flexibility a call provision provides to a financial manager, you might expect all bonds to be callable. However, that is not the case and to see why, we must consider how the investor views the call provision. The financial manager will choose to call the bonds only when the coupon rate the investor is receiving exceeds the market interest rate. By calling the bond, the firm is forcing the investor to relinquish the bond at a price below the value it would have were it to remain outstanding. Naturally, investors view this possibility negatively and pay less for callable bonds than for otherwise identical non-callable bonds. This means that a firm raising capital by issuing callable bonds instead of non-callable bonds will either have to pay a higher coupon rate or accept lower proceeds. A firm will choose to issue callable bonds despite their higher yield if they find the option to refinance the debt in the future particularly valuable.

yield to call (YTC) The yield of a callable bond calculated under the assumption that the bond will be called on the earliest call date.

Yield to Call. A financial manager needs to understand how investors are evaluating the firm's callable bonds. For callable bonds, the **yield to call (YTC)**, the annual yield of a callable bond calculated under the assumption that the bond is called on the earliest call date, is most often quoted. In Chapter 6, we learned how investors evaluate a firm's bonds

TABLE 15.6

Call Features of Hertz's Bonds

Call Features	Tranche 1: Senior Dollar-Denominated Note	Tranche 2: Senior Euro-Denominated Note	Tranche 3: Senior Subordinated Dollar-Denominated Note
	Up to 35% of the outstanding principal callable at 108.875% in the first three years.	Up to 35% of the outstanding principal callable at 107.875% in the first three years.	Up to 35% of the outstanding principal callable at 110.5% in the first three years.
	After four years, fully callable at:	After four years, fully callable at:	After five years, fully callable at:
	• 104.438% in 2010.	• 103.938% in 2010.	• 105.25% in 2011.
	• 102.219% in 2011.	• 101.969% in 2011.	• 103.50% in 2012.
	• Par thereafter.	• Par thereafter.	• 101.75% in 2013.

by computing their yield to maturity. The yield to maturity is always calculated on the assumption that the bond will remain outstanding until maturity and make all of its promised payments. In the case of a callable bond, that assumption is not realistic. Thus, the yield to maturity of a callable bond is the interest rate the bondholder receives if the bond is not called and repaid in full. When the bond's coupon rate is above the yield for similar securities, the yield to call is less than the yield to maturity. However, when the bond's coupon rate is below the yield for similar securities, the bond is unlikely to be called (the firm would not call a bond when it is paying a below-market interest rate). In that case, calling would actually be good for the bondholders and the yield to call would be above the yield to maturity. To keep all this straight, most bond traders quote **yield to worst**, which is the lower of the yield to call or yield to maturity. Table 15.7 summarizes the yield to call and yield to worst.

yield to worst Quoted by bond traders as the lower of the yield to call or yield to maturity.

TABLE 15.7

Bond Calls and Yields

Bond coupons relative to market yields	Bond price is . . .	Likelihood of call is . . .	Yield to Worst is . . .
Coupons are higher	At a premium	High	Yield to call
Coupons are lower	At a discount	Low	Yield to maturity

New York City Calls Its Municipal Bonds

In November 2004, New York City announced plans to call $430 million of its municipal bonds. New York City was an AAA-rated borrower, and these bonds paid relatively high interest rates of 6% to 8%. The city would be refinancing the bonds with new bonds that paid interest rates between 3% and 5%. In total, New York City called 63 individual bond issues with original maturities between 2012 and 2019.

Investors were attracted to the older municipal bonds because of their higher yields. Despite these yields, they did not expect New York City to call these bonds, so the market price for these bonds earlier in the year was 10% to 20% higher than their face value. When New York City announced its plans to call the bonds at

prices slightly higher than the face value investors were caught off guard and the market value of the bonds fell accordingly. Investors suffered losses of 15% or more on their AAA-rated investment.

Investors did not expect New York City to call these bonds because it had already refinanced the debt in the early 1990s. According to Internal Revenue Service rules, the city could not refinance again with another tax-exempt issue. However, New York City surprised the market when it decided to refinance the bonds by issuing taxable bonds instead. Although it happens rarely, this example illustrates that investors are sometimes surprised by issuer call strategies.

Source: A. Lucchetti, Copyright 2005 by DOW JONES & COMPANY, INC. Reproduced with permission of DOW JONES & COMPANY, Inc. via Copyright Clearance Center.

EXAMPLE 15.2

Calculating the Yield to Call

MyFinanceLab

PROBLEM

IBM has just issued a callable (at par) five-year, 8% coupon bond with annual coupon payments. The bond can be called at par in one year or anytime thereafter on a coupon payment date. It has a price of $103 per $100 face value, implying a yield to maturity of 7.26%. What is the bond's yield to call?

SOLUTION

PLAN

The timeline of the promised payments for this bond (if it is not called) is:

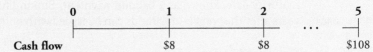

0	1	2	5
Cash flow	$8	$8	$108

If IBM calls the bond at the first available opportunity, it will call the bond at year 1. At that time, it will have to pay the coupon payment for year 1 ($8 per $100 of face value) and the face value ($100). The timeline of the payments if the bond is called at the first available opportunity (at year 1) is:

(Continued)

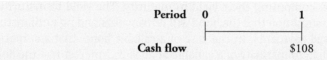

	Period	0	1
Cash flow			$108

To solve for the yield to call, we use these cash flows and proceed as shown in Chapter 6, setting the price equal to the discounted cash flows and solving for the discount rate.

EXECUTE

For the yield to call, setting the present value of these payments equal to the current price gives:

$$103 = \frac{108}{(1 + YTC)}$$

Solving for the yield to call gives:

$$YTC = \frac{108}{103} - 1 = 4.85\%$$

We can use a financial calculator or spreadsheet to derive the same result:

	N	I/Y	PV	PMT	FV
Given:	1		−103	8	100
Solve for:		4.85			

Excel Formula: =RATE(NPER,PMT,PV,FV)=RATE(1,8,−103,100)

EVALUATE

The yield to maturity is higher than the yield to call because it assumes that you will continue receiving your coupon payments for five years, even though interest rates have dropped below 8%. Under the yield to call assumptions, since you are repaid the face value sooner, you are deprived of the extra four years of coupon payments resulting in a lower total return.

Sinking Funds

sinking fund A method for repaying a bond in which a company makes regular payments into a fund administered by a trustee over the life of the bond. These payments are then used to repurchase bonds, usually at par.

Some bonds are repaid through a **sinking fund**, a provision that allows the company to make regular payments into a fund administered by a trustee over the life of the bond instead of repaying the entire principal balance on the maturity date. These payments are then used to repurchase bonds, usually at par. In this way, the company can reduce the amount of outstanding debt without affecting the cash flows of the remaining bonds.

Sinking fund provisions usually specify a minimum rate at which the issuer must contribute to the fund. In some cases, the issuer has the option to accelerate these payments. Because the sinking fund allows the issuer to repurchase the bonds at par, the option to accelerate the payments is another form of a call provision. As with all call provisions, this option is not free—including this provision lowers the price the company would get for the bonds initially.

balloon payment A large payment that must be made on the maturity date of a bond when the sinking fund payments are not sufficient to retire the entire bond issue.

The manner in which an outstanding balance is paid off using a sinking fund depends on the issue. Some issues specify equal payments over the life of the bond, ultimately retiring the issue on the maturity date of the bond. In other cases, the sinking fund payments are not sufficient to retire the entire issue and the company must make a large payment on the maturity date, known as a **balloon payment**. Sinking fund payments often start only a few years after the bond issue. Bonds can be issued with both a sinking fund and a call provision.

Convertible Provisions

convertible bonds Corporate bonds with a provision that gives the bondholder an option to convert each bond owned into a fixed number of shares of common stock.

Another way to retire bonds is by converting them into equity. **Convertible bonds** are corporate bonds with a provision that gives the bondholder an option to convert each bond owned into a fixed number of shares of common stock at a ratio called the **conversion ratio**. The provision

conversion ratio The number of shares received upon conversion of a convertible bond, usually stated per $1000 of face value.

usually gives bondholders the right to convert the bond into stock at any time up to the maturity date for the bond.[4] The conversion ratio is usually stated per $1000 of face value.

Convertible Bond Pricing. Consider a convertible bond with a $1000 face value and a conversion ratio of 20. If you converted the bond into stock on its maturity date, you would receive 20 shares. If you did not convert, you would receive $1000. Hence, by converting the bond you essentially "paid" $1000 for 20 shares, implying a price per share of $1000/20 = \$50$. This implied price per share equal to the face value of the bond divided by the number of shares received in conversion is called the **conversion price**. If the price of the stock exceeds $50, you would choose to convert; otherwise, you would take the cash. Thus, as shown in Figure 15.2, the value of the bond on its maturity date is the maximum of its face value ($1000) and the value of 20 shares of stock.

conversion price The face value of a convertible bond divided by the number of shares received if the bond is converted.

Often companies issue convertible bonds that are callable. With these bonds, if the issuer calls them, the holder can choose to convert rather than let the bonds be called. When the bonds are called, the holder faces exactly the same decision as he or she would face on the maturity date of the bonds: He or she will choose to convert if the stock price exceeds the conversion price and let the bonds be called otherwise. Thus, by calling the bonds a company can force bondholders to make their decision to convert earlier than they would otherwise have preferred.

straight bond A non-callable, non-convertible bond (also called a plain-vanilla bond).

The option (which is not an obligation) to convert the bonds into equity is worth something to a bondholder. Thus, prior to the bond maturity date a convertible bond is worth more than an otherwise identical **straight bond**, a non-callable, non-convertible bond (also called a *plain-vanilla bond*). Consequently, if both bonds are issued at par, the

FIGURE 15.2

Convertible Bond Value

At maturity, the value of a convertible bond is the maximum of the value of a $1000 straight bond (a non-convertible, non-callable bond) and 20 shares of stock, and it will be converted if the stock is above the conversion price. Prior to maturity, the value of the convertible bond will depend upon the likelihood of conversion, and will be above that of a straight bond or 20 shares of stock.

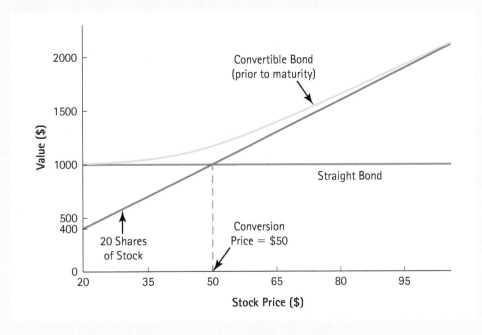

---

[4]Some convertible bonds do not allow conversion for a specified amount of time after the issue date.

straight bond must offer a higher interest rate. Similarly, the option to receive the bond's face value means the convertible bond is also worth more than 20 shares of stock. This relationship is illustrated in Figure 15.2, where the convertible bond's value prior to maturity (the yellow curve) exceeds the value of both the straight bond and the stock (the red and blue lines). The company (meaning its existing shareholders) must weigh the benefit of the lower interest rate on the convertible bond against the cost of giving those bondholders the option to buy new shares of stock at a fixed price.

Convertible Bonds and Stock Prices. Note that the likelihood of eventually converting a convertible bond depends upon the current stock price. When the stock price is low, conversion is unlikely, and the value of the convertible bond is close to that of a straight bond. When the stock price is much higher than the conversion price, conversion is very likely and the convertible bond's price is close to the price of the converted shares. Finally, when the stock price is in the middle range, near the conversion price, there is the greatest uncertainty about whether it will be optimal to convert or not. In this case, the bondholder's option to decide later whether to convert is most valuable, and the value of the convertible bond exceeds the value of straight debt or equity by the greatest amount.

Combining Features. Companies have flexibility in setting the features of the bonds they issue. As we mentioned, companies will often add a call provision to convertible bonds or bonds with sinking funds. Another example of flexibility is to add convertibility to subordinated bonds. Subordinated bonds typically have a higher yield because of their riskier position relative to senior bonds. But if the subordinated bond contains a convertibility feature that the senior bonds do not have, the yield on the subordinated bond could be lower than the senior bonds. One example is RealNetworks, which issued $100 million in subordinated convertible debt in 2003 with a zero coupon rate. As described in Table 15.8, the debt also contained a provision allowing the company to call the debt at par anytime after July 1, 2008. RealNetworks exercised its option to call the debt in 2008, paying $100 million to repurchase the debt from the debtholders.

Leveraged Buyouts. Recall from Chapter 14 our discussion of how private companies become public companies. The deal in which CDR bought Hertz is an example of the opposite transition—a public company becoming private, in this case through a *leveraged buyout*. In a **leveraged buyout (LBO)**, a group of private investors purchases all the equity of a public corporation and finances the purchase primarily with debt.[5] With a total value of $15.2 billion,[6] the leveraged buyout of Hertz was the second largest transaction of its kind at the time of its announcement. This left Hertz with a substantial amount of debt on its balance sheet. As with most LBOs, Hertz's long-term plan was to reduce its leverage through continued profitability. In November 2006, Hertz went public again by selling new stock through an IPO. In 2012, Hertz increased its debt to acquire Dollar/Thrifty, and refinanced some of its senior debt from the LBO by calling the notes due in 2014. In June 2016, the parent company spun off the rental car business so that it trades under HTZ and the equipment rental business trades as a separate company under HRI. Recent LBOs include Michael Dell's purchase of Dell Computer in 2013 and Carlyle Group's buyout of Symantec in 2015. In Chapter 16, we will examine the tradeoffs a financial manager faces in deciding how much of a company to finance with debt and how much to finance with equity.

leveraged buyout (LBO) When a group of private investors purchases all the equity of a public corporation and finances the purchase primarily with debt.

---

[5]At the time of the deal, Hertz was a wholly owned subsidiary of Ford Motor Company, which itself is a public company. Prior to Ford's acquisition of Hertz's outstanding shares in 2001, Hertz was publicly traded.

[6]The total value includes $14.7 billion for Hertz, and $0.5 billion in fees and expenses. In addition to $11.1 billion in new debt, the transaction was financed using $1.8 billion of Hertz's own cash and securities (including a $1.2 billion obligation from Ford, which was forgiven as part of the payment to Ford). The remaining $2.3 billion in private equity was contributed by Clayton, Dubilier & Rice, The Carlyle Group, and Merrill Lynch Global Private Equity.

TABLE 15.8

RealNetworks' 2003
Convertible Debt Issue

Convertible Subordinated Notes	
Issued under Rule 144A	
Aggregate principal amount:	$100 million
Proceeds net of offering costs:	$97.0 million
Coupon:	0%
Conversion ratio:	107.5650 shares per $1000 principal amount
Call date:	July 1, 2008
Call price:	100%
Maturity:	July 1, 2010

CONCEPT
CHECK

8. Do callable bonds have a higher or lower yield than otherwise identical bonds without a call feature? Why?

9. What is a sinking fund?

MyFinanceLab

Here is what you should know after reading this chapter. MyFinanceLab will help you identify what you know, and where to go when you need to practice.

KEY POINTS AND EQUATIONS	KEY TERMS	ONLINE PRACTICE
15.1 Corporate Debt • Companies can raise debt using different sources. Typical kinds of debt are public debt, which trades in a public market, and private debt, which is negotiated directly with a bank or a small group of investors. The securities that companies issue when raising debt are called corporate bonds. • Private debt can be in the form of term loans or private placements. A term loan is a bank loan that lasts for a specific term. A private placement is a bond issue that is sold to a small group of investors. • For public offerings, the bond agreement takes the form of an indenture, a formal contract between the bond issuer and a trust company. The indenture lays out the terms of the bond issue. • Four types of corporate bonds are typically issued: notes, debentures, mortgage bonds, and asset-backed bonds. Notes and debentures are unsecured. Mortgage bonds and asset-backed bonds are secured. • Corporate bonds differ in their level of seniority. In case of bankruptcy, senior debt is paid in full before subordinated debt is paid. • International bonds are classified into four broadly defined categories: domestic bonds that trade in foreign markets; foreign bonds that are issued in a local market by a foreign entity; Eurobonds that are not denominated in the local currency of the country in which they are issued; and global bonds that trade in several markets simultaneously.	asset-backed bonds, p. 471 asset-backed line of credit, p. 468 debentures, p. 471 domestic bonds, p. 472 Eurobonds, p. 472 foreign bonds, p. 472 global bonds, p. 472 indenture, p. 469 mortgage bonds, p. 471 notes, p. 471 original issue discount (OID) bond, p. 470 private debt, p. 468 private placement, p. 469 revolving line of credit, p. 468 secured debt, p. 471 seniority, p. 472 subordinated debenture, p. 472 syndicated bank loan, p. 468 term loan, p. 468 tranches, p. 472 unsecured debt, p. 471	MyFinanceLab Study Plan 15.1

15.2 Other Types of Debt

- Governments, states, and other state-sponsored enterprises issue bonds as well.
- The U.S. Treasury has issued four different kinds of securities: Treasury bills, Treasury notes, Treasury bonds, and TIPS.
- Municipal bonds ("munis") are issued by state and local governments. Their distinguishing characteristic is that the income on municipal bonds is not taxable at the federal level.
- An asset-backed security (ABS) is a security that is made up of other financial securities, that is, the security's cash flows come from the cash flows of the underlying financial securities that "back" it.
- A mortgage-backed security (MBS) is an asset-backed security backed by home mortgages. U.S. government agencies, such as the Government National Mortgage Association (GNMA, or "Ginnie Mae"), are the largest issuers in this sector.
- Holders of agency-issued mortgage-backed securities face prepayment risk, which is the risk that they will find that the bond will be partially (or wholly) repaid earlier than expected. Holders of privately issued mortgage-backed securities also face default risk.
- A collateralized debt obligation is an asset-backed security that is backed by other asset-backed securities.

asset-backed security (ABS), p. 475
asset pools, p. 476
asset securitization, p. 475
collateralized debt obligation (CDO), p. 477
collateralized mortgage obligations (CMOs), p. 476
double-barreled, p. 475
general obligation bonds, p. 475
long bonds, p. 473
mortgage-backed security (MBS), p. 475
municipal bonds, p. 474
prepayment risk, p. 477
revenue bonds, p. 475
serial bonds, p. 474
sovereign debt, p. 473
stop-out yield, p. 474
STRIPS, p. 474
subprime mortgages, p. 476
TIPS, p. 474

15.3 Bond Covenants

- Covenants are restrictive clauses in the bond contract that help investors by limiting the issuer's ability to take actions that will increase its default risk and reduce the value of the bonds.

covenants, p. 478

MyFinanceLab Study Plan 15.2

15.4 Repayment Provisions

- A call provision gives the issuer of the bond the right (but not the obligation) to retire the bond after a specific date (but before maturity).
- A callable bond will generally trade at a lower price than an otherwise equivalent non-callable bond.
- The yield to call is the yield of a callable bond assuming that the bond is called at the earliest opportunity.
- Another way in which a bond is repaid before maturity is by periodically repurchasing part of the debt through a sinking fund.
- Some corporate bonds, known as convertible bonds, have a provision that allows the holder to convert them into equity.
- Convertible debt carries a lower interest rate than other comparable non-convertible debt.

balloon payment, p. 482
call date, p. 479
call price, p. 479
callable bonds, p. 479
conversion price, p. 483
conversion ratio, p. 483
convertible bonds, p. 482
leveraged buyout (LBO), p. 484
sinking fund, p. 482
straight bond, p. 483
yield to call (YTC), p. 480
yield to worst, p. 481

MyFinanceLab Study Plan 15.3

**CRITICAL
THINKING**

1. What are the different types of corporate debt and how do they differ?

2. Explain some of the differences between a public debt offering and a private debt offering.

3. Explain the difference between a secured corporate bond and an unsecured corporate bond.

4. Why do bonds with lower seniority have higher yields than equivalent bonds with higher seniority?

5. What is the difference between a foreign bond and a Eurobond?

6. Why would companies voluntarily choose to put restrictive covenants into a new bond issue?

7. Why would a call feature be valuable to a company issuing bonds?

8. What is the effect of including a call feature on the price a company can receive for its bonds?

9. When will the yield to maturity be higher than the yield to call for a callable bond?

10. How does a sinking fund provision affect the cash flows associated with a bond issue from the company's perspective? From a single bondholder's perspective?

11. Why is the yield on a convertible bond lower than the yield on an otherwise identical bond without a conversion feature?

PROBLEMS

All problems are available in MyFinanceLab. *The* ⬛×⬛ *icon indicates problems that are easier to solve using Excel and have data in an Excel format available in* MyFinanceLab.

Corporate Debt

1. You are finalizing a bank loan for $200,000 for your small business and the closing fees payable to the bank are 2% of the loan. After paying the fees, what will be the net amount of funds from the loan available to your business?

2. Your firm is considering two one-year loan options for a $500,000 loan. The first carries fees of 2% of the loan amount and charges interest of 4% of the loan amount. The other carries fees of 1% of the loan amount and charges interest of 4.5% of the loan amount.
   a. What is the net amount of funds from each loan?
   b. Based on the net amount of funds, what is the true interest rate of each loan?

3. Your firm is issuing $100 million in straight bonds at par with a coupon rate of 6% and paying total fees of 3%. What is the net amount of funds that the debt issue will provide for your firm?

Other Types of Debt

4. Describe the kinds of securities the U.S. government uses to finance the federal debt.

5. Suppose on January 15, 2013, the U.S. Treasury issued a five-year inflation-indexed note with a coupon of 3%. On the date of issue, the consumer price index (CPI) was 250. By January 15, 2018, the CPI had increased to 300. What principal and coupon payment was made on January 15, 2018?

6. On January 15, 2020, the U.S. Treasury issued a 10-year inflation-indexed note with a coupon of 6%. On the date of issue, the CPI was 400. By January 15, 2030, the CPI had decreased to 300. What principal and coupon payment was made on January 15, 2030?

7. Describe what prepayment risk in a GNMA is.

8. What is the distinguishing feature of how municipal bonds are taxed?

Bond Covenants

9. Your firm successfully issued new debt last year, but the debt carries covenants. Specifically, you can only pay dividends out of earnings made after the debt issue and you must maintain a minimum quick (acid-test) ratio

$$((\text{current assets} - \text{inventory})/\text{current liabilities})$$

of 1:1. Your net income this year was $70 million. Your cash is $10 million, your receivables are $8 million, and your inventory is $5 million. You have current liabilities of $19 million. What is the maximum dividend you could pay this year and still comply with your covenants?

10. Your firm has tangible assets of $100 million. You are planning to acquire a firm that is half your firm's size. You have bonds with a merger & acquisition covenant that requires the combined firm to have a minimum ratio of net tangible assets to debt of 1.5:1. Your firm has a ratio of 2:1 and the target firm has a ratio of 1.2:1. Can you acquire this firm (and thus take on more debt) without violating your covenant?

Repayment Provisions

11. General Electric has just issued a callable (at par) 10-year, 6% coupon bond with annual coupon payments. The bond can be called at par in one year or anytime thereafter on a coupon payment date. It has a price of $102.
    a. What is the bond's yield to maturity?
    b. What is its yield to call?
    c. What is its yield to worst?

12. Boeing Corporation has just issued a callable (at par) three-year, 5% coupon bond with semiannual coupon payments. The bond can be called at par in two years or anytime thereafter on a coupon payment date. It has a price of $99.
    a. What is the bond's yield to maturity?
    b. What is its yield to call?
    c. What is its yield to worst?

13. You own a bond with a face value of $10,000 and a conversion ratio of 450. What is the conversion price?

14. A $1000 face value bond has a conversion ratio of 40. You estimate the transaction costs of conversion to be 3% of the face value of the bond. What price must the stock reach in order for you to convert?

15. You are thinking about buying Dovia Co.'s convertible bonds. You plan to convert to equity at the end of the year and you think that Dovia's common equity will be priced at $35 per share at that point. What conversion ratio should Dovia's bonds have in order for you to expect to be able to convert them at the end of the year?

16. You are the CFO of RealNetworks on July 1, 2008. The company's stock price is $6.74 and its convertible debt (as shown in Table 15.8) is now callable.
    a. What is the value of the shares the bondholders would receive per $1000 bond if they convert?
    b. What is the value per $1000 bond they would receive under the call?
    c. If you call the bonds, will the bondholders convert into shares or accept the call price?

DATA CASE

You are working for Home Depot and have been asked to help explore the impact of a potential debt issue. The CFO and other top managers in the finance division are all aware that increasing the debt load will have ramifications in the credit markets. Specifically, they realize that the firm's debt rating could change, which will raise the cost of borrowing as well as possibly lower the value of the existing debt. No one is exactly sure what the impact will be, but they all agree that it deserves investigation.

You have been summoned to an executive-level meeting and asked to estimate the impact of increasing the debt of the firm. You are to consider four different scenarios: issuing $1 billion, $10 billion, $20 billion, and $30 billion in new debt. In each case, proceeds from the debt will be used to repurchase stock (so the total amount of financing for the firm will not change—just the balance between debt and equity). The CFO believes that the $1 billion level will not affect the firm's credit rating. However, each larger increase in debt will cause the debt to be downgraded one letter grade (e.g., from Baa to Ba). For example, the $10 billion scenario will lower the current debt rating one level, the $20 billion scenario would lower the rating still another level, and so on. Your job is to determine the impact of additional debt on borrowing costs at each debt level. Assume the new debt will be raised by issuing 10-year bonds.

1. Determine the current debt rating for The Home Depot.
   - Research the current bond rating at FINRA (finra-markets.morningstar.com/BondCenter/). Select the "Corporate" toggle, enter the symbol for Home Depot (HD), and click "Show Results."
   - What is the Moody's bond rating on the Home Depot bond with the maturity closest to 10 years from today? What is the yield on this bond?

2. Because lower bond ratings will lead to higher interest costs, you will need to determine those costs. Go to Bonds Online (www.bondsonline.com) and click "Today's Market." Next, click "US Corporate Bond Spreads." You will see a table of bond spreads prepared by Reuters and the date the table was prepared right below it. These spreads represent the increased yield a bond must pay over the U.S. Treasury of the same maturity. Choose the 10-year spread for Home Depot's current rating and the three ratings below it. The spreads are in basis points; a basis point is 1/100th of a percentage point (thus, 50 basis points is 0.5%). We will adjust these old spreads to estimate the current spread.
   - Because these spreads are dated, you will need to create new yield spreads for the various ratings. Use the current difference between the Home Depot bond's yield and the 10-year Treasury as the true spread for the rating. Using Excel, compute the spreads for the other ratings, by adding the *difference* in spreads from the table to the new true spread for Home Depot's rating. Finally, determine the yield for each rating by adding the new spread to the yield on the 10-year Treasury bond.
   - Compute the required yields on 10-year bonds at each of the new debt levels requested.

3. What factors cause the bond rating to fall, and the bond yields to increase, as Home Depot increases its debt levels?

Note: Updates to this data case may be found at www.berkdemarzo.com.

<table>
<tr><td>**Chapter 15**
APPENDIX</td><td># Using a Financial Calculator
to Calculate Yield to Call</td></tr>
</table>

Calculate the yield to call of the bond from Example 15.2. In the example, the bond is called at year one; however, this can be generalized and solved for longer periods than one year.

HP-10BII

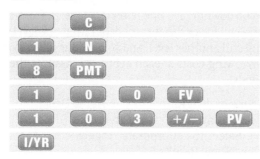

Press [Orange Shift] and then the [C] button to clear all previous entries.

Enter the Number of periods.

Enter the Payment amount per period.

Enter the price you would receive when it is called.

Enter the present value or price of the bond.

Solve for yield to call.

TI-BAII Plus Professional

Press [2nd] and then the [FV] button to clear all previous entries.

Enter the Number of periods.

Enter the Payment amount per period.

Enter the price you would receive when it is called.

Enter the present value or price of the bond.

Solve for yield to call.

If the bond were called after two years, you would simply use 2 instead of 1 for the number of periods.

5 Integrative Case

This case draws on material from Chapters 14 and 15.

On May 8, 1984, Hannah Eisenstat graduated from Louisiana State University. She set to work opening a coffee shop in Baton Rouge called HannaH and found a perfect location in a new development. Using a $50,000 inheritance to finance the venture together with her own sweat equity, she started the business on August 1, 1984 as a sole proprietorship.

The shop was profitable in the first year. Hannah found, however, that the quality of her coffee was not as high as she had initially envisioned. She discussed this issue with one of her regular customers, Natasha Smith. On the spot, Natasha offered to help finance the purchase of a roasting machine. By roasting the beans herself, Hannah could produce higher-quality coffee and, in addition, expand the business by offering beans for sale.

Expansion

After looking carefully at the financials, Hannah determined that she would need an investment of $75,000 from Natasha to undertake this expansion. In exchange for this investment, Hannah offered her a 40% share in the business. Natasha accepted the offer and the business was incorporated with two owners. The equity consisted of 1,000,000 shares in total, with Natasha owning 400,000 shares and Hannah owning 600,000 shares.

By the end of the second year, the business was doing extremely well. Revenue from the sale of beans soon began to rival beverage sales. In response to this success, Hannah and Natasha decided to expand to five stores over the next two years. Rather than using equity financing, they decided to seek bank financing. Each new store required an investment of $100,000. Opening the stores took longer than planned, but by the end of 1999, there were five HannaHs in Baton Rouge employing 30 people. As planned, this expansion was financed solely with debt that was ultimately consolidated into a $500,000 term loan due in 2004.

Venture Capital

In early 2000, the two owners decided to take a weekend retreat and reevaluate their initial business plan. Perhaps the biggest surprise was the popularity of beans; almost 80% of revenue was attributable to bean sales alone. Furthermore, a buyer from a local supermarket chain had approached HannaH with a proposal to sell the beans in the chain's stores. However, HannaH was currently at its capacity limits—it could barely roast enough coffee for its five stores. More importantly, to enhance the coffee quality further, Hannah proposed that they buy beans directly from coffee farmers in Costa Rica, where she would be able to monitor quality closely. However, the supermarket proposal would require a significant increase in the production of roasted beans. By the end of the retreat, Hannah and Natasha had decided to change the focus of the business from retail beverage and bean sales to wholesale roasted coffee beans. Rather than build new stores, they decided to invest in a state-of-the-art roasting facility.

In the next few weeks, Hannah approached Dixie Partners, a local venture capital firm. On the strength of the commitment from the supermarket chain to carry the coffee, Dixie agreed to invest $3 million to finance the construction of a high-capacity roasting facility in exchange for a 50% share of the company. To accomplish this, 1,000,000 new shares in HannaH were issued to Dixie.

Further Expansion

Hannah's intuition was correct—the quality of the coffee increased significantly. Within eight years, the company had grown to almost 200 employees and its strong reputation allowed it to sell its coffee for a 50% premium over other brands. To finance the expansion, Dixie made two more equity investments: It paid $4 million for 1,200,000 shares in 2003 and $8 million for 1,500,000 shares in 2006. Furthermore, the term loan was renewed for another five years when it came due in 2004, and in 2007 an additional 400,000 shares were issued to employees as part of their compensation.

IPO

At the beginning of 2008, the board of directors decided to expand the distribution of the coffee throughout the United States and finance this expansion from the proceeds of an IPO. The plan was to initially raise $20 million in new capital at the IPO and then, within a year or two, raise an additional $20 million in an SEO. Dixie planned on selling 10% of its stake in HannaH at the IPO and subsequently liquidating the rest of its investment by the end of 2009. The IPO was successfully undertaken in August 2008. All told, the company sold 2,000,000 shares for $12 per share at the IPO, including 10% of Dixie's stake (no other existing shareholder sold any shares at the IPO).

SEO

A year later, in August 2009, the company did a cash offer SEO, selling an additional 4,000,000 shares for $20 per share, which included 400,000 shares from each original owner, Hannah and Natasha, and 2,000,000 of Dixie's shares. Thus, of the shares sold, 2,800,000 shares were existing shares and the rest were new shares. Some of the proceeds were used to repay the term loan that matured at the same time as the SEO and the remaining proceeds were used to finance the continued national expansion. Dixie had been selling additional shares in the secondary market over the prior year, so that issue represented the liquidation of Dixie's final stake—after the sale, Dixie no longer owned shares in HannaH. During this time, an additional 50,000 shares were issued to employees as part of their compensation.

LBO

By 2010, the fortunes of the company had changed. Although HannaH coffee still had a strong brand name and sales continued to grow the company, it was experiencing significant growing pains. Hannah herself was no longer directly involved in operations. Soon after the SEO a new CEO, Luke Ignion, was hired to take over the day-to-day running of the company, but he proved to be a poor fit. By late 2010, the company's share price had dropped to $5 per share. Hannah was distressed to see the value of her remaining stake drop to this level, so she decided to take advantage of what she saw as a buying opportunity. Together with six other key employees, she undertook an LBO of HannaH. At the time of the LBO, the firm had 8,000,000 shares outstanding because an additional 20,000 shares had been given to key employees. Hannah and the other key employees had already started purchasing shares, so by the time of the LBO announcement Hannah owned 500,000 shares and the other key employees together owned an additional 100,000 shares. The group issued a tender offer to repurchase the remaining 7,400,000 shares for $7.50 per share. To finance the repurchase, the group combined an additional equity investment of $7,000,000, bank debt, and a (rule 144A) private placement of a $30 million semiannual, 10-year coupon bond. The plan was to register this privately placed debt publicly within a year. The debt was convertible and callable (at par) in five years. It had a conversion ratio of 50, a face value of $1000, and coupon rate of 5%.

Case Questions

1. Natasha is an example of what kind of an investor?
2. At each funding stage prior to the IPO (i.e., 1985, 2000, 2003, and 2006), calculate the pre-money and post-money valuation of the *equity* of the company.
3. What fraction of the IPO was a primary offering and what fraction was a secondary offering?
4. Immediately following the IPO the shares traded at $14.50.
   a. At this price, what was the value of the whole company? Expressed in percent, by how much was the deal underpriced?
   b. In dollars, how much did this underpricing cost existing shareholders?
   c. Assuming that none of the owners purchased additional shares at the IPO, what fraction of the equity did Hannah own and what was it worth immediately following the IPO?
   d. What was the company's debt-equity ratio—the ratio of the book value of debt outstanding to the market value of equity—immediately following the IPO?
5. Address the following questions related to the SEO:
   a. What fraction of the SEO was a primary offering and what fraction was a secondary offering?
   b. Assuming that the underwriters charged a 5% fee, what were the proceeds that resulted from Hannah's sale of her stock? How much money did the company raise that would be available to fund future investments and repay the term loan?
6. Immediately following the SEO, the stock price remained at $20 per share.
   a. Once the term loan was repaid, what was the value of the whole company?
   b. What fraction of the equity did Hannah own?
7. Assume the LBO was successful.
   a. How much bank debt was required?
   b. What was the debt-equity ratio immediately following the LBO?
8. A year after the LBO, just after the second payment was made, the convertible debt traded for a price of $950.
   a. What was its yield to maturity?
   b. What was the yield to call?
9. Assume that in the five years following the LBO Hannah was able to turn the company around. Over the course of this period, all the bank debt was repaid and the company went public again. The price per share was now $60/share. Predict what the holders of the convertible debt would do. What would their investment be worth?

Capital Structure and Payout Policy

Valuation Principle Connection. One of the fundamental questions of corporate finance is how a firm should choose its *capital structure*, which is the total amount of debt, equity, and other securities that a firm has outstanding. Does the choice of capital structure affect the value of the firm? Applying the Valuation Principle in perfect capital markets, in Chapter 16 we show that as long as the cash flows generated by the firm's assets are unchanged, then the value of the firm, which is the total value of its outstanding securities, does not depend on its capital structure. Thus, if capital structure has a role in determining the firm's value, it must come from market imperfections. The remainder of Chapter 16 is devoted to exploring those imperfections. At the conclusion of the chapter, you will have a strong foundation for considering the tradeoffs that arise in financing decisions.

We then turn to *payout policy*—the firm's decisions relating to how much, when, and by what method capital is returned to its equity holders—in Chapter 17. Again, we start from a setting of perfect markets and apply the Valuation Principle. We show that unless these decisions alter the future cash flows generated by the firm, they do not affect the total value received by the shareholders. We proceed through the chapter examining market imperfections such as taxes and how they affect payout policy.

16

Capital Structure

LEARNING OBJECTIVES

- Examine how capital structures vary across industries and companies

- Understand why investment decisions, rather than financing decisions, fundamentally determine the value and cost of capital of a firm

- Describe how leverage increases the risk of a firm's equity

- Demonstrate how debt can affect a firm's value through taxes and bankruptcy costs

- Show how the optimal mix of debt and equity trades off the costs (including financial distress costs) and benefits (including the tax advantage) of debt

- Analyze how debt can alter the incentives of managers to choose different projects and can be used as a signal to investors

- Weigh the many costs and benefits to debt that a manager must balance when deciding how to finance the firm's investments

notation

D	market value of debt
E	market value of levered equity
EPS	earnings per share
NPV	net present value
PV	present value
r_D	expected return (cost of capital) of debt
r_E	expected return (cost of capital) of levered equity
r_U	expected return (cost of capital) of unlevered equity
r_{wacc}	weighted average cost of capital
T_c	marginal corporate tax rate
V^L	value of the firm with leverage
V^U	value of the unlevered firm

When a firm needs to raise new funds to undertake its investments, it must decide which type of financing security it will issue to investors. What considerations should guide this decision and how does this decision affect the value of the firm?

Consider the case of Facebook from Chapter 14 issuing new equity in a seasoned equity offering to fund its expansion, or Hertz from Chapter 15 substantially increasing its leverage through its leveraged buyout. In the summer of 2007, Home Depot dramatically changed its capital structure by reducing its equity by $22 billion and increasing its debt by \$12 billion. What led managers at Facebook to rely on equity for its expansion and Hertz and Home Depot to choose to increase their debt instead? How might such capital structure decisions impact the value of these firms?

In this chapter, first we explore these questions in a setting of *perfect capital markets*, in which all securities are fairly priced, there are no taxes or transaction costs, and the total cash flows of the firm's projects are not affected by how the firm finances them. Although in reality capital markets are not perfect, this setting provides an important benchmark.

We devote the remainder of the chapter to exploring how violations of our perfect capital markets assumptions affect our conclusions. We further explore how the tax advantage of debt that we briefly discussed in Chapter 13 makes debt a potentially attractive financing source. Then we discuss the costs of financial distress and bankruptcy faced by firms with debt. This discussion leads us to the insight that managers choose debt by balancing the tax advantages against the distress costs of debt. After discussing other influences on capital structure, including agency problems and differences in information between managers and investors, we conclude with some recommendations for a financial manager making capital structure decisions.

16.1   Capital Structure Choices

Recall that the relative proportions of debt, equity, and other securities that a firm has outstanding constitute its *capital structure*. When corporations raise funds from outside investors, they must choose which type of security to issue and what type of capital structure to have. The most common choices are financing through equity alone and financing through a combination of debt and equity. How do firms arrive at their capital structures and what factors should a financial manager consider when choosing among financing alternatives?

First and foremost, various financing choices will promise different future amounts to each security holder in exchange for the cash that is raised today. But beyond that, the firm may also need to consider whether the securities it issues will receive a fair price in the market, have tax consequences, entail transactions costs, or even change its future investment opportunities. A firm's capital structure is also affected by decisions on whether to accumulate cash, pay off debt or pay dividends, or conduct share repurchases. Before exploring the theory underpinning this analysis, we place these financing decisions in the context of actual firm practices.

Capital Structure Choices Across Industries

debt-to-value ratio The fraction of a firm's total value that corresponds to debt.

Figure 16.1 shows the median debt-to-value ratios across industries for U.S. stocks. A firm's **debt-to-value ratio**—$D/(E + D)$—is the fraction of the firm's total value that corresponds to debt. Notice that the debt levels financial managers choose differ across industries. For example, software companies such as Microsoft are far less levered (have less debt relative to their equity) than are construction equipment manufacturers such as Caterpillar Company.

Capital Structure Choices Within Industries

The differences in capital structures across industries are striking. However, even within industries, two competing firms may make different choices about their debt-to-value ratios. For example, Intel and ARM Holdings, PLC, both members of the semiconductor

FIGURE 16.1

Debt-to-Value Ratio [$D/(E + D)$] for Select Industries

The bars represent debt-to-value ratios across a wide variety of industries. Debt levels are determined by book values, and equity by market values. The average debt financing for all U.S. stocks was about 22%, but note the large differences by industry.

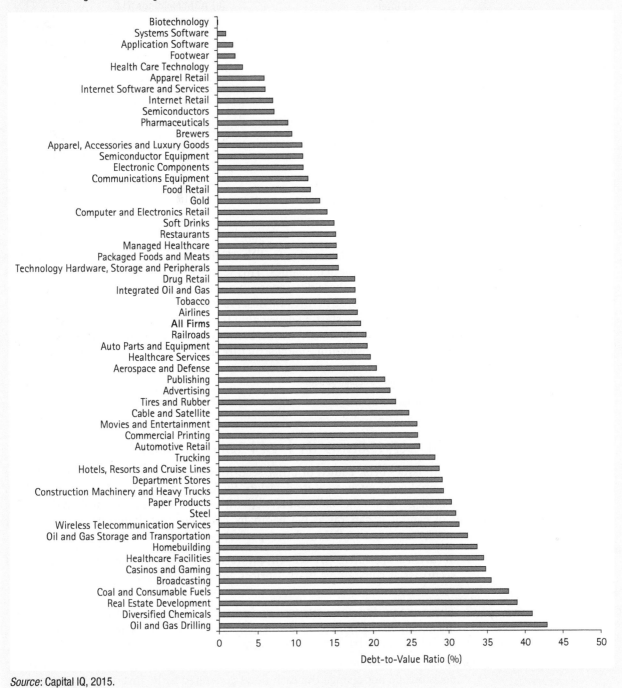

Source: Capital IQ, 2015.

industry, have different capital structures, as depicted in Panels (a) and (b) of Figure 16.2. Intel has 15% debt and 85% equity, as shown in Panel (a), and ARM has no debt, as shown in Panel (b)! Even though the companies are direct competitors, they have very different assets and histories. ARM, which has enjoyed strong growth recently due to the use of its

FIGURE 16.2

Capital Structures of
Intel and ARM Holdings

The pie charts in panels (a) and (b) show the split between debt and equity in two competing firms, Intel and ARM Holdings, PLC. Both are part of the semiconductor industry. Even within an industry, two companies can choose a different mix of debt and equity.

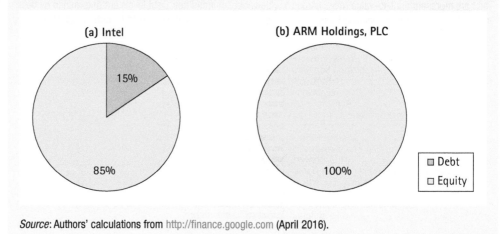

(a) Intel

15%

85%

(b) ARM Holdings, PLC

100%

☐ Debt
☐ Equity

Source: Authors' calculations from http://finance.google.com (April 2016).

chips in tablets, has no chip fabrication facilities. Unlike Intel, ARM licenses its chip designs to be manufactured by other companies. This leaves it with few physical assets. In this chapter, we will learn why these differences in assets and business plans would naturally lead to the different capital structures we observe today.

In the next section, we start by developing the critical theoretical foundation of any capital structure analysis. Then we move on to important real-world factors that managers must trade off when considering capital structure decisions.

**CONCEPT
CHECK**

1. What constitutes a firm's capital structure?

2. What are some factors a manager must consider when making a financing decision?

16.2 Capital Structure in Perfect Capital Markets

When a firm issues debt, equity, or other securities to fund a new investment, there are many potential consequences of its decision. By far the most important question for a financial manager is whether different choices will affect the value of the firm and thus the amount of capital it can raise. We begin by considering this question in a simple environment—a perfect capital market. A **perfect capital market** is a market in which:

**perfect capital
markets** A set of conditions in which investors and firms can trade the same set of securities at competitive market prices; there are no frictions and the firm's financing decisions do not change the cash flows generated by its investments.

1. *Securities are fairly priced.* Investors and firms can trade the same set of securities at competitive market prices equal to the present value of their future cash flows.

2. *There are no tax consequences or transactions costs.* There are no tax consequences, transactions costs, or other issuance costs associated with financing decisions or security trading.

3. *Investment cash flows are independent of financing choices.* A firm's financing decisions do not change the cash flows generated by its investments, nor do they reveal new information about those cash flows.

The assumption of perfect capital markets may seem narrow and unrealistic. We will see, however, that by starting with them we will gain important insight into the true benefits and costs of leverage.

Application: Financing a New Business

Let's begin with an example of a possible financing decision in a perfect capital market. Imagine you have one year left in college and you want to earn some extra money before graduation. You have been offered the opportunity to run the coffee shop in the lobby of a nearby office building. The owner of the building is willing to grant you this right on a one-year basis prior to a major remodeling of the building.

Your research indicates that you will need to make an up-front investment of $24,000 to start the business. After covering your operating costs, including paying yourself a nice wage, you expect to generate a cash flow of $34,500 at the end of the year. The current risk-free interest rate is 5%. You believe, however, that your profits will be somewhat risky and sensitive to the overall market (which will affect the level of activity in the building and demand for your business), so that a 10% risk premium is appropriate, for a total discount rate of 15% (5% + 10%). Therefore, you calculate the NPV of this investment in the coffee shop as:

$$NPV = -\$24{,}000 + \frac{\$34{,}500}{1.15} = -\$24{,}000 + \$30{,}000 = \$6000$$

Thus, the investment has a positive NPV.

Even though the investment looks attractive, you still need to raise the money for the up-front investment. How should you raise the funds, and what is the amount you will be able to raise?

Equity Financing. First, you consider raising money solely by selling equity in the business to your friends and family. Given the cash flow estimates, how much would they be willing to pay for those shares? Recall that the value of a security equals the present value of its future cash flows. In this case, equity holders in your firm will expect to receive the payoff of $34,500 at the end of the year, with the same risk as the cash flows generated by the coffee shop. Therefore, your firm's equity cost of capital will be 15% and the value of its equity today will be:

$$PV \text{ (Equity Cash Flows)} = \frac{\$34{,}500}{1.15} = \$30{,}000$$

unlevered equity Equity in a firm with no debt.

Recall that the absence of debt means the absence of financial leverage. Equity in a firm with no debt is therefore called **unlevered equity**. Because the present value of the equity cash flows is $30,000, you can raise $30,000 by selling all the unlevered equity in your firm. Doing so allows you to keep the NPV of $6000 as profit after paying the investment cost of $24,000. In other words, the project's NPV represents the value to the initial owner of the firm (in this case, you, the entrepreneur) created by the project.

levered equity Equity in a firm with outstanding debt.

Levered Financing. As an alternative, you also consider borrowing some of the money you will need to invest. Suppose the business's cash flow is certain to be at least $16,000. Then you can borrow $15,000 at the current risk-free interest rate of 5%. You will be able to pay the debt of $15,000 × 1.05 = $15,750 at the end of the year without any risk of defaulting.

How much can you raise selling equity in your business now? Equity in a firm that also has outstanding debt is called **levered equity**. After the debt is repaid, equity holders can expect to receive $34,500 − $15,750 = $18,750. What discount rate should we use to value levered equity? What expected return will investors demand?

It is tempting to use the same 15% equity cost of capital as before. In that case, by selling levered equity, you could raise $18,750/1.15 = $16,304. If this result were correct, then using leverage would allow you to raise a total amount, including the debt, of $15,000 + $16,304 = $31,304, or $1304 more than in the case without leverage.

Thus, it would seem that simply financing a project with leverage can make it more valuable. *But if this sounds too good to be true, it is.* Our analysis assumed that your firm's equity cost of capital remained unchanged at 15% after adding leverage. But as we will see shortly, that will not be the case—leverage will increase the risk of the firm's equity and raise its equity cost of capital. To see why, and to understand what will actually happen, we turn to the hallmark work of researchers Franco Modigliani and Merton Miller.

Leverage and Firm Value

In an important paper, researchers Modigliani and Miller (or simply MM) considered whether leverage would increase the total value of the firm. Their answer to this question surprised researchers and practitioners at the time.[1] They argued that with perfect capital markets, the total value of a firm should *not* depend on its capital structure. Their reasoning: Your firm's total cash flows—those paid to both debt and equity holders—still equal the cash flows of the coffee shop, with the same expected value of $34,500 and the same total risk as before, as shown in Figure 16.3. Because the total cash flows of the debt and equity equal the cash flows of the unlevered firm, the Valuation Principle tells us that their market values must be the same. Specifically, we calculated earlier that the value of the unlevered firm, V^U, is:

$$V^U = \$34,500/1.15 = \$30,000$$

FIGURE 16.3

Unlevered Versus Levered Cash Flows with Perfect Capital Markets

When the firm has no debt, as shown in Panel (a), the cash flows paid to equity holders correspond to the free cash flows generated by the firm's assets. When the firm has the debt, shown in Panel (b), these cash flows are divided between debt and equity holders. However, with perfect capital markets, the total amount paid to all investors still corresponds to the free cash flows generated by the firm's assets. Therefore, the value of the unlevered firm, V^U, must equal the total value of the levered firm, V^L, which is the combined value of its debt D and levered equity E.

Panel (a), Unlevered Cash Flows

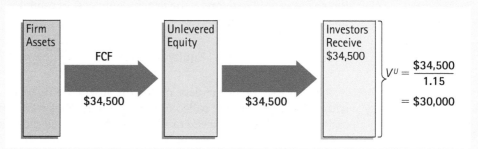

Panel (b), Levered Cash Flows

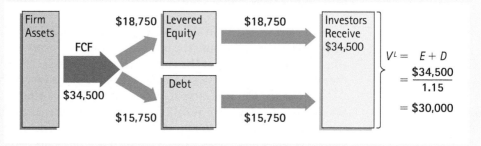

---

[1]F. Modigliani and M. Miller, "The Cost of Capital, Corporation Finance and the Theory of Investment," *American Economic Review*, 48 (3) (1958): 261–297.

Thus, the total value of the levered firm, V^L, which is the combined value of its debt, D, and levered equity, E, must be the same:

$$V^L = D + E = \$30,000$$

Therefore, if the initial market value of the debt is $D = \$15,000$ (the amount borrowed), the initial market value of the levered equity must be $E = \$30,000 - \$15,000 = \$15,000$.

Thus, Modigliani and Miller argued that leverage merely changes the allocation of cash flows between debt and equity without altering the total cash flows of the firm in a perfect capital market. As a result, they concluded that:

MM Proposition I: *In a perfect capital market, the total value of a firm is equal to the market value of the free cash flows generated by its assets and is not affected by its choice of capital structure.*

We can write this result in an equation as follows:

$$V^L = E + D = V^U \tag{16.1}$$

This equation states that the total value of the firm is the same with or without leverage.

Note in our example that because the cash flows of levered equity are smaller than those of unlevered equity, levered equity will sell for a lower price than unlevered equity ($15,000 versus $30,000). However, the fact that the equity is less valuable with leverage does not mean that you are worse off. You will still raise a total of $30,000 by issuing both debt and levered equity, just as you did with unlevered equity alone, and still keep the $6000 difference between the $30,000 you raise and your $24,000 cost as profit. As a consequence, you will be indifferent between these two choices for the firm's capital structure.

The Effect of Leverage on Risk and Return

Modigliani and Miller's conclusion went against the common view that even with perfect capital markets, leverage would affect a firm's value. In particular, it was thought that the value of the levered equity should exceed $15,000, because the present value of its expected cash flow at a 15% discount rate is $18,750/1.15 = $16,304, as we calculated earlier. The reason this is *not* correct is that leverage increases the risk of the equity of a firm. Therefore, it is inappropriate to discount the cash flows of levered equity at the same discount rate of 15% that we used for unlevered equity.

Let's take a closer look at the effect of leverage on the firm's equity cost of capital. If equity holders are only willing to pay $15,000 for the levered equity, then given its expected payoff of $18,750, their expected return is:

$$\text{Expected Return of Levered Equity} = \$18,750/\$15,000 - 1 = 25\%$$

Although this return may seem like a good deal for investors, remember that the coffee shop cash flows are uncertain. Table 16.1 considers the different levels of demand and free

TABLE 16.1

Returns to Equity in Different Scenarios with and Without Leverage

	Coffee Shop	Security Cash Flows			Security Returns		
Demand	Free Cash Flows	Unlevered Equity	Debt	Levered Equity	Unlevered Equity	Debt	Levered Equity
Weak	$27,000	$27,000	$15,750	$11,250	−10%	5%	−25%
Expected	$34,500	$34,500	$15,750	$18,750	15%	5%	25%
Strong	$42,000	$42,000	$15,750	$26,250	40%	5%	75%

cash flows that the coffee shop may generate, and compares the security payoffs and returns with unlevered equity to the case in which you borrow $15,000 and raise an additional $15,000 using levered equity. Note that the returns are very different with and without leverage. With no debt, the returns of unlevered equity range from −10% to 40%, with an expected return of 15%. With leverage, the debt holders receive a risk-free return of 5%, whereas the returns of levered equity are much more volatile, with a range of −25% to 75%. To compensate for this higher risk, levered equity holders receive a higher expected return of 25%.

We further illustrate the effect of leverage on returns in Figure 16.4. By adding leverage, the returns of the unlevered firm are effectively "split" between low-risk debt and much higher-risk levered equity. Note that the returns of levered equity fall twice as fast as those of unlevered equity if the coffee shops cash flows decline. This doubling of the risk justifies a doubling of the risk premium, which is 15% − 5% = 10% for unlevered equity and 25% − 5% = 20% for levered equity. As this example shows, *leverage increases the risk of equity even when there is no risk that the firm will default.*

FIGURE 16.4

Unlevered Versus
Levered Returns
with Perfect Capital
Markets

Leverage splits the firm's return between low-risk debt and high-risk levered equity compared to the equity of an unlevered firm. In this example, the returns of levered equity are twice as sensitive to the firm's cash flows as the returns of unlevered equity. This doubling of risk implies a doubling of the risk premium from 10% to 20%.

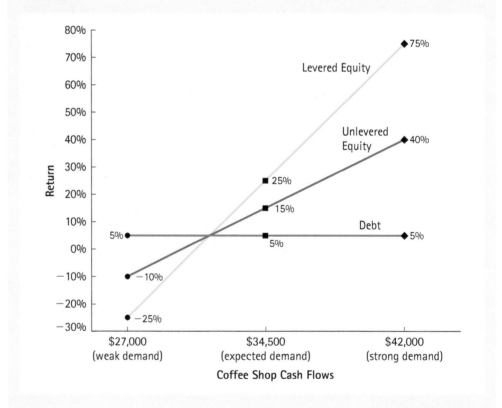

EXAMPLE 16.1

The Risk and Return of
Levered Equity

MyFinanceLab

PROBLEM

Suppose you borrow only $6000 when financing your coffee shop. According to Modigliani and Miller, what should the value of the equity be? What is the expected return?

SOLUTION

PLAN

The value of the firm's total cash flows does not change: It is still $30,000. Thus, if you borrow $6000, your firm's equity will be worth $24,000. To determine the equity's expected return, we will compute the cash flows to equity under the two scenarios. The cash flows to equity are the cash flows of the firm net of the cash flows to debt (repayment of principal plus interest).

EXECUTE

The firm will owe debt holders $6000 × 1.05 = $6300 in one year. Thus, the expected payoff to equity holders is $34,500 − $6300 = $28,200, for a return of $28,200/$24,000 − 1 = 17.5%.

EVALUATE

While the total value of the firm is unchanged, the firm's equity in this case is more risky than it would be without debt, but less risky than if the firm borrowed $15,000. To illustrate, note that if demand is weak, the equity holders will receive $27,000 − $6300 = $20,700, for a return of $20,700/$24,000 − 1 = −13.75%. Compare this return to −10% without leverage and −25% if the firm borrowed $15,000. As a result, the expected return of the levered equity is higher in this case than for unlevered equity (17.5% versus 15%), but not as high as in the previous example (17.5% versus 25%).

Homemade Leverage

MM showed that the firm's value is not affected by its choice of capital structure. But suppose investors would prefer an alternative capital structure to the one the firm has chosen. MM demonstrated that in this case, investors can borrow or lend on their own and achieve the same result. For example, an investor who would like more leverage than the firm has chosen can borrow and thus add leverage to his or her own portfolio. Adding leverage in this way will lower the out-of-pocket cost of the security, but increase the risk of the portfolio. When investors use leverage in their own portfolios to adjust the leverage choice made by the firm, we say that they are using **homemade leverage**. As long as investors can borrow or lend at the same interest rate as the firm, which is true in perfect capital markets, homemade leverage is a perfect substitute for the use of leverage by the firm. Thus, because different choices of capital structure offer no benefit to investors in perfect capital markets, those choices do not affect the value of the firm.

homemade leverage When investors use leverage in their own portfolios to adjust the leverage choice made by a firm.

Leverage and the Cost of Capital

We can use the insight of Modigliani and Miller to understand the effect of leverage on the firm's cost of capital. Recall from Figure 16.3 and Eq. 16.1 that if we look at a portfolio of the equity and debt of a levered firm together, that portfolio has the same value and cash flows as the unlevered firm. Therefore, the expected return of the portfolio should equal the expected return of the unlevered firm. Recall from Chapter 12 that the expected return of the portfolio equity and debt is simply the weighted average of the expected returns of each security. Thus, with r_E representing the expected return of levered equity, r_D the expected return of debt, and r_U the expected return of the unlevered equity, we have:

Weighted Average Cost of Capital (Pretax)

$$\underbrace{r_E \frac{E}{E + D} + r_D \frac{D}{E + D}}_{\text{Pretax WACC}} = r_U$$

(16.2)

The amounts $\frac{E}{E+D}$ and $\frac{D}{E+D}$ represent the fraction of the firm's value financed by equity and debt, respectively. Thus, the left side of Eq. 16.2 is the weighted average cost of capital

pretax WACC The weighted average cost of capitial computed using the pretax cost of debt.

(WACC) of the firm, which we defined in Chapter 13. Note that the cost of debt is not adjusted for taxes, because we are assuming "perfect capital markets" and thus are ignoring taxes. When we compute the weighted average cost of capital without taxes, we refer to it as the firm's **pretax WACC**. Equation 16.2 states that for any choice of capital structure, the firm's pretax WACC is unchanged and remains equal to the firm's unlevered cost of capital.

Let's check this result for our coffee shop example. With leverage, the firm's debt cost of capital was $r_D = 5\%$, and its equity cost of capital rose to $r_E = 25\%$. What about the portfolio weights? In this case, the firm borrowed $D = 15,000$, and issued equity worth $E = 15,000$, for a total value $V^L = E + D = 30,000$. Therefore, its pretax WACC is:

$$r_E \frac{E}{E+D} + r_D \frac{D}{E+D} = 25\% \left(\frac{15,000}{30,000} \right) + 5\% \left(\frac{15,000}{30,000} \right) = 15\%$$

Thus, the pretax WACC does indeed equal the firm's unlevered cost of capital, $r_U = 15\%$.

How is it that the firm's weighted average cost of capital stays the same even after adding leverage? There are two offsetting effects of leverage: We finance a larger fraction of the firm with debt, which has a lower cost of capital, but at the same time adding leverage raises the firm's equity cost of capital. Because the firm's total risk has not changed (it has just been split between these two securities), these two effects should exactly cancel out

---

COMMON MISTAKE

Capital Structure Fallacies

Here, we take a critical look at two incorrect arguments that are sometimes cited in favor of leverage.

Leverage and Earnings per Share

Fallacy 1: Leverage can increase a firm's expected earnings per share; by doing so, leverage should also increase the firm's stock price.

Consider the coffee shop example. In the all-equity case, if you issued 1000 shares, they would each be worth $30 and the expected earnings per share (EPS) would be $34,500/1000 = $34.50. EPS would vary from $27 per share to $42 per share in the case of weak or strong demand. In the case with debt, as shown in Table 16.1, you only need to raise $15,000 in equity and so could issue only 500 shares, each worth $30. In this case, your expected EPS will be $18,750/500 = $37.50, with a range from $22.50 to $52.50. Thus, although the expected EPS

is greater with leverage, the variation in EPS is also much greater, as shown in the blue and yellow bars. With leverage, EPS falls to $22.50 when cash flows are low, which is much further than EPS would have dropped without leverage ($27). Although EPS increases on average, this increase is necessary to compensate shareholders for the additional risk they are taking. As a result, the entrepreneur's share price does not increase as a result of issuing debt.

Equity Issuances and Dilution

Fallacy 2: Issuing equity will *dilute* existing shareholders' ownership, so debt financing should be used instead. *Dilution* means that if the firm issues new shares, the cash flows generated by the firm must be divided among a larger number of shares, thereby reducing the value of each individual share.

This line of reasoning ignores the fact that the cash raised by issuing new shares will increase the firm's assets. Consider Google's September 2005 seasoned equity offering of 14,159,265 Class A shares at $295 apiece. Google priced the shares to match the market price of Class A shares on NASDAQ at the time of the offer. The amount raised was then $4,176,983,175, so the total value of Google increased to $60,560,157,355, which when divided by the new total number of shares (205,288,669), still results in a price of $295 per share.

In general, as long as the firm sells the new shares of equity *at a fair price*, there will be no gain or loss to shareholders associated with the equity issue itself. The money taken in by the firm as a result of the share issue exactly offsets the dilution of the shares. *Any gain or loss associated with the transaction will result from the NPV of the investments the firm makes with the funds raised.*

and leave the firm's WACC unchanged. In fact, we can use Eq. 16.2 to determine the precise impact of leverage on the firm's equity cost of capital. Solving the equation for r_E, we have:

MM Proposition II: The Cost of Capital of Levered Equity

$$r_E = r_U + \frac{D}{E}(r_U - r_D) \tag{16.3}$$

Or, in words:

MM Proposition II: *The cost of capital of levered equity is equal to the cost of capital of unlevered equity plus a premium that is proportional to the debt-equity ratio (measured using market values).*

Let's check MM Proposition II for the coffee shop example. In this case:

$$r_E = r_U + \frac{D}{E}(r_U - r_D) = 15\% + \frac{15,000}{15,000}(15\% - 5\%) = 25\%$$

This result matches the expected return for levered equity we calculated in Table 16.1.

Figure 16.5 illustrates the effect of increasing the amount of leverage in a firm's capital structure on its equity cost of capital, its debt cost of capital, and its WACC. In the

FIGURE 16.5 WACC and Leverage with Perfect Capital Markets

Panel (a) represents the data in Panel (b) for the coffee shop example. As the fraction of the firm financed with debt increases, both the equity and the debt become riskier and their cost of capital rises. Yet because more weight is put on the lower-cost debt, the weighted average cost of capital, r_{wacc}, remains constant.

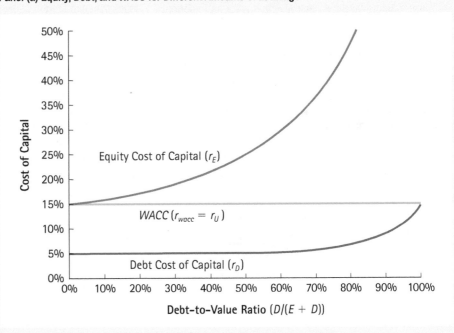

Panel (a) Equity, Debt, and WACC for Different Amounts of Leverage

Panel (b) WACC Data for Alternative Capital Structures

E	D	r_E	r_D	$r_E\dfrac{E}{E+D} + r_D\dfrac{D}{E+D}$	$= r_{wacc}$
30,000	0	15.0%	5.0%	15.0% × 1.0 + 5.0% × 0.0	= 15%
24,000	6,000	17.5%	5.0%	17.5% × 0.8 + 5.0% × 0.2	= 15%
15,000	15,000	25.0%	5.0%	25.0% × 0.5 + 5.0% × 0.5	= 15%
3,000	27,000	75.0%	8.3%	75.0% × 0.1 + 8.3% × 0.9	= 15%

figure, we measure the firm's leverage in terms of its debt-to-value ratio, $D/(E + D)$. With no debt, the WACC is equal to the unlevered equity cost of capital. As the firm borrows at the low cost of capital for debt, its equity cost of capital rises, according to Eq. 16.3. The net effect is that the firm's WACC is unchanged. Of course, as the amount of debt increases, the debt becomes riskier because there is a chance the firm will default; as a result, the debt cost of capital also rises. With close to 100% debt, the debt would be almost as risky as the assets themselves (similar to unlevered equity). But even though the debt and equity costs of capital both rise when leverage is high, because more of the firm is financed with debt (which has lower cost), the WACC remains constant.

GLOBAL FINANCIAL CRISIS

Bank Capital Regulation and the ROE Fallacy

In banking jargon, a "capital requirement" obligates a bank to finance itself with a certain minimum amount of equity to ensure that its debt-to-equity ratio will stay below a set level. The permitted level of leverage is very high—international standards allow common equity to represent as little as 2% of a bank's total funding.[2] To put this number in perspective, the equity of a typical non-financial firm exceeds 50% of firm value. Such extreme leverage makes bank equity very risky.

These extreme levels of bank leverage were an important contributing factor to the financial meltdown in 2008 and the subsequent recession: With such a small equity cushion, even a minor drop in asset values can lead to insolvency. Post-crisis, banks have come under increased pressure to reduce leverage with new international rules more than doubling the required proportion of equity financing. Many policymakers believe capital requirements should be increased much more to reduce the risk of the financial sector and the consequent spillovers to the broader economy.

Bankers counter that decreased leverage will lower their return on equity, limiting their ability to compete effectively.

According to Josef Ackermann, then CEO of Deutsche Bank, new capital requirements would "depress ROE to levels that make investment into the banking sector unattractive relative to other business sectors."[3] The return on equity is indeed a function of the firm's leverage. As with EPS, lower leverage will tend to decrease the firm's ROE on average, though it will raise the ROE in bad times. But this decrease in average ROE is compensated for by a reduction in the riskiness of equity and therefore the required risk premium. Thus, from an investor's perspective, the reduction in ROE that results solely from a decrease in leverage does not make investing in the firm any less attractive. Franco Modigliani and Merton Miller were awarded the Nobel Prize for pointing out that in a perfect market the bank's capital structure cannot affect its competitiveness.

The only way a change in leverage can affect the "attractiveness" of equity (and the competitiveness of banks) is if there is a market imperfection. The most important imperfections come from deposit insurance, too-big-to-fail policies, and the tax deductibility of interest, giving banks a strong incentive to maximize their leverage. These imperfections derive from government subsidies, so the banks' gains from leverage come largely at taxpayer expense.

EXAMPLE 16.2

Computing the Equity Cost of Capital

MyFinanceLab

PROBLEM
Suppose you borrow only $6000 when financing your coffee shop. According to MM Proposition II, what will your firm's equity cost of capital be?

SOLUTION

PLAN

Because your firm's assets have a market value of $30,000, according to MM Proposition I the equity will have a market value of $24,000 = $30,000 − $6000. We can use Eq. 16.3 to compute the cost of equity. We know the unlevered cost of equity is $r_u = 15\%$. We also know that r_D is 5%.

[2]Two percent is the Tier 1 Common Equity Requirement of the Basel II Accord, the global regulatory standard for bank capital. Starting in 2013, the new Basel III Accord will raise this requirement gradually to 4.5% by 2015.

[3]J. Ackermann, "The new architecture of financial regulation: Will it prevent another crisis?" Special Paper 194, FMG Deutsche Bank Conference, London School of Economics, October 2010.

EXECUTE

$$r_E = 15\% + \frac{6000}{24{,}000}\left(15\% - 5\%\right) = 17.5\%$$

EVALUATE

This result matches the expected return calculated in Example 16.1 where we also assumed debt of $6000. The equity cost of capital should be the expected return of the equity holders.

MM and the Real World

Our conclusions so far may seem striking at first: In perfect capital markets, leverage does not affect either the cost of capital or a firm's value, and so the firm's choice of capital structure would be irrelevant! However, capital markets are not perfect in the real world. What then are we to make of Modigliani and Miller's results?

NOBEL PRIZE Franco Modigliani and Merton Miller

Franco Modigliani and Merton Miller, authors of the Modigliani-Miller Propositions, each won the Nobel Prize in Economics for their work in financial economics, including their capital structure propositions. Modigliani won the Nobel Prize in 1985 for his work on personal savings and for his capital structure theorems with Miller. Miller earned his prize in 1990 for his analysis of portfolio theory and capital structure.

Miller once described the MM propositions in an interview this way:

People often ask, "Can you summarize your theory quickly?" Well, I say, you understand the MM theorem if you know why this is a joke: The pizza delivery man comes to Yogi Berra after the game and says, "Yogi, how do you want this pizza cut, into quarters or eighths?" And Yogi says, "Cut it in eight pieces. I'm feeling hungry tonight."

Everyone recognizes that's a joke because obviously the number and shape of the pieces don't affect the size of the pizza. And similarly, the stocks, bonds, warrants, etc., issued don't affect the aggregate value of the firm. They just slice up the underlying earnings in different ways.*

Modigliani and Miller each won the Nobel Prize in large part for their observation that the value of a firm should be unaffected by its capital structure in perfect capital markets. Whereas the intuition underlying the MM propositions may be as simple as slicing pizza, their implications for corporate finance are far-reaching. The propositions imply that the true role of a firm's financial policy is to deal with (and potentially exploit) financial market imperfections such as taxes and transaction costs. Modigliani and Miller's work began a long line of research into these market imperfections, which we will look at in the rest of the chapter.

*Peter J. Tanous, Investment Gurus (New York: Institute of Finance, 1997).

As an analogy, consider Galileo's law of falling bodies. Galileo overturned the conventional wisdom by showing that without friction, free-falling bodies will fall at the same rate, independent of their mass. If you test this law, you will likely find it does not hold exactly. The reason, of course, is that unless we are in a vacuum, air friction tends to slow some objects more than others.

MM's results are similar. In practice, we will find that capital structure can have an effect on a firm's value. Galileo's law of falling bodies reveals that we must look to air friction, rather than any underlying property of gravity, to explain differences in the speeds of falling objects. MM's propositions reveal that any effects of capital structure must similarly be due to frictions that exist in capital markets. We explore the important sources of these frictions, and their consequences, in the remainder of this chapter.

CONCEPT CHECK

3. How does leverage affect the risk and cost of equity for the firm?

4. In a perfect capital market, can you alter the firm's value or WACC by relying more on debt capital?

16.3   Debt and Taxes

So far, we have used the perfect capital markets setting to focus on the fundamental point that the firm's choice of projects and investments is the primary determinant of its value and risk, and hence its overall cost of capital. But in the real world, markets are imperfect and these imperfections can create a role for the firm's capital structure. In this section, we focus on one important market friction—corporate taxes—and show how the firm's choice of capital structure can affect the taxes that it must pay and therefore its value to investors.

The Interest Tax Deduction and Firm Value

As we discussed in Chapter 13, corporations can deduct interest expenses from their taxable income. The deduction reduces the taxes they pay and thereby increases the amount available to pay investors. In doing so, the interest tax deduction increases the value of the corporation.

To illustrate, let's consider the impact of interest expenses on the taxes paid by The Kroger Co., a grocery store chain. In 2015, Kroger had earnings before interest and taxes of $3.58 billion, and interest expenses of $480 million. Given a corporate tax rate of 35%, we can compare Kroger's actual net income with what it would have been without debt, as shown in Table 16.2.

TABLE 16.2

Kroger's Income with and Without Leverage, 2012 ($ million)

	With Leverage	Without Leverage
EBIT	$3580	$3580
Interest expense	−480	0
Income before tax	3100	3580
Taxes (35%)	−1085	−1253
Net income	$2015	$2327

As we can see from Table 16.2, Kroger's net income in 2015 was lower with leverage than it would have been without leverage. Thus, Kroger's debt obligations reduced the value of its equity. But more importantly, the *total* amount available to *all* investors was higher with leverage:

	With Leverage	Without Leverage
Interest paid to debt holders	480	0
Income available to equity holders	2015	2327
Total available to all investors	**$2495**	**$2327**

With leverage, Kroger was able to pay out $2495 million in total to its investors, versus only $2327 million without leverage, representing an increase of $168 million.

It might seem odd that a firm can be better off with leverage even though its earnings are lower. But recall from Section 16.1 that the value of a firm is the total amount it can raise from all investors, not just equity holders who receive the earnings. Thus, if the firm can pay out more in total with leverage, it will be able to raise more total capital initially.

Where does the additional $168 million come from? Looking at Table 16.2, we can see that this gain is equal to the reduction in taxes with leverage: $1253 million − $1085 million = $168 million. Because Kroger does not owe taxes on the $480 million of pretax earnings that were used to make interest payments, this $480 million is *shielded* from the corporate tax, providing the tax savings of $0.35 \times \$480$ million $= \$168$ million.

In general, the gain to investors from the tax deductibility of interest payments is referred to as the **interest tax shield**. The interest tax shield is the additional amount a firm can pay to investors by saving the taxes it would have paid if it did not have leverage. We can calculate the amount of the interest tax shield each year as follows:

$$\text{Interest Tax Shield} = \text{Corporate Tax Rate} \times \text{Interest Payments} \qquad (16.4)$$

interest tax shield The reduction in taxes paid due to the tax deductibility of interest payments.

EXAMPLE 16.3

Computing the Interest Tax Shield

MyFinanceLab

PROBLEM

Shown below is the income statement for E. C. Builders (ECB). Given its marginal corporate tax rate of 35%, what is the amount of the interest tax shield for ECB in years 2010 through 2013?

1	ECB Income Statement ($ million)	2010	2011	2012	2013
2	Total sales	$3369	$3706	$4077	$4432
3	Cost of sales	−2359	−2584	−2867	−3116
4	Selling, general, and administrative expense	−226	−248	−276	−299
5	Depreciation	−22	−25	−27	−29
6	**Operating income**	762	849	907	988
7	Other income	7	8	10	12
8	**EBIT**	769	857	917	1000
9	Interest expense	−50	−80	−100	−100
10	**Income before tax**	719	777	817	900
11	Taxes (35%)	−252	−272	−286	−315
12	**Net income**	$467	$505	$531	$585

SOLUTION

PLAN

From Eq. 16.4, the interest tax shield is the tax rate of 35% multiplied by the interest payments in each year.

EXECUTE

1	($ million)	2010	2011	2012	2013
2	Interest expense	50	80	100	100
3	**Interest tax shield (35% × interest expense)**	17.5	28	35	35

EVALUATE

By using debt, ECB is able to reduce its taxable income and therefore decrease its total tax payments by $115.5 million over the four-year period. Thus, the total amount of cash flows available to all investors (debt holders and equity holders) is $115.5 million higher over the four-year period.

Value of the Interest Tax Shield

When a firm uses debt, the interest tax shield provides a corporate tax benefit each year. To determine the benefit of leverage for the value of the firm, we must compute the present value of the stream of future interest tax shields the firm will receive.

As we saw with Kroger and in Example 16.3, each year a firm makes interest payments, the cash flows it pays to investors will be higher than they would be without leverage by the amount of the interest tax shield:

$$\begin{pmatrix} \text{Cash Flows to Investors} \\ \text{with Leverage} \end{pmatrix} = \begin{pmatrix} \text{Cash Flows to Investors} \\ \text{Without Leverage} \end{pmatrix} + (\text{Interest Tax Shield})$$

Figure 16.6 illustrates this relationship. Notice how each dollar of pretax cash flows is divided. The firm uses some fraction to pay taxes, and it pays the rest to investors. By increasing the amount paid to debt holders through interest payments, the amount of the pretax cash flows that must be paid as taxes decreases. The gain in total cash flows to investors is the interest tax shield.[4]

Because the cash flows of the levered firm are equal to the sum of the cash flows from the unlevered firm plus the interest tax shield, according to the Valuation Principle the same must be true for the present values of these cash flows. Thus, letting V^L and V^U represent the value of the firm with and without leverage, respectively, we have the following change to MM Proposition I in the presence of taxes:

The total value of the levered firm exceeds the value of the firm without leverage due to the present value of the tax savings from debt:

$$V^L = V^U + PV \text{ (Interest Tax Shield)} \qquad (16.5)$$

Clearly, there is an important tax advantage to the use of debt financing. But how large is this tax benefit? To compute the increase in the firm's total value associated with the interest tax shield, we need to forecast how a firm's debt—and therefore its interest payments—will vary over time. Given a forecast of future interest payments, we can determine the interest tax shield and compute its present value by discounting it at a rate that corresponds to its risk.

FIGURE 16.6

The Cash Flows of the Unlevered and Levered Firm

By increasing the cash flows paid to debt holders through interest payments, a firm reduces the amount paid in taxes. The increase in total cash flows paid to investors is the interest tax shield. (The figure assumes a 40% marginal corporate tax rate.)

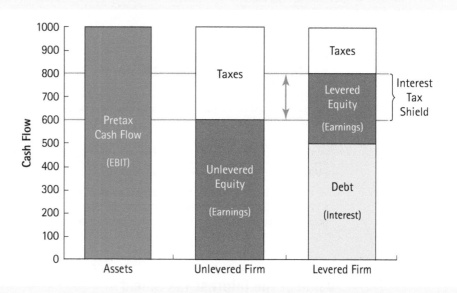

EXAMPLE 16.4

Valuing the Interest Tax Shield

MyFinanceLab

PROBLEM

Suppose ECB from Example 16.3 borrows $2 billion by issuing 10-year bonds. ECB's cost of debt is 6%, so it will need to pay $120 million in interest each year for the next 10 years, and then repay the principal of $2 billion in year 10. ECB's marginal tax rate will remain 35% throughout this period. By how much does the interest tax shield increase the value of ECB?

---

[4]If investors are taxed on interest income at a higher rate than they are on capital gains, this personal tax *disadvantage* of debt will partly offset the corporate tax advantage of debt.

SOLUTION

PLAN

In this case, the interest tax shield lasts for 10 years, so we can value it as a 10-year annuity. Because the tax savings are as risky as the debt that creates them, we can discount them at ECB's cost of debt: 6%.

EXECUTE

The interest tax shield each year is 35% $\times$ $120 million = $42 million. Valued as a 10-year annuity with a discount rate of 0.06, we have:

$$PV\,(\text{Interest Tax Shield}) = \$42 \text{ million} \times \frac{1}{0.06}\left(1 - \frac{1}{1.06^{10}}\right)$$

$$= \$309 \text{ million}$$

Because only interest is tax deductible, the final repayment of principal in year 10 is not deductible, so it does not contribute to the tax shield.

EVALUATE

We know that in perfect capital markets, financing transactions have an NPV of zero—the interest and principal repayment have a present value of exactly the amount of the bonds: $2 billion. However, the interest tax deductibility makes this a positive-NPV transaction for the firm. Because the government effectively subsidizes the payment of interest, issuing these bonds has an NPV of $309 million.

The Interest Tax Shield with Permanent Debt

Many factors can affect the future tax savings from interest. Typically, the level of future interest payments varies due to:

Changes the firm makes in the amount of debt outstanding,
Changes in the interest rate on that debt,
Changes in the firm's marginal tax rate, and
The risk that the firm may default and fail to make an interest payment.

Rather than attempting to account for all possibilities here, we will consider the special case in which the firm issues debt and plans to keep the dollar amount of debt constant forever.

For example, the firm might issue a perpetual consol bond, making only interest payments but never repaying the principal. More realistically, suppose the firm issues short-term debt such as a five-year coupon bond. When the principal is due, the firm raises the money needed to pay it by issuing new debt. In this way, the firm never pays off the principal but simply refinances it whenever it comes due. In this situation, the debt is effectively permanent.

Many large firms have a policy of maintaining a certain amount of debt on their balance sheets. As old bonds and loans mature, they start new loans and issue new bonds. Note that we are considering the value of the interest tax shield with a *fixed* dollar amount of outstanding debt, rather than an amount that changes with the size of the firm.

As we learned in Chapter 6, if the debt is fairly priced, the Valuation Principle implies that the market value of the debt today must equal the present value of the future interest payments:[5]

$$\text{Market Value of Debt} = D = PV\,(\text{Future Interest Payments}) \qquad (16.6)$$

---

[5]Equation 16.6 is valid even if interest rates fluctuate and the debt is risky, as long as any new debt is fairly priced. It requires only that the firm never repay the principal on the debt (it either refinances or defaults on the principal).

If the firm's marginal tax rate (T_c) is constant, then we have the following general formula:

Value of the Interest Tax Shield of Permanent Debt

$$PV \text{ (Interest Tax Shield)} = PV(T_c \times \text{Future Interest Payments})$$

$$= T_c \times PV \text{ (Future Interest Payments)}$$

$$= T_c \times D \tag{16.7}$$

This formula shows the magnitude of the interest tax shield. Given a 35% corporate tax rate, it implies that for every $1 in new permanent debt that the firm issues, the value of the firm increases by $0.35.

Leverage and the WACC with Taxes

There is another way we can incorporate the benefit of the firm's future interest tax shield. Recall from Chapter 13 that for companies without preferred stock (which is most companies), we defined the WACC with taxes as:

Weighted Average Cost of Capital with Taxes

$$r_{wacc} = r_E \frac{E}{E+D} + r_D(1-T_C)\frac{D}{E+D} \tag{16.8}$$

In Eq. 16.8, we incorporate the benefit of the interest tax shield by adjusting the cost of debt to the firm. If the firm pays interest rate r_D on its debt, then because it receives a tax shield of $T_C \times r_D$, the effective after-tax cost of debt is reduced to $r_D(1-T_C)$. Comparing Eq. 16.8 with Eq. 16.2 for the pretax WACC, we can see that corporate taxes lower the effective cost of debt financing, which translates into a reduction in the weighted average cost of capital. In fact, Eq. 16.8 implies:

$$r_{wacc} = \underbrace{r_E \frac{E}{E+D} + r_D \frac{D}{E+D}}_{\text{Pretax WACC}} - \underbrace{r_D T_C \frac{D}{E+D}}_{\substack{\text{Reduction Due} \\ \text{to Interest Tax Shield}}} \tag{16.9}$$

Thus, the reduction in the WACC increases with the amount of debt financing. The higher the firm's leverage, the more the firm exploits the tax advantage of debt and the lower its WACC. Figure 16.7 illustrates this decline in the WACC with leverage. The figure also shows the pretax WACC as shown in Figure 16.5.

Debt and Taxes: The Bottom Line

In this section, we have seen that the deductibility of interest expenses for corporate taxes creates an advantage for debt financing. We can calculate the value of this benefit to the firm in two ways. First, we can forecast the firm's future interest tax shields and determine their present value. This approach is especially simple when the amount of debt is fixed permanently, in which case the value of the tax shield is equal to $T_C \times D$.

A second way to calculate the benefit of the interest tax shield is to incorporate it in the firm's cost of capital by using the WACC. Unlike the pretax WACC, the WACC with taxes declines with leverage because of the interest tax shield. If we use this lower discount rate to compute the present value of the firm's or an investment's free cash flow, the present value will be higher by an amount that reflects the benefit of the future interest tax shields. This approach is simplest to apply when the firm adjusts its debt to keep the fraction of debt financing (its debt-to-value ratio) constant over time.

FIGURE 16.7

The WACC with and Without Corporate Taxes

We compute the WACC as a function of leverage using Eq. 16.9. Whereas the pretax WACC remains constant, with taxes the WACC declines as the firm increases its reliance on debt financing and the benefit of the interest tax deduction grows. The figure assumes a marginal corporate income tax rate of 35%.

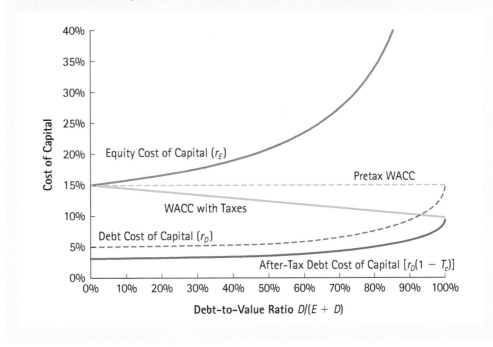

To summarize, we can include the interest tax shield when assessing the value of a firm or an investment by *either* of these methods:

1. Discounting its free cash flow using the pretax WACC, and adding the present value of expected future interest tax shields, or

2. Discounting its free cash flow using the WACC (with taxes).

Using either of these methods, we will find the value of the firm will increase with leverage. Thus, unlike the setting with perfect capital markets, capital structure matters. But now we face a new puzzle: Given the tax benefit, why don't firms use debt financing almost exclusively?

CONCEPT CHECK

5. How does the interest tax deduction affect firm value?

6. How does the firm's WACC change with leverage?

16.4   The Costs of Bankruptcy and Financial Distress

financial distress When a firm has difficulty meeting its debt obligations.

The last section presents us with an interesting question: If increasing debt increases the value of the firm, why not shift to nearly 100% debt? One part of the answer comes from bankruptcy costs. With more debt, there is a greater chance that the firm will be unable to make its required interest payments and will default on its debt obligations. A firm that has trouble meeting its debt obligations is in **financial distress**. Bankruptcy is a long and complicated process that imposes both direct and indirect costs on the firm and its investors that the assumption of perfect capital markets ignores.

Direct Costs of Bankruptcy

Each country has a bankruptcy code that details the process for dealing with a firm in default of its debt obligations (see the appendix to this chapter). The bankruptcy code is designed to provide an orderly process for settling a firm's debts. However, the process is still complex, time-consuming, and costly. When a corporation becomes financially distressed, outside professionals, such as legal and accounting experts, consultants, appraisers, auctioneers, and others with experience selling distressed assets, are generally hired. Investment bankers may also assist with a potential financial restructuring.

In addition to the money spent by the firm, the creditors may incur costs during the bankruptcy process. In the case of reorganization, creditors must often wait several years for a reorganization plan to be approved and to receive payment. To ensure that their rights and interests are respected, and to assist in valuing their claims in a proposed reorganization, creditors may seek separate legal representation and professional advice.

Studies typically report that the average direct costs of bankruptcy are approximately 3% to 4% of the pre-bankruptcy market value of total assets. The costs are likely to be higher for firms with more complicated business operations and for firms with larger numbers of creditors, because it may be more difficult to reach agreement among many creditors regarding the final disposition of the firm's assets. Because many aspects of the bankruptcy process are independent of the size of the firm, the costs are typically higher, in percentage terms, for smaller firms.

 Bankruptcy Can Be Expensive

Outside experts that specialize in aiding distressed firms are costly. At the time Enron entered bankruptcy, it reportedly spent a record $30 million per month on legal and accounting fees, and the total cost ultimately exceeded $750 million. WorldCom paid its advisors $657 million as part of its reorganization to become MCI. Between 2003 and 2005, United Airlines paid a team of more than 30 advisory firms an average of $8.6 million per month for legal and professional services related to its bankruptcy reorganization. Whether paid by the firm or its creditors, these direct costs of bankruptcy reduce the value of the assets that the firm's investors will ultimately receive. In the case of Enron, reorganization costs were expected to approach 10% of the value of the assets.

Source: Julie Johnsson, "UAL a Ch. 11 Fee Machine," *Crain's Chicago Business*, June 27, 2005.

Indirect Costs of Financial Distress

Aside from the direct legal and administrative costs of bankruptcy, many other *indirect* costs are associated with financial distress (whether or not the firm has formally filed for bankruptcy). Whereas these costs are difficult to measure accurately, they are often much larger than the direct costs of bankruptcy.

Indirect bankruptcy costs often occur because the firm may renege on both implicit and explicit commitments and contracts when in financial distress. For example, a bankrupt software manufacturer need not fulfill an obligation to support one of its products. Knowing this, customers who rely on such support might choose to buy software from companies that have a low chance of bankruptcy; that is, companies with lower leverage. Importantly, many of these indirect costs may be incurred even if the firm is not yet in financial distress, but simply faces a significant possibility of bankruptcy in the future. Consider the following examples:

Loss of Customers. Because bankruptcy may enable firms to walk away from future commitments to their customers, those customers may be unwilling to purchase products whose value depends on future support or service from the firm.

Loss of Suppliers. Suppliers may be unwilling to provide a firm with inventory if they fear they will not be paid. For example, Swiss Air was forced to shut down in 2001 because financial concerns caused its suppliers to refuse to fuel its planes.

Cost to Employees. One important cost that often receives a great deal of press coverage is the cost of financial distress to employees. Most firms offer their employees explicit long-term employment contracts, or an implicit promise regarding job security. However, during bankruptcy these contracts and commitments are often ignored and significant numbers of employees may be laid off. In anticipation of this, employees will be less willing to work for firms with significant bankruptcy risk and so will demand a higher compensation to do so. Thus, hiring and retaining key employees may be costly for a firm with high leverage: Pacific Gas and Electric Corporation implemented a retention program costing over $80 million to retain 17 key employees while it was in bankruptcy in 2003.

Fire Sales of Assets. A company in distress may be forced to sell assets quickly to raise cash, possibly accepting a lower price than the assets are actually worth to the firm. This cost is likely to be large when creditors are more pessimistic than management regarding the value of the assets, and so creditors will try to force liquidation even at low prices.

In total, the indirect costs of financial distress may be substantial. A study of highly levered firms by Gregor Andrade and Steven Kaplan estimated a potential loss due to financial distress of 10% to 20% of firm value.[6] Importantly, many of these indirect costs may be incurred even if the firm is not yet in financial distress, but simply faces a significant possibility that it may occur in the future.

**CONCEPT
CHECK**

7. What are the direct costs of bankruptcy?

8. Why are the indirect costs of financial distress likely to be more important than the direct costs of bankruptcy?

16.5   Optimal Capital Structure: The Tradeoff Theory

We can now combine our knowledge of the benefits of leverage from the interest tax shield with the costs of financial distress to determine the amount of debt that a firm should issue to maximize its value. The analysis presented in this section is called the *tradeoff theory* because it weighs the benefits of debt that result from shielding cash flows from taxes against the costs of financial distress associated with leverage. This theory is also sometimes referred to as the *static tradeoff theory*.

tradeoff theory The total value of a levered firm equals the value of the firm without leverage plus the present value of the tax savings from debt, less the present value of financial distress costs.

According to the **tradeoff theory**, the total value of a levered firm equals the value of the firm without leverage plus the present value of the tax savings from debt, less the present value of financial distress costs:

$$V^L = V^U + PV(\text{Interest Tax Shield}) - PV(\text{Financial Distress Costs}) \quad (16.10)$$

Equation 16.10 shows that leverage has costs as well as benefits. Firms have an incentive to increase leverage to exploit the tax benefits of debt. But with too much debt, they are more likely to risk default and incur financial distress costs.

Differences Across Firms

Whereas we have seen in Section 16.3 how to calculate the benefits of the interest tax shield, calculating the precise present value of financial distress costs is very difficult if not impossible. Two key qualitative factors determine the present value of financial distress costs: (1) the probability of financial distress and (2) the magnitude of the direct and indirect costs related to financial distress that the firm will incur.

---

[6]G. Andrade, and S. Kaplan, 1998, "How Costly Is Financial (Not Economic) Distress? Evidence from Highly Leveraged Transactions that Became Distressed," *Journal of Finance* 53: 1443–1493.

What determines each of these factors? The magnitude of the financial distress costs will depend on the relative importance of the sources of these costs and is likely to vary by industry. For example, technology firms are likely to incur high costs associated with financial distress, due to the potential for loss of customers and key personnel, as well as a lack of tangible assets that can be easily liquidated. In contrast, forest products companies are likely to have low costs of financial distress, as much of their value derives from tangible assets (timber land and mills) that can be sold if necessary. Not surprisingly, by reviewing Figure 16.1 we can see that these two industries have very different leverage policies: Technology companies have very low debt, whereas forest products companies tend to be highly levered. Similarly, in Figure 16.2 we saw that Intel has debt whereas ARM Holdings has none. Intel has patents and large chip fabrication facilities that can be sold to meet the claims of lenders. ARM has design facilities and also has patents, but little else that could be sold to meet the demands of creditors.

The probability of financial distress depends on the likelihood that a firm will be unable to meet its debt commitments and therefore default. This probability increases with the amount of a firm's liabilities (relative to its assets). It also increases with the volatility of a firm's cash flows and asset values. Thus, firms with steady, reliable cash flows such as utility companies are able to use high levels of debt and still have a very low probability of default. Firms whose value and cash flows are very volatile (for example, semiconductor firms) must have much lower levels of debt to avoid a significant risk of default.

Optimal Leverage

Figure 16.8 shows how the value of a levered firm, V^L, varies with the level of permanent debt, D, according to Eq. 16.10. With no debt, the value of the firm is V^U. For low levels of debt, the risk of default remains low and the main effect of an increase in leverage is an

FIGURE 16.8

Optimal Leverage with Taxes and Financial Distress Costs

As the level of debt increases, the tax benefits of debt increase until the interest expense exceeds the firm's EBIT. However, the probability of default, and hence the present value of financial distress costs, also increases. The optimal level of debt, D^*, occurs when these effects balance out and the value of the levered firm is maximized. D^* will be lower for firms with higher costs of financial distress.

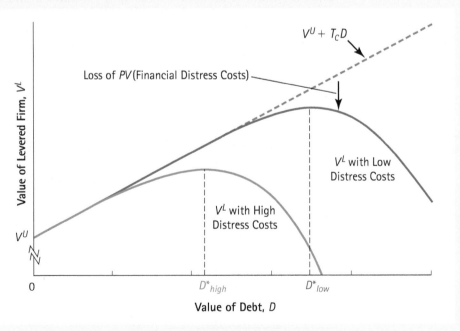

increase in the interest tax shield, which has present value $T_C D$ as shown in Eq. 16.7. If there were no costs of financial distress, the value would continue to increase at this rate until the interest on the debt exceeds the firm's earnings before interest and taxes, and the tax shield is exhausted.

The costs of financial distress reduce the value of the levered firm, V^L. The amount of the reduction increases with the probability of default, which in turn increases with the level of the debt D. The tradeoff theory states that firms should increase their leverage until it reaches the level D^* for which V^L is maximized. At this point, the tax savings that result from increasing leverage are just offset by the increased probability of incurring the costs of financial distress.

Figure 16.8 also illustrates the optimal debt choices for two types of firms. The optimal debt choice for a firm with low costs of financial distress is indicated by D^*_{low}, and the optimal debt choice for a firm with high costs of financial distress is indicated by D^*_{high}. Not surprisingly, with higher costs of financial distress, it is optimal for the firm to choose lower leverage.

The tradeoff theory helps to resolve two important facts about leverage:

1. The presence of financial distress costs can explain why firms choose debt levels that are too low to fully exploit the interest tax shield.

2. Differences in the magnitude of financial distress costs and the volatility of cash flows can explain the differences in the use of leverage across industries.

CONCEPT CHECK

9. According to the tradeoff theory, how should a financial manager determine the right capital structure for a firm?

10. Why would managers in one industry choose different capital structures from those in another industry?

16.6 Additional Consequences of Leverage: Agency Costs and Information

Taxes and financial distress costs are not the only capital market imperfections that arise in practice. In this section, we continue to relax the assumption of perfect capital markets to see other ways in which capital structure can affect a firm's value. We begin by discussing how leverage alters managers' incentives and changes their investment decisions. We then address the complexities of stakeholders in the firm having different information.

Agency Costs

agency costs The costs that arise when there are conflicts of interest among stakeholders.

Agency costs are costs that arise when there are conflicts of interest among stakeholders. In Chapter 1, we briefly mentioned the agency problem that arises when managers put their own interests ahead of shareholders' interest. Here, we discuss how debt can mitigate this problem. However, it may also distort equity holders' preferences for the types of projects pursued by the firm.

Managerial Entrenchment. Although managers often do own shares of the firm, in most large corporations they own only a very small fraction of the outstanding shares. Shareholders, through the board of directors, have the power to fire managers. In practice, they rarely do so unless the firm's performance is exceptionally poor.

management entrenchment A situation arising as a result of the separation of ownership and control, in which managers may make decisions that benefit themselves at investors' expense.

This separation of ownership and control creates the possibility of **management entrenchment**; facing little threat of being fired and replaced, managers are free to run the firm in their own best interests. As a result, managers may make decisions that benefit themselves at investors' expense. Managers may reduce their effort, spend excessively on perks such as corporate jets, or undertake wasteful projects that increase the size of the firm (and their paychecks) at the expense of shareholder value, often called "empire building." If these decisions have a negative NPV for the firm, they are a form of agency cost.

These agency costs are most likely to arise when equity ownership is highly diluted (so that no individual shareholder has an incentive to monitor management closely) and when the firm has a great deal of cash available for managers to spend on wasteful projects. Debt can therefore help in two ways. First, by borrowing rather than raising funds by issuing shares, ownership of the firm may remain more concentrated, improving the monitoring of management. Second, by forcing the firm to pay out cash to meet interest and principal payments, debt reduces the funds available at management's discretion. For managers to engage in wasteful investment, they must have the cash to invest. Only when cash is tight will managers be motivated to run the firm as efficiently as possible. Thus, leverage can provide incentives for managers to run the firm efficiently and effectively. These benefits provide an additional incentive to use debt rather than equity financing.

Airlines Use Financial Distress to Their Advantage

The need to generate cash flows sufficient to make interest payments may also tie managers' hands and commit them to pursue sound business strategies with greater vigor than they would without the threat of financial distress. For example, when American Airlines was in labor negotiations with its unions in April 2003, the firm was able to win wage concessions by explaining that higher costs would push it into bankruptcy. (A similar situation enabled Delta Airlines to persuade its pilots to accept a 33% wage cut in November 2004.) Without the threat of

financial distress, American's managers might not have reached agreement with the union as quickly or achieved the same wage concessions.

A firm with greater leverage may also become a fiercer competitor and act more aggressively in protecting its markets because it cannot risk the possibility of bankruptcy. This commitment to aggressive behavior can scare off potential rivals. (However, this argument can also work in reverse, as a firm weakened by too much leverage might become so financially fragile that it crumbles in the face of competition, allowing other firms to erode its markets.)

Equity-Debt Holder Conflicts. When a firm has leverage, a conflict of interest exists if investment decisions have different consequences for the value of equity and the value of debt. Such a conflict is most likely to occur when the risk of financial distress is high. In some circumstances, managers may take actions that benefit shareholders but harm the firm's creditors and lower the total value of the firm.

To illustrate, put yourself in the place of the shareholders of a company in distress that is likely to default on its debt. You could continue as normal, in which case you will very likely lose the value of your shares and control of the firm to the bondholders. Alternatively, you could:

1. Roll the dice and take on a risky project that could save the firm, even though its expected outcome is so poor that you normally would not take it on.

2. Conserve funds rather than invest in new, promising projects.

3. Cash out by distributing as much of the firm's capital as possible to the shareholders before the bondholders take over.

excessive risk-taking
A situation that occurs when a company is near distress and shareholders have an incentive to invest in risky negative-NPV projects that will destroy value for debt holders and the firm overall.

Why would you roll the dice? Even if the project fails, you are no worse off because you were headed to default anyway. If it succeeds, then you avoid default and retain ownership of the firm. This incentive leads to **excessive risk-taking**, a situation that occurs when a company is near distress and shareholders have an incentive to invest in risky negative-NPV projects that will destroy value for debt holders and the firm overall. Anticipating this behavior, security holders will pay less for the firm initially. This cost is likely to be highest for firms that can easily increase the risk of their investments.

Moral Hazard and Government Bailouts

The term **moral hazard** refers to the idea that individuals will change their behavior if they are not fully exposed to its consequences. Discussion of moral hazard's role in the 2008 financial crisis has centered on mortgage brokers, investment bankers, and corporate managers who earned large bonuses when their businesses did well, but did not need to repay those bonuses later when things turned sour. The agency costs described in this chapter represent another form of moral hazard, as equity holders may take excessive risk or pay excessive dividends if the negative consequences will be borne by bondholders.

How are such abuses by equity holders normally held in check? Bondholders will either charge equity holders for the risk of this abuse by increasing the cost of debt, or, more likely, equity holders will credibly commit not to take on excessive risk by, for example, agreeing to very strong bond covenants and other monitoring.

Ironically, despite the potential immediate benefits of the federal bailouts in response to the 2008 financial crisis, by protecting the bondholders of many large corporations, the government may have simultaneously weakened this disciplining mechanism and thereby increased the likelihood of future crises. With this precedent in place, all lenders to corporations deemed "too big to fail" may presume they have an implicit government guarantee, thus lowering their incentives to insist on strong covenants and to monitor whether those covenants are being satisfied.[7] Without this monitoring, the likelihood of future abuses by equity holders and managers has probably been increased, as has the government's liability.

On the other hand, when default is very likely, a firm may pass up a good project before default because some or most of the benefit will go to bondholders (by reducing the risk or extent of default). For example, if a firm can invest $100 in a project that will increase the value of its debt by $30 and the value of its equity by $90, then the project has a positive NPV of $30 + $90 − $100 = $20. Equity holders will not want to fund it as their gain ($90) is less than the project's cost of $100. In this case, there is an **under-investment problem**: Shareholders choose not to invest in a positive-NPV project because the firm is in financial distress and the value of undertaking the investment opportunity will accrue to bondholders rather than themselves. This failure to invest is costly for debt holders and for the overall value of the firm, because it is giving up the NPV of the missed opportunities. The cost is highest for firms that are likely to have profitable future growth opportunities requiring large investments.

under-investment problem A situation in which shareholders choose not to invest in a positive-NPV project because the firm is in financial distress and the value of undertaking the investment opportunity will accrue to bondholders rather than to shareholders.

The ultimate form of under-investment is cashing out. Knowing that they are likely to lose the firm to the bondholders, shareholders have an incentive to withdraw as much capital from the firm as possible before it enters bankruptcy and transfers to the debt holders. An extreme example of this would be to sell all the assets of the firm and distribute the proceeds to shareholders as a special dividend. The firm would then enter bankruptcy as a worthless shell. As we discussed in Chapter 15, bondholders can anticipate this problem and often require restrictions on the size of dividends and source of funds for those dividends.

Our discussion suggests that we can create a more complete tradeoff model of capital structure by incorporating the possible agency costs and benefits of debt in addition to tax benefits and financial distress costs. This tradeoff model representing optimal leverage is illustrated in Figure 16.9. When debt is too low, adding leverage increases the value of the firm by providing tax benefits and motivating managers to run the firm more efficiently (and avoid wasteful investment). But if debt is too high, the firm will incur financial distress costs and suffer from excessive risk taking and under-investment. The optimal level of debt $D*$ is the point that maximizes firm value by balancing these positive and negative consequences of leverage.

---

[7]As an example, a number of large banks continued to pay dividends during the crisis even after receiving bailout funds. Had the funds been raised from outside investors without any government guarantee, it is very likely the new investors would have restricted such payouts.

FIGURE 16.9

Optimal Leverage with Taxes, Financial Distress, and Agency Costs

As the level of debt increases, the value of the firm increases from the interest tax shield ($T_C D$) as well as improvements in managerial incentives. If leverage is too high, however, the present value of financial distress costs, as well as the agency costs from debt holder–equity holder conflicts, dominates and reduces firm value. The optimal level of debt, D^*, balances these benefits and costs of leverage.

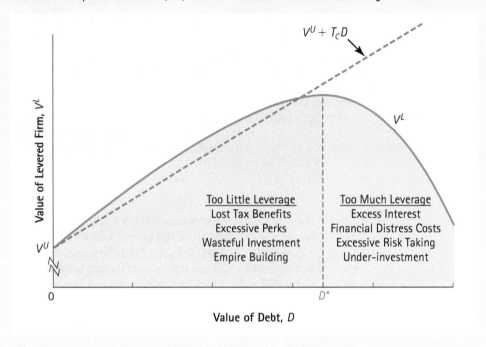

Financial Distress and Rolling the Dice, Literally

Shortly after launching FedEx, founder Frederick Smith was running out of cash and on the verge of shuttering the company's operations. The problem was massive fixed costs (airplanes, sorting facilities, delivery personnel, etc.) and low initial volume.

"By 1973, Smith was so desperate for cash that he flew to Las Vegas to play the blackjack tables. He wired the $27,000 he won back to FedEx."* The company used the winnings to pay its fuel bills, and the rest is history.

*"Frederick W. Smith: No Overnight Success," *Business Week*, September 20, 2004.

Debt and Information

Our final market imperfection is related to the role of information. Throughout this chapter, we have assumed that managers, stockholders, and creditors have the same information. We have also assumed that securities are fairly priced: The firm's shares and debt are priced according to their true underlying value. These assumptions may not always be accurate in practice. Due to **asymmetric information**, managers' information about the firm and its future cash flows is likely to be superior to that of outside investors. This asymmetric information may motivate managers to alter a firm's capital structure.

asymmetric information
A situation in which parties have different information. It can arise when, for example, managers have superior information to that of outside investors regarding the firm's future cash flows.

Leverage as a Credible Signal. To convince the stock market that it has great projects, a firm may commit to large future debt payments. If the projects are great, then the firm will have no trouble making the debt payments. But if the firm is making false claims and then does not grow, it will have trouble paying its creditors and will experience financial distress. This distress will be costly for the firm and also for its managers, who will likely lose their jobs. Thus, the managers can use leverage as a way to convince investors that they do have information that the firm will grow, even if they cannot provide verifiable details about the sources of growth. Investors will interpret the additional leverage as a credible signal of the managers' confidence. The use of leverage as a way to signal good information to investors is known as the **signaling theory of debt**.

signaling theory of debt The use of leverage as a way to signal good information to investors.

Market Timing. When managers have better information than outside investors regarding the value of the firm, they may attempt to engage in **market timing** by selling new shares when they believe the stock is overvalued, and relying on debt and retained earnings (and possibly repurchasing shares) if they believe the stock is undervalued. Managers who successfully time the market in this way benefit long-term shareholders by trading the firm's shares whenever they are mispriced. The firm's capital structure would change as the managers issued new equity (decreasing the leverage) or new debt (increasing the leverage) while attempting to time the market. As a result, the firm's capital structure may deviate above or below the optimal level described by the tradeoff theory, depending on management's view of the share price relative to its true value.

market timing When managers sell new shares because they believe the stock is overvalued, and rely on debt and retained earnings (and possibly repurchasing shares) if they believe the stock is undervalued.

Adverse Selection and the Pecking Order Hypothesis. Suppose managers do try to issue equity when it is overpriced relative to its true value. Knowing this, how would investors react? Recall from Chapter 14 the adverse selection or lemons effect in seasoned equity offerings. Fearful that they are being sold a "lemon," investors will discount the price they are willing to pay for the stock.

The adverse selection problem has implications for capital structure. Managers do not want to sell equity if they have to discount it to find buyers. Therefore, they may seek alternative forms of financing. Debt issues may also suffer from adverse selection. Because the value of low-risk debt is not very sensitive to managers' private information about the firm (but is instead determined mainly by interest rates), the discount needed to attract buyers will be smaller for debt than for equity. Of course, a firm can avoid underpricing altogether by financing investment using its cash (retained earnings) when possible. The **pecking order hypothesis** therefore states that to avoid this "lemons cost":

pecking order hypothesis The idea that managers will have a preference to fund investment using retained earnings, followed by debt, and will only choose to issue equity as a last resort.

Managers will have a preference to fund investment using retained earnings, followed by debt, and will only choose to issue equity as a last resort.

This hypothesis has implications for firms' capital structure. When firms are profitable and generate sufficient cash to fund their investments, they will not issue debt or equity, but just rely on retained earnings. Thus, highly profitable firms will have little debt in their capital structure. Only firms that need to raise external capital will have significant debt financing. According to the pecking order hypothesis, firms should almost never issue equity. In reality, it is likely that multiple forces will shape the firm's capital structure, and firms will issue equity when the agency costs or financial distress costs of debt are too great.

EXAMPLE 16.5

The Pecking Order of Financing Alternatives

MyFinanceLab

PROBLEM

Axon Industries needs to raise $9.5 million for a new investment project. If the firm issues one-year debt, it may have to pay an interest rate of 8%, although Axon's managers believe that 6% would be a fair rate given the level of risk. However, if the firm issues equity, the managers believe the equity may be underpriced by 5%. What is the cost to current shareholders of financing the project out of retained earnings, debt, and equity?

SOLUTION

PLAN

We can evaluate the financing alternatives by comparing what the firm would have to pay to get the financing versus what its managers believe it should pay if the market had the same information they do.

(Continued)

EXECUTE

If the firm spends $9.5 million out of retained earnings, rather than paying that money out to shareholders as a dividend, the cost of financing the project is $9.5 million.

Using one-year debt costs the firm $9.5 × (1.08) = $10.26 million in one year, which has a present value based on management's view of the firm's risk of $10.26 ÷ (1.06) = $9.68 million.

If equity is underpriced by 5%, then to raise $9.5 million the firm will need to issue shares that are actually worth $10 million. (For example, if the firm's shares are each worth $50, but it sells them for 0.95 × $50 = $47.50 per share, it will need to sell $9.5 million ÷ $47.50/share = 200,000 shares. These shares have a true value of 200,000 shares × $50/share = $10 million.) Thus, the cost of financing the project with equity will be $10 million.

EVALUATE

Comparing the three options, retained earnings are the cheapest source of funds, followed by debt, and finally by equity. The ranking reflects the effect of differences in information between managers and investors that result in a lemons problem when they issue new securities, and particularly when they issue new equity.

CONCEPT CHECK

11. How can too much debt lead to excessive risk-taking?

12. What is the "pecking order" hypothesis?

16.7 Capital Structure: Putting It All Together

In this chapter, we have examined a number of factors that might influence a firm's choice of capital structure. What is the bottom line for a financial manager devising the optimal capital structure for a firm? The optimal capital structure depends on market imperfections such as taxes, financial distress costs, agency costs, and asymmetric information, as follows:

1. *Make use of the interest tax shield if your firm has consistent taxable income.* The interest tax shield allows firms to repay investors and avoid the corporate tax.

2. *Balance the tax benefits of debt against the costs of financial distress when determining how much of the firm's income to shield from taxes with leverage.* Whereas the risk of default is not itself a problem, financial distress may lead to other consequences that reduce the value of the firm.

3. *Consider short-term debt for external financing when agency costs are significant.* Too much debt can motivate managers and equity holders to take excessive risks or under-invest in a firm. When free cash flows are high, too little leverage may encourage wasteful spending.

4. *Increase leverage to signal managers' confidence in the firm's ability to meet its debt obligations.* Investors understand that bankruptcy is costly for managers.

5. *Be mindful that investors are aware that you have an incentive to issue securities that you know are overpriced.* Thus, when an issue is announced, investors will lower their valuation of that security. This effect is most pronounced for equity issues because the value of equity is most sensitive to the manager's private information.

6. *Rely first on retained earnings, then debt, and finally equity.* This pecking order of financing alternatives will be most important when managers are likely to have a great deal of private information regarding the value of the firm.

7. *Do not change the firm's capital structure unless it departs significantly from the optimal level.* Actively changing a firm's capital structure (for example, by selling or repurchasing shares or bonds) entails transactions costs. Most changes to a firm's debt-equity ratio are likely to occur passively, as the market value of the firm's equity fluctuates with changes in the firm's stock price.

MyFinanceLab

Here is what you should know after reading this chapter. MyFinanceLab will help you identify what you know, and where to go when you need to practice.

KEY POINTS AND EQUATIONS	KEY TERMS	ONLINE PRACTICE
16.1 Capital Structure Choices • The collection of securities that a firm issues to raise capital from investors is called the firm's capital structure. Equity and debt are the securities most commonly used by firms. • Various financing choices will promise different future amounts to each security holder in exchange for the cash that is raised today. • Managers also need to consider whether the securities that the firm issues will receive a fair price in the market, have tax consequences, entail transactions costs, or even change its future investment opportunities.	debt-to-value ratio, p. 498	MyFinanceLab Study Plan 16.1
16.2 Capital Structure in Perfect Capital Markets • When equity is used without debt, the firm is said to be unlevered. Otherwise, the amount of debt determines the firm's leverage. • The owner of a firm should choose the capital structure that maximizes the total value of the securities issued. • According to MM Proposition II, the cost of capital for levered equity is: $$r_E = r_U + \frac{D}{E}(r_U - r_D) \qquad (16.3)$$ • Debt is less risky than equity, so it has a lower cost of capital. Leverage increases the risk of equity, however, raising the equity cost of capital. The benefit of debt's lower cost of capital is offset by the higher equity cost of capital, leaving a firm's weighted average cost of capital (WACC) unchanged with perfect capital markets. • According to MM Proposition I, with perfect capital markets, the value of a firm is independent of its capital structure. With perfect capital markets, homemade leverage is a perfect substitute for firm leverage.	homemade leverage, p. 505 levered equity, p. 501 perfect capital markets, p. 500 pretax WACC, p. 506 unlevered equity, p. 501	MyFinanceLab Study Plan 16.2 Interactive Leverage Effect Analysis
16.3 Debt and Taxes • Because interest expense is tax deductible, leverage increases the total amount of income available to all investors. The gain to investors from the tax deductibility of interest payments is called the interest tax shield. Interest Tax Shield = Corporate Tax Rate $\times$ Interest Payments $\qquad$ (16.4) • When we consider corporate taxes, the total value of a levered firm equals the value of an unlevered firm plus the present value of the interest tax shield. $$V^L = V^U + PV(\text{Interest Tax Shield}) \qquad (16.5)$$	interest tax shield, p. 511	MyFinanceLab Study Plan 16.3

- When securities are fairly priced, the original shareholders of a firm capture the full benefit of the interest tax shield from an increase in leverage.
- When we introduce corporate taxes, the weighted average cost of capital is:

$$r_{wacc} = r_E \frac{E}{E+D} + r_D(1 - T_C)\frac{D}{E+D} \quad (16.8)$$

- Absent other market imperfections, the WACC declines with a firm's leverage because interest expense is tax deductible.
- To capture the effect of the interest tax deduction on firm value, you can either compute the PV of the future tax shields or use the WACC with taxes to discount the firm's free cash flows, but not both!

16.4 The Costs of Bankruptcy and Financial Distress • Bankruptcy is a costly process that imposes both direct and indirect costs on a firm and its investors. • Some direct costs are fees paid to lawyers and bankruptcy experts. • Some indirect costs are loss of customers, suppliers, and employees or being forced to sell assets at a deep discount to raise money.	financial distress, p. 515	MyFinanceLab Study Plan 16.4
16.5 Optimal Capital Structure: The Tradeoff Theory • According to the tradeoff theory, the total value of a levered firm equals the value of the firm without leverage plus the present value of the tax savings from debt minus the present value of financial distress costs: $$V^L = V^U + PV(\text{Interest Tax Shield}) - PV(\text{Financial Distress Costs}) \quad (16.10)$$ • The optimal leverage is the level of debt that maximizes V^L.	tradeoff theory, p. 517	MyFinanceLab Study Plan 16.5
16.6 Additional Consequences of Leverage: Agency Costs and Information • Leverage has agency benefits and can improve incentives for managers to run a firm more efficiently and effectively. However, when a firm enters financial distress, leverage can create incentives to forgo good projects or to take excessive risks. • When managers have better information than investors, the result is asymmetric information. Given asymmetric information, managers may use leverage as a credible signal to investors of the firm's ability to generate future free cash flow. • Managers who perceive that the firm's equity is underpriced will have a preference to fund investment using retained earnings, or debt, rather than equity. This result is called the pecking order hypothesis.	agency costs, p. 519 asymmetric information, p. 522 excessive risk-taking, p. 520 management entrenchment, p. 519 market timing, p. 523 pecking order hypothesis, p. 523 signaling theory of debt, p. 523 under-investment problem, p. 521	MyFinanceLab Study Plan 16.6

**CRITICAL
THINKING**

1. Absent tax effects, why can't we change the cost of capital of the firm by using more debt financing and less equity financing?

2. Explain what is wrong with the following argument: "If a firm issues debt that is risk-free because there is no possibility of default, the risk of the firm's equity does not change. Therefore, risk-free debt allows the firm to get the benefit of a low cost of capital of debt without raising its cost of capital of equity."

3. What are the channels through which financing choices can affect firm value?

4. How do taxes affect the choice of debt versus equity?

5. What is meant by "indirect costs of financial distress"?

6. Which type of firm is more likely to experience a loss of customers in the event of financial distress:
   a. Campbell Soup Company or Intuit, Inc. (a maker of accounting software)?
   b. Allstate Corporation (an insurance company) or Reebok International (a footwear and clothing firm)?

7. According to the tradeoff theory, how is capital structure determined?

8. For each pair below, which type of asset is more likely to be liquidated for close to its full market value in the event of financial distress:
   a. An office building or a brand name?
   b. Product inventory or raw materials?
   c. Patent rights or engineering "know-how"?

9. Which of the following industries have low optimal debt levels according to the tradeoff theory? Which have high optimal levels of debt?
   a. Tobacco firms
   b. Accounting firms
   c. Established restaurant chains
   d. Lumber companies
   e. Cell phone manufacturers

10. How can leverage alter the incentives of managers?

PROBLEMS

All problems are available in MyFinanceLab. *The* [icon] *icon indicates problems that are easier to solve using Excel and have data in an Excel format available in* MyFinanceLab. *An asterisk * indicates problems with a higher level of difficulty.*

Capital Structure in Perfect Capital Markets

For problems in this section assume no taxes or distress costs.

1. Consider a project with free cash flows in one year of $130,000 or $180,000, with each outcome being equally likely. The initial investment required for the project is $100,000, and the project's cost of capital is 20%. The risk-free interest rate is 10%.
   a. What is the NPV of this project?
   b. Suppose that to raise the funds for the initial investment, the project is sold to investors as an all-equity firm. The equity holders will receive the cash flows of the project in one year. How much money can be raised in this way—that is, what is the initial market value of the unlevered equity?
   c. Suppose the initial $100,000 is instead raised by borrowing at the risk-free interest rate. What are the cash flows of the levered equity, and what is its initial value according to MM?

2. You are an entrepreneur starting a biotechnology firm. If your research is successful, the technology can be sold for $30 million. If your research is unsuccessful, it will be worth nothing. To fund your research, you need to raise $2 million. Investors are willing to provide you with $2 million in initial capital in exchange for 50% of the unlevered equity in the firm.

   a. What is the total market value of the firm without leverage?

   b. Suppose you borrow $1 million. According to MM, what fraction of the firm's equity must you sell to raise the additional $1 million you need?

   c. What is the value of your share of the firm's equity in cases (a) and (b)?

3. Acort Industries owns assets that will have an 80% probability of having a market value of $50 million in one year. There is a 20% chance that the assets will be worth only $20 million. The current risk-free rate is 5%, and Acort's assets have a cost of capital of 10%.

   a. If Acort is unlevered, what is the current market value of its equity?

   b. Suppose instead that Acort has debt with a face value of $20 million due in one year. According to MM, what is the value of Acort's equity in this case?

   c. What is the expected return of Acort's equity without leverage? What is the expected return of Acort's equity with leverage?

   d. What is the lowest possible realized return of Acort's equity with and without leverage?

*4. Suppose there are no taxes. Firm ABC has no debt, and firm XYZ has debt of $5000 on which it pays interest of 10% each year. Both companies have identical projects that generate free cash flows of $800 or $1000 each year. After paying any interest on debt, both companies use all remaining free cash flows to pay dividends each year.

	ABC		XYZ	
FCF	Debt Payments	Equity Dividends	Debt Payments	Equity Dividends
$ 800				
$1000				

   a. Fill in the table above showing the debt payments and equity dividends each firm will receive given each of the two possible levels of free cash flows.

   b. Suppose you hold 10% of the equity of ABC. What is another portfolio you could hold that would provide the same cash flows?

   c. Suppose you hold 10% of the equity of XYZ. If you can borrow at 10%, what is an alternative strategy that would provide the same cash flows?

5. Hardmon Enterprises is currently an all-equity firm with an expected return of 12%. It is considering borrowing money to buy back some of its existing shares, thus increasing its leverage.

   a. Suppose Hardmon borrows to the point that its debt-equity ratio is 0.50. With this amount of debt, the debt cost of capital is 6%. What will be the expected return of equity after this transaction?

   b. Suppose instead Hardmon borrows to the point that its debt-equity ratio is 1.50. With this amount of debt, Hardmon's debt will be much riskier. As a result, the debt cost of capital will be 8%. What will be the expected return of equity in this case?

   c. A senior manager argues that it is in the best interest of the shareholders to choose the capital structure that leads to the highest expected return for the stock. How would you respond to this argument?

6. Suppose Microsoft has no debt and a WACC of 9.2%. The average debt-to-value ratio for the software industry is 5%. What would be its cost of equity if it took on the average amount of debt for its industry at a cost of debt of 6%?

7. Your firm is financed 100% with equity and has a cost of equity capital of 12%. You are considering your first debt issue, which would change your capital structure to 30% debt and 70% equity. If your cost of debt is 7%, what will be your new cost of equity?

8. One of your new employees notes that your debt has a lower cost of capital (5%) than your equity (15%). So, he suggests that the firm swap its capital structure from 30% debt and 70% equity to 70% debt and 30% equity instead. He estimates that after the swap, your cost of equity would be 20%.
   a. What would be your new cost of debt?
   b. Have you lowered your overall cost of capital?

Debt and Taxes

9. Pelamed Pharmaceuticals had EBIT of $325 million in 2013. In addition, Pelamed had interest expenses of $125 million and a corporate tax rate of 40%.
   a. What was Pelamed's 2013 net income?
   b. What was the total of Pelamed's 2013 net income and interest payments?
   c. If Pelamed had no interest expenses, what would its 2013 net income have been? How does it compare to your answer in part (b)?
   d. What was the amount of Pelamed's interest tax shield in 2013?

10. Grommit Engineering expects to have net income next year of $20.75 million and free cash flow of $22.15 million. Grommit's marginal corporate tax rate is 35%.
    a. If Grommit increases leverage so that its interest expense rises by $1 million, how will its net income change?
    b. For the same increase in interest expense, how will its free cash flow change?

11. Braxton Enterprises currently has debt outstanding of $35 million and an interest rate of 8%. Braxton plans to reduce its debt by repaying $7 million in principal at the end of each year for the next five years. If Braxton's marginal corporate tax rate is 40%, what is the interest tax shield from Braxton's debt in each of the next five years?

12. Assume that Microsoft has a total market value of $300 billion and a marginal tax rate of 35%. If it permanently changes its leverage from no debt by taking on new debt in the amount of 13% of its current market value, what is the present value of the tax shield it will create?

13. Suppose the corporate tax rate is 40%. Consider a firm that earns $1000 before interest and taxes each year with no risk. The firm's capital expenditures equal its depreciation expenses each year, and it will have no changes to its net working capital. The risk-free interest rate is 5%.
    a. Suppose the firm has no debt and pays out its net income as a dividend each year. What is the value of the firm's equity?
    b. Suppose instead the firm makes interest payments of $500 per year. What is the value of its equity? What is the value of its debt?
    c. What is the difference between the total value of the firm with leverage and without leverage?
    d. To what percentage of the value of the debt is the difference in part (c) equal?

14. Your firm currently has $100 million in debt outstanding with a 10% interest rate. The terms of the loan require the firm to repay $25 million of the balance each year. Suppose that the marginal corporate tax rate is 40%, and that the interest tax shields have the same risk as the loan. What is the present value of the interest tax shields from this debt?

15. Arnell Industries has $10 million in permanent debt outstanding. The firm will pay interest only on this debt. Arnell's marginal tax rate is expected to be 35% for the foreseeable future.
    a. Suppose Arnell pays interest of 6% per year on its debt. What is its annual interest tax shield?
    b. What is the present value of the interest tax shield, assuming its risk is the same as the loan?
    c. Suppose instead that the interest rate on the debt is 5%. What is the present value of the interest tax shield in this case?

16. Rogot Instruments makes fine violins, violas, and cellos. It has $1 million in debt outstanding, equity valued at $2 million, and pays corporate income tax at a rate of 35%. Its cost of equity is 12% and its cost of debt is 7%.
    a. What is Rogot's pretax WACC?
    b. What is Rogot's (effective after-tax) WACC?

17. Rumolt Motors has 30 million shares outstanding with a price of $15 per share. In addition, Rumolt has issued bonds with a total current market value of $150 million. Suppose Rumolt's equity cost of capital is 10%, and its debt cost of capital is 5%.
    a. What is Rumolt's pretax WACC?
    b. If Rumolt's corporate tax rate is 35%, what is its after-tax WACC?

18. Summit Builders has a market debt-equity ratio of 0.65 and a corporate tax rate of 40%, and it pays 7% interest on its debt. By what amount does the interest tax shield from its debt lower Summit's WACC?

19. Milton Industries expects free cash flows of $5 million each year. Milton's corporate tax rate is 35%, and its unlevered cost of capital is 15%. The firm also has outstanding debt of $19.05 million, and it expects to maintain this level of debt permanently.
    a. What is the value of Milton Industries without leverage?
    b. What is the value of Milton Industries with leverage?

20. NatNah, a builder of acoustic accessories, has no debt and an equity cost of capital of 15%. NatNah decides to increase its leverage to maintain a market debt-to-value ratio of 0.5. Suppose its debt cost of capital is 9% and its corporate tax rate is 35%. If NatNah's pretax WACC remains constant, what will be its (effective after-tax) WACC with the increase in leverage?

*21. Kurz Manufacturing is currently an all-equity firm with 20 million shares outstanding and a stock price of $7.50 per share. Although investors currently expect Kurz to remain an all-equity firm, Kurz plans to announce that it will borrow $50 million and use the funds to repurchase shares. Kurz will pay interest only on this debt, and it has no further plans to increase or decrease the amount of debt. Kurz is subject to a 40% corporate tax rate.
    a. What is the market value of Kurz's existing assets before the announcement?
    b. What is the market value of Kurz's assets (including any tax shields) just after the debt is issued, but before the shares are repurchased?
    c. What is Kurz's share price just before the share repurchase? How many shares will Kurz repurchase?
    d. What are Kurz's market value balance sheet and share price after the share repurchase?

22. Kohwe Corporation plans to issue equity to raise $50 million to finance a new investment. After making the investment, Kohwe expects to earn free cash flows of $10 million each year. Kohwe currently has 5 million shares outstanding, and it has no other assets or opportunities. Suppose the appropriate discount rate for Kohwe's future free cash flows is 8%, and the only capital market imperfections are corporate taxes and financial distress costs.
    a. What is the NPV of Kohwe's investment?
    b. What is Kohwe's share price today?

23. Suppose Kohwe borrows the $50 million instead. The firm will pay interest only on this loan each year, and it will maintain an outstanding balance of $50 million on the loan. Suppose that Kohwe's corporate tax rate is 40%, and expected free cash flows are still $10 million each year. What is Kohwe's share price today if the investment is financed with debt?

24. Now suppose that with leverage, Kohwe's expected free cash flows will decline to $9 million per year due to reduced sales and other financial distress costs. Assume that the appropriate discount rate for Kohwe's future free cash flows is still 8%. What is Kohwe's share price today given the financial distress costs of leverage?

*25. Rally, Inc., is an all-equity firm with assets worth $25 billion and 10 billion shares outstanding. Rally plans to borrow $10 billion and use these funds to repurchase shares. The firm's corporate tax rate is 35%, and Rally plans to keep its outstanding debt equal to $10 billion permanently.
    a. Without the increase in leverage, what would Rally's share price be?
    b. Suppose Rally offers $2.75 per share to repurchase its shares. Would shareholders sell for this price?
    c. Suppose Rally offers $3.00 per share, and shareholders tender their shares at this price. What will Rally's share price be after the repurchase?
    d. What is the lowest price Rally can offer and have shareholders tender their shares? What will be its stock price after the share repurchase in that case?

Optimal Capital Structure: The Tradeoff Theory

26. With its current leverage, Impi Corporation will have net income next year of $4.5 million. If Impi's corporate tax rate is 35% and it pays 8% interest on its debt, how much additional debt can Impi issue this year and still receive the benefit of the interest tax shield next year?

27. Now that your firm has matured, you are considering adding debt to your capital structure for the first time. Your all-equity firm has a market value of $20 million and you are considering issuing $2 million in debt with an interest rate of 7% and using it to repurchase shares. You pay a corporate tax rate of 40%. Assume taxes are the only imperfection and the debt is expected to be permanent.
    a. What will be the total value of the firm after the change in capital structure?
    b. What will be the value of the remaining equity after the change in capital structure?

28. Hawar International is a shipping firm with a current share price of $5.50 and 10 million shares outstanding. Suppose that Hawar announces plans to lower its corporate taxes by borrowing $20 million and repurchasing shares, that Hawar pays a corporate tax rate of 30%, and that shareholders expect the change in debt to be permanent.
    a. If the only imperfection is corporate taxes, what will the share price be after this announcement?

b. Suppose the only imperfections are corporate taxes and financial distress costs. If the share price rises to $5.75 after this announcement, what is the PV of financial distress costs Hawar will incur as the result of this new debt?

29. Marpor Industries has no debt and expects to generate free cash flows of $16 million each year. Marpor believes that if it permanently increases its level of debt to $40 million, the risk of financial distress may cause it to lose some customers and receive less favorable terms from its suppliers. As a result, Marpor's expected free cash flows with debt will be only $15 million per year. Suppose Marpor's tax rate is 35%, the risk-free rate is 5%, the expected return of the market is 15%, and the beta of Marpor's free cash flows is 1.10 (with or without leverage).
    a. Estimate Marpor's value without leverage.
    b. Estimate Marpor's value with the new leverage.

*30. Colt Systems will have EBIT this coming year of $15 million. It will also spend $6 million on total capital expenditures and increases in net working capital, and have $3 million in depreciation expenses. Colt is currently an all-equity firm with a corporate tax rate of 35% and a cost of capital of 10%.
    a. If Colt's free cash flows are expected to grow by 8.5% per year, what is the market value of its equity today?
    b. If the interest rate on its debt is 8%, how much can Colt borrow now and still have non-negative net income this coming year?
    c. Is there a tax incentive today for Colt to choose a debt-to-value ratio that exceeds 50%? Explain.

Additional Consequences of Leverage: Agency Costs and Information

31. Dynron Corporation's primary business is natural gas transportation using its vast gas pipeline network. Dynron's assets currently have a market value of $150 million. The firm is exploring the possibility of raising $50 million by selling part of its pipeline network and investing the $50 million in a fiber-optic network to generate revenues by selling high-speed network bandwidth. Whereas this new investment is expected to increase profits, it will also substantially increase Dynron's risk. If Dynron is levered, would this investment be more or less attractive to equity holders than if Dynron had no debt?

32. Consider a firm whose only asset is a plot of vacant land, and whose only liability is debt of $15 million due in one year. If left vacant, the land will be worth $10 million in one year. Alternatively, the firm can develop the land at an up-front cost of $20 million. The developed land will be worth $35 million in one year. Suppose the risk-free interest rate is 10%, assume all cash flows are risk-free, and assume there are no taxes.
    a. If the firm chooses not to develop the land, what is the value of the firm's equity today? What is the value of the debt today?
    b. What is the NPV of developing the land?
    c. Suppose the firm raises $20 million from equity holders to develop the land. If the firm develops the land, what is the value of the firm's equity today? What is the value of the firm's debt today?
    d. Given your answer to part (c), would equity holders be willing to provide the $20 million needed to develop the land?

*33. Zymase is a biotechnology start-up firm. Researchers at Zymase must choose one of three different research strategies. The payoffs (after taxes) and their likelihood for each strategy are shown below. The risk of each project is diversifiable.

Strategy	Probability	Payoff ($ million)
A	100%	75
B	50%	140
	50%	0
C	10%	300
	90%	40

a. Which project has the highest expected payoff?

b. Suppose Zymase has debt of $40 million due at the time of the project's payoff. Which strategy has the highest expected payoff for equity holders?

c. Suppose Zymase has debt of $110 million due at the time of the strategy's payoff. Which strategy has the highest expected payoff for equity holders?

d. If management chooses the strategy that maximizes the payoff to equity holders, what is the expected agency cost to the firm from having $40 million in debt due? What is the expected agency cost to the firm from having $110 million in debt due?

*34. You own a firm, and you want to raise $30 million to fund an expansion. Currently, you own 100% of the firm's equity, and the firm has no debt. To raise the $30 million solely through equity, you will need to sell two-thirds of the firm. However, you would prefer to maintain at least a 50% equity stake in the firm to retain control.

a. If you borrow $20 million, what fraction of the equity will you need to sell to raise the remaining $10 million? (Assume perfect capital markets.)

b. What is the smallest amount you can borrow to raise the $30 million without giving up control? (Assume perfect capital markets.)

*35. Empire Industries forecasts net income this coming year as shown below (in thousands of dollars):

EBIT	$1000
Interest expense	0
Income before tax	1000
Taxes	−350
Net income	$650

Approximately $200,000 of Empire's earnings will be needed to make new, positive-NPV investments. Unfortunately, Empire's managers are expected to waste 10% of its net income on needless perks, pet projects, and other expenditures that do not contribute to the firm. All remaining income will be distributed to shareholders.

a. What are the two benefits of debt financing for Empire?

b. By how much would each $1 of interest expense reduce Empire's distributions to shareholders?

c. What is the increase in the *total* funds Empire will pay to investors for each $1 of interest expense?

*36. Info Systems Technology (IST) manufactures microprocessor chips for use in appliances and other applications. IST has no debt and 100 million shares outstanding. The correct price for these shares is either $14.50 or $12.50 per share. Investors view both possibilities as equally likely, so the shares currently trade for $13.50.

IST must raise $500 million to build a new production facility. Because the firm would suffer a large loss of both customers and engineering talent in the event of financial distress, managers believe that if IST borrows the $500 million, the present value of financial distress costs will exceed any tax benefits by $20 million. At the same time, because investors believe that managers know the correct share price, IST faces a lemons problem if it attempts to raise the $500 million by issuing equity.

a. Suppose that if IST issues equity, the share price will remain at $13.50. To maximize the long-term share price of the firm once its true value is known, would managers choose to issue equity or borrow the $500 million if:

   i.   They know the correct value of the shares is $12.50?
   ii. They know the correct value of the shares is $14.50?

b. Given your answer to part (a), what should investors conclude if IST issues equity? What will happen to the share price?

c. Given your answer to part (a), what should investors conclude if IST issues debt? What will happen to the share price in that case?

d. How would your answers change if there were no distress costs, but only the tax benefits of leverage?

Chapter 16 Appendix	# The Bankruptcy Code

When a firm fails to make a required payment to debt holders, it is in default. Debt holders can then take legal action against the firm to collect payment by seizing the firm's assets. Because most firms have multiple creditors, coordination is required to guarantee that each creditor will be treated fairly. Moreover, because the assets of the firm might be more valuable if kept together, creditors seizing assets in a piecemeal fashion might destroy much of the remaining value of the firm.

The U.S. bankruptcy code was created to organize this process so that creditors are treated fairly and the value of the assets is not needlessly destroyed. According to the provisions of the 1978 Bankruptcy Reform Act, U.S. firms can file for two forms of bankruptcy protection: Chapter 7 or Chapter 11.

In Chapter 7 liquidation, a trustee is appointed to oversee the liquidation of the firm's assets through an auction. The proceeds from the liquidation are used to pay the firm's creditors, and the firm ceases to exist.

In the more common form of bankruptcy for large corporations, Chapter 11 reorganization, all pending collection attempts are automatically suspended, and the firm's existing management is given the opportunity to propose a reorganization plan. While developing the plan, management continues to operate the business. The reorganization plan specifies the treatment of each creditor of the firm. In addition to cash payment, creditors may receive new debt or equity securities of the firm. The value of cash and securities is generally less than the amount each creditor is owed, but more than the creditors would receive if the firm were shut down immediately and liquidated. The creditors must vote to accept the plan, and it must be approved by the bankruptcy court.[8] If an acceptable plan is not put forth, the court may ultimately force a Chapter 7 liquidation of the firm.

---

[8]Specifically, management holds the exclusive right to propose a reorganization plan for the first 120 days, and this period may be extended indefinitely by the bankruptcy court. Thereafter, any interested party may propose a plan. Creditors who will receive full payment or have their claims fully reinstated under the plan are deemed unimpaired, and do not vote on the reorganization plan. All impaired creditors are grouped according to the nature of their claims. If the plan is approved by creditors holding two-thirds of the claim amount in each group and a majority in the number of the claims in each group, the court will confirm the plan. Even if all groups do not approve the plan, the court may still impose the plan (in a process commonly known as a "cram down") if it deems the plan fair and equitable with respect to each group that objected.

17

Payout Policy

LEARNING OBJECTIVES

- Identify the different ways in which corporations can make distributions to shareholders

- Understand why the way in which they distribute cash flow does not affect value absent market imperfections

- Demonstrate how taxes can create an advantage for share repurchases versus dividends

- Explain how increased payouts can reduce agency problems but potentially reduce financial flexibility

- Understand the role of payout policy in signaling information to the market

- Describe alternate non-cash methods for payouts

notation

P_{cum}	cum-dividend (with-dividend) stock price	
P_{ex}	ex-dividend (without-dividend) stock price	

P_{rep}	stock price with share repurchase	
PV	present value	

When a firm's investments generate free cash flow, the firm must decide how to use that cash. If the firm has new positive-NPV investment opportunities, it can reinvest the cash and increase the value of the firm. Many young, rapidly growing firms reinvest 100% of their cash flows in this way. But mature, profitable firms often find that they generate more cash than they need to fund all of their attractive investment opportunities. When a firm has excess cash, it can hold those funds as part of its cash reserves or pay out the cash to shareholders. If the firm decides to follow the latter approach, it has two choices: It can pay a dividend or it can repurchase shares from current owners. These decisions represent the firm's payout policy.

For many years, Microsoft Corporation chose to distribute cash to investors primarily by repurchasing its own stock. During the five fiscal years ending June 2004, for example, Microsoft spent an average of $5.4 billion per year on share repurchases. Microsoft began paying dividends to investors in 2003, with what CFO John Connors called "a starter dividend" of $0.08 per share. Then, on July 20, 2004, Microsoft stunned financial markets by announcing plans to pay the largest single cash dividend payment in history, a one-time dividend of $32 billion, or $3 per share, to all shareholders of record on November 17, 2004. In addition to this dividend, Microsoft announced plans to repurchase up to $30 billion of its stock over the next four years and pay regular quarterly dividends at an annual rate of $0.32 per share. What considerations led financial managers at Microsoft to make this payout? What are the implications of such actions for shareholders and the value of the firm?

In this chapter, we show that as with capital structure, a firm's payout policy is shaped by market imperfections such as taxes, agency costs, transaction costs, and asymmetric information between managers and investors. We look at why some firms prefer to pay dividends, while others pay no dividends and rely exclusively on share repurchases. In addition, we explore why some firms retain cash and build up large reserves, while others tend to pay out their excess cash.

17.1   Cash Distributions to Shareholders

Figure 17.1 illustrates the alternative uses of free cash flow.[1] The primary decision is one of whether to retain the cash flow or distribute it to the firm's capital providers as a return on their investment. The driver of this decision is whether the firm could better employ the cash flow than could its investors. This is the same as asking whether the firm has enough positive-NPV projects to use the free cash flow, because positive-NPV projects are those that are expected to generate value relative to what investors could generate elsewhere in the capital markets. So, the payout and investment decisions are closely linked. If the firm chooses to retain the cash flow, it will invest in new projects now or add to cash reserves to fund future investment. If the firm chooses to distribute the cash flow, it can do so by repurchasing shares or paying dividends. The way a firm chooses between these alternatives is referred to as its **payout policy**. We begin our discussion of a firm's payout policy by considering the choice between paying dividends and repurchasing shares. In this section, we examine the details of these methods of paying cash to shareholders.

payout policy The way a firm chooses between the alternative ways to pay out cash to shareholders.

FIGURE 17.1

Uses of Free Cash Flow

A firm can retain its free cash flow, either investing or accumulating it, or pay out its free cash flow through a dividend or share repurchase. The choice between these options is determined by the firm's payout policy.

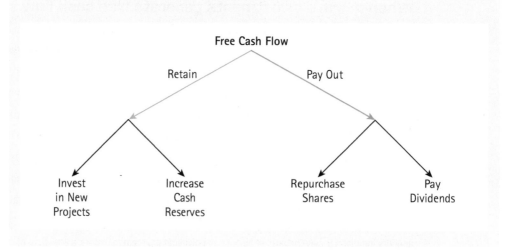

---

[1]Strictly speaking, Figure 17.1 is for an all-equity firm. For a levered firm, we would begin with the firm's free cash flows to equity, which is free cash flows less after-tax payments to debt holders.

Dividends

A public company's board of directors determines the amount of the firm's dividend. The board sets the amount per share that will be paid and decides when the payment will occur. The date on which the board authorizes the dividend is the **declaration date**. After the board declares the dividend, the firm is legally obligated to make the payment.

declaration date The date on which a public company's board of directors authorizes the payment of a dividend.

record date The specific date set by a public company's board of directors such that the firm will pay a dividend to all shareholders of record on this date.

The firm will pay the dividend to all shareholders of record on a specific date set by the board called the **record date**. Because it takes three business days for shares to be registered, only shareholders who purchase the stock at least three days prior to the record date receive the dividend. As a result, the date two business days prior to the record date is known as the **ex-dividend date**. Anyone who purchases the stock on or after the ex-dividend date will not receive the dividend. Finally, on the **payable date** (or **distribution date**), which is generally within a month after the record date, the firm mails dividend checks to the registered shareholders. Figure 17.2 shows these dates for Microsoft's $3 dividend.

FIGURE 17.2

Important Dates for Microsoft's Special Dividend

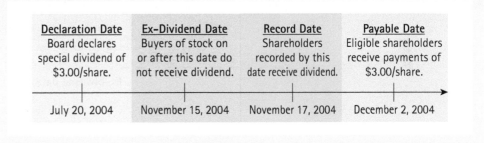

Declaration Date	Ex-Dividend Date	Record Date	Payable Date
Board declares special dividend of $3.00/share.	Buyers of stock on or after this date do not receive dividend.	Shareholders recorded by this date receive dividend.	Eligible shareholders receive payments of $3.00/share.
July 20, 2004	November 15, 2004	November 17, 2004	December 2, 2004

ex-dividend date A date, two days prior to a dividend's record date, on or after which anyone buying the stock will not be eligible for the dividend.

Microsoft declared the dividend on July 20, 2004, payable on December 2 to all shareholders of record on November 17. Because the record date was November 17, the ex-dividend date was two days earlier—November 15, 2004.

payable date (distribution date) A date, generally within a month after the record date, on which a firm mails dividend checks to its registered stockholders.

special dividend A one-time dividend payment a firm makes that is usually much larger than a regular dividend.

Special Dividend. Most companies that pay dividends pay them at regular quarterly intervals. Companies usually do not adjust the amount of their dividends, with little variation in the amount of the dividend from quarter to quarter. Occasionally, a firm may pay a one-time, **special dividend** that is usually much larger than a regular dividend, like Microsoft's $3.00 dividend in 2004. Figure 17.3 shows the dividends paid by GM from 1983 to 2008. In addition to regular dividends, GM paid special dividends in December 1997 and again in May 1999 (associated with spin-offs of subsidiaries, discussed further in Section 17.6).

Whereas GM raised its dividends throughout the 1980s, it cut its dividends during the recession in the early 1990s. GM raised its dividends again in the late 1990s but was forced to cut them again in early 2006 and suspend them altogether in July 2008 in response to financial difficulties. One year later GM filed for Chapter 11 bankruptcy and its existing shareholders were wiped out. GM has since emerged from bankruptcy (in 2009) and issued new shares, but did not reintroduce a dividend payment until 2014.

return of capital When a firm, instead of paying dividends from current earnings (or accumulated retained earnings), pays dividends from other sources, such as paid-in capital or the liquidation of assets.

Accounting Implications. Dividends are a cash outflow for the firm. From an accounting perspective, dividends generally reduce the firm's current (or accumulated) retained earnings. In some cases, dividends are attributed to other accounting sources, such as paid-in capital or the liquidation of assets. In this case, the dividend is known as a **return of capital** or a **liquidating dividend**. Although the source of the funds makes little difference to a firm or to investors directly, there is a difference in tax treatment: A return of capital is taxed as a capital gain rather than as a dividend for the investor.

FIGURE 17.3

Dividend History for
GM Stock, 1983–2008

Starting in 1983, GM paid a regular dividend each quarter until July 2008, when it suspended its dividend due to financial difficulties. GM paid additional special dividends in December 1997 and May 1999.

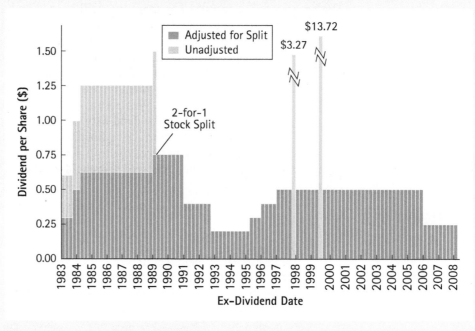

Share Repurchases

liquidating dividend A return of capital to shareholders from a business operation that is being terminated.

An alternative way to pay cash to investors is through a share repurchase or buyback. In this kind of transaction, the firm uses cash to buy shares of its own outstanding stock. These shares are generally held in the corporate treasury and they can be resold if the company needs to raise money in the future. We now examine three possible transaction types for a share repurchase.

open market repurchase When a firm repurchases its own shares by buying them on the open market over time.

Open Market Repurchase. With an **open market repurchase**, the most common way that firms repurchase shares, a firm announces its intention to buy its own shares on the open market and then proceeds to do so over time similar to any other investor. The firm may take a year or more to buy the shares and it is not obligated to repurchase the full amount it originally stated. Also, the firm must not buy its shares in a way that might appear to manipulate the price. For example, SEC guidelines recommend that the firm not purchase more than 25% of the average daily trading volume in its shares on a single day, nor make purchases at the market open or within 30 minutes of the close of trade.[2]

While open market share repurchases represent about 95% of all repurchase transactions,[3] other methods are available to a firm that wants to buy back its stock. These methods are used when a firm wishes to repurchase a substantial portion of its shares, often as part of a recapitalization.

tender offer A public announcement of an offer to all existing security holders to buy back a specified amount of outstanding securities at a prespecified price over a short time period, generally 20 days.

Tender Offer. A firm can repurchase shares through a **tender offer** in which it offers to buy shares at a prespecified price during a short time period, generally within 20 days. The price

---

[2]SEC Rule 10b-18, introduced in 1983, defines the guidelines for open market share repurchases.

[3]G. Grullon and D. Ikenberry, "What Do We Know About Stock Repurchases?" *Journal of Applied Corporate Finance,* 13 (1) (2000): 31–51.

Dutch auction Shareholders indicate prices and quantities of shares for sale. The firm pays the lowest possible price to repurchase its desired number of shares.

targeted repurchase A firm purchases shares directly from a specific shareholder at a negotiated price.

greenmail When a firm avoids takeover and removal of its management by a major shareholder by buying-out that shareholder, often at a premium.

is usually set at a substantial premium (10%–20% is typical) to the current market price. The offer often depends on shareholders tendering a sufficient number of shares. If shareholders do not tender enough shares, the firm may cancel the offer and no buyback occurs.

A related method is the **Dutch auction** share repurchase, in which the firm lists different prices at which it is prepared to buy shares, and shareholders in turn indicate how many shares they are willing to sell at each price. The firm then pays the lowest price at which it can buy back its desired number of shares.

Targeted Repurchase. A firm may also purchase shares directly from a major shareholder in a **targeted repurchase**. In this case, the purchase price is negotiated directly with the seller. A targeted repurchase may occur if a major shareholder desires to sell a large number of shares but the market for the shares is not sufficiently liquid to sustain such a large sale without severely affecting the price. Under these circumstances, the shareholder may be willing to sell shares back to the firm at a discount to the current market price. Alternatively, targeted repurchases may be used if a major shareholder is threatening to take over the firm and remove its management. With **greenmail**, the firm may decide to eliminate the threat by buying out the shareholder—often at a large premium over the current market price.

CONCEPT CHECK

1. How is a stock's ex-dividend date determined, and what is its significance?
2. What is an open market share repurchase?

17.2 Dividends Versus Share Repurchases in a Perfect Capital Market

If a corporation decides to pay cash to shareholders, it can do so through either dividend payments or share repurchases. How do firms choose between these alternatives? In this section, we show that in the perfect capital markets setting of Modigliani and Miller, the method of payment does not matter.

Consider the case of Genron Corporation, a hypothetical firm. Genron has $20 million in excess cash and no debt. The firm expects to generate additional free cash flows of $48 million per year in subsequent years. If Genron's unlevered cost of capital is 12%, then the enterprise value of its ongoing operations is:

$$\text{Enterprise Value} = PV(\text{Future FCF}) = \frac{\$48 \text{ million}}{12\%} = \$400 \text{ million}$$

Including the cash, Genron's total market value is $420 million.

Genron's board is meeting to decide how to pay out its $20 million in excess cash to shareholders. The board is considering three options:

1. Use the $20 million to pay a $2 cash dividend for each of Genron's 10 million outstanding shares.
2. Repurchase shares instead of paying a dividend.
3. Raise additional cash to pay an even larger dividend today and in the future.

Will the amount of the current dividend affect Genron's share price? Which policy would shareholders prefer?

To provide a baseline for our discussion of payout policy, we will analyze the consequences of each of these three alternative policies in the following sections and compare them in a setting of perfect capital markets. We will also explore how market imperfections such as taxes and transaction costs affect payout policy.

Alternative Policy 1: Pay a Dividend with Excess Cash

Suppose the board opts for the first alternative and uses all excess cash to pay a dividend. With 10 million shares outstanding, Genron will be able to pay a $2 dividend immediately. Because the firm expects to generate future free cash flows of $48 million per year, it anticipates paying a dividend of $4.80 per share each year thereafter. The board declares the dividend and sets the record date as December 14, so that the ex-dividend date is December 12. To determine the impact of this decision, let's compute Genron's share price just before and after the stock goes ex-dividend.

Recall from Chapter 7 and the Valuation Principle that the fair price for the shares is the present value of the expected dividends given Genron's equity cost of capital. Because Genron has no debt, its equity cost of capital equals its unlevered cost of capital of 12%. Just before the ex-dividend date, the stock is said to trade **cum-dividend** ("with the dividend") because anyone who buys the stock will be entitled to the dividend. In this case:

cum-dividend When a stock trades before the ex-dividend date, entitling anyone who buys the stock to the dividend.

$$P_{cum} = \text{Current Dividend} + PV(\text{Future Dividends}) = 2 + \frac{4.80}{0.12} = 2 + 40 = \$42$$

After the stock goes ex-dividend, new buyers will not receive the current dividend. At this point, the share price will reflect only the dividends in subsequent years:

$$P_{ex} = PV(\text{Future Dividends}) = \frac{4.80}{0.12} = \$40$$

The share price will drop on the ex-dividend date, December 12, from $42 to $40. The amount of the price drop is equal to the amount of the current dividend, $2. We can also determine this change in the share price using the market value balance sheet (values in millions of dollars):

	December 11 (Cum-Dividend)	December 12 (Ex-Dividend)
Cash	20	0
Other assets	400	400
Total market value	420	400
Shares (millions)	10	10
Share price	$42	$40

As the market value balance sheet shows, the share price falls when a dividend is paid because the reduction in cash decreases the market value of the firm's assets. Although the stock price falls, holders of Genron stock do not incur a loss overall. Before the dividend, their stock was worth $42. After the dividend, their stock is worth $40 and they hold $2 in cash from the dividend, for a total value of $42. Our analysis of both the stock price and the market value balance sheet shows that:

> *In a perfect capital market, when a dividend is paid, the share price drops by the amount of the dividend when the stock begins to trade ex-dividend.*

Alternative Policy 2: Share Repurchase (No Dividend)

Suppose that Genron does not pay a dividend this year, but instead uses the $20 million to repurchase its shares on the open market. How will the repurchase affect the share price?

With an initial share price of $42, Genron will repurchase $20 million ÷ $42 per share = 0.476 million shares, leaving only 10 − 0.476 = 9.524 million shares outstanding. Once again, we can use Genron's market value balance sheet to analyze this transaction:

	December 11 (Before Repurchase)	December 12 (After Repurchase)
Cash	20	0
Other assets	400	400
Total market value of assets	420	400
Shares (millions)	10	9.524
Share price	$42	$42

In this case, the market value of Genron's assets falls when the company pays out cash, but the number of shares outstanding also falls from 10 million to 9.524 million. The two changes offset each other, so the share price remains the same at $42.

Genron's Future Dividends. We can also see why the share price does not fall after the share repurchase by considering the effect on Genron's future dividends. In future years, Genron expects to have $48 million in free cash flow, which can be used to pay a dividend of $48 million ÷ 9.524 million shares = $5.04 per share each year. Thus, with a share repurchase, Genron's share price today is:

$$P_{rep} = \frac{5.04}{0.12} = \$42$$

In other words, by not paying a dividend today and repurchasing shares instead, Genron is able to raise its dividends *per share* in the future. The increase in future dividends compensates shareholders for the dividend they give up today. This example illustrates the following general conclusion about share repurchases:

> *In perfect capital markets, an open market share repurchase has no effect on the stock price, and the stock price is the same as the cum-dividend price if a dividend were paid instead.*

Investor Preferences. Would an investor prefer that Genron issue a dividend or repurchase its stock? Both policies lead to the same *initial* share price of $42. But is there a difference in shareholder value *after* the transaction? Consider an investor who currently holds 2000 shares of Genron stock. Assuming the investor does not trade the stock, the investor's holdings after a dividend or share repurchase are as follows:

Dividend	Repurchase
$40 × 2000 = $80,000 stock	$42 × 2000 = $84,000 stock
$2 × 2000 = $4000 cash	

In either case, the value of the investor's portfolio is $84,000 immediately after the transaction. The only difference is the distribution between cash and stock holdings. Thus, it might seem the investor would prefer one approach or the other based on whether she needs the cash.

But if Genron repurchases shares and the investor wants cash, she can raise cash by selling shares. For example, she can sell 95 shares to raise 95 × $42 per share = $3990 in cash. She will then hold 1905 shares, or 1905 × $42 = $80,010 in stock. Thus, in the case of a share repurchase, by selling shares an investor can create a *homemade dividend*.

Repurchases and the Supply of Shares

There is a misconception that when a firm repurchases its own shares, the price rises due to the decrease in the supply of shares outstanding. This intuition follows naturally from the standard supply and demand analysis taught in microeconomics. Why does that analysis not apply here?

When a firm repurchases its own shares, two things happen. First, the supply of shares is reduced. At the same time, however, the value of the firm's assets declines when it spends its cash to buy the shares. If the firm repurchases its shares at their market price, these two effects offset each other, leaving the share price unchanged.

This result is similar to the dilution fallacy discussed in Chapter 16: When a firm issues shares at their market price, the share price does not fall due to the increase in supply. The increase in supply is offset by the increase in the firm's assets that results from the cash it receives from the issuance.

Similarly, if Genron pays a dividend and the investor does not want the cash, she can use the $4000 proceeds of the dividend to purchase 100 additional shares at the ex-dividend share price of $40 per share. As a result, she will hold 2100 shares, worth $2100 \times \$40 = \$84,000$. In fact, many firms allow investors to register for a dividend reinvestment program, or *DRIP*, that automatically reinvests any dividends into new shares of the stock.

We summarize these two cases below:

Dividend + Buy 100 Shares	Repurchase ÷ Sell 95 Shares
$40 × 2100 = $84,000 stock	$42 × 1905 = $80,010 stock
	$42 × 95 = $3990 cash

By selling shares or reinvesting dividends, the investor can create any combination of cash and stock desired. As a result, the investor is indifferent between the various payout methods the firm might employ:

In perfect capital markets, investors are indifferent between the firm distributing funds via dividends or share repurchases. By reinvesting dividends or selling shares, they can replicate either payout method on their own.

Alternative Policy 3: High Dividend (Equity Issue)

Let's look at a third possibility for Genron. Suppose the board wishes to pay an even larger dividend than $2 per share right now. Is that possible and, if so, will the higher dividend make shareholders better off?

Genron plans to pay $48 million in dividends starting next year. Suppose the firm wants to start paying that amount today. Because it has only $20 million in cash today, Genron needs an additional $28 million to pay the larger dividend now. It could raise cash by scaling back its investments. But if the investments have positive NPV, reducing them would lower the firm's value. An alternative way to raise more cash is to borrow money or sell new shares. Let's consider an equity issue. Given a current share price of $42, Genron could raise $28 million by selling $28 million ÷ $42 per share = 0.67 million shares. Because this equity issue will increase Genron's total number of shares outstanding to 10.67 million, the amount of the dividend per share each year will be:

$$\frac{\$48 \text{ Million}}{10.67 \text{ Million Shares}} = \$4.50 \text{ per Share}$$

Under this new policy, Genron's cum-dividend share price is:

$$P_{cum} = 4.50 + \frac{4.50}{0.12} = 4.50 + 37.50 = \$42$$

As in the previous examples, the initial share value is unchanged by this policy, and increasing the dividend has no benefit to shareholders.

EXAMPLE 17.1

Homemade
Dividends

MyFinanceLab

PROBLEM

Suppose Genron does not adopt the third alternative policy and instead pays a $2 dividend per share today. Show how an investor holding 2000 shares could create a homemade dividend of $4.50 per share × 2000 shares = $9000 per year on her own.

SOLUTION

PLAN

If Genron pays a $2 dividend, the investor receives $4000 in cash and holds the rest in stock. She can raise $5000 in additional cash by selling 125 shares at $40 per share just after the dividend is paid.

EXECUTE

The investor creates her $9000 this year by collecting the $4000 dividend and then selling 125 shares at $40 per share. In future years, Genron will pay a dividend of $4.80 per share. Because she will own 2000 − 125 = 1875 shares, the investor will receive dividends of 1875 × $4.80 = $9000 per year from then on.

EVALUATE

Again, the policy that the firm chooses is irrelevant—the investor can transact in the market to create a homemade dividend policy that suits her preferences.

Modigliani-Miller and Dividend Policy Irrelevance

In our analysis, we considered three possible dividend policies for the firm: (1) pay out all cash as a dividend, (2) pay no dividend and use the cash instead to repurchase shares, or (3) issue equity to finance a larger dividend. These policies are illustrated in Table 17.1.

Table 17.1 shows an important tradeoff: If Genron pays a higher *current* dividend per share, it will pay lower *future* dividends per share. For example, if the firm raises the current dividend by issuing equity, it will have more shares and therefore smaller free cash flows per share to pay dividends in the future. If the firm lowers the current dividend and repurchases its shares, it will have fewer shares in the future, so it will be able to pay a higher dividend per share. The net effect of this tradeoff is to leave the total present value of all future dividends, and hence the current share price, unchanged at $42.

The logic of this section matches that in our discussion of capital structure in Chapter 16. There, we explained that in perfect capital markets, buying and selling equity and debt are zero-NPV transactions that do not affect firm value. Moreover, any choice of leverage by a firm could be replicated by investors using homemade leverage. As a result, the firm's choice of capital structure is irrelevant. Here, we have established the same principle for a firm's choice of a dividend. Regardless of the amount of cash the firm has on hand, it can pay a smaller dividend (and use the remaining cash to repurchase shares) or a larger dividend (by selling equity to raise cash). Because buying or selling shares is a zero-NPV transaction, such transactions have no effect on the initial share price.

TABLE 17.1

Genron's Dividends
per Share Each Year
Under the Three
Alternative Policies

		Dividend Paid ($ per share)			
	Initial Share Price	Year 0	Year 1	Year 2	...
Policy 1:	$42.00	2.00	4.80	4.80	...
Policy 2:	$42.00	0	5.04	5.04	...
Policy 3:	$42.00	4.50	4.50	4.50	...

MM Dividend Irrelevance In perfect capital markets, holding fixed the investment policy of a firm, the firm's choice of dividend policy is irrelevant and does not affect the initial share price.

Furthermore, shareholders can create a homemade dividend of any size by buying or selling shares themselves.

Modigliani and Miller developed this idea in another influential paper published in 1961.[4] As with their result on capital structure, it went against the conventional wisdom that dividend policy could change a firm's value and make its shareholders better off even if there were no market imperfections. We state here their important proposition:

MM Dividend Irrelevance: *In perfect capital markets, holding fixed the investment policy of a firm, the firm's choice of dividend policy is irrelevant and does not affect the initial share price.*

COMMON MISTAKE

The Bird in the Hand Fallacy

"A bird in the hand is worth two in the bush."

The bird in the hand hypothesis states that firms choosing to pay higher current dividends will enjoy higher stock prices because shareholders prefer current dividends to future ones (with the same present value). According to this view, alternative policy 3 would lead to the highest share price for Genron.

This view is a misconception. Modigliani and Miller showed that with perfect capital markets, shareholders can generate an equivalent homemade dividend at any time by selling shares. Thus, the dividend choice of the firm should not matter.

Dividend Policy with Perfect Capital Markets

The examples in this section illustrate the idea that by using share repurchases or equity issues a firm can easily alter its dividend payments. Because these transactions do not alter the value of the firm, neither does dividend policy.

This result may at first seem to contradict the idea that the price of a share should equal the present value of its future dividends. As our examples have shown, however, a firm's choice of dividend today affects the dividends it can afford to pay in the future in an offsetting fashion. Thus, although dividends *do* determine share prices, a firm's choice of dividend policy does not.

As Modigliani and Miller made clear, the value of a firm ultimately derives from its underlying free cash flows. A firm's free cash flows determine the level of payouts that it can make to its investors. In a perfect capital market, whether these payouts are made through dividends or share repurchases does not matter. Of course, in reality capital markets are not perfect. As with capital structure, it is the imperfections in capital markets that should determine the firm's payout policy. The main imperfection we will discuss is taxes: Repurchases and dividends have different tax implications and investors also face different tax rates. In addition, when managers have information investors do not, payout policy decisions can help signal that information. We start with taxes.

CONCEPT CHECK

3. Explain the misconception that when a firm repurchases its own shares, the price rises due to the decrease in the supply of shares outstanding.

4. In a perfect capital market, how important is the firm's decision to pay dividends versus repurchase shares?

---

[4]See F. Modigliani and M. Miller, "Dividend Policy, Growth, and the Valuation of Shares," *Journal of Business*, 34 (4) (1961): 411–433. See also J. B. Williams, *The Theory of Investment Value* (Cambridge, MA: Harvard University Press, 1938).

17.3   The Tax Disadvantage of Dividends

As with capital structure, taxes are an important market imperfection that influences a firm's decision to pay dividends or repurchase shares.

Taxes on Dividends and Capital Gains

Shareholders typically must pay taxes on the dividends they receive. They must also pay capital gains taxes when they sell their shares. Table 17.2 shows the history of U.S. tax rates from 1971–2016 applied to dividends and long-term capital gains for investors in the highest tax bracket.

TABLE 17.2

Long-Term Capital Gains Versus Dividend Tax Rates in the United States, 1971–2016

Year	Capital Gains	Dividends
1971–1978	35%	70%
1979–1981	28%	70%
1982–1986	20%	50%
1987	28%	39%
1988–1990	28%	28%
1991–1992	28%	31%
1993–1996	28%	40%
1997–2000	20%	40%
2001–2002	20%	39%
2003–2012	15%	15%
2013–2016*	20%	20%

The tax rates shown are for financial assets held for one year. For assets held less than one year, capital gains are taxed at the ordinary income tax rate (currently 39.6% for the highest bracket); the same is true for dividends if the assets are held for less than 61 days. Because the capital gains tax is not paid until the asset is sold, for assets held for longer than one year the *effective* capital gains tax rate is equal to the present value of the rate shown, when discounted by the after-tax risk-free interest rate for the additional number of years the asset is held.

* Rates were still current when this book went to press in late 2016.

Do taxes affect investors' preferences for dividends versus share repurchases? When a firm pays a dividend, shareholders are taxed according to the dividend tax rate. If the firm repurchases shares instead, and shareholders sell shares to create a homemade dividend, the homemade dividend will be taxed according to the capital gains tax rate. If dividends are taxed at a higher rate than capital gains, which had been true until the change to the tax code in 2003, shareholders will prefer share repurchases to dividends. Recent changes to the tax code have equalized the tax rates on dividends and capital gains. It is probably not coincidental that Microsoft started paying dividends shortly after these changes. Furthermore, a number of U.S. companies issued special dividends and accelerated regular dividends in December 2012 right before dividend tax rates were set to increase in 2013. Nonetheless, because long-term investors can defer the capital gains tax until they sell, *there is still a tax advantage for share repurchases over dividends*.

Not all countries tax dividends at a higher rate than capital gains. Figure 17.4 shows the dividend and capital gains tax rates for different countries. In Finland, for example, capital gains are taxed at a 33% rate, while dividends are taxed at 29%. A similar tax preference for dividends exists in Estonia and the Slovak Republik.

Optimal Dividend Policy with Taxes

When the tax rate on dividends exceeds the tax rate on capital gains, shareholders will pay lower taxes if a firm uses share repurchases for all payouts rather than dividends. This tax savings will increase the value of a firm that uses share repurchases rather than dividends.

FIGURE 17.4

Dividend and Capital Gains Tax Rates Around the World

The capital gains tax rate (red bar) and dividend tax rate (blue bar) for different countries are shown. A missing bar indicates that the distribution is exempt from taxation in that country. Whereas most countries tax dividends at rates greater than or equal to the rate for capital gains, providing a tax preference for share repurchases, some countries, such as Finland, tax capital gains at a higher rate. Several countries, including Singapore and Hong Kong (not pictured), do not tax either.

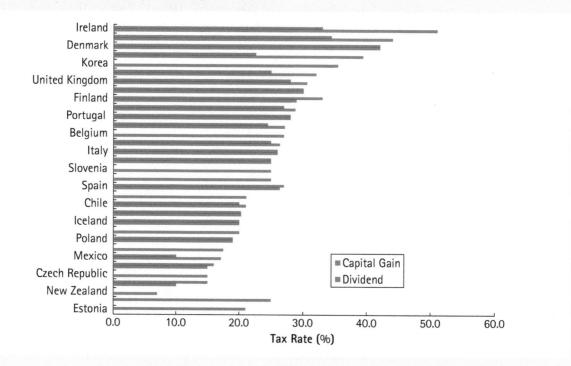

Source: OECD 2015, www.oecd.org; capital gains rates based on marginal rate for an investor with $100,000 in income exceeding any initial exemption.

We can also express the tax savings in terms of a firm's equity cost of capital. Firms that use dividends will have to pay a higher pretax return (and thus a higher equity cost of capital) to offer their investors the same after-tax return as firms that use share repurchases. As a result, the optimal dividend policy when the dividend tax rate exceeds the capital gain tax rate is to *pay no dividends at all*.

Dividends in Practice. While firms do still pay dividends, substantial evidence shows that many firms have recognized their tax disadvantage. For example, prior to 1980, most firms used dividends exclusively to distribute cash to shareholders (see Figure 17.5). But by 2000, only about 20% of firms relied exclusively on dividends. Starting in the early 2000's, this trend has partially reversed. By 2015 the fraction of firms that relied exclusively on dividends rose to about 40%, most likely driven by the Bush administration's dramatic lowering of the dividend tax rate in 2003 (see Table 17.2). A relatively stable 30% of all firms (and more than half of firms making payouts to shareholders) used share repurchases exclusively or in combination with dividends.

FIGURE 17.5

The Rise of Repurchases

This figure shows the percentage of U.S. firms making payouts to shareholders. The shaded regions show the firms that used dividends exclusively (*blue*), repurchases exclusively (*green*), or both (*red*). Because firms that repurchase shares do not usually do so every year, we classify a firm as using repurchases if it repurchased that year or the previous year. Note that after steadily declining for more than 20 years, dividend use has been on the rise since 2000. However, as Figure 17.6 shows, repurchases now account for the largest part of the total value of distributions.

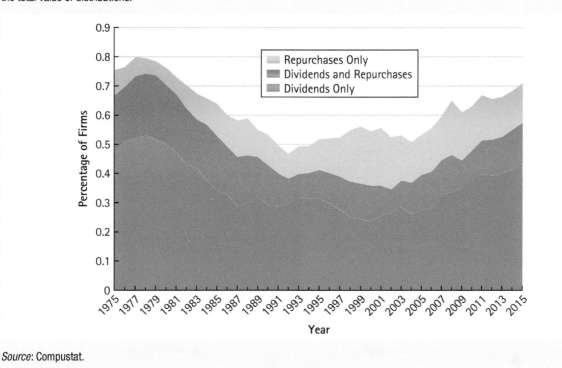

Source: Compustat.

We see a more dramatic trend if we consider the relative magnitudes of both forms of corporate payouts. Figure 17.6 shows the relative importance of share repurchases as a proportion of total payouts to shareholders. Although dividends accounted for more than 80% of corporate payouts until the early 1980s, the importance of share repurchases grew dramatically in the mid-1980s. Repurchase activity slows during recessions (see 1990–1991, 2001–2002, and 2009). This fact highlights the flexibility companies have to adjust repurchase payouts as their profits fluctuate. At the same time, there is a strong expectation that companies will maintain dividend payouts unless they are near distress. Partly due to this flexibility and the tax advantages, by the end of the 1990s distributions through repurchasing surpassed those through dividends.

While this evidence is indicative of the growing importance of share repurchases as a part of firms' payout policies, it also shows that dividends remain a key form of payouts to shareholders. The fact that firms continue to issue dividends despite their tax disadvantage is often referred to as the **dividend puzzle**.[5] Table 17.3 summarizes dividends versus repurchases, highlighting the differences between the two ways to distribute cash to shareholders. In the next section, we consider some factors that may mitigate this tax disadvantage. In Section 17.5, we examine alternative motivations for using dividends based on differences in information between managers and investors.

dividend puzzle When firms continue to issue dividends despite their tax disadvantage.

---

[5]See F. Black, "The Dividend Puzzle," *Journal of Portfolio Management*, 2 (1976): 5–8.

FIGURE 17.6

The Changing
Composition of
Shareholder
Payouts

This figure shows the value of share repurchases as a percentage of total payouts to shareholders (dividends and repurchases). Although initially small, the total dollar amount of share repurchases has grown faster than dividends, so that by the late 1990s share repurchases surpassed dividends to become the largest form of corporate payouts for U.S. industrial firms.

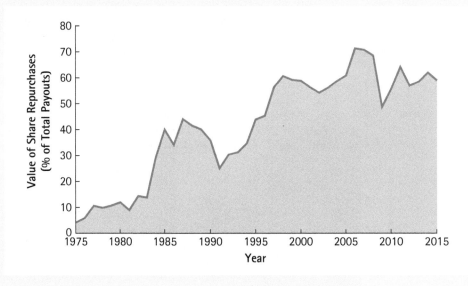

Source: Compustat/CRSP data for U.S. firms, excluding financial firms and utilities.

TABLE 17.3 Summary of Dividends Versus Repurchases

	Dividends	**Share Repurchases**
How cash is distributed to shareholders	Cash payment made on a per-share basis to all shareholders	Shares are bought back from some shareholders
Participation	Involuntary (everyone with a share receives a dividend)	Voluntary (shareholders choose whether to sell their shares)
Taxation for ordinary investors	Generally taxed as ordinary income, but taxed at 20% as of 2016	Taxed as capital gains, 20% as of 2016
Effect on share price	Share price drops by the amount of the dividend	Share price is unaffected as long as shares are repurchased at a fair (market) price

Tax Differences Across Investors

Even though many investors have a tax preference for share repurchases rather than dividends, the strength of that preference depends on the difference between the dividend tax rate and the capital gains tax rate that they face. Tax rates vary by income, by jurisdiction, and by whether the stock is held in a retirement account. Because of these differences, firms may attract different groups of investors depending on their dividend policy. In this section, we highlight the differences in the tax treatment of dividends across investors and discuss how that leads different groups of investors to prefer different payout policies.

Dividend Tax Rate Factors. Tax rates on dividends and capital gains differ across investors for a variety of reasons:

Income Level.   Investors with different levels of income fall into different tax brackets and face different tax rates.

Investment Horizon.   Capital gains on stocks held less than one year, and dividends on stocks held for less than 61 days, are taxed at higher ordinary income tax rates. Long-term investors can defer the payment of capital gains taxes (lowering their effective capital gains tax rate even further). Investors who plan to bequeath stocks to their heirs avoid the capital gains tax altogether.

Tax Jurisdiction.   U.S. investors are subject to state taxes that differ by state. For example, New Hampshire imposes a 5% tax on income from interest and dividends, but no tax on capital gains. Foreign investors in U.S. stocks are subject to 30% withholding for dividends they receive (unless that rate is reduced by a tax treaty with their home country). There is no similar withholding for capital gains.

Type of Investor or Investment Account.   Stocks held by individual investors in a retirement account are not subject to taxes on dividends or capital gains. Similarly, stocks held through pension funds or nonprofit endowment funds are not subject to dividend or capital gains taxes. Corporations that hold stocks are able to exclude 70% of dividends they receive from corporate taxes, but are unable to exclude capital gains.[6]

As a result of their different tax rates, these investors have varying preferences regarding dividends:

1. Long-term investors are more heavily taxed on dividends, so they would prefer share repurchases to dividend payments.

2. One-year investors, pension funds, and other non-taxed investors have no tax preference for share repurchases over dividends; they would prefer a payout policy that most closely matches their cash needs. For example, a non-taxed investor who desires current income would prefer high dividends so as to avoid the brokerage fees and other transaction costs of selling the stock.

3. Corporations enjoy a tax *advantage* associated with dividends due to the 70% exclusion rule. For this reason, a corporation that chooses to invest its cash will prefer to hold stocks with high dividend yields.

clientele effects When the dividend policy of a firm reflects the tax preferences of its investor clientele.

Clientele Effects.   Table 17.4 summarizes the different preferences across investor groups. These differences in tax preferences create **clientele effects**, in which the dividend policy of a firm is optimized for the tax preference of its investor clientele. Individuals in the highest tax brackets have a preference for stocks that pay no or low dividends, whereas tax-free investors and corporations have a preference for stocks with high dividends. In this case, a firm's dividend policy is optimized for the tax preference of its investor clientele.

TABLE 17.4

Differing Dividend Policy Preferences Across Investor Groups

Investor Group	Dividend Policy Preference	Proportion of Investors
Individual investors	Tax disadvantage for dividends Prefer share repurchase	~52%
Institutions, pension funds, retirement accounts	No tax preference Prefer dividend policy that matches income needs	~47%
Corporations	Tax advantage for dividends	~1%

Source: Proportions based on *Federal Reserve Flow of Funds Accounts*, 2015.

---

[6]Corporations can exclude 80% if they own more than 20% of the shares of the firm paying the dividend.

Evidence supports the existence of tax clienteles. For example, Professors Franklin Allen and Roni Michaely[7] report that in 1996 individual investors held 54% of all stocks by market value, yet received only 35% of all dividends paid, indicating that individuals tend to hold stocks with low dividend yields. Of course, the fact that high-tax investors receive any dividends at all implies that the clienteles are not perfect—dividend taxes are not the only determinants of investors' portfolios.

5. Under what conditions will investors have a tax preference for share repurchases rather than dividends?

6. What is the dividend puzzle?

17.4 Payout Versus Retention of Cash

Looking back at Figure 17.1, we have thus far considered only one aspect of a firm's payout policy: the choice between paying dividends and repurchasing shares. But how should a firm decide the amount it should pay out to shareholders and the amount it should retain?

To answer this question, first we must consider what the firm will do with cash that it retains. It can invest the cash in new projects or in financial instruments. In the next section, we will examine these options in the context of perfect capital markets.

Retaining Cash with Perfect Capital Markets

Once a firm has taken all positive-NPV projects, it is left with the question of whether to retain any remaining cash or distribute it to shareholders. If the firm retains the cash, it can hold the cash in the bank or use it to purchase financial assets. The firm can then pay the money to shareholders at a future time or invest it when positive-NPV investment opportunities become available.

What are the advantages and disadvantages of retaining cash and investing in financial securities? In perfect capital markets, buying and selling securities is a zero-NPV transaction, so it should not affect a firm's value. On their own, shareholders can make any financial investment a firm makes if the firm pays out the cash. Thus, it should not be surprising that with perfect capital markets, the retention versus payout decision—just like the dividend versus share repurchase decision—is irrelevant.

EXAMPLE 17.2

Payout Decisions in a Perfect Capital Market

MyFinanceLab

PROBLEM

Barston Mining has $100,000 in excess cash. Barston is considering investing the cash in one-year Treasury bills paying 2% interest, and then using the cash to pay a dividend next year. Alternatively, the firm can pay a dividend immediately and shareholders can invest the cash on their own. In a perfect capital market, which option would shareholders prefer?

SOLUTION

PLAN

We need to compare what shareholders would receive from an immediate dividend ($100,000) to the present value of what they would receive in one year if Barston invested the cash.

---

[7]F. Allen and R. Michaely, "Payout Policy," in *Handbook of the Economics of Finance: Corporate Finance*, G. M. Constantinides, M. Harris, and R. M. Stulz, Eds., Vol. 1A (Amsterdam, The Netherlands: Elsevier, 2003), Chap. 7.

EXECUTE

If Barston retains the cash, at the end of one year the company would be able to pay a dividend of $100,000 \times (1.02) = \$102,000$. Note that this payoff is the same as if shareholders had invested the $100,000 in Treasury bills themselves. In other words, the present value of this future dividend is exactly $102,000 \div (1.02) = \$100,000$, which is the same as the $100,000 shareholders would receive from an immediate dividend. Thus, shareholders are indifferent about whether the firm pays the dividend immediately or retains the cash.

EVALUATE

Because Barston is not doing anything that the investors could not have done on their own, it does not create any value by retaining the cash and investing it for the shareholders versus simply paying it to them immediately. As we showed with Genron in Example 17.1, if Barston retains the cash, but investors prefer to have the income today, they could sell $100,000 worth of shares.

As the example illustrates, there is no difference for shareholders if the firm pays the cash immediately or retains the cash and pays it out at a future date. This example provides yet another illustration of Modigliani and Miller's fundamental insight regarding financial policy irrelevance in perfect capital markets:

MM Payout Irrelevance
In perfect capital markets, if a firm invests excess cash flows in financial securities, the firm's choice of payout versus retention is irrelevant and does not affect the initial value of the firm.

MM Payout Irrelevance: *In perfect capital markets, if a firm invests excess cash flows in financial securities, the firm's choice of payout versus retention is irrelevant and does not affect the initial value of the firm.*

Retaining Cash with Imperfect Capital Markets

Based on MM Payout Irrelevance, it is clear that the decision of whether to retain cash depends on market imperfections, which we now address.

Taxes and Cash Retention. The Barston example assumed perfect capital markets, and so ignored the effect of taxes. How would our result change with taxes?

EXAMPLE 17.3
Retaining Cash with Corporate Taxes

MyFinanceLab

PROBLEM

Recall Barston Mining from Example 17.2. Suppose Barston must pay corporate taxes at a 35% rate on the interest it will earn from the one-year Treasury bill paying 2% interest. Would pension fund investors (who do not pay taxes on their investment income) prefer that Barston use its excess cash to pay the $100,000 dividend immediately or retain the cash for one year?

SOLUTION

PLAN

As in the original example, the comparison is between what shareholders could generate on their own and what shareholders will receive if Barston retains and invests the funds for them. The key question then is: What is the difference between the after-tax return that Barston can earn and distribute to shareholders versus the pension fund's tax-free return on investing the $100,000?

EXECUTE

Because the pension fund investors do not pay taxes on investment income, the results from the prior example still hold: They would get $100,000, invest it, and earn 2% to receive a total of $102,000 in one year.
   If Barston retains the cash for one year, it will earn an after-tax return on the Treasury bills of:

$$2\% \times (1 - 0.35) = 1.30\%$$

Thus, at the end of the year Barston will pay a dividend of $100,000 \times (1.013) = \$101,300$.

(Continued)

EVALUATE

This amount is less than the $102,000 the investors would have earned if they had invested the $100,000 in Treasury bills themselves. Because Barston must pay corporate taxes on the interest it earns, there is a tax disadvantage to retaining cash. Pension fund investors will therefore prefer that Barston pays the dividend now.

As Example 17.3 shows, corporate taxes make it costly for a firm to retain excess cash. This effect is the very same effect we identified in Chapter 16 with regard to leverage: When a firm pays interest, it receives a tax deduction for that interest, whereas when a firm receives interest, it owes taxes on the interest. Cash can be thought of as equivalent to *negative* leverage, so the tax advantage of leverage implies a tax disadvantage to holding cash.

Investor Tax Adjustments. The decision to pay out versus retain cash may also affect the taxes paid by shareholders. Although pension and retirement fund investors are tax exempt, most individual investors must pay taxes on interest, dividends, and capital gains. How do investor taxes affect the tax disadvantage of retaining cash?

Because the dividend tax will be paid whether the firm pays the cash immediately or retains the cash and pays the interest over time, the dividend tax rate does not affect the cost of retaining cash. However, when a firm retains cash, it must pay corporate tax on the interest it earns. In addition, the investor will owe capital gains tax on the increased value of the firm. In essence, the interest on retained cash is taxed twice. If the firm paid the cash to its shareholders instead, they could invest it and be taxed only once on the interest that they earn. The cost of retaining cash therefore depends on the combined effect of the corporate and capital gains taxes, compared to the single tax on interest income. Under most tax regimes there remains a substantial tax *disadvantage* for the firm to retaining excess cash even after adjusting for investor taxes.

Issuance and Distress Costs. If there is a tax disadvantage to retaining cash, why do some firms accumulate large cash balances? Generally, they retain cash balances to cover potential future cash shortfalls. For example, if there is a reasonable likelihood that future earnings will be insufficient to fund future positive-NPV investment opportunities, a firm may start accumulating cash to make up the difference. This motivation is especially relevant for firms that may need to fund large-scale research and development projects or large acquisitions.

The advantage of holding cash to cover future potential cash needs is that this strategy allows a firm to avoid the transaction costs of raising new capital (through new debt or equity issues). As we showed in Figure 14.7, for larger new capital issuances the direct costs of issuance range from 1% to 3% for debt issues and from 3.5% to 7% for equity issues. There can also be substantial indirect costs of raising capital due to the agency and adverse selection (lemons) costs discussed in Chapter 16. A firm must therefore balance the tax costs of holding cash with the potential benefits of not having to raise external funds in the future. Firms with very volatile earnings may also build up cash reserves to enable them to weather temporary periods of operating losses. By holding sufficient cash, these firms can avoid financial distress and its associated costs.

Agency Costs of Retaining Cash. There is no benefit to shareholders when a firm holds cash above and beyond its future investment or liquidity needs, however. In fact, in addition to the tax cost, there are likely to be agency costs associated with having too much cash in the firm. As discussed in Chapter 16, when firms have excessive cash, managers may use the funds inefficiently by continuing money-losing pet projects, paying excessive executive perks, or overpaying for acquisitions. Leverage is one way to reduce a firm's excess cash; dividends and share repurchases perform a similar role by taking cash out of the firm.

Thus, paying out excess cash through dividends or share repurchases can boost the stock price by reducing managers' ability and temptation to waste resources. For example, on April 23, 2004, Value Line announced it would use its accumulated cash to pay a special dividend of $17.50 per share. Value Line stock increased by roughly $10 on the announcement of its special dividend, very likely due to the perceived tax benefits and reduced agency costs that would result from the transaction.

EXAMPLE 17.4

Cutting Negative-NPV Growth

MyFinanceLab

PROBLEM

Rexton Oil is an all-equity firm with 100 million shares outstanding. Rexton has $150 million in cash and expects future free cash flows of $65 million per year. Management plans to use the cash to expand the firm's operations, which will in turn increase future free cash flows to $72.8 million per year. If the cost of capital of Rexton's investments is 10%, how would a decision to use the cash for a share repurchase rather than the expansion change the share price?

SOLUTION

PLAN

We can use the perpetuity formula to value Rexton under the two scenarios. The repurchase will take place at market prices, so the repurchase itself will have no effect on Rexton's share price. The main question is whether spending $150 million now (instead of repurchasing) to increase cash flows by $7.8 million per year is a positive-NPV project.

EXECUTE

Invest: Using the perpetuity formula, if Rexton invests the $150 million to expand, its market value will be $72.8 million ÷ 10% = $728 million, or $7.28 per share with 100 million shares outstanding.

Repurchase: If Rexton does not expand, the value of its future free cash flows will be $65 million ÷ 10% = $650 million. Adding the $150 million in cash it currently has, Rexton's market value is $800 million, or $8.00 per share.

If Rexton repurchases shares, there will be no change to the share price: It will repurchase $150 million ÷ $8.00 per share = 18.75 million shares, so it will have assets worth $650 million with 81.25 million shares outstanding (100 million shares − 18.75 million shares repurchased). That implies a share price of $650 million ÷ 81.25 million shares = $8.00 per share.

In this case, cutting investment and growth to fund a share repurchase increases the share price by $0.72 per share ($8.00 − $7.28).

EVALUATE

The share price is higher with the repurchase because the alternative of expansion has a negative NPV: It costs $150 million, but increases future free cash flows by only $7.8 million per year forever, for an NPV of:

$$-\$150 \text{ million} + \$7.8 \text{ million}/10\% = -\$72 \text{ million, or } -\$0.72 \text{ per share}$$

Thus, by avoiding the expansion, the repurchase keeps the shares from suffering the $0.72 loss.

Ultimately, firms should choose to retain cash for the same reasons they would use low leverage—to preserve financial slack for future growth opportunities and to avoid financial distress costs. These needs must be balanced against the tax disadvantage of holding cash and the agency cost of wasteful investment. It is not surprising then that high-tech and biotechnology firms, which typically choose to use little debt, also tend to retain and accumulate large amounts of cash. See Table 17.5 for a list of selected firms with large cash balances.

As with capital structure decisions, however, even though a firm's board of directors sets its payout policy, that policy is generally heavily influenced by managers whose

TABLE 17.5

Selected Firms with
Large Cash Balances

Ticker	Company	Cash & Marketable Securities ($ billion)	Percentage of Market Capitalization	Mkt Cap
AAPL	Apple Inc.	215.7	37%	586.8
GE	General Electric	113.8	39%	294
MSFT	Microsoft	102.3	23%	443.2
GOOGL	Alphabet (Google)	73.1	14%	528.4
CSCO	Cisco Systems	59.1	43%	137.8
ORCL	Oracle Corporation	52.3	34%	153.5
AMGN	Amgen, Inc.	31.4	26%	122.5
GM	General Motors	20.3	38%	52.9

Source: Google Finance, January 2016.

incentives may differ from those of shareholders. Managers may prefer to retain and maintain control over the firm's cash rather than pay it out. The retained cash can be used to fund investments that are costly for shareholders but have benefits for managers (for instance, pet projects and excessive salaries), or it can simply be held as a means to reduce leverage and the risk of financial distress that could threaten managers' job security. According to the managerial entrenchment theory of payout policy, managers pay out cash only when pressured to do so by the firm's investors.

CONCEPT CHECK

7. Is there an advantage for a firm to retain its cash instead of paying it out to shareholders in perfect capital markets?

8. How do corporate taxes affect the decision of a firm to retain excess cash?

17.5 Signaling with Payout Policy

One market imperfection that we have not yet considered is asymmetric information. When managers have better information than investors regarding the future prospects of the firm, their payout decisions may signal this information. In this section, we look at managers' motivations when setting a firm's payout policy, and we evaluate what these decisions may communicate to investors.

Dividend Smoothing

Firms can change dividends at any time, but in practice they vary the sizes of their dividends relatively infrequently. For example, General Motors (GM) changed the amount of its regular dividend only eight times over a 20-year period. Yet during that same period, GM's earnings varied widely, as shown in Figure 17.7.

The pattern seen with GM is typical of most firms that pay dividends. Firms adjust dividends relatively infrequently, and dividends are much less volatile than earnings. This practice of maintaining relatively constant dividends is called **dividend smoothing**. Firms also increase dividends much more frequently than they cut them. For example, from 1971 to 2001, only 5.4% of dividend changes were decreases.[8] In a classic survey of corporate executives, John Lintner suggested that these observations resulted from (1) management's belief that investors prefer stable dividends with sustained growth and (2) management's

dividend smoothing The practice of maintaining relatively constant dividends.

---

[8]F. Allen and R. Michaely, "Payout Policy," in G. Constantinides, M. Harris, and R. Stulz, eds., *Handbook of the Economics of Finance* (2003).

desire to maintain a long-term target level of dividends as a fraction of earnings.[9] Thus, firms raise their dividends only when they perceive a long-term sustainable increase in the expected level of future earnings, and cut them only as a last resort. While this is perhaps a good description of how firms *do* set their dividends, as we have shown in this chapter there is no clear reason why firms *should* smooth their dividends. One explanation is that it contributes to signaling with dividends, as discussed in the next section.

How can firms keep dividends smooth as earnings vary? As we have already discussed, firms can maintain almost any level of dividend in the short run by adjusting the number of shares they repurchase or issue and the amount of cash they retain. However, due to the tax and transaction costs of funding a dividend with new equity issues, managers do not wish to commit to a dividend that the firm cannot afford to pay out of regular earnings. For this reason, firms generally set dividends at a level they expect to be able to maintain based on the firm's earnings prospects.

Dividend Signaling

If firms smooth dividends, the firm's dividend choice will contain information regarding management's expectations of future earnings.

1. When a firm increases its dividend, it sends a positive signal to investors that management expects to be able to afford the higher dividend for the foreseeable future.

2. When managers cut the dividend, it may signal that they have given up hope that earnings will rebound in the near term and so need to reduce the dividend to save cash.

FIGURE 17.7

GM's Earnings and Dividends per Share, 1985–2008

Compared to GM's earnings, its dividend payments were relatively stable until it finally suspended them in 2008 prior to filing for bankruptcy the next year. (Data adjusted for splits, earnings exclude extraordinary items.)

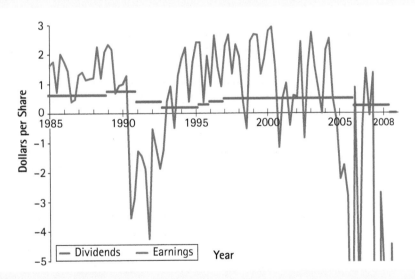

Source: Compustat and Capital IQ.

[9]J. Lintner, "Distribution of Incomes of Corporations Among Dividends, Retained Earnings and Taxes," *American Economic Review*, 46 (1956): 97–113.

dividend signaling hypothesis The idea that dividend changes reflect managers' views about a firm's future earnings prospects.

The idea that dividend changes reflect managers' views about a firm's future earnings prospects is called the **dividend signaling hypothesis**.

While an increase of a firm's dividend may signal management's optimism regarding its future cash flows, it might also signal a lack of investment opportunities. For example, Microsoft's move to initiate dividends in 2003 was largely seen as a result of its declining growth prospects as opposed to a signal about its increased future profitability.[10] Conversely, a firm might cut its dividend to exploit new positive-NPV investment opportunities. In this case, the dividend decrease might lead to a positive—rather than negative—stock price reaction (see the box about Royal & SunAlliance's dividend cut). In general, we must interpret dividends as a signal in the context of the type of new information managers are likely to have.

Royal & SunAlliance's Dividend Cut

In some quarters, Julian Hance must have seemed like a heretic. On November 8, 2001, the finance director of Royal & SunAlliance, a U.K.-based insurance group with £12.6 billion ($20.2 billion) in annual revenue, did the unthinkable—he announced that he would cut the firm's dividend.

Many observers gasped at the decision. Surely, they argued, cutting the dividend was a sign of weakness. Didn't companies cut their dividend only when profits were falling?

Quite the contrary, countered Hance. With insurance premiums rising around the world, particularly following the World Trade Center tragedy, Royal & SunAlliance believed that its industry offered excellent growth opportunities.

"The outlook for business in 2002 and beyond makes a compelling case for reinvesting capital in the business rather than returning it to shareholders," explained Hance.

The stock market agreed with him, sending Royal & SunAlliance's shares up 5% following its dividend news. "Cutting the dividend is a positive move," observed Matthew Wright, an insurance analyst at Credit Lyonnais. "It shows the company expects future profitability to be good."

Source: Justin Wood, http://CFOEurope.com, December 2001.

Signaling and Share Repurchases

Share repurchases, similar to dividends, may also signal managers' information to the market. However, several important differences distinguish share repurchases and dividends:

1. Managers are much less committed to share repurchases than to dividend payments. As we noted earlier, when firms announce authorization for an open market share repurchase, they generally announce the maximum amount they plan to spend on repurchases. The actual amount spent, however, may be far less. Also, it may take several years to complete the share repurchase.

2. Firms do not smooth their repurchase activity from year to year, as they do with dividends. Thus, announcing a share repurchase today does not necessarily represent a long-term commitment to repurchase shares. In this regard, share repurchases may be less of a signal than dividends are about future earnings of a firm.

3. The cost of a share repurchase depends on the market price of the stock. If managers believe the stock is currently over-valued, a share repurchase will be costly to the firm. That is, buying the stock at its current (over-valued) price is a negative-NPV investment. By contrast, repurchasing shares when managers perceive the stock to be under-valued is a positive-NPV investment. Managers will clearly be more likely to repurchase shares if they believe the stock to be under-valued.

---

[10]See "An End to Growth?" *The Economist* (July 22, 2004): 61.

JOHN CONNORS

John Connors was Senior Vice President and Chief Financial Officer of Microsoft. He retired in 2005 and is now a partner at Ignition Partners, a Seattle venture capital firm.

QUESTION: *Microsoft declared a dividend for the first time in 2003. What goes into the decision of a company to initiate a dividend?*

ANSWER: Microsoft was in a unique position. The company had never paid a dividend and was facing shareholder pressure to do something with its $60 billion cash buildup. The company considered five key questions in developing its distribution strategy:

1. Can the company sustain payment of a cash dividend in perpetuity and increase the dividend over time? Microsoft was confident it could meet that commitment and raise the dividend in the future.

2. Is a cash dividend a better return to stockholders than a stock buyback program? These are capital structure decisions: Do we want to reduce our shares outstanding? Is our stock attractively priced for a buyback, or do we want to distribute the cash as a dividend? Microsoft had plenty of capacity to issue a dividend and continue a buyback program.

3. What is the tax effect of a cash dividend versus a buyback to the corporation and to shareholders? From a tax perspective to shareholders, it was largely a neutral decision in Microsoft's case.

4. What is the psychological impact on investors, and how does it fit the story of the stock for investors? This is a more qualitative factor. A regular ongoing dividend put Microsoft on a path to becoming an attractive investment for income investors.

5. What are the public relations implications of a dividend program? Investors don't look to Microsoft to hold cash but to be a leader in software development and provide equity growth. So they viewed the dividend program favorably.

QUESTION: *How does a company decide whether to increase its dividend, have a special dividend, or repurchase its stock to return capital to investors?*

ANSWER: The decision to increase the dividend is a function of cash flow projections. Are you confident that you have adequate cash flow to sustain this and future increases? Once you increase the dividend, investors expect future increases as well. Some companies establish explicit criteria for dividend increases. In my experience as a CFO, the analytic framework involves a set of relative comparables. What are the dividend payouts and dividend yields of the market in general and of your peer group, and where are we relative to them? We talk to significant investors and consider what is best for increasing shareholder value long-term.

A special dividend is a very efficient form of cash distribution that generally involves a nonrecurring situation, such as the sale of a business division or a cash award from a legal situation. Also, companies without a comprehensive distribution strategy use special dividends to reduce large cash accumulations. For Microsoft, the 2004 special dividend and announcement of the stock dividend and stock buyback program resolved the issue of what to do with all the cash and clarified our direction going forward.

QUESTION: *What other factors go into dividend decisions?*

ANSWER: Powerful finance and accounting tools help us to make better and broader business decisions. But these decisions involve as much psychology and market thinking as math. You have to consider non-quantifiable factors such as the psychology of investors. Not long ago, everyone wanted growth stocks; no one wanted dividend-paying stocks. Now dividend stocks are in vogue. You must also take into account your industry and what the competition is doing. In many tech companies, employee ownership in the form of options programs represents a fairly significant percentage of fully diluted shares. Dividend distributions reduce the value of options.*

At the end of the day, you want to be sure that your cash distribution strategy helps your overall story with investors.

---

*We discuss options in Chapter 21. The key point here is that employee stock options increase in value when the stock price goes up, but as we learned in this chapter, a dividend reduces the stock price on the ex-dividend day.

Thus, share repurchases may signal that managers believe the firm to be under-valued (or at least not severely over-valued). Share repurchases are a credible signal that the shares are underpriced, because if they are overpriced a share repurchase is costly for current shareholders. If investors believe that managers have better information regarding the firm's prospects and act on behalf of current shareholders, then investors will react favorably to share repurchase announcements.

In a 2004 survey, 87% of CFOs agreed that firms should repurchase shares when their stock price is a good value relative to its true value.[11] Investors also appear to interpret share repurchases as a positive signal. The average market price reaction to the announcement of an open market share repurchase program is about 3% (with the size of the reaction increasing in the portion of shares outstanding sought).[12]

9. What possible signals does a firm give when it cuts its dividend?

10. Would managers be more likely to repurchase shares if they believe the stock is under- or over-valued?

17.6   Stock Dividends, Splits, and Spin-Offs

In this chapter, we have focused on a firm's decision to pay cash to its shareholders. But a firm can pay another type of dividend that does not involve cash: a stock dividend. In this case, each shareholder who owns the stock before it goes ex-dividend receives additional shares of stock of the firm itself (a stock split) or of a subsidiary (a spin-off). Here, we briefly review these two types of transactions.

Stock Dividends and Splits

stock dividend (stock split) When a company issues a dividend in shares of stock rather than cash to its shareholders.

In a **stock dividend** or **stock split**, the company issues additional shares rather than cash to its shareholders. If a company declares a 10% stock dividend, each shareholder will receive one new share of stock for every 10 shares already owned. Stock dividends of 50% or higher are generally referred to as stock splits. For example, with a 50% stock dividend, each shareholder will receive one new share for every two shares owned. Because a holder of two shares will end up holding three new shares, this transaction is also called a 3:2 ("3-for-2") stock split. Similarly, a 100% stock dividend is equivalent to a 2:1 stock split.

With a stock dividend, a firm does not pay out any cash to shareholders. As a result, the total market value of the firm's assets and liabilities, and therefore of its equity, is unchanged. The only thing that is different is the number of shares outstanding. The stock price will therefore fall because the same total equity value is now divided over a larger number of shares.

Unlike cash dividends, stock dividends are not taxed. Thus, from both the firm's and shareholders' perspectives, there is no real consequence to a stock dividend. The number of shares is proportionally increased and the price per share is proportionally reduced so that there is no change in value.

Stock Splits and Share Price. Why, then, do companies pay stock dividends or split their stock? The typical motivation for a stock split is to keep the share price in a range thought to be attractive to small investors. Stocks generally trade in lots of 100 shares, and in any case do not trade in units of less than one share. As a result, if the share price rises significantly, it might be difficult for small investors to afford one share, let alone 100. Making the stock more attractive to small investors can increase the demand for and the

---

[11]A. Brav, J. Graham, C. Harvey, and R. Michaely, "Payout Policy in the 21st Century," *Journal of Financial Economics*, 77 (3) (2005): 483–527.

[12]See D. Ikenberry, J. Lakonishok, and T. Vermaelen, "Market Underreaction to Open Market Share Repurchases," *Journal of Financial Economics*, 39 (2) (1995): 181–208.

Berkshire Hathaway's A and B Shares

Many managers split their stock to keep the price affordable for small investors, making it easier for them to buy and sell the stock. Warren Buffett, chairman and chief executive of Berkshire Hathaway, disagrees. As he commented in Berkshire's 1983 annual report, "We are often asked why Berkshire does not split its stock . . . we want [shareholders] who think of themselves as business owners with the intention of staying a long time. And, we want those who keep their eyes focused on business results, not market prices." In its 40-year history, Berkshire Hathaway has never split its stock.

As a result of Berkshire Hathaway's strong performance and the lack of stock splits, the stock price climbed. By 1996, it exceeded $30,000 per share. Because this price was much too expensive for some small investors, several financial intermediaries created unit investment trusts whose only investment was Berkshire shares. (Unit investment trusts are similar to mutual funds, but their investment portfolio is fixed.) Investors could buy smaller interests in these trusts, effectively owning Berkshire stock with a much lower initial investment.

In response, Buffett announced in February 1996 the creation of a second class of Berkshire Hathaway stock, the Class B shares. Each owner of the original shares (now called Class A shares) was offered the opportunity to convert each A share into 30 B shares. "We're giving shareholders a do-it-yourself split, if they care to do it," Buffett said. Through the B shares, investors could own Berkshire stock with a smaller investment, and they would not have to pay the extra transaction costs required to buy stock through the unit trusts.

In June 2016, the price of one share of Berkshire Hathaway Class A shares was $208,000.*

*We should note that Buffett's logic for not splitting the stock is a bit puzzling. It is unclear why allowing the stock price to rise to a very high level would attract the kind of investors Buffet wanted. If indeed this was the motivation for Buffet's policies, he could have obtained the desired results much earlier by simply doing a reverse stock split, where a company issues, for example, 1 new share for every 10 old shares.

liquidity of the stock, which may in turn boost the stock price. On average, announcements of stock splits are associated with a 2% increase in the stock price.[13]

Most firms use splits to keep their share prices from exceeding $100. From 1990 to 2000, Cisco Systems split its stock nine times, so that one share purchased at the IPO split into 288 shares. Had it not split, Cisco's share price at the time of its last split in March 2000 would have been 288 × $72.19, or $20,790.72.

Spin-Offs

spin-off When a firm sells a subsidiary by selling shares as a non-cash special dividend in the subsidiary alone.

Rather than pay a dividend using cash or shares of its own stock, a firm can also distribute shares of a subsidiary in a transaction referred to as a **spin-off**, where non-cash special dividends are used to spin off assets or a subsidiary as a separate company. For example, after selling 15% of Monsanto Corporation in an IPO in October 2000, Pharmacia Corporation announced in July 2002 that it would spin off its remaining 85% holding of Monsanto Corporation. The spin-off was accomplished through a special dividend in which each Pharmacia shareholder received 0.170593 share of Monsanto per share of Pharmacia owned. After receiving the Monsanto shares, Pharmacia shareholders could trade them separately from the shares of the parent firm.

Alternatively, Pharmacia could have sold the shares of Monsanto and distributed the cash to shareholders as a cash dividend. The transaction Pharmacia chose offers two advantages over the cash dividend strategy: (1) It avoids the transaction costs associated with such a sale and (2) the special dividend is not taxed as a cash distribution. Instead, Pharmacia shareholders who received Monsanto shares are liable for capital gains tax only at the time they sell the Monsanto shares.

CONCEPT CHECK
11. What is the difference between a stock dividend and a stock split?
12. What are some advantages of a spin-off as opposed to selling the division and distributing the cash?

[13]S. Nayak and N. Prabhala, "Disentangling the Dividend Information in Splits: A Decomposition Using Conditional Event-Study Methods," *Review of Financial Studies*, 14 (4) (2001): 1083–1116.

17.7 Advice for the Financial Manager

Payout policy decisions are related to the capital structure decisions we discussed in Chapter 16. The amount of debt the firm has determines how much cash flow is precommitted to debt holders as interest payments and how much will be left for possible distribution to shareholders or reinvestment in the firm. Furthermore, distributing capital to shareholders reduces the equity left in the firm, increasing leverage. When setting the amount of the payout to shareholders, the financial manager needs to carefully weigh the future investment plans of the firm. If the manager expects to make large investment expenditures in the near future, then it does not make sense to make a large distribution to shareholders only to quickly return to the markets for new capital financing (either through debt or additional equity as discussed in Chapters 14 and 15). Overall, as a financial manager you should consider the following when making payout policy decisions:

1. For a given payout amount, try to maximize the after-tax payout to the shareholders. Repurchases and dividends are often taxed differently and one can have an advantage over the other.

2. Repurchases and special dividends are useful for making large, infrequent distributions to shareholders. Neither implies any expectation of repeated payouts.

3. Starting and increasing a regular dividend is seen by shareholders as an implicit commitment to maintain this level of regular payout indefinitely. Only set regular dividend levels that you are confident the firm can maintain.

4. Because regular dividends are seen as an implicit commitment, they send a stronger signal of financial strength to shareholders than do infrequent distributions such as repurchases. However, this signal comes with a cost because regular payouts reduce a firm's financial flexibility.

5. Be mindful of future investment plans. There are transaction costs associated with both distributions and raising new capital, so it is expensive to make a large distribution and then raise capital to fund a project. It would be better to make a smaller distribution and fund the project internally.

Table 17.6 briefly summarizes these considerations as a series of questions you should ask yourself when deciding whether to make a distribution and what form it should take.

TABLE 17.6

Navigating the Payout Decision

Payout or Not	Dividend or Repurchase
Do we have any unfunded positive-NPV projects?	What are the tax implications for our shareholder base?
What are our future investment plans?	Do we value the flexibility that repurchases allow?
Do we have sufficient cash reserves to weather a recession without distress?	Do we need to send the stronger signal that dividends would convey?
Would we benefit from signaling financial strength to the market?	

MyFinanceLab

Here is what you should know after reading this chapter. MyFinanceLab will help you identify what you know, and where to go when you need to practice.

KEY POINTS AND EQUATIONS	KEY TERMS	ONLINE PRACTICE
17.1 Cash Distributions to Shareholders • When a firm wants to distribute cash to its shareholders, it can pay a cash dividend or it can repurchase shares. • Most companies pay regular, quarterly dividends. Sometimes firms announce one-time, special dividends. • Firms repurchase shares using an open market repurchase, a tender offer, a Dutch auction repurchase, or a targeted repurchase. • On the declaration date, firms announce that they will pay dividends to all shareholders of record on the record date. The ex-dividend date is the first day on which the stock trades without the right to an upcoming dividend; it is usually two trading days prior to the record date. Dividend checks are mailed on the payment date.	declaration date, p. 539 Dutch auction, p. 541 ex-dividend date, p. 539 greenmail, p. 541 liquidating dividend, p. 539 open market repurchase, p. 540 payable date (distribution date), p. 539 payout policy, p. 538 record date, p. 539 return of capital, p. 539 special dividend, p. 539 targeted repurchase, p. 541 tender offer, p. 540	MyFinanceLab Study Plan 17.1
17.2 Dividends Versus Share Repurchases in a Perfect Capital Market • In perfect capital markets, the stock price falls by the amount of the dividend when a dividend is paid. An open market share repurchase has no effect on the stock price, and the stock price is the same as the cum-dividend price if a dividend were paid instead. • The Modigliani-Miller dividend irrelevance proposition states that in perfect capital markets, holding fixed the investment policy of a firm, the firm's choice of dividend policy is irrelevant and does not affect the initial share price. • In reality, capital markets are not perfect, and market imperfections affect firm dividend policy.	cum-dividend, p. 542 MM Dividend Irrelevance, p. 546	MyFinanceLab Study Plan 17.2
17.3 The Tax Disadvantage of Dividends Taxes are an important market friction that affects dividend policy. • Considering taxes as the only market imperfection, when the tax rate on dividends exceeds the tax rate on capital gains, the optimal dividend policy is for firms to pay no dividends. Firms should use share repurchases for all payouts. • The tax impact of a dividend varies across investors for several reasons, including income level, investment horizon, tax jurisdiction, and type of investment account. • Different investor taxes create clientele effects, in which the dividend policy of a firm suits the tax preference of its investor clientele.	clientele effects, p. 551 dividend puzzle, p. 549	MyFinanceLab Study Plan 17.3

17.4 Payout Versus Retention of Cash • Modigliani-Miller payout policy irrelevance says that in perfect capital markets, if a firm invests excess cash flows in financial securities, the firm's choice of payout versus retention is irrelevant and does not affect the initial share price. • Corporate taxes make it costly for a firm to retain excess cash. Even after adjusting for investor taxes, retaining excess cash brings a substantial tax disadvantage for a firm. • Even though there is a tax disadvantage to retaining cash, some firms accumulate cash balances. Cash balances help firms minimize the transaction costs of raising new capital when they have future potential cash needs. However, there is no benefit to shareholders from firms holding cash in excess of future investment needs. • In addition to the tax disadvantage of holding cash, agency costs may arise, as managers may be tempted to spend excess cash on inefficient investments and perks. Without pressure from shareholders, managers may choose to horde cash to spend in this way or as a means of reducing a firm's leverage and increasing their job security. • Dividends and share repurchases help minimize the agency problem of wasteful spending when a firm has excess cash.	MM Payout Irrelevance, p. 553	MyFinanceLab Study Plan 17.4
17.5 Signaling with Payout Policy • Firms typically maintain relatively constant dividends. This practice is called dividend smoothing. • The idea that dividend changes reflect managers' views about a firm's future earnings prospects is called the dividend signaling hypothesis. • Managers usually increase dividends only when they are confident the firm will be able to afford higher dividends for the foreseeable future. • When managers cut the dividend, it may signal that they have lost hope that earnings will improve. • Share repurchases may be used to signal positive information, as repurchases are more attractive if management believes the stock is under-valued at its current price.	dividend signaling hypothesis, p. 558 dividend smoothing, p. 556	MyFinanceLab Study Plan 17.5
17.6 Stock Dividends, Splits, and Spin-Offs • In a stock dividend or a stock split, a company distributes additional shares rather than cash to shareholders. • With a stock dividend, shareholders receive either additional shares of stock of the firm itself (a stock split) or shares of a subsidiary (a spin-off). The stock price generally falls proportionally with the size of the split.	spin-off, p. 561 stock dividend (stock split), p. 560	MyFinanceLab Study Plan 17.6

CRITICAL THINKING	

1. What are the ways in which a corporation can distribute cash to its shareholders?

2. Describe the different mechanisms available to a firm for the repurchase of shares.

3. Without taxes or any other imperfections, why doesn't it matter how the firm distributes cash?

4. What kind of payout preference do tax codes typically create?

5. What are the advantages and disadvantages of retaining excess cash?

6. How can dividends and repurchases be used to signal managers' information about their firms' prospects?

7. Explain under which conditions an increase in the dividend payment can be interpreted as a signal of good news or bad news.

8. Why is an announcement of a share repurchase considered a positive signal?

9. Why do managers split their firms' stock?

PROBLEMS

All problems are available in MyFinanceLab. *An asterisk * indicates problems with a higher level of difficulty.*

Cash Distributions to Shareholders

1. ABC Corporation announced that it would pay a dividend to all shareholders of record as of Monday, April 5, 2010. It takes three business days after a purchase for the new owners of a share of stock to be registered.
   a. What was the date of the ex-dividend day?
   b. When was the last day an investor could have purchased ABC stock and still received the dividend payment?

2. RFC Corp. has announced a $1 dividend. If RFC's last price while trading cum-dividend is $50, what should its first ex-dividend price be (assuming perfect capital markets)?

3. ECB Co. has 1 million shares outstanding selling at $20 per share. It plans to repurchase 100,000 shares at the market price. What will its market capitalization be after the repurchase? What will its stock price be?

4. KMS corporation has assets of $500 million, $50 million of which are cash. It has debt of $200 million. If KMS repurchases $20 million of its stock:
   a. What changes will occur on its balance sheet?
   b. What will its new leverage ratio be?

5. Suppose that KMS in Problem 4 decides to initiate a dividend instead, but it wants the present value of the payout to be the same $20 million. If its cost of equity capital is 10%, to what amount per year in perpetuity should it commit (assuming perfect capital markets)?

Dividends Versus Share Repurchases in a Perfect Capital Market

6. EJH Company has a market capitalization of $1 billion and 20 million shares outstanding. It plans to distribute $100 million through an open market repurchase. Assuming perfect capital markets:
   a. What will the price per share of EJH be right before the repurchase?
   b. How many shares will be repurchased?
   c. What will the price per share of EJH be right after the repurchase?

7. Natsam Corporation has $250 million of excess cash. The firm has no debt and 500 million shares outstanding with a current market price of $15 per share. Natsam's board has decided to pay out this cash as a one-time dividend.
   a. What is the ex-dividend price of a share in a perfect capital market?
   b. If the board instead decided to use the cash to do a one-time share repurchase, in a perfect capital market, what is the price of the shares once the repurchase is complete?
   c. In a perfect capital market, which policy in part (a) or (b) makes investors in the firm better off?

8. Suppose the board of Natsam Corporation decided to do the share repurchase in Problem 7(b), but you as an investor would have preferred to receive a dividend payment. How can you leave yourself in the same position as if the board had elected to make the dividend payment instead?

The Tax Disadvantage of Dividends

9. The HNH Corporation will pay a constant dividend of $2 per share, per year, in perpetuity. Assume all investors pay a 20% tax on dividends and that there is no capital gains tax. The cost of capital for investing in HNH stock is 12%.
   a. What is the price of a share of HNH stock?
   b. Assume that management makes a surprise announcement that HNH will no longer pay dividends but will use the cash to repurchase stock instead. What is the price of a share of HNH stock now?

10. You purchased CSH stock for $40 and it is now selling for $50. The company has announced that it plans a $10 special dividend.
    a. Assuming 2016 tax rates, if you sell the stock or wait and receive the dividend, will you have different after-tax income?
    b. If the capital gains tax rate is 20% and the dividend tax rate is 40%, what is the difference between the two options in part (a)?

11. Using Table 17.2, for each of the following years, state whether dividends were tax disadvantaged or not for individual investors with a one-year investment horizon:
    a. 1985
    b. 1989
    c. 1995
    d. 1999
    e. 2005

Payout Versus Retention of Cash

12. Clovix Corporation has $50 million in cash, 10 million shares outstanding, and a current share price of $30. Clovix is deciding whether to use the $50 million to pay an immediate special dividend of $5 per share, or to retain and invest it at the risk-free rate of 10% and use the $5 million in interest earned to increase its regular annual dividend of $0.50 per share. Assume perfect capital markets.
    a. Suppose Clovix pays the special dividend. How can a shareholder who would prefer an increase in the regular dividend create it on her own?
    b. Suppose Clovix increases its regular dividend. How can a shareholder who would prefer the special dividend create it on her own?

13. You manage a (tax-free) pension fund that is invested in KOA Corporation. KOA's managers have just announced that they unexpectedly generated an extra $50 million in cash flow this year. They are considering paying it out now as a special dividend or

investing it in one-year Treasury securities that will earn 1% interest over the next year. They would then distribute the $50 million plus interest earned as a special dividend. If KOA pays a 35 corporate tax rate, would you prefer they pay the $50 million as a special dividend now or wait a year?

14. Assume perfect capital markets. Kay Industries currently has $100 million invested in short-term Treasury securities paying 7%, and it pays out the interest payments on these securities as a dividend. The board is considering selling the Treasury securities and paying out the proceeds as a one-time dividend payment.
    a. If the board went ahead with this plan, what would happen to the value of Kay stock upon the announcement of a change in policy?
    b. What would happen to the value of Kay stock on the ex-dividend date of the one-time dividend?
    c. Given these price reactions, will this decision benefit investors?

15. Redo Problem 14, but assume that Kay must pay a corporate tax rate of 35%, and that investors pay no taxes.

16. Redo Problem 14, but assume that investors pay a 15% tax on dividends but no capital gains taxes, and that Kay does not pay corporate taxes.

17. AMS Company has unexpectedly generated a one-time extra $5 million in cash-flow this year. After announcing the extra cash flow, AMS stock price was $55 per share (it has 1 million shares outstanding). The managers are considering spending the $5 million on a project that would generate a single cash flow of $5.5 million in one year, which they would then use to repurchase shares. Assume the cost of capital for the project is 12%.
    a. If they decide on the investment, what will happen to the price per share?
    b. If they instead use the $5 million repurchase stock immediately, what will be the price per share?
    c. Which decision is better and why?

Signaling with Payout Policy

Use the following information to answer Problems 18 through 22:

AMC Corporation currently has an enterprise value of $400 million and $100 million in excess cash. The firm has 10 million shares outstanding and no debt. Suppose AMC uses its excess cash to repurchase shares. After the share repurchase, news will come out that will change AMC's enterprise value to either $600 million or $200 million.

18. What is AMC's share price prior to the share repurchase?

19. What would AMC's share price be after the repurchase if its enterprise value goes up? What would AMC's share price be after the repurchase if its enterprise value declines?

*20. Suppose AMC waits until after the news comes out to do the share repurchase. What would AMC's share price be after the repurchase if its enterprise value goes up? What would AMC's share price be after the repurchase if its enterprise value declines?

21. Suppose AMC management expects good news to come out. Based on your answers to Problems 19 and 20, if management wants to maximize AMC's ultimate share price, will they undertake the repurchase before or after the news comes out? When would management undertake the repurchase if they expect bad news to come out?

*22. Given your answer to Problem 21, what effect would you expect an announcement of a share repurchase to have on the stock price? Why?

Stock Dividends, Splits, and Spin-Offs

23. FCF Co. has 20,000 shares outstanding and a total market value of $1 million, $300 thousand of which is debt and the other $700 thousand is equity. It is planning a 10% stock dividend.
    a. What is the stock price before the dividend and what will it be after the dividend?
    b. If an investor owns 1000 shares before the dividend, what will be the total value of her investment in FCF before and after the dividend?

24. Suppose the stock of Host Hotels & Resorts is currently trading for $20 per share.
    a. If Host issues a 20% stock dividend, what would its new share price be?
    b. If Host does a 3:2 stock split, what would its new share price be?

25. If Berkshire Hathaway's A shares are trading at $120,000, what split ratio would it need to bring its stock price down to $50?

26. After the market close on May 11, 2001, Adaptec, Inc., distributed a dividend of shares of the stock of its software division, Roxio, Inc. Each Adaptec shareholder received 0.1646 share of Roxio stock per share of Adaptec stock owned. At the time, Adaptec stock was trading at $10.55 per share (cum-dividend), and Roxio's share price was $14.23 per share. In a perfect market, what would be Adaptec's ex-dividend share price after this transaction?

DATA CASE

In your role as a consultant at a wealth management firm, you have been assigned a very powerful client who holds 1 million shares of Cisco Systems, Inc., purchased on February 28, 2003. In researching Cisco, you discovered that they are holding a large amount of cash. Additionally, your client is upset that the Cisco stock price has been somewhat stagnant as of late. The client is considering approaching the Board of Directors with a plan for half of the cash the firm has accumulated, but can't decide whether a share repurchase or a special dividend would be best. You have been asked to determine which initiative would generate the greatest amount of money after taxes, assuming that with a share repurchase your client would keep the same proportion of ownership. Because both dividends and capital gains are taxed at the same rate (20%), your client has assumed that there is no difference between the repurchase and the dividend. To confirm, you need to "run the numbers" for each scenario.

1. Go to finance.yahoo.com, enter the symbol for Cisco (CSCO), and click "Key Statistics."
   a. Record the current price and the number of shares outstanding.
   b. Click "Balance Sheet" under "Financials." Copy and paste the balance sheet data into Excel.

2. Using one-half of the most recent cash and cash equivalents reported on the balance sheet (in thousands of dollars), compute the following:
   a. The number of shares that would be repurchased given the current market price.
   b. The dividend per share that could be paid given the total number of shares outstanding.

3. Go to http://finance.yahoo.com to obtain the price at which your client purchased the stock on February 28, 2003.
   a. Enter the symbol for Cisco and click "Get Quotes."
   b. Click "Historical Prices," enter the date your client purchased the stock as the start date and the end date, and hit "Enter." Record the adjusted closing price.

4. Compute the total cash that would be received by your client under the repurchase and the dividend both before taxes and after taxes.

5. The calculation in step 4 reflects your client's immediate cash flow and tax liability, but it does not consider the final payoff for the client after any shares not sold in a repurchase are liquidated. To incorporate this feature, you first decide to see what happens if the client sells all remaining shares of stock immediately after the dividend or the repurchase. Assume that the stock price will fall by the amount of the dividend if a dividend is paid. What are the client's total after-tax cash flows (considering both the payout and the capital gain) under the repurchase of the dividend in this case?

6. Under which program would your client be better off before taxes? Which program is better after taxes, assuming the remaining shares are sold immediately after the dividend is paid?

7. Because your client is unlikely to sell all 1 million shares today, at the time of dividend/repurchase, you decide to consider two longer holding periods: Assume that under both plans the client sells all remaining shares of stock 5 years later, or the client sells 10 years later. Assume that the stock will return 10% per year going forward. Also assume that Cisco will pay no other dividends over the next 10 years.
   a. What would be the stock price after 5 years or 10 years if a dividend is paid now?
   b. What would be the stock price after 5 years or 10 years if Cisco repurchases shares now?
   c. Calculate the total after-tax cash flows at both points in time (when the dividend payment or the share repurchase takes place, and when the rest of the shares are sold) for your client if the remaining shares are sold in 5 years under both initiatives. Compute the difference between the cash flows under both initiatives at each point in time. Repeat assuming the shares are sold in 10 years.

8. Repeat Question 7 assuming the stock will return 20% per year going forward. What do you notice about the difference in the cash flows under the two initiatives when the return is 20% and 10%?

This case draws on material from Chapters 16 and 17.

Maria Suarez returned to her office after spending the afternoon meeting with her firm's investment bankers. Suarez was CFO of Midco Industries, a mid-sized manufacturing firm, and she was taking a hard look at its capital structure and payout policy. Suarez felt that Midco was underlevered and potentially not taking full advantage of the tax benefits of debt. Further complicating matters, Midco's institutional investors had been clamoring for either a repurchase or a special dividend.

One possibility floated by her investment bankers was a "leveraged recap," in which Midco would issue debt and use the proceeds to repurchase shares. Midco Industries has 20 million shares outstanding with a market price of $15 per share and no debt. The firm has had consistently stable earnings and pays a 35% tax rate. Midco's investment bankers proposed that the firm borrow $100 million on a permanent basis through a leveraged recap in which it would use the borrowed funds to repurchase outstanding shares.

As Suarez sat down at her desk, she stared at her notepad. She had written down several questions that she would need to answer before making her decision.

Case Questions

1. What are the tax consequences of the recap?
2. Based only on the tax effects and the Valuation Principle, what will be the total value of the firm after the recap?
   a. How much of the new value will be equity?
   b. How much will be debt?
3. At what price should Midco be able to repurchase its shares?
4. Who benefits from the recap? Who loses?
5. What other costs or benefits of the additional leverage should Midco's managers consider?
6. If Midco's managers decide to issue the debt and distribute the tax shield as a special dividend instead of repurchasing shares, what will the dividend per share be?

Financial Planning and Forecasting

Valuation Principle Connection. In Part 7, we turn to the details of running the financial side of a corporation and focus on forecasting and short-term financial management. We begin in Chapter 18 by developing the tools to forecast the cash flows and long-term financing needs of a firm. We then turn our attention to the important decisions a financial manager makes about the short-term financing and investments of a firm. In Chapter 19, we discuss how firms manage their working capital requirements, including accounts receivable, accounts payable, and inventory. In Chapter 20, we explain how firms finance their short-term cash needs.

In a perfect capital market, the Valuation Principle—in particular, the Law of One Price—and the Modigliani-Miller propositions imply that how a firm chooses to manage its short-term financial needs does not affect the value of the firm. In reality, short-term financial policy does matter because of the existence of market frictions. In Part 7, we identify these frictions and explain how firms set their short-term financial policies.

18

Financial Modeling and Pro Forma Analysis

LEARNING OBJECTIVES

- Understand the goals of long-term financial planning

- Create pro forma income statements and balance sheets using the *percent of sales method*

- Develop financial models of the firm by directly forecasting capital expenditures, working capital needs, and financing events

- Distinguish between the concepts of sustainable growth and value-increasing growth

- Use pro forma analysis to model the value of the firm under different scenarios, such as expansion

notation

FCF	free cash flow
PV	present value
ROA	return on assets

ROE	return on equity
SGR	sustainable growth rate

Most decisions a financial manager makes have long-term consequences. For example, in the late 1990s, Airbus managers decided to bet the future of the company on the market for mega-jets, giving the green light to development of the 555-seat A380. Shortly thereafter, Boeing managers bet that airlines would favor improvements in fuel efficiency and gave the go-ahead to the all-composite, technologically advanced 787. The outcomes of these decisions are still playing out today. In this chapter, we will learn how to build a financial model to analyze the consequences of our financial decisions well into the future. In particular, we will use these models to forecast when the firm will need to secure additional external funding and to determine how the decision will affect the value of the firm.

We will start by explaining the goals of forecasting through financial modeling and pro forma analysis, and how this analysis relates to the overall goal of maximizing firm value. Then, we will move to a basic forecasting technique based on projections of the firm's future sales. Next, we will develop an improved approach to forecasting that produces a more realistic financial model of the firm. We will end with a discussion of value-increasing versus value-decreasing growth. Putting the elements of the chapter together, we will see the connection between the role of forecasting, NPV analysis, and the Valuation Principle that underlies all of finance.

18.1   Goals of Long-Term Financial Planning

The goal of the financial manager is to maximize the value of the stockholders' stake in the firm. One tool to help with this goal is long-term financial planning and modeling. In the following sections, we will develop specific methods to forecast the financial statements and cash flows for the firm as a whole. For context, in this section we discuss the objectives of long-term planning.

Identify Important Linkages

As you will see in Sections 18.2 and 18.3, when you build a model of the future course of the firm, by necessity you will uncover important linkages between, for example, sales, costs, capital investment, and financing. A well-designed spreadsheet model will allow you to examine how a change in your cost structure will impact your future free cash flows, financing needs, and other items in the firm's budget. Some links may be obvious, but others are much more difficult to determine without building a forecast of the entire firm's financial statements years into the future. For example, technological improvements leading to reduced costs could allow the firm to reduce prices and sell more product. However, increased production will require more equipment and facilities, and the associated capital expenditures will require financing and create additional depreciation tax shields. None of these links would be easy to see without a careful forecasting model. This is an important outcome of long-term planning because it allows the financial manager to understand the business and, through that understanding, to increase its value.

Analyze the Impact of Potential Business Plans

Perhaps your firm is planning a big expansion or considering changes in how it manages its inventory. By building a long-term model of your firm's financials, you can examine exactly how such business plans will impact the firm's free cash flows and hence value. In Chapter 9, we developed the tools of capital budgeting with the goal of deciding whether to invest in a new project. To consider a fundamental change in the firm's business plan, the financial manager models the firm as a whole, rather than just a single project. In Section 18.3, we will analyze the impact of a firm-wide expansion plan, including necessary capital investment and debt financing. In Section 18.5, we will determine whether the expansion is a good idea by forecasting changes in free cash flows and calculating the change in firm value.

Plan for Future Funding Needs

Building a model for long-term forecasting reveals points in the future where the firm will need additional external financing—for example, where its retained earnings will not be enough to fund planned capital investment. Identifying the firm's funding needs in advance gives financial managers enough time to plan for them and line up the source of financing that is most advantageous for the firm. In a perfect capital market, this would be unnecessary—you would be able to secure financing instantaneously for any positive-NPV project and the source of financing would have no effect on the firm's value. However, in reality, market frictions mean that you need time to issue debt or new equity and, as we learned in Chapter 16, that financing decisions impact firm value. Thus, identifying and planning for these financing decisions far in advance is a valuable exercise.

1. How does long-term financial planning support the goal of the financial manager?
2. What are the three main things that the financial manager can accomplish by building a long-term financial model of the firm?

18.2 Forecasting Financial Statements: The Percent of Sales Method

We will illustrate our discussion of forecasting financial statements via an application: the fictional company KMS Designs. Assume KMS Designs is a boutique women's fashion house, specializing in affordable fashion-forward separates, with its own production facility. KMS Designs is a growing firm and its financial managers predict that it will need external financing to fuel its growth. In order to predict when KMS will need this financing and the amount the managers will need to secure, we need to prepare a financial model in Excel for KMS that will allow us to produce pro forma income statements and balance sheets. After developing a technique for forecasting, we will turn to the steps involved in preparing the pro forma income statement and balance sheet.

Percent of Sales Method

percent of sales method A forecasting method that assumes that as sales grow, many income statement and balance sheet items will grow, remaining the same percent of sales.

A common starting point for forecasting is the *percent of sales method*. The **percent of sales method** assumes that as sales grow, many income statement and balance sheet items will grow, remaining the same percent of sales. For example, Table 18.1 shows that KMS's costs excluding depreciation were 78% of sales in 2016. There were sales of $74,889 (in thousands). If KMS forecasts that sales will grow by 18% in 2017, then:

- Sales will grow to $74,889 \times 1.18 = \$88,369$.
- Costs excluding depreciation will remain 78% of sales, so that costs will be $88,369 \times 0.78 = \$68,928$ in 2017.[1]

We are essentially assuming that KMS will maintain its profit margins as its sales revenues grow. We proceed by making similar assumptions about working capital items on the balance sheet such as cash, accounts receivable, inventory, and accounts payable. The far-right column of Table 18.1 shows what percent of sales each of these items was in 2016. We can use those percentages to forecast part of the balance sheet in 2017. For example, if sales grow to $88,369 as we predict, then our inventory will need to grow to $88,369 \times 0.20 = \$17,674$ to support those sales.

Some of the items in the percent of sales column are marked "NM" for "Not Meaningful." For example, our assets and accounts payables might reasonably be expected to grow in line with sales, but our long-term debt and equity will not naturally grow in line with sales. Instead, the change in equity and debt will reflect choices we make about dividends and net new financing.

---

[1] For ease of exposition, we will base our forecast on a single year, 2016. Companies often take into account averages and trends over several years in forecasting for the future.

TABLE 18.1

KMS Designs' 2016
Income Statement and
Balance Sheet

	Year	2016	% of Sales
1			
2	**Income Statement ($000s)**		
3	**Sales**	74,889	100%
4	Costs Except Depreciation	−58,413	78%
5	**EBITDA**	16,476	22%
6	Depreciation	−5,492	7.333%
7	**EBIT**	10,984	15%
8	Interest Expense (net)	−306	NM*
9	**Pretax Income**	10,678	14%
10	Income Tax (35%)	−3,737	NM
11	**Net Income**	6,941	9%

*NM indicates representing the item as a percent of sales is not meaningful.

	Year	2016	% of Sales
1			
2	**Balance Sheet ($000s)**		
3	**Assets**		
4	Cash and Equivalents	11,982	16%
5	Accounts Receivable	14,229	19%
6	Inventories	14,978	20%
7	**Total Current Assets**	41,189	55%
8	Property, Plant, and Equipment	49,427	66%
9	**Total Assets**	90,616	121%
10	**Liabilities and Stockholders' Equity**		
11	Accounts Payable	11,982	16%
12	Debt	4,500	NM
13	**Total Liabilities**	16,482	NM
14	**Stockholders' Equity**	74,134	NM
15	**Total Liabilities and Equity**	90,616	121%

Pro Forma Income Statement

Table 18.2 shows KMS's pro forma income statement for 2017 along with how each line was determined. KMS is forecasting 18% growth in sales from 2016 to 2017. In addition to the sales forecast, we require three other details to prepare the pro forma income statement: costs excluding depreciation in 2016 as a percent of sales, depreciation as a percent of sales, and the tax rate. KMS's info from Table 18.1 is as follows:

- Costs excluding depreciation were 78% of sales.
- Depreciation was 7.333% of sales in 2016.
- KMS pays a 35% tax rate.

TABLE 18.2

KMS Designs' Pro
Forma Income
Statement for 2017

	Year	2016	2017	Calculation
1				
2	**Income Statement ($000s)**			
3	**Sales**	74,889	88,369	74,889 × 1.18
4	Costs Except Depreciation	−58,413	−68,928	78% of Sales
5	**EBITDA**	16,476	19,441	Lines 3 + 4
6	Depreciation	−5,492	−6,480	7.333% of Sales
7	**EBIT**	10,984	12,961	Lines 5 + 6
8	Interest Expense (net)	−306	−306	Remains the same
9	**Pretax Income**	10,678	12,655	Lines 7 + 8
10	Income Tax (35%)	−3,737	−4,429	35% of Line 9
11	**Net Income**	**6,941**	**8,226**	Lines 9 + 10

The one final assumption we need to make is about our interest expense.[2] We assume for now that it will remain the same as in 2016 because we will determine if our debt needs will change as part of the forecasting process.

Based on our pro forma balance sheet, we are forecasting an increase in net income of $8226 − $6941 = $1285, which represents an 18.5% increase over 2016 net income.[3] We now turn to forecasting the balance sheet to determine whether we will need any new financing in 2017 to pay for our growth. The net income we forecast in Table 18.2 will be one of the inputs to the pro forma balance sheet. The part of that net income not distributed as dividends will add to stockholders' equity on the balance sheet.

EXAMPLE 18.1

Percent of Sales

MyFinanceLab

PROBLEM

KMS has just revised its sales forecast downward. If KMS expects sales to grow by only 10% next year, what are its costs, except for depreciation, projected to be?

SOLUTION

PLAN

Forecasted 2017 sales will now be: $74,889 × (1.10) = $82,378. With this figure in hand and the information from Table 18.1, we can use the percent of sales method to calculate KMS's forecasted costs.

EXECUTE

From Table 18.1, we see that costs are 78% of sales. With forecasted sales of $82,378, that leads to forecasted costs except depreciation of $82,378 × (0.78) = $64,255.

EVALUATE

If costs remain a constant 78% of sales, then our best estimate is that they will be $64,255.

Pro Forma Balance Sheet

Forecasting the balance sheet using the percent of sales method requires a few iterating steps. In any balance sheet analysis, we know that assets and liabilities/equity must be equal. The assets and liabilities/equity sides of the pro forma balance sheet will not balance, however, until we make assumptions about how our equity and debt will grow with sales. We see this point in Table 18.3, where we have taken a first stab at the pro forma balance sheet (we will explain the details of the calculation below). Our assets are projected to be $8396 more than our liabilities and equity. The imbalance indicates that we will need $8396 in *net new financing* to fund our growth. **Net new financing** is the amount of additional external financing we will need to secure to pay for the planned increase in assets. It can be computed as:

net new financing The amount of additional external financing a firm needs to secure to pay for the planned increase in assets.

$$\text{Net New Financing} = \text{Projected Assets} - \text{Projected Liabilities and Equity}$$

Let's take a closer look at how we arrived at the $8396 figure. Because we are using the percent of sales method, we assume that assets increase in line with sales. Thus, total assets have increased by 18%, the same as sales. The liabilities side of the balance sheet is more complicated. The amount of dividends a company pays will affect the retained earnings it has to finance growth. Furthermore, any increases in debt or equity reflect capital

---

[2]The interest expense should be interest paid on debt, net of interest earned on any invested cash—just as interest paid is tax deductible, interest earned is taxable—so KMS's tax shield comes from its net interest expense. In order to focus on forecasting, we will assume that all cash held by KMS is a necessary part of its working capital needed for transactions. Thus, we assume that KMS holds all of its cash in a non-interest-bearing account. In Chapter 19, we will discuss alternative ways to invest cash.

[3]This is higher than the sales growth of 18% because we assumed that interest expenses would not increase.

TABLE 18.3

First-Pass Pro Forma Balance Sheet for 2017

	Year	2016	2017	Calculation
1	Year	2016	2017	Calculation
2	**Balance Sheet ($000s)**			
3	**Assets**			
4	Cash and Cash Equivalents	11,982	14,139	16% of Sales
5	Accounts Receivable	14,229	16,790	19% of Sales
6	Inventories	14,978	17,674	20% of Sales
7	**Total Current Assets**	41,189	48,603	Lines 4 + 5 + 6
8	Property, Plant, and Equipment	49,427	58,324	66% of Sales
9	**Total Assets**	90,616	106,927	Lines 7 + 8
10	**Liabilities**			
11	Accounts Payable	11,982	14,139	16% of Sales
12	Debt	4,500	4,500	Remains the same
13	**Total Liabilities**	16,482	18,639	Lines 11 + 12
14	**Stockholders' Equity**	74,134	79,892	74,134 + 70% of 8,226
15	**Total Liabilities and Equity**	90,616	98,531	Lines 13 + 14
16	**Net New Financing**		8,396	Line 9 − Line 15

structure decisions and require managers to actively raise capital, as discussed in Chapters 14 and 15. The bottom line is that we cannot simply assume debt and equity increase in line with sales.

In KMS's case, it has a policy of paying out 30% of its net income as dividends. Thus, $2468 of its forecasted $8226 net income will be distributed to stockholders as dividends:

2017 Net Income:	$8,226
−2017 Dividends (30% of NI)	−$2,468
=2017 Retained Earnings	= $5,758

The $5758 in retained earnings (the remaining 70% of net income after dividends are paid) adds to stockholders' equity on the balance sheet. As a result, stockholders' equity is forecast to increase from $74,134 to $79,892 in Table 18.3.

2016 Stockholders' Equity:	$74,134
+2017 Retained Earnings	+$5,758
=2017 Stockholders' Equity	= $79,892

We also assume that accounts payable will grow along with sales, remaining at 16% of sales as they were in 2016, so they are forecast to grow to $14,139. However, our initial assumption is that debt will remain the same, so our forecasted growth in liabilities and equity falls short of our forecasted growth in assets by $8396.

COMMON MISTAKE

Confusing Stockholders' Equity with Retained Earnings

It is easy to confuse new retained earnings, total retained earnings, and stockholders' equity. As in the example above, new retained earnings are the amount of net income left over after paying dividends. These new retained earnings are then added to the *total* accumulated retained earnings from the life of the firm. Total retained earnings makes up one part of stockholders' equity, which also includes the par value of the stock and any paid-in capital.

Making the Balance Sheet Balance: Net New Financing

How do we address this $8396 difference between assets and liabilities? The projected difference between KMS's assets and liabilities in the pro forma balance sheet indicates that KMS will need to obtain new financing from its investors. The net new financing of $8396 in this case is the amount we have to add to the liabilities and equity side of the pro forma balance sheet to make it balance.

While KMS definitely has to secure $8396 in new financing, it could come from new debt or new equity. We discussed the issues involved in the equity versus debt decision in Chapter 16. It is a complex decision weighing many factors. Rather than complicating our analysis here, we assume that KMS's financial managers have evaluated these factors and decided that the best way to finance the growth is through additional debt. Table 18.4 shows our second-pass pro forma balance sheet including the $8396 in additional debt financing that brings the sheet into balance.

TABLE 18.4

Second-Pass Pro Forma Balance Sheet for KMS

	Year	2016	2017	Calculation
1				
2	**Balance Sheet ($000s)**			
3	**Assets**			
4	Cash and Cash Equivalents	11,982	14,139	16% of Sales
5	Accounts Receivable	14,229	16,790	19% of Sales
6	Inventories	14,978	17,674	20% of Sales
7	**Total Current Assets**	41,189	48,603	Lines 4 + 5 + 6
8	Property, Plant, and Equipment	49,427	58,324	66% of Sales
9	**Total Assets**	90,616	106,927	Lines 7 + 8
10	**Liabilities**			
11	Accounts Payable	11,982	14,139	16% of Sales
12	Debt	4,500	**12,896**	4,500 + 8,396
13	**Total Liabilities**	16,482	27,035	Lines 11 + 12
14	**Stockholders' Equity**	74,134	79,892	74,134 + 70% of 8,226
15	**Total Liabilities and Equity**	90,616	106,927	Lines 13 + 14

We should note that the decision to take on additional debt in 2017 makes our initial assumption that our interest expense would remain constant in 2017 potentially incorrect. If KMS takes on the debt before the end of the year, then there will be a partial-year interest expense from the debt. We would need to adjust the pro forma income statement and iterate with the pro forma balance sheet to get the exact amount of new debt needed. However, we have achieved our primary objective: to identify a future funding need and determine approximately how much we will need and how we will fund it. This will give KMS's managers enough time to begin the debt-issuance process with its bankers. We also note that debt has more than doubled, which justifies our original decision not to assume that it will increase in proportion to sales.

EXAMPLE 18.2

Net New Financing

MyFinanceLab

PROBLEM

If instead of paying out 30% of earnings as dividends, KMS decides not to pay any dividend and instead retains all its 2016 earnings, how would its net new financing change?

SOLUTION

PLAN

KMS currently pays out 30% of its net income as dividends, so rather than retaining only $5758, it will retain the entire $8226. This will increase stockholders' equity, reducing the net new financing.

EXECUTE

The additional retained earnings are $8226 − $5758 = $2468. Compared to Table 18.3, stockholders' equity will be $79,892 + $2468 = $82,360 and total liabilities and equity will also be $2468 higher, rising to $100,999. Net new financing, the imbalance between KMS's assets and liabilities and equity, will decrease to $8396 − $2468 = $5928.

(Continued)

Year	2016	2017
Balance Sheet ($000s)		
Liabilities		
Accounts Payable	11,982	14,139
Debt	4,500	4,500
Total Liabilities	16,482	18,639
Stockholders' Equity	74,134	82,360
Total Liabilities and Equity	90,616	100,999
Net New Financing		5,928

EVALUATE

When a company is growing faster than it can finance internally, any distributions to shareholders will cause it to seek greater additional financing. It is important not to confuse the need for external financing with poor performance. Most growing firms need additional financing to fuel that growth as their expenditures for growth naturally precede their income from that growth. We will revisit the issue of growth and firm value in Section 18.4.

Choosing a Forecast Target

Forecasting by assuming fixed ratios of sales is very common. Another approach is to forecast by targeting specific ratios that the company either wants or needs to maintain. For example, debt covenants (such as those discussed in Chapter 15) often require a company to maintain certain levels of liquidity or minimum interest coverage. The lender does this by specifying, for example, a minimum current ratio (current assets/current liabilities) of 1.5, or a minimum cash flow to interest ratio of 1.2. The company would then incorporate these target ratios into its forecasts to ensure it will be in compliance with its loan covenants.

The need to consider other target ratios is an example of a larger issue in forecasting—that the firm's investment, payout, and financing decisions are linked together and cannot be treated separately. As we saw in Table 18.4, the balance sheet must balance. So a financial manager must understand that the firm can set an investment budget and a financing plan, and those will then determine what is available to pay out. Alternatively, a firm could decide on an investment budget and payout policy, and those will then determine the firm's financing position—perhaps in unintended ways. The bottom line is that a financial manager must balance all these linked decisions, and a careful forecast allows him or her to see the consequences of decisions.

CONCEPT CHECK

3. What is the basic idea behind the percent of sales method for forecasting?
4. How does the pro forma balance sheet help the financial manager forecast net new financing?

18.3 Forecasting a Planned Expansion

The percent of sales method is a useful starting point and may even be sufficient for mature companies with relatively stable but slow growth. Its shortcoming is handling the realities of fast growth requiring "lumpy" investments in new capacity. The typical firm cannot smoothly add capacity in line with expected sales. Instead, it must occasionally make a large investment in new capacity that it expects to be sufficient for several years. This kind of capacity expansion also implies that new funding will happen in large, infrequent financing rounds, rather than small increments each year as sales grow. However, we can address these realities in our long-term forecasting by modeling our capacity needs and capital expenditures directly. In this section, we consider a planned expansion by KMS and generate pro forma statements that allow us to decide whether the expansion will increase the value of KMS. First, we identify capacity needs and how to finance that capacity. Next, we construct pro forma income statements and forecast future free cash flows. Finally, we use those forecasted free cash flows to assess the impact of the expansion on firm value.

KMS's managers have constructed a detailed sales forecast by first forecasting the size of the market and what market share KMS can expect to capture. While the size of the market is generally based on demographics and the overall economy, KMS's market share will depend on the appeal of its product and its price, which KMS has forecast as well. KMS currently has the capacity to produce a maximum of 1.1 million units (i.e., 1100 thousand units). However, as detailed in Table 18.5, KMS expects both the total market size and its share of the market to grow to the point where the company will quickly exceed that capacity. Thus, KMS is considering an expansion that will increase its capacity to 2 million units—enough to handle its projected requirements through 2021.

TABLE 18.5

KMS's Forecasted Production Capacity Requirements

1	Year	2016	2017	2018	2019	2020	2021
2	**Production Volume (000s units)**						
3	Market Size	10,000	10,500	11,025	11,576	12,155	12,763
4	Market Share	10.0%	11.0%	12.0%	13.0%	14.0%	15.0%
5	Production Volume (Line 3 × Line 4)	1,000	1,155	1,323	1,505	1,702	1,914
6	**Additional Market Information**						
7	Average Sales Price	$ 74.89	$ 76.51	$ 78.04	$ 79.60	$ 81.19	$ 82.82

KMS Designs' Expansion: Financing Needs

The first step in our analysis is estimating KMS's financing needs based on the capital expenditures required for the expansion.

Capital Expenditures for the Expansion. The new equipment to increase KMS's capacity will cost $20 million and will need to be purchased in 2017 to meet the company's production needs. Table 18.6 details KMS's forecasted capital expenditures and depreciation over the next five years. Based on the estimates for capital expenditures and depreciation, this spreadsheet tracks the book value of KMS's plant, property, and equipment starting from the book value level at the beginning of 2016.[4] The depreciation entries in Table 18.6 are based on the appropriate depreciation schedule for each type of property. Those calculations are quite specific to the nature of the property; they are not detailed here but follow the conventions discussed in the appendix to Chapter 9. The depreciation shown will be

TABLE 18.6

KMS's Forecasted Capital Expenditures

1	Year	2016	2017	2018	2019	2020	2021
2	**Fixed Assets and Capital Investment ($000s)**						
3	Opening Book Value	49,919	49,427	66,984	67,486	67,937	68,344
4	Capital Investment	5,000	25,000	8,000	8,000	8,000	8,000
5	Depreciation	−5,492	−7,443	−7,498	−7,549	−7,594	−7,634
6	Closing Book Value	49,427	66,984	67,486	67,937	68,344	68,709

---

[4]In this table and elsewhere in the chapter, we display rounded numbers. Calculations such as Closing Book Value are based on the actual numbers in the spreadsheet with all significant digits. As a result, there will occasionally be a small discrepancy between the Excel-calculated value shown and the hand-calculated value using the rounded numbers displayed.

used for tax purposes.[5] KMS has ongoing capital investment requirements to cover the replacement of existing equipment—these were expected to be $5 million per year without the new equipment. The additional $20 million is reflected in 2017, bringing the total to $25 million for 2017 and increasing expected recurring investment to $8 million per year in years 2018–2021.

Financing the Expansion. While KMS believes it can fund recurring investment from its operating cash flows, as shown in Table 18.7, it will have to seek external financing for the $20 million in new equipment. KMS plans to finance the new equipment by issuing 10-year coupon bonds with a coupon rate of 6.8%. Thus, KMS will pay only interest on the bonds until the repayment of principal in 10 years. The principal on its outstanding debt of $4500 is also not due before 2021.

TABLE 18.7

KMS's Planned Debt
and Interest Payments

1	Year		2016	2017	2018	2019	2020	2021
2	Debt and Interest Table ($000s)							
3	Outstanding Debt		4,500	24,500	24,500	24,500	24,500	24,500
4	Net New Borrowing		—	20,000	—	—	—	—
5	Interest on Debt	6.80%	306	306	1,666	1,666	1,666	1,666

Given KMS's outstanding debt, its interest expense each year is computed as:[6]

$$\text{Interest in Year } t = \text{Interest Rate} \times \text{Ending Balance in Year } (t-1) \qquad (18.1)$$

As we saw in Chapter 16, the interest on the debt will provide a valuable tax shield to offset KMS's taxable income.

KMS Designs' Expansion: Pro Forma Income Statement

The value of any investment opportunity arises from the future cash flows it will generate. To estimate the cash flows resulting from the expansion, we begin by projecting KMS's future earnings. We then consider KMS's working capital and investment needs and estimate its free cash flows. With its free cash flows and projected interest tax shields, we can compute the value of KMS with and without the expansion to decide whether the benefit of the new equipment is worth the cost.

Forecasting Earnings. To build the pro forma income statement, we begin with KMS's sales. We calculate sales for each year from the estimates in Table 18.5 as follows:

$$\text{Sales} = \text{Market Size} \times \text{Market Share} \times \text{Average Sales Price} \qquad (18.2)$$

For example, in 2017, KMS has projected sales (in thousands) of 10,500 units × 11% market share × $76.51 average sales price = $88,369. We will assume that costs except depreciation will continue to be 78% of sales, so that our projected costs, except depreciation in 2017, will be 78% × $88,369 = $68,928. To arrive at forecasted earnings, we take the following steps:

- Deducting these operating expenses from KMS's sales, we can project EBITDA over the next five years, as shown in Table 18.8.

---

[5]Firms often maintain separate books for accounting and tax purposes, and they may use different depreciation assumptions for each. Because depreciation affects cash flows through its tax consequences, tax depreciation is more relevant for valuation.

[6]Equation 18.1 assumes that changes in debt occur at the end of the year. If debt changes during the year, it is more accurate to compute interest expenses based on the average level of debt during the year.

TABLE 18.8

Pro Forma Income
Statement for KMS
Expansion

	Year	2016	2017	2018	2019	2020	2021
1							
2	**Income Statement ($000s)**						
3	**Sales**	74,889	88,369	103,247	119,793	138,167	158,546
4	Costs Except Depreciation	−58,413	−68,928	−80,533	−93,438	−107,770	−123,666
5	**EBITDA**	16,476	19,441	22,714	26,354	30,397	34,880
6	Depreciation	−5,492	−7,443	−7,498	−7,549	−7,594	−7,634
7	**EBIT**	10,984	11,998	15,216	18,806	22,803	27,246
8	Interest Expense (net)	−306	−306	−1,666	−1,666	−1,666	−1,666
9	**Pretax Income**	10,678	11,692	13,550	17,140	21,137	25,580
10	Income Tax	−3,737	−4,092	−4,742	−5,999	−7,398	−8,953
11	**Net Income**	**6,941**	**7,600**	**8,807**	**11,141**	**13,739**	**16,627**

- Subtracting the depreciation expenses we estimated in Table 18.6, we arrive at KMS's earnings before interest and taxes.
- Next, we deduct interest expenses according to the schedule given in Table 18.7.
- The final expense is the corporate income tax. KMS pays a 35% tax rate, and the income tax is computed as:

$$\text{Income Tax} = \text{Pretax Income} \times \text{Tax Rate} \qquad (18.3)$$

After subtracting the income tax from the pretax income, we arrive at the forecasted net income as the bottom line in Table 18.8.

Working Capital Requirements. We have one more step before we are ready to forecast the free cash flows for KMS. Recall that increases in working capital reduce free cash flows. Thus, we still need to forecast KMS's working capital needs. The spreadsheet in Table 18.9 lists KMS's current working capital requirements and forecasts the firm's future working capital needs. (See Chapter 19 for a further discussion of working capital requirements and their determinants.) We have forecast that the minimum required cash will be 16% of sales, accounts receivable will be 19% of sales, inventory will be 20% of sales, and accounts payable will be 16% of sales, all as they were in 2016.

The minimum required cash represents the minimum level of cash needed to keep the business running smoothly, allowing for the daily variations in the timing of income and expenses. Firms generally earn little or no interest on these balances, which are held in cash or in a checking or short-term savings account. As a consequence, we account for this opportunity cost by including the cash balance as part of the firm's working capital. We will make the assumption that KMS distributes all cash in excess of the minimum required cash as dividends. If our forecast shows that KMS's cash flows will be insufficient to

TABLE 18.9

KMS Projected Working
Capital Needs

	Year	2016	2017	2018	2019	2020	2021
1							
2	**Working Capital ($000s)**						
3	**Assets**						
4	Cash	11,982	14,139	16,520	19,167	22,107	25,367
5	Accounts Receivable	14,229	16,790	19,617	22,761	26,252	30,124
6	Inventory	14,978	17,674	20,649	23,959	27,633	31,709
7	**Total Current Assets**	41,189	48,603	56,786	65,886	75,992	87,201
8	**Liabilities**						
9	Accounts Payable	11,982	14,139	16,520	19,167	22,107	25,367
10	**Total Current Liabilities**	11,982	14,139	16,520	19,167	22,107	25,367
11	**Net Working Capital**						
12	Net Working Capital (7 − 10)	29,207	34,464	40,266	46,719	53,885	61,833
13	Increase in Net Working Capital		5,257	5,802	6,453	7,166	7,948

fund the minimum required cash, then we know that we need to plan to finance those cash needs. Again, identifying these future funding needs is one of the advantages of forecasting.

If KMS instead retained some cash above the amount needed for transactions, the company would likely invest it in some short-term securities that earn interest. Most companies choose to do this to provide funds for future investment so that they do not need to raise as much capital externally. In this case, the excess amount of cash would not be included in working capital. We will discuss cash management in Chapter 19.

COMMON MISTAKE

Treating Forecasts as Fact

Forecasts, like much of finance, give the illusion of precision—we can produce an answer down to dollars and cents. As a result, it is easy to lose sight of the fact that the answer depends on a number of big assumptions that could easily turn out to be wrong. Although it is the financial manager's job to build the forecast and analyze it, he or she is highly dependent on all the other functional areas for input. Good financial managers will talk to operations, marketing, and sales people to develop reliable estimates of future production costs and potential revenues for each product. However, even the best forecasts can be wrong. That's why it is so important to perform sensitivity and scenario analysis as we did in Chapter 9.

Forecasting the Balance Sheet

We have enough data now to forecast the balance sheet for our planned expansion. Recall from Section 18.2 with the percent of sales method that forecasting the balance sheet helps us identify any future funding needs because the balance sheet must balance. Here, we have explicitly planned for the funding of the expansion in 2017. Nonetheless, we can check to make sure that our debt issue will be enough and then forecast past the expansion to see if we will need any future financing. Table 18.10 shows the balance sheet for 2016 and 2017 filled in with the information we have so far. The only piece of information we are missing is the dividend amount, so we assume for now that we will not pay any dividends in 2017.

As we can see from the column for 2017 in the pro forma balance sheet, KMS's balance sheet does not initially balance: the liabilities and equity are greater than the assets. In Section 18.2, KMS faced the opposite situation—its assets were greater than its liabilities

TABLE 18.10

Pro Forma Balance Sheet for KMS, 2017

	Year	2016	2017	Source for 2017 Data	2017 (Revised)
2	**Balance Sheet ($000s)**				
3	**Assets**				
4	Cash and Cash Equivalents	11,982	14,139	Table 18.9	14,139
5	Accounts Receivable	14,229	16,790	Table 18.9	16,790
6	Inventories	14,978	17,674	Table 18.9	17,674
7	**Total Current Assets**	41,189	48,603	Lines 4 + 5 + 6	48,603
8	Property, Plant, and Equipment	49,427	66,984	Table 18.6	66,984
9	**Total Assets**	90,616	115,587	Lines 7 + 8	115,587
10	**Liabilities**				
11	Accounts Payable	11,982	14,139	Table 18.9	14,139
12	Debt	4,500	24,500	Table 18.7	24,500
13	**Total Liabilities**	16,482	38,639	Lines 11 + 12	38,639
14	**Stockholders' Equity**				
15	Starting Stockholders' Equity	69,275	74,134	2016 Line 18	74,134
16	Net Income	6,941	7,600	Table 18.8	7,600
17	Dividends	−2,082	0	**Assumed**	**−4,786**
18	**Stockholders' Equity**	74,134	81,734	Lines 15 + 16 + 17	76,948
19	**Total Liabilities and Equity**	90,616	120,373	Lines 13 + 18	115,587

and equity—and this told KMS's managers that they needed external financing. When liabilities and equity are greater than the assets, we have generated more cash than we had planned to consume and we need to decide what to do with it. KMS's options are:

- Build-up extra cash reserves (which would increase the cash account to bring assets in line with liabilities and equity).
- Pay down (retire) some of its debt.
- Distribute the excess as dividends.
- Repurchase shares.

Let's assume KMS's managers choose to distribute the excess as dividends. The excess is the amount by which liabilities and equity exceeds assets: $120,373 − $115,587 = $4786. The final column of Table 18.10, labeled "2017 (Revised)," shows the new pro forma balance sheet, including KMS's planned dividend. The balance sheet now balances! We can do this for the full forecast horizon (2017–2021). The completed pro forma balance sheet is shown in the appendix to this chapter.

The general lesson from the example in Section 18.2, as well as from this section, is summarized in Table 18.11.

TABLE 18.11

Pro Forma Balance
Sheets and Financing

Liabilities and equity are . . .	less than assets	greater than assets
	New financing is needed—the firm must reduce dividends, borrow, or issue new equity to fund the shortfall.	Excess cash is available—the firm can retain it as extra cash reserves (thus increasing assets), pay dividends, or reduce external financing by retiring debt or repurchasing shares.

CONCEPT CHECK

5. What is the advantage of forecasting capital expenditures, working capital, and financing events directly?
6. What role does minimum required cash play in working capital?

18.4 Growth and Firm Value

We just analyzed an expansion for KMS that involved an expensive capital investment. For KMS, this forecast would be a starting point for the capital budgeting analysis necessary to decide whether the expansion is a positive-NPV project. It is important to remember that not all growth is worth the price. It is possible to pay so much to enable growth that the firm, on net, is worth less. Even if the cost of the growth is not an issue, other aspects of growth can leave the firm less valuable. For example, expansion may strain managers' capacity to monitor and handle the firm's operations. It may surpass the firm's distribution capabilities or quality control or even change customers' perceptions of the firm and its brand.

For example, in Starbucks' 2005 annual report, Chairman Howard Schultz and CEO Jim Donald wrote to shareholders that Starbucks planned to continue opening new stores—1800 in 2006 alone—and planned revenue growth of approximately 20% for the next five years. Around the time Starbucks' shareholders were reading this (early 2006), the price of the company's stock was about $36. By the end of 2007, Starbucks' stock price had fallen to $21, Jim Donald had been fired as CEO, and chairman and founder Howard Schultz had written a memo to employees that Starbucks' recent expansion had caused it to "lose its soul," meaning that the Starbucks experience—the key to its success and the loyalty of its customers—had been watered down. To distinguish between growth that adds to or detracts from the value of the firm, we will discuss two growth rates that factor in financing needs and revisit our top decision rule: NPV analysis.

Sustainable Growth Rate and External Financing

The Starbucks example makes the point that not all growth is valuable growth. The distinction between value-enhancing and value-destroying growth can be made only through careful NPV analysis such as we perform in the next section. However, this distinction is often confused with the concept of a firm's **internal growth rate**—the maximum growth rate a firm can achieve without resorting to external financing. Intuitively, this is the growth the firm can support by reinvesting its earnings. A closely related and more commonly used measure is the firm's **sustainable growth rate**—the maximum growth rate the firm can sustain without issuing new equity or increasing its debt-to-equity ratio. Let's discuss each of these in turn.

internal growth rate The maximum growth rate a firm can achieve without resorting to external financing.

sustainable growth rate The maximum growth rate a firm can achieve without issuing new equity or increasing its debt-to-equity ratio.

Internal Growth Rate Formula. Both these benchmark growth rates are aimed at identifying how much growth a firm can support based on its existing net income. For a firm that does not pay any dividends, its internal growth rate is its return on assets, because that tells us how fast it could grow its assets using only its net income. If the firm pays some of its net income out as a dividend, then its internal growth rate is reduced to only the growth supported by its retained earnings. This reasoning suggests a more general formula for the internal growth rate:

$$\text{Internal Growth Rate} = \left(\frac{\text{Net Income}}{\text{Beginning Assets}} \right) \times (1 - \text{Payout Ratio})$$

$$= \text{ROA} \times \text{Retention Rate} \tag{18.4}$$

Recall from Chapter 7 that the fraction of net income retained for reinvestment in the firm is called the retention rate. In the context of internal and sustainable growth rates, the retention rate is often called the **plowback ratio**. The internal growth rate is simply the ROA multiplied by the retention rate (plowback ratio).[7]

plowback ratio One minus the payout ratio of the firm, also called the *retention rate.*

Sustainable Growth Rate Formula. The sustainable growth rate allows for some external financing. It assumes that no new equity will be issued and that the firm's managers want to maintain the same debt-to-equity ratio. Thus, it tells us how fast the firm can grow by reinvesting its retained earnings and issuing only as much new debt as can be supported by those retained earnings. The formula for the sustainable growth rate is:[8]

$$\text{Sustainable Growth Rate} = \left(\frac{\text{Net Income}}{\text{Beginning Equity}} \right) \times (1 - \text{Payout Ratio})$$

$$= \text{ROE} \times \text{Retention Rate} \tag{18.5}$$

Sustainable Growth Rate Versus Internal Growth Rate. Because your ROE will be larger than your ROA any time you have debt, the sustainable growth rate will be greater than the internal growth rate. While the internal growth rate assumes no external financing, the sustainable growth rate assumes you will make use of some outside financing equal to the amount of new debt that will keep your debt-to-equity ratio constant as your equity grows through reinvested net income.

---

[7]It is common to define ROA as Net Income / End-of-Period Assets. If that is the case, the formula is more complicated but still has the same intuition: (ROA × Retention Rate)/(1 − ROA × Retention Rate).

[8]Just as with the internal growth rate, if you define ROE using end-of-period equity, the formula changes but maintains its intuition: (ROE × Retention Rate)/(1 − ROE × Retention Rate).

EXAMPLE 18.3

Internal and
Sustainable Growth
Rates and Payout
Policy

MyFinanceLab

PROBLEM

Your firm has $70 million in equity and $30 million in debt and forecasts $14 million in net income for the year. It currently pays dividends equal to 20% of its net income. You are analyzing a potential change in payout policy—an increase in dividends to 30% of net income. How would this change affect your internal and sustainable growth rates?

SOLUTION

PLAN

We can use Eqs. 18.4 and 18.5 to compute your firm's internal and sustainable growth rates under the old and new policy. To do so, we'll need to compute its ROA, ROE, and retention rate (plowback ratio). The company has $100 million (= $70 million in equity + $30 million in debt) in total assets.

$$\text{ROA} = \frac{\text{Net Income}}{\text{Beginning Assets}} = \frac{14}{100} = 14\% \quad \text{ROE} = \frac{\text{Net Income}}{\text{Beginning Equity}} = \frac{14}{70} = 20\%$$

$$\text{Old Retention Rate} = (1 - \text{Payout Ratio}) = (1 - 0.20) = 0.80$$

$$\text{New Retention Rate} = (1 - 0.30) = 0.70$$

EXECUTE

Using Eq. 18.4 to compute the internal growth rate before and after the change, we have:

Old Internal Growth Rate = ROA × Retention Rate = 14% × 0.80 = 11.2%

New Internal Growth Rate = 14% × 0.70 = 9.8%

Similarly, we can use Eq. 18.5 to compute the sustainable growth rate before and after:

Old Sustainable Growth Rate = ROE × Retention Rate = 20% × 0.80 = 16%

New Sustainable Growth Rate = 20% × 0.70 = 14%

EVALUATE

By reducing the amount of retained earnings available to fund growth, an increase in the payout ratio necessarily reduces your firm's internal and sustainable growth rates.

Whenever you forecast growth greater than the internal growth rate, you will have to reduce your payout ratio (increase your plowback ratio), plan to raise additional external financing, or both. If your forecasted growth is greater than your sustainable growth rate, you will have to increase your plowback ratio, raise additional equity financing, or increase your leverage (increase your debt faster than keeping your debt-to-equity ratio constant would allow). Table 18.12 compares internal and sustainable growth rates.

While the internal and sustainable growth rates are useful in alerting you to the need to plan for external financing, they cannot tell you whether your planned growth increases or decreases the firm's value. The growth rates do not evaluate the future costs and benefits of the growth, and the Valuation Principle tells us that the value implications of the growth can be assessed only by doing so.

TABLE 18.12

Summary of Internal
Growth Rate Versus
Sustainable Growth
Rate

	Internal Growth Rate	Sustainable Growth Rate
Formula:	ROA × Retention Rate	ROE × Retention Rate
Maximum growth financed only by:	Retained earnings	Retained earnings and new debt that keeps D/E ratio constant
To grow faster, a firm must:	Reduce payout or raise external capital	Reduce payout, raise new equity, or increase leverage

There is nothing inherently bad or unsustainable about growth greater than your sustainable growth rate as long as that growth is value-increasing. Your firm will simply need to raise additional capital to finance the growth.

For example, in the 1990s, Starbucks' average growth was above 60% even though its average ROE was 20%. Until 2010, Starbucks never paid dividends, so its retention rate was 1, making its sustainable growth rate (SGR) at the time also 20%.

$$SGR = ROE \times \text{Retention Rate} = 20\% \times 1 = 20\%$$

Despite expanding at three times its sustainable growth rate, Starbucks' value increased almost 10 times (1000%) during that period.

Conversely, Starbucks' recent experience illustrates that sustainable growth need not be value-increasing growth, as seen in Figure 18.1. We noted at the beginning of this section that starting in 2006, Starbucks was aiming for annual growth of 20%. How does this compare to its sustainable growth rate at the time? When Schultz and Donald wrote their letter to shareholders, Starbucks' ROE was 20% (based on its 2005 annual report). Again, until 2013, Starbucks never paid dividends, so its retention rate was 1, making its sustainable growth rate also 20%. Thus, 20% growth was sustainable—it just wasn't value-increasing.[9]

FIGURE 18.1

Starbucks' Stock Price During Periods of Growth At, Above, and Below Its SGR

The figure graphs Starbucks' stock price since 2000. During most of its early years, Starbucks grew at well above its sustainable growth rate (SGR) and its value increased substantially. In 2006, it planned growth at its SGR but suffered a share decrease in value. Following a change in strategy to slow growth, it grew below its SGR and saw a turnaround in its stock price performance. The figure demonstrates that there is no necessary relationship between a firm's growth relative to its SGR and whether that growth is valuable.

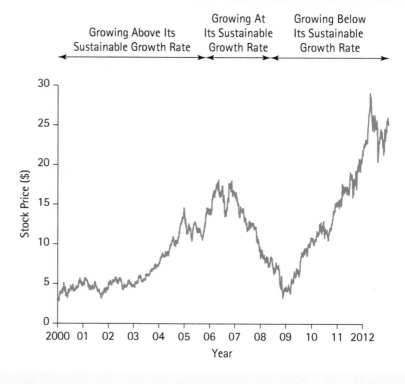

Source: http://finance.yahoo.com, Compustat, and authors' calculations.

---

[9]The book's Web site (www.myfinancelab.com) contains a spreadsheet with a proposed expansion of KMS Designs that allows you to explore the differences between sustainable growth, internal growth rate, and value-increasing growth.

As we discussed in Chapters 14 and 15, there are costs to seeking external financing—the flotation and issuance costs associated with issuing new equity or new bonds. Thus, the internal growth rate indicates the fastest growth possible without incurring any of these costs. The sustainable growth rate still assumes some new debt will be sought, so the company reduces, but does not eliminate entirely, its costs of external financing when growing at the sustainable growth rate. Thus, managers, especially those at small firms, concerned with these costs might track these growth rates. However, for most value-enhancing investment decisions, one would expect these costs to be small relative to the NPV of the decision.

While these costs are usually small relative to the NPV of expanding the business, it would be wrong to ignore them completely. The proper way to incorporate them is to calculate the cash outflow associated with these costs and subtract it from the NPV of the expansion. The point remains that growth above a firm's internal or sustainable growth rates is not necessarily bad but will require external financing and the costs associated with that financing.

CONCEPT
CHECK
7. What is the difference between internal growth rate and sustainable growth rate?

8. If a firm grows faster than its sustainable growth rate, is that growth value decreasing?

18.5   Valuing the Expansion

As the last section made clear, growth can increase or decrease the value of the firm. Planning for and forecasting the impact of growth is just the first step in the analysis of whether the growth will make sense for the shareholders. Our forecasting exercise in Section 18.3 gave us estimates of the implications of the planned expansion for the debt, net income, and working capital of KMS. Now we are ready to determine whether the expansion is a good idea. The Valuation Principle guides us here—we need to forecast the cash flows and compute their present value.

Forecasting Free Cash Flows

We now have the data needed to forecast KMS's free cash flows over the next five years. KMS's earnings are available from the income statement (Table 18.8), as are its depreciation and interest expenses. Capital expenditures are available from Table 18.6, and changes in net working capital can be found in Table 18.9. We combine these items to estimate the free cash flows in the spreadsheet shown in Table 18.13.

To compute KMS's free cash flows, which exclude cash flows associated with leverage, we first adjust net income by adding back the after-tax interest payments associated with the net debt in its capital structure. Our net interest expense is interest paid on debt minus

TABLE 18.13

KMS Forecasted Free
Cash Flows

1	Year	2017	2018	2019	2020	2021
2	**Free Cash Flow ($000s)**					
3	**Net Income**	7,600	8,807	11,141	13,739	16,627
4	Plus: After-Tax Interest Expense	199	1,083	1,083	1,083	1,083
5	**Unlevered Net Income**	7,799	9,890	12,224	14,822	17,710
6	Plus: Depreciation	7,443	7,498	7,549	7,594	7,634
7	Less: Increases in NWC	−5,257	−5,802	−6,453	−7,166	−7,948
8	Less: Capital Expenditures	−25,000	−8,000	−8,000	−8,000	−8,000
9	**Free Cash Flow of Firm**	−15,015	3,586	5,320	7,250	9,396

interest earned on excess cash balances. Recall that interest *paid* is tax deductible, and interest *earned* is taxable, so we adjust each by $(1 - \text{Tax Rate})$:[10]

$$\text{After-Tax Interest Expense} = (1 - \text{Tax Rate}) \times (\text{Interest on Debt})$$
$$- (1 - \text{Tax Rate}) \times (\text{Interest on Excess Cash}) \quad (18.6)$$

Because KMS has no excess cash, its after-tax interest expense in 2017 is $(1 - 35\%) \times \$306 = \$199$ (thousand), providing unlevered net income of $\$7600 + 199 = \$7799$. We could also compute the unlevered net income in Table 18.13 by starting with EBIT and deducting taxes. For example, in 2017 EBIT is forecasted as $11.998 million (Table 18.8), which amounts to:

$$\$11.998 \times (1 - 35\%) = \$7.799 \text{ million after taxes}$$

To compute KMS's free cash flows from its unlevered net income, we add back depreciation (which is not a cash expense), and deduct KMS's increases in net working capital and capital expenditures. The free cash flows on line 9 of Table 18.13 show the cash the firm will generate for its investors, both debt and equity holders.[11] While KMS will generate substantial free cash flows over the next five years, the level of free cash flows varies substantially from year to year. They are even forecasted to be negative in 2017 (when the expansion takes place).

As we noted, free cash flows compute the total cash available to all investors (debt and equity holders). To determine the amount that can be paid out to equity holders, we can adjust the free cash flows to account for all (after-tax) payments to or from debt holders. For example, in 2017 KMS will pay after-tax interest of $199,000 and receive $20 million by issuing new debt as follows:

	2017
Free Cash Flows	−15,015
Less: After-Tax Interest Expense	−199
Plus: Increase in Debt	+20,000
= Free Cash Flows to Equity	= 4,786

Note that the free cash flows that are available to equity holders in 2017, $4.786 million, are exactly the amount of dividends we forecast at the end of Section 18.3. This is no coincidence—we chose in that section to pay out all excess available cash flows as a dividend. This is exactly what the free cash flows to equity tell us—the total amount of excess cash flows that belongs to the equity holders for them to use to pay dividends, repurchase shares, retain in the firm as cash, or retire debt. (See the appendix to this chapter for a forecast of free cash flows to equity and dividends through 2021.)

---

[10]If KMS had some interest income or expenses from working capital, we would *not* include that interest here. We adjust only for interest that is related to the firm's *financing*—that is, interest associated with debt and excess cash (cash not included as part of working capital).

[11]While we are maintaining the assumption that after paying the interest on its debt, KMS will distribute any excess funds to shareholders as dividends, this payout decision has no impact on the amount of free cash flows the firm generates in the first place, and hence has no impact on the value we will compute for KMS.

Confusing Total and Incremental Net Working Capital

When calculating free cash flows from earnings, students often make the mistake of subtracting the firm's *total* net working capital each year rather than only the incremental change in net working capital. Remember that only a change in net working capital results in a new cash inflow or outflow for the firm. Subtracting the entire *level* of net working capital will reduce the free cash flows, often even making them negative, and lead the student to understate the NPV of the decision.

KMS Designs' Expansion: Effect on Firm Value

We've accomplished a lot by carefully forecasting the impact of the planned expansion on KMS's net income, capital expenditures, and working capital needs. First, we identified future financing needs, allowing us ample time to plan to secure the necessary funding. Next, in order to construct our pro forma statements, we built an Excel model of the interactions between sales growth, costs, capital investment, working capital needs, and financing choices. This model allows us to study how changes in any of these factors will affect the others and our expansion plans.[12] Remember the lesson from sensitivity and scenario analysis in Chapter 9—these numbers are only forecasts, and as such you need to see how reasonable deviations from the forecast would affect the value of the expansion. Nonetheless, as a starting point, we use these forecasts to provide our best estimate of whether the expansion plan is a good idea—does it increase the value of KMS? There are two ways of doing this: (1) value the whole company with and without the expansion and compare the values or (2) value only the incremental changes to the company caused by the expansion, as we did in Chapter 9's capital budgeting exercise. We will go the first route to provide an example of how to do whole-company valuation. However, you could arrive at the same answer by following the incremental approach.

As we learned in Chapter 16, absent distress costs, the value of a firm with debt is equal to the value of the firm without debt plus the present value of its interest tax shields. Our careful forecast of the financing of KMS's expansion allows us to apply the same approach to valuing the expansion: We compute the present value of the *unlevered* free cash flows of KMS and add to it the present value of the tax shields created by our planned interest payments.[13] However, we have only forecast cash flows out to 2021, so we will need to account for the remaining value of KMS at that point. We do so using the tools developed in Chapter 10 for valuing common stock.

Multiples Approach to Continuation Value. Practitioners generally estimate a firm's continuation value (also called the *terminal value*) at the end of the forecast horizon using a valuation multiple. Explicitly forecasting cash flows is useful in capturing those specific aspects of a company that distinguish the firm from its competitors in the short run. However, because of competition between firms, the long-term expected growth rates, profitability, and risk of firms in the same industry should move toward one another. As a consequence, long-term expectations of multiples are likely to be relatively homogeneous across firms. Thus, a realistic assumption is that a firm's multiple will eventually move toward the industry average. Because distant cash flows are difficult to forecast accurately,

---

[12]You can download a copy of the forecasting model in Excel from the book's Web site and experiment with changes in these factors.

[13]This approach is called the *adjusted present value* because it adjusts the present value of the unlevered free cash flows for the effect of the interest tax shields.

estimating the firm's continuation or terminal value based on a long-term estimate of the valuation multiple for the industry is a common (and, generally, reasonably reliable) approach.

Of the different valuation multiples available, the EBITDA (earnings before interest, taxes, depreciation, and amortization) multiple is most often used in practice. In most settings, the EBITDA multiple is more reliable than sales or earnings multiples because it accounts for the firm's operating efficiency and is not affected by leverage differences between firms. We discussed the use of multiples in valuation in Chapter 10. As in that context, here we estimate the continuation value using an EBITDA multiple as follows:

$$\text{Continuation Enterprise Value at Forecast Horizon}$$
$$= \text{EBITDA at Horizon} \times \text{EBITDA Multiple at Horizon} \qquad (18.7)$$

From the income statement in Table 18.8, KMS's EBITDA in 2021 is forecast to be $34.880 million. Firms in KMS's industry are valued at an average EBITDA multiple of 9. If we assume that the appropriate EBITDA multiple in 2021 is unchanged from the current value of 9, then KMS's continuation value in 2021 is $34.880 \times 9 = \$313.920$ million. This assumption is important—the EBITDA multiple at the horizon will have a large impact on our value calculation. A careful analysis of the prospects for industry growth (which tends to be related to higher multiples) at the horizon is important. Here, we assume that the design and apparel industry is mature and will remain relatively stable, but this assumption can be probed, especially in sensitivity analysis.

KMS Designs' Value with the Expansion. Assume that KMS's financial managers have estimated KMS's unlevered cost of capital to be 10% (specifically, 10% is their pretax WACC; see the details regarding the estimation of the cost of capital in Chapter 13). Now we have all the inputs we need to value KMS with the expansion. Table 18.14 presents the calculation. First, we compute the present value of the forecasted free cash flows of the firm over the next five years. These are the cash flows available to both bondholders and equity holders, so they are free of any effects of leverage. Because they represent cash flows to both debt and equity holders, and because we will account for the benefits of the interest tax shield separately, we discount KMS's free cash flows at the firm's pretax WACC of 10%. Using the free cash flows we forecasted for 2017–2021 in Table 18.13, we get a present value of $4096:

$$PV(FCF) = \frac{-15{,}015}{(1.10)^1} + \frac{3586}{(1.10)^2} + \frac{5320}{(1.10)^3} + \frac{7250}{(1.10)^4} + \frac{9396}{(1.10)^5} = 4096 \quad (18.8)$$

Even though the PV of the cash flows over the next five years is small, the expansion pays off in the long run by providing higher free cash flows from 2021 onward. This growth results in a higher EBITDA in 2021 than would otherwise be possible, and thus a higher continuation value once that EBITDA is multiplied by the continuation multiple of 9. The

TABLE 18.14

Calculation of KMS Firm Value with the Expansion

	Year		2017	2018	2019	2020	2021
1							
2	Free Cash Flow of Firm		−15,015	3,586	5,320	7,250	9,396
3	**PV Free Cash Flow** (at 10%)	4,096					
4	Continuation Value						313,920
5	**PV Continuation Value** (at 10%)	194,920					
6	Net Interest Expense		−306	−1,666	−1,666	−1,666	−1,666
7	Interest Tax Shield		107	583	583	583	583
8	**PV Interest Tax Shield** (at 6.8%)	1,958					
9	**Firm Value (3 + 5 + 8)**	200,974					

$313,920 continuation value in 2021 that we calculated is included in Table 18.14. However, because it is a 2021 value, we need to discount it to the present:

$$PV \text{ Continuation Value} = \frac{313,920}{(1.10)^5} = 194,920 \qquad (18.9)$$

Finally, because we are financing the expansion with debt, we will have additional interest tax shields. The total net interest expense is included in the table and the interest tax shield in the table is calculated as we did in Chapter 16, by multiplying the interest expense by the tax rate (35% for KMS):

$$\text{Interest Tax Shield} = \text{Net Interest Expense} \times \text{Tax Rate} \qquad (18.10)$$

Also as we did in Chapter 16, we calculate the present value of the interest tax shield using the interest rate on debt as the discount rate, *not* using the WACC. Recall that the reason for doing so is that the tax shield is only as risky as the debt that creates it, so that the proper discount rate is the debt's interest rate, here at 6.8%:[14]

$$PV \text{ Interest Tax Shield} = \frac{107}{(1.068)^1} + \frac{583}{(1.068)^2} + \frac{583}{(1.068)^3} + \frac{583}{(1.068)^4}$$

$$+ \frac{583}{(1.068)^5} = 1,958 \qquad (18.11)$$

The total value of KMS with the expansion is the sum of the present values of the forecasted unlevered free cash flows, the continuation value of the firm, and the interest tax shields. As shown in Table 18.14, the total firm value is $200,974 million.

KMS Designs' Value Without the Expansion. But how do we know if the expansion is a good idea? We can compare KMS's value with the expansion to its value without the expansion. If KMS does not invest in the new equipment, it will be stuck with a maximum capacity of 1100 units. While its sales revenue will grow due to price increases, its main source of growth will be cut off. Table 18.15 shows the sales revenue without the expansion. By 2017, KMS reaches maximum production capacity and can no longer expand. Comparing the sales revenue in the table to the sales revenue with the expansion given in Table 18.8, we see how much higher sales are forecasted to be with the expansion.

TABLE 18.15

Sales Forecast
Without Expansion

1	Year	2016	2017	2018	2019	2020	2021
2	Production Volume	1,000	1,100	1,100	1,100	1,100	1,100
3	Sales Price		$ 74.89	$ 76.51	$ 78.04	$ 79.60	$ 81.19	$ 82.82
4	Sales Revenue		$74,889	$84,161	$85,844	$87,561	$89,312	$91,099

We can complete the same process for forecasting the free cash flows of the firm without the expansion as we did for the firm with the expansion. In this case, we would find that the 2021 EBITDA would only be $20,042, so that the continuation value would drop to $20,042 × 9 = $180,378. Also, KMS will not be taking on any additional debt, so the interest expense will remain constant at $306 per year. The final result of the valuation is presented in Table 18.16.

---

[14]We have not ignored the rest of the interest tax shields from the new debt. The value of those shields is subsumed in the continuation value of the firm. When we say that the firm will be worth 9 times EBITDA, we are saying that the total value at that point, including all unused tax shields, will be 9 times EBITDA.

TABLE 18.16

KMS's Value Without
the Expansion

	Year		2017	2018	2019	2020	2021
1	Year		2017	2018	2019	2020	2021
2	Free Cash Flow of Firm		5,324	8,509	8,727	8,952	9,182
3	**PV Free Cash Flow** (at 10%)	30,244					
4	Continuation Value						180,378
5	**PV Continuation Value** (at 10%)	112,001					
6	Net Interest Expense		−306	−306	−306	−306	−306
7	Interest Tax Shield		107	107	107	107	107
8	**PV Interest Tax Shield** (at 6.8%)	441					
9	**Firm Value (3 + 5 + 8)**	142,686					

While the PV of the free cash flows over the next five years is higher because we don't have to spend $20 million for the new equipment, the lower growth substantially reduces our continuation value and the reduced debt (because we do not need to borrow to fund the equipment) produces a much lower present value of interest tax shields as well. The resulting firm value is almost $60 million lower without the expansion than it is with the expansion. Thus, the expansion is certainly a good idea for KMS.

Optimal Timing and the Option to Delay

We just showed that if the alternative is not to expand at all, KMS should definitely expand in 2017. However, what if it also has the option to simply delay expansion to 2018 or later, rather than not expand at all? If we repeat the valuation analysis above for expansion in each year from 2017 to 2021, we get the following firm values in 2016:[15]

Expand in ...	2017	2018	2019	2020	2021
KMS's Firm Value in 2016:	200,974	203,553	204,728	204,604	203,277

KMS's firm value is maximized by delaying the expansion to 2019. The reason is that while delaying expansion means that KMS cannot produce enough units to meet demand, the shortfall is not too great until 2019. The value gained from putting off such a large financial outlay is greater than the value lost from forgone sales.

The timing analysis recalls an important point from Chapter 9: Managers often have real options embedded in capital budgeting decisions. In this case, it is important for KMS's managers to realize that the alternative is not expand or do nothing. Rather, it is expand or delay expansion for another year (or more). As we see here, this option is valuable, allowing KMS's managers to add almost $4 million in additional value to the firm.

CONCEPT CHECK

9. What is the multiples approach to continuation value?

10. How does forecasting help the financial manager decide whether to implement a new business plan?

---

[15]Interested students may perform this analysis using the spreadsheet that accompanies this chapter on the book's Web site.

MyFinanceLab
Here is what you should know after reading this chapter. MyFinanceLab will help you identify what you know, and where to go when you need to practice.

KEY POINTS AND EQUATIONS	KEY TERMS	ONLINE PRACTICE
18.1 Goals of Long-Term Financial Planning Building a financial model to forecast the financial statements and free cash flows of a firm allows the financial manager to: • Identify important linkages. • Analyze the impact of potential business plans. • Plan for future funding needs.		MyFinanceLab Study Plan 18.1
18.2 Forecasting Financial Statements: The Percent of Sales Method • One common approach to forecasting is the percent of sales approach, where you assume that costs, working capital, and total assets will remain a fixed percent of sales as sales grow. • A pro forma income statement projects the firm's earnings under a given set of hypothetical assumptions. • A pro forma balance sheet projects the firm's assets, liabilities, and equity under the same assumptions used to construct the pro forma income statement. • Forecasting the balance sheet with the percent of sales method requires two passes. • The first pass reveals by how much equity and liabilities would fall short of the amount needed to finance the expected growth in assets. • In the second pass, the pro forma balance sheet shows the necessary financing from the planned sources and is in balance.	net new financing, p. 577 percent of sales method, p. 575	MyFinanceLab Study Plan 18.2 Spreadsheet Tables 18.1–18.4
18.3 Forecasting a Planned Expansion • An improvement over the percent of sales method is to forecast the firm's working capital and capital investment, along with planned financing of those investments directly. • Such a financial model will have the correct timing of external financing and capital investment so that we can estimate the firm's future free cash flows.		MyFinanceLab Study Plan 18.3 Spreadsheet Tables 18.5–18.10
18.4 Growth and Firm Value • Two common concepts are internal growth rate and sustainable growth rate. • The internal growth rate identifies the maximum rate at which the firm can grow without external financing: Internal Growth Rate $= \text{ROA} \times \text{Retention Rate}$ (18.4) • The sustainable growth rate identifies the maximum rate at which the firm can grow if it wants to keep its D/E ratio constant without any new equity financing: Sustainable Growth Rate $= \text{ROE} \times \text{Retention Rate}$ (18.5)	internal growth rate, p. 586 plowback ratio, p. 586 sustainable growth rate, p. 586	MyFinanceLab Study Plan 18.4

- Neither the internal growth rate nor the sustainable growth rate indicates whether planned growth is good or bad. Only an NPV analysis can tell us whether the contemplated growth will increase or decrease the value of the firm.

18.5 Valuing the Expansion - In addition to forecasting cash flows for a few years, we need to estimate the firm's continuation value at the end of the forecast horizon. - One method of estimating the continuation value is to use a valuation multiple based on comparable firms. - Given the forecasted cash flows and an estimate of the cost of capital, the final step is to combine these inputs to estimate the value of the firm based on the business plan. We can compare this to the value of the firm without the new plan to determine whether to implement the plan.	MyFinanceLab Study Plan 18.5 Interactive Financial Statement Model Spreadsheet Tables 18.13–18.16

CRITICAL THINKING

1. What is the purpose of long-term forecasting?

2. What are the advantages and disadvantages of the percent of sales method?

3. What is gained by forecasting capital expenditures and external financing specifically?

4. What can the sustainable growth rate tell a financial manager and what can it not tell?

5. How can the financial manager use the long-term forecast to decide on adopting a new business plan?

PROBLEMS

All problems are available in MyFinanceLab. *The* ⊞ *icon indicates problems that are easier to solve using Excel and have data in an Excel format available in* MyFinanceLab.

Forecasting Financial Statements: The Percent of Sales Method

1. Your company has sales of $100,000 this year and cost of goods sold of $72,000. You forecast sales to increase to $110,000 next year. Using the percent of sales method, forecast next year's cost of goods sold.

2. For the next fiscal year, you forecast net income of $50,000 and ending assets of $500,000. Your firm's payout ratio is 10%. Your beginning stockholders' equity is $300,000 and your beginning total liabilities are $120,000. Your non-debt liabilities such as accounts payable are forecasted to increase by $10,000. What is your net new financing needed for next year?

3. Assume your beginning debt in Problem 2 is $100,000. What amount of equity and what amount of debt would you need to issue to cover the net new financing in order to keep your debt-equity ratio constant?

For Problems 4–7, use the following income statement and balance sheet for Jim's Espresso:

Income Statement	
Sales	200,000
Costs Except Depreciation	(100,000)
EBITDA	100,000
Depreciation	(6,000)
EBIT	94,000
Interest Expense (net)	(400)
Pretax Income	93,600
Income Tax	(32,760)
Net Income	60,840

Balance Sheet	
Assets	
Cash and Equivalents	15,000
Accounts Receivable	2,000
Inventories	4,000
Total Current Assets	21,000
Property, Plant, and Equipment	10,000
Total Assets	31,000
Liabilities and Equity	
Accounts Payable	1,500
Debt	4,000
Total Liabilities	5,500
Stockholders' Equity	25,500
Total Liabilities and Equity	31,000

4. Jim's expects sales to grow by 10% next year. Using the percent of sales method, forecast (*see* MyFinanceLab *for the data in Excel format*):
   a. Costs
   b. Depreciation
   c. Net income
   d. Cash
   e. Accounts receivable
   f. Inventory
   g. Property, plant, and equipment

5. Assume that Jim's pays out 90% of its net income. Use the percent of sales method to forecast (*see* MyFinanceLab *for the data in Excel format*):
   a. Stockholders' equity
   b. Accounts payable

6. What is the amount of net new financing needed for Jim's (*see* MyFinanceLab *for the data in Excel format*)?

7. If Jim's adjusts its payout policy to 70% of net income, how will the net new financing change?

For Problems 8–11, use the following income statement and balance sheet for Global Corp.:

Figures in $ millions

Net sales	186.7	**Assets**	
Costs Except Depreciation	−175.1	Cash	23.2
EBITDA	11.6	Accounts Receivable	18.5
Depreciation and Amortization	−1.2	Inventories	15.3
EBIT	10.4	Total Current Assets	57
Interest Income (expense)	−7.7		
Pretax Income	2.7	Net Property, Plant, and Equipment	113.1
Taxes	−0.7	Total Assets	170.1
Net Income	2.0		
		Liabilities and Equity	
		Accounts Payable	34.7
		Long-Term Debt	113.2
		Total Liabilities	147.9
		Total Stockholders' Equity	22.2
		Total Liabilities and Equity	170.1

8. Global expects sales to grow by 8% next year. Using the percent of sales method, forecast (*see* MyFinanceLab *for the data in Excel format*):
   a. Costs except depreciation
   b. Depreciation
   c. Net income
   d. Cash
   e. Accounts receivable
   f. Inventory
   g. Property, plant, and equipment
   h. Accounts payable

9. Assume that Global pays out 50% of its net income. Use the percent of sales method to forecast stockholders' equity (*see* MyFinanceLab *for the data in Excel format*).

10. What is the amount of net new financing needed for Global (*see* MyFinanceLab *for the data in Excel format*)?

11. If Global decides that it will limit its net new financing to no more than $9 million, how will this affect its payout policy (*see* MyFinanceLab *for the data in Excel format*)?

Forecasting a Planned Expansion

For problems in this section, you should download the KMS spreadsheets available on the book's Web site.

12. Assume that KMS's market share will increase by 0.25% per year rather than the 1% used in the chapter (see Table 18.5) and that its prices remain as in the chapter. What production capacity will KMS require each year? When will an expansion become necessary (that is, when will production volume exceed 1100)?

13. Under the assumption that KMS's market share will increase by 0.25% per year, you determine that the plant will require an expansion in 2018. The expansion will cost $20 million. Assuming that the financing of the expansion will be delayed accordingly, calculate the projected interest payments and the amount of the projected interest tax shields (assuming that KMS still uses a 10-year bond and interest rates remain the same as in the chapter) through 2021.

14. Under the assumption that KMS's market share will increase by 0.25% per year (and the investment and financing will be adjusted as described in Problem 13), you project the following depreciation:

Year	2016	2017	2018	2019	2020	2021
Depreciation	5,492	5,443	7,398	7,459	7,513	7,561

Using this information, project net income through 2021 (that is, reproduce Table 18.8 under the new assumptions).

15. Assuming that KMS's market share will increase by 0.25% per year (implying that the investment, financing, and depreciation will be adjusted as described in Problems 13 and 14), and that the working capital assumptions used in the chapter still hold, calculate KMS's working capital requirements through 2021 (that is, reproduce Table 18.9 under the new assumptions).

Growth and Firm Value

16. Using the information in the following table, calculate this company's:

Net Income	50,000
Beginning Total Assets	400,000
Beginning Stockholders' Equity	250,000
Payout Ratio	0%

a. Internal growth rate.
b. Sustainable growth rate.
c. Sustainable growth rate if it pays out 40% of its net income as a dividend.

17. Did KMS's expansion plan call for it to grow slower or faster than its sustainable growth rate?

18. Your firm has an ROE of 12%, a payout ratio of 25%, $600,000 of stockholders' equity, and $400,000 of debt. If you grow at your sustainable growth rate this year, how much additional debt will you need to issue?

19. IZAX, Co. had the following items on its balance sheet at the beginning of the year:

Assets		Liabilities and Equity	
Cash	50,000	Debt	100,000
PPE	350,000	Equity	300,000

Its net income this year is $20,000 and it pays dividends of $5,000. If its assets grew at its internal growth rate, what is its new D/E ratio?

Valuing the Expansion

20. Forecast KMS's free cash flows (reproduce Table 18.13), assuming KMS's market share will increase by 0.25% per year; investment, financing, and depreciation will be adjusted accordingly; and working capital will be as you projected in Problem 15.

21. Calculate the continuation value of KMS using your reproduction of Table 18.8 from Problem 14, and assuming an EBITDA multiple of 8.5.

22. Assuming a cost of capital of 10%, compute the value of KMS under the 0.25% growth scenario.

The Balance Sheet and Statement of Cash Flows

The information we have calculated so far can be used to project KMS's balance sheet and statement of cash flows through 2021. While these statements are not critical for our valuation of the expansion, they often prove helpful in providing a more complete picture of how a firm will grow during the forecast period. These statements for KMS are shown in the spreadsheets in Tables 18.17 and 18.18.

TABLE 18.17

Pro Forma Balance Sheet for KMS, 2016–2021

	Year	2016	2017	2018	2019	2020	2021
1	Year	2016	2017	2018	2019	2020	2021
2	**Balance Sheets ($000s)**						
3	**Assets**						
4	Cash and Cash Equivalents	11,982	14,139	16,520	19,167	22,107	25,367
5	Accounts Receivable	14,229	16,790	19,617	22,761	26,252	30,124
6	Inventories	14,978	17,674	20,649	23,959	27,633	31,709
7	**Total Current Assets**	41,189	48,603	56,786	65,886	75,992	87,201
8	Property, Plant, and Equipment	49,427	66,984	67,486	67,937	68,344	68,709
9	**Total Assets**	90,616	115,587	124,272	133,823	144,335	155,910
10							
11	**Liabilities**						
12	Accounts Payable	11,982	14,139	16,520	19,167	22,107	25,367
13	Debt	4,500	24,500	24,500	24,500	24,500	24,500
14	**Total Liabilities**	16,482	38,639	41,020	43,667	46,607	49,867
15							
16	**Stockholders' Equity**						
17	Starting Stockholders' Equity	69,275	74,134	76,948	83,252	90,156	97,729
18	Net Income	6,940	7,600	8,807	11,141	13,739	16,627
19	Dividends	−2,082	−4,786	−2,503	−4,237	−6,167	−8,313
20	**Stockholders' Equity**	74,134	76,948	83,252	90,156	97,729	106,042
21	**Total Liabilities and Equity**	90,616	115,587	124,272	133,823	144,335	155,910

TABLE 18.18

Pro Forma Statement of Cash Flows for KMS, 2016–2021

	Year	2016	2017	2018	2019	2020	2021
1	Year	2016	2017	2018	2019	2020	2021
2	**Statement of Cash Flows ($000s)**						
3	**Net Income**		7,600	8,807	11,141	13,739	16,627
4	Depreciation		7,443	7,498	7,549	7,594	7,634
5	**Changes in Working Capital**						
6	Accounts Receivable		−2,561	−2,827	−3,144	−3,491	−3,872
7	Inventory		−2,696	−2,976	−3,309	−3,675	−4,076
8	Accounts Payable		2,157	2,381	2,647	2,940	3,261
9	**Cash from Operating Activities**		11,942	12,884	14,884	17,107	19,574
10	Capital Expenditures		−25,000	−8,000	−8,000	−8,000	−8,000
11	Other Investment		—	—	—	—	—
12	**Cash from Investing Activities**		−25,000	−8,000	−8,000	−8,000	−8,000
13	Net Borrowing		20,000	—	—	—	—
14	Dividends		−4,786	−2,503	−4,237	−6,167	−8,313
15	**Cash from Financing Activities**		15,214	−2,503	−4,237	−6,167	−8,313
16							
17	**Change in Cash (9 + 12 + 15)**		2,157	2,381	2,647	2,940	3,261

The balance sheet (Table 18.17) continues the work we started in Table 18.10. Current assets and liabilities come from the net working capital spreadsheet (Table 18.9). The inventory entry on the balance sheet includes both raw materials and finished goods. Property, plant, and equipment information comes from the forecasted capital expenditure spreadsheet (Table 18.6), and the debt comes from Table 18.7.

KMS's book value of equity will steadily grow as it expands and remains profitable, paying out only a portion of its net income each year. Its debt will jump from $4500 to $24,500 in 2017 when it finances its expansion. KMS's other liabilities—accounts payable—will grow steadily with sales. KMS's book debt-equity ratio will jump from $4500/74,134 = 6\%$ in 2016 to $24,500/76,948 = 32\%$ in 2017, and then will steadily decline to 23% by 2021.

The statement of cash flows in Table 18.18 starts with net income. Cash from operating activities includes depreciation as well as *changes* to working capital items (other than cash) from Table 18.9. Cash from investing activities includes the capital expenditures in Table 18.6. Cash from financing activities includes net borrowing from Table 18.7, and dividends are equal to free cash flows to equity because we assume KMS pays out all excess cash. We can compute FCF to equity from Table 18.13 using the following equation:

$$\text{FCF to Equity} = \text{FCF of the Firm} + \text{Net Borrowing}$$
$$- \text{After-Tax Interest Expense} \qquad (18.12)$$

KMS is not planning to raise any additional equity financing, so there are no capital contributions on the cash flow statement. As a final check on the calculations, note that the change in the minimum cash balance shown on the balance sheet (Table 18.17). For example, in 2017, the change in cash and cash equivalents is 2157, which is the amount by which 2017 cash exceeds 2016 cash on the balance sheet.

19

Working Capital Management

LEARNING OBJECTIVES

- Understand the cash cycle of the firm and why managing working capital is important

- Use trade credit to the firm's advantage

- Make decisions on extending credit and adjusting credit terms

- Manage accounts payable

- Know the costs and benefits of holding additional inventory

- Contrast the different instruments available to a financial manager for investing cash balances

notation

CCC	cash conversion cycle		*NPV*	net present value
EAR	effective annual rate		*PV*	present value
g	perpetuity growth rate		*r*	discount rate

In Chapter 2, we defined a firm's net working capital as its current assets minus its current liabilities. Net working capital is the capital required in the short term to run the business. Thus, working capital management involves short-term asset accounts such as cash, inventory, and accounts receivable, as well as short-term liability accounts such as accounts payable. The level of investment in each of these accounts differs from firm to firm and from industry to industry. It also depends on factors such as the type of business and industry standards. Some firms, for example, require heavy inventory investments because of the nature of their business.

Consider The Kroger Company, a retail grocery chain, and Southwest Airlines, a regional airline. Inventory amounted to over 18% of Kroger's total assets in early 2016 whereas Southwest's investment in inventory was just over 1%. A grocery store requires a large investment in inventory, but an airline's profitability is generated primarily from its investment in plant, property, and equipment—that is, its airplanes.

There are opportunity costs associated with investing in inventories and accounts receivable, and from holding cash. Excess funds invested in these accounts could instead be used to pay down debt or returned to shareholders in the form of a dividend or share repurchase. This chapter focuses on the tools firms use to manage their working capital efficiently and thereby minimize these opportunity costs. We begin by discussing why firms have working capital and how it affects firm value. In a perfect capital market, many of the working capital accounts would be irrelevant. Not surprisingly, the existence of these accounts for real firms can be traced to market frictions. We discuss the costs and benefits of trade credit and evaluate the tradeoffs firms make in managing various working capital accounts. Finally, we discuss the cash balance of a firm and provide an overview of the short-term investments in which a firm may choose to invest its cash.

19.1 Overview of Working Capital

Most projects require the firm to invest in net working capital. The main components of net working capital are cash, inventory, receivables, and payables. Working capital includes the cash that is needed to run the firm on a day-to-day basis. It does not include excess cash, which is cash that is not required to run the business and can be invested at a market rate. As we discussed in Chapter 13, excess cash may be viewed as part of the firm's capital structure, offsetting firm debt. In Chapter 9, we discussed how any increases in net working capital represent an investment that reduces the cash that is available to the firm. The Valuation Principle tells us that the value of the firm is the present value of its free cash flows. Therefore, working capital alters a firm's value by affecting its free cash flows. In this section, we examine the components of net working capital and their effects on the firm's value.

The Cash Cycle

The level of working capital reflects the length of time between when cash goes out of a firm at the beginning of the production process and when it comes back in. Take Intel, for example. Let's trace the path of $1000 worth of inventory and raw materials through Intel's production process.

- First, Intel buys $1000 of raw materials and inventory from its suppliers, purchasing them on credit, which means that the firm does not have to pay cash immediately at the time of purchase.
- About 36 days later, Intel pays for the materials and inventory, so five weeks have passed between when Intel purchased the materials and when the cash outflow occurred.
- After another 55 days, Intel sells the materials (now in the form of finished microprocessors) to a computer manufacturer, but the sale is on credit, meaning that the computer manufacturer does not pay cash immediately. A total of 91 days have passed between when Intel purchased the materials and when it sold them as part of the finished product.
- About 32 days later, the computer manufacturer pays for the microprocessors, producing a cash inflow for Intel.

operating cycle The average length of time between when a firm originally receives its inventory and when it receives the cash back from selling its product.

A total of $36 + 55 + 32 = 123$ days have passed from when Intel originally bought the raw materials until it received the cash from selling the finished product. Thus, Intel's *operating cycle* is 123 days: a firm's **operating cycle** is the average length of time between when the firm originally purchases its inventory and when it receives the cash back from

cash cycle The length of time between when a firm pays cash to purchase its initial inventory and when it receives cash from the sale of the output produced from that inventory.

selling its product. A firm's **cash cycle** is the length of time between when the firm pays cash to purchase its initial inventory and when it receives cash from the sale of the output produced from that inventory. For Intel, the cash cycle is 87 days: the 55 days it holds the material after paying for it plus the 32 days it waits to receive cash after selling the finished product. Some companies actually have a *negative* cash cycle; they are paid for the product before they have to pay for the cost of producing it! This is generally possible only if companies keep very low inventory and have the size to force their suppliers to wait to be paid. Example 19.1 goes through an example of this for Apple. Figure 19.1 illustrates the operating and cash cycle.

cash conversion cycle A measure of the cash cycle calculated as the sum of a firm's inventory days and accounts receivable days, less its accounts payable days.

Some practitioners measure the cash cycle by calculating the *cash conversion cycle*. The **cash conversion cycle (CCC)** is defined as:

$$CCC = \text{Inventory Days} + \text{Accounts Receivable Days} - \text{Accounts Payable Days} \quad (19.1)$$

where

$$\text{Inventory Days} = \frac{\text{Inventory}}{\text{Average Daily Cost of Goods Sold}}$$

$$\text{Accounts Receivable Days} = \frac{\text{Accounts Receivable}}{\text{Average Daily Sales}}$$

$$\text{Accounts Payable Days} = \frac{\text{Accounts Payable}}{\text{Average Daily Cost of Goods Sold}}$$

All these ratios can be computed from the firm's financial statements. We discussed how to compute and use them in Chapter 2. Even though the cash conversion cycle is an important metric on its own, a financial manager needs to keep an eye on each of its components, because they all contain valuable information about how efficiently the firm is managing its working capital. Higher accounts receivable days may signal that the firm is having trouble collecting from its customers, and low accounts payable days might suggest it is not taking full advantage of opportunities to delay payment to suppliers. Finally, high inventory days would focus a manager on why the firm needs to have its inventory on hand so long before it sells the product.

FIGURE 19.1

The Cash Cycle and Operating Cycle for a Firm

The cash cycle is the average time between when a firm pays for its inventory and when it receives cash from the sale of its product. If the firm pays cash for its inventory, this period is identical to the firm's operating cycle. However, most firms buy their inventory on credit, which reduces the amount of time between the cash investment and the receipt of cash from that investment.

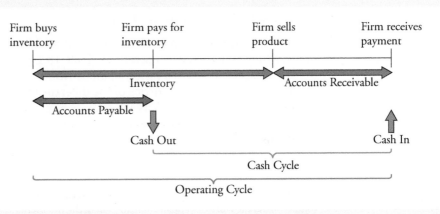

EXAMPLE 19.1

Computing the Cash
Conversion Cycle

MyFinanceLab

PROBLEM

The following information is from Apple's 2015 income statement and balance sheet (numbers are in $ millions). Use it to compute Apple's cash conversion cycle.

Sales	233,715
Cost of Goods Sold	140,089
Accounts Receivable	16,849
Inventory	2,349
Accounts Payable	35,490

SOLUTION

PLAN

The CCC is defined in Eq. 19.1 as Inventory Days + Accounts Receivable Days − Accounts Payable Days. Thus, we need to compute each of the three ratios in the CCC. In order to do that, we need to convert Sales and COGS into their average daily amounts simply by dividing the total given for the year by 365 days in a year.

EXECUTE

Average Daily Sales = Sales/365 Days = 233,715/365 = 640.32

Average Daily COGS = COGS/365 Days = 140,089/365 = 383.81

$$\text{Inventory Days} = \frac{\text{Inventory}}{\text{Average Daily Cost of Goods Sold}} = \frac{2,349}{383.81} = 6.12$$

$$\text{Accounts Receivable Days} = \frac{\text{Accounts Receivable}}{\text{Average Daily Sales}} = \frac{16,849}{640.32} = 26.31$$

$$\text{Accounts Payable Days} = \frac{\text{Accounts Payable}}{\text{Average Daily Cost of Goods Sold}} = \frac{35,490}{383.81} = 92.47$$

Thus, Dell's CCC = 6.12 + 26.31 − 92.47 = −60.04!

EVALUATE

Apple actually has a *negative* cash conversion cycle, meaning that it generally receives cash for its computers and other products *before* it pays its suppliers for the parts in its products. Apple is able to do this because its combination of direct sales to the consumer (it charges your credit card as soon as you order) and sales through retailers keep its receivables low. Due to its size and bargaining power, its suppliers allow it to wait nearly 93 days before paying them!

Working Capital Needs by Industry

The longer a firm's cash cycle, the more working capital it has, and the more cash it needs to carry to conduct its daily operations. Table 19.1 provides data on the working capital needs for selected firms in a variety of industries.

Because of the characteristics of the different industries, working capital levels vary significantly. For example, a large portion of a retail grocery store's customers pay cash when they buy their groceries, so you would expect accounts receivable to be a very small percentage of its sales.[1] For Kroger, accounts receivable represent only four days worth of

---

[1]When you use your credit card to pay for your groceries, it is a cash sale for the store. The credit card company pays the store cash upon confirmation of the transaction, even if you do not pay your credit card bill on time.

TABLE 19.1

Cash Conversion Cycles of Various Companies (2015)

Cash Conversion Cycle (CCC)	Company	Industry	Accounts Receivable Days	Inventory Days	Accounts Payable Days	CCC
	Molson Coors Brewing Company	Brewing	48	37	184	−99
	Pepsico	Beverages	40	40	164	−84
	Verizon Communications	Telecommunications	37	8	117	−72
	Apple	Computer Hardware	26	6	92	−60
	Bristol-Myers Squibb	Pharmaceuticals	72	126	223	−25
	Southwest Airlines	Airlines	9	9	32	−14
	Amazon.com	Internet Retail	19	45	73	−9
	Chipotle Mexican Grill	Restaurants	2	2	10	−6
	The Kroger Co.	Grocery Stores	4	24	23	5
	Walmart Stores	Superstores	4	47	39	12
	Microsoft	Software	62	33	77	18
	Macy's	Department Stores	4	147	133	18
	FedEx	Air Freight	43	5	22	26
	Starbucks	Restaurants	12	30	16	26
	Nordstrom	Department Stores	29	79	62	46
	Nike	Footwear	36	91	41	86
	AGL Resources	Gas Utilities	150	76	132	94
	Brown-Forman	Distillers and Vintners	72	440	90	422
	Lennar	Homebuilding	3	463	23	443
	Tiffany & Co.	Luxury Goods	17	546	66	497

Source: www.capitaliq.com.

sales. Similar results hold for Southwest Airlines, because many of its customers pay in advance for airline tickets with cash or credit cards. Inventory represents a large percentage of sales for firms such as Lennar, which have a long development and sales cycle. Note also the wide variation in the firms' cash conversion cycles. For example, Southwest's cash conversion cycle is negative, reflecting the fact that it receives cash from its customers before having to pay its suppliers.

Firm Value and Working Capital

To understand why working capital management can increase firm value, recall that any funds your company has from investors need to earn an opportunity cost of capital for those investors. Working capital ties up funds that could be deployed elsewhere in the firm to earn a return. For example, imagine $50,000 in raw materials sitting in a factory waiting to be used. That $50,000 needs to earn a return, so any delay in converting that material into a product that can be sold reduces its return. If you could improve your production process so that only $30,000 of raw material was waiting to be used at any one time, you would have freed up $20,000 to be invested elsewhere or returned to the shareholders. Similarly, when you allow your customers to pay within 30 days, you are giving them a 30-day interest-free loan. However, your investors and banks have not given you interest-free funds! If you can reduce the time it takes customers to pay without reducing sales, you can improve the return your investors earn on the business.

Any reduction in working capital requirements generates a positive free cash flow that the firm can distribute immediately to shareholders. For example, if a firm is able to reduce its required net working capital by $50,000, it will be able to distribute this $50,000 as a dividend to its shareholders immediately.

Recall that the Valuation Principle implies that the value of the firm is the present value of its free cash flows. Managing working capital efficiently will increase those free cash flows, allowing a manager to maximize firm value. We now turn our attention to some specific working capital accounts.

EXAMPLE 19.2

The Value of Working
Capital Management

MyFinanceLab

PROBLEM

The projected net income and free cash flows next year for Emerald City Paints are given in the following table in $ thousands:

Net Income	20,000
+ Depreciation	+5,000
− Capital Expenditures	−5,000
− Increase in Working Capital	−1,000
= Free Cash Flow	19,000

Emerald City expects capital expenditures and depreciation to continue to offset each other, and for both net income and increase in working capital to grow at 4% per year. Emerald City's cost of capital is 12%. If Emerald City were able reduce its annual increase in working capital by 20% by managing its working capital more efficiently without adversely affecting any other part of the business, what would be the effect on Emerald City's value?

SOLUTION

PLAN

A 20% decrease in required working capital increases would reduce the starting point from $1,000,000 per year to $800,000 per year. The working capital increases would still grow at 4% per year, but each increase would then be 20% smaller because of the 20% smaller starting point. We can value Emerald City using the formula for a growing perpetuity from Chapter 4 (Eq. 4.7):

$$PV = \frac{Cash\ Flow}{r - g}$$

As shown in the table above, we can determine Emerald City's free cash flow as:

Net Income + Depreciation − Capital Expenditures − Increases in Working Capital.

EXECUTE

Currently, Emerald City's value is:

$$\frac{20,000,000 + 5,000,000 - 5,000,000 - 1,000,000}{.12 - .04} = 237,500,000$$

If they can manage their working capital more efficiently, the value will be:

$$\frac{20,000,000 + 5,000,000 - 5,000,000 - 800,000}{.12 - .04} = 240,000,000$$

EVALUATE

Although the change will not affect Emerald City's earnings (net income), it will increase the free cash flow available to shareholders and increase the value of the firm by $2.5 million.

**CONCEPT
CHECK**

1. What is the difference between a firm's cash cycle and operating cycle?

2. How does working capital impact a firm's value?

19.2 Trade Credit

When a firm allows a customer to pay for goods at some date later than the date of purchase, it creates an account receivable for the firm and an account payable for the customer. Accounts receivable represent the credit sales for which a firm has yet to receive payment. The accounts payable balance represents the amount that a firm owes its suppliers for goods that it has received but for which it has not yet paid. The credit that the firm is extending to its customer is known as **trade credit**—the difference between receivables

trade credit The difference between receivables and payables that is the net amount of a firm's capital consumed as a result of those credit transactions; the credit that a firm extends to its customers.

and payables that is the net amount of a firm's capital consumed as a result of those credit transactions. A firm would, of course, prefer to be paid in cash at the time of purchase. A "cash-only" policy, however, may cause it to lose its customers to competition. Even after a customer decides to pay a bill, there is a delay before the money is credited to the firm because of processing and mailing the payment. In this section, we demonstrate how managers can compare the costs and benefits of trade credit to determine optimal credit policies.

Trade Credit Terms

To see how the terms of trade credit are quoted, let's consider some examples. If a supplier offers its customers terms of "net 30," payment is not due until 30 days from the date of the invoice. Essentially, the supplier is letting the customer use its money for an extra 30 days. (Note that "30" is not a magic number; the invoice could specify "net 40," "net 15," or any other number of days as the payment due date.)

cash discount The percentage discount offered if the buyer pays early.

discount period The number of days a buyer has to take advantage of the cash discount.

credit period The total length of time credit is extended to the buyer.

Sometimes the selling firm will offer the buying firm a discount if payment is made early. The terms "2/10, net 30" mean that the buying firm will receive a 2% discount if it pays for the goods within 10 days; otherwise, the full amount is due in 30 days. The **cash discount** is the percentage discount offered if the buyer pays early, in this case 2%. The **discount period** is the number of days the buyer has to take advantage of the cash discount; here it is 10 days. Finally, the **credit period** is the total length of time credit is extended to the buyer—the total amount of time the buyer has to pay. It is 30 days in our example. Firms offer discounts to encourage customers to pay early so that the selling firm gets cash from the sale sooner. However, the amount of the discount also represents a cost to the selling firm because it does not receive the full selling price for the product. This timeline shows the terms of our 2/10, net 30 example:

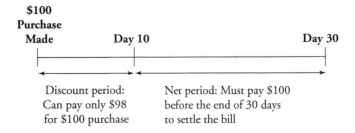

Trade Credit and Market Frictions

In a perfectly competitive market, trade credit is just another form of financing. As we learned in Chapter 16, financing decisions are irrelevant under the assumptions of perfect capital markets. In reality, product markets are rarely perfectly competitive, so firms can maximize their value by using their trade credit options effectively.

Cost of Trade Credit. Trade credit is, in essence, a loan from the selling firm to its customer. The price discount represents an interest rate. Often, firms offer favorable interest rates on trade credit as a price discount to their customers. Therefore, financial managers should evaluate the terms of trade credit to decide whether to use it.

How do we compute the interest rate on trade credit? Suppose a firm sells a product for $100 but offers its customer terms of 2/10, net 30. The customer doesn't have to pay anything for the first 10 days, so it effectively has a zero-interest loan for this period. If the customer takes advantage of the discount and pays within the 10-day discount period, the customer pays only $98 for the product. The cost of the discount to the selling firm is equal to the discount percentage times the selling price. In this case, it is $0.02 \times \$100$, or $2.

COMMON MISTAKE

Using APR Instead of EAR to Compute the Cost of Trade Credit

Some managers fail to fully recognize the cost of trade credit by using APR (simple interest) rather than EAR to compute the annual cost for comparison with other financing options. Recall from Chapter 5 that whereas the EAR appropriately accounts for the compounding "interest on interest" effect over the year, APR ignores compounding. Thus, in our example below with 2.04% interest over 20 days, the corresponding APR would be $(365/20) \times 2.04\% = 37.23\%$, which is less than the true effective annual cost of this credit: 44.6%.

Rather than pay within 10 days, the customer has the option to use the $98 for an additional 20 days $(30 - 10 = 20)$. The interest rate for the 20-day term of the loan is $2/$98 = 2.04\%. To compare this 20-day interest rate with interest rates available from other financing sources, we convert it to an effective annual rate using Eq. 5.1 from Chapter 5, where n is the number of 20-day periods in a year:

$$EAR = (1 + r)^n - 1$$

With a 365-day year, there are 365/20 (18.25) 20-day periods in a year. Thus, this 2.04% rate over 20 days corresponds to an effective annual rate of:

$$EAR = (1.0204)^{365/20} - 1 = 44.6\%$$

Therefore, by not taking the discount, the firm is effectively paying 2.04% to borrow the money for 20 days, which translates to an effective annual rate of 44.6%! If the firm can obtain a bank loan at a lower interest rate, it would be better off borrowing at the lower rate and using the cash proceeds of the loan to take advantage of the discount offered by the supplier.

EXAMPLE 19.3

Estimating the Effective Cost of Trade Credit

MyFinanceLab

PROBLEM

Your firm purchases goods from its supplier on terms of 1/15, net 40. What is the effective annual cost to your firm if it chooses not to take advantage of the trade discount offered?

SOLUTION

PLAN

Using a $100 purchase as an example, 1/15, net 40 means you get a 1% discount if you pay within 15 days, or you can pay the full amount within 40 days. 1% of $100 is a $1 discount, so you can either pay $99 in 15 days, or $100 in 40 days. The difference is 25 days, so you need to compute the interest rate over the 25 days and then compute the EAR associated with that 25-day interest rate.

EXECUTE

$1/$99 = 0.0101, or 1.01% interest for 25 days. There are 365/25 = 14.6 25-day periods in a year. Thus, your effective annual rate is $(1.0101)^{14.6} - 1 = 0.158$, or 15.8%.

EVALUATE

If you really need to take the full 40 days to produce the cash to pay, you would be better off finding a bank that would lend you the $99 at a lower rate so you could take advantage of the discount.

Benefits of Trade Credit. For a number of reasons, trade credit can be an attractive source of funds. First, trade credit is simple and convenient to use, and it has lower transaction costs than alternative sources of funds. For example, no paperwork must be completed, as would be the case for a loan from a bank. Second, it is a flexible source of funds and can be used as needed. Finally, it is sometimes the only source of funding available to a firm.

Trade Credit Versus Standard Loans. You might wonder why companies would ever provide trade credit. After all, most companies are not banks, so why are they in the business of making loans? Several reasons explain their willingness to offer trade credit. First, providing financing at below-market rates is an indirect way to lower prices for only certain customers. Consider, for example, an automobile manufacturer. Rather than lowering prices on all cars, the financing division may offer specific credit terms that are attractive to customers with bad credit, but unattractive to customers with good credit. In this way, the car manufacturer is able to discount the price only for those customers with bad credit who otherwise might not be able to afford the car.

Second, because a supplier may have an ongoing business relationship with its customer, it may have more information about the credit quality of the customer than a traditional outside lender such as a bank would have. The supplier may also be able to increase the likelihood of payment by threatening to cut off future supplies if payment is not made. Finally, if the buyer defaults, the supplier may be able to seize the inventory as collateral. This inventory is likely to be more valuable to a company within the industry such as the supplier (which presumably has other customers) than to an outsider.

Managing Float

One factor that contributes to the length of a firm's receivables and payables is the delay between the time a bill is paid and the cash is actually received. This delay, or *processing float*, will impact a firm's working capital requirements.

collection float The amount of time it takes for a firm to be able to use funds after a customer has paid for its goods.

Collection Float. The amount of time it takes for a firm to be able to use funds after a customer has paid for its goods is referred to as **collection float**. Firms can reduce their working capital needs by reducing their collection float. Collection float is determined by three factors, as shown in Figure 19.2:

mail float The time it takes a firm to receive a customer's payment check after the customer has mailed it.

- **Mail float:** The time it takes the firm to receive a payment check after the customer has mailed it.

processing float The time it takes a firm to process a customer's payment check and deposit it in the bank.

- **Processing float:** The time it takes the firm to process a customer's payment check and deposit it in the bank.

availability float The time it takes a bank to give a firm credit for customer payments the firm has deposited in the bank.

- **Availability float:** The time it takes a bank to post the funds from customer payments the firm has deposited in the bank.

FIGURE 19.2

Collection Float

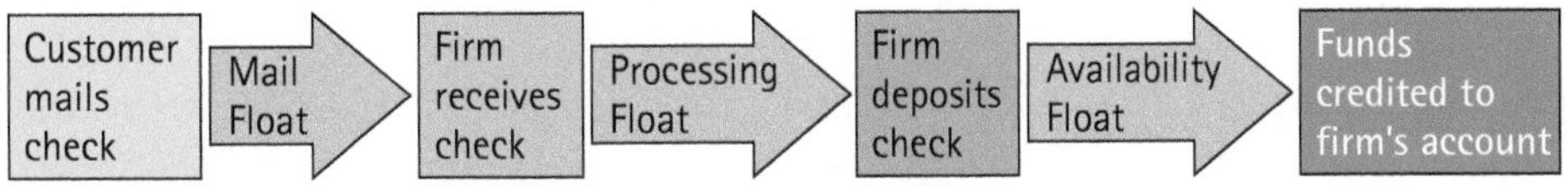

Customer mails check → Mail Float → Firm receives check → Processing Float → Firm deposits check → Availability Float → Funds credited to firm's account

disbursement float The time it takes before a firm's payments to its suppliers actually result in a cash outflow for the firm.

Disbursement Float. The time it takes before payments to suppliers actually result in a cash outflow for the firm is referred to as **disbursement float**. Similar to collection float, it is a function of mail time, processing time, and check-clearing time. Although a firm may try to extend its disbursement float in order to lengthen its payables and reduce its working capital needs, it risks making late payments to suppliers. In such a case, the firm may be charged an additional fee for paying late or may be required to pay cash before delivery (CBD) or cash on delivery (COD) for future purchases. In some cases, the supplier may refuse to do business in the future with the delinquent firm.

Electronic Check Processing. Firms can employ several methods to reduce their collection and disbursement floats. The **Check Clearing for the 21st Century Act (Check 21)**, which became effective on October 28, 2004, eliminated the part of the disbursement float due to the check-clearing process. Under the act, banks can process check information

Check Clearing for the 21st Century Act (Check 21) Eliminates the disbursement float due to the check-clearing process. Banks can process check information electronically and, in most cases, the funds are deducted from a firm's checking account on the same day that the firm's supplier deposits the check in its bank.

electronically and, in most cases, the funds are deducted from a firm's checking account on the same day the firm's supplier deposits the check in its bank. Unfortunately, even though the funds are taken out of the check writer's account almost immediately under Check 21, the check recipient's account is not credited as quickly. As a result, the act does not serve to reduce collection float.

There are, however, several ways that a firm *can* reduce its collection float. For example, the firm may streamline its in-house check-processing procedures. In addition, with electronic collection, funds are automatically transferred from the customer's bank account to the firm's bank account on the payment date, reducing the collection float to zero. The methods a firm employs to reduce its collection float are not without costs, of course. New check-processing systems could be expensive and disruptive, and hiring a collection agency to speed up collections generates costs such as fees to the agency as well as bad will with the firm's customers. Therefore, to decide which method, if any, to employ, the firm must compare the costs and benefits of systems that allow it to use its cash for a longer period.

CONCEPT CHECK

3. What does the term "2/10, net 30" mean?

4. List three factors that determine collection float.

19.3 Receivables Management

So far, we have discussed the costs and benefits of trade credit in general. Next, we look at some issues that arise specifically from the management of a firm's accounts receivable. In particular, we focus on how a firm adopts a policy for offering credit to its customers and how it monitors its accounts receivable on an ongoing basis.

Determining the Credit Policy

Establishing a credit policy involves three steps that we will discuss in turn:

1. Establishing credit standards
2. Establishing credit terms
3. Establishing a collection policy

 The 5 C's of Credit

Lenders have coined the phrase "The 5 C's of Credit" to summarize the qualities they look for before granting credit:

Character: Is the borrower trustworthy, with a history of meeting its debt obligations?

Capacity: Will the borrower have enough cash flow to make its payments?

Capital: Does the borrower have enough capital (net worth) to justify the loan?

Collateral: Does the borrower have any assets that can secure the loan?

Conditions: How are the borrower and the economy performing and how are they expected to perform?

Establishing Credit Standards. Management must first decide on its credit standards. Will it extend credit to anyone who applies for it? Or will it be selective and extend credit only to those customers who have very low credit risk? Unless the firm adopts the former policy, it will need to assess the credit risk of each customer before deciding whether to grant credit. Large firms perform this analysis in-house with their own credit departments. Small firms purchase credit reports from credit rating agencies such as Dun & Bradstreet.

Many firms will consider additional factors when deciding whether to grant credit to a particular customer. For example, in order to win sales a firm may be more likely to grant credit if the customer is expected to be a repeat customer. If the cost of the credit is small relative to the purchase price, it may also adopt a less restrictive policy. Thus, while credit risk is the starting point, the firm's managers may choose to extend credit strategically when dealing with potentially important customers or high-margin sales.

The decision of how much credit risk to assume plays a large role in determining how much money a firm ties up in its receivables. Although a restrictive policy can result in a lower sales volume, the firm will have a smaller investment in receivables. Conversely, a less selective policy will produce higher sales, but the level of receivables will also rise.

Establishing Credit Terms. After a firm decides on its credit standards, it must next establish its credit terms. The firm decides on the length of the period before payment must be made (the "net" period) and chooses whether to offer a discount to encourage early payments. If it offers a discount, it must also determine the discount percentage and the discount period. If the firm is relatively small, it will probably follow the lead of other firms in the industry in establishing these terms.

EXAMPLE 19.4

Evaluating a Change in
Credit Policy

MyFinanceLab

PROBLEM

Your company currently sells its product with a 1% discount to customers who pay cash immediately. Otherwise, the full price is due within 30 days. Half of your customers take advantage of the discount. You are considering dropping the discount so that your new terms would just be net 30. If you do that, you expect to lose some customers who were only willing to pay the discounted price, but the rest will simply switch to taking the full 30 days to pay. Altogether, you estimate that you will sell 20 fewer units per month (compared to 500 units currently). Your variable cost per unit is $60 and your price per unit is $100. If your required return is 1% per month, should you switch your policy?

SOLUTION

PLAN

To decide whether to change your policy, compute the NPV of the change. It costs you $30,000 to make the 500 units. You receive payment for half of the units immediately at a price of $99 per unit (1% discount). The other half comes in 30 days at a price of $100 per unit. At that point, you are starting over again with the next set of product. Thus, you can think of your cash flows in any 30-day period as:

	Now	30 days	
Produce first set of 500 units at $60 apiece	−30,000		
Customers pay for 250 units at $99 apiece	+24,750		
Customers pay for 250 units at $100 apiece		+25,000	. . .
Produce next set of 500 units at $60 apiece		−30,000	. . .
Customers pay for 250 units at $99 apiece		+24,750	. . .
Total	−5,250	+25,000 − 5,250	. . .

Under the new policy, your cash flows would switch to:

	Now	30 days	
Produce first set of 480 units at $60 apiece	−28,800		
Customers pay for 480 units at $100 apiece		+48,000	. . .
Produce next set of 480 units at $60 apiece		−28,800	. . .
Total	−28,800	+48,000 − 28,800	

With these cash flows, we are ready to compute the NPV of the policy change.

(Continued)

EXECUTE

$$NPV_{current} = -5250 + \frac{25,000 - 5250}{.01} = 1,969,750$$

$$NPV_{new} = -28,800 + \frac{48,000 - 28,800}{.01} = 1,891,200$$

So the NPV of the switch will be $1,891,200 - $1,969,750 = -$78,550.

EVALUATE

You shouldn't make the switch because you will lose too many customers, even though your remaining customers will be paying the full price. The NPV helps us weigh this tradeoff—the present value of the costs outweighs the present value of the benefits, so the decision is not a good one.

Establishing a Collection Policy. The last step in the development of a credit policy is to decide on a collection policy. The content of this policy can range from doing nothing if a customer is paying late (generally not a good choice), to sending a polite letter of inquiry, to charging interest on payments extending beyond a specified period, to threatening legal action at the first late payment.

Monitoring Accounts Receivable

After establishing a credit policy, a firm must monitor its accounts receivable to analyze whether its credit policy is working effectively. Two tools that firms use to monitor the accounts receivable are the *accounts receivable days* (or average collection period) and the *aging schedule*.

Accounts Receivable Days. The accounts receivable days is the average number of days that it takes a firm to collect on its sales. A firm can compare this number to the payment policy specified in its credit terms to judge the effectiveness of its credit policy. If the credit terms specify "net 30" and the accounts receivable days outstanding is 50 days, the firm can conclude that its customers are paying 20 days late, on average.

The firm should also look at the trend in the accounts receivable days over time. If the accounts receivable days ratio of a firm has been approximately 35 days for the past few years and it is 43 days this year, the firm may want to reexamine its credit policy. Of course, if the economy is sluggish, the entire industry may be affected. Under these circumstances, the increase might have little to do with the firm itself.

Accounts receivable days can be calculated from the firm's financial statements. Outside investors commonly use this measure to evaluate a firm's credit management policy. A major weakness of the accounts receivable days is that it is merely one number and conceals much useful information. Seasonal sales patterns may cause the number calculated for the accounts receivable days to change depending on when the calculation takes place. The number can also look reasonable even when a substantial percentage of the firm's customers are paying late.

aging schedule
Categorizes a firm's accounts by the number of days they have been on the books. It can be prepared using either the number of accounts or the dollar amount of the accounts receivable outstanding.

Aging Schedule. An **aging schedule** categorizes a firm's accounts by the number of days they have been on the books. It can be prepared using either the number of accounts or the dollar amount of the accounts receivable outstanding. For example, assume that a firm selling on terms of 2/15, net 30 has $530,000 in accounts receivable that has been on the books for 15 or fewer days in 220 accounts. Another $450,000 has been on the books for 16 to 30 days and is made up of 190 accounts, and $350,000 has been on the books for 31 to 45 days and represents 80 accounts. The firm has $200,000 that has been on the books for 46 to 60 days in 60 accounts. Yet another $70,000 has been on the books for more than 60 days and is made up of 20 accounts. Table 19.2 includes aging schedules based on the number of accounts and dollar amounts outstanding.

In this case, if the firm's average daily sales are $65,000, its accounts receivable days is $1,600,000/$65,000 = 25 days. But on closer examination, using the aging schedules in Table 19.2, we can see that 28% of the firm's credit customers (and 39% by dollar amounts) are paying late.

TABLE 19.2

Aging Schedules

(a) Number of Accounts

Days Outstanding	Number of Accounts	Percentage of Accounts (%)
1–15	220	38.6
16–30	190	33.3
31–45	80	14.0
46–60	60	10.5
60+	20	3.5
	570	100.0

(b) Dollar Amounts Outstanding

Days Outstanding	Amount Outstanding ($)	Percentage Outstanding (%)
1–15	530,000	33.1
16–30	450,000	28.1
31–45	350,000	21.9
46–60	200,000	12.5
60+	70,000	4.4
	1,600,000	100.0

EXAMPLE 19.5

Aging Schedules

MyFinanceLab

PROBLEM

Financial Training Systems (FTS) bills its accounts on terms of 3/10, net 30. The firm's accounts receivable include $100,000 that has been outstanding for 10 or fewer days, $300,000 outstanding for 11 to 30 days, $100,000 outstanding for 31 to 40 days, $20,000 outstanding for 41 to 50 days, $10,000 outstanding for 51 to 60 days, and $2000 outstanding for more than 60 days. Prepare an aging schedule for FTS.

SOLUTION

PLAN

An aging schedule shows the amount and percent of total accounts receivable outstanding for different lengths outstanding. With the available information, we can calculate the aging schedule based on dollar amounts outstanding. (The numbers don't add to exactly 100% because of rounding.)

EXECUTE

Days Outstanding	Amount Outstanding ($)	Percentage Outstanding (%)
1–10	100,000	18.8
11–30	300,000	56.4
31–40	100,000	18.8
41–50	20,000	3.8
51–60	10,000	1.9
60+	2,000	0.4
	532,000	100.0

(Continued)

If the aging schedule gets "bottom-heavy"—that is, if the percentages in the lower half of the schedule representing late-paying firms begin to increase—the firm will likely need to revisit its credit policy. The aging schedule is also sometimes augmented by analysis of the **payments pattern**, which provides information on the percentage of monthly sales that the firm collects in each month after the sale. By examining past data, a firm may observe that 10% of its sales are usually collected in the month of the sale, 40% in the month following the sale, 25% two months after the sale, 20% three months after the sale, and 5% four months after the sale. Management can compare this normal payments pattern to the current payments pattern. Knowledge of the payments pattern is also useful for forecasting the firm's working capital requirements.

> **payments pattern**
> Provides information on the percentage of monthly sales that the firm collects in each month after the sale.

CONCEPT CHECK

5. Describe three steps in establishing a credit policy.

6. What is the difference between accounts receivable days and an aging schedule?

19.4 Payables Management

A firm should choose to borrow using accounts payable only if trade credit is the cheapest source of funding. The cost of the trade credit depends on the credit terms. The higher the discount percentage offered, the greater the cost of forgoing the discount. The cost of forgoing the discount is also higher with a shorter loan period. When a company has a choice between trade credit from two different suppliers, it should take the less expensive alternative.

In addition, a firm should always pay on the latest day allowed. For example, if the discount period is 10 days and the firm is taking the discount, payment should be made on day 10, not on day 2. If the discount is not taken and the terms are 2/10, net 30, the full payment should be made on day 30, not on day 16. A firm should strive to keep its money working for it as long as possible without developing a bad relationship with its suppliers or engaging in unethical practices. In this section, we examine two techniques that firms use to monitor their accounts payable: determining the accounts payable days outstanding and stretching accounts payable.

Determining Accounts Payable Days Outstanding

Similar to the situation with its accounts receivable, a firm should monitor its accounts payable to ensure that it is making its payments at an optimal time. One method is to calculate the accounts payable days outstanding and compare it to the credit terms. The accounts payable days outstanding is the accounts payable balance expressed in terms of the number of days of cost of goods sold. If the accounts payable outstanding is 40 days and the terms are 2/10, net 30, the firm can conclude that it generally pays late and may be risking supplier difficulties. Conversely, if the accounts payable days outstanding is 25 days and the firm has not been taking the discount, the firm is paying too early. It could be earning another five days' interest on its money.

EXAMPLE 19.6

Accounts Payable Management

MyFinanceLab

PROBLEM

The Rowd Company has an average accounts payable balance of $250,000. Its average daily cost of goods sold is $14,000, and it receives terms of 2/15, net 40 from its suppliers. Rowd chooses to forgo the discount. Is the firm managing its accounts payable well?

SOLUTION

PLAN

Given Rowd's AP balance and its daily COGS, we can compute the average number of days it takes to pay its vendors by dividing the average balance by the daily costs. Given the terms from its suppliers, Rowd should either be paying on the 15th day (the last possible day to get the discount), or on the 40th day (the last possible day to pay). There is no benefit to paying at any other time.

EXECUTE

Rowd's accounts payable days outstanding is $250,000/$14,000 = 17.9 days. If Rowd made payment three days earlier, it could take advantage of the 2% discount. If, for some reason, it chose to forgo the discount, it should not be paying the full amount until the 40th day.

EVALUATE

The firm is not managing its accounts payable well. The earlier it pays, the sooner the cash leaves Rowd. Thus, the only reason to pay before the 40th day is to receive the discount by paying before the 15th day. Paying on the 18th day not only misses the discount, but costs the firm 22 days (40–18) use of its cash.

Stretching Accounts Payable

stretching the accounts payable When a firm ignores a payment due period and pays later.

Some firms ignore the payment due period and pay the amount owed later, in a practice referred to as **stretching the accounts payable**. Given terms of 2/10, net 30, for example, a firm may choose not to pay the amount owed until 45 days have passed. Doing so reduces the direct cost of trade credit because it lengthens the time that a firm has use of the funds. Although the interest rate per period remains the same—$2/$98 = 2.04\%$—the firm is now using the $98 for 35 days beyond the discount period, rather than 20 days as provided by the trade credit terms.

EXAMPLE 19.7

Cost of Trade Credit with Stretched Accounts Payable

MyFinanceLab

PROBLEM

What is the effective annual cost of credit terms of 1/15, net 40 if the firm stretches the accounts payable to 60 days?

SOLUTION

PLAN

First, we need to compute the interest rate per period. The 1% discount means that on a $100 purchase, you can either pay $99 in the discount period, or keep the $99 and pay $100 later. Thus, you pay $1 interest on the $99. If you pay on time, then this $1 in interest is over the 25-day period between the 15th day and the 40th day. If you stretch, then this $1 in interest is over the 45-day period between the 15th day and the 60th day.

EXECUTE

The interest rate per period is $1/$99 = 1.01\%$. If the firm delays payment until the 60th day, it has use of the funds for 45 days beyond the discount period. There are $365/45 = 8.11$ 45-day periods in one year. Thus, the effective annual cost is $(1.0101)^{8.11} - 1 = 0.0849$, or 8.49%.

EVALUATE

Paying on time corresponds to a 25-day credit period and there are $365/25 = 14.6$ 25-day periods in a year. Thus, if the firm pays on the 40th day, the effective annual cost is $(1.0101)^{14.6} - 1 = .1580$, or 15.8%. By stretching its payables, the firm substantially reduces its effective cost of credit.

Firms may also make a payment on the 30th day but pay only the discounted price. Some may pay only the discounted price and pay even later than the 30th day. Although all these actions will reduce the effective annual rate associated with the trade credit, the firm may incur costs as a result of these actions. Suppliers may react to a firm whose payments are always late by imposing terms of cash on delivery (COD) or cash before delivery (CBD). The delinquent firm then bears the additional costs associated with these terms and may have to negotiate a bank loan to have the cash available to pay. The supplier may also discontinue business with the delinquent customer, leaving the customer to find another source, which may be more expensive or of lower quality. A poor credit rating might also result, making it difficult for the firm to obtain good terms with any other supplier. Moreover, when a firm explicitly agrees to the terms of the sale, violating these terms constitutes unethical business behavior.

CONCEPT
CHECK

7. What is the optimal time for a firm to pay its accounts payable?

8. What do the terms COD and CBD mean?

19.5   Inventory Management

As we discussed, in a perfect capital markets setting, firms would not need to have accounts payable or receivable. Interest rates on trade credit would be competitive, and firms could use alternative sources of financing. However, unlike trade credit, inventory represents one of the required factors of production. Therefore, even in a perfect markets setting, firms still need inventory.

Inventory management receives extensive coverage in a course on operations management. Nevertheless, it is the firm's financial manager who must arrange for the financing necessary to support the firm's inventory policy and who is responsible for ensuring the firm's overall profitability. Therefore, the role of the inventory manager is to balance the costs and benefits associated with inventory. Because excessive inventory uses cash, efficient management of inventory increases firm value.

Benefits of Holding Inventory

A firm needs its inventory to operate for several reasons. First, inventory helps minimize the risk that the firm will not be able to obtain an input it needs for production. If a firm holds too little inventory, **stock-outs**, the situation when a firm runs out of inventory, may occur and lead to lost sales. Disappointed customers may switch to one of the firm's competitors.

stock-outs The situation that occurs when a firm runs out of inventory.

Second, firms may hold inventory because factors such as seasonality in demand mean that customer purchases do not perfectly match the most efficient production cycle. Consider the case of the Sandpoint Toy Company. As is typical for many toy manufacturers, 80% of Sandpoint's annual sales occur between September and December, in anticipation of the holiday gift season. It is more efficient for Sandpoint to manufacture toys at relatively constant levels throughout the year. If Sandpoint produces its toys at a constant rate, its inventory levels will increase to very high levels by August, in anticipation of the increase in sales beginning in September. In contrast, Sandpoint may consider a seasonal manufacturing strategy, producing more toys between September and December when sales are high. Under this strategy, inventory would not accumulate, freeing up cash flow from working capital and reducing the costs of inventory. However, seasonal manufacturing incurs additional costs, such as increased wear and tear on the manufacturing equipment during peak demand and the need to hire and train seasonal workers. Sandpoint must weigh the costs of the inventory buildup under constant production against the benefits of more efficient production. The optimal choice is likely to involve a compromise between the two extremes, so that Sandpoint will carry some inventory.

Costs of Holding Inventory

As suggested by the Sandpoint Toy example, tying up capital in inventory is costly for a firm. We can classify the direct costs associated with inventory into three categories:

- *Acquisition costs* are the costs of the inventory itself over the period being analyzed (usually one year).
- *Order costs* are the total costs of placing an order over the period being analyzed.
- *Carrying costs* include storage costs, insurance, taxes, spoilage, obsolescence, and the opportunity cost of the funds tied up in the inventory.

Minimizing these total costs involves some tradeoffs. For example, if we assume no quantity discounts are available, the lower the level of inventory a firm carries, the lower its carrying cost, but the higher its annual order costs because it needs to place more orders during the year.

"just-in-time" (JIT) inventory management
When a firm acquires inventory precisely when needed so that its inventory balance is always zero, or very close to it.

Some firms seek to reduce their carrying costs as much as possible. With **"just-in-time" (JIT) inventory management**, a firm acquires inventory precisely when needed so that its inventory balance is always zero, or very close to it. This technique requires exceptional coordination with suppliers as well as a predictable demand for the firm's products. In 2007, Boeing established a global production system for its new 787 "Dreamliner." Very little of the new plane is actually produced at its plant in Everett, Washington. Rather, all of its major systems, including the fuselage and wings, are produced elsewhere and are flown to the final assembly plant using a specially modified 747 cargo plane. The pieces arrive very shortly before they are needed in the final assembly of the airplane, so Boeing does not have to face the carrying costs of maintaining a large inventory. However, such a plan has risks, as Boeing initially had substantial troubles with its contracted producers finishing their parts on time. Consequently, it delayed the delivery of the first planes and suffered financial penalties from doing so. By 2010, with the 787 in flight-testing, Boeing remained committed to the new production system, although it had to send thousands of its own engineers out to suppliers to help solve bottleneck problems. In some cases, it even bought its suppliers.

Inventory Management Adds to the Bottom Line at Gap

In 2003, the apparel chain GAP reduced its investment in inventory significantly by reducing its inventory days outstanding by 24%. This change freed up $344 million for other purposes. GAP invested some of this cash in short-term securities—primarily in U.S. government and agency securities and in bank certificates of deposit with maturities between three months and one year. The firm reported an increase of *$1.2 million* in interest income in fiscal year 2003 compared with fiscal year 2002. It attributed the increase in interest income to increases in the average cash balances available for investment.

Source: GAP 2003 annual report.

Even if your company does not practice JIT inventory management, it may be forced to adopt it if a major customer does so. For example, in 1999, Toys "R" Us instituted JIT, which caused one of its suppliers, toy manufacturer Hasbro, to make changes in its production schedule.[2]

CONCEPT CHECK
9. What are the direct costs of holding inventory?
10. Describe "just-in-time" inventory management.

---

[2]Hasbro 1999 annual report.

19.6 Cash Management

In the perfect markets setting, the level of cash is irrelevant. With perfect capital markets, a firm is able to raise new money instantly at a fair rate, so it can never be short of cash. Similarly, the firm can invest excess cash at a fair rate to earn an NPV of zero.

In the real world, of course, markets are not perfect. Liquidity has a cost; for example, holding liquid assets may earn a below-market return, and a firm may face transaction costs if it needs to raise cash quickly. Similarly, recall from Chapter 16 that holding excess cash has a tax disadvantage. In these cases, the optimal strategy for a firm is to hold cash in anticipation of seasonalities in demand for its products and random shocks that affect its business. Risky firms and firms with high-growth opportunities tend to hold a relatively high percentage of assets as cash. Firms with easy access to capital markets (for which the transaction costs of accessing cash are therefore lower) tend to hold less cash.[3] In this section, we examine the firm's motivation for holding cash, tools for managing cash, and the short-term securities in which firms invest.

Motivation for Holding Cash

There are three reasons why a firm holds cash:

- To meet its day-to-day needs
- To compensate for the uncertainty associated with its cash flows
- To satisfy bank requirements

We will now examine each of these motivations for holding cash in detail.

transactions balance
The amount of cash a firm needs to pay its bills.

Transactions Balance. Just like you, a firm must hold enough cash to pay its bills. The amount of cash a firm needs to be able to pay its bills is sometimes referred to as a **transactions balance**. The amount of cash a firm needs to satisfy the transactions balance requirement depends on both the average size of the transactions made by the firm and the firm's cash cycle, discussed earlier in the chapter.

precautionary balance
The amount of cash a firm holds to counter the uncertainty surrounding its future cash needs.

Precautionary Balance. The amount of cash a firm holds to counter the uncertainty surrounding its future cash needs is known as a **precautionary balance**. The size of this balance depends on the degree of uncertainty surrounding a firm's cash flows. The more uncertain future cash flows are, the harder it is for a firm to predict its transactions need, so the larger the precautionary balance must be.

compensating balance
An amount a firm's bank may require the firm to maintain in an account at the bank as compensation for services the bank performs.

Compensating Balance. A firm's bank may require it to hold a **compensating balance** in an account at the bank as compensation for services that the bank performs. Compensating balances are typically deposited in accounts that earn either little or no interest. This arrangement is similar to a bank offering individuals free checking as long as their balances do not fall below a certain level—say, $1000. Essentially, the customer has $1000 cash that she cannot use unless she is willing to pay a service charge. Similarly, the cash that a firm has tied up to meet a compensating balance requirement is unavailable for other uses.

Alternative Investments

In our discussion of collection and disbursement floats, we assumed that the firm will invest any cash in short-term securities. In fact, the firm may choose from a variety of

---

[3]See T. Opler, L. Pinkowitz, R. Stulz, and R. Williamson, "The Determinants and Implications of Corporate Cash Holdings," *Journal of Financial Economics*, 52 (1) (1999): 3–46.

money market Market for safe, short-term debt issued by high-quality borrowers, such as governments or high credit quality firms.

short-term securities that differ somewhat with regard to their default risk and liquidity risk. The greater the risk, the higher the expected return on the investment. The financial manager must decide how much risk she is willing to accept in return for a higher yield. If her firm expects to need the funds within the next 30 days, the manager will probably avoid the less liquid options. Table 19.3 briefly describes the most frequently used short-term investments; these short-term debt securities are collectively referred to as **money market securities**.

TABLE 19.3

Money Market Investment Options

Investment	Description	Maturity	Risk	Liquidity
Treasury Bills	Short-term debt of the U.S. government.	Four weeks, three months (91 days), six months (182 days), or 52 weeks when newly issued.	Default risk free.	Very liquid and marketable.
Certificates of Deposit (CDs)	Short-term debt issued by banks. Minimum denomination of $100,000.	Varying maturities up to one year.	If the issuing bank is insured by the FDIC, any amount up to $250,000 is free of default risk because it is covered by the insurance. Any amount in excess of $250,000 is not insured and is subject to default risk.	Unlike CDs purchased by individuals, these CDs sell on the secondary market, but are less liquid than Treasury bills.
Repurchase Agreements	Essentially a loan arrangement wherein a securities dealer is the "borrower" and the investor is the "lender." The investor buys securities, such as U.S. Treasury bills, from the securities dealer, with an agreement to sell the securities back to the dealer at a later date for a specified higher price.	Very short term, ranging from overnight to approximately three months in duration.	The security serves as collateral for the loan, and therefore the investor is exposed to very little risk. However, the investor needs to consider the creditworthiness of the securities dealer when assessing the risk.	No secondary market for repurchase agreements.
Banker's Acceptances	Drafts written by the borrower and guaranteed by the bank on which the draft is drawn. Typically used in international trade transactions. The borrower is an importer who writes the draft in payment for goods.	Typically one to six months.	Because both the borrower and a bank have guaranteed the draft, there is very little risk.	When the exporter receives the draft, he may hold it until maturity and receive its full value or he may sell the draft at a discount prior to maturity.
Commercial Paper	Short-term, unsecured debt issued by large corporations. The minimum denomination is $25,000, but most commercial paper has a face value of $100,000 or more.	Typically one to six months.	Default risk depends on the creditworthiness of the issuing corporation.	No active secondary market, but issuer may repurchase commercial paper.
Short-Term Tax Exempts	Short-term debt of state and local governments. These instruments pay interest that is exempt from federal taxation, so their pretax yield is lower than that of a similar-risk, fully taxable investment.	Typically one to six months.	Default risk depends on the creditworthiness of the issuing government.	Moderate secondary market.

Hoarding Cash

Corporate liquidity is measured as corporate investments in short-term, marketable securities. In the United States, it rose from $3.9 trillion in 1999 to $9.7 trillion in 2013, for an increase of nearly 150%. Indeed, in 2015 more than 39% of U.S. publicly traded firms were net investors, having more cash and short-term investments than debt outstanding.

Why have companies been accumulating more cash? Factors include a shift away from industries such as manufacturing that spend heavily on plant and equipment, strength in sectors such as financial services that have low capital expenditures and high cash flows, avoidance of repatriation taxes by multinational firms, and a desire by companies to preserve liquidity and maintain financial flexibility. As a result, corporate savings have reached an all-time high.

How are companies investing their cash? A 2007 survey by Treasury Strategies indicated that 20% is invested in money market funds and accounts, 18% is invested in bonds and notes, and

the remainder is invested directly in commercial paper, CDs, repurchase agreements, and other investments.

During the 2008 financial crisis, short-term credit markets froze and many businesses that relied on short-term credit found themselves unable to conduct business, You might expect that businesses that held a lot of cash were in good shape. However, cash-holding firms during the crisis did not know what to do with the cash. Before it became clear that governments were going to bail out large banks, firms had to worry about how secure their cash was. In the event of a bank bankruptcy, the firm risked losing access to its cash in the short term and perhaps ultimately losing the cash altogether. For firms that relied on cash balances to conduct business, the impact of the breakdown in financial markets was potentially as big as for firms that relied on credit.

Source: Authors' calculations from Internal Revenue Service Data and Treasury Strategies 2007 Corporate Liquidity Research Overview.

Thus, a financial manager who wants to invest the firm's funds in the least risky security will choose to invest in Treasury bills. However, if a financial manager wishes to earn a higher return on the firm's short-term investments, she may opt to invest some or all of the firm's excess cash in a riskier alternative, such as commercial paper.

CONCEPT CHECK

11. List three reasons why a firm holds cash.

12. What tradeoff does a firm face when choosing how to invest its cash?

MyFinanceLab

Here is what you should know after reading this chapter. MyFinanceLab will help you identify what you know, and where to go when you need to practice.

KEY POINTS AND EQUATIONS	KEY TERMS	ONLINE PRACTICE
19.1 Overview of Working Capital • Working capital management involves managing a firm's short-term assets and short-term liabilities. • A firm's cash cycle is the length of time between when the firm pays cash to purchase its initial inventory and when it receives cash from the sale of the output produced from that inventory. The operating cycle is the average length of time between when a firm originally purchases its inventory and when it receives the cash back from selling its product.	cash conversion cycle, p. 605 cash cycle, p. 605 operating cycle, p. 604	MyFinanceLab Study Plan 19.1

19.2 Trade Credit

- Trade credit is effectively a loan from the selling firm to its customer. The cost of trade credit depends on the credit terms. The cost of not taking a discount that is offered by a supplier implies an interest rate for the loan.
- Firms provide trade credit to their customers for two reasons: (a) as an indirect way to lower prices and (b) because they may have advantages in making loans to their customers relative to other potential sources of credit.
- A firm should compare the cost of trade credit with the cost of alternative sources of financing in deciding whether to use the trade credit offered.
- Collection float is the amount of time it takes for a firm to be able to use funds after a customer has paid for its goods. Firms can reduce their working capital needs by reducing their collection float.

availability float, p. 611
cash discount, p. 609
Check Clearing for the 21st Century Act (Check 21), p. 611
collection float, p. 611
credit period, p. 609
disbursement float, p. 611
discount period, p. 609
mail float, p. 611
processing float, p. 611
trade credit, p. 609

19.3 Receivables Management

- Establishing a credit policy involves three steps: establishing credit standards, establishing credit terms, and establishing a collection policy.
- The accounts receivables days and aging schedule are two methods used to monitor the effectiveness of a firm's credit policy.

aging schedule, p. 614
payments pattern, p. 616

MyFinanceLab Study Plan 19.3

19.4 Payables Management

- Firms should monitor accounts payable to ensure that they are making payments at an optimal time.
- Paying late, known as stretching accounts payable, can reduce the direct costs of trade credit, but may result in worse terms from suppliers.

stretching the accounts payable, p. 617

MyFinanceLab Study Plan 19.4

19.5 Inventory Management

- Because excessive inventory uses cash, efficient inventory management increases the firm's free cash flow and thus increases firm value.
- Firms hold inventory to avoid lost sales due to stock-outs and because of factors such as seasonal demand.
- The costs of inventory include acquisition costs, order costs, and carrying costs.

"just-in-time" (JIT) inventory management, p. 619
stock-outs, p. 618

MyFinanceLab Study Plan 19.5

19.6 Cash Management

- If a firm's need to hold cash is reduced, the funds can be invested in a number of different short-term securities, including Treasury bills, certificates of deposit, commercial paper, repurchase agreements, banker's acceptances, and short-term tax exempts.

compensating balance, p. 620
precautionary balance, p. 620
transactions balance, p. 620

MyFinanceLab Study Plan 19.6

CRITICAL THINKING

1. What does a firm's cash cycle tell us?

2. Answer the following:
   a. What is the difference between a firm's cash cycle and its operating cycle?
   b. How will a firm's cash cycle be affected if it increases its inventory, all else being equal?
   c. How will a firm's cash cycle be affected if it begins to take the discounts offered by its suppliers, all else being equal?

3. Does an increase in a firm's cash cycle necessarily mean that the firm is managing its cash poorly?

4. Why is trade credit important?

5. What are the ways that receivables management can affect a firm's value?

6. What are the three steps involved in establishing a credit policy?

7. What factors determine how a firm should manage its payables?

8. What is meant by "stretching the accounts payable"?

9. What are the tradeoffs involved in reducing inventory?

10. What are the different ways you can invest your firm's cash?

11. Which of the following short-term securities would you expect to offer the highest before-tax return: Treasury bills, certificates of deposit, short-term tax exempts, or commercial paper? Why?

PROBLEMS

All problems are available in MyFinanceLab. *The* ⊞ *icon indicates problems that are easier to solve using Excel and have data in an Excel format available in* MyFinanceLab. *An asterisk * indicates problems with a higher level of difficulty.*

Overview of Working Capital

1. Homer Boats has accounts payable days of 20, inventory days of 50, and accounts receivable days of 30. What is its operating cycle?

2. FastChips Semiconductors has inventory days of 75, accounts receivable days of 30, and accounts payable days of 90. What is its cash conversion cycle?

3. Westerly Industries has the following financial information. What is its cash conversion cycle?

Sales	100,000
Cost of Goods Sold	80,000
Accounts Receivable	30,000
Inventory	15,000
Accounts Payable	40,000

4. Aberdeen Outboard Motors is contemplating building a new plant. The company anticipates that the plant will require an initial investment of $2 million in net working capital today. The plant will last 10 years, at which point the full investment in net working capital will be recovered. Given an annual discount rate of 6%, what is the net present value of this working capital investment?

5. Your firm currently has net working capital of $100,000 that it expects to grow at a rate of 4% per year forever. You are considering some suggestions that could slow that growth to 3% per year. If your discount rate is 12%, how would these changes impact the value of your firm?

6. The Greek Connection had sales of $32 million in 2015, and a cost of goods sold of $20 million. A simplified balance sheet for the firm appears below:
   a. Calculate The Greek Connection's net working capital in 2015.
   b. Calculate the cash conversion cycle of The Greek Connection in 2015.
   c. The industry average accounts receivable days is 30 days. What would have been the cash conversion cycle for The Greek Connection in 2015 had it matched the industry average for accounts receivable days (see MyFinanceLab *for the data in Excel format*)?

The Greek Connection
Balance Sheet as of December 31, 2015
(thousands of dollars)

Assets		Liabilities and Equity	
Cash	$ 2,000	Accounts payable	$ 1,500
Accounts receivable	3,950	Notes payable	1,000
Inventory	1,300	Accruals	1,220
Total current assets	$ 7,250	Total current liabilities	$ 3,720
Net plant, property, and equipment	8,500	Long-term debt	$ 3,000
		Total liabilities	$ 6,720
Total assets	$ 15,750	Common equity	$ 9,030
		Total liabilities and equity	$ 15,750

Trade Credit

7. Assume the credit terms offered to your firm by your suppliers are 3/5, net 30. Calculate the cost of the trade credit if your firm does not take the discount and pays on day 30.

8. Your supplier offers terms of 1/10, net 45. What is the effective annual cost of trade credit if you choose to forgo the discount and pay on day 45?

*9. The Fast Reader Company supplies bulletin board services to numerous hotel chains nationwide. The owner of the firm is investigating the desirability of employing a billing firm to do her billing and collections. Because the billing firm specializes in these services, collection float will be reduced by 20 days. Average daily collections are $1200, and the owner can earn 8% annually (expressed as an APR with monthly compounding) on her investments. If the billing firm charges $250 per month, should the owner employ the billing firm?

*10. The Saban Corporation is trying to decide whether to switch to a bank that will accommodate electronic funds transfers from Saban's customers. Saban's financial manager believes the new system would decrease its collection float by as much as five days. The new bank would require a compensating balance of $30,000, whereas its present bank has no compensating balance requirement. Saban's average daily collections are $10,000, and it can earn 8% on its short-term investments. Should Saban make the switch? (Assume the compensating balance at the new bank will be deposited in a non-interest-earning account.)

Receivables Management

11. The Manana Corporation had sales of $60 million this year. Its accounts receivable balance averaged $2 million. How long, on average, does it take the firm to collect on its sales?

12. The Mighty Power Tool Company has the following accounts on its books:

Customer	Amount Owed ($)	Age (days)
ABC	50,000	35
DEF	35,000	5
GHI	15,000	10
KLM	75,000	22
NOP	42,000	40
QRS	18,000	12
TUV	82,000	53
WXY	36,000	90

The firm extends credit on terms of 1/15, net 30. Develop an aging schedule using 15-day increments through 60 days, and then indicate any accounts that have been outstanding for more than 60 days.

Payables Management

13. Simple Simon's Bakery purchases supplies on terms of 1/10, net 25. If Simple Simon's chooses to take the discount offered, it must obtain a bank loan to meet its short-term financing needs. A local bank has quoted Simple Simon's owner an interest rate of 12% on borrowed funds. Should Simple Simon's enter the loan agreement with the bank and begin taking the discount?

14. Your firm purchases goods from its supplier on terms of 3/15, net 40.
    a. What is the effective annual cost to your firm if it chooses not to take the discount and makes its payment on day 40?
    b. What is the effective annual cost to your firm if it chooses not to take the discount and makes its payment on day 50?

*15. Use the financial statements supplied below and on the next page for International Motor Corporation (IMC) to answer the following questions (*see* MyFinanceLab *for the data in Excel format*):
    a. Calculate the cash conversion cycle for IMC for both 2015 and 2016. What change has occurred, if any? All else being equal, how does this change affect IMC's need for cash?
    b. IMC's suppliers offer terms of net 30. Does it appear that IMC is doing a good job of managing its accounts payable?

International Motor Corporation
Income Statement (in millions)
for the Years Ending December 31

	2015	2016
Sales	$60,000	$75,000
Cost of goods sold	52,000	61,000
Gross profit	$ 8,000	$14,000
Selling, general, and administrative expenses	6,000	8,000
Operating profit	$ 2,000	$ 6,000
Interest expense	1,400	1,300
Earnings before taxes	$ 600	$ 4,700
Taxes	300	2,350
Earnings after taxes	$ 300	$ 2,350

International Motor Corporation

Balance Sheet (in millions) as of December 31

	2015	2016		2015	2016
Assets			**Liabilities**		
Cash	$ 3,080	$ 6,100	Accounts payable	$ 3,600	$ 4,600
Accounts			Notes payable	1,180	1,250
receivable	2,800	6,900	Accruals	5,600	6,211
Inventory	6,200	6,600	Total current		
Total current assets	$12,080	$19,600	liabilities	$10,380	$12,061
Net plant, property,			Long-term debt	$ 6,500	$ 7,000
and equipment	$23,087	$20,098			
			Total liabilities	$16,880	$19,061
Total assets	$35,167	$39,698	**Equity**		
			Common stock	$ 2,735	$ 2,735
			Retained earnings	$15,552	$17,902
			Total equity	$18,287	$20,637
			Total liabilities and equity	$35,167	$39,698

Inventory Management

16. Your company had $10 million in sales last year. Its cost of goods sold was $7 million and its average inventory balance was $1,200,000. What was its average days of inventory?

17. Happy Valley Homecare Suppliers, Inc. (HVHS), had $20 million in sales in 2015. Its cost of goods sold was $8 million, and its average inventory balance was $2 million.
    a. Calculate the average number of days inventory outstanding ratios for HVHS.
    b. The average days of inventory in the industry is 73 days. By how much would HVHS reduce its investment in inventory if it could improve its inventory days to meet the industry average?

DATA CASE [4]

You are the Chief Financial Officer (CFO) of Walmart. This afternoon you played golf with a member of the company's board of directors. Somewhere during the back nine, the board member enthusiastically described a recent article she had read in a leading management journal. This article noted several companies that had improved their stock price performance through effective working capital management, and the board member was intrigued. Even though Walmart was known for working capital management, she wondered if it could do even better. How was Walmart managing its working capital, and how does it compare to Costco, another company well known for working capital management?

Upon returning home, you decide to do a quick preliminary investigation using information freely available on the Internet.

1. Obtain Costco's financial statements for the past four years from
   http://moneycentral.msn.com.
   a. Enter the stock symbol (COST) in the box and click "Get Quote."
   b. Next click "Income Statement" in the left column.

---

[4]If the data sets on the Web sites indicated for this case become unavailable in the future, the data sets will be posted on the book's Web site.

    c. Select "Annual," and if you are using Internet Explorer, place the cursor in the statement and right-click the mouse. Select "Export to Microsoft Excel" from the menu. If you do not have that option, you can copy and paste the data into Excel.

    d. Go back to the Web page and click "Balance Sheet" at the left of the page; repeat the download procedure for the balance sheets.

    e. Copy and paste the balance sheet so that it is on the same worksheet as the income statement.

2. Following the same steps as you did for Costco, Obtain Walmart's (WMT) financial statements for comparison from http://moneycentral.msn.com.

3. Compute the cash conversion cycle for Walmart and Costco for each of the last four years.
    a. Compute the inventory days using "Cost of Revenue" as cost of goods sold and a 365-day year.
    b. Compute accounts receivable days using a 365-day year.
    c. Compute accounts payable days using a 365-day year.
    d. Compute the cash conversion cycle for each year.

4. How has Walmart's CCC changed over the last few years?

5. Compare Walmart's inventory and receivables turnover ratios for the most recent year to Costco's.
    a. Compute the inventory turnover ratio as cost of revenue/inventory.
    b. Compute the receivable turnover ratio as total revenue/net receivables.

6. Now assume Walmart matches Costco's inventory and receivables turnover ratios without changing its payable days.
    a. How much would Walmart's free-cash flow change relative to its current situation?
    b. What would Walmart's CCC be in this case?

7. What are your impressions regarding Walmart's working capital management based on this preliminary analysis? Discuss any advantages and disadvantages of attempting to match Costco's cash conversion cycle.

20

Short-Term Financial Planning

LEARNING OBJECTIVES

- Forecast cash flows and short-term financing needs

- Understand the principle of matching short-term needs to short-term funding sources

- Know the types of different bank loans and their tradeoffs

- Understand the use of commercial paper as an alternative to bank financing

- Use financing secured by accounts receivable or inventory

- Know how to create a short-term financial plan

notation

APR	annual percentage rate
EAR	effective annual rate

Hasbro is a company in Standard & Poor's 500 index, with year-end 2015 assets of $4.7 billion. Hasbro designs and manufactures toys throughout the world; its major product lines include the Playskool, Tonka, and Transformers brands. Typically, the demand for toys is highly seasonal, with demand peaking during the fall in anticipation of December's holiday retailing season. As a result, Hasbro's revenues vary dramatically throughout the calendar year. For example, revenues during the fourth quarter of the calendar year are typically more than twice as high as revenues in the first quarter.

Hasbro's varying business revenues cause its cash flows to be highly cyclical. The firm generates surplus cash during some months; it has a great demand for capital during other months. These seasonal financing requirements are quite different from its ongoing, long-term demand for permanent capital. How does a company such as Hasbro manage its short-term cash needs within each calendar year?

In this chapter, we analyze short-term financial planning. We begin by showing how companies forecast their cash flows to determine their short-term financing needs, and we explore the reasons why firms use short-term financing. Next, we discuss the financing policies that guide these financing decisions. Finally, we compare alternative ways a company can finance a shortfall during periods when it is not generating enough cash, including short-term financing with bank loans, commercial paper, and secured financing.

20.1   Forecasting Short-Term Financing Needs

The first step in short-term financial planning is to forecast the company's future cash flows. This exercise has two distinct objectives. First, a company forecasts its cash flows to determine whether it will have surplus cash or a cash deficit for each period. Second, management needs to decide whether that surplus or deficit is temporary or permanent. If it is permanent, it may affect the firm's long-term financial decisions. For example, if a company anticipates an ongoing surplus of cash, it may choose to increase its dividend payout. Deficits resulting from investments in long-term projects are often financed using long-term sources of capital, such as equity or long-term bonds.

In this chapter, we focus specifically on short-term financial planning. With this perspective, we are interested in analyzing the types of cash surpluses or deficits that are temporary and, therefore, short-term in nature. When a company analyzes its short-term financing needs, it typically examines cash flows at quarterly intervals.

Application: Springfield Snowboards, Inc.

To illustrate, let's assume that it is currently December 2017 and consider the case of Springfield Snowboards, Inc. Springfield manufactures snowboarding equipment, which it sells primarily to sports retailers. Springfield anticipates that in 2018 its sales will grow by 10% to $20 million and its total net income will be $1,950,000. Assuming that both sales and production will occur uniformly throughout the year, management's forecast of its quarterly net income and statement of cash flows for 2018 is presented in the spreadsheet in Table 20.1.[1] (Also shown, in gray, is the income statement from the fourth quarter of 2017.)[2]

From this forecast, we see that Springfield is a profitable company. Its projected quarterly net income is almost $500,000. Springfield's capital expenditures are equal to depreciation. While Springfield's working capital requirements increase in the first quarter due to the increase in sales, they remain constant thereafter and so have no further cash flow consequences. Based on these projections, Springfield will be able to fund projected sales growth from its operating profit and, in fact, will accumulate excess cash on a continuing basis. Given similar growth forecasts for next year and beyond, this surplus is likely to be long-term. Springfield could reduce the surplus by paying some of it out as a dividend or by repurchasing shares.

Let's now turn to Springfield's potential short-term financing needs. Firms require short-term financing for three reasons: negative cash flow shocks, positive cash flow shocks, and seasonalities.

Negative Cash Flow Shocks

Occasionally, a company will encounter circumstances in which cash flows are temporarily negative for an unexpected reason. These situations, which we refer to as *negative cash flow shock*, can create short-term financing needs.

Returning to the Springfield Snowboards example, assume that during April 2018 management learns that some manufacturing equipment has broken unexpectedly. If replacing the equipment is costly enough, Springfield's cash reserves would be insufficient

---

[1]In this table, and elsewhere in the chapter, we display rounded numbers. Calculations such as net income are based on the actual numbers in the spreadsheet with all significant digits. As a result, occasionally there will be a small discrepancy between the Excel-calculated value shown and the hand-calculated value using the rounded numbers displayed.

[2]Given the coverage we have provided in Chapters 2 and 18 on how to construct pro forma financial statements, we do not discuss those details here. For simplicity, we have assumed Springfield has no debt, and earns no interest on retained cash.

TABLE 20.1

Projected Financial
Statements for
Springfield
Snowboards, 2018,
Assuming Level Sales

1	Quarter	2017Q4	2018Q1	2018Q2	2018Q3	2018Q4
2	**Income Statement ($000)**					
3	Sales	10,909	5,000	5,000	5,000	5,000
4	Cost of Goods Sold	−7,091	−3,250	−3,250	−3,250	−3,250
5	Selling, General, and Administrative	−773	−500	−500	−500	−500
6	**EBITDA**	3,045	1,250	1,250	1,250	1,250
7	Depreciation	−455	−500	−500	−500	−500
8	**EBIT**	2,590	750	750	750	750
9	Taxes	−907	−263	−263	−263	−263
10	**Net Income**	1,683	488	488	488	488
11	**Statement of Cash Flows**					
12	Net Income		488	488	488	488
13	Depreciation		500	500	500	500
14	Changes in Working Capital					
15	Accounts Receivable		−136	—	—	—
16	Inventory		—	—	—	—
17	Accounts Payable		48	—	—	—
18	**Cash from Operating Activities**		900	988	988	988
19	Capital Expenditures		−500	−500	−500	−500
20	Other Investment		—	—	—	—
21	**Cash from Investing Activities**		−500	−500	−500	−500
22	Net Borrowing		—	—	—	—
23	Dividends		—	—	—	—
24	Capital Contributions		—	—	—	—
25	**Cash from Financing Activities**		—	—	—	—
26	Change in Cash and Equivalents (18 + 21 + 25)		400	488	488	488

to pay for a replacement. Springfield will have to borrow (or arrange for another financing source) to cover the shortfall. However, once the equipment is replaced, the company will continue to generate positive cash flow in subsequent quarters, and will soon have generated enough in cumulative cash flow to repay the loan. Therefore, this negative cash flow shock has created the need for short-term financing.

Positive Cash Flow Shocks

Next, we analyze a case in which a positive cash flow shock affects short-term financing needs. Although this surprise is good news, it still creates demand for short-term financing.

During the first quarter of 2018, a major sporting goods chain agrees to exclusively sell Springfield Snowboards. The opportunity to grow comes with large up-front marketing, working capital, and production capacity expenses.

The unexpected event in this case—the opportunity to grow more rapidly—is positive. It would result, however, in a negative net cash flow during the first quarter, due primarily to the new marketing expenses and capital expenditures. Because the company will be even more profitable in subsequent quarters, this financing need is temporary.

Seasonalities

For many firms, sales are seasonal. Figure 20.1 shows the seasonal pattern of sales for department stores, sporting goods, and building materials. Department store and sporting good sales are concentrated during the Christmas holiday season, while for building materials, sales peak in the spring ahead of the summer building season. When sales are concentrated during a few months, sources and uses of cash are also likely to be seasonal. Firms in this position may find themselves with a surplus of cash during some months that is sufficient to compensate for a shortfall during other months. However, because of timing differences, such firms often have short-term financing needs.

FIGURE 20.1

Sales Seasonality
(2010–2015)

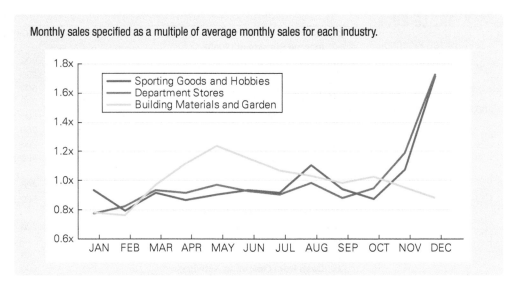

Monthly sales specified as a multiple of average monthly sales for each industry.

Legend:
- Sporting Goods and Hobbies
- Department Stores
- Building Materials and Garden

To illustrate, let's return to the example of Springfield Snowboards. In Table 20.1, management assumed that Springfield's sales occur uniformly throughout the year. In reality, for a snowboard manufacturer, sales are likely to be highly seasonal. Assume that 20% of sales occur during the first quarter, 10% during each of the second and third quarters (largely Southern Hemisphere sales), and 60% during the fourth quarter, in anticipation of the Northern Hemisphere winter snowboarding season. The spreadsheet in Table 20.2 presents the resulting statement of cash flows. These forecasts continue to assume production occurs uniformly throughout the year.

TABLE 20.2

Projected Financial
Statements
for Springfield
Snowboards, 2018,
Assuming Seasonal
Sales

	Quarter	2017Q4	2018Q1	2018Q2	2018Q3	2018Q4
1	**Quarter**	2017Q4	2018Q1	2018Q2	2018Q3	2018Q4
2	**Income Statement ($000)**					
3	Sales	10,909	4,000	2,000	2,000	12,000
4	Cost of Goods Sold	−7,091	−2,600	−1,300	−1,300	−7,800
5	Selling, General, and Administrative	−773	−450	−350	−350	−850
6	**EBITDA**	3,045	950	350	350	3,350
7	Depreciation	−455	−500	−500	−500	−500
8	**EBIT**	2,590	450	−150	−150	2,850
9	Taxes	−907	−158	53	53	−998
10	**Net Income**	1,683	292	−97	−97	1,852
11	**Statement of Cash Flows**					
12	Net Income		292	−97	−97	1,852
13	Depreciation		500	500	500	500
14	Changes in Working Capital					
15	Accounts Receivable		2,073	600	—	−3,000
16	Inventory		−650	−1,950	−1,950	4,550
17	Accounts Payable		48	—	—	—
18	**Cash from Operating Activities**		2,263	−947	−1,547	3,902
19	Capital Expenditures		−500	−500	−500	−500
20	Other Investment		—	—	—	—
21	**Cash from Investing Activities**		−500	−500	−500	−500
22	Net Borrowing		—	—	—	—
23	Dividends		—	—	—	—
24	Capital Contributions		—	—	—	—
25	**Cash from Financing Activities**		—	—	—	—
26	Change in Cash and Equivalents (18 + 21 + 25)		1,763	1,447	−2,047	3,402

From Table 20.2, we see that Springfield is still a profitable company, and its annual net income still totals $1,950,000. However, the introduction of seasonal sales creates some dramatic swings in Springfield's short-term cash flows. There are two effects of seasonality on cash flows. First, although the cost of goods sold fluctuates proportionally with sales, other costs (such as administrative overhead and depreciation) do not, leading to large changes in the firm's net income by quarter. Second, net working capital changes are more pronounced. In the first quarter, Springfield receives cash by collecting the receivables from last year's high fourth quarter sales. During the second and third quarters, the company's inventory balance increases. Given capacity constraints in its manufacturing equipment, Springfield produces snowboards throughout the year, even though sales during the summer are low. Because production occurs uniformly, accounts payable do not vary over the year. Inventory, however, builds up in anticipation of fourth quarter sales—and increases in inventory use up cash. As a consequence, Springfield has negative net cash flows during the second and third quarters, primarily to fund its inventory. By the fourth quarter, high sales recover the cash spent on inventory for the company.

Seasonal sales create large short-term cash flow deficits and surpluses. During the second and third quarters, the company will need to find additional short-term sources of cash to fund inventory. During the fourth quarter, Springfield will have a large short-term surplus. Given that its seasonal cash flow needs are likely to recur next year, Springfield may choose to invest this cash in one of the short-term investment options discussed in Chapter 19. Management can then use this cash to fund some of its short-term working capital needs during the following year.

The Cash Budget

The statement of cash flows section of Table 20.2 reflects assumptions made by Springfield's managers about the timing of cash receipts and disbursements throughout the year. Once Springfield's managers forecast the sales and production costs for the year, they must also forecast when Springfield will actually receive the cash for those sales and when it will need to pay its suppliers. They do this in a **cash budget**, a forecast of cash inflows and outflows on a quarterly (or sometimes monthly) basis used to identify potential cash shortfalls.

cash budget A forecast of cash inflows and outflows on a quarterly (or sometimes monthly) basis used to identify potential cash shortfalls.

For example, based on past experience, Springfield assumes that it will receive payment for 70% of its sales in the quarter they are made, with the remaining 30% coming in the following quarter (this corresponds with an accounts receivable payment period of about one month). So each quarter, cash receipts will be 30% of last quarter's sales in receivables plus 70% of the current quarter's sales:

$$\text{Springfield's Quarterly Cash Receipts} =$$
$$30\% \times \text{Last Quarter's Sales} + 70\% \times \text{This Quarter's Sales}$$

Using this assumption and the sales forecast from Table 20.2, we can forecast Springfield's cash receipts. Note that sales in 2017Q4 were 10,909, so beginning receivables are $30\% \times 10{,}909 = 3273$. Table 20.3 presents the projected cash receipts.

TABLE 20.3

Projected Cash Receipts for Springfield Snowboards, Assuming Seasonal Sales

	Quarter	2018Q1	2018Q2	2018Q3	2018Q4
1					
2	Beginning Receivables	3,273	1,200	600	600
3	Sales	4,000	2,000	2,000	12,000
4	Cash Collections (Line 2+70% of Line 3)	6,073	2,600	2,000	9,000
5	Ending Receivables (30% of Line 3)	1,200	600	600	3,600

TABLE 20.4

Projected Cash
Disbursements
for Springfield
Snowboards, Assuming
Seasonal Sales

Panel (a) Calculating Payments to Suppliers

	Quarter	2018Q1	2018Q2	2018Q3	2018Q4
1					
2	**Payment to Suppliers**				
3	Last Quarter's AP	477	525	525	525
4	This Quarter's Payments	2,725	2,725	2,725	2,725
5	Total Payments	3,202	3,250	3,250	3,250
6					
7	Ending AP (3250 − Line 4)	525	525	525	525

Panel (b) Total Cash Disbursements

	Quarter	2018Q1	2018Q2	2018Q3	2018Q4
1					
2	Cash Collections (from Line 4 of Table 20.3)	6,073	2,600	2,000	9,000
3					
4	**Disbursements**				
5	Payments to Suppliers (from Line 5 of Panel a)	−3,202	−3,250	−3,250	−3,250
6	SG&A+Taxes+Interest (from Line 5 of Table 20.2)	−608	−297	−297	−1,848
7	Capital Expenditures (from Line 19 of Table 20.2)	−500	−500	−500	−500
8	Total Disbursements	−4,310	−4,047	−4,047	−5,598
9					
10	Net Cash Flow (Line 2 + Line 8)	1,763	−1,447	−2,047	3,402

The next step is to forecast cash disbursements. As we mentioned earlier, although Springfield's sales are seasonal, it produces a constant amount each quarter and simply builds up inventory. Thus, each quarter it pays its suppliers a level amount for materials. These costs are reflected in the income statement when the sales occur, but the cash outflow happens when they pay their suppliers. This can be seen by adding the inventory line to the cost of goods sold line in Table 20.2. In 2018Q1 it is $-2600 - 650 = -3250$, and it is -3250 for the rest of the quarters in 2018 as well, reflecting the steady production of snowboards. Springfield's managers forecast that of the 3250 of cost of goods sold in each quarter, they will need to pay 2725 in the quarter, carrying 525 in accounts payable into the next quarter. Each quarter, their cash disbursements on materials will be last quarter's accounts payable plus 2725 of the current quarter's costs. Because Springfield's production was lower in 2017, it had lower costs and so it ended 2017 with lower accounts payable than it will have going forward. Table 20.4 shows that it will have 477 in accounts payable for the first quarter of 2018 only, before it rises to 525 for the rest of the quarters. Using that fact and the assumption we just made, we can forecast their disbursements on materials. The other cash disbursements will be selling, general, and administrative expenses (SG&A), taxes and interest, as well as any capital expenditures, each of which is forecast in Table 20.2 The table also shows Springfield's forecasted cash disbursements.

Now that we have the quarterly net cash flow, we can generate Springfield's cash budget. We need two more pieces of information: the amount of cash Springfield will start 2018 with and the minimum amount of cash it needs on hand for transactions purposes. Springfield will start 2018 with $1 million in cash and its managers have set $500,000 as the minimum acceptable cash balance. Putting it all together, we have Springfield's cash budget in Table 20.5.

TABLE 20.5

Springfield
Snowboards' Cash
Budget

	Quarter	2018Q1	2018Q2	2018Q3	2018Q4
1					
2	Beginning Cash Balance	1,000	2,763	1,316	−731
3	Net Cash Flow	1,763	−1,447	−2,047	3,402
4	Ending Cash Balance	2,763	1,316	−731	2,671
5	Minimum Cash Balance	500	500	500	500
6	Surplus (Deficit)	2,263	816	−1,231	2,171

Looking at the cash budget, we can immediately see that there will be a substantial cash shortfall in the third quarter. Having identified the shortfall, Springfield's managers can prepare external financing to cover it. We discuss the factors that determine how to cover such a shortfall in the next two sections.

1. How do we forecast the firm's future cash requirements?
2. What is the effect of seasonalities on short-term cash flows?

20.2 The Matching Principle

In a perfect capital market, the choice of financing is irrelevant; thus, how the firm chooses to finance its short-term cash needs cannot affect the firm's value. In reality, important market frictions exist, including transaction costs. For example, one transaction cost is the opportunity cost of holding cash in accounts that pay little or no interest. Firms also face high transaction costs if they need to negotiate a loan on short notice to cover a cash shortfall. Firms can increase their value by adopting a policy that minimizes these kinds of costs. One such policy is known as the *matching principle*. The **matching principle** states that short-term cash needs should be financed with short-term debt and long-term cash needs should be financed with long-term sources of funds.

matching principle States that a firm's short-term cash needs should be financed with short-term debt and long-term cash needs should be financed with long-term sources of funds.

Permanent Working Capital

Permanent working capital is the amount that a firm must keep invested in its short-term assets to support its continuing operations. Because this investment in working capital is required as long as the firm remains in business, it constitutes a long-term investment. The matching principle indicates that the firm should finance this permanent investment in working capital with long-term sources of funds. Such sources have lower transaction costs than short-term sources of funds that have to be replaced more often.

permanent working capital The amount that a firm must keep invested in its short-term assets to support its continuing operations.

Temporary Working Capital

Another portion of a firm's investment in its accounts receivable and inventory is temporary and results from seasonal fluctuations in the firm's business or unanticipated shocks. This **temporary working capital** is the difference between the firm's actual level of investment in short-term working capital needs and its permanent working capital investment. Because temporary working capital represents a short-term need, the firm should finance this portion of its investment with short-term financing.

temporary working capital The difference between the firm's actual level of investment in short-term working capital needs and its permanent working capital requirements.

Permanent Versus Temporary Working Capital

To illustrate the distinction between permanent and temporary working capital, we return to the Springfield Snowboards example. Table 20.2 presented cash flow forecasts assuming seasonal sales. In the spreadsheet in Table 20.6, we report the underlying levels of working capital that correspond to these forecasts.

TABLE 20.6

Projected Levels of Working Capital for Springfield Snowboards, 2018, Assuming Seasonal Sales

1	Quarter	2017Q4	2018Q1	2018Q2	2018Q3	2018Q4
2	**Net Working Capital Requirements ($000)**					
3	Minimum Cash Balance	500	500	500	500	500
4	Accounts Receivable	3,273	1,200	600	600	3,600
5	Inventory	300	950	2,900	4,850	300
6	Accounts Payable	−477	−525	−525	−525	−525
7	**Net Working Capital**	3,596	2,125	3,475	5,425	3,875

In Table 20.6, we see that working capital for Springfield varies from a minimum of $2,125,000 in the first quarter of 2018 to $5,425,000 in the third quarter. The minimum level of working capital, or $2,125,000, can be thought of as the firm's permanent working capital. The difference between this minimum level and the higher levels in subsequent quarters (for example, $5,425,000 − $2,125,000 = $3,300,000 in the third quarter) reflects Springfield's temporary working capital requirements.

Financing Policy Choices

Following the matching principle should, in the long run, help minimize a firm's transaction costs.[3] But what if, instead of using the matching principle, a firm financed its permanent working capital needs with short-term debt? When the short-term debt comes due, the firm will have to negotiate a new loan. This new loan will involve additional transaction costs, and it will carry whatever market interest rate exists at the time. As a result, the firm is also exposed to interest rate risk.

aggressive financing policy Financing part or all of a firm's permanent working capital with short-term debt.

Aggressive Financing Policy. Financing part or all of the permanent working capital with short-term debt is known as an **aggressive financing policy**. An ultra-aggressive policy would involve financing even some of the plant, property, and equipment with short-term sources of funds.

When the yield curve is upward sloping, the interest rate on short-term debt is lower than the rate on long-term debt. In that case, short-term debt may appear cheaper than long-term debt. However, we know that with perfect capital markets, Modigliani and Miller's results from Chapter 16 apply: The benefit of the lower rate from short-term debt is offset by the risk that the firm will have to refinance the debt in the future at a higher rate. This risk is borne by the equity holders, and so the firm's equity cost of capital will rise to offset any benefit from the lower borrowing rate.

Why, then, might a firm choose an aggressive financing policy? Such a policy might be beneficial if the market imperfections mentioned in Chapter 16, such as agency costs and asymmetric information, are important. The value of short-term debt is less sensitive to the firm's credit quality than long-term debt; therefore, its value will be less affected by management's actions or information. As a result, short-term debt can have lower agency and lemons costs than long-term debt, and an aggressive financing policy can benefit shareholders. On the other hand, by relying on short-term debt the firm exposes itself to **funding risk**, which is the risk of incurring financial distress costs if it cannot refinance its debt in a timely manner or at a reasonable rate. The box on the commercial paper and the financial crisis (page 641) highlights exactly this risk.

funding risk The risk of incurring financial distress costs if a firm cannot refinance its debt in a timely manner or at a reasonable rate.

conservative financing policy When a firm finances its short-term needs with long-term debt.

Conservative Financing Policy. Alternatively, a firm could finance its short-term needs with long-term debt, a practice known as a **conservative financing policy**. For example, when following such a policy, a firm would use long-term sources of funds to finance its fixed assets, permanent working capital, and some of its seasonal needs. The firm would use short-term debt very sparingly to meet its peak seasonal needs. To implement such a policy effectively, there will necessarily be periods when excess cash is available—those periods when the firm requires little or no investment in temporary working capital. In an imperfect capital market, this cash will earn a below-market interest rate, thereby reducing the firm's value. It also increases the possibility that managers of the firm will use this excess cash nonproductively—for example, on perquisites for themselves.

---

[3]Some evidence indicates that most firms appear to follow the matching principle. See W. Beranek, C. Cornwell, and S. Choi, "External Financing, Liquidity, and Capital Expenditures," *Journal of Financial Research* (Summer 1995): 207–222; and M. H. Stohs and D. C. Mauer, "The Determinants of Corporate Debt Maturity Structure," *Journal of Business*, 69 (3) (1996): 279–312.

In Figure 20.2, we illustrate aggressive and conservative financial policies for Springfield. With an aggressive policy, Springfield relies entirely on short-term financing to fund its inventory buildup, so its borrowing reaches a peak along with its inventory in the third quarter. With a conservative policy, it uses long-term borrowing to ensure that it will have enough cash to pay for its peak inventory. In this case, Springfield's borrowing does not

FIGURE 20.2

Financing Policy Choices for Springfield Snowboards

Assuming $25,000 in fixed assets, the figure shows the levels of fixed assets (green), permanent working capital ($2,125, yellow), and seasonal inventory (gray) for Springfield Snowboards. In Panel (a), each quarter shows the mix of long-term financing (purple) and short-term debt (red) used to finance the assets and working capital. In the aggressive policy illustrated in Panel (a), Springfield maintains no excess cash reserves and instead finances its working capital entirely through short-term borrowing. The amount of borrowing must match the amount of working capital.

Panel (b) illustrates a conservative policy, in which Springfield maintains enough cash reserves to cover its peak temporary financing needs. Springfield does this with $30,425 in long-term financing, which is enough to finance its fixed assets, permanent working capital, and peak inventory. Its total working capital is constant at $5,425, but the composition of the working capital varies over the year as it draws down its cash reserves (blue) to build inventory and then replenishes the cash reserves when it sells the inventory.

Panel (a): Aggressive financing policy: All working capital is financed with short-term debt.

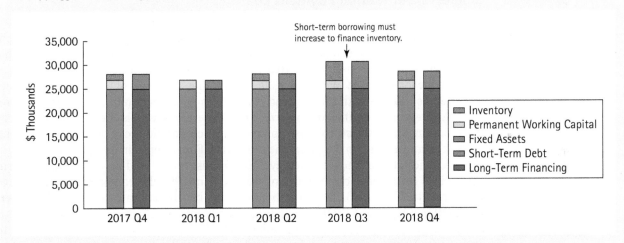

Panel (b) Conservative financing policy: Working capital is financed with long-term debt.

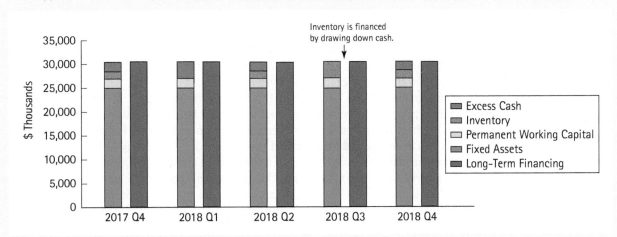

fluctuate at all, but rather it draws down its cash reserves so that its cash reserves are at a minimum when its inventory is at its peak.

Once a firm determines its short-term financing needs, it must choose which instruments it will use for this purpose. In the rest of this chapter, we survey the specific financing options that are available: bank loans, commercial paper, and secured financing.

3. What is the matching principle?

4. What is the difference between temporary and permanent working capital?

20.3 Short-Term Financing with Bank Loans

promissory note A written statement that indicates the amount of a loan, the date payment is due, and the interest rate.

One of the primary sources of short-term financing, especially for small businesses, is the commercial bank. Bank loans are typically initiated with a **promissory note**, which is a written statement that indicates the amount of the loan, the date payment is due, and the interest rate. In this section, we examine three types of bank loans: a single, end-of-period payment loan; a line of credit; and a bridge loan. In addition, we compare the interest rates of these bank loans and present the common stipulations and fees associated with them.

prime rate The rate banks charge their most creditworthy customers.

London Inter-Bank Offered Rate (LIBOR) The rate of interest at which banks borrow funds from each other in the London interbank market.

line of credit A bank loan arrangement in which a bank agrees to lend a firm any amount up to a stated maximum. This flexible agreement allows the firm to draw upon the line of credit whenever it chooses.

uncommitted line of credit A line of credit that is an informal agreement and does not legally bind a bank to provide the funds a borrower requests.

committed line of credit A legally binding written agreement that obligates a bank to provide funds to a firm (up to a stated credit limit) regardless of the financial condition of the firm (unless the firm is bankrupt) as long as the firm satisfies any restrictions in the agreement.

Single, End-of-Period Payment Loan

The most straightforward type of bank loan is a single, end-of-period-payment loan. Such a loan agreement requires that the firm pay interest on the loan and pay back the principal in one lump sum at the end of the loan. The interest rate may be fixed or variable. With a fixed interest rate, the specific rate that the commercial bank will charge is stipulated at the time the loan is made. With a variable interest rate, the terms of the loan may indicate that the rate will vary with some spread relative to a benchmark rate, such as the yield on one-year Treasury securities or the *prime rate*. The **prime rate** is the rate banks charge their most creditworthy customers. However, large corporations can often negotiate bank loans at an interest rate that is *below* the prime rate. For example, in its 2009 annual report, Hasbro indicated that the weighted average interest rate it paid on average short-term borrowings from domestic institutions was 1.2% in 2009. By comparison, the average prime rate in 2009 was 3.25%.[4] Another common benchmark rate is the **London Inter-Bank Offered Rate,** or **LIBOR**, which is the rate of interest at which banks borrow funds from each other in the London interbank market. It is quoted for maturities of one day to one year for 10 major currencies. As it is a rate paid by banks with the highest credit quality, most firms will borrow at a rate that exceeds LIBOR.

Line of Credit

Another common type of bank loan arrangement is a **line of credit**, in which a bank agrees to lend a firm any amount up to a stated maximum. This flexible agreement allows the firm to draw upon the line of credit whenever it chooses.

Firms frequently use lines of credit to finance seasonal needs. An **uncommitted line of credit** is an informal agreement that does not legally bind the bank to provide the funds. As long as the borrower's financial condition remains good, the bank is happy to advance additional funds. A **committed line of credit** consists of a legally binding written agreement that obligates the bank to provide funds to a firm (up to a stated credit limit) regardless of the financial condition of the firm (unless the firm is bankrupt) as long as the firm satisfies any restrictions in the agreement. These arrangements are typically accompanied by a compensating balance requirement (that is, a requirement that the firm maintain a minimum level of

---

[4]Hasbro 2009 annual report and *Federal Reserve Statistical Release* Web site. On the other hand, in 2015 Hasbro was paying nearly 4% while the prime rate was only 3.25%.

deposits with the bank) and restrictions regarding the level of the firm's working capital. The firm pays a commitment fee of $\frac{1}{4}$% to $\frac{1}{2}$% of the unused portion of the line of credit in addition to interest on the amount that the firm borrowed. The line of credit agreement may also stipulate that at some point the outstanding balance must be zero. This policy ensures that the firm does not use the short-term financing to finance its long-term obligations.

revolving line of credit A line of credit, which a company can use as needed, that involves a solid commitment from a bank for a longer time period, typically two to three years.

Banks usually renegotiate the terms of a line of credit annually. A **revolving line of credit** is a committed line of credit, which a company can use as needed, that involves a solid commitment from the bank for a longer period of time, typically two to three years. A revolving line of credit with no fixed maturity is called **evergreen credit**. In its 2012 annual report, Hasbro reported that it relied on a $700 million revolving credit facility as the primary source of financing for its seasonal working capital requirements.

evergreen credit A revolving line of credit with no fixed maturity.

Bridge Loan

bridge loan A type of short-term bank loan that is often used to "bridge the gap" until a firm can arrange for long-term financing.

A **bridge loan** is another type of short-term bank loan that is often used to "bridge the gap" until a firm can arrange for long-term financing. For example, a real estate developer may use a bridge loan to finance the construction of a shopping mall. After the mall is completed, the developer will obtain long-term financing. Other firms use bridge loans to finance plant and equipment until they receive the proceeds from the sale of a long-term debt or an equity issue. After a natural disaster, lenders may provide businesses with short-term loans to serve as bridges until they receive insurance payments or long-term disaster relief.

discount loan A type of bridge loan in which the borrower is required to pay the interest at the beginning of the loan period. The lender deducts interest from the loan proceeds when the loan is made.

Bridge loans are often quoted as discount loans with fixed interest rates. With a **discount loan**, the borrower is required to pay the interest at the *beginning* of the loan period. The lender deducts interest from the loan proceeds when the loan is made.

Common Loan Stipulations and Fees

We now turn to common loan stipulations and fees that affect the effective interest rate on a loan. Specifically, we look at loan commitment fees, loan origination fees, and compensating balance requirements.

Commitment Fees. Various loan fees charged by banks affect the effective interest rate that the borrower pays. For example, the commitment fee associated with a committed line of credit increases the effective cost of the loan to the firm. The "fee" can really be considered an interest charge under another name. Suppose that a firm has negotiated a committed line of credit with a stated maximum of $1 million and an interest rate of 10% (EAR) with a bank. The commitment fee is 0.5% (EAR). At the beginning of the year, the firm borrows $800,000. It then repays this loan at the end of the year, leaving $200,000 unused for the rest of the year. The total cost of the loan is:

Interest on borrowed funds = 0.10 ($800,000)	$80,000
Commitment fee paid on unused portion = 0.005 ($200,000)	$ 1,000
Total cost	$81,000

loan origination fee A common type of fee, which a bank charges to cover credit checks and legal fees. A borrower must pay this fee to initiate a loan.

Loan Origination Fee. Another common type of fee is a **loan origination fee**, which a bank charges to cover credit checks and legal fees. The firm pays the fee when the loan is initiated; similar to a discount loan, it reduces the amount of usable proceeds that the firm receives. And similar to the commitment fee, it is effectively an additional interest charge.

To illustrate, assume that Timmons Towel and Diaper Service is offered a $500,000 loan for three months at an APR of 12%. This loan has a loan origination fee of 1%. The loan origination fee is charged on the principal of the loan; thus, the fee in this case amounts to $0.01 \times \$500,000 = \$5000$, so the actual amount borrowed is $495,000. The interest payment for three months is $500,000 \left(\frac{0.12}{4} \right) = \$15,000$. These cash flows are shown here on a timeline:

Thus, the actual three-month interest rate paid is:

$$\frac{515,000 - 495,000}{495,000} = 4.04\%$$

Expressing this rate as an EAR gives $1.0404^4 - 1 = 17.17\%$

Compensating Balance Requirements. Regardless of the loan structure, the bank may include a compensating balance requirement in the loan agreement that reduces the usable loan proceeds. Recall from Chapter 19 that a compensating balance requirement means that the firm must hold a certain percentage of the principal of the loan in an account at the bank. Assume that rather than charging a loan origination fee, Timmons Towel and Diaper Service's bank requires that the firm keep an amount equal to 10% of the loan principal in a non-interest-bearing account with the bank as long as the loan remains outstanding. The loan is for $500,000, so this requirement means that Timmons must hold $0.10 \times 500,000 = \$50,000$ in an account at the bank. Thus, the firm has only $450,000 of the loan proceeds actually available for use, although it must pay interest on the full loan amount. At the end of the loan period, the firm owes $500,000 \times (1 + 0.12/4) = \$515,000$, so it must pay $515,000 - 50,000 = \$465,000$ after applying its compensating balance to the repayment. These cash flows are shown here on a timeline:

The actual three-month interest rate paid is:

$$\frac{465,000 - 450,000}{450,000} = 3.33\%$$

Expressing this as an EAR gives $1.0333^4 - 1 = 14.01\%$

We assumed that Timmons' compensating balance is held in a non-interest-bearing account. Sometimes a bank will allow the compensating balance to be held in an account that pays a small amount of interest to offset part of the interest expense of the loan.

EXAMPLE 20.1

Compensating Balance Requirements and the Effective Annual Rate

MyFinanceLab

PROBLEM

Assume that Timmons Towel and Diaper Service's bank pays 1% (APR with quarterly compounding) on its compensating balance accounts. What is the EAR of Timmons' three-month loan?

SOLUTION

PLAN

The interest earned on the $50,000 will reduce the net payment Timmons must make to pay off the loan. Once we compute the final payment, we can determine the implied three-month interest rate and then convert it into an EAR.

EXECUTE

The balance held in the compensating balance account will grow to $50,000(1 + 0.01/4) = \$50,125$. Thus, the final loan payment will be $500,000 + 15,000 - 50,125 = \$464,875$. Notice that the interest on the compensating balance accounts offsets some of the interest that Timmons pays on the loan. The new cash flows are shown here on a timeline:

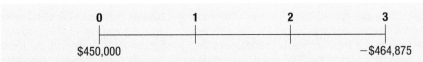

The actual three-month interest rate paid is:

$$\frac{464{,}875 - 450{,}000}{450{,}000} = 3.31\%$$

Expressing this as an EAR gives $1.0331^4 - 1 = 13.89\%$.

EVALUATE

As expected, because the bank allowed Timmons to deposit the compensating balance in an interest-bearing account, the interest earned on the compensating balance reduced the overall interest cost of Timmons for the loan.

CONCEPT CHECK

5. What is the difference between an uncommitted line of credit and a committed line of credit?

6. Describe common loan stipulations and fees.

20.4 Short-Term Financing with Commercial Paper

commercial paper
Short-term, unsecured debt issued by large corporations.

Commercial paper is short-term, unsecured debt used by large corporations that, as shown in the box below, is usually a cheaper source of funds than a short-term bank loan. The minimum face value is $25,000, and most commercial paper has a face value of at least $100,000. Similar to long-term debt, commercial paper is rated by credit rating agencies. The interest on commercial paper is typically paid by selling it at an initial discount.

Short-Term Financing and the Financial Crisis of the Fall of 2008

Large companies with high-quality credit ratings can access the commercial paper market as an alternative to bank loans. This figure shows the comparatively low cost of commercial paper relative to the prime rate. During most of the period, interest rates on commercial paper were less than half a percent higher than the rates paid by the U.S. government on Treasury bills. The figure also shows how unusual the financial crisis was. One of the biggest problems firms faced during the financial crisis in the fall of 2008 was short-term financing. In the weeks following the bankruptcy of Lehman Brothers, the short-term credit markets froze. Many investors lost confidence in money market mutual funds and withdrew their capital. In response, fund managers liquidated their short-term investments, causing the availability of short-term credit to contract dramatically and short-term yields to skyrocket. Nowhere was this more evident than in the commercial paper market.

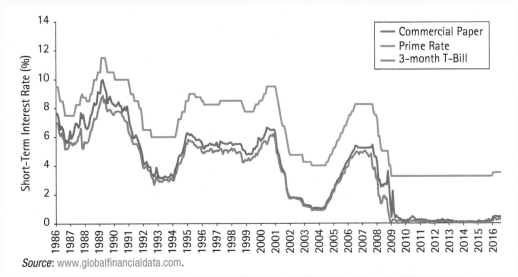

Source: www.globalfinancialdata.com.

(Continued)

By October 2008, the spread between the commercial paper rate and the Treasury rate was almost 3%. The new year brought more calm to the short-term debt markets—by July 2009 spreads were back to their fall 2007 levels. Spreads like those seen in 2008 effectively shut many firms out of the commercial paper market and severely hampered their ability to conduct business—the effect was particularly serious for those pursuing aggressive financing policies like those described in Section 20.2. In addition, the increased uncertainty in financial markets made firms less likely to invest. Both effects were significant contributors to the global recession that accompanied the financial crisis.

direct paper Commercial paper that a firms sells directly to investors.

dealer paper Commercial paper that dealers sell to investors in exchange for a spread (or fee) for their services.

The average maturity of commercial paper is 30 days and the maximum maturity is 270 days. Extending the maturity beyond 270 days triggers a registration requirement with the Securities and Exchange Commission (SEC), which increases issue costs and creates a time delay in the sale of the issue. Commercial paper is referred to as either *direct paper* or *dealer paper*. With **direct paper**, the firm sells the security directly to investors. With **dealer paper**, dealers sell the commercial paper to investors in exchange for a spread (or fee) for their services. The spread decreases the proceeds that the issuing firm receives, thereby increasing the effective cost of the paper. Similar to long-term debt, commercial paper is rated by credit rating agencies.

EXAMPLE 20.2

The Effective Annual Rate of Commercial Paper

MyFinanceLab

PROBLEM

A firm issues three-month commercial paper with a $100,000 face value and receives $98,000. What effective annual rate is the firm paying for its funds?

SOLUTION

PLAN

First, put the firm's cash flows on a timeline:

0	3
$98,000	−$100,000

The three-month rate can be computed by comparing the present value received ($98,000) with the future value paid ($100,000). From there, we can convert it into an EAR using Eq. 5.1:

$$\text{EAR} = \text{equivalent one-year rate} = (1 + r)^n - 1,$$

where n is the number of three-month periods in a year.

EXECUTE

The actual three-month interest rate paid is:

$$\frac{100,000 - 98,000}{98,000} = 2.04\%$$

Expressing this as an EAR gives $1.0204^4 - 1 = 8.42\%$

EVALUATE

The financial manager needs to know the EAR of all of the firm's funding sources to be able to make comparisons across them and choose the least costly way to finance the firm's short-term needs.

CONCEPT CHECK

7. What is commercial paper?

8. What is the maximum maturity of commercial paper?

20.5 Short-Term Financing with Secured Financing

secured loan A type of corporate loan in which specific assets, most typically a firm's accounts receivable or inventory, are pledged as the firm's collateral.

Businesses can also obtain short-term financing by using a **secured loan**, a type of corporate loan in which specific assets, most typically the firm's accounts receivables or inventory, are pledged as a firm's collateral. Commercial banks, finance companies, and **factors**, which are firms that purchase the receivables of other companies, are the most common sources for secured short-term loans.

Accounts Receivable as Collateral

factors Firms that purchase the receivables of other companies.

Firms can use accounts receivable as security for a loan by *pledging* or *factoring*. We'll examine these uses of accounts receivable to secure loans in the following sections.

pledging of accounts receivable An agreement in which a lender reviews the credit sales of the borrowing firm and decides which credit accounts it will accept as collateral for the loan, based on its own credit standards.

Pledging of Accounts Receivable. In a **pledging of accounts receivable** agreement, the lender reviews the invoices that represent the credit sales of the borrowing firm and decides which credit accounts it will accept as collateral for the loan, based on its own credit standards. The lender then typically lends the borrower some percentage of the value of the accepted invoices—say, 75%. If the borrowing firm's customers default on their bills, the firm is still responsible to the lender for the money.

factoring of accounts receivable An arrangement in which a firm sells receivables to the lender (i.e., the factor), and the lender agrees to pay the firm the amount due from its customers at the end of the firm's payment period.

Factoring of Accounts Receivable. In a **factoring of accounts receivable** arrangement, the firm sells receivables to the lender (i.e., the factor), and the lender agrees to pay the firm the amount due from its customers at the end of the firm's payment period. For example, if a firm sells its goods on terms of net 30, then the factor will pay the firm the face value of its receivables, less a factor's fee, at the end of 30 days. The firm's customers are usually instructed to make payments directly to the lender. In many cases, the firm can borrow as much as 80% of the face value of its receivables from the factor, thereby receiving its funds in advance. In such a case, the lender will charge interest on the loan in addition to the factor's fee. The lender charges the factor's fee, which may range from $\frac{3}{4}$% to $1\frac{1}{2}$% of the face value of the accounts receivable, whether or not the firm borrows any of the available funds. Both the interest rate and the factor's fee vary, depending on such issues as the size

 A Seventeenth-Century Financing Solution

In recent years, it has become more difficult for small businesses to obtain funding so as to purchase inventory. Several factors have contributed to this trend. First, bigger banks have acquired many small, regional banks that were traditionally important sources of loans to small businesses. Second, large banks have tightened lending requirements for small borrowers. Third, many small businesses rely increasingly on foreign suppliers that demand payment up front, increasing the immediate demand for capital by small businesses.

Some small businesses have started to rely on a 400-year-old solution: venture merchant financing. This type of financing arrangement began in the seventeenth century, when groups of investors would provide capital for the voyages of Dutch sea captains. The captains would sail the seas, using the capital to purchase exotic merchandise. On their return, the merchant bankers would take about one-third of the captains' profits when the goods were sold as compensation for the financing.

Now consider the Kosher Depot, which sells exotic kosher foods to restaurants and supermarkets in Westbury, New York. It wanted to grow but lacked access to capital to purchase more specialty-foods inventory. Kosher Depot arranged a two-year, $3.3 million venture merchant financing arrangement with Capstone Business Credit. Kosher Depot would prearrange sales and notify Capstone, which would use its capital to buy the goods for Kosher Depot. Capstone would purchase and import the goods, storing them in its own warehouses. The warehouses then filled the orders received by Kosher Depot. For its services, Capstone received about 30% of the profits.

The cost of this arrangement—the 30% margin charged by the venture merchant—may be expensive relative to some of the alternative financing arrangements discussed in this chapter. However, the price may be worthwhile for a small business with no other short-term alternatives.

Source: Marie Leone, "Capital Ideas: A Little Cash'll Do Ya," http://CFO.com, March 3, 2005.

of the borrowing firm and the dollar volume of its receivables. The dollar amounts involved in factoring agreements may be substantial. In 2015, for example, Mattel has sold nearly $20 million of its accounts receivable under factoring arrangements.

A financing arrangement may be **with recourse**, meaning that the lender can seek payment from the borrower should the borrower's customers default on their bills. Alternatively, the financing arrangement may be **without recourse**, in which case the lender's claim on the borrower's assets in the event of a default is limited to explicitly pledged collateral only. In this latter case, the factor will pay the firm the amount due regardless of whether the factor receives payment from the firm's customers. If the arrangement is with recourse, the lender may not require that it approve the customers' accounts before sales are made. If the factoring agreement is without recourse, the borrowing firm must receive credit approval for a customer from the factor prior to shipping the goods. If the factor gives its approval, the firm ships the goods and the customer is directed to make payment directly to the lender.

with recourse
A financing arrangement in which the lender can claim all the borrower's assets in the event of a default, not just explicitly pledged collateral.

without recourse A financing arrangement in which the lender's claim on the borrower's assets in the event of a default is limited to explicitly pledged collateral only.

Inventory as Collateral

Inventory can be used as collateral for a loan in one of three ways: as a *floating lien*, as a *trust receipt*, or in a *warehouse arrangement*. These options are discussed in the following sections.

floating lien (general or blanket lien) A financial arrangement in which all of a firm's inventory is used to secure a loan.

Floating Lien. In a **floating lien**, **general lien**, or **blanket lien** arrangement, all of the firm's inventory is used to secure the loan. This arrangement is the riskiest setup from the standpoint of the lender because the value of the collateral used to secure the loan dwindles as inventory is sold. When a firm becomes financially distressed, management may be tempted to sell the inventory without making payments on the loan. In such a case, the firm may not have enough funds to replenish its inventory. As a result, the loan may become under-collateralized. To counter this risk, this type of loan bears a higher interest rate than the next two arrangements that we discuss. In addition, lenders will lend a low percentage of the value of the inventory.

trust receipts loan (floor planning) A type of loan in which distinguishable inventory items are held in a trust as security for the loan. As these items are sold, the firm remits the proceeds from their sale to the lender in repayment of the loan.

Trust Receipt. With a **trust receipts loan** or **floor planning**, distinguishable inventory items are held in a trust as security for the loan. As these items are sold, the firm remits the proceeds from their sale to the lender in repayment of the loan. The lender will periodically have its agent verify that the borrower has not sold some of the specified inventory and failed to make a repayment on the loan. Car dealerships often use this type of secured financing arrangement to obtain the funds needed to purchase vehicles from the manufacturer.

Loan Guarantees: The Ex-Im Bank Controversy

Exporters looking to finance working capital needs often face difficulty obtaining loans from domestic lenders. Lenders may feel unable to evaluate adequately the credit risk of foreign customers, for example, making them unwilling to lend against the exporter's accounts receivables, or to finance its purchases of inventory.

The Export-Import Bank of the United States, or Ex-Im Bank, was established in 1934 by President Franklin D. Roosevelt as an independent export credit agency that serves to "assist in financing the export of U.S. goods and services to international markets." It does so by providing loan guarantees which insure exporters' receivables against the risk of default by foreign customers, as well as risks of non-payment due to war or inconvertibility of the foreign currency. After obtaining such a loan guarantee, it is then usually possible for the exporter to arrange for short-term financing of its working capital needs from traditional lenders.

Critics of the Ex-Im Bank argue that because the bank is government sponsored, these loan guarantees implicitly pass the risk of the loans to U.S. taxpayers. If defaults were to exceed the bank's reserves, the federal government would need to bail out the bank. Supporters of the bank emphasize that the bank creates U.S. jobs by supporting the growth of U.S. exporters, and that without these guarantees the firms it serves would be unable to obtain competitive financing terms.

After facing controversial reauthorization votes in 2012 and 2014, the U.S. Congress let the Ex-Im Bank's authorization expire on June 30, 2015, closing the bank. After months of strong lobbying by U.S. businesses, Congress voted in a rare bipartisan effort to reauthorize and reopen the bank in December 2015.

warehouse arrangement When the inventory that serves as collateral for a loan is stored in a warehouse.

public warehouse A business that exists for the sole purpose of storing and tracking the inflow and outflow of inventory, providing the lender tighter control over the inventory.

field warehouse A warehouse arrangement that is operated by a third party, but is set up on the borrower's premises in a separate area so that the inventory collateralizing the loan is kept apart from the borrower's main plant.

Warehouse Arrangement. In a **warehouse arrangement**, the inventory that serves as collateral for the loan is stored in a warehouse. A warehouse arrangement is the least risky collateral arrangement from the standpoint of the lender. This type of arrangement can be set up in one of two ways.

The first method is to use a **public warehouse**, which is a business that exists for the sole purpose of storing and tracking the inflow and outflow of the inventory. The lender extends a loan to the borrowing firm, based on the value of the inventory stored. When the borrowing firm needs the inventory to sell, it returns to the warehouse and retrieves it upon receiving permission from the lender. This arrangement provides the lender with the tightest control over the inventory. Public warehouses work well for some types of inventory, such as wine and tobacco products, which must age before they are ready to be sold. It is not practical for items that are subject to spoilage or are bulky and, therefore, difficult to transport to and from the warehouse.

The second option, a **field warehouse**, is operated by a third party, but is set up on the borrower's premises in a separate area so that the inventory collateralizing the loan is kept apart from the borrower's main plant. This type of arrangement is convenient for the borrower but gives the lender the added security of having the inventory that serves as collateral controlled by a third party.

Warehouse arrangements are expensive. The business operating the warehouse charges a fee on top of the interest that the borrower must pay the lender for the loan. However, the borrower may also save on the costs of storing the inventory herself. Because the warehouser is a professional at inventory control, there is likely to be little loss due to damaged goods or theft, which in turn lowers insurance costs. Because the control of the inventory remains in the hands of a third party, lenders may be willing to lend a greater percentage of the market value of the inventory than they would under other inventory arrangements.

EXAMPLE 20.3
Calculating the Effective Annual Cost of Warehouse Financing

MyFinanceLab

PROBLEM

The Row Cannery wants to borrow $2 million for one month. Using its inventory as collateral, it can obtain a 12% (APR) loan. The lender requires that a warehouse arrangement be used. The warehouse fee is $10,000, payable at the end of the month. Calculate the effective annual rate of this loan for Row Cannery.

SOLUTION

PLAN

The monthly interest rate is 12%/12 = 1%. We need to compute the total cash flows Row will owe at the end of the month (including interest and the warehouse fee). By scaling those cash flows by the amount of the loan, we will have a total monthly cost for the loan that we can then convert to an EAR.

EXECUTE

At the end of the month, Row will owe $2,000,000 \times 1.01 = $2,020,000 plus the warehouse fee of $10,000. The cash flows are shown here on a timeline:

The actual one-month interest rate paid is:

$$\frac{2,030,000 - 2,000,000}{2,000,000} = 1.5\%$$

Expressing this as an EAR gives $1.015^{12} - 1 = 0.196$, or 19.6%

EVALUATE

The warehouse arrangement is quite costly: The EAR on the loan itself is $(1.01)^{12} - 1 = .1268$, or 12.68%, but the warehouse arrangement raises it to 19.6%!

The method that a firm adopts when using its inventory to collateralize a loan will affect the ultimate cost of the loan. The blanket lien agreement exposes the lender to the most risk and will, therefore, carry the highest interest rate of the three types of arrangements discussed. Although a warehousing arrangement provides the greatest amount of control over the inventory to the lender, resulting in a lower interest rate on the loan itself, the borrowing firm must pay the additional fees charged by the warehouser and accept the inconvenience associated with the loss of control. Although a trust receipts arrangement may offer a lower interest rate than a blanket lien and allows the firm to avoid the high fees associated with a warehouse arrangement, it can be used only with certain types of inventory.

CONCEPT CHECK

9. What is factoring of accounts receivable?

10. What is the difference between a floating lien and a trust receipt?

20.6 Putting It All Together: Creating a Short-Term Financial Plan

Let's return to Springfield Snowboards. In Table 20.2, we found that due to the seasonal nature of its sales, there would be wide swings in its forecasted cash flows—with large positive cash flows in the first and fourth quarters of the year and big negative ones in the second and third quarters. A financial manager at Springfield would need to plan for how to deal with those cash flow swings, and in particular how to finance any shortfalls. To do so, she would prepare a spreadsheet tracking Springfield's cash balance and short-term financing such as the one shown in Table 20.7. Springfield will end the fourth quarter of 2017 with $1 million in cash, and it needs to maintain a minimum cash balance of $500,000 to meet its basic transaction needs. Given the cash flows projected in Table 20.2, it will have a cash deficit by the third quarter of 2018.

The analysis identifies two decisions facing the financial manager: what to do with the excess cash generated in the first quarter, and how to finance the third quarter deficit. The analysis currently assumes that the excess cash is held as just that—cash. However, as we discussed in Chapter 19, there are many different options for investing excess cash, even over short horizons, which would generate (taxable) interest income. With such investments, the beginning cash in a quarter would be equal to the ending cash in the previous quarter plus the after-tax portion of the interest received.

Turning to the third quarter deficit, we see that cash flows in the fourth quarter will be large enough to pay off any financing of the third quarter deficit. After reviewing their options, Springfield's managers decide to obtain a one-quarter bank loan with a single repayment. Their bank charges them 3% interest per quarter, so they will need to repay $1231(1.03) = 1268$ in the fourth quarter, which they will easily be able to do given their excess cash flow at that time. By creating a short-term financial plan, the managers can anticipate upcoming shortfalls, allowing them enough time to investigate the least costly way to finance those shortfalls.

TABLE 20.7

Projected Cash Balance and Short-Term Financing at Springfield Snowboards

1	Quarter	2017Q4	2018Q1	2018Q2	2018Q3	2018Q4
2	**Cash Balance and Short-Term Financing ($000)**					
3	Starting Cash Balance		1,000	2,763	1,316	500
4	Change in Cash and Equivalents		1,763	−1,447	−2,047	3,402
5	Minimum Cash Balance		500	500	500	500
6	**Surplus (Deficit) Relative to Minimum** (3 + 4 − 5)		2,263	816	−1,231	3,402
7	Increase (Decrease) in Short-Term Financing		0	0	1,231	−1,268
8	Existing Short-Term Financing	0	0	0	0	1,268
9	Total Short-Term Financing (7 + 8)	0	0	0	1,231	0
10	**Ending Cash Balance** (3 + 4 + 7)	1,000	2,763	1,316	500	2,634

MyFinanceLab

Here is what you should know after reading this chapter. MyFinanceLab will help you identify what you know, and where to go when you need to practice.

KEY POINTS AND EQUATIONS	KEY TERMS	ONLINE PRACTICE
20.1 Forecasting Short-Term Financing Needs • The first step in short-term financial planning is to forecast future cash flows. The cash flow forecasts allow a company to determine whether it has a cash flow surplus or deficit, and whether the surplus or deficit is short-term or long-term. • Firms need short-term financing to deal with seasonal negative cash flow shocks, positive cash flow shocks, or working capital requirements. • Using forecasted inflows and outflows of cash, a cash budget allows managers to identify any potential cash shortfalls.	cash budget, p. 633	MyFinanceLab Study Plan 20.1 Spreadsheet Tables 20.1–20.5
20.2 The Matching Principle • The matching principle specifies that short-term needs for funds should be financed with short-term sources of funds, and long-term needs should be financed with long-term sources of funds.	aggressive financing policy, p. 636 conservative financing policy, p. 636 funding risk, p. 636 matching principle, p. 635 permanent working capital, p. 635 temporary working capital, p. 635	MyFinanceLab Study Plan 20.2 Spreadsheet Table 20.6
20.3 Short-Term Financing with Bank Loans • Bank loans are a primary source of short-term financing, especially for small firms. • The most straightforward type of bank loan is a single, end-of-period payment loan. • Bank lines of credit allow a firm to borrow any amount up to a stated maximum. The line of credit may be uncommitted, which is a nonbinding, informal agreement or, more typically, may be committed. • A bridge loan is a short-term bank loan that is used to bridge the gap until the firm can arrange for long-term financing. • The number of compounding periods and other loan stipulations, such as commitment fees, loan origination fees, and compensating balance requirements, affect the effective annual rate of a bank loan.	bridge loan, p. 639 committed line of credit, p. 638 discount loan, p. 639 evergreen credit, p. 639 line of credit, p. 638 loan origination fee, p. 639 London Inter-Bank Offered Rate (LIBOR), p. 638 prime rate, p. 638 promissory note, p. 638 revolving line of credit, p. 639 uncommitted line of credit, p. 638	MyFinanceLab Study Plan 20.3

20.4 Short-Term Financing with Commercial Paper • Commercial paper is a method of short-term financing that is usually available only to large companies with high-quality credit ratings. It is a low-cost alternative to a short-term bank loan for those firms with access to the commercial paper market.	commercial paper, p. 641 dealer paper, p. 642 direct paper, p. 642	MyFinanceLab Study Plan 20.4
20.5 Short-Term Financing with Secured Financing • Short-term loans may also be structured as secured loans. The accounts receivable and inventory of a firm typically serve as collateral in short-term secured financing arrangements. • Accounts receivable may be either pledged as security for a loan or factored. In a factoring arrangement, the accounts receivable are sold to the lender (or factor), and the firm's customers are usually instructed to make payments directly to the factor. • Inventory can be used as collateral for a loan in several ways: a floating lien (also called a general or blanket lien), a trust receipts loan (or floor planning), or a warehouse arrangement. These arrangements vary in the extent to which specific items of inventory are identified as collateral; consequently, they vary in the amount of risk the lender faces.	factoring of accounts receivable, p. 643 factors, p. 643 field warehouse, p. 645 floating lien (general or blanket lien), p. 644 pledging of accounts receivable, p. 643 public warehouse, p. 645 secured loan, p. 643 trust receipts loan (floor planning), p. 644 warehouse arrangement, p. 645 with recourse, p. 644 without recourse, p. 644	MyFinanceLab Study Plan 20.5
20.6 Putting It All Together: Creating a Short-Term Financial Plan • A short-term financial plan tracks a firm's cash balance and new and existing short-term financing. The plan allows managers to forecast shortfalls and plan to fund them in the least costly manner.		MyFinanceLab Study Plan 20.6 Spreadsheet Table 20.7

CRITICAL THINKING

1. What are the objectives of short-term financial planning?

2. What are seasonalities and what role do they play in short-term financial planning?

3. Which of the following companies are likely to have high short-term financing needs? Why?
   a. A clothing retailer
   b. A professional sports team
   c. An electric utility
   d. A company that operates toll roads
   e. A restaurant chain

4. Why is it important to distinguish between permanent and temporary shortfalls?

5. What is the difference between permanent working capital and temporary working capital?

6. Describe the different approaches a firm could take when preparing for cash flow shortfalls.

7. What are the different bank financing options and what are their relative advantages?

8. What is the difference between evergreen credit and a revolving line of credit?

9. What is the difference between direct paper and dealer paper?

10. What is the difference between pledging accounts receivable to secure a loan and factoring accounts receivable? What types of short-term secured financing can a firm use to cover shortfalls?

11. What will a short-term financial plan enable a financial manager to do?

PROBLEMS

All problems are available in MyFinanceLab. *The* *icon indicates problems that are easier to solve using Excel and have data in an Excel format available in* MyFinanceLab.

Forecasting Short-Term Financing Needs

1. Sailboats Etc. is a retail company specializing in sailboats and other sailing-related equipment. The following table contains financial forecasts as well as current (month 0) working capital levels (*see* MyFinanceLab *for the data in Excel format*).

($000)				Month			
	0	1	2	3	4	5	6
Net Income		$10	$12	$15	$25	$30	$18
Depreciation		2	3	3	4	5	4
Capital Expenditures		1	0	0	1	0	0
Levels of Working Capital							
Accounts Receivable	$2	3	4	5	7	10	6
Inventory	3	2	4	5	5	4	2
Accounts Payable	2	2	2	2	2	2	2

a. During which month are the firm's seasonal working capital needs the greatest?
b. When does the firm have surplus cash?

2. Emerald City Umbrellas sells umbrellas and rain gear in Seattle, so its sales are fairly level across the year. However, it is branching out to other markets where it expects demand to vary across the year. It expects sales in its new market of:

Q1	Q2	Q3	Q4
$20,000	$50,000	$10,000	$50,000

It carries inventory equal to 20% of next quarter's sales, has accounts payable of 10% of next quarter's sales, and accounts receivable of 20% of this quarter's sales.
a. Assume that it starts with $4000 in inventory, $2000 in accounts payable, and no accounts receivable for the new market. Forecast its working capital levels and changes over the four quarters.
b. If Emerald City Umbrellas has net income equal to 20% of sales, what will be its financing needs over the quarter?

The Matching Principle

The following table includes quarterly working capital levels for your firm for the next year. Use it to answer Problems 3–7.

($000)	Quarter			
	1	2	3	4
Cash	$100	$100	$100	$100
Accounts Receivable	200	100	100	600
Inventory	200	500	900	50
Accounts Payable	100	100	100	100

 3. What are the permanent working capital needs of your company? What are the temporary needs (*see* MyFinanceLab *for the data in Excel format*)?

 4. If you chose to use only long-term financing, what total amount of borrowing would you need to have on a permanent basis? Forecast your excess cash levels under this scenario (*see* MyFinanceLab *for the data in Excel format*).

 5. If you hold only $100 in cash at any time, what is your maximum short-term borrowing and when (*see* MyFinanceLab *for the data in Excel format*)?

 6. If you choose to enter the year with $400 total in cash, what is your maximum short-term borrowing (*see* MyFinanceLab *for the data in Excel format*)?

 7. If you want to limit your maximum short-term borrowing to $500, how much excess cash must you carry (*see* MyFinanceLab *for the data in Excel format*)?

Short-Term Financing with Bank Loans

 8. Hand-to-Mouth (H2M) is currently cash-constrained, and must make a decision about whether to delay paying one of its suppliers, or take out a loan. They owe the supplier $10,000 with terms of 2/10 Net 40, so the supplier will give them a 2% discount if they pay today (when the discount period expires). Alternatively, they can pay the full $10,000 in one month when the invoice is due. H2M is considering three options:

Alternative A: Forgo the discount on its trade credit agreement, wait and pay the full $10,000 in one month.

Alternative B: Borrow the money needed to pay its supplier today from Bank A, which has offered a one-month loan at an APR of 12%. The bank will require a (no-interest) compensating balance of 5% of the face value of the loan and will charge a $100 loan origination fee. Because H2M has no cash, it will need to borrow the funds to cover these additional amounts as well.

Alternative C: Borrow the money needed to pay its supplier today from Bank B, which has offered a one-month loan at an APR of 15%. The loan has a 1% loan origination fee, which again H2M will need to borrow to cover.

Which alternative is the cheapest source of financing for Hand-to-Mouth?

9. Your firm has a committed line of credit with your bank with a commitment fee of 0.5% (EAR) and an interest rate of 6% (EAR). The total line is $500,000 and you borrowed $300,000 at the beginning of the year. If you repay the $300,000 at the end of

the year, what is your total cost, in dollars of the interest and commitment fee? What is this cost as a percentage of the amount you borrowed?

10. Your firm's bank has offered you two options for short-term financing in the amount of $400,000. The first option is a committed line of credit with a commitment fee of 0.5% (EAR) and an interest rate of 8% (APR, compounded quarterly). The second option is a loan with a 5% compensating balance and an interest rate of 7.6% (APR, compounded quarterly). If you need $380,000 in financing at the beginning of the year and plan to pay it back at the end of the year, which option has a lower effective annual rate of interest?

11. Consider two loans with one-year maturities and identical face values: an 8% loan with a 1% loan origination fee and an 8% loan with a 5% (no-interest) compensating balance requirement. Which loan would have the higher effective annual rate? Why?

12. Which of the following one-year, $1000 bank loans offers the lowest effective annual rate?
    a. A loan with an APR of 6%, compounded monthly
    b. A loan with an APR of 6%, compounded annually, with a compensating balance requirement of 10% (on which no interest is paid)
    c. A loan with an APR of 6%, compounded annually, with a 1% loan origination fee

13. The Needy Corporation borrowed $10,000 from Bank Ease. According to the terms of the loan, Needy must pay the bank $400 in interest every three months for the three-year life of the loan, with the principal to be repaid at the maturity of the loan. What effective annual rate is Needy paying?

Short-Term Financing with Commercial Paper

14. The Treadwater Bank wants to raise $1 million using three-month commercial paper. The net proceeds to the bank will be $985,000. What is the effective annual rate of this financing for Treadwater?

15. Magna Corporation has an issue of commercial paper with a face value of $1 million and a maturity of six months. Magna received net proceeds of $973,710 when it sold the paper. What is the effective annual rate of the paper to Magna?

16. Assume that the prime rate is 8% APR, compounded quarterly. How much dollar savings in interest did Treadwater (Problem 14) and Magna (Problem 15) achieve by accessing the commercial paper market?

17. The Signet Corporation has issued four-month commercial paper with a $6 million face value. The firm netted $5,870,850 on the sale. What effective annual rate is Signet paying for these funds?

Short-Term Financing with Secured Financing

18. The Ohio Valley Steel Corporation has borrowed $5 million for one month at a stated annual rate of 9%, using inventory stored in a field warehouse as collateral. The warehouser charges a $5000 fee, payable at the end of the month. What is the effective annual rate of this loan?

19. The Rasputin Brewery is considering using a public warehouse loan as part of its short-term financing. The firm will require a loan of $500,000. Interest on the loan will be 10% (APR, annual compounding) to be paid at the end of the year. The warehouse

charges 1% of the face value of the loan, payable at the beginning of the year. What is the effective annual rate of this warehousing arrangement?

Putting It All Together: Creating a Short-Term Financial Plan

20. Construct a short-term financial plan for Springfield Snowboards based on its expansion opportunity described in the "Positive Cash Flow Shocks" part of Section 20.1. Base the plan on the following table, which forecasts additional capital expenditures, marketing (SG&A), and working capital in Q1 and Q2 along with higher sales in Q2–Q4. Assume that Springfield ends 2017 with $1 million in cash and that its bank will offer it a short-term loan at the rate 2.5% per quarter (see MyFinanceLab for the data in Excel format).

	Quarter	2017Q4	2018Q1	2018Q2	2018Q3	2018Q4
1						
2	**Income Statement ($000)**					
3	Sales	4,545	5,000	6,000	6,000	6,000
4	Cost of Goods Sold	−2,955	−3,250	−3,900	−3,900	−3,900
5	Selling, General, and Administrative	−455	−1,000	−600	−600	−600
6	**EBITDA**	1,136	750	1,500	1,500	1,500
7	Depreciation	−455	−500	−525	−525	−525
8	**EBIT**	682	250	975	975	975
9	Taxes	−239	−88	−341	−341	−341
10	**Net Income**	443	162	634	634	634
11	**Statement of Cash Flows**					
12	Net Income		162	634	634	634
13	Depreciation		500	525	525	525
14	Changes in Working Capital					
15	Accounts Receivable		−136	−300	—	—
16	Inventory		—	—	—	—
17	Accounts Payable		48	105	—	—
18	**Cash from Operating Activities**		574	964	1,159	1,159
19	Capital Expenditures		−1,500	−525	−525	−525
20	Other Investment		—	—	—	—
21	**Cash from Investing Activities**		−1,500	−525	−525	−525
22	Net Borrowing		—	—	—	—
23	Dividends		—	—	—	—
24	Capital Contributions		—	—	—	—
25	**Cash from Financing Activities**		—	—	—	—
26	**Change in Cash and Equivalents** (18 + 21 + 25)		−926	439	634	634

Integrative Case

This case draws on material from Chapters 18–20. See MyFinanceLab for the data in Tables 1, 2, 3, and 4 and the spreadsheet referenced in the case questions.

Idexo Corporation is a privately held designer and manufacturer of licensed college apparel in Cincinnati, Ohio. In late 2016, after several years of lackluster performance, the firm's owner and founder, Rebecca Ferris, returned from retirement to replace the current CEO, reinvigorate the firm, and plan for its eventual sale or possible IPO. She has hired you to assist with developing the firm's financial plan for the next five years.

In 2016, Idexo had total assets of about $103 million and annual sales of $100 million (see Table 1). The firm was profitable, with expected 2016 earnings of more than $9 million, for a net profit margin of 9.1%.[1] However, revenue growth has slowed dramatically in recent years and the firm's net profit margin has actually been declining. Ferris is convinced the firm can do better. After only several weeks at the helm, she has already identified a number of potential improvements to drive the firm's future growth.

TABLE 1

Idexo's 2016 Income Statement and Balance Sheet

	Year	2016
1	Year	2016
2	**Income Statement ($000s)**	
3	Sales	100,000
4	Cost of Goods Sold	
5	Raw Materials	−21,333
6	Direct Labor Costs	−24,000
7	**Gross Profit**	54,667
8	Sales and Marketing	−15,000
9	Administration	−18,000
10	**EBITDA**	21,667
11	Depreciation	−6,667
12	**EBIT**	15,000
13	Interest Expense (net)	−1,021
14	**Pretax Income**	13,979
15	Income Tax	−4,893
16	**Net Income**	9,086

	Year	2016
1	Year	2016
2	**Balance Sheet ($000s)**	
3	**Assets**	
4	Cash and Cash Equivalents	15,000
5	Accounts Receivable	20,000
6	Inventories	8,219
7	**Total Current Assets**	43,219
8	Property, Plant, and Equipment	60,000
9	Goodwill	—
10	**Total Assets**	103,219
11	**Liabilities and Stockholders' Equity**	
12	Accounts Payable	6,205
13	Debt	20,000
14	**Total Liabilities**	26,205
15	**Stockholders' Equity**	77,014
16	**Total Liabilities and Equity**	103,219

---

[1]See Table 1 for further projected income and balance sheet information for 2016.

Operational Improvements

On the operational side, Ferris is quite optimistic regarding the company's prospects. The market is expected to grow by 6% per year, and Idexo produces a superior product. Idexo's market share has not grown in recent years because prior management devoted insufficient resources to product development, sales, and marketing. At the same time, Idexo has overspent on administrative costs. Indeed, from Table 1, Idexo's current administrative expenses are $18 million/$100 million = 18% of sales, which exceeds its expenditures on sales and marketing (15% of sales). Competitors spend less on administrative overhead than on sales and marketing.

Ferris plans to cut administrative costs immediately to 15% of sales and redirect resources to new product development, sales, and marketing. By doing so, she believes Idexo can increase its market share from 10% to 14% over the next four years. Using the existing production lines, the increased sales demand can be met in the short run by increasing overtime and running some weekend shifts. The resulting increase in labor costs, however, is likely to lead to a decline in the firm's gross margin to 53%. Table 2 shows sales and operating-cost projections for the next five years based on this plan, including the reallocation of resources from administration to sales and marketing over the five-year period, and an increase in Idexo's average selling price at a 2% inflation rate each year.

TABLE 2

Idexo's Sales and Operating Cost Projections

	Year		2016	2017	2018	2019	2020	2021
1								
2	**Sales Data**	Growth/Yr						
3	Market Size (000s units)	6.0%	20,000	21,200	22,472	23,820	25,250	26,765
4	Market Share	*1.0%	10.0%	11.0%	12.0%	13.0%	14.0%	14.0%
5	Average Sales Price ($/unit)	2.00%	50.00	51.00	52.02	53.06	54.12	55.20
6								
7	**Operating Expense and Tax Data**							
8	Gross Margin		54.7%	53.0%	53.0%	53.0%	53.0%	53.0%
9	Sales and Marketing (% sales)		15.0%	16.5%	18.0%	19.5%	20.0%	20.0%
10	Administration (% sales)		18.0%	15.0%	15.0%	14.0%	13.0%	13.0%
11	Tax Rate		35.0%	35.0%	35.0%	35.0%	35.0%	35.0%

*Market Share growth is expected through 2020 only.

Expansion Plans

Table 3 shows the forecast for Idexo's capital expenditures over the next five years. Based on the estimates for capital expenditures and depreciation, this spreadsheet tracks the book value of Idexo's plant, property, and equipment starting from its level at the end of 2016. Note that investment is expected to remain relatively low over the next two years—slightly below depreciation. Idexo will expand production during this period by using its existing plant more efficiently.

TABLE 3

Idexo's Capital Expenditure Forecast

	Year	2016	2017	2018	2019	2020	2021
1							
2	**Fixed Assets and Capital Investment ($000s)**						
3	Opening Book Value	60,167	60,000	58,500	57,150	73,935	77,341
4	Capital Investment	6,500	5,000	5,000	25,000	12,000	8,000
5	Depreciation	−6,667	−6,500	−6,350	−8,215	−8,594	−8,534
6	Closing Book Value	60,000	58,500	57,150	73,935	77,341	76,807

However, once Idexo's volume grows by more than 50% over its current level, the firm will need to undertake a major expansion to increase its manufacturing capacity. Based on the projections in Table 2, sales growth exceeds 50% of current sales in 2019. Therefore, Table 3 budgets for a major expansion of the plant at that time, leading to a large increase in capital expenditures in 2019 and 2020.

Working Capital Management

To compensate for its weak sales and marketing efforts, Idexo has sought to maintain the loyalty of its retailers, in part through a very lax credit policy. This policy affects Idexo's working capital requirements: For every extra day that customers take to pay, another day's sales revenue is added to accounts receivable (rather than received in cash). From Idexo's current income and balance sheet (Table 1), we can estimate the number of days of receivables as:

$$\text{Accounts Receivable Days} = \frac{\text{Accounts Receivable (\$)}}{\text{Sales Revenue (\$/yr)}} \times 365 \text{ Days/Yr}$$

$$= 20 \text{ Million/100 Million} \times 365 = 73 \text{ Days}$$

The standard for the industry is 45 days. Ferris believes that Idexo can tighten its credit policy to achieve this goal without sacrificing sales.

Ferris does not foresee any other significant improvements in Idexo's working capital management, and expects inventories and accounts payable to increase proportionately with sales growth. The firm will also need to maintain a minimum cash balance equal to 30 days' sales revenue to meet its liquidity needs. It earns no interest on this minimal balance, and Ferris plans to pay out all excess cash each year to the firm's shareholders as dividends.

Capital Structure Changes: Levering Up

Idexo currently has $20 million in debt outstanding with an interest rate of 6.8%, and it will pay interest only on this debt during the next five years. The firm will also obtain additional financing at the end of years 2019 and 2020 associated with the expansion of its manufacturing plant, as shown in Table 4. While Idexo's credit quality will likely improve by that time, interest rates may also increase somewhat. You expect that rates on these future loans will be about 6.8% as well.

Given Idexo's outstanding debt, its interest expense each year is computed as:

$$\text{Interest in Year } t = \text{Interest Rate} \times \text{Ending Balance in Year } t - 1$$

The interest on the debt will provide a valuable tax shield to offset Idexo's taxable income.

TABLE 4

Idexo's Debt and
Interest Forecast

1	Year		2016	2017	2018	2019	2020	2021
2	Debt and Interest Table ($000s)							
3	Outstanding Debt		20,000	20,000	20,000	35,000	40,000	40,000
4	Interest on Term Loan	6.80%		−1,360	−1,360	−1,360	−2,380	−2,720

Case Questions

1. Based on the forecasts in this case, use the following spreadsheet to construct a pro forma income statement for Idexo over the next five years. What is the annual growth rate of the firm's net income over this period?

1	Year	2016	2017	2018	2019	2020	2021
2	**Income Statement ($000s)**						
3	Sales	100,000					
4	Cost of Goods Sold	−45,333					
5	**Gross Profit**	54,667					
6	Sales and Marketing	−15,000					
7	Administration	−18,000					
8	**EBITDA**	21,667					
9	Depreciation	−6,667					
10	**EBIT**	15,000					
11	Interest Expense (net)	−1,021					
12	**Pretax Income**	13,979					
13	Income Tax	−4,893					
14	**Net Income**	9,086					

2. Use the following spreadsheet to project Idexo's working capital needs over the next five years. Why is the increase in net working capital negative in 2017? Why does the increase in net working capital decline from 2017 to 2018?

1	Year	2016	2017	2018	2019	2020	2021
2	**Working Capital ($000s)**						
3	**Assets**						
4	Accounts Receivable	20,000					
5	Inventories	8,219					
6	Minimum Cash Balance	8,219					
7	Total Current Assets	36,438					
8	**Liabilities**						
9	Accounts Payable	6,205					
10	**Net Working Capital**	30,233					
11	Increase in Net Working Capital						

3. Based on the forecasts you have already developed, use the following spreadsheet to project Idexo's free cash flow for 2017–2021. Will the firm's free cash flow steadily increase over this period? Why or why not?

1	Year	2017	2018	2019	2020	2021
2	**Free Cash Flow ($000s)**					
3	**Net Income**					
4	Plus: After-Tax Interest Expense					
5	**Unlevered Net Income**					
6	Plus: Depreciation					
7	Less: Increases in NWC					
8	Less: Capital Expenditures					
9	**Free Cash Flow of Firm**					
10	Plus: Net Borrowing					
11	Less: After-Tax Interest Expense					
12	**Free Cash Flow to Equity**					

4. (Optional) Recall that Idexo plans to maintain only the minimal necessary cash and pay out all excess cash as dividends.

Year	2016	2017	2018	2019	2020	2021
2 Balance Sheet ($000s)						
3 Assets						
4 Cash and Cash Equivalents						
5 Accounts Receivable						
6 Inventories						
7 Total Current Assets						
8 Property, Plant, and Equipment						
9 Goodwill						
10 Total Assets						
11 Liabilities and Stockholders' Equity						
12 Accounts Payable						
13 Debt						
14 Total Liabilities						
15 Stockholders' Equity						
16 Starting Stockholders' Equity						
17 Net Income						
18 Dividends						
19 Capital Contributions						
20 Stockholders' Equity						
21 Total Liabilities and Equity						

a. Suppose that at the very end of 2016 Ferris plans to use all excess cash to pay an immediate dividend. How much cash can the firm pay out at this time? Compute a new 2016 balance sheet reflecting this dividend using the spreadsheet on page 656.

b. Forecast the cash available to pay dividends in future years—the firm's *free cash flow to equity*—by adding any *new* borrowing and subtracting *after-tax* interest expenses from free cash flow each year. Will Idexo have sufficient cash to pay dividends in all years? Explain.

c. Using your forecast of the firm's dividends, construct a pro forma balance sheet for Idexo over the next five years.

5. In late 2016, soon after Ferris's return as CEO, the firm receives an unsolicited offer of $210 million for its outstanding equity. If Ferris accepts the offer, the deal would close at the end of 2016. Suppose Ferris believes that Idexo can be sold at the end of 2018 for an enterprise value equal to nine times its final EBITDA. Idexo's unlevered cost of capital is 10% (specifically, 10% is the pretax WACC). Based on your forecast of Idexo's free cash flow in 2017–2021 in Question 3, and its final enterprise value in 2021, estimate the following:

a. Idexo's unlevered value at the end of 2016.

b. The present value of Idexo's interest tax shields in 2017–2021. (Recall that these tax shields are fixed and so have the same risk level as the debt.)

c. Idexo's enterprise value at the end of 2016. (Add the present value of the interest tax shield in (b) to the unlevered value of the firm in (a).)

d. Idexo's equity value today. (Adjust the enterprise value in (c) to reflect the firm's debt and excess cash at the end of 2016.)

e. Based on your analysis, should Ferris sell the company now?

Special Topics

Valuation Principle Connection. In Part 8, the final section of the text, we address special topics in corporate financial management. The Valuation Principle continues to provide a unifying framework as we consider these topics. Chapter 21 discusses options; the key to understanding how to value them comes from the Law of One Price application of the Valuation Principle. In Chapter 22, we provide an overview of mergers and acquisitions. Chapter 23 introduces the issues a firm faces when making a foreign investment, and addresses the valuation of foreign projects. We will see that the Law of One Price generates several important relations that will drive our valuation of foreign cash flows.

Chapter 21
Option Applications
and Corporate Finance

Chapter 22
Mergers and Acquisitions

Chapter 23
International Corporate
Finance

21

Option Applications and Corporate Finance

LEARNING OBJECTIVES

- Understand basic option terminology

- Explain the difference between *calls* and *puts*, how they pay off, and the profit from holding each to expiration

- Analyze the factors that affect option prices

- Become familiar with the Black-Scholes option pricing formula

- Describe the relationship that must hold between the prices of similar *calls* and *puts* on the same stock

- Demonstrate how options are applied in corporate finance

notation   *NPV*   net present value

               PV   present value

Since the introduction of publicly traded options on the Chicago Board Options Exchange (CBOE) in 1973, financial options have become one of the most important and actively traded financial assets. Today, options are everywhere. Over 2000 companies in the United States alone have options on their stock— including Google, Amazon.com, and Apple. Many public companies such as Nike pay their executives partly in stock options. The 1997 Nobel Prize in Economics was awarded for an option pricing formula. Huge quantities of commodities such as corn, wheat, oil, soybeans, and gold are traded through options. Companies such as Dell spend millions of dollars each year buying options on foreign currencies. Even the plot of the James Bond film *Casino Royale* featured the villain losing a fortune when his options expired worthless. As the use of options grows, so does the value of understanding them.

In this chapter, we introduce the financial option, a financial contract between two parties. In Chapter 9, we briefly discussed the idea of *real options*, or the value of flexibility when managing projects. Here, we delve further into understanding what options are and what factors affect their value. To start, we provide an overview of the basic types of financial options, introduce important terminology, and describe the payoffs of various option-based strategies. Next, we discuss the factors that affect option prices. Finally, we model the equity and debt of the firm as options to gain insight into the conflicts of interest between equity and debt holders, as well as the pricing of risky debt.

21.1   Option Basics

financial option A contract that gives its owner the right (but not the obligation) to purchase or sell an asset at a fixed price at some future date.

call option A financial option that gives its owner the right to buy an asset.

put option A financial option that gives its owner the right to sell an asset.

option writer The seller of an option contract.

derivatives Securities whose cash flows depend solely on the prices of other marketed assets.

warrant A call option written by a company itself on new stock.

exercising (an option) When a holder of an option enforces the agreement and buys or sells a share of stock at the agreed-upon price.

strike (exercise) price The price at which an option holder buys or sells a share of stock when the option is exercised.

American options The most common kind of option, they allow their holders to exercise the option on any date up to and including the expiration date.

expiration date The last date on which an option holder has the right to exercise the option.

European options Options that allow their holders to exercise the option only on the expiration date.

A **financial option** contract gives its owner the right (but not the obligation) to purchase or sell an asset at a fixed price at some future date. There are two distinct kinds of option contracts: *call options* and *put options*. A **call option** gives the owner the right to *buy* the asset; a **put option** gives the owner the right to *sell* the asset. An option is a contract between two parties. For every owner of a financial option, there is also an **option writer**, the seller of an option contract, who is the person who takes the other side of the contract. Options are part of a broader class of securities called **derivatives** because they derive their value solely from the price of another asset.

The most common option contracts are options on shares of stock. A stock option gives the holder the option to buy or sell a share of stock on or before a given date for a given price. For example, a call option on 3M Corporation stock might give the holder the right to purchase a share of 3M for $180 per share at any time up to, for example, January 18, 2019. Similarly, a put option on 3M stock might give the holder the right to sell a share of 3M stock for $175 per share at any time up to, say, February 15, 2019.

When a company writes a call option on *new* stock in the company, it is called a **warrant**. A regular call option is written by a third party on existing stock. When a holder of a warrant exercises it and thereby purchases stock, the company delivers this stock by issuing new stock. In all other respects, a warrant is identical to a call option.

Option Contracts

Practitioners use specific words to describe the details of option contracts. When a holder of an option enforces the agreement and buys or sells a share of stock at the agreed-upon price, he is **exercising** the option. The price at which the option holder buys or sells the share of stock when the option is exercised is called the **strike price** or **exercise price**.

There are two kinds of options. **American options**, the most common kind, allow their holders to exercise the option on any date up to and including a final date called the **expiration date**. **European options** allow their holders to exercise the option *only* on the expiration date—holders cannot exercise before the expiration date. The names *American* and *European* have nothing to do with the location where the options are traded: Both types are traded worldwide. For options on equity (stock), the expiration date is the Saturday following the third Friday of the expiration month. However, trading of the option stops on that Friday.

As with other financial assets, options can be bought and sold. Standard stock options are traded on organized exchanges, while more specialized options are sold through dealers. The oldest and largest options exchange is the Chicago Board Options Exchange (CBOE). By convention, all traded options expire on the Saturday following the third Friday of the month. The market price of the option is also called the *option premium*.

The *option buyer*, also called the *option holder*, holds the right to exercise the option and has a *long* position in the contract. The *option seller*, also called the *option writer*, sells (or

writes) the option and has a *short* position in the contract. Because the long side has the option to exercise, the short side has an *obligation* to fulfill the contract. For example, suppose you own a call option on Hewlett-Packard stock with an exercise price of $25. Hewlett-Packard stock is currently trading for $40, so you decide to exercise the option. The person holding the short position in the contract is obligated to sell you a share of Hewlett-Packard stock for $25. Your $15 gain—the difference between the price you pay for the share of stock and the price at which you can sell the share in the market—is the short position's loss.

Investors exercise options only when they stand to gain something. Consequently, whenever an option is exercised, the person holding the short position funds the gain. That is, the obligation will be costly. Why, then, do people write options? The answer is that when you sell an option you get paid for it—options always have positive prices. This up-front payment compensates the seller for the risk of loss in the event that the option holder chooses to exercise the option. If all this new terminology is confusing, rest assured that you will become comfortable with it as you proceed through the chapter. We provide a summary of the new terms in Table 21.1.

Stock Option Quotations

Table 21.2 shows near-term options on Amazon.com taken from the CBOE Web site (www.cboe.com) on July 18, 2016. Call options are listed on the left and put options on the right. Each line corresponds to a particular option. The first two digits in the option name refer to the year of expiration. The option name also includes the month of expiration and the strike or exercise price. Looking at Table 21.2, the first line of the left column is a call option with an exercise price of $715 that expires on the Saturday following the third Friday of August 2016 (Saturday, August 20, 2016). The columns to the right of the name display market data for the option. The first of these columns shows the last sale price, followed by the net change from the previous day's last reported sale price, the current bid and ask prices, and the daily volume. The final column is the **open interest**, the total number of contracts of that particular option that have been written and not yet closed.

open interest The total number of contracts of a particular option that have been written and not yet closed.

The top line of the option quote displays information about the stock itself. In this case, Amazon's stock last traded at a price of $736.07 per share, which is $0.63 less than where it closed the previous day (red indicates a decline).

at-the-money Describes options whose exercise prices are equal to the current stock price.

When the exercise price of an option is equal to the current price of the stock, the option is said to be **at-the-money**. Notice that much of the trading occurs in options that are closest to being at-the-money—that is, calls and puts with exercise prices of $735. Note how the August 735 calls have high volume. They last traded for $34.04, which is above the

TABLE 21.1

The Language of Options

Call option	Option to <u>buy</u> the stock at a prespecified price
Put option	Option to <u>sell</u> the stock at a prespecified price
Strike (exercise) price	The prespecified price in the option contract
Write an option	Sell an option
Exercise (an option)	Enforce your right to buy or sell the stock as specified in the option contract
Short/Long position	The writer (seller) has a short position and the buyer has a long position in the option
American option	You can exercise the option any time on or before the expiration date
European option	You can exercise the option only on the expiration date
Warrant	A call option written by the firm whereby new stock will be issued if the warrant is exercised

TABLE 21.2

Option Quotes for Amazon.com Stock

The description of each traded option can be read as: year and month of expiration, followed by the strike price. For example, the first call listed expires in August 2016 and has an exercise (strike) price of 715.00.

AMZN (AMAZON.COM INC)   736.07 0.63
Jul 18 2016 @ 17:47 ET

Calls	Last Sale	Net	Bid	Ask	Vol	Open Int	Puts	Last Sale	Net	Bid	Ask	Vol	Open Int
16 Aug 715.00	44.20	0.09	43.55	44.35	44	1253	16 Aug 715.00	22.10	−1.47	22.05	22.75	97	590
16 Aug 720.00	41.79	0.52	40.55	41.35	135	806	16 Aug 720.00	24.00	−1.87	24.05	24.70	158	610
16 Aug 725.00	38.79	0.74	37.60	38.45	149	602	16 Aug 725.00	25.60	−2.09	26.15	26.80	37	624
16 Aug 730.00	36.07	0.47	34.95	35.65	168	1496	16 Aug 730.00	27.81	−2.24	28.40	29.15	49	714
16 Aug 735.00	34.04	1.26	32.20	33.00	156	656	16 Aug 735.00	30.31	−2.04	30.70	31.40	28	318
16 Aug 740.00	30.36	0.16	29.70	30.40	185	669	16 Aug 740.00	33.10	−1.12	33.10	33.65	65	657
16 Aug 745.00	28.65	0.71	27.30	27.95	51	602	16 Aug 745.00	35.70	−1.65	35.70	36.50	19	338
16 Aug 750.00	25.70	0.10	24.80	25.60	378	1671	16 Aug 750.00	38.60	−1.50	38.35	39.10	25	615
16 Aug 755.00	24.20	0.75	22.90	23.35	57	682	16 Aug 755.00	41.00	−1.41	41.10	41.90	8	305

Source: Chicago Board Options Exchange at www.cboe.com.

current bid price ($32.20) and the ask price ($33.00). This indicates that the trade likely did not occur recently because the last traded price is not a current market price.

Stock option contracts are always written on 100 shares of stock. If, for instance, you decided to purchase one August 715 call contract, you would be purchasing an option to buy 100 shares at $715 per share. Option prices are quoted on a per-share basis, so the ask price of $44.35 implies that you would pay $100 \times 44.35 = \$4,435$ for the contract. Similarly, if you decide to buy an August 715 put contract, you would pay $100 \times 22.75 = \$2,275$ for the option to sell 100 shares of Amazon's stock for $715 per share.

Note from Table 21.2 that for the August 2016 expiration date, call options with lower strike prices have higher market prices—the right to buy the stock at a lower price is more valuable than the right to buy it for a higher price. Conversely, because the put option gives the holder the right to sell the stock at the strike price, puts with higher strikes are more valuable (for the same expiration date). On the other hand (not shown in the table), holding fixed the strike price, both calls and puts are more expensive for a longer time to expiration. Because these options are American-style options that can be exercised at any time, having the right to buy or sell for a longer period is valuable.

in-the-money Describes an option whose value if immediately exercised would be positive.

out-of-the-money Describes an option that if exercised immediately results in a loss of money.

deep in-the-money Describes options that are in-the-money and for which the strike price and the stock price are very far apart.

deep out-of-the-money Describes options that are out-of-the-money and for which the strike price and the stock price are very far apart.

If the payoff from exercising an option immediately is positive, the option is said to be **in-the-money**. Call options with strike prices below the current stock price are in-the-money, as are put options with strike prices above the current stock price. At the time of the quotes in Table 21.2, Amazon's stock price was $736.07, so any call option with a strike price below $736.07 would be in-the-money, such as the August 715 through 735 calls, and any put option with a strike price above $736.07 would be in the money, such as the August 740 through 755 puts. Conversely, if the payoff from exercising the option immediately is negative, the option is **out-of-the-money**. Call options with strike prices above the current stock price are out-of-the-money, as are put options with strike prices below the current stock price. In Table 21.2, the August 740 through August 755 calls are out-of-the money, as are the August 715 through 735 puts. Of course, a holder would not exercise an out-of-the-money option. Options where the strike price and the stock price are very far apart are referred to as **deep in-the-money** or **deep out-of-the-money**.

EXAMPLE 21.1

Purchasing Options

MyFinanceLab

PROBLEM

It is July 18, 2016, and you have decided to purchase 10 August call contracts on Amazon's stock with an exercise price of $740. Because you are buying, you must pay the ask price. How much money will this purchase cost you? Is this option in-the-money or out-of-the-money?

SOLUTION

PLAN

From Table 21.2, the ask price of this option is $30.40. Remember that the price quoted is per share and that each contract is for 100 shares.

EXECUTE

You are purchasing 10 contracts and each contract is on 100 shares, so the transaction will cost $30.40 \times 10 \times 100 = \$30,400$ (ignoring any commission fees). Because this is a call option and the exercise price is above the current stock price ($736.07), the option is currently out-of-the-money.

EVALUATE

Even though the option is currently out-of-the-money, it still has value. During the time left to expiration, the stock could rise above the exercise (strike) price of $740.

Options on Other Financial Securities

hedging To reduce risk by holding contracts or securities whose payoffs are negatively correlated with some risk exposure.

speculate When investors use securities to place a bet on the direction in which they believe the market is likely to move.

Although the most commonly traded options are written on stocks, options on other financial assets do exist. Perhaps the most well known are options on stock indexes such as the S&P 100 index, the S&P 500 index, the Dow Jones Industrial Average index, and the NYSE index. These popular options allow investors to protect the value of their investments from adverse market changes. As we will see shortly, a stock index put option can be used to offset the losses on an investor's portfolio in a market downturn. Using an option to reduce risk by holding contracts or securities whose payoffs are negatively correlated with some risk exposure is called **hedging**. Options also allow investors to **speculate**, or place a bet on the direction in which they believe the market is likely to move. By purchasing a call, for example, investors can bet on a market rise with a much smaller investment than they could by investing in the market index itself.

Options Are for More Than Just Stocks

Although the examples in this chapter are mainly about options on stocks, there are options on a wide variety of other assets. For example, options are also traded on Treasury securities. These options allow investors to bet on or hedge interest rate risk. There are also options on currencies (we discuss these in more detail in Chapter 23), gold, platinum, and other commodities such as copper or oil. There are also many options on agricultural products such as wheat, soybeans, livestock, cotton, orange juice, and sugar. These options allow both farmers and large agribusinesses to hedge their risks from fluctuations in production and prices.

CONCEPT CHECK

1. Does the holder of an option have to exercise it?
2. What is the difference between an American option and a European option?

21.2 Option Payoffs at Expiration

With our new understanding of the basics of puts and calls, we are now prepared to examine their values. From the Valuation Principle, the value of any security is determined by the future cash flows an investor receives from owning it. Therefore, before we can assess what an option is worth, we must determine an option's payoff at the time of expiration.

The Long Position in an Option Contract

Assume you own an option with a strike price of $20. If, on the expiration date, the stock price is greater than the strike price, say $30, you can make money by exercising the call (by paying $20, the strike price for the stock) and immediately selling the stock in the open market for $30. The $10 difference is what the option is worth. Consequently, when the stock price on the expiration date exceeds the strike price, the value of the call is the difference between the stock price and the strike price. When the stock price is less than the strike price at expiration, the holder will not exercise the call, so the option is worth nothing. These payoffs are plotted in Figure 21.1.

Thus, the value of the call at expiration is:

Call Value at Expiration

Call Value = Stock Price − Strike Price, if Stock Price > Strike Price

$\qquad\qquad = 0,\qquad\qquad\qquad\qquad$ if Stock Price ≤ Strike Price $\quad$ (21.1)

The holder of a put option will exercise the option if the stock price is below the strike price. Because the holder receives the strike price when the stock is worth less, the holder's gain is equal to Strike Price − Stock Price. Thus, the value of a put at expiration is:

Put Price at Expiration

Put Value = Strike Price − Stock Price, if Stock Price < Strike Price

$\qquad\qquad = 0,\qquad\qquad\qquad\qquad$ if Stock Price ≥ Strike Price $\quad$ (21.2)

FIGURE 21.1

Payoff of a Call Option with a Strike Price of $20 at Expiration

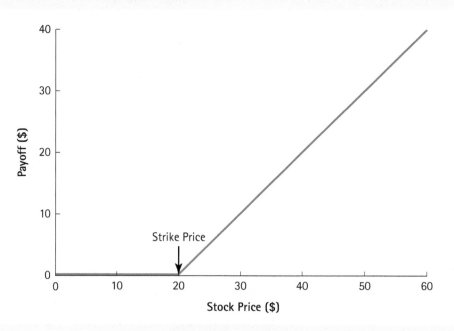

If the stock price is greater than the strike price ($20), the call will be exercised. The holder's payoff is the difference between the stock price and the strike price. If the stock price is less than the strike price, the call will not be exercised, and so has no value.

EXAMPLE 21.2

Payoff of a Put Option at Maturity

MyFinanceLab

PROBLEM

You own a put option on Oracle stock with an exercise price of $20 that expires today. Plot the value of this option as a function of the stock price.

SOLUTION

PLAN

From Eq. 21.2, and the fact that the strike price is $20, we see that the value of the put option is:

Put Value $= 20 -$ Stock Price, if Stock Price $< 20; = 0$, if Stock Price ≥ 20

EXECUTE

Plotting this function gives:

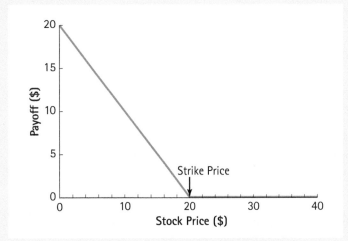

EVALUATE

Because the put option allows you to force the put writer to buy the stock for $20, regardless of the current market price, we can see that the put option payoff increases as Oracle's stock price decreases. For example, if Oracle's price were $10, you could buy a share of Oracle in the market for $10 and then sell it to the put writer for $20, making a profit of $10.

The Short Position in an Option Contract

An investor holding a short position in an option has an obligation: This investor takes the opposite side of the contract to the investor who is long. Thus, the short position's cash flows are the negative of the long position's cash flows. Because an investor who has a long position in an option can only receive money at expiration—that is, the investor will not exercise an option that is out-of-the-money—a short investor can only pay money.

To demonstrate, assume you have a short position in a call option with an exercise price of $20. If the stock price is greater than the strike price of a call—for example, $25—the holder will exercise the option. You then have the obligation to sell the stock for the strike price of $20. Because you must purchase the stock at the market price of $25, you lose the difference between the two prices, or $5. However, if the stock price is less than the strike price at the expiration date, the holder will not exercise the option, so in this case you lose nothing; you have no obligation. These payoffs are plotted in Figure 21.2.

FIGURE 21.2

Short Position in a
Call Option at
Expiration

If the stock price is greater than the strike price, the call will be exercised. A person on the short side of a call will lose the difference between the stock price and the strike price. If the stock price is less than the strike price, the call will not be exercised, and the seller will have no obligation.

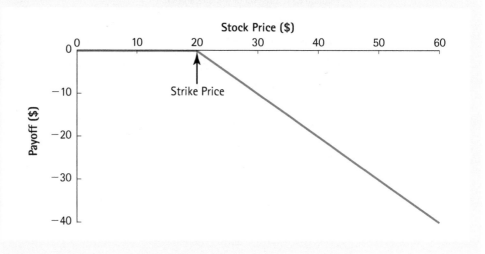

EXAMPLE 21.3

Payoff of a
Short Position in
a Put Option

MyFinanceLab

PROBLEM

You are short a put option on Oracle stock with an exercise price of $20 that expires today. Plot the value of this option as a function of the stock price.

SOLUTION

PLAN

Again, the strike price is $20 and in this case your cash flows will be opposite of those from Eq. 21.2, as depicted in the previous example. Thus, your cash flows will be

$$-(20 - \text{Stock Price}) = -20 + \text{Stock Price, if Stock Price} < 20$$
$$= 0, \text{ if Stock Price} \geq 20$$

EXECUTE

The graph plots
your cash flows:

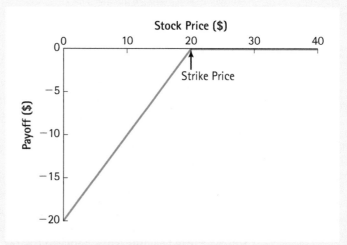

EVALUATE

If the current stock price is $30, the put will not be exercised and you will owe nothing. If the current stock price is $15, the put will be exercised and you will lose $5. Comparing the graph here and in Example 21.2, we see that the payoffs are mirror images of each other.

Notice that because the stock price cannot fall below zero, the downside for a short position in a put option is limited to the strike price of the option. A short position in a call, however, has no limit on the downside (see Figure 21.2).

Profits for Holding an Option to Expiration

Although payouts on a long position in an option contract are never negative, the *profit* from purchasing an option and holding it to expiration could be negative. That is, the payout at expiration might be less than the initial cost of the option.

To illustrate, let's consider the potential profits from purchasing the "16 August 735" call option on Amazon's stock quoted in Table 21.2. The option costs $33.00 \times 100 = \$3,300$ and expires on Saturday, August 20, 2016 (33 days). Assume you choose to finance the purchase by borrowing $3,300 at an interest rate of 3% per year. At the end of 33 days, you will need $3,308.83 to pay off the loan $(3,300 \times 1.03^{33/365} = 3,308.83)$. The profit is the call payoff minus the $3,308.83 owed on the loan, shown as the brick-colored curve in Figure 21.3. Once the cost of the position is taken into account, you make a positive profit only if the stock price exceeds $768.09. For example, if the price of the stock is $768.10, then you can exercise your option to buy at $735, sell at $768.10, gaining $33.10 per share. With 100 shares, you have a total gain of $3,310, which will be enough to pay off your loan. As we can see from Table 21.2, the further in-the-money the option is, the higher its initial price and thus the larger your potential loss. An out-of-the-money option has a smaller

FIGURE 21.3

Profit from Holding a Call Option to Expiration

The curves show the profit per share from purchasing a few of the August call options in Table 21.2 on July 18, 2016, paying for this purchase by borrowing at 3%, and holding the position until the expiration date. Note that all of the payoff diagrams are shifted down by the amount of the option's premium. Thus, even if the payoff is positive, if it is not enough to offset the premium you paid to acquire the option, your profit will be negative.

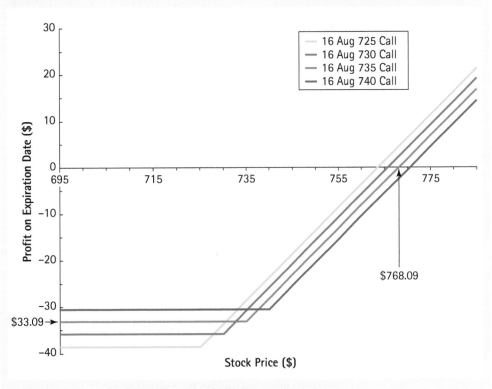

initial cost and hence a smaller potential loss. The probability of a gain, however, is also smaller because the point where profits become positive is higher.

Because a short position in an option is the other side of a long position, the profits from a short position in an option are the negative of the profits of a long position. For example, a short position in an out-of-the-money call such as the "16 August 740" Amazon call in Figure 21.3 produces a small positive profit if Amazon's stock is below $770.49, but leads to losses if the stock price is above $770.49.

EXAMPLE 21.4

Profit on Holding a Position in a Put Option Until Expiration

MyFinanceLab

PROBLEM

Assume you decided to purchase the August 725 through 740 put options quoted in Table 21.2 on July 18, 2016, and you financed each position by borrowing at 3% for 33 days. Plot the profit of each position as a function of the stock price on expiration.

SOLUTION

PLAN

Suppose P is the price of each put option on August 21. Then your cash flows on the expiration date will be:

$$(\text{Strike Price} - \text{Stock Price}) - P \times 1.03^{33/365}, \text{ if Stock Price} < \text{Strike Price}$$

$$\text{or } 0 - P \times 1.03^{33/365}, \text{ if Stock Price} \geq \text{Strike Price}$$

EXECUTE

The graph plots your profits:

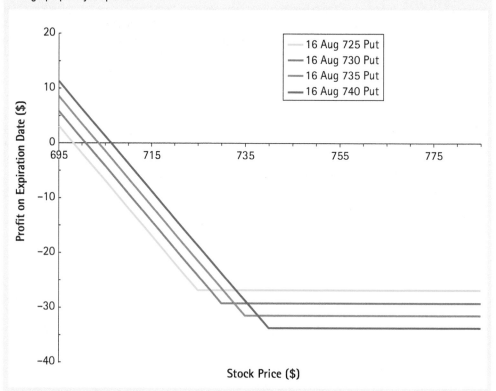

EVALUATE

The graph illustrates the same tradeoff between the maximum loss and the potential for profit as for the call options in Figure 21.3. The greatest profit potential comes from the most expensive option, so if that option expires worthless, you have lost the greatest amount.

Returns for Holding an Option to Expiration

We can also compare options based on their potential returns. Figure 21.4 shows the return from purchasing one of the August 2016 options in Table 21.2 on July 18, 2016, and holding it until the expiration date. Let's begin by focusing on call options, shown in Panel (a). In all cases, the maximum loss is 100%—the option may expire worthless. Notice how the curves change as a function of the strike price—the potential returns for out-of-the-money call options are more extreme than those for in-the-money calls. That is, an out-of-the money call option is more likely to have a −100% return. If the stock goes up sufficiently, however, it will also have a much higher return than an in-the-money call option. Similarly, all call options have more extreme returns than the stock itself (given Amazon's initial price of $736.07, the range of stock prices shown in the plot represent returns from about −10% to +10%). Consequently, the risk of a call option is amplified relative to the risk of the stock. The amplification is greater for deeper out-of-the-money calls. Thus, if a stock had a positive beta, call options written on the stock will have even higher betas and expected returns than the stock itself.

Now consider the returns for put options. Look carefully at Panel (b) in Figure 21.4. The put position has a higher return in states with *low* stock prices; that is, if the stock has a positive beta, the put has a negative beta. Hence, put options on positive beta stocks have lower expected returns than the underlying stocks. The deeper out-of-the-money the put option is, the more negative its beta, and the lower its expected return. As a result, put options are generally not held as an investment, but rather as insurance to hedge other risk in a portfolio. We explore the idea of using options for insurance further in Section 21.5.

At this point, we have discussed the cost (premium) of buying an option, the payoffs at expiration, and the profits. It is a lot to keep track of, but it is usually helpful to remember

FIGURE 21.4

Option Returns from Purchasing an Option and Holding It to Expiration

Panel (a) shows the return on the expiration date from purchasing one of the August call options in Table 21.2 on July 18, 2016, and holding the position until the expiration date. Panel (b) shows the same return for the September put options in the table. Notice how the returns are more sensitive to a change in the stock price the further out-of-the-money the option is. For example, in Panel (a), the slope of the return line after the strike price is reached is steeper for options that are further out-of-the-money. For the August 740 call, a small change in the stock price can lead to a large change in the return. A similar effect is seen for puts in Panel (b).

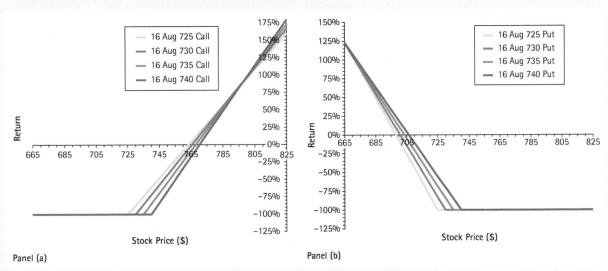

Panel (a)

Panel (b)

that there are only three things being exchanged: (1) the option premium, (2) the strike price, and (3) the share of stock. Furthermore, because an option is a contract between two parties, the losses of one party are the gains of the other. We summarize these relationships in Table 21.3 for the "16 August 735" calls and puts on Amazon.com stock from Table 21.2. When reading the table, keep in mind that if you own the option and exercising it would create a negative payoff, you will choose not to exercise, so the payoff will be zero (see Eqs. 21.1 and 21.2).

TABLE 21.3

Payoffs, Profits, and Returns to Buying or Writing Options in Table 21.2

	At Purchase	At Expiration If Stock Price = 695		At Expiration If Stock Price = 775	
		Payoff	**Profit**	**Payoff**	**Profit**
Buy a 16 Aug 735 Call	Pay 33.00	0	**−33.00** −100% return	775 − 735 = **40**	40 − 33 = **7** 7/33 = 21% return
Write a 16 Aug 735 Call	Receive 33.00	0	**33.00**	735 − 775 = **−40**	33.40 = **−7**
Buy a 16 Aug 735 Put	Pay 31.40	735 − 695 = **40**	40 − 31.40 = **8.60** 8.60/31.40 = 27% return	0	**−31.40** −100% return
Write a 16 Aug 735 Put	Receive 31.40	695 − 735 = **−40**	31.40 − 40 = **−8.60**	0	**31.40**

Contracts are for 100 shares. Payoffs shown are per share.

CONCEPT CHECK
3. How are the profits from buying an option different from the payoff to the option at expiration?

4. How are the payoffs to buying a call option related to the payoffs from writing a call option?

21.3 Factors Affecting Option Prices

When we discussed Table 21.2, we noted some relations between the option prices and different characteristics of the options. In this section, we identify and explain all the factors that affect the price of an option.

Strike Price and Stock Price

As we noted earlier for the Amazon.com option quotes in Table 21.2, the value of an otherwise identical call option is higher if the strike price the holder must pay to buy the stock is lower. Because a put is the right to sell the stock, puts with a lower strike price are less valuable.

For a given strike price, the value of a call option is higher if the current price of the stock is higher, as there is a greater likelihood the option will end up in-the-money. Conversely, put options increase in value as the stock price falls.

Option Prices and the Exercise Date

For American options, the longer the time to the exercise date, the more valuable the option. To see why, let's consider two options: an option with one year until the exercise date and an option with six months until the exercise date. The holder of the one-year option can turn her option into a six-month option by simply exercising it early. That is, the one-year option has all the same rights and privileges as the six-month option, so by the Valuation Principle, it cannot be worth less than the six-month option. That is, *an American option with a later exercise date cannot be worth less than an otherwise identical American option with an earlier exercise date*. Usually the right to delay exercising the option is worth something, so the option with the later exercise date will be more valuable.

What about European options? The same argument will not work for European options, because a one-year European option cannot be exercised early at six months. As a consequence, a European option with a later exercise date may potentially trade for less than an otherwise identical option with an earlier exercise date. For example, think about a European call on a stock that pays a liquidating dividend in six months (a *liquidating dividend* is paid when a corporation chooses to go out of business, sells off all of its assets, and pays out the proceeds as a dividend). A one-year European call option on this stock would be worthless, but a six-month call would have value.

Option Prices and the Risk-Free Rate

The value of a call option is increasing in the risk-free rate, but the value of a put option is decreasing in the risk-free rate. The intuition is that a higher discount rate reduces the present value of the strike price: Because you must pay the strike price to exercise a call option, reducing the present value of your payment increases the value of the option. However, because you *receive* the strike price when you exercise a put, reducing the present value decreases the value of the put option. We note, however, that given normal swings in the risk-free rate, they would be unlikely to change enough over the life of an option to have a substantial impact on the price of the option—that is, option values are not particularly sensitive to changes in the risk-free rate.

Option Prices and Volatility

An important criterion that determines the price of an option is the volatility of the underlying stock. In fact, *the value of an option generally increases with the volatility of the stock*.[1] The intuition for this result is that an increase in volatility increases the likelihood of very high and very low returns for the stock. The holder of a call option benefits from a higher payoff when the stock goes up and the option is in-the-money, but earns the same (zero) payoff no matter how far the stock drops once the option is out-of-the-money. *Because of this asymmetry of the option's payoff, an option holder generally gains from an increase in volatility*. Consider the following example.

EXAMPLE 21.5
Option Value and Volatility

MyFinanceLab

PROBLEM

Two European call options with a strike price of $50 are written on two different stocks. Suppose that tomorrow, the *low-volatility* stock will have a price of $50 for certain. The *high-volatility* stock will be worth either $60 or $40, with each price having equal probability. If the exercise date of both options is tomorrow, which option will be worth more today?

SOLUTION

PLAN

The value of the options will depend on the value of the stocks at expiration. The value of the options at expiration will be the stock price tomorrow minus $50 if the stock price is greater than $50, and $0 otherwise.

(Continued)

---

[1]This relation between the stock's volatility and the value of an option holds for realistic distributions of stock prices assumed by practitioners, in which an increase in volatility implies a more "spread out" distribution for the entire range of future stock prices. That said, it need not hold, for example, if the volatility of the stock increases in some ranges but falls in others.

EXECUTE

The low-volatility stock will be worth $50 for certain, so its option will be worth $0 for certain. The high-volatility stock will be worth either $40 or $60, so its option will pay off either $0 or $60 − $50 = $10. Because options have no chance of a negative payoff, the one that has a 50% chance of a positive payoff has to be worth more than the option on the low-volatility stock (with no chance of a positive payoff).

EVALUATE

Because volatility increases the chance that an option will pay off, the options have very different values even though the expected value of *both* stocks tomorrow is $50—the low-volatility stock will be worth this amount for sure, and the high-volatility stock also has an expected value of $40 $\left(\frac{1}{2}\right)$ + $60 $\left(\frac{1}{2}\right)$ = $50.

Example 21.5 confirms our intuition that the value of a call option is increasing in the volatility of the underlying stock. The same holds for puts. Recall that adding a put option to a portfolio is akin to buying insurance against a decline in value. Insurance is more valuable when there is higher volatility—hence, put options on more volatile stocks are also worth more. Table 21.4 summarizes the factors that affect option values and how an increase in each factor affects those values.

TABLE 21.4

How an Increase in Each Factor Affects Option Values

	American		European	
	Call	**Put**	**Call**	**Put**
Stock Price	Increases Value	Decreases Value	Increases Value	Decreases Value
Strike Price	Decreases Value	Increases Value	Decreases Value	Increases Value
Time to Expiration	Increases Value	Increases Value	Uncertain	Uncertain
Risk-Free Rate	Increases Value	Decreases Value	Increases Value	Decreases Value
Volatility of Stock Price[2]	Increases Value	Increases Value	Increases Value	Increases Value

CONCEPT CHECK

5. Can a European option with a later exercise date be worth less than an identical European option with an earlier exercise date?

6. Why are options more valuable when there is increased uncertainty about the value of the stock?

21.4 The Black-Scholes Option Pricing Formula

In Nobel Prize-winning research, Professors Fischer Black and Myron Scholes derived a formula for the price of a European-style call option for a non-dividend-paying stock. The formula now serves as the basis of pricing for options contracts traded worldwide. Their formula is:

Black-Scholes Price of a Call Option on a Non-Dividend-Paying Stock

$$\text{Call Price} = \text{Stock Price} \times N(d_1) - PV(\text{Strike Price}) \times N(d_2) \qquad (21.3)$$

The present value is calculated using the risk-free rate and $N(d_1)$ and $N(d_2)$ are probabilities. The expressions for d_1 and d_2 are complicated and explaining them is better left to your later finance courses.[3] However, we note here that they contain only the stock price,

---

[2]See footnote 1 on page 673.

[3]For the curious student, they are:

$$d_1 = \frac{\ln[\text{Stock Price}/PV(\text{Strike Price})]}{\sigma\sqrt{T}} + \frac{\sigma\sqrt{T}}{2} \text{ and } d_2 = d_1 - \sigma\sqrt{T},$$

where σ is the annual standard deviation of the stock return and T is the time to expiration of the option (in years). We also note that $N(\cdot)$ in Eq. 21.3 refers to the cumulative normal distribution function.

strike price, risk-free rate, time to expiration of the option, and volatility of the stock. Thus, Black and Scholes confirmed our discussion from the last section that these five factors are the only ones relevant to the value of an option. What is just as notable is what is *not* relevant: We do not need to know the expected return of the stock. You might wonder how it is possible to compute the value of a security such as an option that appears to depend critically on the future stock price without knowing the expected return of the stock. In fact, the expected return of the stock is already incorporated into the current stock price, and the value of the option today depends on the stock price today.

Fortunately, you do not need to understand the Black-Scholes formula to use it. There are many online option pricing calculators and even add-ins for Excel based on the formula. In Figure 21.5, we show one such calculator from the Options Industry Council.

So far, we have discussed the factors affecting the prices of individual calls and puts. You may have noticed in Figure 21.5 that the prices of both the put and call for the stock are displayed. In fact, those prices cannot move independently of each other. In the next section, we will demonstrate a powerful relation that links the price of a put to the price of a call on the same stock.

FIGURE 21.5

Online Option
Pricing Calculator

This option pricing calculator is based on the Black-Scholes option pricing formula. Here, we selected "Black-Scholes (European)" in the "Model/Exercise" box and then entered a stock price of $46, a strike price of $45, expiration in September 2016, a risk-free interest rate of 1%, annual volatility (standard deviation) of the stock return of 25%, and no dividends. The right side of the screen shows that the call value is $2.42 (and the put value is $1.35). The other outputs on the right side of the screen are called "the Greeks" because they are mostly Greek letters (vega is not a real Greek letter). Interested students can go to the Web site and click the question mark next to each Greek letter to learn its meaning. Note that the option values will vary depending on how close you are to the expiration date, so you should not expect to get the same values shown when you try the calculator.

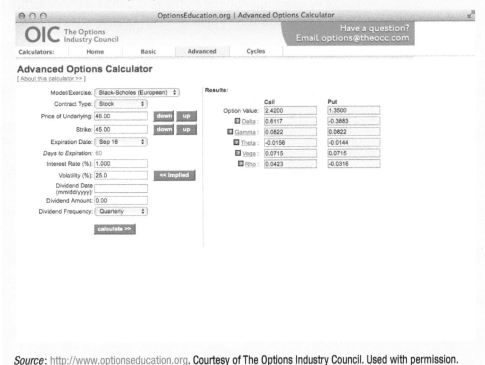

Source: http://www.optionseducation.org. Courtesy of The Options Industry Council. Used with permission.

**CONCEPT
CHECK**

7. What factors are used in the Black-Scholes formula to price a call option?

8. How can the Black-Scholes formula not include the expected return on the stock?

21.5 Put-Call Parity

As we have seen, the payoffs to both puts and calls depend on the price of the underlying stock. The expected payoffs determine the prices of the options, so the prices of puts and calls depend partly on the price of the underlying stock. Because the prices of both a put and a call on a given stock are influenced by the price of that same stock, their prices are related. In this section, we develop that relation by showing that both puts and calls can be packaged in different ways to achieve the same objective—to provide insurance against a drop in the price of a stock. Then we use the Valuation Principle's Law of One Price to show that if the two packages provide exactly the same payoffs, they must have the same price.

Portfolio Insurance

Let's see how we can use combinations of options to insure a stock against a loss. Assume you currently own a stock worth $80 and you would like to insure the stock against the possibility of a price decline. To do so, you could simply sell the stock, but you would also give up the possibility of making money if the stock price increases. How can you insure against a loss without relinquishing the upside? You can purchase a put option while still holding the stock, sometimes known as a **protective put**.

protective put
Purchasing a put option on a stock you already own.

For example, suppose you want to insure against the possibility that the stock price will drop below $75. You decide to purchase a European put option with a strike price of $75. The yellow line in Figure 21.6, Panel (a), shows the value of the combined position on the expiration date of the option. If the stock price is above $75 at expiration, you keep the stock. If it is below $75, you exercise your put and sell it for $75. Thus, you get the upside, but are insured against a drop in the price of the stock.

You can use the same strategy to insure against a loss on an entire portfolio of stocks by using put options on the portfolio as a whole rather than just a single stock.

FIGURE 21.6

Portfolio Insurance

The plots show two different ways with identical payoffs for insuring against the possibility of a stock's price falling below $75. The yellow line in Panel (a) indicates the value on the expiration date of a position that consists of buying one share of the stock and one European put option with a strike of $75 (the blue dashed line is the payoff of the stock itself). The yellow line in Panel (b) shows the value on the expiration date of a position that consists of buying a zero-coupon risk-free bond with a face value of $75 and a European call option on the stock with a strike price of $75 (the green dashed line is the bond payoff).

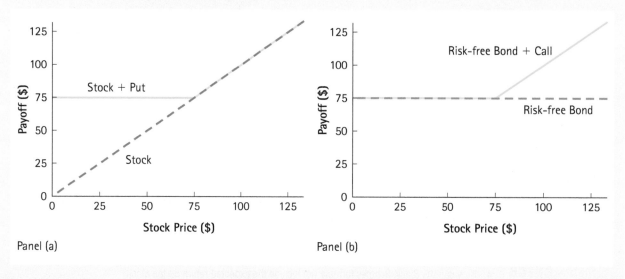

Panel (a)

Panel (b)

portfolio insurance A protective put written on a portfolio rather than a single stock.

Consequently, holding stocks and put options in this combination is known as **portfolio insurance**.

Put-Call Parity: Non-Dividend-Paying Stock. You can also achieve portfolio insurance by purchasing a bond and a call option. Let's return to the insurance we purchased on the $80 stock. Assume that the stock does not pay dividends, so there are no cash flows before the expiration of the option. Thus, instead of holding a share of stock and a put, you could get the same payoff by purchasing a risk-free zero-coupon bond with a face value of $75 and a European call option with a strike price of $75. In this case, if the stock price is below $75, you receive the payoff from the bond. If the stock price is above $75, you can exercise the call and use the payoff from the bond to buy the stock for the strike price of $75. The yellow line in Figure 21.6, Panel (b), shows the value of the combined position on the expiration date of the option; it achieves exactly the same payoffs as owning the stock itself and a put option.

Consider the two different ways to construct portfolio insurance illustrated in Figure 21.6: (1) Purchase the stock and a put or (2) purchase a bond and a call. Because both positions provide exactly the same payoff, the Valuation Principle and, in particular, the Law of One Price, requires that they must have the same price:

$$\text{Stock Price} + \text{Put Price} = PV(\text{Strike Price}) + \text{Call Price}$$

The left side of this equation is the cost of buying the stock and a put; the right side is the cost of buying a zero-coupon bond with face value equal to the strike price of the put and a call option (with the same strike price as the put). Recall that the price of a zero-coupon bond is the present value of its face value, which we have denoted by PV(Strike Price). Rearranging terms gives an expression for the price of a European call option for a non-dividend-paying stock:

put-call parity (for non-dividend paying stocks) The relationship that gives the price of a call option in terms of the price of a put option plus the price of the underlying stock minus the present value of the strike price.

$$\text{Call Price} = \text{Put Price} + \text{Stock Price} - PV(\text{Strike Price}) \qquad (21.4)$$

This relationship between the value of the stock, the bond, and the call and put options is known as **put-call parity**. It says that the price of a European call equals the price of the stock plus an otherwise identical put minus the price of a bond with a face value equal to the strike price that matures on the exercise date of the option. In other words, you can think of a call as a combination of a levered position in the stock, Stock Price − PV(Strike Price), plus insurance against a drop in the stock price, the put.

EXAMPLE 21.6
Using Put-Call Parity

MyFinanceLab

PROBLEM

You are an options dealer who deals in non-publicly traded options. One of your clients wants to purchase a one-year European call option on HAL Computer Systems stock with a strike price of $20. Another dealer is willing to write a one-year European put option on HAL stock with a strike price of $20, and sell you the put option for a price of $2.50 per share. If HAL pays no dividends and is currently trading for $18 per share, and if the risk-free interest rate is 6%, what is the lowest price you can charge for the call option and still guarantee yourself a profit?

SOLUTION

PLAN

We can use put-call parity to determine the price of the option:

$$\text{Call Price} = \text{Put Price} + \text{Stock Price} - PV(\text{Strike Price}).$$

In order to price a one-year European call with a strike price of $20, we need to know the price of a one-year European put with the same strike price, the current stock price, and the risk-free interest rate. We have all of that information, so we're ready.

(Continued)

EXECUTE

$$\text{Call Price} = \text{Put Price} + \text{Stock Price} - PV(\text{Strike Price})$$
$$= \$2.50 + \$18 - \$20/1.06 = \$1.632.$$

EVALUATE

Put-call parity means that we can replicate the payoff of the one-year call option with a strike price of $20 by holding the following portfolio: Buy the one-year put option with a strike price of $20 from the dealer, buy the stock, and sell a one-year, risk-free zero-coupon bond with a face value of $20. With this combination, we have the following final payoff, depending on the final price of HAL stock in one year, S_1:

		Payoff	
		Final HAL Stock Price	
		$S_1 < \$20$	$S_1 \geq \$20$
	Buy Put Option	$20 - S_1$	0
+	Buy Stock	S_1	S_1
+	Sell Bond	-20	-20
=	Portfolio	0	$S_1 - 20$
+	Sell Call Option	0	$-(S_1 - 20)$
=	Total Payoff	0	0

Note that the final payoff of the portfolio of the three securities matches the payoff of a call option. Therefore, we can sell the call option to our client and have future payoff of zero no matter what happens. Doing so is worthwhile as long as we can sell the call option for more than the cost of the portfolio, which we found to be $1.632.

Put-Call Parity: Dividend-Paying Stock. What happens if the stock pays a dividend? In that case, the two different ways to construct portfolio insurance do not have the same payout because the stock will pay a dividend while the zero-coupon bond will not. Thus, the two strategies will cost the same to implement only if we add the present value of future dividends to the combination of the bond and the call:

$$\text{Stock Price} + \text{Put Price} = PV(\text{Strike Price}) + PV(\text{Dividends}) + \text{Call Price}$$

The left side of this equation is the value of the stock and a put; the right side is the value of a zero-coupon bond, a call option, and the future dividends paid by the stock during the life of the options. Rearranging terms gives the general put-call parity formula:

Put-Call Parity

$$\text{Call Price} = \text{Put Price} + \text{Stock Price} - PV(\text{Strike Price}) - PV(\text{Dividends}) \quad (21.5)$$

In this case, the call is equivalent to having a levered position in the stock without dividends plus insurance against a fall in the stock price.

CONCEPT CHECK

9. Explain put-call parity.

10. If a put option trades at a higher price from the value indicated by the put-call parity equation, what action should you take?

21.6 Options and Corporate Finance

We briefly explored real options in capital budgeting in Chapter 9. There, we stressed the value of the flexibility provided by a real option—the option to delay, change, or abandon a project. These are options because, like the ones discussed in this chapter, you would only exercise a real option if doing so would make you better off.

We also noted in Chapter 15 that the ability to retire (or call) a bond early is a valuable option for a firm, and that the ability to convert the bond into shares of stock is an option for the bondholders. We can now say more formally that when a firm issues a callable bond, it is selling a bond that has a call option on it with a strike price equal to the call price. Because the buyers of the bond are granting a valuable call option to the firm, they will pay less for a callable bond than they would for an equivalent non-callable bond. Similarly, when a firm issues a convertible bond, it is essentially issuing a package of a straight bond and warrants on its stock. Those warrants are valuable options, so buyers of convertible bonds will pay more than they would for similar non-convertible bonds.

Options are plentiful in corporate finance. In Chapter 14, we described another one—the "greenshoe option," which gives the underwriter the option to sell additional shares in an oversubscribed equity offering. Many start-up and high-tech firms compensate their employees by granting them options on the firm's stock, and it is common for the majority of a CEO's compensation to come in this form.

One other very important corporate finance application of options is interpreting the capital structure of the firm as options on the firm's assets. Specifically, a share of stock can be thought of as a call option on the assets of the firm with a strike price equal to the value of debt outstanding.[4] To illustrate, consider a single-period world in which at the end of the period the firm is liquidated. If the firm's value does not exceed the value of debt outstanding at the end of the period, the firm must declare bankruptcy and the equity holders receive nothing. Conversely, if the value exceeds the value of debt outstanding, the equity holders get whatever is left once the debt has been repaid. Figure 21.7 illustrates this payoff. Note how the payoff to equity looks exactly the same as the payoff of a call option.

Viewed this way, a share of equity is a call option on the firm's assets. In fact, debt holders can be thought of as owning the firm, but they have *written* to equity holders a call option on the firm's assets with a strike price equal to the required debt payment. Recall that the price of an option increases with the volatility level of the underlying security. That means equity holders benefit from high-volatility investments. Because the price of equity is increasing with the volatility of the firm's assets, equity holders benefit from a zero-NPV project that increases the volatility of the firm's assets. However, debt holders, as lenders to the firm, do not benefit from an increase in the risk of the firm's assets. Thus, the project increases the value of equity, but decreases the value of the debt claims. In fact, because the project is zero-NPV, taking it on does not change the value of the firm as a whole. The value of the debt claims decreases by exactly the amount the value of the equity increases. This effect creates a conflict of interest between equity holders and debt holders. Options pricing theory helps us understand why this conflict of interest arises.

---

[4]This insight has been known at least since Black and Scholes wrote their pathbreaking option valuation paper. See F. Black and M. Scholes, "The Pricing of Options and Corporate Liabilities," *Journal of Political Economy*, 81 (3) (1973): 637–654.

FIGURE 21.7

Equity as a Call Option

If the value of the firm's assets exceeds the required debt payment, the equity holders receive the value that remains after the debt is repaid. Otherwise, the firm is bankrupt and its equity is worthless. Thus, the payoff to equity is equivalent to a call option on the firm's assets with a strike price equal to the required debt payment.

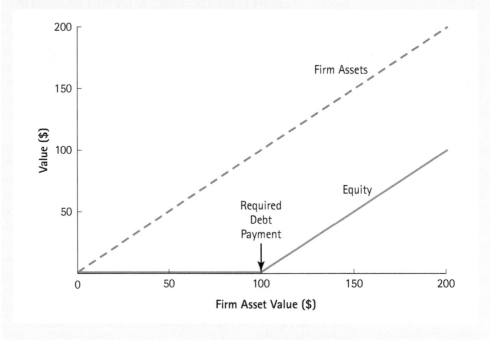

The option price is more sensitive to changes in volatility for at-the-money options than it is for in-the-money options. In the context of corporate finance, equity is at-the-money when a firm is close to bankruptcy. In this case, the loss in equity value that results from taking on a negative-NPV investment might be outweighed by the gain in equity value from the increase in volatility. Hence, equity holders have an incentive to take on negative-NPV, high-volatility investments. As we saw in Chapter 16, this excessive risk-taking problem is of concern to debt holders, who bear its cost.

CONCEPT CHECK

11. Explain how equity can be viewed as a call option on the firm.

12. Under what circumstances would equity holders have a possible incentive to take on negative-NPV investments?

MyFinanceLab

Here is what you should know after reading this chapter. MyFinanceLab will help you identify what you know, and where to go when you need to practice.

KEY POINTS AND EQUATIONS	KEY TERMS	ONLINE PRACTICE

21.1 Option Basics

- An option that gives the holder the right (but not the obligation) to purchase an asset at some future date is known as a call option.
- An option that gives the holder the right to sell an asset at some future date is known as a put option.
- When a holder of an option enforces the agreement and buys or sells the share of stock at the agreed price, the holder is exercising the option.
- The price at which the holder agrees to buy or sell the share of stock when the option is exercised is known as the strike price or exercise price.
- The last date on which the holder has the right to exercise the option is known as the expiration date.
- An American option can be exercised on any date up to, and including, the exercise date. A European option can be exercised only on the expiration date.
- If you would make money by exercising an option immediately, the option is in-the-money. Conversely, if you would lose money by exercising an option immediately, the option is out-of-the-money.

Key Terms: American options, p. 662; at-the-money, p. 663; call option, p. 662; deep in-the-money, p. 664; deep out-of-the-money, p. 664; derivatives, p. 662; European options, p. 662; exercising (an option), p. 662; expiration date, p. 662; financial option, p. 662; hedging, p. 665; in-the-money, p. 664; open interest, p. 663; option writer, p. 662; out-of-the-money, p. 664; put option, p. 662; speculate, p. 665; strike (exercise) price, p. 662; warrant, p. 662

Online Practice: MyFinanceLab Study Plan 21.1

21.2 Option Payoffs at Expiration

- The value of a call option at expiration
  = Stock Price − Strike Price, if Stock Price > Strike Price;
  = 0, if Stock Price ≤ Strike Price   (21.1)
- The value of a put option at expiration
  = Strike Price − Stock Price, if Stock Price < Strike Price;
  = 0, if Stock Price ≥ Strike Price   (21.2)
- An investor holding a short position in an option has an obligation; he or she takes the opposite side of the contract to the investor who holds the long position.

Online Practice: MyFinanceLab Study Plan 21.2

21.3 Factors Affecting Option Prices

- Call options with lower strike prices are more valuable than otherwise identical calls with higher strike prices. Conversely, put options are more valuable with higher strike prices.
- Call options increase in value, and put options decrease in value, when the stock price rises.
- The value of an option generally increases with the volatility of the stock.

Online Practice: MyFinanceLab Study Plan 21.3

21.4 The Black-Scholes Option Pricing Formula		MyFinanceLab
• The Black-Scholes option pricing formula shows that the price of an option on a non-dividend-paying stock is a function of only the current stock price, the strike price, the time to expiration, the volatility of the stock, and the risk-free rate.		Study Plan 21.4
21.5 Put-Call Parity	portfolio insurance, p. 677	MyFinanceLab
• Put-call parity relates the value of the European call to the value of the European put and the stock: Call Price = Put Price + Stock Price − PV(Strike Price) − PV(Dividends) (21.5)	protective put, p. 676 put-call parity, p. 677	Study Plan 21.5
21.6 Options and Corporate Finance		MyFinanceLab
• Equity can be viewed as a call option on the firm. • The debt holders can be viewed as owning the firm *and* having sold a call option with a strike price equal to the required debt payment.		Study Plan 21.6

CRITICAL THINKING

1. Explain the meanings of the following financial terms:
   a. Option
   b. Expiration date
   c. Strike price
   d. Call
   e. Put

2. What is the difference between a European option and an American option?

3. Explain the difference between a long position in a put and a short position in a call.

4. What position has more downside exposure: a short position in a call or a short position in a put? That is, in the worst case, in which of these two positions would your losses be greater?

5. If you own a call option at expiration and the stock price equals the strike price, is your *profit* zero?

6. Is an increase in a stock's volatility good for the holder of a call option? Is it good for the holder of a put option?

7. Why are the prices of puts and calls on the same stock related?

8. Explain why an option can be thought of as an insurance contract.

9. Explain why equity can be viewed as a call option on a firm.

PROBLEMS

All problems are available in MyFinanceLab. *An asterisk * indicates problems with a higher level of difficulty.*

Option Basics

1. See the option quote on IBM from the CBOE Web site on the next page.
   a. Which option contract had the most trades today?
   b. Which option contract is being held the most overall?

    c. Suppose you purchase one option with symbol IBM1616I155-E. How much will you need to pay your broker for the option (ignoring commissions)?

    d. Suppose you sell one option with symbol IBM1619H165-E. How much will you receive for the option (ignoring commissions)?

    e. The calls with which strike prices are currently in-the-money? Which puts are in-the-money?

IBM (INTL BUSINESS MACHINES)

Jul 20 2016 @ 17:21 ET   Bid 161.11   Ask 161.3 Size 3 × 1   161.36 1.78

                                                                            Vol 4372921

Calls	Last Sale	Net	Bid	Ask	Vol	Open Int	Puts	Last Sale	Net	Bid	Ask	Vol	Open Int
16 Aug 155.00 (IBM1619H155-E)	6.45	0.75	6.95	7.25	9	7640	16 Aug 155.00 (IBM1619T155-E)	1.18	−0.75	1.17	1.25	61	4505
16 Aug 160.00 (IBM1619H160-E)	3.3	0.85	3.15	3.3	101	12811	16 Aug 160.00 (IBM1619T160-E)	2.76	−1.24	2.71	2.84	61	2114
16 Aug 165.00 (IBM1619H165-E)	1.05	0.3	0.96	1.06	178	27064	16 Aug 165.00 (IBM1619T165-E)	7.1	−0.4	5.7	5.9	1	332
16 Aug 170.00 (IBM1619H170-E)	0.21	−0.01	0.21	0.27	20	6086	16 Aug 170.00 (IBM1619T170-E)	12.25	0	9.95	10.3	0	393
16 Sep 155.00 (IBM1616I155-E)	7.77	1.58	7.5	7.7	2	122	16 Sep 155.00 (IBM1616U155-E)	2.34	−0.59	2.13	2.22	3	251
16 Sep 160.00 (IBM1616I160-E)	4.05	0.76	4	4.2	6	380	16 Sep 160.00 (IBM1616U160-E)	4	−1.09	3.8	4	1	476
16 Sep 165.00 (IBM1616I165-E)	1.87	0.47	1.76	1.88	161	297	16 Sep 165.00 (IBM1616U165-E)	6.65	−2.1	6.55	6.75	1	27
16 Sep 170.00 (IBM1616I170-E)	0.65	0.07	0.63	0.71	2	498	16 Sep 170.00 (IBM1616U170-E)	12.35	0	10.4	10.7	0	47

Source: Chicago Board Options Exchange at www.cboe.com.

Option Payoffs at Expiration

2. You own a call option on Intuit stock with a strike price of $40. The option will expire in exactly three months.

    a. If the stock is trading at $55 in three months, what will be the payoff of the call?

    b. If the stock is trading at $35 in three months, what will be the payoff of the call?

    c. Draw a payoff diagram showing the value of the call at expiration as a function of the stock price at expiration.

3. Assume that you have shorted the call option in Problem 2.

    a. If the stock is trading at $55 in three months, what will you owe?

    b. If the stock is trading at $35 in three months, what will you owe?

    c. Draw a payoff diagram showing the amount you owe at expiration as a function of the stock price at expiration.

4. You own a put option on Ford stock with a strike price of $10. The option will expire in exactly six months.

    a. If the stock is trading at $8 in six months, what will be the payoff of the put?

    b. If the stock is trading at $23 in six months, what will be the payoff of the put?

    c. Draw a payoff diagram showing the value of the put at expiration as a function of the stock price at expiration.

5. Assume that you have shorted the put option in Problem 4.

    a. If the stock is trading at $8 in three months, what will you owe?

    b. If the stock is trading at $23 in three months, what will you owe?

    c. Draw a payoff diagram showing the amount you owe at expiration as a function of the stock price at expiration.

6. You are long both a call and a put on the same share of stock with the same exercise date. The exercise price of the call is $40 and the exercise price of the put is $45. Plot the value of this combination as a function of the stock price on the exercise date.

7. You are long two calls on the same share of stock with the same exercise date. The exercise price of the first call is $40 and the exercise price of the second call is $60. In addition, you are short two otherwise identical calls, both with an exercise price

of $50. Plot the value of this combination as a function of the stock price on the exercise date.

*8. A *forward contract* is a contract to purchase an asset at a fixed price on a particular date in the future. Both parties are obligated to fulfill the contract. Explain how to construct a forward contract on a share of stock from a position in options.

9. You own a share of Costco stock. You are worried that its price will fall and would like to insure yourself against this possibility. How can you purchase insurance against a fall in the price of the stock?

Factors Affecting Option Prices

10. What is the maximum value that a call option and a put option can have?

11. Why is an American option with a longer time to expiration generally worth more than an otherwise identical option with a shorter time to expiration?

Put-Call Parity

12. Dynamic Energy Systems stock is currently trading for $33 per share. The stock pays no dividends. A one-year European put option on Dynamic with a strike price of $35 is currently trading for $2.10. If the risk-free interest rate is 10% per year, what is the price of a one-year European call option on Dynamic with a strike price of $35?

13. You happen to be checking the newspaper and notice an arbitrage opportunity. The current stock price of Intrawest is $20 per share and the one-year risk-free interest rate is 8%. A one-year put on Intrawest with a strike price of $18 sells for $3.33, while the identical call sells for $7. Explain what you must do to exploit this arbitrage opportunity.

Options and Corporate Finance

*14. Express the position of an equity holder in terms of put options.

15. Express the position of a debt holder in terms of put options.

DATA CASE

Your uncle owns 10,000 shares of Walmart stock. He is concerned about the short-term outlook for Walmart's stock due to an impending "major announcement." This announcement has received much attention in the press so he expects the stock price will change significantly in the next month, but is unsure whether it will be a profit or a loss. He hopes the price will increase, but he also doesn't want to suffer if the price were to fall in the short term.

His broker recommended he buy a "protective put" on the stock, but your uncle has never traded options before and is not much of a risk taker. He wants you to devise a plan for him to capitalize if the announcement is positive but still be protected if the news causes the price to drop. You realize that a protective put will protect him from the downside risk, but you think a strategy of purchasing a call and a put with the same exercise price (known as a "straddle") may offer similar downside protection, while increasing the upside potential. You decide to show him both strategies and the resulting profits and returns he could face from each.

1. Download option quotes on options that expire in approximately one month on Walmart from the Chicago Board Options Exchange (www.cboe.com) into an Excel spreadsheet. If you choose to download "near-term at-the-money" options you will get a range of options expiring in about a month. You can only get active quotes while the exchange is open; bid or ask prices are not available when it is closed.

2. Determine your uncle's profit and return using the protective put.
   a. Identify the expiring put with an exercise price closest to, but not below, the current stock price. Determine the investment required to protect all 10,000 shares.
   b. Determine the put price at expiration for each stock price at $5 increments within a range of $20 above and below Walmart's current price using Eq. 21.2.
   c. Compute the profit (or loss) on the put for each stock price used in (b).
   d. Compute the profit on the stock from the current price for each stock price used in (b).
   e. Compute his overall profit (or loss) of the protective put; that is, combining the put and his stock for each price used in (c) and (d).
   f. Compute the overall return of the protective put.

3. Determine your uncle's profit and return using the straddle.
   a. Compute the investment your uncle would have to make to purchase the call and put with the same exercise price and expiration as the put option in Question 2, to cover all 10,000 of his shares.
   b. Determine the value at expiration of the call and the put options at each $5 increment of stock prices within a range of $20 above and below Walmart's current price using Eqs. 21.1 and 21.2.
   c. Determine the profit (or loss) on the options at each stock price used in (b).
   d. Determine the profit (or loss) on the stock from the current price for each stock price used in (b).
   e. Compute his overall profit (or loss) of the stock plus the straddle; that is, combining the position in both options and his stock for each price used in (c) and (d).
   f. Compute the overall return of this position.

4. Was the broker correct that the protective put would prevent your uncle from losing if the announcement caused a large decrease in the stock value? What is your uncle's maximum possible loss using the protective put?

5. What is the maximum possible loss your uncle could experience using the straddle?

6. Which strategy, the protective put or the straddle, provides the maximum upside potential for your uncle? Why does this occur?

22

Mergers and Acquisitions

LEARNING OBJECTIVES

- Discuss the types of mergers and trends in merger activity

- Understand the stock price reactions to takeover announcements

- Critically evaluate the different reasons to acquire

- Follow the major steps in the takeover process

- Discuss the main takeover defenses

- Identify factors that determine who gets the value-added in a merger

notation					
	A	premerger total value of acquirer		P_A	premerger share price of acquirer
	EPS	earnings per share		P_T	premerger share price of target
	N_A	premerger number of shares of acquirer outstanding		S	value of all synergies
				T	premerger total value of target
	N_T	premerger number of shares of target outstanding		x	number of new shares issued by acquirer to pay for target
	P/E	price-earnings ratio			

On July 14, 2008, St. Louis-based Anheuser-Busch agreed to an acquisition by Belgium-based beer giant InBev for $70 per share in cash. The agreement ended 150 years of independence for the brewer of iconic Budweiser beer. In fact, Anheuser-Busch's board had flatly rejected InBev's initial $65 per share offer, preferring to remain independent. However, the sweetened offer, valuing the company at $60 billion, was too compelling a deal for Anheuser's board to pass up. Next, InBev's managers faced the daunting task of integrating Anheuser's organization and brands into their global company and generating enough value from the transaction to justify the price they paid. Given the complexity and potential sums of money at stake, it is clear that some of the most important decisions financial managers make concern mergers and acquisitions.

In this chapter, first, we provide some historical background about the market for mergers and acquisitions. Next, we discuss some of the reasons why a corporate financial manager may decide to pursue an acquisition.

Then, we review the takeover process. Finally, we address the question of who benefits from the value that is added when a takeover occurs.

22.1 Background and Historical Trends

acquirer (or bidder) A firm that, in a takeover, buys another firm.

target A firm that is acquired by another in a merger or acquisition.

takeover Refers to two mechanisms, either a merger or an acquisition, by which ownership and control of a firm can change.

Mergers and acquisitions are part of what is often referred to as "the market for corporate control." When one firm acquires another, typically there is a buyer, the **acquirer** or **bidder**, and a seller, the **target** firm. There are two primary mechanisms by which ownership and control of a public corporation can change: Either another corporation or group of individuals can acquire the target firm, or the target firm can merge with another firm. In both cases, the acquiring entity must purchase the stock or existing assets of the target either for cash or for something of equivalent value (such as shares in the acquiring or newly merged corporation). For simplicity, we refer to either mechanism as a **takeover**.

The global takeover market is highly active, averaging more than $1 trillion per year in transaction value. Table 22.1 lists the twenty largest transactions completed during the 13-year period from August 2000 through July 2016. As the table indicates, many takeovers happen between well-known companies, and individual transactions can involve huge sums of money.

TABLE 22.1

Twenty Largest Merger Transactions, August 2000–July 2016

Date Announced	Date Completed	Target Name	Acquirer Name	Value ($ billions)
Apr. 2007	Nov. 2007	ABN-AMRO Holding NV	RFS Holdings BV	98
Mar. 2006	Dec. 2006	BellSouth Corp	AT&T Inc	89
Oct. 2004	Aug. 2005	Shell Transport & Trading Co	Royal Dutch Petroleum Co	80
Feb. 2006	July 2008	Suez SA	Gaz de France SA	75
Apr. 2015	Feb. 2016	BG Group PLC	Royal Dutch Shell PLC	69
Nov. 2014	Mar. 2015	Allergan Inc	Actavis PLC	68
Jan. 2004	Aug. 2004	Aventis SA	Sanofi-Synthelabo SA	65
Jan. 2009	Oct. 2009	Wyeth	Pfizer Inc	64
July 2002	Apr. 2003	Pharmacia Corp	Pfizer Inc	60
June 2008	Nov. 2008	Anheuser-Busch Cos Inc	InBev NV	60
Jan. 2004	July 2004	Bank One Corp, Chicago, IL	JPMorgan Chase & Co	58
Jan. 2005	Oct. 2005	Gillette Co	Procter & Gamble Co	57
May 2015	May 2016	Time Warner Cable Inc	Charter Communications Inc	56
Oct. 2003	Apr. 2004	FleetBoston Financial Corp, MA	Bank of America Corp	49
Sep. 2008	Jan. 2009	Merrill Lynch & Co Inc	Bank of America Corp	48
May 2014	July 2014	DirecTV Inc	AT&T Inc	48
Feb. 2004	Oct. 2004	AT&T Wireless Services Inc	Cingular Wireless LLC	47
Dec. 2004	Aug. 2005	Nextel Communications Inc	Sprint Corp	46
Mar. 2015	July 2015	Kraft Foods Group	HJ Heinz Co	46
Mar. 2009	Nov. 2009	Schering-Plough Corp	Merck & Co Inc	45

Source: Thomson Financials' SDC M&A Database.

Merger Waves

merger waves Peaks of heavy activity followed by quiet troughs of few transactions in the takeover market.

The takeover market is also characterized by **merger waves**—peaks of heavy activity followed by quiet troughs of few transactions. Figure 22.1 displays the time series of takeover activity from 1926 to 2015. Merger activity is greater during economic expansions than during contractions and correlates with bull markets. Many of the same technological and economic conditions that lead to bull markets also motivate managers to reshuffle assets through mergers and acquisitions. Thus, the same economic activities that drive expansions most likely also drive peaks in merger activity.[1]

Figure 22.1 shows that the periods of the greatest takeover activity occurred in the 1960s, 1980s, 1990s, and 2000s. Each merger wave was characterized by a typical type of deal. The increase in activity in the 1960s is known as the "conglomerate wave" because firms typically acquired firms in unrelated businesses. At the time, it was thought that managerial expertise was portable across business lines and that the conglomerate business form offered great financial advantages. This conglomerate fad eventually fell out of favor, and the 1980s were known for hostile, "bust-up" takeovers, in which the acquirer purchased a poorly performing conglomerate and sold off its individual business units for more than the purchase price. The 1990s, in contrast, were known for "strategic" or "global" deals that were more likely to be friendly and to involve companies in related businesses; these mergers often were designed to create strong firms on a scale that would allow them to compete globally. At the end of 2004, takeover activity began to pick up again, starting the next big merger wave, marked by consolidation in many industries such as telecommunications and software. This wave also saw private equity playing a larger role than it had in the past, with some private equity groups such as KKR, TPG, Blackrock, and

FIGURE 22.1

Percentage of Public Companies Taken Over Each Quarter, 1926–2015

Mergers appear to occur in distinct waves, with the most recent waves occurring in the 1980s, 1990s, and 2000s.

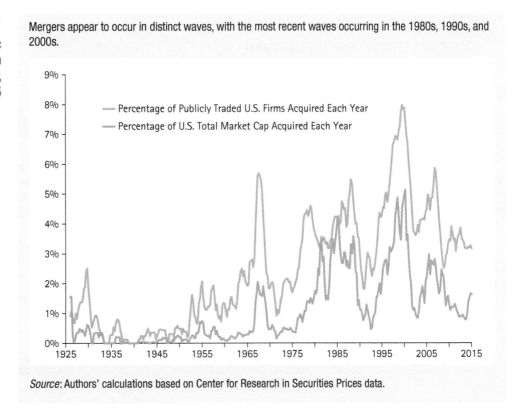

Source: Authors' calculations based on Center for Research in Securities Prices data.

---

[1]See J. Harford, "What Drives Merger Waves," *Journal of Financial Economics*, 77 (2005): 529–560, for an analysis of why these waves occur.

horizontal merger The type of merger when the target and acquirer are in the same industry.

vertical merger The type of merger when the target's industry buys or sells to the acquirer's industry.

conglomerate merger The type of merger when the target and acquirer operate in unrelated industries.

stock swap Merger deal when the target shareholders receive stock as payment for target shares.

term sheet Summary of the structure of a merger transaction that includes details such as who will run the new company, the size and composition of the new board, the location of the headquarters, and the name of the new company.

Cerberus taking ever-larger firms such as Hertz (see Chapter 15), Chrysler, and Harrah's private. The financial crisis and severe contraction of credit in 2008 brought an abrupt end to that merger wave.

Types of Mergers

While we tend to talk about merger waves and mergers in general, the term "merger," as commonly used, encompasses several types of transactions that vary by the relation between the target and the acquirer and by the method of payment used in the transaction. If the target and acquirer are in the same industry, the merger is typically called a **horizontal merger**, whereas if the target's industry buys or sells to the acquirer's industry, it is called a **vertical merger**. Finally, if the target and acquirer operate in unrelated industries, the deal is called a **conglomerate merger**. Conglomerate mergers, while popular in the 1960s, have generally fallen out of favor with shareholders because of the difficulty in creating value when combining two unrelated businesses.

Deals also vary based on whether the target shareholders receive stock or cash as payment for target shares. When they receive stock, the deal is often called a **stock swap**, because target shareholders are swapping their old stock for new stock in either the acquirer or a newly created merged firm. The consideration paid to target shareholders can be very complex, including debt instruments, options, and mixes of any of these with cash and/or stock. Commonly, however, target shareholders receive stock, cash, or a mix of the two.

While news reports understandably focus on the price and method of payment, the structure of a merger transaction, summarized in a **term sheet**, can be simple or incredibly complex. The items to negotiate include, among other things, who will run the new company, the size and composition of the new board, the location of the headquarters, and the name of the new company.

CONCEPT CHECK

1. What are merger waves?

2. What is the difference between a horizontal and a vertical merger?

22.2 Market Reaction to a Takeover

acquisition premium Paid by an acquirer in a takeover, it is the percentage difference between the acquisition price and the premerger price of a target firm.

In most U.S. states, the law requires that when existing shareholders of a target firm are forced to sell their shares, they receive a fair value for their shares. Typically this concept is interpreted as the value exclusive of any value that arises because of the merger itself. For practical purposes, this principle translates into the share price prior to the merger. As a consequence, a bidder is unlikely to acquire a target company for less than its current market value. Instead, most acquirers pay a substantial **acquisition premium**, which is the percentage difference between the acquisition price and the premerger price of the target firm.

Table 22.2 lists the average historical premium and market reaction to a takeover.[2] As the table shows, acquirers pay an average premium of 43% over the premerger price

TABLE 22.2

Average Acquisition Premium and Stock Price Reactions to Mergers

Premium Paid over Premerger Price	Announcement Price Reaction	
	Target	Acquirer
43%	15%	1%

Source: Data based on all U.S. deals from 1980 to 2005, as reported in *Handbook of Corporate Finance: Empirical Corporate Finance*, Vol. 2, Chapter 15, pp. 291–430, B. E. Eckbo, ed., Elsevier/North-Holland Handbook of Finance Series, 2008.

---

[2]The original research done in the 1970s and 1980s documented that shareholders experience significant gains (between 20% and 30%) upon a successful takeover of their firms. More recent papers have found combined losses on the order of $240 billion in capitalization at the announcement of takeover bids. This finding appears to be driven by spectacular losses from some large takeovers of public targets, especially in the late 1990s.

of the target. When a bid is announced, the target shareholders enjoy a gain of 15% on average in their stock price. Although acquirer shareholders see an *average* gain of 1%, in half of the transactions, the bidder price *decreases*. These facts raise three important questions:

1. Why do acquirers pay a premium over the market value for a target company?
2. Although the price of the target company rises on average upon the announcement of the takeover, why does it rise less than the premium offered by the acquirer?
3. If the transaction is a good idea, why does the acquirer not consistently experience a large price increase?

Let's start with the first question—why do acquirers pay a premium over market value? In fact, this question has two parts: (1) Why is the target worth a premium over the current market value? and (2) Even if the target is worth more than its premerger value, why do acquirers pay more than the premerger market price? In the next section, we answer the first part of this question. We delay the discussion of the second part until the end of the chapter, when we fully understand the mechanics of the takeover process.

CONCEPT CHECK

3. On average, what happens to the target share price on the announcement of a takeover?
4. On average, what happens to the acquirer share price on the announcement of a takeover?

22.3 Reasons to Acquire

For most investors, an investment in the stock market is a zero-NPV investment. How, then, can an acquirer pay a premium for a target and still satisfy the requirement that the investment be a positive-NPV investment opportunity? The answer is that an acquirer might be able to add economic value, as a result of the acquisition, that an individual investor cannot add. The basis of the assumption that value of the combined companies will be worth more than the sum of the two companies' individual values is the assumption that they will create *synergies*. We discuss some examples of synergies below, but for simplicity in this section we refer to any additional value created as **synergies**.

synergies Value obtained from an acquisition that could not be obtained if the target remained an independent firm (i.e., value in excess of the firms' stand-alone value).

Large synergies are by far the most common justification that bidders give for the premium they pay for a target. An extreme example is SBC's acquisition of AT&T in 2005 for more than $15 billion. In interviews immediately after the announcement, SBC's Chairman Ed Whitacre was quick to point out that the projected synergies of $15 billion alone could justify the price SBC agreed to pay for AT&T, let alone AT&T's assets.

Such synergies usually fall into two categories: cost reductions and revenue enhancements. Cost-reduction synergies are more common and easier to achieve because they generally translate into layoffs of overlapping employees and elimination of redundant resources. This was the case in the SBC/AT&T acquisition, which forecasted 13,000 layoffs in the first year. If the merger will create possibilities to expand into new markets or gain more customers, then the merger partners will predict synergies that enhance their revenue. For example, when Delta and Northwest airlines announced their merger agreement in April 2008, they forecasted $200–$300 million per year in revenue-enhancement synergies because their expanded network and flight options would bring in more customers and increase customer loyalty.

Let's examine in detail the synergies most often cited by acquirers to justify takeovers.

economies of scale The savings a large company can enjoy from producing goods in high volume, that are not available to a small company.

Economies of Scale and Scope

A large company can enjoy **economies of scale**, or savings from producing goods in high volume, that are not available to a small company. For example, in Stride Rite's acquisition of sports shoemaker Saucony in 2005, one motivation was to reduce Saucony's manufacturing costs because, due to its larger size, Stride Rite could negotiate superior manufacturing contracts in China. Larger firms can also benefit from **economies of scope**, which are savings that come from combining the marketing and distribution of different types of related products (e.g., soft drinks and snack foods).

economies of scope Savings large companies can realize that come from combining the marketing and distribution of different types of related products.

There may also be costs associated with size. Chief among these is that larger firms are more difficult to manage. In a small firm, the CEO is often close to the firm's operations. She can keep in touch with the firm's largest customers and most important personnel, thereby keeping abreast of changing market conditions and potential problems. Because they receive information quickly, small firms are often able to react in a timely way to changes in the economic environment.

Vertical Integration

vertical integration Refers to the merger of two companies that make products required at different stages of the production cycle for the final good. Also, refers to the merger of a firm and its supplier or a firm and its customer.

Vertical integration refers to the merger of two companies that make products required at different stages of the production cycle of the final good. A company might conclude that it can enhance its product if it has direct control of the inputs required to make the product. Similarly, another company might not be happy with how its products are being distributed, so it might decide to take control of its distribution channels.

The principal benefit of vertical integration is coordination. By putting two companies under central control, management can ensure that both companies work toward a common goal. For example, oil companies are often vertically integrated. They generally own all stages of the production process, from the oil fields to the refineries and so on, even down to the gas stations that distribute their primary product—gasoline. Many also have divisions that prospect for new oil.

Vertically integrated companies are large, and as we have already pointed out, large corporations are more difficult to run. Consequently, not all successful corporations are vertically integrated. A good example is Microsoft Corporation. Microsoft has chosen to make the operating system that the vast majority of computers use, but not the computers themselves. Many experts have argued that a key factor in Microsoft's early success over rivals IBM and Apple was its decision not to integrate vertically.

Expertise

Firms often need expertise in particular areas to compete more efficiently. Faced with this situation, a firm can enter the labor market and attempt to hire personnel with the required skills. However, hiring experienced workers with the appropriate talent might be difficult with an unfamiliar, new technology. A more efficient solution may be to purchase the talent as an already functioning unit by acquiring an existing firm. For example, in 2000, Paris-based AXA bought Sanford C. Bernstein, a Wall Street private partnership, to gain expertise and a preexisting client base in the huge U.S. asset management market. Similarly, U.K. builder Amec bought a large stake in Spie Batignolles, a French contractor, to gain local contacts and expertise in the French building industry. Such mergers are common in high-tech industries. Networking firm Cisco Systems is known for its strategy of buying young start-up firms that have developed promising new networking technologies.

Monopoly Gains

It is often argued that merging with or acquiring a major rival enables a firm to substantially reduce competition within the industry and thereby increase profits. Society as a whole bears the cost of monopoly strategies, so most countries have antitrust laws that limit such activity.

The extent to which these laws are enforced tends to vary across countries and over time depending on the policy of current leaders. When General Electric (GE) agreed to buy Honeywell in October 2000, the U.S. Justice Department approved the deal with limited conditions. However, the European Commission (EC) determined that putting GE's aircraft leasing division and Honeywell's extensive avionics product line under the same management would lead to unacceptable anticompetitive effects in the avionics market. Despite substantial concessions by GE and top-level political lobbying by U.S. officials, the EC refused to approve the deal, and it was eventually called off. The GE/Honeywell deal was the first time a merger of two U.S. companies that had been approved by U.S. authorities was blocked by European officials. The EC had no direct jurisdiction over the merger of the companies, but it was in the position to impose crippling restrictions on sales inside the European Union.

Monopoly power could be very valuable, and we would expect that in the absence of strong antitrust laws, many companies would merge. However, while all companies in an industry benefit when competition is reduced, only the merging company pays the associated costs (from, for instance, integrating the target and managing a larger corporation). Perhaps this reason, along with existing antitrust regulation, accounts for the lack of convincing evidence that monopoly gains result from the reduction of competition following takeovers. For example, financial researchers have found that the share prices of other firms in the same industry did not significantly increase following the announcement of a merger within the industry.[3]

Efficiency Gains

Another justification acquirers cite for paying a premium for a target is efficiency gains, which are often achieved through an elimination of duplication—for example, as in the SBC/AT&T merger mentioned earlier. Acquirers also often argue that they can run the target organization more efficiently than existing management could.

Although in theory a chief executive of an inefficiently run corporation can be ousted by current shareholders voting to replace the board of directors, very few managers are replaced in this way. Instead, unhappy investors typically sell their stock, so the stock of a corporation with an inept chief executive trades at a discount relative to the price at which it would trade if it had more capable leadership. In such a situation, an acquirer could purchase shares at the discounted price to take control of the corporation and replace the chief executive with a more effective one. Once the benefits of the new management team become obvious to investors, the discount for the old management will likely disappear and the acquirer can resell its shares for a profit.

Although identifying poorly performing corporations is relatively easy, fixing them is another matter entirely. Takeovers relying on the improvement of target management are difficult to complete, and post-takeover resistance to change can be great. Thus, not all inefficiently run organizations necessarily become more efficient following a takeover.

Tax Savings from Operating Losses

When a firm makes a profit, it must pay taxes on the profit. However, when it incurs a loss, the government does not rebate taxes. Thus, it might appear that a conglomerate has a tax advantage over a single-product firm simply because losses in one division can be offset by profits in another division. Let's illustrate this scenario with an example.

---

[3]See B. E. Eckbo, "Horizontal Mergers, Collusion and Stockholder Wealth," *Journal of Financial Economics*, 11(1) (1983): 241–273, and R. Stillman, "Examining Antitrust Policy Toward Horizontal Mergers," *Journal of Financial Economics*, 11(1) (1983): 225–240.

EXAMPLE 22.1

Taxes for a Merged
Corporation

MyFinanceLab

PROBLEM

Consider two firms, Yin Corporation and Yang Corporation. Both corporations will either make $50 million or lose $20 million every year with equal probability. The only difference is that the firms' profits are perfectly negatively correlated. That is, any year Yang Corporation earns $50 million, Yin Corporation loses $20 million, and vice versa. Assume that the corporate tax rate is 34%. What are the total expected after-tax profits of both firms when they are two separate firms? What are the expected after-tax profits if the two firms are combined into one corporation called Yin-Yang Corporation, but are run as two independent divisions? (Assume it is not possible to carry back or carry forward any losses.)

SOLUTION

PLAN

We need to calculate the after-tax profits of each firm in both the profitable and unprofitable states by multiplying profits by $(1 - \text{tax rate})$. We can then compute expected after-tax profits as the weighted average of the after-tax profits in the profitable and unprofitable states. If the firms are combined, their total profits in any year would always be $50 million − $20 million = $30 million, so the after-tax profit will always be $30 \times (1 - \text{tax rate})$.

EXECUTE

Let's start with Yin Corporation. In the profitable state, the firm must pay corporate taxes, so after-tax profits are $50 \times (1 - 0.34) = $33 million. No taxes are owed when the firm reports losses, so the after-tax profits in the unprofitable state are −$20 million.

Thus, the expected after-tax profits of Ying Corporation are $33(0.5) + (-20)(0.5) = $6.5 million. Because Yang Corporation has identical expected profits, its expected profits are also $6.5 million. Thus, the total expected profit of both companies operated separately is $13 million.

The merged corporation, Yin-Yang Corporation, would have after-tax profits of $30 \times (1 - 0.34) = $19.8 million.

EVALUATE

Yin-Yang Corporation has significantly higher after-tax profits than the total stand-alone after-tax profits of Yin Corporation and Yang Corporation. This is because the losses on one division reduce the taxes on the other division's profits.

Although Example 22.1 is an extreme case, it illustrates a benefit of conglomeration. In the United States, however, these benefits are mitigated because the IRS allows companies to carry back losses up to two years, or forward up to 20 years, to offset earnings. While that rule would reduce the tax benefit in Example 22.1, it also creates a motive for profitable firms to acquire targets with large tax loss carryforwards in order to reap the tax savings from them. However, the IRS will disallow a tax break if it can show that the principal reason for a takeover is tax avoidance, so it is unlikely that such a tax benefit could, by itself, be a valid reason to acquire another firm.

Diversification

The benefits of diversification are frequently cited as a reason for a conglomerate merger. The justification for these benefits comes in three forms: direct risk reduction, lower cost of debt or increased debt capacity, and liquidity enhancement. We discuss each in turn.

Risk Reduction. Like a large portfolio, large firms bear less idiosyncratic risk, so often mergers are justified on the basis that the combined firm is less risky. The problem with this argument is that it ignores the fact that investors can achieve the benefits of diversification themselves by purchasing shares in the two separate firms. Because most stockholders will already be holding a well-diversified portfolio, they get no further benefit from the firm diversifying through acquisition. Moreover, as we have already pointed out, there are costs associated with merging and with running a large diversified firm. Because it may be harder to measure performance accurately in a conglomerate, agency costs may increase and resources may be inefficiently allocated across divisions. As a result, it is cheaper for investors to diversify their own portfolios than to have the corporation do it through acquisition.

Debt Capacity and Borrowing Costs. All else being equal, larger more diversified firms have a lower probability of bankruptcy given the same degree of leverage. Consequently, such firms can increase leverage further and enjoy greater tax savings without incurring significant costs of financial distress. Thus, increased tax benefits and reduction in bankruptcy costs from leverage are potential benefits of diversifying mergers. Of course, to justify a merger, these gains must be large enough to offset any disadvantages of running a larger, less-focused firm.

Liquidity. Shareholders of private companies are often under-diversified: They have a disproportionate share of their wealth invested in the private company. Consequently, when an acquirer buys a private target, it provides the target's owners with a way to reduce their risk exposure by cashing out their investment in the private target and reinvesting in a diversified portfolio. This liquidity that the bidder provides to the owners of a private firm can be valuable and often is an important incentive for the target shareholders to agree to the takeover.

Earnings Growth

It is possible to combine two companies with the result that the earnings per share of the merged company exceed the premerger earnings per share of either company, *even when the merger itself creates no economic value*. Let's look at how this can happen.

EXAMPLE 22.2

Mergers and Earnings per Share

MyFinanceLab

PROBLEM

Consider two corporations that both have earnings of $5 per share. The first firm, OldWorld Enterprises, is a mature company with few growth opportunities. It has 1 million shares that are currently outstanding, priced at $60 per share. The second company, NewWorld Corporation, is a young company with much more lucrative growth opportunities. Consequently, it has a higher value: Although it has the same number of shares outstanding, its stock price is $100 per share. Assume NewWorld acquires OldWorld using its own stock, and the takeover adds no value. In a perfect market, what is the value of NewWorld after the acquisition? At current market prices, how many shares must NewWorld offer to OldWorld's shareholders in exchange for their shares? Finally, what are NewWorld's earnings per share after the acquisition?

SOLUTION

PLAN

Because the takeover adds no value, the post-takeover value of NewWorld is just the sum of the values of the two separate companies: 100×1 million + 60×1 million = $160 million. To acquire OldWorld, NewWorld must pay $60 million. First, we need to calculate how many shares NewWorld must issue to pay OldWorld shareholders $60 million. The ratio of NewWorld shares issued to OldWorld Shares will give us the exchange ratio. Once we know how many new shares will be issued, we can divide the total earnings of the combined company by the new total number of shares outstanding to get the earnings per share.

EXECUTE

At its pre-takeover stock price of $100 per share, the deal requires issuing 600,000 shares ($60 million/$100 = 600,000). As a group, OldWorld's shareholders will then exchange 1 million shares in OldWorld for 600,000 shares in NewWorld. The exchange ratio is the ratio of issued shares to exchanged shares: 600,000/1 million = 0.6. Therefore, each OldWorld shareholder will get 0.6 shares in NewWorld for each 1 share in OldWorld. Notice that the price per share of NewWorld stock is the same after the takeover: The new value of NewWorld is $160 million and there are 1.6 million shares outstanding, giving it a stock price of $100 per share.

(Continued)

However, NewWorld's earnings per share have changed. Prior to the takeover, both companies earned $5/share $\times$ 1 million shares = $5 million. The combined corporation thus earns $10 million. There are 1.6 million shares outstanding after the takeover, so NewWorld's post-takeover earnings per share are

$$EPS = \frac{\$10 \text{ million}}{1.6 \text{ million shares}} = \$6.25/\text{share}$$

By taking over OldWorld, NewWorld has raised its earnings per share by $1.25.

EVALUATE

Because no value was created, we can think of the combined company as simply a portfolio of NewWorld and OldWorld. Although the portfolio has higher total earnings per share, it also has lower growth because we have combined the low-growth OldWorld with the high-growth NewWorld. The higher current earnings per share has come at a price—lower earnings per share growth.

As Example 22.2 demonstrates, by acquiring a company with low growth potential (and thus a low P/E multiple), a company with high growth potential (and high P/E multiple) can raise its earnings per share. In the past, people have cited this increase as a reason to merge. Of course, a savvy investor will see that the merger *adds no economic value*. All that has happened is that the high-growth company, by combining with a low-growth company, has lowered its overall growth rate. As a result, its P/E multiple should fall, which results from its earnings per share rising. Thus, we can draw no conclusion regarding whether a merger was beneficial solely by looking at its impact on the acquirer's earnings.

EXAMPLE 22.3

Mergers and the Price-Earnings Ratio

MyFinanceLab

PROBLEM

Calculate NewWorld's price-earnings ratio, before and after the takeover described in Example 22.2.

SOLUTION

PLAN

The price-earnings ratio is price per share / earnings per share. NewWorld's price per share is $100 both before and after the takeover, and its earnings per share is $5 before and $6.25 after the takeover.

EXECUTE

Before the takeover, NewWorld's price-earnings ratio is

$$P/E = \frac{\$100/\text{share}}{\$5/\text{share}} = 20$$

After the takeover, NewWorld's price-earnings ratio is

$$P/E = \frac{\$100/\text{share}}{\$6.25/\text{share}} = 16$$

EVALUATE

The price-earnings ratio has dropped to reflect the fact that after taking over OldWorld, more of the value of NewWorld comes from earnings from current projects than from its future growth potential.

Managerial Motives to Merge

Most of the reasons given so far are economically motivated, shareholder-driven incentives to merge. However, managers sometimes have their own reasons to merge. Studies have consistently found that the stock price of large bidders drops on average when a bid is announced, especially when the target is publicly traded. Two possible explanations might be conflicts of interest with their shareholders and overconfidence.

Conflicts of Interest. Managers may prefer to run a larger company due to the additional pay and prestige it brings. Because most CEOs hold only a small fraction of their firm's stock, they may not bear enough of the cost of an otherwise bad merger that increases their personal benefits.[4] For example, a CEO who owns 1% of her firm's stock bears 1% of every dollar lost on a bad acquisition, but enjoys 100% of the gains in compensation and prestige that come with being the CEO of a larger company. If the acquisition destroys $100 million in shareholder value, but increases the present value of her compensation by more than $1 million, she will prefer to execute the merger anyway. Why would the board of directors create these incentives? Either due to poor monitoring of the manager, or belief that the strategy is correct even if the stock market disagrees, boards typically increase the pay of CEOs along with the size of the firm, even if the size comes at the expense of poorly performing acquisitions.[5]

Overconfidence. As explained in Chapter 10, people in general tend to be overconfident in their abilities. Psychological research has shown that it takes repeated failures for a person to change his belief that he is above average at some activity. Most CEOs perform at most one large acquisition during their tenure as CEO. In a well-known 1986 paper,[6] Richard Roll proposed the "hubris hypothesis" to explain takeovers, which maintains that overconfident CEOs pursue mergers that have low chance of creating value because they truly believe that their ability to manage is great enough to succeed. The critical distinction between this hypothesis and the incentive conflict discussed above is that overconfident managers believe they are doing the right thing for their shareholders, but irrationally overestimate their own abilities. Under the incentive conflict explanation, managers know they are destroying shareholder value, but personally gain from doing so.

CONCEPT CHECK

5. What are the reasons most often cited for a takeover?

6. Explain why risk diversification benefits and earnings growth are not good justifications for a takeover intended to increase shareholder wealth.

22.4 The Takeover Process

In this section, we explore how the takeover process works. We begin by establishing how a bidder determines the initial offer. We then review the tax and accounting issues specific to a takeover and explain the regulatory approval process. We end by discussing board approval, including defensive strategies that boards implement to discourage takeovers.

Valuation

In Chapters 7 and 10, we demonstrated how to value the stock of a company. Recall that there are two broad categories of valuation approaches, which can be applied here to valuing a target company. The first—and simplest—approach compares the target to other comparable companies. Although this approach is easy to implement, it gives at best a rough estimate of value. Valuing the target using a multiple based on comparable firms does not directly incorporate the operational improvements and other synergistic efficiencies that the acquirer intends to implement. Purchasing a corporation usually constitutes

---

[4]M. Jensen highlighted the agency conflict in acquisition decisions in his 1986 paper, "Agency Costs of Free Cash Flow, Corporate Finance and Takeovers," *American Economic Review*, 76 (1986): 323–329.

[5]J. Harford and K. Li, "Decoupling CEO Wealth and Firm Performance: The Case of Acquiring CEOs," *Journal of Finance*, 62 (2007): 917–949, shows that in 75% of mergers where the acquiring shareholders lose money, acquiring CEOs are financially better off.

[6]R. Roll, "The Hubris Hypothesis of Corporate Takeovers," *Journal of Business*, 59(2) (1986): 197–216.

a very large capital investment decision, so it requires a more accurate estimate of value including careful analysis of both operational aspects of the firm and the ultimate cash flows the deal will generate. Thus, the second approach to valuation requires making a projection of the expected cash flows that will result from the deal, and valuing those cash flows.

A key issue for takeovers is quantifying and discounting the value added as a result of the merger. As demonstrated in Section 22.3, a takeover can generate many different sources of value, which we can characterize as the takeover synergies.

We know that the price paid for a target is equal to the target's pre-bid market capitalization plus the premium paid in the acquisition. If we view the pre-bid market capitalization as the stand-alone value of the target,[7] then from the bidder's perspective, the takeover is a positive-NPV project only if the premium it pays does not exceed the synergies created. Although the premium that is offered is a concrete number, the synergies are not—investors might well be skeptical of the acquirer's estimate of their magnitude. The bidder's stock price reaction to the announcement of the merger is one way to gauge investors' assessments of whether the bidder overpaid or underpaid for the target. As Table 22.2 shows, the average stock price reaction is 1%, but as we noted, the median is closer to zero. Thus, the market, on average, believes that the premium is approximately equal to the synergies. Nonetheless, there is large variation in the premium across deals. One recent large-scale study of the value effects of mergers found that positive reactions to bids are concentrated in smaller bidders. In fact, during the 1990s, 87 large public acquirers announced bids that resulted in $1 billion or more in value reduction at announcement.[8] This finding is likely related to some of the managerial motives discussed in the previous section.

The Offer

Once the acquirer has completed the valuation process, it is in the position to make a tender offer—that is, a public announcement of its intention to purchase a large block of shares for a specified price. A bidder can use either of two methods to pay for a target: cash or stock. In a cash transaction, the bidder simply pays for the target, including any premium, in cash. In a stock-swap transaction, the bidder pays for the target by issuing new stock and giving it to the target shareholders. The "price" offered is determined by the **exchange ratio**—the number of bidder shares received in exchange for each target share—multiplied by the market price of the acquirer's stock.

> **exchange ratio** In a takeover, the number of bidder shares received in exchange for each target share.

A stock-swap merger is a positive-NPV investment for the acquiring shareholders if the share price of the merged firm (the acquirer's share price after the takeover) exceeds the premerger price of the acquiring firm. We can write this condition as follows. Let A be the premerger, or stand-alone, value of the acquirer, and T be the premerger (stand-alone) value of the target. Let S be the value of the synergies created by the merger. If the acquirer has N_A shares outstanding before the merger, and issues x new shares to pay for the target, then the acquirer's share price should increase post-acquisition if

$$\frac{A + T + S}{N_A + x} > \frac{A}{N_A} \tag{22.1}$$

---

[7]Rumors about a potential bid for the target will often push its share price up in anticipation of the premium offer. Practitioners refer to the "unaffected" target price, meaning the target's share price before it was affected by rumors of a takeover. This price would be used to compute the stand-alone value of the target.

[8]S. Moeller, R. Stulz, and F. Schlingemann, "Wealth Destruction on a Massive Scale: A Study of Acquiring Firm Returns in the Recent Merger Wave," *Journal of Finance*, 60(2) (2005): 757–782.

The left side of Eq. 22.1 is the share price of the merged firm. The numerator indicates the total value of the merged firm: the stand-alone value of the acquirer and target plus the value of the synergies created by the merger. The denominator represents the total number of shares outstanding once the merger is complete. The ratio is the post-merger share price. The right side of Eq. 22.1 is the premerger share price of the acquirer: the total premerger value of the acquirer divided by the premerger number of shares outstanding.

Solving Eq. 22.1 for x gives the maximum number of new shares the acquirer can offer and still achieve a positive NPV:

$$x < \left(\frac{T+S}{A}\right) N_A \tag{22.2}$$

We can express this relationship as an exchange ratio by dividing by the premerger number of target shares outstanding, N_T:

$$\text{Exchange Ratio} = \frac{x}{N_T} < \left(\frac{T+S}{A}\right)\frac{N_A}{N_T} \tag{22.3}$$

We can also rewrite Eq. 22.3 in terms of the *premerger* target and acquirer share prices, $P_T = T/N_T$ and $P_A = A/N_A$:

$$\text{Exchange Ratio} < \frac{P_T}{P_A}\left(1 + \frac{S}{T}\right) \tag{22.4}$$

EXAMPLE 22.4

Maximum Exchange Ratio in a Stock Takeover

MyFinanceLab

PROBLEM

At the time Sprint announced plans to acquire Nextel in December 2004, Sprint stock was trading for $25 per share and Nextel stock was trading for $30 per share. If the projected synergies were $12 billion, and Nextel had 1.033 billion shares outstanding, what is the maximum exchange ratio Sprint could offer in a stock swap and still generate a positive NPV? What is the maximum cash offer Sprint could make?

SOLUTION

PLAN

We can use Eq. 22.4 to compute the maximum shares Sprint could offer and still have a positive NPV. To compute the maximum cash offer, we can calculate the synergies per share and add that to Nextel's current share price.

EXECUTE

Using Eq. 22.4,

$$\text{Exchange Ratio} < \frac{P_T}{P_A}\left(1 + \frac{S}{T}\right) = \frac{30}{25}\left(1 + \frac{12}{31}\right) = 1.665$$

That is, Sprint could offer up to 1.665 shares of Sprint stock for each share of Nextel stock and generate a positive NPV.

For a cash offer, given synergies of $12 billion/1.033 billion shares = $11.62 per share, Sprint could offer up to $30 + 11.62 = $41.62.

EVALUATE

Both the cash amount and the exchange offer ($25 × 1.665 = $41.62) have the same value. That value is the most that Nextel is worth to Sprint—if Sprint pays $41.62 for Nextel, it is paying full price plus paying Nextel shareholders for all the synergy gains created—leaving none for Sprint shareholders. Thus, at $41.62, buying Nextel is exactly a zero-NPV project.

Merger "Arbitrage"

Once a tender offer is announced, there is no guarantee that, in fact, the takeover will take place at this price. Often acquirers have to raise the price to consummate the deal. Alternatively, the offer may fail. When an acquirer bids for a target, the target firm's board may not accept the bid and recommend that existing shareholders not tender their shares, even when the acquirer offers a significant premium over the pre-offer share price. Even if the target board supports the deal, there is also the possibility that regulators might not approve the takeover. Because of this uncertainty about whether a takeover will succeed, the market price generally does not rise by the amount of the premium when the takeover is announced.

risk arbitrageurs Traders who, once a takeover offer is announced, speculate on the outcome of the deal.

This uncertainty creates an opportunity for investors to speculate on the outcome of the deal. Traders known as **risk arbitrageurs**, who believe that they can predict the outcome of a deal, take positions based on their beliefs. While the strategies these traders use are sometimes referred to as arbitrage, they are actually quite risky, so they do not represent a true arbitrage opportunity in the sense we have defined in this book. Let's illustrate the strategy using the 2002 stock-swap merger of Hewlett-Packard (HP) and Compaq.

In September 2001, HP announced that it would purchase Compaq by swapping 0.6325 shares of HP stock for each share of Compaq stock. After the announcement, HP traded for $18.87 per share, so the implied value of HP's offer was $18.87 \times 0.6325 = $11.9353. Yet, the price of Compaq was only $11.08 per share after the announcement, $0.8553 below the value of HP's offer. Thus, a risk arbitrageur who simultaneously purchased 10,000 Compaq shares and sold short 6325 HP shares, would net $6325 \times $18.87 - 10,000 \times $11.08 = 8553 immediately. Then, if the takeover was successfully completed on the original terms, the 10,000 Compaq shares would convert into 6325 HP shares, allowing the risk arbitrageur to cover the short position in HP and be left with no net exposure. Thus, the arbitrageur would pocket the original $8553 as a profit.[9]

merger-arbitrage spread In a takeover, the difference between a target stock's price and the implied offer price.

The potential profit described above arises from the difference between the target's stock price and the implied offer price, and is referred to as the **merger-arbitrage spread**. However, it is not a true arbitrage opportunity because there is a risk that the deal will not go through. If the takeover did not ultimately succeed, the risk arbitrageur would eventually have to unwind his position at whatever market prices prevailed. In most cases, these prices would have moved against him (in particular, the price of Compaq would be likely to decline if the takeover did not occur), so he would face losses on the position.

The HP-Compaq takeover was distinctive in that the uncertainty about the success of the deal stemmed largely from acquirer discomfort with the deal rather than from target shareholder discomfort. Although initially supportive of the merger, the Hewlett family got cold feet. About two months after the deal was announced, Walter Hewlett disclosed his family's opposition to it. On the day of Walter Hewlett's announcement, the price of HP stock rose to $19.81, while Compaq's stock price fell to $8.50, causing the merger-arbitrage spread to widen to $19.81 \times 6325 - $8.5 \times 10,000 = $40,298$. We plot the merger-arbitrage spread for the HP-Compaq merger in Figure 22.2. The risk-arbitrage strategy outlined above is effectively a short position on this spread, which pays off if the spread declines. Thus, an arbitrageur who opened the strategy when the deal was announced and closed it after Walter Hewlett announced his opposition would face a loss of $40,298 - $8553 = $31,745$.

---

[9]For simplicity, we are ignoring dividend payments made during the period. HP paid $0.24 and Compaq paid $0.075 in dividends prior to the completion of the merger, reducing slightly the profit from the trade by $10,000 \times $0.075 - 6325 \times $0.24 = -$768$.

FIGURE 22.2

Merger-Arbitrage
Spread for the Merger
of HP and Compaq

The plot shows the potential profit, given that the merger was ultimately successfully completed, from purchasing 10,000 Compaq shares and short-selling 6325 HP shares on the indicated date. A risk arbitrageur who expects the deal to go through can profit by opening the position when the spread is large, and closing the position after it declines.

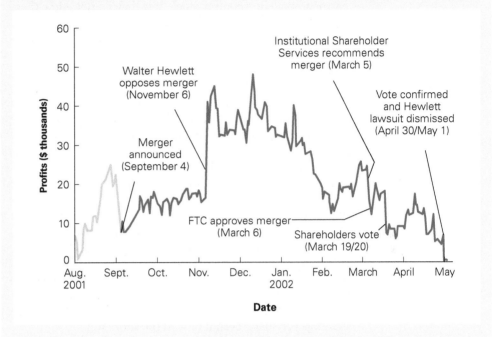

Although the Hewlett family members were large shareholders of HP, they were not controlling shareholders; they did not have enough shares to block the deal single-handedly. Hence, a battle for control of HP ensued between the Hewlett family and then-CEO Carly Fiorina, the driving force behind the acquisition of Compaq. This conflict was only resolved months later when HP shareholders, by a slim margin, voted in favor of issuing new shares, thereby effectively approving the merger and netting a profit for any risk arbitrageur who stayed the course. As is clear from Figure 22.2, arbitrageurs who did not have the stomach to hold on would have faced large losses at several points during the roller-coaster ride. And while HP CEO Carly Fiorina survived this early challenge to her authority, the performance of HP following the merger vindicated Hewlett's position. HP's board ultimately fired Fiorina in 2005.

Tax and Accounting Issues

Once the terms of trade have been decided, the tax and accounting implications of a merger can be determined. How the acquirer pays for the target affects the taxes of both the target shareholders and the combined firm. Any cash received in full or partial exchange for shares triggers an immediate tax liability for target shareholders. They will have to pay a capital gains tax on the difference between the price paid for their shares in the takeover and the price they paid when they first bought the shares. If the acquirer pays for the takeover entirely by exchanging bidder stock for target stock, then the tax liability is deferred until the target shareholders actually sell their new shares of bidder stock.

If the acquirer purchases the target assets directly (rather than the target stock), then it can **step up** the book value of the target's assets to the purchase price. This higher depreciable basis reduces future taxes through larger depreciation charges. Furthermore, any goodwill created could also be amortized for tax purposes over 15 years. The same treatment applies

step up Refers to an increase in the book value of a target's assets to the purchase price when an acquirer purchases those assets directly instead of purchasing the target stock.

to a *forward cash-out merger*, where the target is merged into the acquirer and target shareholders receive cash in exchange for their shares.

Many transactions are carried out as acquisitive reorganizations under the tax code. These structures allow the target shareholders to defer their tax liability on the part of the payment made in acquirer stock, but they do not allow the acquirer to step up the book value of the target assets. However, they provide a mechanism for isolating the target's assets and liabilities in a subsidiary of the acquirer. This can be very attractive for an acquirer that does not want to be exposed to the known (or unknown) liabilities of the target.

While the method of payment (cash or stock) affects how the value of the target's assets is recorded for tax purposes, it does not affect the combined firm's financial statements for financial reporting. The combined firm must mark up the value assigned to the target's assets on the financial statements by allocating the purchase price to target assets according to their fair market value. If the purchase price exceeds the fair market value of the target's identifiable assets, then the remainder is recorded as goodwill and is examined annually by the firm's accountants to determine whether its value has decreased. For example, in HP's takeover of Compaq, HP recorded more than $10 billion in goodwill. The footnotes to the statements attributed the goodwill to the value of the Compaq brand name, which is assumed to have an indefinite life.

Even when a merger has a positive NPV, bidding managers are typically very concerned with the effect of the merger on earnings. This is the other side of the earnings-growth argument as a reason to merge. Just as merging two companies can increase earnings without affecting economic value, it can also decrease earnings without affecting economic value. Nevertheless, acquirers are hesitant to commit to a deal that would be dilutive to earnings per share, even if only in the short run.

Board and Shareholder Approval

For a merger to proceed, both the target and the acquiring board of directors must approve the deal and put the question to a vote of the shareholders of the target (and, in some cases, the shareholders of the acquiring firm as well).

friendly takeover When a target's board of directors supports a merger, negotiates with potential acquirers, and agrees on a price that is ultimately put to a shareholder vote.

In a **friendly takeover**, the target board of directors supports the merger, negotiates with potential acquirers, and agrees on a price that is ultimately put to a shareholder vote. Although it is rare for acquiring boards to oppose a merger, target boards sometimes do not support the deal even when the acquirer offers a large premium. In a **hostile takeover**, the board of directors (together with upper-level management) fights the takeover attempt. To succeed, the acquirer must garner enough shares to take control of the target and replace the board of directors. When a takeover is hostile, the acquirer is often called a **corporate raider** (or **raider**).

hostile takeover A situation in which an individual or organization, sometimes referred to as a corporate raider, purchases a large fraction of a target corporation's stock and in doing so gets enough votes to replace the target's board of directors and its CEO.

corporate raider (or raider) The acquirer in a hostile takeover.

If the shareholders of a target company receive a premium over the current market value of their shares, why would a board of directors ever oppose a takeover? There are a number of reasons. The board might legitimately believe that the offer price is too low. In this case, a suitor that is willing to pay more might be found or the original bidder might be convinced to raise its offer. Alternatively, if the offer is a stock-swap, target management may oppose the offer because they feel the acquirer's shares are overvalued, and therefore that the value of the offer is actually less than the stand-alone value of the target. Finally, managers (and the board) might oppose a takeover because of their own self-interests, especially if the primary motivation for the takeover is efficiency gains. In this case, the acquirer most likely plans to undertake a complete change of leadership of the corporation. Upper-level managers could view opposing the merger as a way of protecting their jobs (and the jobs of their employees). In fact, this concern is perhaps the single biggest reason for the negative associations that hostile takeovers generate. Bear in mind that if substantial efficiency gains are indeed possible, current management is not doing an effective job. A takeover, or threat thereof, might be the only recourse investors have to fix the problem.

In theory, the duty of the target board of directors is to choose the course of action that is in the best interests of the target shareholders. In practice, the courts have given target directors wide latitude under what is called the "business judgment rule" to determine the best course for their companies, including spurning a premium offer if the directors can reasonably argue that more value will eventually be realized for their shareholders by remaining independent. The premise of this rule is that absent evidence of misconduct or self-dealing, the court will not substitute its judgment for that of the elected, informed directors.

In merger transactions, however, there is heightened judicial scrutiny under what is commonly referred to as the "Revlon duties" and "Unocal," named after the cases in which they were established. The Revlon duties state that if a change of control is going to occur, then directors must seek the highest value (they cannot favor one controlling entity over another based on anything other than value to shareholders). The Unocal case established that when the board takes actions deemed as defensive (we discuss these in detail in the next section), its actions are subject to extra scrutiny to ensure that they are not coercive or designed simply to preclude a deal. The board must believe that there is a threat to its corporate strategy and its defenses must be proportional to the magnitude of the threat.

CONCEPT CHECK

7. What are the steps in the takeover process?

8. What do risk arbitrageurs do?

22.5 Takeover Defenses

For a hostile takeover to succeed, the acquirer must go around the target board and appeal directly to the target shareholders. The acquirer can do this by making an unsolicited offer to buy target stock directly from the shareholders (a tender offer). The acquirer will usually couple this with a **proxy fight**: The acquirer attempts to convince target shareholders to unseat the target board by using their proxy votes to support the acquirers' candidates for election to the target board. Target companies have a number of strategies available to them to stop this process. These strategies can force a bidder to raise its bid or entrench management more securely, depending on the independence of the target board. We begin with the most effective defensive strategy, the poison pill.

Poison Pills

A **poison pill** is a rights offering that gives existing target shareholders the right to buy shares in the target at a deeply discounted price once certain conditions are met. The acquirer is specifically excluded from this right. Because target shareholders can purchase shares at less than the market price, the rights offering dilutes the value of any shares held by the acquirer. This dilution makes the takeover so expensive for the acquiring shareholders that they choose to pass on the deal.

The poison pill was invented in 1982 by a takeover lawyer, Martin Lipton, who successfully warded off a takeover attempt of El Paso Electric by General American Oil.[10] Because the original poison pill goes into effect only in the event of a complete takeover (that is, a purchase of 100% of the outstanding shares), one way to circumvent it is to not do a complete takeover. The first time this work-around was used was by Sir James Goldsmith, who took control of Crown Zellerbach by purchasing slightly more than 50% of the outstanding stock. Because he did not purchase the rest, Crown Zellerbach's poison pill was ineffective.

proxy fight In a hostile takeover, when the acquirer attempts to convince the target's shareholders to unseat the target's board by using their proxy votes to support the acquirers' candidates for election to the target's board.

poison pill A defense against a hostile takeover. It is a rights offering that gives the target shareholders the right to buy shares in either the target or an acquirer at a deeply discounted price.

---

[10]For a brief history, see Len Costa, "The Perfect Pill," *Legal Affairs* (March 2005), www. legalaffairs. org.

In response to the takeover of Crown Zellerbach, corporate lawyers have perfected the original poison pill. Most poison pills now specify that if a raider acquires more than a trigger amount (typically 20%) of the target shares (but chooses not to execute a complete takeover by purchasing all outstanding shares), existing shareholders—with the exception of the acquirer—have the right to buy more shares in the target at a discounted price.

The name *poison pill* comes from the world of espionage. Once caught, a spy is supposed to take his own life by swallowing a poison pill rather than give up important secrets. Poison pills are very effective in stopping takeovers, but where is the suicide analogy? The answer is that by adopting a poison pill, a company effectively entrenches its management by making it much more difficult for shareholders to replace bad managers, thereby potentially destroying value. Financial research has verified this effect. A firm's stock price typically drops when it adopts a poison pill. Furthermore, once adopted, firms with poison pills have below-average financial performance.[11]

Not surprisingly, companies adopting poison pills are harder to take over, and when a takeover occurs, the premium that existing shareholders receive for their stock is higher. Therefore, because a poison pill increases the cost of a takeover, all else being equal, a target company must be in worse shape (there must be a greater opportunity for profit) to justify the expense of waging a takeover battle.

Poison pills also increase the bargaining power of the target firm when negotiating with the acquirer because they make it difficult to complete the takeover without the cooperation of the target board. If used effectively, this bargaining power can allow target shareholders to capture more of the takeover gains by negotiating a higher premium than they would get if no pill existed. Numerous studies on the impact of antitakeover provisions on takeovers have found that such provisions result in higher premiums accruing to existing shareholders of the target company.[12]

Staggered Boards

staggered (classified) board In many public companies, a board of directors whose three-year terms are staggered so that only one-third of the directors are up for election each year.

A determined bidder in the face of a poison pill has another available option: get its own slate of directors elected to the target board, which it can submit at the next annual shareholders meeting. If the target shareholders elect those candidates, then the new directors can cancel the poison pill and accept the bidder's offer. To prevent such a coup from happening, about two-thirds of public companies have a **staggered** (or **classified**) **board**. In a typical staggered board, every director serves a three-year term and the terms are staggered so that only one-third of the directors are up for election each year. Thus, even if the bidder's candidates win board seats, it will control only a minority of the target board. A bidder's candidate would have to win a proxy fight two years in a row before the bidder had a majority presence on the target board. The time required to execute this maneuver can deter a bidder from making a takeover attempt when the target board is staggered. Most experts consider a poison pill combined with a staggered board to be the most effective defense available to a target company.

---

[11]P. Malatesta and R. Walkling, "Poison Pill Securities: Stockholder Wealth, Profitability and Ownership Structure," *Journal of Financial Economics*, 20(1) (1988): 347–376; and M. Ryngaert, "The Effects of Poison Pills Securities on Stockholder Wealth," *Journal of Financial Economics*, 20(1) (1988): 377–417.

[12]R. Comment and G. W. Schwert, "Poison or Placebo: Evidence on the Deterrence and Wealth Effects of Modern Antitakeover Measures," *Journal of Financial Economics*, 39(1), (1995): 3–43; N. Varaiya, "Determinants of Premiums in Acquisition Transactions," *Managerial and Decision Economics*, 8(3) (1987): 175–184; and R. Heron and E. Lie, "On the Use of Poison Pills and Defensive Payouts by Takeover Targets," *Journal of Business*, 79(4) (2006): 1783–1807.

White Knights

When a hostile takeover appears to be inevitable, a target company will sometimes look for another, friendlier company to acquire it. This company that comes charging to the target's rescue is known as a **white knight**. The white knight will make a more lucrative offer for the target than the hostile bidder. Incumbent managers of the target maintain control by reaching an agreement with the white knight to retain their positions.

One variant on the white knight defense is the **white squire** defense. In this case, a large investor or firm agrees to purchase a substantial block of shares in the target with special voting rights. This action prevents a hostile raider from acquiring control of the target. The idea is that the white squire itself will not choose to exercise its control rights.

Golden Parachutes

A **golden parachute** is an extremely lucrative severance package that is guaranteed to a firm's senior managers in the event that the firm is taken over and the managers are let go. For example, when Ronald Perelman successfully acquired Revlon Corporation, the firm's former chairman, Michael Bergerac, was reported to have received a golden parachute compensation package worth in excess of $35 million.

Golden parachutes have been criticized because they are seen both as excessive and a misuse of shareholder wealth. In fact, the empirical evidence does not support this view.[13] If anything, it supports the view that an adoption of a golden parachute actually creates value. If a golden parachute exists, management will be more likely to be receptive to a takeover. This means the existence of golden parachutes lessens the likelihood of managerial entrenchment. Researchers have found that stock prices rise on average when companies announce that they plan to implement a golden parachute policy, and that the number of firms bidding against one another for the target and the size of the takeover premium are higher if a golden parachute agreement exists.

Recapitalization

Another defense against a takeover is a recapitalization, in which a company changes its capital structure to make itself less attractive as a target. For example, a company with a lot of cash might choose to pay out a large dividend. Companies without a lot of cash might instead choose to issue debt and then use the proceeds to pay a dividend or repurchase stock.

Why does increasing leverage make a firm less attractive as a target? In many cases, a substantial portion of the synergy gains that an acquirer anticipates from a takeover are from tax savings from an increase in leverage as well as other cost reductions. By increasing leverage on its own, the target firm can reap the benefit of the interest tax shields. In addition, the need to generate cash to meet the debt service obligations provides a powerful motivation to managers to run a corporation efficiently. In effect, the restructuring itself can produce efficiency gains, often removing the principal motivation for the takeover in the first place.

Other Defensive Strategies

Corporate managers and defense advisors have devised other mechanisms to forestall a takeover. A corporation's charter can require a supermajority (sometimes as much as 80%) of votes to approve a merger. It can also restrict the voting rights of very large shareholders. Finally, a firm can require that a "fair" price be paid for the company, where the

---

[13]M. Narayanan and A. Sundaram, "A Safe Landing? Golden Parachutes and Corporate Behavior," *University of Michigan Business School Working Paper No. 98015* (1998).

determination of what is "fair" is up to the board of directors or senior management. Beauty is always in the eye of the beholder, so "fair" in this case usually implies an optimistic determination of value.

We might expect the presence of defensive strategies to reduce firm value. However, Gregg Jarrell and Annette Poulsen[14] found that, on average, the public announcement of antitakeover amendments by 600 firms in the period 1979–1985 had an insignificant effect on the value of announcing firms' shares.

Regulatory Approval

All mergers must be approved by regulators. In Section 22.3, we discussed monopoly gains from takeovers and the use of antitrust regulations to limit them. In the United States, antitrust enforcement is governed by three main statutes: the Sherman Act, the Clayton Act, and the Hart-Scott-Rodino Act. The Sherman Act of 1890, which was passed in response to the formation of huge oil trusts such as Standard Oil, prohibits mergers that would create a monopoly or undue market control. The Clayton Act, enacted in 1914, strengthened the government's hand by prohibiting companies from acquiring the stock (or, as later amended, the assets) of another company if it would adversely affect competition. Under both the Sherman and Clayton acts, the government had to sue to block a merger. Often by the time a decision was rendered, the merger had taken place and it was difficult to undo it. The Hart-Scott-Rodino (HSR) Act of 1976 put the burden of proof on the merging parties. Under HSR, all mergers above a certain size (the formula for determining whether a transaction qualifies is complicated, but it comes out to approximately $60 million) must be approved by the government before the proposed takeovers occur. The government cannot delay the deal indefinitely, however, because it must respond with approval or a request for additional information within 20 days of receiving notification of the proposed merger.

 ### Weyerhaeuser's Hostile Bid for Willamette Industries

In November 2000, Weyerhaeuser, a forest products company based in Federal Way, Washington, announced a hostile bid of $48 per share for its smaller neighbor, Willamette Industries, based in Portland, Oregon. Weyerhaeuser had been pursuing Willamette in private since 1998, when Steve Rogel unexpectedly resigned as CEO of Willamette to become CEO of Weyerhaeuser. Each time Rogel approached his old employer in private, he was rebuffed. The response to the hostile tender offer was no different. Despite the fact that the bid represented a substantial premium to the firm's pre-bid stock price, the Willamette board rejected the offer and urged its shareholders not to tender their shares to Weyerhaeuser.

Willamette's defenses included a staggered board and a poison pill, so Weyerhaeuser made its tender offer conditional on Willamette's board canceling the poison pill. Consequently, Weyerhaeuser initiated a proxy fight at the next annual shareholders' meeting in June 2001. One of the directors up for reelection at

that time was Duane McDougall, Willamette's CEO. One month before the meeting, Weyerhaeuser increased its offer to $50 per share, but Willamette's board still believed that the offer was too low and worried that too many of its long-time employees would face layoffs after the merger. Nonetheless, at the annual meeting, Weyerhaeuser's slate received 1.4% more votes than Willamette's, thereby removing Willamette's CEO from its board.

The loss of the board seats did not change Willamette's position. Willamette unsuccessfully searched for a white knight to generate a bidding contest that would force Weyerhaeuser to up its bid. It also entered into talks to buy Georgia-Pacific's building products division. Such a deal would have increased its size and added enough debt to its balance sheet to render the firm unattractive to Weyerhaeuser.

In the end, Weyerhaeuser increased its offer to $55.50 per share in January 2002, and Willamette finally agreed to a deal and called off its negotiations with Georgia-Pacific. Even without the presence of other bidders, Willamette's board was able to get what it considered to be a fair price from Weyerhaeuser.

---

[14]G. Jarrell and A. Poulsen, "Shark Repellents and Stock Prices: The Effects of Antitakeover Amendments Since 1980," *Journal of Financial Economics*, 19 (1988): 127–168.

The European Commission has established a process similar to the HSR process, which requires merging parties to notify the EC, provide additional information if requested about the proposed merger, and wait for approval before proceeding. As discussed in the Honeywell/GE example, even though the EC technically lacks legal authority to block a merger of U.S. companies, it can stop a takeover by imposing restrictions on the combined firm's operations and sales in Europe. Although globally a proposed takeover might have to satisfy antitrust rules in more than 80 jurisdictions, practically the most important jurisdictions besides the home jurisdiction of the firm are Europe and the United States.

CONCEPT CHECK

9. What defensive strategies are available to help target companies resist an unwanted takeover?

10. How can a hostile acquirer get around a poison pill?

22.6 Who Gets the Value Added from a Takeover?

Now that we have explained the takeover process, we can return to the remaining questions posed at the beginning of this chapter: why the price of the acquiring company does not rise at the announcement of the takeover and why the bidder is forced to pay a premium for the target.

You might imagine that the people who acquire the corporation and replace its management will capture the value created by the merger. Based on the average stock price reaction, it does not appear that the acquiring corporation generally captures this value. Instead, the premium the acquirer pays is approximately equal to the value it adds, which means the *target* shareholders ultimately capture the value added by the acquirer. To see why, we need to understand how market forces react to a takeover announcement.

The Free Rider Problem

Assume you are one of the 1 million shareholders of HighLife Corporation, all of whom own 1 share of stock. HighLife has no debt. Its chief executive is not doing a good job, preferring to spend his time using the company's jets to fly to the corporate condo in Aspen, Colorado, rather than running the company in Chicago. As such, the shares are trading at a substantial discount. They currently have a price of $45 per share, giving HighLife a market value of $45 million. Under a competent manager, the company would be worth $75 million. HighLife's corporate charter specifies that a simple majority is required to make all decisions, so to take control of HighLife a shareholder must purchase half the outstanding shares.

T. Boone Icon decides to fix the situation (and make a profit at the same time) by making a tender offer to buy half the outstanding shares for $60 per share in cash. If fewer than 50% of the shareholders tender their shares, the deal is off.

In principle, this idea could land T. Boone a handsome profit. If 50% of shareholders tender their shares, those shares will cost him $60 × 500,000 = $30 million. Once he has control of the firm, he can replace the managers. When the executive jets and the Aspen condo are sold and the market realizes that the new managers are serious about improving performance, the market value of the firm will rise to $75 million. Hence, T. Boone's shares will be worth $75 per share, netting him a profit of $15 × 500,000 = $7.5 million. But will 50% of the shareholders tender their shares?

The offer price of $60 per share exceeds the value of the firm if the takeover does not go through ($45 per share). Hence, the offer is a good deal for shareholders overall. But if all shareholders tender their shares, as an individual shareholder, you could do better by not tendering your share. Then, if T. Boone takes control, each of your shares will be worth

$75 rather than the $60 you would get by tendering. In this case, it is wiser not to tender. Of course, if all shareholders think this way no one will tender their shares, and T. Boone's deal will not get off the ground. The only way to persuade shareholders to tender their shares is to offer them at least $75 per share, which removes any profit opportunity for T. Boone. The problem here is that existing shareholders do not have to invest time and effort, but still participate in all the gains from the takeover that T. Boone Icon generates—hence the term "free rider problem." By sharing the gains in this way, T. Boone Icon is forced to give up substantial profits and thus will likely choose not to bother at all.

Toeholds

One way for T. Boone to get around the problem of shareholders' reluctance to tender their shares is to buy the shares in the market anonymously. However, SEC rules make it difficult for investors to buy much more than about 10% of a firm in secret.[15] After T. Boone acquires such an initial stake in the target, called a **toehold**, he would have to make his intentions public by informing investors of his large stake. To successfully gain control of HighLife, he would have to announce a tender offer to buy an additional 40% of the shares for $75 per share. Once in control, he would be able to sell his stake for $75 per share. Assuming he accumulated the first 10% for $50 per share, his profits in this case will be $25 \times 100,000 = \$2.5$ million. Not bad, but substantially less than the value he is adding.

toehold An initial ownership stake in a firm that a corporate raider can use to initiate a takeover attempt.

Why should investors care whether T. Boone's profits are substantially lower than the value he is adding? The answer is that people like T. Boone perform an important service. Because of the threat that such a person might attempt to take over their company and fire them, chief executives are less likely to shirk their duties. Thus, the more profitable we make this activity, the less likely we will have to resort to it. If $2.5 million is not enough to justify T. Boone's time and effort, he will not try to acquire HighLife. Current management will remain entrenched and T. Boone will think about acquiring the company only if further erosion in the stock price makes the deal lucrative enough for him.

A number of legal mechanisms exist that allow acquirers to avoid the free rider problem and capture more of the gains from the acquisition. Next, we describe the two most common mechanisms: the leveraged buyout and the freezeout merger.

The Leveraged Buyout

The good news for shareholders is that another significantly lower-cost mechanism allows people like T. Boone Icon to take over companies and fire underperforming managers. Recall from Chapter 15 that this mechanism is called the leveraged buyout (LBO). Let's illustrate how it works by returning to HighLife Corporation.

Assume that T. Boone chooses not to buy any shares in the market secretly, but instead announces a tender offer for half the outstanding shares at a price of $50 per share. However, instead of using his own cash to pay for these shares, he borrows the money through a shell corporation (one that is created for the sole purpose of making the acquisition) by *pledging the shares themselves as collateral on the loan*. The only time he will need the money is if the tender offer succeeds, so the banks lending the money can be certain that he will have control of the collateral. Even more important, if the tender offer succeeds, with control of the company, T. Boone can merge the target with the shell corporation, effectively attaching the loans directly to the target—that is, it is as if the target corporation, and not T. Boone, has borrowed the money. At the end of this process, T. Boone still owns half the shares, but the *corporation* is responsible for repaying the loan. T. Boone has effectively acquired half the shares without paying for them!

---

[15]The rules actually require that any shareholder who owns more than 5% of a firm publicly disclose this fact, but the time delays in the disclosure process allow investors to accumulate more than 5% of the firm before this information is made public.

You might imagine that no shareholder would be willing to tender her shares under these circumstances. Surprisingly, this conclusion is wrong. If you tender your shares, you will receive $50 for each of them. If you do not tender your shares, but enough other shareholders do, then T. Boone will take control of the company. After he replaces the managers, the enterprise value of the company will be $75 million. What will your shares be worth if you did not tender them?

For simplicity, assume that there are no frictions or taxes. To gain control of the firm, T. Boone borrowed $25 million to purchase half the outstanding shares ($50 × 500,000). Because this debt is now attached to HighLife, the total value of HighLife's equity is just the total value of the company, minus the value of debt:

$$\text{Total Value of HighLife Equity} = \$75 \text{ million} - \$25 \text{ million} = \$50 \text{ million}$$

The total number of outstanding shares is the same (remember that T. Boone purchased existing shares), so the price per share is $50 million ÷ 1 million = $50/share. If the tender offer succeeds, you will be indifferent. Whether you tender your shares or keep them, each is always worth $50. If you keep your shares and the tender offer fails, the price per share stays at $45. Clearly, it is always in your best interests to tender your shares, so T. Boone's tender offer will succeed. T. Boone also makes substantially more profits than he would if he used a toehold strategy—his profits are the value of his shares upon completion of the takeover: $50 × 500,000 = $25 million.

EXAMPLE 22.5

Leveraged Buyout

MyFinanceLab

PROBLEM

FAT Corporation stock is currently trading at $40 per share. There are 20 million shares outstanding, and the company has no debt. You are a partner in a firm that specializes in leveraged buyouts. Your analysis indicates that the management of this corporation could be improved considerably. If the managers were replaced with more capable ones, you estimate that the value of the company would increase by 50%. You decide to initiate a leveraged buyout and issue a tender offer for at least a controlling interest—50% of the outstanding shares. What is the maximum amount of value you can extract and still complete the deal?

SOLUTION

PLAN

Currently, the value of the company is $40 × 20 million = $800 million, and you estimate you can add an additional 50%, or $400 million. If you borrow $400 million and the tender offer succeeds, you will take control of the company and install new management. The total value of the company will increase by 50% to $1.2 billion. You will also attach the debt to the company, so the company will now have $400 million in debt. You can then compute the value of the post-takeover equity and your gain. You can repeat this computation assuming you borrow more than $400 million and confirming that your gain does not change.

EXECUTE

The value of the equity once the deal is done is the total value minus the debt outstanding:

$$\text{Total Equity} = \$1200 \text{ million} - \$400 \text{ million} = \$800 \text{ million}$$

The value of the equity is the same as the premerger value. You own half the shares, which are worth $400 million, and paid nothing for them, so you have captured the value you anticipated adding to FAT.

What if you borrowed more than $400 million? Assume you were able to borrow $450 million. The value of equity after the merger would be

$$\text{Total Equity} = \$1200 \text{ million} - \$450 \text{ million} = \$750 \text{ million}$$

This is lower than the premerger value. Recall, however, that in the United States, existing shareholders must be offered at least the premerger price for their shares. Because existing shareholders anticipate that the share price will be lower once the deal is complete, all shareholders will tender their shares. This implies that you will have to pay $800 million for these shares, and so to complete the deal, you will have to pay

(Continued)

$800 million − $450 million = $350 million out of your own pocket. In the end, you will own all the equity, which is worth $750 million. You paid $350 million for it, so your profit is again $400 million.

EVALUATE

In each case, the most you can gain is the $400 million in value you add by taking over FAT. Thus, you cannot extract more value than the value you add to the company by taking it over.

The examples we have illustrated are extreme in that the acquirer takes over the target without paying any premium and with no initial investment. In practice, premiums in LBO transactions are often quite substantial—while they can avoid the free rider problem, acquirers must still get board approval to overcome other defenses such as poison pills, as well as outbid other potential acquirers. Also, lenders typically require that the acquirer have a substantial equity stake as protection for the debt holders, in case the claimed post-acquisition benefits do not materialize. In the $15.2 billion Hertz LBO (at the time, the second largest in history), which we described in Chapter 15, the acquirers contributed $2.3 billion in cash out of a total of $5.6 billion that was paid for Hertz's equity.

From 2003 to 2007, there was a surge in leveraged buyout activity, fueled by a combination of huge flows of capital to buy out (private equity) firms, and increased appetite for risk by lenders willing to allow buyout groups to leverage their equity investment at attractive terms. Buyout firms took many companies private with the stated goal of increasing their performance without concern for perceived pressure from public investors to meet short-term earnings targets. They also employed so-called "roll-up" strategies whereby they would buy many smaller, already private firms in a particular industry and consolidate them into a larger player. The typical LBO has a planned exit in five years, either by taking the firm public again, or selling it to an operating firm or another private equity group. In 2008, the financial crisis and contraction of credit put an almost

 The Leveraged Buyout of RJR-Nabisco by KKR

By the summer of 1988, Ross Johnson, CEO of RJR Nabisco (RJR), was becoming increasingly worried about the poor stock price performance of the conglomerate. Despite a strong earnings record, management had not been able to shake loose its image as a tobacco company, and the stock price was languishing at $55 per share. In October 1988, Johnson and a small team of RJR's executives, backed by the Wall Street firms of Shearson Lehman Hutton and Salomon Brothers, announced a bid of $75 per share for the company. At this price, the deal would have been valued at $17.6 billion, more than twice as large as the largest LBO completed up to that point. Because this deal involved the current management of the company, it falls into a special category of LBO deals called **management buyouts (MBOs)**.

The announcement focused Wall Street's attention on RJR. Even at this substantial premium, the MBO appeared to be a good deal for Johnson and his team, because soon after the offer went public, it became hotly contested. Foremost among the contenders was the firm of Kohlberg, Kravis, and Roberts (KKR). KKR launched its own bid with a cash offer of $90 per share. A bidding war ensued that saw the offer price ultimately rise to $109 per share,

valuing the deal at more than $25 billion. In the end, both Johnson and KKR offered very similar deals, although management's final bid was slightly higher than KKR's. Eventually, RJR's board accepted KKR's bid of $109 per RJR share. The offer price comprised $81 per share in cash, $18 per share in preferred stock, and $10 per share in debenture securities.

From an economic point of view, this outcome is surprising. One would think that given their inside knowledge of the company, management would be in the best position not only to value it, but also to run it. Why, then, would an outsider choose to outbid an insider for a company? The answer in RJR's case appeared to point to the managers themselves. As the deal proceeded, it became increasingly obvious to investors that executives (and members of the board of directors) enjoyed perks that were unprecedented. For example, Johnson had the personal use of numerous corporate apartments in different cities and literally a fleet of corporate jets that he, the top executives, and members of the corporate board used for personal travel. In their leveraged buyout proposal, they had obtained a 4% equity stake for top executives that was worth almost $1 billion, $52.5 million in golden parachutes, and assurances that the RJR air force (the fleet of corporate jets) and the flamboyant Atlanta headquarters would not be subject to budget cutting.

management buyout (MBO) A leveraged buyout in which the buyer group includes the firm's own management.

complete halt to private equity activity. Some highly levered private equity transactions from the peak faltered under their debt load during the recession. For example, Chrysler, which had been purchased and taken private from DaimlerChrysler AG by private equity firm Cerberus Group, declared bankruptcy in 2009, wiping out Cerberus's stake in the firm.

The Freezeout Merger

freezeout merger A situation in which the laws on tender offers allow an acquiring company to freeze existing shareholders out of the gains from merging by forcing non-tendering shareholders to sell their shares for the tender offer price.

Although a leveraged buyout is an effective tool for a group of investors to use to purchase a company, it is less well suited to the case of one company acquiring another. An alternative is the **freezeout merger**: The laws on tender offers allow the acquiring company to freeze existing shareholders out of the gains from merging by forcing non-tendering shareholders to sell their shares for the tender offer price. Let's see how this is accomplished.

An acquiring company makes a tender offer at an amount slightly higher than the current target stock price. If the tender offer succeeds, the acquirer gains control of the target and merges its assets into a new corporation, which is fully owned by the acquirer. In effect, the non-tendering shareholders lose their shares because the target corporation no longer exists. In compensation, non-tendering shareholders get the right to receive the tender offer price for their shares. The bidder, in essence, gets complete ownership of the target for the tender offer price.

Because the value the non-tendering shareholders receive for their shares is equal to the tender price (which is more than the premerger stock price), the law generally recognizes it as fair value and non-tendering shareholders have no legal recourse. Under these circumstances, existing shareholders will tender their stock, reasoning that there is no benefit to holding out: If the tender offer succeeds, they get the tender price anyway; if they hold out, they risk jeopardizing the deal and forgoing the small gain. Hence, the acquirer is able to capture almost all the value added from the merger and, as in a leveraged buyout, is able to effectively eliminate the free rider problem.

The freezeout tender offer has a significant advantage over a leveraged buyout because an acquiring corporation need not make an all-cash offer. Instead of paying the target's shareholders in cash, it can use shares of its own stock to pay for the acquisition. In this case, the bidder offers to exchange each shareholder's stock in the target for stock in the acquiring company. As long as the exchange rate is set so that the value in the acquirer's stock exceeds the premerger market value of the target stock, the non-tendering shareholders will receive fair value for their shares and will have no legal recourse.

Competition

The empirical evidence in Table 22.2 suggests that, despite the availability of both the freezeout merger and the leveraged buyout as acquisition strategies, most of the value added still appears to accrue to the target shareholders. That is, on average, acquirers do not have a positive price reaction on the announcement of a takeover. Why do acquirers choose to pay so large a premium that they effectively hand the value they create to the target company's shareholders?

In addition to the presence of the takeover defenses we have previously discussed, the most likely explanation is the competition that exists in the takeover market. Once an acquirer starts bidding on a target company and it becomes clear that a significant gain exists, other potential acquirers may submit their own bids. The result is effectively an auction in which the target is sold to the highest bidder. Even when a bidding war does not result, most likely it is because, rather than participate in a bidding war, an acquirer offered a large enough initial premium to forestall the process. In essence, it must give up most of the value added to the target shareholders.

CONCEPT
CHECK

11. What mechanisms allow corporate raiders to get around the free rider problem in takeovers?

12. Based on the empirical evidence, who gets the value added from a takeover? What is the most likely explanation of this fact?

MyFinanceLab

Here is what you should know after reading this chapter. MyFinanceLab will help you identify what you know, and where to go when you need to practice.

KEY POINTS AND EQUATIONS	KEY TERMS	ONLINE PRACTICE
22.1 Background and Historical Trends • Mergers can be horizontal, vertical, or conglomerate. • The global takeover market is active, averaging more than $1 trillion per year in transaction value. The periods of greatest activity have been the 1960s, 1980s, 1990s, and 2000s. • During the 1960s, deals were aimed at building conglomerates. In the 1980s, the trend reversed and conglomerates were split into individual businesses. The 1990s saw a rise in "strategic" or "global" deals designed to create firms that could compete globally. From 2004–2008, further consolidation and global-scale deals contributed to the most recent merger wave.	acquirer (or bidder), p. 688 conglomerate merger, p. 690 horizontal merger, p. 690 merger waves, p. 689 stock swap, p. 690 takeover, p. 688 target, p. 688 term sheet, p. 690 vertical merger, p. 690	MyFinanceLab Study Plan 22.1
22.2 Market Reaction to a Takeover • While on average the shareholders of the acquiring firm obtain small or no gains, shareholders from the acquired firm typically enjoy gains of 15% on the announcement of a takeover bid.	acquisition premium, p. 690	MyFinanceLab Study Plan 22.2
22.3 Reasons to Acquire • The most common justifications given for acquiring a firm are the synergies that can be gained through an acquisition. • The most commonly cited sources of synergies are economies of scale and scope, the control provided by vertical integration, gaining monopolistic power, the expertise gained from the acquired company, improvements in operating efficiency, and benefits related to diversification such as increased borrowing capacity and tax savings. • Shareholders of a private company that is acquired gain by switching to a more liquid investment. • Some mergers are motivated by incentive conflicts or overconfidence of the acquirer management.	economies of scale, p. 691 economies of scope, p. 692 synergies, p. 691 vertical integration, p. 692	MyFinanceLab Study Plan 22.3

22.4 The Takeover Process

- From the bidder's perspective, a takeover is a positive-NPV project only if the premium paid does not exceed the synergies created. The bidder's stock price reaction to the announcement of the merger is one way to gauge investors' assessments of whether the bidder overpaid or underpaid for the target.
- A tender offer is a public announcement of an intention to purchase a large block of shares for a specified price. Making a tender offer does not guarantee that a deal will take place.
- Bidders use either of two methods to pay for a target: cash or stock. In a cash transaction, the bidder simply pays for the target in cash. In a stock-swap transaction, the bidder pays for the target by issuing new stock and giving it to the target shareholders. The method used by the bidder to pay for the acquired firm has tax and accounting implications.
- For a merger to proceed, both the target and the acquiring boards of directors must approve the merger and put the question to a vote of the shareholders of the target (and, in some cases, the shareholders of the acquiring firm as well).
- In a friendly takeover, the target board of directors supports the merger and negotiates with the potential acquirers.
- If the target board opposes the merger, then the acquirer must go around the target board and appeal directly to the target shareholders, asking them to elect a new board that will support the merger.

corporate raider (or raider), p. 702
exchange ratio, p. 698
friendly takeover, p. 702
hostile takeover, p. 702
merger-arbitrage spread, p. 700
risk arbitrageurs, p. 700
step up, p. 701

MyFinanceLab
Study Plan 22.4

22.5 Takeover Defenses

- A target board of directors can defend itself in several ways to prevent a merger. The most effective defense strategy is the poison pill, which gives target shareholders the right to buy shares in either the target or the acquirer at a deeply discounted price. The purchase is effectively subsidized by the existing shareholders of the acquirer, making the takeover very expensive.
- Another effective defense strategy is having a staggered board, which prevents a bidder from acquiring control over the board in a short period of time.
- Other defenses include looking for a friendly bidder (a white knight), making it expensive to replace management, and changing the capital structure of the firm.

golden parachute, p. 705
poison pill, p. 703
proxy fight, p. 703
staggered (classified) board, p. 704
white knight, p. 705
white squire, p. 705

MyFinanceLab
Study Plan 22.5

22.6 Who Gets the Value Added from a Takeover?
- When a bidder makes an offer for a firm, the target shareholders can benefit by keeping their shares and letting other shareholders sell at a low price. However, because all shareholders have the incentive to keep their shares, no one will sell. This scenario is known as the free rider problem.
- To overcome this problem, bidders can acquire a toehold in the target, attempt a leveraged buyout, or, in the case when the acquirer is a corporation, offer a freezeout merger.

freezeout merger, p. 711
management buyout (MBO), p. 711
toehold, p. 708

MyFinanceLab
Study Plan 22.6

CRITICAL THINKING

1. What are the two primary mechanisms under which ownership and control of a public corporation can change?

2. Why do you think mergers cluster in time, causing merger waves?

3. What are some reasons why a horizontal merger might create value for shareholders?

4. Why do you think shareholders from target companies enjoy an average gain when acquired, while acquiring shareholders often do not gain anything?

5. If you are planning an acquisition that is motivated by trying to acquire expertise, you are basically seeking to gain intellectual capital. What concerns would you have in structuring the deal and the post-merger integration that would be different from the concerns you would have when buying physical capital?

6. Do you agree that the European Union should be able to block mergers between two U.S.-based firms? Why or why not?

7. How do the carryforward and carryback provisions of the U.S. tax code affect the benefits of merging to capture operating losses?

8. Diversification is good for shareholders. So why shouldn't managers acquire firms in different industries to diversify a company?

9. How does a toehold help overcome the free rider problem?

PROBLEMS

All problems are available in MyFinanceLab.

Reasons to Acquire

1. Your company has earnings per share of $4. It has 1 million shares outstanding, each of which has a price of $40. You are thinking of buying TargetCo, which has earnings per share of $2, 1 million shares outstanding, and a price per share of $25. You will pay for TargetCo by issuing new shares. There are no expected synergies from the transaction.
   a. If you pay no premium to buy TargetCo, what will be your earnings per share after the merger?
   b. Suppose you offer an exchange ratio such that, at current pre-announcement share prices for both firms, the offer represents a 20% premium to buy TargetCo. What will be your earnings per share after the merger?
   c. What explains the change in earnings per share in (a)? Are your shareholders any better or worse off?

    d. What will be your price-earnings ratio after the merger (if you pay no premium)? How does this compare to your P/E ratio before the merger? How does this compare to TargetCo's premerger P/E ratio?

2. If companies in the same industry as TargetCo (from Problem 1) are trading at multiples of 14 times earnings, what would be one estimate of an appropriate premium for TargetCo?

3. You are invested in GreenFrame, Inc. The CEO owns 3% of GreenFrame and is considering an acquisition. If the acquisition destroys $50 million of GreenFrame's value, but the present value of the CEO's compensation increases by $5 million, will he be better or worse off?

The Takeover Process

4. Loki, Inc., and Thor, Inc., have entered into a stock-swap merger agreement whereby Loki will pay a 40% premium over Thor's premerger price. If Thor's premerger price per share was $40 and Loki's was $50, what exchange ratio will Loki need to offer?

5. The NFF Corporation has announced plans to acquire LE Corporation. NFF is trading at $35 per share and LE is trading at $25 per share, implying a premerger value of LE of $4 billion. If the projected synergies are $1 billion, what is the maximum exchange ratio NFF could offer in a stock swap and still generate a positive NPV?

6. Let's reconsider Problem 1 (b). The actual premium that your company will pay for TargetCo when it completes the transaction will not be 20%, because on the announcement the target price will go up and your price will go down to reflect the fact that you are willing to pay a premium for TargetCo without any synergies. Assume that the takeover will occur with certainty and all market participants know this on the announcement of the takeover (ignore time value of money).
    a. What is the price per share of the combined corporation immediately after the merger is completed?
    b. What is the price of your company immediately after the announcement?
    c. What is the price of TargetCo immediately after the announcement?
    d. What is the actual premium your company will pay?

7. ABC has 1 million shares outstanding, each of which has a price of $20. It has made a takeover offer of XYZ Corporation, which has 1 million shares outstanding and a price per share of $2.50. Assume that the takeover will occur with certainty and all market participants know this. Furthermore, there are no synergies to merging the two firms.
    a. Assume ABC made a cash offer to purchase XYZ for $3 million. What happens to the price of ABC and XYZ on the announcement? What premium over the current market price does this offer represent?
    b. Assume ABC makes a stock offer with an exchange ratio of 0.15. What happens to the price of ABC and XYZ this time? What premium over the current market price does this offer represent?
    c. At current market prices, both offers are to purchase XYZ for $3 million. Does that mean that your answers to (a) and (b) must be identical? Explain.

Takeover Defenses

8. BAD Company's stock price is $20, and the firm has 2 million shares outstanding. You believe you can increase the company's value if you buy it and replace the management. Assume that BAD has a poison pill with a 20% trigger. If it is triggered, all BAD's shareholders—other than the acquirer—will be able to buy one new share in

BAD for each share they own at a 50% discount. Assume that the price remains at $20 while you are acquiring your shares. If BAD's management decides to resist your buyout attempt, and you cross the 20% threshold of ownership:

a. How many new shares will be issued and at what price?

b. What will happen to your percentage ownership of BAD?

c. What will happen to the price of your shares of BAD?

d. Do you lose or gain from triggering the poison pill? If you lose, where does the loss go (who benefits)? If you gain, from where does the gain come (who loses)?

Who Gets the Value Added from a Takeover?

9. You work for a leveraged buyout firm and are evaluating a potential buyout of UnderWater Company. UnderWater's stock price is $20, and it has 2 million shares outstanding. You believe that if you buy the company and replace its management, its value will increase by 40%. You are planning on doing a leveraged buyout of UnderWater, and will offer $25 per share for control of the company.

a. Assuming you get 50% control, what will happen to the price of non-tendered shares?

b. Given the answer in (a), will shareholders tender their shares, not tender their shares, or be indifferent?

c. What will be your gain from the transaction?

23

International Corporate Finance

LEARNING OBJECTIVES

- Explain the basics of foreign exchange

- Identify and hedge exchange rate risk

- Understand integrated capital markets and their implication for prices

- Determine how to handle cash flows in foreign currencies in capital budgeting

- Analyze the impact of different countries' tax rates on investment decisions and firm value

- Show how to exploit opportunities from segmented international markets

- Demonstrate how to address exchange rate risk in your capital budgeting approach

notation

C_{FC}	foreign currency cash flow
D	market value of debt
E	market value of equity
F	forward exchange rate
$r_{\$}$	dollar risk-free interest rate
$r_{\$}^{*}$	dollar cost of capital
r_{FC}	foreign currency risk-free interest rate

r_{FC}^{*}	foreign currency cost of capital
r_{D}	required return on debt
r_{E}	required return on equity
r_{wacc}	weighted average cost of capital
S	spot exchange rate

In the 1990s, Starbucks Coffee Company identified Japan as a potentially lucrative new market for its coffee products and decided to invest as much as $10 million in fiscal year 1996 to begin operations there. Because Starbucks realized it needed specialized knowledge of the Japanese market, it established a joint venture with Sazaby, Inc., a Japanese retailer and restaurateur. This venture, called Starbucks Coffee Japan Ltd., intended to open as many as 12 stores in its initial phase. Although stores opened more slowly than expected, the venture had more than 200 stores and sales of ¥29 billion ($252 million) by 2001, and it opened its 500th store in November 2003. To finance this growth, Starbucks Coffee Japan Ltd. used the Japanese capital markets. It held an initial public offering of shares on the Osaka Stock Exchange in October 2001 with a market capitalization of ¥90.88 billion ($756 million), raising ¥18.8 billion ($156 million) in additional capital for expansion. As of 2016, Starbucks had over 1000 stores in Japan. How did Starbucks' managers decide to undertake this investment opportunity? Why did they decide to use the Japanese domestic market to finance it rather than using U.S. markets?

This chapter focuses on some of the special factors a firm faces when making a foreign investment. There are three key issues that arise when considering an investment in a foreign project such as Starbucks Coffee Japan Ltd.:

- The project will most likely generate foreign currency cash flows, although the firm cares about the home currency value of the project.
- Interest rates and costs of capital will likely be different in the foreign country as a result of the macro-economic environment.
- The firm will probably face a different tax rate in the foreign country and will be subject to both foreign and domestic tax codes.

We begin this introduction to international finance with an overview of foreign exchange markets and the risk that comes from exchange rate fluctuations. From there, we examine how a firm can manage exchange rate risk. Next, we explain how a financial manager should evaluate foreign projects by first examining the case when the local and foreign capital markets are integrated. This case provides a useful benchmark for comparing the different methods that can be used to value a foreign project as well as the implications, on valuation, of foreign and domestic tax codes. Finally, we explain how to value a foreign project when capital markets are segmented.

23.1 Foreign Exchange

In Chapter 3, we showed the following list of McDonald's Big Mac prices, reproduced here in Figure 23.1. In Chapter 3, we pointed out that with free transportation, you would buy as many Big Macs as you could in Venezuela and try to sell them for a profit in Switzerland. But how would you do this? Assuming you are starting in the United States, you would need to exchange U.S. dollars for bolivares fuertes to buy Big Macs in Venezuala. Then you would sell them in Switzerland, receiving Swiss Francs. Finally, for your profit, you would exchange those Swiss Francs into U.S. dollars again. Figure 23.2 summarizes your transactions.

As the figure indicates, you start by "buying" bolivares fuertes with U.S. dollars. At first, buying money usually strikes students as odd, but that is exactly what happens every day in the foreign exchange markets—every currency has a price in terms of other currencies. Specifically, a **foreign exchange rate** is a price for a currency denominated in another currency. For example, it might cost you $1 to buy 200 bolivares fuertes and $1.10 to buy 1 euro. Whereas you can buy small amounts of euros at any currency exchange such as those found in international airports, much larger sums of currencies are bought and sold around the clock on the *foreign exchange market*.

foreign exchange rate The price for a currency denominated in another currency.

The Foreign Exchange Market

Imagine a market that is open 24 hours a day during the business week, has no central physical location, and experiences *daily* turnover of around $5 trillion. The **foreign exchange (FX or forex) market**, in which currencies are traded, is such a market. There are many reasons to trade currencies, but we will focus on those of a financial manager in a firm doing business in more than one country (a multinational firm). Consider Starbucks or Apple. Each has retail outlets in many different countries and so collects revenue in many different currencies. However, both are U.S. firms, so they will eventually want to exchange their profits in euros, yen, pounds, and other currencies into dollars. In addition to revenues, each firm has costs incurred in other countries. For example, Starbucks buys coffee all over the world and sources most of its inventory locally (milk, pastries, and so on). Similarly, Apple manufactures iPods and MacBooks outside the United States and must pay for parts and labor in other currencies.

foreign exchange (FX or forex) market A market in which currencies are traded that has no central physical location.

FIGURE 23.1

Prices of Big Macs in Different Currencies

This table, reproduced from Chapter 3, shows the retail price of a Big Mac, in January 2016, in different countries and in different currencies. Note that once the amounts are converted into U.S. dollars, we see a wide range of prices.

Country	Local Cost	U.S. Dollar Cost
Switzerland	6.50 Swiss francs	$6.44
Sweden	45 Swedish Krona	$5.23
United States	4.93 US dollars	$4.93
Britain	2.89 pounds	$4.22
Canada	5.84 Canadian dollars	$4.14
Australia	5.30 Australian dollars	$3.74
U.A.E.	13 dirhams	$3.54
Brazil	13.50 reals	$3.35
Japan	370 yen	$3.12
Mexico	49 pesos	$2.81
China	17.60 yuan	$2.68
Hong Kong	19.20 HK dollars	$2.48
Poland	960 zlotys	$2.37
Indonesia	30,500 rupiahs	$2.19
Russia	114 rubles	$1.53
Venezuela	132 bolivares fuertes	$0.66

Source: Economist.com.

The main players in the foreign exchange market are the very large, global investment banks such as Deutsche Bank, UBS, and Citibank. These banks trade on their own account as well as for client multinational firms. Some large multinational firms trade for themselves as well. Other players in the market are government central banks, hedge

FIGURE 23.2

McDonald's Big Macs Round-the-World Transactions

This figure summarizes the transactions necessary to take advantage of the opportunity to make money by buying and selling McDonald's Big Macs at different prices around the world.

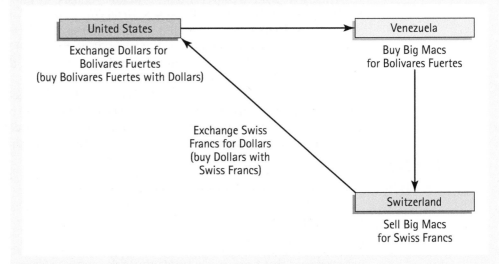

FIGURE 23.3

The Most Traded
Currencies

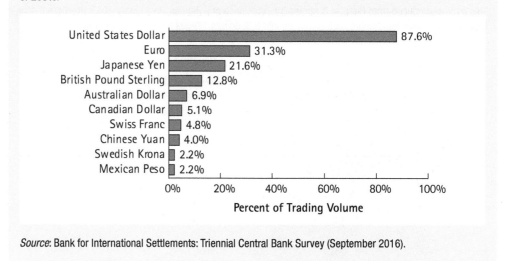

Counting 100% of buying currencies and 100% of selling currencies, for a total of 200%, this table lists the top 10 traded currencies in 2016. Note that these 10 currencies accounted for more than 178% of the total of 200%.

Source: Bank for International Settlements: Triennial Central Bank Survey (September 2016).

funds and other investment managers, and retail brokers. Even though there are over 150 currencies in the world, just two of them, the U.S. dollar and the euro, account for more than half of all trading volume in the foreign exchange market. Figure 23.3 shows the 10 most traded currencies. Note that the total volume sums to 200%, not 100%, because there is a currency on the buy and sell side of every transaction.

Exchange Rates

Figure 23.4 shows the foreign exchange rates quoted in the *Wall Street Journal* for July 29, 2016. These rates are all between a particular foreign currency and the U.S. dollar. For example, the first line indicates that one Argentine peso can be purchased for $0.0667, or equivalently, 14.9925 pesos buys one U.S. dollar (see column 3):

$$1 \text{ peso} = \$0.0667, \text{ so } \frac{\$1}{\$0.0667/\text{peso}} = 14.9925 \text{ pesos per dollar}$$

Thus, if we want to convert from 100 pesos to dollars, we multiply the number of pesos by the $/peso exchange rate: 100 pesos × $0.0667/peso = $6.67. Conversely, if we want to convert from $6.67 to pesos, we multiply the number of dollars by the pesos/$ exchange rate: $6.67 × 14.9925 pesos/dollar = 100 pesos. (Note we are off slightly due to rounding, but that this is the same as dividing the number of dollars by the $/peso exchange rate: $6.67 ÷ $0.0667/peso = 100 pesos.)

Because most exchange rates are market prices, they change from day to day and even within the day. This means that just as it will be hard for you to plan your budget for your semester abroad, companies doing business abroad face considerable risk from changes in exchange rates. We discuss those risks and how to mitigate them in the next section.

CONCEPT   1. What is an exchange rate?

CHECK   2. Why would multinational companies need to exchange currencies?

23.2 Exchange Rate Risk

Multinational firms face the risk of exchange rate fluctuations. In this section, we consider two strategies that firms use to hedge this risk: currency forward contracts and currency options.

FIGURE 23.4

U.S. Dollar Foreign Exchange Rates

Currencies   July 29, 2016

Exchange Rates: New York Closing Snapshot for Friday

U.S.-dollar foreign-exchange rates in late New York trading

Country/currency	USD equiv Friday	Currency per USD (inverse)	US$ vs. YTD % chg	Country/currency	USD equiv Friday	Currency per USD (inverse)	US$ vs. YTD % chg
Americas				**Europe**			
Argentina peso	0.0667	14.9925	15.9	Bulgaria lev	0.572	1.749	-2.8
Brazil real	0.308	3.249	-18	Croatia kuna	0.149	6.698	-4.5
Canada dollar	0.767	1.304	-5.8	Czech Rep. koruna	0.041	24.190	-2.8
Chile peso	0.002	655.31	-7.5	Denmark krone	0.150	6.658	-3.1
Colombia peso	0.000	3069	-3.3	Euro area euro	1.118	0.895	-2.8
Ecuador US dollar	1	1	unch	Hungary forint	0.004	278.560	-4.1
Mexico peso	0.053	18.762	9	Iceland krona	0.008	121.021	-7
Peru new sol	0.298	3.352	-1.8	Norway krone	0.118	8.446	-4.5
Uruguay peso	0.033	29.878	-0.1	Poland zloty	0.257	3.899	-0.6
Venezuela b. fuerte	0.100	9.990	58.4	Romania leu	0.250	3.997	-3.9
				Russia ruble	0.015	66.007	-8.2
Asia-Pacific				Sweden krona	0.117	8.562	1.4
Australian dollar	0.760	1.317	-4.1	Switzerland franc	1.032	0.969	-3.3
China yuan	0.150	6.653	2.5	Turkey lira	0.335	2.989	2.4
Hong Kong dollar	0.129	7.758	0.1	Ukraine hryvnia	0.040	24.814	3.4
India rupee	0.015	66.711	0.7	U.K. pound	1.323	0.756	11.4
Indonesia rupiah	0.000	13089.005	-5.5				
Japan yen	0.010	102.041	-15.1	**Middle East/Africa**			
Kazakhstan tenge	0.003	352.113	4				
Macau pataca	0.125	7.989	-0.2	Bahrain dinar	2.652	0.377	unch
Malaysia ringgit	0.248	4.026	-6.4	Egypt pound	0.113	8.881	13.4
New Zealand dollar	0.720	1.388	-5.1	Israel shekel	0.262	3.815	-2
Pakistan rupee	0.010	104.822	unch	Kuwait dinar	3.307	0.302	-0.4
Philippines peso	0.021	47.170	0.5	Oman sul rial	2.597	0.385	unch
Singapore dollar	0.746	1.340	-5.5	Qatar rial	0.275	3.640	-0.1
South Korea won	0.001	1112.347	-5.4	Saudi Arabia riyal	0.267	3.751	-0.1
Sri Lanka rupee	0.007	145.400	0.8	South Africa rand	0.072	13.889	-10.3
Taiwan dollar	0.031	31.817	-3.3				
Thailand baht	0.029	34.771	-3.5				
Vietnam dong	0.000	22296.544	0.7				

Note: Based on trading among banks of $1 million and more, as quoted at 4 p.m. ET by Reuters.

Source: *Wall Street Journal*, July 29, 2016.

Exchange Rate Fluctuations

Consider the relationship between the U.S. dollar and the euro. In April 2008, the value of the euro (€) relative to the dollar reached its highest value to date at an exchange rate of 0.625 euros per dollar or, equivalently:

$$\frac{1}{€0.625/\$} = \$1.600 \text{ per euro}$$

Brexit

On Thursday, June 23, 2016, voters in the UK surprised financial markets by voting to leave the EU. This vote for a British-Exit, or "Brexit," as it is called, sent the British Pound plunging more than 11% in dollar terms when the result was announced. The European Union's currency, the Euro, dropped at the same time. The large currency swings reflected currency traders' concerns about the uncertainty surrounding future trade, economic activity, and consumer confidence in both regions. The equity markets tumbled as well, reflecting the same concern that future economic growth would be stunted by the decision.

The chart below shows that the Pound appreciated leading-up to the vote as traders grew confident that the UK would stay. It then plunged when the results revealed the decision to leave.

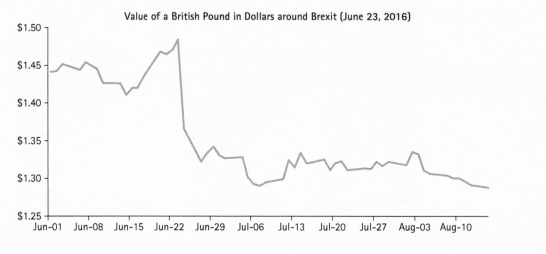

Value of a British Pound in Dollars around Brexit (June 23, 2016)

floating rate An exchange rate that changes constantly depending on the supply and demand for each currency in the market.

Like most foreign exchange rates, the dollar/euro rate is a **floating rate**, which means it changes constantly depending on the quantity supplied and demanded for each currency in the market. The supply and demand for each currency is driven by three factors:

- *Firms trading goods:* A U.S. dealer exchanges dollars for euros to buy cars from a German automaker.

- *Investors trading securities:* A Japanese investor exchanges yen for dollars to purchase U.S. bonds.

- *The actions of central banks in each country:* The British central bank may exchange pounds for euros in an attempt to keep down the value of the pound.

Because the supply and demand for currencies varies with global economic conditions, exchange rates are volatile. Figure 23.5 shows the dollar price of euros from 2001 through July 2016. Notice that the price of the euro often varies by as much as 10% over periods as short as a few months. From 2002 to 2004, the value of the euro climbed more than 50% relative to the dollar. More recently, from March 2014 to March 2015, the value of the euro fell by more than 20% relative to the dollar.

Fluctuating exchange rates cause a problem known as the *importer-exporter dilemma* for firms doing business in international markets. To illustrate, consider the problem faced by Manzini Cyclery, a small U.S. maker of custom bicycles. Manzini needs to import parts from an Italian supplier, Campagnolo. If Campagnolo sets the price of its parts in euros, then Manzini faces the risk that the dollar may fall, making euros, and therefore the parts it needs, more expensive. If Campagnolo sets its prices in dollars, then Campagnolo faces the risk that the dollar may fall and it will receive fewer euros for the parts it sells to the U.S. manufacturer.

FIGURE 23.5

Dollars per Euro ($/€),
Jan. 2001–Jul. 2016

Note the dramatic changes in the exchange rate over short periods.

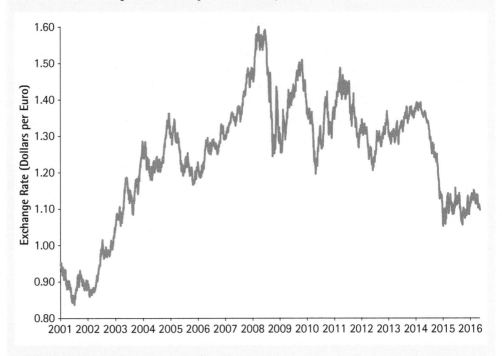

Source: Federal Reserve Board (H.10 Release).

EXAMPLE 23.1

The Effect of
Exchange Rate Risk

MyFinanceLab

PROBLEM

In January 2009, when the exchange rate was $1.30 per euro, Manzini ordered parts for next year's production from Campagnolo. They agreed to a price of 500,000 euros, to be paid when the parts were delivered in one year's time. One year later, the exchange rate was $1.45 per euro. What was the actual cost in dollars for Manzini when the payment was due? If the price had instead been set at $650,000 (which had equivalent value at the time of the agreement: 500,000 euros × $1.30/euro), how many euros would Campagnolo have received?

SOLUTION

PLAN

The price is set in euros, 500,000, but the $/€ exchange rate will fluctuate over time and the problem asks us to consider what would happen if it goes to $1.45/euro, which means that dollars are worth less (it takes more dollars to buy one euro).

We can always convert between dollars and euros at the going exchange rate by multiplying the $/€ exchange rate by the number of euros or by dividing the number of dollars by the $/€ exchange rate.

EXECUTE

With the price set at 500,000 euros, Manzini had to pay ($1.45/euro) × (500,000 euros) = $725,000. This cost is $75,000, or about 12%, higher than it would have been if the price had been set in dollars.

If the price had been set in dollars, Manzini would have paid $650,000, which would have been worth only $650,000 ÷ ($1.45/euro) = 448,276 euros to Campagnolo, or about 10% less.

EVALUATE

Whether the price was set in euros or dollars, one of the parties would have suffered a substantial loss. Because neither knows which will suffer the loss ahead of time, each has an incentive to hedge.

The problem of exchange rate risk is a general problem in any import-export relationship. If neither company will accept the exchange rate risk, the transaction may be difficult or impossible to negotiate. Example 23.1 demonstrates the potential magnitude of the problem.

Hedging with Forward Contracts

Exchange rate risk naturally arises whenever transacting parties use different currencies: One of the parties will be at risk if exchange rates fluctuate. The most common method firms use to reduce the risk that results from changes in exchange rates is to hedge the transaction using *currency forward contracts*.

A **currency forward contract** is a contract that sets the exchange rate and an amount to exchange in advance. It is usually written between a firm and a bank, and it fixes a currency exchange rate for a transaction that will occur at a future date. A currency forward contract specifies (1) an exchange rate, (2) an amount of currency to exchange, and (3) a delivery date on which the exchange will take place. The exchange rate set in the contract is referred to as the **forward exchange rate**, because it applies to an exchange that will occur in the future. By entering into a currency forward contract, a firm can lock in an exchange rate in advance and reduce or eliminate its exposure to fluctuations in a currency's value.

currency forward contract A contract that sets a currency exchange rate, and an amount to exchange, in advance.

forward exchange rate The exchange rate set in a currency forward contract; it applies to an exchange that will occur in the future.

EXAMPLE 23.2
Using a Forward Contract to Lock in an Exchange Rate

MyFinanceLab

PROBLEM
Assume that in January 2009, banks were offering one-year currency forward contracts with a forward exchange rate of $1.29/€. Suppose that at that time, Manzini placed the order with Campagnolo with a price of 500,000 euros and simultaneously entered into a forward contract to purchase 500,000 euros at a forward exchange rate of $1.29/€ in January 2010. What payment would Manzini be required to make in January 2010?

SOLUTION

PLAN
If Manzini enters into a forward contract locking in an exchange rate of $1.29/€, then it doesn't matter what the actual exchange rate is in January 2010—Manzini will be able to buy 500,000 euros for $1.29/€.

EXECUTE
Even though the exchange rate rose to $1.45/€ in January 2010, making the euro more expensive, Manzini would obtain the 500,000 euros using the forward contract at the forward exchange rate of $1.29/€. Thus, Manzini must pay:

$$500{,}000 \text{ euros} \times \$1.29/€ = \$645{,}000 \text{ in January 2010}$$

Manzini would pay this amount to the bank in exchange for 500,000 euros, which are then paid to Campagnolo.

EVALUATE
This forward contract would have been a good deal for Manzini. Without the hedge, it would have had to exchange dollars for euros at the prevailing rate of $1.45/€, raising its cost to $725,000. However, the exchange rate could have moved the other way. If the exchange rate had fallen to $1.15/€, the forward contract would still commit Manzini to pay $1.29/€. In other words, the forward contract locks in the exchange rate and eliminates the risk—whether the movement of the exchange rate is favorable or unfavorable.

If the forward contract allows the importer to eliminate the risk of a stronger euro, where does the risk go? At least initially, the risk passes to the bank that has written the forward contract. Because the bank agrees to exchange dollars for euros at a fixed rate, it will experience a loss if the euro increases in value. In Example 23.2, the bank receives only $645,000 in the forward contract, but gives up euros that are worth $725,000.

FIGURE 23.6

The Use of Currency
Forwards to Eliminate
Exchange Rate Risk

In this example, the U.S. importer and the U.S. exporter both hedge their exchange rate risk by using currency forward contracts (shown in blue). By writing offsetting contracts, the bank bears no exchange rate risk and earns a fee from each transaction.

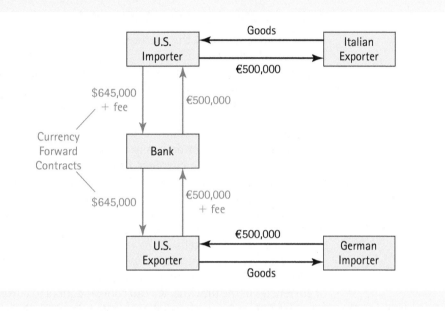

Why is the bank willing to bear this risk? First, the bank is much larger and has more capital than a small importer, so it can bear the risk without being in jeopardy of financial distress. More importantly, in most settings the bank will not even hold the risk. Instead, the bank will find another party willing to trade euros for dollars. By entering into a second forward contract with offsetting risk, the bank can eliminate its risk altogether.

This situation is illustrated in Figure 23.6. A U.S. importer, who must pay for goods with euros, purchases euros from the bank through a forward contract with a forward exchange rate of $1.29 per euro. This transaction locks in the importer's cost at $645,000. Similarly, a U.S. exporter, who will receive payment in euros, uses a forward contract to sell the euros to

FIGURE 23.7

Currency Timeline
Showing Forward
Contract and Cash-
and-Carry Strategy

The cash-and-carry strategy (the three transactions in black) replicates the forward contract (in blue) by borrowing in one currency, converting to the other currency at the spot exchange rate, and investing in the new currency.

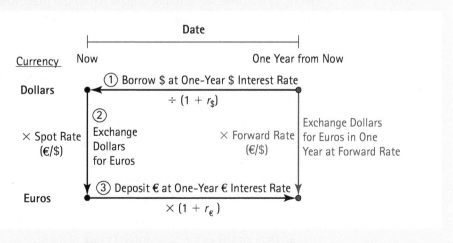

the bank, locking in the exporter's revenue at $645,000. The bank holds both forward contracts—the first to exchange dollars for euros and the second to exchange euros for dollars. The bank bears no exchange rate risk and earns fees from both the exporter and the importer.

Cash-and-Carry and the Pricing of Currency Forwards

An alternative method, the *cash-and-carry strategy*, also enables a firm to eliminate exchange rate risk. Because this strategy provides the same cash flows as the forward contract, we can use it to determine the forward exchange rate using the Law of One Price. Let's begin by considering the different ways investors can exchange foreign currency in the future for dollars in the future.

currency timeline Indicates time horizontally by dates (as in a standard timeline) and currencies (as in dollars and euros) vertically.

Currency Timeline. Currency forward contracts allow investors to exchange a foreign currency in the future for dollars in the future at the forward exchange rate. We illustrate such an exchange in the **currency timeline** shown in Figure 23.7, which indicates time horizontally by dates (as in a standard timeline) and currencies (dollars and euros) vertically. Thus, "dollars in one year" corresponds to the upper-right point in the timeline and "euros in one year" corresponds to the lower-right point in the timeline. To convert cash flows between points, we must convert them at an appropriate rate. The forward exchange rate, indicated by $F€/\$$, tells us the rate at which we can exchange dollars for euros in one year using a forward contract.

spot exchange rate The current foreign exchange rate.

Figure 23.7 also illustrates other transactions that we can use to move between dates or currencies in the timeline. We can convert dollars to euros today at the current exchange rate, also referred to as the **spot exchange rate**, $S€/\$$. By borrowing or lending at the dollar interest rate $r_\$$, we can exchange dollars today for dollars in one year. Finally, we can convert euros today for euros in one year at the euro interest rate $r_€$, which is the rate at which banks will borrow or lend on euro-denominated accounts.

cash-and-carry strategy A strategy used to lock in the future cost of an asset by buying the asset for cash today, and storing (or "carrying") it until a future date.

Cash-and-Carry Strategy. As Figure 23.7 shows, combining these other transactions provides an alternative way to convert euros to dollars in one year. The **cash-and-carry strategy**, used to lock in the future cost of a currency by buying it today and depositing it in a risk-free account (or "carrying") it until a future date, consists of the following three simultaneous transactions:

1. Borrow dollars today using a one-year loan at the dollar interest rate.
2. Exchange the dollars for euros today at the spot exchange rate.
3. Deposit the euros today for one year at the euro interest rate.

In one year's time, we will owe dollars (from the loan in transaction 1) and receive euros (from the deposit in transaction 3). That is, we have converted dollars in one year to euros in one year, just as with the forward contract. This method is called a cash-and-carry strategy because we borrow cash that we then carry (invest) in the future.

Covered Interest Parity. Because the forward contract and the cash-and-carry strategy accomplish the same conversion, by the Law of One Price they must do so at the same rate. Let's return to Manzini's problem in Example 23.2. In January 2009, the spot exchange rate was $1.30/€ (or equivalently 0.769 €/$), while one-year interest rates were 1.2% for dollars and 2.4% for euros. Rather than entering into the forward contract from that example, Manzini could have followed the cash-and-carry strategy described in Figure 23.7. To do so, Manzini would:

1. Borrow dollars at an interest rate of 1.2%, receiving $1/1.012 = $0.988 in January 2009 per $1 in January 2010.
2. Exchange them for euros at 0.769 euros per dollar.
3. Deposit the euros at an interest rate of 2.4%.

For every $1 owed in January 2010, Manzini starts with $0.988 in January 2009. Exchanging those dollars for euros at 0.769 euros per dollar gets Manzini 0.760 euros ($0.988 × 0.769 €/$). Finally, in one year, Manzini's euro deposit has grown to 0.778 euros (€0.760 × 1.024). The end result is that in one year, Manzini owes $1 and receives 0.778 euros, so it has exchanged dollars for euros at 0.778 €/$ or, equivalently, $1.29/€, which is the forward rate offered by the bank. We can write the three transactions as follows:

$$\frac{\$1.00}{1.012} \times (\text{€}0.769/\$) \times 1.024 = \text{€}0.778$$

Rearranging terms, we have a more general statement about the relation between interest rates, spot exchange rates, and forward rates:

$$\text{€}0.778 = (\text{€}0.769/\$) \times \frac{1.024}{1.012}$$

If we use $r_\$$ to represent the dollar interest rate and $r_\text{€}$ for the euro interest rate, we have the following no-arbitrage formula for the forward exchange rate:

Covered Interest Parity

$$\underbrace{\text{Forward Rate}}_{\substack{\text{€ in one year} \\ \text{$ in one year}}} = \underbrace{\text{Spot Rate}}_{\substack{\text{€ today} \\ \text{$ today}}} \times \underbrace{\frac{1 + r_\text{€}}{1 + r_\$}}_{\substack{\text{€ in one year/€ today} \\ \text{$ in one year/$ today}}} \qquad (23.1)$$

Equation 23.1 expresses the forward exchange rate in terms of the spot exchange rate and the interest rates in each currency. Note that on both sides of the equation, the ultimate units are €/$ in one year.

covered interest parity equation States that the difference between the forward and spot exchange rates is related to the interest rate differential between the currencies.

Equation 23.1 is referred to as the **covered interest parity equation**; it states that the difference between the forward and spot exchange rates is related to the interest rate differential between the currencies. When the interest rate differs across countries, investors have an incentive to borrow in the low-interest rate currency and invest in the high-interest rate currency. Of course, there is always the risk that the high-interest rate currency could depreciate while the investment is held. Suppose you try to avoid this risk by locking in the future exchange rate using a forward contract. Equation 23.1 implies that the forward exchange rate will exactly offset any benefit from the higher interest rate, eliminating any arbitrage opportunity.

Equation 23.1 easily generalizes to a forward contract longer than one year. Using the same logic, but investing or borrowing for T years rather than one year, the no-arbitrage forward rate for an exchange that will occur T years in the future is:

$$\text{Forward Rate}_T = \text{Spot Rate} \times \frac{(1 + r_\text{€})^T}{(1 + r_\$)^T} \qquad (23.2)$$

In this equation, the spot and forward rates are in units of €/$, and the interest rates are the current risk-free T-year rates from the yield curve for each currency.

EXAMPLE 23.3

Computing the No-Arbitrage Forward Exchange Rate

MyFinanceLab

PROBLEM
Suppose that the spot exchange rate for the Japanese yen is ¥116/$. At the same time, the one-year interest rate in the United States is 4.85% and the one-year interest rate in Japan is 0.10%. Based on these rates, what forward exchange rate is consistent with no arbitrage?

(Continued)

SOLUTION

PLAN

We can compute the forward exchange rate using Eq. 23.1. Because the exchange rate is in terms of ¥/$, we need to make sure we are dividing 1 plus the yen rate by 1 plus the dollar rate:

$$\text{Forward Rate}_{\text{¥/\$}} = \text{Spot Rate}_{\text{¥/\$}} \times \left(\frac{1 + r_{\text{¥}}}{1 + r_{\text{\$}}} \right)$$

(A useful rule to remember is that the ratio of interest rates must match the units of the exchange rate. Because the exchange rate is ¥/$, we multiply by the yen interest rate and divide by the dollar interest rate. We could also solve the problem by converting all the rates to $/¥.)

EXECUTE

$$\text{Forward Rate}_{\text{¥/\$}} = \text{Spot Rate}_{\text{¥/\$}} \times \frac{1 + r_{\text{¥}}}{1 + r_{\text{\$}}} = \text{¥116/\$} \times \frac{1.0010}{1.0485} = \text{¥110.7/\$ in one year}$$

EVALUATE

The forward exchange rate is lower than the spot exchange rate, offsetting the higher interest rate on dollar investments. If the forward exchange rate were anything other than ¥110.7/$, such as ¥111/$, arbitrage profits would be available. We could have borrowed ¥1 billion at 0.10% interest, exchanged it into $8,620,690 (¥1 billion ÷ ¥116/$) and deposited the dollars, earning 4.85% interest. In one year, we would have $9,038,793 ($8,620,690 × (1.0485)) and owe ¥1.0010 billion (¥1 billion × (1.0010)). If we had locked in a forward exchange rate of ¥111/$, we would need $9,018,018 (¥1.0010 billion ÷ ¥111/$) to pay off our loan, leaving us with a no-risk profit of $20,775! We (and everyone else) would do this until the forward rate came into line with the no-arbitrage rate of ¥110.7/$.

Advantages of Forward Contracts. Why do firms use forward contracts rather than the cash-and-carry strategy? First, the forward contract is simpler, requiring one transaction rather than three, so it may have lower transaction fees. Second, many firms are not able to borrow easily in different currencies and may pay a higher interest rate if their credit quality is poor. Generally speaking, cash-and-carry strategies are used primarily by large banks, which can borrow easily and face low transaction costs. Banks use such a strategy to hedge their currency exposures that result from commitments to forward contracts.

Hedging Exchange Rate Risk with Options

Currency options are another method that firms commonly use to manage exchange rate risk. Currency options, as with the stock options introduced in Chapter 21, give the holder the right—but not the obligation—to exchange currency at a given exchange rate. Currency forward contracts allow firms to lock in a future exchange rate; currency options allow firms to insure themselves against the exchange rate moving beyond a certain level.

Forward Contracts Versus Options. To demonstrate the difference between hedging with forward contracts and hedging with options, let's examine a specific situation. In May 2008, the one-year forward exchange rate was $1.55 per euro. Instead of locking in this exchange rate using a forward contract, a firm that will need euros in one year can buy a call option on the euro, giving it the right to buy euros at a maximum price.[1] Suppose a one-year European call option on the euro with a strike price of $1.55 per euro trades for $0.05 per

---

[1]Currency options can be purchased over the counter from a bank or on an exchange. The Philadelphia Stock Exchange is one exchange offering currency options.

TABLE 23.1

Cost of Euros ($/€)
When Hedging with a
Currency Option with a
Strike Price of $1.55/€
and an Initial Premium
of $0.05/€

May 2009 Spot Exchange Rate	Exercise Option?	Exchange Rate Taken	+	Cost of Option	=	Total Cost
1.35	No	1.35		0.05		1.40
1.50	No	1.50		0.05		1.55
1.65	Yes	1.55		0.05		1.60
1.80	Yes	1.55		0.05		1.60

euro. That is, for a cost of $0.05 per euro, the firm can buy the right—but not the obligation—to purchase euros for $1.55 per euro in one year's time. By doing so, the firm protects itself against a large increase in the value of the euro but still benefits if the euro declines.

Table 23.1 shows the outcome from hedging with a call option if the actual exchange rate in one year is one of the values listed in the first column. If the spot exchange rate is less than the $1.55 per euro strike price of the option, then the firm will not exercise the option and will convert dollars to euros at the spot exchange rate. If the spot exchange rate is more than $1.55 per euro, the firm will exercise the option and convert dollars to euros at the rate of $1.55 per euro (see the second and third columns). We then add the initial cost of the option (fourth column) to determine the total dollar cost per euro paid by the firm (fifth column).[2]

We plot the data from Table 23.1 in Figure 23.8, where we compare hedging with options to the alternative of hedging with a forward contract or not hedging at all. If the firm does not hedge at all, its cost for euros is simply the spot exchange rate. If the firm hedges with a forward contract, it locks in the cost of euros at the forward exchange rate and the

FIGURE 23.8

Comparison of Hedging
the Exchange Rate
Using a Forward
Contract, an Option, or
No Hedge

The forward hedge locks in an exchange rate and so eliminates all risk. Not hedging leaves the firm fully exposed. Hedging with an option allows the firm to benefit if the exchange rate falls and protects the firm from a very large increase.

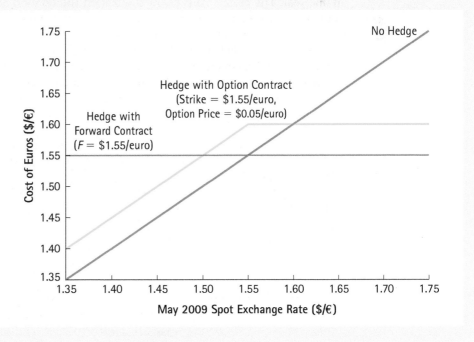

---

[2]In computing the total cost, we have ignored the small amount of interest that could have been earned on the option premium.

firm's cost is fixed. As Figure 23.8 shows, hedging with options represents a middle ground: The firm puts a *cap* on its potential cost but will benefit if the euro depreciates in value.

Advantages of Options. Why might a firm choose to hedge with options rather than forward contracts? Many managers want the firm to benefit if the exchange rate moves in its favor, rather than being stuck paying an above-market rate. Firms also prefer options to forward contracts if the transaction they are hedging might not take place. In this case, a forward contract could commit them to making an exchange at an unfavorable rate for currency they do not need, whereas an option allows them to walk away from the exchange. In any case, it is worth noting that an option holder can always sell the position at a gain rather than demanding delivery of the currency, so if the transaction does not take place and the option is in-the-money, the company need not actually demand delivery of the foreign currency.

CONCEPT CHECK

3. How can firms hedge exchange rate risk?

4. Why might a firm prefer to hedge exchange rate risk with options rather than forward contracts?

23.3 Internationally Integrated Capital Markets

Does the value of a foreign investment depend on the currency we use in the analysis? To address this important question, we will develop a conceptual benchmark based on the assumptions that any investor can exchange either currency in any amount at the spot rate or forward rates and is free to purchase or sell any security in any amount in either country at their current market prices. Under these conditions, which we term **internationally integrated capital markets**, the value of an investment does *not* depend on the currency we use in the analysis.

internationally integrated capital markets When any investor can exchange currencies in any amount at the spot or forward rates and is free to purchase or sell any security in any amount in any country at its current market prices.

Consider a share of Vodafone Group, PLC, trading on the London Stock Exchange. Vodafone does not pay dividends and you expect the share of stock to have a value of £260 in one year. The price of this share of stock on the London Stock Exchange is the present value of this cash flow using the cost of capital of a local investor. Assuming that the appropriate cost of capital for Vodafone is 13%, then we have: £260/1.13 = £230.09. If the spot exchange rate between dollars and pounds is $1.33/£, then the dollar cost to a U.S. investor who wants to purchase this share of stock will be $306.02 (£230.09 × $1.33/£).

Now any U.S. investor who actually purchased a share of Vodafone would have to convert the future pounds cash flow when they sell it into dollars, so the payoff to such an investor is the dollar cash flow it produces. To value this cash flow, assume that the U.S. investor contracts today to convert the *expected* cash flow in one period at the forward rate, for example $1.36/£. If we assume that spot exchange rates and the foreign currency cash flows of the security are uncorrelated, then this U.S. investor's expected dollar cash flow is $353.60 (£260 × $1.36/£). If 15.55% is the appropriate cost of capital from the standpoint of a U.S. investor, the present value of this expected cash flow is $353.60/1.1555 = $306.02, which is the dollar cost of buying a share of Vodafone today. In fact, the Valuation Principle tells us that the dollar present value of the expected cash flow must be equal to what the U.S. investor paid for the security:

$$\underbrace{\$1.33/\pounds}_{\text{Spot exchange rate}} \times \underbrace{\frac{\pounds 260}{(1.13)}}_{\substack{\text{Expected } \pounds \text{ cash flow} \\ \text{discounted at } \pounds \\ \text{discount rate}}} = \underbrace{\frac{\overbrace{\$1.36/\pounds \times \pounds 260}^{\text{Forward rate times expected } \pounds \text{ cash flow}}}{\underbrace{1.1555}_{1 + \$ \text{ discount rate}}}}_{\substack{\$ \text{ cash flow discounted at} \\ \$ \text{ discount rate}}}$$

Using $r_\$^*$ for dollar discount rate and r_{FC}^* for foreign currency discount rate, we can write this more generally as:

$$\text{Spot Rate} \times \frac{\text{Foreign Cash Flow}}{(1 + r_{FC}^*)} = \frac{\text{Forward Rate} \times \text{Foreign Cash Flow}}{(1 + r_\$^*)}$$

Rearranging terms we have:

$$\text{Forward \$/FC Rate} = \frac{(1 + r_\$^*)}{(1 + r_{FC}^*)} \times \text{Spot \$/FC Rate} \qquad (23.3)$$

This condition ought to look familiar, because Eq. 23.3 is simply covered interest parity (Eq. 23.1), here derived for risky cash flows rather than risk-free cash flows.

EXAMPLE 23.4

Present Values and Internationally Integrated Capital Markets

MyFinanceLab

PROBLEM

You are a U.S. investor trying to calculate the present value of a ¥10 million cash flow that will occur one year in the future. The spot exchange rate is ¥110/$ and the one-year forward rate is ¥105.8095/$. The appropriate dollar cost of capital for this cash flow is $r_\$^* = 5\%$ and the appropriate yen cost of capital for this cash flow is $r_¥^* = 1\%$. What is the dollar present value of the ¥10 million cash flow from the standpoint of a Japanese investor? What is the present value of the ¥10 million cash flow from the standpoint of a U.S. investor who first converts the ¥10 million into dollars and then applies the dollar discount rate?

SOLUTION

PLAN

For the Japanese investor, we can compute the present value of the future yen cash flow at the yen discount rate and use the spot exchange rate to convert that amount to dollars.

For the U.S. investor, we can convert the future yen cash flow to dollars at the forward rate and compute the present value using the dollar discount rate.

We know:

$$\text{Future CF} = \text{¥10 million}, \quad \text{one-year forward rate} = \text{¥105.8095/\$}$$

$$r_\$^* = 0.05 \qquad\qquad \text{spot rate} = \text{¥110/\$}$$

$$r_¥^* = 0.10$$

EXECUTE

For the Japanese investor, the dollar present value of the yen cash flow is:

$$\frac{\text{Yen Cash Flows}}{(1 + \text{Yen Discount Rate})} \times \text{Spot Rate} = \frac{\text{¥10,000,000}}{1.01} \times (\text{\$1/¥110}) = \$90,009$$

For a U.S. investor who first converts the ¥10 million into dollars using the forward rate and then applies the dollar cost of capital:

$$\frac{\text{Yen Cash Flows} \times \text{Forward Rate}}{(1 + \text{Dollar Discount Rate})} = \frac{\text{¥10,000,000} \times (\text{\$1/¥105.8095})}{1.05} = \$90,009$$

EVALUATE

Because the U.S. and Japanese capital markets are internationally integrated, both methods produce the same result.

COMMON MISTAKE

Forgetting to Flip the Exchange Rate

Note that in Example 23.4 we had exchange rates in terms of yen per dollar, for example ¥110/$. However, we needed to convert yen into dollars, so we multiplied the present value in yen by the *reciprocal* of the exchange rate: $1/¥110. Note that this is the same as dividing the yen present value by ¥110/$ to find the number of dollars. It is common when working with exchange rates to lose track of which currency should be in the numerator and which should be in the denominator. It is best to always write

down the cash flows along with their currency signs so that you can keep track of them. Then by crossing out currency signs as you go, you can be sure that you will be left with an answer in the correct currency:

$$\frac{\text{Yen Cash Flows}}{(1 + \text{Yen Discount Rate})} \times \text{Spot Rate}$$

$$= \frac{10,000,000}{1.01} \times \left(\frac{\$1}{110}\right) = \$90,009$$

CONCEPT CHECK

5. What assumptions are needed to have internationally integrated capital markets?

6. What implication do internationally integrated capital markets have for the value of the same asset in different countries?

23.4 Valuation of Foreign Currency Cash Flows

The most obvious difference between a domestic project and a foreign project is that the foreign project will most likely generate cash flows in a foreign currency. If the foreign project is owned by a domestic corporation, managers and shareholders need to determine the home currency value of the foreign currency cash flows.

In an internationally integrated capital market, two equivalent methods are available for calculating the NPV of a foreign project:

1. Calculate the NPV in the foreign country and convert it to the local currency at the spot rate.

2. Convert the cash flows of the foreign project into the local currency and then calculate the NPV of these cash flows.

The first method is essentially what we have done throughout this book (calculating the NPV of a project in a single currency) with the added step at the end of converting the NPV into the local currency using spot rates. Because this method should be familiar to you at this stage, we will concentrate on the second method. The second valuation method requires converting the expected dollar value of the foreign currency cash flows and then proceeding to value the project as if it were a domestic project.

Application: Ityesi, Inc.

Ityesi, Inc., a manufacturer of custom packaging products headquartered in the United States, wants to apply the weighted average cost of capital (WACC) technique to value a project in the United Kingdom. Ityesi is considering introducing a new line of packaging in the U.K. that will be its first foreign project. The project will be completely self-contained in the U.K., such that all revenues are generated and all costs are incurred there.

Engineers expect the technology used in the new products to be obsolete after four years. The marketing group expects annual sales of £37.5 million per year for this product line. Manufacturing costs and operating expenses are expected to total £15.625 million and £5.625 million per year, respectively. Developing the product will require an up-front investment of £15 million in capital equipment that will be obsolete in four years and an initial marketing expense of £4.167 million. Ityesi pays a corporate tax rate of 40%, no matter in which country it manufactures its products. The spreadsheet in Table 23.2 projects the expected pound free cash flows of the proposed project.

TABLE 23.2

Expected Foreign Free
Cash Flows from
Ityesi's U.K. Project

	Year	0	1	2	3	4
1	Year	0	1	2	3	4
2	**Incremental Earnings Forecast (£ million)**					
3	Sales	—	37.500	37.500	37.500	37.500
4	Cost of Goods Sold	—	−15.625	−15.625	−15.625	−15.625
5	**Gross Profit**	—	21.875	21.875	21.875	21.875
6	Operating Expenses	−4.167	−5.625	−5.625	−5.625	−5.625
7	Depreciation	—	−3.750	−3.750	−3.750	−3.750
8	**EBIT**	−4.167	12.500	12.500	12.500	12.500
9	Income Tax at 40%	1.667	−5.000	−5.000	−5.000	−5.000
10	**Unlevered Net Income**	−2.500	7.500	7.500	7.500	7.500
11	**Free Cash Flow**					
12	Plus: Depreciation	—	3.750	3.750	3.750	3.750
13	Less: Capital Expenditures	−15.000	—	—	—	—
14	Less: Increases in NWC	—	—	—	—	—
15	**Pound Free Cash Flow**	−17.500	11.250	11.250	11.250	11.250

Ityesi's managers have determined that there is no correlation between the uncertainty in these cash flows and the uncertainty in the spot dollar–pound exchange rate. As we explained in the last section, under this condition, the expected value of the future cash flows in dollars is the expected value in pounds multiplied by the forward exchange rate. Obtaining forward rate quotes for as long as four years in the future is difficult, so Ityesi's managers have decided to use the covered interest rate parity formula (Eq. 23.2) to compute the forward rates.

Forward Exchange Rates. The current spot exchange rate, S, is \$1.60/£. Suppose that the yield curve in both countries is flat: The risk-free rate on dollars, $r_\$$, is 4%, and the risk-free interest rate on pounds, $r_£$, is 7%. Using the covered interest parity condition for a multiyear forward exchange rate (Eq. 23.2), we have:

$$F_1 = S \times \frac{(1+r_\$)}{(1+r_£)} = (\$1.60/£)\frac{(1.04)}{(1.07)} = \$1.5551/£$$

$$F_2 = S \times \frac{(1+r_\$)^2}{(1+r_£)^2} = (\$1.60/£)\frac{(1.04)^2}{(1.07)^2} = \$1.5115/£$$

$$F_3 = S \times \frac{(1+r_\$)^3}{(1+r_£)^3} = (\$1.60/£)\frac{(1.04)^3}{(1.07)^3} = \$1.4692/£$$

$$F_4 = S \times \frac{(1+r_\$)^4}{(1+r_£)^4} = (\$1.60/£)\frac{(1.04)^4}{(1.07)^4} = \$1.4280/£$$

Free Cash Flow Conversion. Using these forward exchange rates, we can now calculate the expected free cash flows in dollars by multiplying the expected cash flows in pounds by the forward exchange rate, as shown in the spreadsheet in Table 23.3.

TABLE 23.3

Expected Dollar Free
Cash Flows from
Ityesi's U.K. Project

	Year	0	1	2	3	4
1	Year	0	1	2	3	4
2	**Dollar Free Cash Flow ($ million)**					
3	Pound FCF (£ million)	−17.500	11.250	11.250	11.250	11.250
4	Forward Exchange Rate ($/£)	1.6000	1.5551	1.5115	1.4692	1.4280
5	**Dollar Value of Pound FCF (3 × 4)**	−28.000	17.495	17.004	16.528	16.065

TABLE 23.4

Ityesi's Current Market Value Balance Sheet ($ million) and Cost of Capital Without the U.K. Project

Assets		Liabilities		Cost of Capital	
Cash	20	Debt	320	Debt	6%
Existing Assets	600	Equity	300	Equity	10%
	620		620		

The Value of Ityesi's Foreign Project with WACC. With the cash flows of the U.K. project now expressed in dollars, we can value the foreign project as if it were a domestic U.S. project. We proceed, as we did in Chapter 12, under the assumption that the market risk of the U.K. project is similar to that of the company as a whole; as a consequence, we can use Ityesi's costs of equity and debt in the United States to calculate the WACC.[3]

Ityesi has built up $20 million in cash for investment needs and has debt of $320 million, so its net debt is $D = \$320 - \$20 = \$300$ million. This amount is equal to the market value of its equity (E), implying a (net) debt-equity ratio of 1. Ityesi intends to maintain a similar (net) debt-equity ratio for the foreseeable future. The WACC thus assigns equal weights to equity and debt, as shown in Table 23.4.

With Ityesi's cost of equity (r_E) at 10% and its cost of debt (r_D) at 6%, we calculate Ityesi's WACC as follows:

$$r_{wacc} = r_E \frac{E}{E+D} + r_D(1 - T_C)\frac{D}{E+D}$$

$$= (10.0\%)(0.5) + (6.0\%)(1 - 40\%)(0.5) = 6.8\%$$

We can now determine the value of the foreign project, including the tax shield from debt, by calculating the present value of the future free cash flows using the WACC:

$$\frac{17.495}{1.068} + \frac{17.004}{1.068^2} + \frac{16.528}{1.068^3} + \frac{16.065}{1.068^4} = \$57.20 \text{ million}$$

Because the up-front cost of launching the product line in dollars is only $28 million, the net present value is $57.20 - $28 = $29.20 million. Thus, Ityesi should undertake the U.K. project.

The Law of One Price as a Robustness Check

To arrive at the NPV of Ityesi's project required making a number of assumptions—for example, that international markets are integrated, and that the exchange rate and the cash flows of the project are uncorrelated. The managers of Ityesi will naturally worry about whether these assumptions are justified. Luckily, there is a way to check the analysis.

Recall that there are two ways to compute the NPV of the foreign project. Ityesi could just as easily have computed the foreign NPV by discounting the foreign cash flows at the foreign cost of capital and converting this result to a domestic NPV using the spot rate. Except for the last step, this method requires doing the same calculation we have performed throughout this book—that is, calculate the NPV of a (domestic) project. Determining the NPV requires knowing the cost of capital—in this case, the cost of capital for an investment in the United Kingdom. Recall that to estimate this cost of capital we use

---

[3]The risk of the foreign project is unlikely to be *exactly* the same as the risk of domestic projects (or the firm as a whole), because the foreign project contains residual exchange rate risk that the domestic projects often do not contain. In Ityesi's case, managers have determined that the additional risk premium for this risk is small, so for practical purposes they have chosen to ignore it and just use the domestic cost of capital.

return data for publicly traded single-product companies—in this case, U.K. firms. For this method to provide the same answer as the alternative method, the estimate for the foreign cost of capital, $r_£^*$, must satisfy the Law of One Price, which from Eq. 23.3 implies:

$$(1 + r_£^*) = \frac{\text{Spot \$/£ Rate}}{\text{Forward \$/£ Rate}} (1 + r_\$^*) \qquad (23.4)$$

If it does not, then Ityesi's managers should be concerned that the simplifying assumptions in their analysis are not valid: Market frictions exist so that the market integration assumption is not a good approximation of reality, or perhaps there is a significant correlation between spot exchange rates and cash flows.

We can rewrite Eq. 23.4 as follows. Using the covered interest rate parity relation (Eq. 23.1), we have:

$$\frac{\text{Spot \$/£ Rate}}{\text{Forward \$/£ Rate}} = \frac{1 + r_£}{1 + r_\$} \qquad (23.5)$$

Here, $r_£$ and $r_\$$ are the foreign and domestic risk-free interest rates, respectively. Combining Eqs. 23.4 and 23.5, and rearranging terms gives the foreign cost of capital in terms of the domestic cost of capital and interest rates:

The Foreign-Denominated Cost of Capital

$$r_£^* = \frac{1 + r_£}{1 + r_\$} (1 + r_\$^*) - 1 \qquad (23.6)$$

If the simplifying assumptions Ityesi made in calculating the NPV of its U.K. project are valid, then the cost of capital estimate calculated using Eq. 23.6 will be close to the cost of the capital estimate calculated directly using comparable single-product companies in the United Kingdom.

EXAMPLE 23.5

Internationalizing the Cost of Capital

MyFinanceLab

PROBLEM

Use the Law of One Price to infer the pound WACC from Ityesi's dollar WACC. Verify that the NPV of Ityesi's project is the same when its pound free cash flows are discounted at this WACC and converted at the spot rate.

SOLUTION

PLAN

We can use Eq. 23.6 to compute the pound WACC. The market data we need is:

$$r_£ = 0.07, \ r_\$ = 0.04, \ r_\$^* = 0.068.$$

Finally, we'll need the spot exchange rate ($1.60/£) to convert the pound NPV to dollars.

EXECUTE

Applying Eq. 23.6, we have

$$r_£^* = \frac{1 + r_£}{1 + r_\$} (1 + r_\$^*) - 1 = \left(\frac{1.07}{1.04}\right)(1.068) - 1 = 0.0988$$

The pound WACC is 9.88%.

We can now use Ityesi's pound WACC to calculate the present value of the pound free cash flows in Table 23.3:

$$\frac{11.25}{1.0988} + \frac{11.25}{1.0988^2} + \frac{11.25}{1.0988^3} + \frac{11.25}{1.0988^4} = £ \ 35.75 \text{ million}$$

(Continued)

> The NPV in pounds of the investment opportunity is £35.75 − £17.5 = £18.25 million. Converting this amount to dollars at the spot rate gives £18.25 million × $1.6/£ = $29.20 million, which is exactly the NPV we calculated before.
>
> **EVALUATE**
>
> The U.S. and U.K. markets are integrated and our simplifying assumptions for the WACC valuation method are valid.

7. Explain two methods we use to calculate the NPV of a foreign project.

8. When do these two methods give the same NPV of the foreign project?

23.5 Valuation and International Taxation

In this chapter, we assume that Ityesi pays a corporate tax rate of 40% no matter where its earnings are generated. In practice, determining the corporate tax rate on foreign income is complicated because corporate income taxes must be paid to two national governments: the host government (the United Kingdom in this example) and the home government (the United States). If the foreign project is a separately incorporated subsidiary of the parent company, the amount of taxes a firm pays generally depends on the amount of profits **repatriated** (brought back to the home country). International taxation is a complex subject to which specialized experts devote considerable time. In this introductory setting, we aim only to provide a broad overview and sense of the issues involved.

repatriated Refers to the profits from a foreign project that a firm brings back to its home country.

A Single Foreign Project with Immediate Repatriation of Earnings

We begin by assuming that the firm has a single foreign project and that all foreign profits are repatriated immediately. The general international arrangement prevailing with respect to taxation of corporate profits is that the host country gets the first opportunity to tax income produced within its borders. The home government then gets an opportunity to tax the income to the domestic firm from a foreign project. In particular, the home government must establish a tax policy specifying its treatment of foreign income and foreign taxes paid on that income. In addition, it needs to establish the timing of taxation.

Tax policy in the United States requires U.S. corporations to pay taxes on their foreign income at the same rate as profits earned in the United States. However, a full tax credit is given for foreign taxes paid *up to* the amount of the U.S. tax liability. In other words, if the foreign tax rate is less than the U.S. tax rate, the company pays total taxes equal to the U.S. tax rate on its foreign earnings. It does this by first paying the foreign tax rate and then paying the *additional* amount of tax due up to the U.S. rate. In this case, all the company's earnings are taxed at the same rate no matter where they are earned—the working assumption we used for Ityesi.

If the foreign tax rate exceeds the U.S. tax rate, companies must pay this higher rate on foreign earnings. Because the U.S. tax credit exceeds the amount of U.S. taxes owed, no tax is owed in the United States. Note that U.S. tax policy does not allow companies to apply the part of the tax credit that is not used to offset domestic taxes owed, so this extra tax credit is wasted. In this scenario, companies pay a higher tax rate on foreign income and a lower (U.S.) tax rate on income generated in the United States.

Multiple Foreign Projects and Deferral of Earnings Repatriation

Thus far, we have assumed that the firm has only one foreign project and that it repatriates earnings immediately. Neither assumption is realistic. Firms can lower their taxes by pooling multiple foreign projects and deferring the repatriation of earnings. Let's begin by considering the benefits of pooling the income on all foreign projects.

Pooling Multiple Foreign Projects. Under U.S. tax law, a multinational corporation may use any excess tax credits generated in high-tax foreign countries to offset its net U.S. tax liabilities on earnings in low-tax foreign countries. In this way, it pools all foreign taxes together and compares the total to its total U.S. tax liability on foreign income. Thus, if the U.S. tax rate exceeds the combined tax rate on all foreign income, it is valid to assume that the firm pays the same tax rate on all income no matter where it is earned. Otherwise, the firm must pay a higher tax rate on its foreign income.

Deferring Repatriation of Earnings. Now consider an opportunity to defer repatriation of foreign profits. This consideration is important because if the foreign operation is set up as a separately incorporated subsidiary (rather than as a foreign branch), U.S. tax liability is not incurred until the profits are brought back home. If a company chooses not to repatriate £12.5 million in pretax earnings, for example, it effectively reinvests those earnings abroad and defers its U.S. tax liability. When the foreign tax rates exceed the U.S. tax rates, there are no benefits to deferral because in such a case there is no additional U.S. tax liability.

When the foreign tax rate is less than the U.S. tax rate, deferral can provide significant benefits. Deferring repatriation of earnings lowers the overall tax burden in much the same way as deferring capital gains lowers the tax burden imposed by the capital gains tax. Other benefits from deferral arise because the firm effectively gains a real option to repatriate income at times when repatriation might be cheaper. For example, we have already noted that by pooling foreign income, the firm effectively pays the combined tax rate on all foreign income. Because the income generated across countries changes, this combined tax rate will vary from year to year. In years in which it exceeds the U.S. tax rate, the repatriation of additional income does not incur an additional U.S. tax liability, so the earnings can be repatriated tax free.

CONCEPT CHECK

9. What tax rate should we use to value a foreign project?

10. How can a U.S. firm lower its taxes on foreign projects?

23.6 Internationally Segmented Capital Markets

To this point, we have worked under the assumption that international capital markets are integrated. Often, however, this assumption is not appropriate. In some countries, especially in the developing world, all investors do not have equal access to financial securities. In this section, we consider why countries' capital markets might not be integrated—a case called **segmented capital markets**.

segmented capital markets Capital markets that are not internationally integrated.

Many of the interesting questions in international corporate finance address the issues that result when capital markets are internationally segmented. In this section, we briefly consider the main reasons for segmentation of the capital markets and the implications for international corporate finance.

Differential Access to Markets

In some cases, a country's risk-free securities are internationally integrated but markets for a specific firm's securities are not. Firms may face differential access to markets if there is any kind of asymmetry with respect to information about them. For example, Ityesi may be well known in the United States and enjoy easy access to dollar equity and debt markets there because it regularly provides information to an established community of analysts tracking the firm. It may not be as well known in the United Kingdom and, therefore, may have difficulty tapping into the pound capital markets because it has no track record there. For this reason, investors in the United Kingdom may require a higher rate of return to persuade them to hold pound stocks and bonds issued by the U.S. firm.

With differential access to national markets, Ityesi would face a higher pound WACC than the pound WACC implied by Eq. 23.6. Ityesi would then view the foreign project as less valuable if it raises capital in the United Kingdom rather than in the United States. In fact, to maximize shareholder value, the firm should raise capital at home; the method of valuing the foreign project as if it were a domestic project would then provide the correct NPV. Differential access to national capital markets is common enough that it provides the best explanation for the existence of **currency swaps**, in which two parties agree to "swap" bond payments in different currencies. Specifically, the holder of the swap receives coupons in one currency and pays coupons denominated in a different currency. Currency swaps generally also have final face value payments, also in different currencies. Using a currency swap, a firm can borrow in the market where it has the best access to capital, and then "swap" the coupon and principal payments to whichever currency it would prefer to make payments in. Thus, swaps allow firms to mitigate their exchange rate risk exposure between assets and liabilities, while still making investments and raising funds in the most attractive locales.

currency swaps A contract in which parties agree to exchange coupon payments and a final face value payment that are in different currencies.

Macro-Level Distortions

Markets for risk-free instruments may also be segmented. Important macroeconomic reasons for segmented capital markets include capital controls and foreign exchange controls that create barriers to international capital flows and thus segment national markets. Many countries regulate or limit capital inflows or outflows, and many do not allow their currencies to be freely converted into dollars, thereby creating capital market segmentation. Similarly, some countries restrict who can hold financial securities.

Political, legal, social, and cultural characteristics that differ across countries may require compensation in the form of a country risk premium. For example, the rate of interest paid on government bonds or other securities in a country with a tradition of weak enforcement of property rights is not likely to truly be a risk-free rate. Instead, interest rates in the country will reflect a risk premium for the possibility of default, so relations such as covered interest rate parity will likely not hold exactly.

EXAMPLE 23.6

Risky Government Bonds

MyFinanceLab

PROBLEM

For May 23, 2008, *The Financial Times* reported a spot ruble–dollar exchange rate of R23.5937/$ and a one-year forward exchange rate of R24.2316/$. At the time, the yield on short-term Russian government bonds was about 5.7%, while the comparable one-year yield on U.S. Treasury securities was 2.1%. Using the covered interest parity relationship, calculate the implied one-year forward rate. Compare this rate to the actual forward rate, and explain why the two rates differ.

SOLUTION

PLAN

Using the covered interest parity formula, the implied forward rate is:

$$\text{Forward Rate} = \text{Spot Rate} \times \frac{(1 + r_R)}{(1 + r_\$)}$$

Thus, we need the spot exchange rate (R23.5937/$), the dollar interest rate ($r_\$ = 0.021$), and the ruble interest rate ($r_R = 0.057$).

EXECUTE

$$\text{Forward Rate} = \text{Spot Rate} \times \frac{(1 + r_R)}{(1 + r_\$)} = (\text{R23.5937/\$}) \frac{1.057}{1.021} = \text{R24.4256/\$}$$

The implied forward rate is higher than the current spot rate because Russian government bonds have higher yields than U.S. government bonds. The actual forward rate, however, is lower than the implied forward rate. The difference between the implied forward rate and the actual forward rate likely reflects the default risk in Russian government bonds (the Russian government defaulted on its debt as recently as 1998). A holder of 100,000 rubles seeking a true risk-free investment could convert the rubles to dollars, invest in U.S. Treasuries, and convert the proceeds back to rubles at a rate locked in with a forward contract. By doing so, the investor would earn:

$$\frac{R100{,}000}{R23.5937/\$ \text{ today}} \times \frac{\$1.021 \text{ in 1 yr}}{\$ \text{ today}} \times (R24.2316/\$ \text{ in 1 yr}) = R104{,}860 \text{ in 1 yr}$$

The effective ruble risk-free rate would be 4.860%.

EVALUATE

The higher rate of 5.7% on Russian bonds reflects a credit spread of $5.7\% - 4.860\% = 0.840\%$ to compensate bondholders for default risk.

Implications of Internationally Segmented Capital Markets

A segmented financial market has an important implication for international corporate finance: One country or currency has a higher rate of return than another country or currency, when the two rates are compared in the same currency. If the return difference results from a market friction such as capital controls, corporations can exploit this friction by setting up projects in the high-return country/currency and raising capital in the low-return country/currency. Of course, the extent to which corporations can capitalize on this strategy is naturally limited: If such a strategy was easy to implement, the return difference would quickly disappear as corporations competed to use the strategy. Nevertheless, certain corporations might realize a competitive advantage by implementing such a strategy. For example, as an incentive to invest, a foreign government might strike a deal with a particular corporation that relaxes capital controls for that corporation alone.

EXAMPLE 23.7

Valuing a Foreign Acquisition in a Segmented Market

MyFinanceLab

PROBLEM

Camacho Enterprises is a U.S. company that is considering expanding by acquiring Xtapa, Inc., a firm in Mexico. The acquisition is expected to increase Camacho's free cash flows by 21 million pesos the first year; this amount is then expected to grow at a rate of 8% per year. The price of the investment is 525 million pesos, which is $52.5 million at the current exchange rate of 10 pesos/$. Based on an analysis in the Mexican market, Camacho has determined that the appropriate after-tax peso WACC is 12%. If Camacho has also determined that its after-tax dollar WACC for this expansion is 7.5%, what is the value of the Mexican acquisition? Assume that the Mexican and U.S. markets for risk-free securities are integrated and that the yield curve in both countries is flat. The U.S. risk-free interest rates are 6%, and Mexican risk-free interest rates are 9%.

SOLUTION

PLAN

We can calculate the NPV of the expansion in pesos and convert the result into dollars at the spot rate. The free cash flows (in millions) are:

```
        0            1              2                3
        |            |              |                |          ...
  −525 pesos    21 pesos    21 (1.08) pesos   21 (1.08)² pesos
```

We can also compute the NPV in dollars by converting the expected cash flows into dollars using forward rates. The N-year forward rate (Eq. 23.2) expressed in pesos/$ is:

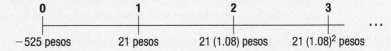

$$F_N = S \times \frac{(1 + r_{\text{p}})^N}{(1 + r_{\$})^N} = 10 \times \left(\frac{1.09}{1.06}\right)^N = 10 \times 1.0283^N = 10.283 \times 1.0283^{N-1}$$

(Continued)

EXECUTE

The net present value of the peso cash flows at the peso WACC is:

$$NPV = \frac{21 \text{ pesos}}{0.12 - 0.08} - 525 \text{ pesos} = 0$$

Thus, the purchase is a zero-NPV transaction. Presumably, Camacho is competing with other Mexican companies for the purchase.

To compute the NPV using the dollar WACC, we need to convert the peso cash flows to dollar cash flows. The dollar-expected cash flows are the peso cash flows, denoted C^N_{pesos}, (from the earlier timeline) converted at the appropriate forward rate, F_N. We divide by the forward rate because it is in pesos/$:

$$C^N_{pesos}/F_N = \frac{21\,(\,1.08\,)^{N-1}}{10.283 \times 1.0283^{N-1}} = 2.0422 \times 1.0503^{N-1}$$

The dollar-expected cash flows are therefore:

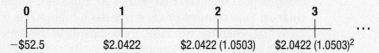

Thus, the dollar cash flows grow at about 5% per year. The NPV of these cash flows is:

$$NPV = \frac{\$2.0422}{0.075 - 0.0503} - \$52.5 = \$30.18 \text{ million}$$

EVALUATE

We calculated two different NPVs, but which NPV more accurately represents the benefits of the expansion? The answer depends on the source of the difference. To compute the dollar-expected cash flows by converting the peso-expected cash flows at the forward rate, we must accept the assumption that spot rates and the project cash flows are uncorrelated. The difference might simply reflect that this assumption failed to hold. Another possibility is that the difference reflects estimation error in the respective WACC estimates.

If Camacho is relatively confident in its assumptions about spot rates and its WACC estimates, a third possibility is that Mexican and U.S. capital markets are not integrated. In this case, Camacho, because of its access to U.S. capital markets, might have a competitive advantage. Perhaps other companies with which it is competing for the purchase of Xtapa are all Mexican firms that do not have access to capital markets outside of Mexico. Hence, Camacho can raise capital at a cheaper rate. Of course, this argument also requires that other U.S. companies not be competing for the purchase of Xtapa. Camacho, however, might have special knowledge of Xtapa's markets that other U.S.-based companies lack. This knowledge would give Camacho a competitive advantage in the product market over other U.S. companies and would put it on an equal footing in the product market with other Mexican companies. Because it would have a competitive advantage in capital markets over other Mexican companies, the NPV of the purchase would be positive for Camacho, but zero for the other bidders for Xtapa.

As Example 23.7 demonstrates, the existence of segmented capital markets makes many decisions in international corporate finance more complicated but potentially more lucrative for a firm that is well positioned to exploit the market segmentation.

CONCEPT CHECK

11. What are the reasons for segmentation of capital markets?

12. What is the main implication for international corporate finance of a segmented financial market?

23.7   Capital Budgeting with Exchange Rate Risk

The final issue that arises when a firm is considering a foreign project is that the cash flows of the project may be affected by exchange rate risk. The risk is that the cash flows generated by the project will depend upon the future level of the exchange rate. A large part of international corporate finance addresses this foreign exchange risk. This section offers an overview with respect to valuation of foreign currency cash flows.

The working assumptions made thus far in this chapter are that the project's free cash flows are uncorrelated with the spot exchange rates. Such an assumption often makes sense if the firm operates as a local firm in the foreign market—it purchases its inputs and sells its outputs in that market, and price changes of the inputs and outputs are uncorrelated with exchange rates. However, many firms use imported inputs in their production processes or export some of their output to foreign countries. These scenarios alter the nature of a project's foreign exchange risk and, in turn, change the valuation of the foreign currency cash flows.

Application: Ityesi, Inc.

As an example, let's reconsider what happens if the Ityesi project in the United Kingdom imports some materials from the United States. In this case, the project's pound free cash flows will be correlated with exchange rates. Assuming the cost of the material in the United States remains stable, if the value of a dollar appreciates against the pound, the pound cost of these materials will increase, thereby reducing the pound free cash flows. The reverse is also true: If the dollar depreciates, then the pound free cash flows will increase. Hence, our working assumption that changes in the free cash flows are uncorrelated with changes in the exchange rate is violated. It is no longer appropriate to calculate the expected dollar free cash flows by converting the expected pound free cash flows at the forward rate.

Whenever a project has cash flows that depend on the values of multiple currencies, the most convenient approach is to separate the cash flows according to the currency they depend on. For example, a fraction of Ityesi's manufacturing costs may be for inputs whose costs fluctuate with the value of the dollar. Specifically, suppose £5.625 million of the costs are denominated in pounds, and an additional $16 million (or £10 million at the current exchange rate of $1.60/£) is for inputs whose price fluctuates with the value of the dollar. In this case, we would calculate Ityesi's pound-denominated free cash flows excluding these dollar-based costs, as shown in Table 23.5.

TABLE 23.5

Ityesi's Pound-Denominated Free Cash Flows

1	**Year**	**0**	**1**	**2**	**3**	**4**
2	**Incremental Earnings Forecast (£ million)**					
3	Sales	—	37.500	37.500	37.500	37.500
4	Cost of Goods Sold	—	−5.625	−5.625	−5.625	−5.625
5	**Gross Profit**	—	31.875	31.875	31.875	31.875
6	Operating Expenses	−4.167	−5.625	−5.625	−5.625	−5.625
7	Depreciation	—	−3.750	−3.750	−3.750	−3.750
8	**EBIT**	−4.167	22.500	22.500	22.500	22.500
9	Income Tax at 40%	1.667	−9.000	−9.000	−9.000	−9.000
10	**Unlevered Net Income**	−2.500	13.500	13.500	13.500	13.500
11	**Free Cash Flow**					
12	Plus: Depreciation	—	3.750	3.750	3.750	3.750
13	Less: Capital Expenditures	−15.000	—	—	—	—
14	Less: Increases in NWC	—	—	—	—	—
15	**Pound Free Cash Flow**	**−17.500**	**17.250**	**17.250**	**17.250**	**17.250**

If the revenues and costs in the spreadsheet in Table 23.5 are not affected by changes in the spot exchange rates, it makes sense to assume that changes in the free cash flows are uncorrelated with changes in the spot exchange rates. Hence, we can convert the pound-denominated free cash flows to equivalent dollar amounts using the forward exchange rate, as we did in Section 23.4. The spreadsheet shown in Table 23.6 performs this calculation, with the dollar value of the pound-denominated free cash flow shown in line 5.

Next, we add the dollar-based cash flows to determine the project's aggregate free cash flow in dollar terms. This calculation is done in lines 6 through 8 of Table 23.6. Note that

TABLE 23.6

Expected Dollar Free
Cash Flows from
Ityesi's U.K. Project

	Year	0	1	2	3	4
1						
2	**Dollar Free Cash Flow ($ million)**					
3	Pound FCF (£ million)	−17.500	17.250	17.250	17.250	17.250
4	Forward Exchange Rate ($/£)	1.6000	1.5551	1.5115	1.4692	1.4280
5	**Dollar Value of Pound FCF** (3 × 4)	−28.000	26.825	26.073	25.344	24.633
6	Dollar Costs	—	−16.000	−16.000	−16.000	−16.000
7	Income Tax at 40%	—	6.400	6.400	6.400	6.400
8	**Free Cash Flow**	**−28.000**	**17.225**	**16.473**	**15.744**	**15.033**

we deduct Ityesi's dollar-denominated costs, and then add the tax shield associated with these costs. Even if the taxes will be paid in pounds in the U.K., they will fluctuate with the dollar cost of the inputs and so can be viewed as a dollar-denominated cash flow.

Given the dollar-denominated free cash flow in line 8 of Table 23.6, we can now compute the NPV of the investment using Ityesi's dollar WACC:[4]

$$\frac{\$17.225}{1.068} + \frac{\$16.473}{1.068^2} + \frac{\$15.744}{1.068^3} + \frac{\$15.033}{1.068^4} - \$28.000 = \$27.05 \text{ million.}$$

Conclusion

The Ityesi example was simplified because we could easily isolate the cash flows that would vary perfectly with the dollar-pound exchange rate from those that would be uncorrelated with the exchange rate. In practice, determining these sensitivities may be difficult. If historical data are available, the tools of regression can be used to identify the exchange rate risk of project cash flows, in much the same way that we used regression to identify the market risk of security returns in Part 4 of the text.

International capital budgeting is sufficiently complicated that entire textbooks have been devoted to it. Hence, it is difficult to do justice to this issue in a single chapter's treatment. Nonetheless, we have provided a basic framework for approaching the problem.

CONCEPT
CHECK

13. What conditions cause the cash flows of a foreign project to be affected by exchange rate risk?

14. How do we make adjustments when a project has inputs and outputs in different currencies?

MyFinanceLab

Here is what you should know after reading this chapter. MyFinanceLab will help you identify what you know, and where to go when you need to practice.

KEY POINTS AND EQUATIONS	KEY TERMS	ONLINE PRACTICE
23.1 Foreign Exchange • The foreign exchange market is where currencies are traded. • It has very high volume, is dominated by large international banks, and operates 24 hours a day during the business week. • An exchange rate is a price for one currency denominated in another currency.	foreign exchange (FX or forex) market, p. 718 foreign exchange rate, p. 718	MyFinanceLab Study Plan 23.1

---

[4]We again use the domestic WACC to discount the cash flows because we continue to assume that any additional risk premium for the exchange rate risk is small. If this assumption does not hold, then the dollar costs and the dollar value of the expected pound free cash flows would have to be discounted at different rates to reflect the additional exchange rate risk in the pound free cash flows.

23.2 Exchange Rate Risk

- Firms can manage exchange rate risk in financial markets using currency forward contracts to lock in an exchange rate in advance, and using currency options contracts to protect against an exchange rate moving beyond a certain level.
- The cash-and-carry strategy is an alternative strategy that provides the same cash flows as the currency forward contract. By the Law of One Price, we determine the forward exchange rate by the cost-of-carry formula, called the covered interest parity equation. Using "FC" to represent any foreign currency, for an exchange that will take place in 1 year, the corresponding forward exchange rate in FC per $ is:

$$\text{Forward Rate} = \text{Spot Rate} \times \frac{(1 + r_{FC})}{(1 + r_\$)} \quad (23.1)$$

- Currency options allow firms to insure themselves against the exchange rate moving beyond a certain level. A firm may choose to use options rather than forward contracts if:
  - It would like to benefit from favorable exchange rate movements but not be obligated to make an exchange at unfavorable rates.
  - There is some chance that the transaction it is hedging will not take place.

23.3 Internationally Integrated Capital Markets

- The condition necessary to ensure internationally integrated capital markets is that the value of a foreign investment does not depend on the currency (home or foreign) used in the analysis.
- Two methods are used to value foreign currency cash flows when markets are internationally integrated and uncertainty in spot exchange rates are uncorrelated with the foreign currency cash flows:
  - Compute the expected value of the foreign currency cash flows in the home currency by multiplying the expected value in the foreign currency by the forward exchange rates, and then compute the NPV of these home currency cash flows using the domestic cost of capital.
  - Calculate the foreign currency value of a foreign project as the NPV of the expected foreign currency future cash flows discounted at the foreign cost of capital, and then convert the foreign currency NPV into the home currency using the current spot exchange rate.

23.4 Valuation of Foreign Currency Cash Flows • When markets are internationally integrated and uncertainty in spot exchange rates is uncorrelated with the foreign currency cash flows, the foreign and domestic WACCs are related as follows (using "FC" for the foreign currency): $$r^*_{FC} = \frac{1 + r_{FC}}{1 + r_{\$}}(1 + r^*_{\$}) - 1 \qquad (23.6)$$		MyFinanceLab Study Plan 23.4 Spreadsheet Table 23.2
23.5 Valuation and International Taxation • A U.S. corporation pays the higher of the foreign or domestic tax rate on its foreign project, so project valuation should use the higher of these two rates as well. The U.S. corporation may be able to reduce its tax liability by undertaking foreign projects in other countries whose earnings can be pooled with those of the new project or by deferring the repatriation of earnings.	repatriated, p. 736	MyFinanceLab Study Plan 23.5
23.6 Internationally Segmented Capital Markets • Capital markets might be internationally segmented. The implication is that one country or currency has a higher cost of capital than another country or currency, when the two are compared in the same currency.	currency swaps, p. 738 segmented capital markets, p. 737	MyFinanceLab Study Plan 23.6
23.7 Capital Budgeting with Exchange Rate Risk • When a project has inputs and outputs in different currencies, the foreign-denominated cash flows are likely to be correlated with changes in spot rates. To correctly value such projects, the foreign and domestic cash flows should be valued separately.		MyFinanceLab Study Plan 23.7 Spreadsheet Table 23.5 Spreadsheet Table 23.6

CRITICAL THINKING

1. How is an exchange rate used?

2. What are some reasons a financial manager would need to access the foreign exchange market?

3. What are the differences between hedging exchange rate risk with options versus forwards?

4. What does it mean to say that international capital markets are integrated?

5. What assumptions are necessary to value foreign cash flows using the domestic WACC method?

6. How are U.S. firms taxed on their foreign earnings?

7. If international markets are segmented, how does that change the way the financial manager approaches valuation problems?

8. How does exchange rate risk affect our approach to valuation?

PROBLEMS   *All problems are available in* MyFinanceLab. *The* *icon indicates problems that are easier to solve using Excel and have data in an Excel format available in* MyFinanceLab. *An asterisk * indicates problems with a higher level of difficulty.*

Foreign Exchange

1. You have just landed in London with $500 in your wallet. Stopping at the foreign exchange booth, you see that pounds are being quoted at $1.95/£. For how many pounds can you exchange your $500?

2. Your firm needs to pay its French supplier €500,000. If the exchange rate is €0.65/$, how many dollars will you need to make the exchange?

Exchange Rate Risk

3. Your start-up company has negotiated a contract to provide a database installation for a manufacturing company in Poland. That firm has agreed to pay you $100,000 in three months when the installation will occur. However, it insists on paying in Polish zloty (PLN). You don't want to lose the deal (the company is your first client!), but you are worried about the exchange rate risk. In particular, you are worried the zloty could depreciate relative to the dollar. You contact Fortis Bank in Poland to see if you can lock in an exchange rate for the zloty in advance.
   a. Assume that the current spot exchange rate is 2.3117 PLN per U.S. dollar and that the three-month forward exchange rate is 2.2595 PLN per U.S. dollar. How many zloty should you demand in the contract to receive $100,000 in three months if you hedge the exchange rate risk with a forward contract?
   b. Given the bank forward rates in (a), were short-term interest rates higher or lower in Poland than in the United States at the time? Explain.

4. You are a broker for frozen seafood products for Choyce Products. You just signed a deal with a Belgian distributor. Under the terms of the contract, in one year you will deliver 4000 kilograms of frozen king crab for 100,000 euros. Your cost for obtaining the king crab is $110,000. All cash flows occur in exactly one year.
   a. Plot your profits in one year from the contract as a function of the exchange rate in one year, for exchange rates from $0.75/€ to $1.50/€. Label this line "Unhedged Profits."
   b. Suppose the one-year forward exchange rate is $1.25/€, and that you enter into a forward contract to sell the euros you will receive at this rate. In the figure from (a), plot your combined profits from the crab contract and the forward contract as a function of the exchange rate in one year. Label this line "Forward Hedge."
   c. Suppose that instead of using a forward contract, you consider using options. A one-year call option to buy euros at a strike price of $1.25/€ is trading for $0.10/€. Similarly, a one-year put option to sell euros at a strike price of $1.25/€ is trading for $0.10/€. To hedge the risk of your profits, should you buy or sell the call or the put?
   d. In the figure from (a) and (b), plot your "all in" profits using the option hedge (combined profits of crab contract, option contract, and option price) as a function of the exchange rate in one year. Label this line "Option Hedge." (*Note*: You can ignore the effect of interest on the option price.)
   e. Suppose that by the end of the year, a trade war erupts, leading to a European embargo on U.S. food products. As a result, your deal is cancelled, and you don't receive the euros or incur the costs of procuring the crab. However, you still have the profits (or losses) associated with your forward or options contract. In a new figure, plot the profits associated with the forward hedge and the options hedge

(labeling each line). When there is a risk of cancellation, which type of hedge has the least downside risk? Explain briefly.

Internationally Integrated Capital Markets

5. You are a U.S. investor who is trying to calculate the present value of a €5 million cash inflow that will occur one year in the future. The spot exchange rate is $S = \$1.25/€$ and the forward rate is $F_1 = \$1.215/€$. You estimate that the appropriate dollar discount rate for this cash flow is 4% and the appropriate euro discount rate is 7%.
   a. What is the present value of the €5 million cash inflow computed by first discounting the euro and then converting it into dollars?
   b. What is the present value of the €5 million cash inflow computed by first converting the cash flow into dollars and then discounting?
   c. What can you conclude about whether these markets are internationally integrated, based on your answers to (a) and (b)?

6. Mia Caruso Enterprises, a U.S. manufacturer of children's toys, has made a sale in India and is expecting a 400 million rupee cash inflow in one year. (The currency of India is the rupee). The current spot rate is $S = \$0.022/\text{rupee}$ and the one-year forward rate is $F_1 = \$0.021/\text{rupee}$.
   a. What is the present value of Mia Caruso's 400 million rupee inflow computed by first discounting the cash flow at the appropriate rupee discount rate of 10% and then converting the result into dollars?
   b. What is the present value of Mia Caruso's rupee 400 million inflow computed by first converting the cash flow into dollars and then discounting at the appropriate dollar discount rate of 5%?
   c. What can you conclude about whether these markets are internationally integrated, based on your answers to (a) and (b)?

Valuation of Foreign Currency Cash Flows

7. Etemadi Amalgamated, a U.S. manufacturing firm, is considering a new project in Portugal. You are employed in Etemadi's corporate finance department and are responsible for deciding whether to undertake the project. The expected free cash flows, in euros, are shown here:

Year	0	1	2	3	4
Free Cash Flow (€ million)	−15	9	10	11	12

You know that the spot exchange rate is $S = \$1.15/€$. In addition, the risk-free interest rate on dollars is 4% and the risk-free interest rate on euros is 6%.

Assume that these markets are internationally integrated and the uncertainty in the free cash flows is not correlated with uncertainty in the exchange rate. You determine that the dollar WACC for these cash flows is 8.5%. What is the dollar present value of the project? Should Etemadi Amalgamated undertake the project?

8. Etemadi Amalgamated, the U.S. manufacturing company in Problem 7, is still considering a new project in Portugal. All information presented in Problem 7 is still accurate, except the spot rate is now $S = \$0.85/€$, about 26% lower. What is the new present value of the project in dollars? Should Etemadi Amalgamated undertake the project?

9. You work for a U.S. firm, and your boss has asked you to estimate the cost of capital for countries using the euro. You know that $S = \$1.20/€$ and $F_1 = \$1.157/€$. Suppose the dollar WACC for your company is known to be 8%. If these markets are internationally

integrated, estimate the euro cost of capital for a project with free cash flows that are uncorrelated with spot exchange rates. Assume the firm pays the same tax rate no matter where the cash flows are earned.

10. Maryland Light, a U.S. manufacturer of light fixtures, is considering an investment in Japan. The dollar cost of equity for Maryland Light is 11%. You are in the corporate treasury department, and you need to know the comparable cost of equity in Japanese yen for a project with free cash flows that are uncorrelated with spot exchange rates. The risk-free interest rates on dollars and yen are $r_\$ = 5\%$ and $r_¥ = 1\%$, respectively. Maryland Light is willing to assume that capital markets are internationally integrated. What is the yen cost of equity?

11. The dollar cost of debt for Healy Consulting, a U.S. research firm, is 7.5%. The firm faces a tax rate of 30% on all income, no matter where it is earned. Managers in the firm need to know its yen cost of debt because they are considering launching a new bond issue in Tokyo to raise money for a new investment there. The risk-free interest rates on dollars and yen are $r_\$ = 5\%$ and $r_¥ = 1\%$, respectively. Healy Consulting is willing to assume that capital markets are internationally integrated and that its free cash flows are uncorrelated with the yen–dollar spot rate. What is Healy Consulting's after-tax cost of debt in yen? (*Hint*: Start by finding the after-tax cost of debt in dollars and then find the yen equivalent.)

12. Manzetti Foods, a U.S. food processing and distribution company, is considering an investment in Germany. You are in Manzetti's corporate finance department and are responsible for deciding whether to undertake the project. The expected free cash flows, in euros, are uncorrelated to the spot exchange rate and are shown here:

Year	0	1	2	3	4
Free Cash Flow (€ million)	−25	12	14	15	15

The new project has similar dollar risk to Manzetti's other projects. The company knows that its overall dollar WACC is 9.5%, so it feels comfortable using this WACC for the project. The risk-free interest rate on dollars is 4.5% and the risk-free interest rate on euros is 7%.
   a. Manzetti is willing to assume that capital markets in the United States and the European Union are internationally integrated. What is the company's euro WACC?
   b. What is the present value of the project in euros?

Valuation and International Taxation

13. Tailor Johnson, a U.S. maker of fine menswear, has a subsidiary in Ethiopia. This year, the subsidiary reported and repatriated earnings before interest and taxes (EBIT) of 100 million Ethiopian birrs. Assume the current exchange rate is 8 birr/$ or $S_1 = \$0.125/\text{birr}$. The Ethiopian tax rate on this activity is 25%. Tax law in the United States requires Tailor Johnson to pay taxes on the Ethiopian earnings at the same rate as profits earned in the United States, which is currently 45%. However, the United States gives a full tax credit for foreign taxes paid up to the amount of the U.S. tax liability. What is Tailor Johnson's U.S. tax liability on its Ethiopian subsidiary?

*14. Tailor Johnson, the menswear company with a subsidiary in Ethiopia described in Problem 13, is considering the tax benefits resulting from deferring repatriation of the earnings from the subsidiary. Under U.S. tax law, the U.S. tax liability is not incurred until the profits are brought back home. Tailor Johnson reasonably expects to defer repatriation for 10 years, at which point the birr earnings will be converted into dollars at the prevailing spot rate, S_{10}, and the tax credit for Ethiopian taxes paid will still be converted at the exchange rate $S_1 = \$0.125/\text{birr}$. Tailor Johnson's after-tax cost of debt is 5%.

a. Suppose the exchange rate in 10 years is identical to this year's exchange rate, so $S_{10} = \$0.125/\text{birr}$. What is the present value of deferring the U.S. tax liability on Tailor Johnson's Ethiopian earnings for 10 years?

b. How will the exchange rate in 10 years affect the actual amount of the U.S. tax liability? Write an equation for the U.S. tax liability as a function of the exchange rate S_{10}.

15. Peripatetic Enterprises, a U.S. import-export trading firm, is considering its international tax situation. Tax law in the Unites States requires U.S. corporations to pay taxes on their foreign earnings at the same rate as profits earned in the United States; this rate is currently 45%. However, a full tax credit is given for the foreign taxes paid up to the amount of the U.S. tax liability. Peripatetic has major operations in Poland, where the tax rate is 20%, and in Sweden, where the tax rate is 60%. The profits, which are fully and immediately repatriated, and foreign taxes paid for the current year are shown here:

	Poland	Sweden
Earnings before interest and taxes (EBIT)	$80 million	$100 million
Host country taxes paid	$16 million	$60 million
Earnings before interest and after taxes	$64 million	$40 million

a. What is the U.S. tax liability on the earnings from the Polish subsidiary assuming the Swedish subsidiary did not exist?

b. What is the U.S. tax liability on the earnings from the Swedish subsidiary assuming the Polish subsidiary did not exist?

c. Under U.S. tax law, Peripatetic is able to pool the earnings from its operations in Poland and Sweden when computing its U.S. tax liability on foreign earnings. Total EBIT is thus $180 million and the total host country taxes paid are $76 million. What is the total U.S. tax liability on foreign earnings? Show how this relates to the answers in (a) and (b).

Internationally Segmented Capital Markets

*16. Suppose the interest on Russian government bonds is 7.5%, and the current exchange rate is 28 rubles per dollar. If the forward exchange rate is 28.5 rubles per dollar, and the current U.S. risk-free interest rate is 4.5%, what is the implied credit spread for Russian government bonds?

Capital Budgeting with Exchange Rate Risk

*17. For Ityesi Inc.'s U.K. project example in Table 23.2, assume all sales actually occur in the United States and are projected to be $60 million per year for four years. The risk-free rate on dollars is 4% and the risk-free rate on pounds is 7%. Ityesi's WACC is 6.8%. The current spot exchange rate is $1.60 per pound. The tax rate is 40% in both countries. Keep all of the other assumptions embedded in Table 23.2 and calculate the NPV of the investment opportunity.

As discussed in the text, there are multiple ways to handle analyses that have both foreign and domestic cash flows. The most straightforward way to perform this analysis is to convert the pound expenses to dollars using forward rates and combine them with the dollar revenues and expenses to compute dollar EBIT. Also remember that when the EBIT is negative the resulting negative taxes are added to EBIT when calculating FCF because they are tax shields. Assume all tax shields are used in the current year and are not carried forward.

DATA CASE

You are a senior financial analyst with IBM in its capital budgeting division. IBM is considering expanding in Australia due to its positive business atmosphere and cultural similarities to the United States.

The new facility would require an initial investment in fixed assets of $5 billion Australian and an additional capital investment of 3% would be required each year in years 1–4. All capital investments would be depreciated straight line over the five years that the facility would operate. First-year revenues from the facility are expected to be $6 billion Australian and grow at 10% per year. Cost of goods sold would be 40% of revenue; the other operating expenses would amount to 12% of revenue. Net working capital requirements would be 11% of sales and would be required the year prior to the actual revenues. All net working capital would be recovered at the end of the fifth year. Assume that the tax rates are the same in the two countries, that the two markets are internationally integrated, and that the cash flow uncertainty of the project is uncorrelated with changes in the exchange rate. Your team manager wants you to determine the NPV of the project in U.S. dollars using a cost of capital of 12%.

1. Go to the NASDAQ Web site.
   a. Enter the stock symbol for IBM (IBM) in one of the boxes and click "Summary Quotes."
   b. Click "Income Statement" on the left, place the cursor inside the statement and right click. Select "Export to Microsoft Excel" from the menu. If this option does not appear, then copy and paste the information.

2. Obtain exchange rates and comparable interest rates for Australia at Bloomberg's Web site (www.bloomberg.com).
   a. Place the cursor on "Markets" and click "Currencies from the drop-down menu. Copy the "AUD_USD" exchange rate (the U.S. dollars per Australian dollar) from the table and paste it into the same spreadsheet as the IBM Income Statement.
   b. Go to www.investing.com, click "Markets," then click "World Markets," and select Australia from the drop-down menu. Click "Bonds" at the top of the "Australia Indices" panel to get the interest rates for Australia. Copy and paste the data into Excel.
   c. Go to www.investing.com, click "Markets," then click "United States." Click "Bonds" at the top of the "United States Indices" panel to get the interest rates for the United States. Copy and paste the data into Excel.

3. You may have noticed that the four-year rate is not available at www.investing.com for the U.S. Treasury. To find an estimate of the four-year yield, calculate the average of the three and five-year yields.

4. In your Excel spreadsheet, create a new worksheet with a timeline for the project's expected cash flows.
   a. Compute the tax rate as the four-year average of IBM's annual income tax divided by annual earnings before tax.
   b. Determine the expected free cash flows of the project.

5. Note that the free cash flows you calculated in Question 4 are in Australian dollars. Use Eq. 23.2 to determine the forward exchange rates for each of the five years of the project. Then use the forward rates to convert the cash flows to U.S. dollars.

6. Compute the NPV of the project in U.S. dollars using the 12% required return given by your team manager.

Index

	INTERVIEWS WITH notable practitioners highlight leaders in the field and address the financial crisis.	COMMON MISTAKE boxes alert students to common mistakes stemming from misunderstanding core concepts and calculations.	GLOBAL FINANCIAL CRISIS boxes reflect the reality of the recent financial crisis and ongoing sovereign debt crisis, noting lessons learned.	GENERAL INTEREST boxes highlight timely material from financial publications that shed light on business problems and real company practices, with a focus on the recent financial crisis and lessons learned.	USING EXCEL boxes describe Excel techniques and include screenshots to serve as a guide for students using this technology.
CHAPTER 1 Corporate Finance and the Financial Manager	Frank Hatheway, Nasdaq		The Dodd-Frank Act The Dodd-Frank Act on Corporate Governance	Corporate Taxation Around the World Shareholder Value Versus Stakeholder Value Citizens United v. Federal Election Commission NYSE, BATS, DJIA, S&P 500: Awash'in Acronyms	
CHAPTER 2 Introduction to Financial Statement Analysis	Ruth Porat, Google/Alphabet	Mismatched Ratios	Bernard Madoff's Ponzi Scheme	International Financial Reporting Standards	
CHAPTER 3 Time Value of Money: An Introduction		Summing Cash Flows Across Time		Your Personal Financial Decisions Rule of 72 Using a Financial Calculator	
CHAPTER 4 Time Value of Money: Valuing Cash Flow Streams		Discounting One Too Many Times		Using a Financial Calculator: Solving for Present and Future Values of Cash Flow Streams Historical Examples of Perpetuities	
CHAPTER 5 Interest Rates	Kevin M. Warsh, former Governor of the Federal Reserve Board	Using the EAR in the Annuity Formula Using the Annuity Formula When Discount Rates Vary States Dig a $3 Trillion Hole by Discounting at the Wrong Time	Teaser Rates and Subprime Loans	How Is Inflation Actually Calculated? Interest Rates, Discount Rates, and the Cost of Capital	
CHAPTER 6 Bonds	Lisa Black, Teachers Insurance and Annuity Association		Negative Bond Yields	The U.S. Treasury Market Finding Bond Prices on the Web Clean and Dirty Prices for Coupon Bonds Are Treasuries Really Default-Free Securities? The Credit Crisis and Bond Yields	
CHAPTER 7 Stock Valuation		Forgetting to "Grow" This Year's Dividend			
CHAPTER 8 Investment Decision Rules	Dick Grannis, QUALCOMM	IRR Versus the IRR Rule		Why Do Rules Other Than the NPV Rule Persist?	Computing NPV and IRR
CHAPTER 9 Fundamentals of Capital Budgeting	David Holland, Sports and Entertainment Solutions	The Opportunity Cost of an Idle Asset The Sunk Cost Fallacy			Capital Budgeting Using a Spreadsheet Program Project Analysis Using Excel
CHAPTER 10 Stock Valuation: A Second Look	Douglas Kehring, Oracle			Forms of Market Efficiency	
CHAPTER 11 Risk and Return in Capital Markets		Mistakes When Computing Standard Deviation A Fallacy of Long-Run Diversification	Diversification Benefits During Market Crashes	Arithmetic Average Returns Versus Compound Annual Returns	Computing the Standard Deviation of Historical Returns